also by Walter Korn

MODERN CHESS OPENINGS (8th through 12th Editions), *Editor*

AMERICA'S CHESS HERITAGE

AMERICAN CHESS ART

THE BRILLIANT TOUCH IN CHESS

MODERN CHESS OPENINGS

MCO-13

THIRTEENTH EDITION

MODERN CHESS OPENINGS

MCO-13

COMPLETELY REVISED BY

NICK DEFIRMIAN

UNDER THE EDITORSHIP OF

WALTER KORN

DAVID MCKAY COMPANY, INC.
NEW YORK

Library of Congress Cataloging-in-Publication Data

Korn, Walter.
  Modern chess openings / Walter Korn, editor.—13th ed. / Nick
DeFirmian, reviser.
      p.   cm.
  Bibliography: p.
  Includes index.
  ISBN 0-8129-1730-8—ISBN 0-8129-1785-5 (pbk.)
  1. Chess—Openings.   I. DeFirmian, Nick   II. Title.
GV1450.K67   1990
794.1'22—dc20   88-40493
                                                          CIP

Manufactured in the United States of America

Thirteenth Edition
2nd Printing
Designed by M 'N O Production Services, Inc.

EDITOR'S PREFACE

After having been responsible for *Modern Chess Openings*—often called "The Chessplayer's Bible"—for the past fifty years, I decided to widen its scope and analytical prowess by engaging Nick DeFirmian to do a complete revision, and Mr. DeFirmian in turn employed a number of other practicing chessmasters to assist him. Their and my respective contributions are itemized in the reviser's preface.

Another innovation is the switch from the descriptive to the algebraic notation, which has now firmly established itself in the English-speaking world, allowing for greater compatibility with global chess literature.

MCO strives for completeness and clarity while avoiding the minutiae of an encyclopedia. The lastest nuances of the day are taken care of by essays in chess magazines and by specialized monographs—many of them quoted in the Bibliography. Nevertheless, the enormous proliferation of opening theory, with newer analysis often reaching into the middle game, has led to a substantial increase in volume in this edition.

I have also maintained MCO's more articulate style, in addition to simply symbols, to evaluate moves and positions in both the individual introductions and the notes. Importantly, MCO 13 reaches beyond the scope of the usual manuals by including a multitude of complete game scores. While they are not fully annotated, they illustrate the underlying themes of major lines, to render a total conception of how the game develops from the opening.

Many of the modern systems, especially of closed "Indian" nature, are interconnected and thus pose the challenge of properly noting transpositions. I have therefore augmented the texts wherever feasible with cross references to other openings and have also added much recent data. Sources of analyses have been stated wherever practical; otherwise the evaluations are those of the collaborators and the reviser. In transcribing Slavic names, in Cyrillic characters, I have generally followed the usage of the Library of Congress.

I am grateful to Robert Burger and to Burt Hochberg, former editor of *Chess Life*, for valuable linguistic pointers; to computer scientist Hans Berliner, and to Grandmasters Arthur Bisguier and Edmar Mednis and to many other aficionados for varied useful advice. Some changes in design and layout from the previous editions will, I trust, meet with the reader's approval. I also appreciate the patience shown by my editor, Ruth Fecych, and production editor, Nancy Inglis, in dealing with this impatient author.

WALTER KORN

REVISER'S PREFACE

In the last few decades, chess activity has undergone an upsurge—in the United States partly due to America's Robert J. Fischer, but also universally. Competitions and participants have grown dramatically in number, and thus also the complexity of chess technique and of chess openings theory. With far more material to cover, MCO 13 required even more selective treatment to keep the book a comprehensive one-volume work. The choice of material is mostly based on the best line(s) (in the reviser's judgment) and includes demanding though less desirable variations and illustrations of common mistakes or misjudgments.

This work would have been difficult to complete within a reasonable time without the contributions of the following people:

John Donaldson, International Master, who wrote the Slav and Semi-Slav Defense.

John Grefe, Internationasl Master, who wrote the Queen's Indian Defense.

Marc Leski, International Master, who prepared the Pirc Defense.

Elliott Winslow, International Master, who did the King's Indian Defense.

Bruce Leverett, Senior Master, who handled the English and the Regular Flank Openings.

Stephen Brandwein, National Master, who supplied the work on the Queen's Gambit Declined and several Double King's Pawn Openings.

Dr. Hans Baruch, who contributed the Catalan and the Neo-Grünfeld.

Walter Korn, Editor, who revised, specifically, the Budapest and the Latvian Gambits, the Center Counter and the Nimzowitsch Defense, the Unusual Semi-Open King's Pawn and Unusual Flank Openings, and the Queen's Pawn Games.

Danny Olim, who suggested innovations in the Sicilian Defense and did proofreading.

Eileen Doran, who did many long hours of typing.

National Master Vladimir Pafnutieff did research on the French Defense and proofreading. Special thanks go to National Master Robert Burger, without whom I would not have written this book, and Nicholas Carlin, Esq., for advice and support.

—GRANDMASTER NICK DeFIRMIAN

CONTENTS

	page
Editor's Preface	vii
Reviser's Preface	ix
Bibliography	xv
Explanatory Notes	xvii

SCHEMATIC CHART OF OPENINGS AND DEFENSES
For alphabetical listings, also of subordinate variants, see *Index*

I. SYMMETRICAL KING'S PAWN OPENINGS

1 e4 e5

2 f4			King's Gambit	3
2 Nc3 Nc6			Vienna Game	18
2 .... Nf6	3 f4		Vienna Gambit	20
	3 Nf3		*see* Three Knights' Game	
2 Nf3 Nc6	3 Bb5		Ruy Lopez	24
	3 Nc3		Three Knights' Defense	87
	3 .... Nf6		Four Knights' Defense	90
	3 Bc4 Bc5		Giuoco Piano	97
	3 .... Be7		Hungarian Defense	152
	3 .... Nf6		Two Knights' Defense	107
	3 d4 exd4		Scotch Game	117
		4 c3	Göring Gambit	125
	3 c3		Ponziani's Opening	128
2 .... Nf6			Petrov's Defense	131
2 .... d6	3 d4		Philidor's Defense	137
2 .... d5			Queen's Pawn Counter Gambit	152
2 .... f5			Latvian (or Greco Counter-) Gambit	140
2 Bc4			Bishop's Opening	143
2 d4			Center Game	146
2 .... exd4 3 c3			Danish Gambit	149
2 Ne2			Alapin's Opening	152

II. SEMI-OPEN KING'S PAWN DEFENSES

1 e4

1 .... Nf6		Alekhine's Defense	157
1 .... c6		Caro-Kann Defense	171
1 .... e6		French Defense	197
1 .... c5		Sicilian Defense	243
1 .... d6	2 d4	Pirc Defense	326
1 .... g6	2 d4	Robatsch (or Modern) Defense	340
1 .... d5		Center Counter Defense	345
1 .... Nc6		Nimzowitsch Defense	350

(also *see* 1 d4 Nc6—Queen's Knight Defense)

1 .... g5	(2 d4)	Basman's Defense	353
1 .... b6	(2 d4)	Owen's Defense	354
1 .... a6	(2 d4)	Baker's Defense	353

III. QUEEN'S PAWN OPENINGS

(A) Symmetrical Queen's Pawn Openings

```
1 d4    d5                                                               page
2 c4    e6 ------------------------ Queen's Gambit Declined ................. 359
              3 g3 (Nf6) ------- see Catalan Opening
2  .... dxc4 ----------------------- Queen's Gambit Accepted ................. 404
2  .... c6 ------------------------- Slav, and Semi-Slav Defense ............ 414
2  .... Nc6 ----------------------- Queen's Gambit, Chigorin Defense ....... 402
2  .... e5 ------------------------- Queen's Gambit, Albin Counter Gambit ... 442
2 Nf3 Nf6  3 e3 ------------------ Colle System .............................. 441
2  .... Nc6 ----------------------- see Kevitz-Trajković Defense
2 e3 ------------------------------ Stonewall System ......................... 441
2 Bg5 ----------------------------- Queen's Bishop Attack .................... 441
2 e3 ------------------------------ see Colle System
2 Nc3 (Nf6 3 Bg5) --------------- see Richter-Veresov Attack
2 f3 ------------------------------ see Blackmar-Diemer Attack
2 e4 ------------------------------ Blackmar-Diemer Gambit ................... 441
```

(B) Asymmetrical Queen's Pawn Games
(Excluding Indian Systems in Section IV)

```
(i) 1 d4 Nf6
2 c4    e5 ------------------------ Budapest (Counter) Gambit ............... 453
2  .... e6   3 Nf3 Ne4 ----------- Döry Defense .............................. 446
                      c5 ------------ Blumenfeld (Counter) Gambit ............. 442
2  .... Nc6 ----------------------- Kevitz-Trajković Defense ................ 442
2 Nc3 d5  3 Bg5 ------------------ Richter-Veresov Attack .................. 441
2 Bg5 ----------------------------- Trompowski (or Opočensky or Ruth) Attack .......... 441
2 Nf3 e6  3 Bg5 ----------------- Torre Attack ............................. 441
          3 ----------- c5 4 e4 -------------------- (H.) Wagner Gambit .................... 446
2  .... Ne4 ----------------------- see Döry Defense
2  .... b5 ------------------------ Polish Defense Deferred I ................ 685
2 f3 ------------------------------ see Blackmar-Diemer Gambit

(ii) 1 d4, Various (other than 1 ... Nf6)
1  .... e6   2 c4 Bb4† ---------- Franco-Indian Defense ................... 448
             2 ........ b6 -------- see Queen's Indian or Fianchetto Defenses
             2 .......... c5 3 d5 see Benoni Defense
             2 e4 ----------------- see French Defense
1  .... g6 ------------------------ see Robatsch Defense
1  .... b6 (2 e4) ----------------- see Owen's Defense
1  .... b5 ------------------------ Polish Defense ........................... 441
1  .... Nc6 ----------------------- Queen Knight's Defense .................. 442
             2 e4 ----------------- see Nimzowitsch Defense
1  .... e5 ------------------------ Englund Gambit ........................... 450
1  .... f5 ------------------------ Dutch Defense ............................ 456
             2 e4 ----------------- Staunton Gambit .......................... 464
1  .... c5 (2 d5) ----------------- see Benoni Defense
1  .... a6 (2 e4) ----------------- see Baker's Defense
1  .... d6 (2 e4) ----------------- see Pirc Defense
```

IV. INDIAN DEFENSE SYSTEMS

```
1 d4 Nf6 2 c4
2  .... b6    3 Nf3   ⎫
                      ⎬ -------- Queen's Indian Defense ................... 469
2  .... e6    3 Nf3 b6 ⎭
```

3 .... Bb4† ------- Bogolyubov (Bogo-) Indian Defense 490

3 Nc3 Bb4 ---------- Nimzowitsch (Nimzo-) Indian Defense 495

3 g3 (..... d5) ----- Catalan Opening 530

2 .... g6   3 Nc3 d5 ----------- Grünfeld (Indian) Defense 548

3 .... Bg7 ⎫
3 g3 Bg7 4 Bg2 0-0 ⎬ King's Indian Defense 570

4 ....d5 --------- Neo-Grünfeld Defense 550

2 .... d6   3 Nc3 ⎫
3 Nf3 ⎬ ------------ Old Indian Defense 602

2 .... c5   3 g3 ------------------ see Catalan, or English, Opening

3 d5 ----------------- Benoni Defense 604

3 .... b5 -------- Benko Gambit 618

(1 d4 Nf6) 2 Nf3 b6 -------------- see Queen's Indian Defense

V. FLANK OPENINGS

1 Nf3 d5   2 c4 ------------------ Reti Opening—Classical 675

2 ..... e6 3 g3 ----- Reti-(or Neo-) Catalan 677

2 .... d4 -------- Reti Opening-Benoni Reversed 673

2 g3 ------------------ Reti Opening-Barcza System 674

2 b3 ----------------- Nimzowitsch Attack 685

2 b4 ----------------- Santasiere's Folly 700

1 Nf3 & g3 & Bg2 & d3 & 0-0 -- King's Indian Attack 679

1 .... Nf6   2 g3 b5 -------------- Polish Defense Deferred II 685

1 .... f5   2 e4 ------------------ Lisitsin Gambit 685

1 c4 ------------------------------ English Opening 625

1 .... e5   2 Nc3 Nf6 3 g3 ---- Carls' Bremen System 626

1 .... c5   2 Nc3 Nf6 3 Nf3 ⎫
2 Nf3 Nf6 3 Nc3 ⎬ e6 4 g3 b6 ------------- Hedgehog System 628

1 f4 ------------------------------ Bird's Opening 685 693

1 g3 ------------------------------ King's Fianchetto Opening 686

1 b3 ------------------------------ Larsen's (or Queen's Fianchetto) Opening 685

1 g4 ------------------------------ Grob's Attack 696

1 b4 ------------------------------ Sokolsky Opening 697

1 Na3 ----------------------------- Durkin's Opening 699

1 c3 ------------------------------ Saragossa Opening 699

1 Nc3 ----------------------------- Dunst Opening (or Queen's Knight Attack) 696

1 Nh3 (d5 2 g3 e5 3 f4 Bxh3 4 Bxh3 exf4 5 0-0) ------------- Paris Gambit 699

Index... 701

BIBLIOGRAPHY

Listed below are some of the sources from which references have been quoted. This will enable the reader to consult the more detailed treatises on openings of particular interest and possibly locate them at well-stocked chess book dealers or the library. For practical reasons some preference is given to titles that are also listed in the widely available R.R. Bowker's *Publishers' List of Books in Print* (U.S.) and Whitaker's *British Books in Print* (U.K.).

J. ADORJAN & J. DÖRY: *Winning with the Grünfeld.*
J. ADORJAN & T. HORVATH: *Sicilian Sveshnikov Variation.*
L. ALBURT & E. SCHILLER: *Alekhine for the Tournament Player.*
L. BARDEN, W. HARTSTON & R. KEENE: *The King's Indian Defense.*
R. BELLIN: *Trompowski Opening and Torre Attack.*
F. BILGUER: *Handbuch des Schachspiels* (German) and H. KMOCH'S *Nachtrag* ("Supplement") (German)—referred to as *Bilguer.*
L. BLACKSTOCK: *The Ruy Lopez: Breyer System.*
O. BORIK: *Budapest Gambit.*
R. BURGER: *The Chess of Bobby Fischer.*
B. CAFFERTY & D. HOOPER: *A Complete Defence to e4* (The Petroff).
CHESS INFORMANT: Semiannual (multilingual) publication, Vols. 1 onward— referred to as *Informant.*
J. DONALDSON: *Meran Defense.*
ENCYCLOPEDIA OF CHESS OPENINGS (Multilingual), Vols. A–E: referred to as ECO.
L. EVANS: *The Chess Opening for You.*
R.J. FISCHER: *My 60 Memorable Games.*
S. GLIGORIĆ: *Play the Nimzo-Indian Defense.*
J. GREFE & J. SILMAN: *Center Counter.*
K. GRIVAINIS: *The Latvian Gambit.*
E. GUFELD: *Benkö Gambit Accepted.*
J. HALL & K. SMITH: *Attacking the Sicilian With 2 f4* and *Winning With the Colle System.*
P. JANICKI: *Anglo Benoni: Two Knights System* and *Anglo Benoni: Four Knights System.*
P. JANICKI & J. KONIKOWSKI: *English: Flohr–Mikenas System.*
T. KAPITANIAK: *The Polish Defense 1 . . . b5.*
G. KASPAROV & R. KEENE: *Batsford Chess Openings*—referred to as BCO.
G. KOLTANOWSKI: *The Colle System,* 12th edition.
J. KONIKOWSKI: *Queen's Gambit: Tartakower System* and *Queen's Indian: Petrosian System* and *Modern Benoni: Four Pawns Attack.*
V. KORCHNOI & V. ZAK: *King's Gambit.*
W. KORN, Editor: MODERN CHESS OPENINGS (MCO), analyses from previous editions (7th–12th) and varied essays—referred to as *Comments.*
A. LAMFORD: *Albin Counter Gambit.*
B. LEVERETT: *Sicilian Defense: Velimirović Attack.*
D. N. LEVY: *Sicilian Dragon: Classical and Levenfish Variation.*
J. MOLES: *The French Defense: Main Line Winawer.*

H. MYERS: *Myers' Openings Bulletin* (quarterly).

Ya. NEISHTADT: *Play the Catalan, Open Variation* and *Play the Catalan, Closed Variation*.

NEW IN CHESS: (Semiannual) Yearbook, Vols. 1984–1989.

J. NUNN: *The Najdorf for the Tournament Player* and *The Pirc for the Tournament Player* and *The Benoni for the Tournament Player*.

Yu. RAZUVAEV & A. MATSUKEVICH: *The Anti-Sicilian 3 Bb5†*.

SCHACH-ARCHIV: Monthly Loose-leaf (German).

E. SCHILLER: *The Blackmar–Diemer Gambit*.

A. SOLTIS: *Winning with the Bird Opening*.

S.G. TARTAKOWER: (aka Xavier Tartakover): *Die Hypermoderne Schachpartie*, et al. (German).

H. TIEMANN & H. VETTER: *Lettisches Gambit* (German).

J. WATSON: *Symmetrical English* and *English: Franco, Slav & Flank Defenses*.

M. YUDOVICH: *Spanish without . . . a6*.

Other references, often individually acknowledged, have been extracted from annotations of a general nature in magazines such as *Chess Life, Inside Chess*, (Correspondence-) *Chess International, The Chess Correspondent* (all U.S.); *The British Chess Magazine, Pergamon Chess* (all British); *Europa-Rochade* and *Deutsche Schachzeitung* (all German); *64* (Russian) and various chess columns, e.g. *The New York Times* (R. Byrne), the *Los Angeles Times* (J. Peters) and others.

EXPLANATORY NOTES

The symbols used to evaluate the variations are:

+   after White's (or Black's) move: White (or Black) has a clear winning advantage.

±   White has a distinct superiority, although there is no immediate forced win.

∓   Black has a distinct superiority, although there is no immediate win.

⩲   White has slightly better chances.

⩱   Black has slightly better chances.

=   The position offers even chances.

∞   Unclear position, with judgment reserved, or open to further experimentation.

†   check.

!   Good move, or best choice among several alternatives.

!?   Acceptable move, but open to further research.

?   Weak move.

?!   Speculative attempt to complicate.

Chp.   Championship

Corr.   Correspondence

Comments: quotations carried over from previous MCO editions and concurring with Reviser's present evaluations.

En passant moves are reproduced thus (for White): . . . f5 exf6; (for Black): c4 dxc3, and similarly.

The above symbols of evaluation are guideposts based on contemporary opinion and may change in the light of later developments. However, readers should not forgo their own judgment, as temperament, personal style, and preference each plays a role in selecting a specific line or variation. "Transpositions" of opening moves have become a frequent tactical weapon, and thus cross-references of one line to another, as explained in the introductions or footnotes, should be given careful attention.

As a practical suggestion, two chessboards and men (or pocket sets) may be used when playing through MCO columns, making identical moves until reaching an important note. The note may then be examined on one board, leaving the main position on the other board intact until proceeding to the next note.

ALGEBRAIC NOTATION

Algebraic notation is a simple grid-reference system for recording chess moves. Each square on the board is identified by a combination of a letter and a number, as seen on the accompanying diagram. The files (vertical columns) are lettered *a* to *h* from left to right as seen from White's side of the board; the ranks (horizontal rows) are numbered 1 to 8 starting with the rank closest to White's edge of the board.

A move is recorded by giving the abbreviation of the piece that is moving (K for king, Q for queen, R for rook, N for knight, B for bishop), followed by its destination square. For example, Nf3 indicates a Knight move to the f3 square. A pawn move is usually recorded by giving only its destination square (although the square it is moving from is also occasionally given to indicate that it is a move, not the name of a square). The letter x indicates a capture.

a8	b8	c8	d8	e8	f8	g8	h8
a7	b7	c7	d7	e7	f7	g7	h7
a6	b6	c6	d6	e6	f6	g6	h6
a5	b5	c5	d5	e5	f5	g5	h5
a4	b4	c4	d4	e4	f4	g4	h4
a3	b3	c3	d3	e3	f3	g3	h3
a2	b2	c2	d2	e2	f2	g2	h2
a1	b1	c1	d1	e1	f1	g1	h1

I
SYMMETRICAL
KING'S PAWN
OPENINGS

KING'S GAMBIT

1 e4 e5 2 f4

Diagram 2

WHAT IS THE KING'S GAMBIT? Is it an attempt to overwhelm one's opponent by starting an attack as early as the second move? Or is it a well-judged positional attempt to undermine Black's position in the center? The nineteenth century was the time of chess romanticism, when sacrifices and quick attacks were routine. The King's Gambit saw constant use, but even then players like Steinitz and Chigorin played it with positional considerations in mind.

Claims of the gambit's unsoundness have frequently been made. Six decades ago, Spielmann wrote a mournful article entitled "From the Sickbed of the King's Gambit," and Bobby Fischer's article from the sixties, "A Bust to the King's Gambit," is well known. Yet even in the modern era of chess, the honor roll of players who have ventured 2 f4 is quite impressive: Keres, Spassky, Bronstein, Tal, and Fischer, among others. A number of younger stars, including Mark Hebden of England and the amazing Polgar sisters, employ this old gambit in these days of enormous theoretical opening knowledge. As long as there are players with venturesome spirits, or players willing to improve upon the old analyses, the King's Gambit will continue to be played.

With 2 f4 White stakes a pawn for a dominating center, better development, and a rapid attack on f7, which utilizes the open king's bishop file. White may have problems with his own king's safety, though. Black has four choices in response. He can: (1) decline the gambit, which is safe but unenterprising; (2) accept the gambit and hold on to the pawn; (3) accept the pawn and quickly return it for equality; (4) gambit a pawn himself (2 . . . d5).

Black plays 2 . . . exf4, accepting the gambit in cols. 1–24. The first six columns cover the defense 3 . . . g5 (to 3 Nf3), holding on to the pawn. Most attention is paid to the *Kieseritzky Gambit*, cols. 1–3. Less common defenses on the third move are covered in cols. 7–12. These lines are complicated and less reliable than 3 . . . g5.

Black returns the pawn with 3 . . . d5 (cols. 13–16). This is a safe way to ensure a playable game. *Cunningham's Variation* is the peculiar 3 . . . Be7 (cols. 17–18).

The KING'S BISHOP GAMBIT, 3 Bc4, and other moves which allow 3 . . . Qh4† are seen in cols. 19–24. This check is double-edged because the black queen must often lose time retreating. 3 Qf3 (col. 24) is the *Breyer Gambit.*

Diagram 3

The FALKBEER COUNTERGAMBIT, 2 . . . d5, (cols. 25–30), is the most aggressive counterthrust to the King's Gambit. (See diagram.) Black attempts to rip the position wide open. The old main line of the Falkbeer (col. 26) is under a cloud, so Nimzowitsch's 3 . . . c6 (cols. 28–29) is played more often.

Declining the gambit with 2 . . . Bc5 is an old and respected way to respond. Whether White plays 4 Nc3 or 4 c3 Black seems to hold his own. Column 36 examines less usual defenses.

KING'S GAMBIT

1 e4 e5 2 f4 exf4 3 Nf3 g5

	1	2	3	4	5	6
				Philidor Gambit	Hanstein Gambit	Muzio Gambit
	Kieseritzky Gambit					
4	h4................................Bc4					
	g4			Bg7.....................g4		
5	Ne5(a)			h4..........d4		0–0(s)
	Bg7.........Nf6(d)			h6	h6	gxf3
6	d4(b)	d4..........Bc4		d4	0–0(o)	Qxf3
	d6	d6	d5	d6	d6	Qf6
7	Nxg4(c)	Nd3	exd5	hxg5(l)	g3	e5
	Bxg4	Nxe4	Bd6	hxg5	Nc6	Qxe5
8	Qxg4	Bxf4	d4(h)	Rxh8	c3(p)	d3
	Bxd4	Qe7(e)	0–0(i)	Bxh8	g4(q)	Bh6
9	c3	Qe2(f)	0–0(j)	Nc3	Nh4	Nc3
	Be5	Bg7	Nh5	c6(m)	f3	Ne7
10	Bxf4	c3	Nxg4	g3	Nd2	Bd2
	Nf6	Bf5	Qxh4	g4	Nf6	Nbc6
11	Qf3	Nd2	Nh2	Bxf4	Nf5	Rae1
	Nbd7 =	Nxd2(g)	Ng3(k)	gxf3(n)	Bxf5(r)	Qf5(t)

(a) 5 Ng5 is the Allgaier Gambit. After 5 . . . h6 6 Nxf7 Kxf7 7 Bc4† (if 7 d4 f3 forces White to play 8 Bc4† anyway) 7 . . . d5 8 Bxd5† Kg7 9 d4 f3 10 gxf3 Nf6 Black is better.

(b) If 6 Nxg4 d5 7 d4 dxe4 8 Bxf4 Qxd4 9 Qxd4 Bxd4 =.

(c) 7 Nxf7, played in Pillsbury–Marco, Vienna 1903, is speculative. 7 Nc4 Nf6 8 Bxf4 Nxe4 Nbd2 Qf6 was good for Black in Hebden–Hawksworth, London 1985. The column is *Comments*.

(d) Other moves at this point—5 . . . d5, 5 . . . Qe7, 5 . . . h5, 5 . . . Nc6, and 5 . . . d6—all give White the advantage.

(e) 8 . . . Bg7 9 c3 (Spassky–Fischer, Mar del Plata 1960, saw 9 Nc3 Nxc3 10 bxc3 c5 $\overline{\mp}$) 9 . . . 0–0 10 Nd2 Re8 11 Nxe4 Rxe4† is approximately even.

(f) 9 Be2, suggested by Korchnoi and Zak, is possible.

(g) After 12 Qxe7† Kxe7 13 Kxd2 White has enough for the pawn (Keres).

(h) 8 0–0 is the Rice Gambit. After 8 . . . Bxe5 9 Re1 Qe7 10 c3 Nh5 play becomes wild and messy, but it tends to favor Black.

(i) 8 . . . Nh5 (Staunton) 9 0–0 Qxh4 10 Qe1 Qxe1 11 Rxe1 0–0 =.

(j) Not 9 Bxf4 Nh5 10 g3 f6 11 Nd3 Nxg3 $\mp$, Pillsbury–Chigorin, Vienna 1903.

(k) Better than 11 . . . Re8 recommended by *Bilguer*. Black has the advantage.

(l) (A) 7 Qd3 Nc6 8 hxg5 hxg5 9 Rxh8 Bxh8 10 e5 Bg7 11 Qh7 Kf8 is bad for White, Anderssen–Neumann, Berlin 1865. (B) 7 c3 Nc6 8 Qb3 Qe7 9 0–0 Nf6 also favors Black.

(m) 9 . . . Nc6 is worth a try.

(n) White has attacking chances for his lost material. Play is sharp and probably balanced, but this type of position is what King's Gambit players strive for.

(o) 6 g3 is interesting. On 6 . . . Nc6, the risky 7 gxf4 has been played (instead of transposing to the column with 7 0–0), but after 7 . . . g4 8 Ng1 Qh4† 9 Kf1 Nf6 Black achieves an advantage.

(p) 8 gxf4 g4 9 d5 ∞, Arnason–Larsen, Reykjavik 1978.

(q) After 8 . . . Bh3 9 gxf4 Bxf1 10 Qxf1 White has value for the exchange due to his strong center and initiative.

(r) 12 exf5 0–0, Heuer–Villard, Tallinn 1964. Black stands well.

(s) 5 Ne5, the Salvio Gambit, was favored at one time by Steinitz. After 5 . . . Qh4† 6 Kf1 Nc6 7 Nxf7 Bc5 8 Qe1 g3 9 Nxh8 Bf2 Black has a terrific attack. Other entertaining but dubious tries are 5 Bxf7† (Lolli Gambit), 5 Nc3 (McDonnell Gambit), and 5 d4 (Ghulam Kassim Gambit).

(t) 12 Nd5 Kd8 13 Qe2 Qe6 14 Qf2 Qf5 used to be thought a forced draw, but Black plays 13 . . . b5 14 Nxe7 Qc5† 15 Rf2 Nxe7 and obtains the advantage.

KING'S GAMBIT

1 e4 e5 2 f4 exf4 3 Nf3

	7	8	9	10	11	12
	d6(a)	Ne7	f5	Nf6		
4	d4(b)	d4	e5	e5		
	g5	d5	d5(f)	Nh5(g)		
5	h4	Nc3	d4	Be2	d4	Qe2
	g4	dxe4	g5	g6(h)	d6(j)	Be7
6	Ng1	Nxe4	h4	d4	Qe2	d4
	Bh6(c)	Ng6	g4	Bg7	d5(k)	0–0(m)
7	Ne2	h4	Ng1	0–0	c4	g4
	Qf6	Be7(d)	f3	d6	Be6	fxg3
8	Nbc3	h5	Bg5	Nc3	cxd5	Qg2(n)
	Ne7	Nh4	fxg2	0–0	Bxd5	d6
9	Qd2	Bxf4	Bxg2	Nd5(i)	Nc3	hxg3
	Nbc6	Bg4	Be7	dxe5	Nc6	Bg4
10	g3	h6	Nc3 ±	dxe5	Bd2	Nh2(o)
	Bd7 =	0–0(e)		Nc6 =	Bb4(l)	Nxg3(p)

(a) Fischer's Variation. He called 3 . . . d6 "a high-class waiting move." The idea is to hold the pawn while preventing the Ne5 as in col. 1.

(b) (A) 4 Bc4 transposes to col. 5. (B) Interesting is 4 d3 g5 5 h4 g4 6 Ng1 or 6 Nd4 with little-explored possibilities.

(c) (A) Risky is 6 . . . Nf6, as in the miniature Gallagher–Sanz, Gijon 1988: 7 Qd3! d5 (7 . . . Nc6 8 c3) 8 e5 Nh5 9 Ne2 Be7 10 Bxf4 c5 (10 . . . Bxh4† 11 g3 +) 11 dxc5 Nc6 12 Nbc3 Nxf4 13 Nxf4 Nxe5 14 Qe3 Bf6 15 Ncd5 0–0 16 0–0–0 Bg7 17 Nh5 Nd7 18 Ne7† Kh8 19 Nxg7 Resigns. The column is Planinc–Portisch, Portorož 1973. (B) 6 . . . f3 7 gxf3 Be7 8 Be3 Bxh4† 9 Kd2 c5! 10 Kc1 (or 10 Bb5†) 10 . . . cxd4 11 Qxd4 Bf6 ∞, Gallagher–Conquest, British Chp. 1988.

(d) Bad is 7 . . . Qe7? 8 Kf2! Bg4 (8 . . . Qxe4 9 Bb5† Kd8 10 Re1 wins) 9 h5 Nh4 10 Bxf4 +, Spassky–Seirawan.

(e) Kuznetsov–Bonch-Osmolovsky, USSR 1964. White has a substantial advantage.

(f) After 4 . . . d6, Alapin's 5 Qe2 with the idea of 5 . . . dxe5 6 Nxe5 Qe7 7 d4 gives White the advantage.

(g) 4 . . . Ne4 might be playable, although after 5 d3 Ng5 6 Bf4 Ne6 7 Bg3 d5 White stood freer in Tolush–Averbakh, USSR 1960.

(h) On (A) 5 . . . g5 White plays 6 0–0 (rather than 6 Nxg5) so that 6 . . . Rg8 7 d4 d5 8 c4 or 8 Qd3 gives White a plus. (B) 5 . . . d6 6 0–0 dxe5 7 Nxe5 and neither 7 . . . Bc5† nor 7 . . . Qd4† allows Black an equal game.

(i) 9 Ne1 was disadvantageous for White in Chigorin–Steinitz, Havana 1892. The text is Korchnoi's idea.

7

(j) 5 . . . d5 6 c4 Nc6 7 cxd5 Qxd5 8 Nc3 Bb4 9 Be2 Bg4 10 0–0 ⩲.

(k) 6 . . . dxe5 7 Nxe5 Qh4† 8 g3 is not playable for Black.

(l) 11 Nxd5 Qxd5 12 0–0–0 Qxa2 13 d5! gives White a plus after 13 . . . Bxd2† 14 Qxd2 and 13 . . . Qa1† 14 Kc2 Qa4† 15 Kb1.

(m) Weak is 6 . . . Bh4† 7 Kd1 0–0 8 g4 fxg3 9 Qg2 ±, Randviir–Tepaks, Tallinn 1946.

(n) Aggressive is 8 hxg3 Nxg3 9 Qh2 Nxh1 10 Bd3, but 10 . . . f5 11 exf6 Bb4† makes this choice risky for White. *Comments.*

(o) Deserving of study is Keres' suggestion 10 Bd3, which should give White enough play for his pawn, e.g., 10 . . . Nc6 11 c3 Qd7 12 Nh2 (Korn).

(p) 11 Rg1 Bf5 12 Nf3 Nh5 13 Rh1 Bg6 14 Nc3 Nc6 ∞. *Comments.*

KING'S GAMBIT

1 e4 e5 2 f4 exf4 3 Nf3

	13	14	15	16	17	18
					Cunningham Variation	
	d5				Be7	
4	exd5				Bc4	Nc3
	Nf6			Bd6	Nf6(m)	Nf6(p)
5	Nc3	Bb5†	c4	Nc3	e5(n)	e5(q)
	Nxd5(a)	c6	c6	Ne7	Ng4	Ng4
6	Nxd5	dxc6	d4(h)	d4	Nc3	d4
	Qxd5	bxc6(f)	Bb4†(i)	0–0	d6	Ne3
7	d4	Bc4	Nc3	Bd3	d4	Bxe3
	Be7(b)	Nd5	cxd5	Nd7	dxe5	fxe3
8	c4(c)	Nc3(g)	Bxf4	0–0	dxe5	Bc4
	Qe4†	Be7	0–0	h6(k)	Qxd1†	d6
9	Kf2(d)	0–0	Be2	Ne4	Nxd1	0–0
	Bf5	0–0	dxc4	Nxd5	Be6	0–0
10	Be2(e)	d4	Bxc4	c4	Bxe6	Qd3
	Nc6 =	Nb6 ±	Nd5(j)	Ne3(l)	fxe6(o)	Nc6(r)

(a) After 5 ... Bd6 6 Bc4 0–0 7 0–0 Nbd7 8 d4 Nb6 9 Bb3 h6 10 Ne5 g5, White makes a promising exchange sacrifice with 11 g3 Bh3 12 gxf4!.

(b) Both (A) 7 ... Bd6 8 c4 Qe4† 9 Kf2 and (B) 7 ... Bg4 8 Bxf4 are better for White.

(c) 8 Bd3 g5 and not Rubinstein's 9 Qe2?!, but 9 c4 (Euwe) produces an interesting game.

(d) 9 Be2 Bf5 10 0–0 Nc6 = , Spielmann–Milner-Barry, Margate 1938.

(e) 10 c5 Nc6 11 Bb5 Qd5 12 Re1 Be4 is good for Black. *Comments.*

(f) 6 ... Nxc6, played in Hartston–Spassky, Hastings 1966 is all right, but after 7 d4 Bd6 8 0–0 0–0 9 Nbd2 Bg4 10 Nc4 Bc7 11 Bxc6 White has a slight plus.

(g) The text is an improvement over 8 0–0 Bd6 9 Nc3 Be6, since 8 Nc3 Bd6 9 Qe2! is strong. The column is Muchnik–Lilienthal, USSR 1967.

(h) 6 dxc6 Nxc6 7 d4 Bg4 gives Black too much play.

(i) 6 ... cxd5 7 c5 Nc6 8 Bxf4 Be7 9 Nc3 0–0 = .

(j) With no difficulties and good pawn structure Black has at least equality.

(k) 8 ... Nf6 is an improvement which gives chances for equality. If Black wants to play 4 ... Bd6 he must find something better than the continuation in the column.

(l) 11 Bxe3 fxe3 12 c5 Be7 13 Bc2 Re8 14 Qd3 e2 15 Nd6! Nf8 16 Nxf7 exf1=Q† 17 Rxf1 Bf5 18 Qxf5 Qd7 19 Qf4 Bf6 20 N3e5 Qe7 21 Bb3 Bxe5 22 Nxe5† Kh7 23 Qe4† Resigns, Spassky–Bronstein, USSR 1960; a truly brilliant game.

(m) 4 ... Bh4† 5 Kf1 (better than the speculative 5 g3) d5 6 Bxd5 Nf6 and now Glazkov's 7 Bb3 gives White chances for an edge.

(n) (A) 5 Nc3 Nxe4 6 Ne5 Ng5 $\mp$. (B) 5 Qe2 and (C) 5 d3 produce only equality.

(o) 11 h3 Nh6 12 Bxf4 Nf5 = (Korchnoi).

(p) 4 ... Bh4† is also logical. After 5 Ke2 d5 6 Nxd5 Nf6 7 Nxf6† Qxf6 8 d4 the question is whether White's center is worth more than his exposed king.

(q) 5 d4 d5 6 Bd3 (or 6 exd5) gives White little chance for an edge.

(r) 11 exd6 Bxd6 12 Ne4 Be7 =.

KING'S GAMBIT

1 e4 e5 2 f4 exf4

	19	20	21	22	23	24
3	Bc4...(Bishop's Gambit) d5	Nc3......... Nf6(c)	Nc3......... Qh4†(h)	d4 .... d5	Be2......... d5	Qf3 Nc6(q)
4	Bxd5 Nf6	Nc3 c6(d)	Ke2 d5!(i)	exd5 Qh4†	exd5 Nf6	c3 Nf6
5	Nc3 Bb4(a)	Bb3(e) d5	Nxd5 Bg4†	Ke2(m) Bd6	Nf3(n) Be7	d4 d5
6	Nf3(b) Bxc3	exd5 cxd5	Nf3 Bd6(j)	Nf3 Bg4	0–0 0–0	e5 Ne4
7	dxc3 c6	d4 Bd6	d4 Nc6(k)	c4 c5	c4(o) Ne8(p)	Bxf4 Be7(r)
8	Bc4 Qxd1†	Nge2 0–0	e5 0–0–0	Nc3 Nf6	d4 g5	Nd2 f5
9	Kxd1 0–0	Bxf4(f) Bxf4	Bxf4 Nge7	dxc5 Bxc5	Bd3 Ng7	exf6 Nxf6
10	Bxf4 Nxe4 =	Nxf4 Re8†(g)	c4 Bb4(l)	Kd2 ∞	Qc2 f5 ±	Bd3 0–0 ∓

(a) Other tries do not seem as good: (A) 5 . . . Nxd5 6 Nxd5 Qh4† 7 Kf1 ±; (B) 5 . . . c6 6 Bb3 Bg4 7 Nf3 ±.

(b) Both (A) 6 Nge2 Bxc3 7 bxc3 Nxd5, and (B) 6 Qf3 0–0 7 Nge2 Re8, lead to complete equality. The column is an old analysis by *Bilguer*.

(c) (A) 3 . . . Qh4† is playable, but after 4 Kf1 White will later gain time in development by attacking Black's queen with Nf3. (B) 3 . . . d6 4 Nc3 Be6 5 Bxe6 fxe6 6 d4 Qh4† 7 Kf1 Nh6 8 Nf3 Qf6 is roughly equal, Hjartarson–Beliavsky, Reykjavik 1988.

(d) 4 . . . Bb4 is all right after 5 e5 d5 6 Bb5† c6 7 exf6 cxb5 8 fxg7 Rg8 = (Castro–Karpov, Stockholm 1969), but 5 Nf3 Nc6 7 Nd5 makes it unreliable.

(e) 5 d4 Bb4 6 Qf3 d5 7 exd5 0–0 8 Nge2 cxd5 9 Bd3 Bg4 ∓, Spielmann–Bogolyubov, Carlsbad 1923. Surprisingly, this line was repeated 62 years later in Hartmann–Spassky, West Germany 1985.

(f) Equality results from 9 0–0 g5 10 Nxd5 Nc6 11 h4 h6.

(g) 11 Nfe2 Ng4 12 Nd5 Be6 13 h3 was suggested by Fischer as good for White, but Keres's 13 . . . Nh6 or 12 . . . Nc6 (instead of 12 . . . Be6) should produce counterplay.

(h) Black may play 3 . . . Nc6 with an acceptable position, yet there is no reason to avoid giving the queen check.

(i) The text move is the sharpest plan. Less incisive is 4 . . . d6 5 Nf3 Bg4 6 Nd5 Bxf3† 7 gxf3 Kd8 8 d3 ±.

(j) The text move is probably strongest, but possible is 6 . . . Nc6 7 Nxc7† Kd8 8 Nxa8 Ne5 (8 . . . Nd4† 9 Kd3 Qf6 ∞, Jago–J. E. Littlewood, England 1965) 9 h3 Bxf3† 10 gxf3 Qg3 11 d4 when Black can give perpetual check.

(k) Adequate alternatives are 7 . . . Ne7 and 7 . . . Nf6.

(l) This position was reached in Spassky–Furman, USSR 1959, where Black played 10 . . . Nf5? and was much worse. Instead, 10 . . . Bb4 assures him of a big advantage.

(m) The other reasonable way to escape from check is 5 Kd2. If then 5 . . . Bd6 6 Qe1† is about equal (Keres). The column is Mason–Kürschner, Nürnberg 1882.

(n) Better than 5 c4 c6 6 d4 Bb4† 7 Kf1 (else 7 . . . Ne4) cxd5 $\overline{\overline{\mp}}$, Tartakower–Capablanca, New York 1924.

(o) 7 Nc3 Nxd5 8 Nxd5 Qxd5 9 d4 g5 ∞. Korchnoi evaluated this position as better for Black, then changed his mind to prefer the White side. The text move is better than 7 Nc3.

(p) The text looks odd, but the tries 7 . . . b5 (Nei) and 7 . . . c6 (Estrin) have both failed to shake White's advantage. The column is Biaux–Buy, corr. 1984.

(q) A good alternative is 3 . . . d5. After 4 exd5 Nf6 5 Bb5† c6 6 dxc6 Nxc6 7 d4 Bg4 Black stands at least equal, Spielmann–Nimzowitsch, Carlsbad 1907.

(r) 7 . . . f6 8 exf6 Nxf6 9 Bd3 =. *Comments.* The column is Drimer–Unzicker, Hastings 1969.

KING'S GAMBIT

Falkbeer Counter Gambit

1 e4 e5 2 f4 d5

	25	26	27	28	29	30
3	exd5..Nf3					
	e4...............................c6					dxe4
4	d3			Nc3(l)		Nxe5
	Nf6			exf4		Nd7(p)
5	Nd2(a)......dxe4.......Nc3			Nf3		d4
	exd3	Nxe4	Bb4	Nf6........Bd6		exd3
6	Bxd3	Nf3(d)	Bd2	d4	Bc4(o)	Nxd3
	Nxd5(b)	Bc5	e3(i)	Bd6(m)	Ne7	Ngf6
7	Qf3(c)	Qe2	Bxe3	Qe2†	dxc6	Nc3
	Nc6	Bf5(e)	0–0	Qe7(n)	Nbxc6	Nb6
8	a3	Nc3(f)	Bd2(j)	Qxe7†	d4	Be2
	Bc5	Qe7	Bxc3	Kxe7	0–0	Bd6
9	Ne2	Be3	bxc3	Ne5	0–0	0–0
	0–0	Bxe3(g)	Re8†	Nxd5	Bg4	0–0
10	Nb3	Qxe3	Be2	Nxd5†	Ne4	Bf3
	Be7 =	Nxc3(h)	Bg4(k)	cxd5 ±	Bc7 ∞	c6 =

(a) This move avoids the complications that can arise from 5 . . . Bf5 and 5 . . . e3, as those moves are weak here. 5 Nd2 is safe, but not ambitious.

(b) Also reasonable is 6 . . . Qxd5 7 Ngf3 Nc6 8 Qe2† Be7 =.

(c) 7 Ne4 Nb4 8 Bb5† c6 also produces an equal game.

(d) (A) 6 Be3 Qh4† 7 g3 Nxg3 8 Nf3 (8 hxg3 was played by Tal, but it is not a sound sacrifice) 8 . . . Qe7 9 hxg3 Qxe3† 10 Qe2 gives White a minute endgame edge, Spassky–Matanović, Belgrade 1964. (B) Charousek's 6 Qe2 fails to 6 . . . Qxd5 7 Nd2 f5 8 g4 Nc6 9 c3 Be7 10 Bg2 Qf7 ∓, Bardeleben–Pillsbury, Hanover 1902.

(e) 7 . . . Bf2† 8 Kd1 Qxd5† 9 Nfd2! wins.

(f) 8 g4 0–0 9 gxf5 Re8 is too dangerous for White, Spielmann–Tarrasch, Mor. Ostrava 1923.

(g) 9 . . . Nxc3? 10 Bxc5 Nxe2 11 Bxe7 Nxf4 12 Ba3 +, Bronstein–Tal, USSR 1968.

(h) 11 Qxe7† Kxe7 12 bxc3 makes it difficult for Black to equalize. Foune–Mathieu, corr. 1985, continued 12 . . . Be4 13 Ng5 Bxd5 14 0–0–0 Bxa2 15 c4 b5 16 cxb5 a6? (Estrin suggested 16 . . . h6 as a better try. Black has an uphill struggle in any case, but now he faces a strong attack.) 17 Bd3 axb5 18 Rhe1† Be6 19 f5 Kf6 20 fxe6 Kxg5 21 exf7 Rf8 22 Re8 Rxf7 23 Kb2 c6 24 Bxh7 Rfa7 25 Rdd8 g6 26 Bg8 Rb7 27 g3 Kf6 28 h4 c5 29 Bd5 Resigns.

(i) 6 . . . 0–0 7 Nxe4 Re8 8 Bxb4 Nxe4 9 dxe4 Rxe4† 10 Be2 Rxb4 11 Nf3 ±, Spassky–Bronstein, Moscow 1971.

(j) 8 Be2?! Bxc3† 9 bxc3 Nxd5 10 Bd2 Qf6 gives Black too much play, Gruzman–Kimelfeld, Moscow 1966.

(k) 11 Kf2 (better than 11 c4?! of Schulten–Morphy, New York 1857) 11 . . . Bxe2 12 Nxe2 Qxd5 gives Black chances for his pawn.

(l) The text move is considered best. Both (A) 4 Qe2 cxd5 5 fxe5 Nc6 6 c3 d4 Alekhine– Johner, Carlsbad 1908, and (B) 4 dxc6 Nxc6 5 Bb5 exf4 6 Nf3 Bd6 Ree–Short, Wijk aan Zee 1986, are risky for White.

(m) 6 . . . Nxd5 7 Nxd5 Qxd5 8 Bxf4 Qe4† 9 Qe2 $\pm$, Stoltz–Brinckmann, Swinemünde 1932.

(n) The alternative is worse: 7 . . . Kf8 8 Ne5 cxd5 9 Bf4 $\pm$.

(o) This is an improvement over 6 d4 Ne7 7 dxc6 Nbxc6 8 d5 Nb4 9 Bc4 (Hebden–Henley, New York 1983) when 9 . . . Bf5 would be good for Black. The column is Illescas–Nunn, Dubai 1986.

(p) 4 . . . Bd6 is well playable. If then the sharp 5 Bc4, Black obtains the better game with 5 . . . Bxe5 6 fxe5 Nc6 7 e6 Bxe6 8 Bxe6 fxe6 9 Qh5† g6 10 Qg4 Nd4 11 Qxe4 Nf6, Delaney–Mortensen, Thessaloniki 1984. The column is Lutikov–Nikitin, Tbilisi 1959.

KING'S GAMBIT DECLINED

1 e4 e5 2 f4

	31	32	33	34	35	36
	Bc5..Qh4†(n)					
3	Nf3					g3
	d6(a)					Qe7
4	Nc3 ....c3					Nc3(o)
	Nf6		Nf6(f)			exf4(p)
5	Bc4		fxe5 ....d4			gxf4(q)
	Nc6		dxe5		exd4(k)	Qh4†
6	d3		d4 ....Nxe5		cxd4	Ke2
	Bg4.........a6(d)		exd4	Qe7(i)	Bb4†(l)	d5
7	Na4(b)	f5	cxd4	d4	Bd2	Nxd5
	Bb6(c)	h6(e)	Bb4†	Bd6	Bxd2†	Bg4†
8	Nxb6	Qe2	Bd2	Nf3(j)	Nbxd2	Nf3
	axb6	Bd7	Qe7	Nxe4	Qe7	Bxf3†
9	c3	Be3	Bd3(g)	Be2	Bd3	Kxf3
	0–0 =	Nd4 =	Nxe4(h)	0–0 =	Nd5(m)	Qh5†(r)

(a) 3 . . . Nc6, intending to play a gambit after 4 fxe5 d6, is handled simply by Zaitsev's 4 Nxe5 Nxe5 5 d4 Bxd4 6 Qxd4 ±.

(b) 7 h3 Bxf3 8 Qxf3 exf4 (8 . . . Nd4 is playable but riskier) 9 Bb5 (9 Bxf4 Nd4 and 9 Qxf4 Ne5 are worse) 0–0 =.

(c) Other possibilities are (A) 7 . . . Bxf3 8 Qxf3 Nd4 9 Qg3 and (B) 7 . . . Nd4 8 Nxc5 dxc5 9 c3. White has the edge in both cases.

(d) (A) 6 . . . Na5 7 f5 h6 8 Qe2 c6 9 Be3 =. (B) 6 . . . Ng4?! 7 Ng5 h6 8 f5 ±. (C) 6 . . . Be6 7 Bb5 a6 8 Bxc7† ±.

(e) 7 . . . Na5 deserves consideration. If 8 Bg5 then 8 . . . Nxc4 9 dxc4 Bb5 followed by capturing on c3. If 8 Nd5 Nxc4 9 Nxf6† gxf6 10 dxc4 Bd7 produces a complicated fight, Valvo–Sherwin, Boston 1964. The column is Tolush–Furman, Leningrad 1946.

(f) (A) On 4 . . . Bg4 either Marshall's maneuver 5 fxe5 dxe5 6 Qa4† or the simple 5 h3 gives White the better game. (B) 4 . . . f5 is another risky attempt best met by 5 fxe5 dxe5 6 d4 exd4 7 Bc4 (Reti).

(g) 9 e5 is the more usual move here, yet this sacrifice is very interesting.

(h) 10 Bxe4 Qxe4† 11 Kf2 Bxd2 12 Nbxd2 (So. Polgar–Flear, Brussels 1987); now 12 . . . Qd5 13 Re1 Be6 14 Re5 Qd6 (Flear) would produce a complicated struggle.

(i) 6 . . . 0–0 7 d4 Bd6 8 Nf3 Nxe4 9 Bd3 ∞ (Keres).

(j) 8 Nc4 Nxe4 9 Nxd6† Nxd6† is fine for Black, Prandstetter–Augustin, Czechoslovakia 1974. The column is Charousek–Janowski, Berlin 1897.

15

(k) 5 Bb6 6 fxe5 dxe5 7 Nxe5 0–0 8 Bg5 (8 Bc4 Qe8 9 Qf3 c5 =, Rellstab–Ahues, Bad Nauheim 1936) 8 . . . c5 9 dxc5 Qxd1† 10 Kxd1 Bc5 11 Bxf6 ±, So. Polgar–Sharif, Brussels, 1987.

(l) 6 . . . Bb6 7 Nc3 (7 e5 is worth a try) 7 . . . 0–0 8 e5 Ng4 (8 . . . dxe5 9 fxe5 Nd5 10 Bg5 is difficult for Black) 9 h3 Nh6 10 g4 Nc6 with chances for both sides, Filtser–Khachaturov, USSR 1965.

(m) If instead 9 . . . 0–0, not 10 0–0 Nd5!, but 10 Qe2 with a plus. After the text White also has a small plus.

(n) 2 . . . Nf6 3 fxe5 Nxe4 4 Nf3 Ng5 5 d4 Nxf3† 6 Qxf3 Qh4† 7 Qf2 Qxf2† 8 Kxf2 Nc6 9 c3 d6 10 exd6 Bxd6 11 Nd2 ±, Fischer–Wade, Vincovči 1968.

(o) 4 fxe5 d6 5 exd6 (5 Nc3 dxe5 6 d3 c6 =, Lundvall–Harding, Wijk aan Zee 1972) 5 . . . Qxe4† 6 Qe2 Qxe2† 7 Nxe2 Bd6 with complete equality, Robertson–O'Connell, London 1972.

(p) 4 . . . d6 is more solid. After 5 Nf3 Bg4 6 h3 Bxf3 7 Qxf3 Nf6 the game is equal, Milner-Barry–Keene, London 1969.

(q) For the bold, the gambit 5 d4 fxg3 6 Bf4 is attractive.

(r) 10 Kf2 Qxd1 11 Bb5† Kd8 12 Rxd1 c6 13 Bc4 cxd5 14 Bxd5 results in a complex, roughly even endgame, Stewart–Dobrev, Groningen 1984.

VIENNA GAME

1 e4 e5 2 Nc3

Diagram 4

T HE GOLDEN DAYS OF THE VIENNA GAME corresponded with the halcyon years of the city itself. It was the opening staple of many strong players, from Chigorin to Spielmann. But after World War I its popularity waned, as a more modern era of chess openings began. The 1940s and '50s saw a revival of the Vienna, due largely to Weaver Adams, who fashioned it into an ideology: "White to Play and Win." Otherwise it has only seen occasional use.

The Vienna is played with a view to a direct kingside attack. Weaver Adams wrote, "2 Nc3 conforms to most principles, develops naturally, prepares f4, prevents . . . d5, keeps the d1–h5 diagonal open, and fortifies the e-pawn." With such virtues there shouldn't be much wrong with the move; yet it fails to do one important thing: threaten something. This lack of impetus allows Black to develop naturally and equalize in a number of ways.

2 . . . Nf6 (cols. 1–12) is the most forceful defense. On 3 Bc4 (cols. 1–6) Black has a choice of defenses, but most interesting is the line 3 . . . Nxe4 and 5 . . . Nc6 (cols. 1–2), in which Black sacrifices the exchange, leading to complications that remain unsolved despite many years of testing. In cols. 3–6 Black seeks equality by more tranquil methods.

The positional line 3 g3 (cols. 7–8) has been used recently by Spassky and deserves attention.

3 f4 (cols. 9–12), a delayed King's Gambit, gives Black little trouble after 3 . . . d5!. White must be careful to avoid getting the worst of it.

Alternatives to 2 . . . Nf3 are considered in cols. 13–18. Against 2 . . . Nc6 White can play 3 f4 with a choice of gambits—the *Pierce* (col. 14), *Hamppe–Allgaier* (col. 15) or *Steinitz* (cols. 16–17). Black gets fine play against all of these, so 3 Bc4 (col. 13) is a sounder choice. 2 . . . Bc5 (col. 18) is unusual and probably allows White an edge.

17

VIENNA GAME

1 e4 e5 2 Nc3 Nf6 3 Bc4

	1	2	3	4	5	6
	Nxe4.............................			Nc6		Bc5
4	Qh5			d3(j)		d3
	Nd6			Na5.........Bb4		d6
5	Bb3(a)			Nge2	Bg5(m)	Bg5(p)
	Nc6		Be7	Nxc4(k)	h6	Be6(q)
6	Nb5(b)		Nf3(g)	dxc4	Bxf6(n)	Qd2
	g6		Nc6	d6	Bxc3†	Nbd7
7	Qf3		Nxe5	0–0	bxc3	Nge2
	f5		0–0	Be6	Qxf6	Bxc4
8	Qd5		0–0	b3	Ne2	dxc4
	Qe7(c)		Nd4	c6	d6	h6
9	Nxc7†		Nd5	Ng3(l)	Qd2(o)	Be3
	Kd8		Nxb3	g6	Be6	Qe7
10	Nxa8		axb3	h3	Bb5	Ng3
	b6		Ne8	h5	Qg5	Bxe3
11	d3 ....Nf3(e)		Qe2(h)	Qd3	Ng3	fxe3
	Bb7(d)	Bb7(f)	Nf6(i)	Be7 =	0–0 =	g6 =

(a) 5 Qxe5† Qe7 6 Qxe7† Bxe7 7 Bb3 Nf5 8 Nd5 Bd8 =, Suttles–Tarjan, Venice 1974.

(b) Weaver Adams' 6 d4 is met by 6 . . . Nxd4! 7 Nd5 Ne6 8 Qxe5 c6 9 Nf4 Qe7 10 Nc3 Nc5 11 0–0 Qxe5 12 Nxe5 Be7 13 Re1 Ne6 ∓. *Comments.*

(c) After 8 . . . Qf6 play is similar to the column, but worse for Black.

(d) 12 h4 f4 13 Qf3 Bh6 and Black has good compensation for his lost material. A recent game Wibe–Bryson, corr. 1985, continued 14 Qg4? (14 Bd5 is better) e4 15 Bxf4 exd3† 16 Kf1 Bxf4 17 Qxf4 Rf8 18 Qg3 Ne4! 19 Qc7† Ke8 20 Nf3 Qc5 21 Kg1 Rxf3 22 Kh2 Qh5 23 Rhf1 Nd4 24 Rae1 d2 25 Resigns.

(e) 11 Nxb6 axb6 12 d3 Bb7 13 Qf3 Nd4 14 Qh3 g5 (better than 14 . . . e4) allows Black good attacking chances.

(f) 12 d4 Nxd4 13 Bg5 Nxf3† 14 Qxf3 Qxg5 15 Bd5 e4 16 Qb3 Ba6 produces a sharp position with chances for both sides.

(g) (A) 6 Qxe5 0–0 7 d4 Nc6 is completely equal, McCormick–Hartels, USA 1959. (B) 6 d3?! Nc6 7 Nf3 g6 8 Qh3 Nf5 with a big advantage in Jaffe–Alekhine, Carlsbad 1911.

(h) 11 d4 d6 12 Nf3 Be6 = (Alekhine).

(i) 12 Nxe7† Qxe7 13 Re1 d6 14 Nc4 Qxe2 15 Rxe2 Bf5 =.

(j) 4 f4 Nxe4 5 Nf3 can be met either by 5 . . . Nd6 (when neither 6 Bb3 nor 6 Bd5 give White anything) or 5 . . . Nxc3 6 dxc3 Qe7 with sharp play that is probably good for Black, Kuindzi–Razuvaev, USSR 1973.

(k) (A) 5 . . . Be7 6 0–0 0–0 7 a4 Nxc4 8 dxc4 d6 $\pm$, Vogt–Mikhalchishin, Baku 1980. (B) 5 . . . c6 6 a3 Nxc4 7 dxc4 d6 8 Qd3 Be7 is equal, Ivanović–Vl. Kovačević, Bugojno 1984.

(l) After 9 Qd3 Be7 10 Bg5 h6 11 Bxf6 Bxf6 12 Rad1 (Schlechter–Steinitz, Cologne 1898) Black can gain the upper hand with 12 . . . Qa5!. The column is Westerinen–Boey, Siegen 1970.

(m) 5 Ne2 d5 6 exd5 Nxd5 7 Bxd5 Qxd5 8 0–0 Qd8 (or 8 . . . Qa5) is equal.

(n) It's best to exchange the bishop, since 6 Bh4 d6 7 Ne2 Be6 8 0–0 g5 favors Black.

(o) 9 0–0 g5 10 d4 Ne7 11 Rb1 Ng6 equalizes (Alekhine). The column is Bronstein–Tal, Amsterdam 1964.

(p) Many moves are plausible here—5 Na4, 5 Be3 and Larsen's 5 Qf3!?.

(q) 5 . . . h6 6 Be3 Bxe3 7 fxe3 c6 was about equal, Larsen–Dehmelt, New York 1986. The column is Khavin–Sokolsky, USSR 1944.

VIENNA GAME

1 e4 e5 2 Nc3 Nf6

	7	8	9	10	11	12
3	g3 . . . . .f4 (Vienna Gambit)					
	d5 . . . . Bc5(e)		d5			
4	exd5	Bg2	fxe5(g)			
	Nxd5	0–0(f)	Nxe4			
5	Bg2	d3	Nf3 . . . . .d3 . . . . .Qf3			
	Nxc3(a)	Re8	Be7 . . . . Bg4		Nxc3(l)	f5
6	bxc3	Nge2	d4(h)	Qe2(j)	bxc3	d3
	Bd6(b)	c6	0–0	Ng5	d4(m)	Nxc3
7	Nf3(c)	0–0	Bd3	h4(k)	Nf3	bxc3
	0–0	d5	f5	Nxf3†	Nc6(n)	d4
8	0–0	exd5	exf6	gxf3	cxd4	Qg3(p)
	Nd7	Nxd5	Bxf6	Be6	Bb4†	Nc6
9	d3	Kh1	0–0	d4	Bd2	Be2
	Rb8	Bg4	Nc6	Nc6	Bxd2†	Be6
10	a4	h3	Nxe4	Be3	Qxd2	Bf3
	b6(d)	Be6 =	dxe4(i)	Be7 =	Nxd4(o)	Qd7(q)

(a) 5 . . . Be6 6 Nf3 Nc6 7 0–0 Be7 8 Re1 Bf6 9 Ne4 ±, Smyslov–Polugaevsky, USSR 1961.

(b) (A) 6 . . . Be7 7 Nf3 Nc6 8 0–0 0–0 9 Re1 Bf6 and now 10 Rb1 would give White the edge, Soltis–Ljubojević, New York 1985. (B) 6 . . . Nc6 and (C) 6 . . . Nd7 are also possible.

(c) 7 Ne2 0–0 8 0–0 c6 9 d3 Nd7 10 f4 exf4 11 Bxf4 =, Spassky–Karpov, Tilburg 1979.

(d) After 11 a5 Bb7 12 axb6 the game Benko–Smyslov, Las Palmas 1971, was equal and agreed a "grandmaster draw."

(e) An enterprising try is (A) 3 . . . h5. After 4 Nf3 h4 5 Nxh4 Rxh4 6 gxh4 Qxh4 Black had play for the exchange, Dreev–Khalifman, USSR 1984. (B) 3 . . . Bb4 and (C) 3 . . . c6 are also playable here.

(f) 5 . . . Nc6 6 Nf3 d6 7 d3 a6 8 0–0 0–0 with just a tiny edge for White, Vorotnikov–Havsky, USSR 1973. The column is Portisch–Toran, Malaga 1961.

(g) Steinitz's 4 d3 should be met by 4 . . . exf4 5 exd5 (5 Bxf4 Bb4 6 exd5 Nxd5 7 Bd2 Bxc3 8 bxc3 0–0 [Spielmann–Lasker, St. Petersburg 1909] and 5 e5 d4! both favor Black) 5 . . . Bb4 with good play.

(h) (A) 6 d3 Nxc3 7 bxc3 0–0 8 c4 f6! 9 Be3 fxe5 10 Nxe5 Bf5 =, Spielmann–Kaufman, 1917. (B) 6 Qe2 f5! or 6 . . . Nxc3 7 dxc3 c5! Comments.

(i) After 11 Bxe4 Nxd4 12 Ng5 Bf5 13 c3 (13 Bxf5 Nxf5 14 Ne6 Qxd1 15 Rxd1 Rfe8 16 Nxc7 Rad8 ∓,) 13 . . . Bxg5 with an equal position, Spielmann–Reti, Vienna 1922.

(j) (A) 6 Be2 Nc6 7 d3 Bxf3! is dangerous for White, Wolf–Vidmar, Carlsbad 1907. (B) 6 d3 Nxc3 7 bxc3 Be7 =.

20

(k) 7 d4 is more thematic, but after 7 . . . Nxf3† 8 gxf3 Be6 the game is also equal.

(l) (A) 5 . . . Qh4†?! 6 g3 Nxg3 7 Nf3 Qh5 8 Nxd5 is not recommended for Black. (B) A sharp line is 5 . . . Bb4 6 dxe4 Qh4† 7 Ke2 Bxc3 8 bxc3 Bg4† 9 Nf3 dxe4 10 Qd4, but White should be better.

(m) Besides the text Black can play simply 6 . . . Be7 or 6 . . . c5 and achieve a reasonable position.

(n) 7 . . . dxc3 8 Be2 Be7 9 0–0 Be6 10 Qe1 Nc6 11 Qxc3 0–0 is about equal, Sax–Plaskett, Lugano 1986.

(o) After 11 c3 Nxf3† 12 gxf3 f6! Black held the advantage in Terentiev–Kaidanov, USSR 1984.

(p) 8 Bd2 bxc3 9 Bxc3 Bb4! 10 Bxb4 Qh4† ∓, Spielmann–Duras, Coburg 1904.

(q) 11 Ne2 Bc5 12 c4 0–0 13 0–0 Bxc4 and Black is better, Spielmann–Romanovsky, Moscow 1925.

VIENNA GAME

1 e4 e5 2 Nc3

	13	Pierce Gambit 14	Hamppe–Allgaier Gambit 15	Steinitz Gambit 16	17	18
	Nc6					Bc5
3	Bc4 Bc5(a)	f4 exf4(e)				Nf3(n) d6
4	Qg4 g6(b)	Nf3 g5(f)		d4 Qh4†		d4(o) exd4
5	Qf3 Nf6	d4 g4	h4 g4	Ke2 d6	d5	Nxd4 Nf6
6	Nge2 d6(c)	Bc4(g) gxf3	Ng5 h6(i)	Nf3 Bg4	exd5 Bg4†	Bg5 h6
7	d3 Bg4	0–0 d5	Nxf7 Kxf7	Bxf4(k) 0–0–0(l)	Nf3 0–0–0	Bh4 Nc6
8	Qg3 h6	exd5 Bg4!	d4(j) d5	Ke3 Qh5	dxc6 Bc5	Nxc6 bxc6
9	f4 Qe7	Qd2 Nce7(h)	Bxf4 Bb4	Be2 g5!	Qe1 Qh5	Bd3 Qe7
10	Nd5 Nxd5(d)	Qxf4 Qd7 ∓	Be2 Bxc3† ∓	Nxg5 Nf6 ∓	cxb7† Kb8(m)	0–0 g5(p)

(a) 3 ... f5 is provocative. Kivisto–Pyhala, Pori 1986, continued 4 exf5 (4 d3 is better) 4 ... Nf6 5 d3 Bb4 6 Bg5 d5 7 Bxf6 gxf6 8 Qh5† Ke7 9 Bb3 Nd4 with advantage to Black.

(b) Other moves: (A) 4 ... Kf8 5 Qf3 Nf6 6 Nge2 d6 7 d3 ±, Hennings–Korchnoi, Sarajevo 1969; (B) 4 ... Qf6 5 Nd5! Qxf2† 6 Kd1 and neither 6 ... Kf8 7 Nh3 Qd4 8 d3 ±, Mieses–Chigorin, Ostend 1906, nor 6 ... Nf6 7 Qxg7 Nxd5 8 Qxh8† Bf8 (Fidelity S.2. computer–Shirazi, USA 1986) 9 Qg8 ±, solves Black's problems.

(c) Keres suggested the regrouping 6 ... Bf8 followed by ... Bg7. As the column is better for White, this is worth a try.

(d) After 11 Qxg4 White held a slight advantage in Larsen–Portisch, Santa Monica 1966.

(e) 3 ... Bc5 is interesting. White can accept the gambit with 4 fxe5 d6 5 exd6 Qxd6 6 Nf3 Bg4 ∞, or play 4 Nf3 forcing Black into the King's Gambit Declined where White retains the option of playing his Bishop to c4 or b5.

(f) 4 ... Nf6 and 4 ... Be7 are playable alternatives, but the text is more incisive.

(g) 6 Ne5 Nxe5 7 dxe5 Qh4† is clearly better for Black, L. Paulsen–Gunsberg, Breslau 1889.

(h) After 9 ... Bg7 10 Qxf4 Bxd4† 11 Kh1 Qh4 12 dxc6 fxg2† 13 Kxg2 0–0–0 (Eger–Weinitsch, corr. 1985) 14 cxb7† White has the more dangerous attack.

(i) 6 ... d6?! 7 d4 h6 8 Nxf7 Kxf7 9 Bc4† Kg7 10 Bxf4 Nf6 is a wild, unclear game, Hellers–Akesson, Sweden 1985. It is better for Black to force the sacrifice immediately.

(j) 8 Bc4† d5 9 Bxd5† Kg7 10 d4 f3 also leaves Black on top. White's sacrifice creates too little compensation for the lost material.

(k) 7 Nd5 0–0–0 8 Kd3 Qh6 9 Bxf4 Qh5 10 c4 f5 leaves Black with a large plus, Kavalek–Stein, Tel Aviv 1964.

(l) 7 ... f5 is also good. The column is Barle–Portisch, Portorož/Ljubljana 1974.

(m) Black has a strong attack, but it is not clear who is better after 11 Kd2 or 11 Bxf4.

(n) 3 Qg4 Nf6 4 Qxg7 Rg8 5 Qh6 Bxf2!† is bad for White.

(o) 4 Na4 Bb6 5 Nxb6 axb6 6 d4 exd4 7 Qxd4 Qf6 =, Kan–Capablanca, Moscow 1936.

(p) Not 10 ... Qe5 11 Na4 Bb6 12 Bg3 ±, Horowitz–Kupchik, Syracuse 1934. After 10 ... g5 Larsen rates White as slightly better.

RUY LOPEZ

1 e4 e5 2 Nf3 Nc6 3 Bb5

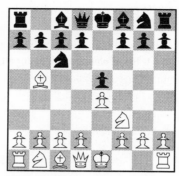

Diagram 5

T HIS OPENING, HALF A MILLENNIUM OLD, represents the classic play of the game of chess. It was first mentioned in the historic Göttingen manuscript of 1490, but the Spanish priest Ruy Lopez, in his *Libro del Ajedrez* of 1561, was the first to treat the opening systematically. Hence the opening bears his name, although in other languages it is usually called "Spanish Game."

The Ruy Lopez came to the fore in the late nineteenth century, when chess strategy reached a deeper level than the sharp gambits of the romantic era. Early attacks tested Black's defenses only tactically; after several accurate moves Black could generally attain equality. The Ruy Lopez, instead of aiming a quick blow at the weak f7 point, puts pressure on the Black center with a once-removed attack on the black e-pawn. Though this pawn is not in immediate danger, Black must patiently defend for a long while, which explains the opening's nickname, "Spanish torture."

Over the last century chess thinkers have searched for good defenses for Black to combat the Ruy Lopez, producing many deeply analyzed variations. The result is a bitter struggle for the center which commonly spreads to attack against the kings. The long analyses of variations in many lines have turned some players away from this opening, yet those who choose it will reach rich and fascinating positions.

I. Systems without 3 . . . a6 (cols. 1–33) are not as common, since 3 . . . a6 usually gives Black more options. Nonetheless, many of these systems are routinely played by grandmasters.
    A. The CORDEL (or *Classical*) DEFENSE, 3 . . . Bc5 (cols. 1–6) begins with a logical developing move. Though the oldest defense to the Ruy, it still sees use today. 4 c3 f5 (cols. 1–2) is a very sharp line.
    B. The BERLIN DEFENSE, 3 . . . Nf6 (cols. 7–12), has been faithfully played

24

by GM Arthur Bisguier. This is a solid opening, but it tends to leave Black with less scope for maneuvering.

C. The COZIO DEFENSE, 3 . . . Nge7 (cols. 13–15), is rarely seen in modern play, and then usually in conjunction with . . . g6.

D. BIRD'S DEFENSE, 3 . . . Nd4 (cols. 16–18), is experiencing a brief renaissance. The idea is to capitalize at once on 3 Bb5. It is doubtful, however, that Black can achieve equality against best play.

E. The SCHLIEMANN DEFENSE (also called the *Jaenisch Gambit*), 3 . . . f5 (cols. 19–23), is frequently employed by players looking for a real slugfest. Black aims to open the f-file for the purpose of attack, in the course of which he frequently sacrifices a pawn or two. The opening is probably not quite sound, but proving this over the board is no easy matter. White can play safe with 4 d3 (col. 23), forgoing the win of material as in other lines. Column 24 is the Schliemann Deferred (3 . . . a6 4 Ba4 f5).

F. The OLD STEINITZ DEFENSE, 3 . . . d6 (cols. 25–29), gives Black a cramped but solid game. Black defends his center in the most straightforward manner, simply leaving White a little freer. While playable, this defense is considered archaic.

G. 3 . . . g6 (cols. 31–33) is currently in vogue, especially the line 4 c3 a6 (col. 32). Black solidifies the kingside and tries to keep the position closed.

II. Morphy's 3 . . . a6 gives Black more elbow room. If White plays 4 Ba4 (as usual), then Black can always break the pin with . . . b5.

A. The EXCHANGE VARIATION, 4 Bxc6 (cols. 34–42), has the strategic idea of obtaining a kingside pawn majority after playing d4 and exchanging for Black's e-pawn. White would have an endgame edge because Black's queenside pawn majority would be difficult to mobilize. Fischer was very successful with this variation in the 1960's. However, Black's two bishops and easy development give him play, and the variation is no longer considered dangerous.

The following CLOSED SYSTEMS constitute the main lines of defense against the Ruy Lopez.

Diagram 6

25

B. The FIANCHETTO VARIATION, 9 h3 (see diagram) Bb7 10 d4 Re8 (cols. 43–48), is currently much in use, being the favorite defense of ex-World Champion Karpov. Black develops all his pieces before moving more pawns. This variation has similarities with the Breyer and Smyslov variations, into which it can transpose.

C. In the BREYER VARIATION, 9 h3 Nb8 (cols. 49–54), Black redevelops the queen's knight at d7, centralizing all his pieces and maintaining control of the center. This allows White time to choose his plan of play on the kingside, queenside or both. Column 49 is probably White's best line.

D. The SMYSLOV VARIATION, 9 h3 h6 (cols. 55–60), is slightly out of fashion now, but for no distinct reason.

E. The CHIGORIN VARIATION, 9 h3 Na5 10 Bc2 c5 (cols. 61–78), is still the most common system. Black gains a tempo attacking the white bishop and puts pressure on d4. He has play on the c-file in the lines following . . . cxd4 (cols. 61–66), but he opens the position for White, too. In Keres's line (cols. 74–76) the strange-looking 11 . . . Nd7 is holding up well. Probably still best is Fischer's 12 dxc5 (col. 76).

Playing 9 d4 without the preparatory h3 is seen in cols. 85–88. Black holds his own in these lines. Anti-Marshall lines and less common moves are covered in cols. 91–96. Black has little to fear, except that 8 a4 (cols. 92–93) requires good defense.

The MARSHALL (COUNTER) ATTACK (cols. 97–102) is a remarkable pawn sacrifice (8 . . . d5!) introduced by Frank Marshall against Capablanca in New York 1918. New ideas against it continue to be introduced, but Black seems to remain comfortable. Black's compensation for the pawn is mostly positional—based on creating weaknesses in the White kingside and slowing White's development—hence the gambit is hard to refute.

Unusual sixth moves including the *Worrall Attack* (6 Qe2), the *Center Variation* (6 d4) and the *Exchange Variation Doubly Deferred* (6 Bxc6) are seen in cols. 103–114. Theoretically Black is secure in these variations, but they are at least worth some surprise value.

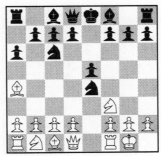

Diagram 7

III. The OPEN DEFENSE, 3 . . . a6 4 Ba4 Nf6 5 0–0 Nxe4 (cols. 115–138), is a major branch of the Ruy Lopez. (See diagram.) It is logical for Black to take the unprotected pawn, with the idea that while White is recapturing it Black gets a stake in the center. The chief disadvantage is that Black's position becomes a trifle loose. Korchnoi has been a champion of the Open Defense.

White's main response is 6 d4 b5 7 Bb3 d5 8 dxe5 Be6 9 c3 (cols. 115–126). Black then has two main replies: (1) 9 . . . Bc5 (cols. 115–120) offers Black tactical mobility and pressure on f2, although it removes the bishop from the defense of the kingside. Column 118 (11 . . . Nxf2), the *Dilworth Attack,* is a promising line for Black. (2) 9 . . . Be7 (cols. 121–126) is safe but perhaps too passive, as White obtains some advantage with 10 Nbd2 (cols. 121–122).

The *Howell Attack,* 9 Qe2 (cols. 127–130), is an aggressive alternative. White seeks to cause trouble on the d-file with 10 Rd1. Play becomes tactical and Black must be careful. 9 Nbd2 (cols. 131–132) is the current fashion. White immediately attacks Black's strong knight on e4. White seems to maintain a small advantage. Less common play for both sides is seen in cols. 133–138. Generally these moves are inferior to the main lines. In col. 137 Black tries to keep the pawn he took on move 5 but slips into an inferior endgame. Col. 138 is innocuous.

The *Counterthrust Variation* with an earlier 5 . . . b5 is covered in cols. 139–144 and has its even quicker parallel in the *Accelerated Counterthrust Variation* (see cols. 154–156).

Apparently within the normal course, yet unusual, are the variations starting with 3 . . . a6 4 Ba4 Nf6 covered in cols. 145–153.

Diagram 8

The compact complex of THE MODERN STEINITZ DEFENSE, 3 . . . a6 4 Ba4 d6 is shown in cols. 157–174. (See diagram.) The addition of the moves 3 . . . a6 4 Ba4 makes the Old Steinitz Defense much more interesting (see cols. 25–29). Some of the characteristics in these defenses are the same, but the ability to break the pin on the knight with . . . b5 allows more dynamic possibilities.

The replies 5 0–0, 5 Bxc6†, 5 c4, and 5 d4 are given in cols. 157–162. The first of these two are no worse than the main line, 5 c3, but are not played as much.

The *Siesta Variation*, 5 c3 f5 (cols. 163–168), produces wild play. White's best response is seen in col. 166.

In the variations arising from 5 c3 Bd7 6 d4 (cols. 169–174), Black follows a strong-point strategy, maintaining firm control of e5. The positions take on a closed nature similar to those in the King's Indian Defense. Some may be arrived at from the move 3 . . . g6.

RUY LOPEZ

Cordel's (Classical) Defense

1 e4 e5 2 Nf3 Nc6 3 Bb5 Bc5

	1	2	3	4	5	6
4	c3					.0–0
	f5		Nge7	Nf6		Qf6(p)
5	d4(a)	0–0!(i)		d4	0–0	c3
	fxe4	Bb6		exd4(j)	0–0(m)	Nge7
6	Bxc6		d4	e5	d4	Re1
	dxc6(b)		exd4	Ne4	Bb6	h6
7	Nfd2.......Nxe5		cxd4	0–0	Bg5(n)	d4
	Bd6(c)	Bd6	d5	d5(k)	h6	Bb6
8	dxe5	Qh5†	exd5	Nxd4(l)	Bh4	Na3
	e3	g6	Nxd5	0–0	d6	0–0
9	exd6(d)	Qe2(f)	Re1†	f3	a4	Nc4 ±
	exd2†	Qh4(g)	Be6	Ng5	a5	
10	Nxd2	h3	Bg5 ±	Be3	Qd3	
	Qxd6(e)	Be6(h)		f6 ∞	exd4(o)	

(a) 5 exf5?! e4 6 d4 exf3 7 dxc5 Qe7† 8 Be3 fxg2 9 Rg1 Nf6 =, Vasiukov–Arsenyev, Rostov 1962.

(b) 6 ... exf3 7 Bxf3 exd4 8 0–0! Nf6 9 Re1† is good for White, Torre–Tatai, Haifa 1976.

(c) A very tricky move is 7 ... Qg5?! 8 dxc5 Nf6 (8 ... Qxg2 9 Qh5†) when White must play carefully. On the natural 9 0–0 Bh3 10 g3 then 10 ... 0–0–0! gives Black a big attack. Best is 9 Qe2! Qxg2 10 Qf1 Qg4 11 Nc4 Qh5 12 Be3 Be6 13 Nbd2 0–0–0 14 Qg2 when Black does not have enough for the piece, de Firmian–Rodgers, Philadelphia 1986.

(d) 9 fxe3 Bc5 10 Qh5† g6 11 Qf3 also gives White an edge.

(e) 11 0–0 Be6 12 Qh5† ±, Stern–Snyder, corr. 1978.

(f) An old line is 9 Nxg6?! Nf6 10 Qh6 Rg8 11 Ne5 Qe7 12 Bg5 Bxe5 13 dxe5 Ng4 14 Qh5† Qf7 = (Tarrasch).

(g) 9 ... Bf5 10 Bf4 Nf6 11 Nd2 0–0 12 0–0 Qe7 13 f3 exf3 14 Ndxf3 and White has a grip in the center, Mestel–Plaskett, Brighton 1984.

(h) 11 Nd2 Bxe5 12 dxe5 Qg5 13 0–0 Bxh3 14 Qxe4 ±, Vasiukov–Miagmasuren, Havana 1967.

(i) 5 d4 exd4 6 cxd4 Bb4† 7 Bd2 Bxd2† 8 Qxd2 a6! 9 Ba4 d5 10 exd5 Qxd5 11 Nc3 Qe6† 12 Kf1 Qc4† =, Alekhine–Bogolyubov, St. Petersburg 1913.

(j) 5 ... Bb6 6 dxe5 (6 Nxe5 Nxe5 7 dxe5 Nxe4 8 Qg4 Bxf2† 9 Ke2 Qh4 10 Qxg7 Rf8 11 Nd2 Nxd2 12 Bxd2 Bc5 13 Rhf1 [Short–Gulko, Linares 1989] 13 ... Qe4† 14 Kd1 Qg6 =) 6 ... Nxe4 7 Qe2 d5 8 exd6 0–0 9 dxc7 Bxc7 10 0–0 Re8 11 Be3 Bg4 12 Nbd2 Nxd2 13 Qxd2 Qf6 with play for the pawn, Ivanchuk–Gulko, Linares 1989.

(k) On 7 . . . dxc3 8 Qd5 is very strong.

(l) 8 exd6 0–0! 9 dxc7 Qxc7 10 cxd4 Nxd4! 11 Nxd4 Qb6 12 Bd3 Nxf2 with excellent chances for Black, Hesse–Beyen, corr. 1975.

(m) 5 . . . Nxe4?! 6 Qe2 f5 7 d3 is bad for Black.

(n) (A) 7 Bxc6 dxc6 8 Nxe5 Nxe4 = , O'Kelly–Karaklajić, Bognor Regis 1960. (B) 7 Re1 exd4 8 cxd4 d5 9 e5 Ne4 10 Nc3 Bg4 11 Bxc6 bxc6 12 Nxe4 dxe4 13 Rxe4 Bxf3 14 Qxf3 Bxd4 = , Unzicker–Fischer, Leipzig 1960.

(o) 11 Bxc6! bxc6 12 Nxd4 gives White the edge, Kavalek–Spassky, Solingen 1977.

(p) (A) 4 . . . Nf6 transposes to the Berlin Defense (col. 7). (B) 4 . . . Nd4 5 b4! (Zaitsev) Bxb4 6 Nxd4 exd4 7 Bb2 ±. (C) 4 . . . d6 5 c3 Bd7 6 d4 Bb6 7 Bg5 ±.

RUY LOPEZ

Berlin Defense

1 e4 e5 2 Nf3 Nc6 3 Bb5 Nf6

	7	8	9	10	11	12
4	0–0				Qe2	d4(q)
	Bc5	Nxe4			Be7!(m)	exd4(r)
5	Nxe5(a)	d4		Re1	c3	e5
	Nxe5(b)	Nd6	Be7	Nd6!(k)	0–0	Ne4
6	d4	Bxc6(d)	Qe2	Nxe5	Bxc6(n)	0–0
	a6!	dxc6	Nd6	Be7(l)	bxc6(o)	a6
7	Be2(c)	dxe5	Bxc6	Bd3	Nxe5	Bxc6(s)
	Ba7	Nf5(e)	bxc6	0–0	Re8	dxc6
8	dxe5	Qxd8†	dxe5	Nc3	0–0	Qe2
	Nxe4	Kxd8	Nb7(h)	Nxe5	Bd6	Bf5
9	Bd3	b3(f)	Bf4(i)	Rxe5	f4	Rd1
	Qh4	h6	0–0	Bf6	Bxe5	Bc5
10	Qf3	Nc3	Nc3	Re3	fxe5	Be3
	d5	Be6	Nc5	g6	Rxe5	Qe7
11	exd6	Bb2	Ne4	b3	d3	Nxd4
	Nxd6 $\mp$	Kc8(g)	Ne6(j)	Bd4 =	Ba6(p)	Bxd4 =

(a) 5 c3 transposes to column 5.

(b) On 5 . . . Nxe4 6 Qe2 Nxe5 7 Qxe4 Qe7 8 d4 Nc6 White can play a slightly better ending with 9 Qxe7† Bxe7 10 c3 or the complicated 9 Qg4 h5 10 Qxg7 Bxd4 ∞.

(c) A better try is 7 Ba4 Nxe4 8 Qe2 Be7 9 Qxe4 Ng6 10 c4 (10 f4 0–0 11 f5 d5 12 Qd3 Nh4 13 g3 c5 14 dxc5 Bxc5† 15 Kh1 Qa5 ∞, Zapata–Torre, Thessaloniki 1988) 10 . . . 0–0 11 Nc3 d6 12 Nd5 with a small edge, de Firmian–Fishbein, New York 1989. The column is Chandler–Spassky, London 1984.

(d) Amusing is 6 dxe5 Nxb5 7 a4 winning back the knight. After 7 . . . Nbd4 8 Nxd4 Nxd4 9 Qxd4 d5 Black is equal, Suetin–Bannik, Vladimir 1960.

(e) Bisguier has often played 7 . . . Ne4, yet Gulko–Reshevsky, Vilnius 1978, continued 8 Qe2 Nc5 (8 . . . Bf5 9 Rd1 Qc8 10 Rd4!, Lobron–Lombardy, New York 1987) 9 Be3 Bg4 10 Nc3 Qe7 11 Rfe1 with an edge for White.

(f) Also giving White a slightly better ending is 9 Nc3 Ke8 10 Ne2 Be6 11 Nf4 Bd5 12 Nxd5, Fischer–Bisguier, US Chp. 1963.

(g) 12 Ne2 Bd5 13 Nd2 c5 14 Nf4 $\pm$, Tseshkovsky–Romanishin, USSR Chp. 1976.

(h) 8 . . . Nf5 9 Qe4 g6 10 b3 0–0 11 Bb2 Bb7 12 Nbd2 is better for White, Morović–Spassky, New York 1987.

(i) Another good plan is 9 Nc3 0–0 10 Re1 Nc5 11 Nd4 Ne6 12 Be3.

(j) 12 Bg3 f5 13 exf6 Bxf6 14 c3 Be7 15 Rad1 gives White more firepower in the center, de Firmian–Knežević, Reykjavik 1984.

(k) 5 . . . Nf6 6 Nxe5 Be7?! (6 . . . Nxe5 $\pm$) 7 d4 0–0 8 Nc3 leaves Black in a bind, Müller–Behting, Riga 1899.

(l) Also reasonable is 6 . . . Nxe5 7 Rxe5† Be7. The column is Sherwin–Bisguier, US Chp. 1962.

(m) 4 . . . d6 allows 5 d4 exd4 6 e5! dxe5 7 Nxe5 with some advantage, A. Ivanov–Romanishin, USSR Chp. 1980.

(n) It is probably better to play 6 d4 exd4 7 cxd4 d5 8 e5 Ne4 9 0–0.

(o) In Kupreichik–Levin, Kiev 1976, Black achieved equality with 6 . . . dxc6 7 Nxe5 Bd6 8 d4 c5 9 0–0 Re8 10 f4 cxd4 11 cxd4 c5.

(p) 12 c4 d5 13 Nc3 dxe4 14 dxe4 Qd4†, Dzindzichashvili–Shamkovich, New York 1983. Black is better.

(q) In the last century 4 d3 was commonly seen. This is playable, of course, but it does not set Black any problems. 4 . . . d6 5 c3 and either 5 . . . Be7 or 5 . . . g6! Gives Black an equal game.

(r) 4 . . . Nxe4 5 0–0 transposes to 4 0–0 Nxe4 5 d4 (col. 2).

(s) 7 Ba4 transposes to col. 106. Column 12 is Kuindzi–Tseitlin, USSR 1977.

RUY LOPEZ

1 e4 e5 2 Nf3 Nc6 3 Bb5

	13	14	15	16	17	18
	Nge7 (Cozio Defense) . . . . Nd4 (Bird's Defense)					
4	d4	0–0	c3	Nxd4		Bc4(o)
	exd4	g6(c)	a6	exd4		Bc5(p)
5	Nxd4	c3	Ba4	0–0		Nxd4
	g6(a)	Bg7	b5(f)	Bc5	c6	Bxd4
6	Nc3(b)	d4	Bb3	d3(i)	Bc4(l)	c3
	Bg7	exd4	d5	c6	Nf6	Bb6
7	Be3	cxd4	d3(g)	Bc4(j)	Re1	d4
	0–0	d5	f6	d5	d6	Qh4
8	Qd2	exd5	Nbd2	exd5	c3	0–0
	d5	Nxd5	Be6	cxd5	Ng4	Nf6
9	0–0–0	Bg5	0–0	Bb5†	h3	Nd2
	dxe4	Qd6	Ng6	Bd7	Ne5	d6
10	Nxe4	Qe2†(d)	a4	Bxd7†	d3!(m)	Nf3
	Nxd4	Be6	b4	Qxd7	Nxc4	Qh5
11	Bxd4	Nbd2	a5	Nd2	dxc4	Ng5
	Qxd4 =	0–0(e)	Be7(h)	Ne7(k)	dxc3(n)	Qxd1 ±

(a) 5 . . . Nxd4 6 Qxd4 Nc6 7 Qd5 Nb4 8 Qb3 Bc5 9 a3 Nc6 10 Qg3 0–0 11 Bg5 f6 12 Bc4† with a minimal advantage.

(b) 6 Nxc6 Nxc6 7 Bxc6 bxc6 8 Qd4 f6 and Black is no worse according to Larsen. The column is analysis by Mechkarov.

(c) 4 . . . Ng6 5 d4 exd4 6 Nxd4 Bc5 7 Nb3 Bb6 8 Nc3 is a little better for White, Dzindzichashvili–Larsen, Tilburg 1978.

(d) White can get a small advantage with 10 Re1† Be6 11 Nc3 0–0 12 Ne4 Qb4 13 Bxc6† bxc6 14 Qc1, Minić-Dely, Belgrade 1968.

(e) Timman–Spassky, Bugojno 1986, which continued 12 Ne4 Qb4 13 a3 Qa5 14 Bxc6 bxc6 15 Ne5?! (With 15 Rac1 the game would be level. Spassky now gets the opportunity to play aggressively, disrupting White's pieces.) 15 . . . Rae8 16 Rac1 f6! 17 Nxc6 Qb6 18 Bd2 Bd7 19 Nb4 Qxd4 20 Rc4 Qe5 21 Nd3 Qe7 22 Qf3 Bb5 23 Rd4 c6 24 Ng3 Qd8 25 a4 Ba6 26 Nb4 Qb6 27 Rxd5 (For 10 moves White has saved all his pieces, but finally he must lose the exchange.) 27 . . . cxd5 28 Nxa6 Qxa6 29 Qxd5† Qe6 30 Qxe6† Rxe6 31 Rc1 f5 32 b4 f4 33 Nf1 Bd4 34 Rc4 Re4 35 Kh1 Rfe8 36 h3 Bxf2 37 Rc6 Re1! 38 Bxe1 Rxe1 39 g4 f3 40 Rc8† Kf7 41 Resigns.

(f) Safer is 5 . . . d6 or 5 . . . g6 which gives White only a slight edge.

(g) 7 exd5 Nxd5 8 d4 exd4 9 Nxd4 Nxd4 10 Qxd4 Be6 was equal in Medlev–Morphy, London 1858.

(h) 12 Ba4 with a big advantage, Ornstein–Rantanen, Norway 1978.

(i) 6 Qh5!? Qe7 7 d3 Nf6 8 Qh4 c6 (Kuzmin–Malanyuk, USSR 1986) and now 9 Ba4 looks promising.

(j) 7 Ba4 Ne7 8 Nd2 d5 9 exd5 Nxd5 10 Re1† Be6 =, Karpov–Kupreichik, Leningrad 1976.

(k) 12 Nb3 Bb6 13 Bg5 f6 14 Bd2 a5 with equal chances, Rohde–Christiansen, US Chp. 1986.

(l) 6 Ba4 Nf6 7 c3 Be7 8 d3 0–0!? 9 cxd4 d5 is an interesting variation shown by McCormick and Soltis.

(m) Very dangerous for White is 10 Bf1?! d3 11 f4 Qd6† 12 Kh1 h5! threatening 13 . . . Bg4, Milić–Nikolać, Yugoslavia 1951.

(n) 12 Nxc3 Be7 13 Bf4, Matanović–Gliksman, Zagreb 1967. Despite Black's two bishops, White is better due to his extra space and the target to attack on d6.

(o) 4 Ba4 Bc5 5 0–0 Nxf3† 6 Qxf3 Ne7 7 d3 0–0 8 Be3 Bb6 =, Reti–Spielmann, Vienna 1913.

(p) 4 . . . Nxf3† 5 Qxf3 Qf6 6 Qg3 d6 7 Nc3 c6 8 0–0 Be6 and White has only a small advantage (Yudovich). The column is Böök–Prins, Munich 1936.

RUY LOPEZ

Schliemann Defense

1 e4 e5 2 Nf3 Nc6 3 Bb5

	19	20	21	22	23	24
	f5.......	....	....	....	....	a6
4	Nc3	....	....	d4	d3	Ba4
	fxe4	....	Nd4(h)	fxe4	fxe4	f5
5	Nxe4		exf5(i)	Nxe5	dxe4	d4!
	d5	Nf6	Nf6(j)	Nxe5	Nf6	exd4
6	Nxe5(a)	Qe2(e)	Nxe5	dxe5	Bg5(o)	e5
	dxe4	d5	Bc5	c6	Bc5	Bc5
7	Nxc6	Nxf6†	0–0	Nc3(l)	Nc3	0–0
	Qd5(b)	gxf6	0–0	cxb5(m)	d6	Nge7
8	c4	d4	Nf3	Nxe4	0–0	c3(q)
	Qd6	Bg7(f)	c6	d5	0–0	dxc3
9	Nxa7†	dxe5	Nxd4	exd6	Nd5	Nxc3
	c6(c)	0–0	Bxd4	Nf6	Kh8	d5
10	Nxc8	Bxc6	Ba4	Qd4	c3	Bg5!
	Rxc8	bxc6	d5	Nxe4	Ne7	Kf8(r)
11	Ba4	e6	Ne2	Qxe4†	b4	Rc1
	Nf6(d)	Re8(g)	Bb6(k)	Kf7(n)	Nexd5(p)	Ba7(s)

(a) 6 Ng3 Bg4 7 0–0 (Geller) gives Black some trouble defending his advanced center.

(b) (A) An important alternative is 7 . . . Qg5 8 Qe2 Nf6 (8 . . . Qxg2 9 Qh5†) 9 f4! Qxf4 (9 . . . Qh4† 10 g3 Qh3 11 Ne5† c6 12 Bc4 Bc5 13 d3 Ng4 14 Nf7! Bf2† 15 Kd1 e3 16 Qf3 Nxh2 17 Qe4† Kf8 18 Bxe3 with a winning advantage, Kavalek–Ljubojević, Amsterdam 1975) 10 Ne5† c6 11 d4 Qh4 12 g3 Qh3 13 Bc4 Be6 14 Bg5 Bd6 15 0–0–0 0–0–0 16 Nf7 Bxf7 17 Bxf7 with some advantage to White, Yudovich–Boey, corr. 1975. (B) Dubious is 7 . . . bxc6?! 8 Bxc6† Bd7 9 Qh5† Ke7 10 Qe5† Be6 11 Bxa8 Qxa8 12 Qxc7† ±.

(c) 9 . . . Bd7 10 Bxd7† Qxd7 11 Qh5† g6 12 Qe5† Kf7 13 Nb5 (13 Qxh8 Nf6) c6 14 Qd4 and White's two pawns are worth more than Black's activity and open lines.

(d) White is two pawns ahead, but he is only slightly better. White's backward d-pawn and Black's open lines ensure active play for Black.

(e) A good alternative is 6 Nxf6† Qxf6 7 Qe2 Be7! 8 Bxc6 dxc6 9 Nxe5 0–0 10 0–0 Bd6 11 d4 c5 12 Be3 Be6 13 f4, Liberzon–Parma, Athens 1976. Black's activity and bishop pair almost compensate for White's extra pawn.

(f) 8 . . . e4 9 Nh4 Qe7 10 Bf4 Be6 11 g3 a6 12 Bxc6† bxc6 13 Bh6 ±, Monticelli–Spielmann, Warsaw 1935.

(g) 12 Be3, de Firmian–Rizzitano, New York Open 1983. White has a pull; although Black is active, his pawn structure is broken.

(h) 4 . . . Nf6 5 exf5 e4 (5 . . . Bc5 6 0–0 0–0 7 Nxe5 Nxe5 8 d4 ±) 6 Ng5 d5 7 d3 Bxf5 8 dxe4 dxe4 9 Qe2 Bb4 10 Bd2 Qe7 11 Qc4 ±, Aronin–Klaman, Leningrad 1947.

(i) There are several other choices here. (A) 5 Ba4 Nf6 6 0–0 Bc5 7 Nxe5 0–0 8 Nd3 (8 exf5 d5 9 Nf3 Bxf5 10 Nxd4 Bxd4 11 Ne2 Bg4 =) 8 . . . fxe4! 9 Nxc5 d5 with an attack worth the sacrificed piece, Lehmann–Spassky, Vienna 1957. (B) 5 Bc4 c6 6 0–0 Nf6 7 Nxe5 fxe4 8 Nf7 Qc7 9 Nxh8 d5 10 Be2 ± (Geller). (C) 5 Nxe5 Qf6 6 Nf3 Nxb5 7 Nxb5 fxe4 ∞. (D) 5 0–0 Nf6 is untested.

(j) 5 . . . Nxb5 6 Nxb5 d6 7 d4 e4 8 Ng5 Bxf5 9 d5 c5?! 10 Nc3 Nf6 11 f3 exf3 12 Qxf3 ±, Belokurov–Lutikov, corr. 1969.

(k) 12 d4 ±, Unzicker–Nievergelt, Zürich 1959.

(l) 7 Be2 Qa5† wins the e-pawn.

(m) 7 . . . Qe7 8 Bf4 cxb5 9 0–0 Qc5 10 Nxe4 Qc6 11 Re1 b6 12 Qf3 Be7 ∞.

(n) 12 Bf4 Qe8 13 Be5 Bxd6 14 Qd5† Qe6 15 Qxd6 Qxd6 16 Bxd6 Re8† 17 Kf1 Bf5, Gonzalez–Montalvo, Havana 1978. Black, though a pawn down, is slightly better in the endgame.

(o) 6 0–0 Bc5 7 Nc3 d6 8 Be3 Bb6 9 Nd5 0–0 10 Bc4† Kh8 11 Ng5 Bg4 =, Hulak–Tatai, Stip 1979.

(p) 12 exd5 Bb6 13 a4 a6 =, Rigo–Meleghegyi, Tapolca 1981.

(q) 8 Bb3 d5 9 exd6 Qxd6 10 Re1 h6 11 Nbd2 ±.

(r) Black cannot free his position with 10 . . . b5 because of 11 Nxb5! axb5 12 Bxb5 and White wins the piece back (Rc1 is coming).

(s) 12 Bxc6 bxc6 13 Ne2 c5 14 Nf4 c6 15 e6 and Black is in dire straits, W. Watson–Nunn, London 1984.

RUY LOPEZ

1 e4 e5 2 Nf3 Nc6 3 Bb5

	25	26	27	28	29	30
3	d6 (Old Steinitz Defense)					Bb4(o)
4	d4 / Bd7(a)					c3(p) / Ba5
5	Nc3 / exd4		Nf6		Nge7	0–0 / Nge7
6	Nxd4 / g6		0–0(g) / Be7		Bc4(m) / exd4	Bxc6(q) / Nxc6
7	Be3 .... / Bg7	0–0 / Bg7	Re1 .... / exd4(h)	Bxc6 / Bxc6	Nxd4 / Nxd4	b4 / Bb6
8	Qd2 / Nf6	Bxc6 / bxc6	Nxd4 / 0–0	Qd3 / exd4	Qxd4 / Nc6	b5 / Na5
9	f3(b) / 0–0	Re1(e) / Ne7	Bxc6 / bxc6	Nxd4 / Bd7	Qe3 / Ne5	Nxe5 / 0–0
10	Bxc6(c) / bxc6	Bf4 / c5	Bg5(i) / h6	b3(k) / 0–0	Bb3 / c6	d4 / Qe8
11	0–0–0 / Re8(d)	Nf3 / 0–0(f)	Bh4 / Re8(j)	Bb2 / c6(l)	Qg3 / Ng6(n)	Nd2 / d6(r)

(a) 4 ... exd4 5 Qxd4 Bd7 6 Bxc6 is a line from Philidor's Defense that is better for White.

(b) *Archives* consider 9 Bxc6 bxc6 10 Bh6 Bxh6 11 Qxh6 c5 12 Nde2 Bc6. White may be a bit better here.

(c) 10 0–0–0 Nxd4 11 Bxd4 Nxe4! 12 Nxe4! (12 fxe4 Bxd4 13 Qxd4 Bxb5 14 Nxb5 Qg5†) 12 ... Bxb5 13 Bxg7 Kxg7 14 Qc3† f6 =, *Comments.*

(d) 12 Bh6 Bh8 13 h4 Qb8 14 h5 Qb4! =, Tseitlin–Kimelfeld, USSR 1967.

(e) 9 f4 c5 10 Nde2 f5 11 e5 Bc6 ∞, *Comments.*

(f) 12 e5 and Black has difficulties (Keres).

(g) Note that this position may arise by the move order 3 ... Nf6 4 0–0 d6 5 d4 Bd7 6 Nc3.

(h) A famous trap is 7 ... 0–0? 8 Bxc6 Bxc6 9 dxe5 dxe5 10 Qxd8 Raxd8 11 Nxe5 Bxe4 12 Nxe4 Nxe4 13 Nd3 f5 14 f3 Bc5† 15 Nxc5 Nxc5 16 Bg5 Rd5 17 Be7 and White wins the exchange since if the rook on f8 moves then 18 c4 wins a piece, Tarrasch–Marco, Dresden 1892.

(i) (A) 10 b3 d5! 11 e5 Bb4 is equal, Forgacs–Wolf, Nürnberg 1906. (B) 10 Bf4 Rb8 11 Nb3 is given by ECO as leading to a slight advantage for White, but this evaluation is debatable.

(j) 12 Qd2 Nh7 13 Bxe7 Rxe7 =, Capablanca–Lasker, World Chp. 1921.

(k) 10 Bg5 0–0 11 Rae1 h6 12 Bh4 Nh7 13 Bxe7 Qxe7 14 Nd5 also gives White some advantage, Lasker–Capablanca, World Chp. 1921.

(l) 12 Rad1 Qc7 13 Rfe1, Pillsbury–Steinitz, Vienna 1898. White has more space and a harmonious position. Black's position is solid but passive.

(m) Moving the bishop again is justified here because f7 is weak. Also reasonable is 6 0–0 Ng6 7 b3 Be7 8 Bb2 0–0 9 Nd5, Rogulj–Orlov, Yugoslav Chp. 1980.

(n) The column is Lasker–Steinitz, World Chp. 1894. Now 12 Be3 gives White the advantage.

(o) This queer-looking move of Alapin's is not that bad; it at least has surprise value.

(p) 4 0–0 Nge7 5 d4 exd4 6 Nxd4 leaves the Black bishop at b4 vulnerable and the kingside subject to attack, R. Burger–H. Steiner, Hollywood, 1953.

(q) On the natural 6 d4 then 6 . . . exd4 7 cxd4 d5 equalizes.

(r) 12 Nd3 (C. Hansen–Dreyev, Kiljava 1984). According to Hansen, best is now 12 . . . f5 13 e5 Qxb5 14 c4 Nxc4 15 a4 Qd5 16 Nxc4 Qxc4 17 a5 Bxd4 18 Ra4 Qd5 19 Nf4 Bxf2† 20 Kxf2 Qxd1 21 Rxd1 dxe5 22 Nd5 when White has some advantage.

RUY LOPEZ

1 e4 e5 2 Nf3 Nc6 3 Bb5

	31	32	33	34	35	36
	g6......................................a6					
4	c3.......................d4			Bxc6 (Exchange Variation)		
	d6(a) ....a6(d)		exd4(i)	dxc6(k)		
5	d4	Ba4(e)	Bg5	d4(l).......Nc3.........0–0		
	Bd7	d6	f6(j)	exd4	f6(n)	Ne7
6	0–0	d4	Bf4	Qxd4	d3(o)	Nxe5(p)
	Bg7	Bd7	Bg7	Qxd4	Bd6	Qd4
7	dxe5(b)	0–0	0–0	Nxd4	Be3	Nf3(q)
	dxe5(c)	Bg7	Nge7	Bd7(m)	c5	Qxe4
8	Be3	Re1(f)	Re1	Be3	Ne2	Re1
	Nf6	Nge7(g)	0–0	0–0–0	Ne7	Qg6
9	Nbd2	Be3	Nxd4	Nd2	Ng3	Ne5
	0–0	0–0	f5	Ne7	Be6	Qf6
10	Bc5	Nbd2	e5	0–0–0	c3	Nc3
	Re8	Qe8	Nxd4	Re8	Qd7	Bf5
11	Re1	Bb3	Qxd4	Rhe1	0–0	g4
	Nh5 ±	b6(h)	d5 =	Ng6 =	0–0 =	Bg6(r)

(a) Not 4 . . . Bg7?! 5 d4 ± and Black must give up the center.

(b) 7 Qb3!? deserves attention. After 7 . . . a5 8 Qa4 c6 9 Be2 b5 10 Qc2 Ne7 11 Be3 0–0 12 dxe5 dxe5 13 a4! Qc7 14 b4 White had the advantage, Kupreichik–Smyslov, Moscow 1976.

(c) 7 . . . Nxe5?! 8 Nxe5 dxe5 (8 . . . Bxb5 9 Qd5) 9 Qb3 ±.

(d) The move order 3 . . . a6 4 Ba4 g6 allows 5 d4 exd4 6 Nxd4 Bg7 7 Nxc6! bxc6 8 0–0 ±, de Firmian–Smyslov, Copenhagen 1985.

(e) (A) Nothing comes of 5 Bxc6 dxc6 6 0–0 (6 Nxe5 Qg5) 6 . . . Bg7 7 d4 exd4 8 cxd4 Ne7 9 Nc3 Bg4 10 Be3 0–0 11 h3 Bxf3 =, Chandler–Spassky, Vienna 1986. (B) 5 Bc4 d6 6 d4 Bg7 7 Bg5 Nge7 8 dxe5 dxe5 9 Qe2 h6 =, Timman–Smyslov, Tilburg 1982.

(f) (A) 8 dxe5 dxe5 9 Be3 Nf6 is covered in col. 171. It is similar to col. 31, but slightly improved for Black because the white bishop on a4 cannot retreat to the good square f1. (B) 8 d5 Nb8 9 c4 Nf6 is similar to a King's Indian Defense; Black is all right.

(g) 8 . . . Nf6 puts the knight on a more active square, but then comes 9 Bxc6 Bxc6 10 dxe5 dxe5 11 Qxd8† Rxd8 12 Nxe5 Bxe4 13 f3 Bxb1 14 Nxg6† winning. Playable is 8 . . . b5 9 Bb3 Nf6.

(h) 12 dxe5 dxe5 13 Nc4 Kh8 14 Qcl ±, Karpov–Spassky, Bugojno 1986. See also cols. 171–172 for more on this variation.

(i) 4 . . . Nxd4 5 Nxd4 exd4 6 Qxd4 Qf6 7 e5 Qb6 8 Qd3 c6 9 Bc4 Qa5† 10 Nc3 Qxe5† 11 Be3 gives White too much development for the pawn, Zaitsev–Suteyev, Moscow 1968.

(j) 5 ... Be7 6 h4 h6 7 Bxe7 Qxe7 8 Bxc6 dxc6 9 Qxd4 is good for White, Juares–Sugulski, Dubai 1986. The column is Cleghorn–Bisguier, Lone Pine 1976.

(k) 4 ... bxc6?! 5 d4 exd4 6 Qxd4 leaves White in control of the center.

(l) On 5 Nxe5 either 5 ... Qd4 or 5 ... Qg5 wins the pawn back with an equal game.

(m) 7 ... Bd6 8 Nc3 Ne7 9 Be3 c5 10 Nde2 Ng6 11 0–0 0–0 12 f3 Re8 =, Melsen–Ahues 1934. The column is Peterson–Alekhine, Örebro 1935.

(n) Also good is 5 ... Qd6 6 d4 exd4 7 Nxd4 Qg6 8 Qf3 Bg4 9 Qg3 0–0–0 10 h3 Bd7 11 Qxg6 hxg6 =, Goldenov–Bronstein, USSR Chp. 1952.

(o) 6 d4 exd4 7 Qxd4 Qxd4 is equal, similar to the previous column. This column is Romanovsky–Botvinnik, Moscow 1935.

(p) 6 d4 exd4 7 Nxd4 c5 8 Nb3 Qxd1 9 Rxd1 Ng6 10 Nc3 Bd7 11 Be3 b6 12 a4 a5 13 Nd2 0–0–0 14 Nc4 with a small pull for White, Adorjan–Wittman, Teesside 1974.

(q) 7 Qh5 g6 8 Nf3 Qxe4 9 Qa5 Qf4 10 d3 Qd6 11 Nbd2 Nd5 12 Ne4 Qb4 13 Qxb4 Nxb4 14 Bd2 Be7 15 a3 Nd5 16 c4 is also better for White, Timman–P. Nikolić, Brussels 1988.

(r) 12 d4 h5 13 Ne4 Bxe4 14 Rxe4 ±, Gruchasz–Biyiasas, Lone Pine 1976.

RUY LOPEZ

Exchange Variation

1 e4 e5 2 Nf3 Nc6 3 Bb5 a6 4 Bxc6 dxc6 5 0–0

	37	38	39	40	41	42
	f6 ....Bd6.........Qd6 ....Bg4(m) $\pm$					
6	d4			d4	d3(k)	h3
	Bg4.....................		exd4	exd4	f6	h5(n)
7	dxe5........c3		Nxd4(f)	Qxd4	Be3	d3
	Qxd1	Bd6(d) $\pm$	c5(g)↵	f6	c5(l) $\pm$	Qf6
8	Rxd1	Be3	Nb3	b3(j)=	Nbd2	Nbd2
	fxe5(a)↵↵	Qe7	Qxd1	Be6	Be6	Ne7
9	Rd3	Nbd2	Rxd1	Ba3	a3	Re1
	Bd6(b) $\pm$	0–0–0	Bg4(h)	Nh6	Qd7	Ng6
10	Nbd2	Qc2	f3	Bxd6	Qe2	d4
	b5	exd4	Be6	cxd6	Rd8	Bd6
11	b3	cxd4	Be3	c4	Rfd1	hxg4
	Ne7	Re8	b6	0–0	Bd6	hxg4
12	Bb2	e5	a4	Nc3	c3	Nh2
	Ng6(c)=	Bb4(e)=	Bd6(i)=	Nf7 $\pm$	Ne7 =	Rxh2!(o) $\pm$

(a) 8 . . . Bxf3 9 gxf3 fxe5 10 Be3 Bd6 11 Nd2 Ne7 12 Nc4 0–0–0 13 Rd3 (White is slightly better out of the opening. Black must now weaken his position due to the threat of 14 Rad1.) 13 . . . b5 14 Na5 Bb4 15 Nb3 Rxd3 16 cxd3 Ng6 17 Kf1 Rf8 18 Ke2 Nf4+ 19 Bxf4 Rxf4 20 Rg1 Rh4? (20 . . . g6, keeping a more solid pawn structure, is better) 21 Rxg7 Rxh2 22 a3 Bd6 23 f4! exf4 24 d4 Kd8 25 Na5 c5 26 e5 Bf8 27 Nc6+ Ke8 28 Rxc7 Resigns (because of 29 e6 and 30 Rc8 mate), Fischer–Rubinetti, Buenos Aires 1970.

(b) on 9 . . . Bxf3 10 gxf3! still gives White some advantage.

(c) 13 g3 0–0 14 Kg2 Rf6 =, Nunn–Portisch, Wijk aan Zee 1985.

(d) 7 . . . exd4?! 8 cxd4 Qd7 9 h3 Be6 (9 . . . Bxf3 10 Qxf3 Qxd4 11 Rd1 Qc4 12 Bf4 Bd6 13 Bxd6 cxd6 14 Rxd6 $\pm$, Timman–Beliavsky, Linares 1988) 10 Nc3 0–0–0 11 Bf4 Ne7?! 12 Rc1 Ng6 13 Bg3 Bd6 14 Na4 $\pm$, Fischer–Gligorić, Havana 1966.

(e) 13 h3 Be6 14 Ne4 Qf7 15 a3 Bb3 16 Qb1 Bf8 =, Smyslov–Geller, USSR Chp. 1973.

(f) 7 Qxd4 Qxd4 8 Nxd4 is less good since White would prefer to castle queenside in this particular endgame.

(g) Inferior are: (A) 7 . . . Ne7 8 Be3 Ng6 9 Nd2 Bd6 10 Nc4 0–0 11 Qd3 Ne5 12 Nxe5 Bxe5 13 f4, Fischer–Unzicker, Siegen 1970; (B) 7 . . . Bd6 8 Qh5+ g6 9 Qf3.

(h) 9 . . . Bd6 10 Na5! b5 11 c4 Ne7 12 Be3 f5 13 Nc3 f4 14 e5! Bxe5 15 Bxc5 $\pm$, Fischer–Portisch, Havana 1966.

(i) 13 a5 0–0–0 14 Nc3 Kb7 =, Quinteros–Kavalek, Manila 1976.

(j) (A) 8 Re1 Ne7 9 e5 fxe5 10 Nxe5 0–0 11 Bg5 Be6 12 Nc3 Qe8 =, Adorjan–Rumens, Hastings 1976–77. (B) Mirković's 8 c4 is worth a try. The column is Kagan–Zwaig, Hastings 1976–77.

(k) (A) 6 d4 cxd4 7 Nxd4 Bd7 8 Be3 0–0–0 9 Nd2 Nh6 10 h3 Qg6 11 Qf3 f5 12 Rad1 fxe4 13 Qxe4 Nf5 14 Nc4 Re8 15 Ne5 Rxe5! 16 Qxe5 Bd6 17 Nxf5 Bxf5 18 Qa5 h6 19 Kh1 Bxh3 20 gxh3 Qe4† 21 Kg1 Qg6† draw, Kurtenkov–Sergiev, corr. 1982. (B) 6 c3 Bg4 7 h3 Bxf3 8 Qxf3 0–0–0 9 d4! exd4 10 Bf4 Qg6 11 cxd4 Rxd4 12 Nc3 is a promising pawn sacrifice, Pilipian–Korolev, corr. 1986.

(l) 7 ... Bg4 8 Nbd2 0–0–0 9 Qb1!? Qd7 (Krogius prefers 9 ... Nh6 10 Bxh6 gxh6) 10 b4 g5 11 a4 ±, Petrushin–Kaidanov, USSR 1984. The column is Grefe–Bisguier, US Chp. 1975.

(m) 5 ... Qf6 6 d4 exd4 7 Bg5 Qg6 8 Qxd4 Be7 9 Bxe7 Nxe7 10 Ne5 Qd6 11 Rd1 Qxd4 12 Rxd4 gave White a slightly better endgame in Poutianen–Takemoto, Teesside 1974.

(n) 6 ... Bxf3 7 Qxf3 Qd7 8 d3 Bd6 9 Nd2 Ne7 10 Nc4 0–0 11 Be3 f5 12 exf5 Rxf5 13 Qe2 Ng6 14 Nd2 Raf8 15 Ne4 ±, Nunn–Korchnoi, Wijk aan Zee 1985.

(o) 13 Qxg4! (13 Kxh2? Qxf2 14 Re2 exd4† ∓) 13 ... Qh4 14 Qxh4 Rxh4 15 Nf3 with a slightly better endgame, Pachman–Lengyel, Vrnjačka Banja 1967.

RUY LOPEZ

Closed Defense, Fianchetto Variation

1 e4 e5 2 Nf3 Nc6 3 Bb5 a6 4 Ba4 Nf6 5 0–0 Be7 6 Re1 b5 7 Bb3 d6 8 c3 0–0 9 h3 Bb7 10 d4 Re8

	43	44	45	46	47	48
11	Ng5	a4			Nbd2	
	Rf8	Bf8	h6		Bf8	
12	f4(a)	d5	Nbd2		Bc2(m)	a3
	exf4	Na5(c)	Bf8(f)		g6(n)	h6(o)
13	Bxf4	Ba2	Bc2		d5	Bc2
	Na5	c6	exd4(g)		Nb8	Nb8
14	Bc2	Na3	cxd4		b3	b3(p)
	Nd5	cxd5	Nb4		c6	Nbd7
15	exd5	exd5	Bb1		c4	Bb2
	Bxg5	bxa4(d)	c5	bxa4	a5	g6
16	Qh5	Qxa4	d5	Rxa4	Nf1	a4
	h6	Nxd5	Nd7(h)	a5	Nbd7	c6(q)
17	Nd2	Ng5!	Ra3(i)	Ra3	Bg5	Qb1
	Bxd5	Re7	c4	Ra6(k)	Be7	Bg7
18	Ne4	b4	Nd4	Rae3	Be3	axb5
	Bxf4(b)	Nxc3(e)	Qf6(j)	a4(l)	Qc7 =	axb5 ±

(a) Several games have ended 12 Nf3 Re8 13 Ng5 Rf8 14 Nf3 draw. This is a problem with the Fianchetto Variation if Black must play to win.

(b) 19 Qf5 g6 20 Nf6† Kg7 21 Nh5† Kh8 22 Qxf4 Qg5 23 Qxg5 hxg5 24 Nf6 and White had compensation for his pawn in Y. Gruenfeld–P. Nikolić, Lugano 1987.

(c) 12 . . . Nb8 13 axb5 axb5 14 Rxa8 Bxa8 15 Na3 c6 16 Bg5 Nbd7 17 dxc6 Bxc6 18 Nc2 Qa8 19 Bxf6 Nxf6 20 Nb4! Bxe4 21 Rxe4! Qxe4 22 Ng5 Qb7 23 Bxf7† Kh8 24 Bxe8 Nxe8 25 Nxh7 ± .

(d) In de Firmian–Granda-Zuniga, Los Angeles 1987, Black complicated matters with 15 . . . Qd7 16 Bg5 e4 17 Nh2 bxa4 18 Bxf6 gxf6 19 Nc4 Nxc4 20 Bxc4 f5 21 Rxa4 Bh6. Probably 16 axb5 axb5 17 Bg5 leaves White with a safe advantage.

(e) 19 Qc2 g6 20 Qxc3 Rc8 21 Qg3 Nc6 22 Qh4 h5 23 Qe4 Bg7 24 Qxg6 d5 25 Qh7† Kf8 26 Ne4! Re6 27 Nc5 Rg6 28 Nxb7 Qd7 29 Qxh5 Nxb4 30 Na5 Nd3 31 Bd2 Qa4 32 Qf5 Resigns, Karpov–Miles, London 1984.

(f) 12 . . . exd4 13 cxd4 Nb4 14 axb5 axb5 15 Rxa8 Qxa8 16 e5 dxe5 17 dxe5 Nfd5 18 Ne4 c5 19 e6! fxe6 20 Ne5 ± , de Firmian–P. Nikolić, Tunis, 1985.

(g) 13 . . . Rb8 14 axb5 axb5 15 Bd3 Bc8 16 Nf1 Bd7 17 Ng3 Qc8 18 Be3 Qb7 (Hjartarson–Karpov, Dubai 1986). Now 19 Qe2! exd4 20 cxd4 Nb4 21 Bb1 c5 22 dxc5 dxc5 23 e5 is better for White (Hjartarson).

(h) 16 . . . g6 17 Nf1 Bg7 18 a5 Nd7 19 Ra3 ± .

43

(i) 17 Nf1 f5! 18 exf5 Nf6 left White with weak pawns in de Firmian–Beliavsky, Tunis 1985.

(j) Worse are (A) 18 . . . Qb6?! 19 Nf5 Ne5 20 Rg3 Kh7 21 Nf3 Bc8 22 Nxg7!! Bxg7 23 Qd2 Nbd3 24 Bxd3 Nxd3 25 Rxg7† Kxg7 26 Qxh6† Kb8 27 Be3 Qc7 28 Bd4 f6 29 Bxf6 Re7 30 Qh8† Resigns, Sax–P. Nikolić, Lugano 1987, and (B) 18 . . . Ne5 19 axb5 Qb6 20 Nxc4! Nxc4 21 Rg3 Bc8 22 b3! Ne5 23 Be3 with a strong attack, A. Sokolov–Portisch, Brussels 1988. After (C) 18 . . . Qf6 19 N2f3 Nc5 20 axb5 axb5 21 Nxb5 Rxa3 22 Nxa3 Ba6 Black had equal chances in this complex position, Kasparov–Karpov, World Chp. 1986.

(k) (A) 17 . . . Qd7 18 Nh4 Qb5 19 Rf3 Nh7 20 Rg3 ±, Ehlvest–Beliavsky, USSR Chp. 1984. (B) 17 . . . g6 18 e5 dxe5 19 dxe5 Nh5 20 Qb3!? ± (Kasparov).

(l) 19 Nf5 d5 20 e5 Ne4 21 N1d2 ±, Balashov–Karpov, USSR Chp. 1983.

(m) 12 a4 Qd7 (12 . . . h6 is cols. 3 and 4) 13 axb5 axb5 14 Rxa8 Bxa5 15 d5 should be a little better for White, although Karpov reached a good position against Kasparov in the 1985 World Chp. after 15 . . . Na5 16 Ba2 c6 17 b4 Nb7 18 c4 Rc8 19 dxc6?! Qxc6.

(n) 12 . . . Nb8 is often played, similar to the Breyer Variation, but 13 a4 Nbd7 14 Bd3 c6 15 Nf1 gives White an edge. The column is Karpov–Beliavsky, USSR Chp. 1983.

(o) 12 . . . Nb8 13 dxe5 dxe5 14 Bxf7† Kxf7 15 Qb3† Ke7 16 Nxe5 Qd6 17 Ndf3 Qe6 18 c4 gives White a dangerous attack, Epstein–Bielova, USSR 1980.

(p) 14 b4 Nbd7 15 Bb2 (A) 15 . . . g6 16 c4 exd4 17 cxb5 axb5 18 Nxd4 c6 19 a4 bxa4 20 Bxa4 Qb6 =, Timman–Kasparov, match 1985. (B) 15 . . . c5 16 bxc5 exd4 17 cxd4 dxc5 18 Rc1 (also (1) 18 Bb1! Nh5! 19 e5 Nf4! 20 Qc2 g6 =, Čabrilo–Hazai, Vrnjačka Banja 1988, or (2) 18 d5 Qc7 19 Rc1 c4 ∞) 18 . . . Rc8 19 Bb1 Nh5 20 Nf4 21 e5 Ne4 with a slight advantage, Nunn–Greenfeld, Groningen 1988. (C) 15 . . . a5!? 16 Bd3 c6 17 Nb3 axb4 18 cxb4 exd4 19 Nfxd4 c5! 20 bxc5 dxc5 21 Nxb5 Nxe4 =, Hjartarson–Karpov, match 1989.

(q) 16 . . . c5 17 d5 Qb6 18 Qe2 also gave White a small edge in Hort–van der Sterran, Wijk aan Zee 1986. The column is Short–Hjartarson, Reykjavik 1987.

RUY LOPEZ

Closed Defense, Breyer Variation

1 e4 e5 2 Nf3 Nc6 3 Bb5 a6 4 Ba4 Nf6 5 0–0 Be7 6 Re1
b5 7 Bb3 d6 8 c3 0–0 9 h3 Nb8

	49	50	51	52	53	54
10	d4					d3
	Nbd7(a)					Nbd7
11	Nbd2			Nh4	c4(l)	Nbd2
	Bb7			g6(j)	c6!	Bb7
12	Bc2			Bh6	c5!(m)	Nf1
	Re8			Re8	Qc7	Nc5
13	Nf1	b4	b3	Nf3(k)	cxd6	Bc2
	Bf8(b)	Bf8	Bf8	c5	Bxd6	Re8
14	Ng3	a4(f)	d5(i)	Nbd2	Bg5	Ng3(p)
	g6	Nb6(g)	c6	Bf8	exd4!	Bf8
15	a4(c)	a5	c4	Be3	Bxf6	b4(q)
	c5(d)	Nbd7	Qc7	Bb7	gxf6	Ncd7
16	d5	Bb2	Nf1	d5	Qxd4	d4
	c4	Rb8	Rec8	Nb6	Ne5(n)	g6(r)
17	Bg5	Rb1	Ne3	Bc2	Nbd2	a4
	h6(e)	Ba8(h)	g6 =	Bc8 =	Rd8(o)	Bg7(s)

(a) Counterattacking the white e-pawn doesn't work well: 10 . . . Bb7 11 dxe5! dxe5 (11 . . . Nxe4 12 e6 fxe6 13 Bxe6† Kh8 14 Bd5 ±, Gligorić–Benko, Zürich 1959) 12 Qxd8 Bxd8 13 Nxe5 Nxe4 14 Be3 Bf6 15 Ng4 Nd7 16 Nd2 Nxd2 17 Bxd2 Re8 18 Bf4 Rxe1†?! 19 Rxe1 Re8 20 Bc2 g6 21 Rd1 Resigns, Keres–Benko, Zürich 1959.

(b) 13 . . . d5? 14 Nxe5 Nxe5 15 dxe5 Nxe4 16 f3 Ng5 17 Ng3 Bc5† 18 Kh2 f6 19 Bxg5 fxg5 20 Qb1! h6 21 Qd1 ±, Lobron–Portisch, Wijk aan Zee 1985.

(c) Many other moves have been played, none giving White any advantage; e.g., 15 Bg5 h6 16 Bd2 c5 17 dxe5 Nxe5 18 Nxe5 dxe5 19 Qe2 Nh7 =, Lein–Krogius, Sochi 1965. White needs queenside play, too.

(d) 15 . . . Bg7 16 Bd3 forces the passive 16 . . . c6 since 16 . . . d5?! 17 Bg5 was very good for White in Karpov–O'Kelly, Caracas 1970.

(e) This well-studied position is slightly better for White. (A) Short–Spassky, Montpellier 1985, continued 18 Be3 Nc5 19 Qd2 h5 20 Ng5 Bg7 21 axb5 axb5 22 Rxa8 Bxa8 23 f4 ±. (B) de Firmian–Beliavsky, Thessaloniki 1988, continued 18 Be3 Nc5 19 Qd2 h5 20 Bg5 Be7 21 Bh6 Nfd7 22 Rf1 Bf6 23 Qe3 ±.

(f) 14 Bb2 Nb6 15 a3 h6 is an equal position from the Smyslov Variation.

(g) 14 . . . a5 15 bxa5 Rxa5 16 Rb1 Ba6 17 d5 Qa8 18 Ba3 ±, Beliavsky–A. Petrosian, USSR 1973.

(h) 18 Ba1 g6 19 c4 bxc4 20 dxe5 Nxe5 21 Nxe5 dxe5 22 Bc3 Bc6 was equal in Browne–Karpov, Amsterdam 1976.

(i) 14 Bb2 g6 15 a4 c6 16 Bd3 Bg7 17 Qc2 Rc8 18 Rad1 Qb6 19 Qb1 Nh5 20 Bf1 draw, Spassky–Smejkal, Thessaloniki 1984. The column is Psakhis–Smejkal, Szirak 1986.

(j) (A) 11 . . . Re8 12 Nf5 Bf8 13 Nd2 c5 14 Nf3 exd4 is also playable, Zaitsev–Averbakh, USSR Chp. 1968. (B) Risky is the pawn grab 11 . . . Nxe4 12 Nf5 N7f6 13 Nxe7† Qxe7 14 Re2! (Bronstein), planning 15 Qe1 and 16 f3.

(k) 13 f4 c5! 14 Nf3 c4 15 Bc2 Bb7 16 Nbd2 Bf8 17 Bxf8, agreed drawn here in R. Byrne–Portisch, Amsterdam 1969. The column is R. Byrne–Unzicker, Ljubljana 1969.

(l) Or 11 Bg5 Bb7 12 Nbd2 h6 13 Bh4 c5 14 a4 Qc7 15 Qe2 c4 16 Bc2 Rfe8 =, Fuchs–Matanović, Vrnjačka Banja 1967.

(m) Less energetic is (A) 12 Nc3 b4 13 Na4 c5 14 d5 Re8 15 Bc2 a5 16 b3 Nf8 17 Nb2 Ng6 =, R. Byrne–Darga, Amsterdam 1969. More determined is (B) 12 Qc2!? Bb7 13 Nc3 b4 14 Ne2 exd4 15 Nxd4 Re8 16 Nf5 ±, Hjartarson–Beliavsky, Linares 1989.

(n) 16 . . . Bc5 17 Qc3 a5 (Zaitsev) is a more active way.

(o) 18 Qe3 Nd3 19 Qh6 Bf4 20 Qxf6 Rd6 21 Qc3 Nxe1 22 Rxe1 Qd8 with an exciting position, Fischer–Portisch, Santa Monica 1966.

(p) 14 Ne3 g6 15 b4 Ne6 16 Bb3 a5 17 Ng4 Nxg4 18 hxg4 Bf6 =, Westerinen–Tringov, Leningrad 1967.

(q) 15 Nh2 Ne6 16 Nf5 h6 17 Ng4 Nxg4 18 Qxg4 Kh7 draw, Matanović–Ivkov, Palma de Mallorca 1966.

(r) Or 16 . . . Nb6 17 Bd3 g6 18 Bd2 Bg7 19 Qc2 Rc8 20 Rad1 Qe7 21 Nh2 Nfd7 22 d5 c5 ∓, Krauss–Korn, corr. 1975.

(s) 18 Bd3 bxa4 19 dxe5 Nxe5 20 Nxe5 Rxe5 is equal (Matanović).

RUY LOPEZ

Closed Defense, Smyslov Variation

**1 e4 e5 2 Nf3 Nc6 3 Bb5 a6 4 Ba4 Nf6 5 0–0 Be7 6 Re1
b5 7 Bb3 d6 8 c3 0–0 9 h3 h6 10 d4 Re8**

	55	56	57	58	59	60
11	Nbd2					Be3
	Bf8					Bf8
12	Nf1				a3(l)	Nbd2
	Bd7(a)		Bb7(g)		Bd7(m)	Bd7(o)
13	Ng3(b)		Ng3		Ba2	a3
	Na5		Na5		a5	Rc8(p)
14	Bc2		Bc2		Nf1	Bc2
	Nc4	c5	Nc4(h)		a4	g6
15	b3!(c)	b3	b3	Bd3(j)	Ng3	b4
	Nb6	Nc6	Nb6	Nb6	Na5	Bg7
16	Nh2	d5(e)	Bb2(i)	Bd2	Be3	Rc1
	c5	Ne7	c5	c5	c6!	Nh5
17	f4	Be3	dxe5	d5	Rc1	Nb3
	cxd4	g6	dxe5	Bc8	Be6	Qf6 =
18	cxd4	Qd2	c4	Nh2	Bxe6	
	Rc8(d)	Kh7(f)	Nbd7 =	Nh7(k)	Rxe6(n)	

(a) Not 12 . . . exd4 13 cxd4 Nxe4? 14 Bd5 winning a knight.

(b) Simplification with 13 dxe5 Nxe5 14 Nxe5 dxe5 15 Qf3 c5 16 Rd1 c4 was completely equal in Keres–Spassky, match 1965.

(c) Initiating queenside play gives no advantage here: 15 a4 c5 16 b3 Na5 17 axb5 axb5 18 d5 Qc7 19 Be3 Ra7 20 Nd2 Rae8 21 f4 Nb7 with full equality, Kavalek–Reshevsky, Netania 1969.

(d) 19 Nf3 Qc7 20 Bd3 exd4 21 Bb2 with strong play in the center, Minić–Savon, Skopje vs. Ochrid 1968.

(e) 16 Be3 cxd4 17 cxd4 exd4 18 Nxd4 d5! 19 exd5 Nb4 (simpler than 19 . . . Nxd5 20 Nxc6 Bxc6 21 Be4) 20 Nc6 Nxc6 21 dxc6 Bxc6 = , Schmidt–Smyslov, Monaco 1969.

(f) 19 Nh2 Bg7 20 f4 exf4 21 Bxf4 c4 22 Nf3 $\pm$, Sigurjonsson–Smejkal, Raach 1969.

(g) This position is similar to the Fianchetto Variation, but with White's queen knight heading for g3.

(h) 14 . . . c5 15 d5! leaves both the bishop on b7 and the knight on a5 badly placed.

(i) 16 a4 was successfully used by Fischer, but 16 . . . bxa4 17 bxa4 a5 led to equality in Kurajica–Mecking, Yugoslavia 1970. In the column, White plays for pressure on e5.

(j) 15 a4 d5! 16 b3 dxe4 17 Nxe4 Nxe4 18 Rxe4 Bxe4 19 Bxe4 Nb6 20 Bxa8 Nxa8 =, Stein–Reshevsky, Los Angeles 1968.

(k) 19 Rf1 Be7 20 f4 exf4 21 Bxf4 Bg5 with equal chances, Hecht–Gligorić, Büsum 1969.

(l) 12 Bc2 Bd7 (12 . . . Bb7! 13 a4 is the Fianchetto Variation, col. 3) 13 Bd3 Qb8 14 b3 g6 15 Bb2 Bg7 16 d5 Nd8 17 c4 gave White an edge in Savon–Geller, Lvov 1978.

(m) For 12 . . . Bb7 see col. 6 in the Fianchetto Variation.

(n) The position is equal, Keres–Portisch, Moscow 1967.

(o) 12 . . . Bb7 13 Qb1! Qb8 14 a3 Nd8 15 Bc2 c6 16 b4 was quite good for White in Fischer–Ivkov, Palma de Mallorca 1970.

(p) 13 . . . a5?! 14 d5 Na7 15 a4 c6 16 axb5 cxb5 17 c4 gave White the advantage in Tseshkovsky–Smyslov, USSR 1974. The column is Hort–Pietzsch, Havana 1966.

RUY LOPEZ

Closed Defense, Chigorin Variation

1 e4 e5 2 Nf3 Nc6 3 Bb5 a6 4 Ba4 Nf6 5 0–0 Be7 6 Re1 b5 7 Bb3 d6 8 c3 0–0 9 h3 Na5 10 Bc2 c5 11 d4 Qc7 12 Nbd2 cxd4 13 cxd4

	61	62	63	64	65	66
	Bb7			Nc6		Bd7(o)
14	d5′.........	Nf1		Nb3′.......	a3(l)	Nf1
	Rac8(a)	Rac8		a5	Bd7	Rac8
15	Bd3(b)	Re2(e)	Bb1	Be3	d5(m)	Ne3
	Nd7	Nh5(f)	Rfe8(h)	a4	Na5	Nc6(p)
16	Nf1	Bd3	Ng3(i)	Nbd2	Nf1	d5(q)
	Nc4(c)	Nc6	Bf8	Bd7(j)	Rfc8	Nb4
17	Ng3	Rc2	b3	Rc1	Bd3	Bb1
	g6	Qd7	Nc6	Qb7	g6!	a5
18	b3	d5	Bb2	Qe2	Bh6	a3
	Ncb6	Nb4	g6	Rfe8	Nh5	Na6
19	Bh6	Rxc8	Qd2	Bd3	Ne3	b4!
	Rfe8(d)	Rxc8(g)	Bg7 =	Rab8(k)	Qd8(n)	g6(r)

(a) 14 ... Bc8 15 b4! Nc4 16 Nxc4 Qxc4 17 Rb1 Bd7 (17 ... Qxa2 18 Nd2 traps the queen) 18 Bd3 Qc7 19 Be3 Ne8 20 Nd2 Qd8 21 Nb3 ±, Tseshkovsky–van Riemsdijk, Riga 1979.

(b) Also 15 Bb1 Nd7 (15 ... Nh5 16 Nf1 Nf4 17 Kh2! and Black gets pushed back, Thipsay–P. Littlewood, London 1985) 16 Nf1 Nc4 17 Ng3 g6 18 Nh2 Qa5 19 Ng4 with the attack, Savon–Geller, USSR 1969.

(c) 16 ... f5 17 exf5 Nc5 (17 ... Bxd5 18 Bb1 Nc4 19 Ne3 Bf6 20 Nxc4 bxc4 21 Ng5 was good for White in Tolnai–Pinter, Hungary 1987) 18 Ng5 Bxg5 19 Bxg5 Nf6 20 Bxf6 Rxf6 21 Bxb5 ±, Liberzon–Suetin, USSR 1960.

(d) 20 Bd2 ±, Parma–Hennings, Kapfenberg 1970.

(e) 15 Bd3 d5 16 dxe5 Nxe4 17 Ng3 f5 18 exf6 Bxf6 19 Bxe4 dxe4 20 Nxe4 Rcd8 21 Qe2 h6 22 Rb1 Kh8 and Black had active pieces for the pawn in Simagin–Heemsoth, corr. 1960-62.

(f) Now 15 ... d5 is not so good: 16 dxe5 Nxe4 17 Ng3 f5 (17 ... Nxg3 18 fxg3 ±) 18 exf6 Bxf6 19 Nxe4! dxe4 20 Bxe4 Rfd8 21 Qe1 (a good square for the queen) ±, Beliavsky–Diesen, Hastings 1974–75.

(g) 20 Be2 Nc2 21 Rb1 f5 =, Savon–Bronstein, Petropolis 1973.

(h) Not so good here is 15 ... d5 16 exd5! exd4 17 Bg5 h6 18 Bxh6! gxh6 19 Qd2 Rfd8 (19 ... Kg7 20 Ng3) 20 Qxh6 (Telen) with a strong attack.

(i) Noteworthy is Bronstein's suggestion 16 d5 Nc4 17 Ng3 g6 18 a4!?. The column is Unzicker–Bronstein, Krems 1967, where 17 ... Qc3?! 18 Qd2 Qxd2 (18 ... Qxa1?? 19 Bb2) 19 Bxd2 Nc6 20 d5 allows White a favorable endgame.

49

(j) (A) 16 . . . Nb4 17 Bb1 Bd7 18 a3 Nc6 19 Qe2! Qb7 20 Bd3 Rfe8 21 Rac1 $\pm$, Karpov–Hort, Lucerne 1982. (B) 16 . . . Be6 17 a3 Na5 18 Ng5 Bc8 19 f4 $\pm$.

(k) 20 a3 h6 21 dxe5 dxe5 22 Bc5, Spassky–Torre, Hamburg 1982. Black is weak on the queenside.

(l) 14 d5 Nb4 15 Bb1 a5 16 a3 Na6 17 b4 Bd7 18 Qb3 Nh5 19 Ra2, Yudovich–Levenfish, USSR 1939. White stands somewhat better.

(m) 15 Nb3 a5 16 d5 Nb8 17 Bd2 a4 18 Nc1 Rc8 19 Bc3 Na6, Timman–Torre, Tilburg 1982: Chances are about equal in this complicated position.

(n) Smyslov–Botvinnik, USSR Chp. 1940. The position is equal. ECO recommends 19 . . . Nf4 20 Bf1 Qb6.

(o) 13 . . . Rd8 14 b3 (on 14 Nf1 exd4 15 Nxd4 d5 should equalize) Nc6 15 Bb2 exd4 16 Nxd4 Nxd4 17 Bxd4 $\pm$, Kavalek–Balashov, Tilburg 1977.

(p) More passive is 15 . . . Rfe8 16 b3 exd4 17 Nxd4 Bf8 18 Bb2 Qd8 19 Ndf5 $\pm$, Spassky–Keres, match 1965.

(q) 16 a3? Nxd4 17 Nxd4 exd4 18 Qxd4 d5! 19 e5 Bc5 20 Qf4 Rfe8 21 Nf5 Nh5 22 Qf3 Bxf2† 23 Qxf2 Qxc2 is good for Black (Pytel).

(r) 20 Bd2 axb4 21 axb4 Qb7 22 Bd3 Nc7 23 Nc2 $\pm$, Tal–Hjartarson, Reykjavik 1987.

RUY LOPEZ

Closed Defense, Chigorin Variation

1 e4 e5 2 Nf3 Nc6 3 Bb5 a6 4 Ba4 Nf6 5 0–0 Be7 6 Re1 b5 7 Bb3 d6 8 c3 0–0 9 h3 Na5 10 Bc2 c5 11 d4 Qc7 12 Nbd2

	67	68	69	70	71	72
	Nc6			Bd7		Re8(q)
13	d5	dxc5(e)		Nf1		Nf1(r)
	Nd8(a)	dxc5		Nc4	Rfe8(n)	Bf8
14	a4(b)	Nf1	a4(i)	Ng3(k)	b3!	Bg5
	Rb8	Be6(f)	Be6	Rfe8(l)	g6	Nd7
15	b4	Ne3	Ng5	b3	Bg5	b3
	Nb7(c)	Rad8	Rad8	Nb6	Nh5(o)	Nb6(s)
16	axb5	Qe2	axb5	Be3	Bxe7	Rc1
	axb5	c4	axb5	h6	Rxe7	Nc6
17	Nf1	Nf5	Nxe6	Nd2	Ne3	Bb1
	Bd7	Rfe8(g)	fxe6	c4	Nf6	Ne7
18	Be3	Bg5	Qe2	Rc1	Rc1	Ng3
	Ra8(d)	Nd7(h)	c4(j)	a5(m)	Nb7(p)	a5 ±

(a) Black's other choice is 13 . . . Na5 14 b3 Bd7 15 Nf1 Nb7 16 c4 Rfb8 17 Ne3 Bf8 18 Nf5 Nd8 19 Nh2 ±, Karpov–Andersson, Stockholm, 1969.

(b) Playing only on the kingside is not so promising: 14 Nf1 Ne8 15 g4 g6 16 Ng3 Ng7 17 Kh2 f6 18 Be3 Bd7 19 Qd2 Nf7 =, Robatsch–Padevsky, Amsterdam 1972. White has more space, but the black position is solid.

(c) (A) 15 . . . Ne8 16 Nf1 g6 17 bxc5 dxc5 18 Bh6 Ng7 19 Ne3 ±, Fischer–Gore, New York (blitz tournament) 1971. (B) 15 . . . c4 16 Nf1 Ne8 17 axb5 axb5 18 N3h2 f6 19 f4 ±, Karpov–Spassky, USSR Chp. 1973.

(d) 19 Qd2 Rfc8 20 Bd3 g6 21 Ng3 Bf8 22 Ra2, Karpov–Unzicker, Nice 1974. White is better, with play on both sides of the board.

(e) (A) 13 dxe5?! Nxe5 14 Nxe5 dxe5 equalizes. (B) 13 a3 Bd7 14 b4 cxd4 15 cxd4 Rfc8 16 Bb3 a5 =, Gufeld–Karpov, USSR 1971.

(f) (A) 14 . . . Rd8 15 Qe2 Nh5 16 a4! Rb8 17 axb5 axb5 18 g3 g6 19 h4 Be6 20 Ne3 c4 21 Ng5 Bxg5 22 hxg5 ±, Fischer–Eliskases, Mar del Plata 1966. (B) 14 . . . Bd6 15 Nh4 Ne7 16 Qf3 Rd8 17 Ne3 Qb7 18 Ng4 Nxg4 19 hxg4 Ng6 20 Nf5 ±, Fischer–Filip, Curaçao 1962.

(g) 17 . . . Bxf5?! 18 exf5 Rfe8 19 Bg5 Nd5 20 Be4 and the use of the e4 square offers White more leeway.

(h) 19 Bxe7 (better than 19 Nxe7†; the bishop pair is not worth much here) 19 . . . Nxe7 20 Ng5 Nf8 and Black achieved equality, Rubinetti–Filip, Palma de Mallorca 1970.

(i) 14 Nh2 Be6 15 Ndf1 Rad8 16 Qf3 c4 17 Ng4 Nxg4 18 hxg4 Bc5 draw, Tringov–Matanović, Belgrade 1969.

51

(j) 19 b3 Bc5 and Black had full equality in Kuijpers–Zuidema, Amsterdam 1966. The doubled black e-pawns control important center squares, and Black also has play on the f-file.

(k) 14 b3 Nb6 15 Ne3 c4 16 bxc4 Nxc4 17 Nxc4 bxc4 gives White a slight pull, but Petrosian used to play this way for Black.

(l) 14 . . . g6 15 b3 Nb6 16 dxe5 dxe5 17 Nh2 Ne8 18 Ng4 ±, Yelagin–Bocalo, corr. 1966.

(m) 19 bxc4 Nxc4 20 Nxc4 Qxc4 21 Bb3 Qc7 22 a4 bxa4 23 Bxa4 Reb8 24 Bxd7 Qxd7 25 f4 exf4 26 Bxf4 Nh7 27 Nf5 Bg5 (de Firmian–Djurić, Vrsać 1983); now 28 Bxd6! Bxc1 (28 . . . Rb5 29 Bc5 Bxc1 30 Qg4 g6 31 Nxh6† Bxh6 32 Qxd7) 29 Bxb8 wins a pawn.

(n) 13 . . . cxd4 14 cxd4 transposes into column 66.

(o) 15 . . . Be6 16 Ne3 Rad8 17 Rc1 Nh5 18 b4 Nc4 19 Bxe7 Rxe7 20 Nxc4 Bxc4 21 bxc5 dxc5 22 d5 is much better for White, Geller–Ivkov, Havana 1963.

(p) 19 b4 c4 20 a4 Rae8 21 axb5 axb5 22 Ra1 Bc6 23 Ra6 Qc8 24 d5 ±, Stein–Matanović, Tel Aviv 1964.

(q) Other less frequently played moves are: (A) 12 . . . Bb7 13 dxe5 dxe5 14 Nh2 Rad8 15 Qf3 Bc8 16 Ndf1 Nc4 17 Ng3 g6 18 b3 ±, Stein–Bannik, USSR Chp. 1961. (B) 12 . . . Be6 13 d5 Bd7 14 b3 Nb7 15 Bd2 a5 16 Qe2 b4 17 a4 ±, Mukhin–Ivanov, Tashkent 1977.

(r) Sharp is 13 b4 cxb4 14 cxb4 Nc6 15 Bb2 Nxb4 16 Bb3 Nd7 17 Rc1 Qb7 18 Re3 ± (Keres).

(s) 15 . . . Nc6 16 Ne3 Ne7 17 dxe5 dxe5 18 Bxe7 Bxe7 19 Nd5 ±, Sigurjonsson–Kristiansen, Skopje 1972. The column is R. Byrne–Ivkov, Skopje 1972.

RUY LOPEZ

Closed Defense, Chigorin Variation

1 e4 e5 2 Nf3 Nc6 3 Bb5 a6 4 Ba4 Nf6 5 0–0 Be7 6 Re1 b5 7 Bb3
d6 8 c3 0–0 9 h3 Na5 10 Bc2 c5 11 d4

	73	74	75	76	77	78
	(Qc7) Nd7		(Keres Variation) ....Bb7.........Nc6			
12	b4(a)⌐......Nbd2...................dxc5				Nbd2(m)	d5
	cxb4	cxd4		dxc5	cxd4	Na5(p)
13	cxb4	cxd4		Nbd2	cxd4	b3
	Nc4(b)⌐	Nc6(d)		f6(k)	Rc8	g6
14	Nbd2	Nb3 ....Nf1		Nh4	Nf1(n)	a4
	Bb7	a5	exd4(h)	Nb6	d5!	Bd7
15	Nxc4	Be3(e)	Nxd4	Nf5	dxe5	axb5
	bxc4	a4	Nxd4	Ra7(l)	Nxe4	axb5
16	d5	Nbd2	Qxd4	Qf3	Ng3	Nxe5
	a5	Bf6(f)	Ne5	Kh8	f5	dxe5
17	b5	d5	Rd1(i)	h4	exf6	d6
	a4	Nd4	Bb7	Be6	Bxf6	Nh5
18	Bxa4	Rc1!	Ng3	h5	Nxe4	dxe7
	Qa5(c)⌐	Bb7(g)	Bf6!(j)	Rd7 ±	dxe4(o)	Qxe7(q)

(a) 12 d5 Nc4 13 a4 Bd7 14 b3 Na5! 15 axb5 axb5 16 Bb2 c4 17 b4 Nb7 18 Rxa8 Rxa8 =,
Levchenkov–Eingorn, Nikolaev 1981.

(b) Riskier but playable is 13 . . . Nc6 14 Bb2 Nxb4 15 Bb3 Nc6 16 Nc3 Bb7 17 Rc1 Qd8 18
Nd5 Na5, Vasiukov–Kholmov, USSR Chp. 1966.

(c) 19 Bc2 Qxb5 =, Tal–Sanguinetti, Munich 1958.

(d) Black should not give up his strongpoint in the center quite yet: after 13 . . . exd4 14
Nxd4 Bf6 15 Nf1 Ne5 16 Ne3 g6 17 Nd5 Bg7 18 a4 White is better, Kotkov–Zhukhovitsky,
USSR 1964.

(e) 15 Bd3 Ba6 16 d5 Nb4 17 Bf1 a4 18 a3 Nxd5 19 Qxd5 axb3 20 Bxb5 Nf6 21 Qd3 Bxb5
22 Qxb5 Qb8 23 Qxb8 Raxb8 24 Bg5 Rfc8 is usually regarded as an equal ending.

(f) 16 . . . exd4 17 Nxd4 Nxd4 18 Bxd4 Ne5 19 Nf1 Be6 20 Ne3 Bg5 21 b3 ±, Tarjan–
Karklins, US Chp. 1974.

(g) 19 Bb1 Qb6 20 Nf1 Rfc8 21 Qd2 ±, Gufeld–Romanishin, Vilnius 1975.

(h) 14 . . . Bf6 15 Be3 Nb6 16 b3 d5 17 dxe5 Nxe5 18 Nd4 dxe4 19 Bxe4 Nd5 20 Qc2 ±,
Zakharov–Zwaig, World Junior Chp. 1963.

(i) 17 Ne3? Bxh3 18 gxh3? Nf3† wins. But after 17 Rd1 Bxh3? 18 Qxe5 dxe5 19 Rxd8 Rxd8
20 gxh3 White is much better.

(j) 19 Qxd6 Qc8 with compensation for the pawn, Spragget–Romanishin, Wijk aan Zee
1985.

53

(k) (A) 13 . . . Qc7 14 Nf1 Nb6 15 Ne3 Rd8 16 Qe2 Be6 17 Nd5! Nxd5 18 exd5 Bxd5 19 Nxe5 Ra7 20 Bf4 Qb6 21 Rad1 g6 22 Ng4 Nc4 23 Bh6 Be6 24 Bb3 Qb8 25 Rxd8† Bxd8 26 Bxc4 bxc4 27 Qxc4! Qd6 28 Qa4 Qe7 29 Nf6† Kh8 30 Nd5 Qd7 31 Qe4 (again working on the weak back rank) 31 . . . Qd6 32 Nf4 Re7 33 Bg5 Re8 34 Bxd8 Rxd8 35 Nxe6 Qxe6 36 Qxe6 fxe6 37 Rxe6 Rd1† 38 Kh2 Rd2 39 Rb6 Rxf2 40 Rb7 Rf6 41 Kg3 Resigns, Fischer–Keres, Curaçao 1962. (B) 13 . . . Bb7 14 Qe2 Qc7 15 Nf1 Nc4 16 b3 Nd6 17 c4 Rfe8 18 Bb2 $\pm$, Short–Portisch, Tilburg 1988.

(l) Or 15 . . . Rf7 16 Qg4 Kh8 17 h4 g6 18 Nh6 Rg7 19 Qf3 and White is better (Fischer). The column is Tringov–Barle, Yugoslavia 1974, where again White obtains pressure on the kingside.

(m) 12 d5 Bc8 is possible, transposing into col. 36.

(n) 14 d5! Qc7 is back in col. 19.

(o) 19 Qxd8 Rfxd8 20 Bxe4 Bxe4 21 Rxe4 Rc2 22 Rb1 Nc4 23 b3 Nd6 =, de Firmian–Arnason, Oslo 1984.

(p) 12 . . . Na7 13 a4 Nd7 14 Be3 Qc7 15 Nbd2 Nb6 16 a5 $\pm$, Nunn–van der Wiel, Amsterdam 1988.

(q) 19 Be3 Be6 20 Nd2 Nc6 21 Qe2 with a small advantage, Benjamin–Romanishin, Moscow 1987.

RUY LOPEZ

Closed Defense

1 e4 e5 2 Nf3 Nc6 3 Bb5 a6 4 Ba4 Nf6 5 0–0 Be7 6 Re1 b5 7 Bb3 d6 8 c3 0–0 9 h3

	79	80	81	82	83	84
	(Na5) ......Be6.....................			Nd7		Qd7
10	(Bc2) c6	d4(c) Bxb3		d4 Nb6 ....Bf6		d4 Re8
11	d4(a) Qc7	Qxb3 ....axb3 d5(d)	exd4(g)	Nbd2(i) exd4	Be3(l) Na5	Nbd2 Bf8
12	Nbd2 Re8	exd5 Na5	cxd4 d5	cxd4 d5(j)	Bc2 Nc4	d5 Ne7
13	Nf1 Nc4	Qc2 exd4	e5 Ne4	Bc2 Be6	Bc1 c5(m)	Nf1 h6(o)
14	Ng3 h6	cxd4(e) Nxd5	Nc3 f5	e5 Qd7	b3 Ncb6	c4 c6
15	Nh2 Bf8	Nc3 Nxc3(f)	exf6 Nxf6(h)	Nf1 Nb4	Be3 c4	dxc6 Nxc6
16	b3 Nb6(b)	Qxc3 Nc4 ±	Bg5 ±	Bb1 Bf5(k)	d5 Bb7(n)	cxb5 axb5(p)

(a) 11 a4 may be better. Gligorić–Lombardy, Munich 1958 continued 11 . . . Rb8 12 axb5 axb5 13 d4 Nd7 14 Nbd2 Bf6 15 Nf1 Nc4 16 b3 Ncb6 17 Ne3 g6 18 Ng4 Bg7 19 dxe5 Nxe5 20 Nfxe5 dxe5 21 Nh6† Bxh6 22 Bxh6 with clear advantage to White.

(b) 17 Qf3 Nh7 18 dxe5 dxe5 19 Nf5 ±, Scholl–Ree, Dutch Chp. 1969.

(c) 10 Bxe6 fxe6 leaves Black with solid central squares and the open f-file.

(d) 11 . . . Qd7 12 Nbd2 Rfe8 (12 . . . Na5 13 Qc2 exd4 14 cxd4 c5 15 d5 ±) 13 a4 Na5 14 Qd1 Bf8 15 b3 ±, Spassky–Kholmov, USSR Chp. 1962.

(e) 14 Nxd4 Re8 (14 . . . Nxd5 15 Nd2 Re8 16 Ne4 Qd7 17 Bg5 ±) 15 a4 Qxd5 16 axb5 axb5 17 Bd2 ±, A. Sokolov–P. Nikolić, Brussels 1988.

(f) 15 . . . Bb4 16 Bd2 Bxc3 17 Bxc3 Nc4 18 b3 ±. The column is Short–van der Sterren, Wijk aan Zee 1986.

(g) 11 . . . Re8 12 d5 Nb8 13 c4 Nbd7 14 Nc3 leaves White strongly placed in the center, Gufeld–Forintos, Kecskemét 1968.

(h) For the adventurous, the pawn sacrifice 15 . . . Bxf6 16 Nxe4 dxe4 17 Rxe4 Qd5 can be tried. The column is Ivanchuk–Serper, Irkutsk 1986.

(i) 11 Be3 exd4 12 cxd4 Na5 13 Bc2 c5 14 Nc3 Nac4 15 Bc1 cxd4 16 Nxd4 Bf6 =, Gligorić–F. Olafsson, Bled 1959.

(j) 12 . . . Nb4 13 Nf1 c5 14 a3 Nc6 15 Be3 Na5 16 Bc2 Ncb4 17 Bc1 ±, Karpov–Ivkov, Bugojno 1980.

(k) 17 Bg5! Bxg5 18 Nxg5 Nc4 (Byrne gives 18 . . . h6 as better) 19 Ng3 Bxb1 20 Qxb1 f5 21 exf5 gxf6 22 Ne6 Rfe8 23 Qf5 Nd6 24 Qxf6 Ne4 25 Rxe4 dxe4 26 Nf5 Resigns, Byrne–Janetschek, Baden 1980.

(l) 11 a4 Na5 12 Bc2 Nb6 13 b4 Nac4 14 a5 Nd7 15 Bb3 and White obtained the advantage in Fischer–Matanović, Vinkovći 1968.

(m) 13 . . . Bb7 14 a4 exd4 15 Nxd4 $\pm$, P. Popović–Lengyel, Pecs 1980.

(n) 17 b4 a5 18 a4, Karpov–Torre, Hannover 1983, White is clearly better.

(o) 13 . . . g6 14 c4 Bg7 15 c5 Nh5 16 a4 dxc5 17 axb5 left Black with an ugly position in Fischer–Wade, Buenos Aires 1960.

(p) 17 Ne3 Na5 (Timoshenko–Lanc, Děčín 1978); now 18 Nd5 Nxd5 19 Bxd5 should be better for White.

RUY LOPEZ
Closed Defense

1 e4 e5 2 Nf3 Nc6 3 Bb5 a6 4 Ba4 Nf6 5 0–0 Be7 6 Re1 b5 7 Bb3 d6 8 c3 0–0

	85	86	87	88	89	90
9	d4				d3	a4
	Bg4				Na5(m)	Bg4(o)⋚
10	Be3		d5		Bc2	h3
	exd4 .... d5(e)⋚		Na5		c5	Bxf3
11	cxd4	exd5	Bc2		Nbd2	Qxf3
	Na5(a)⋚	exd4	c6		Nd7	Na5
12	Bc2	Bxd4(f)⋤	dxc6	h3	Nf1	Ba2
	c5(b)⋜	Nxd4	Qc7(i)⋚	Bxf3(k)⁼	Nb6	b4!(p)⋨
13	dxc5(c)⋜	cxd4	Nbd2	Qxf3	Ne3	cxb4
	dxc5	Bb4	Qxc6	cxd5	Nc6	Nc6
14	Nbd2	Nc3	h3(j)⋝	exd5	h3	Qc3
	Re8	Bxc3(g)⋚	Be6	Nc4	Be6	Qd7
15	Qb1	bxc3	Ng5	a4	d4	Na3
	Nd7	Nxd5	Bc8	g6	cxd4	d5
16	e5	Qd3	Nf1	Bd3	cxd4	b5
	Nf8(d)⋝	g6(h)⋚	Nc4 =	Qd7(l)⋝	Nxd4(n)⋜	axb5(q) ♙

(a) 11 . . . d5 12 e5 Ne4 13 h3 Bh5 14 Nc3 Nxc3 15 bxc3 Na5 16 Bc2 Nc4 17 g4 Bg6 18 Bf5 ±, Sznapik–van der Wiel, Copenhagen 1984.

(b) 12 . . . Nc4 13 Bc1 c5 14 b3 Nb6 15 Nbd2 Rc8 16 Bb2 Nfd7! gives good chances for equality, Yates–Ed. Lasker, New York 1924.

(c) 13 Nbd2 cxd4 14 Bxd4 Nc6 15 Be3 d5 =, Unzicker–Keres, match 1956.

(d) 17 h3 Bh5 18 Bf5 Bg6 with equality, Chandler–Hodgson, Bath 1987.

(e) The tricky 10 . . . Nxe4 11 Bd5 Qd7 12 Bxe4 d5 would give Black a lot of play after 13 Bc2 e4, but 13 Bxh7†! Kxh7 14 dxe5 wins a pawn.

(f) 12 bxc6 dxe3 13 Rxe3 Bc5 14 Qxd8 Rfxd8 15 Re1 Bxf3 16 gxf3 Rab8 going after the pawn on c6 gives Black the better of it.

(g) 14 . . . a5?! 15 Qd3 a4 16 Bc2 a3 17 Ne5! Bd7 18 bxa3 Rxa3 19 Bb3 ± (van der Wiel).

(h) 17 Re5 c6 18 Rae1 ±, van der Wiel–P. Nikolić, Novi Sad 1982.

(i) 12 . . . Nxc6 13 Bg5 gives White a better chance of controlling d5.

(j) 14 Nf1 Nc4 15 Ne3 Nxe3 16 Bxe3 h6 17 Qe2 Rfc8 =, Karastoichev–Kolarov, Bulgarian Chp. 1960. The column is Tringov–Sokolov, Belgrade 1967.

(k) Also playable is 12 . . . Bc8 13 dxc6 Qc7 14 a4 Be6 15 axb5 axb5 16 Ng5 Qxc6 17 Nxe6 fxe6 =, Schrancz–Hardicsay, Hungary 1978.

(l) 17 Qe2 Qb7 18 Rd1 Nb6 with a complex but balanced position, Benjamin–Short, match 1983.

(m) 9 . . . Be6 is another good way to play against the slow 9 d3. After 10 Nbd2 Bxb3 11 Qxb3 Nd7 12 Nf1 Nc5 13 Qc2 d5 (Wade), Black is equal.

(n) 17 Nxd4 exd4 18 Qxd4 Rc8 =, Korchnoi–Petrosian, Curaçao 1962.

(o) (A) 9 . . . b4 10 a5 Be6!? (10 . . . Rb8 11 Bc4! bxc3 12 dxc3 ±) 11 Bxe6 fxe6 12 d3 bxc3 13 bxc3 Rb8 14 Nbd2 Rb5 draw, Ljubojević–Spassky, Dubai 1986. (B) 9 . . . Bb7 10 d4 should be better for White since he has saved a tempo by not playing h3.

(p) 12 . . . bxa4 13 Qd1 Qd7 14 d3 Rfb8 15 Nd2 Qb5 16 Bc4 Nxc4 17 Nxc4 Nd7 18 Rxa4 gave White a solid advantage in Ljubojević–Karpov, Dubai 1986.

(q) 17 axb5 Nd4 18 exd5 Nxd5 with a complicated position, Ljubojević–Smejkal, Dubai 1986.

RUY LOPEZ

1 e4 e5 2 Nf3 Nc6 3 Bb5 a6 4 Ba4 Nf6 5 0–0 Be7 6 Re1 b5 7 Bb3
(Anti-Marshall and Unusual Lines)

	91	92	93	94	95	96
	(d6)........	0–0(b)				
8	(c3)	a4		.d4	.h3	.c3
	Bg4?!	Bb7........	.b4	Nxd4(h)	Bb7(l)	d5
9	d3	d3	a5(f)	Nxd4(i)	d3	d4
	Na5	d6(c)	d6	exd4	d6	exd4
10	Bc2	Nc3	d3	e5	c3	e5
	c5	Na5	Rb8	Ne8	Na5	Ne4
11	Nbd2	Ba2	Nbd2	c3(j)	Bc2	cxd4(n)
	0–0	b4	Kh8	dxc3	c5	Bg4
12	h3	Ne2	c3	Nxc3	Nbd2	Nc3
	Bh5	c5	Nh5	d6	Qc7	Bxf3
13	g4	Ng3	d4	Bf4	Nf1	gxf3
	Bg6	Bc8(d)	Bf6	dxe5	Rfe8	Nxc3
14	Nf1	h3	d5	Bxe5	Ng3	bxc3
	Nc6(a)	Be6(e)	Ne7(g)	Qxd1(k)	Rad8(m)	Qd7 $\overline{\overline{\mp}}$

(a) 15 Ng3 with a bind on the kingside; Maróczy–Rubens, Copenhagen 1927.

(b) Delaying . . . d6 to answer c3 with . . . d5—the Marshall Counter Attack; White now avoids the move c3, hence "anti-Marshall." Note that the Marshall occurs in good form below, after 9 c3 d5 10 exd5 Nxd5.

(c) 9 . . . Re8!?, trying to play d7–d5 in one move has been a favorite of Nunn's. Zapata–Nunn, Dubai 1986, continued 10 Ng5?! d5 11 exd5 Nd4! 12 Ba2 Nxd5 13 Rxe5 Bxg5 14 Bxg5 Qd7 15 Rxe8+ Rxe8 16 Nd2 Nb4 17 Bb1? (White's position is bad in any case, but now Black's great lead in development leads to a quick kill.) 17 . . . Ne2+ 18 Kf1 Bxg2+! 19 Kxg2 Qg4+ 20 Kh1 Ng3+ (winning the queen) 21 Resigns.

(d) The pawn sacrifice 13 . . . b3!? 14 Bxb3 Nxb3 15 cxb3 Nd7 16 b4! cxb4 17 d4 was slightly better for White in Matulović–Jansa, Kapfenberg 1970.

(e) 15 Bxe6 fxe6 16 c3 bxc3 17 bxc3 Rb8 18 Be3 $\pm$, Chandler–Tal, World vs. USSR 1984.

(f) 9 d4 d6 10 dxe5 Nxe5 11 Nbd2 Bb7 12 Nxe5 dxe5 13 Qf3 Kh8 14 g4 Bc5 15 Nc4 Nxe4!? 16 Rxe4 f5 17 gxf5 Rxf5 18 Qxf5 Qd1+ 19 Kg2 Rf8 20 Ne3 with complications, Ehlvest–Kupreichik, USSR Chp. 1987. After a hard struggle, Black blundered and White won.

(g) 15 Nf1 $\pm$, Kapengut–I. Ivanov, USSR 1975.

(h) (A) Safe is 8 . . . d6! 9 c3 Bg4 transposing to cols. 85–88. (B) 8 . . . exd4 9 e5 Ne8 10 Bd5 gives Black problems.

(i) Sharp is 9 Bxf7+ Rxf7 10 Nxe5 Nc6 11 Nxf7 Kxf7 ∞.

(j) Innocuous is 11 Qxd4 Bb7 12 c3 d6 $=$, L. Steiner–Marshall, New York 1929.

(k) 15 Raxd1 with compensation for the pawn (Vogt).

(l) 8 . . . d6 9 c3 is back in normal channels, but White has avoided the Marshall Attack.

(m) Tal–Geller, Kislovodsk 1966. White obtained no advantage with this slow buildup.

(n) 11 Nxd4 Nxe5 12 f3 c5 13 fxe4 cxd4 14 Bxd5 dxc3 15 Bxa8 Bc5† 16 Kh1 (Neikirch–Zinn, East Germany 1966) now 16 . . . Nd3 gives Black a winning game. The column, declining the gambit, is analysis by Tal and Gutman.

RUY LOPEZ

Marshall (Counter) Attack

**1 e4 e5 2 Nf3 Nc6 3 Bb5 a6 4 Ba4 Nf6 5 0–0 Be7 6 Re1
b5 7 Bb3 0–0 8 c3 d5 9 exd5**

	97	98	99	100	101	102
	Nxd5					e4
10	Nxe5					dxc6(p)
	Nxe5					exf3
11	Rxe5					d4!(q)
	c6!				Nf6(l)	fxg2(r)
12	d4		Bxd5	g3(h)	d4	Qf3
	Bd6		cxd5	Bd6(i)	Bd6	Be6
13	Re1	Re2	d4	Re1	Re1	Bf4
	Qh4	Bg4(c)	Bd6	Qd7!(j)	Ng4	Nd5
14	g3	f3	Re3	d3	h3	Bg3
	Qh3	Bh5	Qh4(f)	Qh3	Qh4(m)	a5
15	Be3(a)	Bxd5(d)	h3	Re4	Qf3	Nd2 ±
	Bg4	cxd5	Qf4	Qf5	Nxf2	
16	Qd3	Nd2	Re5	Nd2	Re2(n)	
	Rae8(b)	Qc7(e)	Qf6(g)	Qg6(k)	Ng4(o)	

(a) 15 Re4? g5 16 Qf3 (16 Bxg5?? Qf5) 16 . . . Bf5 17 Bc2 (17 Bf4!?) 17 . . . Bxe4 18 Bxe4 Qe6 19 Bxg5 (19 Bf5? Qe1† 20 Kg2 Qxc1 21 Na3 Qd2 wins) 19 . . . f5 20 Bd3 h6 $\overline{\overline{\mp}}$ (Gutman).

(b) Short–Pinter, Rotterdam, 1988 continued 17 Nd2 Re6 18 a4 bxa4 19 Rxa4 f5 20 Qf1 Qh5 21 f4 Rb8 22 Bxd5 cxd5 23 Rxa6 Rbe8 24 Qb5 Qf7 25 h3! with complications favoring White.

(c) 13 . . . Qh4 14 g3 Qh5 (14 . . . Qh3 15 Nd2 Bf5 16 Ne4!?) 15 Nd2 Bg4 16 f3 Bxf3 17 Nxf3 Qxf3 18 Rf2 Qe4 19 Qf3 $\stackrel{+}{=}$, Sax–P. Nikolić, Plovdiv 1983.

(d) If 15 Nd2 Nf4 is annoying.

(e) 17 Nf1 Rfe8 18 Be3 Qc4 ∞, van der Sterren–Pein, Brussels 1984. Black has good play for the pawn.

(f) 14 . . . f5 15 Nd2 f4 16 Re1 Qg5 17 Nf3 Qh5 18 Ne5 f3 19 gxf3 Bh3 20 f4 ± (Tal).

(g) 17 Re1 Qg6 18 Qf3 Be6 19 Bf4 Bxf4 20 Qxf4 Bxh3 21 Qg3 Qxg3 = , Tal–Spassky, match 1965.

(h) 12 d3 Bd6 13 Re1 (13 . . . Qh4 14 g3 Qh3 transposes back into the column) 13 . . . Bf5! 14 Nd2 Nf4 15 Ne4 Nxd3 16 Bg5 Qd7 17 Re3 Bxe4 18 Rxe4 Rae8 = , Kir. Georgiev–Nunn, Dubai 1986.

(i) Geller's 12 . . . Bf6 13 Re1 c5 14 d4 Bb7, playing for central control, is a reasonable alternative.

(j) 13 . . . Nf6 14 d4 Bg4 15 Qd3 c5 16 Bc2 is better for White, according to Fischer.

(k) 17 a4 f5 (or 17 . . . Bf5 18 axb5 axb5 18 Rxa8 Rxa8 20 Re1 Bd3 21 Nf3 with advantage) 18 Rd4! f4 19 Ne4 Bg4 20 Qf1 with a clear plus, Zapata–M. Pavlović, Belgrade, 1988.

(l) A passable variant is 11 . . . Bb7 12 d4 Qd7 13 Nd2 Nf4 14 Ne4 Bd6! 15 Nd6 cxd6 16 Rg5 Ng6 17 Rg3! Rae8 18 Bg5 Qf5 19 Bc2 Be4 20 Bxe4 Rxe4 21 a4 bxa4 22 Rxa4 Rfe8 (22 . . . Qe6 23 Re3±, Kudrin—Hebden, Las Palmas 1989) 23 Be3 Qd7= (Byrne).

(m) The best try in this old line is 14 . . . Bh2† 15 Kf1 Nxf2 16 Qf3 (16 Kxf2? Qh4† 17 Kf1 Bxh3) 16 . . . Nh1!, Eslon–Barczay, Kecskemét 1983. In spite of complications, White should get the advantage.

(n) (A) 16 Bd2 Bb7 17 Qxb7 Nd3 18 Re2 Qg3 19 Kf1 Nf4 20 Rf2! (Wedberg) should be good for White. (B) Not 16 Qxf2? Bh2† 17 Kf1 Bg3 18 Qe2 Bxh3 19 gxh3 Rae8 +, Matanović–Matulović 1954.

(o) Capablanca–Marshall, New York 1918, continued 16 . . . Bg4?! 17 hxg4 Bh2† 18 Kf1 Bg3 19 Rxf2 Qh1† 20 Ke2 Bxf2 21 Bd2! Bh4 22 Qh3 Rae8† 23 Kd3 Qf1† 24 Kc2 Bf2 25 Qf3 +; White has a decisive material advantage and a safe king. After 16 . . . Ng4, Grefe's 17 g3! Qxh3 (17 . . . Bxg3 18 Qxf7†! Rxf7 19 Re8 mate) 18 Qxh8 gives Black too little for his rook.

(p) 10 Ng5?! Bg4 11 f3 exf3 12 Nxf3 (12 gxf3 Nxd5) 12 . . . Na5 13 Bc2 Re8 14 d4 Qxd5 15 Qd3 Bd6 leaves Black far ahead in development, Morley–Harding, Teesside 1972.

(q) Risky is 11 Qxf3 Bg4 12 Qg3 Re8 13 d4 Bd6 14 Rxe8† Qxe8 15 Qe3 Qxc6 16 f3 Re8 17 Qf2 Re7! 18 Bg5 Qe8 with a turbulant position.

(r) 11 . . . Bg4 12 gxf3! Bh3 13 Bf4 is very good for White. The column is analysis by Tal and Gutman, but 9 . . . e4 was originated by Herman Steiner.

RUY LOPEZ

1 e4 e5 2 Nf3 Nc6 3 Bb5 a6 4 Ba4 Nf6 5 0–0 Be7

	103	104	105	106	107	108
6	Qe2 (Worrall Attack) b5			d4 (Center Variation) exd4		 Nxe4
7	Bb3 0–0(a)			e5 . . . . Ne4	Re1 b5(i)	Qe2 f5
8	c3 . . . . d5	 d6	a4 b4(f)	Nxd4 Nxd4(g)	e5(j) Nxe5	dxe5 0–0
9	d3(b) Re8	Rd1 Be6(d)	a5 d6	Qxd4 Nc5	Rxe5 d6	c3(l) Qe8
10	Re1 Bb7	Bc2 d5	c3 Rb8	Nc3 0–0	Re1 bxa4	Nbd2 Nc5
11	Nbd2 Qd7	d3 Re8	Bc4 d5! =	Bg5 Bxg5	Nxd4 Bd7	Bc2 Ne6
12	Nf1 Rad1	Nbd2 Bd6		Qxc5 Be7	Qf3 0–0	Nb3 Qh5
13	Bg5 Na5(c)	Nf1 h6(e)		Qe3 d5(h)	Nc6 Bxc6(k)	Re1 d6(m)

(a) 7 . . . Qd6 8 Nbd2 Be6 9 b3 Nd7 10 Bb2 c5 11 Nc4 Bxc4 12 dxc4 Qxd1 13 Rfxd1 f6 14 Nd2 Rd8 15 Nf1, Draw, Hjartarson–Karpov, match 1989.

(b) 9 exd5 Bg4 10 dxc6 e4 11 d4 exf3 12 gxf3 Bh5! 13 Bf4 Re8 14 Bg3 Bd6 15 Qd3 Bg6 =, Borisov–Zhuravlev, USSR 1960.

(c) 14 Bc2 dxe4 15 dxe4 Nc4 =, Keres–Geller, Budapest 1952.

(d) 9 . . . Na5 10 Bc2 c5 11 d3 Nc6 12 Nbd2 Re8 13 Nf1 Bf8 14 a4 Bb7 15 Bg5 gave White good play on the central light squares in Barlov–G. Agzamov, Sochi 1984.

(e) 14 h3 Qc8!? 15 Ng3 dxe4 =, Barlov–Velimirović, Vrsać 1985.

(f) 8 . . . Rb8 9 axb5 axb5 10 Nc3 d6 11 h3 Bd7, Treybal–Alekhine, Pistyan 1922, is also fine for Black. The column is Tringov–Smyslov, Amsterdam 1964.

(g) Equally satisfactory is 8 . . . 0–0 9 Nf5 d5 10 Bxc6 bxc6 11 Nxe7† Qxe7 12 Re1 f6 13 f3 Ng5 14 Nc3 Bf5 15 exf6 Qxf6 =. *Comments.*

(h) 14 Rad1 c6 15 Ne2 Qa5 16 Bb3 Bg4 =, Honfi–Krogius, Hamburg 1965.

(i) 7 . . . 0–0 8 e5 Ne8 9 c3 dxc3 10 Nxc3 d6 11 exd6 Nxd6 12 Nd5 Re8 is equal. Pia Cramling–Korchnoi, London 1982, continued 11 . . . cxd6?! 12 Nd5 Bf6 13 Be3 Be6 14 Bb6 Qd7 15 Rc1 Bxb2 16 Rc2 Bf6 17 Nb4 Bd8 18 Rxc6 bxc6 19 Bxc6 Qc8 20 Bxd8 Qxd8 21 Bxa8 Qxa8 22 Ng5 a5 23 Qc2 Nf6 24 Nc6 Re8 25 h3 a4 26 Rd1 h6 27 Nxe6 Rxe6 28 Rb1 Nd7 29 Rb4 Qe8 30 Qxa4 Nc5 31 Qb5 Kh7 32 Rd4 Rg6 33 Kh2 Qe1 34 Qb2 Qf1 (34 . . . Ne4 is better) 35 Rg4 Nd3 36 Qc2 Ne1? 37 Qf5 Nxg2 38 Ne7 Ne3 39 fxe3? (with both players in time pressure, Cramling misses 39 Qxf7 Nxg4† 40 hxg4 Rg5 41 Qg8 mate!) 39

. . . Qe2† 40 Kh1 Qe1† 41 Kh2 Qe2† 42 Kh1 Draw. This game was a milestone in the progress of women's chess.

(j) Tame is 8 Bb3 d6 9 Bd5 Bd7 10 Bxc6 (10 Nxd4 Nxd5 is all right for Black) 10 . . . Bxc6 11 Nxd4 Bd7 = , Matulović–Hecht, Hamburg 1965.

(k) 14 Qxc6 d5 15 Bf4 Bd6 16 Bxd6 Qxd6 = , Nicholson–Hjartarson, Dubai 1986.

(l) 9 Be3 Kh8 10 Nbd2 d5 ∞.

(m) 14 exd6 Bxd6 = , Plaskett–Pyhala, Jarvenpaa 1985.

RUY LOPEZ

1 e4 e5 2 Nf3 Nc6 3 Bb5 a6 4 Ba4 Nf6 5 0–0 Be7

	109	110	111	112	113	114
6	Bxc6 (Exchange Variation Doubly Deferred) .....Nc3........d3(l)					
	dxc6				b5	d6(m)
7	d3......................Qe1........Nc3				Bb3	c3
	Nd7(a)		c5(g)	Bg4	d6	0–0
8	Nbd2		Nxe4	h3	Nd5(j)	Nbd2
	0–0		Qd4	Bh5	Bb7	Bd7
9	Nc4		Nd3	Qe2(i)	Nxf6†	Re1
	f6(b)		c4	Qc8	Bxf6	Re8
10	Nh4		Nf4	Qe3	Bd5	d4
	Nc5(c)		g5	Nd7	Qc8	b5
11	Nf5 ....Qf3		Nd5(h)	g4	Re1	Bc2
	Bxf5	Be6(e)	Nxd5	Bg6	0–0	Bf8
12	exf5	Ne3	exd5	d4	c3	Nb3
	Qd7	g6	Qxd5 =	f6	Na5(k)	h6
13	Qg4	Qg3		Ne2	Bxb7	h3
	b5(d)	Kh8(f)		h5 =	Qxb7 =	Qb8(n)

(a) 7 ... Bd6 8 Nbd2 0–0 9 Nc4 Re8 10 b3 b5 11 Ne3! ± (Pickett).

(b) 9 ... Bf6?! 10 b3 Re8 11 Bb2 c5 12 h3 b5 13 Ne3 Nb6 14 a4 gave White a good edge in Benko–Rossolimo, US Chp. 1968.

(c) Lukacs' 10 ... g6 is the best try to keep winning chances for Black. The column is drawish.

(d) 14 Ne3 Rfe8 15 h3 Qd4 16 Rd1 Rad8 17 Rb1 Qxg4 =, Hort–Reshevsky, Los Angeles 1968.

(e) 11 ... Ne6 12 Nf5 Nd4 13 Nxd4 Qxd4 (13 ... exd4 is also good) 14 Be3 Qd8 was equal in Hort–Spassky, match 1977.

(f) 14 b3 Bf7 15 f4 exf4 16 Rxf6 Ne6! (on 16 ... Bd6 Wedberg gives 17 Bb2 Bxf4 18 Qxf4 Nd7 19 Ng4 +) 17 Rf2 Bd6 =, Wedberg–Reshevsky, Reykjavik 1984.

(g) In order to stop d2–d4 at some time.

(h) 11 Ne2 Qxe4 12 d3 cxd3 13 cxd3 Qxd3 14 Bxg5 Rg8 = (Keres). The column is Schmid–Puig, Bern 1962.

(i) 9 g4 Nxg4!? (9 ... Bg6 10 Nxe5 Nxe4 11 Nxg6 Nxc3 =, Matulović–Spassky, USSR vs. Yugoslavia 1965) 10 hxg4 Bxg4 11 Kg2 Bc5 is unclear, Large–P. Littlewood, London 1983. The column is Wolff–Kavalek, US Chp. 1985.

(j) 8 a4 b4 9 Nd5 Na5 10 Nxe7 Qxe7 11 d4 Nxb3 12 cxb3 Bg4 13 Bg5 0–0 =, Thomas–Alekhine, Hastings 1922.

(k) 12 . . . Ne7 13 Bb3 c5 14 d4 Qc7 15 a4 allows White some advantage. Keres–Gligorić, USSR vs. Yugoslavia 1958. The column is by the same opponents in a later round of the match; Gligorić improved by eliminating the light-square bishop.

(l) For 6 Re1 see col. 149.

(m) 6 . . . b5 7 Bb3 Bb7 8 Nc3 0–0 transposes to the game Chandler–A. Rodriguez, Minsk 1982, where White held the advantage after 9 Bd2 d6 10 a4 Na5 11 Ba2 b4 12 Nd5 c5 13 Nxe7† Qxe7 14 Nh4.

(n) Lutikov–Ornstein, Tirana 1976; the position is equal.

RUY LOPEZ

Open Defense

1 e4 e5 2 Nf3 Nc6 3 Bb5 a6 4 Ba4 Nf6 5 0–0 Nxe4 6 d4 b5 7 Bb3 d5 8 dxe5 Be6 9 c3 Bc5

	115	116	117	118	119	120
10	Nbd2					Qd3(o)
	0–0			Dilworth		0–0
11	Bc2			Attack		Nbd2(p)
	Bf5		f5	Nxf2	Nxd2	f5
12	Nb3		Nb3(f)	Rxf2	Qxd2	exf6
	Bg6	Bg4	Bb6	f6	f6	Nxf6
13	Nfd4	h3(d)	Nfd4	exf6	exf6(m)	a4(q)
	Bxd4	Bh5	Nxd4	Bxf2†	Rxf6	Bf7(r)
14	cxd4(a)	g4	Nxd4	Kxf2	Ng5!	Ng5
	a5	Bg6	Bxd4(g)	Qxf6	Bf5	Ne5
15	Be3	Bxe4	Qxd4!(h)	Nf1	a4!	Qg3
	a4(b)	dxe4	c5	Ne5	Ne7	Qd6
16	Nd2	Nxc5	Qd1	Be3(k)	Bxf5	Bc2
	a3	exf3	f4	Rae8	Nxf5	Bg6(s)
17	Nxe4	Bf4	f3	Bd4	Qd3	Bxg6
	axb2(c)	Qxd1(e)	Ng5(i)	Qh4†(l)	h6(n)	Nxg6 =

(a) 14 Nxd4 Qd7 (14 . . . Nxe5? 15 f4 Nc4 16 f5 +) 15 Nxc6 Qxc6 =, Korchnoi–Karl, Swiss Chp. 1982.

(b) 15 . . . Nb4 16 Bb1 a4 17 Nd2 a3 18 Qc1 axb2 19 Qxb2 ±, Karpov–Savon, Moscow 1971.

(c) 18 Rb1 Bxe4 19 Rxb2 Qd7 20 Bd3 Bxd3 21 Qxd3 Rfb8 22 Rfb1 b4 23 Rc1 and White has the advantage due to Black's queenside weaknesses, P. Popović–Timman, Sarajevo 1984.

(d) 13 Nxc5 Nxc5 14 Re1 Re8 15 Be3 Ne6 16 Qd3 g6 17 Bh6 Ne7 18 Nd4 Bf5 19 Nxf5 Nxf5 20 Bd2 Qh4 =, Fischer–Larsen, Santa Monica 1966.

(e) 18 Raxd1 Nd8 19 Rd7 ±, Karpov–Korchnoi, World Chp. 1978.

(f) Leading only to equality is 12 exf6 Nxf6 13 Nb3 Bb6 14 Ng5 Qd7 15 Nxe6 Qxe6 16 Nd4 Nxd4 17 cxd4 Rae8 = (Larsen).

(g) 14 . . . Qd7 15 f3 Nc5 16 Kh1 ±, Kieninger–Bogolyubov, Krakow 1941.

(h) 15 cxd4 f4 16 f3 Ng3! 17 hxg3 hxg3 18 Qd3 Bf5 19 Qxf5 Rxf5 20 Bxf5 Qh4 21 Bh3 Qxd4† 22 Kh1 Qxe5 is a very difficult position for both sides, but Black should not be worse.

(i) 18 a4 b4 19 cxb4 ±.

(j) It is best to take the rook immediately; if 12 . . . Qxf6?! 13 Qf1 Bg4 14 h3 Ne5 15 Nd4.

(k) Morović–Yusupov, Tunis 1985, went 16 Kg1?! Nxf3† 17 gxf3 Qxf3 18 Qxf3 Rxf3 and Black was slightly better in the endgame.

(l) 18 Kg1 Nxf3 19 gxf3 Qg5† 20 Ng3 Bh3 21 a4 $\pm$, Tseshkovsky–Chekhov, Rostock 1984. But 17 . . . Bg4 may be better.

(m) On Simagin's 13 Qd3 there is 13 . . . g6 14 exf6 Bf5 15 Qe2 Re8 16 Qd1 Bxc2 17 Qxc2 Qxf6 =.

(n) 18 axb5! axb5 19 Rxa8 Qxa8 20 Qxb5 $\pm$, Suetin–Antoshin, Sochi 1974.

(o) 10 Qe2 0–0 11 Be3 f6 12 exf6 Qxf6 13 Nbd2 Bd6 14 a4 Nxd2 15 Qxd2 Ne5 16 Nxe5 Qxe5 17 f4 Qh5 =, Bertok–Geller, Stockholm 1962.

(p) 11 Be3 f6! 12 exf6 Qxf6 13 Bxd5 Rad8 14 Bxe6† Qxe6 with good play for the pawn.

(q) 13 Ng5 Ne5! 14 Qg3 Qd6 15 Re1?! (15 Bc2!) Nfg4 16 Nde4 dxe4 17 Bxe6† Kh8 18 Be3 Nxf2 19 Qh4 h6 20 Nxe4 Nxe4 21 Qxe4 Rae8 $\mp$, Schelfout–Euwe, Amsterdam 1942.

(r) Also possible is 13 . . . Rb8 14 axb5 axb5 15 Ng5 Ne5 16 Qg3 Qd6 17 Bc2 Bd7 18 Nb3 Bb6 19 Bf4 Rbe8 20 Nd4 Nh5! 21 Bxe5 Rxe5 22 Bxh7† Kh8 23 Qh4 g6 24 f4 Rxg5 25 Qxg5 Kxh7 =, A. Sokolov–Timman, Reykjavik 1988.

(s) 16 . . . h6?! 17 Nxf7 Nxf7 18 Nb3 was good for White in A. Sokolov–Yusupov, match 1986. 16 . . . Bg6 is Sokolov's suggested improvement for Black.

RUY LOPEZ

Open Defense

**1 e4 e5 2 Nf3 Nc6 3 Bb5 a6 4 Ba4 Nf6 5 O–O Nxe4
6 d4 b5 7 Bb3 d5 8 dxe5 Be6 9 c3 Be7**

	121	122	123	124	125	126
10	Nbd2............	........Be3(f)	....	....	....Bc2........	..Qe2(l)
	O–O		Nc5........	....Qd7	O–O(j)	Nc5
11	Qe2........	Bc2	Bc2	Nbd2	Qe2	Bc2
	Nc5(a)	f5	Bg4(g)	Rd8(i)	Qd7	d4
12	Nd4	Nb3	Nbd2	Nxe4	Rd1(k)	Rd1
	Nxb3(b)	Qd7	Ne6(h)	dxe4	f5	Bc4
13	Nxc6!	Nfd4	Qb1	Qxd7†	Nbd2	Qe1
	Nxc1	Nxd4	Bh5	Bxd7	Kh8	d3
14	Raxc1	cxd4(d)	b4	Ng5	Nb3	Na3(m)
	Qd7	a5	Qd7	Nxe5	Bf7	Qc8
15	Nxe7†	f3	a4	Bd4	Nbd4	Bb1
	Qxe7	a4	Rb8	Bxg5	Bh5 =	Bd5
16	f4	fxe4	axb5	Bxe5		Bxd3
	f5	axb3	axb5	O–O		Bxf3
17	exf6	Bxb3	Bf5	Bxc7		gxf3
	Qxf6(c)	fxe4(e)	Bg6 ±	Rc8 =		Nxd3(n)

(a) 11 . . . Nxd2 12 Qxd2 Na5 13 Bc2 Nc4 14 Qd3 g6 15 Bh6 gave White strong play on the kingside in Tal–Korchnoi, USSR 1955.

(b) 12 . . . Qd7 13 Bc2 f6 14 Nxe6 Qxe6 15 b4! Nd7 16 Qd3 is strong. Reti–Euwe, Vienna 1928.

(c) After 18 Qe3 Bf5 19 Qd4 (Janošević–Lukić, Yugoslavia 1955), Korchnoi rates White as slightly better.

(d) 14 Nxd4 c5 15 Nxe6 Qxe6 16 f3 Ng5 17 a4 g6 18 Qe2 worked out well for White in A. Rodriguez–Passerotti, Malta 1980.

(e) 18 Be3 Rxf1† 19 Qxf1 Rf8 20 Qe2 h6 was played in Gruenfeld–Tal, Riga 1979. Miles now gives 21 Rc1 ±.

(f) Nowadays this position usually arises by 9 Be3 Be7 10 c3 in order to avoid 9 c3 Bc5.

(g) Tal–Timman, 3rd match game 1985, saw 11 . . . Nd7!? 12 Nd4 Ndxe5 13 f4 Nc4 14 Nxc6 Nxe3 15 Nxd8 Nxd1 16 Nxe6 Ne3 17 Nxc7† Kd7 18 Nxa8 Nxc2 19 Nd2 Bc5† 20 Kh1 Nxa1 21 Rxa1 Rxa8 22 Re1 Kd6 23 g3 Rc8 Draw.

(h) 12 . . . Nxe5? 13 Bxc5 Bxc5 14 Qe1 f6 15 Nxe5 fxe5 16 Qxe5†. The column is Zapata–G. Garcia, Columbia 1986.

(i) 11 . . . Nxd2 12 Qxd2 Na5 13 Bg5 ±, Keres–Pilnik, Buenos Aires 1964. The column is Timman–Korchnoi, Reykjavik 1987.

(j) 10 . . . Bg4 11 h3 Bh5 (11 . . . Bxf3 12 gxf3) 12 g4 Bg6 13 Bb3 Na5 14 Bxd5 c6 15 Bxe4 ±, Fischer–Olafsson, Havana 1966.

(k) (A) 12 Nd4 Nc5 13 Nd2 f6 14 exf6 Bxf6 15 Nxe6 Nxe6 16 Nf3 Nc5 17 Rd1 Rae8 =, Stein–Savon, USSR 1963. (B) 12 Bxe4?! dxe4 13 Qxe4 Bd5 gives Black good play for the pawn. The column is Tal–Keres, Moscow 1966.

(l) 10 a4 b4! 11 Nd4 Nxe5 12 f4 Bg4! 13 Qc2 c5 14 fxe5 cxd4 15 cxd4 0–0 16 Nd2 Be2 17 Re1 Rc8 18 Qb1 Bh5 19 Qd3 Bg6 =, Evans–Hanauer, New York 1949.

(m) 14 b3? Qc8! 15 bxc4 dxc2 wins a piece.

(n) 18 Rxd3 Qf5! (Euwe), Black stands well.

RUY LOPEZ

Open Defense

**1 e4 e5 2 Nf3 Nc6 3 Bb5 a6 4 Ba4 Nf6 5 0–0 Nxe4 6 d4
b5 7 Bb3 d5 8 dxe5 Be6**

	127	128	129	130	131	132
9	Qe2 (Howell Attack)				Nbd2	
	Be7			Bc5(j)	Nc5(n)	
10	Rd1(a)			Be3	c3	
	Nc5		0–0	0–0(k)	d4	Bg4(r)
11	c4	Bxd5(e)	c4	Nbd2(l)	Bxe6(o)	Bc2
	d4(b)	Bxd5	bxc4	Nxd2	Nxe6	Be7
12	cxb5	Nc3	Bxc4	Qxd2	cxd4	Re1
	d3(c)	Bc4!	Qd7(g)	d4	Ncxd4	Qd7
13	Qf1	Rxd8†	Nc3	Bg5	Ne4(p)	Nf1
	Nxb3	Rxd8	Nxc3	Qd7	Be7	Rd8
14	axb3	Qe3	bxc3	h3	Be3	Ne3
	Nb4	b4	f6	Rfe8	Nf5	Bh5
15	Bd2	b3	exf6	Qf4(m)	Qc2	Nf5
	Nc2	Be6	Bxf6	h6	0–0	0–0
16	Rxa6	Ne4	Bg5	Bh4 ∞	Rad1	Nxe7†
	Rxa6	Rd1†	Kh8(h)		Nxe3	Nxe7
17	bxa6	Ne1	Bxf6		fxe3	Be3
	Bxb3(d)	Nd4(f)	Rxf6(i)		Qc8!(q)	Ne6(s)

(a) Aggressive but speculative is 10 c4!? bxc4 11 Ba4 Bd7 12 Nc3 Nc5 13 e6 fxe6 14 Bxc6 Bxc6 15 Ne5 Qd6 16 Qh5† g6 17 Nxg6 hxg6 18 Qxh8† Kd7 19 Qg7 d4 with ample compensation for the exchange, Abrosin–Radchenko 1954.

(b) 11 . . . bxc4 12 Bxc4 0–0 13 Nc3 d4 14 Be3 is clearly better for White.

(c) 12 . . . Nxb3 13 axb3 axb5 14 Rxa8 Qxa8 15 Bg5 Bxb3 16 Rc1 Bxg5 17 Nxg5 h6 18 Nd2! hxg5 19 Nxb3 0–0 20 e6 ±, A. Rodriguez–Agzamov, Cienfuegos 1984.

(d) 18 Bg5! Bc4 (18 . . . Bxg5 19 Rxd3) 19 Bxe7 Qxe7 20 a7 0–0 21 Nbd2 Ba6 22 b3 ±, Greenfeld–Pernik, Israel 1983.

(e) (A) 11 Be3 0–0 12 c4 bxc4 13 Bxc4 Na5 14 Bxd5! Bxd5 15 Nc3 Bxf3 16 Qxf3 Qe8 17 b4 is slightly better for White, Jansa–Milev, Tel Aviv 1964. (B) 11 Nc3 Nxb3 12 axb3 0–0 = .

(f) 18 Bb2 Nxc2 19 Qe2 Rxa1 20 Bxa1 Nxa1 21 Nxc5 Bxc5 22 Nd3 Bb6 23 Nxb4 0–0 24 Nc6 f6 25 h4 fxe5 26 Qxe5 Rf6 27 Nd8! Bf7 28 Nxf7 Kxf7 29 Qxa1 Rxf2 30 Kh2 and White held a slight material advantage in the endgame, Timman–Yusupov, Montpellier 1985.

(g) 12 . . . Bc5 13 Be3 Bxe3 14 Qxe3 Qb8 15 Bb3 Na5 16 Nbd2 Qa7 17 Nxe4! Qxe3 18 fxe3 Nxb3 19 axb3 dxe4 20 Nd4 and despite the doubled pawns White has the more comfortable endgame, Timman–Tal, Wijk aan Zee 1982.

(h) 16 ... Bxc3 17 Rac1 Bf6 18 Bxf6 Rxf6 19 Ng5 Ne7 20 Re1! dxc4 21 Nxe6 (Euwe) gives White an edge.

(i) 18 Ng5 Na5 19 Bxa6 Bg4 20 f3 Rfxa6 21 fxg4 h6 22 Nf3 Nb3 23 Rab1 Rxa2 24 Rb2 Rxb2 25 Qxb2 Nc5 draw, Sigurjonsson–F. Olafsson, Geneva 1977.

(j) 9 ... Nc5 10 Rd1 Nxb3 11 axb3 Qc8 12 c4 Nb4 13 cxb5 axb5 14 Rxa8 Qxa8 15 Bd2! c6 16 Nd4 Na6 17 b4 Nc7 18 Rc1 Bd7 19 Qd3 ±, Písek–Ratoliska, Prague 1957.

(k) 10 ... Qe7 11 Nbd2 Bxe3 12 Qxe3 Nxd2 13 Qxd2 ±̱.

(l) 11 Rd1 Na5 12 Nbd2 Bxe3 13 Qxe3 Nxd2 14 Rxd2 leaves Black a bit weak on the dark squares, Minić–Honfi, Vrnjačka Banja 1966.

(m) 15 Rfe1?! Bb4 16 c3 dxc3 17 bxc3 Qxd2 18 Bxd2 Ba3 =, Schmid–Korchnoi, Lucerne 1982.

(n) 9 ... Be7 10 Nxe4 dxe4 11 Bxe6 fxe6 12 Ng5 Bxg5 13 Qh5† g6 14 Qxg5 ±̱.

(o) Spectacular, but not advantageous for White, is 11 Ng5!? Qxg5 12 Qf3 0–0–0! 13 Bxe6† fxe6 14 Qxc6 Qxe5 15 b4 Qd5! 16 Qxd5 exd5 17 bxc5 dxc3 with good compensation for the piece, Timman–Smyslov, East Germany 1979.

(p) 13 a4 Be7 14 Nxd4 Qxd4 15 axb5 Qxe5 16 bxa6 0–0 17 Nf3 Qb5 18 Qa4 Qxa4 19 Rxa4 Nc5 =, Psakhis–Dolmatov, USSR Chp. 1981.

(q) (A) 18 Nd4 Nxd4 19 exd4 Qe6! 20 Qxc7 (20 Ng3 c6 21 Nf5 Rfe8 22 Rd3 Bf8 23 Rh3 g6 =, Short–Yusupov, Montpellier 1985) 20 ... Rac8 21 Qa5 Rc2 22 Rf2 Rfc8 23 Qe1, Hübner–Ljubojević, Tilburg 1985. According to Hübner, 23 ... Rxf2 24 Qxf2 Qxa2 leads to equality. (B) 18 h3 Rd8 19 Nh2 Rxd1 20 Qxd1 Qe8 21 Qh5 Nc5 22 Ng3 a5 23 Nf5 Ra6 ∞, Tal–Korchnoi, Reykjavik 1987.

(r) 10 ... Nxb3 11 Nxb3 Be7 12 Nfd4 Nxe5 13 Re1 Ng6 14 Nxe6 fxe6 15 Nd4! was very good for White in Kuzmin–Beliavsky, USSR Chp. 1977.

(s) 18 Bxh7†! Kxh7 19 Ng5† Kg6 20 g4 Bxg4 21 Qxg4 ±, Geller–Hazai, Sochi 1982.

RUY LOPEZ

Open Defense

1 e4 e5 2 Nf3 Nc6 3 Bb5 a6 4 Ba4 Nf6 5 0–0 Nxe4

	133	134	135	136	137	138
6	(d4)..Re1?!					
	(b5)..exd4					Nc5
7	(Bb3)				Re1	Bxc6(l)
	(d5)				d5	dxc6
8	(dxe5)(a)..........................Nxe5				Nxd4	Nxe5
	(Be6)			Nxe5	Bd6	Be7
9	c3.........Be3.........a4			dxe5	Nxc6	d4
	Nc5	Nc5(e)	b4	c6(i)	Bxh2†	Ne6
10	Bc2	c3(f)	a5	Be3	Kh1!	Be3
	Bg4	Nxb3	Nc5	Be7	Qh4	0–0
11	Re1	axb3	Bg5	Nd2	Rxe4†	Nc3
	d4(b)	Be7	Qd7	Nxd2	dxe4	f6
12	h3	Nd4(g)	Nbd2	Qxd2	Qd8†	Nf3
	Bh5	Nxd4	h6	0–0	Qxd8	Re8 =
13	e6!	cxd4	Bh4	Qc3	Nxd8†	
	fxe6(c)	0–0	Rb8(h)	Bb7	Kxd8	
14	cxd4	f4 =	c3	f4	Kxh2	
	Bxf3(d)		Bg4 ∞	a5(j)	Be6(k)	

(a) 8 a4 Nxd4 9 Nxd4 exd4 10 axb5 Bc5 11 c3 0–0 12 cxd4 Bb6 13 Nc3 Bb7 =, Lasker–Schlechter, World Chp. 1910.

(b) 11 ... Be7 12 Nbd2 transposes into col. 132.

(c) 13 ... Nxe6 14 Be4 ±, Gutkin–Klavins, USSR 1968.

(d) 15 Qxf3 Nxd4 16 Qh5† g6 17 Bxg6† hxg6 18 Qxh8 Nc2 19 Bh6 with advantage, Unzicker–Lehmann, Berlin 1953.

(e) (A) 9 ... Bc5 10 Qd3 0–0 11 Nc3! Nb4 12 Qe2 Bxe3?! (12 ... Nxc3 13 bxc3 ⩲) 13 Qxc3 c5 14 a3 ±, Nunn–Murey, Brighton 1983. (B) 9 ... Be7 10 Nbd2 Nc5 11 Nd4 Nxd4 12 Bxd4 Qd7 13 c3 Na4! =, Tseshkovsky–Balashov, USSR 1983.

(f) 10 Qe2!? Nxb3 11 axb3 Be7 12 Rd1 Qc8 13 Nc3 Nb4 14 Bg5 c5 15 Bxe7 Kxe7 16 Qd2 Rd8 17 Ne2!, Horvath–Agzamov, Sochi 1985, is an interesting line for White.

(g) 12 Nbd2 0–0 13 b4 Bg4 ∞. The column is Ghinda–Yusupov, Dubai 1986, including Yusupov's suggestion 14 f4! instead of 14 Nc3 as played.

(h) 13 ... Be7 14 Bxe7 Nxe7 15 Nd4 0–0 =, J. Kristiansen–Murey, Beersheba 1985.

(i) 9 ... Be6 10 c3 Bc5 11 Qe2 0–0 12 Be3 is good for White (Keres).

(j) Black is completely equal, Fischer–Addison, US Chp. 1966/67. The game continued 15 a3 b4 16 Qd2 a4 17 Ba2 bxa3 18 bxa3 Bxa3 19 Rfb1 Bc8 20 Bxd5 Qxd5 21 Rxa3 Qxd2

22 Bxd2 Bf5 23 Rb2 Rfd8 24 Be3 h5 25 h3 Rdb8 26 Rxb8† Rxb8 27 Rxa4 Bxc2 28 Rc4 Rb1† 29 Kf2 Rb2 30 Kg3 Bf5 31 Rxc6 Rxg2†! Draw.

(k) 15 Be3 f5 16 Nc3 Ke7 17 g4 and White has the advantage in the ending, Capablanca–Ed. Lasker, New York 1915.

(l) 7 Nxe5 Nxe5 8 Rxe5† Be7 leaves Black with easy equality. The column is Soler–Mitchell, England 1932.

RUY LOPEZ

Counterthrust Variation

1 e4 e5 2 Nf3 Nc6 3 Bb5 a6 4 Ba4 Nf6 5 0–0 b5 6 Bb3

	139	140	141	142	143	144
	Bb7..d6					
7	Re1.................... Bc5		c3 .... Nxe4(f)	d4 .... Nxd4	d3 .... Bc5	Ng5(m) d5
8	c3 d6 0–0		d4 Na5(g)	Bxf7†(j) Kxf7	Nc3 d6	exd5 Nd4
9	d4 Bb6	d4 Bb6	Bc2 exd4	Nxe5† Kg8	a4 Na5	Re1(n) Bc5
10	Bg5(a) h6	Bg5(d) h6	b4(h) Nc4	Qxd4 c5	Ba2 b4	Rxe5† Kf8
11	Bh4 Qd7(b)	Bh4 Re8	Bxe4 Bxe4	Qd1(k) Qe8	Nd5 b3!?	c3 Ng4
12	a4 0–0–0	Qd3 d6	Re1 d5	Ng4 Nxg4	Nxf6† Qxf6	cxd4 Bxd4
13	axb5 axb5(c)	Nbd2 Na5(e)	Nxd4 Bd6(i)	Qxg4 h5(l)	cxb3 Nc6 ∞	Re2 Qg5(o)

(a) 10 a4 h6 11 Nh4 Ne7 12 Qd3 Qd7 13 h3 0–0–0 14 axb5 axb5 15 Bxf7 Rhf8 16 Bb3 d5 ∞, Arnason–Timman, Reykjavik 1987.

(b) 11 . . . 0–0 12 a4 exd4 13 axb5 axb5 14 Rxa8 Bxa8 15 cxd4 Re8 16 Nc3 g5 17 Qd2! Na5 (17 . . . gxh4 18 Qxh6 Nh7 19 Bxf7† Kh8 20 Nxh4 Ne7 21 Nd5 Bxd5 22 exd5 ±, Bouwmeester) 18 Bc2 ±, Penrose–Vukcević, corr. 1984.

(c) 14 Bxf6! gxf6 15 Bd5, Rogers–Flear, Szirak 1986. White has the better chances in this sharp position.

(d) 10 a4 d6 11 axb5 axb5 12 Rxa8 Bxa8 13 d5 Ne7 14 Bg5 Ng6 15 Nh4 Nxh4 16 Bxh4 h6 17 Na3 g5 18 Bg3 Qd7 =, Bednarski–Levi, Polish Chp. 1969.

(e) 14 Bc2 c5 15 d5 c4 16 Qe2 Kh7 17 b4 ±, Savon–Gipslis, USSR Chp. 1970.

(f) 7 . . . h6 8 d4 d6 9 Qe2! g6 10 a4 Bg7 11 dxe5 dxe5 12 axb5 axb5 13 Rxa8 Qxa8 14 Na3 ±, P. Popović–Tal, Subotica 1987.

(g) 8 . . . Be7 9 Re1 d5 10 dxe5 Na5 11 Bc2 0–0 12 Qe2 c5 13 Nbd2 ±.

(h) 10 Bxe4 Bxe4 11 Re1 d5 12 Nxd4 c5 13 f3 cxd4 14 fxe4 dxe4 15 Qg4! Ra7! 16 Rxe4† Re7 17 Rxd4 Qa8 ∞ (Flear).

(i) 14 f3 Qh4 15 h3 Qg3 16 Nf5! Qh2† 17 Kf2 0–0–0 18 fxe4 dxe4 19 Qg4 Ne5!? (also 19 . . . Kb8 20 Qxe4 Rhe8 21 Qxe8 Rxe8 22 Rxe8† Kb7 ∞, Kindermann) 20 Qxe4 (20 Nxd6† Kb8 21 Qxe4 Rxd6 22 Qxe5 Rf6† 23 Qxf6 gxf6 [Yakovich] leaves Black much better due to White's lagging development) 20 . . . Rhe8 21 Bg5! g6 (21 . . . f6 22 Nxd6† Rxd6 23 Bf4 and 23 . . . Rf6 is not possible) 22 Nd2! (giving back the piece to imprison Black's queen!) 22 ... gxf5 23 Qxf5† Rd7 24 Nf1 Qh1 25 Rad1 Re6 26 Bf4 Ng6 27 Bxd6 Rdxd6 28 Rxd6 cxd6 29 Rxe6 fxe6 30 Qxe6† Kc7 31 Qf7† Kb6 32 Qd7 Resigns, Abramović–Flear, Brussels 1986.

(j) 8 Nxd4 exd4 9 e5 Ne4 10 c3 dxc3 11 Qf3 d5 12 exd6 Qf6! 13 d7† (van der Wiel–Gonzalez, Biel 1985) and now 13 ... Kd8! 14 Qxf6 Nxf6 15 Nxc3 Kxd7 is equal (Ligterink).

(k) 11 Qe3?! Qc7! 12 Qg3 Ne4 13 Qf4 d5 14 Nf3 Bd6 15 Qf5 Qf7 ∓, Hecht–Malanyuk, Moscow 1985.

(l) 14 Qe2 Qxe4 15 Qxe4 Bxe4 16 c3 h4 17 h3 Rh5 =, Gragger–Matsukević, corr. 1967.

(m) It is better to transpose into normal lines of the Closed Defense with 7 c3 Be7 8 Re1, though Black has the option of 7 ... Bg4. Compare col. 149.

(n) Safer than the text is 9 c3 Nxb3 10 Qxb3 Bd6! 11 d3 Bf5 12 c4 0–0 13 cxb5 Rb8 =, Kupper–Lombardy, Zürich 1960.

(o) 14 h3 Nxf2 15 Rxf2 Bxh3 ∓ (Hort).

RUY LOPEZ

1 e4 e5 2 Nf3 Nc6 3 Bb5 a6 4 Ba4 Nf6

	145	146	147	148	149	150
5	O–O..Nc3(q)					
	d6 ....Be7					b5(r)
6	c3 ....Bxc6† ......Re1(g)				Re1(l)	Bb3
	Bd7(a)	bxc6	b5 ....Be7(i)		d6(m)	Be7(s)
7	d4	d4	Bb3	Bxc6†	c3	O–O
	Be7	Nxe4!(d)	Na5	bxc6	Bg4(n)	d6
8	Re1	dxe5(e)	d4	d4	d3(o)	Nd5
	O–O	d5	Nxb3	Nd7(j)	O–O	Na5
9	Nbd2	Nbd2	axb3	Na3	Nbd2	Nxe7
	Re8	Nxd2	Bb7!	f6	Re8	Qxe7
10	Nf1(b)	Bxd2	Bg5	Nc4	Nf1	d4
	h6	Bg4	h6	Nf8	Bf8	O–O(t)
11	Ng3	h3	Bh4	Na5	h3	Bg5
	Bf8	Bh5	Be7	Bd7	Bd7	Bg4
12	h3	Re1	Nc3	Qd3	Ng3	dxe5
	g6(c)	Bc5(f)	Nd7(h)	Ne6(k)	g6(p)	dxe5 =

(a) 6 ... Nxe4 7 d4 gives Black more than a pawn's worth of problems.

(b) 10 a3 transposes to column 174.

(c) 13 Bc2 Bg7 14 Be3 Kh7 15 Qd2 ±, Tal–Rellstab, Hastings 1973–74.

(d) 7 ... exd4 8 Nxd4 (8 Qxd4! is also good) 8 ... c5 9 Nf3 Be7 10 Nc3 O–O 11 Re1 Bb7 12 Bg5 with a pull for White, Smyslov–Botvinnik, World Chp. 1954.

(e) 8 Re1 allows the sharp line 8 ... f5 9 dxe5 d5 10 Nd4 Bc5 11 c3 Qh4 12 f3 Nf2! ∞ (Belavenets).

(f) 13 b4 Bb6 14 e6 ±, Bellin–Bisguier, Hastings 1975–76.

(g) Satisfactory for Black is 6 d4 b5! 7 Bb3 Nxd4 8 Nxd4 exd4. Compare col. 162 where the moves 4 ... Nf6 5 O–O were not played.

(h) 13 Bxe7 Qxe5 14 dxe5 dxe5 15 Nd5 Qd6 =. *Comments.*

(i) 6 ... Bd7 7 Bxc6! Bxc6 8 d4 Be7 (8 ... Bxe4 9 Nc3) 9 Nc3 exd4 10 Nxd4 O–O 11 b3 Nd7 12 Bb2 Bf6 13 Nxc6 bxc6 14 Qd2 ±.

(j) 8 ... exd4 9 Qxd4 O–O 10 e5 Nd5 11 Nc3 Be6 12 Nxd5 cxd5 13 Bf4 ±, Kir. Georgiev–A. Petrosian, Sarajevo 1986.

(k) 13 Be3 Qb8 14 a4! (preventing 14 ... Qb5) with the advantage, Lobron–Kavalek, Reggio Emilia 1985–86.

(l) (A) 6 Qe2 transposes into col. 103, and (B) 6 d4 transposes into col. 106.

(m) Note that the same position as in the previous column has been reached by a different order of moves. 6 . . . b5 leads to the main variations of the Closed Defense.

(n) 7 . . . Bd7 8 d4 0–0 transposes into cols. 145 or 174.

(o) 8 h3 gives Black a chance to mix things up: 8 . . . Bh5 9 d3 Qd7 10 Nbd2 g5!? 11 g4?! (11 Nf1 is better) 11 . . . Bg6 12 Nf1 h5 13 N3h2 hxg4 14 hxg4 0–0–0 with excellent attacking chances, Kots–Spassky, USSR 1961.

(p) 13 d4 Bg7 14 a3 ±, Gufeld–A. Petrosian, USSR 1979.

(q) For 5 d4 exd4 6 0–0 Be7 see col. 106.

(r) 5 . . . d6 6 Bxc6† bxc6 7 d4 gives White chances for an edge, as in col. 159.

(s) 6 . . . Bc5 7 Nxe5 Nxe5 8 d4 Bd6 9 dxe5 Bxe5 10 f4 Bxc3† 11 bxc3 Bb7 12 e5 Ne4 13 0–0 d5 14 Qg4 Qe7! =, Bisguier–Turner, New York 1955.

(t) Also 10 . . . Bb7 11 Bg5 0–0 =, Keres–Euwe, Varna 1962.

RUY LOPEZ

1 e4 e5 2 Nf3 Nc6 3 Bb5 a6 4 Ba4

	151	152	153	154	155	156
	Wormald Variation	Duras Variation	Exchange Var. Deferred	Accelerated Counterthrust Variation		
	Nf6			b5		
5	Qe2......... b5(a)	d3.......... d6	Bxc6 dxc6	Bb3 Na5		
6	Bb3 Be7	c4(c) g6	d3(f) Bd6	0–0..................... d6		Bxf7†?! Kxf7
7	a4 Rb8	d4(d) exd4	Nbd2 Be6	d4 Nxb3	exd4(j)	Nxe5† Ke7
8	axb5 axb5	Nxd4 Bd7	Qe2 Nh5	axb3 f6	Nxd4 Bb7(k)	d4(n) Nf6
9	d4 d5	Nxc6 bxc6	Nc4 Bxc4	Nh4(h) Ne7	Bd2 Nxb3(l)	Qf3 Bb7
10	c3 Nxe4	0–0 Bg7	dxc4 Qf6	f4 Bb7	Nxb3 Nf6	b4?! Nc4
11	Nxe5 Nxe5(b)	c5 0–0(e)	g3 Qe6(g)	d5 c6(i)	Re1 Be7(m)	Qe2 Nxe5(o)

(a) 5 . . . Bc5 6 Bxc6 (6 0–0 =) bxc6! 7 Nxe5 0–0 8 0–0 Re8 9 Nxf7 Qe7 10 Ng5 d5 11 d3 Bg4 ∓, Kholmov–Zhu. Polgar, Budapest 1979.

(b) 12 dxe5 0–0 13 0–0 Bf5 =, Spassky–Kholmov, Leningrad 1954.

(c) 6 c3, the old Anderssen line, is met by 6 . . . g6! (6 . . . Be7 is playable but less active) 7 0–0 Bg7 8 d4 and now either 8 . . . 0–0 9 d5 Ne7 = or 8 . . . exd4! 9 cxd4 b5 10 Bb3 0–0 with play against the center, Romanishin–Dorfman, Lvov 1984.

(d) A recent try in this old line went 7 Nc3 Bg7 8 Nd5 Nd7?! (8 . . . Be6 is better) 9 0–0 Nc5 10 b4! Ne6 11 b5 with advantage, Kuzmin–Kuligowski, Poland 1984.

(e) 12 Nc3 Qe7 13 cxd6 cxd6 14 f3 d5 =, Duras–Cohn, Carlsbad 1911.

(f) 6 0–0 Bg4 7 h3 Bh5 8 g4 Bg6 9 Nxe5 Nxe4! 10 Nxe4 Bxe4 11 Qe2 Qd4 ∓, *Comments.*

(g) 12 Be3 c5 =, Flohr–Reshevsky, Kemeri 1937.

(h) Also good are (A) 9 c4 Bb7 10 Nc3 Ne7 11 Qe2 c6 12 Rd1 Qc7 13 Be3 Ng6 14 Rac1 ±, Fischer–Johannessen, Havana 1966; and (B) 9 Nc3 Bb7 10 Nh4 Qd7 11 f4 0–0–0 12 Nf3 ±, Tolush–Johannessen, Riga 1959. In the column, if 9 . . . Qd7 10 c4 or 10 Nc3.

(i) 12 c4 exf4 13 Rxf4 g5 14 Qh5† Kd7 15 Rxf6 ±, Arnason–Agdestein, Gausdal 1987; after 15 . . . gxh4 White has a strong attack for the piece.

(j) On 7 . . . f6 8 Nh4! play will usually transpose to the previous column since Black will eventually have to take the bishop on b3.

(k) (A) 8 . . . c5?! 9 Bd5!; (B) 8 . . . Nxb3 9 axb3 Bb7 10 Re1 Ne7 11 Nc3 Nc6 12 Nd5 Be7 13 Nf5 ± (Parma).

(l) 9 . . . c5 10 Bd5! Bxd5 11 exd5 cxd4 12 Qe1† Qe7 13 Bxa5 Qxe1 14 Rxe1† Ne7 15 Nd2 Kd7 16 Nb3 ±, Smyslov–Evans, Havana 1964.

(m) 12 Na5 Rb8 (12 . . . Bxe4? 13 Bg5 wins) 13 Nxb7 ±, Simagin–Kupreichik, Minsk 1985.

(n) 8 Nc3 Qe8 9 Nd5† Kd8 10 Qf3 Bb7 11 Nf7† Kc8 12 0–0 Nf6 13 Nxh8 Bxd5 14 exd5 Bd6 ∓ (Pachman).

(o) 12 dxe5 Nxe4 13 f3 Ke8! ∓ (Taimanov). In the column, an improvement is 10 Nc3 (Rabar and Gipslis). Black is still for choice: 10 . . . Qe8 11 Bg5 d6 12 0–0–0 h6.

RUY LOPEZ

Modern Steinitz Defense

1 e4 e5 2 Nf3 Nc6 3 Bb5 a6 4 Ba4 d6

	157	158	159	160	161	162
5	0–0.....................Bxc6†....................c4..........d4					
	Bg4........Bd7		bxc6		Bd7(n)	b5
6	h3	d4	d4		Nc3	Bb3
	h5(a)	b5	f6..........exd4		g6	Nxd4
7	d4!(b)	Bb3	Be3(h)	Qxd4	d4	Nxd4
	b5	Nxd4(e)	Ne7	c5	exd4	exd4
8	Bb3	Nxd4	Nc3	Qd3	Nxd4	c3(o)
	Nxd4(c)	exd4	Ng6	g6(k)	Bg7	dxc3
9	hxg4	c3(f)	Qe2(i)	Nc3	Be3	Nxc3
	hxg4	dxc3	a5	Bg7	Nge7	Bb7
10	Ng5	Qh5	h4	Bf4(l)	0–0	Qe2
	Nh6	g6	Ba6	Ne7	0–0	c5
11	Bd5	Qd5	Qd2	Qd2	h3	Bf4
	c6(d)	Be6(g)	h5(j)	0–0(m)	Nxd4 =	Ne7 =

(a) 6 ... Bh5 7 c3 Nf6 8 d4 Nd7 9 Be3 Be7 10 Nbd2 0–0 11 a3 Bf6 12 g4 Bg6 13 d5 Ncb8 14 Bc2 with more active play for White (Pachman).

(b) 7 c4 Qf6 8 Qb3 0–0–0 9 Bxc6 bxc6 10 hxg4 hxg4 11 Nh2 d5! 12 Nxg4 Qe6 13 Qg3 dxe4 with a strong attack for the piece.

(c) 8 ... Bxf3 9 Qxf3 Qf6 10 Qc3 Nge7 11 dxe5 dxe5 12 Be3 g5 13 a4 ± , Nikolaevsky–Shiyanovsky, USSR 1962.

(d) 12 c3 cxd5 13 cxd4 Be7 14 dxe5 is better for White (Stoica).

(e) 7 ... exd4 8 c3 dxc3 (8 ... d3 9 Qxd3 $\pm$) 9 Nxc3 also gives White fine play for the pawn.

(f) A well-known trap is 9 Qxd4?? c5 10 Qd5 c4 winning a piece.

(g) 12 Qc6† Bd7 13 Qxc3 and White has excellent prospects for the pawn, de Firmian–Haring, San Jose 1980.

(h) On 7 Nc3 Bg4 8 Be3 Qb8 is sufficient for equality.

(i) 9 Qd2 Be7 10 h4 h5 11 0–0–0 Be6 12 dxe5 fxe5 13 Ng5 Bxg5 14 Bxg5 Qb8 = , Ivkov–Smyslov, Yugoslavia vs. USSR, 1956.

(j) 12 0–0–0 Qc8 ∞ , Short–Smyslov, Subotica 1987.

(k) 8 ... Ne7 9 Nc3 Rb8 10 b3 Ng6 11 0–0 Be7 12 Nd5 with a small advantage, Mecking–Keres, Petropolis 1973.

(l) 10 Bg5 f6 11 Bh4 Ne7 12 0–0–0 Be6 $\overline{\overline{+}}$, Timman–Spraggett, Taxco 1985.

(m) 12 0–0–0 Re8 13 Bh6 Bh8 was better for Black in Timman–Spassky, Linares 1983. Timman suggests 12 Bh6, but 12 . . . Bg4 should be equal.

(n) Also reasonable is 5 . . . Bg4 6 d3 Nf6 7 Be3 Be7 8 Nbd2 0–0 9 h3 Be6 =, Browne–F. Olafsson, Las Palmas 1974. The column is Keres–Capablanca, Buenos Aires 1939.

(o) 8 Bd5 Rb8 9 Bc6† Bd7 10 Bxd7† Qxd7 11 Qxd4 Nf6 12 Nc3 Be7 13 0–0 0–0 =, Hort–Keres, Oberhausen 1961. The column is Stoltz–Flohr, match 1931.

Modern Steinitz Defense, Siesta Variation

1 e4 e5 2 Nf3 Nc6 3 Bb5 a6 4 Ba4 d6 5 c3 f5

	163	164	165	166	167	168
6	d4	exf5				
	fxe4	Bxf5				
7	Nxe5(a)	d4		0–0		
	dxe5	e4		Bd3		
8	Qh5†	Ng5(c)		Re1		
	Ke7!	d5		Be7		
9	Bxc6	f3	c4	Bc2	c4	Re3(l)
	bxc6	h6!(d)	dxc4(g)	Bxc2	Rb8	e4
10	Bg5†	fxe4	Bxc6†	Qxc2	Qb3	Ne1
	Nf6	hxg5	bxc6	Nf6	e4	Bg5
11	dxe5	exf5	Qa4	d4	Nd4	Rh3(m)
	Qd5	Bd6	Qd7	exd4(i)	Nf6	Nh6(n)
12	Bh4	Nd2(e)	Nc3	cxd4	Nf5	Nxd3
	Kd7(b)	Qf6(f)	Nf6(h)	0–0(j)	Kf7(k)	exd3(o)

(a) 7 Ng5 exd4 8 Nxe4 Bf5 9 Qxd4 Qe7 10 f3 b5 11 Qd5 Bb7 12 Bb3 Nf6 $\overline{\overline{\mp}}$, *Comments*.

(b) 13 Qg5 h6 14 Qg5† Ke8 15 Qg6† Qf7 16 Qxf7† Kxf7 17 exf6 gxf6 $\overline{\overline{\mp}}$ (Capablanca).

(c) (A) The original appearance of this variation was in Capablanca–Marshall, 14th match game 1909. It continued 8 Qe2 Be7 9 Nfd2 Nf6 10 h3 d5 11 Nf1 b5 12 Bc2 Na5 13 Ne3 Bg6 14 Nd2 0–0 15 b4 Nc4 16 Nxc4 dxc4 17 a4 Nd5 18 Nxd5 Qxd5 19 axb5 e3! 20 0–0 Rxf2 21 Rxf2 exf2† 22 Qxf2 Rf8 23 Qe2 Bxc2 24 Qxc2 axb5 25 Be3 Bd6 26 Bf2 Qg5 27 Qe4 h6 28 Re1 Rxf2 29 Kxf2 Bg3† 30 Kg1 Bxe1 31 Qxe1 Draw. (B) 8 d5 exf3 9 dxc6 b5 10 Qxf3 Bxb1 11 Bb3 Bg6 12 0–0 Nf6 13 Bg5 Be7 14 Rae1 Kf8 15 Re3 h6 16 Bxf6 Bxf6 17 Qd5 h5 18 g3 Qc8 19 Re6 Qd8 20 Re3 Qc8 Draw, Capablanca–H. Steiner, New York 1931.

(d) 9 . . . e3 10 f4 Nf6 11 Nf3 Bd6 12 Bxe3 0–0 13 0–0 Ng4 14 Qd2 Na5 15 Bb3 Nxb3 16 axb3 Nxe3 17 Qxe3 Bxf4 18 Qxf4 Bxb1 = (Suetin).

(e) 12 Qg4 Nf6 13 Qxg5 Kf8 14 Bf4 Rh5 15 Qg3 Qe7† $\pm$, Baturinsky–Estrin, Moscow 1947.

(f) 13 Nf3 Bg3† 14 Ke2 Bf4 15 Bxf4 gxf4 16 Qd3 Nh6 with a double-edged position, Rasanen–Aulaskari, corr. 1980.

(g) Interesting is 9 . . . h6 10 cxd5 Qxd5 11 Bb3 Qxd4 12 Qh5† g6 13 Bf7† Ke7 14 Bxg6 Bxg6 15 Qxg6 hxg5 16 Bxg5† Kd7 17 Qf5† Ke8 18 Qg6† Kd7 =, *Comments*.

(h) 13 0–0 c5 14 Qxd7† Kxd7 15 Be3 cxd4 16 Bxd4 Bd6 17 Rad1 Kc6 =, Shamkovich–Shiyanovsky, USSR Chp. 1961.

(i) On 11 . . . Qd7 12 dxe5 or 11 . . . 0–0 12 dxe5 Black gets an isolated pawn. Sharper, but also good for White, is 11 . . . e4 12 Ng5 d5 13 f3 h6 14 Nh3 0–0 15 Nd2, Lebedev–Lutikov, Kharkov 1963.

(j) 13 Nc3 Kh8! 14 Ng5 Nxd4 15 Qd3 h6 16 Qxd4 hxg5 17 Bxg5 Qd7 18 Nd5! Nxd5 19 Bxe7 ±, Glek–Vorotnikov, USSR 1986.

(k) 13 Na3 Re8 = (Radchenko).

(l) 9 Qb3 Rb8 10 Qd5 e4 produces an obscure position.

(m) 11 Rg3 Bh4 12 Qh5† g6 13 Rxg6 Bxf2† 14 Kh1 hxg6 15 Qxh8 Kf8 16 Nxd3 exd3 17 Bxc6 Qe7 winning, Harms–Kalish, corr. 1970.

(n) 11 . . . Nf6 12 Nxd3 exd3 13 Rxd3 0–0 14 Rh3 Ne4?! (14 . . . Qe7 =) 15 f3 Qf6 16 Bxc6 bxc6 17 d3! Bxc1 18 dxe4 ±, Kurtentov–Angelov, corr. 1985.

(o) 13 Rxd3 0–0 14 Rh3 Qe7 15 Na3 Rae8 16 Nc2 Qe2 17 Qf1 Bxd2 =, Fodor–Bubenko, corr. 1981.

RUY LOPEZ

Modern Steinitz Defense

1 e4 e5 2 Nf3 Nc6 3 Bb5 a6 4 Ba4 d6 5 c3 Bd7 6 d4

	169	170	171	172	173	174
	Nge7		g6(f)		Nf6	
7	Bb3	0–0	0–0	Bg5	0–0	
	h6	Ng6	Bg7	f6	Qe7	Be7(m)
8	Nbd2(a)	Nbd2	dxe5(g)	Be3	Bb3(k)	Re1
	Ng6	Be7	dxe5(h)	Nh6	h6	0–0
9	Nc4	Re1	Be3	h3(i)	Re1	Nbd2
	Be7	0–0	Nf6	Bg7	g6	Re8
10	Ne3	Nf1	Nbd2	Nbd2	Bd5	a3(n)
	0–0(b)	Bg4	0–0	Nf7	Bg7	Bf8
11	0–0	d5(d)	Bc5	0–0	dxe5	b4
	Kh7?!	Nh4	Re8	0–0	dxe5	d5!
12	g3!	Ne3	Ba3	Re1	b3	Bb3
	Bf6	Bxf3	Qc8	Qe7	Nh5	Bg4
13	Re1	gxf3	Bc2	b4	a4	h3
	Kh8(c)	Na7(e)	b6 =	Kh8(j)	Qf6(l)	Bh5(o)

(a) 8 Nh4 exd4 9 cxd4 Nxd4! 10 Qxd4 Nc6 11 Qd5 Qxh4 12 Qxf7† Kd8 13 Nc3 Ne5 14 Qd5 Bc6 15 Qd4 Be7 =, Tukmakov–Larsen, Leningrad 1973.

(b) 10 . . . Bg5 11 Nxg5 hxg5 12 g3 Nce7 13 Qf3 f6 14 Bd2 Qc8 15 0–0–0 ±, Balashov–R.Ye, Hangshou 1983.

(c) 14 a3 Qe8 15 h4 ±, Fischer–F. Olafsson, Bled 1959. Black would be only slightly worse after 11 . . . Re8.

(d) 11 Bxc6 Nh4 (Petrosian) 12 Bxb7 Bxf3 13 gxf3 Qd7 14 Kh1 Qh3 15 Ne3 Nxf3 16 Nf1 Nh4 (Byrne and Mednis) ends in only a sharp draw.

(e) 14 Kh1 Bg5 15 Rg1 Bf4 16 Ng2 Nxg2 17 Rxg2 Bxc1 18 Qxc1 Qh4 19 Qe3 f5? (Black is worse in any case, but this move leads to great trouble) 20 Rag1 Rf7 21 exf5! Nc8 (21 . . . Qxa4 22 Qh6 Qd7 23 f6 g6 24 Rxg6† wins) 22 f4 Ne7 23 Bd7 Nxd5 24 Be6! Nxe3 25 Rxg7† Kh8 26 Bxf7 h5 27 fxe3?! (better is 27 Bg8 Rxg8 28 Rxg8† Kh7 29 R1g7† Kh6 30 Rg6† Kh7 31 f6!) 27 . . . Qf2 28 Bd5 e4? (28 . . . c6, trying to drive the bishop off the long diagonal, gives Black drawing chances) 29 Bxe4 Qxe3 30 Bxb7 Rf8 31 R7g5 Qh3 32 f6 Resigns, Rohde–Kogan, US Chp. 1986.

(f) This position may arise via 3 . . . g6 (col. 32).

(g) (A) 8 Re1 transposes to col. 32. (B) 8 d5 Nce7 9 Bxd7† Qxd7 10 c4 h6 11 Nc3 f5 (11 . . . 0–0 may be stronger) 12 exf5 gxf5 13 f4 ±, A. Rodriguez–J. Reyes, Havana 1988.

(h) 8 . . . Nxe5 9 Nxe5 dxe5 10 f4 Ne7 11 f5!? gxf5 12 exf5 Nd5! 13 Bb3 Nf6 is equal, Bronstein–Westerinen, Yurmala 1978.

85

(i) Odd, but possibly good, is 9 b4!? Bg7 10 Bb3 Qe7 11 0–0 Nf7 12 Bd5 exd4 13 Nxd4 0–0 14 Nd2 with a good position, Romanishin–Torre, Brussels 1986.

(j) 14 Bc2 Ncd8 15 Nf1 Ne6 = , A. Sokolov–Spassky, Montpellier 1985.

(k) More normal play is 8 Re1 g6 9 Nbd2 Bg7 10 Nf1 0–0 11 Bg5 h6 12 Bh4 Qe8 13 Bc2 Kh8 14 Ne3 when White may have an advantage, Lein–Ciocaltea, Novi Sad 1973.

(l) 14 Ba3 Nf4 15 Nbd2 is an unclear position, de Firmian–Ivkov, Baden–Baden 1981.

(m) 7 . . . Nxe4 8 Re1 f5 9 dxe5 dxe5 10 Nbd2 Nxd2 11 Nxe5! Nxe5 12 Rxe5† Be7 13 Bxd2 gives White the edge, Ivkov–Jovanović, Yugoslav Chp. 1965.

(n) 10 Nf1 is seen in column 145, where this position is reached by a different order of moves. Also compare column 149.

(o) 14 dxe5 Nxe5 15 g4 Nxf3† 16 Nxf3 dxe4 17 gxh5 exf3 18 Rxe8 Qxe8 19 Qxf3 Qe1† 20 Kg2 Re8 21 h6 c6 = , Fischer–Gligorić, Bled 1959.

THREE KNIGHTS' GAME

1 e4 e5 2 Nf3 Nc6 3 Nc3

Diagram 9

THE THREE KNIGHTS' GAME is an attempt by Black to avoid the solid yet drawish lines of the Four Knights' Game. Playing unsymmetrically is somewhat risky, but no more so than in other aggressive openings. It has been favored by Steinitz, Alekhine, Keres, and Larsen, but is now rarely encountered in tournament practice.

3 . . . g6 (cols. 1–4) is now the main line. 5 Nd5 (cols. 1–2), formerly thought to be the most aggressive, has been analyzed out to even chances. 5 Nxd4 (cols. 3–4) leads to more complicated play, perhaps favoring White.

3 . . . Bb4 (col. 5) allows White a safe, if small, edge as he gains the bishop pair.

3 . . . Bc5 (col. 6) is suspect after 4 Nxe5, but analysis is still incomplete.

THREE KNIGHTS' GAME

1 e4 e5 2 Nf3 Nc6 3 Nc3

	1	2	3	4	5	6
	g6..Bb4........Bc5(o)					
4	d4				Nd5	Nxe5
	exd4				Nf6(l)	Nxe5
5	Nd5		Nxd4		Nxb4	d4
	Bg7(a)		Bg7		Nxb4	Bd6(p)
6	Bg5		Be3		Nxe5	dxe5
	Nce7(b)		Nf6.........d6(j)		Qe7(m)	Bxe5
7	Nxd4	e5	Nxc6(h)	Qd2	d4	f4
	c6(c)	h6	bxc6	Nf6	d6	Bxc3†
8	Nc3	Bxe7(f)	e5	f3	a3	bxc3
	h6	Nxe7	Ng8	0–0	dxe5	Nf6
9	Bf4(d)	Qxd4	Bd4(i)	0–0–0	axb4	e5(q)
	d5	Nxd5	Qe7	Nxd4	exd4(n)	Qe7(r)
10	Qd2	Qxd5	Qe2	Bxd4	Qxd4	Be2
	Nf6	d6	f6	Be6	Qxe4†	Ne4
11	0–0–0	0–0–0	exf6	g4	Qxe4	Qd4
	Nxe4(e)	0–0(g)	Nxf6 ±	c5(k)	Nxe4 ±	Qh4†(s)

(a) (A) 5 . . . h6 6 Nxd4 Nf6 7 Nb5 Nxd5 8 exd5 a6 9 Qe2† is much better for White, Volchok–Kots, USSR 1962. (B) 5 . . . Nb4 6 Bg5 f6 7 Nxf6† Nxf6 8 e5 Nbd5 is a sharp approach.

(b) 6 . . . f6 7 Bf4 d6 8 Nxd4 Nge7 9 Bc4 ±, Gershman–Tukmakov, USSR 1966.

(c) 7 . . . h6 is possible. After 8 Bh4 c6 9 Nxe7 Nxe7 10 Qd2 d5 =, Karlsson–Geller, Reykjavik 1986.

(d) 9 Be3 Nf6 10 Qe2 0–0 11 0–0–0 b5 and Black has the initiative, Utasi–Westerinen, Havana 1985.

(e) 12 Nxe4 dxe4 13 Bc4 Nf5 =, Lehmann–Keres, West Germany vs. USSR 1960.

(f) It is best to trade the bishop: 8 Bh4 g5 9 Nxe7 Qxe7 led to a clear advantage for Black in Winawer–Steinitz, London 1883.

(g) 12 exd6 Be6 is risky for White, so best is 12 Be4 Bd6 with equality.

(h) 7 Qd2 d6 8 0–0–0 Ng4 =, Bellon–Karpov, Las Palmas 1977.

(i) Better than 9 Bf4 Qe7 10 Qf3 f6 when White is worse, Chernin–Radashkovich, USSR 1971.

(j) 6 . . . Nge7 7 Qd2 d6 8 h4 Be6 9 Nxe6 fxe6 10 h5 is slightly better for White, Weinzettl–Kwatschewski, Vienna 1986.

(k) After 12 Be3 Qa5 the position is unclear, Yurtayev–Gulko, Frunze 1985.

(l) 4 . . . Be7 5 d4 d6 6 Bb5 exd4 7 Nxd4 $\pm$, Znosko-Borovsky–Alekhine, 1922.

(m) 6 . . . d6 7 Nf3 Nxe4 8 d3 is preferable for White (Tartakower).

(n) (A) 9 . . . Nxe4 10 dxe5 Qxe5 11 Qe2 Qe6 12 f3 $\pm$ (Fine). (B) 9 . . . Qxb4† 10 c3 is also worse for Black.

(o) (A) 3 . . . f5?! was harshly dealt with in A. Marić–Hoiberg, Smederevska Palanka 1985: 4 d4 fxe4 5 Nxe5 Nf6 6 Bc4 d5 7 Nxd5! Nxd5 8 Qh5† g6 9 Nxg6 Nf6 10 Bf7†! Kxf7 11 Ne5† Ke6 12 Qf7† Kf5 13 g4 mate. (B) 3 . . . Nge7 and (C) 3 . . . d6 are little-known possibilities, but they are passive and unpromising.

(p) 5 . . . Bxd4 6 Qxd4 d6 (6 . . . Qf6 7 Nb5! $\pm$) 7 f4 c5 8 Bb5† is a distinct plus for White.

(q) More circumspect is 9 Bd3 d5 10 e5 Bg4 11 Qd2 with advantage, Yurkov–Natapov, USSR 1959.

(r) 9 . . . Ne4 (Martorelli–Bellia, Italy 1985) leaves White slightly better after 10 Qd5.

(s) After 12 g3 Nxg3 13 hxg3 Qxh1† 14 Kf2 the position is unclear; White has good attacking chances, but Black has extra material.

FOUR KNIGHTS' GAME

1 e4 e5 2 Nf3 Nc6 3 Nc3 Nf6

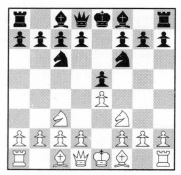

Diagram 10

TARRASCH, SCHLECHTER, AND MAROCZY played the Four Knights' regularly, with every intention of winning. But to the modern master the opening is a dinosaur; lifeless, dull, and seen only in the history books. The opening is solid enough—but the lack of threats and the symmetrical structure allow little chance for initiative. It still has use as a "drawing weapon" and, like other archaic openings, has surprise value; such grandmasters as Spassky and Bisguier have occasionally chosen it for this reason.

Black can continue the symmetry for several moves or break it immediately. The main line is the *Symmetrical Variation*, 4 Bb5 Bb4 5 0–0 0–0 6 d3 d6 (cols. 1–6). Both sides develop routinely and White hopes that his extra move will give him some edge. After 7 Bg5 Bxc3 8 bxc3 (cols. 1–5) Black has a choice of equalizing continuations. Departures by Black in columns 7 and 8 are risky, while White's deviations in cols. 6 and 9 are unimpressive. Cols. 7–12 are also described as the *Spanish Four Knights' Game*.

The *Rubinstein Variation*, 4 . . . Nd4 (cols. 10–13), immediately tries to unbalance the position. Strangely enough, White can force a drawish endgame by 5 Nxd4 (col. 10). Columns 14 and 15 cover 4 . . . a6 and 4 . . . Bc5, seldom-used options that are not as bad as their reputations.

The *Scotch Four Knights' Variation* is 4 d4 (cols. 16–18). After 4 . . . exd4 White may transpose into the Scotch Game with 5 Nxd4, but in this chapter the enterprising 5 Nd5!? (the *Belgrade Gambit*) is investigated (cols. 16–17). Black can also avoid this gambit with 4 . . . Bb4 (col. 18). For 4 Be2 *see* Unusual King's Pawn Games.

90

FOUR KNIGHTS' GAME
Symmetrical Variation

1 e4 e5 2 Nf3 Nc6 3 Nc3 Nf6 4 Bb5 Bb4 5 O–O O–O(a) 6 d3 d6

	1	2 ✓	3	4	5	6
7	Bg5..Ne2					
	Bxc3					Ne7(n)
8	bxc3					c3
	Qe7................................			Bd7.........	Ne7	Ba5
9	Re1.....................	Nd2	d4(h)	Nh4(k)	Ng3	
	Nd8	h6(g)	h6	Bg4(l)	c6	
10	d4		Bh4	Bh4	f3	Ba4
	Bg4?!........Ne6		Nd8	Re8(i)	Bd7	Ng6
11	h3	Bc1	Re1	Re1	Bc4	d4
	Bh5(b)	c5(d)	Ne6	a6	Be6	Re8(o)
12	g4	dxe5(e)	Nf1	Bd3	Bb3	Bb3
	Bg6	dxe5	Nf4	Bg4	Bxb3	h6(p)
13	d5	Bc4	Ne3	d5	axb3	h3
	c6(c)	Rd8(f)	c6 =	Nb8(j)	Nd7(m)	Be6 =

(a) Both (A) 5 . . . d6 6 Nd5 Bc5 7 d4 exd4 8 Nxd4, Tarrasch–Lasker, Munich 1908 and (B) 5 . . . Nd4 6 Nxd4 exd4 7 e5! are bad for Black.

(b) 11 . . . Bxf3 12 Qxf3 gives White a simple edge.

(c) 14 Bd3 cxd5 15 exd5 e4 16 Bxe4! Bxe4 17 Qd4 and White is much better, Spassky–Gligorić, Sarajevo 1986. If 15 . . . Rc8 16 c4 e4 not 17 Bf1 Ne6! Belavenets–Panov, USSR 1934, but again 17 Bxe4 ±.

(d) Other possibilities are: (A) 11 . . . Rd8 12 a4 c5 13 Bf1 Nf8 14 d5 ±, Spassky–Yusupov, Bugojno 1986; (B) 11 . . . c6 12 Bf1 Rd8 (12 . . . Qc7 13 g3 Rd8 14 Nh4 ±, Teichmann–Cohn, Vienna 1908) 13 g3 Qc7 14 Bg2 ±, Louma–Blatný, Czechoslovakia 1953.

(e) 12 d5 Nc7 13 Bd3 b5 14 Bg5 h6 15 Bh4 Bd7 = (Keres).

(f) After 15 Bd5 Nc7 16 c4 Bg4 the game is equal, Alexander–Pachman, Dublin 1957.

(g) 9 . . . Nd8 10 f4 exf4 11 Bxf4 Bg4 12 Qe1 ±, Richter–Teschner, 1948. The column is Smyslov–Bagirov, Lvov 1978.

(h) 9 Qd2 h6 10 Bh4 Bg4 11 Qe3 Bxf3 12 Qxf3 g5 13 Bg3 Kg7 =.

(i) 10 . . . Qe7 11 Re1 Rad8 12 h3 Nb8 is equal, Curdo–Winston, US 1976.

(j) Black is at least equal, Urzica–Karpov, Stockholm 1969. 8 . . . Bd7 is a good choice for Black.

(k) If 9 Bxf6 gxf6 10 Nh4 f5 11 f4, then not 11 . . . Ng6?! 12 Nxf5 Bxf5 13 exf5 ±, but 11 . . . exf4 12 Rxf4 Ng6 13 Nxg6 hxg6 =, Lawrence–Teichmann, London 1900.

(l) 9 . . . c6 10 Bc4 d5 11 Bb3 is risky as White may become very active.

(m) White has only a minute advantage, Soultanbeieff–O'Kelly, Belgium 1934.

(n) 7 . . . Bb4 and 7 . . . Bc5 are feasible alternatives; Black need not play symmetrically.

(o) 11 . . . d5 12 exd5 e4 13 Ne5 cxd4 is also sufficient for equality, Schlechter–Duras, Vienna 1908.

(p) The text is preferable to 12 . . . cxd4 13 cxd4 Be6 14 Ng5 Bxb3 15 Qxb3 when White is slightly better, Alekhine–Euwe, Amsterdam 1936. The column is Sveshnikov–Yusupov, USSR 1979.

FOUR KNIGHTS' GAME

1 e4 e5 2 Nf3 Nc6 3 Nc3 Nf6 4 Bb5 (Spanish Four Knights' Game)

	7	8	9	10	11	12
	(Bb4)................................Nd4 (Rubinstein Variation)					
5	(0–0)			Nxd4	Nxe5	Ba4
	(0–0)			exd4	Qe7(m)	Bc5(r)
6	(d3) Bxc6			e5(k)	f4(n)	Nxe5
	Bxc3........Nd4(e)		dxc6(h)	dxc3	Nxb5	0–0
7	dxc3	Nxd4	d3	exf6	Nxb5	Nd3
	d5(a)	exd4	Bd6(i)	Qxf6(l)	d6	Bb6
8	exd5(b)	Ne2	Bg5	dxc3	Nf3	e5(s)
	Qxd5(c)	c6(f)	h6	Qe5†	Qxe4†	Ne8
9	c4	Ba4	Bh4	Qe2	Kf2	0–0
	Qd6	d5	c5	Qxe2†	Ng4†	d6
10	Bxc6	e5	Nd2(j)	Bxe2	Kg1(o)	exd6
	bxc6	Ng4		d5	Qc6	Nxd6(t)
11	Bb2	c3		Bf4	N5d4(p)	Kh1(u)
	Re8(d)	dxc3(g)		c6 =	Qc5(q)	c6(v)

(a) The Svenonius Variation.

(b) 8 Bxc6 bxc6 9 Nxe5 dxe4 yields White a smaller edge than the column.

(c) 8 ... Nxd5 9 Bxc6 bxc6 10 Nxe5 Nxc3 11 Qd2 Nd5 12 c4 ± (Keres).

(d) 12 Qe1 Bg4 13 Nxe5 Nd7 14 f4 f6 15 Qg3 +, Korn–Frydman, corr. 1938.

(e) If 6 ... d5 then 7 Nxd5 Nxd5 8 exd5 Qxd5 9 Bc4 Qd6 10 c3 Bc5 11 b4 Bb6 12 a4 with a considerable advantage, Sterk–Marshall, Pistyan 1912.

(f) If 8 ... d5 then 9 e5! followed by c3 gives White a central wedge.

(g) 12 bxc3 Ba5 13 d4 was good for White in Perlis–Alekhine, Carlsbad 1911.

(h) 6 ... bxc6 7 Nxe5 Qe8 8 Nd3 Bxc3 9 dxc3 Qxe4 10 Re1 with a lead in development, Bisguier–Kalme, US 1959.

(i) 7 ... Qe7, 7 ... Nd7, and 7 ... Re8 are all possible. The text leads to a positional trap on move 10.

(j) 10 Nd5? g5! 11 Nxf6† Qxf6 12 Bg3 Bg4 was played in Winter–Capablanca, Hastings 1919, after which Black had all the chances. 10 Nd2 keeps the game level.

(k) 6 Nd5 Nxd5 7 exd5 Qf6 is satisfactory for Black, Wolf–Alekhine, Carlsbad 1923.

(l) 7 ... cxd2† is too hazardous. A recent game continued 8 Bxd2 Qxf6 9 0–0 Be7 10 Bc3 Qg5 11 Re1! Qxb5 (11 ... 0–0 12 Re5 Qf6 13 Bd3 g6 14 Rh5 wins) 12 Qg4 Rg8 13 Rxe7†! Kxe7 14 Qe4† Kd8 15 Qh4† f6 16 Bxf6† Ke8 17 Re1† Kf7 18 Re7† Kg6 19 Be5 d6 20 Qg3† Kh5 21 Qf3† Kh6 22 Qf4† g5 23 Qf6† Rg6 24 Rxh7†! Kxh7 25 Qh8 mate, J. Shipman–Weber, New York 1985. The column is Petrosian–O'Kelly, Bucharest 1953.

93

(m) Neither (A) 5 ... Nxe4 6 Nxe4 Nxb5 7 Nxf7 nor (B) 5 ... Bb4 6 Be2 Qe7 7 Nd3 equalizes for Black.

(n) 6 Nf3 Nxb5 7 Nxb5 Qxe4† is completely equal.

(o) 10 Kg3?! Qg6 turned out to be perilous for White in Spielmann–Rubinstein, Baden-Baden 1925.

(p) Better than 11 Qe2† Be7 12 h3 Qb6† 13 d4 Nf6 ∓. *Comments.*

(q) 12 h3 Nf6 13 Kh2 Be6 14 Re1 0–0–0 ∞, Bisguier–Soltis (Blitz Tournament), New York 1971.

(r) 5 ... Nxf3† 6 Qxf3 hands White a lead in development.

(s) 8 0–0 d5 9 Nxd5 Nxd5 10 exd5 Qxd5 11 Nf4 Qg5 allows Black dangerous attacking chances.

(t) 10 ... Nf6 11 d7 Bxd7 12 Bxd7 Qxd7 13 Ne1 Rae8 14 Nf3 ±, Stertinbrink–B. Vukcević, corr. 1983.

(u) 11 Ne1 h5! is less clear, Franzoni–Bhend, Berne 1987.

(v) After 12 Nf4 White's pawn outweighs Black's attacking chances.

FOUR KNIGHTS' GAME

1 e4 e5 2 Nf3 Nc6 3 Nc3 Nf6

	13	14	15	16	17	18
4	(Bb5)............................d4 (Scotch Four Knights' Var.)					
	(Nd4)......a6 ....Bc5			exd4 ....Bb4		
5	Bc4	Bxc6	0–0	Nd5 (Belgrade Gambit)		Nxe5(o)
	Bc5	dxc6	0–0(g)	Nxe4(i)	.....Be7	Nxe4
6	Nxe5(a)	Nxe5	Nxe5	Qe2(j)	Bf4	Qg4
	Qe7	Nxe4	Nxe5	f5	d6	Nxc3
7	Nf3(b)	Nxe4	d4	Ng5(k)	Nxd4	Qxg7
	d5	Qd4	Bd6	d3	Nxd5(m)	Rf8(p)
8	Nxd5	0–0	f4	cxd3	exd5	a3
	Qxe4†	Qxe5	Nc6	Nd4	Nxd4	Ba5(q)
9	Ne3	Re1(d)	e5	Qh5†	Qxd4	Nxc6
	Bg4	Be6	Be7(h)	g6	Bf6(n)	dxc6
10	Be2	d4	d5	Qh4	Bb5†	Qe5†
	Nxe2	Qf5(e)	Nb4	c6	Bd7	Qe7
11	Qxe2	Bg5	exf6	dxe4	Qe3†	Qxe7†
	0–0–0(c)	h6(f)	Bxf6 ∞	cxd5(l)	Qe7 =	Kxe7 =

(a) Campora–Seirawan, Dubai 1986, went 6 0–0 d6 7 Nxd4 Bxd4 8 d3 Be6 9 Nd5 c6 drawn.

(b) Both (A) 7 Bxf7† Kf8 and (B) 7 Nxf7 Rf8 are bad for White. (C) 7 Nd3 d5 and with either capture, 8 Bxd5 or 8 Nxd5, Black will regain one pawn and have good play for the one sacrificed.

(c) Black has more freedom in return for the lost pawn (Schubert–Hendrikson, corr. 1960) but it might not suffice (Korn).

(d) 9 d4 Qf5 10 Qe2 Be6 11 Ng5 = , Sliwa–Szabo, Munich 1958.

(e) 10 . . . Qd5 11 Ng5 is less solid than the text.

(f) Not 11 . . . Bd6? 12 g4 Qg6 13 f4 f5 14 Nxd6 cxd6 15 d5 winning, Znosko-Borovsky–Rubinstein, Ostend 1907. After 11 . . . h6 12 Qd3 Kd7 13 Bh4 White has an edge.

(g) On 5 . . . d6 6 d4 cxd4 7 Nxd4 Bd7 8 Nf5 is troublesome.

(h) 9 . . . Bb4?! 10 d5 a6 11 Be2 Bc5† 12 Kh1 Nxd5 13 Qxd5 ± , Shaposhnikov–Borisenko, corr. 1956. The column is Feodorov–Tseitlin, USSR 1978.

(i) 5 . . . Nxd5, 5 . . . h6 and 5 . . . Nb4 are less explored answers and worth investigating.

(j) 6 Bc4, played by Trajković, is a bold try. White simply develops and ignores his two-pawn deficit, hoping Black will lose time regrouping.

(k) 7 Bf4 d6 8 0–0–0 Be6 9 Nxd4 Nxd4 10 Rxd4 c6 ∓.

(l) After 12 exd5 Qa5† 13 Kd1 Qxd5 14 Bc4 Qxc4 15 Re1† Be7 16 Rxe7† a draw is forced. If 13 Bd2 Qa4 14 Qg3 f4 is unclear.

95

(m) 7 . . . 0–0 8 Nb5 Nxd5 9 exd5 Ne5 should also equalize.

(n) 9 . . . 0–0 10 Qd2 Bf6 11 0–0–0 $\pm$, Tal–Stolyar, USSR 1955. The column is Cuderman–Karaklajić, Yugoslavia 1961.

(o) 5 d5 Ne7 6 Nxe5 0–0 (6 . . . d6 7 Bb5† Kf8 8 Nd3 Bxc3† 9 bxc3 Nxe4 10 Qf3 Nf6 11 Bc4 $\pm$, Perić–Rothgen, corr. 1967) 7 Bd3 Nexd5 8 exd5 Re8 =.

(p) 7 . . . Qf6 8 Qxf6 Ne4† 9 c3 Nxf6 10 Nxc6 $\pm$, Minev–P. Ivanov, Bulgaria 1960.

(q) (A) 8 . . . Na2† 9 axb4 Nxc1 and (B) 8 . . . Nxd4† 9 axb4 Nxc2† are playable alternatives. The column is analysis by Bogolyubov.

GIUOCO PIANO

1 e4 e5 2 Nf3 Nc6 3 Bc4 Bc5, incorporating 4 b4, the EVANS GAMBIT

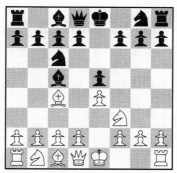

Diagram 11

THE GIUOCO PIANO (or "Italian Opening") can mean different things to different players. For some, it is an attempt to advance in the center and start a quick attack. For others, the name is taken literally: the "Quiet Game," an opportunity to outmaneuver the opponent in a positional way. Since it was mentioned in the Göttingen manuscript of 1490, one would think that five hundred years of analysis would have resolved these issues. Yet innovations continue to occur in several lines (e.g., in the sharp Möller Attack), challenging old conclusions. In the quiet variations, Karpov, Ljubojević, and others have tested their opponents on less familiar ground.

White's 3 Bc4 is a logical developing move, posting the bishop aggressively to attack the weak f7 square. Yet it does not exert the long-term pressure that 3 Bb5 has on the center. The bishop is also on a somewhat exposed square: when Black plays . . . d5 he attacks the bishop and so forces White to trade the e-pawn. Black's 3 . . . Bc5 aims to equalize development and achieve a balanced game without entering the complications of the Two Knights' Defense.

4 c3 (cols. 1–16) is White's main attacking plan, preparing 5 d4 to capture the center. 4 . . . Nf6 5 d4 exd4 6 cxd4 Bb4† 7 Nc3!? is the *Möller Attack* (cols. 1–6), where White sacrifices a pawn for the attack. With accurate play Black has equal chances, but the combinative nature of the position appeals to aggressive players.

7 Bd2 (cols. 7–8), an old Rossolimo favorite, seems to have been knocked out as a winning attempt (see col. 7). Lesser-known tries by both sides are covered in cols. 9–12. These are somewhat inferior to the main lines, but lead to unusual positions.

In the *Giuoco Pianissimo* (cols. 13–16) White plays d3 instead of preparing for d4, taking the game into positional channels. This strategy is so slow that Black should equalize, but delaying the central confrontation allows the position to become complex. The *Canal Variation* (cols. 17–18), characterized by 4 d3 and 6 Bg5, had been long out of favor but was recently revived by the Yugoslav grandmaster Ivanović.

Diagram 12

THE EVANS GAMBIT 4 b4 (see diagram) was introduced by Captain W. D. Evans in 1830; this true gambit produced many of the finest attacking games of the nineteenth century. Its glorious days seem past, and who knows if they will return. Fischer once said he would love to play it against a modern grandmaster who had spent most of his life in the positional intricacies of the Ruy Lopez.

Like most gambits, the Evans offers material in return for rapid mobilization and open lines. Black should return the pawn in order to reach an endgame where he can exploit White's pawn structure. Holding the pawn is also possible if Black is willing to defend patiently.

Upon accepting the gambit (cols. 19–23), Black has adequate resources in both the main variation, 5 c3 Ba5 (cols. 19–22), and with the less common 5 . . . Be7 (col. 23). The *Compromised Defense*, 7 . . . dxc3, (col. 21) is probably too ambitious and seems to give White a distinct advantage. If Black wants to avoid complications he can decline the gambit (col. 24), which is safe but less promising.

GIUOCO PIANO

1 e4 e5 2 Nf3 Nc6 3 Bc4 Bc5 4 c3 Nf6 5 d4 exd4 6 cxd4 Bb4† 7 Nc3 (Möller Attack)

	1	2	3	4	5	6
	Nxe4					d5
8	0–0					exd5
	Bxc3...				Nxc3	Nxd5
9	d5(a)				bxc3	0–0
	Bf6.................................			Ne5(j)	d5(m)	Be6(q)
10	Re1			bxc3	cxb4	Bg5
	Ne7			Nxc4	dxc4	Be7
11	Rxe4			Qd4	Re1†	Bxd5(r)
	d6......................		0–0	0–0(k)	Ne7	Bxd5
12	Bg5(b)		d6	Qxe4	Bg5(n)	Nxd5
	Bxg5		cxd6	Nd6	f6	Qxd5
13	Nxg5		Bg5(g)	Qd3(l)	Qe2	Bxe7
	h6..........	0–0(e)	Ng6(h)	Ne8	Bg4(o)	Nxe7
14	Qe2(c)	Nxh7	Qd5	c4	Bf4	Re1
	hxg5(d)	Kxh7(f)	Ne5(i)	d6 ∞	Kf7(p)	f6(s)

(a) 9 bxc3 is most simply met by 9 ... d5 10 Ba3 dxc4 11 Re1 Be6 12 Rxe4 Qd5 13 Qe2 0–0–0 ∓, Steinitz–Lasker, St. Petersburg 1896.

(b) Too loose is 12 g4 0–0 13 g5 Be5 14 Nxe5 dxe5 15 Rxe5 Ng6 ∓.

(c) 14 Bb5† Bd7 (not 14 ... c6 15 Nxf7! with a strong attack) 15 Qe2 Bxb5 16 Qxb5† Qd7, when everything favors Black: 17 Qe2 Kf8; 17 Qxb7 0–0; or 17 Rxe7† Kxe7 18 Re1† Kd8.

(d) 15 Re1 Be6 16 dxe6 f6 17 Re3 c6 (better than 17 ... d5?! 18 Rh3! Rf8 19 Bd3 with a strong attack, Szecsi–Heinrich, corr. 1986) 18 Rh3!? Rxh3 19 gxh3 g6 produces a sharp position which may favor Black, Szecsi–Szarka, corr. 1987.

(e) 13 ... Bf5 is smashed by 14 Qf3! Bxe4 15 Qxf7† Kd7 16 Qe6† Ke8 17 Qxe4 Qd7 18 Re1 a6 19 Nxh7 Kd8 20 Ng5 Re8 21 Ne6† Kc8 22 Nxg7 Resigns, Emery–Menchik, Biarritz 1939.

(f) 14 ... Bf5 is possible, resulting either in simplification (15 Rxe7 Qxe7 16 Nxf8 =) or in complications (15 Rh4 Re8 16 Qh5 Ng6 17 Rd4 Re5 18 Rd4 Rc5 ∞). After the text comes 15 Qh5† Kg8 16 Rh4 f6 17 g4 Re8 18 Bd3 Kf8 19 Qh8† Ng8 20 Bh7 Kf7 21 Bg6† Kf8 22 Bh7 with repetition of moves.

(g) 13 Qxd6 Nf5 14 Qd5 Ne7 repeats the position or allows ... d6 with development. On 14 ... d6 15 Ng5! White seizes the attack; e.g., 15 ... Bg5 16 Bxg5 (16 ... Qxg5? 17 Qxf7†) Qc7 17 Qd3, or 15 ... Nh6 16 Re1.

(h) 13 ... Bxg5 14 Nxg5 d5 15 Bxd5 Nxd5 16 Qxd5 h6 17 Nxf7 Rxf7 18 Rae1 Qf6 19 Re7 Qxf2† 20 Kh1 g5 leads to a draw after 21 Rxf7 Qxf7 22 Re8† (Botterill).

99

(i) Opinions differ over which side is better, but this is a matter of taste: White's initiative or Black's extra pawns.

(j) The alternatives, (A) 9 . . . Na5 10 Bd3 Nc5 11 bxc3, (B) 9 . . . Ne7 10 bxc3 Nd6 11 Bd3, and (C) 9 . . . Ba5 10 dxc6 bxc6 11 Ne5, are all bad for Black.

(k) (A) 11 . . . f5 12 Qxc4 d6 13 Nd4 0–0 14 f3 Nc5 (if 14 . . . Nf6 15 Bg5 h6 16 Bh4 is good for White [Schlechter]) 15 Re1 leaves White with a dangerous initiative. (B) 11 . . . Ncd6 12 Qxg7 Qf6 13 Qxf6 Nxf6 14 Re1† ±.

(l) 13 Qf4 Ne8 14 d6 cxd6 15 Ba3 b6 and Black's material outweighs White's initiative. The column is Mieses–Süchting, Vienna 1908.

(m) After 9 . . . Bxc3, either 10 Qb3 or 10 Ba3 give White excellent play.

(n) 12 Qe2 Be6 13 Bg5 (or 13 Ng5) is playable, but allows Black better defensive chances than the text.

(o) (A) 13 . . . fxg5?! 14 Qxc4 ±. (B) 13 . . . 0–0 14 Qxe7 fxg5 15 Qc5 Qf6 16 d5 ±.

(p) 15 Qxc4† Nd5 16 Nd2 Be6 17 Bg3 Qe7 = (Korn).

(q) 9 . . . Nxc3 10 bxc3 Be7 11 Bf4 is better for White (*Bilguer*).

(r) 12 Bxe7 Ncxe7 13 Ne4 0–0 14 Qb3 ±.

(s) After 15 Qe2 Qd7 16 Qe4! White has a pull (16 Rac1 was played in Steinitz–von Bardeleben, Hastings 1895, but then 16 . . . Kf7 equalizes).

GIUOCO PIANO

1 e4 e5 2 Nf3 Nc6 3 Bc4 Bc5 4 c3

	7	8	9	10	11	12
	(Nf6)..				Bb6........	d6
5	(d4)				d4	d4
	(exd4)				Qe7	exd4
6	(cxd4).............................		e5		0–0(o)	cxd4
	(Bb4†)		d5		Nf6	Bb4†(r)
7	Bd2		Kf1(f)	Bb5	Re1	Nc3(s)
	Bxd2†		d5(g)	Ne4	d6	Nf6
8	Nbxd2(a)		exd5	cxd4	h3	Bg5
	d5		Nxd5	Bb6(k)	0–0	h6
9	exd5		Nc3(h)	Nc3(l)	Na3(p)	Bxf6
	Nxd5		Be6(i)	0–0	Kh8(q)	Qxf6
10	Qb3	0–0	Qe2	0–0(m)	Nc2	0–0
	Na5(b)	0–0	0–0(j)	Bg4	Nd8	Bxc3
11	Qa4†	Ne5(d)	Bg5	Be3	b3	bxc3
	Nc6(c)	Nxd4(e)	Qd7 $\mp$	f5(n)	Be6 $\pm$	Bg4(t)

(a) 8 Qxd2 was tried in Rogers–Shaw, Itoh 1978, but 8 ... Nxe4 (instead of 8 ... d5 as played in the game) results in equality.

(b) The older 10 ... Nce7 is playable, but the text is more forcing.

(c) The position is equal and could be agreed drawn after 12 Qb3 (12 ... Nb6 was threatened) 12 ... Na5 13 Qa4† Nc6. White played to win in Sveshnikov–Mortensen, Leningrad 1984, with 14 Bb5 Bd7 15 Qd3?! (15 0–0 =) 15 ... Qe7† 16 Kf1 Be6 but Black ended up with the advantage. Black can avoid the draw with 12 ... Nce7, achieving a solid position but leaving White somewhat more mobile.

(d) White's slower (and less forcing) alternatives—11 Rc1, 11 Qc2, and 11 h3—result in complete equality.

(e) 12 Nb3 Nxb3 13 Bxd5 Qf6 (not 13 ... Nxa1? 14 Bxf7† Kh8 15 Qh5 h6 16 Rd1 +) 14 Bxf7† Rxf7 15 Qxb3 =, Khasin–Zagorovsky, USSR 1955.

(f) The Cracow Variation, a brash attempt to avoid simplification.

(g) 7 ... Nxe4?! Is very dangerous for Black; Marshall–Burn, Ostend 1905, continued 8 d5 Ne7 9 Qd4 Nf6 10 Bg5 Ng6 11 Nbd2 h6 12 Re1† Kf8 13 Bd3! Be7 14 Bxg6 hxg5 15 Ne5! fxg6 16 Nxg6† Kf7 17 Rxe7† Kxg6 18 Qd3† Kh6 19 h4 g4 20 h5 Nxh5 21 Qf5 Resigns.

(h) 9 Bg5 Qd6 10 Nc3 Bxc3 11 bxc3 0–0 $\mp$, Linschoten–Dietrich, Vienna 1911.

(i) Bad is 9 ... Nxc3?! 10 bxc3 Bxc3 11 Bxf7†! $\pm$.

(j) 10 ... Bxc3 11 bxc3 Nxc3 12 Qe1 Nd5 is unclear.

(k) (A) 8 ... Bb4† 9 Bd2 Nxd2 10 Nbxd2 Bd7 11 Qb3 $\pm$, Hernandez–Knežević, Havana 1986. (B) 8 ... Be7 9 0–0 0–0 10 Nc3 Bg4 =, Edelman–Boog, Ghent 1986.

(l) Other reasonable tries for White are 9 h3 and 9 Be3.

(m) 10 Bxc6 bxc6 11 Be3 Bg4 12 Qa4 c5 =, Sveshnikov–Dautov, Pinsk 1986.

(n) 12 exf6 Nxc3 with a roughly equal position.

(o) 6 d5 Nd8 7 a4 a6 8 d6 Qxd6 9 Qxd6 cxd6 is a speculative gambit. Black has to play accurately, but should then gain the upper hand.

(p) 9 a4 a6 and now (A) 10 Bg5 h6 11 Be3 Qd8 =, Tarrasch–Alekhine, Baden-Baden 1925, or (B) 10 b4 Kh8 11 Be3 exd4 12 cxd4 Nxe4 =, Klovans–Aronin, USSR 1963.

(q) 9 ... Nd8 10 Bf1 Ne8 11 Nc4 f6 12 a4 was very good for White in Tartakower–Euwe, Venice 1948. The column is Bouwmeester–Euwe, Holland 1952.

(r) 6 ... Bb6 7 Nc3 Nf6 8 Be3 Bg4 9 Bb5 0–0 10 Be3 ±.

(s) (A) 7 Kf1 Ba5 8 Qa4 a6 =. (B) 7 Bd2 Bxd2† 8 Qxd2 Nf6 9 Nc3 ⩲.

(t) After 12 Re1 White's position is preferable.

GIUOCO PIANO

1 e4 e5 2 Nf3 Nc6 3 Bc4 Bc5

	13	14	15	16	17	18
4	(c3) (Giuoco Pianissimo).....................d3 (Canal Variation)					
	Nf6				Nf6	
5	b4.....................d3				Nc3	
	Bb6		d6		d6(j)	
6	d3		0–0		Bg5	
	d6.........a6		0–0........a6		h6.........Na5(p)	
7	a4	0–0	Re1	Bb3	Bxf6(k)	Nd5(q)
	a5(a)	d6(e)	a6	Ba7	Qxf6	Nxc4
8	b5	Nbd2	Bb3	Nbd2	Nd5	dxc4
	Ne7	0–0	Ba7	0–0	Qd8(l)	c6(r)
9	Nbd2(b)	Bb3(f)	h3	Nc4	c3	Nxf6†
	Ng6	Ne7	h6(g)	h6(i)	Ne7(m)	gxf6
10	0–0	Re1	Nbd2	a4	d4	Be3
	0–0	Ng6	Nh5	Be6	Nxd5(n)	Qb6
11	Bb3(c)	h3	Nf1	a5	dxc5	Qd2
	c6(d)	Be6 =	Qf6(h)	Re8 =	Nf4(o)	Be6(s)

(a) 7 . . . a6, leaving the queenside pawn structure more fluid, is a reasonable option.

(b) White could also try 9 Na3 with the possibility of Nc2–e3 controlling f5 and d5.

(c) 11 Qb3 Bg4 12 h3 Bh5 13 Nh2 Nf4 =, Torre–Tukmakov, Leningrad 1987.

(d) 11 . . . d5?! 12 Ba3 Re8 13 exd5 Nxd5 14 Ne4 ±, Ljubojević–Korchnoi, Brussels 1987. After 11 . . . c6 12 d4 Bg4 13 Bb2 White may have an edge (Dolmatov).

(e) 7 . . . 0–0 8 Nbd2 d5 9 exd5 Nxd5 10 Qb3 Nf4 11 d4 (Short–Korchnoi, Belgrade 1987); now 11 . . . exd4 12 Ne4 Ne6 13 Bb2 dxc3 is a sharp, unclear position.

(f) 9 a4 h6 10 a5 Ba7 11 Re1 Kh8 12 h3 Be6 =, Lau–Short, Solingen 1986. The column is Short–Portisch, Brussels 1986.

(g) Also 9 . . . Qe7 10 Nbd2 Be6 11 Nf1 Rad8 12 Ng3 d5 =, Dzindzichashvili–Korchnoi, Chicago 1982.

(h) 12 Be3 Bxe3 13 Nxe3 Nf4 = (Karpov).

(i) 9 . . . Ne7 10 Bg5 Ng6 11 Nh4 Bg4 12 Qc2 Nf4 (12 . . . Qd7 is better) 13 Ne3 ±, Dolmatov–Kruppa, USSR 1986. The column is Romanishin–Smejkal, Szirak 1986.

(j) 5 . . . 0–0 is premature, e.g., 6 Bg5 Bb4 (6 . . . h6 7 h4 hxg5 8 hxg5 Ng4 9 g6 Nxf2 10 Nxe5 wins, Hermann–Wagerheim, Riga 1897) 7 0–0 Bxc3 8 bxc3 ±, Larsen–Kuzmin, Reykjavik 1978.

(k) 7 Bh4 Bg4 8 h3 Bxf3 9 Qxf3 Nd4 =, Romanovsky–Levenfish, USSR 1923.

(l) 8 . . . Qg6 9 Qe2 Bg4 10 c3 is risky for Black, Foltys–Keres, Munich 1936.

(m) 9 . . . a6 10 d4 exd4 11 cxd4 Ba7 12 Rc1 $\pm$, Ivanović–Ilinčić, Yugoslavia 1986.

(n) Also playable is 10 . . . exd4 11 cxd4 Bb6, Timman–Nunn, Amsterdam 1986.

(o) (A) 12 Bb5† Bd7 13 Bxd7† Qxd7 =, Tartakower–Fine, Hastings 1936. (B) 12 g3 Nh3 also leads to nothing for White, Ivanović–Kir. Georgiev, Vrsać 1987.

(p) 6 . . . Be6, providing additional control of d5, is a good alternative and should also result in an even game.

(q) 7 Bb3 c6 8 Nd2 h6 with a balanced position, Becker–Bogolyubov, Karlovy Vary 1929. This is more circumspect than the text.

(r) 8 . . . Bxf2† 9 Kxf2 Nxe4† 10 Kg1 Nxg5 11 Nxg5 c6 = (Unzicker).

(s) 12 0–0–0 0–0–0 and Black has the advantage, Korchnoi–Bronstein, USSR 1952.

GIUOCO PIANO

Evans Gambit

1 e4 e5 2 Nf3 Nc6 3 Bc4 Bc5 4 b4

	19	20	21	22	23	24
	Bxb4 (Evans Gambit Accepted)					Bb6
5	c3					a4(t)
	Ba5				Be7	a6
6	0–0........	d4			d4(q)	Bb2(u)
	d6(a)	exd4		d6	Na5	d6
7	d4	0–0		Qb3(n)	Nxe5(r)	b5
	Bb6(b)	Nge7 ....dxc3		Qd7	Nxc4	axb5
8	dxe5	cxd4(e)	Qb3	dxe5	Nxc4	axb5
	dxe5	d5	Qf6(j)	Bb6(o)	d5	Rxa1
9	Qb3(c)	exd5	e5	Bb5(p)	exd5	Bxa1
	Qf6	Nxd5	Qg6	Nge7	Qxd5	Nd4
10	Bg5	Ba3(f)	Nxc3	0–0	Ne3	Nxd4
	Qg6	Be6	Nge7	Qg4	Qa5	exd4
11	Bd5	Bb5(g)	Ba3(k)	exd6	0–0	c3
	Nge7	f6(h)	0–0(l)	cxd6	Nf6	Nf6
12	Bxe7	Qa4	Rad1	Ba3	c4	0–0
	Kxe7(d)	Bb6(i)	Re8(m)	Be6 =	0–0(s)	0–0(v)

(a) (A) 6 . . . Nge7 and (B) 6 . . . Qf6 are dubious tries, but worth looking at is (C) Chigorin's 6 . . . Nf6 7 d4 Nxe4 8 Nxe5 0–0 9 Ba3 d6 10 Nxc6 bxc6 11 Qa4 Qg5 ∞.

(b) (A) 7 . . . exd4 8 cxd4 Bb6, commonly seen in older times, allows White too much mobility in the center. (B) 7 . . . Bg4 and (C) 7 . . . Bd7 are reasonable choices, with fair chances for Black.

(c) 9 Qxd8† Nxd8 10 Nxe5 Be6 is equal.

(d) 13 Bxc6 Qxc6 14 Nxe5 Qe6 15 Nc4 Rd8 is a complicated, roughly equal position, Botterill–Williams, Pontypridd, 1978.

(e) 8 Ng5?! is met by 8 . . . d5 9 exd5 Ne5 and Black has the edge.

(f) 10 Qb3 Be6 11 Qxb7 Ndb4 12 Bb5 0–0 13 Bxc6 Rb8 14 Qxa7 Nxc6 with at least equality, Anderssen–S. Mieses, Breslau 1867.

(g) 11 Qb3 is met by 11 . . . Qd7 when White cannot capture the b-pawn.

(h) 11 . . . Bb4 12 Bxc6† bxc6 =.

(i) 13 Bxc6† bxc6 14 Qxc6† Kf7 leaves Black on top (Botterill).

(j) 8 . . . Qe7?! 9 Nxc3 Nf6 (9 . . . Qb4 10 Bxf7† Kd8 11 Bb2 ±) 10 Nd5 Nxd5 11 exd5 Ne5 12 Nxe5 Qxe5 13 Bb2 Qg5 14 h4 Qxh4 15 Bxg7 Rg8 16 Rfe1† Kd8 17 Qg3! Resigns, Fischer–Fine (offhand game), New York 1963.

(k) 11 Ne2 b5 12 Bd3 Qe6 ∞, Dupré–Zukertort 1886.

(l) The text leads to trouble, but 11 . . . b5, 11 . . . Rb8, and 11 . . . a6 are also disagreeable.

(m) 13 Bd3 with a strong attack. The column is the *Compromised Defense*, which is hazardous for Black.

(n) 7 Bg5 f6 8 Qb3 fxg5 9 Bxg8 Qf6 leaves Black ahead.

(o) 8 . . . dxe5 is also possible. After 9 0–0 Bb6 10 Rd1 Qe7 the position is unclear.

(p) 9 Nbd2 Na5 10 Qc2 Nxc4 11 Nxc4 d5 12 Nxb6 axb6 ∓, Estrin–Palciauskas, corr. 1984–85. The column is Cafferty–Mariott, corr. 1957.

(q) 6 Qb3 Nh6 7 d4 Na5 8 Qb5 Nxc4 9 Bxh6 gxh6 10 Qxc4 results in an unbalanced position.

(r) (A) 7 Bd3 exd4 8 cxd4 d5 9 Qa4† Nc6 10 exd5 Qxd5 11 Nc4 Bb4 ∓. (B) 7 Bxf7† looks appealing, but after 7 . . . Kxf7 8 Nxe5† Kf8 Black should win.

(s) 13 d5 with an advantage in space.

(t) Bad is 5 b5?! Na5 6 Nxe5? Qf6 ∓. The column is the Evans Gambit Declined.

(u) 6 Nc3 is an equally popular continuation. After 6 . . . Nf6 7 Nd5 Nxd5 8 exd5 Nd4! Black equalizes easily.

(v) 13 d3 d5 14 exd5 Nxd5 and White has only a minimal advantage, Tartakower–Rubinstein, The Hague 1921.

TWO KNIGHTS' DEFENSE

1 e4 e5 2 Nf3 Nc6 3 Bc4 Nf6 (incorporating 4 d4 exd4 5 0–0 Bc5, the
***Max Lange Attack*)**

Diagram 13

T HE TWO KNIGHTS' DEFENSE is another centuries-old opening, dating back to analysis by Polerio in 1580. However, modern lines involving a pawn sacrifice were developed only in the middle of the last century; they give the Two Knights' its aggressive character. It is ideal for players willing to take risks in order to dictate the tempo of play. Rather than defend against the Möller Attack (of the Giuoco Piano) or the Evans Gambit, they throw the gauntlet back to White, inviting him to play 4 Ng5, when it is Black who offers the gambit.

Tarrasch called 4 Ng5 a "duffer's" move that neglects development. Steinitz, however, would play it and accept the pawn sacrifice as a matter of principle, trying in several games with Chigorin to prove the gambit unsound. Later Fischer, a great admirer of Steinitz, devoted his attention to this question. The verdict is still in doubt, but the murky channels one must navigate have deterred many players from taking either side.

The main line is 4 Ng5 d5 5 exd5 Na5 (cols. 1–8). After 6 Bb5† c6 7 dxc6 bxc6 Black obtains a lead in development and open lines for the pawn. White's best counter is probably column 6 (9 Nh3!?), which was Fischer's choice.

Black tries other than 5 . . . Na5 are covered in columns 9–11. Though more speculative, they may be playable.

The *Wilkes-Barre Variation,* 4 . . . Bc5!? (col. 12), looks crazy—Black ignores White's threats to f7—yet there is no known refutation of it. In Europe, it is known as the Traxler Variation.

Avoiding 4 Ng5 with 4 d4 may well be sensible, as Tarrasch insisted. After 4 d4 exd4 5 0–0 White is the aggressor. 5 . . . Bc5 (cols. 13–15) is the *Max Lange Attack.* Both this and 5 . . . Nxe4 (cols. 16–18) result in sharp tactical play which in its final analysis evens out.

The thrust 5 e5 is the subject of cols. 19–20. 5 . . . d5 is the tried and tested response, but Black may have other ways to hold the balance—see note (b).

The modern favorite is 4 d3 (cols. 21–22). This positional line avoids an immediate confrontation and allows the game to build up slowly. Kudrin and Short have scored well with it.

4 Nc3 (col. 23) and 4 0–0 (col. 24) are lesser-known variations which give Black little trouble.

TWO KNIGHTS' DEFENSE

1 e4 e5 2 Nf3 Nc6 3 Bc4 Nf6 4 Ng5 d5 5 exd5 Na5 6 Bb5† c6(a) 7 dxc6 bxc6 8 Be2 h6

	1	2	3	4	5	6
9	Nf3					Nh3
	e4					Bc5(m)
10	Ne5					0–0
	Bd6		Bc5	Qc7	Qd4	0–0(n)
11	d4 . . . . f4		c3(h)	f4	f4	d3
	exd3(b)	exf3(e)	Bd6	Bc5	Bc5	Nb7
12	Nxd3	Nxf3	f4	c3(j)	Rf1	Nc3
	Qc7	0–0	Qc7	Nb7	Bd6(k)	Nd5(o)
13	b3	d4	d4	b4	c3	Bf3
	0–0	c5	exd3	Bd6	Qb6	Bb6
14	Bb2	0–0(f)	Qxd3(i)	d4	Qa4	Qe2
	Nd5(c)	Re8	0–0	exd3	0–0	Re8
15	Nc3	Kh1	0–0	Qxd3	b4	Re1
	Nf4	Bb7	Rd8	0–0	Nb7	Nxc3
16	Nxf4(d)	Nc3	Qc2	0–0	Qxc6	bxc3
	Bxf4 ∞	cxd4(g)	Nd5 =	a5 =	Qd8(l)	Bd7 =

(a) 6 . . . Bd7 is an obscure possibility. After 7 Qe2 Bd6 8 Nc3 0–0 9 Bxd7 Qxd7 10 0–0 c6 Black had play for the pawn, Paoli–Johannessen, Skopje 1972.

(b) 11 . . . Qc7 12 Bd2 Nb7 13 0–0 0–0 14 Na3 ± , Bogolyubov–Zimmermann, Zürich 1928.

(c) On 14 . . . Bf5 15 Nd2 is good.

(d) Tal recommends 16 0–0 as better, but the position is messy in any case. The column is Honfi–Tal, Sarajevo 1966.

(e) 11 . . . Qc7 12 0–0 0–0 13 Nc3 Bf5! ∞, Timman–Gligorić, Bad Lauterberg 1977, is an improvement on 13 . . . Bxe5?! 14 fxe5 Qxe5 15 d4 exd3 16 Qxd3 ⩲ , Fine–Reshevsky, US 1940.

(f) 14 dxc5 Bxc5 15 Qxd8 Rxd8 16 Bd2 Nc6 (Timman–Bisguier, Sombor 1974) and Black fares well after 17 Nc3 Ng4.

(g) 17 Qxd4 Nc6 18 Qh4 Ne5 = , M. Vukcević–Romanishin, Hastings 1977.

(h) If 11 0–0, either 11 . . . Qd4 12 Ng4 Bxg4 13 Bxg4 0–0 or 11 . . . Qd6 allows Black even chances.

(i) 14 Nxd3 0–0 15 0–0 Bf5 is unclear. The column is Skrobek–Sydor, Lodž 1980.

(j) 12 d4 exd3 13 cxd3 0–0 14 Bd2 Nd5 is all right for Black, Gilezedinov–Klovans, corr. 1969. The column is Mednis–Spassky, Antwerp 1955.

(k) The old 12 . . . Qd8 is met by 13 c3 Nd5 14 Qa4 0–0 15 Qxe4 Qh4† (Keres suggests 15 . . . Re8!? 16 d4 Bb6) 16 Kd1 ± , Nestorenko–Mosin, USSR 1963.

(l) After 17 Na3 a5 chances are roughly even, Estrin–Leonidov, corr. 1978.

(m) 9 . . . Bd6 is Black's main alternative. Bobkov–Korelov, corr. 1975, continued 10 d3 0–0 11 Nc3 Nd5 12 Bd2 Rb8 13 Qc1 Bxh3 14 gxh3 Nf4 15 Rg1 f5 ∞.

(n) 10 . . . g5 11 Kh1 g4 12 Ng1 Ne4 13 Bxg4 Nxf2† 14 Rxf2 and White gets good compensation for the exchange (Fischer, citing Gottschall).

(o) 12 . . . Bb6 13 Kh1 Nc5 14 Bf3 Nd5 15 Ng1 f5 ∞, Kuindzi–Klovans, USSR 1973. The column is Nunn–Hardicsay, Budapest 1978.

TWO KNIGHTS' DEFENSE

1 e4 e5 2 Nf3 Nc6 3 Bc4 Nf6 4 Ng5

			Fritz Var.		Ulvestad Var.	Wilkes-Barre Var.
	7	8	9	10	11	12
	(d5)..Bc5					
5	(exd5)					Bxf7†(r)
	(Na5)...................Nd4........b5..........Nxd5					Ke7
6	(Bb5†)......d3		c3(g)	Bf1(k)	d4(n)	Bd5
	(c6)	h6	b5	h6	Bb4†(o)	d6(s)
7	(dxc6)	Nf3	Bf1	Nf3(l)	c3	c3
	(bxc6)	e4	Nxd5	Qxd5!	Be7	Qe8!(t)
8	Qf3	Qe2(d)	Ne4(h)	Nc3	Nxf7(p)	d4
	Rb8(a)	Nxc4	Ne6(i)	Qe6	Kxf7	exd4
9	Bd3(b)	dxc4	Bxb5†	Bxb5	Qf3	cxd4
	h6	Bc5!	Bd7	Bb7	Ke6	Nxd4
10	Ne4	h3(e)	Bxd7†	0–0(m)	Qe4	Nc3
	Nd5	0–0	Qxd7	0–0–0	b5	Qh5
11	Ng3(c)	Nh2	0–0	Qe2	Bxb5	Qd3
	g6	c6	Be7	e4	Bb7	Rf8
12	0–0	dxc6	d4	Bxc6	f4	b4
	Bg7 =	e3(f)	exd4(j)	Qxc6 ∓	g6(q)	Bb6 =

(a) This move of Coleman's has superseded the older 8 . . . Qc7 and 8 . . . cxb5.

(b) 9 Bxc6† Nxc6 10 Qxc6† Nd7 11 d3 (11 d4 Be7 12 Ne4 Rb6 13 Qa4 0–0 14 0–0 f5 ∓, Kahgren–Axelsson, Örebro 1949) Be7 with good play, Howlend–Brown, corr. 1952.

(c) 11 b3 g6 12 Qg3 Bg7 13 Ba3 Nb4 with excellent chances for Black, Van der Wiel–Torre, Sochi 1980. The column is Estrin–Ragozin, Moscow 1955.

(d) 8 dxe4?!, Bronstein's piece sacrifice, is best met by 8 . . . Nxc4 9 Qd4 Nd6 10 Nc3 (10 e5 Nf5 is no better) 10 . . . Nfxe4! 11 Nxe4 Qe7 12 0–0 Nxe4 ∓ (Euwe).

(e) 10 Nfd2 0–0 11 Nb3 Bg4 12 Qf1 Bb4† 13 c3 (13 Nc3 c6 was also bad for White in Luckis–Keres, Buenos Aires 1939) 13 . . . Be7 ∓, Salwe–Marshall, Vienna 1908.

(f) 13 Bxe3 Bxe3 14 fxe3 Ne4 15 0–0 Ng3 with a small plus for Black, Kopylov–Kondratiev, USSR 1955.

(g) 6 d6 Qxd6 7 Bxf7† Ke7 8 Bb3 Nxb3 9 axb3 h6 10 Nf3 e4 puts White on the run, Bogolyubov–Rubinstein, Stockholm 1919.

(h) 8 cxd4 Qxg5 9 Bxb5† Kd8 10 0–0 exd4 11 Qf3 Bb7 12 Qxf7? Nf6! 13 Resigns, Fischer–R. Burger, simultaneous game, San Francisco 1963. This is Fischer's shortest recorded loss. Hans Berliner played the Fritz in his ascent to first place in the Correspondence World Championship in the 1970s, and has written extensively in Chess Review et al. on this obscure defensive gambit so typical of the Two Knights'.

(i) 8 . . . Qh4?! 9 Ng3 Bg4 10 f3 e4 11 cxd4 Bd6 12 Bxb5 Kd8 13 0–0 exf3 14 Rxf3 Rb8, Estrin–Berliner, 5th World Corr. Chp. 1965–68, is a sharp, speculative sacrifice.

(j) After 13 cxd4 0–0 14 Nbc3 Rad8 15 Be3 $\pm$, Petik–Sukov, corr. 1967, Black lacks full compensation for the pawn.

(k) 6 Bxb5 Qxd5 7 Nc3 Qxg2 8 Qf3 Qxf3 9 Nxf3 Bd7 =.

(l) 7 Nxf7 Kxf7 8 dxc6 Bc5 leaves Black very active, Kirilov–Shebenyuk, corr. 1985.

(m) Keres gave 10 d3 as clearly better for White, but after 10 . . . 0–0–0 11 Qe2 Qg4 12 Be3 Nd4 13 Bxd4 exd4 14 Ne4 Bb4† Black had a raging attack in Tiemann–Zmokly, corr. 1981. The column is Ginko–Shebenyuk, corr. 1986.

(n) 6 Nxf7 (the "Fried Liver Attack") is unclear after 6 . . . Kxf7 7 Qf3† Ke6 8 Nc3 Nb4 9 Qe4 (9 a3 Nc2† 10 Kd1 Nd4! ∞) c6 10 a3 Na6 11 d4 Nc7.

(o) This is the Pincus Variation, which was thought to be refuted but has recently been resurrected.

(p) 8 0–0 0–0 is too slow to achieve any advantage, Fink–Adams, New York 1947.

(q) After 12 f4 old theory prefers White, but 12 . . . g6! puts it into question. After 13 fxe5 (13 dxe5 Bc5) Rf8 14 Qg4† Rf5 15 Bd3 Nxd4 the best for White is probably 16 cxd4 Nb4 17 Bxf5† gxf5 ∞. In the game Kalvach–Drtina, corr. 1986, White played 16 Rf1? which was met by 16 . . . Ne3! 17 Bxe3 Nf3† 18 gxf3 Qd3 19 Qd4 Bh4† 20 Qxh4 Qxe3† 21 Resigns.

(r) (A) 5 d4 is met by 5 . . . d5 6 Bxd5 Nxd4 7 Bxf7† Ke7 8 Bc4 b5 9 Bd3 Rf8 with active play, Zinn–Nunn, corr. 1966. (B) 5 Nxf7 leads to head-splitting complications after 5 . . . Bxf2†! 6 Kxf2 (6 Kf1 Qe7 7 Nxh8 d5 8 exd5 Bg4 ∞) Nxe4† 7 Kg1 (or 7 Ke3 Qh4) Qh4 8 g3 Nxg3 9 Nxh8 d5 10 Qf3 Nf5 11 Bb5 Be6 when best play might lead to a draw.

(s) 6 . . . Rf8?! 7 0–0 d6 8 c3 Bg4 9 Qb3 h6 10 d4 Bd6 11 h3 and White has a big edge, Estrin–W. Schmidt, corr. 1972.

(t) 7 . . . Rf8 8 d4 exd4 9 Bxc6 cxb6 10 0–0 $\pm$, Estrin–Zaitsev, USSR 1970. The column is Karpov–Beliavsky, USSR 1983.

TWO KNIGHTS' DEFENSE

1 e4 e5 2 Nf3 Nc6 3 Bc4 Nf6 4 d4 exd4 5 0–0

	13	14	15	16	17	18
	Bc5	(Max Lange Attack)...........Nxe4				
6	e5(a)			Re1		
	d5......................Ng4			d5		
7	exf6		Bf4(i)	Bxd5(m)		
	dxc4		d6(j)	Qxd5		
8	Re1†........fxg7		exd6	Nc3		
	Be6(b)	Rg8	Bxd6	Qa5 ....Qh5(q)		
9	Ng5	Bg5	Re1†	Nxe4		Nxe4
	Qd5	Be7(f)	Kf8(k)	Be6		Be6
10	Nc3	Bxe7	Bxd6†	Neg5 ....Bd2		Bg5
	Qf5	Kxe7!(g)	Qxd6	0–0–0	Qd5(o)	Bd6
11	Nce4(c)	Nbd2(h)	c3	Nxe6	Bg5	Bf6
	0–0–0(d)	Rxg7	Qc5	fxe6	Bd6	0–0
12	g4	Nc4	Nbd2	Rxe6	Bf6	Nxd6
	Qe5(e)	Be6 ∓	d3(l)	Bd6(n)	0–0(p)	cxd6(r)

(a) 6 c3 Nxe4 7 cxd4 d5 8 dxc5 dxc4 9 Qxd8† Kxd8 is equal.

(b) 8 ... Kf8?! 9 Bg5 gxf6 10 Bh6† Kg8 11 Nc3 Bf8 12 Bxf8 Kxf8 13 Ne4 ±. *Comments.*

(c) 11 g4?! Qg6 12 Nce4 Bb6 13 f4 0–0 14 f5 Bxf5 gave Black too much for the piece in Blackburne–Teichmann, Nürnberg, 1895.

(d) Development is the best course here. 11 ... Bf8 and 11 ... Bd6 were proved inferior in old games.

(e) 13 Nxe6 fxe6 and now: (A) 14 fxg7 Rhg8 15 Bh6 d3 16 c3 Be7 (16 ... d2?! 17 Re2 Rd3 18 Qf1 Qd5 19 Rd1 Ne5 20 Qg2 ±) 17 f4 Qd5 18 Qd2 ∞, Markelov–Ostroverkov, corr. 1952; (B) 14 Bg5 g6 (14 ... Rd7 and 14 ... h6 are also possible) 15 f7 Be7 16 f4 Qg7 17 Bxe7 Nxe7 18 Ng5 d3 19 Nxe6 Qxf7 with play for the exchange.

(f) Bad are (A) 9 ... f6 10 Re1† Kf7 11 Bh6 and (B) 9 ... Qd5 10 Ne3 Qf5 11 Ne4.

(g) 10 ... Qxe7 11 Nxd4 Rxg7 12 Nxc6 is slightly better for White.

(h) 11 Re1† Be6 12 Re4 d3 13 Nc3 Rxg7 14 cxd3 Qxd3 15 Nd5† Kf8 16 Qxd3 cxd3 17 Nxc7 Bh3 ∓ (Lisitsyn). The column is Foltys–Štulík, Czechoslovakia 1940.

(i) 7 Re1 is complicated. The game Garrilo–Perfiliev, corr. 1951, continued 7 ... d3 8 Bxf7† Kf8 9 Qxd3 Bxf2† 10 Kf1 Bxe1 11 Qf5 Nf6 12 exf6 Qxf6 with an unbalanced game.

(j) 7 ... 0–0!? 8 h3 Nh6 9 Bxh6 gxh6 10 c3 d5 11 Bb3 Bf5 12 cxd4 Bb6 =, is an old analysis of Bardeleben's.

(k) (A) 9 ... Be7 10 Bb5 0–0 11 Bxc6 is ±. (B) 9 ... Ne7 10 Bxd6 Qxd6 11 Qd4 ±.

(l) 13 Nd4 Nxd4 14 cxd4 Qxd4 15 Qf3 Qf6 16 Qg3 and White has the edge.

(m) 7 Nc3, the *Canal Variation*, is most simply met by 7 . . . dxc3 8 Bxd5 Be6 9 Bxe4 (not 9 Rxe4? Ne7 ∓) 9 . . . Bb4 with equality.

(n) 12 . . . Qf5 is also playable. On 13 Qe2 h6 14 Bd2 Qxc2 15 Rc1 Qxb2 16 Rexc6 is complicated but probably even. After 12 . . . Bd6 13 Bg5 (13 Qe2 Qh5 14 h3 Rde8 =∓) 14 . . . Rde8 15 Qe2 Kd7 16 Re1 Qxe1† 17 Nxe1 Rxe6 the game is equal, Estrin–Krogius, USSR 1949.

(o) Other, less explored, choices are (A) 10 . . . Qf5, (B) 10 . . . Bb4 and (C) 10 . . . Qa4 played in Estrin–Zaitsev, USSR 1983. After 11 Bg5 h6 12 Bh4 Bb4 13 Re2 g5 14 Nf6† Kf8 the position was unclear.

(p) 13 Nxd4 Nxd4 14 Qxd4 Qxd4 15 Bxd4 Rfd8 =, Zaitsev–Averbakh, USSR 1964.

(q) 8 . . . Qd8 9 Rxe4† Be7 10 Nxd4 f5 11 Rf4 (the sacrifice 11 Bh6 gxh6 is only equal) 0–0 12 Nxc6 Qxd1† is complicated but probably leads eventually to an even ending.

(r) 13 Bxd4 Bg4 =.

TWO KNIGHTS' DEFENSE

1 e4 e5 2 Nf3 Nc6 3 Bc4 Nf6

	19	20	21	22	23	24
4	(d4)		d3		Nc3	0–0
	(exd4)		Be7		Nxe4	Nxe4(m)
5	e5(a)		0–0		Nxe4	Nc3
	d5(b)		0–0		d5	Nxc3(n)
6	Bb5		Bb3(g)		Bd3(k)	dxc3
	Ne4		d6		dxe4	f6(o)
7	Nxd4		c3		Bxe4	Nh4
	Bd7	Bc5	Bg4	Na5	Bd6	g6
8	Bxc6	Be3(d)	h3	Bc2	d4	f4
	bxc6	Bd7	Bh5	c5	exd4(l)	f5
9	0–0	Bxc6	Re1	Nbd2(i)	Bxc6†	Nf3(p)
	Bc5	bxc6	Nd7	Be6	bxc6	e4
10	f3	0–0	Be3	Re1	Qxd4	Ng5
	Ng5	Qe7	Bxf3(h)	Qc7	0–0	Bc5†
11	Be3	Re1(e)	Qxf3	Nf1	0–0	Kh1
	Bb6(c)	0–0(f)	Bg5 $\pm$	Rad8(j)	c5 $=$	Qe7(q)

(a) 5 Ng5 can be met by 5 . . . d5 6 exd5 Qe7† 7 Kf1 Ne5 8 Qxd4 Nxc4 9 Qxc4 h6 10 Nf3 Qc5 with promising play.

(b) Two other considerations are: (A) 5 . . . Ne4 6 Bd5 Nc5 7 0–0 Ne6 8 c3 dxc3 9 Nxc3 with some attacking prospects, Janošević–Gligorić, Yugoslavia 1960; and (B) 5 . . . Ng4 6 0–0 d6 7 exd6 Bxd6 8 Re1† Kf8 9 Na3 Qf6 or 6 Qe2 Qe7 7 Bf4 f6 8 exf6 Nxf6 ∞.

(c) 12 f4 Ne4 13 Nd2!? (13 Nc3 =) 13 . . . Nxd2 14 Qxd2 c5 15 Nb3 d4 16 Bf2 Bb5 leads to sharp play most likely favoring Black, Sveshnikov–Agzamov, Tashkent 1984.

(d) 8 Nxc6 Bxf2† 9 Kf1 bxc6! 10 Bxc6† Kf8 11 c4 Qh4!, Karklins.

(e) Here 11 f3 Nd6 12 Bf2 Nf5 gives Black an excellent game, Liskov–Ragozin, USSR 1951.

(f) After 12 f3 Ng5 practice has established that Black is superior.

(g) 6 c3 d5 7 exd5 Nxd5 8 Re1 Bg4 9 h3 Bh5 10 Nbd2 Nb6 11 Bb3 $\pm$, Radulov–Spassky, Solingen 1984.

(h) 10 . . . Nc5 11 g4, now 11 . . . Bg6?! allows 12 Bxc5 dxc5 13 Bd5 $\pm$, Psakhis–Kupreichik, Sverdlovsk 1984, so Black should try 11 . . . Nxb3 12 axb3 Bg6 with an unclear position, Gavrikov–Malanchuk, USSR 1987. The column is Dolmatov–Kupreichik, Sverdlovsk 1984.

(i) 9 b4 cxb4 10 cxb4 Nc6 11 b5 Na5 =, Armas–Ciolac, Bucharest 1986.

(j) After 12 h3 Nc6 13 Ng3 with a pull for White, Yudashin–Romanishin, Lvov 1987.

(k) 6 Bb5 dxe4 7 Nxe5 Qg5! is bad for White.

(l) 8 . . . Nxd4 is playable too, e.g. 9 Nxd4 exd4 10 Qxd4 0–0 11 Be3 Qe7 =, Tarrasch–Marshall, Breslau 1912. The column is Tartakower–Bogolyubov, Pistyan 1922.

(m) If 4 . . . Bc5 White can play the daring 5 d4!? Bxd4 6 Nxd4 Nxd4 7 Bg5 d6 8 f4 when either 8 . . . Qe7 or 8 . . . Be6 leaves the situation obscure.

(n) 5 . . . Nf6 6 d4 e4 7 Bg5 d5 8 Nxd5 Be6 =, Basagić–Gligorić, Yugoslavia 1984.

(o) 6 . . . Qe7 7 Ng5 Nd8 8 Be3 h6 9 Ne4 d6 10 f4 is also plausible.

(p) Tempting is 9 Nxf5?, but 9 . . . d5 makes it regrettable.

(q) 12 Bf7† Kf8 Murka–Sanenko, corr. 1963. The game is unbalanced but should ultimately favor Black.

SCOTCH GAME

1 e4 e5 2 Nf3 Nc6 3 d4

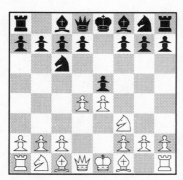

Diagram 14

THE SCOTCH GAME received its name from a celebrated correspondence match between London and Edinburgh in 1824. However, the moves had been analyzed as early as 1750 by Ercole del Rio in his "Sopra il giuoco degli scacchi osservazioni pratiche d'anonimo autore Modenese." It became a favorite of Blackburne and Chigorin and later was kept alive by Spielmann, Tartakower, and Mieses, but then entered a dry period of many years when it was thought to be too sterile to give winning chances. Recently it has regained favor and is used occasionally by top players.

The Scotch is similar to the Center Game in that 3 d4 opens lines for development and takes away Black's central outpost. Yet it also frees Black's game: Black's easy development and the lack of central tension should produce quick equality. At least temporarily, White has more space and control of the d5 square. The obvious advantage of the Scotch over the Center Game is that White loses no time moving his queen. This adherence to developing principles makes the Scotch a respectable modern opening.

After 3 . . . exd4 4 Nxd4 Black has two main replies, 4 . . . Nf6 and 4 . . . Bc5. On 4 . . . Nf6 the classical 5 Nc3 (cols. 1–4) is an old line in which Black can equalize by known methods. Recent attention has therefore focused on Mieses' 5 Nxc6 (cols. 5–6), which is less explored.

White has three counters to 4 . . . Bc5 (cols. 7–14), the modern 5 Nb3 (cols. 7–9), the classical 5 Be3 (cols. 10–13), and the speculative 5 Nf5 (col. 14). Black can hold his own against all three, but 5 Nb3 requires more care.

Steinitz's 4 . . . Qh4 (cols. 15–16) is a brazen attempt at pawn-

117

grabbing. White maintains pressure, but this century-old line will appeal to materialists.

Columns 17–18 cover the *Scotch Gambit,* 4 Bc4 Bc5 5 c3, a kin to the Göring and Danish Gambits. White obtains a strong initiative in these columns, so Black might be wise to transpose into the Two Knights' Defense (col. 17, note q) or the Giuoco Piano (note r).

SCOTCH GAME

1 e4 e5 2 Nf3 Nc6 3 d4 exd4 4 Nxd4 Nf6

	1	2	3	4	5	6
5	Nc3				Nxc6	
	Bb4(a)			Nxe4	bxc6	
6	Nxc6			Nxe4(k)	e5	
	bxc6			Qe7	Qe7(n)	
7	Bd3			f3	Qe2	
	d5(b)			d5	Nd5	
8	exd5(c)			Bb5(l)	c4(o)	
	Qe7†	cxd5		Bd7	Ba6	
9	Qe2	0–0		0–0	Nd2	b3
	cxd5(d)	0–0		dxe4	0–0–0(p)	0–0–0
10	Qxe7†	Bg5(f)		Bxc6	b3(q)	Bb2(s)
	Kxe7	Be6	c6	bxc6	Re8	f6
11	0–0	Nb5	Qf3(h)	fxe4(m)	Bb2	exf6
	Rd8	c5	Bd6(i)	0–0–0	f6	Qb4†
12	Nb5	a3	Bxf6	Qd3 ±	Qe4	Qd2
	c6(e)	Ba5(g)	Qxf6(j)		Nb6(r)	Nxf6 =

(a) 5 . . . Bc5 is a relatively untested possibility. After 6 Be3 Bd6 7 Be2 d6 8 0–0 0–0 9 Nxc6 bxc6 10 Bg5 White was more comfortable in Klovans–Razuvaev, USSR 1974.

(b) 7 . . . 0–0 8 0–0 Re8 9 Bg5 h6 10 Bh4 d6 11 f4 Bb7 12 Qf3 $\stackrel{+}{=}$.

(c) On 8 e5 Ng4 both 9 Bf4 f6 and 9 0–0 f6 are good for Black.

(d) Other choices are no better: (A) 9 . . . Qxe2† 10 Kxe2 cxd5 11 Nb5 $\stackrel{+}{=}$; (B) 9 . . . Nxd5 10 Qxe7† Kxe7 11 a3! with advantage.

(e) 13 Nd4 Bd7 14 Bf4 with a pull, Hort–Spassky, Varna 1962.

(f) 10 Ne2 Re8 11 c3 Bd6 is fully equal, McCormick–Bisguier, US 1966.

(g) 13 b4 and instead of 13 . . . cxb4?! 14 axb4 Bxb4 15 Rxa7 Rxa7 16 Nxa7 h6 17 Nc6 Qd6 18 Bxf6 $\stackrel{+}{=}$ (Salazar–Sanchez Guirado, Vigo 1985), Black can equalize with 13 . . . Bb6!.

(h) 11 Ne2 Re8 12 Nd4 Qd6 13 Qf3 Ne4, poses no problems for Black.

(i) 11 . . . Be7 12 Rae1 h6 13 Bc1! and White has pressure. Note that 13 Bxh6 gxh6 14 Qe3 d4 15 Qxh6 Qd6 16 Qg5† Kh8 is only a draw (17 Qh6† Kg8) since 17 Rxe7? Qxe7 18 Ne4 Ng8! puts Black on top.

(j) 13 Qxf6 gxf6 14 Rad1 Be6 = , Hort–Portisch, Monte Carlo 1968.

(k) 6 Nxc6 Nxc3 7 Nxd8 Nxd1 8 Nxf7 Bogolyubov–Schmid, Bad Pyrmont 1949, and now Euwe's 8 . . . Kxf7 equalizes.

(l) 8 Nxc6 bxc6 9 Qe2 is safe but too tame to achieve any advantage.

(m) 11 Re1 0–0–0 12 Rxe4 Qf6 is unclear, Popov–Hershman, USSR 1965.

(n) Moving the knight (6 ... Ne4 or 6 ... Nd5) hands White the initiative.

(o) 8 h4 is a surprising idea. After 8 ... f6 9 c4 Ba6 10 Rh3 fxe5 11 Ra3 Nb4 12 Nc3 Qxh4†
13 g3 Qd4 14 Rxa6 Nxa6 15 Bf4 0–0–0 the position is unclear, van der Wiel–Timman,
Amsterdam 1987.

(p) 8 ... Nb6, 8 ... Nb4 and 8 ... f6 are alternatives, but the text seems most active.

(q) 10 Qe4 Nb6 11 a4 d5! ∓, Timman–Karpov, Amsterdam 1985.

(r) 13 f4 fxe5 14 fxe5 Bb7 results in equality.

(s) Overly creative is 10 Qb2?! Nb6 11 Be2 Re8 12 Bf4 g5! 13 Bg3 Bg7 ∓, Ljubojević–
Seirawan, Wijk aan Zee 1986.

SCOTCH GAME

1 e4 e5 2 Nf3 Nc6 3 d4 exd4 4 Nxd4 Bc5

	7	8	9	10	11	12
5	Nb3 ....Be3					
	Bb6 ....Bb4†		Qf6			
6	a4 ....Bd2(g)		c3 ....Nb5			
	a5 ....a6		a5(h)	Nge7		Bxe3
7	Nc3	Nc3	a3	g3 ....Nc2(m)		fxe3
	Qf6(a)	Nf6(d)	Bxd2†	d5(j)	Bxe3	Qh4†
8	Qe2	Bg5(e)	Qxd2	Bg2	Nxe3	g3
	Nge7	d6	Nf6	Bxd4(k)	Qe5	Qd8(o)
9	Be3(b)	Qe2(f)	Nc3	cxd4	Nd2(n)	Qg4
	Bxe3(c)	h6	0–0	dxe4	d5	Kf8
10	Qxe3	Bh4	0–0–0	Nc3	exd5	Qf4
	0–0	Nd4	d6	0–0	Nxd5	d6
11	0–0–0	Nxd4	Be2	Nxe4	Nc4	Bc4
	Nb4	Bxd4	Bd7	Qg6	Nxe3	Ne5
12	Nb5	Qc4	Rhe1	0–0	Nxe3	0–0
	b6 =	Be5 =	Re8(i)	Be6(l)	Be6 =	Nf6 $\mp$

(a) An example of 7 . . . d6?! was van der Wiel–Gulko, Amsterdam 1987 which continued 8 Nd5 Ba7 9 Bb5 Bd7 10 0–0 Ne5 11 Bd2! Nf6 (11 . . . c6 12 Bxa5 b6 13 Bc3 also favors White) 12 Bxa5 Nxd5 13 exd5 Bxb5 14 axb5 0–0 15 Bc3 Qg5? (15 . . . Qd7 would avoid the following combination) 16 Rxa7 Rxa7 17 f4 Qh6 18 Qd4 Ng4 19 h3 Raa8 20 hxg4 Rfe8 21 Nd2 Re2 22 Ne4 Resigns.

(b) White can try 9 Nd5 Nxd5 10 exd5† Ne7 and either 11 c4 or 11 h4 with an unclear position.

(c) 9 . . . Nb4 10 0–0–0 0–0 11 g3 may give White a slight edge. The column is Mesing–Papapostolou, Athens 1969.

(d) Other moves are also reasonable: 7 . . . Qf6, 7 . . . Nge7 and 7 . . . d6.

(e) Prandstetter's 8 g3, fianchettoing the bishop, takes the game into more unusual channels.

(f) 9 Qd2 and 9 Bd3 are alternatives. The column is Tseitlin–Geller, Leningrad 1971.

(g) 6 c3 Be7 is roughly equal since 7 Nc3 is not possible.

(h) 6 . . . Bxd2† 7 Qxd2 Nf6 8 Nc3 0–0 9 0–0–0 leaves Black with a disadvantage similar to the column, Petrosian–Trifunović, Belgrade 1964.

(i) After 13 f3 White has more space.

(j) 7 . . . d6 8 Bg2 Bd7 9 0–0 Ne5 10 h3 Nc4 11 Bc1 Nc6 was soon agreed drawn in the game Pazos–Spassky, Dubai 1986, although White is more comfortable.

(k) 8 . . . Nxd4 9 cxd4 Bb4† 10 Nc3 Bxc3† 11 bxc3 dxe4 12 Bxe4 $\pm$, Campora–Rubinetti, Buenos Aires 1986.

(l) 13 Nc3 Rad8 14 Qa4 Nd5 =, Timmerman–Pliester, Amsterdam 1982.

(m) 7 f4, 7 Bc4, 7 Be2, and 7 Qd2 are all reasonable alternatives White may wish to try.

(n) 9 Qf3 0–0 also offers White a few chances for advantage, Tartakower–Tarrasch, Vienna 1922. The column is Sveshnikov–Korchnoi, USSR 1973.

(o) Possible is 8 . . . Qxe4 9 Nxc7† Kd8 10 Nxa8 Qxh1 11 Qd6 Nf6 12 Nd2 Ne8 13 Qf4 Qd5 14 0–0–0 ∞ (Botterill).

SCOTCH GAME

1 e4 e5 2 Nf3 Nc6 3 d4 cxd4

	13	14	15	16	17	18
4	(Nxd4)..Bc4					
	(Bc5) Qh4				Bc5(p)	
5	(Be3) Nf5		Nb5(g)		c3	
	Bb6	d6!(d)	Bb4+(h).....Bc5		dxc3(q).....d3	
6	Nc3	Nxg7+(e)	Bd2	Qf3(m)	Nxc3	0–0
	d6(a)	Kf8	Qxe4+	Nf6(n)	d6	d6(s)
7	Be2	Nh5	Be2	Nxc7+	Bg5	b4
	Nf6	Qh4	Kd8(i)	Kd8	Nge7	Bb6
8	Qd2	Ng3	0–0	Nxa8	Nd5	a4
	Ng4(b)	Nf6	Bxd2(j)	Re8	f6	a6
9	Bxg4	Be2	Nxd2	Bd3	Bxf6	a5
	Bxg4	Ne5	Qf4(k)	Nxe4	gxf6	Ba7
10	f3	b4(f)	g3	Bxe4	Nxf6+	Qb3
	Bd7	Bxb4+	Qh6	Rxe4+	Kf8	Qf6
11	Nd5	c3	Nc4	Kf1	Qc1	b5
	0–0(c)	Bc5 ∓	Nge7(l)	Nd4(o)	Ng8(r)	Ne5(t)

(a) 6 . . . Nf6 7 Be2 d6 transposes back into the column.

(b) 8 . . . Qe7 9 0–0–0 0–0 10 f3 Re8 11 g4 ±, Khasin–Ragosin, USSR 1956.

(c) 12 0–0–0 with excellent attacking prospects, Spielmann–Tarrasch, Breslau 1912.

(d) Older ideas such as Steinitz's 5 . . . d5 and Smyslov's 5 . . . g6 allow White good play, but the text seems to be the cure to 5 Nf5.

(e) White can play less ambitiously with 6 Ng3 or 6 Ne3 avoiding a disadvantage, but 5 Nf5 is not played with that intention.

(f) The text looks strange, but White has trouble with the threat of 10 . . . Nfg4, e.g. 10 0–0? Nfg4 +, or 10 Qd2? Bxf2+ +, or 10 f3 Rg8 (Handoko–Timman, Zagreb 1985) threatening 11 . . . Rxg3. The column is Timman–Borm, Holland 1985.

(g) White has other choices—5 Nf3, 5 Qd3, and 5 Nc3—but the text is the sharpest response.

(h) 5 . . . Qxe4+ 6 Be2 (better than 6 Be3 Qe5 with an easier defense) 6 . . . Kd8 7 0–0 a6 8 N1c3 is strong for White.

(i) If 7 . . . Qe5 8 0–0 Nf6 9 Re1 0–0 10 Bd3 ±.

(j) 8 . . . Nf6 9 N1c3 Qh4 10 g3 Qh3 11 Nd5 Bxd2 12 Nxf6 gxf6 13 Qxd2 d6 14 Rad1 ± (Botterill).

(k) On 9 . . . Qg6 White should again continue 10 Nc4 and Bf3 with a promising position.

(l) 12 Bf3 and White maintains pressure, Botterill–Staples, Manchester 1974.

(m) 6 Qe2 is quieter. After 6 . . . Nd4 7 Nxd4 Bxd4 8 c3 Bb6 9 g3 Qe7 10 Bg2 White has a pull.

(n) 6 . . . Nd4 7 Nxd4 Bxd4 8 c3 $\pm$, Sibarević–Chiburdanidze, Banja Luka 1985.

(o) After 12 Qd3 Nb3 13 Be3 Bxe3 14 fxe3 Nxa1 White has won his rook back, but still has difficulties.

(p) 4 . . . Nf6 transposes into the Two Knights' Defense.

(q) 5 . . . Nf6 transposes into the Giuoco Piano.

(r) After 13 Nh5 White has a strong attack for the piece.

(s) On 6 . . . Nf6 7 e5 d5 8 Bxd3 Ne4 9 Nbd2 Nxd2 10 Bxd2 Bg4 11 Re1 White is for choice.

(t) 11 . . . axb5 12 a6! is strong for White. After 12 Nxe5 dxe5 13 bxa6 Black's queenside is weak.

GÖRING GAMBIT

1 e4 e5 2 Nf3 Nc6 3 d4 cxd4 4 c3

Diagram 15

T HE GÖRING GAMBIT is a near relation of the Danish Gambit. White develops his king's knight before proceeding with the pawn sacrifice, and then usually gives up only one pawn (the main line is 4 . . . dxc3 5 Nxc3). The sacrifice clears away Black's central outpost, opens lines, and facilitates White's development. This is fair compensation for a pawn, hence the opening continues to see occasional use in modern times by tacticians such as Penrose and Ljubojević. Yet Black can reach a reasonable position by either accepting or declining the gambit.

Columns 1–2 investigate 4 . . . dxc3 5 Nxc3 Bb4. Column 1 reaches a complex position with equal material (8 . . . Bg4), while in column 2 Black plays for keeps, trying to hold on to his booty.

By playing 5 . . . d6 and 6 . . . Be6 (col. 3) Black gives back the pawn to avoid problems.

White's 5 Bc4 (col. 4) offers a second pawn as in the Danish Gambit. The line favors Black unless White can improve on the analysis.

Declining the gambit with (A) 4 . . . Nf6 (col. 5) leads to complicated and little explored positions, or (B) 4 . . . d5 (col. 6), which is Capablanca's placid but safe equalizing method.

GÖRING GAMBIT

1 e4 e5 2 Nf3 Nc6 3 d4 exd4 4 c3

	1	2 √	3	4	5	6
	dxc3..Nf6........d5					
5	Nxc3.............................Bc4				e5	exd5
	Bb4 ....d6			cxb2	Ne4	Qxd5
6	Bc4		Bc4	Bxb2	Qe2	cxd4
	d6(a)		Be6(h)	d6(k)	f5(o)	Bb4†(s)
7	0–0(b)		Bxe6	0–0(l)	exf6(p)	Nc3
	Bxc3		fxe6	Be6	d5	Bg4
8	bxc3		Qb3	Bxe6	Nbd2(q)	Be2
	Bg4........Nf6(e)		Qd7(i)	fxe6	Qxf6(r)	Bxf3
9	Qb3	e5	Qxb7	Qb3	Nxe4	Bxf3
	Bxf3	Nxe5	Rb8	Qd7	dxe4	Qc4
10	Bxf7†	Nxe5	Qa6	Ng5	Qxe4	Qb3(t)
	Kf8	dxe5	Be7	Nd8	Qe6	Qxb3
11	gxf3	Qb3(f)	0–0	f4	Bd3	axb3
	Ne5	Qe7	Bf6	Nf6	dxc3	Nge7(u)
12	Bxg8(c)	Ba3	e5	Nc3(m)	0–0	0–0
	Rxg8(d)	c5(g)	Nxe5(j)	Be7(n)	Qxe4 ±	a6 =

(a) (A) 6 ... Nf6 7 e5 d5 8 exf6 dxc4 9 Qxd8† ±, Ljubojević–Lombardy, Manila 1973. (B) 6 ... Qe7 and (C) 6 ... Nge7 both allow White good attacking chances.

(b) (A) 7 Qb3 has been tried. After 7 ... Bxc3† 8 bxc3 (8 Qxc3) 8 ... Qd7 9 Qc2 Nf6 10 0–0 0–0 White doesn't have quite enough for the pawn, Ciocaltea–M. Kovacs, Baja 1971. (B) 7 Ng5 is interesting and merits further exploration.

(c) 12 Be6? Nxf3† 13 Kg2 Qf6 14 Qxb7 Nh5† 15 Kg3 Qf3† 16 Kxh4 h6 leads to mate (O'Kelly).

(d) After 13 f4 Nf3† 14 Kg2 Nh4† 15 Kh1 Qd7 16 c4 (better than 16 f5?! Qc6, Cargnel–Hegeler, corr. 1986) the position is unclear.

(e) 8 ... Be6 9 Bxe6 fxe6 10 Qb3 Qd7 11 Qxb7 Rb8 12 Qa6 Nge7 =, Bjerring–Lein, Varna 1974.

(f) 11 Qxd8† Kxd8 12 Bxf7† Ke7 13 Bb3 Be6 ∓, Yuchtman–Furman, USSR 1959.

(g) 13 Bb5† Kf8 (13 ... Nd7 is drawish, 13 ... Bd7 is interesting but risky) 14 f4 e4 15 f5 Kg8 and the onus is on White to show compensation for his material.

(h) 6 ... Nf6 7 Qb3 Qd7 8 Ng5 Ne5 9 Bb5† c6 is tenable for Black, but quite complicated after 10 f4.

(i) 8 ... Qc8 9 Ng5 Nd8 10 f4 Be7 11 f5 gives White attacking chances.

(j) 13 Nxe5 Bxe5 14 Qxa7 Rc8 results in an unbalanced position, Levy–Feller, Praia da Rocha 1969.

126

(k) 6 . . . Bb4† 7 Nc3 Nf6 8 Qc2 d6 9 0–0–0 0–0 10 e5 Ng4 11 Nd5 is unclear, but White has attacking chances.

(l) (A) 7 Nc3 Be7 9 Qb3 Nh6 = , Csom–Barczay, Hungary 1967. (B) 7 Qb3?! Na5 8 Bxf7† Ke7 9 Qd5 c6 ∓.

(m) 12 f5 e5 13 Nc3 h6 is clearly better for Black, Szabó–Kocsis, corr. 1970.

(n) 13 e5 Ng4 14 exd6 cxd6 ∓.

(o) 6 . . . d5 7 exd6 f5 8 Nxd4 Nxd4 9 cxd4 Bd6 10 f3 ± , Velimirović–Trifunović, Yugoslavia, as 10 . . . Qh4† 11 g3 Bxg3† 12 hxg3 Qxh1 13 Nc3 0–0 14 fxe4 is bad.

(p) 7 Nxd4 Be5 8 Nxf5 0–0 9 Qxe4 d5 10 exd6 Bxf2†! wins for Black.

(q) 8 Nxd4 Nxd4 9 cxd4 Kf7 with at least equality, Levy–Boey, Siegen 1970.

(r) 8 . . . d3 and 8 . . . Bf5 are both possible and lead to complications. The column is Velimirović–Ree, Amsterdam 1976.

(s) 6 . . . Nf6 and 6 . . . Bg4 are natural tries, but are less clear than the text.

(t) 10 Bxc6† bxc6 11 Qe2† Qxe2† 12 Kxe2 0–0–0 = , Ghizdavu–Sidor, Skopje 1972.

(u) 11 . . . Nxd4 12 Bxb7 Rb8 (safer than 12 . . . Nc2†) is an alternative. The column is Ljubojević–Ree, Amsterdam 1972.

PONZIANI'S OPENING

1 e4 e5 2 Nf3 Nc6 3 c3

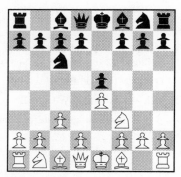

Diagram 16

H ISTORICALLY, PONZIANI'S OPENING was part of the mainstream of opening theory, almost as popular as the Evans Gambit or the Ruy Lopez. Chigorin, for instance, used it frequently and had a theoretical feud with Steinitz over the validity of the defense 3 . . . d5 4 Qa4 f6. Yet for the past eighty years it has more or less languished. Players with a taste for offbeat lines, like Bisguier and Ljubojević (who has ventured it against no less than Karpov), play the Ponziani occasionally, but it is not unusual for a year or two to pass without a single occurrence in master tournaments.

3 c3 is logical in striving for a strong center, but the delay in development allows Black to equalize in a number of ways. The most common defense is 3 . . . Nf6 (cols. 1–4), attacking the e-pawn. After 4 d4 Nxe4 5 d5 Black has three choices: 5 . . . Ne7 (col. 1) leading to a quiet, balanced game; 5 . . . Nb8 (col. 2) with a sharper struggle; or 5 . . . Bc5 (col. 3), resulting in a melee. The line 4 . . . d5 (col. 4) was once considered bad, but recent postal games have revived it. Columns 5–6 deal with 3 . . . d5, a natural response since on 4 exd5 Qxd5 White cannot play 5 Nc3. After 4 Qa4 Black has a choice of gambiting a pawn with 4 . . . Nf6 or 4 . . . Bd7 (col. 5), or solidifying his position with Steinitz's 4 . . . f6 (col. 6).

PONZIANI'S OPENING

1 e4 e5 2 Nf3 Nc6 3 c3

	1	2	3	4	5	6
	Nf6 .... d5(p)					
4	d4				Qa4(q)	
	Nxe4(a) d5				Nf6(r)......f6	
5	d5			Bb5	Nxe5	Bb5
	Ne7 .... Nb8 .... Bc5			exd4(l)	Bd6	Nge7
6	Nxe5	Nxe5(d)	dxc6	e5(m)	Nxc6	exd5
	Ng6	Bc5(e)	Bxf2†(g)	Ne4	bxc6	Qxd5
7	Bd3(b)	Qg4	Ke2	Nxd4	d3(s)	d4
	Nxe5(c)	0–0	bxc6(h)	Bc5	0–0	Bd7(v)
8	Bxe4	Qxe4	Qa4	0–0	Be2	Be3
	Bc5	d6	f5	0–0	Rfe8(t)	exd4
9	Qh5	Bd3	Nbd2(i)	Bxc6	Bg5	cxd4
	d6	f5	0–0	bxc6	Bd7	Ne5
10	Bg5	Qc4	Nxe4	Be3(n)	Nd2	Nc3
	Qd7	b5	fxe4	Qe8(o)	Rb8	Nxf3†
11	0–0	Qxb5	Qxe4(j)	f3	Qc2	gxf3
	Qg4 =	Qe7(f)	Bb6(k)	Nd6 =	h6(u)	Qf5(w)

(a) 4 . . . exd4 transposes into the Göring Gambit.

(b) 7 Nxg6 hxg6 8 Qe2 Qe7 9 Be3 Rh5 10 c4 Qe5 gives Black a good position, Makropoulos–Pr. Nikolić, Athens 1985.

(c) 7 . . . Nxf2? 8 Bxg6! Nxd1 9 Bxf7† Ke7 10 Bg5† Kd6 11 Nc4† Kc5 12 Nba3 Nxb2 13 Be3 mate, Bachmann–Kunsman 1906, is a good trap to know.

(d) 6 Bd3 Nc5 7 Nxe5 Nxd3† 7 Nxd3 d6 is equal.

(e) 6 . . . Qe7 7 Qd4 d6 8 Qxe4 Qxe5 9 Bd3 Nd7 ±, Sveshnikov–Agzamov, Riga 1985. White may achieve a more substantial edge with 8 Bb5† Bd7 9 Nxd7 Nxd7 10 Bxd7† Kxd7 11 0–0.

(f) 12 0–0 dxe5 13 Bg5 Qd6 14 Qb3 Kh8 15 Nd2 Nd7 16 Rad1 Qg6 17 Be3 Rb8 18 Qc2 e4 with good attacking chances for the pawn, Usunov–Morchev, Sofia 1979.

(g) Not 6 . . . Nxf2? 7 Qd5 Qe7 8 cxb7 Bxb7 9 Qxb7 0–0 10 Rg1 ±.

(h) 7 . . . d5 (Staunton) is met by 8 cxb7 Bxb7 9 Qa4† c6 10 Nbd2 f5 11 Nxe4 fxe4 12 Kxf2 with a distinct advantage.

(i) White has other tries—9 Bg5, 9 Be3 and 9 Kd1—but these allow Black the advantage.

(j) 11 Kxf2?! d5 12 Ke1 (12 Qxc6 exf3) 12 . . . exf3 13 gxf3 c5 with a strong attack, Minev–Sax, Bahia 1971.

(k) After 12 Kd1 d5 13 Qxe5 Bf5 Black's attack should be enough for his sacrificed piece.

(l) 5 ... Nxe4 6 Nxe5 Bd7 is possible. If 7 Qb3 Nxe5 8 Qxd5 Qe7 9 Qxe4 Bxb5 10 Qxe5 Qxe5† 11 dxe5 0–0–0 with counterplay.

(m) 6 Nd4 Bd7 7 exd5 Nxd4 =, Tartakower–Bogolyubov, Berlin 1928.

(n) 10 b4 Bxd4 11 cxd4 Ba6 12 Re1 Qh4 $\overline{\mp}$, Bator–Berkell, Sweden 1986.

(o) Better than 10 ... Bd7 11 Nd2 Nxd2 12 Qxd2 Qe7 13 Rfe1 $\pm$, Fuderer–Pachman, Goteborg 1955.

(p) (A) 3 ... f5 4 d4 fxe4 5 Nxe5 Nf6 (or 5 ... Qf6) is possible but less popular. (B) 3 ... d6 is a quiet and little-analyzed alternative.

(q) 4 Bb5 dxe4 5 Nxe5 Qd5 (5 ... Qg5 6 Qa4 Qxg2 7 Bxc6† bxc6 8 Qxc6† Kd8 is complicated and obscure) 6 Qa4 Nge7 7 f4 Bd7 8 Nxd7 Kxd7 produces a sharp but equal position.

(r) 4 ... Bd7 is another promising gambit. After 5 exd5 Nd4 6 Qd1 Nxf3† Black has good play for his pawn.

(s) Both (A) 7 Qxc6† Bd7 8 Qa6 dxe4, and (B) 7 d4 dxe4 8 Ba6 Bd7 9 Bb7 c5 leave White with a poor game.

(t) 8 ... Qe8 9 Nd2 Rb8 10 0–0 c5 (Noval–Kaikamdzozov, Sofia 1970) with good play for the pawn.

(u) After 12 Bh4 Qe7 Black has compensation for the pawn, Kwiatkowski–Yakovlev, Sofia 1955.

(v) 7 ... Bg4 8 Bc4 Qa5 9 Qxa5 Nxa5 10 Bb5† c6 11 Be2 results in a good endgame for White, Eales–Belyavsky, Groningen 1970.

(w) After 12 0–0–0 a6 13 d5 0–0–0 14 Bxd7† Rxd7 15 d6 White had a strong attack in Maas–Michael, London 1912.

PETROV'S DEFENSE

1 e4 e5 2 Nf3 Nf6

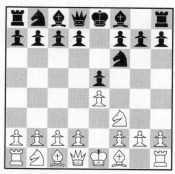

Diagram 17

T HIS DEFENSE BEARS the name of the Russian master who practiced it in the nineteenth century; in Europe it is called the Russian Game. The Petrov is a safe defense. Black's second move counters White's threat with a threat of his own, usually leading to the capture of both e-pawns. This produces a symmetrical pawn structure and the possibility of exchanges on the open e-file. Hence the opening has a drawish character.

In recent times it has gained great respectability. It was featured in many world championship games between Kasparov and Karpov, inspiring other leading players to use it. Yet Petrov's Defense has one severe disadvantage: if White wants a draw, it is almost impossible for Black to avoid. See, for example, column 7, where the game heads into a symmetrical ending with White slightly ahead in development. If Black is not afraid to draw, Petrov's is as good as any other defense.

Diagram 18

The main line is 3 Nxe5 d6 4 Nf3 Nxe4 5 d4 (cols. 1–6). See diagram. Black's 5 . . . d5 (cols. 1–5) supports the Ne4 and stakes out central territory. White tries to undermine the Ne4 with 6 Bd3 and later c4 or Re1. If he achieves this without too many exchanges, he will have the initiative. Black has two choices: 6 . . . Be7 (cols. 1–2) and 6 . . . Nc6 (cols. 3–4), but 6 . . . Bd6 (col. 5) is suspect, as is 5 . . . Be7 (col. 6).

Unusual continuations are covered in columns 7–9. None of these is a serious try for the advantage.

A sharp continuation is 3 d4!? (cols. 10–12). After 3 . . . Nxe4 4 Bd3 d5 5 Nxe5 (cols. 10–11), the position is similar to the main line but with White's knight at a more aggressive post at e5. This may not be good, however, as Black is able to attack it there. 3 . . . exd4 4 e5 Ne4 (col. 12) allows White a small edge.

PETROV'S DEFENSE

1 e4 e5 2 Nf3 Nf6 3 Nxe5 d6 4 Nf3 Nxe4 5 d4

	1	2	3	4	5	6
	d5					Be7(n)
6	Bd3 Be7		Nc6		Bd6	Bd3 Nf6
7	0–0 Nc6	h3 . . . . Be7	0–0 Bg4(i)	0–0 0–0		h3 0–0
8	c4 . . . . Nb4	Re1 Bg4!(e)	0–0 0–0	c4 Nf6	c4 c6	0–0 Re8
9	Be2(a) Be6	c3(f) f5	Re1 Bf5	cxd5(j) Bxf3	Nc3(l) Nxc3	c4 Nc6(o)
10	Nc3 0–0	Nbd2 0–0	Nc3(h) Nxc3	Qxf3 Qxd5	bxc3 dxc4!	Nc3 h6
11	Be3(b) f5(c)	Qb3 Kh8	bxc3 Bxd3	Qe2† Be7	Bxc4 Bg4	Re1 Bf8
12	a3 Nxc3(d)	Qxb7 Rf6(g)	Qxd3 Re8 =	Bb5 Qd6(k)	Qd3 Nd7(m)	Rxe8 Qxe8(p)

(a) 9 cxd5 Nxd3 10 Qxd3 Qxd5 11 Re5 Bf5 12 Nc3 Nxc3 13 Qxc3 Be6! 14 Qxc7 Bd6 15 Qc2 0–0 16 Bd2 Bf5 with enough play for the pawn, Hübner–Smyslov, match 1983. 12 Ne5!? is trickier; after 12 . . . f6 13 Nc3 Nxc3 14 Qxf5 Nb5! 15 Qg4 Nxd4 16 Nd3 Kf7! Black is doing well.

(b) 11 cxd5 Nxc3 12 bxc3 Nxd5 13 Qc2 c5 14 c4 Nb4 =, Ljubojević–Seirawan, Brussels 1986.

(c) (A) 11 . . . Bf5 12 a3 Nxc3 13 bxc3 Nc2 14 Ra2 Nxa3 15 Rxa3 Bxa3 16 c5 and 17 Qb3 wins the bishop, giving White an edge, A. Ivanov–Arkhipov, USSR 1985. (B) 11 . . . Bf6 12 Nxe4 dxe4 13 Ne1 c6 14 Qb3 Qe7 15 a3 Na6 16 Nc2 ±, Ljubojević–Karpov, Bugojno 1986.

(d) 13 bxc3 Nc6 14 Qa4 f4 15 Bc1! Kh8 16 Rb1 Rb8 17 Re1 ±, Kayumov–Serper, USSR 1987.

(e) 8 . . . Bf5 9 c4 Nb4 (9 . . . 0–0 10 Nc3 Nxc3 11 bxc3 ±) 10 Bf1 0–0 11 a3 Nc6 12 cxd5 Qxd5 13 Nc3 Nxc3 14 bxc3 Bf6 15 Bf4 Rac8 16 Re3 Na5 17 Ne5 c5 18 g4! Bg6 19 Bg2 and White is active, Tal–G. Garcia, Yurmala 1983.

(f) (A) 9 Bxe4 dxe4 10 Rxe4 Bxf3 11 Qxf3 Nxd4 =. (B) On 9 c4 Black has 9 . . . Nf6! 10 cxd5 Bxf3 11 Qxf3 Qxd5 12 Qg3 (12 Qxd5 Nxd5 13 Be4 0–0–0 14 Nc3 Bb4 =, Ljubojević–Tal, Bugojno 1984) 12 . . . Qxd4 13 Nc3 0–0 14 Nb5 Qg4 with equality, Sax–Yusupov, Thessaloniki 1984.

(g) 13 Qb3 Rg6 14 Be2 Qd6 15 Nf1 f4 and Black has an attack for his pawn, Tukmakov–Dvoretsky, Leningrad 1974.

(h) 10 c3 Nd6 11 Ne5 Nxe5 12 Bxf5 Nxf5 13 Rxe5 g6 gives Black at least equality, Barlov–Knežević, Yugoslavia 1976.

(i) 7 . . . Be7 transposes into col. 1.

(j) 9 Nc3 Bxf3 10 Qxf3 Nxd4 11 Qe3† (Kupreichik's 11 Qh3 is interesting) 11 . . . Ne6 12 cxd5 Nxd5 13 Nxd5 Qxd5 14 Be4 Qb5 15 a4 Qa6 16 Rd1 Be7 17 b4 0–0 18 Qh3 g6 19 Bb2 Qc4! with equal chances, Kasparov–Karpov, World Chp. 1986.

(k) 12 . . . Qxd4?! 13 Nc3 allows White a strong initiative. After 12 . . . Qd6 13 Nc3 0–0 14 Bxc6 bxc6 15 Be3 Nd5 16 Rac1 Rfe8 White has the better pawn structure, but that has little meaning here, Timman–Yusupov, match 1986.

(l) (A) 9 Qc2 Na6! 10 Bxe4 (10 a3 f5 =) 10 . . . dxe4 11 Qxe4 Re8 12 Qd3 Bg4 gives Black good play for the pawn. (B) Promising is 9 cxd5!? cxd5 10 Nc3 Nxc3 11 bxc3 Bg4 12 h3 Bh5 13 Rb1 Nd7 14 Rb5 Nb6 15 c4! Bxf3 16 Qxf3 dxc4 17 Bc2 with attacking chances for the pawn; Kudrin–Machado, Thessaloniki 1988, continued 17 . . . Rb8 18 a4 a6?! 19 Bg5 Qc7 20 Bxh7†! Kxh7 21 Qh5† Kg8 22 Bf6 Bh2† 23 Kh1 Qd6?! (23 . . . Qf4 holds out longer) 24 Bxg7! Kxg7 25 Rg5† Kf6 26 Re1 Qe6 27 Rxe6† fxe6 28 Rg6† Ke7 29 Rg7† Resigns.

(m) 13 Ng5 Nf6 14 h3 Bh5 15 f4 h6 16 g4 hxg5 17 fxg5 Nxg4 18 hxg4 Qd7 (18 . . . Bxg4 19 Qe4 Qd7 20 g6 Be6 21 Bxe6 wins, Capablanca–Northrop, New York Handicap Tournament 1909) 19 gxh5 Qg4† 20 Kf2 Rae8 21 Rg1 Qh4† 22 Kg2 b5 23 Bb3, Short–Hübner, Tilburg 1988; now best is 23 . . . Re4 24 Qf3 Bh2, but after 25 Bd2! Rg4† 26 Qxg4 Qxg4† 27 Kxh2 (Keene) White is clearly on top.

(n) 5 . . . Nf6 6 Bd3 Bg4?! 7 Nbd2 Be7 8 h3 Bh5 9 Nf1! 0–0 10 Ng3 with a kingside initiative, de Firmian–Shirazi, US Chp. 1983.

(o) Slightly better is 9 . . . Nbd7 10 Nc3 Nf8 11 d5 Ng6 12 Re1 ±, Tal–Smyslov, USSR 1981, but in any case Black has a passive position.

(p) 13 Bf4 Bd7 14 Qd2 with an advantage in space and mobility, Fischer–Gheorghiu, Buenos Aires 1978.

PETROV'S DEFENSE

1 e4 e5 2 Nf3 Nf6

	7	8	9	10	11	12
3	(Nxe5).................Bc4(g) d4					
	(d6)(a)		Nxe4(h)	Nxe4 ....exd4(s)		
4	(Nf3)(b)		Nc3	Bd3(j)		e5
	(Nxe4)		Nxc3	d5		Ne4
5	Qe2........c4(d)		dxc3	Nxe5		Qxd4
	Qe7	Nc6(e)	f6	Bd6........Nd7(o)		d5
6	d3	Nc3(f)	0–0(i)	c4(k)	Nxd7(p)	exd6
	Nf6	Nxc3	d6!	0–0(l)	Bxd7	Nxd6
7	Bg5	dxc3	Nh4	0–0	0–0	Nc3
	Qxe2†	Be7	g6	Bxe5	Qh4(q)	Nc6
8	Bxe2	Bd3	f4	dxe5	c4	Qf4
	Be7	Bg4	Qe7	Nc6	0–0–0	g6
9	Nc3	Be4	f5	cxd5(m)	c5	Be3
	c6!	Qd7	Qg7	Qxd5	g5	Bg7
10	0–0–0	Be3	Qf3	Qc2	Nc3	Bd3
	Na6(c)	Bf5 =	Be7 ∓	Nb4(n)	Bg7(r)	0–0(t)

(a) 3 . . . Nxe4? 4 Qe2 Qe7 5 Qxe4 d6 6 d4 wins a pawn.

(b) Ineffective is 4 Nc4 Nxe4 5 d4 d5 6 Ne3 Be6 7 Bd3 f5 8 0–0 Bd6 with equal chances, Paulsen–Schallopp, Frankfort 1887.

(c) 11 Rhe1 Nc7 12 Bf1 Ne6 13 Bd2 Bd7 =, Spassky–Petrosian, World Chp. 1969. Against reasonable defense, 5 Qe2 produces no advantage. White gains two tempi in development, but this has little meaning in the endgame.

(d) 5 Nc3 Nxc3 6 dxc3 Be7 7 Be3 has surprise value, e.g. 7 . . . d5 8 c4 dxc4 9 Qxd8† Bxd8 10 Bxc4 Bf6 11 0–0–0 ±, Nunn–Mascarinas, Thessaloniki 1984. A good plan is 7 . . . Nc6 8 Qd2 Bg4! 9 Be2 (9 Nd4 Bf6 10 Bb5 Bd7 =) 9 . . . Qd7 10 0–0–0 0–0 =, Nimzowitsch–Marshall, St. Petersburg 1914.

(e) 5 . . . Be7 6 d4 0–0 7 Bd3 d5 8 0–0 Nc6 9 cxd5 Qxd5 10 Re1 Nf6 11 Nc3 ±, Kupreichik–Mikhalchishin, Minsk 1985.

(f) The natural (A) 6 d4?! is bad: 6 . . . d5 7 Nc3 Bb4 8 Qc2 Qe7† 9 Be3 Bf5 with threats, Kupreichik–Mikhalchishin, Kuybyshev 1986. (B) 6 Be2 Be7 7 0–0 0–0 8 d4 Bf6 9 h3 Re8 =, Chiburdanidze–Makarychev, Frunze 1985. The column is Timman–Yusupov, match 1986.

(g) 3 Nc3 Nc6 transposes to the Four Knights' Defense. Black can also play 3 . . . Bb4 4 Bc4 0–0 5 0–0 Nc6 6 d3 Bxc3 =.

(h) 3 . . . Nc6 is the Two Knights' Defense.

(i) (A) 6 Nh4 g6 7 f4 c6! ∓. (B) 6 Nxe5? Qe7 +. The column is analysis by Polugaevsky.

135

(j) 4 dxe5 d5 5 Nbd2 Nxd2 6 Bxd2 Be7 7 Bf4 c5 8 c3 Nc6 9 Bd3 Be6 =, Short–Seirawan, Lugano 1986.

(k) (A) 6 0–0 0–0 7 Nc3 Nxc3 8 bxc3 Nd7 9 f4 c5 10 Qf3 c4 11 Be2 Qa5 =, Tal–Benko, Hastings 1973–74. (B) 6 Nd2 Bxe5 7 dxe5 Nc5 8 Nf3 Bg4 9 h3 Nxd3† 10 Qxd3 Bxf3 =, Nunn–Toth, Lugano 1984.

(l) 6 . . . c6?! allows White to build his initiative easily: 7 0–0 0–0 8 Nc3 Nxc3 9 bxc3 Bxe5 (else White plays f4 with a strong attack) 10 dxe5 dxc4 11 Bxc4 Qxd1 12 Rxd1 Bf5 13 Ba3 with a distinct endgame advantage, Maróczy–Marshall, Paris 1900.

(m) 9 Bf4 Nb4 10 Na3 Nc5 11 Bb1 dxc4 12 Nxc4 Be6 = (van der Wiel).

(n) 11 Bxe4 Nxc2 12 Bxd5 Bf5 13 g4! Bxg4 with a sharp game, but with roughly equal chances, e.g. 14 Be4 Nxa1 15 Nc3 Bh3 16 Re1 f5 17 exf6 Rae8 18 Be3 Rxe4 19 Nxe4 Nc2 20 Rc1 Nxe6 21 fxe3 c6 22 Ng5 Bf5 23 f7† Kh8 ∞, Tal–Timman, Reykjavik 1987.

(o) 5 . . . Be7 6 Nd2 Nxd2 7 Bxd2 Nc6 8 Nxc6 bxc6 9 0–0 0–0 10 Qh5 ±, Spassky–Hort, match 1977.

(p) 6 Qe2 Nxe5 7 Bxe4 dxe4 8 Qxe4 Be6 9 Qxe5 Qd7 10 Be3 Bb4† 11 c3 Bd6 12 Qa5 0–0 13 Nd2 f5 gives Black fair compensation for the pawn.

(q) (A) 7 . . . Bd6?! 8 c4 c6 9 cxd5 cxd5 10 Nc3 Nxc3 11 bxc3 a6 12 Re1† Be6 13 Qh5 Qd7 14 c4 ±, Hellers–Wolff, World Junior Chp. 1987. (B) 7 . . . Nf6!? looks like a good try. (C) 7 . . . Qf6 8 Nc3 Qxd4 9 Qh5! Nf6 10 Re1† Be7 11 Qg5 Qg4?! was played in Shirazi–Kogan, US Chp. 1985, where White found the spectacular 12 Rxe7†! Kxe7 13 Nxd5† Kf8 14 Nxf6 gxf6 15 Qxf6 with a strong attack. The game continued 15 . . . Rg8 16 Bh6† Ke8 17 Re1† Be6 18 g3 Kd7 19 Bxh7 Rge8 20 Bf4 Qh5 21 Qc3! Re7 22 Be4 c6 23 Bf3 Qh3 24 Qc5 Rc8 25 Bg5 f6 26 Qd4† Ke8 27 Qxf6 Rcc7 28 Rxe6! Qxe6 29 Bh5† Kd7 30 Bg4! Resigns.

(r) 11 Ne2 f5 12 f3 Rhf8! 13 a4 Rde8 14 Qe1 Qxe1 15 Rxe1 f4 16 fxe4 dxe4 17 Bc4 f3 18 Be3! fxe2 19 Rxe2 c6 results in a level position, Sax–Salov, Brussels 1988.

(s) 3 . . . d5 4 exd5 exd4 5 Bb5† c6 6 Qe2† Be7 7 dxc6 bxc6 8 Bc4 0–0 9 0–0 Bg4 10 c3! leaves White with the better pawn structure, Pruess–Butler, corr. 1960.

(t) 11 0–0–0 Be6 12 Bc5 ±, Matanović–Trifunović, Yugoslav Chp. 1958.

136

PHILIDOR'S DEFENSE

1 e4 e5 2 Nf3 d6

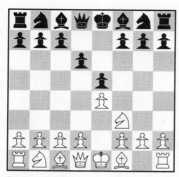

Diagram 19

T HIS DEFENSE WAS FIRST PROPOSED by Philidor in his "L'analyse" (1749). It led a haphazard existence until the beginning of this century, though used occasionally by a number of great players. Its brightest period came with the rise of such masters as Alekhine and Nimzowitsch, and the Viennese analyst Marco played it regularly. Since then it has been rarely seen in grandmaster practice except when Larsen revived the 3 . . . exd4 variation in his pamphlet "Why Not Philidor's Defense?"

There are answers to this question. Black's second move locks in his king's bishop and commits him to a passive game. By playing 3 d4 followed by natural developing moves, White should gain space and mobility. Nonetheless the defense appeals to players who are satisfied to play a cramped but solid game and to wait patiently for their chances.

Columns 1–2 explore Black's most promising variation in the Philidor's, 3 . . . Nf6, which limits White to a small advantage. Column 3, the *Hanham Variation* (3 . . . Nd7), is inadequate unless improvements are found. The 3 . . . exd4 line (cols. 4–5) is the most common choice in modern grandmaster play, but White keeps a spatial advantage. Column 6, 3 Bc4, is an old but little-tested move which takes the play into uncharted territory.

PHILIDOR'S DEFENSE

1 e4 e5 2 Nf3 d6

	1	2	3	4	5	6
3	d4		............Nd7	..exd4(j)		....Bc4
	Nf6					Qf6(q)
4	Nc3(a)		Bc4	Qxd4	Nxd4	d3(r)
	Nbd7		c6	Bd7(k)	g6(n)	Bg4
5	Bc4		Nc3	Bf4	Nc3	Nbd2
	Be7		Be7(g)	Nc6	Bg7	Nc6
6	0–0(b)		dxe5	Qd2	Be3	c3
	0–0		dxe5	Be7(l)	Nf6	Nge7
7	Qe2		Ng5	Nc3	Qd2	h3
	c6 ....exd4		Nh6(h)	Nf6	0–0	Bd7
8	a4	Nxd4	Ne6	0–0–0	0–0–0	b4
	Qc7(c)	Ne5	fxe6	0–0	Re8	Ng6
9	h3	Bb3	Bxh6	e5(m)	f3	Nf1
	b6(d)	c5	Nb6	dxe5	a6(o)	Nf4
10	Rd1	Nf5(e)	Qh5†	Nxe5 ±	g4	Ne3
	Bd7 ±	Bxf5(f)	Kf8(i)		b5(p)	h6 ∞

(a) 4 dxe5 Nxe4 5 Qd5 Nc5 6 Bg5 Be7 or 6 . . . Qd7 leads to only a tiny White edge.

(b) 6 dxe5 dxe5 (6 . . . Nxe5 7 Be2 ±) 7 Bxf7† Kxf7 8 Ng5† Kg8 9 Ne6 Qe8 10 Nxc7 Qg6 11 Nxa8 Qxg2 12 Rf1 Nc5 13 Qe2 Bh3 is murky but probably equal.

(c) 8 . . . exd4 9 Nxd4 Ne5 10 Ba2 c5 is an interesting try as good as the text, Prah–Brglez, corr. 1983. Or 9 . . . Re8 10 Be3 (10 Ba2 Bf8 11 Qf3 g6) 10 . . . Bf8 11 Nf3 Nb6 ∞ (Adams).

(d) 9 . . . exd4 10 Nxd4 Re8 11 Bf4 Ne5 12 Bb3 ±, Grefe–Najdorf, Lone Pine 1976.

(e) Not recommended is 10 Ndb5?! a6 11 Na3 b5 12 Bd5 Ra7 ∓, but 10 Nf3 Bg4 11 Bf4 Nxf3† 12 gxf3 Bh3 13 Rfd1 Nh5 14 Bg3 may be good for White.

(f) After 11 exf5 Qd7 (not 11 . . . Rc8? 12 Bd5 Qd7 13 f4 ±, Boleslavsky–Furman, USSR 1961) 12 Nd5 Rfe8 =, Palciauskas–Staal, corr. 1975. Stronger is 12 f4 Nc6 13 g4 ±.

(g) 5 . . . h6 6 a4 Qf6 7 h4 g6 8 Be3 ±, Unzicker–Blau, Lucerne 1948.

(h) 7 . . . Bxg5 8 Qh5 g6 (or 8 . . . Qf6 9 Bxg5 Qg6 10 Qh4 ±, Schlechter–Alekhine, Hamburg 1910) 9 Qxg5 also gives White a big plus.

(i) After 11 Bb3 gxh6 12 Rd1 Qe8 13 Qxh6† Kf3 14 Rd3 White had a winning attack in Matulović–Tomović, Yugoslavia 1956.

(j) 3 . . . f5 is an old move Mestel revived in the 1970s. It seems most simply met by 4 Nc3 fxe4 5 Nxe4 d5 6 Nxe5 dxe4 7 Qh5† g6 8 Nxg6 Nf6 9 Qe5† Kf7 10 Bc4† Kg7 11 Bh6† Kxh6 12 Nh8 Bb4† 13 c3 Qxh8 14 cxb4 ±.

(k) Other moves are: (A) 4 . . . Nc6 5 Bb5 Bd7 6 Bxc6 Bxc6 7 Nc3 Nf6 8 Bg5 Be7 9 0–0–0 ±; (B) 4 . . . Nf6 5 e5 dxe5 (5 . . . Qe7 6 Be2 dxe5 7 Nxe5 Nbd7 8 Nd3 ±, Jansa–Ermenkov,

138

Prague 1985) 6 Qxd8† Kxd8 7 Ne5 Bd6 ±; (C) 4 . . . a6 5 Bf4 Nc6 6 Qd2 Nf6 ±, Matulović–Barlov, Vrnjačka Banja 1983.

(l) 6 . . . Nge7 7 Nc3 Ng6 8 Bg5 ±, Kurajica–Westerinen, Solingen 1974.

(m) The more patient moves 9 Bd3 (*Bilguer*) and 9 h3 also give White better chances.

(n) 4 . . . Nf6 5 Nc3 Be7 6 Be2 0–0 7 0–0 leaves Black less active, Abramović–Franić, Bela Crkva 1987.

(o) 9 . . . Nc6 10 h4 Ne5 11 Kb1 a6 12 Bg5 allows White attacking chances and more control of the center, Hardicsay–Prinz, Boblingen 1985.

(p) 11 Bg5 ±, Joksić–Lehmann, Plovdiv 1975.

(q) Other moves are: (A) 3 . . . Be6 4 Bxe6 fxe6 5 d4 exd4 6 Nxd4 e5 7 Ne6 ±, Chandler–Large, Hastings 1986; (B) 3 . . . Be7 4 0–0 Nf6 5 Re1 0–0 6 d4 exd4 ∞, Mestel–Georgadze, Hastings 1979; (C) the unexplored pawn sacrifice 3 . . . Nf6 4 Ng5 d5.

(r) 4 d4 and 4 Nc3 take play back into normal channels. The column is Chandler–Hodgson, Hastings 1986.

LATVIAN GAMBIT

1 e4 e5 2 Nf3 f5

Diagram 20

T HIS REVERSE FORM OF THE KING'S GAMBIT was originated by Gioacchino Greco more than three centuries ago. It was called the Greco Counter Gambit until Latvian analysts revived it in this century, notably Karl Behting in the 1920s, and gave it a new lease on life. Yet White has several ways of getting the advantage, so Black must play new or obscure moves to achieve the wild, unbalanced positions the player of this gambit seeks. Tournament experience is rare, but the opening is intriguing enough to have inspired a wealth of analytical research.

It is in the nature of this opening to be favored mostly by correspondence players; some Latvian chess circles have conducted regular tourneys with the gambit as their theme.

3 Bc4 (cols. 1–2) is one of the sharper attempts to refute the gambit; Keres subjected it to searching analyses, with resulting fireworks, but much of it has lost its sparkle and impact by now. 4 . . . d5 has become a more intriguing resource, and 3 . . . b5 (col. 2) also seems to maintain the counterattack.

3 d4 (col. 3) opens lines quickly, but if Black survives the first attack he will be in satisfactory shape.

3 exf5 (col. 4), as old as *Bilguer*, is of interest because White strives for a good variation of the King's Gambit Accepted with colors reversed.

3 Nxe5 (cols. 5–6) is the most difficult move for Black to meet and maintain an equilibrium. 3 . . . Nc6 (col. 5) is an alternative to Black's usual replies.

LATVIAN GAMBIT

1 e4 e5 2 Nf3 f5

	1	2	3	4	5	6
3	Bc4		d4	exf5	Nxe5	
	fxe4(a)	b5!?(e)	fxe4	e4(l)	Nc6(q)	Qf6
4	Nxe5	Bxb5(f)	Nxe5	Ne5(m)	Nxc6(r)	d4(u)
	d5!(b)	fxe4	Nf6	Nf6	dxc6	d6
5	Qh5†	Nxe5	Bg5(h)	Be2	Nc3(s)	Nc4
	g6	Qg5	d6(i)	d6(n)	Qe7	fxe4
6	Nxg6	d4	Nc3(j)	Bh5†	d3	Nc3(v)
	hxg6	Qxg2	dxe5	Ke7	Nf6	Qg6
7	Qxg6†(c)	Rf1	dxe5	Nf7	Bg5	f3(w)
	Kd7	Nf6	Qxd1†	Qe8	Bd7	exf3
8	Bxd5	Bf4	Rxd1	Nxh8(o)	f3	Qxf3
	Nf6	c6	h6!	Qxh5	0–0–0	Nc6
9	Nc3	Be2	Bxf6	Qxh5	Be2	Bd3(x)
	Qe7	d6	gxf6	Nxh5	h6	Qg4
10	0–0	Nc4	Nd5	g4	Bd2	Qf2
	Nxd5(d)	d5(g)	Kd7(k)	Nf6(p)	g5(t)	Qxd4(y)

(a) (A) 3 . . . d6 4 d4 see Philidor's Defense. (B) 3 . . . Nf6 (1) 4 Nxe5 Qe7 5 d4 Nc6 6 Nc3 Nxe5 7 dxe5 Qxe5 8 0–0 fxe4 9 Nd5 Nxd5 10 Bxd5 c6 11 Be4 Be7 12 Re1 Qf6 ∞, Gunderam–Grivainis, corr. 1970–72. (2) 4 d4 fxe4 5 Nxe5 d5 6 Be2 Bd6 ∞.

(b) Designed to bypass the myriad complications arising from the risky 4 . . . Qg5 5 d4 Qxg2 6 Qh5† g6 7 Bf7† Kd8 8 Bxg6! Qxh1† 9 Ke2 c6! 10 Nc3!, e.g. 10 . . . e3 11 Be3 Qxa1 12 Qg5† Kc7 13 Nf7 b5—see comment in note (e)—14 Qd8† Kb7 15 Ne4 Nf6 16 Qa5 Na6 17 Nd8† Kb8 18 Bf4† winning, Grava–Alberts, corr. 1968.

(c) 7 Qxh8 Kf7 8 Qd4 Be6 9 Bb3 Nc6 10 Qh8 Bg7 11 Qh7 Qg5 12 0–0 Nf6 13 d4! Nxh7 14 Bxg5 Nxg5 15 Nc3 Nxd4 16 Bxd5 Ne2† 17 Nxe2 Bxd5 18 c3 Rh8 19 Nf4 Be5 20 Nxd5 Bxh7† Draw, Slater–Karsch, corr. 1987–88.

(d) 11 Nxd5 Qe5 12 Nf6† Kd8 13 g3 Bf5 14 d4! exd3 15 Qf7 (threatening 16 Bf4) 15 . . . Qe6 16 Qxe6 Bxe6 17 Re1 Bf7 18 cxd3 Bh6 19 Be3 Bxe3 20 Rxe3 Rh6 21 Ng4 Rb6 22 b3 Nc6 (Ballenilla–Kozlov, corr. 1979–81) 23 Ne5 ±. White's three pawns may prove stronger than Black's piece, but the whole variation is open to further scrutiny.

(e) This intriguing thrust would seem to provide a loophole for Black's king in the variations following 10 Nc3 in note (b) if White were to continue 4 Bb3 fxe4 5 Nxe5. However, White aborts the whole line by 5 d4! or 5 Nc3! ± instead.

(f) 4 Bb3 is more constricting, whereupon Black might try to build a precarious fence with, e.g., 4 . . . Nc6 5 d3 Nf6 6 exf5 d5 7 Bg5 Bxf5 8 Nc3 Bb4 (Korn).

(g) 11 Ne3 Qg6 12 c4 Bb4† 13 Nc3 Bh3 14 Rh1 Bxc3† 15 bxc3 0–0 =, Strelis–Eglitis, corr. 1977–80.

141

(h) (A) 5 Bc4 d5 6 Bb3 Be6 7 Bg5 Be7 = (7 . . . Nbd7 8 Nd2 Be7 =). (B) 5 Be2! c6 6 0–0 (6 Ng4 Be7) 6 . . . d5 7 c4 Be6 8 cxd5 cxd5 9 Nc3 0–0 with a tight but solid position (Korn). (C) 5 Nc3 d6 6 Nc4 d5 7 Ne5 Bd6 8 Be2 0–0 9 f4 exf3 10 Bxf3 c6 11 0–0 Qc7 12 Bf4 Be6 =, Van den Bosch–Apscheneek, Hamburg 1930

(i) Or 5 . . . Be7! 6 Be2 with the option 6 . . . d5 7 f3 exf3 8 Bxf3 c6 9 0–0 0–0 =.

(j) 6 Nc4 Be7 7 Be2 0–0 8 0–0 d5 9 Ne3 Be6 10 c4 c6 =.

(k) 11 Nb6† Kc6 ∞, Pupols' analysis of Pupols–Kotek, corr. 1970, which went 8 . . . Nfd7? (instead of 8 . . . h6) 9 Nd5 Nc5 10 Nxc7† Kf7 11 Nxa8 Ne6 12 Bc4 Na6 13 Be3 b6 14 Bxa6 Bxa6 15 Nc7 Nxc7 16 Rd7† Resigns.

(l) (A) 3 . . . Nc6 4 d4 exd4 5 Nxd4 Nf6 6 Nxc6 bxc6 7 Be2 Qe7 8 0–0 Qf7 9 Bf4 d5 10 Bd3 ±, Richter–Petrov, Poděbrady 1936. (B) 3 . . . d6 4 d4 (see Philidor's Defense) 4 . . . e4 5 Ng5 Bf5 (5 . . . Nf6 6 Ne6 Bxe6 7 fxe6 and 8 f4?!) 6 f3!? e3 or 6 . . . Qe7 ∞ (Gunderam).

(m) Adventurous is 4 Ng1!? Qg5 5 d3 Qxf5 6 dxe4 Qxe4† 7 Be2 (Bücker).

(n) Playable are 5 . . . d5 6 Bh5† Ke7 7 b3 c5 ∞ (Tiemann), or 5 . . . Be7.

(o) 8 Nc3 g6! (8 . . . Nxh5 9 Nd5† Kxf7 10 Qxh5† g6 11 fxg6† Kg7 12 Nxc7 Qe5! (Grivainis' 12 . . . Qc6 is refuted by 13 b3—Korn) 9 fxg6 hxg6 10 Bxg6 Reg8 11 Bh5 Rxg2 ∞.

(p) 11 Rg1 (Bilguer!) 11 . . . Nc6 12 Rg3 Nd4 13 Kd1 d5 14 d3 Nf3 15 dxe4 dxe4 16 g5 (Garcia–Kapitaniak, corr. 1978) 16 . . . Nh5 =. Also, 13 . . . g6 is good.

(q) The historical line is 3 . . . Qe7 4 Qh5† g6 5 Nxg6 Qxe4† 6 Kd1? (nowadays 6 Be2 would be played with advantage, but the old "Italian" rules did not allow a check to be met by interposition—the king had to move) 6 . . . Nf6 7 Qh3 hxg6 8 Qxh8 Ng4 9 d3 Nf2† 10 Kd2 Qg4 11 Be2 Qf4† 12 Kc3 Qb4 mate, Da Cutri–Greco, 1620.

(r) 4 Qh5† g6 (A) 5 Nxg6 Nf6 6 Qh3 hxg6 7 Qxh8 Qe7 8 Qh4 d5 9 Bb5 Kf7 10 Bxc6 bxc6 ∞, Kurtovich–Atars, corr. 1974. (B) 5 Nxc6 dxc6 6 Qf3 Nf6 = (Kudrin).

(s) 5 d4 Qh4! 6 e5 Be6 7 c3 0–0–0 ∞, Ruben–H. Sörensen, Copenhagen 1967.

(t) 11 exf5 Bxf5 12 0–0 Bg7 =.

(u) 4 Nc4 fxe4 5 Nc3 (A) 5 . . . Qg6 6 d3 Bb4 7 Bd2 Bxc3 8 Bxc3 Nf6 9 Bxf6 gxf6 10 dxe4 Qxe4 11 Ne3 Qb4 12 c3 Qxb2 13 Nd5 (Grobe–Eglitis, corr. 1977–78) 13 . . . c6 ∞. (B) 5 . . . Qe6 6 Ne3 c6 7 d3 Bb4 8 dxe4 Qxe4 9 Bd3 Qh4 10 g3 ±, Grobe–Krustkains, corr. 1977–78. (C) 5 . . . Qf7 6 Ne3 c6 7 Nxe4 d5 8 Ng5 Qf6 9 Nf3 Bd6 10 d4 Ne7 entails complications; e.g. (1) 11 Bd3 0–0 12 Ng6! 0–0 13 Bxg6 hxg6 14 Ne1 g5; or (2) 11 g3 Be6 12 Bg2 Nd7 13 0–0 0–0–0 14 b3 a5 15 c4 g5 16 h4 gxh4 17 Nxh4 Ng6 18 Nxg6 hxg6 ∞. In here, 6 d4!? Bb4 7 Bd2 Nf6 8 Qe2 Bxc3 9 Bxc3 d6 10 0–0–0 ± is an alternative.

(v) Sound is 6 Be2 Qd8 7 d5 Nf6 8 Ne3 g6 9 c4 Bg7 10 Nc3.

(w) 7 Bf4 Nf6 8 Ne3 Be7 9 Nc4 c6 10 d5 Nh5 11 Ng3 Nxg3 12 hxg3 Nd7 = (Dreibergs).

(x) 9 d5 Nb4 10 Ne3 Nf6 11 a3 Na6 12 Bd3 is also solid.

(y) 11 Be3 Qf6 12 Qe2 Be6 13 0–0–0 0–0–0 14 Ne4 Qe7 15 Ng5 d5 = (Grivainis).

BISHOP'S OPENING

1 e4 e5 2 Bc4

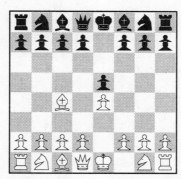

Diagram 21

A S ONE MAY EXPECT, considering the obviousness of White's second move, this is an old opening. It was analyzed by Ruy Lopez and Lucena, but Philidor deserves credit for developing it into a system. 2 Bc4 is played by beginners in the hope that their opponents will kindly allow 3 Qh5 and 4 Qxf7 mate. The Bishop's Opening is much more sophisticated than this, but less so than contemporary openings.

Black's most aggressive reaction is 2 . . . Nf6 (cols. 1–5), after which White has a distinct choice, the positional 3 d3 or the gambit 3 d4.

3 d3 (cols. 1–3) attempts to reach favorable versions of other openings, such as the Giuoco Pianissimo, Vienna Game, or King's Gambit. This calm approach appeals to modern grandmasters who wish to avoid the drawish Petrov's Defense. Black's best response is 3 . . . c6 followed by 4 . . . d5 (col. 1), immediately hitting the Bc4.

3 d4 (cols. 4–5) is an entertaining gambit leading to an open and lively game. White has attacking chances, but Black's extra pawn puts the burden of proof on White.

The ancient 2 . . . Bc5 (col. 6) is less forcing but certainly playable.

BISHOP'S OPENING

1 e4 e5 2 Bc4

	1	2	3	4	5	6
	Nf6...Bc5(o)					
3	d3(a)			d4		c3(p)
	c6		d5	exd4		Nf6(q)
4	Nf3(b)		exd5	Nf3		d4
	d5	d6	Nxd5	Nxe4(i)		exd4
5	Bb3	0–0	Nf3	Qxd4		e5
	Bd6(c)	Be7	Nc6	Nf6(j)		d5
6	Nc3	Nc3(e)	0–0(f)	Bg5		exf6
	dxe4(d)	0–0	Bc5(g)	Be7		dxc4
7	dxe4	Qe2	Re1	Nc3		Qh5
	Na6	Nbd7	0–0	Nc6	c6	0–0
8	Be3	a4	Nc3(h)	Qh4	0–0–0	Qxc5
	Qe7	b6	Nxc3	d6(k)	d5	Re8†
9	Nd2	Rd1	bxc3	0–0–0	Rhe1	Ne2(r)
	Bc5	Bb7	Bg4	Be6	Be6(m)	d3
10	Qe2	d4	h3 ±	Bd3	Bd3	Be3
	Bxe3 =	Qc7 =		Qd7(l)	Nbd7(n)	dxe2(s)

(a) 3 f4 is harmless after either 3 . . . Nxe4 or 3 . . . d5 4 exd5 e4 (a good variation of the Falkbeer Counter Gambit).

(b) 4 Qe2 Be7 5 Nf3 0–0 6 Bb3 d5 =, Ubilava–Gulko, Batumi 1969. Alekhine's 5 Nc3 d5 6 Bb3 0–0 7 Bg5 is equal after 7 . . . d4.

(c) 5 . . . Bb4† 6 Bd2 (6 c3 Bd6 7 Nbd2 0–0 =, Hartston–Romanishin, Skara 1980) 6 . . . Bxd2† 7 Nbxd2 dxe4 8 Nxe5 0–0 9 dxe4 Nxe4 10 Ndf3 ±, Larsen–Nunn, London 1986.

(d) 6 . . . Be6 7 Bg5 Nbd7 (7 . . . Qa5 is riskier) 8 0–0 Qc7 is about equal, Chistiakov–Ravinsky, Moscow 1955. The column is Honfi–Kholmov, Kecskemét 1975.

(e) 6 Nbd2 0–0 7 Bb3 Be6 8 c3 with a small advantage in space, Dvoretsky–Kholmov, USSR 1975. The column is Skora–Antoshin, 1978.

(f) 6 Qe2 Bg4 7 h3 Bh5 8 g4 Bg6 9 Nxe5 Nd4! is good for Black.

(g) 6 . . . Bg4 is not good now due to 7 h3 Bh5 (7 . . . Bxf3 8 Qxf3) 8 Re1 ± .

(h) 8 Nxe5 Qh4! 9 Qf3 Nf6 10 g3 Nxe5! 11 Rxe5 Qd4 allows Black good play.

(i) (A) 4 . . . Nc6 transposes into the Two Knights' Defense. (B) 4 . . . d5 is intriguing. After 5 exd5 Bb4† 6 c3 Qe7† 7 Be2 dxc3 8 bxc3 Bc5, Vinogradov–Rovner, Leningrad 1956, or 7 Kf1 dxc3 8 Nxc3 0–0, Estrin–Vatnikov, Vilnius 1961, the chances are equal.

(j) (A) 5 . . . Nc5 6 Bg5 f6 7 Be3 c6 8 Nc3 d5 9 0–0–0 left White the advantage in Estrin–Taimanov, Leningrad 1949. (B) 5 . . . d5 6 Bxd5 Nf6 7 Bxf7† Kxf7 8 Qxd8 Bb4† 9 Qd2 Re8† with some play for the pawn.

144

(k) 8 . . . d5 9 0–0–0 Be6 10 Rhe1 is dangerous. To play . . . d5 Black should have a pawn on c6 for support.

(l) 11 Bb5 0–0 12 Nd4 (12 Ne5 Qe8 13 Nxc6 bxc6 14 Bd3 h6 15 f4 Nd5 = —Estrin) 12 . . . a6 13 Bd3 h6 (13 . . . Ne5?! 14 f4 Nxd3† 15 Rxd3 is dangerous for Black, Mieses–Rubinstein, Breslau 1912) 14 Bxh6 gxh6 and White will be able to draw by perpetual check, but no more.

(m) 9 . . . 0–0 10 Qh4 Be6 11 Bd3 g6 12 Re2 (or 12 Nd4) gives White good attacking chances.

(n) 11 Qh4 Nc5 12 Nd4 Ng8 13 Bxe7 Qxe7 14 Qg3 g6 and now Keres's 15 Nce2 creates sufficient attacking chances for the pawn.

(o) 2 . . . f5?! is risky. White can play 3 d3 Nf6 4 f4 d6 5 Nf3 ± (Jaenisch).

(p) 3 b4 Bxb4 4 f4 (MacDonnell's double gambit) 4 . . . d5 5 exd5 e4 ∓ was an experimental failure, MacDonnell–Labourdonnais, London 1834. (B) 3 Nf3 is of course a reasonable choice.

(q) 3 . . . d5 4 Bxd5 Nf6 5 Qf3 0–0 6 d4 exd4 7 Bg5 Be7 = is a good alternative.

(r) 9 Kf1 dxc3 10 Nxc3 Qd3† is disastrous for White.

(s) After 11 Nd2 Na6 the game is equal.

CENTER GAME

1 e5 e5 2 d4 exd4 3 Qxd4

Diagram 22

THE CENTER GAME is a primitive attempt to knock out Black's central strongpoint and secure a spatial advantage. Moving the queen to the center on the third move exposes it to harassment from Black's minor pieces. After 3 . . . Nc6, the time lost in relocating the queen allows Black effortless equality.

First analyzed by Stamma in 1737, this opening was played sporadically in the nineteenth century. Its most notable advocate was the British champion Blackburne. At the turn of the century it saw occasional use by players wanting a change of pace, but it has now fallen into disuse in master play.

The main variation is 3 . . . Nc6 4 Qe3 Nf6 5 Nc3 (cols. 1–3). White attempts to maintain his temporary advantages—extra space and a grip on the d5 square—but Black has several adequate counters based on the weakness of the White e-pawn and the ability to play . . . d5.

Displacing the black knight with 5 e5 (cols. 4–5) is worth investigation. The exposed position of White's queen again costs him a tempo, but 6 Qe4 (col. 4) at least leads to interesting play.

4 Qa4 (col. 6) is a reasonable idea: White plays a Center Counter Defense with colors reversed and an extra tempo. It is White's safest line in the Center Game, but again Black has little trouble equalizing.

CENTER GAME

1 e4 e5 2 d4 exd4 3 Qxd4 Nc6

	1	2	3	4	5	6
4	Qe3..Qa4					
	Nf6					Nf6
5	Nc3................................e5(k)					Bg5(p)
	Bb4....................Be7		Ng4			Be7
6	Bd2(a)		Bd2(h)	Qe4........Qe2		Nc3
	0–0		d5	d5	d6	0–0
7	0–0–0		exd5	exd6†	f3(n)	Nf3
	Re8		Nxd5	Be6	Nh6!	d6
8	Qg3........Bc4		Nxd5	Ba6(l)	Bxh6(o)	0–0–0
	Rxe4!(b)	Na5(d)	Qxd5	Qxd6	Qh4†	Bd7
9	Bg5(c)	Bd3(e)	Ne2(i)	Bxb7	g3	Qc4
	Bxc3	d5	Bg4	Qb4†	Qxh6	Be6
10	Qxc3	Nge2(f)	Nf4	Qxb4	exd6†	Qe2
	h6	c5	Qd7	Nxb4	Be6 ∓	Nd7
11	Be3	a3	f3	Na3	h4	
	d6 ∓	d4(g)	0–0–0(j)	Rb8(m)	Nde5 =	

(a) 6 Bc4?! 0–0 7 Bd2 Bxc3 8 Bxc3 Nxe4! is strong, Kupreichik–Lein, USSR 1970.

(b) 8 ... Nxe4 9 Nxe4 Rxe4 (Mieses–Capablanca, Berlin 1913) 10 c3 Bf8 11 Bd3 is less clear than the column.

(c) (A) 9 Bd3 Rg4 10 Qh4 (Zinn–Sax, Baja 1971) is good for Black after 10 ... d6. (B) 9 Nh3 Rg4 10 Qd3 Rd4 also leaves Black on top, Oszvath–Kluger, Hungary 1960. The column is Ciocaltea–Kluger, Bucharest 1954.

(d) 8 ... d6 is also playable, but the text is more dynamic.

(e) 10 Be2 d5 11 Nxd5 Nxd5 12 Qd3 Qf6 13 exd5 Bf5 ∓, Jacobson–Urzica, Groningen 1970.

(f) 10 Qg3 dxe4 11 Nxe4 Nxe4 12 Bxe4 Qe7 gives Black the initiative.

(g) After 11 Qg3 not 11 ... dxc3?, opening lines and leading to trouble (Korolev–A. Geller, USSR 1966), but 11 ... Bxc3 with chances for both sides.

(h) White should consider 6 Bc4 Nb4 7 Qd2 0–0 8 a3 Nc6 =, Soloviev–Yudovich, USSR 1955.

(i) (A) 9 Nf3 0–0 10 c4 Qc5 ∓, and (B) 9 Bc3 0–0 10 Qg3 g6 are better for Black.

(j) 12 fxg4? Bh4† 13 Kd1 Rhe8 ∓. The lesser evil is 12 0–0–0 Bf5 ∓.

(k) (A) 5 Bd2 should be met by 5 ... Ng4 6 Qg3 d5. (B) 5 Be2 Qe7 6 Nc3 d5 7 exd5 Nb4 ∓.

(l) 8 Bc4 and 8 Bb5 are reasonable choices, but not 8 dxc7? Qd1†! 9 Kxd1 Nxf2† ∓.

(m) After 12 Bf3 Ne5 Black had good compensation for the pawn, Mieses–Burn, Breslau 1912.

(n) (A) 7 exd6† Be6 8 dxc7 Qxc7 9 Nf3 Bc5 gave Black too much play in Makovec–Maróczy, Budapest 1895. (B) 7 h3? Ngxe5 8 f4 Qh4† 9 Kd1 Nd4 is bad for White.

(o) 8 exd6† Be6 9 Bxb6 Qh4† ∓. *Comments.*

(p) 5 Nf3 d5 6 Nc3 dxe4 =, Sokolov–Michalek, corr. 1976. The column is A. Milev–Cipev, Bulgaria 1961.

DANISH GAMBIT

1 e4 e5 2 d4 exd4 3 c3

Diagram 23

IRST ANALYZED by the Danes O. Krause and M. From, this straight-forward gambit became a favorite of nineteenth-century roman-tics. White's quick development and raking bishops led to many a brilliancy, but safe ways to decline the gambit have since been developed. It is now rarely seen in serious competition. However, a recent study of the Danish by the American grandmaster Larry Christiansen has uncovered new ideas which make White's chances more appealing, so perhaps this opening may yet be revived.

Accepting the Danish (3 . . . dxc3 4 Bc4 cxb2 5 Bxb2) looks fright-ening, but returning a pawn with 5 . . . d5 (cols. 1–2) is considered the surest way to at least equalize. The columns reflect established theory, but the notes include some interesting, untested ideas for White to try.

5 . . . Nf6 (col. 3) looks risky, but might equalize.

5 . . . d6 (col. 4) avoids immediate tactics, so Black remains two pawns ahead while White keeps a strong initiative. The line is unclear, with scope for original play.

Declining the gambit with 3 . . . d5 is Black's safest course. 4 exd5 Qxd5 (col. 5) is the classical way to equalize. 4 . . . Nf6 (col. 6) is sharper but may allow White a small edge.

DANISH GAMBIT

1 e4 e5 2 d4 exd4 3 c3

	1	2	3	4	5	6
	dxc3 . . . . d5(l)					
4	Bc4 cxb2				exd5 Qxd5	Nf6
5	Bxb2 d5	Nf6(e)	d6	cxd4 Nf6	Bb5†(o) c6(p)
6	Bxd5 Bb4†	Nf6	e5 d5(f)	f4(i) Be6	Nf3 Bb4†	dxc6 bxc6
7	Nc3(a) Bxc3†	Bxf7†(c) Kxf7	exf6 dxc4	Bxe6 fxe6	Nc3 0–0(m)	Bc4 Bc5
8	Bxc3 Nf6	Qxd8 Bb4†	Qxd8†(g) Kxd8	Qb3 Qc8(j)	Be2(n) Ne4	Qe2† Qe7
9	Qf3(b) Nxd5	Qd2 Bxd2†	fxg7 Bb4†	Nf3 Nc6	Bd2 Bxc3	Qxe7† Kxe7
10	exd5 0–0	Nxd2 Re8(d)	Nc3 Rg8(h)	Ng5 Nd8	bxc3 Nxd2	cxd4 Bxd4
11	Ne2 Re8 ∓	Ngf3 Nc6 =		0–0 h6(k)	Qxd2 Bg4 =	Nf3 Rd8 ±

(a) Other possibilities are: (A) 7 Nd2 Bxd2† 8 Qxd2 Nf6 9 Qg5 Rg8 10 0–0 Nxd5 11 Qh5! and White has good chances (Christiansen); (B) 7 Ke2 Nf6 8 Qa4† c6 9 Bxf7 Kxf7 10 Bxb4 Re8 ∞, Thomas–Teo, Southampton 1986; (C) 7 Kf1?! Nf6 8 Qa4† Nc6 is bad for White.

(b) Poor for White is 9 Nf3 Nxd5 10 exd5 Qe7† , Radevich–Asturian, USSR 1968. The column is Grob–Weishaupt, corr. 1960.

(c) (A) 7 Nf3 Bb4† 8 Kf1 0–0 ∓, Nyholm–Reti, Baden 1914. (B) 7 Nc3 is interesting: 7 . . . Nxd5 8 Nxd5 Nd7 (or 8 . . . Nc6) 9 Nf3 give White some attacking chances; on 7 . . . Be7 White has 8 Qb3 0–0 9 0–0–0 ∞, or 8 Qa4† c6 9 0–0–0 Nbd7 10 Bxf7† with attack (Christiansen).

(d) Schlechter recommended 10 . . . c5, but the endgame is roughly equal in any case.

(e) Of no help is 5 . . . Bb4† 6 Nc3 (or 6 Kf1 Nf6 7 e5 d5 8 Bb5† c6 9 exf6 cxb5 10 fxg7 Rg8 11 Qc2 f5 12 a3 Be7 13 Nc3 a6 14 Rd1 Be6 15 Nge2 ±) 6 . . . Nf6 7 Ne2 (= Keres) 7 . . . Nc6!? 8 Qc2 ±; but not 7 . . . Nxe4 8 0–0 Nc3 9 Nxc3 Nc6!? (9 . . . Bxc3? 10 Bxc3 0–0 11 Qg4 +) 10 Nd5 Be7 (10 . . . 0–0 11 Qg4) 11 Qg4 Rg8 12 Rfe1 d6 13 Qh5 + (Korn).

(f) 6 . . . Bb4†, 6 . . . Qe7, and 6 . . . Ng4 all lead to problems for Black.

(g) On 8 fxg7 Bb4† 9 Nc3 Rg8 equalizes.

(h) Black has difficulties after 10 . . . Re8† 11 Nge2 Bf5 12 0–0–0† ±, Marshall–Duras, New York 1913, but after 10 . . . Rg8 the game is even.

(i) Also playable is 6 Qb3 Qd7 7 Nc3 Nc6 8 Nd5 Na5 9 Qg3 f6 ∞, Mieses–Marshall, Hannover 1902.

(j) 8 . . . Nd7 with the idea 9 Qxe6† Qe7 is another way to defend.

(k) After 12 Qh3 Nf6 13 Nc3 White's attacking chances are fair compensation for his two-pawn deficit.

(l) (A) 3 . . . Qe7 is curious. After 4 cxd4 Qxe4† 5 Be3 Nf6 6 Nc3 Bb4 7 Nf3 Nd5 8 Qd2 Nxe3 9 fxe3 White had attacking chances in Romaskevich–Saburov, Russia 1889. (B) 3 . . . d3 and (C) 3 . . . Ne7 are little-explored possibilities.

(m) (A) 7 . . . Nc6 would tranpose to the Göring Gambit, col. 6. (B) 7 . . . Bg4 8 Be2 0–0 9 0–0 Qa5 gives near equality.

(n) 8 Bd2 Re8† 9 Be2 Bxc3 10 bxc3 Qe4 is annoying since 11 Be3 is met by 11 . . . Nd5. The column is Ghitescu–Puribizab, Varna 1958.

(o) White has a wide choice of moves here—5 Qa4†, 5 Bc4, 5 Nf3, and 5 cxd4—but these alternatives give no advantage.

(p) 5 . . . Bd7 6 Bc4 dxc3 7 Nxc3 ±, Klovans–Zhuravlev, Riga 1962. The column is Gusev–Khachaturov, Moscow 1963, up to 11 Nf3.

UNUSUAL KING PAWN GAMES

1 e4 e5

T HE HUNGARIAN DEFENSE, 2 Nf3 Nc6 3 Bc4 Be7 (cols. 1–2), is a solid but passive choice for Black. It avoids tactical play at the cost of allowing White more mobility. It was first played in an 1842 Paris–Budapest correspondence game and has been used by such luminaries as Smyslov and Hort. White can respond in three ways: exchange queens and try for an endgame advantage (col. 1 note *a*); close the center for a long positional struggle (col. 1); or keep the center open (col. 2) for better flexibility.

Column 3 is the rare 3 . . . d6, leading to little-mapped territory. 3 . . . d6 is similar to 3 . . . Be7 in that it is passive, leaving White with a free hand. Proper play should net White a plus. 3 Be2 would create a Hungarian Defense in reverse.

The QUEEN'S PAWN COUNTER GAMBIT is 2 . . . d5 (cols. 4–5). While it may be a good surprise for an unprepared opponent, it leaves Black with insufficient compensation for the pawn.

ALAPIN'S OPENING, 2 Ne2 (col. 6), poses no real problems for Black.

UNUSUAL KING PAWN GAMES

1 e4 e5

	Hungarian Defense			Queen's Pawn Counter Gambit		Alapin's Opening
	1	2	3	4	5	6
2	Nf3					Ne2
	Nc6			d5(l)		Nf6(r)
3	Bc4			exd5(m)		f4
	Be7		d6(h)	e4		Nxe4
4	d4		c3(i)	Qe2		d3
	d6		Bg4(j)	Nf6	f5	Nc5
5	d5(a)	Nc3	d4(k)	d3	d3	fxe5
	Nb8(b)	Nf6	Qe7	Be7(n)	Nf6	d5
6	Bd3	h3	Be3	dxe4	dxe4	d4
	Nf6	0–0(e)	Nf6	0–0	fxe4	Ne6
7	c4(c)	0–0	Qb3	Nc3(o)	Nc3	Nf4
	0–0	exd4(f)	Nd8	Re8	Bb4	c5(s)
8	h3	Nxd4	Nbd2	Bd2	Qb5†	Nc3
	Nbd7	Nxd4	g6	Bb4	c6	cxd4
9	Nc3	Qxd4	dxe5	0–0–0	Qxb4	Ncxd5
	Ne8(d)	c6(g)	dxe5 ±	Bxc3(p)	exf3(q)	Nc6(t)

(a) 5 dxe5 dxe5 6 Qxd8† Bxd8 7 Nc3 Nf6 8 Be3 Be7 9 Nd5 Bd6 10 Nxf6† with an endgame edge, van der Wiel–P. Nikolić, Malta 1980.

(b) 5 . . . Na5 6 Bd3 c5 7 c4 leaves Black's knight on a5 poorly placed.

(c) 7 h3 c6 8 c4 b5 9 Nc3 b4 10 Ne2 0–0 =, Korchnoi–Smyslov, Leningrad 1950.

(d) White has the edge, but Black gets some counterplay on the kingside with . . . g6 and . . . f5, Fuchs–Kholmov, Leningrad 1967.

(e) 6 . . . a6 is interesting: (A) 7 Be3 b5 8 Bd5 Nxd5 9 Nxd5 (9 exd5 looks better) 9 . . . 0–0 =, Tyler–Thomas, Nottingham 1939; (B) 7 a3 is Alekhine's recommendation.

(f) 7 . . . h6 8 Re1 Re8 9 Be3 ±, Tal–Filip, Miskolc 1963.

(g) The text is better than 9 . . . Be6: (A) 10 Bxe6 fxe6 11 e5 ±, Tarrasch–Taubenhaus, Ostend 1905; after (B) 10 a4 Nd7 11 Be3 b6 White had only a minuscule advantage in Spassky–Hort, Reykjavik 1977.

(h) 3 . . . g6 is worthy of note. After 4 c3 d6 5 d4 Qe7 6 dxe5 Nxe5 7 Nxe5 dxe5 Black had drawn even in Mednis–Korchnoi, Vienna 1986.

(i) 4 d4 is also possible, and after 4 . . . Bg4 5 h3 Bxf3 6 Qxf3 Qf6 (or 6 . . . Nf6 7 Qb3) 7 Qb3 Nd8 8 dxe5 White is on top.

(j) More conservative is 4 . . . Nf6 5 d4 Be7 (not 5 . . . Nxe4? 6 d5 Nb8 7 Qa4†) 6 Nbd2 0–0 7 Bd3 ±.

(k) 5 Qb3 Qd7 6 Qxb7 Rb8 7 Qa6 Be7 8 d3 Bxf3 9 gxf3 Bh4 ∞, Brynell–Hector, Malmö 1986. The column is Levenfish–Tolush, USSR 1939.

(l) Other unusual tries are: (A) 2 . . . f6 (Damiano's Defense) 3 Nxe5 Qe7 4 Nf3! d5 (4 . . . Qxe4† 5 Be2 ±) 5 d3 ±, Schiffers–Chigorin, 1897; (B) 2 . . . Qe7 3 Nc3 c6 4 d4 d6 5 Bg5 ±.

(m) 3 Nxe5 Bd6 4 d4 dxe4 5 Nc3 Bf5?! 6 Qh5 g6 7 Qe2 is good for White, Heil–Bücker, Bad Meinberg 1986, but Black should play 5 . . . Bxe5 6 dxe5 Qxd1† with equality.

(n) 5 . . . Qxd5 6 Nfd2 Be7 7 Nxe4 ±.

(o) 7 Bg5 Nxe4 8 Bxe7 Qxe7 9 Nbd2 (Pruss–Wills, corr. 1966) 9 . . . f5 =. 7 Qd3 should be good for White.

(p) 10 Bxc3 Nxe4 11 Qe3 ± (Bücker).

(q) 10 Bg5 cxd5 11 0–0–0 ±, Tal–Lutikov, Tallinn 1964.

(r) Naturally 2 . . . Nc6 is also fine. After 3 Nbc3 Bc5 4 Na4 Be7 5 d4 Nf6 the game Alapin–Chigorin, Berlin 1897, was equal.

(s) 7 . . . Be7 8 Nc3 c6 9 Be3 0–0 =, Bakonyi–Kostić, Špindlerovy Mlíny 1948.

(t) Alapin–Rubinstein, Vienna 1908; now 10 Bb5 Nxf4 would be equal (Fine).

II
SEMI-OPEN
KING'S PAWN
DEFENSES

ALEKHINE'S DEFENSE

1 e4 Nf6

Diagram 24

T HIS DEFENSE, THOUGH COMPLETELY HYPERMODERN IN SPIRIT, was well known for more than a hundred years before Alekhine successfully launched it into twentieth-century master competition against A. Steiner at Budapest in 1921. It was warmly embraced by the hypermoderns, and when Emanuel Lasker used it to defeat Maroczy in the great 1924 New York Tournament, it had really arrived.

Nonetheless, Alekhine's Defense has never held the respect that is accorded the Sicilian Defense and the Ruy Lopez. Most masters find the idea of the defense to be too chancy. Black's strategy is to provoke a White advance in the center at the expense of tempi lost by Black's king's knight. Black then has targets to attack; White's center may become overextended and collapse. Yet with proper care and restraint White should maintain some advantage in space and mobility.

Its adherents maintain that Alekhine's Defense almost always produces double-edged, fighting chess. Thus it is not surprising that Fischer and Korchnoi have played it many times. Its leading advocate today is two-time US Champion Lev Alburt, who uses this defense exclusively in reply to 1 e4.

The MODERN VARIATION, 2 e5 Nd5 3 d4 d6 4 Nf3 (cols. 1–12), is currently considered White's best response. White is content to keep a modest advantage in space until he has developed his pieces. 4 . . . Bg4 (cols. 1–6) is the most common reply for Black; in the main line, col. 1, White maintains a pull. Alburt most often plays 4 . . . g6 (cols. 10–12), which leads to unusual positions that are difficult for both sides to play.

In the EXCHANGE VARIATION, 2 e5 Nd5 3 d4 d6 4 c4 Nb6 5 exd6 (cols. 13–18), White gives up his central point at e5 to avoid problems and then simply develops logically. Black's most enterprising recapture is 5 . . .

cxd6 (cols. 13–16), which preserves the chance for a dynamic central advance. 5 . . . exd6 (cols. 17–18) is more static and safe.

Diagram 25

The FOUR PAWNS' ATTACK, 2 e5 Nd5 3 d4 d6 4 c4 Nb6 5 f4 (cols. 19–27), is a violent attempt to push Black off the board (see diagram). White obtains the initiative and a great advantage in space if Black plays carelessly. But with accurate defense Black counterattacks the white center, balancing the chances. Black has several reasonable plans; the main variation is col. 19, in which White sacrifices the exchange in order to press his initiative.

The TWO PAWNS' ATTACK, 2 e5 Nd5 3 c4 Nb6 4 c5 Nd5, is seen in cols. 28–30. White can obtain attacking prospects, but often at the cost of a pawn. With careful play Black gains full equality.

Cols. 31–36 cover unusual replies to Alekhine's Defense. Each line has its own character, but Black has no great difficulties with any.

ALEKHINE'S DEFENSE

Modern Variation

1 e4 Nf6 2 e5 Nd5 3 d4 d6 4 Nf3 Bg4

	1	2	3	4	5	6
5	Be2					h3
	e6			c6	Nc6	Bxf3
6	0–0			Ng5(j)	0–0	Qxf3
	Be7		Nc6	Bxe2(k)	dxe5(m)	dxe5
7	c4		c4	Qxe2	Nxe5	dxe5
	Nb6		Nb6(h)	dxe5	Bxe2	e6
8	h3	exd6	exd6	dxe5	Qxe2	Qe4(o)
	Bh5(a)	cxd6	cxd6	e6	Qd6(n)	Nd7
9	Nc3	b3(f)	d5	0–0	Qb5	Bc4
	0–0	Nc6	exd5	Nd7	Nb6	Nc5
10	Be3	Nbd2	cxd5	c4	Nxc6	Qe2
	d5(b)	0–0	Bxf3	Ne7	Qxc6	Nb6
11	c5(c)	Bb2	gxf3!	Nc3	Qxc6†	0–0
	Bxf3!	Bf5!(g)	Ne5	Nf5	bxc6	Nxc4
12	gxf3(d)	a3	Bb5†	Rd1	Bf4	Qxc4
	Nc8(e)	a5 =	Ned7(i)	Qc7(l)	Nd5 ±	Qd5 =

(a) 8 . . . Bxf3 9 Bxf3 Nc6 10 Bxc6† gives White a simple advantage in space and pawn structure.

(b) 10 . . . Nc6 11 exd6 cxd6 12 d5 favors White.

(c) 11 cxd5 exd5 (11 . . . Nxd5 12 Qb3 ∞, Lobron–Alburt, New York 1983) 12 Ne1 Bxe2 13 Qxe2 Nc6 14 Nd3 Qd7 15 Rad1 Nd8 16 Nc5 Qc8 17 f4 f5 =, Plachetka–Bagirov, Kirkovan 1978.

(d) White can keep his pawn structure intact at the cost of allowing the black knight to go to c4, e.g. 12 Bxf3 Nc4 13 Bf4 Nc6 14 b3 N4a5 15 Rc1 Qd7 16 Be3 f6 17 exf6 Bxf6 18 Qd2 b6 =, Geller–Bagirov, USSR Chp. 1979.

(e) 13 b4 Bh4 14 f4 Nc6 15 Rb1 Kh8 16 Bd3 g6 17 Qg4 ±, Wolff–Alburt, US Chp. 1985.

(f) 9 Be3 0–0 10 Nc3 d5 11 c5 Bxf3 12 Bxf3 Nc4 13 Bf4 Nc6 14 b3 N4a5 15 Rc1 b6 =, Sax–Hecht, Wijk aan Zee 1973.

(g) On the usual 11 . . . d5 White gets a pull by 12 c5 Nd7 13 b4! b6 (13 . . . Nxb4 14 Qb3 wins the pawn back) 14 Qb3 ±, Kagan–Birnboim, Netanya 1977. The column is Vogt–Bagirov, Tallinn 1981.

(h) Passive but safe is 7 . . . Nde7 8 Qa4 d5 9 Nc3 with a small White edge, Bannik–Mikenas, USSR 1949.

(i) 13 Qd4 Qf6 14 Re1† Be7 15 Qxf6 gxf6 16 Nc3 with a distinct advantage (Boleslavsky).

159

(j) After the natural 6 0–0 Bxf3! 7 Bxf3 dxe5 8 dxe5 e6 9 Qe2 Nd7 10 c4 Ne7 Black has full equality with his pieces heading for good squares, de Firmian–D. Cramling, Gausdal 1980.

(k) 6 . . . Bf5 7 Bg4 (7 e6 fxe6 8 g4 Bg6 is complicated) Qd7 8 Bxf5 Qxf5 9 0–0! $\pm$ dxe5 10 dxe5 Qxe5?! 11 c4 Nf6 12 Qd8† Kxd8 13 Nxf7† Ke8 14 Nxe5 $\pm$, Naumkin–Arkhangelsky, Moscow 1984.

(l) 13 Nce4 Be7 (bad are 13 . . . Qxe5 14 Nxf7 and 13 . . . Nxe5 14 Bf4) 14 Bf4 $\pm$, Novopashin–Agzamov, USSR 1976.

(m) (A) 6 . . . Nb6 7 Nc3! (Alburt), meeting 7 . . . dxe5 with 8 d5, gives White very good play. (B) 6 . . . e6 transposes to col. 3.

(n) 8 . . . Nxd4? 9 Qc4 (Alburt) creates serious problems for Black. The column is Kluss–Braun, Frankfurt 1977.

(o) Other tries also give White few chances for an edge, e.g. 8 Bc4 Nc6 9 Qe4 Nde7 10 Be3 Nf5 11 0–0 Qh4! 12 Qxh4 Nxh4 =, Zhuravlev–Alburt, Odessa 1974. The column is Pavlenko–Bagirov, USSR 1972.

ALEKHINE'S DEFENSE

Modern Variation

1 e4 Nf6 2 e5 Nd5 3 d4 d6 4 Nf3

	7	8	9	10	11	12
	Nc6........dxe5 ....g6					
5	c4 Nb6	Nxe5 Nd7?!.......g6		Bc4(k).................. Nb6(l)		Ng5 c6(s)
6	e6!(a) fxe6	Nxf7! Kxf7	Bc4(h) Be6(i)	Bb3 Bg7		c4 Nc7
7	Nc3(b) g6	Qh5† Ke6	0–0 Bg7	Ng5(m) e6 ....d5	d5	Qf3 f6
8	h4 Bg7	c4 N5f6	Re1 c6	Qf3(n) Qe7(o)	f4 f6	exf6 exf6
9	Be3 d5	d5† Kd6	Bf1 Nd7	Ne4 dxe5	Nf3 Nc6	Ne4 f5(t)
10	c5 Nd7(c)	Qf7 Nb8(e)	Nf3 Bg4	Bg5 Qb4†	c3 0–0	Nec3 Bg7
11	h5 e5	c5† Kd7(f)	c3 0–0	c3 Qa5	0–0 Bf5(q)	d5 0–0
12	h6 Bf6(d)	Bf4 Qe8(g)	Nbd2 e5(j)	Bf6 Bxf6(p)	Nh4 Bxb1(r)	Be2 cxd5 =

(a) White can choose to play safely with 6 exd6 exd6 7 d5 (Alburt) and achieve a small advantage.

(b) Also promising is 7 Ng5 e5 8 d5 Nd4 9 Bd3 Bf5 10 Bxf5 Nxf5 11 Ne6 with good play for the pawn, Baran–Podgorný, corr. 1975.

(c) 10 ... Nc4? 11 Bxc4 dxc4 12 Qa4 Qd7 13 0–0–0 leaves Black all bound up, Nunn–Vaganian, London 1986.

(d) 13 Nxd5 exd4 14 Nxf6† exf6 15 Nxd4 $\pm$.

(e) 10 ... Nb6 11 Nc3 Qe8 12 Bf4† Kd7 13 Qe6† Kd8 14 Qe5 Qd7 15 0–0–0 (Shamkovich) gives White a tremendous attack for the piece.

(f) 11 ... Kxc5 12 Be3† Kd6 13 Na3 a6 14 Nc4† Kd7 15 d6 wins (Kapengut).

(g) 13 Qe6† Kd8 14 Qe5 $\pm$.

(h) Also reasonable is 6 c4 Nf6 7 Nc3 Bg7 8 Be2 0–0 9 0–0 c6 10 Bf4 $\pm$, Kindermann–Wolf, West Germany 1984.

(i) (A) 6 ... Bg7? 7 Nxf7! Kxf7 8 Qf3† wins. (B) 6 ... c6 7 0–0 Bg7 8 Re1 0–0 9 Bb3 Be6 10 Nd2 $\pm$, de Firmian–Alburt, Reykjavik 1984.

(j) 13 h3 Bxf3 14 Nxf3 exd4 15 Nxd4 $\pm$, Arnason–Westerinen, Dubai 1986.

161

(k) A major alternative is 5 c4 Nb6 6 exd6 cxd6 transposing into the Exchange Variation, cols. 13–14.

(l) 5 . . . c6 6 0–0 Bg7 7 exd6! Qxd6 8 h3 0–0 9 Nbd2 Nd7 10 Bb3 Qc7 11 Re1 ±, Kavalek–Ljubojević, Las Palmas 1973.

(m) Alburt considers the interpolation of 7 a4 a5 beneficial to White. Short–Alburt, match 1985, went 7 a4 d5!? 8 a5 Nc4 9 Nbd2 Nxd2 10 Bxd2 ±.

(n) 8 f4 dxe5 9 fxe5 c5 10 0–0 0–0 11 c3 cxd4 12 cxd4 Nc6 13 Nf3 f6 14 exf6 Qxf6 15 Be3 Nd5 16 Bf2 Nf4 with an unbalanced position, Shamkovich–Alburt, Reykjavik 1984.

(o) 8 . . . 0–0?! 9 Qh3 h6 10 Ne4 ±.

(p) 13 Qxf6 0–0 14 Qxe5 Qxe5 15 dxe5 Nc6 16 f4 Na5 and Black has only a minimal disadvantage, Timman–Alburt Taxco 1985.

(q) 11 . . . Bg4 12 Nbd2 Bh6 13 h3 ±. White's wedge in the center always gives him an edge in this line.

(r) 13 Rxb1 fxe5 14 fxe5 Rxf1† 15 Qxf1 ±, Donchev–Přibyl, Bratislava 1983.

(s) 5 . . . f6 6 c4 Nb6 7 e6! fxg5 8 d5 gave White good play for his sacrificed knight in O'Kelly–Golombek, Amsterdam 1951.

(t) Alburt recommends 9 . . . Bg7 10 Bf4 0–0. The column is Ivanov–Kakageldyev, USSR 1979.

ALEKHINE'S DEFENSE

Exchange Variation

1 e4 Nf6 2 e5 Nd5 3 d4 d6 4 c4 Nb6 5 exd6

	13	14	15	16	17	18
	cxd6..exd6					
6	Nf3.....................Nc3.........Be3				Nc3	
	g6		g6	Bf5(i)	Be7(j)	
7	Be2(a)		h4(g)	Nc3	Be3........h3	
	Bg7		h5!	e6	Nc6	0–0
8	0–0		Be3	Nf3	Bd3(k)	Nf3
	0–0		Bg7	Be7	Bf6	Bf6
9	h3(b)		Qb3(h)	Be2	Nge2	Be2
	Nc6		Nc6	0–0	0–0	Re8
10	Nc3		Rd1	0–0	0–0	0–0
	Bf5		0–0	Na6	Bg4	Nc6
11	Be3........Bf4(d)		Be2	Qb3	f3	b3(m)
	d5	h6!	e5	Qb8	Bh5	Bf5
12	c5	Rc1(e)	Nf3	Bf4	b3	Be3
	Nc4	e5	exd4	Nc7	Re8	h6
13	Bxc4	Be3	Nxd4	Rac1	Qd2	Qd2
	dxc4(c)	e4(f) ∓	Qe7 =	Rd8 =	Bg6(l)	Bh7 =

(a) 7 h3 Bg7 8 Nc3 0–0 9 Be3 Nc6 10 Rc1 prepares to meet 10 ... Bf5 with 11 d5 Ne5 12 Nxe5 ±, but 10 ... d5 (as in the column) 11 c5 Nc4 12 Bxc4 dxc4 13 0–0 Bf5 14 Qa4 e5 is still equal, Pytel–Gipslis, Lublin 1969. Or 10 ... e5 11 dxe5 dxe5 12 c5 Nd7 13 Bc4 Nd4! 14 Ne4 b6 15 Bg5 Qc7 16 Be7 Bb7! 17 c6 Qxc6 18 Neg5 (18 Bxf7+ Rxf7 19 Rxc6 Bxc6 ∓) 18 ... Kh8 19 Bd3 Nc5 20 Be4 Qb5! 21 Bxf8 Rxf8 ∓, Grzesik–Hartmann, German Bundesliga 1985. In here, White has 11 d5! Ne7 12 Qb3 (if 12 g4 f5; if 12 Qd2 Nf5 or 12 ... f5) 12 ... Nf5 with complications (Korn).

(b) 9 Nc3 Nc6 10 Be3 Bg4! 11 b3 d5 12 c5 Nc8 13 b4! a6 14 Rb1 e6 15 a4 Bxf3 16 Bxf3 N8e7 with equal chances and a sharp position, Klovans–Bagirov, USSR 1969.

(c) 14 Qa4 e5! (14 ... Bd3 15 Rfd1 f5 16 d5 Ne5 17 Ne1 with advantage for White: Boleslavsky) 15 Rfd1 exd4 16 Nxd4 Nxd4 17 Bxd4 Bxd4 18 Qxc4 Bxf2+ =, Sigurjonsson–Alburt, Reykjavik 1982.

(d) 11 b3?! d5 12 c5 Nd7 13 Bb2 Be4! 14 Na4 e5 ∓, Minev–Bobotsov, Varna 1968.

(e) It is best to admit the strength of Black's last move and retreat with 12 Be3 d5 13 b3 (or 13 c5 as in the previous column) dxc4 14 bxc4 Rc8 15 Rc1 Na5 16 c5 Nbc4 =, Karpov–A. Petrosian, USSR 1976.

(f) 14 Nd2 d5 15 cxd5 Nxd5 16 Nxd5 Qxd5 17 Bc4 Qd8 ∓, Geller–Vaganian, Moscow 1985.

(g) 7 Bd3 Bg7 8 Nge2 0–0 9 b3 Nc6 10 Be3 d5 11 c5 Nd7 12 Bb5 was played in Minić–Fischer, Palma de Mallorca 1970. Fischer now achieved active central play: 12 ... e5 13

0–0 Nxc5! 14 dxe5 d4 15 Nxd4 Nxe5 16 h3 Ne6 17 Nxe6 Bxe6 18 f4? (Black would have only a slight advantage after 18 Qxd8 Rfxd8 19 Rac1 a6 20 Be2 Nd3. Minić's move both weakens his kingside pawn structure and allows the black queen to play an active role.) 18 ... Qa5! 19 fxe5 Qxc3 20 Qd4 (White must lose at least a pawn: 20 Bd4 Qb4 threatening 21 ... Rfd8 and 21 ... Qxb5) 20 ... Qa5 21 a4 Bxb3 22 Bf4 a6 23 Be2 Rae8 24 Ra3 Bd5 25 Rb1 Bc6 26 Bf3 Bxe5 27 Bxe5 Rxe5 28 Bxc6 bxc6 29 Rc3 Re2 (29 ... Re6 may be simpler, but Black wins fairly easily in any case) 30 Rxc6 Qg5 31 Qg4 Qxg4 32 hxg4 Rd8 33 g5 Rd5 34 Kf1 R2e5 35 Rxa6 Rxg5 36 Rb2 Rd1† 37 Kf2 Rf5† 38 Kg3 Rd3† 39 Kh2 Ra3 40 Ra7 h5 41 Kg1 Kg7 42 Rb1 Kh6 43 Rf1 Rxf1† 44 Kxf1 f5 45 Ra8 and White resigned.

(h) 9 c5 dxc5 10 dxc5 N6d7 is equal (Alburt). The column is Kurajica–Hecht, Wijk aan Zee 1973.

(i) 6 ... g6 7 d5!? Bg7 8 Bd4 Bxd4 9 Qxd4 0–0 10 Nc3 e5 11 Qd2 f5 ∞, Suttles–Fischer, Palma de Mallorca 1970. The column is Hartston–B. Schmidt, 1974.

(j) 6 ... g6?! 7 Nf3 Bg7 8 Nbd2 Nc6 9 Be2 0–0 10 0–0 Bg4 11 Rc1 ±, A. Steiner–Alekhine, Budapest 1921.

(k) 8 Nf3 0–0 9 Be2 Bg4 10 b3 Bf6 11 0–0 d5 12 c5 Nc8 13 h3 Be6 =, Sigurjonsson–Olafsson, Reykjavik 1970.

(l) 14 Rae1 d5 =, Ilyin-Zhenevsky–Rabinovich, USSR Chp. 1937.

(m) 11 Bf4 Bf5 12 Rc1 h6 was equal in Matanović–Larsen, Palma de Mallorca 1968. The column is Buljovčić–Vukić, Yugoslav Chp. 1975.

ALEKHINE'S DEFENSE

Four Pawns' Attack

**1 e4 Nf6 2 e5 Nd5 3 d4 d6 4 c4 Nb6 5 f4 dxe5 6 fxe5 Nc6 7 Be3 Bf5
8 Nc3 e6 9 Nf3**

	19	20	21	22	23	24
	Be7...................		Bg4........	Qd7.......	Nb4?!......	Bb4
10	d5.........	Be2	Be2(g)	Be2(i)	Rc1	Be2
	exd5(a)	0–0	Bxf3	0–0–0	c5	Na5(n)
11	cxd5(b)	0–0	gxf3	0–0	Be2	c5
	Nb4	f6	Qh4†	Bg4!(j)	Be7(l)	Nd5
12	Nd4	exf6(e)	Bf2	c5	0–0	Bd2
	Bd7(c)	Bxf6	Qf4	Nd5	0–0	Nc6
13	e6	Qd2	c5	Nxd5	dxc5	0–0
	fxe6	Qe7(f)	Nd7	Qxd5	Nd7	0–0
14	dxe6	Rad1	Qd3(h)	Ng5	a3	Bg5
	Bc6	Rad8	Be7	Bxe2	Nc6	f6
15	Qg4	Qe1	Rd1	Qxe2	b4	exf6
	Bh4†	Nb4	Bh4	Nxd4	Ndxe5	gxf6
16	g3	a3	0–0	Bxd4	Nb5	Nxd5
	Bxh1(d)	Nc2 =	Bxf2† =	Qxd4†(k)	Bd3(m)	fxg5(o)

(a) 10 ... Nb4 11 Rc1! exd5 12 a3 c5 13 axb4 d4 14 Bxd4 cxd4 15 Qxd4 Bxb4 16 c5 Nd5 17 Bb5† Bd7 18 Bxd7† Qxd7 19 0–0 Nxc3 20 bxc3 Qxd4 21 cxd4 with an endgame advantage due to the strong center, Vrabec–Jurek, Czechoslovakia 1976.

(b) 11 Bxb6 axb6 12 cxd5 Nb4 13 Nd4 Bg6 14 d6 (14 Bb5† c6 15 dxc6 0–0) 14 ... Bxd6 15 exd6 0–0 gave Black fine play for the piece in Majević–Rogulj, Yugoslavia 1981.

(c) 12 ... Bg6? 13 Bb5† Kf8 14 0–0 Kg8 15 Nf5 Bxf5 16 Rxf5 N4xd5 17 Bxb6 Nxb6 18 Qb3 Bc5† 19 Kh1 Qe7 20 Na4! Nxa4 21 Rxf7 wins (N. Weinstein).

(d) This complex position has been the subject of many games and much analysis. Chances are probably balanced, e.g. 17 0–0–0 Qf6 18 gxh4 0–0 19 Bb5 c5 20 Bg5 Qe5 21 e7 cxd4 22 exf8† Rxf8 23 Rxh1 dxc3! (23 ... a5? 24 Qe2 Qc7 25 Qe6† Kh8 26 Rf1 ±, Klinger–Herndl, Wolfsberg 1985) 24 Qxb4 h6! =, Murey–Alburt, Beersheva 1980.

(e) 12 Qe1 fxe5 13 dxe5 Nd7 14 Rd1 Qe8 =. Comments.

(f) 13 ... Rf7?! 14 Rad1 Rd7 15 c5 Nd5 16 Nxd5 exd5 17 Ne5 Bxe5 18 Rxf5 ±, F. Garcia–Pomar, Barcelona 1984. The column is Rauzer–Fine, Leningrad 1937.

(g) 10 Qd2 Bb4 11 Be2 (11 a3 Be7!) 11 ... Bxf3 12 gxf3 Na5 13 b3 c5 14 dxc5 Nd7 15 0–0–0 Qe7 16 Kb2 Nxc5 =, Urzica–Ghizdavu, Romanian Chp. 1973.

(h) 14 Ne4 0–0–0 15 Qa4 Ndb8 16 Rd1 Be7 17 0–0 f5 18 exf6 gxf6 19 Bc4 Rd5!, Kupreichik–Alburt, Daugavpils 1974. Both sides have chances in this many-faceted position. The column is Böhm–Schmidt, Wijk aan Zee 1975.

(i) Aggressive but risky is 10 d5 exd4 11 cxd5 Nb4 12 Nd4 N6xd5 13 Nxd5 Nxd5 14 Nxf5 Bb4† 15 Ke2 0–0–0 16 Nd6† Bxd6 17 Qxd5 Qf5 and Black has sufficient play for the piece, Tomić–Gipslis, Dortmund 1978.

(j) 11 . . . f6 12 d5! exd5? (12 . . . Nxe5 13 Nxe5 dxe5 14 a4 is strong) 13 Bxb6 axb6 14 cxd5 Nxe5 15 Nxe5 fxe5 16 Rxf5 wins. 12 . . . Qe8 could be tried.

(k) 17 Kh1 Qd2 18 Qxd2 Rxd2 19 Rxf7 Bxc5 20 Nxe6 with a small endgame advantage, Gipslis–Kengis, Jurmala 1983.

(l) Black's most logical move here is 11 . . . cxd4, but then his lack of development tells: 12 Nxd4 Bg6 13 c5! Bxc5 14 Bb5† Nd7 15 Nxe6 with a significant edge (Alburt).

(m) 17 Nxe5 Nxe5 18 Bd4 Bxe2 19 Qxe2 Nc6 20 Bc3 ± (Mikhalchishin).

(n) 10 . . . 0–0 11 0–0 Bxc3 12 bxc3 Na5 13 Nd2 Qd7 14 Rf4 Bg6 15 Qf1 ⩲, Zuidema–Hecht, Amsterdam 1971.

(o) (A) 16 . . . Qxd5? 17 Bh6 Rfd8 18 Be3 left the bishop on b4 in dire straits in Rohde–Shamkovich, New York 1976. (B) After 16 . . . fxg5 Byrne and Mednis give 17 Nxb4 Nxb4 18 Qd2 Nc6 19 Bb5 h6 20 Bxc6 with a slight plus for White.

ALEKHINE'S DEFENSE

1 e4 Nf6 2 e5 Nd5 3 c4 Nb6

	25	26	27	28	29	30
4	(d4) (Four Pawns' Attack)		....	c5 (Two Pawns' Attack)		
	(d6)			Nd5		
5	(f4)			Bc4		Nc3
	(dxe5)	....	Bf5(i)	e6(k)		e6(q)
6	(fxe5)		Nc3	Nc3	d4	Nxd5(r)
	c5	.... Bf5(e)	e6	Nxc3(l)	b6(o)	exd5
7	d5	Nc3	Be3	dxc3	cxb6	d4
	e6	e6	Be7	Nc6	axb6	d6
8	Nc3(a)	Nf3	Nf3	Bf4	Nc3(p)	cxd6
	exd5	Bb4(f)	0–0(j)	Bxc5(m)	Bb7	cxd6
9	cxd5	Bd3!	Bd3!	Qg4	Nxd5	Nf3
	c4	Bg4(g)	Bxd3	g5!	exd5	Nc6
10	Nf3	0–0	Qxd3	Bxg5	Bd3	Be2
	Bg4(b)	Nc6	d5	Rg8	d6	Be7
11	Qd4(c)	c5!	c5 $\pm$	Nh3	Ne2	0–0
	Bxf3(d)	Bxc3(h)		Be7(n)	dxe5 $=$	0–0 $=$

(a) Not 8 d6? Qh4† 9 g3 Qe4† winning.

(b) If 10 . . . Bb4 then 11 Bxc4 Nxc4 12 Qa4† Nc6 13 dxc6 is good for White.

(c) Now (A) 11 Bxc4 Nxc4 12 Qa4† Nd7 13 Qxc4 Bxf3 14 gxf3 Nxe5 15 Qe4 Qh4† is fine for Black, Cursoux–Letzelter, Le Tourquet 1977. White can play safely with Bagirov's (B) 11 Be2 Bb4 (11 . . . Bc5 12 Bf4 0–0 13 Qd2 and 14 0–0–0) 12 0–0 Bxc3 13 bxc3 Qxd5 14 Qxd5 Nxd5 15 Bxc4 $\pm$.

(d) 12 gxf3 Bb4 13 Bxc4 0–0 14 Rg1 g6 15 Bg5 Qc7 16 Bb3 Bc5 17 Qf4 Bxg1 18 d6 Qc5 19 Ne4 Qd4 20 Rd1 Qxb2 21 Nf6† Kh8 22 Rd2 Qa1† 23 Ke2 Nc6 with unclear chances, Y. Gruenfeld–Wiemer, Tecklenburg 1984. White has a very dangerous attack, but he is a whole rook down.

(e) 6 . . . g6 7 Nc3 Bg7 8 c5 Nd5 9 Bc4 $\pm$.

(f) 8 . . . Be7 9 Be3 0–0?! (9 . . . Nc6 transposes to cols. 19–20) 10 Bd3! Bg4 11 0–0 Nc6 12 h3 Bxf3 13 Qxf3 Nxe5 (13 . . . Nxd4 14 Qe4 Nf5 15 g4) 14 Bxh7† Kxh7 15 dxe5 Qd3 16 Rad1 Qd6 17 Rd4 $\pm$, Velimirović–Marović, Yugoslavia 1972.

(g) 9 . . . Bxd3 10 Qxd3 c5 11 0–0 cxd4 12 Ne4! N6d7 13 Nfg5 Nxe5 14 Qg3 Nbd7 15 Bf4 is terrible for Black, Ivkov–Timman, Amsterdam 1974.

(h) 12 bxc3 Nd5 13 Qe1 with a big edge due to White's strong center and bishop pair, Velimirović–Martz, Vrnjačka Banja 1973.

(i) 5 . . . g6 6 Nc3 Bg7 7 Be3 0–0 8 c5! dxc5 9 dxc5 N6d7 10 h4 $\pm$, Rogers–Depasquale, Australian Chp. 1985/86.

167

(j) 8 . . . Na6 9 exd6! cxd6 10 Be2 leaves the black knight on a6 badly placed. The column is Marjanović–Cooper, Teesside 1973.

(k) 5 . . . c6 6 Qe2 b6 7 Nc3 Nxc3 8 dxc3 bxc5 9 Nf3 e6 10 Ng5 f5 11 Bf4 ±, Shirazi–Alburt, Lone Pine 1981.

(l) 6 . . . d6 7 Nxd5 exd5 8 Bxd5 c6 9 Bxf7†! Kxf7 10 cxd6 Qe8 11 Qf3† Kg8 12 Qe3 Be6 13 Ne2 Nd7 14 Nf4 is promising. *Comments.*

(m) 8 . . . Qh4 9 g3 Qe7 10 Nf3 h6 11 Nf3 h6 12 Be3 b6! is an interesting try, Hegedus–Grunberg, Romanian Chp. 1985.

(n) 12 Bxe7 Rxg4 13 Bxd8 Kxd8 14 f4 Rxg2 15 0–0–0 Ke7 16 Rdg1 Rg6 and Black's extra pawn balances his lack of development, Gertsch–Rosell, corr. 1984.

(o) 6 . . . d6 7 cxd6 cxd6 8 Nf3 Nc6 9 0–0 Be7 10 Qe2 0–0 is a playable position arising also in the Sicilian Defense.

(p) 8 Nf3 Ba6 9 Bxa6 Nxa6 produced equality in Machulsky–Gurgenidze, USSR 1973. The column is Rausis–Shirov, Riga 1986.

(q) Alburt suggests 5 . . . c6 6 Bc4 d6 7 cxd6 exd6 8 Nf3 Be7 9 0–0 Nxc3 10 dxc3 0–0 with an equal game.

(r) 6 Bc4 transposes to col. 28. This column is Westerinen–Hecht, Helsinki 1972.

Unusual Lines

1 e4 Nf6

	31	32	33	34	35	36
2	(e5)				Nc3	
	(Nd5)				d5(j)	
3	(d4).....................		Nc3		e5	exd5
	(d6)		Nxc3(f)		d4(k)	Nxd5
4	Bc4........	f4	bxc3........	dxc3	exf6	g3(m)
	Nb6(a)	dxe5(d)	d5(g)	Nc6(i)	dxc3	Nxc3
5	Bb3	fxe5	d4	Nf3	fxg7	bxc3
	dxe5	c5	c5	d6	cxd2†	Qd5!
6	Qh5	Bb5†(e)	Nf3	Bb5	Qxd2	Nf3
	e6	Bd7	Nc6	Bd7	Qxd2†	Qe4†
7	dxe5	Bxd7†	Be2(h)	Qe2	Bxd2	Be2
	a5	Qxd7	Bg4	a6	Bxg7	Bh3
8	a4	Nf3	0–0	Bc4	0–0–0	Rg1
	Nc6(b)	cxd4	e6	e6	Bg4!(l)	Bg4
9	Nf3	Qxd4	Rb1	Bf4	Be2	d3
	Nd7!	e6	Rb8	dxe5	Bxe2	Qc6
10	Bg5	0–0	h3	Nxe5	Nxe2	c4
	Be7(c)	h6 =	Bh5 =	Bd6 =	Nc6 =	e6 =

(a) 5 . . . Bf5 6 Qf3 Qc8 7 Nh3 Nc6 8 c3 e6 ∞ is a provocative reply, Arnason–Alburt, Lone Pine 1980.

(b) 8 . . . Na6 9 Nc3 Nc5 10 Bg5! Be7 11 Rd1 Bd7 12 Be3 0–0 13 Nf3 gives White play on the kingside, Hecht–Hartmann, West Germany 1985/86.

(c) 11 Bxe7 (11 Bxe6 Ndxe5) 11 . . . Qxe7 12 Nc3 b6 13 0–0 Bb7 14 Rfe1 0–0–0 = , Borlov–Hazai, Hungary 1974.

(d) Black can also play as in the Four Pawns' Attack with 4 . . . Bf5 5 Nf3 e6, but the column is a more direct attack on the center.

(e) Bad is the impetuous 6 c4? Nb4 7 d5 Bf5 8 Na3 e6 9 Qa4† Qd7 10 Qxd7† Nxd7 and White is overextended in the endgame, Zapata–Tal, Subotica 1987.

(f) 3 . . . e6 4 Nxd5 exd5 5 d4 d6 6 Nf3 Nc6 7 Be2?! (7 Bd3 is more aggressive) 7 . . . Be7 8 Bf4 0–0 = , Sämisch–Alekhine, Budapest 1922.

(g) 4 . . . g6 5 d4 d6 6 f4 Bg7 7 Bd3 c5 8 Nf3 0–0 9 0–0 (9 dxc5 dxe5!) 9 . . . Qc7 10 Qe1 gives White a pull because of his central wedge, Grob–Grünfeld, Meran 1926.

(h) 7 Bd3 Bg4 8 Rb1 c4 9 Be2 Qd7 10 h3 Bxf3 11 Bxf3 e6 12 0–0 0–0–0 = , Zaitsev–Bagirov, Minsk 1983. The column is Vaisman–Alburt, Bucharest 1978.

(i) (A) Also good is 4 . . . d5 5 c4 c6 6 Nf3 Bg4 7 h3 Bxf3 8 Qxf3 e6 9 cxd5 Qxd5 =, Kuzmin–Alburt, USSR 1974. (B) 4 . . . d6 5 Nf3 dxe5?! 6 Qxd8† Kxd8 7 Nxe5 gave White a more comfortable ending in Biyiasis–Nezhni, Los Angeles 1975.

(j) 2 . . . e5 transposes to the Vienna Game. 2 . . . d6 3 d4 is the Pirc Defense.

(k) (A) 3 . . . Nfd7 4 d4 e6 is a French Defense, but 4 f4 keeps the game in unusual channels. (B) 3 . . . Ne4 4 Nce2 d4 5 c3 Nc6 6 cxd4 Ng5 7 h4 Ne6 8 Nf3 a6? (8 . . . Nexd4 9 Nexd4 Nxd4 10 Qa4† ±, Bellon–Schmidt, Pula 1975) 9 d5! Qxd5 10 d4 forced a wholesale Black retreat: 10 . . . Ned8 11 Nc3 Qd7 12 d5 Na7 13 e6 with a winning position, Shulman–Shabalov, Riga 1986.

(l) 8 . . . Nc6 9 Bb5 Bd7 10 Nf3 0–0–0 11 Rhe1 allows White a small edge. The column is Spassky–Kirov, Pernik 1976.

(m) 4 Bc4 Nb6 5 Bb3 Nc6 6 Nf3 Bf5 =. The column is Benko–Martz, US Chp. 1972.

CARO-KANN DEFENSE

1 e4 c6

Diagram 26

Mentioned by Polerio in 1590, this defense was little understood and scarcely played until H. Caro of Berlin and M. Kann of Vienna analyzed it seriously in the 1890s. It gained respect during the reign of Capablanca, who frequently employed it to avoid book lines. Other luminaries who have favored it include Botvinnik, Karpov, and Seirawan. Its greatest successes are usually against aggressive opponents who do not sense the danger in the quills of this porcupine-like defense. Its drawback is that it lacks attacking possibilities. Black must usually have patience and endgame skill in order to try for a win—but all openings, of course, have combinational potential.

The plan behind 1 . . . c6 is to support the advance 2 . . . d5 without imprisoning the queen's bishop. Black gets simple development at the cost of allowing White more freedom of play than in other openings. White's challenge is how to make use of his extra mobility.

Diagram 27

The MAIN LINE is 2 d4 d5 3 Nc3 dxe4 4 Nxe4 (cols. 1–30). See diagram.
4 . . . Bf5 (cols. 1–12) is still the most solid response. White often obtains
a small kingside bind when he advances his pawn to h5, but this is
difficult to exploit. 4 . . . Nd7 (cols. 13–21) used to be considered a drawing line, but now it can lead to exciting attacking chess with castling on
opposite sides and complicated piece sacrifices. 4 . . . Nf6 5 Nxf6† exf6
(cols. 22–24) doubles Black's f-pawns to give him extra protection on the
king's wing, but allows White a queenside pawn majority. More interesting is 4 . . . Nf6 5 Nxf6† gxf6 (cols. 25–30). This unbalanced line produces
sharp attacking play—it is the norm rather than the exception to castle on
opposite wings and see whose attack arrives first. Currently, however,
White has the upper hand and Black must find new ideas.

The ADVANCE VARIATION, 2 d4 d5 3 e5 (cols. 31–36), is a direct attacking
scheme which leads to tactical fights. Theoretically Black is fine, but he
must proceed carefully.

The TWO KNIGHTS' VARIATION, 2 Nc3 d5 3 Nf3 (cols. 37–48), was once
favored by Fischer as a sort of reverse King's Indian. White delays (or
avoids) d4 in favor of flexible piece play. Black has a freer hand here than
in the main line, allowing several equalizing choices.

Diagram 28

The PANOV–BOTVINNIK ATTACK, 2 d4 d5 3 exd5 cxd5 4 c4 (cols. 49–60),
is a time-honored plan to turn the defense into an open game (see diagram). Play is often similar to the Queen's Gambit Accepted or the Semi-
Tarrasch Variation. 4 . . . e6 (cols. 55–60) still seems to be Black's best
defense.

The EXCHANGE VARIATION (cols. 61–63) aims for simple development
and a kingside initiative, but it holds few prospects for an advantage. The
Fantasy Variation (cols. 64–65) is not theoretically critical; it is not as
outlandish as it looks and can be a surprise weapon.

Unusual lines are the subject of cols. 66–72. This includes the King's
Indian Attack (col. 71–72, cf. col. 37) and the interesting new line 2 c4.

CARO-KANN DEFENSE

Main Line

1 e4 c6 2 d4 d5 3 Nc3 dxe4 4 Nxe4 Bf5 5 Ng3 Bg6 6 h4 h6 7 Nf3 Nd7 8 h5 Bh7 9 Bd3 Bxd3 10 Qxd3

	1	2	3	4	5	6
	Qc7..					e6
11	Bd2(a)					Bf4(r)
	e6					Ngf6(s)
12	0–0–0..............................			Qe2		0–0–0
	Ngf6			Ngf6		Be7
13	Ne4(b)...................		Kb1	0–0–0		Ne5
	0–0–0(c)		c5!(i)	0–0–0	Bd6(o)	a5
14	g3		Qe2(j)	Ne5	Nf5	Rhe1
	Nxe4	Nc5	Be7	Nb6(k)	Bf4	a4?!
15	Qxe4	Nxc5	Bc1	Ba5	Bxf4(p)	Ng6!
	Nf6(d)	Bxc5	cxd4	Rd5	Qxf4†	Nd5(t)
16	Qe2	c4(f)	Nxd4	Bxb6(l)	Ne3	Nf5!
	Bd6	Bb6(g)	0–0 =	axb6	0–0–0	Bf8
17	c4	Kb1		c4(m)	Kb1	Bd6
	c5(e)	c5(h)		Rd8(n)	Kb8(q)	Rg8(u)

(a) 11 Rh4 e6 12 Bf4 Qa5† (Pomar's 12 . . . Bd6 13 Bxd6 Qxd6 14 Ne4 Qe7 15 Qa3! Qxa3 16 bxa3 Ke7 17 Rb1 Rb8 18 Nc5 Nxc5 19 dxc5 a5 is playable but unenterprising) 13 Bd2 Qb6 14 0–0–0 Be7 15 Rhh1 Ngf6 16 c4 Qa6 17 Kb1 Bd6 =, Gilezhdetinov–Shakarov, corr. 1976.

(b) 13 c4 b5! = wins the d5 square for Black's knight.

(c) (A) 13 . . . Rd8 14 Nxf6† Nxf6 15 Ne5! a6 (15 . . . Bc5 16 Qg3 Bxd4 17 Qxg7 ±) 16 Bf4 Bf6 17 Qg3 ±, Wedberg–Stean, Lucerne 1982. (B) 13 . . . Be7 14 Nxf6† Bxf6 15 Qe4 0–0–0 16 Bf4 ±, Karpov–Seirawan, Linares 1983.

(d) 15 . . . Be7 16 Kb1 Rhe8 17 Qe2 Bf8 18 c4 c5 19 Bc3 ±, Balashov–Hübner, Wijk aan Zee 1982.

(e) 18 Bc3 cxd4 19 Nxd4 with a pull for White, Benko–Kagan, Israel 1967.

(f) 16 Qe2 Bxd4 17 Nxd4? (17 Bf4 e5 =) 17 . . . Rxd4 18 Bf4 Rxd1† 19 Qxd1 e5 ∓, Tal–Chandler, Wijk aan Zee 1982.

(g) (A) 16 . . . Bxd4? 17 Nxd4 c5 18 Nb5 Rxd3 19 Nxc7 +. (B) 16 . . . Rhe8 17 Bc3 Kb8 18 Qe2 Bf8 19 Ne5 ±, Christiansen–Chandler, Wijk aan Zee 1982.

(h) 18 Bf4 Qe7 19 d5 Rhe8 20 Rhe1 Qf8 21 Ne5 Be7 22 Qf3 with more space, de Firmian–Miles, Tunis 1985.

(i) 13 . . . 0–0–0 14 c4 c5 15 Bc3 Bd6 16 Nxe4 Nxe4 17 Qxe4 Nf6 can be played, but it does not give Black full equality. The column is more dynamic.

(j) 14 Ne5 cxd4 15 Nxd7 Qxd7 = (Kasparov).

(k) 14 . . . Nxe5 15 dxe5 Nd7 16 f4 favors White because of the kingside pressure.

(l) 16 b4 Rxa5 17 bxa5 Ba3† 18 Kb1 Na4 allows Black an attack worth the sacrificed exchange.

(m) 17 f4 Bd6 18 Kb1 Rd8 19 c3 (Romanishin–Bagirov, USSR 1978); now Kasparov gives 19 . . . c5! loosening White's center and creating equal chances.

(n) 18 Ne4 Nxe4 19 Qxe4 Bd6 20 Nf3, Spassky–Pomar, Palma de Mallorca 1968. Here Bagirov's idea of 20 . . . Be7 intending 21 . . . Bf6 would give Black an even game.

(o) A good try is 13 . . . c5 14 Nf5 0–0–0 15 Ne3 Nb8 16 Rh4 Nc6 17 Bc3 Be7 18 dxc5 Bxc5 19 Rc4 Bxe3† 20 Qxe3 Rxd1† =, Faibisovich–Okhotnik, USSR 1979.

(p) W. Watson–Miles, British Chp. 1984, took the exciting route 15 Nxg7†!? Kf8 16 Nxe6† fxe6 17 Qxe6 Re8 18 Qf5 Bxd2† 19 Rxd2 Qd6 with a sharp but balanced game.

(q) 18 Nc4 Qc7 19 Nfe5 ±, Magerramov–Vdovin, USSR 1978.

(r) 11 Bd2 Ngf6 12 0–0–0 Be7 (12 . . . Qc7 transposes to col. 1) 13 Qe2 Rc8 14 Ne5 c5 15 Rhe1 0–0 16 Ng6 Re8 17 Nxe7† ±, Y. Gruenfeld–Lobron, New York 1986.

(s) 11 . . . Qa5† 12 c3 (12 Bd2 Qc7 transposes to col. 1) 12 . . . Ngf6 13 a4 c5 14 0–0 Be7 15 Rfe1 0–0 = , Vitolins–Klovans, Latvian Chp. 1978.

(t) 15 . . . fxg6 16 Qxg6† Kf8 17 Rxe6 Qe8 18 Rde1 wins for White (Beliavsky).

(u) 18 c4 Nb4 19 Qh3 fxg6 20 Rxe6 Kf7 21 hxg6† Kxe6 22 Re1† Ne5 23 Bxe5 Resigns, Beliavsky–Larsen, Tilburg 1981.

CARO-KANN DEFENSE

Main Line

1 e4 c6 2 d4 d5 3 Nc3 dxe4 4 Nxe4 Bf5

	7	8	9	10	11	12
5	(Ng3)..Nc5					
	(Bg6)					Qb6(m)
6	(h4)........Bc4......................Ne2(h)......Nf3					Nf3
	(h6)	e6		Nf6	Nd7	e6
7	f4(a)	N1e2(c)		Nf4(i)	Bd3(k)	Nb3
	e6	Nf6(d)		e5	e6	Nd7
8	Nf3	0–0........Nf4(f)		Nxg6	Bxg6(l)	Bd3
	Nd7	Bd6	Bd6	hxg6	hxg6	Bg6
9	h5	f4	Bb3	dxe5	Qe2	0–0
	Bh7	Qd7!	Qc7	Qa5†	Ngf6	Ngf6
10	Bd3	Bd3	Qf3	Bd2	Bd2	c4
	Bxd3	Bxd3	Nbd7	Qxe5†	Qc7	Qc7
11	Qxd3	Qxd3	Be3(g)	Qe2	0–0–0	Re1
	Qc7	g6	0–0–0	Qxe2†	c5!	Bb4
12	Bd2	b3	0–0–0	Bxe2	Kb1	Re3
	Ngf6(b)	Na6(e)	c5 =	Nbd7(j)	Be7 =	Bd6 =

(a) White can play 7 Bd3 Bxd3 8 Qxd3 and reach the same positions as in cols. 1–6 with the difference that his h-pawn is at h4 instead of h5. The pawn is more cramping at h5, but also more exposed.

(b) 13 0–0–0 c5 14 Qe2 0–0–0 15 Ne5 Nb6 =, Kavalek–Saidy, Las Palmas 1973.

(c) For 7 Nf3 see col. 11 note (k).

(d) 7 ... Bd6 8 h4 h6 9 Nf4 Bxf4 10 Bxf4 cedes White the bishop pair, Tal–Botvinnik, World Chp. 1960.

(e) Chances are equal. The game van der Wiel–Seirawan, Baden 1980, continued 13 Bb2 Be7 14 c4 Nc7 15 Qf3 0–0 16 Nc1 Nce8 17 Nd3 Ng7 18 Ne5 Qc7 19 h3 Rad8 20 Rad1 h5 21 Ne2 h4! (now White has a "hole" at g3) 22 Ng4 Nfh5 23 Qc3 Kh7 24 Rf3 Nf5 25 Ne3?! Bf6 (the bishop is strong on the long diagonal, so the white knight should not have left g4) 26 Ng4 Bh8 27 Ne5? (after positionally outplaying his opponent Black now cashes in tactically) 27 ... Nxf4! 28 Rxf4 Bxe5 29 Re4 Bf6 30 Rf1 c5! 31 Qd2 cxd4 32 Resigns.

(f) White can sharpen the game with 8 h4 h6 9 Nf4 Bh7 10 0–0 Bd6 11 Nxe6 fxe6 12 Bxe6, Tal–Botvinnik, World Chp. 1960. The position is unclear, but Black should not be worse.

(g) 11 h4 e5! 12 dxe5?! (12 Nxg6 =) 12 ... Nxe5 13 Qe2 0–0–0 14 h5 Neg4 15 hxg6 hxg6 16 Rxh8 Rxh8 (Kasparov) puts White in difficulties. The column is Kupreichik–Chandler, Hastings 1981–82.

(h) Since the knight is headed toward f4, 6 Nh3 will lead to the same position.

(i) (A) 7 Nxg6?! hxg6 gives White the bishop pair, but Black obtains a compact pawn formation and the open h-file. (B) 7 h4 h6 8 Nf4 Bh7 9 Bc4 e6 transposes to col. 9 note (f).

(j) 13 0–0–0 Bc5 14 f4 0–0 =, Tseshkovsky–Bagirov, USSR 1978.

(k) Insipid is 7 Bc4 Ngf6 8 0–0 e6 9 Qe2 Be7 10 Re1 0–0 =.

(l) Perhaps a better plan is 8 0–0 Ngf6 9 b3 Bd6 10 Bb2 0–0 11 Bxg6 hxg6 12 c4 Qc7 (Spassky–Karpov, match 1974), although White has no advantage here either. The column is de Firmian–Seirawan, Lone Pine 1981.

(m) (A) 5 ... e5 6 Nxb7 Qb6 7 Nc5 Bxc5 8 dxc5 Qxc5 9 c3 ±, Fischer–Petrosian, blitz tournament, Bled 1961. (B) 5 ... b6 6 Nb3 e6 7 Nf3 Nf6 8 g3 Nd7 9 Bg2 Bd6 10 Qe2 Qc7 11 Nh4 ± (Arnason). The column is Arnason–Miles, Esbjerg 1984, with 12 ... Bd6 instead of Miles's 12 ... 0–0–0.

CARO-KANN DEFENSE

Main Line

1 e4 c6 2 d4 d5 3 Nc3 dxe4 4 Nxe4 Nd7

	13	14	15	16	17	18
5	Bc4				Nf3	
	Ngf6				Ngf6	
6	Ng5			Nxf6†	Nxf6†	
	e6(a)			Nxf6	Nxf6	
7	Qe2			Nf3	Ne5(m)	
	Nb6(b)			Bf5	Be6	Nd7(p)
8	Bd3		Bb3	Qe2(l)	Be2	Bf4
	h6		h6(h)	e6	g6	Nxe5
9	N5f3		N5f3	Bg5	0–0	Bxe5
	c5		a5(i)	Be7	Bg7	Qd5
10	dxc5(c)		a3	0–0–0	c4	Be2!?(q)
	Bxc5	Nbd7	a4(j)	Bg4	0–0	Qxg2
11	Ne5(d)	b4!	Ba2	h3	Be3	Bf3
	Nbd7	b6(f)	c5	Bxf3	Ne4!(n)	Qg5
12	Ngf3	Nd4	c3	Qxf3	Qc2	Qe2(r)
	Nxe5(e)	Nd5(g)	Bd7(k)	Nd5 =	Nd6(o)	

(a) 6 . . . Nd5 7 N1f3 h6 8 Ne4 N7b6 9 Bd3 Nb4 10 0–0 Nxd3 11 Qxd3 e6 12 Ne5 gives White an edge (Fischer).

(b) Not 7 . . . Be7? 8 Nxf7!.

(c) 10 Be3 Nbd5 11 Ne5 a6 12 c3 cxd4 13 Bxd4 Nf4 14 Qf3 Nxd3† =, Wedberg–Adorjan, Reykjavik 1982.

(d) 11 Bd2 Nbd7 12 0–0–0 Qc7 is an aggressive setup for White, but his tangled knights balance the chances.

(e) 13 Nxe5 0–0 with two distinct plans: (A) the wild 14 Bd2 Qd5 15 0–0–0 (15 0–0 Bd4 16 Nf3 Bxb2 17 Rb1 Ba3 =, P. Popović–Christiansen, Portorož 1985) 15 . . . Qxa2 16 c3 b5! 17 Bxh6 Bb7 18 Nd7 (18 Bb1 Qa4 =) 18 . . . Nxd7 19 Qg4 Qa1† 20 Bb1 g6 21 Rxd7 Ba3! 22 bxa3 Qxc3† 23 Kd1 Rfd8 24 Rd2! Rxd2† 25 Bxd2 Rd8 26 Qg5 Bf3†! 27 gxf3 (27 Ke1? Qc1†!) 27 . . . Qxf3† ∓; (B) the safe 14 0–0 Qc7 15 Bf4 Bd6 16 Rfe1 b6 with a minimal plus for White, Barlov–Radulov, Belgrade 1982.

(f) 11 . . . Nd5 12 Bd2 Qf6 13 Rb1 a5 14 a3 g5 15 Be4 Nc3 16 Bxc3 Qxc3† 17 Qd2 Qxa3 18 Qd4 ±, A. Rodriguez–Tal, Subotica 1987.

(g) Black is in great danger. Note that 12 . . . bxc5? 13 Nc6 Qc7 14 Qxe6†! fxe6 15 Bg6 is checkmate! After 12 . . . Nd5 Sapirov gives 13 Bb2 Nxb4 14 Nxe6! Nxd3† 15 Qxd3 Qe7 16 0–0–0 fxe6 17 Qe4 Rb8 18 c6 Nc5 19 Qg6† Qf7 20 c7 Ra8 21 Rd8† Ke7 22 Qxf7† Kxf7 23 Nf3 Na6 24 Ne5† with great advantage to White.

(h) The d-pawn is poisoned: 8 . . . Qxd4? 9 N1f3 Qg4 10 Nxf7!.

177

(i) 9 . . . c5 10 Bf4 Nbd5 11 Be5 Qa5† 12 Nd2 b5 13 c4 bxc4 14 Bxc4 Nb6 is also roughly equal, Short–Speelman, Hastings 1988–89.

(j) In Tal–Speelman, Subotica 1987, Black played 10 . . . Be7 and failed to generate counterplay: 11 Bd2 Nbd5 12 c4 Nc7 13 Bc2 0–0 (now Tal shows his famous attacking virtuosity!) 14 Ne5! Qxd4 15 Bc3 Qd8 16 Ngf3 Nce8 17 g4! b5 18 g5 hxg5 19 Nxg5 Ra6 20 Qf3 b4 (finally Black has counterplay, but it comes too late) 21 Qh3 g6 22 Bxg6! bxc3 (22 . . . hxg6 23 Nxg6 Kg7 24 Qh7 mate) 23 Nexf7 Qd2† 24 Kf1 Rxf7 25 Bxf7† Kg7 26 Rg1 Qxg5 27 Rxg5† Kxf7 28 bxc3 e5? (Black is lost in any case, but after this blunder he saw 29 Qxc8 coming and so resigned).

(k) 13 Ne5 cxd4 14 cxd4 Be7 15 Ngf3 0–0 with near equality, Karpov–Petrosian, Tilburg 1982.

(l) 8 0–0 e6 9 h3 Be7 10 Qe2 0–0 11 Rd1 Qc7 12 Nh4 Be4 13 Bg5 Bd5 14 Bd3 b5 =, Reshevsky–Smyslov, Palma de Mallorca 1970. The column is Fischer–Petrosian, Bled 1961.

(m) 7 h3 has served Spassky well, but 7 . . . Bf5 8 Bd3 Bxd3 9 Qxd3 e6 is equal.

(n) Browne–Rogoff, US Chp. 1975, saw instead 11 . . . Qc8 12 Bf3 Rd8 13 Qe2 Nd7 14 Ng4! when White kept an edge.

(o) 13 b3 c5 14 Rad1 Nf5 15 d5 Bxe5 16 dxe6 Qc7 17 exf7† Rxf7 18 g3 Raf8 19 Bg4 Nxe3 20 fxe3 Rxf1† draw, A. Sokolov–Karpov, match 1987.

(p) 7 . . . Bf5 8 c3 e6 9 g4 Bg6 10 h4 h5 11 g5 Nxd5 12 Nxg6 ruins Black's kingside, Karpov–Hort, Bugojno 1978.

(q) 10 c4 Qe4† 11 Qe2 Bf5 levels the chances, Hulak–Speelman, Wijk aan Zee 1983.

(r) Here the game Kavalek–Christiansen, US Chp. 1986, was agreed drawn, yet White has good play for his pawn and his position is preferable.

CARO-KANN DEFENSE

Main Line

1 e4 c6 2 d4 d5 3 Nc3 dxe4 4 Nxe4

	19	20	21	22	23	24
	(Nd7)			Nf6		
5	(Nf3)		Bd3(e)	Nxf6		
	(Ngf6)		Ngf6(f)	exf6		
6	Ng3		Ng5	c3	Bc4	g3(p)
	e6 .... c5		e6	Bd6(i)	Bd6(m)	c5
7	Bd3	Bd3(c)	N1f3	Bd3	Qe2†(n)	Nf3
	c5	cxd4	Qc7?(g)	0–0	Qe7	Bd6
8	c3(a)	Nxd4	Qe2	Qc2	Qxe7†	Be3
	Qc7(b)	g6!	h6	Re8†	Kxe7	Qc7
9	Qe2	Bg5?!	Bg6!	Ne2	Ne2	dxc5
	Be7	Bg7	hxg5	g6(j)	Be6	Bxc5
10	0–0	0–0	Bxf7†	h4	Bd3	Bxc5
	0–0	0–0	Kd8!	f5(k)	Nd7	Qxc5
11	Re1	Re1	Nxg5	h5	Bf4	Qe2†
	b6	h6	Nb6	Qf6	Rhe8	Kf8!(q)
12	Bg5	Bc1(d)	Bxe6?	hxg6	0–0–0	Bg2
	h6 =	Nc5 $\overline{\overline{+}}$	Rxh2(h)	fxg6(l)	f5(o)	Nc6(r)

(a) 8 0–0 cxd4 9 Nxd4 Bc5 10 Nf3 0–0 11 Qe2 b6 12 Bf4 Bb7 13 Rad1 Nd5 =, Ivanović–Speelman, Thessaloniki 1984.

(b) 8 ... cxd4 9 Nxd4 Bc5 10 Bc2 b6 11 Ne4 Bb7 12 Nxc5 and the bishop pair gives White a pull, Tseitlin–Bagirov, USSR Chp. 1982. The column is Zapata–Dlugy, Tunis 1985.

(c) Several games have continued 7 c3 e6 transposing to the previous column. Black can answer 7 ... cxd4 8 Nxd4 g6 with play similar to this column.

(d) White has no better retreat for the bishop. The column is Tal–Spiridonov, Albania 1984.

(e) 5 Ng5 will transpose to the column after 5 ... Ngf6 6 Bd3, but Black must avoid (A) 5 ... h6? 6 Ne6! Qa5† 7 Bd2 Qb6 8 Bd3 fxe6? 9 Qh5† Kd8 10 Ba5 winning the queen, Nunn–Kir. Georgiev, Linares 1988, and (B) 5 ... Ndf6 6 N1f3 h6 7 Nxf7! Kxf7 8 Ne5† Ke8 9 Bd3. If White wishes to avoid 5 ... Ndf6, 5 Ng5 discourages it more strongly than 5 Bd3. (C) 5 ... g6 has also been suggested.

(f) 5 ... Ndf6 6 Ng5 Bg4 7 N1f3 Bh5! (7 ... h6 8 Nxf7 Bxf3 9 Bg6! Qa5† 10 Bd2 wins) 8 c3 Qc7 9 Qc2 h6 10 Ne6! Qd6 11 Nxf8 ±, Reimersma–van der Wiel, Dutch Chp. 1987.

(g) (A) 7 ... h6 8 Nxe6! Qe7 9 0–0 fxe6 10 Bg6† Kd8 11 Bf4 Qb4 12 a3 Qxb2 13 Qe2 Nd5 14 Bd2 Bd6 15 Qxe6 Kc7 16 Rfb1 Qxa1 17 Rxa1 Ne5 18 Qxd6† Kxd6 19 Nxe5 with a distinct advantage despite being down the exchange, Geller–Meduna, Sochi 1986. (B) 7 ... Bd6 8 Qe2 h6 9 Ne4 Nxe4 10 Qxe4 Nf6 11 Qe2 b6 12 Bd2 Bb7 13 0–0–0 Qc7 14 Rhe1 0–0–0 15 Ba6 ±, A. Sokolov–Karpov, Belfort 1988.

179

(h) 13 0–0 Rh5 14 g3 Qe7 15 Re1 Rxg5 16 Bxg5 Bxe6 17 Qxe6 Qxe6 18 Rxe6 with rook and two pawns against two knights, van der Wiel–Karpov, Amsterdam 1987. 12 g3 was best.

(i) 6 ... Bf5 7 Nf3 Bd6 8 Bd3 Bxd3 9 Qxd3 0–0 10 Be3 Nd7 (Ivanović–Matulović, match 1985); now with the simple 11 0–0 White has the edge due to his queenside pawn majority.

(j) 9 ... Kh8!? 10 h4 h6 11 Be3 Be6 12 Qd2 h5 ∞, Lukacs–Möhring, Trnava 1986. This idea may be Black's best try.

(k) 10 ... Nd7 11 h5 Nf8 12 Bh6 ±, Spassky–Barcza, Leipzig 1960.

(l) 13 Qb3† Kh8 14 Bg5! Qg7 (14 ... Qxg5? 15 Qf7 wins) 15 0–0–0 with good attacking chances, Sznapik–Plachetka, Bratislava 1983.

(m) (A) 6 ... Nd7 7 Ne2 Bd6 8 0–0 0–0 9 Ng3 Nb6 10 Bb3 ±, Zapata–Boersma, Amsterdam 1986. (B) 6 ... Qe7† 7 Qe2 Be6 8 Bb3 Na6 9 c3 Bxb3 10 axb3 ±, Keres–Smyslov, Amsterdam 1971.

(n) White can also play a preferable middlegame: 7 Ne2 Qc7 8 Ng3 0–0 9 0–0 Nd7 10 Re1 c5 11 Nf5! Bxh2†? (11 ... Nb6 at once is better) 12 Kh1 Nb6 13 Ne7† Kh8 14 Qh5 Nxc4 15 Re4! with the decisive threat of 16 Qxh7† Kxh7 17 Rh4 mate, Kaplan–Donner, San Juan 1969.

(o) Klovans–Kholmov, USSR 1966. Black's doubled f-pawns are not important. Chances are about level.

(p) 6 Nf3 Na6 7 Be2 Bd6 8 0–0 Nc7 9 c4 0–0 10 Be3 Re8 11 Qd2 Bf5 12 Rad1 Be4 =, Wedberg–Lechtinský, Malta 1980.

(q) 11 ... Be6?! 12 Bh3! gave Black trouble in Tal–Lechtinský, USSR 1979.

(r) 13 0–0 g6 with equality (Lechtinský).

CARO-KANN DEFENSE

Main Line

1 e4 c6 2 d4 d5 3 Nc3 dxe4 4 Nxe4 Nf6 5 Nxf6†(a) gxf6

	25	26	27	28	29	30
6	c3		Nf3	Ne2	Bc4	Be2(p)
	Bf5		Bg4(h)	h5(k)	Bf5(m)	Na6(q)
7	Nf3	Ne2	Be2	Qd3	Bf4(n)	Nf3
	Qc7(b)	Nd7(f)	Qc7(i)	Qa5	e6	Bg4
8	g3(c)	Ng3	h3	Bd2	Nf3	0–0
	Nd7	Bg6	Bh5	Qf5	Na6	Nc7
9	Bg2	h4	0–0	Qb3	0–0	c4
	e6	h5	Nd7	Bh6	Nc7	Qd7
10	0–0	Be2	d5	0–0–0	Bg3	Be3
	0–0–0(d)	Qa5	Rd8	Qxf2	Bd6	Bg7
11	Re1!	b4	c4	Bxh6	Re1	Nh4
	Bg4	Qc7	Nb6	Rxh6	Qd7	f5
12	b4	Nxh5	Be3	Nc3	Nh4	h3
	h5	e5!	Bxf3	e6	Bg6	Bxe2
13	Qa4	Ng3	Bxb6!	Be2(l)	c3	Qxe2
	Bf3(e)	0–0–0(g)	axb6(j)	Qe3† ∞	0–0–0(o)	f4(r)

(a) 5 Ng3 g6 6 Nf3 Bg7 7 Be2 0–0 8 0–0 Qb6 9 b3 a5 =, Sax–Larsen, Tilburg 1979.

(b) 7 ... Nd7 8 Bf4!? Qb6 9 Bd3! Bxd3 10 Qxd3 Qxb2 11 0–0 ±, Karpov–Miles, Oslo 1984.

(c) 7 ... e6 8 g3 Qd5 9 Bg2 Qc4 10 Be3 Nd7 11 Nh4 Bg6 12 Nxg6 hxg6 13 Qd2 Rd8 14 b3 Qb5 15 c4 Qb4 16 Qxb4 Bxb4† 17 Ke2 ∓ (A. Rodriguez).

(d) 10 ... Bd6 11 Be3 Bg4 12 Qb3 is preferable for White, Arnason–Christiansen, Lone Pine 1980.

(e) 14 Bxf3 Kb8 15 Bf4 Bd6 16 Bxd6 Qxd6 17 Rad1 h4 18 c4 and White has the more dangerous attack, de Firmian–Conquest, London 1986.

(f) 7 ... h5 8 Ng3 Bg4 9 f3 Be6 10 Bf4 Qa5 11 Bd3 h4 12 Ne4 ±, Estrin–Stecko, USSR 1974.

(g) 14 h5 Bh7 15 Qb3 Nb6 with full value for the pawn due to White's scattered position, Peters–Seirawan, US Chp. 1984.

(h) 6 ... Bf5 7 Bd3 Bxd3 8 Qxd3 gives White a simple edge. Early exchanges highlight the weakness of the black pawn structure.

(i) 7 ... e6 8 h3 Bh5 9 0–0 Bd6 10 Be3 Nd7 11 c4 Bg6?! 12 d5! exd5 13 cxd5 with the initiative as well as the better pawn structure, Tringov–Opočenský, Bratislava 1957.

(j) 14 Bxf3 cxd5 15 cxd5 ±, Smyslov–Pachman, Amsterdam 1964.

(k) 6 ... Bf5 7 Ng3 Bg6 8 h4 h6 9 h5 Bh7 10 c3 e6 11 Be3 Nd7 12 Qd2 Qa5 13 Be2 0–0–0 14 Bxh6 Bxh6 15 Qxh6 e5 produced an obscure position in Mecking–Larsen, San Antonio 1972.

181

(l) This is van der Berg–Pachman, Wijk aan Zee 1965. After 13 ... Qe3† the position is sharp but roughly even.

(m) 6 ... h5?! 7 Qd3! Qd6 8 Ne2 Be6 9 Bb3 Na6 10 0–0 Nb4 11 Qc3 Nd5 12 Qf3 Bg4 13 Qd3 Nb4 14 Qe4 f5 15 Qe3 and despite many queen moves White has a very good game, Miles–Hort, match 1983.

(n) 7 Ne2 h5 8 Nf4 h4 9 c3 e6 10 Qe2 Bd6 = , Rigo–Skembris, Rome 1984.

(o) 14 Qf3 f5 15 Be5 Bxe5 16 Rxe5 Rhe8 = , Tal–Larsen, Riga 1979.

(p) 6 g3 h5 7 Bg2 Bg4 8 Qd3 e6 9 Bf4 Bd6 10 Bxd6 Qxd6 11 Nf3 Nd7 = , Aratovsky–M. Tseitlin, USSR 1988.

(q) Also good is the natural 6 ... Bf5, e.g. 7 Nf3 Qc7 8 0–0 Nd7 9 c4 0–0–0 10 Be3 e6 11 Qa4 Kb8 = , Hort–Hodgson, Lugano 1983.

(r) 14 Bxf4 Nxe6 and Black wins back the d-pawn with a level game, Yangarber–Kopilov, corr. 1968.

CARO-KANN DEFENSE

Advance Variation

1 e4 c6 2 d4 d5 3 e5

	31	32	33	34	35	36
	Bf5 ....c5					
4	Nc3		h4	Bd3	c3(l)	dxc5
	e6(a)		h5(g)	Bxd3	e6	e6
5	g4		c4	Qxd3	Be3	Be3(n)
	Bg6		e6	e6	Nd7(m)	Ne7
6	Nge2		Nc3	Nc3	Nd2	c3
	c5(b)		Be7!(h)	Qa5	Ne7	Nf5
7	h4	Be3	Nf3	Nge2	f4	Bd4
	h6!(c)	Nc6	Bg4	Qa6	f6	Qc7
8	Be3	dxc5	Be3	Qh3(j)	Ngf3	Bd3
	Qb6	Nxe5	Nh6	b5(k)	fxe5	Bxc5
9	Qd2(d)	Nd4	cxd5	Nf4	Nxe5	Bxc5
	Nc6	Nd7(e)	cxd5	b4	Nxe5	Qxc5
10	0–0–0	f4(f)	Qb3	Nce2	fxe5	Bxf5
	h5	Bxc5	Qd7	c5	Ng6	exf5
11	dxc5	Qf3 ∞	Bd3	dxc5	Qh5	Nf3
	Bxc5 =		Nf5(i)	Bxc5 ±	Qb6 =	Nc6(o)

(a) 4 ... h5?! 5 Bd3 Bxd3 6 Qxd3 e6 7 Nf3 Nh6 8 0–0 Nf5 9 Ne2! Nd7 10 Ng3 $\pm$, Nunn–Dlugy, London 1986.

(b) Complicated is 6 ... f6 7 Nf4 fxe5 8 Nxe6 Qe7 9 Nxf8 exd4† 10 Be2 dxc3 11 Nxg6 hxg6 12 Qd3 Nf6 13 Qxc3 Nbd7 =, Nunn–Anderson, London 1982.

(c) 7 ... cxd4?! 8 Nxd4 h5 9 f4! hxg4 10 Bb5† Nd7 11 f5 Rxh4 12 Rf1 Rh2 (12 ... exf5 13 Bf4 a6 14 e6 axb5 15 Qe2 Be7 ∞ [Adianto]) 13 Bxd7†! Kxd7 14 Qxg4 $\pm$, Moore–Mills, US 1984; White has exactly the kind of attacking chess he wants from the Advance Variation.

(d) Nunn–Seirawan, Lugano 1983, went 9 h5 Bh7 10 Qd2 Nc6 11 0–0–0 c4! and play quickly became tactical: 12 f4 Qa5 13 f5 b5 14 Nxd5! b4! (14 ... Qxd2† 15 Bxd2 exd5 16 Nc3 is at least equal for White since the bishop on h7 is shut out) 15 Nc7†!? Qxc7 16 Nf4 c3 17 Qg2 Nge7 18 Bc4 0–0–0 19 fxe6? (this lets the dead bishop on h7 come back to life; later Nunn gave 19 d5 Nxe5 20 Ba6† Kb8 21 dxe6 as the right way to play) 19 ... Kb8 20 exf7 cxb2† 21 Kb1 Na5 22 Bd3 Nc4 23 Bxc4 Qxc4 24 Rh2 (if 24 d5 Be4 wins the d-pawn) 24 ... Nd5 25 Nxd5 Rxd5 26 e6 b3! (starting the decisive attack—everything is now forced) 27 axb3 Qa6 28 Bf4† Kc8 29 Kxb2 Qa3† 30 Kc3 Qa5† 31 Kb2 Qa3† 32 Kc3 Bb4† 33 Kc4 Be7 34 Kc3 Qa5† 35 Kb2 Ba3†! 36 Kb1 Qc3 37 Bc1 Bxc1 38 Kxc1 Qa1† 39 Kd2 Qxd4† 40 Resigns. The column is A. Sokolov–Karpov, match 1987.

(e) 9 ... Nf6 10 Bb5† Ned7 11 Qe2 ∞ (Timman).

183

(f) 10 Bb5† a6 11 Ba4 Bc5 12 Nxe6 fxe6 13 Bxd7† Qxd7 14 Bxc5 Nf6 15 Qe2 Rc8 left Black clearly better in Biro–Berg, Budapest 1986.

(g) (A) 4 . . . h6 5 g4 Bd7 (5 . . . Bh7 6 e6) 6 h5 e6 7 f4 c5 8 c3 Nc6 9 Nf3 Qb6 10 Kf2 0–0–0 11 Kg3 $\pm$ (Nunn). (B) 4 . . . c5 5 dxc5 Qc7 6 Nc3 Nc6 7 Nf3 Rd8 8 Nb5 $\pm$, Tal–Botvinnik, World Chp. 1961.

(h) 6 . . . Ne7 7 Bg5 dxc4 8 Bxc4 Nd7 9 Qd2 Nb6 10 Bb3 with an aggressive position, Mokrý–Spiridonov, Prague 1985.

(i) The column is Nunn–Miles, Amsterdam 1985. White has difficulties because his pawn on h4 is weak.

(j) 8 Nf4 Qxd3 9 Nxd3 Nd7 10 Be3 Ne7 11 f4 Nf5 12 Bc2 h5 13 Ke2 b6 = (Boleslavsky).

(k) Black does better with 8 . . . Ne7 or 8 . . . Nd7 planning . . . c5 without advancing the b-pawn. The column is Kontronias–Skembris, Kavala 1985.

(l) 4 c4 dxc4 5 Bxc4 e6 6 Nc3 Nd7 7 Nge2 Ne7 8 0–0 Nb6 9 Bb3 Qd7 resulted in equality in Tal–Golombek, Munich 1958. Recently, the line 4 c4 was explored by Minev in *Inside Chess* 1989/No. 15–16.

(m) 5 . . . Qb6 6 Qb3 Bg6 7 Nd2 Nh6 8 Ne2 Nf5 9 Nf4 Be7 10 g3 $\pm$, Gurgenidze–Bagirov, USSR Chp. 1982. The column is Zaichik–Tal, Tbilisi 1986.

(n) 5 Qg4 Nd7 6 Nf3 Ne7 7 Bg5 h6 8 Bxe7 Qxe7 =, Tal–Botvinnik, World Chp. 1961.

(o) 12 0–0 0–0 13 Nbd2 $\pm$ (Boleslavsky). Black has no compensation for his split pawn structure.

CARO-KANN DEFENSE

Two Knights' Variation

1 e4 c6 2 Nc3 d5 3 Nf3 Bg4 4 h3 Bxf3 5 Qxf3

	37	38	39	40	41	42
	Nf6 . . . . .e6					
6	d3. . . . . .g3(h)			d3 . . . . .d4!		
	e6			dxe4	Qf6!?	Nf6(k)
7	g3 . . . . .Bd2. . . . . . . .a3(f)			Qe2	Qe2	Bd3
	Bb4	Nbd7	Bc5(g)	Nbd7	Bb4	dxe4
8	Bd2	g4	Be2	Bg2	Bd2	Nxe4
	d4	Bb4(d)	0–0	g6	Nd7	Qxd4
9	Nb1	a3(e)	0–0	Nxe4	a3	c3(l)
	Qb6(a)	Ba5	Nbd7	Nxe4	Ba4	Qd8
10	b3(b)	0–0–0	Qg3	Qxe4	g3	0–0
	a5	0–0	Bd4	Bg7	d4	Be7
11	a3	h4	Bh6	0–0	Nb8	Rd1
	Bxd2†	b5	Ne8	0–0	Bxd2†	Nbd7
12	Nxd2	g5	Bg5	Re1	Nxd2	Qg3
	Nbd7(c)	Ne8 =	Ndf6 =	e5(i)	Ne7(j)	Nxe4(m)

(a) Also reasonable is 9 . . . Bxd2† 10 Nxd2 e5 11 Bg2 c5 12 0–0 Nc6 =, Fischer–Petrosian, Candidates Bled 1959.

(b) Intriguing is 10 c3 Bc5 11 Bc1 Nbd7 12 Qe2 e5 13 Nd2 a5 14 Bg2 0–0 ∞. *Comments.*

(c) 13 Bg2 Qc5 14 Qd1 h4 =, Fischer–Benko, Candidates Bled 1959.

(d) 8 . . . h6 9 h4!? Ne5 10 Qg3 Nexg4 11 e5 Bc5 12 Nd1 Qc7 13 f4 turned out badly for Black in Timman–Miles, Amsterdam 1985.

(e) 9 g5 Ng8 10 h4 d4 11 Nb6 Qb6 is pleasant for Black, Suetin–Shamkovich, USSR 1972. Minev suggests 9 a3 Ba5 10 g5. The column is Darga–Gereben, Bordeaux 1964.

(f) 7 Be2 Nbd7 8 Qg3 g6 9 0–0 Bg7 10 Bf4 Qb6 11 Rab1 0–0 =, Smyslov–Botvinnik, World Chp. 1958.

(g) 7 . . . Nbd7 8 g4! Bd6 9 g5 Ng8 10 h4 Ne7 11 h5 Qb6 12 Bh3 0–0–0 13 a4 with the initiative, Fischer–Kagan, Netanya 1968. The column is Fischer–Larsen, Zürich 1959.

(h) 6 d4 dxe4 7 Qe3 e6 8 Nxe4 Nxe4 9 Qxe4 Nd7 10 c3 Nf6 11 Qf3 Be7 12 Bd3 0–0 13 0–0 Qb6 14 Bg5 Rfd8 15 Rfe1 Rd5 =, Ghinda–W. Watson, Thessaloniki 1988.

(i) 13 d3 a5 14 Be3 a4 15 Rad1 Re8 and Black has at least even chances, Kudrin–Christiansen, US Chp. 1983.

(j) 13 h4 0–0–0 =, Unzicker–Pomar, Varna 1962.

(k) Black can accept the gambit now or on the previous move (the same position is reached after 6 . . . dxe4 7 Nxe4 Qxd4 8 Bd3). Declining the gambit is not very good: 7 . . . Bb4

8 e5 Nfd7 9 Qg3 Bf8 10 0–0 Qb6 11 Ne2 Na6 12 c3 c5 13 Re1 cxd4 14 Nxd4 Nac5 15 Bc2 with a big advantage, Ghinda–Herzog, Lucerne 1982.

(l) 9 Nxf6† Qxf6 10 Qg3 threatening Qc7 is to be considered. *Comments.*

(m) 13 Bxe4 g6 14 Bf4 with an initiative worth more than the sacrificed pawn, Korchnoi–Spassky, USSR Chp. 1959.

CARO-KANN DEFENSE

Two Knights' Variation

1 e4 c6 2 Nc3 d5 3 Nf3

	43	44	45	46	47	48
	(Bg4)		Nf6	dxe4		
4	(h3)		e5	Nxe4		
	Bh5		Ne4	Nf6	Nd7	Bg4(l)
5	exd5(a)		Ne2(e)	Nxf6†	Bc4	h3
	cxd5		Bg4	gxf6(h)	Ngf6	Bxf3(m)
6	Bb5†		Nfg1(f)	g3(i)	Neg5	Qxf3
	Nc6		Bxe2	Bg4	e6	e6
7	g4		Bxe2	Bg2	Qe2	c3
	Bg6		e6	Qd7	Nd5(k)	Nf6
8	Ne5		d3	h3	d4	d4
	Rc8	Qd6	Nc5	Bf5	h6	Nxe4
9	d4	d4	Nf3	Nh4	Ne4	Qxe4
	e6	f6	Ncd7	Be6	Be7	Bd6
10	Qe2(b)	Nxg6	0–0	d3	0–0	Qg4
	Bb4(c)	hxg6(d)	c5(g)	Na6(j)	Qc7 ±	Qf6 ±

(a) 5 d4!? e6 (5 . . . dxe4 6 Nxe4 Bxf3 7 Qxf3 Qxd4 8 Be3 Qxb2 9 Bc4!) 6 exd5 cxd5 7 g4 Bg6 8 Ne5 Nc6 9 h4 Nxe5 10 dxe5 Bb4 11 h5 Be4 12 Rh3 d4 13 a3 Ba5 14 b4 dxc3 ∞, Ghinda–Lobron, Lucerne 1982.

(b) It doesn't pay to rush matters: 10 h4 f6 11 Nxg6 hxg6 12 Bd3 f5! 13 Ne2 Rxh4 14 Rg1 Nf6 ∓, Kupreichik–Christiansen, Hastings 1981–82.

(c) 11 h4 Ne7 12 h5 Be4 13 f3 0–0 14 Nxc6 Nxc6, and now White should play 15 Bxc6 Rxc6 16 0–0 Bxc3 17 bxc3 Rxc3 18 Bd2 Rxc2 19 fxe4 dxe4 20 Rfc1! Rb2 21 Rcb1 Rc2 22 Rc1 with equality (Varnusz). Instead, the ambitious 15 Be3?! gets into trouble: 15 . . . Qf6 16 fxe4 Nxd4 17 Bxd4 Qxd4 18 Rd1 Bxc3† 19 bxc3 Qxc3† 20 Kf1 dxe4 21 Qxe4 f5! 22 Qxe6† Kh8 23 Bd3 Qd4 24 gxf5 Rce8 ∓, van der Wiel–Timman, Amsterdam 1986.

(d) 11 Qd3 0–0–0 12 Bxc6 Qxc6 13 Qxg6 e5 14 Qd3 Bb4 15 Bd2 (Keres–Bondarevsky, USSR Chp. 1951), and even with 15 . . . Nh6 it is doubtful that Black has enough play for the pawn.

(e) On 5 Be2 Nxc3 6 dxc3 Black solves all his problems with 6 . . . Bg5.

(f) 6 d4 may be strong since on 6 . . . Bxf3 7 gxf3 the black knight is trapped.

(g) 11 c3 Nc6 =, Estrin–Kopylov, Moscow 1951.

(h) 5 . . . exf6 6 g3 Be7 7 Bg2 0–0 8 0–0 Bg4 9 d4 Nd7 10 c4 ±, Byvshev–Ratner, USSR 1949.

(i) Probably best is 6 d4 transposing to col. 27.

(j) 11 Be3 h5 12 Qd2 Bd5 13 0–0 Bxg2 =. Van der Wiel–Miles, Brussels 1986, continued 14 Kxg2 e6 15 f4 f5 16 Nf3 Bg7 17 c4? (this creates a backward d-pawn; 17 c3 and 18 d4 is a better idea) 17 . . . 0–0–0 18 Rad1 c5 19 h4 Kb8 20 Qe2 Bd4 21 a3 Kb8 22 Bxd4 cxd4 (White no longer has the backward pawn, but he is constricted and his king is insecure) 23 b4 Nc7 24 b5 f6 25 a4 Rhg8 26 Rg1 Rde8 27 Kh2 e5! (this break attacks both the center and the kingside; now 28 fxe5 fxe5 29 Nxe5 Qg7 30 Rde1 Re7 followed by 31 . . . Rge8 would win the knight, so White chooses a slower death) 28 fxe5 fxe5 29 Qf2 Rg4 30 Rde1 Qg7 31 a5 Qf6 32 Rg2 f4! 33 Re2 Rf8 34 Re4 Ne6 35 gxf4 Rxf4 36 Rxf4 Qxf4 37 Rg3 Nc5 38 Qe2 e4 39 dxe4 Nxe4 40 Resigns.

(k) 7 . . . Nb6? (7 . . . h6?? 8 Nxf7) 8 Ne5! Nxc4 9 Qxc4 Qd5 10 Qxd5 exd5 11 Ngxf7 wins a pawn, Nezhmetdinov–Livishin, USSR Chp. 1954. The column is Smyslov–Golombek, Venice 1950.

(l) An old trap is 4 . . . Bf5 5 Ng3 Bg6? 6 h4 h6 7 Ne5 Bh7 8 Qh5 g6 9 Bc4! e6 10 Qe2 with a big advantage.

(m) 5 . . . Bh5 6 Ng3 Bxf3 7 Qxf3 Nf6 8 Bc4 e6 9 0–0 Nbd7 10 Re1 Qc7 11 d4 $\pm$, Zaitsev–Bronstein, USSR 1968.

188

CARO-KANN DEFENSE

Panov–Botvinnik Attack

1 e4 c6 2 d4 d5 3 exd5 cxd5 4 c4 Nf6 5 Nc3 Nc6

	49	50	51	52	53	54
6	Bg5				Nf3	
	Qa5	Be6	Qb6(g)	e6	Bg4!	e6
7	Bd2(a)	g3(d)	cxd5	c5(k)	cxd5	c5(q)
	dxc4(b)	Qa5	Nxd4(h)	Be7	Nxd5	Ne4(r)
8	Bxc4	Bg2	Be3	Nf3(l)	Qb3(n)	Qc2
	e6	Ne4	e5	0–0	Bxf3	f5
9	Nf3	Bxe4	dxe6	Rc1	gxf3	Bb5
	Qd8	dxe4	Bc5	Ne4	e6(o)	Bd7
10	Be3	d5	exf7†	Bxe7	Qxb7	0–0
	Be7	0–0–0	Ke7	Qxe7	Nxd4	Be7
11	0–0	Bd2	Bc4!	Be2	Bb5†	Bxc6
	0–0	Nb4	Rd8(i)	Rd8	Nxb5	bxc6
12	a3	Nxe4(e)	Nf3	0–0	Qc6†	Bf4
	b6	Bf5	Bg4	e5	Ke7	0–0
13	Qd3	Qb1	Bxd4	Nxe5	Qxb5	b4 $\pm$
	Bb7(c)	Qb6(f)	Rxd4(j)	Nxe5(m)	Qd7(p)	

(a) (A) 7 Bxf6 exf6 8 cxd5 Bb4! 9 Qd2 Bxc3 10 bxc3 Qxd5 =, Jansa–Bellon, Cirella di Diamante 1976–77. (B) 7 Qd2 Be6 8 c5 Ne4! 9 Nxe4 dxe4 10 Qxa5 Nxa5 =, Ribli–Torre, Alicante 1983.

(b) 7 . . . Qd8 8 Nf3 e6 9 c5 Be7 10 Bb5 0–0 11 0–0 $\pm$, Kindermann–Goldenberg, Trouville 1982. White has control of the e5 square and a good queenside pawn majority.

(c) 14 Ba2 Rc8 15 Rad1 produces a typical isolated-queen-pawn position where White is more active.

(d) (A) 7 Bxf6 gxf6! 8 Qd2?! (8 c5 Qd7 9 Nge2 0–0–0 ∞) 8 . . . Qa5 9 c5 0–0–0 10 Bb5 Rg8 11 f4 Bh6 12 Qf4 Nb4! gave White problems in Miles–Yusupov, Tunis 1985. (B) 7 Nge2!? dxc4 8 Nf4 Nxd4 9 Nxe6 Nxe6 10 Bxc4! Nxg5 11 Qa4† Nd7 12 0–0–0 a6 13 Rxd7 Qxd7 14 Bb5 axb5 15 Qxa8† Qd8 16 Qxb7 (Velimirović–Cirić, Yugoslavia 1966) is a promising sacrifice, but 8 . . . Qxd4 should be an improvement.

(e) 12 dxe6? Qf5! 13 Kf1 e3 wins (Tal).

(f) 14 Ne2 e6 15 Be3 Qa6 16 0–0 Kb8 with balanced chances, Tal–Hodgson, Sochi 1986.

(g) (A) Suspect is 6 . . . dxc4 7 Bxc4! Qxd4 8 Qxd4 Nxd4 9 0–0–0 e5 10 f4 Bc5 11 fxe5 Ng4 12 Nf3 Nc6 13 Rhe1 $\pm$, Paroulek–Lundkvist, corr. 1970.

(h) A quick disaster was 7 . . . Qxb2? 8 Rc1 Nb4 9 Na4 Qxa2 10 Bc4 Bg4 (10 . . . Qa3 11 Ra1) 11 Nf3 Bxf3 12 gxf3 Resigns, Botvinnik–Spielmann, Moscow 1935.

(i) 12 . . . Qxb2 13 Nge2 Nc2† 14 Qxc2! Qxa1† 15 Bc1 b5 16 Bb3 Bb7 17 0–0 +, Dely–Sallay, Hungary 1964.

(j) 14 Qe2† Kf8 15 Bb3 and although Black has active play, it is not enough to compensate for the pawns, Röthgen–Gelenczy, corr. 1967.

(k) 7 cxd5 exd5 8 Bxf6 Qxf6 9 Nxd5 Qd8 10 Bc4 Be6 11 Qe2? b5! wins. *Comments.*

(l) 8 Bb5 0–0 9 Nf3 Ne4 10 Bxe7 Qxe7 11 Qc2 Ng5 12 Nxg5 Qxg5 13 Bxc6 bxc6 =, Keres–Alekhine, AVRO 1938.

(m) 14 dxe5 Nxc3 15 Rxc3 d4 16 Rc2 Qxe5 =, Liberzon–Zaitsev, USSR Chp. 1969.

(n) 8 Bb5 Rc8 9 h3 Bxf3 10 Qxf3 e6 11 0–0 a6 levels the game, Krause–Nimzowitsch, corr. 1925.

(o) 9 . . . Nb6 10 Be3 e6 11 0–0–0 Be7 12 d5 exd5 13 Nxd5 Nxd5 14 Rxd5 Qc7† 15 Kb1 0–0 16 f4 Nb4 17 Rd4 Nc6 18 Rd1 Bf6 19 Bg2 ±, Anand–Karolyi, Frunze 1987.

(p) 14 Nxd5† Qxd5 15 Qxd5 exd5 16 Be3 Ke6 17 0–0–0 Bb4 18 Kb1 Rhd8 19 Rd3 with a minutely better endgame, A. Sokolov–Spraggett, match 1988.

(q) Note the similarity of this position to the Queen's Gambit, Semi-Tarrasch Defense. 7 a3 and 7 cxd5 Nxd5 8 Bc4 or 8 Bd3 transposes to the Semi-Tarrasch.

(r) Straightforward development also leaves White better: 7 . . . Be7 8 Bb5 0–0 9 0–0 (A) 9 . . . Bd7 10 a3 a6 11 Bd3 with control of e5 and a queenside pawn majority. (B) 9 . . . Ne4 10 Qc2 f5 (or 10 . . . Ng5) 11 Bxc6 bxc6 (Wach–Pfleger, Innsbruck 1989) 12 Bf4 g5 13 Be5 g4 14 Nd2 Ng5 15 b4 Ba6 16 Re1 ±. The column is Vasiukov–Padevsky, Varna 1971.

CARO-KANN DEFENSE

Panov–Botvinnik Attack

1 e4 c6 2 d4 d5 3 exd5 cxd5 4 c4 Nf6 5 Nc3

	55	56	57	58	59	60
	e6			g6		
6	Nf3		...Bb4	cxd5	Qb3	
	Be7(a)		Bb4	Nxd5(n)	Bg7(r)	
7	c5	cxd5(f)	cxd5(i)	Qb3	cxd5	
	0–0(b)	exd5(g)	Nxd5(j)	Nxc3(o)	0–0	
8	Bd3	Bb5†	Qc2(k)	Bc4!	Be2	Nge2
	b6	Bd7(h)	Nc6	e6	Nbd7	Nbd7
9	b4	Bxd7†	Bd3	bxc3	Bf3	g3
	a5	Nbxd7	Nf6(l)	Nc6	Nb6	Nb6
10	Na4	Qb3!	0–0	Nf3	Nge2	Bg2
	Nfd7!	Nb6	h6	Bg7	Bf5	Bf5
11	b5(c)	0–0	Rd1	Ba3	0–0(s)	Nf4
	bxc5	0–0	0–0	Bf8	Qd7	h6
12	dxc5	Re1	a3	0–0(p)	a4	a4
	e5(d)	Re8	Bd6	Na5	Bd3	Qd7(u)
13	c6	Bg5 ±	Ne4	Bb5†	d6	a5
	e4(e)		Nxe4(m)	Bd7(q)	Bc4(t)	Nc8(v)

(a) 6 . . . Nc6 transposes to col. 54.

(b) It is dangerous to start immediate counterplay on the queenside: 7 . . . b6?! 8 b4 a5 9 Na4! Nfd7 10 Bb5 0–0 11 Bf4 with grave difficulties for Black, Euwe–Kramer, 1941.

(c) Karlsson–Mahlin, corr. 1970 took an interesting course: 11 h4 f5 (White was threatening 12 Nxb6 Nxb6 13 Bh7† Kxh7 14 Ng5† with a winning attack, but 11 . . . e5 is worth trying since Black would have 14 . . . Kg8 15 Qh5 Bf5 in this variation) 12 Ng5 Qe8 13 Kf1 axb4 14 Nxe6 Nxc5 15 Naxc5 bxc5 16 Nxf8 c4 ∓.

(d) 12 . . . Nxc5? 13 Nxc5 Bxc5 14 Bxh7†! Kxh7 15 Ng5† Kg6 16 Qc2† ±.

(e) 14 cxd7 Nxd7 15 0–0 exf3 16 Qxf3 Ne5 17 Qg3 Nxd3 18 Qxd3 d4 =, Sokolsky–Simagin, corr. 1964.

(f) 7 Bg5 Nc6 8 c5 transposes to col. 52.

(g) 7 . . . Nxd5 transposes to the Queen's Gambit, Semi-Tarrasch Defense, after 8 Bc4 Nc6 (col. 55) or 8 Bd3 Nc6 (col. 49).

(h) 8 . . . Nc6 9 Ne5 Bd7 10 0–0 0–0 11 Bg5 ±, Hübner–Petrosian, match 1971. The column is Gheorghiu–Herrmann, West Germany 1975.

(i) 7 Bd3 dxc4 8 Bxc4 Qc7 9 Qd3 0–0 10 0–0 b6 11 Nb5 Qd8 12 Bf4 a6 13 Nc3 Bb7 =. *Comments.*

191

(j) 7 . . . exd5 8 Bd3 0–0 9 h3 gives White a nagging little edge. The black bishop on b4 is not well posted.

(k) 8 Bd2 0–0 9 Bd3 Nc6 10 0–0 Nf6 11 Bg5, Djurić–Tarjan, Vrsać 1983, also gives White chances for an advantage.

(l) Risky but playable is J. Speelman's pawn grab 9 . . . Ba5 10 a3 Nxc3 11 bxc3 Nxd4 12 Nxd4 Qxd4 13 Bb5† Ke7 14 0–0 ∞.

(m) 14 Bxe4 Bd7 15 d5 exd5 16 Bxd5 Qf6 17 Bd2 Rac8 18 Bc3 ±, Sveshnikov–Tal, USSR 1984. In the column, interesting is 9 Be2 0–0 10 0–0 Be7 11 Rd1 Qd6 12 Bg5 with a small edge, Benjamin–Miles, US Chp. 1988.

(n) 6 . . . Bg7 allows White to protect d5 more naturally with 7 Bc4 0–0 8 Nge2 Nbd7 9 Nf4 Nb6 10 Bb3 ±.

(o) 7 . . . Nb6 8 d5 Bg7 9 Be3 0–0 10 Rd1 Na6 11 Be2 Qd6 12 Nf3 Nc5 13 Qb5 Nca4 14 Ne4! ±, K. Schulz–Miles, Bad Kissingen 1983.

(p) 12 Bxf8 Kxf8 13 0–0 Kg7 14 Bb5 Bd7 =, Kochiev–Agapov, USSR 1987.

(q) 14 Qa4 Bxa3 15 Bxd7† Qxd7 16 Qxa3 Nc4 17 Qb4 Rc8 18 Ne5 a5! = *Informant*.

(r) 6 . . . dxc4?! 7 Bxc4 e6 8 Nf3 Bg7 9 0–0 0–0 10 Bg5 is unsavory for Black.

(s) 11 Nf4 g5 12 Nfe2 g4 13 Ng3 Bg6 14 Be2 Nbxd5 15 Qxb7 Rb8 16 Qxa7 Nb4 ∞.

(t) 14 Qb4 (Milos–Christiansen, Szirak 1987), and now 14 . . . Qxd6 15 Qxd6 exd6 16 Bxb7 Rab8 17 Bf3 Nbd5 would give Black reasonable play.

(u) 12 . . . a5 13 0–0 g5 14 Nfe2 Bd3 15 Qd1 ±.

(v) 14 Na4! Nd6 15 0–0 g5 16 Nd3 Bh3 17 Ne5 ±, Suba–Dvoirys, Sochi 1983.

CARO-KANN DEFENSE

1 e4 c6 2 d4 d5

	61	62	63	64	65	66
3	exd5 Exchange Variation			f3 Fantasy Variation		Nd2
	cxd5			dxe4 . . . . g6(k)		g6(l)
4	Bd3			fxe4	c3	Ngf3
	Nc6			e5	Bg7	Bg7
5	c3			Nf3	Na3	h3
	Nf6		Qc7(f)	Be6(h)	Nd7	dxe4(m)
6	Bf4(a)		Ne2	Bg5(i)	Be3	Nxe4
	Bg4 . . . . g6(d)		e6	Be7	dxe4	Nf6
7	Qb3	Nf3	Bf4	Bxe7	fxe4	Bd3
	Qd7(b)	Bg7	Bd6	Qxe7	Ngf6	Nxe4
8	Nd2	Nbd2(e)	Bxd6	Nc3	Qf3	Bxe4
	e6	Bf5!	Qxd6	Bg4	0–0	0–0
9	Ngf3	Bxf5	Nd2	Bc4	0–0–0	0–0
	Bxf3	gxf5	Nf6	Nd7	Qa4	Nd7
10	Nxf3	Ne5	f4!	d5	Nh3	Bg5!
	Bd6(c)	Qb6 =	Ng4(g)	Ngf6(j)	b5 =	h6(n)

(a) 6 Nf3 looks more natural, but 6 . . . Bg4 7 0–0 e6 gives Black quick equality.

(b) (A) 7 . . . Qc8 is also good, but the text is more active. (B) 7 . . . Na5 8 Qa4† Bd7 9 Qc2 e6 10 Nf3 Qb6 11 a4!, avoiding the exchange of light-squared bishops secures an edge, Fischer–Petrosian, USSR vs. Rest of the World 1970. This great confrontation continued 11 . . . Rc8 12 Nbd2 Nc6 13 Qb1 Nh5? (White's pieces are more actively placed, but this move only aggravates Black's problem) 14 Be3 h6 15 Ne5 Nf6 16 h3 Bd6 17 0–0 Kf8 (17 . . . 0–0 would place Black's king in serious danger, but the ugly text move is no better) 18 f4! Be8 (18 . . . Nxe5? 19 fxe5 Bxe5 20 a5 wins a piece) 19 Bf2 Qc7 20 Bh4 Ng8 21 f5 Nxe5 22 dxe5 Bxe5 23 fxe6 Bf6 24 exf7 Bxf7 25 Nf3 Bxh4 26 Nxh4 Nf6 27 Ng6† Bxg6 28 Bxg6 Ke7! (Black is lost because his king is caught in the middle, yet Petrosian makes a fight out of it by heading toward a haven on the queenside) 29 Qf5 Kd8 30 Rae1 Qc5† 31 Kh1 Rf8 32 Qe5 (keeping the king in the center; now the end comes quickly) 32 . . . Rc7 33 b4 Qc6 34 c4! dxc4 35 Bf5 Rff7 36 Rd1† Rfd7 (36 . . . Nd7 37 Rfe1 wins) 37 Bxd7 Rxd7 38 Qb8† Ke7 39 Rde1† Resigns.

(c) 11 Bxd6 Qxd6 12 0–0 0–0 13 Rae1 Rab8 14 Ne5 b5 15 a3 a5 16 f4 (16 Bxb5 Na7 wins back the pawn) 16 . . . b4 17 axb4 axb4 =, Benjamin–Christiansen, US Chp. 1981.

(d) 6 . . . e6 7 Nd2 Bd6 8 Bxd6 Qxd6 9 Ngf3 0–0 10 0–0 e5 11 dxe5 Nxe5 12 Nxe5 Qxe5 13 Nf3 ±, Lein–Arnason, Iceland 1985. Black is worse because of his isolated d-pawn.

(e) 8 0–0 Bg4 9 h3 Bxf3 10 Qxf3 Qb6 =, Gusev–Bronstein, Moscow Chp. 1947. The column is Spielmann–Sämisch, Berlin 1920.

(f) Inferior is 5 . . . g6 6 Nf3 Bg4?! 7 Qb3! Bxf3 8 Qxb7 Qc8 9 Qxc8† Rxc8 10 gxf3 Nxd4 11 Be3! Nc6 12 Bb5 ±, Rossolimo–Bronstein, Monte Carlo 1969.

(g) 11 Nf3 f5 12 Qd2 Bd7 13 Ne5 Nf6 14 Qe3 0–0 15 0–0 $\pm$, Meyer–Lein, Berlin 1984.

(h) Risky is 5 . . . exd4?! 6 Bc4 when White has quick play against the f7-square.

(i) Not 6 Nxe5? Qh4†. The older line is 6 c3 Nf6 7 Bd3 Nbd7 8 Qe2 Bd6 9 Nbd2 Qe7 10 0–0 0–0–0 =, Kasparian–Kholmov, USSR Chp. 1949.

(j) 11 h3 Bxf3 12 Qxf3 Nb6 13 Bb3 0–0 14 0–0–0 Rad8 =, Murey–Seirawan, New York 1985.

(k) Also possible is 3 . . . e6 when the position is a French Defense with the non-constructive moves f3 and . . . c6. The column is Vinogradov–Kopylov, USSR 1946.

(l) 3 . . . dxe4 4 Nxe4 transposes to the main variations covered in cols. 1–30. The idea of 3 Nd2 is to have the option to move the c-pawn when Black chooses the closed variation 3 . . . g6.

(m) Black can keep the position closed with the odd-looking 5 . . . Nh6 6 Bd3 0–0 7 0–0 f6! 8 Re1 Nf7, but after 9 c4 Na6 10 Bf1 Nc7 11 b3 White has a more harmonious position, Sax–Garcia Gonzales, Rio de Janeiro 1979.

(n) 11 Be3 c5 (Chandler–Christiansen, Thessaloniki 1984) 12 Qd2! cxd4 13 Bxh6 $\pm$.

CARO-KANN DEFENSE

1 e4 c6

	67	68	69	70	71	72
2	(d4)........c4................................d3					
	(d5)	d5(d)			d5	
3	Nc3	exd5			Nd2	
	g6(a)	cxd5			e5 ....g6(l)	
4	e5(b)	cxd5(e)			Ngf3	Ngf3
	Bg7	Nf6.....................Qxd5			Bd6(k)	Bg7
5	f4	Nc3........Bb5†(h)		Nc3	g3	Be2(m)
	h5	Nxd5	Nbd7	Qd6	Nf6	e5
6	Be3	Nf3	Nc3	d4	Bg2	0–0
	Nh6	Nxc3(f)	a6	Nf6	0–0	Ne7
7	Nf3	bxc3	Qa4	Nge2	0–0	Re1
	Bg4	g6	g6	e6	Re8	0–0
8	Be2	d4(g)	Nf3	g3	Re1	Bf1
	Nd7	Bg7	Bg7	Be7(j)	Nbd7	d4
9	Qd2	Bd3	d4	Bg2	c3	b4
	e6	Nc6	0–0	0–0	dxe4	Na6
10	g3	0–0	Bxd7	0–0	dxe4	a3
	Bf8(c)	0–0 =	Qxd7(i)	Rd8 =	Qc7 =	c5 ±

(a) 3 . . . b5?! 4 a3! simply leaves Black with a queenside weakness.

(b) 4 h3 Bg7 5 Nf3 dxe4 6 Nxe4 transposes to col. 66.

(c) 11 h3 Bxf3 12 Bxf3 Nf5 13 Bf2 and although the bishop pair means little in this position, White's possibility of breaking with g4 makes his game preferable, Arnason–Christiansen, Reykjavik 1986.

(d) 2 . . . e5 3 d4 Bb4† 4 Bd2 Bxd2† 5 Qxd2 d6 6 Nc3 Nf6 7 f4! ± with the initiative in the center, Tal–Nei, Parnu 1971.

(e) 4 d4 transposes to the Panov–Botvinnik Attack, cols. 49–60.

(f) 6 . . . Nc6 7 d4 Bg4 transposes to col. 53.

(g) In A. Sokolov–Karpov, match 1987, White played the original 8 h4!? Bg7 9 h5 Nc6 10 Rb1?! Qc7 11 Ba3 Bf5 12 Rb5 a6 13 Rc5 Qd7 14 Qb3 0–0, but Black's position is to be preferred.

(h) 5 Qa4† Nbd7 6 Nc3 g6 7 d4 Bg7 8 Qb3 0–0 9 Bg5 Nb6 10 Bxf6 Bxf6 =, Larsen–Karpov, Montreal 1979.

(i) 11 Qxd7 Bxd7 12 0–0 Rad8 13 Re1 Rfe8 14 Bg5 Kf8 =, Kindermann–Dückstein, Vienna 1986.

(j) Trying to contest the long white diagonal leads to trouble: 8 . . . Bd7 9 Bf4 Qc6?! 10 d5! exd5 11 Bg2 Be6 12 0–0 Qd7 13 Bg5 Be7 14 Nf4 Nc6 15 Bxf6 Bxf6 16 Ncxd5 ±, A. Rodriguez–Dlugy, Athens 1984. The column is Nunn–Miles, Biel 1986.

(k) 4 . . . Nd7 5 Qe2!? dxe4 6 Nxe4 Be7 7 Bd2 Ngf6 8 Bc3 Nd5 9 Nxe5 Nxc3 10 Nxc3 Nxe5 11 Qxe5 0–0 with good play for the pawn because Black has control of the dark squares, Ljubojević–Christiansen, Szirak 1987. The column is Ljubojević–Karpov, Buenos Aires 1980.

(l) 3 . . . Nd7 4 Ngf3 Qc7 5 exd5! cxd5 6 d4 g6 7 Bd3 Bg7 8 0–0 e6 9 Re1 Ne7 10 Nf1 ±, Fischer–Marović, Zagreb 1970.

(m) White can also continue in the style of the King's Indian Attack with 5 g3 e5 6 Bg2 Ne7 7 0–0, but the unsymmetrical placement of the king's bishop allows White better chances for an advantage. The column is Lobron–Johannesson, Reykjavik 1984.

FRENCH DEFENSE

1 e4 e6

Diagram 29

ALTHOUGH ANALYZED BY THE ITALIAN LUCENA in the fifteenth century, the French Defense was named for the Parisian players who adopted the move 1 . . . e6 in an 1834 correspondence game against London. Every world champion since Steinitz (with the stark exception of Fischer, who stumbled against it as White quite a few times) has employed it, though it was Botvinnik who was instrumental in transforming it into the sharp counterattacking weapon it is today. Many prominent masters are listed among its adherents, as seen from the quoted games and analyses.

It is more a defense than most Black choices: Black blocks the a2–g8 diagonal with his first move and prepares to occupy the light central squares, intending to deal with the dark squares later. Far and away Black's biggest problem in this opening is the queen's bishop, blocked in by Black's first move—many games revolve around this one feature. The tension created by the combat between e4 and d5 usually results in some central concession by one of the players. The choices here run the range from quiet defense to raging gambit play.

Diagram 30

THE CLASSICAL VARIATION, 1 e4 e6 2 d4 d5 3 Nc3 Nf6 4 Bg5 (see diagram) Be7 5 e5 Nfd7 6 Bxe7 Qxe7 (cols. 1–6), was for decades the orthodox approach for Black, but it has taken a back seat to the Winawer Variation. The White plan combining Qd2, 0–0–0, and f4 left White better in the center. However, in the mid-1980s Korchnoi took up this line, winning with sharp queenside play, and now it is White who has been avoiding it, preferring the Steinitz Variation.

THE ALEKHINE–CHATARD ATTACK, 6 h4 (cols. 7–9), remains unsolved. Black may either take the pawn on g5 and suffer through a tenuous equality, or just sidestep the offer with moves like 6 . . . a6, 6 . . . f6, or 6 . . . c5 with unclear play.

THE BURN VARIATION, 4 . . . dxe4 (cols. 10–12), while more solidly structured than the Rubinstein Variation with the earlier 3 . . . dxe4, is one of the quieter lines. White gets a slight advantage in space, which Black can aim to dissipate with . . . c5.

THE MACCUTCHEON VARIATION, 4 . . . Bb4 (cols. 13–18), is the oldest of the sharp French systems. Theory gives no clear advantage to either side, and it does fairly well on its relatively rare appearances.

Diagram 31

THE STEINITZ VARIATION, 4 e5 (cols. 19–24)—see diagram—has seen an outburst of ideas led by the resilience of the line 4 . . . Nfd7 5 f4 c5 6 Nf3 Nc6 7 Be3 Qb6 8 Na4 Qa5† 9 c3 cxd4 10 b4 Nxb4!? (cols. 19–20). But many players are retreating to the quiet of 7 . . . cxd4 8 Nxd4 Bc5 or 8 . . . Nxd4 9 Bxd4 Nb8 and 10 . . . Nc6. 5 Qg4 (col. 23) is Gledhill's sharp variation.

THE RUBINSTEIN VARIATION, 3 . . . dxe4 (cols. 25–30), is generally avoided in these days of active counterplay, since Black gives up the center without provocation. White needs to combine play on both sides of the board to utilize his space advantage.

Diagram 32

THE WINAWER VARIATION, 1 e4 e6 2 d4 d5 3 Nc3 Bb4 (cols. 31–66), is one of the epic lines (see diagram). The battles of bishops vs. knights and space vs. structure has riled the emotions of the greatest combatants. The choices for White are whether to play 4 e5 (cols. 31–58) or one of the lines in cols. 59–66. After 4 e5 c5 5 a3 Bxc3† 6 bxc3 Ne7 White may proceed positionally with 7 Nf3 or 7 a4 or gamble on the French Poisoned Pawn with 7 Qg4 (cols. 31–36). Black can again vary with 6 . . . Qc7 (cols. 43–48), 5 . . . Ba5!? (cols. 49–54), 4 . . . b6 (cols. 55–58), or 4 . . . Qd7.

Diagram 33

THE TARRASCH VARIATION, 3 Nd2 (cols. 67–102)—see diagram—is seen by some as an avoidance of the complications of allowing the pin . . . Bb4 (and possibly weakened pawns) after 3 Nc3. But since 3 Nd2 exerts no pressure on d5, it permits Black to play 3 . . . c5 more freely. After 4 exd5 exd5 (cols. 73–78) Black often ends up with the classic isolated d-pawn but also with free play; Korchnoi has played versions of this for decades. Still, the trials of this position have prompted many players to prefer 4 . . . Qxd5 (cols. 79–84), when the absence of weak pawns makes it hard for White to claim much. 3 . . . Nf6 (cols. 85–92), meanwhile, is also in fashion, e.g. 4 e5 Nfd7 5 f4 c5 6 c3 Nc6 7 Ndf3 Qb6 8 g3 cxd4 9 cxd4 Bb4† 10 Kf2 g5!? and 5 Bd3 c5 6 c3 Nc6 7 Ne2 cxd4 8 cxd4 f6. These lines are

difficult to evaluate at this time. A refined version of 3 . . . c5 is to first play
3 . . . a6 (cols. 93–96), an idea popular a few years ago; the loss of a little
less than a move to prevent the pin on b5 is no worse than the slightly
passive position of a knight on d2 for the same reason. *The Guimard
Variation*, 3 . . . Nc6 (cols. 97–102), is no longer popular.

THE EXCHANGE VARIATION, 3 exd5 exd5 (cols. 103–108), looks drawish,
but its simple formation should not be underestimated; see Tatai–
Korchnoi, note (a).

Diagram 34

THE ADVANCE VARIATION, 3 e5 (cols. 109–114), was the soul of the French
Defense according to Nimzowitsch, who seemed to derive a number of his
theories of chess from its immediately defined pawn structure (see diagram). Dormant for many years, it has considerably advanced in theoretical stature, in good part through its heavy use by Soviet tactician
Y. Sveshnikov.

Other moves include Chigorin's 2 Qe2 (cols. 115–117), which is
unusual but requires consideration; the Two Knights' Variation, 2 Nf3 d5
3 Nc3 (col. 120); and the King's Indian Attack via the French, 2 d3 d5 3
Nd2 (col. 118). This last was Fischer's answer to the French Defense for
many years.

FRENCH DEFENSE
Classical Variation

1 e4 e6 2 d4 d5 3 Nc3 Nf6 4 Bg5 Be7 5 e5 Nfd7 6 Bxe7 Qxe7

	1	2	3	4	5	6
7	Qd2..Qg4.........Bd3.........f4					
	0–0			0–0	0–0	0–0
8	Nce2(a)	.....Nd1	.......f4	Nf3	Nce2	Nf3
	c5	f6	c5	c5	c5(h)	c5
9	c3	f4	Nf3	Bd3	c3	dxc5(j)
	f6	c5	Nc6	f6(f)	f6	Nc6
10	f4	c3	0–0–0	exf6	f4	Bd3
	cxd4	Nc6	f6!?	Rxf6	fxe5	f6
11	cxd4	Nf3	exf6	Qh4	fxe5	exf6
	fxe5	cxd4	Qxf6(d)	Nf8	cxd4	Qxf6
12	fxe5	cxd4	g3	dxc5	Nexd4	g3
	Nc6(b)	fxe5	cxd4	Qxc5	Nxe5!	Nc5
13	Nf3	fxe5	Nxd4	0–0	Bxh7†	0–0!
	Nb6	Rxf3!	Nc5	Nc6	Kxh7	Bd7(k)
14	Ng3	gxf3	Bg2	Rae1	Qh5†	
	Qb4 =	Qh4†(c)	Bd7(e)	Bd7(g)	Kg8(i)	

(a) To protect pawns d4 and e5 with pawns c3 and f4. 8 Nd1 has the same idea.

(b) If 12 ... Qh4† 13 Ng3 Nc6 14 Rd1 = (not 14 Nf3 Rxf3 15 gxf3 Nxd4 ∓).

(c) If 15 Qf2 Nxd4! 16 Ne3 Nxf3† 17 Ke2 Ndxe5 18 Qxh4 Nxh4 19 Rc1 Nc6 ∓, Harmonist–Tarrasch, 1887.

(d) 11 ... Nxf6 12 dxc5 Qxc5 13 g3 ±, Fuderer–Wade, Munich 1954.

(e) Stahlberg–Keres, Kemeri 1937, continued 15 Rhe1 Rac8 16 Nxc6 Rxc6 17 Bxd5 exd5 18 Nxd5 Qh6 19 Ne7† Kh8 20 Nxc6 Bxc6 21 Qa5 ±. In the column, instead of 10 ... f6, direct queenside play may be considered, e.g. 10 ... a6 11 h4 b5 ∞, de Firmian–Oreyev, New York Open 1989.

(f) Black, playing simply, reaches equality. Also good is 9 ... cxd4 10 Bxh7† Kxh7 11 Qh5† Kg8 12 Ng5 Qxg5 13 Qxg5 dxc3 and three minor pieces are worth more than a queen in this position (Alekhine).

(g) 15 Ne5 Nxe5 16 Rxe5 Qb6 ∓, Bernstein–Lasker, Zürich 1934.

(h) 8 ... Qb4 9 c3 Qxb2 10 f4 and Nf3 ± with an attack on Black's king.

(i) 15 Qxe5 Nc6 16 Nxc6 bxc6 ± (Keres). 7 Bd3 was Tarrasch's suggestion.

(j) 9 Qd2 transposes to col. 3.

(k) (A) 14 Qd2 Nd4 15 Nxd4 Qxd4 16 Qf2 Qb4 17 a3 Qb6 18 b4 Nd3 =, or (B) 14 Qd2 Nxd3 15 cxd3 e5 16 Rae1 Bh3! 17 Rf2 d4 18 Ne4 Qf5 =, de Firmian–Chernin, New York Open 1988. (C) 14 Bb5!? Nb4 15 Qd4! Qxd4† 16 Nxd4 Bxb5 17 Ncxb5 a6 18 c3! Nbd3 19 Nc7 gives White an initiative into the endgame, Fernandez Garcia–Vera, Las Palmas 1988.

FRENCH DEFENSE
Classical Variation

1 e4 e6 2 d4 d5 3 Nc3 Nf6 4 Bg5

	7	8	9	10	11	12
	(Be7).............................dxe4 (Burn's Variation)					
5	(e5) (Nfd7)			Nxe4! Be7		
6	h4 (Alekhine-Chatard Attack) Bxg5 ....f6(h)			Bxf6(l) Bxf6........gxf6		
7	hxg5 Qxg5		Qh5†! Kf8(i)	Nf3 Nd7	Nf3(o) f5..........b6	
8	Nh3 Qe7(a)		exf6 Nxf6	Bc4 Be7(m)	Nc3 Bf6	Qd2(s) Nd7
9	Nf4(b) a6(c).......Nc6		Qf3 c5	Qe2 c6	Qd2 c5!	Qh6! Bf8
10	Qg4 g6(d)	Qd2 Nb6	dxc5 b6(j)	0–0–0 Qc7	0–0–0(p) cxd4	Qf4 Bb7
11	0–0–0 Nb6	Nh5 Rg8(f)	h5 h6	Kb1 b6	Nxd4 Nc6(q)	0–0–0 h5
12	Bd3 Nbd7	Bd3 Bd7	Bxf6 Bxf6	h4 h6	Bb5 Bd7	Kb1 Be7
13	Rh6 Nf8	Bxh7 Rh8	Nh3 Nc6	Ng3 Bb7	Nxf5!? exf5	Qg3 Nf8 ±
14	Rdh1 Bd7(e)	Nxg7 Kd8(g)	Nf4 Nd4!(k)	Ne5 Rf8(n)	Qd6! Be5!(r)	

(a) If 8 ... Qh6 9 g3 c6 10 Bd3 g6 11 f4 b6 12 Qe2 followed by 0–0–0 ±, Ryumin–Makaganov, 9th USSR Chp. 1934. Also good is 9 Nb5 Na6 10 f4 (Keres).

(b) 9 Qg4!? may well be a better try; 9 ... f5 10 Qh5† g6 11 Qh6, or 10 ... Qf7 11 Qxf7† Kxf7 12 Ng5† ±, Keres and Euwe.

(c) 9 ... g6?! 10 Bd3 Nf8 11 Nfxd5! led to hot water for Black in Agaichenko–Estrin, USSR 1967.

(d) If 10 ... Kf8 11 Qf3 (threatening 12 Ng6†) 11 ... Kg8 12 Bd3 or 12 Ncxd5 exd5 13 Nxd5 Qd8 14 Bc4 Nf8 15 Nb6 Be6 16 Bxe6 Nxe6 17 Qxb7 ±.

(e) 15 Nh3 Bb5 16 Ng5 Bxd3 17 cxd3 Nbd7 18 Nxh7 0–0–0 =, Roider–Müller, Vienna 1931.

(f) 11 ... Kf8?! is wrong as the king belongs on the queenside. 11 ... f5!? is a try, though.

(g) 15 Ne2! Nc4! (15 ... f6? 16 exf6 Qxf6 17 Qh6 Qxh6 18 Rxh6 Ke7 19 Nf4 ±, Unzicker–Donner, Lenzerheide 1964) 16 Qf4 when White has a slight advantage in a complicated position.

(h) (A) 6 ... h6?! 7 Be3 c5 8 Qg4 Kf8 9 Nf3 Nc6 10 0–0–0 gave White chances for a fast attack in Dubinin–Rabinovich, USSR 1934. (B) Best may be 6 ... a6 7 Qg4 Bxg5 8 hxg5 c5! 9 g6 f5! 10 Qg3 (10 exf6 Nxf6 11 Rxh7 Rf8! led to Black's advantage in Murey–Shilov, USSR 1968) 10 ... h6 11 0–0–0 with central complications, Kliavin–Osnos, USSR 1959.

(i) If 7 ... g6?! 8 exf6! (Alexander) Nxf6 9 Qe2 c5 10 dxc5 Nc6 11 0–0–0 0–0 12 Nh3 ±, Sanguinetti–Benko, Buenos Aires 1954.

(j) If 10 ... Bxc5 11 0–0–0 Nc6 12 Nge2 ±; or 10 ... Nbd7 11 0–0–0 Nxc5 12 Nh3 Bd7 13 Qe3 Rc8 (Alexander–Tylor, Brighton 1938) 14 f3! ± (Fine).

(k) Not 14 ... bxc5 15 Bd3! as in Keres–Stahlberg, Stockholm 1960. After 14 ... Nd4 15 Qd1 bxc5 Keres felt the game would have been ±.

(l) Or 6 Nc3 0–0 7 Nf3 b6 8 Qd2 Bb7 9 Be2 Nbd7 =, Tarrasch–Tartakower, Mor. Ostrava, 1923.

(m) Better is 8 ... 0–0 9 Qe2 Nb6 10 Bb3 Bd7 11 0–0 Qe7 12 Rfe1 ±. *Comments.*

(n) Black is in trouble, e.g. 15 Nxf7 Rxf7 16 Bxe6 Rf8 17 Nf5 Bf6 18 d5 cxd5 19 Bxd5† ±, Short–Nikolaiczuk, Dortmund 1986.

(o) (A) 7 Qd3 b6 8 0–0–0 Bb7 9 Nc3 c6 10 f4 f5 11 g4!? fxg4 12 f5 ±, Bronstein–Chistyakov, Moscow 1978. (B) 7 g3 f5 8 Nc3 Bf6! 9 Nge2 Nc6 10 d5 exd5 11 Nxd5 Bxb2 12 Bg2 0–0 (12 ... Bxa1 13 Qxa1 and Black's dark squares are weak) 13 0–0 Bh8?! (13 ... Be5 is more sensible) 14 Nef4 Ne5 ±, Fischer–Petrosian, match 1971.

(p) 10 Bb5† Ke7 (10 ... Bd7! 11 dxc5 a6 12 Bxd7† Nd7, A. Sokolov) 11 d5 a6 12 Be2 Rg8 (better 12 ... Qd6 or 12 ... e5, Liberzon) 13 0–0–0 Qd6 14 Rhe1 b5 15 Bf1 Bb7 16 Qh6 ±, Peretz–Czerniak, Israel 1976.

(q) Or 11 ... Bxd4 12 Qxd4 Qxd4 13 Rxd4 Bd7 14 Bb5 Bxb5 15 Nxb5 Nc6 =.

(r) 15 Rhe1 Qg5† 16 Kb1 0–0–0 17 Rxe5 Be6! 18 Qc5 Rxd1† 19 Nxd1 Rd8 20 Nc3 Qxg2 21 Re1 Kb8 22 Bxc6 Qxc6 23 Qe5† Qc7 =, Liberzon–Botvinnik, USSR 1966. 14 Qd6 is Fischer's move.

(s) 8 Bc4 Bb7 9 Qe2 c6 10 0–0–0 Qc7 11 Rhe1 Nbd7 12 Kb1 0–0–0 13 Ne4 Bd6 14 Nf3 Bf8 = (Pafnutieff). The column is Botvinnik–Guimard, Groningen 1946.

FRENCH DEFENSE

MacCutcheon Variation

1 e4 e6 2 d4 d5 3 Nc3 Nf6 4 Bg5 Bb4 5 e5 h6

	13	14	15	16	17	18
6	Be3(a) Bd2					
	Ne4	Bxc3(g)				
7	Qg4	Bxc3.......bxc3				
	g6!(b)	Ne4	Ne4			
8	a3!(c)	Ba5(h)	Bd3........Qg4			
	Bxc3†	0–0(i)	Nxd2	Kf8 ....g6		
9	bxc3	Bd3	Qxd2	h4!(l)	Bc1........Bd3!	
	Nxc3!(d)	Nc6	c5	c5(m)	c5	Nxd2
10	Bd3	Bc3	dxc5	Rh3(n)	Bd3	Kxd2
	Nc6	Nxc3	Qc7	Qa5	Nxc3!(r)	c5(u)
11	h4	bxc3	Qe3	Bd3(o)	dxc5	Nf3(v)
	Qe7(e)	f6	0–0	Nxd2	Qa5	Nc6
12	h5	f4	Nf3	Rg3!(p)	Bd2	Rab1(w)
	g5	fxe5	Nd7	g6	Qa4!	cxd4(x)
13	f4	fxe5	0–0	Kxd2	h3	cxd4
	gxf4	Ne7	Nxc5	cxd4	Ne4	Qa5†
14	Qxf4	Nf3	Nd4	Qxd4	Ne2(s)	Ke3!?
	Bd7(f)	c5(j)	Bd7(k)	Nc6(q)	Nc5(t)	b6(y)

(a) Or (A) 6 Bh4 g5 7 Bg3 Ne4 8 Ne2 c5 (8 . . . f5 9 exf6 Qxf6 10 Qd3 Nc6 11 0–0–0 Nxg3 12 Nxg3 Bd7 13 Be2 0–0–0 =, Purdy–Miller, Australia 1955) 9 a3 Bxc3† 10 Nxc3 Qa5 11 Qd3 Nc6 12 dxc5 Bd7 13 0–0–0 Nxc3 14 Qxc3 Qxc3 15 bxc3 Rc8 =, Bernstein–Swiderski, Coburg 1904. (B) 6 Bc1 Ne4 7 Qg4 Kf8 8 a3 Bxc3† 9 bxc3 c5 10 Bd3 Nxc3 11 dxc5 Nc6 12 Bd2 f5! 13 exf6 Qxf6 14 Qf3 Ne4! =, Malich–Fuchs, East Germany 1963. White was unable to gain an advantage.

(b) With 7 . . . Kf8 8 a3 Bxc3† 9 bxc3 c5 10 Bd3 Nd7!? Black has an easier time than with 10 . . . Nxc3 11 dxc5 Nc6 12 Nf3 f5! 13 exf6 Qxf6 with complications.

(c) Not 8 Bd3 Nxc3 9 a3 Na2† 10 Bd2 Bxd2† 11 Kxd2 c5 12 Rxa2 Nc6 ∓.

(d) The standard 9 . . . c5 10 Bd3 Qa5 11 Ne2 cxd4 12 Bxd4 Nc5 13 0–0 Nc6 14 Bxg6! ± falls in with White's plan for a fast attack, Shamkovich–Chistyakov, USSR 1961.

(e) On 11 . . . Ne7 White can just play 12 f3! to save his bishop, as in Kurajica–Dvoretsky, Wijk aan Zee 1976.

(f) In Klovans–Makarichev, USSR 1978, White played 15 Nf3, when after 15 . . . 0–0–0 16 Bf2 Qf8 17 Bh4 Re8 18 0–0 Rg8 Black via a timely . . . Ne7 and . . . Ne4 took over the initiative based on the long diagonal and the g-file. Better was 15 Nh3, and after 15 . . . 0–0–0 16 0–0 Rdg8 17 Qf6! Black's pawns seem the weaker.

(g) 6 . . . Nfd7?! is not in the spirit of the opening, and after 7 Qg4 Bf8, either 8 f4 c5 9 dxc5 Nxc5 10 Nf3 Nc6 11 0–0–0 (Kagan–Chistyakov, USSR 1956), or 8 Nf3 c5 (8 . . . a6 9 b4! ±) 9 Nb5 cxd4 (9 . . . g6 10 Bd3 Rg8 11 c4! ±, Nezhmetdinov–Chistyakov, USSR 1956) 10 c3! dxc3 11 Bxc3 g6 12 0–0–0 ± (Nezhmetdinov) leaves Black completely undeveloped.

(h) 8 Bb4 c5 9 Bxc5 (9 dxc5? Nxf2! ∓) 9 . . . Nxc5 10 dxc5 Nd7 followed by recapture on c5 was the more sober play, as in Spielmann–Nimzowitsch, Göteborg 1920.

(i) 8 . . . b6? 9 Bb4 c5 10 Ba3! cxd4 11 Qxd4 Nc6 12 Bb5 ±.

(j) 15 0–0 Qa5! ∓, Fischer–Petrosian, Curaçao 1962.

(k) Fink–Stoppel, Vienna 1966. Black meets 15 f4 with 15 . . . f5, leaving White with weak pawns.

(l) (A) On 9 Bd3 Nxd2 10 Kxd2 Qg5†! 11 Qxg5 hxg5 Black can play for . . . f6. (B) 9 Bc1 c5 10 Bd3 Nxc3 11 dxc5 Qa5 12 Bd2 Qa4 (12 . . . Qxc5 is also correct) 13 h3 Qg4 14 hxg4 Na4 15 g5 Nxc5! returns the pawn with equality, Klovans–Kiarner, USSR 1968.

(m) 9 . . . f5 10 exf6 Qxf6 11 Nf3 Nc6 12 Qf4 Nxd2 13 Qxd2 e5 14 0–0–0! led to a clear advantage for White in Tringov–Sliwa, Marianské Lázně 1962.

(n) Or 10 Bd3 Nxd2 11 Kxd2 Qa5 (11 . . . c4 12 Be2 Nd7 13 Nf3 b5 14 Qf4 Nb6 15 a3 Na4 16 Rhb1! ±, Fuchs–Barczay, Berlin 1968) 12 Nf3 Nf6 13 Qf4 b6? (13 . . . cxd4 is the only move, to distract White) 14 Ng5! ±, Shabanov–Mnatsakanian, USSR 1971.

(o) 11 Qf4 Nxd2 12 Qxd2 =; 11 Nf3 Nc6 12 Qf4 Bd7 13 g4 Rc8 ∞, Seibold–Keres, corr. 1934.

(p) 12 Kxd2 cxd4 (12 . . . Nc6 13 Nf3?! cxd4 14 Rg3 Qxc3† 15 Ke2 Rg8 16 Rb1 b6 ∓, Jansa–Padevsky, Havana 1963) 13 Rg3 Qxc3† 14 Ke2 Rg8 15 Rb1 b6 16 Kd1 Nd7 17 f4 Nc5 18 Ne2 Nxd3 19 Rxd3 Qc7 ∓ (Ciocaltea).

(q) 15 Qf4 d4 16 Nf3 Qxc3† 17 Ke2 Ne7 (17 . . . Qxa1 18 Qf6 Rg8 19 h5 ±, Maroczy) 18 Qxd4 ±, Sachsenmaier–Keres, corr. 1934.

(r) 10 . . . cxd4?! 11 Ne2 Nc6 (11 . . . Nc5 12 cxd4 Nxd3† 13 cxd3 b6 14 h4 h5 15 Qf3 ±, Bronstein–Goldenov, USSR 1944; 11 . . . Qa5 12 0–0 dxc3 13 Bxe4 dxe4 14 Ng3! Nc6 15 Nxe4 Nxe5 16 Qg3 ±, Boleslavsky–Lisitsin, USSR 1944) 12 Bxe4 dxe4 13 cxd4 Nxd4 14 Qxe4 Nxe2 15 Qxe2 Bd7 16 0–0 with advantage, Liberzon–Faibisovich, USSR 1967.

(s) 14 Bxe4 allows 14 . . . Qd4! followed by 15 . . . Qxe5 with a balanced position, Rantanen–Vooremaa, Tallinn 1979.

(t) 15 Qf3 Qd7 16 0–0 b6 =, Arbakov–Gurevich, USSR 1978.

(u) Now on 10 . . . Qg5†? 11 Qxg5 hxg5 12 g4! leaves Black unable to secure his kingside pawns.

(v) The only other move with any initiative is 11 h4, for example: 11 . . . Nc6 12 Rh3 cxd4 13 cxd4, but after the solid 13 . . . Bd7 Capablanca, against Torre, Moscow 1925, could find nothing better than 14 c3 Qe7 15 Qd1 Na5 16 Qb1 Rc8 17 Ne2 Rc6 =.

(w) 12 Qf4 has been the most popular move, but after 12 . . . cxd4 13 cxd4 Bd7 14 h4 Rc8 15 Qf6 Qa5†! Black creates complications, and after 12 . . . Qa5 13 Rhb1 b6 14 a4 Ba6 15 Bb5 Rc8 16 dxc5 bxc5 17 Bxc6† Rxc6 18 Rb8† Rc8 the game is equal (Fischer).

(x) Barcza mentions 12 . . . c4!?

(y) On 14 . . . Nb4?! 15 Rb2 Qa4 16 Rhb1 a5 17 Ne1! ±, Pilnik–Flores, Mar del Plata 1941, but after the text there is only a slight edge for White.

FRENCH DEFENSE

Steinitz Variation

1 e4 e6 2 d4 d5 3 Nc3 Nf6 4 e5

	19	20	21	22	23	24
	Nfd7..Ne4					
5	f4...Qg4					Nxe4
	c5				c5	dxe4
6	Nf3				Nf3(i)	Bc4
	Nc6				cxd4	a6
7	Be3				Nxd4	a4
	Qb6(a)..................cxd4				Nxe5	b6
8	Na4		Nxd4(d)		Qg3	Nh3
	Qa5		Bc5.........Nxd4		Nbc6	Bb7
9	c3		Qd2	Bxd4	Bb5	Nf4
	cxd4		0–0	Nb8	a6!	Nc6
10	b4		0–0–0	Qd2	Bxc6†	Be3
	Nxb4		Qe7	Nc6	Nxc6	Ne7(j)
11	cxb4		Bb5	0–0–0	Be3	0–0
	Bxb4†		Nxd4(e)	Nxd4	Be7	g6
12	Bd2		Bxd4	Qxd4	Nxc6	Qe2
	Bxd2†		a6	Bd7	bxc6	Nf5
13	Nxd2		Bxd7	f5!	Qxg7	Rfd1
	b6		Bxd7	Qg5†?(g)	Bf6	Bh6
14	Qb3 ....Bd3		Ne2	Kb1	Qh6	a5
	Ba6(b)	Ba6(c)	b6(f)	Qxf5(h)	Rb8	0–0(k)

(a) 7 ... a6 8 a3!? Be7 (8 ... c4?! 9 Ne2 h5 10 Ng5 Ne7 11 Bf2 ∞, Murey–Korchnoi, Beersheba 1984) 9 dxc5 Nxc5 10 b4 Nd7 11 Bd3 ±, Korchnoi–Keller, Switzerland 1984. The text move, . . . Qb6, is sharp also after 7 . . . cxd4 8 Nxd4 (see col. 21) 8 . . . Qb6; e.g. 9 Ncb5 Bc5 10 c3 a6 11 b4 Nxd4 = (Winslow) or 9 Qd2 Qxb2 10 Rb1 Qa3 11 Bb5 Nxd4 12 Bxd4 Bb4 ∞.

(b) 15 Bxa6 Qxa6 16 Nb2 Nc5 17 Qb4 Qd3! 18 Qa4† Nxa4? (18 . . . b5! Yusupov) 19 Nxd3 ±, Timman–Yusupov, Bugojno 1986.

(c) 15 Nb2 Bxd3 16 Nxd3 Nc5 17 Nf2 (17 Nxc5 bxc5 18 0–0 c4 19 f5 exf5 20 Rxf5 d3 ∞) 17 . . . Na4 18 0–0 Nc3 19 Qg4 0–0 20 Nf3 ±, Timman–Korchnoi, Brussels 1987.

(d) If 8 Bxd4!? Bc5 9 Qd2 Nxd4 ∞. Not 8 . . . f6 9 Qe2 fxe5 10 Bxe5 Ndxe5 11 fxe5 Bb4 12 Qd3 Qa5 13 Be2 Bd7 14 0–0 0–0 15 Nb5 ±, Konstantinov–Lerner, Sverdlovsk 1972.

(e) Schranz–Heidenfeld, 9th Corr. Olympiad 1977–78, varied by 11 . . . Bxd4 12 Bxd4 a6 13 Be2 Nxd4 14 Qxd4 f6 15 exf6 Qxf6 16 Bg4! Nb6! 17 Qxf6 Rxf6 18 g3 ±.

(f) 15 Rhf1 Rac8 =, Liberzon–Chistiakov, USSR 1964.

(g) Better 13 ... Qa5. An improvement on move 11 would be 11 ... Qa5 or 11 ... a6.

(h) 15 Bd3! Qg5 16 Rhf1 Be7 17 Nxd5! exd5 (17 ... 0–0? 18 h4! Qxh4 19 Bxh7†! Kh8 20 Rh1 Qxd4 21 Be4† Kg8 22 Nxe7 mate) 18 Qxd5 0–0–0 19 Ba6! bxa6 20 Qa8† Kc7 21 Qxa7† Kc8 22 Qxa6† Kc7 23 Qa7† Kc8 24 Rd6! Qxe5 25 Rb6 Rde8 26 Rd1! Bd6 27 Rb8† Bxb8 28 Qxd7 mate, Hazai–Schmidt, Pula 1975.

(i) 6 Nb5?! cxd4! 7 Nf3 Nc6 8 Nd6† (8 Qg3 Golombek; if 8 Bf4 Bb4† 9 Nd2 Kf8! ∓ Czerniak) 8 ... Bxd6 9 Qxg7 Bxe5 10 Nxe5 Qf6 11 Qxf6 Nxf6 12 Bb5 Bd7 13 Nf3 Ne4! 14 0–0 f6! Bogolyubov–Reti, Mor. Ostrava 1923. The column is Estrin–Lilienthal, Baku 1951.

(j) 10 ... Be7 11 Qg4 g6 ± (11 ... Nxd4 12 Qxg7 Nxc2† 13 Ke2 Rf8 14 Rad1 ±).

(k) 16 Nb2 Nc5 17 Bd3 Bxd3 18 Nxd3 Ne4 19 Ke3! ±, Aseyev–Lputian, USSR 1984.

FRENCH DEFENSE

Rubinstein Variation

1 e4 e6 2 d4 d5 3 Nc3 (or 3 Nd2) 3 ... dxe4 4 Nxe4 Nd7

	25	26	27	28	29	30
5	Nf3				Be3	g3
	Nf6		Be7		Ngf6	Nf6
6	Nxf6†		Bd3		Nxf6†	Nxf6†
	Nxf6		Ngf6		gxf6	Nxf6
7	Bd3(a)	Bg5	Nxf6†		Bc4	Bg2
	c5	c5	Bxf6		c6	Be7
8	dxc5	Bc4(c)	0–0		Nh3	Ne2
	Bxc5	cxd4	c5		Qc7!	0–0
9	Bg5	0–0	c3(f)		Qh5	0–0
	Be7	Be7	0–0		Nb6	c5
10	Qe2	Qe2	Qc2	Qe2	Bb3	c4
	0–0	h6(d)	h6	a6	Bd7	cxd4
11	0–0–0	Bf4	Qe2	Bf4	0–0–0	Qxd4
	Qa5	0–0	cxd4	cxd4	a5	Nd7
12	Kb1	Rad1	cxd4	cxd4	a3	Be3
	Qb6	Bd7	Re8	Nb6	Nd5	Qc7
13	h4	Rxd4	Bf4	Be5	Rhe1	Qc3
	Bd7	Qb6	Nf8	Nd5	a4	Bf6
14	Bxh7†	Qd2!	Be4!	Qe4	Ba2	Bd4
	Nxh7(b)	Bc6(e)	Qb6(g)	g6(h)	b5(i)	e5(j)

(a) 7 Ne5 (Capablanca's move) 7 ... Qd5 =, but not 7 ... Bd6 8 Qf3 ±.

(b) 15 Bxe7 Bb5 16 c4 Re8 17 Bd6 Bc6 18 Be5 Rad8 19 Bc3 Qc5 20 Ne5 f6 21 b4 ±, Spielmann–Petrov, Margate 1938.

(c) 8 Bb5† (Simagin) 8 ... Bd7 9 Bxd7† Qxd7 (A) 10 Qe2 Be7 11 0–0–0 0–0 12 dxc5 Qc7 13 Ne5 Qxc5 14 Bxf6 Bxf6 15 Nd7 Qg5† 16 Kb1 Rfd8 Pachman. (B) 10 Bxf6 gxf6 11 c3 cxd4 12 Nxd4 Bc5 13 Qf3 0–0–0 14 0–0–0 f5! = Kottnauer, but not 14 ... Qe7? 15 Nb3 Bb6 16 g4 ±, Spassky–Petrosian, Moscow 1967.

(d) Also good is 10 ... a6 11 Rad1 Nd7 12 Bxe7 Qxe7 13 Nxd4 0–0 14 Nf5 Qf6 15 Nd6 Ne5 16 Bb3 Ng6 =, Matanović–Barcza, Varna 1962.

(e) 15 Bxh6 Ne4 16 Qf4 gxh6 17 Rxe4 Bxe4 18 Qxe4 Rad8 19 b3 ∞.

(f) 9 ... cxd4 10 cxd4 0–0 11 Qe2 Qa5 12 Bf4 Qh5 13 Rac1 Nb6 14 Be5 Bxe5 15 dxe5 Nd5 16 Rc4 ±.

(g) 15 Rfc1 ±, Shmit–Begun, Latvia 1976.

(h) 15 Bc4 Bg7 16 Bxg7 Kxg7 17 Rac1 Nf6 18 Qe5 Bd7 19 Bb3 Bc6 20 Rc3 Kg8 21 Qf4 Nd5 22 Qh6 Qf6 Draw, Wade–Clarke, British Chp. 1973.

(i) 15 c3 Bd6 16 g3 (better is 16 Bh6) 16 . . . 0–0–0! 17 Qxf7 Rhf8 18 Qh5 (not 18 Qxh7 Rh8 ∓) 18 . . . Be8 19 Qe2 Bd7 20 f4 Rfe8 21 Qh5 Re7 22 Nf2 Bxa3! 23 bxa3 Qd6 24 Kb2 Be8 25 Ne4!? (else 15 . . . Nxc3 is dangerous) 25 . . . Bxh5 26 Nxd6† Rxd6 =.

(j) 15 Be3 Nc5 16 b4! Ne6 17 Rac1 Bd7 18 Qb3 Bc6 19 Nc3 Bxg2 20 Kxg2 Qc6† 21 Nd5 b6 22 Rfd1 ±, Přibyl–Pokorný, Prague 1986.

FRENCH DEFENSE

Winawer (Poisoned Pawn) Variation

**1 e4 e6 2 d4 d5 3 Nc3 Bb4 4 e5 c5 5 a3 Bxc3† 6 bxc3 Ne7 7 Qg4 Qc7(a)
8 Qxg7(b) Rg8 9 Qxh7 cxd4**

	31	32	33	34	35	36
10	Kd1		Ne2			
	Nd7	Nbc6(g)	Nbc6			
11	Nf3(c)	Nf3	f4			
	Nxe5(d)	dxc3	Bd7			
12	Bf4	Bf4!	Qd3			
	Qxc3	Bd7	dxc3			
13	Nxe5	Ng5	Nxc3(i)	Qxc3	Rb1	Ng3
	Qxa1†	Rxg5	a6	Nf5	Nf5	0–0–0
14	Bc1	Bxg5	Rb1(j)	Bd2	Qxc3	Be2
	Rf8	Qxe5	Na5	Qb6!	0–0–0	Nf5
15	Bd3	h4	h4	Rc1	Be3	Nxf5
	Bd7	Rc8	Nf5	Rc8	Be8	exf5
16	Re1(e)	Bd3	Rh3	Qb3	Nd4	0–0
	Nc6	Nd8	0–0–0	Qc7	Nfxd4	d4
17	Nxf7	Re1	h5	Qd3	Bxd4	Rb1
	Rxf7(f)	Qd4(h)	d4!(k)	a6(l)	Nxd4(m)	f6(n)

(a) (A) 7 ... cxd4 8 Qxg7 (8 cxd4 Qc7 9 Kd1 0–0 is equal, Spassky–Korchnoi, match Belgrade 1977–78) 8 ... Rg8 9 Qxh7 Qa5?!, long thought to be inferior because of 10 Rb1 Qxc3† 11 Bd2 Qc7 12 f4 Nbc6 13 Nf3 Bd7 14 Ng5! Rxg5 15 fxg5 Qxe5† 16 Kd1 ±, Alexander–Botvinnik, match 1946, was challenged without success by Timman against Short, Amsterdam 1988: 10 ... Nbc6 11 Nf3 Bd7 12 Rxb7 Qxc3† 13 Kd1 Na5 14 Rb4! ±. 9 ... Qc7, however, just transposes. (B) The dangerous and popular 7 ... 0–0!? is met by two moves: (1) 8 Bd3 Nbc6 (8 ... f5 9 exf6 Rxf6 10 Bg5 Rf7 11 Qh4 ±, J. Arnason–McDonald, Oakham 1988) 9 Qh5 h6 10 Bxh6! (10 g4?! c4 11 Be2 Qa5 12 Bd2 f6! 13 exf6 Rxf6 14 Nf3 Bd7 15 g5 Rf5 16 Qh3 hxg5 17 Nxg5 Rxg5! 18 Bxg5 e5! with a tactical melee, Short–Uhlmann, Thessaloniki 1988) 10 ... gxh6 11 Qxh6 Nf5 12 Bxf5 exf5 13 0–0–0 f4 (13 ... c4 14 Re1 Qe7 15 Re3 f4 16 Qxf4 f5 ∞—Chandler) 14 Nh3 Ne7 15 Ng5 Bf5 16 g4 Be4 17 Rhe1 Qb6 18 e6 Bg6 19 Rd3 Resigns, Maus–Hübner, Lugano 1989 and (2) 8 Nf3 Nbc6 (8 ... f5 9 exf6 Rxf6 10 Bd3!, Winslow) 9 Bd3 f5 10 exf6 Rxf6 11 Bg5 Rf7 12 Bxe7 Rxe7 13 Qh4 h6 14 0–0 c4 15 Bg6 Bd7 16 Rfe1 ±, Hjartarson–Yusupov, Linares 1988.

(b) White can also try to avoid the main line by 8 Bd3 cxd4 9 Ne2 dxc3 10 Qxg7 Rg8 11 Qxh7 Nbc6 12 f4 Bd7 13 0–0 0–0–0 ∞.

(c) 11 Rb1 Nc5 12 Bd3 dxc3 13 Nf3 (Yanofsky–Uhlmann, Havana Olymp. 1966) 13 ... Nxd3! ∞.

(d) 11 ... Nb6 12 Qd3 dxc3 13 Be3 Bd7 14 g3 a6 15 Bd4 Rc8 16 a4 Qa5! 17 Ra3 Bb5 18 Qe3 Nf5 19 Bxb5 axb5 20 Qd3 b4 21 Ra2 Rc4 ∓, N. Store–Larsen Norwegian corr. Chp. 1973.

(e) Or 16 Ke2 Nf5!? (Marić) 17 Nxd7 (17 Nxf7 Rxf7 18 Qg8† Rf8 19 Qg6† Rf7 20 Bxf5?! exf5 21 Re1 0–0–0 ∓) 17 . . . Kxd7 18 Bxf5 exf5 19 Qxf5† Kc6 20 Qf6† Kb5 and the king gets out.

(f) 18 Bg6! 0–0–0 19 Qxf7 (if 19 Bxf7 d3! 20 Bxe6 Bxe6 21 Rxe6 Nd4 ∞) and White is slightly better.

(g) Or 10 . . . dxc3 11 Nf3 Nbc6 transposes.

(h) 18 Ke2 Qg4† 19 Kf1 ±, Scriba–Dahl, corr. 1977. Black must play 11 . . . Nxe5.

(i) Others: (A) 13 h4 Nf5 (13 . . . 0–0–0 14 h5 Nf5 transposes) 14 h5 0–0–0 15 h6 Rg6! 16 h7 Rh8 17 Rb1 (17 Rh3 d4 18 Rb1 Be8 19 Qf3 Qd8 ∓, Bronstein–Uhlmann, Tallin 1977) 17 . . . f6 18 exf6 Be8 19 Qxc3 Rxh7 20 Rxh7 Qxh7 21 Rb3 (Vasiukov–Doroshkevich, USSR 1967) 21 . . . d4! $\overline{\overline{\mp}}$. (B) 13 Be3 Nf5 14 Bf2 (14 Bd4 0–0–0 15 Bxc3 d4! 16 Bd2 f6 17 exf6 e5! ∓, Fichtl–Golz, Dresden 1959) 14 . . . d4 15 Ng3 0–0–0 16 Nxf5 exf5 17 Bh4 Rde8 18 Kf2 Rg4 19 g3?! Rxe5!! 20 fxe5 Nxe5 21 Qd1? (21 Qe2 Pachman) 21 . . . Rxh4! 22 gxh4 Ng4† 23 Ke1 Qf4 24 Qe2 Bb5! 25 Qg2 Qe3† Resigns, Cobo–Ivkov, Havana 1963.

(j) 14 g3 Rc8 15 Ne2 Nf5 16 Bh3 Nce7 17 Nd4 Nxd4 18 Qxd4 Qxc2 = .

(k) 18 Ne4 Bb5 ∓. Black also has (A) 17 . . . Rg4 18 h6 Rh8 ∓, Düball–Uhlmann, Raach 1969. (B) 17 . . . Nc4 18 Rb4 Bc6 19 Ne2 Bb5 20 a4 Qc5 ∞, Hort–Nogueiras, Biel 1988.

(l) 18 Rg1 Nce7 19 g4 Bb5 20 Qh3 Qb6 21 Rg2 Nd4 22 Nxd4 Bxf1 23 Kxf1 Qxd4 24 Qd3 Qa4 and Black stands well, Hartmann–Uhlmann, Budapest 1986.

(m) 18 Qxd4 Qxc2 19 Rb2 Qe4† 20 Qxe4 dxe4 21 Rc2† Kb8 22 Kf2 Rd1 23 g3 Bc6 24 Ke2 Rgd8 $\overline{\overline{\mp}}$, Mork–Agdestein, Steinkier 1986.

(n) 18 exf6 Rgf8 19 Bf3 Rxf6 = , Ivkov–Sofrevski, Yugoslavia 1962.

FRENCH DEFENSE

Winawer Variation

1 e4 e6 2 d4 d5 3 Nc3 Bb4 4 e5 c5 5 a3 Bxc3† 6 bxc3 Ne7

	37	38	39	40	41	42
7	a4		Nf3			
	Qa5		Nbc6		b6	Bd7
8	Qd2	Bd2	Bd3	Be2	a4	a4
	Nbc6	Nbc6	Qa5(g)	Qa5	Ba6	Qa5
9	Nf3	Nf3	0–0	Bd2	Bb5†!?	Qd2
	Bd7	Bd7	c4	cxd4	Bxb5	Nbc6
10	Be2	Bb5(c)	Be2	cxd4	axb5	Bd3
	f6	c4(d)	Qxc3	Qa4	Qd7(j)	f6
11	exf6	0–0	Bd2	Bd3(h)	Qe2	Ba3
	gxf6	f6!(e)	Qb2	b6	c4	cxd4!?
12	dxc5	Re1	Rb1	Qe2	Ba3	cxd4
	0–0–0	f5(f)	Qa3	Nxd4	Qxb5	Qxd2†
13	0–0	Qc1		Nxd4	Ng5	Kxd2
	e5	h6	Ra1 =	Qxd4	Qd7 ∞	Na5
14	c4(a)	h4		0–0		Rhb1
	d4(b)	0–0–0 =		Nc6(i)		Bc6(k)

(a) 14 Qh6 Rdf8 15 c4 d4?! 16 Bd3! f5 17 Nh4 e4 18 Be2 Ne5 19 Rb1 ±, Timman–Nogueiras, Brussels 1988, but 15 . . . Nf5 forces a perpetual.

(b) 15 Qh6 Ng6 (now 15 . . . Nf5 16 Qh5 and White will become active) 16 Nd2! f5 17 Nb3 Qc7 with a complicated position, Bogdanović–Uhlmann, Sarajevo 1965.

(c) A finesse from Robert Byrne; after 10 . . . a6?! 11 Be2 Black's b6 is weak. After the direct 10 Be2 f6! (on 10 . . . c4 the maneuver 11 Ng5! h6 12 Nh3 0–0–0 13 Nf4 develops play on the kingside, Kavalek–Uhlmann, Manila 1976) there are: (A) 11 c4 Qc7 12 exf6 gxf6 13 cxd5 Nxd5 14 c4 Nf4! (14 . . . Nde7 15 Bc3!? 0–0–0 16 d5! exd5 17 Bxf6 Rhg8 18 cxd5 Be6 19 0–0 ±, Kanzler–Fedoruk, USSR 1979) 15 Bxf4 Qxf4 16 d5 Nb4! 17 dxe6 Bxe6 18 0–0 Bd7! favors Black, Spraggett–J. Watson, Columbus 1977; (B) 11 0–0 c4 12 Re1 fxe5 13 dxe5 0–0 14 Bf1 Rf5 15 g3 Raf8 16 Re3 h6 and Black already has the initiative, Pein–Plaskett, Great Britain Chp. 1987; (C) 11 Rb1!? Qc7 12 Bf4 Ng6! 13 Bg3 fxe5! 14 0–0 ∞, Wedberg–Renman, Sweden 1979.

(d) Hemming in the bishop. Others: (A) 10 . . . Qc7 11 0–0 0–0 (11 . . . Na5 12 Bd3! c4 13 Be2 0–0–0 14 Bc1! Kb8 15 Qd2! h6 16 Qf4 and kingside threats coupled with a latent Ba3 gave White a clear plus in Nunn–Farago, Dortmund 1987) 12 Re1 b6 (12 . . . h6 of Byrne–Vaganian, Moscow 1975, should be met by 13 Bc1! and 14 Ba3 ±) 13 Bd3 h6 14 Qc1 c4 15 Bf1 f6 16 g3 rerouting the bishop to g2 with some advantage, Rogers–Nogueiras, Szirak 1986; (B) 10 . . . f6!? 11 exf6 gxf6 12 dxc5 a6 (Hjorth–Garcia Gonzalez, Dubai 1986) 13 Bd3 ±.

(e) (A) 11 . . . Nb8 12 Qb1! Qc7 (Rogers–P. Nikolić, Bor 1986) and now 13 Bc1! and 14 Ba3 ±. (B) 11 . . . 0–0 12 Qb1! again threatening Bc1–a3, Tischbierek–Knaak, Halle 1987. (C)

Even after 11 . . . h6 12 Qe1 Nb8?! White reverted to 13 Qb1! in Wedberg–Hug, Lugano 1988. (D) In Nunn–Hübner, German Bundesliga 1987, Black forced issues with 11 . . . a6 12 Bxc6 Bxc6 attacking a4; after 13 Ng5! h6 14 Qh5 g6 15 Qh3 White had good attacking chances for the pawn on a4.

(f) Another finesse, assuming the rook belongs on f1 to support f4. Now 13 Qb1!? could still be tried, to play Bc1–a3–b4; the column is Garcia Martinez–Vilela, Havana 1986.

(g) 8 . . . Qc7 9 0–0 Bd7 10 a4 c4 11 Be2 f6 12 Re1 Ng6 13 Ba3! fxe5 14 dxe5 Ncxe5 15 Nxe5 Nxe5 16 Qd4! Ng6 17 Bh5 Kf7 18 f4 Rhe8 19 f5 exf5 20 Qxd5† with a complicated position which White went on to win, Fischer–Larsen, match 1971.

(h) (A) 11 c3 Qxd1† 12 Kxd1 Na5 13 Kc2 Bd7 14 a4 0–0 15 Rhb1 Rac8 16 Bb5 Rc7 17 Ne1 = , Pritchett–Garcia Martinez, Dubai 1986; (B) 11 Bc3 b6 12 Qd3 a5 13 Qd2 Ba6 14 Bxa6 Rxa6 15 0–0 0–0 16 Rfe1 Raa8 17 Re3 Rac8 18 h4 Na7! ∓ de Firmian–Garcia Martinez, Dubai 1986.

(i) 15 Rae1! with compensation for the pawn but no more, Ehlvest–Hübner, Belfort 1988.

(j) 10 . . . Qc7 11 0–0 0–0 12 Qd3 h6 13 dxc5 bxc5 14 c4 Nd7 15 cxd5 exd5 16 Re1 ± Tseshkovsky–Vladimirov, USSR 1984.

(k) 15 Bb5?! (better is 15 Ke2 =) 15 . . . Kd7! 16 Bb4 Nc4† 17 Ke2 Ng6 18 Bc3 Rhc8 19 Rb3 Rc7 20 g3 Rac8 ∓, Garcia Gonzales–Knaak, Tunja 1984.

FRENCH DEFENSE
Winawer Variation

1 e4 e6 2 d4 d5 3 Nc3 Bb4 4 e5 c5 5 a3 Bxc3† 6 bxc3 Qc7(a)

	43	44	45	46	47	48
7	Qg4				.Nf3	
	f5(b)		.f6		Nd7	.Ne7
8	Bb5†	Qg3	Nf3?	Qg3	a4	a4
	Kf7(c)	Ne7(e)	c4(h)	Ne7!	Ne7	b6
9	Qh5†	Qxg7	Be2	Bb5†	Be2(k)	Bb5†
	g6	Rg8	Nc6	Bd7	f6	Bd7
10	Qh4	Qxh7	0–0	Bxd7†	exf6	0–0
	Qa5	cxd4	Qf7!	Kxd7!	gxf6	Bxb5
11	Rb1	Kd1!	Qh3	Ne2	c4	axb5
	Qxc3†	Bd7!	Nge7	Nbc6	0–0	a5!
12	Bd2	Qh5†	a4	0–0	0–0	Ng5
	Qxd4	Kd8(f)	Bd7	Rhg8	dxc4	h6
13	f4	Ne2	Ba3	f4	dxc5	Nh3
	Qe4†	dxc3	0–0–0	Na5	Nxc5	Nd7
14	Kf2	Qf3	a5	Be3	Bxc4	Nf4
	Qd4†(d)	Nbc6(g)	h5(i)	h6(j)	Rd8(l)	0–0(m)

(a) The classical Winawer, a very rare line in modern practice.

(b) 7 . . . cxd4? 8 Qxg7 Qxc3† 9 Kd1 Qxa1 10 Qxh8 Kf8 11 Bd3 Nc6 12 Bxh7 Nce7 13 h4 ± .

(c) 8 . . . Nc6 or 8 . . . Kf8 9 Qh5 Qf7 = deserve consideration.

(d) 15 Be3 Qe4 16 Nf3 d4 17 Bd2 Qd5 18 c4! dxc3 19 Bxc3 ±, Lukić–Segi Yugoslavia Chp. 1955.

(e) 8 . . . cxd4 9 cxd4 Ne7 (9 . . . Qxc2?! 10 Bd2 and Rc1 ±) 10 Bd2 g6 11 Bd3 b6 12 Ne2 Ba6 13 Nf4 Qd7 14 Bb4 ±, Hort–T. Petrosian, Kapfenberg 1970.

(f) 12 . . . Ng6 13 Ne2 d3!? 14 cxd3 Ba4†?! (Tal thought 14 . . . Nc6 would give Black real compensation) 15 Ke1 Qxe5? (15 . . . Nd7 16 d4 0–0–0 ± was more prudent) 16 Bg5! Nc6 17 d4 Qc7 18 h4! ± was the historic first game of Tal–Botvinnik, World Chp. 1960.

(g) 15 Qxc3 Nxe5 16 Qxc7† Kxc7 17 Nd4 Ng4 18 Ke1 e5 19 f3! Nf6 (not willing to shred his own central pawns, but now they come under pressure) 20 Nb3 Rac8 21 Bb2 ± (Pachmann).

(h) This was Byrne's improvement over 8 . . . Nc6 9 Qg3 fxe5 10 dxe5 Qf7 =. However, instead of 8 Nf3, better is 8 Bb5† Nc6 and now 9 Nf3 ± (Parma).

(i) 15 Nd2 g5 ∓ Matanović–R. Byrne, Sousse 1967.

(j) 15 dxc5!? Nc4 16 Nd4 g5 =, Karaklajić–Fuchs, Bad Liebenstein 1963.

(k) 9 Bd3 c4 10 Be2 f6! 11 exf6 gxf6 12 0–0 Ng6 13 g3 Nf8 14 Bh6 Rg8 15 Qd2 Bd7 =,
Kuindzhi–Antoshin, Moscow Chp. 1971.

(l) 15 Qe2 Nd5 16 Rh3! Kh8 17 Bb2 ±, Rakić–Lengyel, Belgrade–Budapest 1957.

(m) 15 Nh5 Kh8 16 Qg4 Rg8 =, Ivkov–R. Byrne, Sousse 1967. Watch for transpositions from
cols. 47–48 into col. 40.

FRENCH DEFENSE
Winawer Variation

1 e4 e6 2 d4 d5 3 Nc3 Bb4 4 e5 c5 5 a3 Ba5

	49	50	51	52	53	54
6	b4				Bd2	
	cxd4(a)				Nc6	
7	Qg4(b)..................		Nb5		Nb5	
	Ne7		Bc7		Nxd4	
8	bxa5.......Nb5		f4		Nxd4	
	dxc3	Bc7	Ne7........Bd7		Bxd2†(l)	
9	Qxg7	Qxg7	Nf3	Nf3	Qxd2	
	Rg8	Rg8	Nbc6(i)	Bxb5	cxd4	
10	Qxh7	Qxh7	Bd3	Bxb5†	Nf3	
	Nbc6	a6(f)	a6	Nc6	Ne7	
11	f4	Nxc7†	Nxc7†	0-0	Nxd4	
	Qxa5	Qxc7	Qxc7	Nge7	0-0	
12	Nf3(c)	Ne2	0-0	Bd3	f4	
	Bd7	Bd7(g)	Bd7	a6	Nc6........Bd7	
13	Ng5	Bb2	Bb2	Kh1	0-0-0	h4!?
	Rf8	Nbc6	Qb6	h6	Bd7	a5
14	h4!?(d)	0-0-0	Kh1	Qe2	Be2	g4
	Nd4!?(e)	0-0-0(h)	0-0-0(j)	Qd7(k)	Nxd4 =	Nc6(m)

(a) 6 ... cxb4?! 7 Nb5 Nc6 (7 ... b3† and 7 ... bxa3† are both met by 8 c3 with a dangerous attack) 8 axb4 (8 Bd2!? a6 9 Nd6† Kf8 10 axb4 Bxb4 11 Bxb4 Nxb4 12 Qb1! ±, Napolitano–Endzelins, corr. 1971–72) 8 ... Bxb4† 9 c3 Be7! 10 Bd3! a6 11 Qg4 Kf8 12 Ba3! f5 13 Qf4 Bxa3 14 Rxa3 Nh6 15 Nf3 Nf7 (Liberzon–Khasin, USSR 1960) 16 h4 ± with a kingside attack.

(b) 7 Qxd4? Bc7 8 Nf3 Nc6 9 Bb5 (9 Qg4 Nxe5 10 Qxg7 Nxf3† 11 gxf3 Qf6 12 Bh6 Qe5† and 13 ... Ne7 ∓) 9 ... Ne7 10 Bg5 Bd7 11 Bxc6 Bxc6 12 Qh4 Qd7 13 Rd1 Ng6 14 Qd4 Bb5 ∓.

(c) 12 Rb1 Nd4 13 Nh3 Bd7 14 Ng5 0-0-0 15 Nxf7 Nef5 ∓, or 12 ... Bd7 13 Rxb7 Nd4 14 Qd3 Nef5 15 Nf3 Nxf3† 16 Qxf3, Timman–Vaganian, Montpellier 1985, and now, instead of 16 ... Rc8?, 16 ... Bc6 17 Rb3 Nd4 18 Qxc3 Nxb3 would have given Black a plus.

(d) (A) 14 Be2?! 0-0-0 15 Nxf7 Rxf7 16 Qxf7 Nd4 17 Bd3 Qc5 18 a4 Nef5 ∓. (B) 14 Rb1 0-0-0 15 Bd3!? (Moles; 15 Nxf7 Rxf7! 16 Qxf7 Be8! 17 Qxe6† Bd7 18 Qf6 Bf5 19 Be2 Qc5! ∓, Fichtl–Blatný, Czechoslovakia 1964) 15 ... f6! 16 exf6! Rxf6 17 Nf7 ∞, Dahlem–Crispin, corr. 1984–85.

(e) (A) 14 ... Qa4?! 15 Bd3 Nd4 (15 ... Nb4?! 16 Rb1!) 16 Rb1 Nef5 17 Kd1 ∓, Short–Lputian, Erevan 1984. (B) 14 ... Nd4!? leads to treacherous complications (typical for this line) after 15 Bd3 Ba4 16 g4 (Black was threatening 16 . . . Nef5 17 Kd1 Bxc2† 18 Bxc2 Nxc2 19 Kxc2 Qa4†) 16 . . . 0–0–0 17 Be3 Nec6 18 Nxf7 Rxf7 19 Qxf7 Bxc2 (Stecko).

(f) 10 . . . Bxe5 11 Nf3 Rh8 12 Qd3 Bf6 13 Bf4 Nbc6 (13 . . . Ng6 14 Nc7† Kf8 15 Bg3 e5 16 Nxa8 e4 17 Qb3 exf3 18 0–0–0 ±) 14 Nxc7† Kf8 15 Nxa8 e5 16 b5 ±, Kots–Khasin, USSR 1952.

(g) 12 . . . Qxe5 13 Bb2 Qf6! 14 f4 Nbc6 15 Qd3 Nf5 16 0–0–0 Qh6! =, van de Oudeweetering–Timmer, Holland 1987.

(h) 15 Nxd4 Nxd4 16 Bxd4 Nf5 17 Qh3 Nxd4 18 Rxd4 Qxe5 with compensation.

(i) 9 . . . 0–0 10 Bd3 f6 11 0–0 Bb6 12 Bb2 a6 13 Nbxd4 Nbc6 14 Kh1 f5 15 c4 ±, Zuidema–Enklaar, Holland 1972.

(j) 15 Qd2 f6 16 exf6 gxf6 17 Rae1 Rae8 18 Qf2 ±, Simagin–Chistiakov, USSR 1951.

(k) 15 Bb2 Bb6 16 Rae1 Rc8 17 g4 g6, Chandler–Vaganian, London 1986.

(l) 8 . . . cxd4 9 Bb5† Bd7 10 Bxd7† Kxd7!? ∞.

(m) Better is 14 . . . f6, Kurajica–Vaganian, Sarajevo 1987. The column is Nunn–Hug, Biel 1986.

FRENCH DEFENSE
Winawer Variation
1 e4 e6 2 d4 d5 3 Nc3 Bb4

	55	56	57	58	59	60
4	(e5)..Ne2					
	b6				dxe4	
5	Qg4(a)...........................a3				a3	
	Bf8			Bf8	Be7	
6	Nf3(b)......Bg5.........a4			Nf3	Nxe4	
	Qd7	Qd7	Nc6	Qd7	Nc6(h)......Nbd7	
7	Bb5	f4	Nh3	Bb5!	Be3	N2g3
	c6	Nc6	Qd7	c6	Nf6	Ngf6
8	Be2	0–0–0	Bb5	Ba4	N2c3(i)	Be3
	Ba6	Nge7	a6	Ba6	0–0	Nxe4
9	0–0	Nge2	Bxc6	Ne2	Ng3	Nxe4
	Ne7	Bb7	Qxc6	h5	b6	Nf6
10	Bg5	Ng3(d)	0–0	0–0	Be2	Bd3
	Nf5	h6	a5	Nh6	Bb7	Bd7
11	Nh4	Bxe7	Nf4	Re1	0–0	Nxf6†
	h6(c)	Nxe7(e)	Ba6(f)	Be7(g)	Qd7(j)	Bxf6(k)

(a) (A) 5 Ne2?! Ba6 6 Nf4 Bxf1 7 Kxf1 Qd7 8 h4 Nc6 9 Rh3 0–0–0 10 a3 Bf8 11 a4?! f6 12 a5? fxe5 13 dxe5 Nxa5 ∓, Arseniev–Lutikov, USSR 1960. (B) 5 Bd2 Bf8 6 Nf3 Ne7 7 h4! h5! 8 Bg5 Qd7 9 Bb5 c6 10 Bd3 Ba6 =, van der Wiel–Portisch, Tilburg 1988.

(b) 6 a4?! Nc6 7 h4 Bb7 8 Nb1 Qd7 9 c3 Na5 10 Nd2 c5 11 dxc5 bxc5 12 Ngf3 0–0–0 13 Bd3 f5 14 Qf4 Be7 ∓, Kurajica–Planinć, Yugoslavia 1972.

(c) 12 Nxf5 exf5 13 Qh3 ±, Cherepkov–Mokasian, USSR 1955.

(d) 10 Qh3 Ng6 11 g4 h6 12 Bh4 Nxh4 13 Qxh4 Be7 14 Qh3 ∞.

(e) White stands better, Lputian–Psakhis, Sochi 1985.

(f) 12 Re1 0–0–0 13 Be3 Nh6 14 Qh5 (14 Qd1 Bb4 ∓) 14...b6?! (14...Bb4! 15 Nd3 Bxc3 16 bxc3 Nf5 ∓) 15 Qd1! Nf5 16 Nce2! h5 17 c3 g5 18 Nd3 Qc4 19 Nec1 Be7 20 Qd2 Nxe3 21 Nc5?! Bxc5! (21...bxc5?! 22 b3 Qf1† 23 Rxf1 Nxf1 24 Qc2 cxd4 25 c4 dxc4 26 bxc4 d3 27 Nxd3 Rd4 28 Rxf1 Rhd8! 29 Nb2 Rd2 30 Qb3 Bc5 ∓) 22 b3 Be7 23 bxc4 Nxc4 24 Qc2 g4! 25 Nd3 Rdg8 26 Nb2 Nxb2 27 Qxb2 h4 28 Qc2 Rh5 29 Rab1 Bc4! 30 Re3 Bg5 31 R3 Bh6 32 Rf1 Rf5 33 g3 (33 h3 Rfg5 ∓ or 33 f3 Kb7 34 fxg4 Be3† or 33 Rdd1 h3 34 g3 Rf3 with the plan Rg8–g5–h5 ∓) 33...Rh8 34 Rfd1 Rfh5 35 Qe2 hxg3 36 fxg3 Be3†!! 37 Qxe3 (37 Kh1 Rxh2† 38 Qxh2 Rxh2† 39 Kxh2 Bg5! 40 R3d2 Bxd2 41 Rxd2 Bb3 42 Rf2 Bxa4 43 Rxf7 Bc2 ∓) 37...Rxh2 38 Qg5 Bxd3 39 Rxd3 Rh1† 40 Kf2 R8h2† 41 Ke3 Re1 mate, Chesney–Gulko, Somerset 1986. Notes by Gulko in *Informant* 42.

(g) 12 c3 g6 13 Nf4 Nf5 14 Nh3 Bb5 15 Bc2 c5 16 Bg5 Nc6 17 Bf6 Bxf6 18 exf6 Qd8 19 dxc5 bxc5 20 Nf4 Qxf6 21 Qxd5 Rc8 22 Qxc5 Qa6 23 a4 Nce7 24 Nd5! Resigns, Chandler–Vaganian, Dubai 1986.

(h) 6 ... Nf6 7 Nec3 Nbd7 8 Bf4 Nxe4 9 Nxe4 Nf6 10 Bd3 0–0 11 Nxf6† Bxf6 12 c3 Qd5 13 Qe2 c6 14 0–0 Rfe8 15 Rad1 ±, Lasker–Capablanca, Moscow 1935.

(i) 8 Nxf6† Bxf6 9 Qd2 e5 10 0–0–0 0–0 11 d5 Ne7 12 Ng3 Ng6 =, Lilienthal–Botvinnik, Moscow 1936.

(j) 12 Qd2 Rfd8 13 Rfd1 Qc8 =, Alekhine–Euwe, match 1935.

(k) 12 Be4 Bc6! (Black exchanges his bad bishop for White's good one, but as a result the pawns become weak) 13 Bxc6 bxc6 14 0–0 0–0 15 c3 (better was 15 b4) 15 ... Qd5 16 Qc2 Rfd8 17 Rfd1 a5 18 Bf4 Qd7 (not 18 ... Rd7 19 Be5!) 19 Re1 a4 20 b4 axb3 21 Qxb3 c5! =, Kopec–Pafnutieff, Los Angeles 1985.

FRENCH DEFENSE

Winawer Variation

1 e4 e6 2 d4 d5 3 Nc3 Bb4

	61	62	63	64	65	66
4	(Ne2)......................		Qg4.........	Bd2		
	(dxe4)		Nf6(f)	dxe4(j)		
5	(a3)		Qxg7	Qg4		
	Bxc3†		Rg8	Nf6.........	Qxd4	
6	Nxc3		Qh6	Qxg7	0–0–0	
	Nc6(a)		Rg6(g)	Rg8	h5(m)	
7	Bb5		Qe3	Qh6	Qg3.........	Qh4
	Ne7		c5(h)	Qxd4(k)	Bd6	Be7
8	Bg5(b)		Bd2	0–0–0	Bf4	Bg5
	f6		Ng4	Bf8	h4	Qe5
9	Be3		Qd3	Qh4	Qg4	Nxe4
	0–0		Nc6	Rg4	Qf6	f6
10	Qd2		Nge2	Qh3	Qxf6	Nf3(o)
	f5...........	a6	cxd4	Qxf2	Nxf6	fxg5?!
11	f3	Bxc6(d)	Nxd4	Be2	Bxd6	Nexg5
	Nd5(c)	Nxc6(e)	Nxf2(i)	Rg6(l)	cxd6(n)	Qf6(p)

(a) (A) 6 ... Nf6 7 Bg5 ±. (B) 6 ... f5 7 f3 exf3 8 Qxf3 Qxd4 9 Qg3 Nf6 (9 ... Ne7 10 Be3 Qf6 11 0–0–0 Alekhine) 10 Qxg7 Rg8 (10 ... Qe5† 11 Be2 Rg8 12 Qh6 Rg6 13 Qh4 Bd7 14 Bg5 Bc6 15 0–0–0 ±, Alekhine–Nimzowitsch, Bled 1931) 11 Qxc7 Nc6 12 Bf4 ±.

(b) (A) 8 0–0 0–0 9 Bxc6 Nxc6 10 d5 exd5 11 Qxd5 Nd4 12 Bg5 Qxd5 13 Nxd5 Ne6 ∓, Lasker–Kan, Moscow 1936. (B) 8 Nxe4 0–0 9 c3 e5 =, Tartakower–Bondarevsky, Stockholm 1948.

(c) Alternatives: (A) 11 ... exf3?! 12 gxf3 Nd5 13 Bxc6 Nxe3 14 Qxe3 Qh4† 15 Qf2 Qxf2† 16 Kxf2 bxc6 17 Rhe1 ±, Pilnik–Donner, Beverwijk 1951. (B) 11 ... f4!? 12 Bxf4 exf3 is an untried suggestion from Keres. The column (11 ... Nd5) continued 12 Bxc6 Nxc3 (12 ... bxc6!?) 13 Qxc3 bxc6 14 Bf4 Qd5 15 0–0–0 ±, Pachman–Bondarevsky, Moscow 1947.

(d) 11 Bc4 Nf5! 12 0–0–0 Nd6 13 Ba2 Kh8 14 Bf4 Ne7 15 Bxd6 cxd6 16 Nxe4 d5 ∓, R. Berger–Pafnutieff, San Francisco 1955.

(e) 12 Nxe4 e5 13 dxe5 Qxd2† 14 Kxd2 Nxe5 15 Bf4 Nc4†! =, Gipslis–Casper, Jurmala 1987.

(f) 4 ... e5 5 Qxg7 Qf6 6 Qxf6 Nxf6 7 dxe5 Ne4 8 Nge2 ± (Keres).

(g) Or 6 ... dxe4 7 Ne2 b6! 8 Bg5 Nbd7 9 0–0–0 Bb7 10 d5 Bf8! 11 Qh4 exd5 12 Rxd5! (if 12 Nxd5 Rxg5! 13 Qxg5 Nxd5 14 Rxd5 Qxg5† 15 Rxg5 Bh6 ∓) 12 ... Bxd5 13 Nxd5 Be7 14 Nxf6† Nxf6 15 Nc3 Ng4 ∓, Planinć–Ivkov, Yugoslavia 1970.

(h) 7 ... Ne4 8 Bd3 f5 9 Nge2 c5 10 Bxe4 fxe4 11 Qh3 Nc6 12 Qxh7 ±, Alekhine–Euwe, match 1935.

(i) 12 Kxf2 Bc5 13 Be3 Qf6† $\mp$ (Keres).

(j) 4 ... c5 5 a3 Bxc3 6 Bxc3 Nf6 7 dxc5 Nxe4 8 Bxg7 Rg8 9 Bd4 Nc6 10 Nf3 f6 11 b4 e5 12 Bb2 $\pm$, Boleslavsky–Bronstein, USSR 1950.

(k) 7 ... Nc6 8 0–0–0 Rg6 9 Qh4 Bxc3 10 Bxc3 Qd5 11 b3 Ne7 12 f3 Nd7 13 fxe4 $\pm$, Keres–Botvinnik, 1948.

(l) 12 g4 Qc5 =, Mestrović–Matanović, Yugoslav Chp. 1967.

(m) 6 ... f5 7 Qg3 Bd6 8 Bf4 Bxf4† 9 Qxf4 Qc5 10 f3 Ne7 11 fxe4 0–0 12 Nf3 Nd7 13 exf5 Nxf5 14 Qc4 $\mp$, Keres.

(n) 13 Nxd6† Ke7 $\mp$, Lundquist–Uhlmann, Marianské Lázně 1961.

(o) For a piece White gets an attack. But with 10 ... Qf5! (Timman) and 11 ... Qg4, Black has a clear advantage (Byrne).

(p) Not 11 ... Bxg5† 12 Nxg5 threatening 13 Rd8† and if 12 ... Nc6 13 Bc4 and 14 Rhe1. The game Gulko–Timman, Sombor 1974, continued 12 Bb5†! c6 (12 ... Bd7 13 Qe4! Nc6 14 Rxd7 Kxd7 15 Bxc6† bxc6 16 Ne5† Kc8 17 Ngf7) 13 Bc4 b5 (not 13 ... Nh6 14 Rhe1 Nf5 15 Nxe6!! Nxh4 16 Nc7† Kf8 17 Rd8† Bxd8 18 Re8 mate) 14 Bxb5 e5! 15 Bc4 Bg4 16 Qg3 Nd7 17 Nf7 Nh6! (the point of Black's play—if 18 Rxd7 Nxf7!) 18 Nxh8 Nf5 19 Bf7† Qxf7 20 Nxf7 Nxg3 21 hxg3 Kxf7 22 Rhe1 Bf6 23 Rd6 Rc8 24 Nd2 Ke7 25 Rd3 Bf5 $\mp$.

222

FRENCH DEFENSE

Tarrasch Variation

1 e4 e6 2 d4 d5 3 Nd2 c5

	67	68	69	70	71	72
4	dxc5.......Ngf3					
	Bxc5	Nf6(c) Nc6				
5	Nb3(a)	exd5	Bb5			
	Bb6(b)	Nxd5	Bd6.........dxe4........a6 ....cxd4			
6	exd5	Nb3(d)	e5	Nxe4	exd5	Nxd4
	exd5	cxd4	Bb8	Bd7	axb5(i)	Bd7
7	Nf3	Nbxd4	dxc5	Bg5(h)	dxc6	Nxc6
	Nc6	Be7	Ne7	Qa5†	bxc6	bxc6
8	Bb5	g3!	0–0	Nc3	dxc5	Bd3
	Ne7	0–0	0–0	cxd4	Bxc5	Qc7
9	0–0	Bg2	Re1	Nxd4	0–0(j)	Qe2
	0–0	Bf6(e)	Ng6	Be7	Nf6	Ne7
10	Nfd4	0–0	Bxc6	Qd2	Nb3	Nf3
	a6	Ne7	bxc6	Nf6	Qxd1	Ng6
11	Be2	Bg5 ±	b4(f)	0–0–0 ∞	Rxd1	e5
	Ne5 =		f6(g)		Be7(k)	Rb8(l)

(a) 5 Bd3 Nf6 6 e5 Nfd7 7 Ngf3 Nc6 8 Qe2 Qc7 9 Nb3 Bb6 10 Bf4 f6 ∓, Keres.

(b) 5 ... Nf6 6 Nxc5 Qa5† 7 c3 Qxc5 8 exd5 Qxd5 9 Qxd5 ±, Bronstein–Barcza, Moscow 1962. The column is Haag–Korchnoi, Gyula 1965.

(c) (A) 4 ... a6 *see* 3 ... a6; (B) 4 ... cxd4 5 exd5 Qxd5 *see* 3 exd5 Qxd5 (cols. 79–84). White could try 5 Nxd4 instead.

(d) Or 6 Ne4 cxd4 7 Nxd4 Be7 8 Bb5† Bd7 9 0–0 0–0 10 c4 Nf6 11 Qf3 a6 12 Bxd7 Nbxd7 13 Rd1 ±, Kapengut–Vladimirov, USSR 1974.

(e) After 9 ... Bd7 10 0–0 Nc6 11 Nxc6 Bxc6 12 Ne5 White had a slight but clear advantage, Jansa–Korchnoi, Nice 1974. The column is Parma–Sofrevski, Skopje–Ohrid 1968.

(f) (A) 11 Nb3?! f6 ∞. (B) 11 b3 Qa5 12 Bb2 Qxc5 13 c4 f6 14 Rc1 Qe7 15 exf6 gxf6 16 Nf1 Nf4 ∞, Gufeld–Portisch, Tbilisi 1971.

(g) 12 Bb2 fxe5 13 Nxe5 Nxe5 14 Bxe5 Bxe5 15 Rxe5 Qh4 16 c3 ±, Westerinen–Portisch, Vilnius 1969.

(h) 7 Be3 Qa5† 8 Nc3 cxd4 9 Nxd4 Bb4 10 0–0 Bxc3 11 bxc3 Nge7 12 Rb1 0–0 13 Bd3 Nxd4 14 cxd4 Bc6 15 c4 Rad8 =, Stein–Uhlmann, Moscow 1971. The column is Tal–Gipslis, USSR 1974.

(i) 6 ... Qxd5 7 c4 Qh5 8 Bxc6 bxc6 9 dxc5 Bxc5 10 Ne4 ±.

(j) 9 Qe2 Nf6 10 0–0 Be7 11 Rd1 Qb6 12 c4 0–0 =, Radulov–R. Byrne, Leningrad 1973.

(k) 12 Ne5 Bb7 13 Be3 Nd5 14 Bc5 ±, Tseitlin–Gulko, USSR 1971.

(l) 12 0–0 Be7 13 Re1 c5 14 c4 0–0 =, Tal–Korchnoi, Moscow 1971.

FRENCH DEFENSE

Tarrasch Variation

1 e4 e6 2 d4 d5 3 Nd2 c5 4 exd5 exd5

	73	74	75	76	77	78
5	Ngf3			Bb5†		
	Nc6(a)			Nc6		Bd7
6	Bb5			Qe2†		Qe2†
	Bd6(b)			Qe7(m)	Be7	Be7
7	dxc5		0–0	dxc5	dxc5	dxc5
	Bxc5		cxd4	Qxe2†	Nf6	Nf6
8	0–0		Nb3(j)	Nxe2	Nb3	Nb3(s)
	Ne7		Ne7	Bxc5	0–0	0–0
9	Nb3		Nbxd4	Nb3	Nf3	Be3
	Bb6	Bd6	0–0	Bb6	Ne4	Re8
10	Re1(c)	Re1(f)	Be3(k)	Bd2(n)	Be3	0–0–0
	0–0	0–0	Bg4	Bd7(o)	Re8	a6(t)
11	Be3(d)	Bg5(g)	h3	Bc3	0–0–0(q)	Bxd7
	Bg4	Bg4	Bh5	f6	Nxc5	Nbxd7
12	Bxb6	h3(h)	Qd2	0–0	Bc4	Nh3(u)
	axb6(e)	Bh5(i)	Rc8(l)	Nge7(p)	Nxb3†(r)	Nxc5(v)

(a) Other moves are occasionally played: (A) 5 . . . Nf6 6 Bb5† Bd7 7 Bxd7† (or 7 Qe2† Be7 8 dxc5 0–0 9 Nb3 Re8 10 Be3 Bxc5 11 Nxc5 Qa5† 12 Qd2 Qxb5 13 0–0–0 ±, Karpov–Korchnoi, match 1978) 7 . . . Nbxd7 8 0–0 Be7 9 dxc5 Nxc5 10 Nb3 (or 10 Nd4 0–0 11 Nf5 ±) 10 . . . Nce4 (10 . . . 0–0 11 Nxc5 Bxc5 12 Bg5 ± got uncomfortable in Tal–Benko, Skopje 1972) 11 Nfd4 Qd7 12 Qf3 0–0 13 Nf5 Re8 14 Nxe7†! ±, Keres–Ivkov, Bamberg 1968. (B) 5 . . . a6 transposes into the 3 . . . a6 line. (C) 5 . . . c4 6 b3 (or 6 Be2 and 7 0–0 first with a slight pull) 6 . . . cxb3 7 axb3 Bb4 8 Be2 Ne7 9 0–0 0–0 10 Ba3! Bc3 11 Ra2 Nbc6 12 Nb1 Bb4 13 Ne5! ±, regaining the upper hand in Matulović–Langeweg, Sarajevo 1976.

(b) This leads to one of the classic variations of opening theory. Other moves fall behind: (A) 6 . . . Bd7 7 0–0 Nxd4 8 Nxd4 cxd4 9 Qe2† Be7 10 Nf3 ±, Alekhine–Bartošek, Prague 1943. (B) 6 . . . a6 7 Bxc6† bxc6 8 0–0 Bd6 (or 8 . . . cxd4 9 Re1† Be7 10 Nb3 and 11 Qxd4 pressures dark squares on both sides of the board, Keres–Koberl, Sczawno Zdroj 1950) 9 dxc5 Bxc5 10 Nb3 Bd6 (10 . . . Bb6 11 Be3! Bxe3 12 Re1 ±) 11 Qd4 f6 12 Bf4 again with a bind on the dark squares, Gligorić–Stahlberg, Belgrade 1949. (C) 6 . . . cxd4 7 Qe2† Qe7 8 Nxd4 Qxe2† 9 Kxe2 Bd7 10 N2f3 Nxd4 (10 . . . Nf6 11 Re1 Nxd4 12 Nxd4 0–0–0 13 Bd3 ±) 11 Nxd4 Bc5 12 Rd1 Ne7 13 Be3 Bxd4 14 Bxd7† Kxd7 15 Rxd4 ±, Hübner–Korchnoi, match 1981. (D) 6 . . . Qe7†? 7 Be2! cxd4 8 0–0 Qd8 (8 . . . Qc7 9 Nb3 Bd6 10 Nbxd4 a6 11 c4! catches Black in the center after 11 . . . Nf6? 12 Bg5! ±, Tal–A. Zaitsev, USSR Chp. 1969; better is 9 . . . Nf6 10 Nbxd4 Be7 with a smaller advantage for White) 9 Nb3 Bd6 10 Nbxd4 Nge7 11 b3! 0–0 12 Bb2 Ng6 13 c4 ±, Tal–Holm, Kapfenberg 1970.

(c) Planning to fix the square d4 without weakening his own pawns. Else: (A) 10 c3 (this position often comes out of the 2 c3 e6 variation of the Sicilian) 10 . . . 0–0 11 Nbd4

Nxd4 12 Nxd4 Nf5 leads to swift equality, Krakau–Winslow, Chicago 1976. (B) 10 Be3 Bxe3 11 Bxc6† bxc6 (11 . . . Nxc6 12 Re1!) 12 fxe3 0–0 13 Qd2 Qb6?! (13 . . . a5! is a finesse which equalizes after 14 Qc3 a4 15 Nc5 Qa5 16 Qa3 Ng6; 14 Nc5 a4! 15 Nxa4 Nf5 and 16 . . . Nxe3) 14 Qc3 Rb8 (14 . . . a5 15 Qc5! ±, is a better finesse, Geller–Stahlberg, Copenhagen 1960) 15 Rab1 Re8 16 Rfe1 Ng6 17 Nc5 ± is Botvinnik–Boleslavsky, USSR Chp. 1941.

(d) 11 Bg5 h6! 12 Be3 Bf5 =, Geller–Spassky, match 1968; or 12 Bh4 f6!? followed by 13 . . . Nf5 ∞ (Karpov).

(e) (A) 12 . . . Qxb6 13 Bxc6 Nc6 14 Qxd5 Nb4 15 Qe4 Bxf3 16 gxf3 a5 17 c3! ±, Winslow–Appleberry, Kansas City 1973, or after (B) 12 . . . axb6 13 c3 Qd6 14 Be2 Ng6 15 h3 Be6 16 Bf1 Nf4 17 Qd2 h6 18 Qe3 Bf5 19 Nfd4! Bd7 20 Ne2! White still holds a positional advantage, Beliavsky–Vaganian, USSR 1974.

(f) (A) 10 Nbd4 transposes to the next column. (B) 10 Bxc6† bxc6 (10 . . . Nxc6?! 11 Re1 Be7 12 Nfd4 (or 12 Bg5 ±) 12 . . . 0–0 13 Bf4 ±, Averbakh–Botvinnik, USSR Chp. 1951) 11 Qd4 0–0 12 Bf4 Nf5! 13 Qd2 (13 Qa4 c5!) 13 . . . Qb6! (13 . . . Be6?!, Kir. Georgiev–Gulko, Saint John 1988, and now 14 Bxd6! Qxd6 15 Qc3 would be somewhat better for White) 14 Nfd4 (Stean–Vaganian, Hastings 1977–78) 14 . . . Rd8! ∞. (C) 10 Bg5 0–0 11 Bh4?! (11 Re1 transposes to the main line) 11 . . . Qb6! (11 . . . Bg4 12 Re1 was played for a while before the queen move was found) 12 Bd3 a5 13 a4 Nf5! 14 Bg5!? (14 Bxf5 Bxf5 ∓, 14 Bg3? Bxg3 15 hxg3 Nxg3) 14 . . . h6 15 Bd2 Be6 =, Rozentalis–Psakhis, Sebastopol 1986.

(g) (A) 11 c3 Bg4 12 Be2 Re8 13 Nfd4 Bxe2 14 Rxe2 Ne5 15 Bg5 Qd7 16 Qc2 Neg6 17 Rae1 Qg4 18 Qf5 Nf3† 19 Qxf3 Rxe2 20 Rxe2 Qxg5 21 g3 Rd8 22 Kf1 Be5 23 Nf5 ±, Ljubojević–Hjartarson, Reykjavik 1987. (B) 11 Bd3!? is the latest idea, e.g. 11 . . . h6 (not 11 . . . Bg4? 12 Bxh7†) 12 h3 Nf5 (12 . . . Bc7 met with the blow 13 Be3 Re8 14 Qd2 Qd6 15 Qc3! Nf5? 16 Bxh6! ±, Kruppa–Bareyev, Irkutsk 1986) 13 c3 Qf6 (13 . . . Bc7 14 Bc2 Qd6 15 Qd3 g6 16 Qd2!? [16 g4 Bb6! 17 Kg2 Bxf2! ∞, Yudashin–Moskalenko, Norilsk 1987, could have blown up in White's face] 16 . . . h5 17 Bxf5 Bxf5 18 Qh6 [Smagin–B. Lalić, Sochi 1987] and now 18 . . . Be4 19 Nbd2 f5! would have been unclear, according to Smagin) 14 Bc2 Rd8 15 Qd3 g6 16 Qd2! Bf8 17 Nh2! Nh4 (17 . . . h5 18 Nf3) 18 Qe2! Bf5 19 Ng4 Bxg4 20 Qxg4 d4 21 cxd4 Nxd4 22 Be4! ±, Smagin–Uhlmann, Berlin 1988.

(h) (A) 12 Bh4 a6! (an improvement over 12 . . . Qc7, 12 . . . Re8, 12 . . . Rc8, 12 . . . h6 and 12 . . . a5, all tried previously!) 13 Bd3 h6 14 Bg3 Re8 developed smoothly in Aseyev–Epishin, Sebastopol 1986. (B) 12 Be2 Re8 13 c3 a6 equalized in Khalifman–Uhlmann, Plovdiv 1986.

(i) Now 13 Bxc6 bxc6 14 Nbd4 Rc8 15 c4 Re8 (15 . . . h6 16 Bxe7! Bxe7 17 g4 ±, Peters–Ervin, Lone Pine 1978) 16 cxd5 cxd5 (Ornstein–Unzicker, Buenos Aires 1978) 17 Qa4 ± (Unzicker).

(j) (A) 8 Nxd4 Bxh2†! 9 Kxh2 Qh4† 10 Kg1 Qxd4 =, Geller–Ivkov, USSR–Yugoslavia 1969. (B) 8 Re1†!? Ne7 9 Nxd4 0–0 10 N2b3 Qc7 11 g3!? ∞, Zapata–Agdestein, Thessaloniki 1984.

(k) (A) 10 h3 Nxd4! 11 Qxd4 Bf5 12 c3 Be4 13 Ng5 Nf5 14 Qd1 Qf6! =, Tukmakov–Uhlmann, Hastings 1972–73. (B) 10 c3 Bg4 11 Qa4 was popular for a while, but both (1) 11 . . . Bh5 12 Bd3 h6 13 Be3 a6 =, Karpov–Korchnoi 10th match game, 1974, and (2) 11 . . . Qd7 12 Be3 a6 13 Be2 Nxd4 14 Qxd4 Nc6 =, Karpov–Korchnoi, 16th match game, 1974, were quite equal. (C) 10 Bg5 f6 11 Be3 Ne5 led to intense complications in Geller–Uhlmann, Amsterdam 1970.

(l) 13 Rfe1 (13 c3 Bb8 14 Bf4 ±) 13 . . . a6 14 Be2 Bg6 15 c3 Be4 16 Rad1 Bb8 17 Bf4 Bxf4 18 Qxf4 ±, Marjanović–Gulko, Marseilles 1986.

(m) The best; if 6 . . . Be6 7 Ngf3 Qb6 (7 . . . Be7 8 0–0 Nf6 9 Re1 0–0 10 Bxc6 and 11 Ng5 ±, Iglicky–Verlinsky, USSR 1937) 8 0–0 ±.

225

(n) 10 a4 Ne7 11 a5 Bc7 12 Bf4 $\pm$, Szabo–Barcza, Stockholm 1952.

(o) 10 . . . Ne7 11 Bb4 $\pm$, Euwe–Botvinnik, match 1948.

(p) 13 Bd4 $\pm$ (Keres).

(q) 11 0–0 Nc5 12 Qd1 Ne4 13 Nbd4 Qc7 =, Gerstenfeld–Boleslavsky, USSR 1940.

(r) 13 Bxb3 Be6 =, Florian–Katětov, Prague 1943.

(s) 8 Ngf3 0–0 9 0–0 Bxc5 10 Nb3 Bb6 11 c3 Bg4 12 Qd3 Qd6 13 Nbd4 Ne4 $\overline{\mp}$, Fridstein–Petrosian, USSR 1951.

(t) 10 . . . a5 11 a4 Na6 12 Bxd7 Qxd7 13 Qb5 Qxb5 14 axb5 Nc7 15 c6 bxc6 16 bxc6 a4 17 Nd4 a3 18 bxa3 Ne4 with compensation, Bohnisch–Fuchs, East Germany 1966.

(u) 12 Qf3 a5 13 a4 Qc7 =, Rabar–Matulović, Yugoslavia 1957.

(v) 13 Bxc5 Bxc5 14 Qf3 Ba7 15 Nf4 =, Kuzmin–Korchnoi, USSR 1973.

FRENCH DEFENSE

Tarrasch Variation

**1 e4 e6 2 d4 d5 3 Nd2 c5 4 exd5 Qxd5 5 Ngf3
cxd4(a) 6 Bc4 Qd6(b) 7 0–0 Nc6 8 Nb3 Nf6(c)**

	79	80	81	82	83	84
9	Nbxd4				Re1	
	Nxd4				Bd7	Be7
10	Qxd4	Nxd4			g3!?	Nbxd4
	Qxd4	a6	Bd7		Be7	Nxd4
11	Nxd4	b3	b3	Bb3	Bf4	Nxd4
	Bd7(d)	Qc7	a6	Qc7	Qb4	0–0
12	Be2(e)	Bb2	Bb2	Qf3	Qd3	b3
	Bc5	Bd6	Be7	0–0–0(i)	Rc8	e5(l)
13	Nb3	h3	Qe2		a4!	Nf3(m)
	Bb6	0–0	0–0		0–0	Qxd1(n)
14	a4!	Re1	Rad1		a5!(j)	Rxd1
	a6(f)	b5(g)	Qc5(h)		Bd8(k)	e4(o)

(a) 5 ... Nf6 6 Bc4 Qc6 7 a4 (7 ... a6 8 0–0! ±) 7 ... Qc7 8 0–0 cxd4 9 Nxd4 Bd7 10 Qe2 Nc6 11 N2f3 ±, U. Andersson–Petrosian, Wijk aan Zee 1971.

(b) (A) 6 ... Qc5? 7 Qe2 Nc6 8 Nb3 Qb6 9 0–0 Nge7 ±, Beliavsky–P. Nikolić, Wijk aan Zee 1984. (B) 6 ... Qd8 7 0–0 Nc6 8 Nb3 Nf6 9 Qe2 Be7 10 Rd1 0–0 11 Nbd4 ±, Keres–Eliskases, Noordwijk 1938.

(c) 8 ... e5? 9 Ng5 Nh6 10 f4 ±.

(d) 11 ... a6 12 Be2 Bd7 (12 ... e5 13 Nb3 Bf5 14 c3 0–0–0 15 Bg5 Be7 16 Rfe1 ±) 13 Bf4 Nd5 14 Bg3 Bc5 15 Rfd1 Rc8 16 c3? (better is 16 Nf5! Bf8 17 c4 Nb6 18 Nd6†! Bxd6 19 Rxd6 ⩲) 16 ... Ne7 17 Bf3 Bxd4 18 Rxd4 Bc6 =, van der Wiel–Chernin, Wijk aan Zee 1986.

(e) 12 Bf4 Rc8 13 Be2 (13 Bb3 Bc5 =) 13 ... Nd5 14 Bg3 Bc5 15 Nb3 Bb6 16 c4 Ne7 ∞.

(f) 15 Bf3 0–0–0 16 Re1 ±, van der Wiel–U. Andersson, Reggio Emilia 1986–87.

(g) 15 Bf1?! Rd8! 16 Qe2 Bb7 ∓, Lobron–T. Petrosian, Plovdiv 1983. In the column, also good is 11 c3 Qc7 12 Qe2 Bd6 13 h3 0–0 14 Rd1 b5 15 Bd3 Bb7 16 a4! (A. Sokolov).

(h) 15 a4 Rad8 16 Nf3 Bc6 17 Ne5 Bd5 18 Bd3 a5? (better is 18 ... Qc7, ⩲) 19 Bd4! Qb4 20 c3! ±, P. Popović–Short, Dubai 1986.

(i) 13 Bg5?! e5? (better is 13 ... Qe5 14 Qf4 =).

(j) 14 Bd2?! Qb6 15 Nbxd4 Nxd4 16 Nxd4 Rfd8 17 Bc3?! (better is 17 c3) 17 ... Bc5 ∓, Ljubojević–Nogueiras, Reggio Emilia 1985–86.

(k) Not 14 ... Nb8 15 Ne5 Ng4 16 Nxd7 Nxd7 17 Rxe6! ±, or 14 ... e5 15 Bxe5 Bg4 16 Nfd2 ±. After 14 ... Bd8 (freeing e7 for the queen) 15 Bd2 Qd6 16 Nbxd4 Nxd4 17 Nxd4 ⩲ (Nogueiras).

(l) 12 ... Rd8 accedes to the usual slightly passive position: 13 Bb2 Bd7 14 Qe2.

(m) 13 Nb5 Qxd1 14 Rxd1 Bf5 15 c3 Rfd8 =, Ftáčník.

(n) 13 ... e4 might be more accurate, keeping control of e5. Then 14 Nd4 Ng4 15 g3 Qf6 and 16 ... Rd8 puts pressure on White, while 14 Qxd6 Bxd6 15 Nd4 (15 Ng5 Be5 and then 16 ... Bf5) 15 ... a6 prepares ... b5 and ... Bb7 with the better central control.

(o) 15 Ne5 Ng4 16 Nxg4 Bxg4 17 Re1 ±, Ljubojević–Hübner, Tilburg 1986.

FRENCH DEFENSE

Tarrasch Variation

1 e4 e6 2 d4 d5 3 Nd2 Nf6 4 e5 Nfd7 5 Bd3 c5 6 c3

	85	86	87	88	89	90
	b6 .... Nc6					
7	Ne2(a)	Ngf3 .... Ne2				
	Ba6	Qb6	f6(i) cxd4			
8	Bxa6	0–0	Nf4	cxd4		
	Nxa6	cxd4(e)	Qe7	Qb6 .... f6		
9	0–0	cxd4	exf6	Nf3	Nf4 .... exf6	
	Nc7(b)	Nxd4	Qxf6(j)	f6	Nxd4(s)	Nxf6
10	f4(c)	Nxd4	Nf3	exf6(n)	Qh5†	0–0
	f5	Qxd4	cxd4(k)	Nxf6	Ke7	Bd6
11	exf6	Nf3	0–0!	0–0	exf6†	Nf3(v)
	Nxf6	Qb6	Ndxe5(l)	Bd6	Nxf6	Qc7
12	Ng3	Qa4	Nxe5	Nc3(o)	Ng6†	Nc3(w)
	Bd6	Qb4	Nxe5	0–0	hxg6	a6
13	Nf3	Qc2	Bb5†	Be3(p)	Qxh8	Bg5
	0–0	Qc5(f)	Nc6	Bd7	Kf7(t)	0–0
14	Ne5	Qe2(g)	Re1	a3(q)	0–0	Bh4
	Qe8(d)	Be7(h)	Be7(m)	Qd8(r)	e5(u)	Nh5(x)

(a) (A) 7 Qa4 a5! and 8 ... Ba6 $\overline{\overline{\mp}}$, Keres–Mikenas, USSR 1940. (B) 7 Qe2 cxd4 8 cxd4 Nc6 9 Ndf3 Nb4 $\overline{\overline{\mp}}$, Marić–Ugrinović, Yugoslavia 1959. (C) 7 Nh3 Ba6 8 Bxa6 Nxa6 9 0–0 b5 10 Qg4 Qb6 11 Nf3 h6 12 Nf4 c4 13 h4 0–0–0 14 h5 $\pm$, Zapata–Short, Wijk aan Zee 1987. (D) 7 Qg4 Ba6 8 Bxa6 Nxa6 9 Ne2 b5 10 Nf4 Qb6 11 Nf3 will transpose to 7 Ne2 above.

(b) 9 ... b5!? 10 f4 g6 11 Nf3 Be7 12 g4 h5 13 h3 Qb6 14 Kg2 b4! with strong counterplay, Malisauskas–Shabalov, Vilnius 1988.

(c) 10 Nf4 b5 11 Re1 c4 12 b3 Nb6!? 13 a4! (Stoica–Miralles, Lucerne 1985); now 13 ... a6!? was unclear (Miralles).

(d) 15 a4 (or 15 Qe2 cxd4 16 cxd4 Qb5 17 Qe3 $\pm$, Nićevski–Yoffie, Skopje 1969) 15 ... cxd4 16 cxd4 b5 17 b3 $\pm$, Kavalek–Mednis, US Chp. 1978.

(e) 8 ... Be7!? 9 Re1 g5! was Chernin's novelty against Plaskett, Jarvenpaa 1985; after 10 dxc5?! (better was 10 Nf1 g4 11 dxc5 Bxc5 12 Nd4 with compensation—Korzubov and Shereshevsky) 10 ... Bxc4 11 Qe2 g4 12 Nd4 Ndxe5 $\pm$.

(f) (A) 13 ... h6 14 Bd2 Qb6 15 Rac1 Be7 16 Qa4! (preventing castling) $\pm$, Korchnoi–Udovčić, Leningrad 1967. (B) 13 ... Nc5!? 14 Bd2 (on 14 Bxh7 g6 15 Bxg6 fxg6 16 Qxg6† Black has 16 ... Kd7) 14 ... Qa4 15 b3 Qd7 16 Be2 Be7 17 Be3 b6 18 b4 Na6 19 a3 Bb7 20 Nd4 with full compensation, Estrin–Bergdahl, corr. 1977.

(g) 14 Bxh7 recovers the pawn but is not in the spirit of the opening; after 14 ... b6! 15 Qb1 Ba6 16 Rd1 (Tseitlin–Bukhman, USSR 1972) 16 ... Qb4 is equal. 14 Qb1!?, on the other hand, is worth consideration.

229

(h) 15 Bd2! 0–0 16 Rac1 Qb6 17 Bb1 f5 18 exf6 Nxf6 19 Bc3 White combines threats on the kingside with a central bind, Nunn–Mednis, Budapest 1978.

(i) After 7 . . . Qb6 8 Nf3 f6 (8 . . . cxd4 9 cxd4 is the next column) 9 exf6 Nxf6 10 0–0 Bd6 11 dxc5 Bxc5 12 Ned4 ± , Bolbochan–Wade, Trenčanské Teplice 1949. White avoids the weak d-pawn.

(j) 9 . . . Nxf6 10 Nf3 e5 11 dxe5 Nxe5 12 0–0 Nxf3† 13 Qxf3 Bg4 14 Bb5†! ± , Euwe–Kramer, match 1940.

(k) 10 . . . Bd6 11 Nh5 Qe7 12 Qc2! g6 13 dxc5 Bxc5 14 Bg5 Qf7 15 Nf4 ± , Stoliar–Shagalovich, USSR 1955.

(l) (A) 11 . . . dxc3 12 Nxe6! cxb2 13 Bxb2 Qxb2 14 Re1 with a strong attack for the piece. (B) 11 . . . Nc5 12 Re1 threatens the whole center.

(m) 15 cxd4 0–0 16 Be3 ⩲ , Keres.

(n) (A) 10 Nc3?! fxe5 11 dxe5 g6 (11 . . . Ndxe5? 12 Nxe5 Nxe5 13 Qh5† Nf7 14 Bb5† Ke7 is very good for White, but perhaps 11 . . . Be7!?) 12 Be3!? Qa5?! (12 . . . Qxb2!? 13 Nb5 Bb4† 14 Kf1 0–0! 15 Rb1 Qxa2 16 Nc7 ∞) 13 Bd2 Ndxe5 14 Nxe5 Nxe5 15 Bb5† Bd7! 16 Qe2! with a dangerous attack for the pawn, Shamkovich–J. Watson, US Open 1976. (B) 10 0–0?! is a dubious gambit line: 10 . . . fxe5 11 fxe5 Ndxe5 12 Nxe5 Nxe5 13 Nf4, when Minić recommends 13 . . . g6!

(o) (A) 12 Bf4 Bxf4 13 Nxf4 Qxb2! 14 Rb1 Qxa2 15 Ng5 0–0 16 Ra1 Qb2 17 Rb1 = . (B) The latest attempt is also one of the oldest: 12 b3!? 0–0 (12 . . . e5!? 13 dxe5 Nxe5 14 Nxe5 Bxe5 threatens both . . . Bxa1 and . . . Bxh2†!) 13 Bb2 Bd7 14 Ng3 Kh8 15 Kh1! with the idea 16 Ne5 and 17 f4 ± , Serper–Martin, Baguio City 1987.

(p) 13 Bg5 Bd7 14 Re1 Ng4! 15 Bh4 Nh6 16 Bg3 Be7! (16 . . . Bxg3?! 17 hxg3 just lets White stabilize his control of the dark squares) 17 Na4 Qa5 18 a3 Rxf3! 19 gxf3 Nxd4 20 Nc3 Bf6 with compensation, Keres–Bronstein, Moscow 1956.

(q) 14 Re1 Kh8!? (As always, 14 . . . Qxb2! 15 Nb5! threatens the bishop as well as 16 Rb1 Qxa2 17 Ra1 Qb2 18 Ra4 trapping the queen) 15 a3?! (Tal mentions 15 a3!? and 15 Rc1!?) 15 . . . Be8! 16 Na4?! (16 Nxc6 =) 16 . . . Qa5 17 Bd2 Qc7 18 Rc1 Bh5! 19 f3 Nd7 20 Nxd7 Bxh2†!? (20 . . . Qxd7 would be slightly better for Black, but instead he tries to play like his famous opponent) 21 Kh1 (Tal–Wiedenkeller, European Team Chp. 1986); now 21 . . . Qg3! (instead of 21 . . . Bg3? 22 Re5! ±) 22 Nxf8 Nxd4! 23 Be2 Rxf8 was very dangerous.

(r) On 14 . . . Be8 15 Ng5!? Ne7! indirectly covers e6; now, instead of 16 h3, as in R. Bernard–Wl. Schmidt, Poznan 1987, Schmidt prefers 16 g3, with a slight advantage. After 14 . . . Qd8 15 Re1 (15 b4 e5?—better 15 . . . Rc8—16 Nxd5! Nxd5 17 Bc4 Be6 18 Ng5 ± , Grunfeld–Watson, Gausdal 1980) 15 . . . Rc8 16 h3, the immediate 16 . . . Qe8!? is better than 16 . . . Kh8 17 Rc1 Qe7 18 Rc2 a6 19 Rce2 ⩲ , Geller–Uhlmann, Skopje 1968.

(s) 9 . . . Qe7?! 10 Nf3 = , but not 10 exf6 Qxf6 11 Nf3 Bb4† 12 Kf1 Bd6 13 Nh3 Qe7 ∓ , Niephaus–Stahlberg, Wageningen 1957.

(t) 13 . . . e5 14 Nf3 (14 Bxg6 e4! 15 0–0 Ne2† 16 Kh1 Nf4 17 Bh7 Nd3 18 b3 Qd6! 19 a4—if 19 f3 Ne5 and 20 . . . Nf7—19 . . . Nxc1 and 20 . . . Qf4) 14 . . . Nxf3† 15 gxf3 Bf5 16 Bxf5 gxf5 17 Bg5 Qa5† 18 Kf1 Kf7 19 Kg2! e4 20 Qh3 d4 21 Bxf6 Kxf6 22 Qh4† g5 23 Qh8† ⩲ , Prandstetter–Jurek, Karvina 1986.

(u) Now: (A) 15 Nf3 Nxf3† 16 gxf3 Nh5? (16 . . . Bf5 is better) 17 Bxg6†!! Kxg6 18 Kh1 Qh4 (18 . . . Qe8? 19 Rg1† Kf6 20 Rg5 Nf4 21 Bxf4 exf4 22 Rxg7 wins, or 18 . . . Nf6 19 Rg1† Kf7 20 Rxg7 Ke6 21 Bg5 Be7 22 Rxe7† Qxe7 23 Qa3! ±) 19 Qf8 Bg4 20 Qa3± , Kruszynski–Ehrenfeucht, Poraka 1986. (B) 15 Nb3 Nxb3 16 axb3 Bf5 17 Bxf5 gxf5 18 Bg5 Bc5 19 Qh4 Qd6 20 Bxf6 (20 Rad1 Ne4 21 Qh5 Qg6 22 Qxg6† Kxg6 23 Be3 d4 24 Bc1

230

Kf6 McCambridge) 20 . . . Qxf6 21 Qxf6 Kxf6 22 Ra5 b6 23 Ra6 e4! 24 Rfa1 Rc8 25 Kf1 (25 Rxa7 Bd4! 26 Rd1 Rc2 ∓) 25 . . . Bb4!! ±, Kramer–Chernin, Somerset 1986.

(v) 11 f4 0–0 (11 . . . Qb6 12 Nf3 e5! 13 fxe5 Bxe5 14 Kh1 Bd6 =) 12 Nf3 Bd7 13 a3 Qb6 14 Kh1 Rac8 15 Ne5 Be8 16 g4 Kh8 17 Be3 Ne7 18 Rc1 Rxc1 19 Bxc1 Bb5 20 Nc3 ∓, Afek–S. Agdestein, London 1986.

(w) 12 Bg5 0–0 and now (A) 13 Rc1 Ng4 14 Ng3 (14 h3? Rxf3!) 14 . . . g6 15 Bb5 Bd7 16 Nh4 Nf6 17 Qd3 Kg7?! (17 . . . Rf7!) 18 Bxc6 bxc6 19 Qe2 Rf7 20 Nf3 h6 21 Bd2 Ng4 =, Sokolov–Yusupov, Riga 1986. (B) 13 Bh4 Nh5 14 Qc2! (the knight remains on e2 to control d4 and f4) 14 . . . h6 15 Bg6 Nf4 16 Nxf4 Bxf4 17 Rfe1 ± (Timoshenko).

(x) 15 Re1 a6 16 Rc1 Qg7 17 Bf1 Bd7 18 Bg5 h6 19 Be3 Rf7 20 g3 Raf8 21 Bg2 Nf6 22 h3 g5 23 Kh2 Kh8 24 Na4 Re7 25 Nc5 Be8 ±, Karpov–Mestel, London 1984.

FRENCH DEFENSE

Tarrasch Variation

1 e4 e6 2 d4 d5 3 Nd2

	91	92	93	94	95	96
3	(Nf6)		a6			
4	(e5)		Ngf3			
	(Nfd7)		c5			
5	f4		exd5		dxc5	
	c5		exd5		Bxc5	
6	c3		Be2	dxc5	Bd3	
	Nc6		c4(j)	Bxc5	Nf6	Ne7
7	Ndf3		0–0	Nb3	0–0	0–0
	cxd4(a)	Qa5	Bd6	Be7(o)	Nc6	Nbc6
8	cxd4	Kf2(f)	b3(k)	Bd3(p)	Qe2	a3(s)
	Qb6	Be7(g)	cxb3(l)	Nf6	Qc7!	0–0
9	g3(b)	Bd3	axb3	Bg5	a3	b4
	Bb4†	Qb6	Ne7	Bg4	Ba7!(r)	Ba7
10	Kf2	Ne2	Re1	h3	exd5	Bb2
	g5!?(c)	f6	Nbc6	Bh5	Nxd5	Ng6
11	h3(d)	Kg3!?(h)	Nf1	Qe2	Ne4	
	gxf4	g5!?	Bg4(m)	0–0	0–0	Nb3(t) ±
12	Bxf4	h3!?(i)	Ng3	0–0–0	Ng3	
	f6(e)		0–0(n)	Re8!(q)	=	

(a) (A) 7 ... c4?! 8 g4 b5 9 Ne2 Nb6 10 Ng3 a5 11 Bg2 b4 12 0–0 a4 13 a3! ±, Beliavsky–Bagirov, USSR 1974. (B) 7 ... f5 8 Bd3 Be7 9 Ne2 0–0 10 h3 c4 11 Bc2 b5 12 Ng5 Nb6 13 g4 a5 14 Ng3 Ra7 15 h4 ±, Korchnoi–Larsen, Belgrade 1964. (C) 7 ... Qb6 8 g3 f5 (8 ... cxd4 transposes to the column) 9 Ne2 Be7 10 h3 0–0 11 g4 a5 12 gxf5 exf5 13 Bg2 Rd8 14 0–0 ±, Jansa–Franke, Bad Wörishofen 1988.

(b) Spassky swept away years of convention with 9 h4!? against Yusupov, Belfort 1988; 9 ... f6 10 a3 Be7 11 Bd3 0–0 12 Ne2 h6 13 b4 Kh8 14 Bb1 f5 15 Bd3 Qd8 16 h5 Nb6 17 Kf2 Bd7 18 Qg1! Nc4 19 g4 b5 20 gxf5 exf5 21 Qg6 ±.

(c) This stunning move continues to succeed since its first appearance in 1983. The previously played 10 ... f6 and 10 ... f5 are met by 11 Kg2 followed by 12 Bd3 and pressure on the kingside, with a slight advantage for White.

(d) (A) 11 Be3 f6 12 Bh3 fxe5 13 fxe5 0–0 14 Bg4 Bc5! (Botterill) 15 Bxe6† Kh8 16 dxc5 Qxb2† 17 Bd2! g4! ∓, Emms–Kosten, British Chp. 1985. (B) 11 fxg5 Ndxe5 12 Nxe5 Nxe5 13 Kg2 Nc6 14 Nf3 Bf8! 15 b3 Bg7 16 Bb2 Bd7 ∞, Polancek–Kaplun, USSR 1983.

(e) 13 Kg2 Bf8 14 Rh2!? (similar to an idea by Karpov against Ljubojević) 14 ... Bg7 (14 ... Qxb2† 15 Kh1 followed by Bb5 ∞) 15 Kh1 0–0 16 Re2 fxe5 17 dxe5 Nc5 18 Bg2 Ne4 19 Rxe4!? with complications, Zagrebelny–Barsov, USSR 1988.

(f) Other plans are (A) 8 dxc5 Qxc5 9 Bd3 a5 10 Ne2 Qb6 11 Ned4 Nxd4 12 cxd4 Nb8 13 0–0 Nc6 =, Franzen–Bukal, Starý Smokovec 1980. (B) 8 Be3!? cxd4 (8 . . . b5 fails to 9 dxc5! b4 10 Nd4 Bb7 11 a3! bxc3 12 b4 ±, Tseshkovsky–Vaganian, USSR 1975) 9 Nxd4 Nxd4 10 Bxd4 Nb8 11 Nf3 Bd7 (11 . . . Nc6 12 Be3 ±) 12 Bd3 Bb5 13 0–0 Bxd3 14 Qxd3 ±, Sakharov–Doroshkevich, USSR 1973.

(g) 8 . . . b5 9 Ne2 b4 10 g4 Ba6 11 f5 bxc3 12 bxc3 Bxe2 13 Bxe2 Qxc3 14 Qa4 Nxd4 15 fxe6 fxe6 16 Bd2 Qc2 17 Qxc2 Nxc2 18 Rac1 Na3 19 Ng5 Ke7 20 Rc3 ∞, McCambridge–Shirazi, Los Angeles 1981.

(h) 11 exf6 Bxf6 12 Kg3 cxd4 13 cxd4 0–0 14 Re1? (better is 14 h3! and 15 Kh2 ∞) 14 . . . e5! 15 fxe5 Ndxe5 16 dxe5 Bh4†! 17 Kxh4 Rxf3! 18 Rf1! Qb4† 19 Bf4 Qe7† 20 Bg5 Qe6! 21 Bf5 Rxf5 22 Nf4 Qxe5 ∓, Reshevsky–Vaganian, Skopje 1976.

(i) The idea is 13 Kh2. The game Adorjan–Vaganian, Teesside 1974, went 12 Re1 cxd4 13 Ned4 (better, according to Vaganian, is 13 cxd4 gxf4 14 Nxf4 fxe5 15 dxe5 Nc5 with equality) 13 . . . gxf4 14 Bxf4 fxe5 15 Nxe5 Ndxe5 with already a slight advantage for Black.

(j) 6 . . . cxd4 7 Nxd4 Nc6 8 N2f3 Bd6 9 0–0 Nge7 10 c3! 0–0 11 Bd3! h6?! 12 Bc2! Re8 13 Qd3 with an ideal position for White, A. Rodriguez–Dohojan, Sochi 1988. See col. 74(k) after 10 c3 a6?! 11 Bd3.

(k) 8 Re1 Ne7 9 b3 cxb3 10 axb3 transposes to the column. The quieter 9 Nf1 Nbc6 10 Bg5 0–0 11 c3 f6 12 Bd2 b5 puts less pressure on Black, as in Gipslis–Korchnoi, Tallinn 1967.

(l) 8 . . . b5?! 9 Re1 (Geller has twice succeeded with 9 a4!? c3 10 axb5 cxd2 11 Bxd2, but after 11 . . . Bb7! 12 bxa6 Nxa6 13 Bxa6 Rxa6 14 Qe2† Qe7 15 Qxa6! White should have only a slight advantage, Geller–Kekki, Team match 1986) 9 . . . Ne7 10 a4 b4 11 Nf1 b4 12 Ng3 0–0 13 Bd3 ±, Sherper–Legki, USSR 1986.

(m) On 11 . . . 0–0 White could also continue 12 Ng3 as an improvement on 12 Ne3 Bh5 13 Ba3 0–0, followed by play on the c-file, Dvoiris–Eingorn, USSR Chp. 1986.

(n) 13 c3 Qc7 14 Ra2 Ng6 15 Ng5 Bxe2 16 Raxe2 with some initiative, A. Sokolov–Miralles, Dubai 1986.

(o) 7 . . . Ba7 (A) 8 Bg5 Ne7 9 Qd2!? Nbc6 10 Be3 Bxe3 11 Qxe3 0–0 12 0–0–0 Bf5! ±, van der Wiel–Seirawan, Biel 1985. (B) 8 Bd3 Qe7† 9 Be2 Nf6 10 0–0 0–0 11 Bg5 h6 12 Bh4 g5! 13 Bg3 Ne4 =, Vogt–Lebredo, Cienfuegos 1983.

(p) 8 Be2 Nf6 9 0–0 0–0 10 Nfd4 (10 Bg5 Nc6 11 Re1 h6 12 Bh4 g5! 13 Bg3 Ne4 14 Bd3 Bf6! 15 c3 Bg7! =, Renet–Chernin, Lucerne 1985) 10 . . . Nc6 11 Bf4 Bf5! 12 Nfd4 Be4! =, Kuporosov–Glek, USSR 1986.

(q) 12 . . . Nc6?! 13 Rhe1 ±, Yudasin–M. Gurevich, Baku 1986; 12 . . . Re8 13 Rhe1 Nbd7 is better, intending 14 . . . Qc7 or 14 . . . Bb4.

(r) 9 . . . 0–0?! 10 e5 Ng4 (10 . . . Nd7 is even worse) 11 Bxh7†! Kxh7 12 Ng5† Kg8 13 Qxg4 Qxe5 14 Ndf3 (this is why White avoided 11 Nb3) 14 . . . Qf6? (14 . . . Qf5 was the only chance) 15 c4! Qg6 16 Nh4 Qc2 17 Be3 Ne5 18 Qh5 Bxe3 19 fxe3 f6 20 Nf5! Resigns, Kveinys–Legki, USSR 1987. The column is Gruenfeld–Eingorn, Zagreb 1987.

(s) 8 Qe2 0–0 9 Nb3 Ba7 10 Bg5 Qc7 11 Bh4 dxe4 12 Bxe4 Nf5 ∓, Wittman–Dolmatov, Frunze 1983.

(t) 11 c4 is possible, e.g. 11 . . . d4!? 12 c5!? intending 13 Nc4; 11 . . . dxc4 12 Nxc4 b5 13 Nce5 Nxe5 14 Nxe5 Nf4 is unclear, Bellin–Raičević, Hastings, 1979–80. The column is Matanović–Kupper, Opatja 1953.

233

FRENCH DEFENSE

Tarrasch Variation, Guimard Defense

1 e4 e6 2 d4 d5 3 Nd2 Nc6

	97	98	99	100	101	102
4	c3	Ngf3				
	Nf6(a)	Nf6				
5	e5	e5				
	Nd7	Nd7				
6	Bd3	Be2				Nb3
	f5	Be7(d)..................		f6		a5(j)
7	g4(b)	b3	Nf1	exf6		a4
	Ndxe5	0–0	Ncb8(f)	Nxf6.......	Qxf6	Be7(k)
8	dxe5	0–0	Ng3	0–0	Nf1	Bb5
	Nxe5	f6	c5	Bd6	Bd6	Na7
9	Be2	Bb2	c3	c4	Ne3	Be2
	fxg4	fxe5	b6	0–0	0–0	b6
10	Nf1	Nxe5!	h4	c5	0–0	h4
	Qf6	Ndxe5	Ba6	Bf4	Qg6	h6
11	Ne3	dxe5	Bxa6	Bb5	g3	c3
	Bc5(c)	Bc5(e)	Nxa6(g)	Bd7(h)	Nf6(i)	c5(l)

(a) (A) 4 . . . dxe4 5 Nxe4 Nf6 6 Nxf6† Qxf6 7 Nf3 h6 8 Bd3 Bd6 9 Qe2 ±, Hertel–Blank, East Germany 1975; (B) 4 . . . e5 5 dxe5! (avoiding the complexities of 5 exd5 Qxd5 6 Ngf3 exd4 7 Bc4) 5 . . . Nxe5 6 Ngf3 Nxf3 7 Qxf3 Nf6 8 Bd3 ± (intending 9 e5 Nd7 10 Qe2).

(b) 7 Ne2 Nb6 8 Nf4 g6 9 h4 Qe7 10 Qf3 Qf7 11 Qg3 Rg8 12 Nf3 h6 13 Be3 Bd7 14 0–0–0 0–0–0 15 Nh3 ±, Klinger–Rogers, Biel 1986.

(c) 12 Bxg4 ± (analysis by W. Watson).

(d) 6 . . . exd6 7 exf6 Qf6 8 Nf1 Bd6 9 Ne3 b6 10 Ng4 Qg6 11 Nh4 Qf7 12 f4 0–0! 13 Be3 Bxf4 14 Rf1 Qe7 15 Bxf4 Qxh4† 16 g3 Qe7 17 Qd2 Bb7 18 0–0–0 ±, Kuzmin–Naumkin, USSR 1986.

(e) 12 c4 Qe7 13 Rc1 Nd4 14 Bd3 Nf5 15 Nf3 dxc4 16 Bxc4 Bd7 17 Nd4 Rad8 18 Nxf5 Rxf5 19 Qc2! Qg5 20 Rcd1 Rdf8 ±, Smagin–Johansen, Belgrade 1986.

(f) 7 . . . 0–0 8 Ne3 f6 9 exf6 Nxf6 10 0–0 Bd6 11 c4 b6 12 a3 a5 13 b3 Ne7 14 Bb2 Ne4 15 Bd3 Ng6 16 g3 Bb7 ∓, Smagin–Rogers, Belgrade 1986.

(g) 12 h5 h6 13 0–0 0–0 14 Nh2 f5 15 exf6 Nxf6 16 Ng4 Bd6 17 Ne5 cxd4 18 cxd4 Bxe5 19 dxe5 Nd7 20 Qg4 Qe7 21 f4 Rac8 =, Kindermann–Klinger, Dubai 1986.

(h) 12 Bxc6! Bxc6 13 Nb3 Ne4 14 Bxf4 Rxf4 15 Qe2 a6 16 a4 Qe8 17 Qe3 Rf6? (17 . . . Rf8! ∞, Tseitlin) 18 Ne5 Bxa4 19 f3 Bxb3 20 fxe4 Bc2 21 Qg3 ±, Tseitlin–Gusev, USSR 1986.

(i) 12 Nh4! Qe8 13 f4 Ne7 14 Ng4 Ne4 15 Nf3 c5 16 Bd3 ±, Velimirović–Vaganian, Rio de Janeiro 1979.

(j) 6 . . . f6 (6 . . . Be7 7 Bb5 a5 8 a4 transposes to the next note) 7 Bb5! keeps Black in a bind, for example 7 . . . fxe5 8 dxe5 Be7 9 Nbd4 Ndb8 10 Ng5! Bxg5 11 Qh5† g6 12 Qxg5 Qxg5 13 Bxg5 Bd7 14 Nxc6 Nxc6 15 Bf6 Rg8 16 Be2! with a wretched position for Black, Estrin–Bagirov, match 1958.

(k) 7 . . . f6 8 Bb5 fxe5 9 dxe5 Nc5 10 Bg5 Qd7 11 Nbd4! Ne4 12 Be3 Be7 13 Nd2! Nxd2 14 Qxd2 0–0 15 0–0 ±, Morović–Beliavsky, Tunis 1985.

(l) 7 . . . Be7 8 Bb5 Na7 9 Be2 b6 10 h4 h6 11 c3 c5 12 Be3 Nc6 13 Bb5 Qc7 14 Nbd2 Ba6 when by trading off the light-square bishop Black keeps White's advantage to a minimum, Tseshkovsky–Savon, USSR Chp. 1974.

FRENCH DEFENSE

Exchange Variation

1 e4 e6 2 d4 d5 3 exd5 exd5

	103	104	105	106	107	108
4	Bd3		Nf3			Nc3
	Bd6(a)		Bd6			Bb4
5	c3	Qf3	Bd3			Bd3
	Nc6	Nc6	Ne7........	Nc6........	Nf6	Nc6(i)
6	Nf3	c3	0–0	0–0(f)	0–0	Ne2
	Nge7	Nf6	Bg4	Bg4	0–0	Nge7
7	0–0	h3(c)	c3	c3	Bg5	0–0
	Bg4	0–0	Nbc6	Nge7	Bg4	Bf5
8	h3	Ne2	Re1	Re1	Nbd2	Bxf5
	Bh5	Re8	Qd7	Qd7	Nbd7	Nxf5
9	Re1	Bg5	Nbd2	Nbd2	c3	Qd3
	Qd7	Be7	0–0–0	0–0	c6	Qd7
10	a4	Be3	b4	h3	Qc2	Nb5(j)
	0–0–0	Ne4!	Ng6	Bf5	Qc7	Bd6
11	a5	Bxe4	b5	Nf1	Rfe1	Bf4
	f6(b)	dxe4(d)	Nce7(e)	Rae8(g)	Rfe8(h)	0–0(k)

(a) Korchnoi's daring 4 . . . c5!? succeeded against Tatai, Beersheba 1978: 5 Nf3 Nc6 6 Qe2†? (6 dxc5 Bxc5 7 0–0 was safer) 6 . . . Be7 7 dxc5 Nf6 8 h3?! 0–0 9 0–0 Bc5 (Black will now regain the time lost with interest) 10 c3 Re8 11 Qc2 Qd6 12 Nbd2 Qg3! 13 Bf5 Re2 14 Nd4 Nxd4 15 Resigns.

(b) 12 b4 Rde8 13 b5 Nd8 14 Nbd2 Ng6 15 Rxe8† Rxe8 16 Qc2 (16 Nb3 Nh4! 17 Be2 Rxe2 18 Qxe2 Nxf3† 19 gxf3 Qxh3 ∓) 16 . . . Nf4!? 17 Bf5 Nde6 18 b6 a6 19 c4 (19 Nb3 g6 20 Bxf4 gxf5 21 Bxd6 Bxf3 22 gxf3 Qxd6 23 Qf5† ∞) 19 . . . g6 20 Bxe6 Qxe6 21 cxd5 Qxd5 ∓, Kochiev–Psakhis, Tallinn 1987.

(c) 7 Bg5 Bg4 8 Qe3 Kd7 ∞.

(d) 12 Qxe4 Nb4! 13 Kd1 (13 cxb4 Bxb4† wins) 13 . . . Nd5 14 Nf4 Nxe3† 15 fxe3 Bd6 ∞, Malanyuk–Psakhis, USSR 1983.

(e) 12 Qa4 Kb8 13 Ba3 Nf4 14 Bf1 f6 (the standard move in such positions) 15 Bc5 Nc8 16 Qb3 Bf5 17 Re3 g5 18 a4 g4 19 Nh4 Be6 20 Bxd6 Nxd6 ∓, Nikolić–Barlov, Yugoslavia 1986.

(f) 6 Bg5 f6 7 Bh4 Bg4 8 Qe2 Nge7 9 c3 Qd7 10 Nbd2 0–0–0 11 0–0–0 Rde8 ∓, Zita–Fichtl, 1943.

(g) 12 Bxf5 Qxf5 13 Ne3 Qd7 14 Bd2 Nd8 15 Qc2 c6 ∓, Tal–Korchnoi, USSR 1955.

(h) 12 Bh4 Bh5 13 Bg3 Bg6 14 Bxg6 hxg6 =, Capablanca–Maróczy, Lake Hopatcong 1926.

(i) Provoking White to play 6 Nf3 or 6 Ne2; if 5 . . . Ne7 6 Qf3!

(j) Capablanca–Alekhine, World Chp. 1927, went 10 Nd1 0–0! 11 Ne3? (11 Bf4! =) 11 . . . Nxe3 12 Bxe3 Rfe8 13 Nf4?! Bd6 14 Rfe1?! Nb4 15 Qb3 Qf5 16 Rac1? Nxc2! 17 Rxc2 Qxf4! ∓ and Black won on move 43 (the actual move order was 3 Nc3 Bb4 4 exd5 exd5).

(k) 12 Nxd6 Nxd6 =, Poliak–Bondarevsky, USSR 1946.

FRENCH DEFENSE

Advance Variation

1 e4 e6 2 d4 d5 3 e5 c5

	109	110	111	112	113	114
4	c3					Nf3(t)
	Nc6(a)					Nc6(u)
5	Nf3					Bd3
	Qb6................................			Bd7.........	Nge7	cxd4
6	Be2........	a3	Bd3	Be2(n)	Na3	0–0
	cxd4(b)	c4(f)	cxd4(j)	f6	cxd4	f6(v)
7	cxd4	Nbd2(g)	cxd4	0–0	cxd4	Qe2(w)
	Nh6(c)	f6!(h)	Bd7	fxe5	Nf5	fxe5
8	Nc3	Be2	0–0	Nxe5	Nc2	Nxe5
	Nf5	fxe5	Nxd4	Nxe5	Qa5(q)	Nxe5
9	Na4	Nxe5	Nxd4	dxe5	Bd2	Qxe5
	Bb4†	Nf6	Qxd4	Qc7	Qb6	Nf6
10	Bd2(d)	0–0	Nc3	c4(o)	Bc3	Bb5†
	Qa5	Bd6	Qxe5(k)	Qxe5	Bd7(r)	Kf7
11	Bc3	Ndf3	Re1	Bh5!	Bd3	Qxd4
	b5	0–0	Qb8!(l)	g6	Be7	Bd6(x)
12	a3	Qc2	Nxd5	Bf3	0–0!(s)	
	Bxc3†(e)	Qc7(i)	Bd6(m)	0–0–0(p)		

(a) 4 ... Qb6 5 Nf3 Bd7 intends to trade off the bad bishop but is very slow; 6 Be2 Bb5 7 c4! Bxc4 8 Bxc4 Qb4† (8 ... dxc4 9 d5!) 9 Nbd2 dxc4 10 a3 Qa5 11 0–0 Nc6 12 Nxc4 Qa6 13 Nd6† Bxd6 14 exd6 cxd4 15 d7†! led to a brilliant attack in J. Wolf–Gerbić, corr. 1988.

(b) 6 ... Nh6?! 7 Bxh6 Qxb2 8 Be3! (8 Bc1 Qxa1 9 Qc2 cxd4 10 cxd4 Bd7 11 Nfd2 dxc3! 12 Nb3 Nb4 13 Nxa1 Nxc2 14 Nxc2 b5! ∓, Payne–Plesse, West Germany 1973) 8 ... Qxa1 9 Qxc2 cxd4 10 Nxd4 puts Black's queen in danger, Drvota–B. Schmidt, Děčin 1979; so Black has to play 7 ... gxh6 8 Qd2 Bg7 9 0–0 0–0 10 Na3 (10 dxc5 Qc7!) 10 ... f6?! 11 exf6 Rxf6 12 dxc5! Qxc5 13 b4 with some advantage, Kupreichik–Huzman, Sverdlovsk 1987.

(c) 7 ... Bd7 8 Nc3 Nh6 9 g3! Nf5 10 Na4 Qd8 11 h4 ±, Hübner–Dückstein, Vienna 1972.

(d) 10 Kf1? Qd8 11 Bg4 Be7 12 Bxe7 Qxe7 13 Qd2 0–0 14 g3 Bd7 15 Nc3 f6 16 g4 Nfxd4! ∓, Camilleri–Uhlmann, Raach 1969.

(e) 13 Nxc3 b4 14 axb4 Qxb4 15 Bb5 Bd7 16 Bxc6 Bxc6 17 Qd2 =, Dünhaupt–Rittner, corr. 1974.

(f) 6 ... Bd7 7 b4 cxd4 8 cxd4 Rc8 9 Bb2 Na5!? 10 Nbd2 (10 Bc3 Nc4 ∓̄, Klinger–Arencibia, Gausdal 1986) 10 ... Nc4 11 Bxc4 dxc4 12 Rc1 c3! 13 Rxc3 Rxc3 14 Bxc3 Qa6 15 Ne4!? Bc6 16 Nfd2 f5 17 exf6 led to an unclear game in Subit–Vilela, Cuba Chp. 1987.

238

(g) Might as well be played now: (A) 7 g3 Bd7 8 Nbd2 transposes to the next note, as does 8 h4 Na5 9 Nbd2. (B) 7 Be2 Bd7 8 0–0 Na5 9 Nbd2 also transposes.

(h) 7 . . . Bd7 8 g3 (8 Be2 Na5 9 0–0 Ne7 10 Rb1 h6 11 Re1 Bc6 12 Nf1 Qb3 =, Sveshnikov–Eingorn, USSR 1981) 8 . . . Na5 9 h4, and of all the moves played here (9 . . . h5, 9 . . . Ne7), 9 . . . 0–0–0 10 Bh3 f5 11 0–0 Nh6 12 Ne1 Nf7 turned out well for Black, Klinger–Portisch, Dubai 1986.

(i) 13 Bf4 Nh5 14 Nxc6 Nxf4 15 Nce5 Bd7 16 Rfe1 Rf5 17 Bf1 Ng6 ∓, Teske–Uhlmann, Nordhausen 1986.

(j) 6 . . . Bd7?! 7 dxc5! Bxc5 8 Qe2 a5 9 Nbd2 a4 10 b4 axb3 11 Nxb3 Ba3 12 0–0 Nge7 13 Bd2 Ng6 14 Nbd4 ±, Hort–Andersson, Reykjavik 1972.

(k) 10 . . . a6 (10 . . . Ne7?! 11 Nb5 Qxe5 12 f4! Qb8 13 f5 a6 14 Qf3! ±) 11 Re1 ∞ (Barcza).

(l) 11 . . . Qd6? holds the d-pawn but succumbs to the attack: 12 Nb5 Qb8 (12 . . . Bxb5 13 Bxb5† Kd8 14 Qf3!) 13 Qf3 Bd6 14 Qxd5! ±.

(m) 13 Qg4 Kf8 14 Bd2 h5! (14 . . . f5? 15 Qf3! exd5 16 Bxf5 Bxf5 17 Qxf5 Nf6 18 Bc3 with the attack for a piece—Harding) 15 Qh3 Bc6 16 Nb4 Nf6! ∓, Messere–Endzelins, corr. 1975–77.

(n) 6 a3 c4 is similar to 5 . . . Qb6 6 a3, except that Black can do without Qb6!, e.g. 7 h4 Qc7!? 8 h5 0–0–0 9 Nh4 f6 10 f4 g5! 11 Nf3 g4 12 Nh2 f5 ∓, B. Ivanović–Levitt, Saint John 1988.

(o) 10 Bf4 Ne7 11 Re1 0–0–0 12 Bd3 Be8! 13 Nd2 Bg6 14 Nf3 Bxd3 15 Qxd3 Ng6 and Black has solved all his problems, Jamieson–Tal, Australia–USSR corr. 1977.

(p) 13 Re1 Qd6?! (13 . . . Qf5 14 Nc3 Nf6! 15 cxd5 exd5 16 Nxd5 Bc6 17 g4 Qd7 18 Nxf6 Qf7 19 Qe2 Qxf6 20 Bxc6 Qxc6 21 Be3 ±, Ivanchuk) 14 Nc3! dxc4 15 Qe2! ±, Romanishin–Ivanchuk, Irkutsk 1986. The game ended suddenly: 15 . . . Nf6 (15 . . . Bg7!? 16 Qxc4!) 16 Qxc4 Be7 17 Bf4 Qd4? (17 . . . Qa6! 18 Qxa6 bxa6 19 b4! ±) 18 Nb5!! Bxb5 19 Bxb7†! Resigns.

(q) Many moves have been tried here: (A) 8 . . . Nb4 9 Nxb5 Bxb4† 10 Bd2 Bxd2† 11 Qxd2 Qb6 12 Bd3 ±, Psakhis–Chernin, USSR 1985. (B) 8 . . . Be7 9 Bd3 Qb6! (9 . . . 0–0? 10 g4! Nh4 11 Nxh5 Bxh4 12 g5 Bxg5 13 Qh5 with an enduring attack, Sveshnikov–Farago, Hastings 1985) 10 g4!? Nh4! 11 Nxh4 Bxh4 12 0–0 (12 g5? Nxe5!) 12 . . . Be7 13 Be3 Bd7 14 b4!? a5! 15 bxa5 Nxa5 16 f5 Nc4 ∞, Plaskett–Mestel, Hastings 1986–87. (C) 8 . . . Qb6 9 Bd3 Bb4† 10 Kf1 Be7 11 g3 Bd7 12 Kg2 Rc8 13 Bxf5 exf5 14 b3 0–0 15 Bg5 Bxg5 16 Nxg5 f4 ∓, Short–Vaganian, Montpellier 1985. (D) 8 . . . Bd7 9 Be2 Nb4 10 Nxb4 Bxb4† 11 Bd2 Qa5 12 Bxb4 Qxb4† 13 Qd2 Qxd2† 14 Kxd2 Ne7! 15 Rhc1 f6 16 Rc5 Kd8 17 Bd3 Rc8 (Sieiro–M. Gurevich, Havana 1986) 18 Rxc8† Kxc8 19 Rc1† Kd8 = (Gurevich).

(r) 10 . . . Be7 11 Bd3 a5 12 Ne3 g6 13 0–0 Bd7 14 Bc2 h5 15 Qd2 Kf8 16 g3 Nb4 17 Bxf5! gxf5 18 h4 Bb5 19 Rfd1 Qa6 20 Ng5 ±, Sveshnikov–L. Ortega, Sochi 1987.

(s) This is better than 12 Qd2 a5! 13 a3 (else 13 . . . Nb4) 13 . . . h5 14 h4 (14 Bxf5!?) g6! 15 Qf4 Na7! 16 Ne3? (16 a4 ∓) 16 . . . Bb5 17 Nxf5 gxf5 18 Rd1 Qa6 19 Bc2?! Rc8 20 Qd2 Qc6! ∓, Marjanović–P. Popović, Yugoslavia 1986.

(t) (A) 4 b4?! cxd4? (4 . . . cxb4 5 a3 Qa5! might be a refutation) 5 a3 Nc6 6 f4 a6 7 Nf3 Qb6 8 Bd3 f5 9 g4! Nh6 10 h3 Bd7 11 Rg1 g6 12 Nbd2 with good compensation, F. Frenkel–Winslow, San Jose 1987. (B) 4 Qg4 cxd4 5 Nf3 Nc6 6 Bd3 Nge7 (or 6 . . . Qc7!?) 7 0–0 Ng6 8 Re1 Qc7 9 Qg3 f6! 10 Bxg6† hxg6 11 c3 d3 12 Qxg6† Qf7 13 Qxd3 fxe5 14 Nxe5 Nxe5 15 Rxe5 Bd6 16 Qe2! Bxe5 17 Qxe5 (Yukhtman–Matulović, USSR–Yugoslavia 1959) 17 . . . Qh5! =. (C) 4 dxc5 Nc6 (to force the knight to f3, thus hindering the standard Qg4 maneuver) 5 Nf3 Bxc5 6 Bd3 f6! 7 Qe2 fxe5 8 Nxe5 Nf6 9 Bf4 0–0 10 0–0 Ne4 11 Nxc6 bxc6 12 Be3 Bxe3 =, Becker–Maróczy, Karlovy Vary 1929.

(u) 4 . . . cxd4 gives White the option of 5 Qxd4 Nc6 6 Qf4 or 6 Qg4, but 4 . . . Nc6 permits him one last chance to go into the main lines with 5 c3.

239

(v) (A) 6 . . . Nge7 7 Bf4 Ng6 8 Bg3 Qb6 9 Qc1 Bd7 10 Nbd2 Rc8 11 a3 a5 12 Re1 Bc5 13 Rb1 0–0?! 14 h4! ±, Welsh–Dunning, U.S. Open 1968. (B) 6 . . . Qb6 7 a3?! (7 Re1! prevents 7 . . . f6 because of 8 exf6 Nxf6 9 Bf5!) 7 . . . Nge7?! 8 b4 Ng6 9 Re1 Be7 10 Bb2 a5? (there are many better moves) 11 b5 a4 12 Nbd2 Na7 13 Bxd4 Bc5 14 Bxc5 Qxc5 15 c4 dxc4? (last chance for 15 . . . 0–0) 16 Ne4 Qd5 17 Nd6† Ke7 18 Nxc4 Qc5 19 Bxg6 hxg6 20 Qd6† Qxd6 21 exd6† Resigns. This is the classic game from which all stems, Nimzowitsch–Leonhardt, San Sebastian 1912.

(w) 7 Bb5!? Bd7 8 Bxc6 bxc6 9 Qxd4 Qb6 =. *Comments.*

(x) With equality, Pachman–Dückstein, Munich 1958.

FRENCH DEFENSE

1 e4 e6

	115	116	117	118	119	120
2	Qe2			d3	c4	Nf3
	c5(a)	Nc6	Be7	d5	d5	d5
3	f4	Nf3(e)	b3(g)	Nd2	cxd5	Nc3
	Nc6	e5	d5	Nf6	exd5	d4
4	Nf3	g3(f)	Bb2	g3(j)	exd5	Nce2
	Nge7(b)	Bc5	Bf6	dxe4(k)	Nf6(l)	c5
5	g3	c3	e5(h)	dxe4	Bb5†(m)	c3
	d5	d6	Be7	e5	Nbd7	Nf6
6	d3	Bg2	Qg4	Bg2	Nc3	d3
	g6(c)	Nge7	Bf8	Nc6	Be7	Nc6
7	Bg2	d3	Nf3	Ngf3	Qf3	g3(n)
	Bg7	f5 =	c5	Bc5	0–0	e5
8	0–0		Bb5†	0–0	Bxd7	Bg2
	b6		Bd7	0–0	Qxd7	Be7
9	Nc3		Bxd7†	c3	Nge2	0–0
	0–0		Qxd7	a5 =	Rd8	0–0
10	Bd2		Nc3		Nf4	h3
	Nd4(d)		Nc6(i)		Bd6 =	Ne8(o)

(a) 2 ... e5 3 f4 d6 (3 ... exf4 4 Nf3 g5 5 d4 Bg7 6 c3 h6 7 h4 Nc6 8 hxg5 hxg5 9 Rxh8 Bxh8 10 Qb5 ±, Tolush–Belavenets, USSR 1932) 4 Nf3 Nc6 5 g3? Bg4 6 c3 exf4 7 gxf4 f5! 8 d3 Ne7 ∓, Konstantinopolsky–Bondarevsky, USSR 1939, but 5 Qf2! is better for White.

(b) 4 ... Nf6 5 d3 d6 6 g3 Be7 7 Bg2 0–0 =, Kostich–Sämisch, Brno 1928.

(c) 6 ... b6 7 Bg2 Ba6 (7 ... dxe4? 8 dxe4 Nb4 9 Na3 Ba6 10 Nc4 ±, Keres–Mikenas, Kemeri 1937).

(d) 11 Nxd4 exd4 12 Nd1 = Solmanis–Chistiakov, USSR 1949.

(e) (A) 3 Nc3?! d5! 4 exd5 Nd4 ∓. (B) 3 f4 Nd4 4 Qd1 c5 5 c3 Nc6 =.

(f) 4 c3 Nf6 5 d3 Be7 6 g3 d5 =, Chigorin–Marco, Hastings 1895. The column is Hromadka–Štulik, Zlin 1943.

(g) 3 Qg4? Bf6 4 f4 d5 5 e5 h5 6 Qd1 Be7 ∓, Alapin; 3 Nc3 d5 4 d3 Nf6 5 g3 b6 (5 ... 0–0 6 Bg2 Nc6 7 Nf3 e5 =, Chigorin–Tarrasch, match St. Petersburg 1893) 6 Bg2 Bb7 7 Nh3 dxe4 8 Nxe4 Nxe4 9 Bxe4 Bxe4 10 Qxe4 Qd5 =, Chigorin–Maróczy, Nürnberg 1896.

(h) 5 Bxf6 Nxf6 6 e5 Nfd7 7 Qg4 g6 (7 ... 0–0 8 f4 Nc6 9 c3 d4 10 Nf3 dxc3 11 Nxc3 Nc5 12 d4 ±, Chigorin–Tarrasch, match St. Petersburg 1893) 8 f4 Nc6 9 Nc3 Nb4 10 Kd1 Nc5 11 Qe2 a6 12 a3 Nc6 13 Nf3 b6 14 d4 =, Chigorin–Tarrasch, match St. Petersburg 1893.

(i) 11 0–0 Nge7 =, Chigorin–Tarrasch, match St. Petersburg 1893.

(j) After 4 Ngf3 c5 5 g3 Nc6 6 Bg2 the game has transposed to the King's Indian Attack.

241

(k) Black takes advantage of White's lack of control of e5 by exchanging and placing his pieces directly on good squares.

(l) 4 . . . Qxd5 5 Nc3 Qd8 6 Bc4 Bd6 7 d4 Nf6 8 Nf3 0–0 9 0–0 Bg4 10 h3 Bh5 11 g4 Bg6 12 Ne5 $\pm$, Tartakower–Marshall, Hamburg 1910.

(m) 5 Bc4 Nxd5 6 Nc3 Nb6 7 Bb3 Nc6 8 Nge2 Bc5 9 Ne4 Bd4 $\mp$, Rubinstein–Spielmann, Vienna 1908. The column is analysis by Keres and Minev.

(n) 7 cxd4 cxd4 8 Qa4† Bd7 9 Nexd4 Bb4† 10 Kd1 Bc5 11 Qc4 Nxe4! 12 dxe4 Nxd4 13 Nxd4 Bxd4 $\mp$, Kiriakov–Kapengut, USSR 1965.

(o) 11 Ne1 Be6 12 c4 a6 13 f4 f6 =, Tseitlin–Faibisović, USSR 1967.

SICILIAN DEFENSE

1 e4 c5

Diagram 35

T HE Sicilian DATES BACK to the Italy of four hundred years ago. It was mentioned by Polerio in 1594 and given its name by Greco early in the next century. It was not until the MacDonnell–La Bourdonnais match of 1834 that the chess world began to appreciate the value of the opening, and in the twentieth century the Sicilian has become the most played and most analyzed opening at both the club and master levels. All world champions of this century have used it extensively—a claim true of no other opening.

1 . . . c5 is classically motivated. Black stakes out territory in the center, denying White the pawn duo of e4 and d4. White's most effective counter is Morphy's d4 (after Nf3) gaining space and opening lines. After . . . cxd4 Black has the open c-file for counterplay, but most important is that Black has both center pawns with which to control the critical central squares. Larsen has gone so far as to say that it is a positional error for White to trade the d-pawn, but this is an exaggeration. White's extra space and mobility provide active play and often good attacking chances on the kingside.

An appealing feature of the Sicilian is the asymmetrical positions that arise. This ensures a colorful game in which White has the advantage on the kingside and Black on the queenside. The result—a fierce struggle combining attack, defense, and counterattack—displays all the richness and excitement of modern chess.

There are many variations of the Sicilian. They are all aggressive, but they differ significantly in positional structure. They vary from positional maneuvering to intense tactical struggles. The major variations have several sub-variations and so themselves require some introductory remarks.

Diagram 36

The NAJDORF VARIATION, 2 Nf3 d6 3 d4 cxd4 4 Nxd4 Nf6 5 Nc3 a6 (see diagram), (cols. 1–36), is a favorite of many leading grandmasters. Its most notable exponent is Bobby Fischer, who has used it almost exclusively in reply to 1 e4. The Najdorf is uncompromisingly aggressive and in many variations produces almost unfathomable tactical complications.

6 Bg5 (cols. 1–19) is the sharpest response. After 6 . . . e6 7 f4 Qb6!? we have the *Poisoned Pawn Variation* (cols. 1–6), in which Black grabs the b-pawn while White takes a lead in development. Wild complications may develop, so players should have a good grasp of tactics to play this. 8 Nb3 (col. 6) avoids these complications but offers little chance for advantage. The main line of 6 Bg5 is 6 . . . e6 7 f4 Be7 8 Qf3 Qc7 9 0–0–0 Nbd7 (cols. 7–12). With 10 g4 (cols. 7–9) White initiates a kingside pawn storm, which seems to be the most promising line. 10 Bd3 (cols. 10–11) leads to entertaining positions, but Black can hold the balance. Columns 12–19 cover other lines. Notable is the *Polugaevsky Variation*, 6 . . . e6 7 f4 b5!? (cols. 14–16), which looks suicidal but has so far defied all attempts to refute it.

6 Bc4 (cols. 20–23) is an equally aggressive continuation. Although favored by Fischer in the 1960s, few grandmasters use this variation regularly. After 6 . . . e6 7 Bb3 b5 the positions become so double-edged that White usually loses the advantage conferred by moving first.

6 g3 (col. 24) is a safe, positional treatment in which Black equalizes easily with proper play.

6 Be2 (cols. 25–30) is the most popular positional treatment. Karpov has used this throughout his career with great success. Here combinations and attacks take a back seat to piece maneuvering and strategic concerns. 6 . . . e5 is Black's usual response, whereupon the struggle revolves around the weakened d5 square.

6 f4 (cols. 31–34) can lead to either a positional or an attacking game. Play is not as forced as in the 6 Bg5 and 6 Bc4 variations, but White's strategy usually involves a slow building attack. Black's most direct response is 6 . . . e5 (cols. 31–32), immediately hitting the center.

After 6 Be3 e5 (cols. 35–36) control of the square d5 is a factor as important as in the 6 Be2 variation.

Diagram 37

In the Scheveningen Variation, 2 Nf3 e6 3 d4 cxd4 4 Nxd4 Nf6 5 Nc3 d6 (cols. 37–60), Black creates a backward pawn-center, controlling d5 and e5 (see diagram). A favorite of Kasparov's, this solid formation is difficult to break through, since there are no weak spots in the Black camp, but White has several plans to fight it.

The main line is 6 Be2 Be7 7 0–0 0–0 8 f4 Nc6 9 Be3 a6 (cols. 37–42), when White can play either to restrict Black in space with 10 a4 (cols. 37–38) or to attempt a direct kingside attack with 10 Qe1 (cols. 39–42). In both cases Black will choose between expanding on the queenside and hitting in the center with . . . e5. Other variations of 6 Be2 are covered in cols. 43–48. 9 . . . Bd7 (col. 43) and 9 . . . e5 (col. 44) are reasonable alternatives to the main line, as is 9 Kh1 (col. 45) for White. An early . . . a6 and lines with . . . Nbd7 are seen in cols. 46–48.

The *Keres Attack*, 6 g4 (cols. 49–54), is the sharpest response to the Scheveningen. White immediately begins kingside operations even before developing. Black's safest plan is 6 . . . h6 (cols. 49–51), which seeks to hold up the kingside onslaught. 6 . . . a6 (col. 52), 6 . . . Nc6 (col. 53) and 6 . . . Be7 (col. 54) all allow White to continue his kingside expansion, but maintain a solid pawn structure.

6 f4 (cols. 55–57) is a flexible and logical move. White can develop his pieces in a number of ways and castle on either side. Black has two plans against this: he can play . . . Nc6 and . . . e5 with a struggle in the center, or . . . a6 intending queenside expansion. Both plans are viable with proper play.

Less common sixth moves for White are 6 Be3 (col. 58), leading into little explored territory, and 6 Bc4 (col. 59) and 6 g3 (col. 60), which are not troublesome to Black if he avoids an early . . . a6.

Diagram 38

The DRAGON VARIATION, 2 Nf3 d6 3 d4 cxd4 4 Nxd4 Nf6 5 Nc3 g6 (cols. 61–90), is so named for the serpentlike pawn formation of Black's kingside (see diagram). The name is appropriate also for the aggressive, dangerous character of the defense. Black's fianchettoed bishop exerts a powerful influence on the long diagonal, bearing down on the center and queenside. The drawback of Black's setup is the less flexible role of his center pawns, creating a weakness at the d5 square.

The *Yugoslav Attack,* 6 Be3 Bg7 7 f3 Nc6 8 Qd2 0–0 (cols. 61–78), is White's most successful antidote to the Dragon. White castles on the queenside and thrusts forward his kingside pawns, playing for mate, while Black counterattacks. Cols. 61–66 cover the line 9 Bc4 Bd7 10 0–0–0 Rc8 11 Bb3 Ne5 12 h4 h5!?, where one false slip for either side is usually fatal. If White plays exactly he should have better chances. Other lines with 9 Bc4 are seen in cols. 67–73. Black has several choices safer than the 12 . . . h5 variation, but they make less demands on White. White, too, has calmer options—9 0–0–0 (col. 74) and 9 g4 (col. 76)—but Black gains equality against them.

The *Classical Variation* is 6 Be2 Bg7 7 0–0 0–0 8 Be3 Nc6 (cols. 79–86). As White almost always castles kingside, the strategy is more positional than attacking. 9 Nb3 (cols. 79–82) is the main line, where White seeks to keep a spatial advantage.

6 f4 is the *Levenfish Variation* (cols. 87–89). White plays for a quick central attack, but Black can counter effectively. 6 . . . Nc6 (col. 87) is the surest response.

6 g3 (col. 90) is a quiet continuation that succeeds only against irresolute play.

The *Accelerated Dragon* is 2 Nf3 Nc6 3 d4 cxd4 4 Nxd4 g6 (cols. 91–102). The idea behind this variation, as compared to the Dragon, is to achieve the break . . . d7–d5 in one move. This can happen after 5 Nc3 Bg7 6 Be3 Nf6 7 Be2 or 7 f3 0–0 8 Qd2 d5. In each case Black is a full tempo ahead of the normal Dragon.

For White to attempt to try for an advantage he needs to control d5. He can do this with pieces (Nc3 and Bc4) or pawns (e4 and c4). The former (cols. 91–96) can easily transpose to the Dragon or head for independent waters with 7 . . . Qa5 or 7 . . . 0–0 8 Bb3 d5. The *Maróczy Bind* (cols. 97–102), placing the pawns on c4 and e4, leads to a quieter type of game, yet Black will get strangled if he cannot find active play. For continuations other than 4 . . . g6 see cols. 139–192.

Diagram 39

Systems beginning with 2 Nf3 e6 3 d4 cxd4 4 Nxd4 (see diagram) are covered in cols. 103–138.

The *Taimanov Variation* (cols. 103–120) is 4 . . . Nc6. Black plays flexibly and avoids an early confrontation. Quick attacks against the king or long tactical variations are rare. Instead White usually plays for positional pressure. Transpositions to the Scheveningen and Paulsen variations can easily occur.

5 Nc3 a6 6 g3 (cols. 103–108) attempts to maintain a spatial advantage and to pressure Black on the long diagonal. Black has many different setups to choose from, but all leave him slightly cramped. 6 Be2 (cols. 109–114) pursues classical development. It leads to sharper play than 6 g3. 6 Be3 (cols. 115–116) is as good as 6 Be2 and may transpose to it. 6 Bf4 (col. 117) is tricky but not best. Karpov has favored 6 Nb5 (cols. 118–120) throughout his career. White obtains a definite advantage in space, yet Black has active plans against this.

The *Paulsen* (or *Kan*) *Variation*, 4 . . . a6 (cols. 121–132), is a half-brother of the Taimanov. Black again has a flexible position, and there are many transpositional possibilities. White can play sharply with 5 Bd3 (cols. 121–124), which often leads to a kingside attack. 5 c4 (cols. 125–127) initiates complicated play. 5 Nc3 (cols. 128–131) leads to Taimanov-like positions. 5 Nd2 (col. 132) is offbeat and harmless.

The *Four Knights' Variation*, 4 . . . Nf6 5 Nc3 Nc6 (cols. 133–136), is better than its reputation. White's best try for an edge is 6 Nbd5 Bb4 7 a3 (col. 133). The other lines are double-edged.

The *Sicilian Counter Attack*, 5 . . . Bb4 (cols. 137–138) is tactical, but bad if White knows what to do.

Diagram 40

In the systems beginning with 2 Nf3 Nc6 3 d4 cxd4 4 Nxd4—see diagram—(cols. 139–192), the *Löwenthal Variation*, 4 . . . e5 5 Nb5 a6 (cols. 139–142), has for good reason fallen from favor. White has a number of ways to gain the advantage, although 8 Qd1 (col. 141) seems best. Two unusual lines, 4 . . . e5 5 Nb5 d6 and 4 . . . Qb6, are seen in cols. 143–144.

4 . . . Nf6 5 Nc3 e5 is the *Pelikan Variation* (cols. 145–156). It has gained considerable respectability in recent years due to the devoted work of Sveshnikov. Black accepts a positional defect—the hole at d5—in return for active play. The main line is 6 Nb5 d6 7 Bg5 a6 8 Na3 b5 9 Bxf6 gxf6 10 Nd5 f5 (cols. 145–150). Play is very tactical—two of the columns begin with a piece sacrifice! 9 Nd5 Be7 10 Bxf6 (cols. 151–153) is the positional approach, favored by Karpov. This can be quite dangerous if Black is complacent. Less common (and inferior) lines for both sides are covered in cols. 154–156.

The Richter-Rauzer Attack, 4 . . . Nf6 5 Nc3 d6 6 Bg5 (cols. 157–177), constitutes classical play by both sides. White develops naturally and aggressively while Black makes straightforward, unprovoking moves. Cols. 157–162 cover 6 . . . e6 7 Qd2 Be7 8 0–0–0 0–0, when White has the direct 9 f4 (cols. 157–159) or the restraining 9 Nb3 (cols. 160–162). 7 . . . a6 8 0–0–0 Bd7 (cols. 160–162) is a more aggressive plan. 9 f4 (cols. 163–166) is a good response if White is prepared for all of Black's choices. 8 . . . h6 (cols. 169–174) puts the question to the bishop. The two main choices, 9 Bf4 (cols. 169–170) and 9 Be3 (cols. 171–174) are equally good. Larsen's favorite, 6 . . . Bd7 (cols. 175–176), is not as popular as it was years ago but is still playable.

6 Be2 steers the game into positional channels, but 6 . . . e5!, the *Boleslavsky Variation* (cols. 178–179) gives Black almost immediate equality.

The Velimirovic Attack, 6 Bc4 e6 7 Be3 (cols. 181–186), is known as a direct attacking weapon. White castles queenside and hunts the black king on the opposite wing or in the center, if it remains there. Sacrifices and combinations are par for the course.

The Sozin Variation, 6 Bc4 (cols. 187–192), is, of course, similar to the Velimirović Attack, but White plays to castle kingside, thus the play is not so wild. The Sozin was a Fischer favorite in the 1960s, but it is not considered so fearsome today.

Of the non-open variations, Rossolimo's 2 Nf3 and 3 Bb5† against 2 ... Nc6 (cols. 193–196) and 2 ... d6 (cols. 197–198) is a safe system, avoiding the complications of the open variations. White gains an initiative against imprecise play, but otherwise has few prospects for advantage.

Diagram 41

The CLOSED SICILIAN, 2 Nc3 Nc6 3 g3 g6 4 Bg2 Bg7 5 d3 d6 (cols. 199–204), has been an occasional weapon of Spassky's throughout his career (see diagram). White expands on the kingside without opening a central front as in the open variations. The attack is dangerous against an unwary opponent. Other closed variations are seen in cols. 205–210.

2 f4 and 2 Nc3 followed by 3 f4 are covered in cols. 211–216. This is one of White's most promising lines in the non-open variations and offers much scope for original play.

2 c3 (cols. 217–220) is a safe continuation. 2 ... d5 (cols. 217–218) is the surest road to equality, while 2 ... Nf6 (cols. 219–220) is sharper.

The *Morra Gambit*, 2 d4 cxd4 3 c3 (cols. 221–222), is entertaining but not especially good.

Unusual lines are covered in cols. 223–228. These are Nimzowitsch's 2 Nf3 Nf6!?; 2 Nf3 a6; the Wing Gambit, 2 b4; Keres's 2 Ne2; and 2 b3.

SICILIAN DEFENSE

Najdorf (Poisoned Pawn) Variation

1 e4 c5 2 Nf3 d6 3 d4 cxd4 4 Nxd4 Nf6 5 Nc3 a6 6 Bg5 e6 7 f4 Qb6

	1	2	3	4	5	6
8	Qd2(a)					Nb3
	Qxb2					Be7(s)
9	Rb1				Nb3	Qf3(t)
	Qa3				Nc6(p)	Nbd7
10	f5		Bxf6	e5(k)	Bxf6(q)	0–0–0
	Nc6(b)		gxf6	dxe5(l)	gxf6	Qc7
11	fxe6		Be2	fxe5	Be2	Bd3
	fxe6		Bg7(h)	Nfd7	d5	b5
12	Nxc6		f5(i)	Bc4(m)	Na4(r)	a3
	bxc6		0–0	Qa5(n)	Qa3	Bb7
13	Be2	e5	0–0	0–0	Nb6	Rhe1
	Be7	dxe5(e)	Nc6	Nxe5	Rb8	Nc5
14	0–0	Bxf6	Nxc6!	Rbe1	exd5	Qh3
	0–0	gxf6	bxc6	Nbc6	Na5!	0–0–0
15	Rb3	Ne4	Kh1	Nxc6	Rb1	Nxc5
	Qc5†(c)	Be7(f)	Qa5	Nxc6	Qb4	dxc5
16	Be3	Be2	Rf3	Qf4	Qxb4	e5
	Qe5(d)	h5(g)	exf5(j)	Bc5†(o)	Bxb4† =	Nd5 =

(a) (A) 8 a3 Nc6 =. (B) 8 Qd3 Qxb2 9 Rb1 Qa3 10 f5 Be7 11 Be2 Nc6 12 fxe6 fxe6 13 Nxc6 bxc6 =, Nunn–Kasparov, Brussels 1986.

(b) 10 . . . b5 11 Rb3 Qa5 12 Bxf6 gxf6 13 Be2 b4 14 fxe6! fxe6 15 0–0 Bg7 16 Nd1 0–0 17 Bc4 ± (Hartston).

(c) 15 . . . Qa5 16 Nd5 Qxd2 17 Nxe7† Kf7 18 Bxd2 Kxe7 19 e5 dxe5 20 Bb4† wins.

(d) 17 Bf4 Qc5† 18 Kh1 Ng4 (18 . . . Nxe4 19 Nxe4 Qxe4 20 Bxd6 ±) 19 h3 e5 20 Na4 Qa7 21 Bc4† Kh8 22 hxg4 exf4 23 Nb6 Rb8 =, Spraggett–A. Sokolov, match 1988.

(e) 13 . . . Nd5 14 Nxd5 cxd5 15 Be2 dxe5 16 0–0 gives White attacking chances after either 16 . . . Ra7 17 c4 Qc5† 18 Kh1 d4 19 Bh5† g6 20 Bd1, or 16 . . . Bc5† 17 Kh1 Rf8 18 c4 Rxf1† 19 Rxf1 Bb7 20 Qc2! (Fischer).

(f) 15 . . . Qxa2 16 Rd1 Be7 17 Be2 0–0 18 0–0 f5 or 18 . . . Ra7 is unclear.

(g) 17 Rb3 Qa4 with two choices: (A) 18 c4 f5 19 0–0 fxe4 and Black is all right in this complex position, e.g. 20 Qc3 Qxa2 21 Bd1 Rf8 22 Bxh5† Kd8 23 Rd1† Bd7 24 Qe3 Qa5 25 Rb7 Bc5 26 Rdxd7† Kc8 27 Rdc7† Kd8 with a draw, Kavalek–Fischer, Sousse 1967. (B) 18 Nxf6† Bxf6 19 c4 Ra7! 20 0–0 Rf7 and accurate play should probably lead to a draw, but Black has the easier task.

(h) 11 . . . Nc6 12 Nxc6 bxc6 13 0–0 Qa5 14 Kh1 Be7 15 f5 exf5 16 exf5 Bxf5 17 Bxa6 Qxa6 18 Rxf5 d5 19 Re1 Qb7 (Matanović–Bertok, Yugoslav Chp. 1962) 20 Qh6! (Nunn) with attacking chances.

250

(i) 12 0–0 f5 13 Rfd1 Nc6 14 Nxc6 bxc6 (14 . . . Bxc3 15 Qe3 bxc6 16 Rb3 ±) 15 Rb3 Qc5†
16 Kh1 0–0 17 Qxd6 Qxd6 =, Matanović–Bronstein, Wijk aan Zee 1963.

(j) 17 Qxd6 Be6 18 Rbf1 fxe4 19 Nxe4 Qe5 =, Zinser–Buljovćić, Reggio Emilia 1967. In this
line White may do better with 15 Rf3 Qc5† 16 Kh1 exf5 17 Bd3!?.

(k) An important alternative is 10 Be2 Nbd7 with (A) 11 0–0 Be7 12 e5 dxe5 13 fxe5 Nxe5
14 Bxf6 gxf6 (14 . . . Bxf6?! 15 Rxf6 gxf6 16 Ne4 is a strong attack) 15 Ne4 f5 16 Rb3 Qa4
17 Nxf5 exf5 18 Nd6† Bxd6 19 Qxd6 Qe4 with equal chances, Pogrebniak–Glek, USSR
1986. (B) 11 . . . Qc5 12 Kh1 Be7 13 f5 e5 14 Ne6 fxe6 15 fxe6 0–0 (the simplest) 16 exd7
Bxd7 17 Rxb7 Ng4 =, Hansson–Sigurjonsson, Neskaupstadur 1984.

(l) Less common but satisfactory is 10 . . . h6 11 Bxf6 gxf6 12 Ne4 fxe5 13 Rb3 Qa4 14 fxe5
dxe5 15 Nf6† Ke7 16 Nf5† exf5 leading to a draw.

(m) 12 Ne4 h6 13 Bb5 axb5 14 Nxb5 hxg5 15 Nxa3 Rxa3 ∓, Platonov–Minić, USSR vs.
Yugoslavia 1968.

(n) Black has a good alternative in 12 . . . Bb4 13 Rb3 Qa5 14 0–0 0–0 15 Bf6! Nxf6 16 exf6
Rd8 17 Rxb4 Qxb4 18 Qg5 g6 with equal chances.

(o) 17 Kh1 0–0. Analysis by Boleslavsky, who rates Black as better; but the position is
unclear.

(p) Also possible is 9 . . . Qa3 10 Bxf6 (10 Bd3 Be7 11 0–0 h6! 12 Bh4 Nxe4! ∓, Spassky–
Fischer, World Chp. 1972) 10 . . . gxf6 11 Be2 Nc6 12 0–0 Bd7 13 Kh1 Rc8 with a roughly
balanced game.

(q) 10 Bd3 d5 11 Bxf6 gxf6 12 Na4 (12 Rb1? Qxc3) Qa3 13 Nb6 Rb8 ∞.

(r) Black threatens 13 . . . Bb4 or 13 . . . Qxc3 14 Qxc3 Bb4. If 12 Nd1 Qa3 13 exd5 Na5! is
at least equal. The column is Westerinen–Szekely, Budapest 1976.

(s) (A) 8 . . . Qe3† 9 Qe2 Qxe2† 10 Bxe2 gives White a pull in the ending. (B) 8 . . . Nbd7
allows the setup 9 Qe2 Be7 10 0–0–0 Qc7 11 g4 which gives White chances for the
initiative. After the accurate text, Black has no problems.

(t) 9 Qe2?! h6 10 Bh4? Nxe4! 11 Bxe7 Nxc3 wins a pawn. The column is Spassky–Portisch,
Tilburg 1979.

SICILIAN DEFENSE

Najdorf Variation

1 e4 c5 2 Nf3 d6 3 d4 cxd4 4 Nxd4 Nf6 5 Nc3 a6 6 Bg5 e6 7 f4 Be7 8 Qf3 Qc7 9 0-0-0 Nbd7

	7	8	9	10	11	12
10	g4..................................			Bd3..................... ✓	....	Be2(r)
	b5			h6	b5	b5(s)
11	Bxf6			Bh4(l)	Rhe1	Bxf6
	Nxf6(a)			g5	Bd7	Nxf6
12	g5			fxg5(m)	Nd5(o)	e5
	Nd7			Ne5	Nxd5(p)	Bb7
13	f5		a3(h)	Qe2	exd5	exf6
	Nc5.........	Bxg5†	Rb8!	Nfg4	Bxg5	Bxf3
14	f6(b)	Kb1	h4(i)	Nf3	fxg5(q)	Bxf3
	gxf6	Ne5	b4	hxg5	Ne5	Bxf6
15	gxf6	Qh5	axb4	Bg3(n)	Qh3	Bxa8
	Bf8	Qd8(e)	Rxb4	Nxf3	Bxd5	Bxa4
16	Rg1(c)	Rg1(f)	Bh3	gxf3	g6	Rxd4
	Bd7	Bf6	Qc5(j)	Ne5	0-0-0	d5
17	Rg7	fxe6	Nb3	f4	gxf7	Bxd5
	b4(d)	0-0(g)	Qb6(k)	gxf4 =	Qxf7 =	exd5(t)

(a) 11 . . . gxf6 12 f5 Ne5 13 Qh3 0-0 14 Rg1 (14 Nce2 Kh8 15 Nf4 Rg8 16 fxe6 fxe6 17 Nfxe6 Bxe6 18 Nxe6 Qd7 19 Nd4 Qxg4 =, Spassky–Donner, Leiden 1970) 14 . . . Kh8 15 Nce2 Rg8 16 Rg3! Bd7 17 Nf4 ±, Wolff–de Firmian, N.Y. Open 1989.

(b) (A) 14 h4 b4 15 Nce2?! e5 16 Nb3 Nxe4! 17 Bg2 (17 Qxe4 Bb7 18 Rd5 Rc8 19 c3 Qc4 20 Qxc4 Rxc4 21 Bg2 Bxd5 22 Bxd5 Rxh4! ∓, Nunn–Browne, Gjovik 1983) 17 . . . Bb7 18 Qe3 d5 19 Bxe4 dxe4 20 Ng3 a5 21 f6 gxf6 22 gxf6 Rc8 23 Rh2 Bg8 24 Ne4 Bxe4! 25 Qxe4 Bn6† 26 Kb1 0-0 =, Wedberg–de Firmian, Oslo 1984. (B) 15 Nb1! Bb7 16 fxe6 fxe6 17 Nd2 e5 18 Nf5 0-0 19 Bc4† Kg8 20 g6 Nxe4! (20 . . . hxg6? 21 Qg4) 21 Nxe4 hxg6 22 Be6 Rf8 (Ljubojević–Hodgson, Wijk aan Zee 1986) 23 Qg4 Rxe6 24 Nd4 Rc8 =.

(c) (A) 16 Bh3?! b4 ∓. (B) 16 Qh5 Bd7 (16 . . . b4?! 17 Nd5! exd5 18 exd5 Bb7 19 Re1† Kd8 20 Kb1! with a strong attack) 17 Bh3 (17 a3 Qa5!, threatening 18 . . . b4 19 axb4 Nb3† winning the Queen) 17 . . . b4 18 Nce2 0-0-0 19 Qxf7 Bh6† 20 Kb1·Rdf8 21 Qh5 Rxf6 =, Browne–Mecking, San Antonio 1972.

(d) Too risky is 17 . . . Bxg7 18 fxg7 Rg8 19 e5! 0-0-0! 20 exd6 Qb6 (20 . . . Qb7 21 Qxf7 ±, Perenyi–Browne, New York 1986) 21 Ne4!, Wolff–Browne, Philadelphia 1987. After 17 . . . b4 18 Nd5 exd5 19 exd5 0-0-0 20 Rxf7 Bh6† 21 Kb1 Rdf8 22 Re7, White has compensation for his sacrifice, but perhaps no more than that. Chinchilla–G. Hernandez, Managna 1987, continued 22 . . . Qd8 23 Rxd7! Kxd7 24 Qf5† Kc7 25 Ne6† Nxe6 26 fxe6 and here 26 . . . d5!? is worth investigating, as is, in the column, 16 . . . h5!? 17 Rg7 b4 18 Nd5 exd5.

252

(e) 15 . . . Qe7 16 Nxe6 Bxe6 17 fxe6 g6 18 exf7† ±.

(f) 16 Nxe6 Bxe6 17 fxe6 g6 18 exf7† Kxf7 19 Qh3 Kg7 20 Qe6 Nf7 =, de Firmian–Browne, US Chp. 1987.

(g) 18 Bh3 g6 19 Nd5 ±, Matulović–Gheorgiu, Uraca 1975. 17 . . . g6 may be a better idea.

(h) 13 Bh3?! b4! 14 Nce2 Bb7 15 Kb1 Nc5 16 Ng2 d5! gives Black the initiative, Smyslov–Fischer, Candidates, Bled 1959.

(i) An old line is 14 Bh3 Nc5 15 Rhg1 b4 16 axb4 Rxb4 17 f5 Qb7! with equal chances.

(j) (A) 16 . . . Qb6 17 Nf5! Rxb2! 18 Nxg7† Kf8 19 Nxe6† fxe6 20 Bxe6, Kholmov–Savon, USSR Chp. 1970 and White's game is slightly preferable. (B) 16 . . . 0–0?! 17 Nxe6! fxe6 18 Bxe6† Kh8 19 Nd5 Qc4 20 Bf5 (threatening 21 Bxh7 Kxh7 22 Qh5 Kg8 23 g6) 20 . . . Rxf5 21 exf5 Bb7 22 Rhe1 ±.

(k) 18 h5 Nc5 19 Nxc5 dxc5! 20 g6 fxg6 21 hxg6 h6 22 Nd5 exd5 23 Bxc8 0–0 ∓, Kaplan–Browne, Madrid 1973.

(l) 11 Qh3 Nb6 12 f5 e5 13 Nde2 Bd7 14 Be3 Bc6 =, Chandler–Browne, Bath 1983.

(m) 12 e5 gxh5 13 exf6 Nxf6 14 f5 e5 15 Nde2 Bd7 16 Be4 and now Nunn's 16 . . . Rg8 seems adequate for equality.

(n) 15 Bxg5 Bxg5† 16 Nxg5 Qc5 17 Nf3 (17 Nh3 Bd7 leaves Black with good play for the pawn) 17 . . . Nf2 18 Nxe5 Nxd1 19 Nxf7 Nxc3 20 Qf3 Rf8 is complex, but satisfactory for Black.

(o) 12 Qg3 b4 (12 . . . 0–0–0 13 Bxb5! axb5 14 Ndxb5 Qb6 15 e5 d5 16 f5 ±, Velimirović–Al Kassas, Nice 1974) 13 Nd5 exd5 14 e5 (14 exd5 Kd8 15 Qe3 Nb6 16 Nf5 Nbxd5 17 Qe2 [17 Qd4 Bf8 ∓] 17 . . . Bc8 ∓ Garnett) 14 . . . dxe5 15 fxe5 Nh5 16 Qh4 (16 e6 Nxg3 17 exf7† Kxf7 18 Rxe7† Kg8 19 hxg3 h6 ∓) 16 . . . Bxg5† 17 Qxg5 g6 18 e6 Nc5 19 exf7† Kxf7 20 Rf1† Kg8 21 Nf5 Ne6 =.

(p) Also possible is 12 . . . exd5 13 Nf5 Kf8 14 Qg3 dxe4 15 Bxe4 Bxe4 16 Rxe4 Qc5! 17 Bxf6 Bxf6 18 Nxd6 Qc7 19 Qe3 g6 20 Re8† Kg7 21 Nf5† Kg7 22 Qg3† with a draw, Wibe–Gunarsson, Norway 1973.

(q) 14 Rxe6†?! fxe6 15 Qh5† g6 16 Bxg6† hxg6 17 Qxh8† Nf8 18 Nxe6 Bxf4†! ∓. The column is A. Rodriguez–de Firmian, Mexico City 1977.

(r) 10 Qg3 b5! 11 Bxb5 axb5 12 Nbxb5 Qb8 13 e5 dxe5 14 fxe5 Nxe5 15 Rhe1 (15 Bf4 Nfg4 16 h3 g5!) 15 . . . Ng6 16 Nc7† Kf8 17 Nxa8 Qxa8 ∓, Shirazi–Browne, US Chp. 1983.

(s) 10 . . . h6 11 Bh4 transposes to the Browne system, column 13.

(t) 18 Nxd5 Qc5 19 Re1† Kf8 =, Keres–Fischer, Candidates, Bled 1959.

SICILIAN DEFENSE

Najdorf Variation

1 e4 c5 2 Nf3 d6 3 d4 cxd4 4 Nxd4 Nf6 5 Nc3 a6 6 Bg5 e6

	13	14	15	16	17	18
7	(f4) .... Qf3(s)					
	(Be7) ....b5 (Polugaevsky Variation) ....Nbd7(n)					h6
8	(Qf3)	e5(e)			Qf3(o)	Bxf6(t)
	h6	dxe5			Qc7	Qxf6
9	Bh4	fxe5			0–0–0	Qxf6
	Qc7(a)	Qc7			b5	gxf6
10	0–0–0	Qe2 ....exf6			Bxb5(p)	Be2
	Nbd7	Nfd7		Qe5†	axb5	h5
11	Be2(b)	0–0–0		Be2	Ndxb5	0–0–0
	g5(c)	Bb7(f)		Qxg5	Qb8	Bd7
12	fxg5	Qg4........Nxe6	Qd3(l)	e5	Kb1
	Ne5	Qxe5(g)	fxe6	Qxf6	Ra5(q)	Kd8
13	Qe3	Be2(h)	Qg4(j)	Rf1	exf6	f4
	Nh7	Bc5	Qxe5	Qe5	gxf6	Nc6
14	Rhf1	Rhf1	Bd3	Rd1	Bh6!	Rhf1
	hxg5(d)	Bxd4(i)	Be7(k)	Ra7(m)	Bxh6(r)	Kc7 =

(a) 9 ... g5 is the Göteborg Variation. After 10 fxg5 Nfd7 White has two choices: (A) 11 Nxe6 fxe6 12 Qh5† Kf8 13 Bb5! Rh7! 14 0–0† Kg8 15 g6 Rg7 16 Rf7 Bxh4 17 Qxh6 Qf6! ±, Mikhalchishin–Kupreichik, USSR Chp. 1981. (B) 11 Qh5! Ne5 12 Bg3 Bxg5 13 Be2 Qb6 when the clearest follow-up is 14 Rd1 Qxb2 15 0–0 Rf6 16 Ndb5! with a strong attack, Iskov–Lund, Denmark 1975. 9 ... Qc7 is Browne's system.

(b) (A) 11 Bd3 transposes to column 10. (B) 11 Qg3 g5 12 fxg5 Nh5 (12 ... Rg8 13 Be2 Ne5 14 Nf3 $\pm$) 13 Qe3 Qc5 14 Kb1 hxg5 =, Chiburdanidze–Gavrikov, USSR 1980.

(c) The slower alternatives, 11 ... Rg8 12 Bg3! b5 13 e5 ±, and 11 ... Rb8 12 Qg3 Rg8 13 e5! dxe5 14 Nxe6! fxe6 15 Qg6† Kd8 16 fxe5 Qxe5 17 Bg3 Qe3† 18 Kb1 ±, allow White to utilize his impetus. Better may be 11 ... b5 12 e5 Bb7 13 Qg3, but White is still ahead.

(d) 15 Bg3 Nf8 16 Nf3 f6 17 Nxg5! fxg5 18 Bxe5 dxe5 19 Qf2 ±, Feldman–Lubin, Leningrad 1970.

(e) Alternatives allow Black to develop aggressively: (A) 8 a3 Bb7 =; (B) 8 Qf3 Bb7 9 0–0–0 Nbd7 10 Bd3 Be7 11 Rhe1 Qb6 =, Kupper–Tal, Zürich 1959.

(f) Not (A) 11 ... Qxe5? 12 Qxe5 Nxe5 13 Ndxb5 +. A promising alternative is 11 ... Nc6 12 Nxc6 Qxc6 13 Qd3 b4! 14 Ne4 Bb7 15 Be2 Qd5 ∞, de Firmian–McCambridge, Los Angeles 1976.

(g) 12 ... Qb6 13 Be2 Nxe5 14 Qh3 Nbd7 15 Rhe1 h6 16 Bh4 g5 is an unclear position. As usual in the Polugaevsky, Black's side looks precarious, but it's hard to find a good continuation for White.

(h) (A) 13 Bxb5 axb5 14 Rhe1 h5 15 Qh4 Qc5 is wild and murky. (B) 13 Bd3 h6 14 Bh4 g5 15 Bg3 Qe7† 16 Kb1 h5 17 Rhe1 hxg4 is at least equal for Black (Nunn).

(i) 15 Rxd4 f6 16 Bd2 f5 17 Qh4 0–0 18 Rd3 Qf6 19 Bg5 Qf7 is unclear, according to Polugaevsky, but looks promising for White.

(j) 13 Qh5† g6 14 Qg4 Qxe5 15 Bd3 Nc5 16 Qh4 Nbd7 17 Rhe1 Qg7 18 Be4 h6 gave Black the advantage in Shabanov–Krimerman, corr. 1986.

(k) Not 14 . . . Nf6?! 15 Bxf6 gxf6 16 Kb1! ±, but 14 . . . Be7 15 Bxe7 Kxe7 16 Rhe1 h5! 17 Qb4† (17 Qh4† Qf6 18 Qb4† Kd8 ∞) 17 . . . Qc5 18 Qh4† Nf6! (18 . . . g5 19 Qh3 ±) 19 Qg3 Rg8 20 Re5 Qb6 21 Bf5 Nbd7 22 Rxe6† Qxe6 23 Bxe6 Kxe6 with a probable draw, Olafsson–Polugaevsky, Rejkjavik 1978.

(l) 12 0–0 Ra7 13 Qd3 Rd7 is roughly equal.

(m) 15 Nf3 (15 Ndxb5 Rd7) 15 . . . Qc7 16 Ng5 f5 17 Qd4 Qe7 (17 . . . h5 18 Rxf5! Qd7 19 Nd5 is a strong attack, Tal–Polugaevsky, match 1980) 18 Nge4 h5 19 Nd6† Qxd6 20 Qxa7 Qe5 =, A. Rodriguez–Polugaevsky, Biel 1985.

(n) 7 . . . Qc7 8 Qf3 b5 9 f5 b4 10 Ncb5! axb5 11 Bxb5† Bd7 12 fxe6 Bxb5 13 Nxb5 Qc5 14 Bxf6 Qxb5 15 Bxg7! Bxg7 16 Qxf7† Kd8 17 Qxg7 is sharp, but better for White, Velimirović–Gaprindashvili, Bela Crkva 1984.

(o) 8 Qe2 Qc7 9 0–0–0 b5 10 g4 Bb7 11 Bg2 Nb6 12 Rhe1 Be7 =, Nunn–Britton, Nottingham 1979.

(p) (A) 10 Bd3 Bb7 11 Rhe1 Qb6 (11 . . . Be7 transposes to column 11) 12 Nd5 Qxd4 13 Bxf6 gxf6 14 Bxb5 Qc5 15 Nxf6† Ke7 seems good for Black; or (B) 10 e5 Bb7 11 Qh3 dxe5 12 Nxe6 dxe6 13 Qxe6† Be7 14 Nxb5 axb5 15 Bxb5 Be4 16 Rd2 Kf8 17 Bc4 Bg6 18 Bxf6 Nxf6 19 fxe5 Bb4 20 Rf2 Bf7! 21 Qxf7† Qxf7 ∓, W. Wittman–Gutman, Beersheba 1985.

(q) 12 . . . Bb7 13 Qe2 dxe5 14 Qc4 ±, Tal–Stean, Hastings, 1973–74.

(r) 15 Nxd6† Ke7 16 Kb1 Nb6 17 Nce4 ⩲, Psakhis-Anikaev, USSR 1979.

(s) (A) 7 Qd3 Nbd7 8 0–0–0 b5 9 f4 Bb7 ∓, Katalimov–Gofstein, USSR 1977. (B) 7 Qe2 Be7 8 0–0–0 Nbd7 =.

(t) 8 Bh4 Nbd7 9 0–0–0 Qc7 10 Be2 Be7 =, Liberzon–Portisch, Skara 1980. The column is Bokucheva–Platonov, Gorki 1971.

SICILIAN DEFENSE

Najdorf Variation

1 e4 c5 2 Nf3 d6 3 d4 cxd4 4 Nxd4 Nf6 5 Nc3 a6

	19	20	21	22	23	24
6	(Bg5)	Bc4				g3
	Nbd7(a)	e6				e5(q)
7	Bc4	Bb3(d)				Nde2
	Qa5	b5(e)				b5(r)
8	Qd2	0–0			f4(n)	Bg2(s)
	e6(b)	Be7(f)			Bb7	Bb7
9	0–0–0	f4		Qf3	f5	0–0
	b5	0–0	Bb7	Qc7(l)	e5	Be7
10	Bb3	e5	e5(i)	Qg3	Nde2	h3
	Bb7	dxe5	dxe5	0–0	Nbd7	Nbd7
11	Rhe1	fxe5	fxe5	Re1	Bg5	g4
	0–0–0	Nfd7	Bc5	Nc6	Be7	0–0
12	a3	Be3(g)	Be3	Nxc6	Ng3	Ng3
	Be7	Nxe5!	Nc6(j)	Qxc6	Rc8	b4
13	Kb1	Qh5	exf6	Bh6	Nh5(o)	Nd5
	Qb6(c)	Nc4(h)	Bxd4(k)	Ne8(m)	Nxh5(p)	Nxd5 =

(a) On 6 . . . Nc6 White can play 7 Qd2, transposing to the Richter–Rauzer System, or 7 f4, entering uncharted but promising territory.

(b) 8 . . . h6 9 Bxf6 Nxf6 10 0–0–0 e6 11 Rhe1 Be7 12 f4 0–0 13 Bb3 Re8 14 Kb1 Bf8 15 g4! Nxg4 16 Qg2 gave White a strong attack in Spassky–Petrosian, World Chp. 1969.

(c) 14 f3 Kb8 15 Be3 $\pm$, Gulko–Petrosian, Moscow 1976.

(d) Too slow is 7 a3 Be7 8 Ba2 0–0 9 0–0 b5 10 f4 Bb7 11 f5 e5 12 Nde2 Nbd7 13 Ng3 Rc8 14 Be3 Nb6 15 Bxb6 Qxb6† 16 Kh1 Qe3! $\mp$, Robatsch–Fischer, Havana 1965.

(e) 7 . . . Nc6 transposes to the Sozin Variation.

(f) (A) 8 . . . Bb7 9 Re1! Nbd7 (9 . . . b4 10 Na4 Nbd7 11 a3! Nxe4 [11 . . . bxa3 is good] 12 Nxe6! fxe6 13 Bxe6 is difficult for Black, de Firmian–Hort, Baden-Baden 1981) 10 Bg5 h6 (10 . . . Be7? 11 Bxe6!) 11 Bxf6 Nxf6 12 Qd3 $\pm$. (B) 8 . . . b4 9 Na4 Nxe4 10 Re1 $\pm$.

(g) 12 Qh5 Nc6 13 Nxc6 Qb6† 14 Be3 Qxc6 15 Rf3 Bb7 16 Kh1 Bc5 =, Mallee–Browne, Mannheim 1975.

(h) 13 . . . Nbc6?! 14 Nxc6 Nxc6 15 Rf3 is better for White. After 13 . . . Nc4 14 Bxc4 bxc4 15 Rad1 Qc7 16 Rf3 g6 17 Qh6 f6 the game is equal, Bouaziz–de Firmian, Tunis 1985.

(i) 10 Be3 b4 11 e5 (11 Nd5!? exd5 12 e5 0–0! =, de Firmian–H. Olafsson, New York 1987) 11 . . . bxc3 12 exf6 Bxf6 13 f5 e5 14 Ba4† Ke7! = (Pinter).

(j) Also good is 12 . . . Bxd4 13 Bxd4 Nc6 =, Nunn–Kosten, London 1980.

(k) 14 Qe1 (14 fxg7? Bxe3† 15 Kh1 Rg8 ∓) 14 ... Bxe3† 15 Qxe3 Qd4 16 Rae1 Rd8 =, Zhidkov–Lepeshkin, USSR 1970.

(l) 9 ... Qb6 10 Be3 Qb7 11 Qg3 0–0 (11 ... Nbd7 12 Nf5!? exf5 13 Qxg7 Rf8 14 Nd5 is dangerous, Azmaiparashvili–Novikov, USSR 1986) 12 Bh6 Ne8 13 Rad1 Bd7 14 a3 Nc6 =, Tisdall–Browne, Lone Pine 1976.

(m) 14 Nd5 Bd8 15 Nf4 (Yurtaev–Gavrikov, USSR 1983) 15 ... Kh8 16 Bg5 Bxg5 17 Qxg5 Nf6 =.

(n) 8 Be3 b5 9 Qe2 Nbd7 10 f3 Nc5 =.

(o) The natural 13 0–0?! h5! (threatening 14 ... h4) and Black is much better, R. Byrne–Fischer, Sousse 1967.

(p) 14 Qxh5 0–0 =, R. Byrne–Bouaziz, Sousse 1967.

(q) (A) 6 ... e6 is a Scheveningen Defense, (B) 6 ... g6 is a Dragon.

(r) 7 ... Nbd7 8 a4 b6 9 Bg2 Bb7 10 h3 may give White a pull.

(s) 8 a4 Bb7 9 Bg2 Be7 10 axb5 axb5 11 Rxa8 Bxa8 12 Bg5 Nbd7 =, Peters–Tarjan, US Chp. 1984. The column is Kudrin–Byrne, US Chp. 1984.

SICILIAN DEFENSE

Najdorf Variation

1 e4 c5 2 Nf3 d6 3 d4 cxd4 4 Nxd4 Nf6 5 Nc3 a6 6 Be2

	25	26	27	28	29	30
	e5					Nbd7(p)
7	Nb3					0–0(q)
	Be7				Be6	Nc5
8	0–0			Bg5(l)	f4	Bf3
	0–0			Be6	Qc7(m)	e6
9	Be3(a)		f4	Bxf6	g4!	Be3
	Be6		Qc7(i)	Bxf6	exf4(n)	Be7
10	Qd2	f4(e)	a4	0–0	g5	a4
	Nbd7(b)	exf4(f)	Be6	0–0	Nfd7	0–0
11	a4	Bxf4(g)	f5(j)	Nd5	Bxf4	a5
	Rc8	Nc6	Bc4	Nd7	Nc6	Qc7
12	a5	Kh1	a5	Qd3	Qd2	b4!
	Qc7	Rc8	Nbd7	Rc8	Be7	Ncd7
13	Rfd1(c)	Qe1	Kh1	c3	0–0–0	Na4
	Rfe8(d)	Ne8!(h)	b5(k)	Bg5 =	Nce5(o)	d5(r)

(a) 9 a4 Nc6 10 f4 (10 Be3 Be6 transposes to footnote e) 10 . . . Nb4 11 Kh1 Bd7! 12 Be3 Bc6 13 Bf3 b5 =, Mestal–Tarjan, Buenos Aires 1978.

(b) (A) 10 . . . b5?! 11 a4 b4 12 Nd5 Nxe4 13 Nxe7† Qxe7 14 Qxb4 f5 15 Na5 $\pm$, Yudasin–Gavrikov, Sverdlovsk 1984. (B) 10 . . . Nc6 11 Rfd1 a5 12 a3 a4 13 Nc1 Qa5 14 f3 Rfc8 ∞, Ehlvest–Georgadze, USSR 1983.

(c) 13 Rfc1 Rfe8 14 Nd5 Qc6 15 Bf3 Bxd5 16 exd5 Qc4 17 Qd3 Qh4 =, Chandler–A. Petrosian, Yurmala 1983.

(d) 14 Qe1 Bf8 15 Nc1 h6 =, Barbulescu–de Firmian, Dubai 1986.

(e) (A) 10 a4 Nbd7 (also playable is 10 . . . Nc6 11 a5!? Bxb3 12 cxb3 Nxa5 13 Nd5 Nc6 ∞) 11 a5 Rc8 12 Qd2 transposes to the previous column. (B) 10 Nd5 Nbd7 11 Qd3 Bxd5 12 exd5 Re8 13 a4 Bf8 14 a5 Rc8 15 c4 e4 16 Qd1 Ne5 =, Kosten–Hellers, Esbjerg 1988.

(f) 10 . . . Qc7 11 a4 Nbd7 transposes to note (j).

(g) 11 Rxf4 Nc6 12 Nd5 Bxd5 13 exd5 Ne5 14 Rb4 Qc8 =.

(h) 14 Rd1 Bh4 15 Qd2 Bf6 =, Pritchett–Portisch, Malta 1980.

(i) The column is the old main line, but a good alternative is 9 . . . b5! 10 a4 b4 11 Nd5 Nxd5 12 Qxd5 Qb6† 13 Kh1 Bb7 with an active game, Larsen–Romanishin, Riga 1979.

(j) 11 Be3 Nbd7 12 Kh1 exf4 13 Rxf4 Ne5 14 Nd4 Rad8 =, Karpov–Polugaevsky, match 1974.

(k) 14 axb6 Nxb6 15 Bg5 Rfc8 16 Bxc4 Nxc4 17 Bxf6 Bxf6 18 Nd5 Qd8 19 Ra2 $\pm$, Klovans–Commons, Primorska 1976.

(l) (A) 8 Be3 0–0 9 g4 Be6 10 g5 Nfd7 11 Qd2 Nb6 12 0–0–0 N8d7 =, Röhrl–Kavalek, Skopje 1972. (B) On 8 f4 0–0 9 g4 d5 10 exd5 Bb4 ∓. The column is Unzicker–Fischer, Santa Monica 1966.

(m) Black's best is probably 8 . . . exf4 9 Bxf4 Nc6, playing as in column 26 with a tempo less.

(n) 9 . . . b5 should be met by 10 a3 instead of 10 f5?! Bc4 11 g5 b4! with complications, Tarjan–Cardoso, Orense 1975.

(o) 14 Nd4 g6 15 h4, with attacking chances and greater control of the center, Adorjan–Browne, Wijk aan Zee 1974.

(p) 6 . . . e6 transposes to the Scheveningen Variation.

(q) (A) On 7 f4 Nunn's 7 . . . b5! 8 Bf3 e5 is a promising idea. (B) 7 Be3 Nc5 8 f3 e6 9 a4 b6 10 0–0 Bb7 11 Qd2 Rc8 12 Rfd1 Be7 13 b4 Ncd7 14 b5 axb5 is roughly equal, but Kavalek–Quinteros, Nice 1974, saw instead 14 . . . a5? 15 Nc6! Bxc6?! 16 bxc6 Rxc6 17 Bb5 Rc8 18 e5! dxe5 19 Ne4 Nd5 20 c4 Bb4 and Black resigned, since 21 Qd3 wins a piece.

(r) 14 exd5 exd5 15 c3 Bd6 16 h3 Ne5 17 Nb6 ±, Geller–Quinteros, Baden-Baden 1985.

SICILIAN DEFENSE

Najdorf Variation

1 e4 c5 2 Nf3 d6 3 d4 cxd4 4 Nxd4 Nf6 5 Nc3 a6

	31	32	33	34	35	36
6	f4..Be3(l)					
	e5......................Qc7........g6(i)				e5(m)	
7	Nf3		Bd3	Nf3!	Nb3 ....Nf3	
	Nbd7		g6	Bg7	Be6	Qc7
8	a4(a)		0–0	e5	Qd2	a4
	Be7........Qc7		Bg7	Ng4(j)	Nbd7	Nbd7
9	Bd3(b)	Bd3	Nf3	h3	f3	Bg5
	0–0	0–0	Nbd7	Nh6	b5(n)	h6(p)
10	0–0	0–0	Qe1	Bc4	a4	Bh4
	Nc5(c)	Bg7	0–0(g)	0–0	b4	Be7
11	Kh1	Qe1	f5!	g4!	Nd5	Nd2
	d5	0–0	b5	Nc6	Bxd5	g5
12	Nxe5!	fxe5(e)	Qh4	Be3	exd5	Bg3
	dxe4	dxe5	Bb7	dxe5	Nb6	Nf8
13	Be2	Qh4	fxg6	fxe6	Bxb6	Bc4
	Qc7(d)	b6(f)	fxg6(h)	Be6(k)	Qxb6(o)	Be6(q)

(a) (A) 8 Bd3 b5 9 0–0 Be7 10 Kh1 0–0 =. (B) 8 Bc4 b5 9 Bd5 Rb8 =, Hort–Andersson, Wijk aan Zee 1979. White must stop Black's queenside drive for an advantage.

(b) 9 Bc4 Qa5 10 Bd2 exf4 11 Qe2 Ne5 12 Bb3 Nxf3† 13 gxf3 Qe5 =, Popovych–Tisdall, Gausdal 1985.

(c) (A) 10 ... Qc7 11 Nh4 g6 12 f5 d5 13 exd5 e4 14 Be2 Bd6 15 g3 $\pm$, Sax–Andersson, London 1980. (B) 10 ... exf4 11 Bxf4 Qb6† 12 Kh1 Qxb2 13 Qe1 allows White attacking chances for the pawn.

(d) 13 ... Qxd1 14 Rxd1 Be6 15 Be3 Rfd8 16 g4 $\pm$, Kindermann–de Firmian, Biel 1986. After 13 ... Qc7 14 Be3 b6 15 Qe1 Bb7 16 Qg3 White has an edge, Beliavsky–Chandler, Vienna 1986.

(e) 12 Kh1 b6 13 Qh4 Bb7 14 f5, Rantanen–de Firmian, Gausdal 1982, also gives White play on the kingside.

(f) 14 Bh6 Bb7 15 Ng5 Qd6 (15 ... Nh5? 16 Bxg7 Kxg7 17 Rxf7† Rxf7 18 Ne6†) 16 Rf3 $\pm$.

(g) (A) 10 ... e5 11 a4 transposes to the previous column. (B) 10 ... Nc5 11 a4 $\pm$. (C) 10 ... b5 11 e5 dxe5 12 fxe5 Ng4 13 e6 (13 Qe4 Ndxe5) 13 ... fxe6 14 Be4 $\pm$.

(h) 14 Ng5 Nc5 15 Rxf6! Rxf6 16 Qxh7† Kf8 17 Be3 Nxd3?! 18 cxd3 Qd7 19 Nd5 Bxd5 20 exd5 Qf5 21 Ne6† Rxe6 22 dxe6 Qxe6 23 Bh6 Resigns, Nunn–Gruenfeld, England–Israel Telex Match 1981. Nunn claims 12 ... Nc5 is better in this line, but after 13 Bh6 White still has good attacking chances.

(i) Alternatives are: (A) 6 . . . Nc6?! 7 Nxc6! bxc6 8 e5 $\pm$; (B) 6 . . . Nbd7! (1) 7 Be2 g6 (7 . . . e5!?) 8 0–0 Bg7 9 a4 0–0 10 Kh1 Nc5 11 Bf3 $\pm$, Stoica–Buljovčić, Bajmok 1984; (2) 7 Nf3 e5 8 a4 d5! 9 fxe5 (9 exd5 e4 10 Ng5 Bb4 $\overline{\mp}$) 9 . . . Nxe4 10 Qxd5 Nxc3 11 bxc3 Qc7 12 Bd2 Nc5 $\mp$, Ulybin–Odeyev, USSR 1989. (C) 6 . . . e6 transposes to the Scheveningen Variation.

(j) 8 . . . Nh5 9 Bc4 0–0 10 Ng5 e6?! (Nunn's 10 . . . Qc7 is better) 11 g4 wins material, Kavalek–R. Byrne, US Chp. 1978.

(k) 14 Bxe6 fxe6 15 Qxd8 Nxd8 16 0–0 with an edge, Ghizdavu–Ghitescu, Timisoara 1972.

(l) Uncommon sixth moves are: (A) 6 a4 Nc6 (6 . . . e5 7 Nf3 Qc7 8 Bg5 is more pleasant for White) 7 Be2 e5 8 Nxc6 bxc6 9 f4 Nd7 10 0–0 Be7 11 a5 0–0 12 Qe1 exf4 13 Bxf4 Ne5 =, Benjamin–de Firmian, US Chp. 1984. (B) On 6 h3 either 6 . . . e6 or 6 . . . Nc6 is good, but 6 . . . e5 gives some justification to 6 h3.

(m) 6 . . . e6 transposes to the Scheveningen Variation.

(n) 9 . . . Be7 10 g4 h6 11 0–0–0 b5 12 h4 gives White a kingside initiative, Hazai–Ftáčnik, Tallinn 1981.

(o) 14 a5 Qb7 15 Bc4 Be7 16 Ra4 Rb8 17 Qd3 Qa7 18 Bxa6 0–0 =, Halafyan–Gaprindashvili, USSR 1983.

(p) 9 . . . Be7 10 Nd2 h6 11 Bxf6 Nxf6 12 Bc4 adds control to d5.

(q) 14 Qe2 Rc8 15 Bb3 h5 16 h4 draw, Gipslis–Marjanović, Dortmund 1978.

SICILIAN DEFENSE

Scheveningen Variation

**1 e4 c5 2 Nf3 e6 3 d4 cxd4 4 Nxd4 Nf6 5 Nc3 d6 6 Be2 Be7 7 0–0 0–0
8 f4 Nc6 9 Be3 a6**

	37	38	39	40	41	42
10	a4 . . . . .Qe1(i)				Nxd4 . . . . . . .Bd7	
	Qc7(a)		Qc7			
11	Kh1(b)		Qg3 . . . . .Kh1(n)		Bxd4	Rd1(u)
	Re8 . . . . .Rd8(f)		Nxd4(j)	Bd7(o)	b5	Nxd4
12	Bf3	Qe1(g)	Bxd4	a4(p)	Rd1(r)	Bxd4
	Rb8(c)	Nxd4	b5	Nxd4	Bb7(s)	Bc6
13	Qd2(d)	Bxd4	a3	Bxd4	Bf3	Bf3
	Bd7	e5	Bb7	Bc6	Qc7	Qc7
14	Nb3	Bg1!	Rae1(k)	Qg3	e5	e5
	b6	exf4	Bc6	b6(q)	dxe5	Nd7
15	g4	a5	Kh1!	Rae1	fxe5	exd6
	Bc8	Re8	Qb7(l)	Qb7	Nd7	Bxd6
16	g5	Bb6	Bd3	Bd3	Bxb7	Bxc6
	Nd7	Qb8	b4	b5	Qxb7	Qxc6
17	Qf2	Rxf4	axb4	axb5	Ne4	Qg3
	Bf8(e)	Be6(h)	Qxb4(m)	axb5 $\pm$	Qc7(t)	g6 =

(a) 10 . . . Bd7 transposes to column 43.

(b) 11 Qe1 e5 12 Nb3 Nb4 13 Qf2 Nxc2 14 Bb5 Qb8 15 Rad1 Be6 ∞, Ehlvest–Kasparov, USSR Chp. 1988.

(c) 12 . . . Nxd4 13 Qxd4 e5 14 Qd2 exf4 15 Bxf4 Be6 16 Rfd1 $\pm$. White has pressure on the center.

(d) Other tries are: (A) 13 Bf2 Bf8 14 Re1 Nd7 15 Qe2 Nxd4 16 Bxd4 b6 17 e5 dxe5 18 fxe5 (Razuvaev–Kasparov, USSR Chp. 1978) and now 18 . . . Bc5 (Kasparov's post-mortem suggestion) equalizes. (B) 13 Qe1 e5 14 Nb3 exf4 15 Bxf4 Be6 16 Nd5 Bf8 17 Rd1 with a small pull for White; likewise (C) 13 g4 Nd7 14 g5 Bf8 15 Bg2 g6 16 Rf3 Bg7 17 Rh3 Nb6 18 Nde2 Nc4 19 Bc1 $\pm$, Fishbein–Dorfman, New York Open 1989.

(e) 18 Bg2 Bb7 19 Rad1 g6 20 Bc1 Rdc8 21 Rd3 and White is more active, but Black's position is solid and hard to crack, Karpov–Kasparov, World Chp. 1985.

(f) 11 . . . Na5 12 Qd3 d5 13 e5 Nd2 14 Bf2 Bb4 15 Na2 Be7 16 Qh3 Nc4 17 Bd3 g6 18 Qh6 Nxb2 19 Bxg6! hxg6 20 Nxe6! gave White a winning attack in Peters–Youngworth, Los Angeles 1976.

(g) Here the positional move 12 Bf3 meets the rejoinder 12 . . . Ne5! when 13 fxe5 dxe5 leaves Black with an edge.

(h) Worse is 17 . . . d5?! 18 Qf2 dxe4?! 19 Bc4! Be6 20 Bxe6 fxe6 21 Nxe4 $\pm$, Geller–Tal, Sochi 1977. After 17 . . . Be6 18 Qg3 Nd7 19 Bd4 Ne5 20 Na4 Black has an uncomfortable position, Geller–Kaplan, Lone Pine 1980.

(i) Slow is 10 Kh1 Bd7 11 Qe1 (11 a4 Nxd4 12 Bxd4 Bc6 =) 11 . . . b5 12 a3 Qb8 13 Qg3 b4 14 axb4 Qxb4 =. In this line, Black's queen doesn't waste a tempo going to c7.

(j) 11 . . . Bd7 is a major alternative. White's best response is 12 Rae1 (12 Nf3 Nb4 and 12 e5!? dxe5 13 fxe5 Nxe5 14 Bf4 Bd6 are all right for Black) 12 . . . b5 13 a3! b4 (14 e5 with strong play was threatened) 14 axb4 Nxb4 15 Kh1 Rab8 16 e5 ±, Tal–Kurajica, Wijk aan Zee 1976.

(k) (A) 14 Kh1 Bc6 15 Rae1 transposes to the column. (B) 14 Rad1 is not as good since the d-file has less bearing on White's kingside attack. (C) 14 Bd3 e5! 15 fxe5 Nh5 16 Qh3 dxe5 =.

(l) 15 . . . g6 16 f5 e5 17 Be3 Bxe4 18 fxg6 Bxg6 19 Rxf6! Bxg6 20 Nd5 Qd8 21 Bb6 Bh4 22 Bxd8 Bxg3 23 Bf6! (threatening mate) gives White a material advantage, Kruszynski–Filipowicz, Poland 1977.

(m) 18 Ne2 Qb7 19 e5 Nh5 20 Qh3 g6 21 Ng3 dxe5 22 Bxe5 Ng7 23 f5! exf5 (23 . . . Nxf5?! 24 Bxf5 gxf5 25 Nxf5 ±, Shishmarev–Samarian, corr. 1987) 24 Bxg7 Kxg7 25 Nxf5† gxf5 26 Qxf5 Bxg2† 27 Kg7 Bc5† 28 Qxc5 Bxf1 29 Qg5† Kh8 30 Qf6† Kg8 (Ermenkov–Adamski, Lublin 1976) and now Samarian's 31 Be4 is strong.

(n) 11 a4 transposes to col. 37(b).

(o) Also reasonable is 11 . . . Nxd4 12 Bxd4 b5 13 e5 Ne8 (13 . . . dxe5 14 dxe5 Nd7 15 Bf3 Bb7 16 Bxb7 Qxb7 17 Ne4 ±) 14 Bf3 Bb7 15 Bxb7 Qxb7 =.

(p) 12 Qg3 b5 13 a3 b4 14 axb4 Nxb4 15 e5 Ne6 16 Rad1 dxe5 17 fxe5 f5! 18 exf6 Bxf6 =.

(q) 14 . . . g6 15 f5 e5 16 Be3 Nxe4 17 Nxe4 Bxe4 18 f6 Bd8 19 c4! d5 20 Qh4 Kh8 21 Qh6 Rg8 22 Bg5 ±, Shamkovich.

(r) 12 a3 Bb7 13 Qg3 Bc6 14 Bd3 Qd7! 15 Rae1 a5 and Black's quick queenside play assures him equal chances.

(s) (A) 12 . . . b4?! 13 Na4 Nxe4? 14 Bf3 d5 15 Bxe4 dxe4 16 Bxg7 +. (B) 12 . . . Qc7 13 e5 dxe5 14 fxe5 Nd7 15 Ne4 Bb7 16 Nf6†! Kh8 17 Bd3 h6 18 b4 Rfd8 19 Nh5 gave White a tremendous attack in A. Ivanov–Magerramov, USSR 1980.

(t) (A) 18 Nf6† Kh8! (18 . . . gxf6? 19 Qg3† Kh8 20 exf6 Resigns, was the sudden conclusion of Ivanović–Zapata, New York 1988) 19 Nxd7 Qxd7 20 Rd3 Rac8 =, F. Olafsson–Panno, Buenos Aires 1980. (B) 18 Qg3 Kh8 19 Nd6 Kg8 20 c3 ±.

(u) 11 Qg3 Nxd4 12 Bxd4 Bc6 13 Rae1 b5 14 a3 Qd7! transposes to col. 5 (r). 13 a4, slowing Black on the queenside, may be a good idea. The column is analysis by Kasparov.

SICILIAN DEFENSE

Scheveningen Variation

1 e4 c5 2 Nf3 e6 3 d4 cxd4 4 Nxd4 Nf6 5 Nc3 d6 6 Be2

	43	44	45	46	47	48
	(Be7)..............................a6					
7	(0–0)			0–0....................Be3		
	(0–0)			Qc7........Nbd7		Nbd7(r)
8	(f4)			f4	f4	a4(s)
	(Nc6)			Be7	b5	b6
9	(Be3)...................Kh1			Kh1(l)	Bf3	f4
	Bd7........e5(e)		a6(i)	0–0	Bb7	Bb7
10	Nb3(a)	fxe5(f)	Nxc6!	a4	e5(o)	Bf3
	a6(b)	dxe5	bxc6	b6	Bxf3	Rac8
11	a4	Nf5	e5	e5!	Nxf3	0–0
	Na5(c)	Bxf5	dxe5(j)	dxe5(m)	dxe5	Be7(t)
12	e5	Rxf5	fxe5	fxe5	fxe5	e5
	Ne8	Qxd1(g)	Nd5	Nfd7	b4(p)	Bxf3
13	Nxa5	Raxd1	Ne4	Bf4	exf6	Qxf3
	Qxa5	g6	c5	Bb7	bxc3	dxe5
14	Qd2	Rf2	Qe1	Bf3	fxg7	Nc6
	Qc7(d)	Nd4(h)	Bb7(k)	Nc6(n)	Bxg7(q)	Qc7(u)

(a) 10 Qe1 Nxd4 11 Bxd4 Bc6 12 Qg3 g6 is all right for Black since the thrust 13 f5 e5 14 Be3 Nxe4 15 Nxe4 Bxe4 is less dangerous with the Black queen still on d8 (instead of c7).

(b) Interesting is 10 . . . Qc7 11 Bf3 (11 g4 d5 12 exd5 Nb4! ∞, Pritchett) 11 . . . Rfd8 12 Nb5 Qb8 13 c4 a6 14 Nc3 b5 =, Tal–Beliavsky, Moscow 1975. White may do better with 12 g4 Be8 13 g5 Nd7 14 Bg2.

(c) 11 . . . Rac8 12 a5 Qc7 13 Bb6 Qb8 14 Qd2 (Kasparov) leaves White with more space.

(d) 15 Bd4 f6 16 exf6 Nxf6 17 Qe3 Rae8 18 Kh1 Bd8 19 Rae1 and White has pressure in the center, Karpov–Ljubojević, Tilburg 1986.

(e) 9 . . . Qc7 is noteworthy. On 10 Qe1 Nxd4 11 Bxd4 e5 12 fxe5 dxe5 13 Qg3 Bc5 equalizes, and 10 Ndb5 Qb8 is also fine. White's best is 10 Kh1 when 10 . . . a6 11 a4 would transpose to column 37, but Black can play 10 . . . Bd7.

(f) 10 Nb3 exf4 11 Rxf4 Be6 is the same as column 26 (in the Najdorf Variation) except that here Black's pawn is on a7 instead of a6. After 12 Kh1 d5 13 e5 Nd7 14 Nxd5 Ndxe5 the game is equal, Tal–Kavalek, Wijk aan Zee 1982.

(g) Perhaps the immediate 12 . . . g6 13 Rf2 Nd4 is preferable, although 14 Bh6 looks better for White. Bad, however, is 14 Bc4 Rc8 15 Qf1? Ng4! 16 Rxf7 Kh8 17 Nd5 Nxc2 ∓, Schrafl–Veličković, Graz 1982.

(h) 15 Bh6 Nxc2? (15 . . . Rfc8 16 Bg5 $\pm$) 16 Bg5! Nd5 17 Bxe7 Nxe7 18 Rd7 Nc6 19 Bc4 with a winning endgame, Geller–Tal, USSR Chp. 1983.

(i) Black can transpose to column 37 with 9 . . . Qc7! 10 Be3 a6 11 a4.

(j) 11 . . . Ne8 (A) 12 Be3 Qc7 13 Na4 dxe5 14 Bb6 Qb8 15 Bg1 Qc7 16 Bb6 Qb8 17 Bf2 $\pm$, Romanishin–Dorfman, Lvov 1981. (B) 12 Bd3! g6 13 Qa2 Qc7 14 b3 c5 15 exd5 Nd6 16 Bb2 Rb8 17 f5 $\pm$, van der Wiel–Ehlvest, Rotterdam 1989.

(k) 15 Qg3 Kh8 16 Ng5 Bxg5 17 Bxg5 and White has the bishop-pair, Mestel–Stean, Marbella 1982.

(l) (A) 9 Bf3 0–0 10 Be3 Nc6! (10 . . . Nbd7 11 g4 is unpleasant) 11 a4 Rd8 12 Qe1 Nxd4 13 Bxd4 e5 =. (B) 9 Be3 0–0 10 a4 b6 (10 . . . Nc6 11 Kh1 is back in column 37) 11 Bf3 Bb7 12 Qe1 Nbd7 13 Rd1 Rfe8 14 Kh1 Bf8 =, Nunn–Hartoch, Amsterdam 1976.

(m) 11 . . . Ne8 12 exd6 Bxd6 13 f5! e5 (13 . . . Bxh2 14 Bf3 Ra7 15 Ndb5 $\pm$, Tal) 14 Nd5 Qd8 15 f6 $\pm$, Tal–Ftáčnik, Naestved 1985.

(n) 15 Bxc6 Bxc6 16 Qg4 with an attack, Beliavsky–Yudasin, USSR Chp. 1986.

(o) 10 a3 Rc8 11 Qe1 Rc4 12 Be3 h5!? 13 Kh1 e5 14 Nb3 Ng4 ∞, J. Kristiansen–Mokrý, Malmö 1985–86.

(p) 12 . . . Ng4 13 Qe2 b4 14 Na4 Qa5 15 b3 Rc8 16 Ng5 $\pm$, Bikhovsky–Cheremisin, USSR 1965. 16 . . . Ngxe5 is met by 17 Nxf7!

(q) 15 b3 0–0 16 Be3 and White has a safer king and better pawn structure (Kasparov).

(r) Black can, of course, transpose to the more common lines via 7 . . . Nc6.

(s) 8 g4 Nc5 9 Bf3 h6 10 h4 g6!? = (Kasparov).

(t) The exchange sacrifice isn't best: 11 . . . Rxc3 12 bxc3 Nxe4 13 c4 Qc7 14 Qe2 Be7 15 a5 bxa5 16 f5! e5 17 Nb3 0–0 18 Nxa5 with advantage, Ostojić–Barczay, Sandefjord 1976.

(u) 15 Nxe7 Kxe7 16 Qg3 Rhe8 with at least equality, Tal–Browne, Milan 1975.

SICILIAN DEFENSE

Scheveningen Variation, Keres Attack

1 e4 c5 2 Nf3 e6 3 d4 cxd4 4 Nxd4 Nf6 5 Nc3 d6 6 g4

	49	50	51	52	53	54
	h6................................			a6	Nc6	Be7(p)
7	g5 .... hxg5	h4(e) Nc6........	 Be7	g5 Nfd7	g5 Nd7	g5 Nfd7
8	Bxg5 Nc6(a)	Rg1 h5(f)	Bg2(i) g6(j)	Be3(k) b5	Be3(m) a6	h4 Nc6
9	Qd2 Qb6(b)	gxh5(g) Nxh5	g5 hxg5	a3 Bb7	Qd2 Qc7(n)	Be3 a6
10	Nb3 a6	Bg5 Nf6	Bxg5! a6	h4 Nb6	0–0–0 Nxd4	Qe2(q) Qc7
11	0–0–0 Bd7	Qd2 Qb6	Qd2 e5	h5 N8d7	Qxd4 b5	0–0–0 b5
12	f4(c) 0–0–0	Nb3 a6	Nde2 Be6	Rh3! Ne5	h4 Rb8	Nxc6 Qxc6
13	h4 Qc7	Be2 Qc7	0–0–0 Nbd7	g6 hxg6	Kb1 b4	Bd4 b4
14	Be2 Be7(d)	h5 Nxh5(h)	f4 Qa5 ±	hxg6 Rxh3(l)	Na4 Bb7(o)	Nd5 exd5(r)

(a) 8 . . . a6 9 Bg2 Bd7 10 Qe2! Be7 11 0–0–0 Qc7 12 h4 Nc6 13 f4 leaves White more active than in the column, Geller–Korchnoi, Moscow 1971.

(b) It is best to chase the knight from d4 where it is active. If 9 . . . a6 10 0–0–0 Bd7 11 h4 Qc7 12 Be2 0–0–0 13 f4 Be7 14 h5 ±, Karpov–K. Smith, San Antonio 1972.

(c) 12 Be3 Qc7 13 f4 b5 14 Bg2 Rc8 15 Kb1 Be7 16 Rhe1 Kf8 17 Bg1 Be8 ∞, Kengis–A. Sokolov, USSR 1984.

(d) 15 Bf3 Kb8 16 h5 Bc8 17 Kb1, Karpov–Andersson, Skara 1980; White is slightly freer, but it is difficult to make progress against Black's solid position.

(e) (A) 7 Rg1 Nc6 8 h4 is a common move order to reach the same position as in the column. (B) 7 Bg2 Nc6 8 h3 Be7 9 Be3 Ne5 10 f4 Nc4 11 Bf2 Bd7 12 b3 Qa5 13 Qd3 Na3 is roughly equal, Hort–Andersson, Malta 1980.

(f) 8 . . . d5 9 Bb5 Bd7 10 exd5 Nxd5 11 Nxd5 exd5 12 Be3 Be7 (12 . . . Qxh4 13 Qd2 Be7 14 0–0–0 with the attack—Nunn) 13 Qd2 ±, Karpov–Spassky, Tilburg 1980.

(g) 9 g5 Ng4 10 Be2 d5! 11 Nxc6 bxc6 12 Bxg4 hxg4 13 Qxg4 d4 14 Ne2 Rb8 gives Black good compensation for the pawn, Schmittdiel–Adorjan, Dortmund 1984.

(h) 15 Rh1 g6 16 Bxh5 gxh5 17 Qe2 ±, A. Rodriguez–Douven, Amsterdam 1987.

(i) 8 Rg1 d5 9 exd5 (9 Bb5† Kf8! 10 exd5 Nxd5 11 Bd2 Bf6 =) 9 . . . Nxd5 10 Nxd5 Qxd5 11 Be3 Nc6 12 g5 hxg5 13 hxg5 Bd7 =, Ljubojević–Timman, match 1987.

(j) 8 . . . Nc6 9 g5 hxg5 10 hxg5 Rxh1† 11 Bxh1 Nh7 12 f4 g6 13 Qd2 e5 14 Nxc6 bxc6 gave Black a good game in Kruppa–Razuvaev, Irkutsk 1986, but White can do better with 12 Nxc6 bxc6 13 Qh5. The column is Gufeld–Georgadze, USSR 1981.

(k) Interesting is 8 Bg2 when 8 . . . b5 9 f4 Bb7 10 f5 b4 11 fxe6 bxc3 12 exf7† Kxf7 13 0–0† Ke8 14 Ne6 gives White good attacking chances (Kasparov). Black should play instead 8 . . . Nc6 9 h4 Be7 10 Be3 Qc7 ∞.

(l) 15 gxf7† Nxf7 16 Bxh3 and Black has difficulties because of his weak e-pawn, Torre–Vogt, Polanica Zdroj 1977.

(m) 8 Ndb5 Nb6 9 Bf4 Ne5 10 Qh5 Ng6 11 Bg3 a6 =, Chiburdanidze–Kozlovskaya, USSR 1979.

(n) 9 . . . Be7 10 h4 0–0 11 0–0–0 Nxd4 12 Qxd4 b5 (Pokojowczyk–Timoshchenko, Poland 1979) 13 f4 Qa5 14 Kb1 ±.

(o) Hort–Andersson, Las Palmas 1973. The position is complex, but White's spatial advantage gives him the edge.

(p) An immediate central thrust by Black isn't good: (A) 6 . . . e5 7 Bb5† Bd7 8 Bxd7† Qxd7 9 Nf5 h5 10 f3! hxg4 11 fxg4 ±, Howell–Suba, London 1988. (B) 6 . . . d5 7 exd5 Nxd5 8 Bb5† Bd7 9 Nxd5 gives Black an isolated d-pawn.

(q) 10 Qd2 Qc7 11 0–0–0 0–0 transposes to note (n).

(r) 15 Bxg7 Rg8 16 exd5 Qc7 17 Bf6 Ne5 18 Bxe5 dxe5 19 f4 with good compensation for the piece, Karpov–Dorfman, USSR Chp. 1976.

SICILIAN DEFENSE

Scheveningen Variation

1 e4 c5 2 Nf3 e6 3 d4 cxd4 4 Nxd4 Nf6 5 Nc3 d6

	55	56	57	58	59	60
6	f4			Be3	Bc4	g3
	Nc6		a6(j)	a6	Be7(q)	Nc6(s)
7	Be3		Be3(k)	Qd2(n)	Bb3	Bg2
	Be7 .... e5		b5	b5	0–0	Bd7
8	Qf3	Nf3(f)	Qf3	f3	Be3	0–0
	e5(a)	Ng4	Bb7	Nbd7(o)	Na6!	Be7
9	Nxc6	Bd2(g)	Bd3	g4	f4	Re1(t)
	bxc6	Be7!(h)	Nbd7	h6	Nc5	0–0
10	f5(b)	Qe2	g4	0–0–0	Qf3	Nxc6
	Qa5	exf4	b4	Bb7	e5(r)	Bxc6
11	Bc4	0–0–0	Nce2	Bd3	Nf5	a4
	0–0	Bf6	e5(l)	Ne5	Bxf5	Qd7
12	0–0–0	Nd5	Nb3	Rhe1	exf5	Re3
	Rb8(c)	Ne3	exf4	Be7	e4	Rfd8
13	Bb3(d)	Bxe3	Bxf4	h4	Qe2	Rd3
	Nd7(e)	fxe3(i)	h5!(m)	b4(p)	Qa5 =	b6 =

(a) On 8 ... Qc7 White has two plans: (A) 9 0–0–0 0–0 10 g4 Nxd4 11 Bxd4 e5 12 fxe5 dxe4 13 Qg3 Nxg4! 14 Nd5 Qd8 15 Nxe7† Qxe7 16 Bc3 Qc5 17 Rg1 Qe3† (Sax–Kasparov, Nikšić 1983); now 18 Rd2 Be6 19 Bxe5 Qxg3 20 Bxg3 (Sax) gives White the bishop-pair in the endgame. (B) 9 Bd3 0–0 10 0–0 a6 11 Rae1 Nb4 and 12 ... Nxd3 leads to equality.

(b) 10 fxe5 dxe5 11 Bc4 0–0 12 h3 (12 0–0 Ng4!) 12 ... Be6! 13 Bxe6 fxe6 and Black's open lines make for even chances, Hübner–Petrosian, match 1971.

(c) 12 ... Bb7 13 g4 d5 14 g5 dxc4 15 gxf6 Bxf6 16 Rd6 Rfd8 17 Rxf6 gxf6 18 Qg3† Kf8 19 Na4! with good attacking chances, Fleck–Dankert, West Germany 1985.

(d) White must take care: on 13 g4 d5 14 exd5 Rxb2! is strong.

(e) 14 g4 Nc5 15 Kb1 Nxb3 16 axb3 ±, Tseitlin–Balicky, Hradec Králové 1984–85.

(f) On 8 fxe5 Ng4 9 Bg1 Ngxe5 10 Be2 Be7 is equal.

(g) 9 Qd2 Nxe3 10 Qxe3 exf4 11 Qxf4 Be6 12 Ng5 Be7 13 Nxe6 fxe6 14 Bc4 Bh4† 15 g3 Bg5 16 Qf3 Ne5 17 Bb5† Ke7 18 Qh5 h6 =, Timman–Tal, match 1985.

(h) (A) 9 ... exf4 10 Bxf4 Be7 11 Qd2 ±. (B) 9 ... Qb6? 10 Qe2 Qb2 11 Rb1 Qc2 12 Qc4 Be6 13 Qb5 + (Tal).

(i) 14 Qxe3 0–0 15 Bc4 Be6 =, Tal–Hansen, Naestved 1985.

(j) 6 ... Be7 may transpose to other variations. A noteworthy line of independent significance is 7 Be3 0–0 8 Qf3 e5 9 Nf5 Bxf5 10 exf5 Nbd7 11 0–0–0 Qa5, and now 12 fxe5 should be good but 12 g4?! Rac8 13 g5 Rxc3! 14 gxf6 Nxf6! 15 bxc3 d5 with a tremendous attack, Kamsky–Sakaev, USSR 1986.

(k) White has two other promising plans: (A) 7 Qf3 Qb6 8 Nb3 Qc7 9 g4 b5 10 Bd3 (10 g5 b4!) 10 . . . Bb7 11 g5 Nfd7 with a sharp struggle. (B) 7 Bd3 Be7 8 0–0 0–0 9 Kh1 Nbd7 10 Qf3 Qb6?! (10 . . . Nc5 is better) 11 Nde2 Qc7 12 b4! b6 13 Bb2 Bb7 14 Qh3 d5 15 e5 Ne4 16 Ng3 Nxg3† 17 hxg3 g6 18 a3 b5 19 f5!? exf5 20 Rxf5 d4! 21 Qh6! (White threatens 22 Rh5 with mate on h7; the only defense is 22 . . . Rfc8 so that 23 Rxf7 Kxf7 24 Qxh7†?! Ke8 25 Bxg6† Kd8 escapes the attack; White should play 24 e6† or 23 Raf1 with an unclear position) 21 . . . Bg5? 22 Rxg5 dxc3 23 Rh5 Rfe8 24 Qxh7† Kf8 25 Qh6† Ke7 26 Qg5† Ke6 27 Qg4† Ke7 28 Qg5† Ke6 29 Bxg6 Nxe5 30 Bf5† Kd6 31 Rd1† Bd5 32 Rh6† Re6 33 Bxe6 fxe6 34 Bc1 Kc6 35 Bf4 Nf7 36 Qxd5† Kb6 37 Be3† Resigns, de Firmian–Rhode, US Chp. 1987. (C) 7 Be2 transposes into cols. 46–48.

(l) Also good is 11 . . . Nc5 12 Ng3 Qc7 13 0–0 Nfd7 14 f5 Ne5 =, Trepp–Ribli, Lucerne 1982.

(m) 14 gxh5 (14 g5 Ng4 =) 14 . . . Nxh5 15 0–0–0 Nxf4 =, Micayabas–Browne, New York 1984.

(n) (A) 7 f4 transposes to column 57. (B) 7 Be2 Nc6 8 0–0 Be7 9 f4 0–0 is columns 37–42.

(o) 8 . . . Be7 9 g4 Bb7 10 0–0–0 0–0 11 h4 Nc6 12 Nxc6 Bxc6 13 g5 ±, Short–Ljubojević, Reykjavik 1987.

(p) 14 Na4 Qa5 15 b3 Nfd7 16 Kb1 Nc5 ∞, Ghinda–Marin, Romanian Chp. 1987.

(q) (A) 6 . . . a6 transposes to the Najdorf Variation, and (B) 6 . . . Nc6 transposes to the Sozin Variation.

(r) 10 . . . a6 11 0–0 Qc7 is also playable. The column is Velimirović–Cebalo, Sarajevo 1986.

(s) If Black plays . . . a6 now or on one of the next few moves, the position will transpose to the Taimanov Variation.

(t) 9 Nce2 Rc8 10 c4 0–0 11 b3 a6 12 Bb2 b5 =, Gligorić–Boleslavsky, Zürich 1953. The column is Browne–Petrosian, San Antonio 1972, with 13 . . . b6 instead of Petrosian's 13 . . . Ne8.

269

SICILIAN DEFENSE

Dragon Variation—Yugoslav Attack

1 e4 c5 2 Nf3 d6 3 d4 cxd4 4 Nxd4 Nf6 5 Nc3 g6 6 Be3 Bg7 7 f3 Nc6 8 Qd2 0–0 9 Bc4 Bd7 10 0–0–0 Rc8 11 Bb3 Ne5 12 h4 h5

	61	62	63	64	65	66
13	Bg5...............		Bh6 ✓................		Kb1.........	g4(p)
	Rc5(a)		Bxh6 ......Nc4		Nc4	hxg4
14	Kb1........	f4(e)	Qxh6	Bxc4	Bxc4	h5
	b5	Nc4(f)	Rxc3	Rxc4	Rxc4	Nxh5
15	g4(b)	Qd3	bxc3	Bxg7	Nb3	Bh6
	a5(c)	b5	Qc7(h)	Kxg7	Qc7	e6
16	gxh5!	e5	Kb1	g4(k)	Bd4	Rdg1
	a4	Ng4	a5(i)	hxg4	Bc6!(m)	Qf6
17	Bd5	exd6	f4	h5	Qe2(n)	fxg4(q)
	Nxh5(d)	Rxg5	Nfg4	Rh8	b5	Bxh6
18	Rhg1	hxg5	Qg5	hxg6	e5	Qxh6
	Kh7	Nf2	a4	fxg6	Nd5	Qf4†
19	a3 ±	Qe2	fxe5	f4	Nxd5	Qxf4
		Nxd1(g)	axb3(j)	e5(l)	Bxd5(o)	Nxf4 ∓

(a) 13 ... Nc4 14 Qe2! Na5 15 Kb1, Geller–Miles, Linares 1983, leaves White safe on the queenside and ready for kingside action.

(b) 15 Rhe1 a5 16 f4 Neg4! and Black is at least equal, Boudy–Diaz, Cuba 1987.

(c) 15 ... hxg4 16 h5 Rxc3 (16 ... Nxh5 17 Nd5 Re8 18 Rxh5! gxh5 19 Qh2 Rc4 20 Bxc4 bxc4 21 Qxh5 f6 22 f4 is winning for White, Karpov–Sznapik, Dubai 1986) 17 bxc3 Nxh5 18 Rxh5! gxh5 19 Qh2 Nc4 20 Qxh5 f6 21 Nxb5! Bxb5 22 Bh6 with a dangerous attack, Ulybin–Tiviakov, USSR 1987.

(d) 17 ... b4?! 18 Nce2 e6?! 19 h6! Bh8 20 h7† Kxh7 21 h5 exd5 22 hxg6† Kg8 23 Rxh8† Kxh8 24 Bxf6† Resigns, Sznapik–Komljanović, Biel 1987.

(e) (A) 14 Rhe1 b5 15 f4 Nc4 (15 ... Neg4 is a good alternative) 16 Qd3 Bg4 ∞. If 16 Bxc4?! Rxc4 17 Bxf6 (17 e5 b4 18 exf6 exf6 ∓) 17 ... Bxf6 18 e5 Bg7 19 Nxcb5 Qb8 ∓, Nunn–Miles, London 1980. (B) 14 g4 hxg4 with (1) 15 h5 Nxh5 16 Nd5 Rxd5 17 Bxd5 Qb6! ∓, since 18 Bxe7? is met by 18 ... Nxf3; (2) 15 f4 Nc4 16 Qd3 b5 17 Nd5 f6! 18 Bh4 e6 ∓, Adorjan–Sedrakian, USSR 1986.

(f) Again, 14 ... Neg4 seems to be a good alternative.

(g) 20 Rxd1 Nxd6 ∞, Klovans–Ivanchuk, Tashkent 1987.

(h) 15 ... Qa5 16 Kb1 Rc8 (16 ... Qxc3 17 Ne2 Qc5 18 g4 a5 19 Nf4 e6 20 Nxh5! was good for White in Oltean–Necinger, Romania 1984) 17 g4 Nc4 18 Bxc4 Rxc4 19 gxh5 Qxc3 20 Rd3 Qb4† 21 Nb3 Nxh5 22 Rg1! Qb6 23 Rg2 ± (Nunn).

(i) 16 ... Rc8 17 g4 a5 18 gxh5 a4 19 hxg6 axb3 20 cxb3 Qxc3 21 gxf7† Kxf7 22 Rhg1 Bh3!= , de Firmian–Kudrin, N. Y. Chp. 1988.

270

(j) 20 cxb3 Nf2 21 e6 Nxe4 22 Qh6 Nxc3† 23 Kb2 Nxd1† 24 Rxd1 ±, Short–H. Olafsson, Wijk aan Zee 1987.

(k) 16 Kb1 Qa5 17 Nb3 Qc7 18 g4 hxg4 19 h5 gxf3 20 Rdg1 f2! 21 Qxf2 Rxc3 22 bxc3 Qxc3 23 hxg6 fxg6 = (Nunn).

(l) 20 Nde2! with advantage (Nunn), but Black may do better with 19 . . . Qf8 20 Rxh8 Kxh8.

(m) 16 . . . Be6? 17 g4 Rc8 (17 . . . hxg4 18 h5 ±) 18 Rhg1 and Black's kingside is weak.

(n) (A) 17 g4? e5! 18 Be3 hxg4 19 h5 gxf3 20 h6 Nxe4! +, Popovych–Soltis, New York 1976. This line works for Black because of the bishop on c6. (B) 17 Rhe1 e5! 18 Be3 Rd8 and Black has at least even chances.

(o) 20 exd6 Qxd6 21 Bxg7 Kxg7 =, Kaplan–Miles, Hastings 1976–77.

(p) 13 Rdg1 Qa5 14 Kb1 Rc5! 15 g4 Rxc3 (15 . . . hxg4 16 h5 Nxh5 is also playable) 16 gxh5!? (16 bxc3 hxg4 17 h5 Nxf3! 18 Nxf3 Nxe4 is fun for Black) 16 . . . Rxb3! (16 . . . Rc5 17 Qxa5 Rxa5 18 hxg6 is promising—Christiansen) 17 Qxa5 Rxb2† 18 Kc1 Nxh5 and this wild position is roughly equal.

(q) (A) 17 Bg5? Nxf3 ∓. (B) 17 Bxg7 Qxg7 18 fxg4 Nf6 leaves White with attacking chances, but not enough for the pawn. The column is Goodman–Miles, England 1974.

SICILIAN DEFENSE

Dragon Variation—Yugoslav Attack

1 e4 c5 2 Nf3 d6 3 d4 cxd4 4 Nxd4 Nf6 5 Nc3 g6 6 Be3 Bg7 7 f3 0–0 8 Qd2 Nc6 9 Bc4

	67	68	69	70	71	72
	(Bd7).........	....	....	....	....	..Nxd4
10	(0–0–0)					Bxd4
	(Rc8).........	....	..Qb8	..Qa5		Be6
11	(Bb3)	h4	Bb3			Bb3
	(Ne5)	Rc8(h)	Rfc8			Qa5
12	(h4)(a)	Bb3	Kb1(l)			0–0–0
	Nc4	a5	Ne5			b5(q)
13	Bxc4	h5!	h4.......	..Bg5		Kb1
	Rxc4	a4	Nc4	Nc4		b4
14	h5(b)	Bd5	Bxc4	Bxc4		Nd5
	Nxh5	Nxh5(i)	Rxc4	Rxc4		Bxd5
15	g4	g4	Nb3	Nb3		exd5!
	Nf6	Nf6	Qc7(m)	Qe5		Qb5
16	Nde2 ....e5(e)	Nf5!	Bd4	Bf4(o)		Qd3
	Re8(c)	Nxg4(f)	Bxf5(j)	Be6	Qe6	Qb7
17	Bh6	fxg4	gxf5	h5	Ne2	Rhe1
	Bh8(d)	Bxg4(g)	Nb4(k)	a5(n)	Ba4(p)	a5(r)

(a) 12 g4?! b5! $\mp$ allows Black immediate queenside play.

(b) A good alternative is 14 g4 Qc7 (14 ... Qa5 15 Nb3 Qc7 16 Bd4 $\pm$; 14 ... h5 15 gxh5 $\pm$) 15 h5 Rc8 16 hxg6 fxg6 17 Kb1 (threatening 18 Nd5 and Qh2) 17 ... Qd8 18 Nd5 e6 19 Nxf6† Qxf6 20 Qh2 $\pm$.

(c) 16 ... Qa5 17 Bh6 Bxh6 (17 ... Bh8 18 Bxf8 is not enough play for the exchange) 18 Qxh6 Rfc8 19 Rd3! $\pm$, threatening 20 g5 Nh5 21 Nf4, Karpov–Korchnoi, match 1974.

(d) 18 e5 Nxg4 (18 ... dxe5? 19 g5 $\pm$) 19 fxg4 Bxe5 20 Bf4 Qa5 $=$, Kutianian–Nesis, corr. 1979.

(e) Other choices are: (A) 16 Bh6 Nxe4 17 Qe3 Rxc3! 18 bxc3 Nf6 19 Bxg7 Kxg7 20 Rh2 Qc7 21 Ne2 Qc4 22 Rdh1 Rh8 $=$, Pinkas–Tolnai, Voronež 1987; (B) 16 Nd5 e6 17 Nxf6† Qxf6 18 Qh2 Rfc8 19 Qxh7† Kf8 with enough play for the pawn, Geller–Ivkov, Amsterdam 1974; (C) 16 Nb3!? Re8 17 e5 Nxg4 18 fxg4 Bxg4 19 Rdg1 h5 20 e6 f5 21 Nd5 $\pm$, M. Ivanović–Velimirović, Stara Pazova 1983.

(f) 16 ... dxe5 17 Nb3 (threatening 18 g5) 17 ... Rc7 18 Nc5 $\pm$, or 17 ... Rd6 18 g5 Rd6 19 gxf6! Rxd2 20 Rxd2 Bxf6 21 Rhd1 $\pm$.

(g) 18 Rdg1 dxe5 19 Rxg4 Rxd4! (19 ... h5 20 Qe2 $\pm$, 19 ... exd4 20 Bh6) 20 Bxd4 exd4 and Black has enough compensation for the rook, Hellers–Ernst, Sweden 1987.

(h) Black can open lines by 11 . . . b5 12 Ndxb5 Rc8, but after 13 Bb3 he doesn't have enough for the pawn.

(i) 14 . . . e6 15 hxg6! exd5 16 Bh6 fxg6 17 Bxg7 Kxg7 18 Qh6† Kf7 19 Nxd5 with a very strong attack (Agdestein).

(j) 16 . . . gxf5 17 gxf5 and it is difficult for Black to defend, e.g. 17 . . . Kf8 18 Bh6 Bxh6 19 Qxh6† Kd8 20 Qf7 ± .

(k) 18 fxg6 Nfxd5 19 Bd4! Bxd4 20 Qxd4 e5 21 gxf7† Kf8 22 Qg1 Nf6 23 Rh6 ± , Agdestein–Karlsson, Gausdal 1987.

(l) White should play Kb1 soon or his a-pawn becomes loose e.g. 12 h4 Ne5 13 g4 (13 h5 Nxh5 14 g4 Nf6 15 Bh6 Rxc3 16 bxc3 Bxh6 = , Tal–Wade, Palma de Mallorca 1966) 13 . . . Nc4 14 Bxc4 Rxc4 15 Nb3 Qa6 16 h5 (now on 16 Kb1 Rac8 Black threatens 17 . . . Bxg4! 18 fxg4 Rxc3 19 bxc3 Nxe4 20 Qd3 Nxc3† ∓) 16 . . . Rxc3 17 bxc3 Qxa2 18 hxg6 Be6! 19 gxh7† Kh8 ∓ (Geller).

(m) Black cannot find a good square for the queen. If (A) 15 . . . Qe5 16 Bf4 Qe6 17 Ne2 ± , de Firmian–McCambridge, Berkeley 1982; or (B) 15 . . . Qa6 16 e5! Ne8 (16 . . . dxe5 17 Nc5 Qd6 18 Qe2 wins material—Düball) 17 h5 with good attacking chances.

(n) 18 a4 with advantage, Damjanović–Kaplan, San Juan 1969.

(o) 16 Rhe1 Rxc3 17 bxc3 Be6 gives Black play for the exchange, Blackstock–Hollis, Marlow 1971.

(p) 18 Ned4 Qd7 19 Bh6 Bh8 20 h4 ± .

(q) 12 . . . Bxb3 13 cxb3! Rfc8 14 Kb1 keeps White's king safe on the queenside while he starts a kingside attack with h4, h5, etc.

(r) 18 Ba4! with a plus, Browne–Kastner, US 1970.

SICILIAN DEFENSE

Dragon Variation—Yugoslav Attack

1 e4 c5 2 Nf3 d6 3 d4 cxd4 4 Nxd4 Nf6 5 Nc3 g6 6 Be3 Bg7 7 f3 (a)

	73	74	75	76	77	78
	(0–0) Nc6					
8	(Qd2)					Qd2
	(Nc6)					Bd7
9	(Bc4) . . . . . . .0–0–0 . . . . .g4				. . . . . . .Be6(k)	0–0–0(n)
	(Bd7)(b)	d5! Nxd4		Nxd4		Rc8
10	h4(c)	exd5	Bxd4	Bxd4	0–0–0(l)	g4
	Qc7(d)	Nxd5	Be6	Be6	Ne5	Ne5
11	Bb3	Nxc6	Kb1	0–0–0	h4	Kb1
	Na5	bxc6	Qc7	Qa5	Bc4	Qa5(o)
12	0–0–0	Bd4(e)	h4	a3	Bh3	h4
	Nc4	e5	Rfc8	Rfc8	Ba6	h5
13	Bxc4	Bc5	h5	h4	b3	gxh5
	Qxc4	Re8(f)	Qa5	Rab8	Qa5	Nxh5
14	Bh6 ±	Nxd5	hxg6	Nd5(i)	Kb1	Rg1 ±
		cxd5(g)	hxg6(h)	Qxd2(j)	Rfc8(m)	

(a) 7 Bc4 Ng4! 8 Bb5† Kf8 =.

(b) The older system 9 . . . Nd7 10 0–0–0 Nb6 11 Bb3 Na5 12 Qd3 Bd7 13 h4 Rc8 14 h5 Nbc4 15 hxg6 fxg6 may be all right for Black, Gligorić–Haag, Havana 1962. White can, however, obtain a simple edge with 10 Bb3 Nb6 11 Nd5.

(c) 10 Bb3 Nxd4! 11 Bxd4 b5 12 0–0–0 a5 13 e5 dxe5 14 Bxe5 Bc6 is equal. If 12 Nd5!? e6 13 Bb6 (Sherzer–Petursson, Philadelphia 1986) 13 . . . Qe8 14 Nc7 Qb8 15 Nxa8 a4 is good.

(d) With 10 . . . Rc8, 10 . . . Qa5, or 10 . . . h5 Black leads into the major lines covered in cols. 61–72. Here 10 . . . Qb8?! 11 h5 is bad for Black.

(e) 12 Nxd5 cxd5 13 Qxd5 Qc7 and Black's open lines provide good play in exchange for the pawn, e.g. 14 Qc5 (14 Qxa8 Bf5 15 Qxf8† Kxf8 ∓) 14 . . . Qb7 15 b3 Bf5 16 Bd3 Rac8 17 Qa5 Rc3 ∓, Smirin–Bassin, USSR 1985. Or 15 Qa3 Bf5 16 Ba6 Qc7 17 Qc5 Qb6! 18 Qxb6 axb6 19 Bc4 Rfc8 20 Bb3 Rxa2! 21 Rd8† Rxd8 22 Bxa2 Bd4 = (Averbakh).

(f) 13 . . . Be6 14 Ne4 (14 Bxf8 Qxf8 is fine for Black) 14 . . . Re8 15 h4 h6 16 g4 is sharp but seems to favor White.

(g) 15 Qxd5 Qxd5 16 Rxd5 Be6 17 Rd6 Bxa2 18 b4 a5 19 Bb5 Rec8 20 Bd7 Rc7 21 Bb6 Rb7 22 bxa5 Rxa5! 23 Bc8 Bf8! 24 Bxb7 Rb5! = (van der Wiel).

(h) 15 a3 Rab8 16 g4 ±.

(i) 14 h5 b5 15 h6?! (15 Nd5 =) 15 . . . b4! 16 hxg7 bxa3 17 Qh6 axb2† 18 Kd2 Bxg4! 19 Bxf6 (19 fxg4 e5 wins) 19 . . . Bh5 (Black has avoided mate and his counterattack proves decisive) 20 Bd4 e5 21 Rxh5 gxh5 22 Qg5 Qb4 23 Bd3 Qxd4 24 Nd5 Qf2† 25 Be2 Rxc2†! 26 Kxc2 Qxe2† 27 Kc3 Qxf3† 28 Kc4 Qb3 mate, Plaskett–W. Watson, Brighton 1983.

(j) 15 Rxd2 Nxd5 16 Bxg7 Kxg7 17 exd5 Bd7 18 h5 h6 =, Nunn–Karlsson, Helsinki 1983.

(k) 9 . . . e6 10 0–0–0 d5 11 Be2 Nxd4 12 Bxd4 dxe4 13 g5 Nh5 14 Qe3! Qc7 15 Bxg7 Kxg7 16 Nxe4 ±, Morris–Kudrin, Gausdal 1983.

(l) 10 Nxe6?! fxe6 11 Bc4 Qd7 is at least equal for Black.

(m) If 14 . . . Qa3?! 15 g4 Nh5 16 Bg4 ±, de Firmian–Kudrin, Bor 1984. After 14 . . . Rfc8 15 Nd5 Qxd2 16 Rxd2 Nxd5 17 exd5 Rc3 chances are even.

(n) White can play 9 Bc4 against this delayed-castling system, too. After 9 . . . Rc8 10 Bb3 Ne5 11 0–0–0 Qa5 (11 . . . Nc4 is better) 12 h4 Nc4 13 Bxc4 Rxc4 14 Nb3 Qc7 15 Bd4 Bc6?! 16 e5! dxe5 17 Bxe5 White is much better, Fischer–Camara, Siegen 1970.

(o) (A) 11 . . . 0–0 12 h4 ± with a quick kingside attack. (B) 11 . . . Nc4 12 Bxc4 Rxc4 13 h4 Qc7 14 h5 ±.

SICILIAN DEFENSE

Classical Dragon

1 e4 c5 2 Nf3 d6 3 d4 cxd4 4 Nxd4 Nf6 5 Nc3 g6 6 Be2 Bg7 7 0–0 0–0
8 Be3 Nc6

	79	80	81	82	83	84
9	Nb3				Qd2(l)	
	Be6			a5(j)	Ng4	d5
10	f4			a4	Bxg4	exd5(p)
	Qc8		Na5(g)	Be6	Bxg4	Nxd5
11	Kh1	Bf3(d)	f5	f4(k)	Nd5(m)	Nxc6(q)
	Bg4(a)	Bg4	Bc4	Rc8	Be6(n)	bxc6
12	Bg1	h3(e)	Bd3(h)	Kh1	c4	Rad1
	Bxe2(b)	Bxf3	Bxd3	Nd7	Qd7	Qc7
13	Qxe2	Qxf3	cxd3	Bf3	a4	Bd4
	Qg4	e6	Nxb3	Nb6	Bxd5	e6
14	Qd2	Rad1	Qxb3!	Bxb6	exd5	Bc5
	b5!	Rd8	Ng4	Qxb6	Nxd4	Rd8
15	Rae1	f5	Bg5	Nd5	Bxd4	Ne4
	b4(c)	Ne5(f)	Qa5(i)	Bxd5 =	Bxd4(o)	Bf5(r)

(a) 11 . . . Rd8 12 Bg1 d5 13 e5 Ne4 14 Bd3 g5 15 Qe1 Nxc3 16 bxc3 gxf4 17 Qh4 Bf5 18 Qxf4 Bg6 19 Rae1 $\pm$, Kindermann–Mestel, Beersheba 1984.

(b) 12 . . . b6 13 Bf3 Bxf3 14 Qxf3 Qg4 15 Qf2 Rac8 16 Rae1 is better for White, Nijboer–Sosonko, Dutch Chp. 1985.

(c) 16 Nd5 Qc8 17 Nd4 Nxd5 18 exd5 Nxd4 19 Bxd4 Bxd4 20 Qxd4 Qxc2 21 Rxe7 Rae8 =, Westerinen–Gufeld, Havana 1985.

(d) 11 h3 Rd8 12 Bf3 Bc4 13 Rf2 e5 =, Steinmeyer–Benko, US Chp. 1963.

(e) 12 Nd5 Bxf3 13 Qxf3 Nd7! (13 . . . Nxd5? 14 exd5 Nb4 15 Qe4! Na6 16 c3 $\pm$, Hübner–Miles, Tilburg 1985) 14 Bc1 (14 c3 e6) 14 . . . Re8 15 c3 Nc5 = (Lobron).

(f) 16 Qf2 Nc4 is equal (Fedorowicz).

(g) 10 . . . Rc8 11 Kh1 Na5 12 f5 Nc4 13 Bd4 Bd7 14 Bxc4 Rxc4 15 Qe2 b5 16 a4 $\pm$, Seitaj–Velimirović, Kavala 1985.

(h) 12 Nxa5 Bxe5 13 Nxb7 Bxd1 14 Nxd8 Bxc2 was equal in Lasker–Riumin, Moscow 1936.

(i) If 15 . . . Bd4† 16 Kh1 Nf2† 17 Rxf2 Bxf2 18 Nd5 Re8 19 f6 is strong. After 15 . . . Qa5 16 Kh1 Qc5 17 Bh4 Be5 18 h3 White has an edge, Mortensen–Arnason, Esbjerg 1984.

(j) (A) 9 . . . a6 10 a4 is interesting because the position may arise via the Najdorf Variation after 6 a4 g6. After 9 . . . a6 10 a4, Zapata–Sunye, Dubai 1986, continued 10 . . . b6!? 11 f4 Bb7 12 Bf3 Rb8 13 Qe1 Qc7 14 Rd1 e6 15 Rd2 Ba8 =. (B) 9 . . . Bd7 10 f4 b5! 11 a3 (11 Bxb5 Ng4) 11 . . . a5 12 Bf3 b4 13 axb4 axb4 was here agreed drawn in Short–Miles, Dortmund 1986.

(k) Commonly played, but 11 Nd4 may be better. After 11 . . . d5 12 Nxe6 fxe6 13 exd5 exd5 (13 . . . Nxd5 14 Bd2 $\pm$) 14 Nb5 e5 15 c3 Kh8 16 Qb3 $\pm$, Horowitz–Reshevsky, New York 1941. Black should try 11 . . . Nxd4 12 Bxd4 Rc8 13 f4 Bc4 14 Rf2 e5 ∞, Tolush–Rovner, Leningrad 1939. The column is Shamkovich–de Firmian, New York 1985.

(l) (A) Any slow move such as 9 h3 or 9 Kh1 is met with 9 . . . d5! =. (B) 9 f4 Qb6! 10 Qd3 (White must be careful; if 10 Qd2 Nxe4 wins a pawn, while on 10 e5 dxe5 11 fxe5 Nxe5 12 Nf5 Qxb2! 13 Nxe7† Kh8 14 Bd4 Qb4 15 Bxe5 Qxe7 16 Qd4 Nh5 $\mp$) 10 . . . Ng4 11 Bxg4 (11 Nd5 Bxd4! 12 Nxb6 Bxe3† 13 Kh1 Bxb6 $\mp$) 11 . . . Bxd4 12 Bxd4 Qxd4† 13 Qxd4 Nxd4 =, Mestrović–Hartston, Örebro 1966.

(m) 11 f4 Nxd4 12 Bxd4 e5! 13 Be3 exf4 is equal, Barczay–Rigo, Hungarian Chp. 1978.

(n) 11 . . . Bd7 12 c4 Ne5 13 b3 e6 14 Nc3 Qa5 15 h3 with a pull (Schwarz).

(o) 16 Qxd4 Rfe8 17 Rfe1 b6 18 h3 e5 19 dxe6 Rxe6 20 Rxe6 Qxe6 21 Rd1 Re8 22 b3 Qd7 23 Qd5 with a slight edge, although Black held the draw easily in Timman–Ljubojević, Bugojno 1986.

(p) Neither (A) 10 Rfd1 Nxd4 11 Qxd4 Nxe4 12 Qxd5 Nd6 =, Lisitsin–Katkov, USSR 1956, nor (B) 10 Nxc6 bxc6 11 e5 Ne8 12 f4 f6 13 Bf3 Rb8! = (Gufeld) gives Black much trouble.

(q) 11 Nxd5 Nxd4! 12 c4 e5 =, Honfi–Gufeld, Kecskemet 1958.

(r) 16 Ng3 (16 Nd6 Bf8!—Olthof) 16 . . . Be6 with at least equality.

SICILIAN DEFENSE

Dragon Variation

1 e4 c5 2 Nf3 d6 3 d4 cxd4 4 Nxd4 Nf6 5 Nc3 g6

	85	86	87	88	89	90
6	(Be3) .... f4 .... (Levenfish Variation) .... g3(r)					
	(Bg7)		Nc6! .... Bg7 .... Nbd7			Bg7(s)
7	(0–0) Be3		Nxc6(h)	e5	Be2(p)	Bg2
	(0–0)	Nc6(d)	bxc6	dxe5(m)	Bg7	0–0
8	Nb3	Qd2(e)	e5	fxe5	0–0(q)	0–0
	Nc6	0–0	Nd7(i)	Nfd7	0–0	Bg4!
9	Bg5(a)	0–0–0	exd6(j)	e6	Bf3	Nde2
	a5(b)	Nxd4	exd6	Ne5	a6	Qc8
10	a4	Bxd4	Be3(k)	Bb5†	Nb3	Re1
	Be6	Be6	Be7!	Nbc6	Nb6	Nc6
11	f4	Kb1	Qf3(l)	exf7†	a4!	f3
	Rc8	b5(f)	d5	Kf8(n)	Be6	Bh3
12	Kh1	Bxb5	0–0–0	Nxc6	a5	Bh1
	Nb4	Rb8	Bf6	Qxd1†	Nc4	Be6
13	Bh4	Rhe1	Bd4	Nxd1	g4 ±	Be3
	Nd7(c)	Qa5(g)	0–0 =	Nxc6(o)		Bc4 =

(a) 9 Kh1 a5 10 a4 Be6 11 f4 Qb6 12 f5 (12 Nd5 Bxd5 =) 12 ... Bxb3 13 cxb3 Qb4 14 Be3 Nd7 15 Bc4 Nb6! 16 Na2 Nxc4 17 Nxb4 Nxe3 18 Qe2 Nxf1 with full compensation for the queen, van den Berg–Larsen, Wijk aan Zee 1959.

(b) The immediate 9 ... Be6 is not as good. After 10 f4 Na5 11 f5 Bc4 12 Kh1 Rc8 13 Bd3 b5 14 Qe1 a6 15 Nxa5 Qxa5 16 Nd5 White had the advantage in Zuyev–Taborov, Avangaard 1978.

(c) 14 f5 Bxb3 15 cxb3 Bxc3 16 bxc3 Rxc3 17 fxg6 hxg6 =, A. Sokolov–Short, Biel 1985.

(d) 7 ... Nbd7 leads to a hybrid Najdorf-Dragon where after 8 0–0 a6 9 a4 Black has difficulty freeing his position. 8 f4 transposes to col. 89, note (a).

(e) 8 Nb3 0–0 9 f4 Be6 10 g4 is an attempt to smash Black on the kingside. If 10 ... d5 11 f5 Bc8 12 exd5 Nb4 13 Bf3 gxf5 14 a3! fxg4 15 Bg2 Na6 16 Qd3 Nd7 17 0–0–0 gives White attacking chances for the pawn, Yakovich–Lerner, Kuybyshev 1986. It is better to play 10 ... Na5! 11 g5 Nd7 12 Bd4 f6! 13 h4 fxg5 14 Bxg7 KIxg7 15 Nd4 Bg8 16 f5 Qb6 with good counterchances (Boleslavsky).

(f) 11 ... Rc8 12 h4 Bc4 13 h5 (Levy) may give White the initiative.

(g) 14 Ba4 Rb4 15 Bb3 Rxd4 16 Qxd4 Nd5 17 exd5 Bxd4 18 Rxd4 Bf5 =, Kupreichik–W. Watson, Frunze 1985.

(h) 7 Bb5 Bd7 8 Bxc6 Bxc6 9 e5 dxe5 10 fxe5 Ne4! 11 Nxe4 Bxe4 12 0–0 Bg7 with even chances, Penrose–Barden, Hastings 1957–58.

(i) 8 . . . dxe5?! 9 Qxd8† Kxd8 10 fxe5 Ng4 11 Bf4 Bg7 12 0–0–0† Bd7 13 e6! fxe6 14 Be4 e5 15 Be2! h5 16 Bd2 ± (Heidenfeld).

(j) On 9 Qf3 Black simply develops, sacrificing the soldier on c6 for time: 9 . . . Bg7 10 Bb5 0–0 11 Bxc6 Rb8 =, Bronstein–Vasiukov, USSR Chp. 1959.

(k) 10 Qd4 Nf6 11 Be3 Be7 12 Be2 0–0 13 0–0 c5 14 Qd2 d5 15 Bf3 Bb7 16 Rad1 Rb8 =, Szabó–Reshevsky, Helsinki 1952.

(l) 11 Qd2 0–0 12 0–0–0 Nb6 13 Be2 d5 14 h4 h5! 15 g4?! Bxg4 16 Bxg4 Nc4 17 Qd3 Qb8! 18 b3 (Larsen–Lein, Lone Pine 1979); now 18 . . . Nxe3 19 Qxe3 Re8 20 Qd2 hxg4 21 h5 Qd6 is sharp, but better for Black. The column is Tal–Lisitsin, USSR Chp. 1956.

(m) 7 . . . Nh5 8 Bb5† Bd7 9 e6 fxe6 10 Nxe6 Bxc3† 11 bxc3 Qc8 12 Bxd7† Nxd7 13 0–0 Nhf6 (Lennox–Levy, Scottish Chp. 1974); now 14 Be3 leaves White with a simple plus because his king is safer.

(n) 11 . . . Kxf7 12 0–0† Bf6 13 Nxc6 bxc6 14 Qxd8 Rxd8 15 Ba4 ± (Boleslavsky).

(o) The column is Dzafarov–Guseynov, corr. 1975. After 14 0–0 White has the advantage.

(p) 7 Nf3 Qc7 8 Bd3 a6 9 0–0 Bg7 transposes to the Najdorf Variation, 6 f4 (col. 33).

(q) 8 Be3 0–0 9 Bf3 a6 10 0–0 Qc7 11 Kh1 (Horowitz–Reshevsky, New York 1944) 11 . . . e5 12 Nb3 b5 ∓. White can maintain an equal game with 10 Nb3 Qc7 11 Qe2 e5, but the combination of Be3 and f4 is not best against this system. The column is Eley–Miles, Birmingham 1973.

(r) 6 Bc4 Bg7 7 h3 Nc6 8 Be3 0–0 9 Bb3 transposes to the Accelerated Dragon (col. 93) after 9 . . . Qa5 10 0–0, or Black can play 9 . . . Na5 10 0–0 b6 11 Qd3 Bb7 with near equality, Fedorowicz–Christiansen, US Chp. 1977.

(s) 6 . . . Nc6 7 Nde2! (7 Bg2 Nxd4! 8 Qxd4 Bg7 9 0–0 0–0 is equal) 7 . . . Bg7 8 Bg2 0–0 (8 . . . Bg4 9 h3 ±) 9 0–0 Be6 10 h3 Qd7 11 Kh7 Bc4 12 a4 Rac8 13 Re1 Rfd8 =, Andonov–Gulko, Saint John 1988. As no pieces have been exchanged, Black is somewhat cramped. The column is Sax–Kudrin, New York 1987.

SICILIAN DEFENSE

Accelerated Dragon

1 e4 c5 2 Nf3 Nc6 3 d4 cxd4 4 Nxd4 g6 5 Nc3 Bg7 6 Be3 Nf6

	91	92	93	94	95	96
7	Nxc6		Bc4			
	bxc6		Qa5		0–0	
8	e5		0–0(h)		Bb3(o)	
	Ng8	Nd5	0–0		a5	
9	f4(a)	Nxd5	Bb3	Nb3	f3(p)	
	Nh6	cxd5	d6	Qc7	d5	
10	Qd2(b)	Qxd5	h3	f4	exd5	Bxd5
	0–0	Rb8	Bd7	d6	Nb4	Nxd5
11	0–0–0(c)	Bc4(e)	f4(i)	Be2	Nde2	exd5(s)
	Qa5!	0–0	Nxd4	b6	a4	Nb4
12	Bc4	0–0(f)	Bxd4	g4(m)	Nxa4	Nde2
	Rb8	Qc7	Bc6	Bb7	Nfxd5	Bf5(t)
13	h4	Bf4	Qd3(j)	g5	Bf2(q)	Rc1
	d6	Bb7	Rad8(k)	Nd7	Bf5	b5
14	h5	Qd4	Rad1	Nd5	0–0	0–0(u)
	Nf5(d)	d6(g)	Nd7(l)	Qd8(n)	b5(r)	Rc8(v)

(a) 9 Bd4 Qa5 10 Bc4 Bxe5 11 0–0 Nf6 12 Re1 d6 13 Bxe5 dxe5 14 Qe2 Bf5 =, Tringov–Stein, Sarajevo 1967.

(b) 10 Qf3 0–0 11 Bc4 d5! 12 exd6 exd6 13 Qxc6 Bd7 14 Qf3 Rc8 15 Bd3 Bg4 ∓, Fichtl–Gereben, Warsaw 1956.

(c) 11 h3 d6 12 0–0 Nf5 13 Bf2 c5 14 g4 Nd4 (thematic) 15 Bg2 Rb8 16 Bxd4 cxd4 17 Qxd4 Qa5 18 Rhe1 Be6 19 Kb1?! Rb4 20 Qe3 dxe5 21 fxe5 Rfb8 22 b3 Rc4! 23 Rd3 Rc5! 24 Red1 Bxe5 25 Rd8† Rxd8 26 Rxd8† Kg7 +, Dückstein–Waller, Austria 1969.

(d) 15 hxg6 hxg6 16 g4 Nxe3 17 Qxe3 Bxg4 18 Rdg1 Bf5 ∓.

(e) Two important alternatives are: (A) 11 0–0–0 Bb7 12 Qd4 0–0 13 f4 d6 14 Bc4 Qc7 15 Bb3 dxe5 16 fxe5 Bxg2 =, Stein–Nei, USSR 1960, and (B) 11 Bxa7 Rxb2 12 Bd4 Rxc2 13 Bd3 e6 14 Qa8 Rc6 15 0–0 (15 Bb5 Ra6! 16 Bxa6 Qa5† =, Barczay–Pokojowczyk, Subotica 1981) 15 . . . 0–0 16 Bb5 Ba6 17 Qxd8 Rxd8 18 Bxc6 Bxf1 19 Kxf1 dxc6 20 Bc3 Rd3 21 Rc1 Rd5 22 Re1 Rc5 23 Re3 Rc4 24 Bb2 h5 =, Kupreichik–Petursson, Reykjavik 1980.

(f) 12 f4 d6 13 Bb3 a5 14 0–0 Bb7 15 Qc4 Rc8 16 Qd3 dxe5 17 Qxd8 Rcxd8 18 f5 e4 = (Silman).

(g) 15 Rfe1 Rfd8 16 Qc3 Rbc8 17 Bb3 Qxc3 18 bxc3 dxe5 19 Bxe5 e6 20 Bxg7 Kxg7 21 Re3 Rc7 =.

(h) Black's 7 . . . Qa5 forces White to castle short, as is plainly shown when White tries other 8th moves, e.g. (A) 8 Qd2? Nxe4! 9 Nxc6 Qxc3 +; (B) 8 Nb3? Qb4 9 Bd3 Nxe4!; (C)

8 f3?! Qb4 9 Bb3? (9 Nxc6 bxc6 =) 9 ... Nxe4 10 Nxc6 Bxc3† 11 bxc3 Qxc3† 12 Ke2 dxc6 13 Bd4 e5! winning.

(i) 11 Re1 Rac8 12 Qd3 Ne5 13 Qe2 Qa6! (fighting for c4) 14 Qxa6 bxa6 15 Nd5?! (15 Rad1 Nc4 16 Bc1 =) 15 ... Nxd5 16 Bxd5 Nc4 17 Bxc4 Rxc4 $\mp$, Povah–Silman, England 1978.

(j) 13 Nd5 Rfe8 14 Bxf6 exf6 15 f5 Rxe4 16 fxg6 hxg6 17 Nxf6† Bxf6 18 Rxf6 Qc5† 19 Kh1 d5 20 Qf3 Qe7 =, Hector–Donaldson, Malmö 1986.

(k) Threatening ... e5 followed by ... d5.

(l) 15 Bxg7 Kxg7 16 Kh1 Nc5 17 Qd4† e5 18 Qe3 Nxb3 19 axb3 exf4 20 Rxf4 Qe5! =.

(m) 12 Bf3 Bb7 13 Rf2 Na5! 14 Nxa5 bxa5 15 Bd4 Nd7 16 Nd5 Bxd5 17 exd5 Bxd4 18 Qxd4 Qc5 19 Rd1 Rfb8 20 c3 Rb7 21 Kf1 Rfb8 $\mp$, Hammie–Silman, USA 1975.

(n) 15 Rb1 (15 Kd4 e6! 16 Nc3 Nxd4 17 Bxd4 e5 18 Be3 exf4 19 Bxf4 Bxc3 20 bxc3 Nc5 $\mp$, Savereide–Silman, US 1974) 15 ... e6! 16 Nc3 Bxc3 17 bxc3 Ne7! $\mp$ (Silman).

(o) 8 0–0 Nxe4! 9 Nxe4 d5 10 Nxc6 bxc6 11 Bd3 dxe4 12 Bxe4 Ba6! 13 Qxd8 Rfxd8 14 Rfb1 Bxd4! 15 Bxc6 (15 Bxd4 Rxd4 16 Bxc6 Rc8 17 c3 Rd2 18 Bf3 e5 19 g3 f5 intending ... e4 and ... Bd3) 15 ... Rac8 16 Ba4 Bxe3 17 fxe3 Rd2 18 Rd1 Rcd8 19 c3 Bb7 20 Kf1 Ba6† 21 Kg1 = (Strauss).

(p) 9 a4 Ng4 10 Qxg4 Nxd4 11 Qd1 (11 Bxd4 Bxd4 12 Qg3 d6 13 0–0–0 Bxc3 14 Qxc3 Be6 =, Ivanović–Cebalo, Yugoslav Chp. 1983) 11 ... Nxb3 12 cxb3 d6 13 Qd2 Be6 14 Nd5 Bxd5 15 exd5 Qd7 16 0–0 b5! $\mp$, Gamarro–Petursson, Buenos Aires 1978.

(q) 13 Bd4 Bxd4 14 Qxd4 Bf5 15 Nac3 Nxc2† 16 Bxc2 Nxc3 17 Qxd8 Rfxd8 18 Bxf5 Nxe2 19 Kxe2 gxf5 20 Rhe1 e5 =, Petrushin–Hasin, USSR 1976.

(r) 15 Nac3 Nxc3 16 Nxc3 Qxd1 17 Rfxd1 Bxc2 18 Bxc2 Nxc2 19 Rac1 Bxc3 20 Rxc2 Bf6 21 b3 h5 =, Kuzmin–Tukmakov, Kishinev 1975.

(s) Equally critical is 11 Nxd5, e.g. 11 ... f5 12 c3 fxe4 13 Nxc6 (13 fxe4 Nxe5?! 14 Bg5 Rf7 15 Rf1!? Bf6 16 Nf3 Nxf3† 17 Qxf3 ±, Omelchenko–Widera, corr. 1985. Black should try 13 ... e6!?) 13 ... bxc6 14 Nb6 Rb8 15 Qxd8 Rxd8 16 Nxc8 Rdxc8 17 0–0–0 exf3 18 gxf3 Rb5 =, Klundt–Tielemann, West Germany 1984.

(t) The older move 12 ... e6 is frowned on because after 13 a3 Nxd5 14 Nxd5 exd5 15 Bd4 Bxd4 16 Qxd4 Re8 17 Kf2 it seems that White has a positional edge because of the isolated d-pawn. But matters may not be so simple in view of White's exposed king, e.g. 17 ... Ra6 18 Nc3 Rc6 19 Rad1 Bf5 20 Rd2 Rc4! 21 Qxd5 Qb6† 22 Kg3 Qe3 23 h3 Qf4† 24 Kf2 =, Gruenfeld–Taylor, New York 1985.

(u) An important alternative is 14 a3 Nxc2† 15 Rxc2 Bxc2 16 Qxc2 b4 17 Na4 Qxd5 18 Nb6 Qe6 19 Kf2 Rab8 20 Nf4 Qa2 21 axb4 axb4 22 Qb1 (22 Nfd5 b3 23 Qe2 Rb7 $\mp$) 22 ... b3 23 Qxa2 bxa2 24 Ra1 Bxb2? 25 Rxa2 ±, Lanka–Priedniek, USSR 1980. Black can improve with 24 ... Rb7, when 25 Rxa2 Rfb8 leads to an equal ending after 26 Nc4 Rb7 or 26 Na4 Bxb2 27 Nc5 Rb5.

(v) 15 Nd4 Rxc3!? (nothing is wrong with the older 15 ... Bxd4, e.g. 16 Qxd4 Nxc2 17 Rxc2 Bxc2 18 Bh6 e5 19 Qxe5 f6 20 Qe6† Rf7 21 Ne4 [21 Nxb5 Bf5 22 Qe3 Qxd5 23 Nd4 Rd7 =, Gavrikov–Kouksov, Kaluga 1977] 21 ... Bxe4 22 fxe4 Qd7 23 Rxf6 Re8 24 Qxd7 Rxd7 25 d6 R7d8! 26 Bg5 a4! $\mp$, Kouksov–Pigusov, Nikoliev 1978) 16 bxc3 Nxa2 17 Ra1! Nxc3 18 Qd2 Bxd4 19 Bxd4 Nxd5 20 g4 Be6 21 Rxa5 $\pm$.

SICILIAN DEFENSE

Accelerated Dragon (Maróczy Bind)

1 e4 c5 2 Nf3 Nc6 3 d4 cxd4 4 Nxd4 g6 5 c4

	97	98	99	100	101	102
	Nf6.................Bg7					
6	Nc3		Be3			
	d6		Nh6.......Nf6			
7	f3..........Be2		Nc3	Nc3		
	Nxd4	Nxd4	d6	Ng4.........0–0		
8	Qxd4	Qxd4	Be2(h)	Qxg4	Be2	
	Bg7	Bg7	0–0	Nxd4	b6..........d6	
9	Be3(a)	Bg5(d)	0–0	Qd1	0–0	0–0
	0–0	0–0	f5	Ne6	Bb7	Bd7
10	Qd2	Qd2	exf5	Rc1(k)	Nxc6(o)	Qd2(r)
	Qa5	Be6	gxf5(i)	d6(l)	Bxc6(p)	Nxd4
11	Rc1	Rc1	f4	b4(m)	f3	Bxd4
	Be6	Qa5(e)	Qb6	Bd7	d6	Bc6
12	Nd5(b)	f3(f)	Nf5	Be2	Qd2	f3
	Qxa2(c)	Rfc8(g)	Qxb2(j)	a5(n)	Qd7(q)	a5(s)

(a) 9 Bg5 0–0 10 Qd2 Be6 11 Rc1 Rc8 12 b3 a6 13 Be2 b5 14 cxb5 axb5 15 Nxb5 Rxc1† 16 Qxc1 Qa5† 17 Qd2 Ra8 18 Qxa5 Rxa5 19 a3 Bxb3 20 Rb1 (20 Kf2 Ba4 21 Rb1 h6 22 Bd2 Ra8 =, Tukmakov–Vaganian, USSR 1984) 20 . . . Ba4 21 Rb1 Bxb5 22 Rxb5 Rxa3 23 Rb8† Bf8 24 Bh6 Nd7 25 Rd8 Ra1† 26 Kf2 Ra2 27 g4 f6 28 Ke3 Rc2 29 Bd3 Draw, Mokrý–Kallai, Trnava 1985.

(b) 12 f3 Rfc8 13 b3 a6 14 Na4 Qxd2† 15 Kxd2 Nd7 16 g4 f5 17 gxf5 gxf5 18 Rhg1 Kh8 =, Lau–Zhu.Polgar, New York 1985.

(c) 13 Nxe7† Kh8 14 Be2 (14 Bd4 Rae8 15 Nd5 Bxd5 16 cxd5 Rc8 17 Be2 Rxc1 18 Qxc1 Nd7 19 Bxg7 Kxg7 20 Qc3† Kg8 21 Kf2 Nb6 22 Qf6 Na4 =) 14 . . . Ng8 15 Nd5 (15 Nxg8 Kxg8 16 Bd4 Bxd4 17 Qxd4 Qa5† 18 Kf2 Qe5 19 Rcd1 Rfc8 20 b3 Rc6 21 Qe3 Rb6 22 Rd3 Qc5 =) 15 . . . Bxd5 16 cxd5 Rfc8 17 0–0 a5 18 Bd4 Qa4 19 Bc3 Qb3 ±.

(d) (A) 9 0–0 0–0 10 Qe3 Be6 11 Bd2 Qb6 12 b3 Qxe3 13 Bxe3 Nd7 14 Rac1 Nc5 15 f3 a5 16 Nd5 Bxd5 17 exd5 Bb2 18 Rc2 Ba3 planning . . . a4 =. (B) 9 Qd3 0–0 10 0–0 Be6 11 Be3 Qa5 12 Rac1 Rfc8 13 b3 Nd7 14 Qd2 Nc5 15 f3 a6 16 Bg5 Rc7 17 Rfd1 Rac8 ±, Ornstein–Velikov, Skara 1980.

(e) 11 . . . a6 12 b3 b5 13 cxb5 axb5 14 Bxb5 Qa5 15 Bd3 Rfc8 16 0–0 Rxc3 17 Rxc3 Nxe4 18 Bxe4 Bxc3 19 Qe3 Ra7 20 Bb1 d5 ∓, Formanek–Rind, Lone Pine 1980.

(f) 12 0–0 Rfc8 13 b3 a6 14 f4 Rc5! 15 Bf3 Rac8 16 Qe3 (16 Rcd1 b5 17 Nd5 Qd8 18 cxb5 Bxd5 19 exd5 axb5 ∓̄, Kaiszauri–Spiridonov, Skara 1980) 16 . . . b5! 17 e5 dxe5 18 fxe5 Nd7 19 Nd5 Bxd5 20 Bxd5 e6 ∓, Psakhis–Pigusov, USSR 1979.

(g) 13 b3 a6 14 Na4 (14 Nd5 Qxd2† 15 Kxd2 Nxd5 16 cxd5 Bd7 17 h4 f6 18 Be3 f5 19 exf5 gxf5 20 g4 fxg4 21 fxg4 Bb2 =, Mokrý–Zhu.Polgar, Czechoslovakia 1985) 14 . . . Qxd2†

(14 . . . Qd8!?) 15 Kxd2 Rc6 16 Nc3 Rac8 17 Nd5 Kf8 18 Be3 $\pm$, Karpov–Kavalek, Nice 1974.

(h) 8 h3 f5 9 exf5 Nxf6 10 Nxf5 Bxf5 11 Qd2 Qa5 12 Rc1 0–0 =, Cing Huan–Larsen, Bled/Portorož 1979.

(i) 10 . . . Nxd4 11 Bxd4 Bxd4 12 Qxd4 Nf5 13 Qd2 Bd7 14 Bf3 Bc6 15 Bd5 $\pm$, Tal–Kupreichik, Sochi 1970.

(j) 13 Nxh6† Bxh6 14 Rc1 Bg7 15 Rc2 (15 Nd5 Qxa2 16 c5 Kh8 17 Bf3 Be7 18 cxd6 exd6 19 Nc7 Bb3 $\mp$, Ermolinsky–I. Ivanov, USSR 1980) 15 . . . Qa3 16 Qd2 Be6 17 Kh1 Rac8 is unclear, Spassov–Nicevski, Sofia 1976.

(k) 10 Be2 Bxc3† 11 bxc3 b6 12 0–0 Bb7 13 f3 Qc7 14 Rb1 0–0 15 Qd2 f5 16 exf5 gxf5 $\mp$.

(l) 10 . . . Qa5 11 Bd3 (11 Qd2 b6 12 Qd5 $\pm$) 11 . . . d6 (11 . . . Bxc3† 12 Rxc3 Qxa2 13 Qc1 Qa5 14 c5 $\pm$, Honfi–Szilagyi, Kecskemet 1971) 12 0–0 0–0 13 Bb1 Bd7 14 f4 Nc5 15 Nd5 $\pm$, Mednis–D. Byrne, US Chp. 1973. By avoiding Qd2 White sidesteps the simplifying . . . Nc5–a4.

(m) Taking away c5 from the Black knight. A different type of game arises from 11 Bd3 (11 Qd2 Qa5 12 Be2 Bd7 13 0–0 Nc5 14 f3 Na4 =) 11 . . . 0–0 12 0–0 a5 13 Bb1 Bd7 14 Qe2 Bc6 15 Rfd1 $\pm$, Beliavsky–Velimirović, Reggio Emilia 1986–87.

(n) Worse is 12 . . . b6 13 Qd2 Bb7 14 f3 Kh8 15 0–0 f5 16 exf5 gxf5 17 f4 $\pm$, Suba–Joksić, Zürich 1987. The column is Marjanović–Velimirović, Sarajevo 1984, which continued 13 a3 axb4 14 axb4 Bd7 15 0–0 Bc6 16 Qd2 Ra3 17 Nd5 Re8 18 Rfd1 Nf8 19 h3 Nd7 $\pm$.

(o) (A) 10 Rc1? Nxd4 11 Bxd4 Bh6! 12 Rc2 Nxe4 $\mp$, Tseshkovsky–Bellon, Las Palmas 1976. (B) 10 Qd2?! Nxd4 11 Bxd4 e5! 12 Bxe5 Nxe4 13 Nxe4 Bxe5 14 Nd6 (14 Nc3 Re8 $\mp$, Tal–Hernandez, Las Palmas 1977) 14 . . . Bxd6! 15 Qxd6 Qg5 16 g3? Rae8 17 Rfe1 Re6 $\mp$, J. Fernandez–R. Hernandez, Cuba 1976. (C) 10 f3 Rc8 (10 . . . Nh5!?) 11 Qd2 (11 Rc1 Nxd4 12 Bxd4 Bh6 13 Rc2 Nh5 14 g3 Ng7 15 f4 f5 =, Browne–Benjamin, Lone Pine 1980) 11 . . . d6 12 Rfd1 Qd7 13 Nxc6 Bxc6 14 a4 $\pm$, J. Adamski–Dizdar, Rzeszow 1979.

(p) 10 . . . dxc6 11 c5 $\pm$.

(q) 13 a4 Qb7 14 a5 bxa5 15 Rxa5 Rfb8 16 Rb1 Qb4 17 Nb5 $\pm$, Ghitescu–Gavrilakis, Sofia 1986.

(r) 10 Rc1 Nxd4 11 Bxd4 Bc6 12 f3 a5 13 b3 (13 Qd1 a4) 13 . . . Nd7 14 Be3 (14 Bxg7 Kxg7 15 Qd4† Kg8 16 Rfd1 Nc5 17 e5 Qb6 18 exd6 exd6 19 Rb1 $\pm$, Andersson–Christiansen, Hastings 1978–79) 14 . . . Nc5 15 a3 $\pm$, Marjanović–Kagan, Skara 1980.

(s) 13 Kh1 Nd7 14 Bxg7 Kxg7 15 f4 Nc5 16 Bf3 a4 17 Rae1 $\pm$, Karlsson–Wedberg, Eksjö 1980.

SICILIAN DEFENSE

Taimanov Variation

1 e4 c5 2 Nf3 e6 3 d4 cxd4 4 Nxd4 Nc6 5 Nc3 a6 6 g3

	103	104	105	106	107	108
	Qc7...				d6.........	Nge7(q)
7	Bg2 Nf6				Bg2 Bd7	Nb3(r) b5(s)
8	0–0 Be7(a).................		Nxd4.......	d6	0–0 Nf6(n)	Bg2 d6
9	Re1(b) Nxd4		Qxd4 Bc5	Re1 Be7(k)	a4(o) Be7	Be3 Bb7
10	Qxd4.......e5!? Bc5	Nb5(f)	Bf4 d6(i)	Nxc6 bxc6	Nb3 0–0(p)	f4 g6
11	Qd1(c) d6	exf6 Nxc3(g)	Qd2 h6	e5 dxe5	a5 b5	Qd2 Qc7
12	Na4(d) Ba7	fxg7 Rg8	Rad1 e5	Rxe5 0–0(l)	axb6 Qxb6	Qf2 Bg7
13	b3 0–0(e)	bxc3 Qxc3(h)	Be3 Bg4(j)	Bf4 Qb7(m)	Qe2 Rfb8 =	0–0 ±

(a) 8 . . . h6 has been tried with the idea that after 9 Re1 Nxd4 10 Qxd4 (10 e5 Nb5 =) 10 . . . Bc5 Black has gained . . . h6 for free. White should play 9 Nb3! Be6 10 a4 d6 11 a5 0–0 12 Be3 with a cramp on the queenside, P. Popović–Rajković, Kladovo 1980.

(b) Other choices are: (A) 9 b3 0–0 10 Bb2 d6 11 Nce2 Nxd4 12 Nxd4 e5 13 Nf5 Bxf5 14 exf5 d5! = , Parma–Matanović, Zagreb 1965; (B) 9 Nde2 0–0 10 h3 d6 11 g4 b5 = .

(c) 11 Bf4 d6 12 Qd2 e5 13 Bg5 Ng4 14 Nd5 Qc6 15 Rf1 h6 16 h3 Be6 17 hxg4 hxg5 = , Tal–Barlov, Sochi 1984.

(d) 12 Be3 e5! 13 Qd2 Be6 14 Rad1 Ke7 is equal, Planinć–Matulović, Vrsać 1975.

(e) 14 c4 e5 15 Ba3 Bd4 16 Rc1 Ng4 17 Rf1 f5 18 c5 ± , Mestel–Bischoff, Plovdiv 1983.

(f) 10 . . . Nc6 11 exf6 gxf6 12 Qg4 allows White excellent attacking chances because of his lead in development, e.g. 12 . . . Ne5 13 Qg7 Ng6 14 Bf4 d6 15 Rad1 e5 (15 . . . Bd7 16 Bxd6! Bxd6 17 Nd5 +) 16 Nd5 Qd8 17 Be3 and 18 Bb6 wins, Boudy–Lebredo, Camaguey 1975.

(g) 11 . . . gxf6 12 Nxb5 axb5 13 Qg4 Bf8 14 c3 h5 15 Qf5 Be7 16 Qxb5 ± , Kindermann–Janssen, Baden 1985.

(h) 14 Rb1 d5 15 Bf4 with good attacking chances.

(i) After 10 . . . Bxd4 11 Bxc7 d5 12 exd5 Bxc3 13 bxc3 Nxd5 14 Be5 f6 15 c4! Black has a poor ending, Honfi–Kozma, Wijk aan Zee 1969.

(j) 13 . . . Bg4 (13 . . . Ke7 14 f4 ±) 14 Bxc5 dxc5 15 f3 Be6 16 f4 Rd8 17 Nd5 Bxd5 18 exd5 e4 19 Rfe1! Rxd5 20 Rxe4† Kd8 21 Qe2 Rxd1† 22 Qxd1† Qd7 23 Qxd7† Kxd7 24 Re5 with an endgame plus that was brilliantly converted to a win in Fischer–Taimanov, match, 1971.

(k) 9 . . . Bd7 10 Nxc6 bxc6 (10 . . . Bxc6 11 Nd5 Bxd5 12 exd5 ±) 11 Na4! Rb8 12 c4 c5 13 Nc3 Be7 14 Bf4 e5 (14 . . . Rxb2 15 e5 ±) 15 Bc1 ±, Kavalek–Garcia-Gonzalez, Buenos Aires 1978.

(l) (A) 12 . . . Bb7 13 Bf4 Bd6 14 Rxe6 +! fxe6 15 Bxd6 Qd7 16 Bc5 Qxd1 17 Rxd1 Rd8 18 Re1 Kf7 19 Ne4 Nxe4 20 Bxe4 with the better ending for White despite the material deficit, Browne–Langeweg, Amsterdam 1972; (B) 12 . . . Nd5 13 Nxd5 cxd5 14 Bf4 Bd6 15 Qxd5 ±.

(m) 14 Re1 Nd5 15 Nxd5 exd5! 16 c4 dxc4 17 Qa4 Qb4 =, F. Garcia–Kotronias, Dubai 1986. 16 Qh5 may be an improvement.

(n) 8 . . . Qc7 9 Re1 Be7 10 Nxc6 Bxc6 11 Qg4 h5 12 Qe2 b5 13 b3 h4 14 Bb2 hxg3 15 hxg3 Nf6 16 a4 bxa4 17 Nxa4 ±, Matulović–Barlov, Vrnjačka Banja 1984.

(o) 9 Re1 Be7 10 Nxc6 Bxc6 11 a4 0–0 12 a5 Nd7 13 Be3 Qc7 14 Na4 Rae8 15 Nb6 f5 is completely equal, Nunn–Andersson, Wijk aan Zee 1983.

(p) 10 . . . Na5?! 11 Nxa5 Qxa5 12 Bf4 Bc6 13 Qd2 Qc7 14 Rfd1 ±, Hübner–Andersson, Tilburg 1984. The column is Ostojić–Suetin, USSR vs. Yugoslavia 1975.

(q) 6 . . . Nxd4 7 Qxd4 Ne7 8 Bf4 Nc6 9 Qd2 leaves White in control of d6.

(r) (A) 7 Bg2 allows Black to free his game: 7 . . . Nxd4 8 Qxd4 Nc6 9 Qd1 Bb4 10 0–0 0–0 11 Be3 b5 =, de Firmian–Hort, Lone Pine 1979. (B) 7 Be3 Nxd4 8 Qxd4 b5 =.

(s) (A) 7 . . . Na5 8 Qh5! Nxb3 9 axb3 Nc6 10 Bg5 Be7 11 Bxe7 Qxe7 12 Bg2 0–0 13 0–0–0 with an edge, Timman–Radev, Tbilisi 1971. (B) 7 . . . d6 8 Bg2 Bd7 9 0–0 Nc8 10 a4 Be7 11 a5 ±, Hort–Garcia-Martinez, Madrid 1973. The column is R. Byrne–Taimanov, Leningrad 1973.

SICILIAN DEFENSE

Taimanov Variation

1 e4 c5 2 Nf3 e6 3 d4 cxd4 4 Nxd4 Nc6 5 Nc3 a6 6 Be2

	109	110	111	112	113	114
	Qc7..Nge7					
7	0–0 ....f4(l)				Bf4 ....0–0(p)	
	Nf6(a)			Nxd4(m)	Ng6	Nxd4
8	Be3.....................Kh1			Qxd4	Nxc6!	Qxd4
	Bb4(b)		Bb4(i)	b5	bxc6	Nc6
9	Na4(c)		Qd3(j)	Be3	Bd6	Qd3
	0–0........Be7(g)		b5	Bb7	Bxd6(n)	Qc7(q)
10	Nxc6	Nxc6	Nxc6	0–0	Qxd6	Bg5
	bxc6(d)	bxc6	Qxc6	Rc8	Qe7	Bd6
11	Nb6	Nb6	a4	Rad1	0–0–0	Qh3
	Rb8	Rb8	Bb7	Nf6	Qxd6	0–0
12	Nxc8	Nxc8	axb5	Bf3	Rxd6	Rad1
	Rfxc8(e)	Qxc8	axb5	h5!	Ke7	f6
13	Bxa6	e5	Rxa8	Kh1	Rhd1	Bc1 ±
	Rf8(f)	Nd5(h)	Bxa8(k)	Be7 ∞	Ra7(o)	

(a) 7 . . . b5 8 Nxc6 dxc6 (8 . . . Qxc6 9 Bf3 ±) 9 a4 Rb8 10 f4 Bb7 11 Kh1 ±, Braga–Karpov, Dubai 1986.

(b) 8 . . . d6 transposes to the Scheveningen Variation.

(c) 9 f3 0–0 10 Kh1 Rd8 preparing . . . d5 gives Black full equality, Bouaziz–Matulović, Sousse 1967.

(d) On 10 . . . dxc6 White can play 11 Bb6 Qf4 12 f3 with the better chances (Taimanov).

(e) Holding on to the pawn leads to a different game: 12 . . . Qxc8?! 13 e5 Nd5 14 Ba7 Ra8 15 Bd4 c5 16 c4! cxd4 17 cxd5 ± (Taimanov).

(f) 14 Qd3 Ng4 15 g3 Qa5 16 Bc4 (Hübner–Ribli, West Germany 1987); now 16 . . . Nxe3 17 Qxe3 Bc5 18 Qc1 Qb4 19 b3 Bd4 20 Rb1 f5 is equal (Ribli).

(g) The other alternatives are favorable for White: (A) 9 . . . Ne7 10 c4 Nxe4 11 Qc2 Nf6 12 c5 ±; (B) 9 . . . Bd6 10 Nb6! Rb8 11 g3 Nxe4 12 Nxc6 Qxc6 13 Bf3 f5 14 Bxe4 fxe4 15 Qh5† g6 16 Qh6 ±, Smejkal–Spassov, Örebro 1966.

(h) 14 Bc1 Bc5 15 c4 Ne7 16 b3 Qc7 17 Bb2 Ng6 18 Qd2 0–0 = (Hübner).

(i) (A) 8 . . . d6 and 8 . . . Be7 9 f4 d6 transpose to the Scheveningen Variation. (B) 8 . . . Nxd4 9 Qxd4 Bc5 10 Qd3 b5 11 f4 Bb7 12 Bf3 ±, Liebert–Furman, Poland 1967.

(j) 9 Bg5 Bxc3 10 Bxf6 gxf6 11 bxc3 Ne7 12 Qd2 d5 =, Ivanović–Kurajica, Yugoslav Chp. 1978.

(k) 14 f3 Bxc3 15 bxc3 0–0 16 Ba3 with advantage, Velimirović–Matulović, Vrsać 1985.

(l) 7 Be3 transposes to column 115.

(m) 7 . . . b5 8 Nxc6 Qxc6 9 Bf3 Bb7 10 e5 Qc7 11 Ne4 Rc8 12 0–0 Qxc2 13 Qxc2 Rxc2 14 Nd6† Bxd6 15 Bxb7 Bc5† 16 Kh1 Nh6 17 Bxa6 ±, Chandler–Wilder, London 1987. The column is Nunn–Andersson, Szirak 1987.

(n) 9 . . . Qb6 10 Bxf8 Rxf8 deprives Black of kingside castling, but his position is otherwise sound. After 11 Rb1 d5 12 0–0 Bb7 13 Re1 0–0–0 Black should be all right.

(o) 14 g3 f6 15 f4 Rd8 16 Na4 with a pleasant endgame for White, Psakhis–Romanishin, Irkutsk 1986.

(p) 7 Nb3 Ng5 8 0–0 Be7 9 Be3 0–0 10 Na4 b5 11 Nb6 Rb8 12 Nxc8 Qxc8 13 a4 Rd8 =, Beliavsky–Zapata, Tunis 1985.

(q) 9 . . . Nb4?! 10 Qg3! Nxc2 11 Bg5! f6 12 Bf4 Kf7 (if 12 . . . Nxa1 13 Bh5† g6 14 Bxg6† hxg6 15 Qxg6† Ke7 16 e5 d5 17 Qxf6† Kd7 18 Qxh8 Nc2 19 Qh7† wins–Plaskett) 13 Bc7 Qe8 14 Rad1 ±; Plaskett–Hartston, Uppingham 1986 went 14 . . . b5 15 e5 Bb7 16 exf6 Kg8 17 fxg7 Bxg7 18 Be5 Resigns, since 18 . . . Qg6 19 Qxg6 hxg6 20 Bxg7 Kxg7 21 Rxd7† wins the bishop. The column is Tal–Zapata, Titograd 1984.

SICILIAN DEFENSE

Taimanov Variation

1 e4 c5 2 Nf3 e6 3 d4 cxd4 4 Nxd4 Nc6

	115	116	117	118	119	120
5	(Nc3)............................			Nb5(j)		
	(a6)(a)			d6(k)		
6	Be3.....................		Bf4(g)	c4......................		Bf4
	Qc7		d6	Nf6		e5
7	Be2.........	Bd3	Nxc6(h)	N1c3(l)		Be3
	b5(b)	Nf6	bxc6	a6		Nf6
8	Nxc6	0–0	Bc4	Na3	.....b6	Bg5
	Qxc6	Ne5(e)	Nf6	Be7(m)		Qa5†(q)
9	f4(c)	h3	Qe2	Be2	Be2	Qd2
	Bb7(d)	Bc5(f)	d5!	0–0	Bb7	Nxe4
10	Bf3	Na4	0–0–0	0–0	0–0	Qxa5
	Rc8	Ba7	Bb7	b6	Nb8(o)	Nxa5
11	0–0	c4	Bb3	Be3	f3	Be3
	Bc5	d6	Be7	Bb7	Nbd7	Kd7
12	Qe1	Rc1	exd5	Qb3	Be3	N1c3
	Qb6	Bd7	cxd5	Nd7	Be7	Nxc3
13	Bxc5	Nc3	Ba4†	Rfd1	Qe1	Nxc3
	Qxc5† =	0–0 =	Nd7(i)	Nc5(n)	Qc7(p)	b6(r)

(a) 5 . . . Qc7 has little independent significance, since on 6 g3, 6 Be2 or 6 Be3 Black's most flexible option is 6 . . . a6.

(b) 7 . . . Nf6 8 0–0 transposes to column 109.

(c) 9 0–0 Bb7 10 Bf3 Rd8! 11 e5 Qc7 12 Bxb7 Qxb7 is equal as Black will advance his d-pawn, Petrosian–Taimanov, USSR Chp. 1967.

(d) (A) 9 . . . b4? 10 Bf3 bxc3? 11 e5 wins the rook on a8. (B) 9 . . . Ba3 10 bxa3 Qxc3† 11 Kf2 Nf6 12 Bf3 Bb7 13 Bd4 Qxa3 14 Qd3 Qxd3 is about even, Matanović–Vasiukov, Yugoslavia vs. USSR 1966. The column is Unzicker–Franzoni, Bern 1987.

(e) 8 . . . Bd6 9 Nxc6 bxc6 10 f4 e5 11 f5 Bb7 12 Qf3 Be7 13 Na4 d5 14 Bb6 Qb8 15 c4 ± (Taimanov).

(f) 9 . . . b5 10 f4 Nc4 11 Bxc4 Qxc4 12 e5 Nd5 13 Nxd5 Qxd5 14 Qe2 and White's lead in development gains him the upper hand, Janssen–Zichichi, Siegen 1970. The column is Tal–Eingorn, Sochi 1986.

(g) (A) 6 f4 Qc7 7 Be2 transposes to col. 112. Black should avoid 6 . . . d5 7 Be3 Nf6 8 e5 when White arrives at a good French Defense. (B) 6 Nxc6 bxc6 7 e5 Qc7 8 f4 f5! (8 . . . d5 9 exd6 Bxd6 10 Ne4! ±) 9 Bd3 d5 is equal.

(h) 7 Bg3 Be7 8 Be2 e5 9 Nb3 Nf6 10 0–0 0–0 11 Qd3 Be6 12 a3 d5 =, W. Watson–Portisch, New York 1987.

(i) 14 Qg4 0–0 15 Bh6 Bf6 16 Bxd7 Qxd7 17 Rd3?! (17 Ne4 $\overline{\mp}$) 17 . . . Rac8 18 Re1 (on 18 Rg3 Black has 18 . . . Rc4) 18 . . . d4 19 Red1? Qc7! Resigns, van der Wiel–Polugaevsky, Amsterdam 1984. 20 Rg3 dxc3 21 Bxg7 cxb2† or 20 Rxd4 Bxd4 21 Rxd4 f5! is hopeless.

(j) (A) 5 c4 Nf6 6 Nc3 Bb4 7 Nxc6 bxc6 8 Bd3 d5 = is a variation that also arises from the English Opening. (B) 5 g3 d5 =.

(k) 5 . . . Bc5?! 6 Bf4 Qf6 7 Qc1 Kf8 8 N1c3 a6 9 Bd6 ±, Mokrý–Plaskett, Trnava 1984.

(l) 7 N5c3 Be7 8 Be2 0–0 9 0–0 b6 10 Bf4 Bb7 11 Nd2 a6 12 a3 Nd4 13 Bd3 Nd7 is equal, Ljubojević–Karpov, Madrid 1973.

(m) 8 . . . d5?! 9 cxd5 exd5 10 exd5 Nb4 11 Be2 Bc5 12 Be3! Bxe3 13 Qa4† Nd7 14 Qxb4 Bc5 15 Qe4† ±, Karpov–van der Wiel, Brussels 1986.

(n) 14 Qc2 Qc7 15 Rac1 Rac8 16 Nab1 Ne5 17 Nd2 Ncd7 =, Jadoul–Karpov, Brussels 1986.

(o) Black redeploys the knight to d7 where it doesn't block the bishop on b7. He can also play 10 . . . Ne5, but this allows the variation 11 f4 Ned7 12 Bf3, which is a more aggressive setup.

(p) 14 Qf2 0–0 15 Rfd1 Rac8 with a roughly equal game, Hába–Mokrý, Czechoslovak Chp. 1986. White has more space, but Black has the possible break . . . b5 or . . . d5.

(q) Fischer–Petrosian, match 1971, went 8 . . . Be6 9 N1c3 a6 10 Bxf6 gxf6 11 Na3 d5! 12 exd5 Bxa3 13 bxa3 Qa5 14 Qd2 0–0–0 with advantage to Black. White should play 9 Nd2 with a pull due to the backward Black d-pawn.

(r) 14 0–0–0 Bb7 15 f4 f6 =, Wedberg–Sjöberg, Stockholm 1985.

SICILIAN DEFENSE

Paulsen Variation

1 e4 c5 2 Nf3 e6 3 d4 cxd4 4 Nxd4 a6

	121	122	123	124	125	126
5	Bd3..c4					
	Nc6........	Nf6....................		Bc5(j)	Nf6	
6	Nxc6	0–0		Nb3	Nc3	
	dxc6(a)	d6(d)		Ba7	Bb4	
7	Nd2(b)	c4		Qe2(k)	Bd3(m)	
	e5	Be7........	g6	Nc6	Nc6(n)	
8	Qh5	Nc3	Nc3	Be3	Nxc6	Bc2(q)
	Bd6	0–0	Bg7	Bxe3	dxc6	Qc7
9	Nc4	Qe2	Re1(h)	Qxe3	e5(o)	0–0
	Bc7	Nbd7(e)	0–0	Nf6	Qa5!	0–0(r)
10	Bg5	f4	Be3	Nc3	exf6	Kh1
	Nf6	Qc7	b6	d6	Bxc3†	Nxd4
11	Qe2	Kh1	h3	0–0–0	bxc3	Qxd4
	h6	b6	Bb7	0–0	Qxc3†	Ng4
12	Bh4	Bd2(f)	Qd2	f4	Bd2	f4
	Qe7(c)	Bb7(g)	Nbd7(i)	Qc7(l)	Qxd3(p)	b5(s)

(a) 6 . . . bxc6 has been considered a poor line ever since Fischer–Petrosian, 7th match game 1971, which went 7 0–0 d5 8 c4 Nf6 9 cxd5 cxd5 10 exd5 exd5 11 Nc3 Be7 12 Qa4+ Qd7 13 Re1! Qxa4 14 Nxa4 Be6 15 Be3 0–0 16 Bc5! (the exchange of dark-squared bishops allows White's other pieces to take up active posts) 16 . . . Rfe8 17 Bxe7 Rxe7 18 b4 Kf8 19 Nc5 Bc8 20 f3 Rea7 (Black wants to play 21 . . . Bd7 and 22 . . . Bb5; if 20 . . . a5 21 b5 with a powerful passed pawn) 21 Re5 Bd7 22 Nxd7+! Rxd7 23 Rc1 Rd6 24 Rc7 Nd7 25 Re2 g6 26 Kf2 h5 27 f4 h4 28 Kf3 f5 29 Ke3 d5+ 30 Kd2 Nb6 31 Ree7 Nd5 32 Rf7+ Ke8 33 Rb7 Nxb4 34 Bc4 Resigns, as 35 Rh7 and 36 Rh8 are coming.

(b) 7 f4 e5 8 f5! also gives White better chances, but 8 0–0 exf4! 9 Bxf4 Ne7 is all right for Black.

(c) 13 0–0–0! Be6 14 f4! Bxc4 15 Bxc4 b5 16 Bb3 0–0 17 Bxf6 Qxf6 18 Rd7 ±, Tseshkovsky–Miles, Bled/Portorož 1979.

(d) 6 . . . Qc7 7 c4 Bd6 8 Kh1 Nc6 (8 . . . Bxh2 9 f4 Bg3 10 Qf3 Bh4 11 g3 †) 9 Nxc6 dxc6 10 Be3 e5 11 c5 Be7 12 f3 0–0 13 Nd2 ±, Beliavsky–Smyslov, USSR Chp. 1973.

(e) (A) 9 . . . Re8 10 f4 Nfd7 11 Kh1 g6 12 Nf3! Nc6 13 e5 is good (Sax–Fedorowicz, New York 1986) since 13 . . . dxe5 14 fxe5 Ncxe5 15 Nxe5 Nxe5 16 Qxe5 Qxd3 17 Bh6 f6 18 Rxf6 wins. (B) 9 . . . Bd7 10 f4 Nc6 11 Nf3 e5 12 f5 Nd4 13 Qf2 Nxf3+ 14 gxf3 Nh5 15 Nd5 ±, Fedorowicz–Miles, Lone Pine 1980.

(f) White can also play 12 Be3 or 12 b3 and 13 Bb2. But 12 Bd2 is probably best, as White can play on the queenside with b4, and, with the e-file not blocked, e5 is in the air.

(g) 13 Rac1 g6 14 b4 Rac8 15 a3 $\pm$, Commons–Peev, Plovdiv 1976.

(h) 9 Bg5 0–0 10 Qd2 b6 11 Rad1 Qc7 12 Rfe1 Bb7 13 Bf1 Rc8 14 Nf3 Ne8 15 Bf4 is also more comfortable for White, Sax–Gheorghiu, New York 1987.

(i) 13 Bh6 Bxh6 14 Qxh6 Ne5 15 Bf1 with attacking chances, Geller–Rajković, Novi Sad 1979.

(j) (A) Black can try the immediate 5 . . . g6 6 c4 Bg7 7 Be3 Ne7 (7 . . . Nf6 8 Nc3 d6 9 0–0 0–0 10 Re1 transposes to col. 123) 8 Nc3 0–0 9 0–0 d5 10 exd5 exd5 11 Rc1 $\pm$, Weinstein–Christiansen, US Chp. 1978. (B) 5 . . . Ne7 6 0–0 Nbc6 7 c3 Be7 8 Be3 0–0 9 f4 $\pm$, Kr. Georgiev–Peev, Bulgarian Chp. 1980.

(k) (A) 7 Qg4?! Nf6 8 Qxg7 Rg8 9 Qh6 Bxf2†! $\mp$; (B) 7 0–0 Nc6 8 Qg4 (other moves give Black little trouble) 8 . . . Nf6 9 Qxg7 Rg8 10 Qh6 Ne5 11 Be2 (Ljubojević–Lobron, Plovdiv 1983); now 11 . . . Nxe4 12 Qxh7 Nf6 13 Qh4 b5 gives Black good play, or 12 Qf4 d5 13 Qxe5? Qh4 threatening . . . Bxf2† and . . . Bb8.

(l) 13 Rhg1 b5 14 g4 b4 15 g5 Ne8 16 Nb1 a5 ∞, Wedberg–Spraggett, New York 1987. White still has some initiative, but either side can win this sharp position.

(m) (A) 7 e5 Ne4 8 Qg4 Nxc3 9 a3 Bf8! 10 bxc3 Qa5 with no worries for Black. (B) 7 Nc2!? Bxc3† 8 bxc3 Qa5 (8 . . . Nxe4 9 Qg4) 9 Qd3 Qe5 10 f3 d5 11 Ba3 dxe4 12 Qe3 Nc6 13 f4 Qa5 with even chances in this sharp position, Kurtecz–Forintos, Hungary 1966.

(n) 7 . . . Qc7 8 0–0 Nc6 9 Nf3! 0–0 10 Bd2 b6 11 Rc1 Qb8 12 Qe2 $\pm$, Karpov–Miles, Brussels 1986.

(o) If White delays with 9 0–0 then 9 . . . e5 is completely freeing.

(p) 13 fxg7 Rg8 14 Bh6 Qc3† 15 Kf1 Qf6 with roughly equal chances, Poulsen–Farago, Svendborg 1981.

(q) On 8 Be3 d5 9 exd5 exd5 is equal (Taimanov).

(r) (A) 9 . . . Nxd4 10 Qxd4 Ng4 11 e5 Nxe5 12 Ne4 b6 13 f4 Qxc4 14 Qxe5 Qxc2 15 Qxg7 Qxe4 16 Qxh8† Ke7 17 Qg7 Qe2 18 Qg5† Ke8 19 Qg8† Draw, Mestel–Liberzon, Hastings 1980–81. (B) 9 . . . Ne5 10 f4 Nxc4 11 e5 Bxc3 12 bxc3 Nd5 ∞.

(s) 13 Qd1 (Mestel–Portisch, London 1982); now 13 . . . Bxc3 14 bxc3 Qxc4 gives Black the better game.

SICILIAN DEFENSE

Paulsen Variation

1 e4 c5 2 Nf3 e6 3 d4 cxd4 4 Nxd4 a6

	127	128	129	130	131	132
5	(c4)........	Nc3...				Nd2
	(Nf6)	Qc7			b5	d6
6	(Nc3)	Be2........	g3	Bd3(k)	Bd3	Bd3
	Qc7(a)	b5(f)	Bb4!	Nc6(l)	Bb7	Nf6
7	Be2(b)	0–0	Ne2(i)	Nxc6	0–0	0–0
	Bb4	Bb7	Nf6	bxc6	Ne7(n)	Nbd7(p)
8	Nc2	Bf3(g)	Bg2	0–0	Qh5	c4
	Bxc3†	Nc6	Be7	Nf6	Nbc6	Qc7
9	bxc3	a4!	0–0	Qe2	Nxc6	b3
	Nc6(c)	b4	Nc6	d5	Nxc6	g6
10	f3(d)	Nxc6	h3	Bg5	Bg5	Bb2
	0–0	bxc3(h)	d6	Bb7	Be7	Bg7
11	Ba3	Nd4	f4	f4	Bxe7	Qe2
	Rd8	Nf6	b5	Be7	Qxe7(o)	0–0 =
12	Bd6	e5 ±	a3	e5	f4	
	Qa5(e)		Rb8(j)	Nd7(m)	g6 ∞	

(a) 6 ... d6 7 Bd3 transposes to column 122, but 7 Be2 is better, e.g. 7 ... Be7 8 0–0 0–0 9 f4 Qc7 10 Be3 Re8 11 Qe1 Bf8 12 Qg4 b6 13 Rae1 with attacking chances, Nunn–Gheorghiu, London 1980.

(b) 7 a3, recommended by Alekhine, lets Black play a hedgehog formation, e.g. 7 ... d6 8 Be2 b6 9 0–0 Bb7 10 f3 Nbd7 11 Be3 Be7 12 Qd2 0–0 = .

(c) 9 ... Nxe4?! 10 Qd4 Nf6 11 Bf4 Qa5 12 Bd6 ± .

(d) 10 Qd3 Ne5! 11 Qd4 Nc6 = (Chandler).

(e) 13 Nb4 Ne8 14 0–0 Nxd6 15 Qxd6 Qa3 16 c5 a5! 17 Nxc6 bxc6 18 Qd4 d5 = , Fischer–Portisch, Varna 1962.

(f) (A) 6 ... Nc6 transposes to the Taimanov Variation, cols. 109–114, and (B) 6 ... d6 is a Scheveningen. (C) 6 ... Nf6 7 0–0 Bb4 8 Qd3 ± .

(g) 8 a3 Nf6 9 Qd3 d6 10 Bg5 Nbd7 was equal in Evans–Tal, Amsterdam 1964.

(h) 10 ... Bxc6 11 Nd5! exd5 12 exd5 Bb7 13 Re1† Kd8 14 d6 is strong. The column is Tseshkovsky–Cvitan, Vrsać 1987.

(i) 7 Bd2 Nf6 8 Bg2 Nc6 9 Nxc6 dxc6 10 0–0 0–0 11 f4 Rd8 12 Qe2 b5 13 Rad1 Bb7 = , P. Popović–Cvitan, Vrsać 1987.

(j) 13 g4 a5 14 g5 Nd7 15 Ng3 b4 16 axb4 axb4 with equal chances, Kudrin–Kavalek, US Chp. 1981.

(k) 6 f4 Nc6 7 Be2 transposes to column 112. Black can also play 6 . . . b5 7 Bd3 Bb7 8 Qf3 Nc6 9 Be3 Nf6 10 g4 d6 11 g5 Nd7 12 0–0–0 Nc5 =, van der Wiel–Gheorghiu, Baden 1980.

(l) (A) 6 . . . Nf6 7 f4 d6 8 0–0 Nbd7 9 Qe2 Be7 10 Kh1 Nc5 ∞. (B) 6 . . . b5?! 7 0–0 Bb7 8 Qe2 Nf6 9 Kh1 Be7 10 f4 d6 11 Bd2 leaves White mobile in the center and with the lever a4 coming, Short–Seirawan, Arnhem 1983.

(m) 13 Bxe7 Kxe7 14 Na4 ±, Spassky–Petrosian, Palma de Mallorca 1969.

(n) (A) 7 . . . Nc6 8 Nxc6 Bxc6 9 Qe2 d6 10 a4 b4 11 Nd5 puts Black in great difficulties, Karklins–Evans, USA 1973. (B) 7 . . . d6 8 Qe2 Nf6 9 Bd2 is similar to Short–Seirawan in note (l).

(o) 11 . . . Nxe7 12 f4 0–0 13 f5 allows White a kingside initiative, Dückstein–Polugaevsky, Le Havre 1966.

(p) 7 . . . Be7 8 c4 0–0 9 b3 Nbd7 10 Bb2 gives White more chances for a kingside attack, Bagirov–Gipslis, USSR Chp. 1963.

SICILIAN DEFENSE

1 e4 c5 2 Nf3 e6 3 d4 cxd4 4 Nxd4 Nf6 5 Nc3

	133	134	135	136	137	138
	Nc6 (Four Knights' Variation)....................Bb4					
					(Sicilian Counterattack)	
6	Ndb5....................Nxc6 ....g3(k)				e5	
	Bb4(a)		bxc6	d5(l)	Nd5 ....Ne4	
7	a3 ....Bf4(e)		e5	exd5	Bd2!(m)	Qg4
	Bxc3†	Nxe4	Nd5	exd5	Nxc3	Qa5(p)
8	Nxc3	Qf3	Ne4(h)	Bg2	bxc3	Qxe4
	d5	d5	Qc7	Be7	Ba5(n)	Bxc3†
9	exd5	Nc7†	f4	0–0	Qg4	bxc3
	exd5(b)	Kf8	Qb6	0–0	0–0	Qxc3†
10	Bd3	0–0–0(f)	c4	h3	Bd3	Kd1
	0–0	Bxc3	Bb4†	Re8	d6	Qxa1
11	0–0	bxc3	Ke2	Re1	Nf3	Nb5
	d4	e5!	f5(i)	h6	g6	d5
12	Ne2(c)	Nxd5	exf6	Bf4	h4	Qb4!
	h6(d)	Ng5(g)	Nxf6(j)	a6 =	dxe5(o)	Nc6(q)

(a) 6 . . . d6 7 Bf4 e5 8 Bg5 transposes to the Pelikan Variation (cols. 145–156).

(b) 9 . . . Nxd5 10 Bd2! Nxc3 (10 . . . Qh4 11 Qf3 0–0 12 0–0–0 ±, Tal–Matulović, Kislovodsk 1966) 11 Bxc3 Qxd1† 12 Rxd1 f6 13 f4 Bd7 14 Bc4 with a distinct endgame edge, Fischer–Addison, US Chp. 1962–63.

(c) 12 Ne4 Bf5 13 Bg5 Bxe4 14 Bxe4 h6 15 Bh4 g5 16 Bxc6 bxc6 17 Bg3 also gives White a pull, Kir. Georgiev–Chandler, Leningrad 1987.

(d) 13 Bf4 Re8 (Schmidt–Browne, San Juan 1969) 14 Qd2 $\pm$.

(e) 7 Nd6†?! Ke7 8 Nxc8† Rxc8 gives Black a lead in development.

(f) 10 Nxa8 e5 11 0–0–0 Bxc3 12 bxc3 exf4 13 Bc4 Be6 14 Qxf4 Qxa8 ∞ (Malyshev).

(g) 13 Qe3?! (13 Bxg5 is best, but Black still stands better) 13 . . . exf4 14 Qc5† Ke8 15 Bc4 Ne6†, Ernst–Hector, Swedish Chp. 1985.

(h) 8 Nxd5 cxd5 9 Bd3 g6 10 0–0 Bg7 11 Bf4 0–0 12 Qe2 d6 =, Evans–Seidman, US Chp. 1954.

(i) 11 . . . Ba6 12 Kf3! f5 13 Nf2 Ne7 14 Be3 Bc5 15 Bxc5 Qxc5 16 Qd6 $\pm$, Mokrý–Vukić, Zenica 1986.

(j) 13 Be3 Qa5 14 Nxf6† gxf6 15 Kf2 0–0 16 Bd3 Rf7 17 a3 $\pm$, Timman–Ligterink, Holland 1974.

(k) 6 Be2 Bb4 7 0–0 Bxc3 8 bxc3 Nxe4 9 Bd3 d5 10 Ba3 Nxd4 11 cxd4 Qa5 12 Qc1 Bd7 13 Rb1 Bc6 14 f3 Nf6 is roughly equal, Korelov–Peterson, Riga 1964.

(l) (A) 6 . . . a6 7 Bg2 Qc7 transposes to the Taimanov Variation. (B) 6 . . . Bb4 7 Bg2 d5 8 exd5 Nxd5 9 0–0 Bxc3 10 bxc3 0–0 (Spielmann–Kopa, Barmen 1905); 11 c4! ±. The column is Ligterink–Kouatly, Budel 1987.

(m) 7 Qg4 0–0! 8 Bh6 g6 9 Bxf8 Qxf8 10 Qg3 Qc5 11 Ne2 Nc6 wins the e-pawn and gives Black almost equal chances.

(n) 8 . . . Be7 9 Qg4 0–0 (9 . . . Kf8 10 Bd3 ±) 10 Bh6 g6 11 h4! Qa5 12 Qg3 Rd8 13 h5 d6 14 hxg6 fxg6 15 Bf4 dxe5 16 Bxe5 Rd5 17 f4 Nd7 18 Bc4 ±, Wedberg–Pokojowicz, Copenhagen 1984. Play continued 18 . . . Nxe5 19 Bxd5 Qxd5 20 fxe5 Qe4† 21 Kd2 Bd7 22 Rae1 Qd5 (Black's vulnerable king has forced him to give up material, but White can still attack with 23 Rxh7! Kxh7 24 Rh1† Kg7 25 Qh2 Kf7 26 Qh7† Ke8 27 Qxg6† Kd8 28 Rh8† winning easily—Wedberg) 23 Qh3?! Bg5† 24 Kd1 h6 25 Qd3 Be8 26 c4 Qd7 27 Nb5 Qxd3 28 cxd3 Bxb5? (28 . . . Bd7, keeping the bishop pair, is better) 29 cxb5 Rc8 30 Ke2! Rc2† 31 Kf3 Rxa2 32 Ra1 Rd2 33 Rhd1 Rb2 34 Rdb1 Rd2 35 Rb3 Resigns.

(o) 13 h5 f5 14 Bxf5! exf5 15 Qc4† Rf7 16 hxg6 hxg6 17 Ng5 Qc7 18 Qh4 and wins, Wagman–Barle, Biel 1981.

(p) 7 . . . Nxc3 8 Qxg7! Rf8 9 a3 Nb5† (9 . . . Ba5 10 Bh6 Qe7 11 Nb3 †) 10 axb4 Nxd4 11 Bg5 Qb6 12 Bh6 Qb4† 13 Nf5 14 cxb4 Nxg7 15 Bxg7 with a very favorable endgame, Szabo–Mikenas, Kemeri 1939.

(q) If 12 . . . Qxe5 13 f4 wins. After 12 . . . Na6 13 Nd6† Kd7 14 Bxa6 bxa6 15 Nxf7 Rg8 16 Kd2 d4 17 Bb2! Qxa2 18 Ra1 Qd5 19 Ra5 White is winning (Euwe).

SICILIAN DEFENSE

1 e4 c5 2 Nf3 Nc6 3 d4 cxd4 4 Nxd4

	139	140	141	142	143	144
	e5 ....Qb6(k)					
5	Ndb5					Nb3
	a6 (Löwenthal Variation)........................d6					Nf6
6	Nd6†				c4(h)	Nc3
	Bxd6				Be7	e6
7	Qxd6				N1c3	Bd3
	Qf6				a6	Be7
8	Qxf6........Qc7.........Qd1(d)			Na3	0–0(l)
	Nxf6	Nge7	Qg6		h6(i)	a6
9	Nc3	Nc3	Nc3		Be2	Kh1
	Nb4(a)	Nb4	Nge7 ....d5!?		Be6	Qc7
10	Kd2!	Bd3	h4	Nxd5	0–0	f4
	d5	d5	h5	Qxe4†	Bg5	d6
11	a3	0–0	Bg5	Be3	Nc2	Qf3
	d4	d4	d5	Nd4	Nge7	0–0
12	axb4	Ne2	exd5(e)	Nc7†	b3	Bd2!
	dxc3†(b)	0–0(c)	Nb4(f)	Ke7(g)	Bxc1(j)	b5(m)

(a) 9 ... d5 10 Bg5 d4 11 Bxf6 dxc3 12 Bxg7 Rg8 13 Bh6 is much better for White (Gligorić).

(b) 13 Ke3! and Black has a difficult endgame, Velimirović–Ristić, Yugoslavia 1979.

(c) 13 f4 (13 Bd2 Nxd3 14 cxd3 Nc6 =) 13 ... Bg4! 14 fxe5 Qc6 15 Qxe7 Nxd3 =, Perfors–Baumbach, corr. 1962–64.

(d) White has other good tries: (A) 8 Qd2 Qg6 9 f3 Nge7 10 c4 d6 11 Nc3 f5 12 b3 0–0 13 Bb2 Be6 14 Bd3 ±, Ljubojević–Ivanović, Nikšić 1983; (B) 8 Qa3 Nge7 9 Nc3 Rb8 10 Be3 b5 11 Nd5 ±.

(e) 12 Bxe7 looks strong, but 12 ... d4! is at least equal as 13 Nd5 fails to 13 ... Qxe4†.

(f) 13 Bxe7! Kxe7 14 Bd3 (14 d6†?! Kd8 15 Bd3 Nxd3† 16 Qxd3 Qxd3 17 cxd3 ±) 14 ... Nxd3† 15 Qxd3 Qxd3 16 cxd3 b5 17 a3 ±, Sveshnikov–Panchenko, USSR 1977.

(g) 13 Rc1 Bg4 14 Qd3 Qxd3 15 Bxd3 Rd8 16 h3 Bh5 17 f4 f6 18 Kf2 Kd6 19 c3 ±, Marjanović–Simić, Yugoslavia 1983.

(h) 6 N1c3 a6 7 Na3 b5 8 Nd5 Nge7 (8 ... Nf6 9 Bg5 transposes to the Pelikan Variation). 9 c4 Nd4 10 cxd5 Nxd5 11 exd5 Bd7, Smirin–Shirov, USSR chp. 1988. Black can also try 7 ... Be6 8 Nc4 b5 9 Ne3 Nf6 ∞.

(i) Routine play simply gives Black a backward d-pawn and a weak d5 square: 8 ... Nf6 9 Be2 0–0 10 Be3 Be6 11 0–0 Rc8 12 Rc1 ±, Suetin–Kopaev, USSR 1952.

(j) 13 Rxc1 Ng6 14 Bg4 0–0 15 Ne3 Nd4 16 Ne2 ±, Kuzmin–Sveshnikov, USSR 1987.

(k) (A) 4 . . . Qc7 5 c4 Nf6 6 f3 gives White more space. If 5 . . . Qe5 6 Nf3 Qxe4† 7 Be2 d6 8 Nc3 is a big lead in development, Matanović–Benko, Portorož 1958. (B) For 4 . . . g6 see cols. 91–102.

(l) Also better for White is 8 Be3 Qc7 9 f4 d6 10 Qf3 a6 11 g4 ±, Kavalek–Hübner, Buenos Aires 1978. The game continued 11 . . . b6!? 12 g5 Nfd7 13 0–0–0 Nc5 14 Kb1 Bd7 15 h4 Qb7 16 Be2 Na7 17 f5 Nb5 18 Bd4! (White avoids 18 Nxb5 axb5, giving Black play on the a-file) 18 . . . Bc6 19 fxe6 Nxc3† 20 Bxc3 Nxe6 21 Rhf1 0–0 22 Bd3 b5 23 a3 Nc5 24 Nxc5 dxc5 25 Qf5! (threatening 26 Qe5) 25 . . . Rae8 26 Bxg7! (Black is lost; if 26 . . . Kxg7 27 e5 mates) 26 . . . Bd7 27 Qe5 Bd8 28 Qd6 Kxg7 29 Qh6† Kh8 30 e5 f5 31 exf6 Be6 32 Rde1 c4 33 Bg6 Rf7 34 Bxf7 Qxf7 35 g6! Qxg6 36 f7 Resigns.

(m) 13 Rae1 Bb7 14 Qh3 with attacking chances, Lobron–Gufeld, Dortmund 1983.

SICILIAN DEFENSE

Pelikan Variation

1 e4 c5 2 Nf3 Nc6 3 d4 cxd4 4 Nxd4 Nf6 5 Nc3 e5 6 Ndb5 d6 7 Bg5 a6
8 Na3 b5 9 Bxf6 gxf6! 10 Nd5 f5 (a)

	145	146	147	148	149	150
11	Bd3		Bxb5	Nxb5	exf5	c3(s)
	Be6		axb5	axb5	Bxf5	Bg7(t)
12	Qh5		Nxb5	Bxb5	Bd3(p)	exf5
	Bg7		Ra4(i)	Bd7(m)	e4	Bxf5
13	0–0(b)		Nbc7†	exf5	Qe2	Nc2
	f4(c)		Kd7	Bg7(n)	Nd4	Ne7
14	c4	c3(f)	0–0	a4	Qe3	Nce3
	bxc4	0–0	Rxe4(j)	Nd4	Bg7	Be6
15	Bxc4	Rad1(g)	Qh5	Bxd7†	f3(q)	g3
	0–0	Rb8	Nd4(k)	Qxd7	Qh4†	Nxd5
16	Rac1	Nc2	Qxf7†(l)	c3	g3	Nxd5
	Kh8(d)	Qd7	Kc6	Qc6	Nxf3†	0–0
17	Rfd1	Qe2	Nb4†	Ne3	Qxf3	Bg2
	Rb8(e)	Kh8(h)	Kb7 ∓	Bh6(o)	exf3(r)	a5(u)

(a) The immediate 10 . . . Bg7!? followed by (A) 11 Qh5 Ne7 12 Ne3 f5 13 exf5 e4! 14 0–0–0 0–0 15 g4 ∞ or (B) 11 Bd3 Ne7 12 Nxe7 Qxe7 13 c3 f5 14 Nc2 0–0 15 0–0 Rb8 16 exf5 e4 17 Re1 d5 = is a suggestion by Vaiser and Shipkov in *Inside Chess* II/8.

(b) 13 c4 Qa5† 14 Kf1 fxe4 15 Bxe4 Bg7 16 cxb5 Nd4! ∞.

(c) (A) 13 . . . 0–0? 14 exf5 Bxd5 15 f6 wins. (B) 13 . . . h6 14 c3 0–0 15 Nc2 fxe4 16 Bxe4 f5 17 Nf4! leaves Black with holes in his position, Spassky–Sveshnikov, USSR Chp. 1973.

(d) (A) 16 . . . Ne7 17 Rfd1 Rc8 18 Nxe7† Qxe7 19 Rc3 ±, Short–Sax, match 1988. (B) 16 . . . Rb8 17 b3 Qd7 18 Rfd1! Kh8 transposes to the column. If 18 . . . Bg4 19 Qg5.

(e) 18 b3 Qd7 19 Qh4 Bxd5 20 Bxd5 Nd4 21 Rc4! f5 22 Nc2 ±, Sveshnikov–Vyzmanavin, Moscow 1987.

(f) 14 Kh1 Ne7 15 Nxe7 Qxe7 16 c4 bxc4 17 Bxc4 0–0 18 Rac1 Rac8 19 Rfd1 Rfd8 20 Rc2 Bxc4 21 Rxc4 Qb7 22 Qe2 Rxc4 23 Nxc4 d5 = (Adorjan).

(g) 15 Nc2 f5 16 Ncb4 Nxb4 17 Nxb4 d5 18 exd5 Bd7 19 Bc2 e4! 20 Qe2 f3 21 gxf3 Be5 ∓ (Adorjan).

(h) 18 Rfe1 f5 19 Ncb4 Nxb4 20 Nxb4 a5 21 exf5 Bg8 with equal chances, R. Byrne–Timman, Bugojno 1978.

(i) The text is Black's most reliable response. Some alternatives are: (A) 12 . . . Rb8 13 Nbc7† Kd7 14 Qh5 Ne7 15 Qxf7 Kc6 16 b4 Nxd5 17 b5† Rxb5 18 exd5† Rxd5 19 Qxd5† Kxc7 ∞; (B) 12 . . . Ra7 13 Nxa7 Nxa7 14 exf5 Bxf5 (14 . . . Nc6?! 15 f6 ±) 15 Qf3 Be6 16

298

Nd5† Ke7 17 0–0 $\pm$, Emerson–Quinteros, London 1987. (C) 12 . . . Qa5† 13 c3 Qa4 14 Ndc7† Kd8 15 Qd5 Rb8 ∞, Berg–Povah, Wijk aan Zee 1978.

(j) 14 . . . Qg5 15 c4 Rg8 16 g3 gives White the better attacking chances.

(k) Also playable is 15 . . . Ne7 16 Qxf7 Kc6 17 c4 Qd7 18 Na8! Ng6 19 Nb4† Kb7 20 Qd5† Kb8 21 Nc6† Kxa8 22 Qb5 Qb7 23 Qa5† Qa6 24 Qc7 Qb7 25 Qa5† Draw, Gruenfeld–Fleck, Lugano 1980.

(l) White might do better with 16 c3 Ne2† 17 Kh1 Kc6 18 g3 Rg8 19 Qf3, but after 19 . . . Qxc7! 20 Nxc7 Kxc7 Black has good attacking chances (Horvath). The column is Szabo–Horvath, Oberwart 1979.

(m) 12 . . . Bb7 13 exf5 Bg7 (13 . . . Ra5 14 Qd3 Bg7 15 Qc4 $\pm$) 14 f6 Bxf6 15 Qf3 Kf8 16 Bxc6 Bxc6 17 Qxf6 Qxf6 18 Nxf6 Ke7 19 Ng4 Bxg2 20 Rg1 $\pm$, Opl–Horvath, Baden 1986.

(n) 13 . . . Rb8 14 a5 Nd4 15 Bxd7† Kxd7 16 0–0 Rxb2 17 a5 and the passed a-pawn makes life difficult for Black, Haist–Kindermann, Bad Wörishofen 1987. On 14 . . . Qg5 15 0–0 Rg8 16 g3 Qxf5 17 Ra3 White was better in Wedberg–Nordstrom, Sweden 1980.

(o) 18 cxd4 Bxe3 19 fxe3 Qxg2 20 Rf1 Qxb2, Drawn, Nunn–Adorjan, Skara 1980.

(p) (A) 12 Qf3 Nd4! 13 Nc7† Qxc7 14 Qxa8† Ke7 15 c3 b4! 16 cxb4 Bh6 17 Qd5 (17 Qxh8? Qb7 +; 17 Qxa6 Rb8 $\mp$) 17 . . . Rc8 (threatening 18 . . . Qc1) and White is in dire straits. (B) Best may be 12 c3 Bg7 transposing to the next column, although Black can also try 12 . . . Be6 13 Nc2 Bh6!?.

(q) 15 Bxe4 0–0 16 0–0–0 Bxe4 17 Qxe4 Re8 18 Qg4 h5! 19 Qh3 Qg5† 20 Ne3 Qf6 is very good for Black, Matulović–Rajković, Yugoslavia 1975.

(r) 18 gxh4 Bxd3 19 cxd3 Bxb2 20 Kd2! Bxa3 21 Nc7† Kd7 22 Nxa8 Bc5 =, Speelman–Povah, England 1976.

(s) 11 g3 fxe4 12 Bg2 Be6 (12 . . . Bf5 13 f3! with play on the long diagonal) 13 Bxe4 Bg7 14 Qh5 Rc8 15 0–0 Ne7 16 Rad1 Rc5 17 Ne3 d5 18 b4 (Gaprindashvili–Peters, Lone Pine 1977) 18 . . . Rc3 19 Nb1 Rxe3 20 fxe3 Qb6 $\mp$.

(t) 11 . . . fxe4?! 12 Bxb5! axb5 13 Nxb5 is a good version of column 147, Shamkovich–Wachtel, New York 1977.

(u) 18 0–0 Rb8 19 Qe2 Qd7 with just a slight pull for White, Yakovich–Sveshnikov, Sochi 1983.

SICILIAN DEFENSE

Pelikan Variation

1 e4 c5 2 Nf3 Nc6 3 d4 cxd4 4 Nxd4 Nf6 5 Nc3 e5 6 Ndb5(a) d6

	151	152	153	154	155	156
7	(Bg5)					Nd5(o)
	(a6)					Nxd5
8	(Na3)					exd5
	(b5)				Be6	Nb8(p)
9	Nd5				Nc4	c4
	Be7(b)				Rc8	a6
10	Bxf6			Nxe7	Bxf6	Nc3
	Bxf6			Nxe7(i)	gxf6(l)	Be7
11	c3			Bxf6	Bd3!	Be2
	0–0		Ne7	gxf6	Ne7	0–0
12	Nc2		Nxf6†	Qf3(j)	Ne3	0–0
	Rb8	Bg5	gxf6	f5	Bh6(m)	f5
13	Be2(c)	a4(e)	g3(g)	exf5	0–0	f4
	Bg5	bxa4	Bb7	Bxf5	Bxe3	Bf6
14	0–0	Rxa4	Bg2	Bd3	fxe3	Qc2
	Be6(d)	a5(f)	f5(h)	Be6(k)	Qb6(n)	Nd7(q)

(a) Other moves give little chance for advantage: (A) 6 Nf3 Bb4 7 Bc4 d6 8 0–0 Be6 = (Adorjan); (B) 6 Nb3 Bb4 7 Bg5 h6 8 Bxf6 Bxc3† 9 bxc3 Qxf6 = ; (C) 6 Nf5 d5 7 exd5 Bxf5 8 dxc6 bxc6 = , Sax–Fedorowicz, Dubai 1986.

(b) 9 . . . Qa5† 10 Bd2 Qd8 11 Nxf6† (11 Bg5 repeats the position) 11 . . . Qxf6 12 c4 Qg6 13 f3 Be7 14 cxb5 Bh4† 15 g3 Bxg3† 16 hxg3 Qxg3† 17 Ke2 Nd4† 18 Ke3 f5 19 exf5 Bxf5 (Ginsberger–Manievich, Israel 1976); now Liberzon gives 20 Bc3 0–0 21 Bxd4 exd4† 22 Qxd4 Rae8† 23 Kd2 Qxf3 24 Bc4† Kh8 25 Rag1 ± .

(c) 13 a4 bxa4 14 Ncb4 Nxb4 15 Nxb4 Bb7 16 Bxa6 Bxe4 17 0–0 Qc7 18 Qxa4 Rfd8 = , Zapata–Schmittdiel, Dortmund 1984.

(d) 15 Qd3 Qd7 16 Rfd1 a5 17 Qg3 h6 18 h4 Bd8 19 Nce3 Kh8 20 Rd2 Ne7 21 Rad1 ± , Spassky–Vukić, Reggio Emilia 1983–84.

(e) Too slow is 13 Be2 Ne7 14 Nxe7† Qxe7 15 Nb4 Be6 16 0–0 a5 17 Nd5 Qb7 with full equality, Christiansen–Adorjan, Denmark 1978.

(f) (A) 14 . . . a5 15 Bc4 (15 Bb5 Ne7 16 Ncb4 Be6 17 Nxe7† Qxe7 =) 15 . . . Rb8 16 Ra2 (16 b3 Kh8 17 0–0 f5 18 exf5 Bxf5 19 Nce3 Be6 20 Qd3 Qd7 =) 16 . . . Kh8 17 Nce3 g6 18 0–0 f5 with chances for both sides, Sznapik–Li Zunian, Thessaloniki 1984. (B) 14 . . . Bb7 with the idea of 15 c4(?) Na5 16 Ba2 Bc6 17 Ra3 Bb5 $\mp$ as in Kuzmin–Timoshchenko, USSR 1988.

(g) (A) 13 Nc2 Bb7 14 Qd3 Qb6 15 Ne3 Rd8 16 Be2 d5 = , Mestel–van der Wiel, London 1982. (B) 14 Bd3 Bb7 15 Qe2 d5 16 0–0–0! ± (Adorjan); 14 . . . Rg8 looks better.

(h) 15 Qe2 0–0 16 Nc2 fxe4 17 Bxe4 Bxe4 18 Qxe4 f5 19 Qe2 Qb6 20 0–0–0 $\pm$, Evans–Lombard, Haifa 1976.

(i) 10 ... Qxe7 11 c4! Nd4 12 Nc2 Qb7 13 Nxd4 Nxe4!? 14 Be3 bxc4 15 Nf3 Qxb2 (Sambursky–Sveshnikov, USSR 1968); 16 Bxc4 Qc3† 17 Nd2 Nxd2 18 Rc1 wins.

(j) (A) 12 c4 Bb7 13 cxb5 Bxc4 14 Qa4 d5 15 bxa6† Kf8 and Black's strong center easily compensates for the pawn. (B) 12 Bd3 Bb7 13 Qe2 d5 14 0–0 dxe4 15 Bxe4 Bxe4 16 Qxe4 Qd5 =, Ivanović–Vukić, Yugoslav Chp. 1982.

(k) 15 0–0 0–0 16 Rfd1 f5 17 c4 Ng6! (Adorjan) with an active game.

(l) 10 ... Qxf6 11 Nb6 Rb8 12 Ncd5 Qd8 13 c3 Be7 14 Bc4 0–0 15 0–0 Bg5 16 a4 with a grip on the center and queenside, Karpov–Nunn, London 1982.

(m) 12 ... Qb6 13 0–0 Qxb2 14 Ncd5 Bxd5 15 exd5 $\pm$, Lombardy–Markland, Nice 1974.

(n) 15 Qf3 h5 16 Nd5 Bxd5 17 exd5 Rh6 18 Rab1 Qa5 19 e4 $\pm$, de Firmian– Matulović, Vrnjačka Banja 1983.

(o) (A) 7 a4 is too slow to maintain the initiative. After 7 ... a6 8 Na3 Be7 9 Be3 Be6 10 Nc4 Nxe4 11 Nxe4 d5 12 Nb6 dxe4 13 Nxa8 Qxa8 Black has an active position for the material deficit, Zakharov–Timoshchenko, USSR 1978. (B) 7 Be3 a6 8 Na3 Rb8! 9 Nd5 Nxd5 =, Perenyi–Horvath, Hungarian Chp. 1981.

(p) Black may encounter difficulties after 8 ... Ne7 9 c3 Ng6 10 Qa4 Bd7 11 Qb4, Dolmatov–Chekhov, Moscow 1977.

(q) 15 Kh1 exf4 16 Bxf4 Ne5 17 a4 Ng6 18 Be3 Be5 =, Geller–Yurtaev, USSR 1979.

SICILIAN DEFENSE

Richter–Rauzer Attack

**1 e4 c5 2 Nf3 Nc6 3 d4 cxd4 4 Nxd4 Nf6 5 Nc3 d6 6 Bg5 e6 7 Qd2 Be7
8 0–0–0 0–0**

	157	158	159	160	161	162
9	f4			Nb3(k)		
	Nxd4		h6(h)	a5	Qb6	a6(r)
10	Qxd4		Bh4(i)	a4	f3	Bxf6
	Qa5	h6	e5	d5	a6(o)	gxf6
11	Bc4(a)	Bh4(e)	Nf5	Bb5(l)	h4(p)	Qh6(s)
	Bd7	Qa5	Bxf5	Nb4(m)	Rd8	Kh8
12	e5(b)	Bc4	exf5	e5	g4	Qh5
	dxe5	e5(f)	exf4	Nd7	d5	Qe8
13	fxe5	fxe5	Kb1	Bxe7	exd5	f4
	Bc6	dxe5	d5	Qxe7	Nxd5	b5
14	Bd2(c)	Qd3	Bxf6	f4	Bxe7	Bd3
	Nd7	Qc5(g)	Bxf6	b6	Ndxe7	Rg8
15	Nd5	Bxf6	Nxd5	Rhe1	Bd3	Nd5!
	Qd8	Bxf6	Be5	Nc5	e5	exd5
16	Nxe7†	Kb1 $\pm$	Bc4	Nd4	h5	exd5
	Qxe7(d)		b5!(j)	Bd7(n)	Kh8(q)	Rg7(t)

(a) 11 Kb1 is too slow. After 11 . . . h6 12 Bxf6 (12 Bh4 e5! =) 12 . . . Bxf6 13 Qd2 Bxc3 14 Qxc3 Qxc3 15 bxc3 Rd8 16 e5 b6 (better than 16 . . . d5?! 17 c4 $\pm$) 17 exd6 Bb7 with even chances, Tal–Slugman, USSR 1952.

(b) 12 Bb3 Bc6 13 Rhf1 h6 14 Bh4 Qh5! =.

(c) 14 h4 Rfd8 15 Qf4 Nh5 16 Qg4 Bxg5† 17 Qxg5 g6 =, Liberzon–D. Gurevich, Beersheba 1984.

(d) 17 Rhe1 (17 h4?! Qc5! 18 Qxc5 Nxc5 19 Bb4 Rfc81 20 Bc5 Bxg2 $\mp$, Murey–D. Gurevich, Jerusalem 1986) 17 . . . Nb6 18 Bf1 Rfd8 19 Qg4 Qc5 20 Bh6 Rxd1† 21 Kxd1 Nd7 22 Kc1 $\pm$, Timman–Sosonko, Holland 1985–86. 17 . . . Rfd8 looks better.

(e) 11 Bxf6 Bxf6 12 Qxd6 Qa5 13 e5 Rd8 14 Qa3 Qxa3 is an even endgame.

(f) (A) Of course 12 . . . Bd7 now loses to 13 e5. (B) 12 . . . Rd8 13 Rhf1 Qh5 14 g3! Bd7 15 f5 $\pm$ threatens 16 Be2, Schmid–Boleslavsky, West Germany vs. USSR 1960.

(g) 14 . . . Be6 15 Bxf6! Bxc4 16 Qxc4 wins control of d5. The column is Gligorić–Taimanov, Stockholm 1952.

(h) The immediate 9 . . . e5 10 Nf5 Bxf5 11 exf5 is not so good because . . . exf4 can always be answered with Bxf4 $\pm$.

(i) 10 Bxf6 Bxf6 11 Nxc6 (11 Nbd5 e5! =) 11 . . . bxc6 12 Qxd6 Qb6 13 Qd3 Rb8 14 b3 Rd8 15 Qf3 Bd4 =, A. Rodriguez–van der Wiel, Biel 1985.

(j) 17 Bxb5 Rb8 18 c4 Nd4 19 Rhe1 (19 f6 gxf6 20 g3 f3 ∞, Tseshkovsky–Piket, Wijk aan Zee 1989) 19 . . . f6 20 a4 a6 21 Bxa6 Rb3 22 Bb5 Qa8 with an attack for the pawns, A. Rodriguez–P. Popović, Dubai 1986.

(k) As usual, going after the d-pawn gives Black good play: 9 Ndb5 Qa5 10 Bxf6 (10 Nxd6? Rd8 †) 10 . . . Bxf6 11 Nxd6 Rd8 12 f4 e5! =, Korchnoi–Boleslavsky, USSR Chp. 1952. 9 Nb3 was Alekhine's move at Poděbrady 1936.

(l) 11 exd5 Nxd5 12 Bxe7 Nxce7 13 Bc4 (Kosten–Chandler, British Chp. 1985) 13 . . . Qe8 =.

(m) 11 . . . Nxe4?! 12 Nxe4 dxe4 13 Qxd8 Bxd8 14 Bxd8 Nxd8 15 Nc5 f5 16 Rd6 allows White a strong endgame initiative. Tal–Sisniega, Taxco 1985, concluded 16 . . . Kf7 17 Rhd1 Ke7 18 Bd7 Rf7 (18 . . . Bxd7 19 Rxd7† ±) 19 Nxe6! Bxd7 20 Nc7! Bxa4 21 Nxa8 Ne6 22 Nb6 Be8 23 R6d5 Bc6 24 Rxa5 Kf6 25 Nd5† Kg6 26 Ne3 Resigns.

(n) 17 Kb1 Rac8? 18 g4 ±, Balashov–Khalifman, Minsk 1986; White controls more squares. 17 . . . Rfc8 was better.

(o) 10 . . . Rd8 11 Be3 Qc7 12 Qf2! (A) 12 . . . Nd7 13 Nb5 Qb8 14 g4 a6 15 N5d4 ±, Fischer–Benko, US Chp. 1959–60. White will attack by advancing his kingside pawns, while Black's counterplay will be slow. (B) 12 . . . d5 13 exd5 Nxd5 14 Nxd5 Rxd5 15 Rxd5 ±, Hübner–Piket, Wijk aan Zee 1988.

(p) (A) 11 Bxf6 Bxf6 12 Qxd6 Be7 13 Qg3 Qa7 14 f4 b5 15 e5 ±, Hübner–Kasparov, match 1985; but 12 . . . Rd8 should give Black enough play for the pawn. (B) 11 g4 Rd8 12 Be3 Qc7 13 g5 Nd7 14 h4 g5 =, Spassky–Boleslavsky, USSR Chp. 1958.

(q) 17 h6 g6 18 Ne4 and the Black king is in serious danger, Gipslis–Bielczyk, Riga 1981.

(r) 9 . . . h6?! 10 Bxf6 Bxf6 11 Qxd6 Bxc3 12 bxc3 Qh4 13 f3 Rd8 14 Qc7 Rxd1† 15 Kxd1 Qf6 16 Kc1 Qxc3 17 Bb5 ±, Serper–Reznikov, USSR 1982.

(s) (A) 11 f4 b5 12 f5 Kh8 13 Ne2 (13 g3 b4 14 Ne2 e5 15 g4 a5 16 Kb1 a4 17 Nbc1 Rg8 =) 13 . . . Rg8 14 Nf4 Bf8 15 Kb1 ±, Hübner–Korchnoi, Tilburg 1989. (B) 11 h4 b5 12 g4 b4 13 Ne2 a5 14 Ned4 Bb7 15 Nxc6 Bxc6 16 Nd4 Bb7 17 g5 f5! 18 Rg1 f4 19 h5 c5 =, Sax–van der Wiel, Brussels 1985.

(t) 17 dxc6 Bg4 18 Qd5 Bxd1 19 Rxd1 with a dominating position for a small material sacrifice (Tisdall). However, 15 . . . Bb7 16 Nxe7 Qxe7 is promising.

SICILIAN DEFENSE

Richter–Rauzer Attack

1 e4 c5 2 Nf3 Nc6 3 d4 cxd4 4 Nxd4 Nf6 5 Nc3 d6 6 Bg5 e6 7 Qd2 a6 8 0–0–0 Bd7

	163	164	165	166	167	168
9	f4 . . . . Be2					
	Be7 . . . . h6 . . . . b5			b5 . . . . Nxd4(s)		
10	Nf3		Bh4	Bxf6(l)	Nxc6	Qxd4
	b5(a)		g5(i)	gxf6	Bxc6	Be7(t)
11	Bxf6 . . . . .e5(f)		fxg5	f5(m)	Qe3	f4
	gxf6(b)	b4	Ng4	Nxd4	Be7(o)	Bc6
12	Kb1(c)	exf6	Nxc6(j)	Qxd4	e5	Bf3
	Qb6(d)	bxc3	Bxc6	Bh6†	Nd5	Qc7
13	f5	Qxc3	Be2	Kb1	Nxd5	e5
	0–0–0	gxf6	Ne5	Bf4	Bxg5(p)	dxe5
14	g3	f5(g)	g3	fxe6	Nc7†(q)	Qxe5
	Kb8	d5	Ng6	fxe6	Qxc7	Rc8
15	fxe6	fxe6	Kb1	Ne2	Qg5	Qxc7
	fxe6	fxe6	h5	Be5	dxe5	Rxc7
16	Bh3	Bd2	Qe3	Qd2	Qxg7	Bxc6†
	Bc8(e)	Rc8(h)	Be7(k)	Qb6(n)	Rf8(r)	Rxc6 =

(a) 10 . . . Rc8 11 Kb1 Qc7 12 e5! dxe5 13 fxe5 Nd5 14 Nxd5 ±, Spassky–Taimanov, USSR 1956.

(b) 11 . . . Bxf6?! 12 Qxd6 Be7 13 Qd3 b4 14 Na4 Ra7 15 Qe3 Qa5 16 b3 Rb7 17 Nd2 Na7 18 Nc4 Qc7 19 Rxd7 Qxd7 20 Nc5 regains the initiative, Psakhis–Geller, Moscow 1986.

(c) 12 Bd3 Qa5 13 Kb1 b4 14 Ne2 Qc5 15 f5 a5 16 Nf4 a4 with counterplay, Fischer–Spassky, World Chp. 1972.

(d) Black can also keep his king in the center: 12 . . . Rc8 13 f5 Qb6 14 Bd3 b4 15 Ne2 e5 16 Qh6 with a small plus, Klovans–Mochalov, USSR 1976–77.

(e) 17 Qe1 with a pull due to Black's loose pawn center, Karpov–Liberzon, Bad Lauterberg 1977.

(f) 11 Be2 h6 12 Bh4 Qb6 13 Kb1 0–0 allows Black to mount an attack.

(g) 14 Bh4 d5 15 Kb1 Rb8 should give Black sufficient play on the kingside.

(h) 17 Qe3 e5 18 Bxa6 Ra8 19 Bb7 d4 20 Qh6 Rxa2 ∞, Damjanović–Tischbierek, Třinec 1985.

(i) 10 . . . Nxe4?! 11 Qe1! (11 Bxd8? Nxd2 ∓) 11 . . . Nf6 12 Nf5 ±, Tal–Klavin, USSR 1958.

(j) Equally good is 12 Nf3 hxg5 13 Bg3 (13 Bxg5? f6! 14 Bf4 e5 wins, as 15 Bg3 is met by 15 . . . Bh6) 13 . . . Be7 14 Be2 Nge5 15 Kb1 b5 16 a3 Rb8 17 Na2 a5 18 Nc1 ⩲, Riemersma–A. Rodriguez, Dieren 1987.

(k) 16 . . . Bg7 17 Nd5! exd5 18 exd5† Qe7 19 Qxe7† is a good endgame for White, Chandler–Bellin, Commonwealth Chp. 1985. After 16 . . . Be7 17 Rhf1 Qc7 18 Qf2 Ne5 19 h3 0–0 20 g4! White is better, Jansa–Banas, Czechoslovak Chp. 1986.

(l) 10 e5 dxe5 11 Nxc6 Bxc6 12 Qxd8† Rxd8 13 Rxd8† Kxd8 14 fxe5 h6 15 Bh4 g5 $\mp\mp$.

(m) (A) 11 Kb1 Qb6 12 Nce2 Na5 13 b3 0–0–0! 14 g3 Kb8 15 Bg2 Rc8 with counterplay (Sax). (B) 11 Nxc6 Bxc6 12 Qe1 Qe7! 13 Bd3 Bg7 14 Qg3 Rg8 15 Rhe1 Kf8 16 Qh4 f5! =, Kudrin–Christiansen, US Chp. 1986.

(n) 17 Nf4 Ke7 (17 . . . 0–0–0 18 g3 Kb8 19 Bh3 $\pm$, Tseshkovsky–Ermenkov, Albania 1977) 18 Nd3 Bd4 19 e5! dxe5 20 Nxe5 Be8 (20 . . . fxe5?! 21 c3) 21 Nf3 $\pm$, Beliavsky–van der Wiel, Reggio Emilia 1986–87.

(o) 11 . . . Qe7 12 Bf3 Qa7 13 Qe2 Nd7 gave Black equal chances in Kosanović–Martinović, Yugoslav Chp. 1986, but White can do better with 13 Qxa7 Rxa7 14 Rhe1 $\pm$.

(p) 13 . . . Bxd5?! 14 Bxe7 Qxe7 15 exd6 Qxd6 16 Rxd5! Qxd5 17 Bf3 Qxa2 18 Qc5! f5 19 Bxa8 Kf7 20 Qc7† Kf6 21 Rd1 Rxa8 22 Qc3† Kg6 23 Rd7 Rg8 24 Qg3† Kf6 25 h4! with great advantage (Nunn).

(q) 14 f4 Bxd5 15 fxg5 0–0 16 Bf3 Bxf3 17 gxf3 (17 Rxd6 Qa5 =) 17 . . . d5 =.

(r) 17 Qxh7 Bxg2 18 Rhg1 Bd5 19 Rg7 e4 with even chances, Vladimirov–Granda Zuniga, Gausdal 1986.

(s) (A) 9 . . . Be7 10 Nb3 b5 11 Bxf6 gxf6 12 Bh5 Ne5 13 f4 Nc4 14 Qe2 $\pm$, Lilienthal–Petrosian, USSR Chp. 1954. (B) 9 . . . h6 10 Bh4 Rc8 11 Nxc6 Bxc6 12 Qe3 Be7 13 f4 0–0 14 Rd2 b5 =, Arnason–Barbero, Plovdiv 1986.

(t) 10 . . . Qa5 11 f4 Bc6 12 Bxf6 gxf6 13 Bf3 Be7 14 Rhe1 Qc5 ∞, Jansa–Plachetka, Czechoslovak Chp. 1986. The column is Dutreeuw–van der Wiel, San Bernardino 1986.

SICILIAN DEFENSE

Richter-Rauzer Attack

1 e4 c5 2 Nf3 Nc6 3 d4 cxd4 4 Nxd4 Nf6 5 Nc3 d6 6 Bg5 e6 7 Qd2 a6 8 0–0–0 h6

	169	170	171	172	173	174
9	Bf4		Be3(h)			
	Bd7		Be7		Nxd4	Bd7(q)
10	Nxc6(a)		f3	f4(k)	Qxd4(n)	f3(r)
	Bxc6		Nxd4	Nxd4	Bd7(o)	b5(s)
11	Qe1(b)		Bxd4(i)	Bxd4	Be2	g4
	Qa5	Be7(e)	b5	b5	Qc7	Ne5
12	f3	h4(f)	h4	Bd3(l)	f4	Bd3
	0–0–0(c)	Qc7	Qa5	Bb7	Bc6	b4
13	Bc4	f3	Qf2	Kb1	Bf3	Nce2
	Qc7	b5	Rb8	b4	b5	d5
14	a3!	Bd3	Kb1	Ne2	g4	Ng3
	Nd7	b4	b4	0–0	0–0–0	Qc7
15	Ba2	Ne2	Ne2	Ng3	a3	Kb1
	b5	Qb6	e5	a5	Be7	Nc4
16	Kb1	g4	Ba7	e5	h4	Bxc4
	Nb6(d)	d5(g)	Rb7(j)	dxe5(m)	Rhg8(p)	dxc4(t)

(a) Pressuring the d-pawn is useless: 10 Nf3 b5! 11 a3 e5 with an active game.

(b) 11 f3 d5! 12 Qe1 Bb4 13 a3 Ba5 14 exd5 Nxd5 15 b4 Nxf4! 16 Rxd8† Bxd8 =, Zagorovsky–Rokhlin, corr. 1967; Black has rook and bishop and attacking chances for the queen.

(c) The best way to defend the d-pawn. After 12 . . . Rd8?! 13 h4 b5 14 Kb1 b4 15 Ne2 e5 16 Bd2 Rb8 17 Nc1 White held a solid advantage in Nunn–van der Wiel, Wijk aan Zee 1983.

(d) 17 Ne2 Kb7 18 Nd4 Bd7 19 Bd2 Rc8 20 Ba5 ±, Jansa–Csom, Sarajevo 1981.

(e) (A) 11 . . . b5? 12 e5 Nd5 13 Nxd5 Bxd5 14 Rxd5! exd5 15 Bd3! dxe5 16 Qxe5† Qe7 17 Qxd5 ±, Torre–Ivanović, Vrsać 1977. (B) 11 . . . Nh5 12 Be3 Qc7 13 f3 Be7 14 h4 ±.

(f) (A) 12 e5 is not so strong now: 12 . . . Nh5 13 Be3 Qc7 14 Be2 g6 15 Bxh5 gxh5 with an active game to compensate for the bad pawn structure, Chandler–Ivanović, Plovdiv 1983. (B) 12 Kb1 Qc7 13 e5 dxe5 14 Bxe5 Qb6 =.

(g) 17 g5 Nh5 18 Bd2 dxe4 19 fxe4 ±, Fedorowicz–Dlugy, London 1987.

(h) 9 Bh4? Nxe4! wins a pawn.

(i) 11 Qxd4 b4 12 e5 dxe5 13 Qxe5 Qa5 14 Kb1 Bb7 15 Bd3 0–0 16 Qg3 (Campora–A. Rodriguez, Amsterdam 1987); 16 . . . b4 ∞.

306

(j) 17 Nc1 Be6 18 Nb3 Qc7 19 Be3 a5 with even chances, van der Wiel–Tukmakov, Thessaloniki 1984.

(k) 10 Be2 Nxd4 11 Qxd4 Bd7 12 f4 Bc6 13 g4 Nd7 14 h4 is rated better for White by Benjamin.

(l) 12 Be2!? b4 13 Na4 Nxe4 14 Qe3 Nf6 15 Bf3 d5 16 Kb1 0–0 17 Nb6 Rb8 18 g4 is fair compensation for the pawn, Short–A. Rodriguez, Subotica 1987.

(m) 17 fxe5 Nd5 18 Nh5 Qc7 (Kudrin–Wilder, US Chp. 1987); now Fedorowicz's plan 19 h4 and Rh3 gives White slightly better chances in this complex position.

(n) 10 Bxd4 b5 11 Bd3 (11 f3 Be7 transposes to col. 171) 11 . . . Qa5 12 Bxf6 gxf6 13 Kb1 Bb7 14 f4 0–0–0 = , Martinović–Radulov, Vrnačka Banja 1983.

(o) 10 . . . Ng4 11 e5 Nxe5 12 f4 is interesting.

(p) White has a spatial advantage, Fedorowicz–Dlugy, US Chp. 1987. The game continued 17 g5 Nd7 18 Bg4 hxg5 19 hxg5 Kb8 20 Rh7 e5? (weakening the central squares; Black would do better with 20 . . . Rc8 or 20 . . . Qb7) 21 Qd2 exf4 22 Bxf4 Nf8 23 Rh3 Ng6 24 Be3 Ne5 25 Be2 Rh8 26 Rdh1 Rxh3 27 Rxh3 Qc8 28 Rh7 Rh8?! 29 Qd4! Resigns (29 . . . Bb7 30 Qa7† Kc7 31 Nd5† Kd7 32 Nb6† wins the queen).

(q) 9 . . . Ng4 looks tempting, but after 10 Nxc6 bxc6 11 Bc5 Bb7 12 h3 White is clearly on top, Smyslov–Botvinnik, World Chp. 1957.

(r) 10 f4 b5 11 Bd3 Be7 12 h3 Nxd4 13 Bxd4 b4 14 Ne2 (Murey–Lobron, Lyon 1988) 14 . . . Qb8 = .

(s) 10 . . . Qc7 11 g4 b5 12 Rg1 b4 13 Nce2 Ne5 14 Ng3 d5 15 h4 dxe4 (Kir. Georgiev–Csom, Warsaw 1987); 16 Nxe4 Nxe4 17 fxe4 Bc5 18 Kb1 ± (Sax).

(t) Arnason–Ivanović, Plovdiv 1986; now 17 Qf2 Bd6 18 Nde2 is unclear.

SICILIAN DEFENSE

1 e4 c5 2 Nf3 Nc6 3 d4 cxd4 4 Nxd4 Nf6 5 Nc3 d6

	175	176	177	178	179	180
6	(Bg5)	....	....	Be2	....	f4(p)
		(Larsen			(Boleslavsky	
	Bd7	Variation)	..Qb6(g)	e5!	Variation)	e5
7	Qd2(a)		Nb3	Nb3	Nf3	Nf3(q)
	Rc8(b)		e6	Be7	h6(m)	Be7
8	0-0-0		Bd3(h)	0-0(j)	0-0	Bd3
	Nxd4		Be7	0-0	Be7	Qb6
9	Qxd4		0-0	Be3(k)	Re1(n)	Rb1
	Qa5		a6	Be6	0-0	0-0
10	f4(c)		Kh1	Bf3(l)	h3	Qe2
	e6	Rxd3(e)	Qc7(i)	a5	Re8(o)	Bg4
11	e5	bxc3	f4	Nd5	Bf1	Be3
	dxe5	e5	Bd7	Bxd5	Bf8	Qa5
12	fxe5	Qb4!	Qe2	exd5	Be3	h3
	Bc6	Qxb4	h6	Nb4	Be6 =	Bxf3
13	Bb5	cxb4	Bh4 ±	a3		Qxf3
	Nd5(d)	Nxe4(f)		Na6 =		d5!(r)

(a) (A) 7 Bxf6 gxf6 8 Nf5 Qa5 9 Bb5 a6 =. (B) 7 Be2 e6 8 Qd2 a6 9 0-0-0 transposes to column 167. (C) 7 Nb3 a6 8 f4 e6 9 Qd3 h6 10 Bh4 g5 11 fxg5 Nh5 12 Qd2 Ge7 ∞, Trepp–Csom, Biel 1986.

(b) 7 . . . Nxd4 8 Qxd4 Qa5 9 Bd2 Qc7 10 Bc4 e6 11 Bb3 ±, R. Byrne–Benko, US 1970.

(c) 10 Bd2 e5 11 Qd3 a6 12 a3 Be6 13 Nd5 Qd8 14 Bg5 Bxd5 15 Bxf6 Qxf6 is equal, Timman–Ljubojević, Brussels 1987.

(d) 14 Nxd5 Bxb5 15 Kb1!? with some attack.

(e) 10 . . . e5 11 fxe5 dxe5 12 Qd2 Bc6 13 Bxf6 gxf6 14 a3 Rd8 15 Qxd8† Qxd8 16 Rxd8† Kxd8 17 Bc4 ±, Mokrý–Chiburdanidze, Polanica Zdroj 1984.

(f) 14 Bh4 g5 (14 . . . exf4 15 Bd3 f5 16 Bxe4 fxe4 17 Rhf1 ±) 15 fxg5 Be8 16 Re1 d5 17 Bd3 and Black lacks full compensation for the exchange, Unzicker–Gheorghiu, Ljubjana 1969.

(g) 6 . . . Qa5?! 7 Bxf6 gxf6 8 Nb3 secures an edge.

(h) 8 Bxf6 gxf6 9 Be2 a6 10 0-0 Be7 11 Kh1 0-0 12 f4 Kh8 gives Black fewer problems, Tarjan–Ostojić, Venice 1974.

(i) On 10 . . . 0-0 not 11 f4?! h6 12 Bxf6 (12 Bh4 Nxe4! 13 Bxe4 Bxh4 14 Qxd6 Be7 =) 12 . . . Bxf6 13 Qh5 Qc7 =, R. Byrne–Fedorowicz, US Chp. 1977, but 11 Qe2 and 12 f4 ±. The column is R. Byrne–Benjamin, US Chp. 1984.

(j) 8 Bg5 Nxe4 9 Bxe7 Nxc3 10 Bxd8 Nxd1 11 Rxd1 Kxd8 12 Rxd6† Ke7 =, Böök–Bronstein, Saltsjöbaden 1948.

(k) 9 Kh1 a5 10 a4 Nb4 11 Be3 Bd7 12 Bf3 Bc6 13 Qe2 Qc7 =, Abramovic–Kuzmin, Kladovo 1980.

(l) 10 f4 exf4 11 Bxf4 d5 is completely equal. The column is Ljubojević–P. Popović, Belgrade 1987.

(m) 7 . . . Be7 8 Bg5! 0–0 9 0–0 Be6 10 Bxf6 Bxf6 11 Nd5 with a pull thanks to control of d5, Smyslov–Hort, Tilburg 1977.

(n) White gains no advantage from the natural 9 Be3 Be6 10 Qd2 0–0 11 Rad1 Qd7 12 h3 Rfd8 =.

(o) Now natural moves by Black give White a pull, e.g.: (A) 10 . . . Be6 11 Bf1 Rc8 12 Nd5 ±, or (B) 10 . . . a6 11 Bf1 b5?! 12 a4 b4 13 Nd5 Nxd5 14 exd5 ±, Sigurjonsson–Hjartarson, Reykjavik 1985.

(p) Other rarely used moves are: (A) 6 g3 Nxd4 7 Qxd4 g6 8 Bg2 Bg7 9 0–0 0–0 =, transposing to an insipid line against the Dragon. (B) 6 Be3 Ng4 7 Bb5 Nxe3 8 fxe3 Bd7 9 Bxc6 bxc6 10 0–0 e6 =, Gliksman–Bradvarević, Yugoslav Chp. 1967.

(q) 7 Nxc6 bxc6 8 fxe5 Ng4! 9 exd6 Bxd6 leaves Black very active.

(r) 14 Bd2 (14 exd5 e4 15 Bxe4 Nxe4 16 Qxe4 Bc5! and 17 . . . Rae8 ∓—A. Rodriguez) 14 . . . Nd4 15 Qf2 dxe4 16 Nxe4 Qxa2 ∓, Cabrilo–A. Rodriguez, Pančevo 1987.

SICILIAN DEFENSE

Velimirović Attack

1 e4 c5 2 Nf3 Nc6 3 d4 cxd4 4 Nxd4 Nf6 5 Nc3 d6 6 Bc4 e6 7 Be3

	181	182	183	184	185	186
	Be7					a6
8	Qe2					Qe2
	0–0 . . . . a6					Qc7
9	0–0–0				0–0–0	0–0–0
	a6 . . . . Qa5(j)				Qc7	Na5
10	Bb3			Bb3	Bb3	Bd3(p)
	Qc7(a)			Nxd4	Na5	b5
11	Rhg1 . . . . g4			Bxd4	g4	a3(q)
	Nd7 . . . . Na5(e)		Nxd4(g)	Bd7	b5	Bb7
12	g4	g4	Rxd4	Kb1	g5	g4
	Nc5	b5	b5(h)	Bc6(k)	Nxb3†	d5
13	g5(b)	g5	g5	f4	axb3	exd5
	b5(c)	Nxb3†	Nd7	Rad8	Nd7	Nxd5
14	Nxc6	axb3	Rg1	Rhf1	h4(m)	Ndxb5!
	Nxb3†	Nd7	Bb7	b5	b4	Qb8(r)
15	axb3	f4	f4	f5	Na4(n)	Nxd5
	Qxc6(d)	b4(f)	Rfe8(i)	b4(l)	Nc5(o)	Bxd5(s)

(a) 10 . . . Qe8 11 Rhg1 Nd7 12 g4 Nc5 13 g5 b5 14 Nxc6 Nxb3† 15 axb3 Qxc6 16 Bd4 b4 17 Qh5! Bb7 18 Nd5! exd5 19 Rd3 Rfc8 20 c3 dxe4 21 Rh3 Kf8 22 g6! fxg6 23 Qxh7 ±, Howell–Wahls, Gausdal 1986.

(b) 13 Nf5 b5! (accepting the sacrifice is dangerous, e.g. 13 . . . exf5 14 gxf5 Bd7 15 Nd5 Qd8 16 Qh5 Kh8 17 Rxg7! Kxg7 18 f6† wins [18 . . . Bxf6 19 Qh6† Kh8 20 Nxf6], S. Sokolov–Grigorian, USSR 1978) 14 Bd5 (14 Nxe7† Nxe7 is equal) 14 . . . exd5 15 Nxd5 Qb7 should be good for Black.

(c) 13 . . . Bd7 14 Qh5 Rfc8 15 Rg3 g6 16 Qh6 Bf8 17 Qh4 Nxb3† 18 axb3 Be7 19 f4 b5 20 Nf5! exf5 21 Nd5 Qd8 22 e5 with a strong attack (Leverett).

(d) 16 Bd4 b4 17 Qh5 Bb7 (17 . . . bxc3 18 Qh6! e5 19 Bxe5 wins) 18 Nd5! exd5 19 Rd3 transposes to note (a).

(e) 11 . . . b5 12 g4 b4 13 Nxc6 Qxc6 14 Nd5! exd5 15 g5 Nxe4 16 Bxd5 Qa4 17 Bxa8 Nc3 18 bxc3 Be6 19 Bd5! Bxd5 (19 . . . Qa3† 20 Kb1 Bxd5 21 c4!) 20 Rxd5 Qxa2 21 Bd4 Re8 22 Rxd6! ± (Leverett).

(f) 16 Nf5! exf5 (safer is 16 . . . Nc5 17 Nxe7† Qxe7 18 e5 bxc3 19 exd6 cxb2† 20 Kxb2 Qa7 21 Qf2 Na4† 22 bxa4 ±—Stean) 17 Nd5 Qd8 18 exf5 Re8 19 Bd4 Bf8?! (19 . . . Bb7 20 g6 f6 seems better) 20 Qh5 Re4 (20 . . . Bb7 21 Nf6† Nxf6 22 gxf6—threatening 23 Rxg7†—22 . . . g6 23 fxg6 hxg6 24 Rxg6† mates) 21 Bf6! Qe8 22 Nc7 Nxf6 23 gxf6 Qd8 24 Nd5! Bb7 25 fxg7 Be7 26 Rg3 Bf6 27 Rh3 Bxg7 28 Qxh7† Kf8 29 f6 Bxf6 30 Qxe4 Qa5 31 Qf5 Bg7 32 Qd7 Resigns, Wolff–I. Sokolov, World Junior Chp. 1987.

(g) (A) 11 . . . Nd7 12 f4 (12 Rhg1 transposes to col. 181) 12 . . . b5 13 f5 b5 14 Kb1 Bd7 15 Nxc6 Qxc6 16 g4 ±, Wedberg–Spassov, Eksjo 1981. (B) 11 . . . Na5 12 g5 Nxb3† 13 axb3 Nd7 14 h4 b5 15 g6! gives White kingside play, Romanishin–Vaiser, USSR 1972.

(h) Black should avoid 12 . . . e5?! 13 Rc4 Qd8 14 g5 Ne8 15 Rg1 Bd7 16 Nd5! Bb5 17 Bb6 Qd7 18 Qg4! ±, Spasojević–Ostojić, Belgrade 1966.

(i) 16 f5 Bf8 17 g6 hxg6 18 fxg6 fxg6 19 Rxg6 Nc5 (Cebalo) is roughly equal.

(j) (A) 9 . . . d5 looks suspect, but is not easy to refute. 10 exd5 exd5 11 Nf3 should give White a pull. (B) On 9 . . . Bd7 10 f4 Qc8 11 Nf3 a6 12 e5 Ne8 13 h4 ±, Peters–Dlugy, Los Angeles 1988.

(k) In de Firmian–Dlugy, US Chp. 1987, Black played 12 . . . Rac8 13 f4 e5 14 Nd5 Nxd5 15 exd5 Bf6 16 fxe5 Bxe5 17 Bxe5 Rfe8 and achieved equality. A better test of this idea is 13 Bxf6.

(l) 16 fxe6! bxc3 17 exf7† Kh8 18 Rf5 Qb4 19 Qf1 Nxe4 (Fischer–Geller, Skopje 1967); now Fischer claims that 20 Qf4! leads to a win.

(m) 14 Nf5 is a well-analyzed sacrifice. After 14 . . . exf5 15 Nd5 Qd8 16 exf5 Bb7 17 f6 gxf6 18 Rhe1 Bxd5 19 Rxd5 Rg8! 20 gxf6 Nxf6 21 Rf5 Rb8, or 20 Bf4 Kf8, chances are even.

(n) 15 Na2 a5 16 Nb5 Qc6 17 Qc4 Nc5 18 Nxd6† Bxd6 19 Rxd6 Qxd6 20 Bxc5 Qc7 ∓.

(o) 16 h5 Bd7 17 Kb1 Bxa4 18 bxa4 Qb7 19 g6 Bf6 20 gxf7† Kxf7 =, Quinteros–P. Popović, Novi Sad 1982.

(p) 10 Bb3 b5 forces the concession 11 f3 to defend the e-pawn, after which 11 . . . Be7 12 g4 Nxb3† 13 axb3 b4 14 Na4 Nd7 is fine for Black.

(q) 11 g4 b4 12 Nb1 Bb7 13 Nd2 d5 14 f3 dxe4 15 fxe4 Be7 16 g5 Nd7 17 h4 (de Firmian–J. Kristiansen, Copenhagen 1984); now 17 . . . Nc6 is equal.

(r) 14 . . . axb5?! 15 Bxb5† Kd8 16 Nxd5 exd5 17 d3 gave White a strong attack in Nunn–Sosonko, Thessaloniki 1984.

(s) 16 Nc3 Bxh1 17 Rxh1 Qc7 18 Nd5 (Hawelko–Gaprindashvili, Polanica Zdroj 1986); now, instead of 18 . . . Qc6 19 Bxa6! ±, Black should have played 18 . . . exd5 19 Bb6† Qe7 20 Bxa5 when White has some advantage in the coming endgame.

SICILIAN DEFENSE

Sozin Variation

1 e4 c5 2 Nf3 Nc6 3 d4 cxd4 4 Nxd4 Nf6 5 Nc3 d6 6 Bc4

	187	188	189	190	191	192
	(e6)					Qb6(n)
7	Bb3				Nb3	Ndb5(q)
	Be7			a6	e6	a6
8	Be3(a)			Be3	0–0	Be3
	0–0			Be7(k)	Be7	Qa5
9	0–0(b)			f4	Bg5(o)	Nd4
	a6	Nxd4	Bd7(h)	0–0	a6	e6(r)
10	f4	Bxd4	f4(i)	Qf3(l)	Bxf6	0–0
	Nxd4(c)	b5(f)	Nxd4	Nxd4	gxf6	Be7
11	Bxd4	Nxb5	Bxd4	Bxd4	Qh5	Bb3
	b5	Ba6	Bc6	b5	Nd4	0–0
12	e5(d)	c4	Qe2	Bxf6(m)	Rfd1	f4
	dxe5	Bxb5	b5	Bxf6	Nxb3	Nxd4
13	fxe5	cxb5	Nxb5	e5	axb3	Qxd4!?
	Nd7	Nxe4	Bxb5	Bh4†	Rb8!	Ng4
14	Ne4	Qf3	Qxb5	g3	Qh6	Kh1 ±
	Bb7(e)	Nf6(g)	Nxe4(j)	Rb8 ∞	Qc5(p)	

(a) 8 f4 Nxd4! 9 Qxd4 0–0 10 0–0 b6 11 Qd3 Nd7 12 Be3 Bb7 = (Nikitin).

(b) (A) 9 f4 a6 10 Qf3 Bd7 11 0–0–0 Rc8 12 f5 Nxd4 13 Bxd4 e5 14 Be3?! Rxc3! 15 bxc3 Bc6 ∓, J. Polgar–I. Ivanov, New York 1989. (B) 9 Qe2 and 10 0–0–0 is cols. 181–186.

(c) 10 ... Bd7 11 f5 Qc8? (11 ... Nxd4 12 Bxd4 ± is better) 12 fxe6 Bxe6 13 Nxe6 fxe6 14 Na4! Rb8 15 Nb6 wins a pawn, Fischer–Larsen, match 1971.

(d) 12 a3 Bb7 13 Qd3 a5! 14 e5 dxe5 15 fxe5 Nd7 16 Nxb5 Nc5 17 Bxc5 Bxc5† 18 Kh1 Qg5 with a strong initiative, Fischer–Spassky, World Chp. 1972.

(e) 15 Nd6 Bxd6 16 exd6 Qg5 17 Rf2 a5 18 a4 b4 19 Qd2 Qxd2 20 Rxd2 Rfd8, Draw, de Firmian–Tringov, Niš 1981.

(f) (A) 10 ... b6 11 f4 Ba6 12 Rf3 Bb7 13 Qe2 d5 14 e5 Ne4 15 Rh3 gives White a pull (Kasparov and Nikitin). (B) 10 ... Qa5 11 Kh1 ± .

(g) 15 Qe2 Nd7 (Fischer–Korchnoi, Zagreb 1970); now simply 16 Rfd1 d5 17 Rac1 would leave White with a pull.

(h) 9 ... Na5 10 f4 b6 11 e5 Ne8 12 Qg4 Nxb3 13 axb3 Bb7 14 Rad1 with a clear initiative, Kindermann–D. Gurevich, Beersheba 1986.

(i) Simple development with 10 Qe2 Qa5 11 Rad1 Rad8 12 f4 also puts White on top, Parma–Bradvarević, Yugoslav Chp. 1963.

(j) 15 f5 Bf6 (15 . . . e5 16 Qe2 ±) 16 Qd3 d5 17 Bxf6 Nxf6 18 c4! ±, Fischer–R. Weinstein, US Chp. 1958–59.

(k) 8 . . . Na5 9 f4 b5 10 e5 dxe5 11 fxe5 Nxb3 12 axb3 Nd5 13 Qf3 ±.

(l) (A) 10 0–0 transposes to column 187. (B) 10 Qe2 Nxd4 11 Bxd4 b5 12 0–0–0 (Sigurjonsson–Ligterink, Wijk aan Zee 1980) and now 12 . . . Bb7 =.

(m) 12 e5?! dxe5 13 fxe5?! Qxd4 14 exf6 Bc5 ∓, Hermlin–Shamkovich, USSR 1972. If 15 Qxa8 Qf2† 16 Kd1 Be3 +.

(n) Unusual tries are: (A) 6 . . . g6?! 7 Nxc6 bxc6 8 e5 Ng4 (8 . . . dxe5? 9 Bxf7†) 9 Bf4! ± (Sosonko); (B) 6 . . . Bd7 7 0–0 g6 8 Nxc6 Bxc6 9 Nd5! Bg7 10 Bg5 Bxd5 11 exd5 0–0 12 Re1 ±, Neamtu–Mititelu, Bucharest 1968.

(o) 9 Be3 Qc7 10 f4 a6 11 Bd3 (11 a4 d5! 12 exd5 Nb4 =) 11 . . . b5 12 Qf3 Bb7 =.

(p) 15 Qg7 Rf8 16 Qxh7 b5 17 Bd3 Bb7 and Black has sufficient play for the pawn due to his bishop-pair and open files on the kingside, Nunn–Martinović, Amsterdam 1985.

(q) (A) On 7 Nxc6 bxc6 8 0–0 e6 or 8 . . . e5 is equal. (B) 7 Nde2 e6 8 0–0 Be7 9 Bb3 0–0 10 Kh1 Na5 11 Bg5 Qc5 12 f4 b5 13 Ng3 (Fischer–Benko, Candidates, Bled 1959); now 13 . . . Nxb3 14 axb3 Bb7 is completely equal. Instead Benko played 13 . . . b4? allowing the powerful 14 e5! dxe5 15 Bxf6 gxf6 16 Nce4 Qd4 17 Qh5 Nxb3 18 Qh6! winning. The game concluded 18 . . . exf4 19 Nh5 f5 20 Rad1 Qe5 21 Nef6† Bxf6 22 Nxf6† Qxf6 23 Qxf6 Nc5 24 Qg5† Kh8 25 Qe7 Ba3 26 Qxc5 Bxf1 27 Rxf1 Resigns.

(r) (A) 9 . . . Nxe4?! 10 Qf3 f5 11 Nxc6 bxc6 12 0–0–0 d5 13 Nxe4 fxe4 14 Qh5† g6 15 Qe5 Rg8 16 Rxd5! cxd5 17 Bxd5 Qb5 18 Qxe4 +, Kindermann–Züger, Mendoza 1985. (B) 9 . . . Ng4 10 Nxc6 bxc6 11 Bd2 g6 12 Qe2 Bg7 13 0–0–0 ±.

SICILIAN DEFENSE

(with 3 Bb5)

1 e4 c5 2 Nf3

	193	194	195	196	197	198
	(Nc6) d6					
3	Bb5				Bb5†	
	g6 . . . . .e6 . . . . .Nf6(m)				Bd7 . . . . .Nc6(u)	
4	0–0		0–0	Nc3	Bxd7†(p)	0–0
	Bg7		Nge7	Nd4	Qxd7(q)	Bd7(v)
5	c3 . . . . .Re1		Nc3(i)	e5	0–0	c3
	Nf6(a)	e5(e)	a6(j)	Nxb5	Nc6(r)	Nf6
6	d4(b)	b4(f)	Bxc6	Nxb5	c3	Re1
	cxd4	cxb4(g)	Nxc6	Nd5	Nf6	a6
7	cxd4	a3	d4	Ng5!	d4!(s)	Bxc6(w)
	Nxe4	Nge7	cxd4	f6(n)	Nxe4	Bxc6
8	d5	axb4	Nxd4	Ne4	d5	d4!
	Nd6	0–0!	d6	f5	Ne5!	Bxe4
9	Na3	Ba3	Re1	c4	Nxe5	Bg5
	Ne5(c)	a6	Bd7(k)	Nc7	dxe5	Bd5
10	Nxe5	Bf1	Nxc6	Nxc5	Re1	Nbd2
	Bxe5(d)	d6(h)	Bxc6(l)	Nxb5(o)	Nf6(t)	e6(x)

(a) 5 . . . e5 6 d4! exd4 7 cxd4 cxd4 8 Bf4 a6 9 Bc4 d6 10 Qb3 Qe7 11 Nbd2 e5 12 Bg3 Bxg3 13 hxg3 Nh6 14 Qb6 is better for White, Ciocaltea–Ghitescu, Romania 1975.

(b) (A) 6 e6 Nd5 7 d4 cxd4 8 cxd4 0–0 9 Nc3 Nxc3 10 bxc3 d6 11 exd6 exd6 12 Bf4 Ne7 13 Bc4 Bg4 14 h3 Rc8! 15 Bb3 Be6 16 Rc1 Nd5 is equal, Matanović–Bouaziz, Sousse 1967. (B) 6 Re1 0–0 7 d4 cxd4 8 cxd4 d5 9 e5 Ne4 =, Benko–Stein, Havana 1966.

(c) 9 . . . Nb4 10 Bf4 0–0 11 Qd2 a5 12 Bxd6 exd6 13 Nc4 b6 14 Nxd6 Ba6 = (Mikhal-chishin).

(d) 11 Re1 Bf6 12 Bh6 Nf5 (12 . . . Bxb2?! 13 Nc4 is dangerous) 13 Qd2 a6 ∞.

(e) 5 . . . Nf6 is also reasonable. After 6 Nc3 0–0 7 e5 Ne8 8 Bxc6 dxc6 9 h3 Nc7 10 d3 b6 chances are even, Castro–Robatsch, Rome 1980.

(f) (A) 6 c3 Nge7 effectively stops 7 d4, since 7 d4 cxd4 8 cxd4 exd4 9 Bf4 a6! is better for Black. (B) 6 Bxc6 dxc6! 7 d3 Qc7 8 Be3 b6 9 a4 Nf6 10 a5 Rb8 11 Qc1 Nd7 12 axb6 axb6 13 Bh6 0–0 ∓, Hecht–Adorjan, Hungary 1974.

(g) 6 . . . Nxb4 7 Bb2 Qc7 8 Nc3 Nge7 9 Nd5 Nbxd5 10 exd5 gave White the initiative for his pawn, Andreyev–Korneyev, USSR 1975.

(h) 11 b5 axb5 12 Bxb5 h6 13 d3 Kh7 =, Mestel–Radulov, Hastings 1973.

(i) 5 c3 a6 6 Ba4 b5 7 Bc2 Bb7 8 a4 Ng6 9 axb5 axb5 10 Rxa8 Bxa8 and Black has no problems, Fuchs–Gulko, East Germany 1969.

(j) 5 ... Ng6 6 d4 cxd4 7 Nxd4 a6 8 Be2 Qc7 9 Nxc6 bxc6 10 f4 d5 11 f5 Bd6 ∞, Sax–
Horvath, Hungary 1985.

(k) 9 ... Be7 10 Nxc6 bxc6 11 Qg4 gives Black some trouble, since 11 ... Bf6?! is met by 12
e5! dxe4 13 Ne4 ±.

(l) 11 Nd5 Be7 12 Nxe7 Qxe7 =.

(m) Weaker alternatives are: (A) 3 ... a6 4 Bxc6 bxc6 5 0–0 d6 6 c3 e5 7 d4 cxd4 8 cxd4 Qc7
9 Na3 Ne7 10 Nc4 Ng6 11 Bd2! ±, Hübner–Sypers, Athens 1969. (B) 3 ... Nd4?! 4 Nxd5
cxd4 5 c3 dxc3 6 Nxc3 ±, Asmundsson–Ulrichsen, Nice 1974. (C) 3 ... Qb6 4 Bxc6
Qxc6 5 0–0 d6 6 d4 cxd4 7 Nxd4 Qxe4 8 Nc3 Qg4 9 Qd3 ⩲, Plaskett–Larsen, London
1986. (D) 3 ... d6 transposes to column 198.

(n) White is threatening 8 Nxf7 Kxf7 9 Qf3† Ke6 10 c4 with a winning attack. 7 ... f5 8 0–0
a6 9 Nc3 ±, Khalifman–Varlamov, USSR 1985.

(o) 11 cxb5 (Tal–Mnatsakanian, Erevan 1986); 11 ... d6 12 cxd6 cxd6 13 Nb3 ⩲.

(p) (A) 4 a4 Nf6 5 Qe2 (5 e5 dxe5 6 Nxe5 Bxb5 7 axb5 Qd5 8 Nf3 Qe4† ∓, Alexandria–
Ioseliani, USSR 1977) 5 ... Nc6 6 0–0 e6 7 Rd1 a6 =. (B) 4 c4 Nf6 5 Nc3 Bxb5 6 cxb5
g6 7 d4 cxd4 8 Nxd4 Bg7 =, Romanishin–Savon, Vilnius 1975.

(q) Recapturing with the knight is equally good: 4 ... Nxd7 5 0–0 Ngf6 6 Re1 e6 7 c4 Be7
8 Nc3 0–0 9 d4 cxd4 10 Nxd4 a6 =. If 7 c3 Be7 8 d4 cxd4 9 cxd4 d5 10 e5 Ne4 =.

(r) 5 ... Nf6 6 e5 dxe5 7 Nxe5 Qc7 8 d4 e6 9 Bf4 Qb6 10 Na3 with the initiative, Bisguier–
Browne, US 1971.

(s) 7 Re1 e6 8 d4 cxd4 9 cxd4 d5 10 e5 Ne4 is equal since White cannot play 11 Ne1 and
12 f3.

(t) 11 Rxe5 e6 12 c4 Bd6 13 Re1 0–0–0 =.

(u) 3 ... Nd7 4 d4 Nf6 5 Nc3 cxd4 6 Qxd4 e6 7 Bg5 Be7 8 e5 dxe5 9 Nxe5 ±, Vasiukov–
Beliavsky, Vilnius 1975.

(v) Less reliable is 4 ... Bg4 5 h3 Bh5 6 c3 a6 7 Bxc6† bxc6 8 d4 cxd4 9 cxd4 ⩲, Sax–
Forintos, Budapest 1973.

(w) On (A) 7 Ba4 c4! 8 d4 cxd3 prevents White from creating a pawn center. (B) 9 Bf1 Bg4!
8 d3 g6 9 Nbd2 Bh6 =, Fritzinger–Browne, Saratoga 1977.

(x) 11 c4 Bxf3 12 Qxf3 cxd4 13 Qxb7 Qc8 =, Timoshchenko–Kupreichik, Ashkhabad 1978.

SICILIAN DEFENSE

Closed Variation

1 e4 c5 2 Nc3 Nc6 3 g3 g6 4 Bg2 Bg7 5 d3 d6

	199	200	201	202	203	204
6	f4..			Be3......................		Nge2
	e6 ....e5 ....Nf6			e6 ....Rb8(l)		Nf6(o)
7	Nf3	Nh3(d)	Nf3	Qd2	f4(m)	0–0
	Nge7	Nge7	0–0	Nge7	Nd4	0–0
8	0–0	0–0	0–0	Bh6(i)	Nf3	h3
	0–0	exf4(e)	Rb8	Bxh6	b5	Rb8
9	Be3(a)	Nxf4(f)	h3(g)	Qxh6	Rb1	f4
	Nd4	0–0	b5	Nd4	b4	Bd7
10	Qd2(b)	Be3	a3	0–0–0	Ne2	a3
	Rb8	Rb8	a5	Nec6	e5	Nd4
11	Nh4	Rb1	Be3	Nge2	c3	Nxd4
	b5	b5	b4	Bd7	bxc3	cxd4
12	Nd1	a3	axb4	Nxd4	bxc3	Ne2
	f5	a5	axb4	cxd4(j)	Rxb1	Qb6
13	c3	Ncd5	Ne2	Ne2	Qxb1	Kh2
	Ndc6(c)	b5 =	Bb7(h)	Qa5(k)	Nxe2(n)	Bc6(p)

(a) 9 Bd2 b6 10 Rb1 Bb7 11 a3 Qd7 12 Ne2 Nd4 13 Nexd4 cxd4 14 Qe2 Rac8 =, Balashov–Adorjan, Munich 1979.

(b) (A) 10 Rb1 b6 11 Ne2 Nxf3† 12 Bxf3 Rb8! 13 g4 f5 14 Ng3 Bb7 with at least equality, Spassky–Portisch, Toluca 1982. (B) 10 Bf2 Nxf3† 11 Bxf3 Nc6 =. (C) 10 e5 Qb6! 11 Ne4 Nexf5 12 Bf2 Qxb2 =, Spassky–J. Horvath, Rotterdam 1988.

(c) 14 Nf3 b4 15 c4 Nd4 with even chances, Campora–Greenberg, Buenos Aires 1978.

(d) 7 Nf3 Nge7 8 0–0 0–0 9 Be3 Nd4 10 Qd2 exf4 11 Bxf4 Nxf3† 12 Rxf3 Be6 13 Bh6 Nc6 14 Bxg7 Kxg7 =, Smyslov–Tal, Leningrad 1962.

(e) 8 ... 0–0?! 9 f5! gxf5 10 exf5 Bxf5 11 Rxf5! Nxf5 12 Be4 Nfd4 (12 ... Nfe7 13 Bxh7† Kxh7 14 Qh5† Kg8 15 Ng5 +) 13 Qh5 Re8 14 Qxh7† with a winning attack, Bilek–Gheorghiu, Bucharest 1968.

(f) 9 Bxf4 h6 10 Be3 Ne5 11 Nf4 0–0 12 h3 Kh7 =, A. Rodriguez–Parma, Malta 1980. The column is Christiansen–de Firmian, Palo Alto 1981.

(g) The direct attack 9 Nh4 Nd4 10 f5 b5 11 Bg5 b4 12 Ne2 Nxe2† 13 Qxe2 Nd7 14 Rb1 Ne5 is only equal, Lein–Sakharov, USSR Chp. 1968.

(h) 14 b3 Ra8 15 Rc1 Ra2 16 g4 Qa8 17 Qe1 Qa6 18 Qf2 Na7 19 f5 with a promising attack, Spassky–Geller, match 1966.

(i) 8 Nge2 Nd4 9 0–0 0–0 10 Rae1 Nec6 11 Nd1 Qa5! 12 Qxa5 Nxa5 =, Pokojowicz–Polugaevsky, Sochi 1976.

(j) 12 . . . Nxd4?! 13 Qg7 Ke7 14 e5! ±.

(k) 14 Kb1 Qa4?! 15 c3 dxc3 16 Nxc3 ±, Hort–Hodgson, Wijk aan Zee 1986. 13 . . . Qf6! is a safer idea.

(l) (A) 6 . . . e5 7 Qd2 Nge7 8 Bh6 Bxh6 9 Qxh6 Nd4 10 Rc1 Be6 11 Nf3 Qb6 ∞, Rohde–Dlugy, US Chp. 1986. (B) 6 . . . Nd4 7 Qd2 Qa5 8 f4 e6 9 Nh3 Ne7 10 0–0 Qb6 11 Nd1 ±, Yudasin–Dzhandzhava, Lvov 1986.

(m) 7 Qd2 b5 8 Nf3 b4 9 Nd1 Bg4 10 h3 Bxf3 11 Bxf3 Nf6 12 Bg2 0–0 =, Smyslov–Fischer, Zagreb 1970.

(n) 14 Kxe2 exf4 15 Bxf4 Ne7 16 Qb8 Qa5 17 Qxd6 Qxa2† 18 Bd2 ±, Norwood–Benjamin, Toronto 1985.

(o) 6 . . . e6 7 0–0 Nge7 8 Bg5 h6 9 Be3 Nd4 10 Rb1 Rb8 11 b4 b6 12 bxc5 dxc5 13 a4 0–0 14 Nb5 Nxb5 15 axb5 with the better pawn structure, Spassky–Kindermann, Dubai 1986.

(p) 14 f5 Rbe8! 15 a4 a5 =, Shamkovich–Browne, US Chp. 1977.

SICILIAN DEFENSE

Closed Variations

1 e4 c5

	205	206	207	208	209	210
2	(Nc3)........................			Nf3		
	(Nc6)..................		e6	Nc6........	d6	e6
3	(g3)		g3	Nc3	c3(k)	Nc3
	(g6)........	e6	d5	e5(i)	Nf6	Nc6
4	(Bg2)	Bg2	exd5(f)	Bc4	Bd3(l)	g3
	(Bg7)	Nf6	exd5	Be7	Nc6	d5
5	(d3)	Nge2(c)	Bg2	d3	Bc2	Bg2(m)
	e6	d5	Nf6	d6	Bg4	d4
6	f4(a)	exd5	Nge2	Nd5(j)	d3	Ne2
	Nge7	exd5	d4	Nf6	g6	g6
7	Nf3	d4	Ne4	0–0	0–0	d3
	b6(b)	cxd4	Nxe4	0–0	Bg7	Bg7
8	0–0	Nxd4	Bxe4	c3	Nbd2	0–0
	d5	Bg4(d)	Nd7	Be6	0–0	Nge7
9	Kh1	Qd3	d3(g)	Nxe7†	h3	Nh4
	Ba6	Be7	Nf6	Qxe7	Bd7	e5 =
10	Qe2	h3	Bg2	Bb3 ±	Nh2	
	0–0 =	Be6(e)	Bd6(h)		b5 =	

(a) 6 Be3 Nd4 7 Nce2 b6 8 c3 Nxe2 9 Nxe2 Bb7 10 Qd2 f5 11 0–0 Ne7 12 Rfe1 0–0 =, Medina–Mecking, Palma de Mallorca 1969.

(b) 7 ... d5 8 0–0 0–0 9 Qe1 d4 10 Nd1 e5 11 Nf2 gives White play on the kingside, Bakulin–Nikitin, USSR 1970. The column is Ovchinikov–Spassky, USSR 1960.

(c) 5 f4 d5 6 e5 Nd7 7 d3 Be7 8 Nf3 b5! 9 0–0 (9 Nxb5? Qa5† 10 Nc3 d4 +) 9 ... b4 and Black's queenside play grants him equal chances, Kupreichik–Sveshnikov, USSR Chp. 1979.

(d) 8 ... Bb4 9 0–0 0–0 10 Nce2 gives White a pull.

(e) 11 Nxe6 fxe6 12 0–0 0–0 13 Bg5 h6 14 Bd2 Qd7 15 Rae1 ±, Fischer–Bertok, Rovinj/ Zagreb 1970. The game continued 15 ... Bc5 16 Kh1 Rfe8 17 a3 a6 18 f4 Rad8 19 g4! Qf7 20 g5 Ne4! 21 Nxe4 dxe4 22 Qc3 Bd4 23 Qb3 Bxb2 24 Qxb2 Rxd2 25 gxh6 Re7? (Black should play 25 ... Qg6 26 Bxe4—26 Qxg7† Qxg7 27 hxg7 Rxc2—26 ... Qxh6 27 Qc3 Red8 which retains the g-pawn) 26 Bxe4 Qh5 27 Qc3 Red7 28 Qe3 Ne7 (now 28 ... Qxh6 29 Bd3 wins the exchange) 29 hxg7 Nf5 30 Qb3! Kxg7 31 Bxf5 exf5 32 Rg1† Resigns.

(f) 4 Bg2 dxe4 5 Nxe4 Be7 6 d3 Nf6 7 Nxf6 Bxf6 8 c3 0–0 =, Raicević–Georgadze, Moscow 1979.

(g) 9 0–0 Nf6 10 Bg2 Bd6 11 c3 d3 12 Nf4 0–0 13 Nxd3 Bxg3 14 fxg3 Qxd3 15 Qf3 Qxf3 =, Spassky–Kasparov, Bugojno 1982.

(h) 11 0–0 0–0 12 Bf4 Bg4 13 Bxd6 Qxd6 with even chances, Spassky–Korchnoi, match 1968.

(i) Other moves such as 3 . . . e6, 3 . . . Nf6, or 3 . . . g6 allow 4 d4, transposing to open Sicilian lines.

(j) 6 0–0 Nf6 7 Ng5 0–0 8 f4 exf4 9 Bxf5 h6 10 Nf3 Be6 =, Kupreichik–Sveshnikov, USSR Chp. 1981.

(k) 3 Nc3 Nf6 (3 . . . e5 4 Bc4 Be7 5 d3 Nc6 transposes to the previous column) 4 e5 (4 d4 cxd4 leads to the usual lines) 4 . . . dxe5 5 Nxe5 Nbd7 6 Nc4 g6 7 g3 Nb6 8 Nxb6 Qxb6 9 Bb5†!? Bd7 10 a4 Bxb5 11 axb5 Bg7 12 0–0 0–0 =, P. Popović–Browne, Novi Sad 1979.

(l) 4 Be2 Nc6 5 d4 cxd4 6 cxd4 Nxe4 7 d5 Qa5† 8 Nc3 Ne5 9 Nxe5 dxe5 10 0–0 Nxc3 11 bxc3 e6 12 Bf3 exd5 13 Bxd5 Bc5 14 Re1 0–0 15 Rxe5 Be6! is equal (Palatnik). The column is Bisguier–Fischer, US Chp. 1966–67.

(m) 5 exd5 exd5 6 d4 c4 (6 . . . cxd4 7 Nxd4 Nf6 8 Bg2 transposes to column 206) 7 Bg2 Bb4 8 0–0 Nge7 =. The column is Spassky–Korchnoi, match 1968.

SICILIAN DEFENSE

f4 Attack

1 e4 c5

	211	212	213	214	215	216
2	f4				Nc3	
	g6		e6	d5	Nc6	d6(o)
3	Nf3(a)		Nf3	exd5	f4	f4
	Bg7		d5	Nf6(i)	e6	g6
4	Nc3		Bb5†(g)	Bb5†(j)	Nf3	Nf3
	Nc6		Bd7	Nbd7(k)	d5(m)	Nc6
5	Bc4	Bb5	Bxd7†	c4	Bb5	Bb5
	e6(b)	Nd4	Nxd7	a6	Nf6	Bd7(p)
6	f5(c)	Bd3(f)	d3	Ba4	Bxc6†	0–0
	Nge7(d)	d6	Bd6	b5	bxc6	Bg7
7	fxe6	Nxd4	0–0	cxb5	e5	Bxc6
	fxe6	cxd4	Ne7	Nxd5	Nd7	Bxc6
8	d3	Ne2	c4	Nf3	0–0	d3
	d5	Nf6!	0–0	g6	Ba6	Nf6
9	exd5	0–0	Nc3	Nc3	d3	Qe1
	exd5	0–0	Bc7!	N5b6	c4	0–0
10	Bb3	c3	b3	d4	d4	f5
	b5(e)	e5 =	Ba5(h)	Nxa4(l)	Be7(n)	e6 ∞

(a) (A) 3 d4 cxd4 (or 3 ... d5 4 exd5 Qxd5 5 Nc3 Qxd4 6 Qf3 Nf6 7 Be3—Hodgson–van der Wiel, Wijk aan Zee 1986–87—7 ... Qd6! =) 4 Qxd4 Nf6 5 e5 Nc6 6 Qd3 Nh5 7 Be2 d6 8 Bxh5 Bf5! 9 Qb3 gxh5 10 Nf3 Qd7 11 0–0 e6 =, Westerinin–Arnason, Brighton 1981. (B) For lines with d3 and eventual g3 and c3, see King's Fianchetto Opening, col. 11.

(b) 5 ... d6 6 0–0 Nf6 7 d3 0–0 8 f5 gxf5 9 Qe1 fxe4 10 dxe4 Bg4 11 Qh4 (Hodgson–Nunn, London 1978); 11 ... Bh5! 12 Bh6 Bg6 ∞.

(c) 6 d3 Nge7 7 0–0 d5 8 Bb3 0–0 is fully equal.

(d) It is dangerous to accept the sacrifice. After (A) 6 ... gxf5 7 d3 Nge7 8 0–0 d5 9 exd5 exd5 10 Bb3 Be6 11 Ng5 Qd7 12 Ne2 Black has holes on the kingside, Gik–Kimelfeld, Moscow 1968. (B) 6 ... exf5 7 d3 Nge7 8 0–0 d6 9 Qe1 h6 10 Qg3 Ne5 11 Nxe5 dxe5 12 Bb5† Kf8 13 exf5 with attacking chances, Watson–Ady, London 1982.

(e) 11 0–0 (Hodgson–Strauss, London 1979) 11 ... c4 12 dxc4 bxc4! 13 Ba4 Bb7 ∞.

(f) 6 Nxd4 cxd4 7 Ne2 Qb6 8 Bc4 d6 9 d3 Nf6 10 0–0 0–0 11 Kh1 e6 =, Padevski–Benko, Siegen 1970. The column is Basman–Adorjan, London 1975.

(g) (A) 4 exd5 exd5 5 Bb5† Bd7 6 Bxd7† Nxd7 7 0–0 Bd6 8 d4 Ne7 9 Nc3 0–0 10 Kh1 Nf6 =, Ostojić–Sax, Budapest 1977. (B) 4 Nc3 Nc6 transposes to column 215.

(h) 11 Bb2 a6 12 Qe2 b5 13 cxb5 Bxc3 14 Bxc3 axb5 with equal chances, Hodgson–Gallagher, England 1984.

(i) 3 . . . Qxd5 4 Nc3 Qd8 5 Nf3 Nf6 6 Ne5 e6 (or 6 . . . g6 7 Bc4 e6 8 d3 ∞) 7 b3 Be7 8 Bb2 0–0 9 Bd3 with attacking chances, Bangiev–Petrajtis, corr. 1985.

(j) White can hold the pawn with 4 c4 e6 5 dxe6 Bxe6 6 Nf3 Nc6, but Black has enough compensation because of his more active pieces and the backward White d-pawn.

(k) Also good is 4 . . . Bd7 5 Bxd7† Qxd7 6 c4 e6 7 Qe2 Bd6 8 d3 0–0 9 dxe6 fxe6 10 Nf3 Nc6 11 0–0 Rae8 12 Nc3 e5 with a dangerous initiative, Evans–Hodgson, London 1989.

(l) 11 Qxa4 Bg7 with chances for both sides, Hodgson–Yrjola, Tallinn 1987.

(m) 4 . . . Nge7 5 d4 Nxd4 6 Nxd4 cxd4 7 Qxd4 Nc6 8 Qf2 Be7 or 8 . . . d5 is also playable for Black. The position is like a Taimanov Sicilian.

(n) 11 Be3 Rb8 12 Rb1 g6 13 g4 h5 = , Tarjan–Evans, Lone Pine 1981.

(o) Black should avoid 2 . . . g6 3 d4! cxd4 4 Qxd4 Nf6 5 Bb5! a6 6 e5 axb5 7 exf6 ± . 2 . . . Nc6 3 f4 g6 4 Nf3 Bg7 transposes to column 211.

(p) If 5 . . . Nf6 6 Bxc6† bxc6 7 d3 0–0 8 0–0 the doubled pawns make some trouble for Black.

SICILIAN DEFENSE

2 c3 and Morra Gambit

1 e4 c5

	217	218	219	220	221	222
2	c3..d4 (Morra Gambit)					
	d5.....................Nf6(i)			cxd4		
3	exd5		e5		c3	
	Qxd5		Nd5		dxc3(p)	
4	d4		d4		Nxc3	
	e6 ....Nf6(f)		cxd4		Nc6	
5	Nf3	Nf3	cxd4........Qxd4(m)		Nf3	
	Nf6	Bg4	d6	e6	d6(q)	
6	Bd3(a)	Be2	Nf3	Nf3(n)	Bc4	
	Nc6(b)	e6	Nc6	Nc6	e6(r)	
7	0–0	h3(g)	Bc4(j)	Qe4	0–0	
	cxd4(c)	Bh5	Nb6(k)	d6(o)	Nf6.........a6	
8	cxd4	0–0	Bb5	Nbd2	Qe2	Qe2
	Be7	Be7	dxe5!	dxe5	Be7(s)	b5
9	Nc3	Be3	Nxe5	Nxe5	Rd1	Bb3
	Qd6(d)	cxd4	Bd7	Nxe5	e5	Ra7!?
10	Nb5	cxd4	Bxc6	Qxe5	h3	Rd1
	Qd8(e)	Nc6(h)	Bxc6(l)	Qd6 =	0–0(t)	Rd7(u)

(a) (A) 6 Be2 Be7 7 0–0 0–0 8 Be3 Ng4 9 Bf4 Rd8 10 Qc2 Nc6 11 Rd4 cxd4 = , Hulak–Adorjan, Banja Luka 1983. (B) 6 Na3 Qd8 7 Be2 Nc6 8 0–0 cxd4 9 Nb5 dxc3 10 Qxd8† Kxd8 11 Ng5 Ke7 12 Nc7 Rb8 13 bxc3 Nd5 14 Nxd5† exd5 15 Ba3† Kf6 16 Bxf8 Kxg5 is about equal.

(b) 6 ... Be7 7 0–0 0–0 8 c4 Qd8 9 dxc5 Nbd7 10 Qe2 Nxc5 11 Bc2 ± , Hort–Hartston, Hastings 1974–75.

(c) It is best to exchange pawns now; on 7 ... Be7 8 c4 Qd8 9 dxc5 Nd7 10 a3 Nxc5 11 Bc2 Qxd1 12 Rxd1 a5 13 Nc3 White has the edge, Kantsler–Magerramov, USSR 1981.

(d) 9 ... Qd8 is also possible. After 10 Re1 the position has transposed to the QGD, Semi-Tarrasch, col. 51.

(e) 11 Bf4 Nd5 12 Bg3 0–0 13 Rc1 Bd7 14 Be4 Ncb4 = , Grefe–Dzindzichashvili, Lone Pine 1980.

(f) (A) 4 ... cxd4? 5 cxd4 Nc6 6 Nf3 Bg4 7 Nc3! Bxf3 8 gxf3 Qxd4 9 Qxd4 Nxd4 10 Nb5! puts Black in hot water. If 10 ... Ne6 11 f4 a6 12 f5 axb5 13 Bxb5† Kd8 14 fxe6†, Kirillov–Salati, Riga 1964; 10 ... Nc2† 11 Kd1 Nxa1 12 Nc7† Kd7 13 Nxa8 e5 14 Be3 ± . (B) 4 ... Nc6 5 Nf3 Bg4 6 Be2 cxd4 7 cxd4 e6 8 Nc3 ± .

(g) 7 0–0 Nc6 8 Na3 cxd4 9 Nb5 Rc8 10 Nbxd4 Nxd4 11 Nxd4 Bxe2 12 Qxe2 Be7 = , Buljovčić–F. Olafsson, Novi Sad 1976.

(h) 11 Nc3 Qd7 12 g4 Bg6 13 Ne5 Qd6 with equal chances, Plisetsky–Grachev, Moscow 1976.

(i) (A) 2 . . . e6 3 d4 d5 4 e5 transposes to the French Defense, Advance Variation. (B) 2 . . . b6 3 d4 Bb7 4 Bd3 Nf6 5 f3 $\pm$. (C) 2 . . . d6 3 d4 Nf6 4 f3 (4 dxc4 Nc6 5 cxd6 Nxe4 6 dxe7 Qxd1† 7 Kxd1 Bxe7 $\mp$) 4 . . . Nc6 5 Be3 d5 6 e5 Nd7 7 f4 cxd4 8 cxd4 Nb6 9 Nc3 Bf5 ∞, Smagin–Arnason, Lodri 1988.

(j) 7 Nc3 dxe5 8 dxe5 Ndb4! 9 a3 Qxd1† 10 Kd1 Na6 11 b4 Nc7 12 h3 Be6 13 Bd3 g6 with at least equality, Menveille–Gheorghiu, Las Palmas 1972.

(k) 7 . . . e6 8 0–0 Be7 9 Qe2 0–0 10 Nc3 (10 Qe4 Kh8! 11 Bd3 f5 =, Chekhov–Dorfman, USSR Chp. 1975) 10 . . . Nxc3 11 bxc3 dxe5 12 dxe5 b6 13 Qe4 Bb7 14 Bd3 g6 15 Bh6 with an attack, Sveshnikov–A. Rodriguez, Cienfuegos 1979.

(l) 11 Nxc6 bxc6 12 Nc3 e6 =, Sveshnikov–Browne, Novi Sad 1979.

(m) 5 Bc4 Nb6 6 Bb3 d6 7 cxd4 dxe5 8 Qh5 e6 9 dxe5 Nc6 =, Marić–Radulov, Novi Sad 1974.

(n) 6 Bc4 Nc6 7 Qe4 Nde7! 8 Nf3 Ng6 9 0–0 Qc7 puts White on the defensive, Timoshchenko–Zaichik, USSR 1977.

(o) Sharper is 7 . . . f5 8 Qe2 Qc7 9 g3 d6 10 exd6 Bxd6 11 Bg2 0–0 12 0–0 Nf6 13 Nbd2 e5 ∞, Vorotnikov–Tseitlin, Leningrad 1978. The column is Bronstein–Hort, Monte Carlo 1969.

(p) Black can decline the gambit and reach a reasonable game with (A) 3 . . . d3 4 Bxd3 Nc6 5 c4 d6 6 Nc3 g6 7 h3 Bg7 8 Nf3 Bxc3† 9 bxc3 Nf6 ∞, or (B) 3 . . . Nf6 4 e5 Nd5 transposing to column 219. Bad is 3 . . . d5?! 4 exd5 Qxd5 5 cxd4 transposing to note (f).

(q) (A) 5 . . . e6 6 Bc4 Bb4 7 0–0 Nge7 8 Qe2 0–0 9 Rd1 gives White a strong initiative in the center. (B) 5 . . . g6 6 Bc4 Bg7 7 e5!? Qa5 8 0–0 Nxe5 9 Nxe5 Bxe5 10 Nd5 e6 11 Re1 f6 12 Bb3! Kf7 13 Rxe5 fxe5 14 Qf3† Ke8 15 Bh6! $\pm$, Sokolov–Petek, Kikinda 1954.

(r) 6 . . . a6! 7 0–0 (7 Bg5 Nf6 $\mp$) 7 . . . Nf6 8 Bg5 e6 9 Qe2 h6 (9 . . . Be7 transposes to note s) 10 Bf4 g5! 11 Be3 Ng4 $\mp$, Atwell–Silman, US 1987.

(s) 8 . . . a6 9 Bb5 Be7 10 Rfdl Qc7 11 Rac1 0–0 12 Bb3 (threatening 13 Nd5) 12 . . . h6 13 Bf4 e5 14 Be3 e5 with even chances, Fischer–Korchnoi, Buenos Aires 1960.

(t) 11 Be3 a6 12 Rac1 h6 13 b4 Be6 14 Bxe6 fxe6 =, Frey–Tarjan, California 1980.

(u) 11 Be3 Be7 12 Rac1 Bb7 or 11 Ng5 Qf6 with unclear chances (Garnett, Haras and Mamlet).

SICILIAN DEFENSE

Unusual Lines

1 e4 c5

	223	224	225	226	227	228
2	Nf3 ....b4(j).......Ne2........b3					
	Nf6......................a6			cxb4	d6	e6(m)
3	e5 ....Nc3		c4!(h)	a3	g3	Bb2
	Nd5	Nc6(e)	Nc6	d5(k)	g6	Nf6
4	Nc3	d4	d4	exd5	Bg2	e5
	e6(a)	d5	cxd4	Qxd5	Bg7	Nd5
5	Nxd5	exd5	Nxd4	Nf3	0–0	Nf3
	exd5	Nxd5	Nf6	e5	Nc6	Nc6
6	d4	Nxd5	Nc3	axb4	c3	g3
	Nc6(b)	Qxd5	e5	Bxb4	e5	Be7
7	dxc5	Be3	Nf5	Na3	d3	Bg2
	Bxc5	cxd4	d5	Bxa3	Nge7	0–0
8	Qxd5	Nxd4	cxd5	Bxa3	a3	0–0
	Qb6(c)	Qa5†(f)	Bxf5	Nc6	0–0	d6
9	Bc4	c3	exf5	c4	b4	exd6
	Bxf2†	Nxd4	Nd4	Qd8	b6	Qxd6
10	Ke2	b4!	Bd3	Qb1	f4	Na3
	0–0(d)	Qe5(g)	Nxd5(i)	Nge7 =	exf4(l)	Bf6(n)

(a) 4 ... Nxc3 5 dxc3 Nc6 6 Bf4 e6 7 Qd2 Qc7 8 0–0–0 h6 9 h4 b6 10 Bc4 Bb7 11 Qe2 ± (Nunn).

(b) 6 ... d6?! 7 Bb5† Bd7 8 Bxd7† Qxd7 9 0–0 Nc6 10 exd6 Bxd6 11 Re1† Ne7 12 dxc5 Bxc5 13 Bg5 0–0 14 Qd3 with a clear positional advantage (Boleslavsky).

(c) 8 ... d6 9 exd6 Qb6 10 Qe4† Be6 11 Qh4! Bxd6 12 Be2 leaves Black with little compensation for his pawn since 12 ... Nb4 13 0–0 Nxc2? 14 Qa4† loses (Nunn).

(d) 11 Rf1 Bc5 12 Ng4 Nd4† 13 Kd1 Ne6 14 Ne4 d6 15 exd6 Rd8 16 Bd3 Bxd6 17 Qh5 f5 18 Nxd6 Qxd6 19 Qxf5 ±, Rhine–Sprenkle, US 1981.

(e) 3 ... d5 4 exd5 Nxd5 5 Bb5† Nc6 6 Ne5 Nxc3 7 dxc3 Qxd1† 8 Kxd1 Bd7 9 Bxc6 Bxc6 10 Nxc6 with the better pawn structure.

(f) 8 ... Nxd4 9 Qxd4 Qxd4 10 Bxd4 also leaves White with the better endgame, Ćirić–Rejfíř, Oberhausen 1961.

(g) 11 Qxd4 Qxd4 12 Bxd4 f6 13 f4 e6 14 g3 Bd6 15 0–0–0 and White is on top, Spassky–Přibyl, Tallinn 1973.

(h) Bad is (A) 3 d4?! cxd4 4 Nxd4 Nf6 5 Nc3 e5! 6 Nf3 Bb4 and Black is active, Schmidt–O'Kelly, Beverwijk 1949. (B) 3 c3 gives White an improved version of the 2 c3 lines, as 2 ... a6 is premature, but 3 c4 is sharper.

(i) 11 0–0 Bb4 12 Be4 Nxc3 13 bxc3 Bxc3 14 Rb1 0–0 15 Rxb7 ± (Gligorić and Sokolov).

(j) The delayed wing gambit, 2 Nf3 d6 3 b4, is suspect; 3 . . . cxb4 4 d4 Nf6 5 Bd3 e6 6 0–0 Be7 7 Nbd2 d5 8 e5 Nfd7 ∓, Corden–Gligorić, Hastings 1969–70.

(k) Accepting the gambit is also playable: 3 . . . bxa3 4 Nxa3 d6 5 Bb2 Nc6 6 d4 Nf6 7 Bd3 e6 8 Nf3 Be7 9 0–0 0–0 =, Marshall–Sämisch, Baden–Baden 1925. The column is Bronstein–Benko, Moscow vs. Budapest 1949.

(l) 11 gxf4 d5 12 e5 Bg4 13 h3 Bxe2 14 Qxe2 f6 =, Keres–Fischer Curaçao 1962.

(m) Also reasonable is 2 . . . d6 3 Bb2 Nc6 4 Bb5 e5 5 Ne2 g6 6 0–0 Bg7 7 f4 Nge7 ∞.

(n) 11 Nc4 Qc7 12 Bxf6 Nxf6 13 Re1 b5! 14 Nce5 Nxe5 15 Nxe5 Bb7 Draw, Lombardy–Reshevsky, Lone Pine 1977.

PIRC DEFENSE

1 e4 d6 2 d4 Nf6 3 Nc3 g6

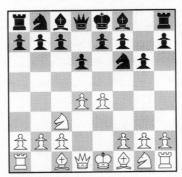

Diagram 42

THIS SYSTEM HAS BEEN KNOWN AS the Pirc Defense since the 1940s. Pioneered by the Yugoslav Vasja Pirc and a group of his compatriots, it is also called the Yugoslav Defense—and sometimes the Ufimtsev Defense in recognition of the Russian master's independent researches.

The Pirc, like the Alekhine, is a hypermodern defense based on counterattack. It sets out right away to create tense positional and tactical situations. Black's strategy is to encourage White to establish a pawn center, which Black will then strive to undermine and annihilate. Black develops his king bishop at g7 and plans pressure against d4 and the black squares in general; to achieve this aim Black must employ his pawns, playing . . . e5 or . . . c5.

It is important to emphasize that Black must not delay organizing his counterplay; if he does he will find his pieces too passively placed to effect any central thrust.

The Pirc is characterized by the move order 1 . . . d6 and 2 . . . Nf6, practically forcing 3 Nc3 and denying White the move c2–c4 as in the Robatsch Defense. After 3 . . . g6 there are several continuations.

Diagram 43

The *Austrian Attack,* 4 f4 (cols. 1–12), is the most aggressive continuation (see diagram). White plans quick development of his troops (Nf3, Bd3, 0–0), then the advance e5 followed by an attack on the kingside. This dangerous line is the most direct attempt to refute the Pirc and was Fischer's favorite choice. It is such a strong plan that Black must counterattack White's center as soon as possible. After 4 . . . Bg7 5 Nf3 Black can play 5 . . . c5 immediately (cols. 1–3) or 5 . . . 0–0, when White has numerous options: 6 e5, 6 Be2, 6 Be3, (cols. 4–7) and the main line 6 Bd3! (cols. 8–12).

Diagram 44

The *Classical System* is 4 Nf3 (cols. 13–18). This unpretentious line is one of White's strongest choices against the Pirc (see diagram). White contents himself with a modest center and develops quickly behind it, posting his pieces on flexible squares and getting ready for Black's . . . e5 or . . . c5. Black has practically no winning chances in this line, so it is no surprise that it is part of Karpov's opening repertoire with White.

After 4 Nf3 Bg7 White's most common choice is 5 Be2 (other choices are seen in cols. 13–14). After 5 . . . 0–0 6 0–0 Black can play 6 . . . Bg4 (cols. 15–16), 6 . . . c6 (col. 17), or rarely played moves (col. 18).

The *Byrne Variation,* 4 Bg5 (col. 19), develops the queen's bishop to pressure the h4–d8 diagonal and sets up attacking chances with Qd2 and

Bh6, exchanging Black's fianchettoed bishop and preparing a pawn storm against the black king.

The *4 f3 System* (col. 20) gives White two options: to prepare Be3, Qd2, 0–0–0, Bh6, h2–h4–h5 attacking the king, or to continue slowly building up a solid center. The best plan depends on where Black's king stands.

4 Be3 (cols. 21–22) is a hybrid of the 4 Bg5 and 4 f3 systems. Play may be similar to those, but White might also transpose into the Classical or Fianchetto variation.

The *Fianchetto Variation*, 4 g3 (col. 23), was invented by Sweden's Gösta Stoltz in 1952. In this positional system the accent is on flexibility.

Unusual systems are covered in col. 24.

PIRC DEFENSE

Austrian Attack

1 e4 d6 2 d4 Nf6 3 Nc3(a) g6 4 f4 Bg7 5 Nf3(b)

	1	2	3	4	5	6
	c5!			0–0		
6	dxc5(c)	Bb5+		e5(o)		Be2
	Qa5	Bd7(f)		dxe5!	Nfd7	c5
7	Bd3	e5(g)		dxe5(p)	h4(t)	dxc5
	Qxc5	Ng4		Qxd1+	c5	Qa5
8	Qe2	e6(h)		Kxd1	h5(u)	0–0
	Bg4!	fxe6!	Bxb5	Nh5(q)	cxd4	Qxc5+
9	Be3	Ng5	exf7+(l)	Bc4	Qxd4(v)	Kh1
	Qa5	Bxb5	Kd7	Nc6	dxe5	Nbd7(y)
10	0–0	Nxe6(i)	Nxb5(m)	Be3(r)	Qf2!	Qe1
	Nc6	Bxd4!	Qa5+	Bg4	e4!	b6
11	h3(d)	Nxd8(j)	Nc3	Rf1	Nxe4(w)	Bd3
	Bxf3	Bf2+	cxd4	Na5	Nf6	Bb7
12	Qxf3	Kd2	Nxd4	Be2	Nxf6+	Be3
	0–0(e)	Be3+(k)	Bxd4(n)	f6(s)	exf6(x)	Qc6(z)

(a) Too tame are (A) 3 Bd3 Nc6 followed by e5!, (B) 3 Nd2 e5!, and (C) 3 f3 c5! 4 d5 e6 5 c4 b5!. In each case Black easily achieves equality.

(b) (A) 5 Bd3 is an interesting alternative to sidestep 5 ... c5: (1) 5 ... e5 6 dxe5 dxe5 7 f5 gxf5 8 exf5 e4 9 Nxe4 Bxf5 10 Nxf6+ Qxf6 11 Qe2+ Be6 12 Nf3 Nc6 13 0–0 (13 Be4!?) 13 ... 0–0–0 14 Ng5 Qd4+ 15 Be3 Qxb2 16 Rab1 Nd4 17 Qh5 Qxa2, Draw, de Firmian–Seirawan, US Chp 1987; (2) 5 ... Nc6! 6 Nf3 Bg4 7 Be2 0–0 (7 ... Bxf3!? 8 Bxf3 e5 is equal) 8 d5 Nb8 ∞, de Firmian–Haik, Biel 1986. (B) 5 e5 Nfd7 may transpose to column 5; playable is 5 ... dxe5 and now (1) 6 fxe5 Nd5 is fine for Black, (2) 6 dxe5 Qxd1+ 7 Kxd1 Ng4 8 Nd5! Kd8 9 Ke1 (Hort–Short, Amsterdam 1982) 9 ... f6! =.

(c) (A) 6 d5 0–0 7 Bd3 e6 8 dxe6 fxe6 9 0–0 Nc6 is fine for Black. (B) 6 e5 Nfd7 7 e6 (7 exd6 0–0! 8 Be3 exd6 9 Qd2 Nc6 =) 7 ... fxe6 8 Ng5 Nf6 (8 ... Bxd4?! 9 Nb5) 9 dxc5 Nc6 10 Bc4 d5 11 Bb5 d4 12 Bxc6+ bxc6 13 Ne2 Qa5+ 14 Qd2 Qxc5 15 Nxd4 Qxd5 16 c3 0–0 17 0–0 Nh5 18 Qe2 e5! = Vasiukov–Tseshkovsky, USSR 1974.

(d) 11 Qf2 Bxf3 12 Qxf3, Sznapik–Pein, Manchester 1982, when 12 ... Nd7! looks fine for Black.

(e) White treads on ice, e.g. (A) 13 Ne2 Nd7 14 c3? Nde5 and Black wins, Ljubojević–Timman, Tilburg 1978. (B) 13 f5 Ne5 14 Qf2 b5! ∓, Botterill–Levy, 1971. (C) 13 a3 Nd7 14 Bd2 Qd8 (14 ... Qb6+ 15 Kh1 Nc5 16 Rab1 Nxd3 17 cxd3 f5! 18 Nd5 Qd8 ±, Balashov–Diesen, Karlovac 1979) 15 Kh1 e6 16 Bc4 a6 17 Ba2 Qc7 18 Rad1 b5 19 Be1 Nb6 20 Qd3 Rad8 21 Bh4 Rd7 22 f5 Ne5 23 Qg3 Re8! 24 fxe6 fxe6 25 Bf6 Nbc4 ∓, Arnason–Kristiansen, Gausdal 1987.

(f) (A) 6 ... Nbd7? 7 e5 Ng4 8 e6 wins. (B) 6 ... Kf8 7 e5 dxe5 8 fxe5 Ng4 9 h3 Nh6 10 dxc5 with a clear plus for White, Lengyel–Ozsvath, Hungary 1972. (C) 6 ... Nfd7 7 Be3 0–0 8 Qd2 a6 9 Bxd7 Nxd7 10 h4 with a strong attack, Pupols–Kampenus, USSR 1978.

(g) 7 Bxd7† Nfxd7 8 d5 0–0 9 0–0 Na6 10 Qe2 (10 f5 Qb6 11 Kh1 Nc7 12 Ne2 c4 $\mp$, Savon–Hort, Petropolis 1973) 10 . . . Nc7 11 a4! (11 Rd1 b5!) 11 . . . a6 12 Rd1 Rb8 13 a5 b5 14 axb6 Nxb6 15 Bd2 and 15 . . . e6 leads to a complex game instead of 15 . . . Qc8 16 Be1! $\pm$, Hort–Torre, Polanica Zdroj 1977.

(h) (A) 8 Bxd7† Qxd7 9 d5 (9 Ng5? cxd4 10 e6 fxe6 11 Qxg4 dxc3 12 Nxe6 cxb2 $\mp$, Purdy–D. Byrne, Lugano 1968) 9 . . . dxe5 10 h3 e4 11 Nxe4 Nf6 12 Ne5 Qd8 13 Nxf6† exf6! =, Smith–Diesen, Fairfax 1980. (B) 8 Ng5 Bxb5 9 Qxg4 Bd7 10 e6 Bxe6 11 Nxe6 fxe6 12 dxc5 Bxc3†! 13 bxc3 Qa5 $\mp$, Lee–Suttles, Havana 1966. (C) 8 h3 Bxb5 9 Nxb5 dxe5! 10 hxg4 Qa5† 11 c3 (11 Bd2 Qxb5 12 dxe5 Qxb2! 13 Rb1 Qxa2 14 Rxb7 Qd5 and Black is well off—Nunn) 11 . . . e4 12 Qe2 exf3 13 Nd6† Kd7 14 Nxb7 Qb6 15 Qxf3 cxd4 with an unclear position, Fedorov–Tseitlin, Leningrad Chp. 1977.

(i) (A) 10 Nxb5 Qa5† 11 c3 Qxb5 12 Nxe6 Na6 13 Qxg4 Bf6 14 d5 Qd3! with a slight edge for Black, Beliavsky–Timman, Belfort 1988. (B) 10 Qxg4! Bc4 11 b3 Bxd4 12 Bd2 Bd5 13 Nxd5 exd5 14 0–0–0 Qd7 15 Ne6 Nc6 16 f5 $\pm$, Nunn–Benjamin, Thessaloniki 1988.

(j) Interesting is 11 Nxb5 (if 11 Nxd4 or 11 Qxg4, then 11 . . . Bd7 wins) 11 . . . Qa5† 12 c3 Bf2† 13 Kd2 Be3† 14 Kc2 Qa4† 15 Kb1! Qe4† 16 Qc2 Qxc2† 17 Kxc2 Kd7 with compensation for the exchange (Seirawan).

(k) Here the game Sax–Seirawan, Brussels 1988, was agreed drawn.

(l) If 9 Ng5? f5 wins.

(m) 10 Ng5 h5 11 Qf3! Bc6 12 d5 Bxc3† 13 bxc3 Bb5 14 Qe4 Kc8 15 Ne6 Qa5 16 Bd2 Nd7 17 Qxg6 b6 18 c4 Qa4 19 cxb5 +, Stader–Vinke, corr. 1983.

(n) (A) 12 . . . h5!? 13 h3 Nc6 14 Nde2 Nh6 15 Be3 Raf8 16 Qd3 Nf5 17 Bf2 Rxf7 18 0–0–0 h4 19 Kb1 Rc8 20 Qe4! b6 21 a3 Nd8 22 Rhe1 Qa6 23 Nd4 Qc4 24 Nd5 and White is better, Beliavsky–Tal, Brussels 1988. (B) After 12 . . . Bxd4 13 Qxd4 Nc6 14 Qc4! Qb6! 15 Qe2 h5 16 Bd2 Nd4 17 Qd3 Nf5 18 Ne4 Rac8 19 0–0–0! Nge3 20 Bxe3 Nxe3 21 c3! Nxd1 22 Rxd1 White has excellent compensation for the exchange, Hellers–Ivanchuk, Champigny 1984.

(o) 6 Bc4 Nxe4 7 Bxf7† Rxf7 8 Nxe4 Rf8 9 0–0 h6 10 Ng3 e6 11 Qd3 Qf6 12 Bd2 Nc6 = (Euwe).

(p) 7 fxe5 Nd5 8 Bc4 Nb6! 9 Bb3 Nc6 10 Be3 Na5 11 Qe2 Nxb3 12 axb3 f6 13 0–0 Be6 14 Rad1 c6 15 Draw, Perecz–Schüssler, Dortmund 1979.

(q) 8 . . . Rd8† and 8 . . . Ng4 are less clear.

(r) 10 Rf1! Bg4 11 Ke1 Na5 12 Bd3 f6 14 exf6 Bxf6 = (Zhuravlev).

(s) 13 exf6 Bxf6 14 Nd2 Bxc3 15 Bxg4 Bxb2 16 Rab1 Bc3 17 Nde4 Bg7 18 Rb5 b6 19 Bxh5 gxh5 20 Rxh5 Nc4 21 Draw, Unzicker–Pfleger, Munich 1979.

(t) (A) 7 Bc4 Nb6 8 Bb3 Nc6 9 Be3 Na5 10 Qe2 Nxb3 11 axb3 f6 =, Unzicker–Tringov, Ljubljana 1979. Both (B) 7 e6 fxe6 8 h4 Nf6 9 Bd3 Nc6 10 h5 gxh5 and (C) 7 Ng5 Nb6 8 Bd3 Nc6 9 d5 Nb4 10 e6 Nxd3† 11 Qxd3 fxe6 12 dxe6 Qe8 leave Black better (Nunn).

(u) 8 e6 fxe6 9 h5 gxh5 10 Rxh5 Nf6 11 Rh4 cxd4 12 Nxd4 Nc6 13 Be3 Qb6 14 Qd3! Nb4 15 Qd2 e5 16 dxe5 dxe5 17 0–0–0! $\pm$, Estrin–Nunn, Lublin 1978.

(v) 9 hxg6 dxc3, with (A) 10 Rxh7!? fxg6 11 Bc4† Kxh7?! (11 . . . e6 ∞) 12 Ng5† Kh8 13 Kf2 Qb6† 14 Kg3 Bh6 15 Qh1 Kg7 16 Ne6† Kh7 (Bussek–Spettel, Saarlouis 1986); now 17 f5 wins. (B) 10 gxf7† Rxf7 11 e6 (11 Ng5? cxb2 12 Bc4 Nxe5 13 Qh5 Qa5† 14 Kf1 Qa6! +, Kirsch–Seret, Epinal 1986) 11 . . . Rf6 12 exd7 Bxd7 13 Bd3 h6! 14 bxc3 Nc6 15 Rh4 Qb6 16 g4 Raf8 17 f5 e6 18 Kf1 (Karlsson–Muchnik, USSR 1967) and Fridstein's 18 . . . Ne5! is better for Black.

(w) 11 Ng5 Nf6 12 hxg6 hxg6 13 Ncxe4! Nxe4 14 Nxe4 Qd4 = (Parma).

(x) 13 hxg6 Re8† 14 Be3 hxg6 15 Bd3 Qa5† (15 . . . Qb6! 16 Kd2 Qxb2? 17 Bc5! f5 18 Ne5 wins, but 16 . . . Qa5† is worth a try) 16 c3 Bg4 17 0–0 Nc6 18 Nd4 f5 19 Nxc6 bxc6 20 Rfe1 ±, Banas–Kindermann, Trnava 1987.

(y) 9 . . . Nc6 10 Bd3 Bg4 11 Qe1 Bxf3 12 Rxf3 Nb4! (12 . . . Nd4 13 Rf1 Qh5 14 Be3 e5 15 Ne2! ±) 13 Be3 Nxd3 14 cxd3 Qb4 15 Rb1 a5 16 f5 Rac8 17 Bg1 a4 18 a3 Qb3 19 Bd4 e6 20 Qg1 b5 21 g4? Nxg4! 22 f6 Nxf6 23 Bxf6 Bxf6 24 Rxf6 b4 25 axb4 a3 (White has trouble with his knight) 26 Qd1 Qxb4 27 Rf2 axb2 28 Na2 Qd4 29 Rfxb2 d5 30 Rb4 Qa7 31 Nc1 dxe4 32 dxe4 Qe3 33 Qg1 Qf3† 34 Qg2 Qd1† 35 Qg1 Rfd8 36 Nb3 Qf3† 37 Qg2 Rd1† 38 Rxd1 Qxd1† 39 Qg1 Qe2 40 h3 Rc2 41 Resigns, Short–Speelman, match 1988.

(z) 13 f5 Nc5 14 fxg6 fxg6 15 Bc4† Kh8 16 Bd5 Qd7 17 Ng5 Ba6! 18 Rf3 Nxd5 ∓, Mortensen–D. Gurevich, Helsinki 1983.

PIRC DEFENSE

Austrian Attack

1 e4 d6 2 d4 Nf6 3 Nc3 g6 4 f4 Bg7 5 Nf3 0–0

	7	8	9	10	11	12
6	Be3........Bd3!					
	Nbd7(a)	Na6		Nc6(n)		
7	Qd2(b)	e5 0–0		e5(o)		0–0!
	c5	Nd7	c5	dxe5		Bg4!(u)
8	0–0–0(c)	Be3(f)	d5(h)	dxe5........fxe5		e5
	Ng4	Nb4	Rb8(i)	Nd5	Nh5!(q)	dxe5(v)
9	Bg1(d)	Be2	Qe2!(j)	Bd2	Be3	dxe5
	cxd4	c5!	Nc7(k)	Bg4	Bg4	Nd5
10	Nxd4(e)	a3	a4	Be4	Be2	Qe1!?(w)
	e5	cxd4	a6(l)	e6	f6	Ndb4!
11	Nde2	Nxd4	a5	h3	exf6	Be4
	exf4	dxe5	b5	Bxf3	exf6	f5
12	Nxf4	fxe5	axb6	Qxf3	Qd2(r)	Bxc6
	Qa5	Nc6	Rxb6	Nd4	f5(s)	Nxc6
13	Bd4	e6	Na4	Qf2	0–0–0	Be3
	Nge5 =	Nxd4(g)	Rb8(m)	c5(p)	f4(t)	Bxf3(x)

(a) (A) 6 . . . c5 7 dxc5 Qa5 8 Qd2! dxc5 9 Nb5 Qa4 (9 . . . Qxd2† 10 Nxd2 Na6 11 0–0–0 $\pm$, Beliavsky–Mednis, Vienna 1986) 10 e5 Ne4 11 Qd3 Qb4† 12 Nd2 Bf5 13 Nc7 Nc6 14 Nxa8 Rd8 15 Qa3! Nxd2 16 0–0–0! $\pm$, Beliavsky–Timman, Tilburg 1986. (B) 6 . . . Nc6 7 Qd2 a6 8 0–0–0 b5 9 e5 Ng4 10 h3 Nxe3 11 Qxe3 Na5 12 Bd3 c6 13 f5 Nc4 14 Qf4 Rb8 15 g4 c5 with a complex position, W. Watson–Norwood, British Chp. 1986. (C) 6 . . . c6 7 Bd3 Nbd7 8 e5 Ng4 9 Bg1 dxe5 10 dxe5 Qa5 11 Nd2 Nh6 12 Nb3 Qc7 13 Qf3 f6 14 e6! with a clear edge for White, Jansa–J. Johansson, Malmö 1986–87.

(b) 7 e5 Ng4 8 Bg1 c5 9 e6 fxe6 10 Ng5 Ndf6 11 Qe2 cxd4 =, L. Schneider–Kaiszauri, Eksjö 1980.

(c) 8 dxc5!? Nxc5 9 e5 Nfe4 10 Nxe4 Nxe4 11 Qb4 d5 12 Bd3 b6 13 0–0 Qc7 14 Rae1 Bb7 is unclear, Khalifman–Azmayparashvili, USSR Chp. 1986.

(d) 9 dxc5 Nxe3 10 Qxe3 Nxc5 11 e5 Qa5 12 Kb1 dxe5 13 Rd5 b6 14 Nxe5 Bb7 15 Nc4 Qxc3! 16 bxc3 Bxd5 with good play, Sideif-Sade–Gipslis, USSR 1983.

(e) 10 Bxd4 e5 11 Bg1 exf4 12 Qxd6 Ne3 = (Keene). The column is Beliavsky–Azmayparashvili, USSR Chp. 1986.

(f) (A) 8 h4 c5 9 h5 cxd4 10 hxg6 hxg6 11 Ng5 Nxe5! 12 fxe5 dxc3 13 Kf2 (de Firmian–van der Wiel, Wijk aan Zee 1986) threatens 14 Rh8† Bxh8 15 Qh1, but 13 . . . Bxe5 should defend. (B) 8 Ng5 dxe5 9 fxe5 Nb6 10 Be4 c5 11 d5 Bxe5 12 Nxh7 Bxc3† 13 bxc3 Kxh7 14 Qh5† Kg8 15 Bxg6 fxg6 16 Qxg6† Kh8 17 c4 Na4 18 Rb1 Rf5 =, Sveshnikov–Davies, Moscow 1987.

(g) 14 exf7† Rxf7 15 Bxd4 Ne5 16 Bxe5 Qxd1† 17 Nxd1 Bxe5 18 Bc4 e6 =, de Firmian–Leski, Vallejo 1987.

(h) 8 dxc5 Nxc5 9 Qe1 b5! 10 a3 Bb7 11 Kh1 a5! $\mp$, Glek–Azmayparashvili, USSR 1986.

(i) (A) 8 . . . Bg4 9 Bc4! Nc7 (9 . . . e6 10 dxe6 Bxe6 11 Bxe6 fxe6 12 Ng5 $\pm$) 10 h3 Bxf3 11 Qxf3 a6 12 a4 Nd7 (Dolmatov–A. Chernin, USSR Chp. 1987) 13 Rd1 Rb8 14 a5 $\pm$ (Chernin). (B) 8 . . . Nc7 9 a4 e6 10 dxe6 fxe6 11 e5 Nfd5 12 Ne4 Ne8 13 Bc4 and White stands better, Sax–Andersson, Manchester 1980.

(j) 9 Kh1 (9 Qe1 Nb4 =) and now: (A) 9 . . . Bg4 10 Bc4! Nc7 11 a4 e6 12 dxe6 fxe6 13 h3 Bxf3 14 Qxf3 d5 15 exd5 Nfxd5 16 Nxd5 exd5 17 Rd1 Re8 18 Be3 b6 19 Bxd5 $\pm$, I. Gurevich–Wolff, Boston 1986. (B) 9 . . . b6 10 a3 Nc7 11 Qe1 b5 (11 . . . e6!?) 12 Qh4 a5 13 f5! b4 14 axb4 axb4 15 Ne2 gxf5 16 Bh6 Bxh6 17 Qxh6 Ng4 18 Qh5 Ne8 19 exf5 Nef6 20 Qh4 Bb7 21 Ng5 c4 22 Nxh7! +, Franzen–Richardson, corr. 1986. (C) 9 . . . Nc7 10 a4 b6 11 Qe1 a6 12 Qh4 b5 13 axb5 axb5 14 f5! c4 15 Be2 Bd7 16 Bh6 $\pm$, Plachetka–Jansa, Trnava 1987.

(k) 9 . . . Nb4 10 Bc4 e6 11 dxe6 Bxe6 12 Bxe6 fxe6 13 e5! dxe5 14 fxe5 Nfd5 15 Bg5 Qc7 16 Nb5 Qb6 17 c4 h6?! 18 cxd5 hxg5 19 Nd6 Nxd5 20 Nxg5 c4† 21 Kh1 Qe3 22 Qg4! Resigns, Kaidanov–Piket, Lvov 1988.

(l) 10 . . . Re8?! 11 f5! gxf5 12 exf5 e6 13 fxe6 fxe6 14 dxe6 Bxe6 15 Qf2! wins, Kaidanov–Davies, Moscow 1987.

(m) 14 c4 e6! 15 e5 Nfe8 16 exd6 Nxd6 17 Ne5 exd5!, with a complex fight, Dolmatov–Gipslis, USSR 1985.

(n) (A) 6 . . . c5 7 dxc5 dxc5 8 Qe2 Nc6 9 e5 Nd5 10 Nxd5 Nxd5 11 Be4 $\pm$, Tan–Pirc, Beverwijk 1963. (B) 6 . . . Nbd7 7 0–0 e5 8 fxe5 dxe5 9 d5 c6 10 dxc6 bxc6 11 Kh1 Qe7 12 b3 Nh5 13 a4 Nf4 14 Ba3 c5 15 Bb5 Nf6 16 Qe1 $\pm$, Matanović–Portisch, Skopje 1968. (C) 6 . . . Bg4 7 h3 Bxf3 8 Qxf3 Nc6 9 Be3 e5 10 dxe5 dxe5 11 f5 $\pm$, Fischer–Benko, US Chp. 1963–64. The game continued 11 . . . gxf5 12 Qxf5! Nd4 13 Qf2 Ne8 14 0–0 Nd6 15 Qg3! Kh8 16 Qg4 c6?! 17 Qh5 Qe8? 18 Bxd4 exd4 19 Rf6! Kg8 20 e5 h6 21 Ne2 Resigns.

(o) (A) 7 Be3 e5 8 fxe5 dxe5 9 d5 Ne7! 10 h3 c6 11 dxc6 Nxc6 =, Martin–Adorjan, Las Palmas 1977. (B) 7 f5 Nb4 8 0–0 Nxd3 9 Qxd3 c5 10 d5 a6 11 a4 Bd7 12 a5 b5 $\mp$, Suetin–Ftáčnik, Sochi 1977. (C) 7 d5 Nb4 8 0–0 c6 9 a3 Nxd3 10 Qxd3 cxd5 $\mp$, Yanofsky–Botvinnik, Tel Aviv 1966.

(p) 14 0–0 f6 15 exf6 Nxf6 16 Bd3 Nh5 $\mp$, Grigorian–Spilker, USSR 1978.

(q) (A) 8 . . . Nd5?! 9 Nxd5 Qxd5 10 c3 Be6 11 Qe2 Rad8 12 Bf4! Qd7 13 0–0 f6 14 exf6 exf6 15 Bxc7 Rde8 16 Bf4 Bxa2 17 Bc4† Kh8 18 Qd3 Bc4 19 Qxc4 with an edge, Petronić–Polihroniade, Wijk aan Zee 1977. (B) 8 . . . Ng4?! 9 Be4 f6 10 h3 Nh6 11 exf6 exf6 12 Bd5† Kh8 13 0–0 Nf5 14 Re1 Ncxd4 15 Nxd4 Nxd4 16 Qxd4 c6 17 Bf4 cxd5 18 Nxd5 $\pm$, Golovei–Borisenko, USSR 1971.

(r) 12 0–0 f5 13 h3 Bxf3 14 Bxf3 f4 15 Bf2 Ng3 16 Re1 Nf5 =.

(s) 12 . . . Qe7 13 0–0–0 Rfe8 14 Rhe1 Kh8 15 Bh6 Bxh6 16 Qxh6 Qg7 17 Qxg7† Kxg7 18 h3 $\pm$, Timman–Nijboer, Dutch Chp. 1985–86.

(t) 14 Bf2 Qd7 is unclear, Barczay–Nagy, Hungary 1973.

(u) 7 . . . e5 8 fxe5 dxe5 9 d5 Ne7 10 Nxe5 and now: (A) 10 . . . Nfxd5 11 Nxf7 Nxc3 12 bxc3 Rxf7 13 Rxf7 Kxf7 14 Bc4† Be6 15 Qf3† Bf6 16 Bxe6 Kxe6 17 Ba3 (O. Efimov–Krasin, USSR 1987) 17 . . . Qd2 =. (B) 10 . . . c6 11 Bg5! cxd5 12 Bxf6 Qb6† 13 Kh1 Bxf6 14 Nxd5 Nxd5 15 Nc4 Qd8 16 exd5 b5 17 Na5! $\pm$, Roos–Messere corr. 1986.

(v) Suspect is 8 . . . Nh5?! 9 Be3 dxe5 10 dxe5 f6 11 exf6 Bxf6 12 h3 Bxf3 13 Qxf3 Bd4 14 Ne2 e5 15 Nxd4 Nxd4? (Black is worse in any case) 16 Qe4 Nxf4 17 Bc4† Resigns (since

333

17 ... Nfe6 is met by 18 Qxe5), Mednis–Vadasz, Budapest 1978.

(w) 10 Nxd5 Qxd5 11 h3 Be6 12 Qe2 Rfd8 13 Be4 Nd4 =, Markland–Portisch, Hastings 1970–71. 12 Qe1 may be better.

(x) 14 Rxf3 e6 15 Bc5 Rf7 16 Rd1 Rd7 17 Rd3 Rxd3 18 Rxd3 Qe8 19 Qd2 a6 20 h4 Bh6 21 Be3 Bf8 22 a3 Be7 23 Bf2 Rd8 24 Kf1 h6 25 Ne2, Draw, Ljubojević–Timman, match 1987.

PIRC DEFENSE

Classical System

1 e4 d6 2 d4 Nf6 3 Nc3 g6 4 Nf3 Bg7

	13	14	15	16	17	18
5	h3	Bc4(f)	Be2			
	0–0	0–0	0–0			
6	Be3	Qe2(g)	0–0			
	c6(a)	Bg4	Bg4		.c6	.c5(t)
7	a4	e5	Be3		h3	d5(u)
	Nbd7(b)	Nh5(h)	Nc6		Nbd7(q)	Na6
8	a5	h3(i)	Qd2(k)✓		a4(r)	Bf4(v)
	e5(c)	Bxf3	e5		e5	Nc7
9	dxe5	Qxf3	dxe5	d5	dxe5	a4
	dxe5	dxe5	dxe5	Ne7(m)	dxe5	a6
10	Qd6	Qxb7	Rad1	Rad1(n)	Be3	Re1(w)
	Ne8(d)	Nd7	Qc8	Bd7!(o)	Qe7	b6
11	Qb4	dxe5	Qc1	Ne1	Qd3!	h3
	Bf6	Nxe5	Rd8	b5(p)	Nh5	Bb7(x)
12	Bc4!	Be2	Rxd8†	f3	Rfd1	Rb1
	Qe7(e)	Nf6(j)	Qxd8(l)	Qb8 =	Nf4(s)	Rb8(y)

(a) (A) 6 ... d5 7 e5 Ne4 8 Nxe4 (8 Bd3!?) dxe4 9 Ng5 (9 Nd2 f5!) 9 ... c5 10 dxc5 Qc7 11 Qd5 h6 12 Nxe4 Rd8 13 Qb3 Qxe5 with compensation (Seirawan). (B) 6 ... a6 7 a4 b6? (7 ... d5! Korn) 8 Bc4 Bb7 9 e5! Ne4 10 Ng5 Nxg5 11 Bxg5 Bxg2 12 Rg1 Bc6 13 Qg4 with a strong attack, Spassky–Seirawan, Zürich 1984. (C) 6 ... Na6 7 Be2 c5 8 dxc5 Nxc5 9 e5! Nfe4 10 Nxe4 Nxe4 11 Qd5 Nc5 12 exd6 ±, Nunn–Davies, London 1985. (D) 6 ... Nbd7 7 e5 Ne8 8 Bc4 Nb6 9 Bb3 c6 10 Qd2 Nc7 11 Bh6 ±, Piket–Hartoch, Wijk aan Zee 1987. (E) 6 ... c5 7 dxc5 Qa5 8 Nd2 dxc5 9 Nc4 Qc7 10 e5 Nfd7 11 f4 ±, Nunn–P. Herzog, Krefeld 1986.

(b) (A) 7 ... a5 8 Be2 Na6 9 0–0 d5 10 exd5 Nxd5 11 Nxd5 Qxd5 12 Bg5 Qd6 13 Re1 Be6 14 Qc1 c5 15 c3 cxd4 16 Nxd4 Bxd4! 17 cxd4 Nb4 =, Ivanović–D. Gurevich, Reykjavik 1982. (B) 7 ... b6 8 Be2 Qc7 9 e5 dxe5 10 Nxe5 Be6 11 Bf4 Qc8 12 Bf3 ±, Benjamin–Wolff, Saint John 1988.

(c) 8 ... d5!? 9 e5 Ne8 10 Be2 (10 Bd3! looks better) f6 11 exf6 exf6 12 0–0 Rf7 13 Bd3 Nf8 14 b3 Nd6 15 Ne2 Bf5 =, Spraggett–Kindermann, Lugano 1988.

(d) 10 ... Re8 11 Bc4 Qe7 12 Qxe7 Rxe7 13 0–0 ±, Nunn–Todorćević, Szirak 1987.

(e) 13 Qxe7 Bxe7 14 Bh6 Ng7 15 0–0 ±, Nunn–Davies, British Chp. 1987.

(f) (A) 5 Bf4 c5! 6 dxc5 Qa5 7 Nd2 Qxc5 8 Nb3 Qb6 9 Qd2 Nc6 10 Be3 Qc7 11 0–0–0 0–0 with a double-edged position, Ivanović–Marangunić, Yugoslavia Chp. 1977. (B) 5 Bg5 Nbd7 6 Qd2 c5 = (Parma).

(g) (A) 6 0–0 Nxe4! 7 Bxf7† (7 Nxe4 d5 8 Bd3 dxe4 9 Bxe4 c5 =) 7 ... Rxf7 8 Nxe4 h6 9 h3 Qf8 10 Re1 Nc6 11 d5? (11 c3 e5 ∓) 11 ... Rxf3! with a clear edge for Black,

335

Honfi–Adorjan, Hungary 1975. (B) 6 e5 dxe5 7 Nxe5 c5 8 dxc5 Qa5 9 0–0 Qxc5 10 Qe2 Nh5! 11 Ng4 Nc6 12 Ne4 Bxg4 $\overline{\mp}$, Keres–Koshanski, Sarajevo 1972.

(h) (A) 7 . . . Ne8?! 8 Bg5 Nc6 9 0–0–0 Kh8 10 Rhe1 Qc8 11 Bd5 Qf5 12 Qe3 dxe5 13 Bxc6! leaves White on top, Hort–Keene, Teesside 1975. (B) 7 . . . Nfd7 8 e6 Nb6 9 exf7† Kh8 10 Be6 Bxe6 11 Qxe6 Qd7 12 Ng5 Nc6 13 Nb5 is strong, Semenova–Gaprindashvili, Tbilisi 1976.

(i) 8 e6?! Nc6 9 exf7† Kh8 $\overline{\mp}$ (Nunn).

(j) 13 0–0 Ne8 14 Be3 Rb8, drawn, Hort–Planinć, Ljubljana–Portorož 1977.

(k) (A) 8 d5!? Bxf3 9 Bxf3 Ne5 10 Be2 c6 11 a4 Qa5 12 Ra3 Rfc8 13 Rb3! $\pm$, Sokolov–Timman, Brussels 1988. (B) 8 Qd3 e5 9 d5 Ne7 10 h3?! Bc8 11 Nd2 Nd7 12 Nc4 f5 13 f4 exf4 14 Rxf4 g5! and Black is better, Gligorić–Nunn, Baden 1980.

(l) 13 Rd1 Qe7 14 h3 Bxf3 15 Bxf3 Rd8 16 Rxd8 Qxd8 17 Qd2 Qxd2 is equal, Karpov–Timman, Amsterdam 1988.

(m) 9 . . . Nb8 10 Rad1 Nbd7 11 h3 with a slight edge for White, Tal–Hort, Montreal 1979.

(n) 10 a4?! Bd7! 11 a5 a6 12 Ne1 Nh5 13 Nd3 f5 14 f3 Nf6 15 b4 f4 16 Bf2 g5 gives Black a pull, Geller–Vasiukov, Kislovodsk 1968.

(o) (A) 10 . . . Kh8 11 h3 Bxf3 12 Bxf3 Nd7 13 Be2 f5 14 f4!. a6 15 fxe5 Nxe5 16 Rf2! Qd7 17 Rdf1 fxe4 18 Nxe4 Rxf2 19 Bxf2 h6 20 b3 Rf8 21 c4 g5 22 Ng3 N7g6 23 Be3! Rxf1† 24 Bxf1 Qf7 25 Qc2 Nh4 26 Be2 Neg6 27 Bd3 Be5 28 Bf2 Nf4 29 Be4 Qf6 30 Qd1! b6 31 Qg4 Kg7 32 Be3 Kf7 33 Qc8 Qe7 34 Bh7! Nxh3† 35 Qxh3 Resigns, Karpov–Smejkal, Leningrad 1977. (B) 10 . . . b5?! 11 Bxb5! is good, but 11 a3 a5 12 b4?! (12 Bxb5!) axb4 13 axb4 Ra3 was fine for Black in Karpov–Azmayparashvili, Moscow 1983.

(p) 11 . . . Ng4 12 Bxg4 Bxg4 13 f3 Bd7 14 f4!. Bg4 15 Rb1! c6 16 fxe5! dxe5 17 Bc5 cxd5? (17 . . . b6 18 Ba3 c5 19 b4! is still much better for White) 18 Qg5! Resigns, Liberzon–Chandler, Hastings 1980–81.

(q) 7 . . . b5?! 8 e5 Ne8 9 a4 b4 10 Ne4 f5 11 Ned2 Nc7 12 Re1 h6 13 h4 with a distinct advantage, Vasiukov–Gurgenidze, USSR 1955.

(r) A reasonable alternative is 8 e5 Ne8 9 Bc4 Nb6 10 Bb3 Nc7 11 Bg5 Ne6 12 Bh4 d5 13 Ne2 f6 14 exf6 exf6 15 Qd2 Bd7 16 Rfe1 $\pm$, Shamkovich–Torre, Rio de Janeiro 1979.

(s) 13 Qd6 Nxe2† 14 Nxe2 Bf6! 15 Qxe7 Bxe7 16 Nd2 Nc5 17 Nc4! $\pm$, Browne–Rohde, US Chp. 1987.

(t) (A) 6 . . . Nc6 7 d5 Nb8 8 Re1 c6 9 h3 Bd7 10 Bg5 and White is better Liberzon–Janetschek, Vienna 1980. (B) 6 . . . Nbd7 7 e5 Ne8 8 Bf4 c6 9 Qd2! $\pm$, (Nunn). (C) 6 . . . a6 7 Re1 Nc6 8 d5 Ne5 9 Nxe5 dxe5 10 Be3 Qd6 11 Qd3 $\pm$, Miles–Kavalek, Amsterdam 1977. (D) 6 . . . b6 7 Re1 Bb7 8 e5 Nd5 9 Nxd5 Nxd5 10 c4 Bb7 11 e6 f5 12 d5 c6 13 Ng5! Na6 14 Bf3 $\pm$.

(u) 7 dxc5 dxc5 8 Be3 b6 9 Qxd8 Rxd8 10 Rfd1 Nc6 11 Rxd8 Nxd8 12 Rd1 Bb7 with equal chances, Andersson–Torre, Leningrad 1987.

(v) 8 Re1 Nc7 9 a4 b6 10 h3 Bb7 11 Bf4 a6 12 Bc4 Qd7 is unclear, Beliavsky–Torre, Moscow 1981.

(w) (A) 10 a5? Nb5!. (B) 10 Qd2 Rb8 11 Rad1 b5 12 axb5 axb5 13 e5 b4 =, Šahović–Veličković, Yugoslavia 1986.

(x) If (A) 11 . . . Rb8?! 12 e5 is strong. (B) 11 . . . Nd7 12 Qd2 Rb8 13 Bh6 $\pm$, Belyavsky–Stoica, Lucerne 1985.

(y) 13 Qd2 b5 14 axb5 axb5 15 b4 c4 with an unclear position, Gavrikov–Torre, Lugano 1988.

PIRC DEFENSE

1 e4 d6 2 d4 Nf6 3 Nc3 g6

	19	20	21	22	23	24
4	Bg5.........f3...........Be3......................g3 ....Bc4(t)					
	Bg7(a)	c6	Bg7.........c6!		Bg7	Bg7(u)
5	Qd2(b)	Be3	Qd2	Qd2(l)	Bg2	Qe2
	c6(c)	Nbd7(e)	0–0(h)	b5	0–0	Nc6(v)
6	f4	Qd2	0–0–0	Bd3	Nge2(o)	e5
	0–0	b5	Nc6(i)	Nbd7	e5(p)	Ng4(w)
7	Nf3	Nh3	f3	Nf3	h3	e6?!(x)
	b5	Bb7(f)	e5	e5	c6	f5!(y)
8	Bd3	Be2	Nge2!	a4(m)	Be3(q)	d5
	Bg4	e5	exd4	b4	b5	Nd4
9	f5	0–0	Nxd4	Ne2	0–0	Qd1
	b4	a6	Nxd4(j)	exd4	Bb7(r)	c6
10	Ne2	Rad1	Bxd4	Nexd4	a3	h3
	Nbd7	Bg7	Be6	c5	Nbd7	b5!
11	0–0	Nf2	Be3!	Ne2	Qd2	Bf1
	c5(d)	0–0(g)	Re8(k)	Bg7(n)	Re8(s)	b4!(z)

(a) (A) 4 ... c6 5 Qd2 b5 6 Bd3 h6 7 Bf4 $\pm$. (B) 4 ... h6 5 Be3 c6 6 Qd2 b5 7 f3 Nbd7 8 a4 b4 9 Nd1 a5 10 Nf2 Bg7 11 Ngh3 Qc7 12 Rd1 $\pm$, Romanishin–Putiainen, Erevan 1976.

(b) (A) 5 e5 dxe5 6 dxe5 Ng4! 7 Qxd8† Kxd8 8 Nf3!? Be6 9 Bh4 Nxe5 10 Ng5 Bd7 11 Bg3 Nbc6 12 Bb5 (Raaste–Parma, Nice 1974) 12 ... h6 =. (B) 5 Qe2 h6 6 Bh4 c6 7 0–0–0 Nh5 8 Qf3 Qc7 9 Kb1 Nd7 10 g4 Nhf6 11 g5 hxg5 12 Bxg5 Nb6 with equality, Parma–Polugaevsky, Yugoslavia–USSR 1969. (C) 5 f4 h6 6 Bh4 c5 7 e5 Nh5 8 dxc5 Nxf4 9 exd6 g5 10 Bf2 0–0 11 Qd2 Nc6 12 0–0–0 exd6 13 cxd6 Qa5 ∞, Olafsson–Kaiszauri, Sweden 1974.

(c) 5 ... h6 6 Bf4 g5 7 Bg3 Nh5 8 0–0–0 Nc6 9 Bb5 Nxg3 10 hxg3 a6 is an interesting suggestion of Nunn's.

(d) 12 c3 bxc3 13 bxc3 Qa5 14 Qf4 cxd4 15 cxd4 Qa4 =, Brown–Hort, Madrid 1973.

(e) 5 ... Qb6 6 Qc1 Bg7 7 Bd3 0–0 8 Nge2 Qc7 9 g4 e5 10 dxe5 dxe5 11 Ng3 b5 12 h4 b4 13 Na4 c5 ∞.

(f) 7 ... Bg7 8 Nf2 0–0 9 a4! b4 10 Ncd1 a5 11 Be2 e5 12 c3 bxc3 13 bxc3 Re8 14 0–0 d5 15 dxe5 with better chances, Kir. Georgiev–Torre, Leningrad 1987.

(g) 12 dxe5 dxe5 13 Nd3 Qc7 14 Nc5 Rad8 =, Jimenez–Botvinnik, Palma de Mallorca 1967.

(h) (A) 5 ... Ng4 6 Bg5 h6 7 Bh4 g5 8 Bg3 f5 9 exf5! Bxf5 10 Bd3 or 10 Bc4 with a clear advantage for White (Chernin). (B) 5 ... Nc6 6 f3 a6 7 0–0–0 e6 8 g4 b5 9 h4 h5 10 gxh5 Nxh5 11 Nge2 Bd7 12 Bh3 b4 13 Nb1 a5 14 Bg5 Qc8 with roughly equal chances, Short–Kavalek, Dubai 1986.

(i) 6 ... Ng4? 7 Bg5 h6 8 Bh4 Nc6 9 h3 Nf6 10 f4 a6 11 g4 b5 12 e5 dxe5 13 dxe5 Qxd2† 14 Rxd2 Nh7 15 Bg2 Bb7 16 Bxe7 +, Yudasin–Zaichik, Lvov 1987.

(j) 9 . . . d5?! 10 exd5 Nxd5 11 Bg5! Qd7 12 Nxc6 bxc6 13 Nxd5 cxd5 14 Qxd5 Qe8 15 Qc5 leaves White a pawn ahead (M. Gurevich).

(k) 12 Bg5! Qe7 (12 . . . c6 13 e5! wins) 13 g4 with a strong attack, Chernin–Zaichik, Lvov 1987.

(l) 5 h3!? followed by 6 g3 is a noteworthy alternative.

(m) Though less tested, 8 0–0 is a more flexible choice.

(n) 12 Rd1 Bb7 13 Ng3 0–0 14 0–0 Re8 15 Bf4 Bf8 16 Rfe1 a6 17 Bc4 d5 18 Ba2 b3! 19 Bxb3 c4 20 Ng5 dxc4 with a clear edge for Black, Balashov–Torre, Lugano 1988.

(o) 6 Nf3 Bg4! 7 Be3 Nc6 8 h3 Bxf3 9 Qxf3 e5 10 dxe5 dxe5 11 0–0 Nd4 12 Qd1 Qe7 13 Nb1 h5 14 Nd2 h4 with a good position, Spassky–Timman, Tilburg 1978.

(p) (A) 6 . . . Nbd7 7 0–0 c5 8 h3 a6 9 Be3 Qc7 10 dxc5! Nxc5 11 Nf4 e6 12 Qd2 Bd7 13 Rfd1 Ne8 14 Nd3 Na4 15 Nxa4 Bxa4 16 Rac1 ±, Barlov–Smyslov, New York 1987. (B) 6 . . . Nfd7 7 0–0 c5 8 h3 cxd4 9 Nxd4 Nc6 10 Nde2 Rb8 11 a4 b6 12 Re1 Bb7 13 b3 Rc8 =, Rukavina–Lević, Vrnjačka Banja 1986.

(q) 8 a4 Re8 9 0–0 exd4 10 Nxd4 Na6 11 Re1 Nb4 12 a5 d5 13 e5 Ne4 14 Nxe4 dxe4 15 Rxe4 Rxe5 16 Rxe5 Bxe5 17 c3 Bxd4 18 cxd4 Be6 19 Ra4, Draw, Gulko–Hort, Biel 1987.

(r) (A) 9 . . . Re8?! 10 dxe5 dxe5 11 Qxd8 Rxd8 12 Rfd1 Re8 13 Nc1! with a clear plus for White. (B) 9 . . . Nbd7 10 d5! cxd5 11 Nxd5 Bb7 12 Nec3 ±, Popović–Chernin, Subotica 1987.

(s) 12 Rfe1 a6 (intending . . . exd4 and . . . c5) 13 d5 cxd5 14 exd5 Nb6 15 b3 Qc7 with good play for Black, Dzhandzhava–M. Gurevich, Lvov 1987.

(t) 4 Be2 Bg7 5 h4 (5 Be3 Nc6 6 g4 e5 7 d5 Nd4! 8 Bxd4 exd4 9 Qxd4 0–0 10 g5 Nd7 11 Qe3 f5 12 gxf6 Bxf6 13 Bg4 Ne5 14 Bxc8 Rxc8! 15 Qxa7 Ra8 16 Qxb7 Ng4! 17 Nge2 Nxf2 18 0–0 Bd4! ∓, Forgacs–Utasi, Hungary 1985–86) followed by: (A) 5 . . . Nc6 6 h5 (6 Be3 e5 7 d5 Nd4!) 6 . . . gxh5 7 Be3 Ng4 8 Rxh5 Nxe3 9 fxe3 e6 10 Qd2 Bd7 11 0–0–0 Qe7 12 Nf3 0–0–0 =, Sax–Simić, Vrnjačka Banja 1974. (B) 5 . . . c5 6 dxc5 Qa5 7 Qd3 Qxc5 8 Be3 Qa5 9 h5 gxh5 10 Nh3 Nc6 11 0–0–0 Bd7 12 a3 ±, Sherzey–Pähtz, Budapest 1988. (C) 5 . . . h5 6 Bg5 (6 Nf3! intending 7 Ng5 is worthy of study) 6 . . . c6 7 Qd2 Qc7 8 0–0–0?! Nbd7 9 f4 b5 10 Bf3 b4 11 Nce2 a5 12 f5 gxf5 13 exf5 Nb6 14 Ng3 Nc4 15 Qe2 d5! 16 Nxh5 Rxh5! 17 Bxh5 a4 18 Nh3 b3 19 cxb3 axb3 20 a3 Rxa3! 21 bxa3 Qa5 22 Rd3 Qxa3† 23 Kb1 Bxf5 24 Nf2 b2 25 Bxf7† Kxf7 26 Bxf6 Qa1† 27 Kc2 b1 = Q† 28 Rxb1 Qa2† 29 Resigns, Sax–Kestler, Nice 1974.

(u) 4 . . . Nc6!? 5 f3 Bg7 6 Nge2 Na5 7 Bb3 (7 Bd3 should be better) Nd7 8 Be3 Nb6 9 Qd3 c6 10 0–0–0 Nxb3† 11 cxb3!? a5 12 Qc2 d5 with chances for both sides, J. Whitehead–Gulko, US Chp. 1987.

(v) 5 . . . c6 (5 . . . 0–0? 6 e5 dxe5 7 dxe5 Ng4 8 e6 +; 5 . . . e5 6 dxe5 dxe5 7 Be3 Qe7 8 Nd5 Nxd5 9 Bxd5 ±, Herbrechtsmeier–Storm, Badenweiler 1985) 6 e5 Nd5! 7 Bd2 0–0 8 h4 b5 9 Bb3 (9 Bxd5 cxd5 10 Nxb5 Qb6 is fair compensation) 9 . . . Nxc3 10 Bxc3 a5 =, Herbrechtsmeier–Smejkal, W. German club match 1985–86.

(w) (A) 6 . . . Nxd4? 7 exf6 Nxe2 8 fxg7 Rg8 9 Ngxe2 Rxg7 10 Bh6 Rg8 11 h4! Be6 12 Bxe6 fxe6 13 0–0–0 Qd7 14 Rhe1 e5 15 f3! 0–0–0 16 Ng3 and White has a clear edge, Klauser–Leski, Geneva 1984. (B) 6 . . . Nh5? 7 Bb5! threatening 8 g4 wins. (C) 6 . . . Nd7 7 Nf3 Nb6 (7 . . . dxe5? 8 Bxf7†!) 8 Bb3 0–0 9 h3 dxe5 10 dxe5 Be6 11 0–0 Nd4 12 Nxd4 Qxd4 13 Re1 Nc4 14 Rd1! ±, Kling–Botterill, London 1980.

(x) 7 Bb5! 0–0 8 Bxc6 bxc6 9 h3 Nh6 10 Nf3 c5! 11 dxc5 Bb7 12 Bd2 Nf5 13 0–0–0 Bxf3 14 Qxf3 Bxe5 15 h4! Qd7 16 Qh3 h5 (Sigurjonsson–Timman, Wijk aan Zee 1980) 17 g4! Ng7 18 gxh5 Qxh3 19 Rxh3 Bxc3 20 Rxc3! with the better endgame for White (Klauser).

(y) (A) 7 . . . Nxd4 8 Qxg4 Nxc2† 9 Kd1 Nxa1 10 exf7† Kf8 11 Qh4 d5 12 Bd3 Bf5 13 Bxf5 gxf5 (Knox–Hindel, Brighton 1977) 14 Bh6! with a strong attack (Boersma). (B) 7 . . . d5

3 3 8

8 Bxd5 Nxd4 9 Qxg4! Nxc2† 10 Ke2 Nxa1 11 Nf3 c6 12 Bc4 fxe6 13 Qe4 Qb6 14 Rd1 Rf8
15 Kf1 with a strong attack for the exchange, Timmerman–van Wijgerden, Dutch Chp.
1983.

(z) 12 Nb1 Nxf2! 13 Kxf2 Qb6 14 Ke1 Qc5 15 c3 bxc3 16 bxc3 Qxd5! 17 Ne2 Nxe6 18 Qxd5
cxd5 19 Be3 0–0 20 Nd2 f4 21 Bf2 Nc5 22 Nd4 Bd7 23 N2b3? Ne4 24 Rc1 Rac8 25 c4 a5!
26 Bg1 a4 27 Nd2 Ng3 28 Rh2 e5 29 N4f3 Re8 30 Be2 Bb5! and wins, Destrebecq–Leski,
Henghien 1982.

ROBATSCH (OR MODERN) DEFENSE

1 e4 g6 2 d4 Bg7

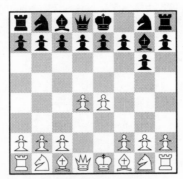

Diagram 45

THIS DEFENSE IS NAMED AFTER THE AUSTRIAN MASTER K. Robatsch, who was the first to analyze it seriously. It gained respectability in the 1950s, but it was not until several young British players explored new avenues for Black twenty years later—they called the opening the "Modern Defense"—that it experienced an upsurge in popularity.

The difference between the Robatsch and the Pirc is that the Robatsch delays or omits . . . Nf6, using the tempo to start queenside action. An early . . . Nf6 often transposes to the Pirc (these transpositions are not specified as they are too numerous); if White plays 3 c4 (cols. 9–11), then an early . . . Nf6 transposes to the King's Indian Defense. The Robatsch is less clearly defined than the Pirc, and it is riskier because it neglects kingside development.

White plays 3 Nc3 in columns 1–5. 4 f4 (cols. 1–2) creates a central pawn front, as in the Austrian Attack of the Pirc, and White obtains good attacking prospects. 4 Ne3 (col. 3) and 4 Bg5 (col. 4), though not as aggressive, may still lead to sharp play. In column 5 White develops classically and tries for a positional advantage. 3 Nf3 and 4 Bc4 (col. 6) leads to play similar to that in the Alekhine Defense in which White maintains a small edge. 3 c3 (col. 7–8) attempts to create a rock-solid center, but Black is able to loosen it.

After 3 c4 (cols. 9–11) the game takes on the character of the King's Indian Defense. White's order of moves is not important—often the position on move three is reached via 1 d4 or 1 c4. After 3 . . . d6 4 Nc3, Black has three choices (besides 4 . . . Nf6, transposing to the King's Indian) that lead to original positions but leave White with some advantage.

Column 12 examines 2 . . . c6 and 3 . . . d5, a hybrid Caro-Kann–Robatsch.

ROBATSCH (OR MODERN) DEFENSE

1 e4 g6 2 d4 Bg7

	1	2	3	4	5	6
3	Nc3.....					Nf3
	d6(a)					d6
4	f4		Be3	Bg5	Nf3	Bc4(p)
	c6 ...	Nc6(e)	c6(i)	Nc6(l)	c6(n)	Nf6
5	Nf3	Nf3(f)	Qd2	Bb5	Be2	Qe2
	Bg4(b)	Bg4	b5	a6	Nd7	0–0(q)
6	Be3	Be3	f3(j)	Bxc6†	0–0	0–0
	Qb6	Bxf3	Nd7	bxc6	Qc7	c6
7	Qd2!	gxf3	Nh3	Nge2	a4	Bb3
	Bxf3	d5!?	Nb6	Rb8	Ngf6	Qc7
8	gxf3	Qd2(g)	Nf2	Rb1	Be3	e5
	Nd7(c)	e6	h5	Nf6	0–0	dxe5
9	0–0–0	0–0–0	Be2	0–0	Qd2	dxe5
	Qa5	Nge7	a5	h6	e5	Nd5
10	f5	h4	a4	Bh4	dxe5	Re1
	b5(d)	h5(h)	b4(k)	g5(m)	dxe5(o)	Na6(r)

(a) 3 . . . c6 4 Bc4 b5 (4 . . . d6 5 Bb3 6 f4 ±) 5 Bb3 b4 6 Nce2 Nf6 7 e5 Nd5 8 Nf4 Nb6 9 Nf3 d5 10 0–0 with kingside play, Kneževič–Kosanski, Yugoslavia 1976.

(b) 5 . . . Qb6 6 Bc4 Nh6 (6 . . . Bg4? 7 Bxf7† Kxf7 8 Ng5†) 7 Bb3 Bg4 8 Be3 Bxf3 9 gxf3 Qa5 10 f5! ±, Kudrin–Soltis, New York 1979.

(c) 8 . . . Qxb2 9 Rb1 Qa3 10 Rxb7 Nd7 11 Rb3 Qa5 12 d5 allows White a strong initiative, de Firmian–Soltis, US Chp. 1983; Black should seek to keep the position closed.

(d) 11 Kb1 ±, as White can meet 11 . . . Nb6 with 12 Bd3 and 11 . . . gxf5?! with 12 Rg1.

(e) 4 . . . a6 5 Nf3 b5 6 a4 b4 7 Na2 Bb7 8 Bd3 a5 9 0–0 Nd7 10 Qe2 ±, Plaskett–Hawelko, European Junior Chp. 1979; also good is 6 Bd3 Bb7 7 Qe2 Nc6 8 e5 ±, Peters–Christiansen, US Chp. 1984.

(f) 5 Be3 e6 6 Nf3 Nge7 7 Qd2 a6 8 0–0–0 d5 9 e5 b6 10 Rg1 Bb7 11 g4 Qd7 12 Ne2 h5 is unclear, Rogulj–Kljako, Citta di Castello 1986.

(g) (A) 8 exd5 Nb4 9 Bb5† Kf8 10 Bc4 Nf6 and (B) 8 Nxd5 e6 allow Black to recapture the pawn with a good game. (C) 8 e5?! e6 and 9 . . . Nge7 gives Black an edge.

(h) 11 Na4 0–0 12 c4 dxc4 13 Bxc4 with more control of the board, de Firmian–J. Kristiansen, Copenhagen 1985. The game continued 13 . . . Qb8 14 Nc5 Rd8 15 Qc3 b6 16 Nxe6!? fxe6 17 Bxe6† Kh7 18 e5 Rf8 19 f5 gxf5? (19 . . . Rxf5! keeps the kingside closed) 20 Rhg1 Qe8 21 Rxg7† Kxg7 22 d5 f4 23 Bd7! Qf7 24 Bf2 Nxd5 25 Qxc6 Ne3 26 Rg1† Kh8 27 e6 Qf6 28 Be1 Nf5 29 Bc3 Nd4 30 e7 Nxc6 31 exf8=Q† Rxf8 32 Bxc6 Resigns.

(i) 4 . . . a6 5 h4 h5 6 f3 Nd7 7 Nh3 b5 8 Ng5 Bb7 9 a4 c6 10 Be2 Ngf6 11 0–0 0–0?! (11 . . . e5 12 Qd2±) 12 f4! and White has serious attacking chances, Kurajica–Adorjan, Pula 1971.

(j) 6 0–0–0 Nd7 7 Kb1 Nb6 8 Bd3 Rb8 9 Nf3 (Keene–Hartston, Cambridge 1968); now 9 . . . e6 and 10 . . . Nge7 would make the position unclear.

(k) 11 Ncd1 Be6 12 b3 c5 13 Bb5†! Bd7 14 Bxd7† Nxd7 15 0–0 cxd4 16 Bxd4 $\pm$, Ciocaltea–Suttles, Siegen 1970.

(l) (A) 4 . . . c6 5 Qd2 b5 6 f4 Nd7 7 Nf3 b4 8 Nd1 Qb6 (Littlewood–Nunn, England 1974) 9 Nf2 $\pm$. (B) 4 . . . a6 5 Qd2 b5 6 a4 b4 7 Nd5 $\pm$.

(m) 11 Bg3 Nh5 12 f4 (Mestel–Botterill, British Chp. 1974); now 12 . . . Bg4 equalizes.

(n) (A) 4 . . . Bg4 5 Be3 Nc6 6 Be2 e5 7 d5 Nce7 8 Nd2 $\pm$, Psakhis–Belov, USSR 1977. (B) 4 . . . a6 5 Bf4 e6 6 Qd2 h6 7 h4 Ne7 8 g3 b5 9 a3 Nd7 10 Rd1 Bb7 11 Bg2 $\pm$, Hecht–Adamski, Raach 1969.

(o) 11 h3 Re8 (Mohrlok–Kurajica, Wijk aan Zee 1974); now 12 Rfd1 Nf8 13 Bc5 and Bd6 is strong.

(p) 4 Nc3 transposes to the previous column. If White plays Nc3 on move 5 or 6, the position transposes to the Pirc Defense, column 14.

(q) 5 . . . Nc6 is sharp: (A) 6 e5 dxe5 7 dxe5 Ng4 8 Bb5 Bd7 9 Bf4 0–0 10 Nc3 a6 11 Bc4 b5 12 Bb3 b4 13 Na4 Na5 14 0–0–0 $\pm$, Vasiukov–Ribli, Wijk aan Zee 1973; (B) 6 c3 0–0 7 0–0 Bg4 8 h3 Bxf3 9 Qxf3 e5 10 Bb5! $\pm$ (Minev).

(r) 11 c3 Nc5 12 Bc2 Bg4 13 Nbd2 b6! (to play . . . Bc8 and . . . Ba6, Nerney–Zlotnikov, US 1985); now 14 a3! Bc8 15 c4 Ba6 16 b4 Ne6 17 Qe4 Ndf4 18 Bb2 is better for White (Alburt).

ROBATSCH (OR MODERN) DEFENSE

1 e4 g6 2 d4(a)

	7	8	9	10	11	12
	Bg7 .... .c6					
3	c3(b) .... .c4 d6(c)		d6			Nc3 d5
4	f4 .... Nf3 Nf6	Nf6(f)	Nc3 Nc6 .... e5	.... Nd7(o)		h3(r) Bg7
5	Bd3(d) e5	Bd3 0–0	d5(i) Nd4	dxe5(l) dxe5	Nf3 e5	Nf6 Nf6
6	Nf3 exd4	0–0 c5(g)	Be3 c5	Qxd8† Kxd8	Be2 c6(p)	Bd3 dxe4
7	cxd4 0–0	dxc5 dxc5	Nge2 Qb6	f4! Nc6(m)	0–0 Nh6	Nxe4 Nxe4
8	Nc3 Nc6	h3 Nc6	Na4(j) Qa5†	Nf3 h6	dxe5 dxe5	Bxe4 0–0
9	0–0 Bg4	Qe2 Qd7	Bd2 Qa6	Be3 exf4	b4 0–0	0–0 Nd7
10	Be3 Re8(e)	Re1 Nd7(h)	Nxd4 Bxd4(k)	0–0–0† Bd7(n)	Rb1 Qe7(q)	Bg5 h6(s)

(a) 2 h4 is unusual. Black should reply 2 ... d5! 3 exd5 Nf6, reaching a Center Counter Defense in which ... g6 is more useful than h4.

(b) 3 f4 c5 4 c3 (4 dxc5 Qa5† ∞) 4 ... cxd4 5 cxd4 Qb6 6 Nf3 Nc6 7 e5 (7 Nc3 Nxd4 8 Nd4 Nxf3† 9 gxf3 Qd8 10 Qc2 Rb8 ∓) 7 ... Nh6 8 Nc3 0–0 9 d5 Nb4 10 a3 Na6 11 Bd3 d6 ±, Caro–Keene, Camaguey 1971.

(c) 3 ... d5 4 exd5 Qxd5 5 Nf3 c5 6 Be3 cxd4 7 cxd4 allows White some initiative.

(d) 5 e5 dxe5 6 fxe5 Nd5 7 Nf3 0–0 8 Bc4 c5! 9 0–0 cxd4 10 cxd4 Nc6 11 Nc3 Be6 12 Bb3 h6 = (Keres).

(e) 11 h3 Bf5! 12 Ng5 Nxe4 13 Bxe4 Bxe4 14 Ncxe4 h6 with even chances, Saidy–Czerniak, Netanya 1973.

(f) 4 ... c6?! 5 Bg5 Nf6 6 Nbd2 0–0 7 a4 h6 8 Bh4 Qc7 9 Qc2 e5 10 dxe5 dxe5 11 Bc4 and White has an aggressive position, Ermenkov–Todorčević, Prokuplje 1987. 4 ... Nf6 is better because White's bishop is less active at d3.

(g) 6 ... Nc6 7 Bg5 Nd7 8 a4 Qe8?! 9 Na3 a6 10 Qd2 f6 11 Bh6 is distinctly better for White, Vaganian–Ermenkov, Thessaloniki 1984.

(h) 11 Bc2 b6 12 a4 Bd7 13 Nbd2 Rad8 =, Korchnoi–Nunn, Brussels 1986.

(i) 5 Be3 is a good alternative; after 5 ... e5 6 d5 Nce7 (6 ... Nd4 7 Nge2 ±) 7 g4 f5 8 f3 Nf6 9 h3 White has more space, Peev–Vogt, Varna 1972.

(j) (A) 8 Nxd4 cxd4 9 Na4 Qa5† 10 Bd2 Qc7 11 Bd3 Nf6 12 b4 Ng4 13 Rc1 0–0 14 0–0 Ne5 15 Nb2 a5! =, Korchnoi–Speelman, Beer-Sheva 1987. (B) 8 Qd2 Nf6! 9 Nxd4 cxd4 10 Qxd4 Qxb2 =, Donner–Ree, Wijk aan Zee 1972.

(k) 11 Nc3 Qb6 (11 . . . Bd7 ±, Polugaevsky) 12 Nb5 Bxb2 13 Rb1 Bg7 14 Qa4 with great advantage, Polugaevsky–Ljubojević, Reykjavik 1987.

(l) 5 Nf3 exd4 (5 . . . Bg4 6 d5 f5 7 h3 Bxf3 8 Qxf3 Ne7 9 h4 0–0 10 h5 fxe4 11 Qh3 ±, Polugaevsky–Seirawan, Lone Pine 1978) 6 Nxd4 Nc6 7 Be3 Nge7 (or 7 . . . Nf6) 8 Be2 0–0 9 g4 Be6 is roughly equal, D. Gurevich–Seirawan, US Chp. 1987.

(m) Black equalized in Karner–Petrosian, Sochi 1977, after 7 . . . Be6 8 Nf3 Nd7 9 g3 h6 10 Be3 c6 11 Bd3 Bh3!; 9 Be3 and 10 0–0–0 look stronger.

(n) 11 Bxf4 g5 12 Bg3 Nge7 13 Nd5 Rc8 14 e5 g4 15 Nf6! Bxf6 16 gxf6 gxf3 17 fxe7† Kxe7 18 Bh4† with an endgame edge, Petursson–Ivkov, New York 1988.

(o) 4 . . . c5 5 Nf3 cxd4 6 Nxd4 Nc6 7 Be3 Nf6 8 Be2 0–0 9 0–0 transposes to the Sicilian Defense, Maróczy Bind.

(p) 6 . . . Ne7 7 d5 0–0 8 h4! Nf6 (8 . . . f5 9 h5 ±) 9 Nh2 followed by g4 is very good for White, according to Polugaevsky.

(q) 11 c5 a5 12 a3 axb4 13 axb4 f6 14 Nd2 Nf7 15 Nc4 ±, Cebalo–V. Kovačević, Yugoslav Chp. 1985.

(r) (A) 4 e5 is sharper; after 4 . . . Bg7 (4 . . . h5 5 h3 ±) 5 f4 h5 6 Be3 Nh6 7 Nf3 Bg4 8 Be2 Nd7 9 Qd2 e6 10 g3! Bf8 11 h3 Bxf3 12 Bxf3 and White is for choice, J. Arnason–Christiansen, Reykjavik 1986. (B) 4 Nf3 Bg4! 5 Be3 Nf6 =.

(s) 11 Be3 c5 (Chandler–Christiansen, Thessaloniki 1984) 12 Qd2! cxd4 13 Bxh6 with some attacking chances.

CENTER COUNTER DEFENSE

1 e4 d5 2 exd5

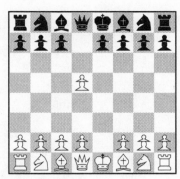

Diagram 46

THE CENTER COUNTER (also known as the Scandinavian Defense) is one of the semi-open king's pawn games that permit Black to choose from the start a defense more familiar to him than to his opponent. He may thereby deny White the opportunity of easy transposition to attacking variations. The sole exception is column 10, which offers White the Panov Attack of the Caro-Kann Defense.

2 Nc3 (instead of 2 exd5) 2 . . . dxe4 3 Nxe4 e5 leaves Black with alternatives dealt with in other sections, and is therefore not considered here.

After 2 . . . Qxd5 3 Nc3 (cols. 1–6) Black's queen is apparently exposed, but 3 . . . Qa5 (cols. 1–5) is safe enough. Col. 3 is the critical line for Black. 3 . . . Qd8 is feasible but rarely seen.

2 . . . Nf6 (cols. 7–12) is a natural move for the development of this knight, but since it permits 3 c4 with transposition to the Caro-Kann, Black should be acquainted with that defense.

3 Bb5† (cols. 11–12), designed to slow down Black's recovery of his gambit pawn, generally leads to equality.

CENTER COUNTER DEFENSE

1 e4 d5 2 exd5 Qxd5 3 Nc3

	1	2	3	4	5	6
	Qa5(a)				Qd8	
4	d4(b)..............................			Nf3	d4	
	Nf6(c)			Bg4	Nf6 ....g6	
5	Bc4........Nf3			h3	Be3	Bf4(k)
	c6	Bg4		Bh5	c6	Bg7
6	Bd2	h3		g4	Bd3	Qd2
	Bf5	Bh5		Bg6	Bg4	Nf6
7	Nd5	Bd2........g4		Bg2	Nge2	0–0–0
	Qd8	e6	Bg6	Nc6	e6	c6(l)
8	Nxf6†	Bc4	Ne5	0–0	Qd2	Bh6
	gxf6	Bb4(e)	e6	0–0–0	Bd6	0–0
9	Bf4	g4	Bg2(g)	a3	Ng3	h4
	Qb6(d)	Bg6(f)	c6(h)	e5(i)	Qc7(j)	Qa4(m)

(a) 3 . . . Qd6 4 d4 Nf6 and now: (A) 5 Nf3 Bg4! 6 h3 (6 g3 e5) Bh5 7 g4 Bg6 8 Ne5 c6 9 Bf4—Psakhis—9 . . . Qb4 10 Qd2 Nbd7 11 0–0–0 0–0–0 ∞ (Korn). (B) 5 Bc4 a6 6 Nge2 is better (Grefe).

(b) (A) Dubious is the Mieses–Kotrč Gambit: 4 b4 Qxb4 5 Rb1 Qd6 6 Nf3 Nf6 7 d4 a6 8 Bc4 e6 9 e5 b5 10 0–0 Be7 $\overline{\overline{\mp}}$. (B) 4 h3 Nf6 (4 . . . Bf5? 5 b4!) 5 Nf3 e6 6 Bc4 has the merit of avoiding the pressure of col. 4 or 2.

(c) 4 . . . e5 5 dxe5 Nc6 6 Nf3 Bb4 7 Bd2 Bg4 8 a3 Nd4 9 Bb5† c6 10 0–0 Bxf3 11 axb4 Bxd1 12 bxa5 Bxc2 13 Ba4 Ne7 14 Bxc2 Nxc2 15 Ra4 Rd8 16 Ne4 Nf5 17 g4 Nfd4 (no better is 17 . . . Rd4 18 b3 Nh4 19 Bc3 Rd3 20 Rc1 ±) 18 Nd6† Ke7 19 Bc3 c5 20 Nxb7 Rd5 21 Rc4 h5 22 Rxc5 Rxc5 23 Nxc5 hxg4 24 Kg2 Nf3 25 Rd1 Rxh2† 26 Kg3 Ke8 27 Ne4 Rh6 28 Kxg4 Nh4 29 Rc1 Resigns, Ivanchuk–Angelov, Varna 1987. The move 4 . . . e5 is attributed to Adolph Anderssen.

(d) 10 Bb3 a5 11 a4 Rg8 12 Ne2! Na6 = (12 . . . Rxg2? 13 Bg3 ±), W. Watson–Rogers, London 1987.

(e) A subtlety is 8 . . . c6 9 Qe2 Bb4 10 g4 Bb6 11 0–0–0 Nbd7 12 Kb1 0–0–0 13 a3 Bxc3 14 Bxc3 Qc7 15 Bd2 Nb6 ∞ (Dolmatov).

(f) 10 Ne5 Nc6! 11 Nxc6 bxc6 12 a3 Bxc3 13 Bxc3 (Miles–Hickl, Zagreb 1987) 13 . . . Qg6 $\overline{\mp}$.

(g) Or (A) at once 9 h4 Bb4 10 Bd2 (10 Rh3 Bxc3 11 bxc3 Nbd7 12 Nxc7 [or 12 Nxg6 hxg6 13 Rb1 0–0–0 =] 12 . . . Nxd7 13 h5 Be4 14 Bd2 0–0–0 15 Re3 Bc6 16 c4 Qg5 17 Rxb6 Qh4 =, Timman–Rogers, Reggio Emilia 1984–85) 10 . . . Qb6 (Myers) 11 h5 Bxc3 12 bxc3 Be4 13 f3 Bc6 14 Rb1 ± (Scoones, Inside Chess I/15). (B) 9 Nc4 Qa6 10 a3 (10 Bf4 Qc6 11 Rg1 Bb4 12 Bd2 Nbd7) 10 . . . Qc6 11 Rg1 Nbd7 12 Qe2 0–0–0 13 Bg5 Kb8 14 0–0–0 ±, Marjanović–Rogers, Niš 1983.

(h) In this position White seems to have more space, e.g.: (A) 10 0–0 Nbd7 11 Qe2 Nxe5 12 dxe5 Nd5 13 Ne4 Bxe4 14 Bxe4 ±. (B) 10 h4 Be4 11 Bxe4 Nxe4 12 Qf3 Nd6 13 Bf4! Nb5 when Rogers suggests 14 Nxf7! Nxd4!; however, 15 Qe4 should win (Korn). Therefore, 13 . . . Be7 is safer. Karpov suggests 10 . . . Bb4 ∞, which remains to be tested.

(i) 10 Ra2 ±, White's notes to Chiburdanidze–Klarić, Banja Luka 1985.

(j) 10 h3 Bxg3 11 hxg4 Nxg4 12 fxg3 Qxg3† 13 Bf2 Qxg2 14 Be4 Qxf2† 15 Qxf2 Nxf2 16 Kxf2 ±. *Comments.*

(k) 5 Bc4 Bg7 6 Nf3 Nf6 7 0–0 0–0 8 h3 Nc6 9 Re1 Nd7 10 Bg5 h6 11 Be3 Nb6 =.

(l) Fischer suggests 7 . . . Nd5 8 Be5 0–0 9 h4 h5 10 Nge2 with only a minute advantage for White.

(m) 10 h5 gxh5 11 Bd3 Nbd7 12 Nge2 Rd8 13 g4 Nf8 14 gxh5 Ne6 15 Rdg1† Kh8 16 Bxg7† Nxg7 17 Qh6 Rg8 18 Rg5 Qd8 19 Rhg1 Nf5 20 Bxf5 Resigns, Fischer–Robatsch, Varna 1962. Fischer considered 8 . . . Bxh6 9 Qxh6 Bf5 as giving Black an equal game.

CENTER COUNTER DEFENSE

1 e4 d5 2 exd5 Nf6

	7	8	9	10	11	12
3	d4............................c4.........Bb5† Nxd5			c6	Bd7	
4	c4 ....Nf3.........g3 Nb6	g6(d)	Bf5	dxc6(h) Nxc6	Bc4(k) Bg4........b5?!	
5	Nf3(a) g6	Bc4(e) Bg7	Bg2 Nc6	d3 e5	f3 Bc8(l)	Be2(n) Nxd5
6	h3(b) Bg7	0–0 0–0	Nf3 Qd7	Nc3 Bf5	Nc3 Nbd7	Bf3 Bc6
7	Nc3 0–0	c3 Nc6	0–0 0–0–0	Nf3 Bb4	Qe2 Nb6	Ne2 Nf6
8	Be3 Nc6	Re1 Nb6	c4 Nb6	Be2 e5	Qd3 g6!	Bxc6† Nxc6
9	Qd2 e5(c)	Bb3 Bg4!(f)	Nc3 e6(g)	dxe4!(i) Qxd1†(j)	Nge2 Bg7(m)	0–0 e6(o)

(a) As against 5 Nc3, the text tries to prevent an early . . . e5. If 5 Nc3 g6 6 c5 Nd5 7 Bc4 Nxd3 8 bxc3 e5 = (Tiviakov in *Informant* 43).

(b) 6 Be2 Bg7 7 0–0 0–0 8 Nc3 Nc6 9 d5 Ne5 10 Nxe5 Nxe5 11 Bh6 ± is more testing, J. Polgar–Stefansson, Egilss Fadir 1988.

(c) 10 d5 Na5! (Suetin–Smagin, USSR 1984) 11 b3 f5 12 Bh6 e4! =.

(d) 4 . . . Bg4 5 Be2 e6 6 0–0 Be7 7 Nbd2 0–0 8 Ne4 Nd7 9 Ng3 ±.

(e) Just as playable are (A) 5 h3 Bg7 6 c4 Nb6 7 Be3 0–0 8 Nc3 Nc6 9 Qd2 e5 10 d5 Ne7 11 g4 f5 12 0–0 (Klovans–Vitolins, Riga 1969) 12 . . . e4 ∞. (B) 5 Be2 Be7 6 0–0 0–0 7 Na3 a5 8 Bc4 a4! 9 Bd2 c5! 10 dxc5 Qc7 11 Qc1 Qc5 =.

(f) 10 Bf4 e5! 11 dxe5 Qxd1 12 Bxd1 Nc4 13 Nbd2 Nxb2 14 Bc2 Rfd8! =, Klovans–Dautov, USSR 1986.

(g) 10 d5! ±, Ničevski–Skrobek, Dembica 1987.

(h) Trying to hold on to the pawn, as in the column, is not fatal, as used to be thought; besides, with 4 d4 White has the Panov Attack in the Caro-Kann if he chooses. Positionally conservative is 4 Nc3 cxd5 5 cxd5 Nxd5 6 Nf3 Nc6 7 d4 Bg4 8 Qb3 Bxf3 9 gxf3 Nb6 10 Be3 e6 11 Rg1 Rc8 =.

(i) 9 Nh4 Be6 10 0–0 exd3 11 Bxd3 Bxc3 12 bxc3 Ne5 13 Be2 Qxd1 14 Rxd1 Rc8 ∓ (Boleslavsky).

(j) 10 Kxd1 0–0–0 11 Kc2 Bxe4 (11 . . . Bxc3 12 exf5 ±; or 11 . . . Nxe4 12 h4 ±) 12 Nxe4 Nxe4 13 Be3 ± (Korn).

(k) 4 Bxd7†? Qxd7 5 c4 c6 6 dxc6 Nxc6 7 Nf3 e5 8 0–0 e4 9 Re1 0–0–0 10 Ng5 Qf5 11 Nxf7 Bc5 12 Rg1 Ng4 ∓.

(l) Shunning the dogmatic . . . Bf5 or . . . Bh5–g6, aiming instead for an eventual queenside fianchetto. Nevertheless, after 5 . . . Bf5!? 6 Nc3 (6 g4 Bc8 7 Nc3 c6 8 dxc6 Nxc6 9 d3 e5 10 g5 Nh5 11 Ne4 Be7 12 Nge2 0–0 13 Be3 Na5 14 Bb3 Nxb3 15 axb3 f5 16 gxf6 Bxf6 with maneuverability in return for the pawn) 6 . . . Nbd7 7 Qe2 Nb6 8 Bb3 Qd7 9 d6 Qxd6 10 Nb5 Qd7 11 Qe5 0–0–0 12 Nxa7† Kb8 13 Nb5 Nfd5 14 a4 f6 (or 14 . . . e6 =, Peters) 15 Qe2 Nf4 16 a5 Nf4 17 axb6 Nxe2 18 bxc7† Qxc7 19 Nxc7 Nd4 20 Na8 Bxc2!! ∓; analysis by Silman.

(m) 10 Ng3 0–0 11 0–0 a6 12 b3 Nxc4 13 bxc4 b5! 14 Rb1 bxc4 15 Qxc4 e6 16 dxe6 Bxe6 =, Belov–Zhilin, USSR 1961.

(n) 5 Bb3 Bg4 6 f3 Bc8 7 Qe2 a6 8 c4 c6 9 Nc3 cxd5 10 cxb5 e6 11 d4 axb5 12 Qxb5† (Evans–Henin, Santa Monica 1965) 12 . . . Nbd7 13 Qe2 Ba6 ∞ (Korn).

(o) 10 d4 Be7 =, Suetin–Bronstein, USSR Chp. 1965.

NIMZOWITSCH DEFENSE

1 e4 Nc6

Diagram 47

A SIDE FROM THE MATERIAL COVERED in this chapter, the most outstanding characteristic of this bizarre defense is its unfathomably widespread misspelling as "Nimzovich" Defense. This defies the Baltic master's own German version of his name, which transcribed into English is correctly pronounced not "Nimzo" but "Nimtso."

The defense was first advocated by the German master Eduard Fischer (b. 1831) in the last century. Nimzowitsch subjected it to deep study and came to the conclusion that it was sound. Many other European masters experimented with it, but Alexander Kevitz of the Manhattan Chess Club probably analyzed and played it more than anyone, including its originator! The underlying idea of some lines of this defense is similar to that of the Kevitz–Trajković Defense 1 d4 Nf6 2 c4 Nc6.

Most masters believe that the defense is too cramped and requires too much patient handling, but Black's move does contain novelty value, and it appeals to players who desire to avoid well-trodden paths or are well-versed in defensive maneuvering.

2 d4, seizing the center, is a healthy and aggressive reaction. Met by 2 ... d5 (cols. 1–2) it leads to old established variations. The reply 2 ... e5 (cols. 3–4) concedes White some space advantage but still preserves a solid setup for Black.

2 Nf3 is White's most neutral, and recently most preferred, treatment, but in sum Black has enough safeguards at his disposal to prevent being overwhelmed.

NIMZOWITSCH DEFENSE

1 e4 Nc6

	1	2	3	4	5	6
2	d4				Nf3	
	d5	e5(g)			d6(l)	
3	e5	Nc3(d)	dxe5	d5	d4	
	f6(a)	dxe4	Nxe5	Nce7	Nf6(m)	
4	f4	d5	Nf3(h)	Bd3	Nc3	
	Bf5	Nb8(e)	Nxf3†	Ng6	Bg4	
5	Ne2	Bf4	Qxf3	Be3	d5	Bb5(q)
	e6	Nf6	Qf6	Bb4†(j)	Nb8(n)	a6
6	Ng3	Bc4	Qg3	c3	Be2(o)	Bxc6
	fxe5	a6	Qg6	Ba5	g6	bxc6
7	fxe5	Qe2	Qxc7	Nf3	Bg5	Bg5
	Qh4(b)	b5	Bd6	Bb6	Bg7	h6
8	c3	Bb3	Qc4	Bxb6	Qd2	Bh4
	Nge7(c)	c5(f)	Nf6(i)	axb6(k)	0–0(p)	g6(r)

(a) 3 . . . Bf5 4 c3 e6 5 Ne2 Nge7 6 Ng3 Bg6 7 Bd3 Qd7 8 0–0 (wasted is 8 Qf3 Bxd3 9 Qxd3 Ng6 10 h4 f5! =) 8 . . . Bxd3 9 Qxd3 Ng6 10 Nd2 0–0–0 11 b4 Be7 12 Nb3 with play for White on both wings.

(b) If 7 . . . Qd7 8 Nxf5 exf5 9 c3 ± (Alekhine).

(c) 9 Bb5 0–0–0 10 0–0 Bg6 11 Be3 (if 11 Nbd2 Nxd4!?) 11 . . . a6 = (Korn).

(d) Enterprising yet inconclusive is the attempt to expose Black's queen with 3 exd5 Qxd5, and now: (A) 4 Nf3 Bg4 5 Be2 0–0–0 6 Nc3 Qa5 7 Be3 Nf6 8 Nd2 Bxe2 9 Qxe2 Qf5 10 Nb3 e5! =. *Comments.* (B) 4 Nc3!? Qxd4 5 Qe2 Bg4! 6 f3 Bf5 7 Be3 Qb4 8 0–0–0 e6 $\overline{\mp}$ (Korn).

(e) 4 . . . Ne5 5 Qd4 Ng6 6 Bb5† Bd7 (6 . . . c6 7 dxc6! +) 7 Nge2 Nf6 8 Bg5 Bxb5 9 Nxb5 a6 10 Nbc3 ±.

(f) 9 dxc6 Nxc6 10 Rd1 Qa5 11 Bd2 Nd4 (or 11 . . . Bg4!? 12 Ne4 Qb6 =, Larsen).

(g) 2 . . . d6 3 d5 Nb8 4 c4 g6 5 Nc3 Bg7 6 Be2 c6 7 Be3 Nf6 ∞ (Larsen) with a stubborn defense.

(h) Sharper, but only by appearance, is 4 f4 Ng6 5 Be3 (5 Nf3 Bc5! 6 Bc4 d6 =) 5 . . . Bb4† 6 c3 Ba5 (6 . . . Be7 7 Bb3 Nh6 8 Ng5 0–0 9 Nd2 ±) 7 Nf3 Bb6 8 Bxb6 axb6 9 f5 (Nunn–Bisguier, Hastings 1975–76) 9 . . . Nh4! =.

(i) 9 Nc3 Be5 10 Bd2 ±.

(j) MCO-12 recommended 5 . . . Be7!.

(k) 9 d6 cxd6 10 c4 d5 11 cxd5 d6 =.

(l) (A) With 2 . . . e5 Black can take a conservative turn into a king's pawn game. (B) 2 . . . Nf6 3 e5 Nd5 4 d4 d6 5 c4 Nb6 transposes to Alekhine's Defense, col. 7, and 3 Nc3 e5

351

results in a Center Counter. (C) Shaky is 2 . . . f5?! 3 exf5 d5 4 d4 Bxf5 5 Bb5† ±. (D) Also in the style of the Center Counter is 2 . . . d5 3 exd5 Qxd5 4 Nc3 Qa5 5 d4 Nf6 6 d5 Nb4 7 Bd2 ±.

(m) The immediate 3 . . . Bg4 4 Bb5 a6 5 Ba4! b5 6 Bb3 Nf6 7 c3 e6 8 Qe2 Be7 9 0–0 0–0 10 Nbd2 occurred in Fine–Mikenas, Hastings 1938, when 10 . . . d5 11 e5 Nd7 12 a4 b4 (MCO-12) 13 a5 Rb8 14 a5! (to prevent . . . Nb6) 14 . . . f6! creates tension in Black's favor.

(n) Ineffective is the more "logical" 5 . . . Ne5, followed by 6 Bb5† c6 7 dxc6 Nxc6 8 e5 dxe5 9 Qxd8† Rxd8 10 Bxc6† bxc6 11 Nxe5 Bd7 12 Be3 ±, Timman–Miles, Tilburg 1981.

(o) Or 6 h3 Bh5 7 Bc4 (7 g4 Bg6 8 Qe2 ∞, Larsen) 7 . . . c6 8 Qe2 Nbd7 9 Bf4 Bxf3 10 Qxf3 Nb6 and White's prospects are minimal.

(p) 9 h3 Bxf3 10 Bxf3 (London–Benjamin, New York 1985) 10 . . . Nbd7 =.

(q) 5 Be2 e5 (5 . . . e6!?) 6 Be3 Bxf3 7 Bxf3 cxd4 8 Bxd4 Nxd4 9 Qxd4 c6 10 0–0–0 Qb6 11 Rhe1 Qxd4 12 Rxd4 0–0–0 13 Rdd1 led to a dead draw in Psakhis–Benjamin, Hastings 1987–88.

(r) 9 h3 Bd7 10 Qe2 Bg7 11 0–0–0 g5 12 Bg3 Qb8 13 Rhe1 ±, Timman–H. Kuijf, Holland 1985.

UNUSUAL KING'S PAWN DEFENSES

A S THE TERM "UNUSUAL" IMPLIES, the usefulness of these defenses is difficult to categorize. Their appeal lies in their unorthodox rejection of conventional wisdom, which has both psychological and surprise value.

Both the Baker and the Basman Defenses owe their recent interest to the British master Michael Basman, while much of the theoretical insight has been provided by strong analyses in Hugh Myers's Opening Bulletin.

Diagram 48

THE BAKER DEFENSE, 1 . . . a6 (cols. 1–2), dubbed the "St. George" by Basman, harbors many technical pitfalls (see diagram). After . . . b5 the system often resembles the Polish Defense.

Diagram 49

THE BASMAN DEFENSE, 1 . . . g5 (cols. 3–4) is a Grob Attack in reverse (see diagram), but there the parallel ends. The move aims to provide a potential dagger against White's kingside if he castles there, and to open a diagonal versus White's queenside.

Diagram 50

OWEN'S DEFENSE, 1 . . . b6 (cols. 5–6), may meld with lines dealt with in the Indian Defenses or some of the Fianchetto Defenses (see diagram).

Note that most of the variations in these defenses may be entered by transposing e4 and d4 on the first and second moves.

UNUSUAL KING'S PAWN DEFENSES

1 e4

	1	2	3	4	5	6
	Baker's Defense		Basman's Defense		Owen's Defense	
	a6 . . . . g5 . . . . b6					
2	d4		d4		d4(q)	
	e6(a)		h6!(j) Bg7		Bb7	
3	Nf3 . . . . .c4		Bd3(k)	Bxg5	Bd3 . . . . .Nc3(t)	
	b5(b)	b5	Bg7(l)	c5	e6(r)	e6
4	Bd3	cxb5	Ne2	Nf3!	Nf3	Bd3
	c5(c)	axb5	c5	Nc6(n)	c5	g6
5	c3(d)	Bxb5	dxc5	Nbd2	c3	Nge2
	Bb7	Bb7	Qa5†	cxd4(o)	Nf6	Bg7
6	0–0	f3(h)	Nbc3	Nb3	0–0	h4
	Nf6	Qh4†	Qxc5	Qb6	Nc6	Nc6
7	Re1(e)	g3	0–0	a4	Nbd2	Bg5
	Be7(f)	Qh5	Nc6	a6	Be7	Nge7
8	a4	Bf1	Be3	a5	Re1	h5
	Qb6(g)	Nc6!(i)	Qa5(m)	Qa7(p)	Qc7(s) ∞	Nxd4(u)

(a) Or first 2 . . . b5 and now (A) 3 Nf3 Bb7 4 Bd3 e6, but not 4 . . . Nf6 5 Qe2 e6 6 c3 (6 a4 b4!—Miles) 6 . . . c5 7 0–0 Nc6 8 e5 ±. (B) 3 Bd3 Bb7 4 Nh3?! e6 5 0–0 c5 6 c3 d5 (6 . . . Nf6!) 7 e5 Nc6 (7 . . . f5!) =, Blackburne (blindfolded)–Baker, simul., London 1868. (C) 3 a4 Bb7 4 axb5 axb5 5 Rxa8 Bxa8 6 Nd2 e6 7 Bxb5 f5 ∞. These variations are often reached via the French Defense after 1 e4 e6 2 d4 a6, reverting to col. 1 or 2.

(b) The position can also arise after 1 d4 e6 (see Franco–Indian) 2 Nf3 (see Reti Opening) 2 . . . b5 3 e4 a6, with features of the Polish Defense.

(c) 4 . . . Bb7 5 Nbd2 Nf6 6 e5 Nd5 7 0–0 Be7 8 a4 b4 9 Nc4 c5 10 c4 bxc3 11 bxc3 Ba6 12 Bxa6 Nxa6 13 c4 Nb6 14 d5 Nxc4 15 d6 cxd6 16 exd6 Bf6 17 Nxf6 Qxf6 18 Bg5 Qf5 19 Qd4 ±, Oll–Bogarts, European Jr. Chp., Groningen, 1984-85.

(d) 5 Nc3 Bb7 (with transposition) 6 dxc5 Bxc5 7 a4 b4! 8 Ne2 Nc6 9 0–0 Nge7 10 Ng3 Qc7 11 Qe2 h5 12 Be3 Bd6 13 Rfe1 f6 14 Nd2 h4 =, Steinitz (blindfolded)–Baker, simul., London 1868.

(e) 7 Qe2 Nc6 8 a3 cxd4 9 cxd4 Na5 10 Nbd2 Rc8 11 b3 d5 12 e5 Ne4! 13 Bb2 Be7 14 Rac1 0–0 15 Bb1! Qb6 ∞, Sowray–Basman, Exeter 1980.

(f) 7 . . . h6! is Basman's recommendation.

(g) 9 axb5 axb5 10 Rxa8 Bxa8 11 Na3 Bc6 12 Qe2 c4 13 Bb1 d6 14 Bg5 Nbd7 (14 . . . h6!) 15 d5! Bb7 16 Nd4 ± (Harding).

(h) 6 Nc3 Bb4 7 Qe2 (7 Nf3!? Nf6 8 e5 =) 7 . . . f5! 8 Nh3 Nf6 =.

(i) 9 Nc3 Bb4 10 Bg2 f5 11 e5 Na5 12 Nh3 Ba6 13 Kf2 Ne7 14 Qf7 ±, Formanek–Basman, London 1982.

(j) The same position arises after 1 d4 h6 2 e4 g5 (see Queen's Pawn Games).

(k) Other choices are (A) 3 Nc3 Bg7 4 Bc4 d6 5 f4 Nc6 6 Nge2 Na5 7 Bd3 a6 8 fxg5 hxg5 9 Bxg5 c5 10 dxc5 dxc5 11 Ng3 Be6 12 Nf5 Be5 ∞, Dighton–Basman, England 1982. (B) 3 Bc4 Bg7 4 Ne2 e6 5 0–0 d5 6 exd5 exd5 7 Bd3 Ne7 8 c3 f5 9 f4 = (Harding). (C) 3 Ne2 e5 4 c3 d5 5 exd5 Qxd5 6 dxc5 Qxc5 7 Be3 Qc7 8 Na3 Nc6 9 Nb5 Qb8 10 Ned4 Nf6 11 Qf3 Bd7 12 Qg3 Nd5 13 0–0–0 Qxg3 14 hxg3 Nxe3 =, Laird–Basman, London 1982.

(l) The fianchetto can be postponed by 3 . . . d6 4 Ne2 c5 5 c3 Nc6 6 0–0 Nf6 (or applied now with 6 . . . Bg7 7 Be3 cxd4 8 cxd4 Nf6 9 Nbc3 Ng4—(Myers) 7 Nd2 Bd7 ∞ (Basman).

(m) 9 Bc4 Nf6 10 f3 d6 11 Qd2 Bd7 12 h3 Rc8 13 Bb3 Ne5 14 Nd4 Ng6 15 Rad1 Nh5 16 Nde2 Be5 =, Whiteley–Basman, London 1982.

(n) 4 . . . cxd4 5 c3 Nc6 6 cxd4 Qb6 7 Nc3 Nxd4 8 Nd5 Qxb2 9 Rc1 Kf8 10 Bc4 d6 11 Be3 ± (Welling).

(o) 5 . . . Nxd4 6 Nxd4 cxd4 7 Nb3 Qb8 ∞ (Myers).

(p) 9 Bd3 d6 10 Nfd2 Nf6 11 Bc4 Be6 12 Nb6 Rd8 13 Bxf6 ±, Jongman–Wind, corr. 1981–82.

(q) 2 c4 Bb7 3 Nc3 e6 4 Nf3 Nf6 5 Bd3 c5 6 0–0 Nc6 7 e5 Ng4 8 Be4 Qc8 9 d3 Ngxe5 10 Nxe5 Nxe5 11 f4 Nc6 ∞, Tal–van der Wiel, Moscow 1982.

(r) 3 . . . Nf6 4 Nc3 (4 f3 or 4 Nd2 have been tried) 4 . . . e6 5 Nf3 d5 is the French Defense; or 5 . . . Bb4 6 Qe2 d5 =.

(s) 9 a3 d5 10 e5 Nd7 11 b4 c4 12 Bc2 0–0–0 13 Nf1 Rdg8 (13 . . . h6! ∞) 14 Ng5 (Torre–Larsen, Geneva 1978) 14 . . . Nd8 ∞.

(t) 3 Nd2 c5 4 c3 cxd4 5 cxd4 g6 6 Bd3 Bg7 7 Ne2 Nc6 8 Nf3 Nb4 9 Qb1 Nf6 10 Nc3 0–0 11 a3 Na6 12 0–0 Rc8 13 Be3 ±, Grefe–Gruenfeld, Lone Pine 1981.

(u) 9 hxg6 (9 h6?!) 9 . . . hxg6 (9 . . . fxg6?!) 10 Rxh8† Bxh8 11 Nxd4 Bxd4 12 Qf2 Bg7 13 0–0–0 Kf8 14 Rh1 Qe8 15 Bf6 Ng8 =, Rogers–Spassky, Reggio Emilia, 1983–84.

III
QUEEN'S PAWN
OPENINGS

QUEEN'S GAMBIT DECLINED

1 d4 d5 2 c4 Including the Tarrasch Defense 2 . . . e6 3 Nc3 c5

Diagram 51

THE QUEEN'S GAMBIT (1 d4 d5 2 c4), one of the oldest openings, dates back to the 1490 Göttingen manuscript and was analyzed in the early seventeenth century by Salvio and by Greco. Rarely a true gambit, it was long considered unenterprising, cautious, dull—not an honorable weapon for the daring combatant. This opinion persisted until the late nineteenth century, when the opening gained wide popularity; it has been on the upsurge ever since.

In his "Analyse nouvelle du jeu des échecs" (1843), Carl von Jaenisch considered 2 . . . e6 to be Black's best defense to the Queen's Gambit, an opinion shared by many masters today. This "declining" of the gambit is the classic line in answer to 1 d4.

There are many branches of the Queen's Gambit Declined, leading to positions suiting players of vastly different styles. Among the popular lines are the Cambridge Springs Defense, Exchange Variation, Lasker's Defense, Manhattan Variation, Petrosian Variation, Ragozin System, Tarrasch Defense, Vienna Variation, and several unorthodox defenses, each with its own peculiar character.

Strategically, White wishes to occupy and control the center with his pawns. His second move (2 c4) aims to undermine Black's outpost in the center (d5) so as to clear the road for the thrust e4. Black's 2 . . . e6 protects d5 but locks in his light-squared bishop. The struggle often revolves around Black's effort to free this bishop with the pawn moves . . . c5 or . . . e5, which also free Black's entire position. White tries either to prevent these advances or to make Black pay for his freedom with a positional concession, such as isolated or "hanging" pawns. Black either allows such weaknesses willingly in exchange for activity, or banks on his solid position to develop his game more soundly and slowly.

Diagram 52

The ORTHODOX DEFENSE, 3 Nc3 Nf6 4 Bg5 Be7 5 e3 0–0 6 Nf3 (see diagram) 6 . . . Nbd7 (cols. 1–18), is one of Black's more solid choices. But it is not very popular today because Black must play patiently to achieve little more than a rather drawish equality. Most contemporary players prefer more active counterchances. The main line is seen in cols. 1–9, where Black trades pieces and plays the liberating . . . e5. White tries to utilize either his pawn majority on the kingside for attack or his superior mobility to get a better ending. In cols. 7–9 White's 11 Ne4 seems to be about as good as the usual 11 0–0. Various attempts by both sides to avoid the main line are shown in cols. 10–18. Though generally inferior, they offer variety. Notable, however, is 7 Qc2 (cols. 17–18), which seems to be as promising as the main line.

In the PETROSIAN VARIATION (cols. 19–28), Black departs from the Orthodox Defense with 6 . . . h6. White's 7 Bxf6 avoids, among other things, the Tartakower Variation. Kasparov is a major adherent of this system and has used it consistently against the world's leading players, including Karpov in world championship matches. Yet now this variation is merely one among the several deviations from classic theory shown in cols. 29–32.

The CAMBRIDGE SPRINGS DEFENSE, 4 Bg5 Nbd7 5 e3 c6 6 Nf3 Qa5 (cols. 33–34), is a time-honored attempt to profit from the absence of White's bishop on the queenside after Bg5. Though not currently popular, it is an effective surprise weapon. It derives its name from its frequent use in the Cambridge Springs tournament of 1904. The DUTCH VARIATION, col. 36, is a sort of gambit version of the Tarrasch.

LASKER'S DEFENSE (cols. 37–42) is an attempt to simplify by trading several minor pieces after . . . Ne4, but, like the Orthodox Defense, it suffers from a lack of counterchances.

The TARTAKOWER VARIATION (cols. 43–48) is characterized by an early queen bishop fianchetto after the preparatory 6 . . . h6. Its exponents are Spassky and Karpov. Black is willing to accept hanging pawns in exchange for active play. Thus it fits in well with contemporary style.

The EXCHANGE VARIATION (cols. 49–60) limits Black's choice of defenses. After 4 cxd5 exd5 (this exchange can take place on move 3 or even later in the game) White has two main strategies: The most common is to castle kingside and continue on the queenside with the "minority attack." The alternative is to castle queenside and attack on the kingside. The disadvantage of the Exchange Variation is that it relieves Black of the problem of freeing his light-squared bishop. Black can attempt to forestall the difficulties caused by White's Bg5 in the Exchange Variation by adopting the move order 3 . . . Be7 (cols. 115–117).

Columns 61–72 consider an important alternative for White to the main variations of the Queen's Gambit Declined, namely the *Classical Variation* with 5 Bf4. This move was played long ago by Steinitz and Nimzowitch and in recent years by Korchnoi.

The RAGOZIN SYSTEM is shown in cols. 73–78. It is an interesting mixture of the Nimzo-Indian and the Queen's Gambit Declined, having characteristics of both, e.g. if 5 e3 0–0, White arrives at a Nimzo-Indian Defense.

Diagram 53

The SEMI-TARRASCH DEFENSE, 4 Nf3 c5 (cols. 79–96), includes many different pawn structures (see diagram). Either White or Black can end up with an isolated d-pawn. Thus White can play positionally or for activity and a kingside attack. In cols. 89–90, White obtains the classic pawn center (pawns on e4 and d4), but it is not easy to make use of it.

Diagram 54

The Tarrasch Defense, 3 Nc3 c5 [see diagram] (cols. 97–114), is enjoying a modest resurgence. After being championed by Tarrasch, Keres, and Spassky at different times, it has been taken up by Kasparov and several other top grandmasters. The Tarrasch Defense gives Black immediate activity at the cost of an isolated pawn, and hence is suitable for aggressive players. The main line for White against the Tarrasch is the *Rubinstein Variation* (cols. 97–108), in which White fianchettoes his king bishop to bear down on the isolated d-pawn. Less common variations, including the *Swedish Variation*, the *Marshall Gambit*, and the *von Hennig-Schara Gambit*, are treated in cols. 109–114. These are usually considered somewhat suspect, although they are certainly entertaining.

Early divergences by either side are covered in columns 114–120. Chigorin's Defense, 2 ... Nc6 (cols. 121–126), goes against traditional principles by not maintaining the central outpost at d5, blocking the c-pawn, and often trading a bishop for a knight. Black develops quickly, however, and this may bring him the initiative or attacking chances against inaccurate play. White's most promising responses are seen in cols. 121 and 124.

The problematical Albin Counter Gambit, 2 ... e5, may be found in the Queen's Pawn Games section.

QUEEN'S GAMBIT DECLINED

Orthodox Variation

1 d4 d5 2 c4 e6 3 Nc3 Nf6 4 Bg5 Be7 5 e3 0–0 6 Nf3 Nbd7 7 Rc1 c6 8 Bd3 dxc4 9 Bxc4 Nd5 10 Bxe7 Qxe7 11 0–0 Nxc3 12 Rxc3 e5

	1	2	3	4	5	6
13	dxe5			h3	Bb3	Qc2
	Nxe5			e4(g)	exd4	cxd4(l)
14	Nxe5			Nd2	exd4	exd4
	Qxe5			Nb6(h)	Nf6	Nf6(m)
15	f4			Qc2	Re1	Re1
	Qe4 .... Qf6(d)			Re8	Qd3	Qd8
16	Qe2	Qe1(b)	e4(e)	Bb3	Rce3(j)	h3
	Bf5	Bf5	Be6	Kh8	Bg4	Nd5
17	Bd3	Bd3	e5	Rc5	h3	Bxd5
	Qe6	Qd5	Qe7	f6	Bxf3(k)	Qxd5
18	e4	e4	Bd3	Rc1	Rxf3 =	Re5
	Rfe8	Qd4†	f5	Bd7		Qd6
19	Re1	Qf2	Qa4	Nf1		Ng5
	Qd6(a)	Qxf2†(c)	a6(f)	Nc8(i)		g6(n)

(a) White is slightly better, Garcia-Gonzales–Toth, Thessaloniki 1984.

(b) 16 Bb3 Be6? (this allows White to gain time for the attack; better is 16 ... Bf5) 17 Bc2 Qb4 18 f5 Qxb2 19 Qe1 Bd7 (19 ... Bd5 20 f6 Rfe8 21 Qh4 h6 22 Qg3 g5 23 e4! Bxe4 24 Qh3 Kh7 25 Qh5 Bg6 26 Bxg6† fxg6 27 Qxh6†! Kxh6 28 Rh3 mate—Prooha) 20 f6 (Black is lost; if 20 ... Rfe8 21 Bxh7† Kxh7 22 Qh4† Kg8 23 Qg5 wins) 20 ... g6 21 Qh4 Kh8 22 Qh6 Rg8 23 Rc4 (threatening 24 Qxh7†) Resigns, Pafnutieff–R. Gross, California Chp. 1953.

(c) After 20 Kxf2 White has some advantage in the ending, Hertneck–Sonntag, West Germany 1985.

(d) Other moves: (A) 15 ... Qe7 is risky after 16 f5 b5 17 Bb3 b4 18 f6. (B) 15 ... Qa5 16 Bd3 Qxa2 17 Qc2 White has good attacking chances (Neistadt).

(e) 16 f5 a5 17 a4 (17 a3 is possible) 17 ... Rb8 18 Qc2 Bd7 19 Rd3 Rdd8 20 Qd2 b5 21 Bxb5 (not 21 axb5 =, Stahlberg–Trifunović, Amsterdam 1950) is better for White, but 16 ... b5 17 Bd3 b4 18 Rc5 Re8 was unclear in Stahlberg–Eliskases, Stockholm 1952.

(f) Black has equalized, Capablanca–Lasker, Moscow 1935.

(g) 13 ... exd4 14 exd4 leads to a small White plus.

(h) 14 ... Nf6 15 Qc2 Bf5 is a better try for level chances (Vaganian).

(i) After 20 d5 White is much better, Vaganian–Radulov, Dubai 1986.

(j) 16 h3 Bd7 17 Rce3 Nd5 18 Re5 f6 =, Ubilava–Kharitonov, USSR 1986.

(k) Better than 17 ... Bh5 18 g4 Bg6 19 Re5 ± (Ubilava).

(l) 13 ... e4 is possible. After 14 Nd2 Nf6 15 Rc1 Bf5 16 a3 Rad8 17 b4 White has a little edge, but Black is solid, Pirc–Jermek, Yugoslavia 1947.

(m) 14 ... Nb6 15 Re1 Qd8 16 b3 Nd5 might be a better equalizing chance, as played in Garcia Gonzales–Ree, Wijk aan Zee 1979.

(n) White is much better, Lputian–Balashov, Erevan 1986, continued 20 Rf3 f6 21 Qb3† Kg7 22 Re8 a5 (22 ... Rxe8 23 Qf7† Kh6 24 Qxh7† Kg5 25 h4† +) 23 Rxc8 Resigns. A crushing victory.

QUEEN'S GAMBIT DECLINED

Orthodox Variation

1 d4 d5 2 c4 e6 3 Nc3 Nf6 4 Bg5 Be7 5 e3 0–0 6 Nf3 Nbd7 7 Rc1 c6 8 Bd3

	7	8	9	10	11	12
	(dxc4)				h6	
9	(Bxc4)				Bf4	Bh4
	(Nd5)		b5		dxc4(i)	dxc4(l)
10	(Bxe7)(a)			Bd3	Bxc4	Bxc4
	(Qxe7)			a6	a6(j)	b5
11	Ne4			a4	Bd3	Bd3
	Qb4†	e5	N5f6	bxa4(g)	c5	a6
12	Qd2	dxe5	Nxf6†(e)	Nxa4(h)	a4	a4
	Qxd2†	Nxe5	Qxf6	Qa5†	cxd4	bxa4
13	Kxd2	Nxe5(c)	Bb3	Nc3	exd4	Nxa4
	Rd8	Qxe5	e5	c5	Nb6	Qa5†
14	Rhd1	Bxd5	0–0	Ra1	0–0	Nd2
	N5f6	cxd5	exd4	Qb4	Nbd5	Bb4(m)
15	Nxf6†	Nc3	Qxd4	0–0	Be5(k)	Nc3
	Nxf6(b)	Rd8(d)	Qxd4(f)	Bb7 $\pm$		c5(n)

(a) 10 Bf4 Nxf4 11 exf4 Nb6 12 Bb3 Nd5 13 Qd2 Qd6 $\overline{\mp}$.

(b) Black has difficulties in the ending, Alekhine–Capablanca, World Chp. 1927.

(c) 13 Bxd5 cxd5 14 Nc3 unexpectedly led to trouble after 14 ... Bg4! 15 Nxd5 Qd6, Michell–Thomas, Edinburgh 1926.

(d) 16 Qd4 Qxd4 17 exd4 leaves White with an endgame edge, Cherepkov–Korelov, USSR 1969.

(e) The famous game Alekhine–Em. Lasker, Zürich 1934, went 12 Ng3 e5 (Capablanca preferred the endgame after 12 ... Qb4† 13 Qd2 Qxd2†, but Lasker's plan is better) 13 0–0 exd4 14 Nf5 Qd8 15 N3xd4 Ne5 16 Bb3 Bxf5 17 Nxf5 Qb6? (as later shown by Flohr, the right move is 17 ... g6, gaining equality) 18 Qd6 N5d7 19 Rfd1 Rac8 20 Qg3 g6 21 Qg5! (Alekhine says the main threat is now Rd6, and Black is horribly tied up in any case) 21 ... Kh8 22 Nd6 Kg7 23 e4 Ng8 24 Rd3 f6 (this allows a beautiful finish, but other moves don't help) 25 Nf5†! Kh8 26 Qxg6! Resigns (26 ... hxg6 27 Rh3 mate).

(f) 16 Nxd4 Rd8 17 Rcd1 Ne5 18 f4 Ng6 19 h3 Bd7 and now 20 Rd2 would be slightly better for White, Korchnoi–Hübner, Biel 1986.

(g) 11 ... b4 12 Ne4 Nxe4 13 Bxe7 Qxe7 14 Bxe4 $\pm$. If 13 ... Nxf2 14 Bxh7† wins.

(h) 12 Qxa4 Nc5 13 dxc5 Qxd3 is unclear (Barcza).

(i) 9 ... Nh5 10 Be4 Nxe5 11 dxe5 $\pm$, Fine–Maróczy, Zandvoort 1936.

(j) If 9 ... Nd5 10 Bg3 White has a small advantage (Polugaevsky).

(k) Tolush–Konstantinopolsky, USSR 1952, White is slightly better.

(l) 9 . . . b6 10 0–0 Bb6 11 Qe2 Ne8 12 Bg3 $\pm$, Portisch–Szily, Vrsać 1971.

(m) 14 . . . c5 15 dxc5 Nxc5 16 Nxc5 Bxc5 17 Bxf6 $\pm$.

(n) Fischer–Spassky, World Chp. 1972. After 16 Nb3 Qd8 17 0–0 cxd4 18 Nxd4 Bb7 19 Be4 Qb8 (19 . . . Rb8 turned out worse after 20 Bxb7 Rxb7 21 Ne4 Qa8 22 Nxf6† Nxf6 23 Bxf6 gxf6 24 Rc4 $\pm$, Christiansen–Cifuentes, Dubai 1986) 20 Bg3 Qa7 21 Nc6 Bxc6 22 Bxc6 Rac8 23 Na4 Rfd8 24 Bf3 a5, Black had gradually equalized and finally drew.

QUEEN'S GAMBIT DECLINED
Orthodox Variation

1 d4 d5 2 c4 e6 3 Nc3 Nf6 4 Bg5 Be7 5 e3 0–0 6 Nf3 Nbd7

	13	14	15	16	17	18
7	(Rc1)..Qc2					
	(c6).........a6......................h6				h6..........c5(m)	
8	Qc2	cxd5(d)	Qc2	Bh4	cxd5	cxd5
	a6	exd5	Ne4	b6(h)	exd5(j)	Nxd5
9	cxd5	Bd3	Bxe7	cxd5	Bf4	Bxe7
	exd5	c6	Qxe7	exd5	c5(k)	Qxe7
10	Bd3	0–0	Bd3(f)	Bb5	Be2	Nxd5
	Re8	Re8	Nxc3	Bb7	b6	exd5
11	0–0	Bb1	bxc3	0–0	0–0	dxc5
	Nf8	Nf8	h6	c5	Bb7	Nxc5
12	h3(a)	Ne5	cxd5	dxc5	Rfd1	Be2
	Be6(b)	N6d7	exd5	bxc5	Rc8	Bg4
13	Ne5	Bf4	0–0	Bxd7	dxc5	Nd4
	N6d7(c)	Nxe5(e)	Nf6(g)	Qxd7(i)	bxc5(l)	Ne6(n)

(a) 12 Rfe1 Be6 13 a3 Nh5 14 Bxe7 Qxe7 15 Na4 Rad8 16 Nc5 Bc8 17 b4 Nf6 18 a4 $\pm$, Andersson–A. Sokolov, Reykjavik 1988.

(b) 12 ... Ng6 13 Ne5 Nd7 14 Bxe7 Qxe7 15 f4 $\pm$ (Alekhine).

(c) 14 Bxe7 Rxe7 15 Na4 Qc7 =, Beliavsky–Hort, Tunis 1985.

(d) 8 c5 c6 9 b4 a5 10 a3 axb4 11 axb4 b6 = (Samarian).

(e) 14 Bxe5 $\pm$, Gligorić–Ivkov, Bugojno 1979.

(f) 10 Nxe4 dxe4 11 Qxe4 Qb4† 12 Nd2 Qxb2 13 Rb1 Qa3 is equal, Agdestein–Prandstetter, Taxco 1985.

(g) White stands slightly better, Timman–Prandstetter, Taxco 1985.

(h) 8 ... c6 9 a3 Ne4 10 Bg3 f5 11 Nxe4 fxe4 12 Nd2 Bh4 =, Seirawan–Korchnoi, Lone Pine 1981. The game continued 13 Qg4 Bxg3 14 Qxg3 (14 Qxe6† Kh7 15 hxg3 Nb6 16 Qe5 Rf5 wins the queen) 14 ... Qf6 15 Be2 e5 16 dxe5 Nxe5 17 cxd5 cxd5 18 0–0 Bf5 19 Nb3 Nc6 20 Rc3 Rad8 21 Rd1 Qe7 22 Nd4 Rd6! (Korchnoi plans to pressure White's kingside with his rooks; Seirawan decides to give up his structural superiority to stop any threats) 23 f4 exf3 24 Nxf5 Rxf5 25 Bxf3 d4 26 exd4 Nxd4 27 Re1 Nxf3† 28 Rxf3 Rxf3 29 Rxe7 Rd1† 30 Qe1 Rxe1† 31 Rxe1 Rb3 32 Re2 Kf7 (the game is now quite drawn, but Korchnoi tries to squeeze the last drop out of his minute advantage, to no avail) 33 Kf1 a5 34 Ke1 a4 35 Kd1 Kf6 36 Kc2 h5 37 Re4 b5 38 Rd4 Ke5 39 Rd3 Rxd3 40 Kxd3 h4 41 Kc3 Kd5 42 Kb4 Kc6 43 b3 axb3 44 Kxb3 Draw.

(i) 14 Bxf6 Bxf6 15 Ne4 $\pm$, Adorjan–Hübner, Oslo 1984 (play would be similar without the interpolation of 7 ... h6 8 Bh4).

(j) 8 . . . hxg5 9 dxe6 fxe6 10 Nxg5 Nb6 11 h4 is probably good for White, with attacking chances for his small material deficit.

(k) 9 . . . c6 10 0–0–0 with a big advantage (Kasparov).

(l) 14 a4 $\pm$, Kasparov–Portisch, Brussels 1986.

(m) 7 . . . c6 8 Rd1 dxc4 9 Bxc4 Nd5 10 Bxe7 Qxe7 11 Ne4 N5f6 12 Ng3 c5 13 0–0 $\pm$, Brinck-Claussen–Norby, Denmark 1976.

(n) 14 Bxg4 Nxd4 is about equal, Polugaevsky–Geller, Portorož 1973. If 14 Nxe6 fxe6 15 Bxg4 Qb4† leads to complete equality (Polugaevsky).

QUEEN'S GAMBIT DECLINED
Petrosian Variation

1 d4 d5 2 c4 e6 3 Nc3 Nf6 4 Bg5 Be7 5 e3 0–0 6 Nf3 h6 7 Bxf6 Bxf6 8 Rc1 c6 9 Bd3 Nd7 10 0–0 dxc4 11 Bxc4

	19	20	21	22	23	24
	e5			c5		b6
12	h3			Qe2	dxc5	e4(m)
	exd4			a6	Nxc5	Bb7
13	exd4			Rfd1	b4	e5
	Nb6			cxd4(g)	Bxc3	Be7
14	Bb3			Nxd4(h)	Rxc3	Qe2
	Re8	Bf5		Qe7	Ne4(k)	Re8
15	Re1	Re1		Ne4	Rd3	Rfd1
	Rxe1†	a5	Bg5	Be5	Qe7	b5
16	Qxe1	a3(c)	Ra1	Qh5(i)	Rd4	Bd3
	Bf5	Re8	Nd7	Rd8	Nf6	Qb6
17	Ne4	Rxe8†	d5	Bf1	Ne5	Qe4
	Bxe4(a)	Qxe8	Rc8(e)	Bb8	Qxb4	Nf8
18	Qxe4	Qd2	Nd4	Qa5	Bxe6	Qe3
	Nd5(b)	Qd7(d)	Bg6(f)	b6(j)	Qe7(l)	c5(n)

(a) An alternative is 17 . . . Qe7, played in Epishin–Faibisovich, USSR 1985, but the text is better.

(b) Shabalov–Klovans, USSR 1987, continued 19 Bxd5 cxd5 20 Qf5 Qb6 21 Rc8† Rxc8 22 Qxc8† Kh7 23 Qf5† Kg8 24 Qxd5 Qxb2 and the position is equal.

(c) 16 Ne5 Bxe5 17 Rxe5 Bg6 18 a3 Qd6 19 Qg4 Nd7 20 Re3 Rae8 =, Andersson–Short, Belfort 1988.

(d) H. Olafsson–van der Sterren, Wijk aan Zee 1987, continued 19 Re1 Re8 20 Rxe8† Qxe8 21 Qf4 Be6 22 Bxe6 Qxe6 23 Qc7 Nc4 24 Qb7 Bxd4 25 Qb8† Kh7 26 Nxd4 Qe1† 27 Kh2 Qxf2 28 Qc8† Draw.

(e) Better is 17 . . . Nc5 18 Nd4 Bg6 19 dxc6 bxc6 20 Nxc6 Qxd1 21 Raxd1 Nb3 and Black is only slightly worse.

(f) Kasparov–Short, Brussels 1986, continued 19 Ne6 fxe6 20 dxe6 Kh7 21 Qxd7 Qb6 22 e7 Rfe8 23 Qg4 Qc5 24 Ne4 Qxe7 25 Bc2 (zugzwang) Rf8 26 g3 Qd8 (26 . . . Bf5 27 Nd6) 27 Rad1 Qa5 28 h4 Be7 29 Nc3 Bxc2 30 Rxe7 Rg8 31 Rdd7 Bf5 32 Rxg7† Kh8 33 Qd4 Resigns.

(g) Not 13 . . . b5 14 dxc5 bxc4 15 c6 (Kasparov).

(h) 14 exd4 b5 15 Bb3, with the idea of d5, is met by 15 . . . Qb6 16 d5 Nc5 ∞, (Kasparov).

(i) An improvement on 16 Nf3 Bb8, after which Black eventually equalized in Kasparov–Karpov, 1986 World Chp.

(j) White has pressure, Kasparov–H. Olafsson, Dubai 1986.

(k) Alternatives leave Black worse: (A) 14 . . . Qf6 15 Rc1 $\pm$. (B) 14 . . . Qxd1 15 Rxd1 $\pm$ (A. Petrosian).

(l) 19 Bxf7 Rxf7 20 Rd8† Rf8 21 Rxf8† Qxf8 22 Qb3† Kh7 23 Qc2† Draw, A. Petrosian–M. Gurevich, Baku 1986. A. Petrosian suggested 18 Nxf7 as being preferable.

(m) 12 Ne4 Be7 13 Qe2 Bb7 14 Rfd1 $\pm$, Polugaevsky–Donner, Havana 1967, may be stronger.

(n) 19 Nxb5 cxd4 20 Qxd4 Red8 21 Qxb6 axb6 22 a3 Bxf3 and Black is not worse, Portisch–Spassky, London 1986.

QUEEN'S GAMBIT DECLINED

Classical Variation

1 d4 d5 2 c4 e6 3 Nc3 Nf6 4 Bg5 Be7 5 e3 0–0

	25	26	27	28	29	30
6	(Nf3)..Rc1					
	(h6)				h6	
7	(Bxf6)				Bh4	
	(Bxf6)				b6	
8	(Rc1) ....Qc2.........Qd2 ....cxd5(i)				Bxf6........cxd5	
	a6	c5	Nc6	exd5	Bxf6	Nxd5
9	Bd3(a)	dxc5	Rc1(f)	Bd3	cxd5	Nxd5
	dxc4	Qa5(c)	a6	c5	exd5	exd5
10	Bxc4	cxd5	Be2	dxc5	Qf3	Bxe7
	Nd7	exd5	dxc4	Bxc3	Bb7	Qxe7
11	Ne4	0–0–0	Bxc4	bxc3	Bc4	Bd3(l)
	c5	Be6(d)	e5	Nd7(j)	c6	c5
12	Nxf6†	Nxd5	d5	Rc1	Bb3	Ne2
	Qxf6	Rc8	Na7(g)	Nxc5	Na6	Bb7
13	0–0	Kb1	Qc2	Bb1	Nge2	0–0
	cxd4(b)	Bxd5(e)	Bd7(h)	b6 =	Nc7(k)	Nd7(m)

(a) Other moves to consider are 9 h3 and 9 Qd2 (Samarian).

(b) After 14 Qxd4 Qxd4 15 Nxd4 White has a small pull in the ending, Speelman–Xu Jun, Subotica 1987.

(c) 9 ... dxc4 10 Bxc4 Qa5 11 0–0 Bxc3 is safer, Karpov–Kasparov, World Chp. 1984.

(d) 11 ... Bxc3 12 Qxc3 Qxc3 13 bxc3 Be6 $\pm$, Novikov–Lputian, Erevan 1984.

(e) 14 Rxd5 $\pm$, Kasparov–Timman, USSR vs. Rest of the World 1984.

(f) 9 cxd5 exd5 10 Be2 Bf5 11 0–0 Ne7 =, Kasparov–Karpov, Moscow 1981.

(g) 12 ... Ne7 13 Ne4 Nf5 14 Be2 Nd6 15 Nxf6† Qxf6 16 0–0 led to a substantial White edge in Karpov–Georgadze, Hannover 1983.

(h) 13 ... Nb5 14 Nxb5 axb5 15 Bb3 gave White only a minimal advantage in game 19 of Karpov–Kasparov, World Chp. 1984. After 15 ... e4!? 16 Nd4 Bxd4 17 exd4 c6 18 dxc6 Qxd4 19 0–0 bxc6 20 Qxc6 Bd7 21 Qd5 Qxd5 22 Bxd5 Ra6 23 Rfd1 Be6 24 a3 Bxd5 25 Rxd5 Rb8 White had a better rook ending, but Black was able to hold the draw.

(i) 8 Qb3 c5 9 dxc5 Nc7 10 cxd5 Qa5 11 Rc1 exd5 12 Qa3 Qxa3 13 bxa3 Rd8 14 Nxd5 Bb2 15 Rd1 Bxa3 =, P. Nikolić–Portisch, Reykjavik 1988.

(j) 11 ... Qa5 12 0–0 Qxc5 is also acceptable. The column is Pfleger–Gligorić, Plovdiv 1983.

(k) Bronstein–Zaitsev, Moscow 1983. The position is even.

(l) (A) 11 Ne2 Bb7 12 Nf4 c5 =. (B) 11 Be2 Be6 12 Bf3 c5 13 Ne2 $\pm$ (Beliavsky).

(m) White is better. Korchnoi–Beliavsky, Tilburg 1986, continued 14 Qa4 a6 (14 . . . c4 is better) 15 Bf5 Nf6 16 Qa3 g6 17 Bh3 Ne4 18 dxc5 Nxc5 19 Qb4 Qd6 20 Rfd1 a5 21 Qf4! Qxf4 22 Nxf4 Rad8 23 g3 Rd6 24 Nd3 Ne4 25 Rc7 Ba6 26 Ne5 Be2 27 Re1 Bb5 28 Bg2 Nc5 29 Bf1 Bxf1 30 Kxf1 (White has a great advantage and should win due to Black's weak pawns and passive pieces, but Beliavsky fights on by giving up a pawn for an active defense) 30 . . . d4 31 Nc4 Rdd8 32 exd4 Rxd4 33 Nb6 Rb8! (heading for a double rook ending) 34 Rxc5 Rxb6 35 Rc2 a4 36 a3 h5 37 Re7 Rd1 38 Kg2 Rd5 39 Ra7 Rd4 40 h4 Kg7 41 Rc3 Rf6 42 Rb7 Rdd6 43 Rc2 Rd4 44 Rb4? (allowing the doubled pawns throws away the win—a mistake brought on by Black's tough resistance) 44 . . . Rxb4 45 axb4 Rd6 46 b3 a3 47 Ra2 Rb6 48 Kf3 Rxb4 49 Rxa3 f6 50 Ke3 g5 51 f4 gxh4 52 gxh4 Kg6 53 Kd3 Kf5 54 Kc3 Rxf4 55 Ra4 Rf3† 56 Kb2 Rh3 57 Rc4 Ke6 58 b4 f5 59 b5 Kd5 60 Rf4 Kd6 61 Kc2 Kc7 Draw.

QUEEN'S GAMBIT DECLINED

1 d4 d5 2 c4 e6 3 Nc3 Nf6 4 Bg5

	31	32	33	34	35	36
	(Be7)............		...Nbd7............			....c5(j)
5	Nf3 h6		e3 c6(c)			cxd5 cxd4(k)
6	Bxf6 Bxf6	Bh4 0–0	Nf3............ Qa5 (Cambridge Springs Defense)		Bd3 dxc4	Qxd4 Be7
7	Qb3 c6	Rc1 dxc4	cxd5....... Nxd5(d)	Nd2 dxc4(g)	Bxc4 Qa5	e4 Nc6
8	0–0–0!? dxc4	e3 c5	Qd2 N7b6	Bxf6 Nxf6	Bh4 b5	Qd2 Nxe4(l)
9	Qxc4 b5	Bxc4 cxd4	Bd3 Nxc3	Nxc4 Qc7	Bb3(h) b4	Nxe4 exd5
10	Qb3 a5	Nxd4 Bd7	bxc3(e) Na4	Be2 Be7	Nce2 Ba6	Bxe7 Qxe7
11	e4 a4(a)	0–0 Nc6(b)	Rc1 Nxc3(f)	0–0 0–0 ±	Nf3 Be7(i)	Qxd5 0–0(m)

(a) With a very unbalanced position, Timman–Yusupov, match, Tilburg 1986. The game continued 12 Qc2 Nd7 13 d5! cxd5 14 exd5 a3 15 dxe6 axb2† 16 Kb1 fxe6 17 Qe4 Bxc3! 18 Qxa8 0–0 19 Qc6?! (19 Bxb5 looks better; White would probably have some advantage even though his king is in danger) 19 ... b4 20 Bc4 Kh8 21 Qe4? (Timman and Yusupov agreed that 21 Rd6 was in order, keeping Black momentarily tied down; now the black pieces come out, to the detriment of the white king) 21 ... Qc7! 22 Nh4 Ne5 23 Bd3 Nxd3! (no fear of checks!) 24 Ng6† Kg8 25 Rxd3 Rxf2 26 Rf3 Rxf3 27 gxf3 Qd6 28 Qc2 e5 (with the light-squared bishop coming out, White is doomed) 29 Nh4 Be6 30 Rd1 Bd4 31 Qa4 Qd8 32 Qc6 Bd5 33 Rxd4 exd4 34 Qb5 Qa8 35 Kxb2 Qxa2† 36 Kc1 Qa1† 37 Kd2 Qc3† 38 Kd1 Bb3† 39 Resigns.

(b) Now 12 Nf3! Rc8 13 a3 Nh5 14 Bxe7 Qxe7 15 Ne4 Rfd8 16 Qd6 with advantage (Uhlmann–Kir. Georgiev, East Germany vs. Bulgaria 1986) improves over 12 Nb3 as played in Karpov–Kasparov, World Chp. 1984–85.

(c) 5 ... Bb4 is the Manhattan Variation. After 6 cxd5 exd5 7 Bd3 c5 8 Ne2! (8 Nf3 c4 9 Bc2 Qa5 gives Black play) 8 ... cxd4 (8 ... c4 9 Bc2 h6 10 Bh4 0–0 11 0–0 Be7 12 f3 ±, Kmoch–Fine, Amsterdam 1936) 9 Nxd4 h6 10 Bh4 0–0 11 0–0 ±, Pleci–Marshall, Liège 1930.

(d) 7 ... Ne4 8 dxe6 fxe6 9 Qa4 Qxa4 10 Nxa4 Bb4† 11 Ke2 b5 12 Nc5 ± (Filip).

(e) 10 0–0, played in Vladimirov–Sabanov, Tashkent 1987, is unclear after 10 ... Nba4 11 a3 h6 12 Bh4 Nxb2.

(f) After 12 0–0 Bb4 either 13 a3 or 13 Qb2 gives White compensation for the pawn.

(g) 7 ... Bb4 8 Qc2 0–0 (8 ... dxc4 9 Bxf6 Nxf6 10 Nxc4 Qc7 11 g3 ±, Capablanca–Alekhine, World Chp. 1927) 9 a3 Ne4 10 Nxce4 dxe4 11 Bh4 ±.

(h) 9 Bd3 Bb7 10 Ne2 a6 =, Capablanca–Alekhine, World Chp. 1927.

(i) 12 0–0 0–0 13 Re1 Rfe8 14 Nf4 c5 15 e4 c4 16 Ba4 Bb5 17 Bc2 Nf8 18 e5 Nd5 19 Nxd5 exd5 20 Bxe7 Rxe7 and White's kingside chances are balanced by Black's on the queen-side, Korchnoi–Ljubojević, Tilburg 1986.

(j) If 4 . . . Bb4 5 cxd5 exd5 6 e3 0–0 7 a3 Bxc3† 8 bxc3 ±, Djurić–Kovačević, Yugoslavia 1983.

(k) 5 . . . Qb6 (the Canal Variation) 6 Bxf6 Qxb2 7 Rc1 gxf6 8 e3 cxd4 9 exd4 Bb4 10 Bb5† Bd7 11 Bxd7† Nxd7 12 Ne2 Bxc3 13 Rxc3 ±, Spassky–Uitumen, Sochi 1966.

(l) (A) 8 . . . exd5 9 Bxf6 Bxf6 10 exd5 ±. (B) 8 . . . Nxd5 9 exd5 Bxg5 10 f4 Bh4† 11 g3 exd5 12 gxh4 Qxh4† 13 Qf2 ± (Filip).

(m) 12 f3 Nb4 13 Qc4 Be6 14 Qc5 Qxc5 15 Nxc5 Nc2† 16 Kd2 with a good edge for White (Korchnoi).

QUEEN'S GAMBIT DECLINED

Lasker's Defense

1 d4 d5 2 c4 e6 3 Nc3 Nf6 4 Bg5 Be7 5 e3 0–0 6 Nf3 h6 7 Bh4 Ne4 8 Bxe7 Qxe7

	37	38	39	40	41	42
9	cxd5...				Qc2(k)......	Rc1
	Nxc3				c6	c6
10	bxc3				Nxe4	Qc2(n)
	exd5				dxe4	Nxc3
11	Qb3..............................			Bd3	Qxe4	Qxc3
	Qd6 ....Rd8.........c6			c5	Qb4†	Nd7(o)
12	c4(a)	c4	Be2(g)	0–0	Nd2	a3
	dxc4	Nc6	Nd7	Nc6(i)	Qb2	dxc4
13	Bxc4	cxd5	0–0	h3	Rb1	Bxc4
	Nd7(b)	Na5(d)	Nf6	Be6	Qa2(l)	b6
14	0–0	Qc3(e)	c4	Re1	Bd3	0–0
	Nb6(c)	b6(f)	dxc4(h)	Rfd8(j)	f5(m)	Bb7(p)

(a) 12 Bd3 Nd7 13 0–0 c5 14 Qa3 Qc7 =, Bilek–Donner, Budapest 1961.

(b) 13 ... Nc6 14 Qc3 Bg4 15 Be2 is worse for Black, Gilg–Keller, West Germany 1970.

(c) After 15 Rfc1 Nxc4 16 Qxc4 c6 17 a4 White has the better of it (Flohr).

(d) 13 ... Qb4† 14 Nd2 Qxb3 15 Nxb3 Nb4 16 Rc1 (P. Nikolić) gives White a small edge in the ending.

(e) 14 Qb5, as in P. Nikolić–Inkiov, Baile Herculaine 1983, also leads to a slightly better ending for White.

(f) 15 Bd3 Bb7 16 0–0 ± (Beliavsky).

(g) 12 Bd3 and 12 c4 are also possible.

(h) After 15 Bxc4 White has a slight pull (Neistadt).

(i) 12 ... Bg4 is a suggestion of Uhlmann's that is worth trying.

(j) The position is better for White, Uhlmann–Averbakh, Polanica Zdroj 1975.

(k) 9 Nxe4 dxe4 10 Nd2 f5 11 Be2 Nd7 12 0–0 c5 is unclear (Beliavsky).

(l) 13 ... Qc3 14 Qd3 Qa5 15 Be2 was disadvantageous for Black in Taimanov–Cvetković, Moscow 1956.

(m) White has play for his pawn, and the game is roughly balanced.

(n) 10 Nxe4 dxe4 11 Nd2 f5 12 c5 Nd7 13 Nc4 e5 =, Capablanca–Rubinstein, Budapest 1929.

(o) 11 ... dxc4 is possible here. Hort–Donner, Wijk aan Zee 1970, continued 12 Bxc4 b6 13 0–0 Bb7 14 e4 c5 15 d5 exd5 16 exd5 Nd7 =.

(p) After 16 Be2 c5 17 dxc5 Nxc5 18 Rfd1 Rfd8 19 b4 Rxd1 20 Bxd1 Nd7, Geller rates the position as equal.

QUEEN'S GAMBIT DECLINED

Tartakower Variation

1 d4 d5 2 c4 e6 3 Nc3 Nf6 4 Bg5 Be7 5 e3 0–0 6 Nf3 h6 7 Bh4 b6

	43	44	45	46	47	48
8	cxd5		Bd3	Rc1	Qc2	Bxf6(m)
	Nxd5		Bb7(f)	Bb7	Bb7	Bxf6
9	Bxe7		0–0	Bxf6	Bxf6	cxd5
	Qxe7		c5	Bxf6	Bxf6	exd5
10	Nxd5		dxc5	cxd5	cxd5	Be2
	exd5		dxc4(g)	exd5	exd5	Be6
11	Rc1	Be2	Bxc4	Be2	0–0–0	0–0
	Be6	Be6	Qxd1	Qe7(i)	c5	c5
12	Qa4(a)	0–0	Rfxd1	0–0	dxc5	Rc1
	c5	c5(d)	Bxc5	Rd8	Nd7(k)	Nd7
13	Qa3	b3	Ne5	Qb3	c6(l)	Ba6
	Rc8	Rc8	Rc8	c5	Bxc6	Qc7
14	Be2(b)	Rc1	Be2	dxc5	Nd4	b4
	Kf8	a5	Be7	bxc5	Bb7	c4
15	dxc5	Bb5	Nc4	Rfd1	g4	e4
	bxc5(c)	Nd7(e)	Nc6(h)	d4(j)	Ne5 $\mp$	dxe4(n)

(a) 12 Be2 c5 13 b3 Rc8 14 0–0 Nd7 = .

(b) 14 Bb5 Qb7 (an improvement on 14 . . . a6 15 dxc5 bxc5 16 0–0 Ra7 17 Be2 Nd7 18 Nd4 $\pm$, Fischer–Spassky, World Chp. 1972) 15 dxc5 bxc5 16 Rxc5 Rxc5 17 Qxc5 Na6 =, Timman–Geller, Hilversum 1973.

(c) 16 0–0 a5 17 Rc3 Nd7 18 Rb3 (Winants–Kasparov, Brussels 1987) and now 18 . . . a4 would have equalized (Kasparov).

(d) 12 . . . Nd7 13 Qa4 c5 14 Rfd1 Rfc8 15 Ne1 c4 with chances for both sides, Larsen–Petursson, Reykjavik 1985.

(e) The position is equal, Najdorf–Gheorghiu, Lugano 1968.

(f) 8 . . . dxc4 and 8 . . . c5 are also playable (Karpov).

(g) 10 . . . bxc5 is probably a better try.

(h) Now 16 Nb5 keeps a big edge. In Beliavsky–Karpov, Tilburg 1986, White erred with 16 Bxf6? gxf6 17 Bf3 Na5 18 Bxb7 Nxb7 19 Rd7 Bb4 20 Rxb7 Rxc4 21 Rd1 Bxc3 22 bxc3 Rxc3 23 g3 Ra3 Draw.

(i) 11 . . . Nd7 and 11 . . . c5 are worth considering.

(j) Garcia-Gonzales–Beliavsky, Moscow 1982. Black has reasonable chances.

(k) 12 . . . Bxc3 13 Qxc3 Nd7 14 c6 Bxc6 15 Kb1 Rc8 16 Qd4 $\pm$, Averkin–Chandler, Sochi 1982.

(l) 13 Nxd5 Nc5 14 Bc4 b5 is dangerous for White, as in Kasparov–Zaitsev, Baku 1980, and Ghitescu–Lputian, West Berlin 1982.

(m) 8 Be2 Bb7 9 Rc1 dxc4 10 Bxc4 Nbd7 is about equal. Kasparov–Karpov, 36th game of the 1984–85 World Chp. match entertainingly continued 11 0–0 c5 12 dxc5 Nxc5 13 Qe2 a6 14 Rfd1 Qe8 15 Ne5 b5 16 Nxb5?! axb5? (16 . . . Qb8! would have cast great doubt on White's bold play; after 17 Bg3 axb5 18 Ng6 fxg6! 19 Bxb8 bxc4 20 Bg3 Rxa2 [Geller], Black's three pieces would be much more effective than White's queen. Now Kasparov is rewarded for his daring) 17 Bxb5 Ba6 18 Rxc5! Bxc5 19 Bxa6 (with aggressive pieces and two pawns for the exchange, White is clearly better) 19 . . . Qa4 20 Bxf6 gxf6 21 Bb5 Qxa2 22 Nd7 Be7 23 Qg4† Kh8 24 Nxf8 Bxf8 25 Qf3 Be7 26 Bc4 (much better is 26 Rd7; White begins to play indecisively and lets Black escape into an ending with bishops of opposite colors) 26 . . . Qa7 27 Qh5 Kg7 28 Qg4† Kf8 29 Bf1 Rd8 30 Rc1 Qb8 31 Rc2 f5 32 Qe2 Kg7 33 g3 Rc8 34 h3 Rxc2 35 Qxc2 (now the draw is certain) 35 . . . Bf6 36 b3 Qb4 37 Qd1 Qc3 38 Kg2 Qc6† 39 Kh2 Qc5 40 Be2 Be7 41 Kg2 Draw. In here, a promising idea is 9 Bxf6 Bxf6 10 cxd5 exd5 11 b4 c5 12 bxc5 bxc5 13 Rb1 Qa5 14 0–0! ±, Seirawan–Karpov, Brussels 1988.

(n) 16 Nxe4 Qc6 =, Dlugy–Alburt, New York 1983.

QUEEN'S GAMBIT DECLINED

Exchange Variation

1 d4 d5 2 c4 e6 3 Nc3 Nf6 4 cxd5 exd5 5 Bg5 c6 6 Qc2

	49	50	51	52	53	54
	Be7					Na6(m)
7	e3					a3(n)
	Nbd7					Nc7
8	Bd3					e3
	0–0			Nf8	Nh5	Be7
9	Nf3			Nf3	Bxe7	Bxf6
	Re8			Ne6	Qxe7	Bxf6
10	0–0		0–0–0	Bh4	Nge2	Bd3
	Nf8(a)		Nf8	g6	Nf8(k)	Qe7
11	Rab1	Rae1	h3	0–0(i)	0–0–0	Nge2
	a5(b)	Be6(d)	Be6(f)	Ng7	Bg4	Bg4
12	a3	Ne5	g4	b4	Kb1	0–0
	Ne4	N6d7	Qa5(g)	a6	Bxe2	Bxe2
13	Bxe7	Bxe7	Kb1	Rab1	Qxe2	Nxe2
	Qxe7(c)	Rxe7(e)	Rac8(h)	Bf5(j)	Nf6(l)	g6(o)

(a) 10 . . . g6!? was played in Izeta–Andersson, Bilbao 1987. After 11 Rae1 Nh5 12 Bxe7 Rxe7 13 b4 Ndf6 14 Ne5 Ng7 Black achieved equality.

(b) 11 . . . Be6 12 b4 a6 13 Na4 Nbd7 14 Bxe7 Qxe7 15 Nc5 $\pm$, Portisch–Yusupov, Bugojno 1986. 11 . . . g6, 11 . . . Bd6, 11 . . . Ng6 and 11 . . . Ne4 are also possible, but White gets a slight pull in every case.

(c) After 14 b4 Bf5 15 Bxe4 dxe4 16 Ne5 White is better, Gligorić–Larsen, Copenhagen 1965. In the column, more comfortable for White is 9 Nge7 Re8 10 0–0 Nf8 11 f3 Be6 12 Rae1 Rc8 13 Kh1 Nbd7 14 Be7 Rxe7 15 Nf4 $\pm$, Kasparov–Andersson, Belfort 1988.

(d) 11 . . . Ng6 12 Ne5 Ng4 13 Bxe7 Qxe7 14 Nxg4 Bxg4 15 f3 $\pm$, Bagirov–Zilberstein, USSR 1972.

(e) The game Razuvaev–Beliavsky, Sochi 1986, continued 14 f4 f6 15 Nf3 Nb6 16 f5 Bf7 17 g4 with a slight plus for White.

(f) 11 . . . a5 12 g4 a4 13 Nxa4 (13 Kb1 may be better) 13 . . . Qa5 14 Bxf6 Bxf6 15 b3 b5 16 Nc5 Qxa2 =, Gheorghiu–Spassky, USSR 1981.

(g) 12 . . . Ne4 13 Bxe7 Qxe7 is also playable, Cebalo–Kovačević, Vinkovći 1982.

(h) After 14 Rc1 Ne4 15 Bxe4 dxe4 16 Bxe7 Rxe7 17 Nd2 Rce8 the position is unclear, Quinteros–Andersson, Mar del Plata 1981.

(i) 11 h3 stops the trade of light-squared bishops. After 11 . . . Ng7 12 g4 0–0 13 0–0–0 White was slightly better in Suetin–Espig, Kecskemet 1972.

(j) 15 b5 axb5 16 axb5 Bxd3 17 Qxd3 $\pm$, Larsen–Smyslov, Copenhagen 1985.

(k) 10 . . . Nb6 11 0–0 g6 12 Na4 gives White a slight plus, R. Byrne–Eliskases, Helsinki 1952.

(l) After 14 Rc1 0–0–0 15 Rc2 Kb8 White enjoyed an edge in Antoshin–Chistiakov, USSR 1960.

(m) 6 . . . Bd6 7 Nf3 0–0 8 e3 Bg4 9 Ne5 Bh5 10 f4 led to a substantial advantage for White in Petrosian–Tolush, USSR 1950.

(n) 7 e3 Nb4 8 Qd2 Bf5 9 Rc1 a5 10 a3 Na6 11 Nge2 Be7 = , Petrosian–Spassky, Amsterdam 1973.

(o) White has a slight edge, Bronstein–Bykhovsky, USSR 1962.

QUEEN'S GAMBIT DECLINED

Exchange Variation

1 d4 d5 2 c4 e6 3 Nc3 Nf6 4 cxd5 exd5

	55	56	57	58	59	60
5	(Bg5)..				Nf3........	Bf4
	(c6)			Be7	c6	Be7
6	e3			e3	Bf4	e3(n)
	Bf5	Nbd7	Be7	Nbd7	Bf5	0–0
7	Qf3	Bd3	Bd3	Bd3	e3	Nf3
	Bg6	Bd6	Ne4	Nf8	Bd6(k)	Bf5
8	Bxf6	Nf3	Bxe7(g)	Nf3	Bxd6	h3
	Qxf6(a)	Nf8(d)	Qxe7	Ne6	Qxd6	c6
9	Qxf6	Qc2	Nf3	Bh4	Be2(l)	g4
	gxf6	Ng6	Nd7	g6	0–0	Bg6
10	Kd2(b)	Nh4(e)	Qc2	0–0	0–0	Ne5
	Nd7	0–0	f5	0–0	Nbd7	Nfd7
11	Bd3	0–0–0	0–0	b4	a3	Nxg6
	Bd6	h6	0–0	Ng7(i)	Rfe8	fxg6
12	h4	Nxg6	Rfe1	b5	b4	Bg2(o)
	h5(c)	fxg6(f)	a5(h)	Bf5(j)	a6(m)	Nb6(p)

(a) 8 ... gxf6 is worse after 9 Qd1 Qb6 10 Qd2 Na6 13 Nf3 ±, Petrosian–Barcza, Budapest 1955.

(b) 10 g3 Nd7 11 Bh3 Nb6 =, Tal–Spassky, Sochi 1973.

(c) White is a little better, Geller–de Grieff, Havana 1963.

(d) 8 ... 0–0 is risky. After 9 Qc2 h6 10 Bh4 Re8 11 g4 White had a very strong attack in Li Zunian–R. Rodriguez, Penang 1984.

(e) 10 0–0–0 h6 11 Bxg6 hxg5 12 Nxg5 fxg6 13 Qxg6† Kd7 is unclear, Cebalo–Ljubojević, Yugoslavia 1982.

(f) White has a small edge, Bagirov–Taimanov, USSR 1977.

(g) 8 Bf4 Bf5 9 f3 Nxc3 10 bxc3 ± (Cebalo).

(h) White is better, Taimanov–Janošević, Vrnjačka Banja 1974.

(i) If 11 ... a6 12 a4 c6 13 Qb3 Ng7 14 b5 ±, Petrosian–Birbrager, USSR 1966.

(j) White has the advantage, Gligorić–Medina, Palma de Mallorca 1967.

(k) 7 ... Qb6 8 Bd3 Bxd3 9 Qxd3 Qxb2 10 0–0 is unclear (Matanović and Ugrinović).

(l) 9 Bd3 Bxd3 10 Qxd3 Nbd7 led to nothing in Cramling–Antunes, Torremolinos 1985.

(m) The position is balanced, Meduna–Panchenko, Sochi 1983.

(n) 6 Qc2 0–0 7 e3 c5 8 dxc5 Bxc5 9 Nf3 Nc6 10 Be2 d4 =, Karpov–Kasparov, World Chp. 1985.

(o) 12 Bd3 Nb6 13 Qe2 c5 and Black has counterplay (Karpov).

(p) The position is about equal. Karpov–Kasparov, World Chp. 1985, continued 13 0–0 Kh8 14 Ne2 g5 15 Bg3 Bd6 16 Qd3 Na6 17 b3 Qe7 18 Bxd6 Qxd6 19 f4 gxf4 20 exf4 Rae8 21 f5 Nc7 22 Rf2 Nd7 23 g5 Qe7 24 h4 Qe3 25 Rd1 Nb5 26 Qxe3 Rxe3 27 Kh2 Nb6 28 Ng3 Nc8 29 Nf1 Re7 (perhaps 29 . . . Rc3 could be tried) 30 Rd3 Ncd6 31 Ng3 Ne4 (probably the losing move; Karpov gives 31 . . . Kg8 as better, but Kasparov actually claims an advantage for Black after 31 . . . Re1) 32 Bxe4 ± dxe4 33 Re3 Nxd4 34 Kh3 Rc5 35 Kg4 h5? (the final error—35 . . . Kg8 is better) 36 Kxh5† Nxf5 37 Rxf5 Rfxf5 38 Nxf5 Rxf5 39 Re4 Kh7 40 Re7 b5 41 Ra7 b4 42 Kg4 Resigns.

QUEEN'S GAMBIT DECLINED

Classical Variation with Bf4

1 d4 d5 2 c4 e6 3 Nc3 Nf6 4 Nf3 Be7 5 Bf4 0–0 6 e3 c5 7 dxc5 Bxc5

	61	62	63	64	65	66
8	Qc2..cxd5........Be2					
	Nc6				Nxd5(l)	dxc4
9	Rd1................................a3				Nxd5	Bxc4
	Qa5				Qa5	exd5	Qxd1†
10	a3(a)			Nd2	Bd3(m)	Rxd1
	Be7			Bb4(j)	Bb4†	a6
11	Nd2....................Rd2			cxd5	Ke2	Bd3
	e5		Ne4	exd5	Nc6	Nbd7
12	Nb3........Bg3		Nxe4	Nb3	Qc2	Rc1
	Qb6(b)	d4(e)	dxe4	Bxc3†	h6	b6
13	Bg5	Nb3	Qxe4	bxc3	Rhd1	Ne4
	d4	Qb6	Rd8(h)	Qa4	Qf6	Bb7
14	Bxf6(c)	exd4	Be2	Bd3	Kf1	Nxc5
	Bxf6	Bf5	Rxd2	b6	Ba5	Nxc5
15	Nd5	Bd3(f)	Nxd2	f3	Be2	Be2
	Qd8(d)	Bxd3(g)	e5(i)	Ba6(k)	Bb6(n)	Rfc8(o)

(a) 10 Nd2 Bb4 11 Nb3 Qb6 12 Bd3 e5 13 Bg5 d4 14 Bxf6 gxf6 is equal, Littlewood–Speelman, Hastings 1981–82.

(b) 12 ... Qc7 13 Bg5 d4 14 Bxf6 Bxf6 15 Nd5 with a minimal advantage for White (Karpov).

(c) 14 c5 Qd8 15 Bb5 Ng4 16 Bxe7 Qxe7 17 exd4 exd4† 18 Ne2 Qh4 19 g3 Qh3 is bad for White, Doroshevich–Plisetsky, USSR 1979.

(d) 16 Bd3 g6 17 exd4 Nxd4 18 Nxd4 exd4 =, Korchnoi–Karpov, World Chp. 1978.

(e) A speculative line is 12 ... Bg4 13 f3 Be6 14 Nb3 Qd8 15 cxd5 Bxd5 16 Bc4 Bxc4 17 Rxd8 Rfxd8, Toth–Barbero, Switzerland 1986.

(f) If 15 Qxf5 Qxb3 16 dxe5 Qxb2 17 Nb5 a6 18 Rb1 Qa2 19 Bd3 g6 Black stands slightly better, B. Archangelsky–S. Nikolov, Sofia 1986.

(g) 16 Rxd3 Nxd4 17 Nxd4 exd4 =, Glek–Averkin, USSR 1983.

(h) Also possible is 13 ... f5 14 Qc2 e5 15 Bg5 Bxg5 16 Nxg5 h6 17 Nf3 e4 18 Nd4 Nxd4 19 exd4 f4, Bareyev–Goldin, USSR 1983. Black has good play for his pawn.

(i) After 16 Bg3 Be6 17 Qc2 Rd8 Black has more than enough for the pawn (Karpov).

(j) 10 ... Be7 is quite playable. After 11 Nb3 Qb6 Black is equal (Karpov).

(k) The position is balanced, according to Agdestein, but 10 0–0–0 Be7 11 g4! is strong (Speelman).

(l) For 8 ... exd5 see columns 91–92.

(m) 10 a3 Nc6 11 Bd3 Bb6 (11 . . . Be7 12 0–0 Be6 13 Ne5 gives White a fairly substantial positional edge, Kraidman–Radashkovich, Netanya 1973) 12 0–0 Bg4 = , Seirawan–Kir. Georgiev, Dubai 1986. After 13 h3 Bh5 14 b4 a6 15 Ra2!? d4 16 e4 Bc7 17 Bxc7 Qxc7 White played the dubious 18 g4?!, weakening his kingside, and went down to defeat. 18 Rc2 intending 19 Rc5 (Georgiev) is a better plan.

(n) With equality, Quinteros–Najdorf, Mar del Plata 1982.

(o) The position is equal, Donner–Benko, Wijk aan Zee 1972. This line is too tame to lead to any advantage for White.

QUEEN'S GAMBIT DECLINED
Classical Variation with Bf4

1 d4 d5 2 c4 e6 3 Nc3 Nf6 4 Nf3 Be7 5 Bf4 0–0 6 e3

	67	68	69	70	71	72
	(c5).............................			b6..........	Nbd7	c6
7	(dxc5)			Rc1(h)	cxd5	h3(n)
	Nc6		Qa5	c5(i)	Nxd5	Nbd7
8	cxd5		a3	cxd5	Nxd5	Qc2
	exd5(a)		dxc4	exd5(j)	exd5	a6
9	Be2		Bxc4	Be2	Bd3	Rd1
	Bxc5		Qxc5	Bb7	c6(l)	b5(o)
10	0–0		Qe2	0–0	0–0	c5
	Be6		a6(f)	Nbd7	Nf6	b4
11	Ne5.........	Rc1	b4	Ne5	Rc8	Na4
	Bd6(b)	Rc8	Qh5	Rc8	Qc2	a5
12	Nxc6	a3(d)	0–0	dxc5	h3	Bd3
	bxc6	h6	b5	Nxc5	Bd6	Ba6
13	Qa4	Bg3	Bd3	Nf3	Be5	Bxa6
	Bxf4(c)	Bb6(e)	Bb7(g)	Nfe4(k)	g6(m)	Rxa6(p)

(a) 8 . . . Nxd5 9 Nxd5 exd5 10 Bd3 (10 a3 Bxc5 is column 89, note m) is better for White.

(b) 11 . . . Ne7 12 Bf3 favors White (Mikhalchishin).

(c) After 14 Qxf4 c5 15 b3 White was a little better in Mikhalchishin–Beliavsky, USSR 1981.

(d) If 12 Nb5 Ne4 13 Nd2 Nxd2 14 Qxd2 Bb4 15 Qd1 Qb6 =, Korchnoi–Kasparov, Brussels 1986.

(e) Fischer–Spassky, World Chp. 1972, White has a small plus.

(f) Two other possibilities are 10 . . . Nd5 (Trifunović) and 10 . . . b6 (Taimanov).

(g) Tal–Zuidema, Wijk aan Zee 1973, White stands much better.

(h) 7 cxd5 exd5 8 Bd3 c5 9 0–0 Bb7 10 Ne5 Na6 offers Black equal prospects, Bagirov–Lputian, Erevan 1982.

(i) 7 . . . Bb7 8 cxd5 Nxd5 9 Bg3 c5 10 Bd3 $\pm$, Rajković–Kapelan, Vrsać 1983.

(j) 8 . . . Nxd5 9 Nxd5 exd5 10 Bd3 Nd7 11 0–0 Bb7 12 Qc2 g6 13 dxc5 was much better for White in Agdestein–Spassky, Gjovik 1983.

(k) White has a slight edge, Gheorghiu–Ree, Wijk aan Zee 1981.

(l) 9 . . . Bd6 10 Bxd6 cxd6 11 0–0 Nf6 12 Qb3 $\pm$, Meduna–Prandstetter, Trnava 1981.

(m) With a small advantage for White (Minev).

(n) 7 Qc2 and 7 Bd3 are both quite possible (Samarian).

(o) 9 . . . Re8 10 a3 Nf8 11 c5 Nbd7 12 Be2 ±, Gheorghiu–Westerinen, Palma de Mallorca 1968.

(p) White has a small edge, Bagirov–A. Petrosian, Riga 1981.

QUEEN'S GAMBIT DECLINED

Ragozin System

1 d4 d5 2 c4 e6 3 Nc3 Nf6 4 Nf3 Bb4

	73	74	75	76	77	78
5	Bg5 ....cxd5 ....Qa4†					
	dxc4 ....h6			exd5		Nc6
6	e4		Bxf6(g)	Bg5		Ne5
	c5		Qxf6	h6 ....Nbd7		Bd7
7	e5 ....Bxc4		e3	Bh4	e3	Nxd7
	cxd4	cxd4	0–0	g5	c5	Qxd7
8	Qa4†(a)	Nxd4	Rc1	Bg3	Bd3	a3(n)
	Nc6	Bxc3†(d)	c6	Ne4	c4	Bxc3†
9	0–0–0	bxc3	a3	Nd2(i)	Bf5	bxc3
	h6(b)	Nbd7	Bxc3†	Nxg3(j)	Qa5	0–0
10	exf6	0–0	Rxc3	hxg3	Qc2	e3
	hxg5	Qa5	Nd7	c5	0–0(l)	a6
11	fxg7	Bxf6(e)	Qc2	a3	0–0	Qc2
	Rg8	Nxf6	dxc4	Bxc3	Re8	Na5
12	Nxd4	Bb5†	Bxc4	bxc3	Nd2	cxd5
	Bxc3(c)	Bd7(f)	e5(h)	Nc6(k)	g6(m)	exd5(o)

(a) Ribli played 8 Nxd4 against Chernin in Subotica 1987, and after 8 . . . Qa5 9 exf6 Bxc3† 10 bxc3 Qxg5 11 fxg7 Qxg7 12 Qf3, even the best reply, 12 . . . 0–0, still slightly favors White after 13 Bxc4 (Ribli).

(b) The older 9 . . . Bd7 favors White after 10 Ne4 Be7 11 exf6 gxf6 12 Bh4 Rc8 13 Kb1 Na5 14 Qc2 e5. After 15 Nxd4 exd4 16 Rxd4 Qb6 17 Rxd7 White's attack is extremely strong (Gipslis).

(c) 13 bxc3 Qa5 14 Qxa5 Nxa5 15 h4 g4 16 h5 $\pm$, Timman–Karpov, Amsterdam 1987.

(d) After 8 . . . Qa5 9 Bxf6 both 9 . . . Bxc3† 10 bxc3 Qxc3† 11 Kf1 and 9 . . . gxf6 10 0–0 are too dangerous for Black, as many old pawns have shown.

(e) 11 Bh4 involves a pawn sacrifice: 11 . . . 0–0 12 Qe2 Qxc3 13 Nb5.

(f) (A) 13 e5 Bxb5 14 Nxb5 Qxb5 15 exf6 gxf6 16 Qf3 Draw, Stempin–Adamski, Poland 1987. (B) 13 Rb1 Rd8 14 e5 Nd5 15 c4 Ne7 is equal, according to Yusupov (Lputian–Yusupov, USSR 1987).

(g) 6 Bh4 dxc4 7 a4 c6 8 Qc2 b5 is better for Black, Aseyev–Novikov, Vilnius 1984.

(h) After 12 d5 c5 White has a small advantage (Gipslis).

(i) Not 9 Rc1 h5 10 Qa4† Nc6 $\mp$ (Korchnoi).

(j) 9 . . . Nxc3 10 bxc3 Bxc3 11 Rc1 Ba5 12 Qc2 Nc6 13 e3 0–0 14 h4 is better for White, Korchnoi–Khasin, USSR Chp. 1961.

(k) On 13 e3 Qa5 14 a4 a6 the position is unclear.

(l) Not 10 . . . Nc5 11 Bxf6 Bxf5 12 Qxf5 Bxc3† 13 bxc3 Qxc3† 14 Ke2 Nd3 15 Bh4 ±.

(m) After 13 Bh3 White has a small advantage, Tukmakov–Kovačević, Hastings 1982–83.

(n) 8 e3 e5 9 dxe5 d4 10 a3 Bxc3† 11 bxc3 dxe3 12 Bxe3 Ng4 is good for Black, Spielmann–Fine, Zandvoort 1936.

(o) The position is balanced, Porreca–Minev, Zagreb 1955.

QUEEN'S GAMBIT DECLINED
Semi-Tarrasch Defense

1 d4 d5 2 c4 e6 3 Nc3 Nf6 4 Nf3 c5 5 cxd5 Nxd5 6 e3 Nc6 7 Bd3

	79	80	81	82	83	84
	cxd4				Be7	
8	exd4				0–0	
	Be7				0–0	
9	0–0				Nxd5	a3
	0–0				Qxd5	Nxc3
10	Re1				e4(h)	bxc3
	Bf6		Nf6	Qd6	Qh5(i)	b6
11	Be4		a3	a3	dxc5	Bb2(k)
	Qd6	Nce7	b6(e)	Rd8	Bxc5	Bb7
12	Nb5(a)	Ne5(c)	Bg5	Qc2	Bf4	Qe2
	Qb8	g6	Bb7	h6	b6	Qc7
13	g3	Bh6	Bc2	Nxd5	a3	Rad1
	Bd7	Bg7	Rc8	Qxd5	Rd8	Bf6
14	Nc3	Bxg7	Qd3	Be3(f)	b4	e4
	Nce7(b)	Kxg7(d)	g6 ±	Bd7(g)	Be7(j)	g6 ±(l)

(a) (A) 12 Bg5 Bxg5 13 Ng5 led to White's advantage in Gheorghiu–Petursson, Lone Pine 1979. (B) 12 Ng5 g6 13 Nxh7 is a draw. (C) 12 Bc2 with the idea of Ne4 is possible (Portisch).

(b) After 15 Bxd5 Nxd5 16 Nxd5 exd5 Black equalized in Beliavsky–Portisch, Reggio Emilia 1986–87.

(c) 12 Qd3 g6 (12 . . . h6 13 Ne5 Nxc3 14 Qxc3 Nf5 15 Be3 ±, Karpov–Timman, Moscow 1981) 13 Bh6 Bg7 14 Bxg7 Kxg7 15 Rfe1 b6 =, Miles–Portisch, Bugojno 1978.

(d) White had an advantage after 15 Rc1 b6 16 Nxd5 Nxd5 17 Bxd5, Smyslov–Ribli, London 1983.

(e) 11 . . . Qd6 12 Be3 Rd8 13 Qc2 Bd7 14 Rad1 Rac8 15 Bg5 led to White's advantage in Karpov–Hort, Malta 1980.

(f) Tal's suggestion, 14 Be4 Nxd4 15 Nxd4 Qxd4 16 Be3 with active play for the pawn, is worth considering.

(g) The position is approximately equal, Spassky–Korchnoi, match 1968.

(h) 10 Qc2 Qh5 11 Be4 cxd4 12 exd4 Bd7 =, Stein–Tukmakov, Reykjavik 1972.

(i) 10 . . . Qd8, played in Kasparov–Begun, USSR 1978, is weaker: 11 dxc5 Bxc5 12 e5 ±.

(j) The position is equal, Keres–Tal, Zürich 1959.

(k) 11 c4 Bf6 12 Bb2 cxd4 13 exd4 Bb7 =, Karpov–Moiseyev, USSR 1971.

(l) Psakhis–Sveshnikov, Sochi 1985. The game continued 15 h4 Rfd8 16 e5 Bg7 17 h5 Rac8 18 Bb1 Qe7 19 Bc1 Na5 20 hxg6 hxg6 21 Be4 cxd4 22 cxd4 Qc7 23 Bxb7 Qxb7 24 Bg5

Rd7 (24 . . . Rd5 is better) 25 Qe3 Nc6 26 Rd3 Rd5 27 Rc1 Qd7 28 Nh2 Bxe5 29 Ng4 Bg7 30 Nf6† Bxf6 31 Bxf6 Rh5 (forced; if 31 . . . Rf5 32 Qh6 Rxf6 33 Rh3) 32 g4 Rh7 33 Rdc3 e5 34 Qe4 Ne7 35 Rxc8† Nxc8 36 dxe5 Rh3 37 Kg2 (37 e6 is better) 37 . . . Rh6 38 Kg3 Kh7 39 Rh1 Qd2 40 Rxh6† Qxh6 41 Qb7 Qf8 42 Kg2 Qe8 43 f4 Kg8 44 f5 Kh7 45 e6 gxf5 46 Qxf7† Resigns. A vigorously prosecuted attack by Psakhis.

QUEEN'S GAMBIT DECLINED

Semi-Tarrasch Defense

1 d4 d5 2 c4 e6 3 Nc3 Nf6 4 Nf3 c5 5 cxd5 Nxd5

	85	86	87	88	89	90
6	(e3)			e4		
	(Nc6)			Nxc3		
7	Bc4			bxc3		
	cxd4		Be7	cxd4		
8	exd4		Bxd5	cxd4		
	Be7		exd5	Bb4†		Nc6
9	0–0		dxc5	Bd2		Bc4
	0–0		Be6	Bxd2†(h)		b5
10	Re1(a)		0–0(f)	Qxd2		Be2(l)
	a6(b)........Nxc3		Bxc5	0–0		Bb4†
11	Bb3	bxc3	b3	Bc4		Bd2
	Nxc3	b6	0–0	Nc6........Nd7		Bxd2†(m)
12	bxc3	Bd3	Bb2	0–0	0–0	Qxd2
	b5	Bb7	a6	b6(i)	Nf6	a6
13	Qd3	h4(d)	Na4	Rad1	Rfe1	a4
	Ra7(c)	Na5(e)	Bb7(g)	Bd7(j)	b6(k)	bxa4(n)

(a) (A) 10 Bxd5 exd5 11 Qb3 Bg4 =. (B) 10 Qe2 Nb6 11 Rd1 Nxc4 =, Uhlmann–Szabó, Moscow 1956.

(b) 10 ... b6 11 Nxd5 exd5 12 Bb5 Bd7 13 Qa4 ±, Botvinnik–Alekhine, AVRO 1938.

(c) Better is 13 ... Bb7. White now has an advantage. The column is A. Sokolov–Karpov, match 1987.

(d) 13 Qe2 Na5 14 Ne5 Rc8 15 Bb2 Bd6 16 Qh5 f5, Larsen–Ribli, Las Palmas 1982. Black has a small edge.

(e) 13 ... Bxh4 14 Nxh4 Qxh4 15 Re3 f5 16 Re6 Nd4 is uncertain, while the position after 13 ... Na5 is unbalanced but equal.

(f) 10 Nd4 0–0 11 Nxc6 bxc6 12 Qd4 Bf6 13 Qa4 d4 =, Uhlmann–Hort, Madrid 1973.

(g) White has the edge, Larsen–Tal, match 1969.

(h) 9 ... a5 10 Rb1 Bxd2† 11 Qxd2 Qxd2† 12 Kxd2 gives White the better ending, Comments.

(i) 12 ... Qd6 13 Rad1 Rd8 14 Rfe1 Bd7 15 d5 exd5 16 exd5 Ne7 17 Ng5 was bad for Black in Browne–H. Olafsson, Reykjavik 1980: 17 ... Ba4? 18 Nxf7! Kxf7 19 Re6! Qxe6 (19 ... Qc5 20 Qf4† Kg8 [20 ... Ke8 21 d6] 21 Rxe7 Qxe7 22 d6† Kh8 23 dxe7 Rxd1† 24 Bf1 wins, Browne) 20 dxe6† Ke8 21 Bd3 Bxd1 22 Qxd1 Rac8 23 h3 Rd5?! 24 Qf3 Resigns.

(j) After 14 Rfe1 Rc8 15 d5 exd5 16 Bxd5 Qc7 17 e5 White has a slight pull (Hort).

(k) The move 13 . . . Bd7 worked out badly after 14 e5 Nd5 15 Bxd5 exd5 16 Rab1 b6 17 b3 ±, Smyslov–Ernst, Subotica 1987. In the column, after 14 a4 Bb7 15 Bd3 White was slightly better in Yusupov–Eslon, Ca'n Picafort 1981.

(l) 10 Bd3 Bb4† 11 Bd2 a6 12 Rc1 Bxd2† 13 Qxd2 Bb7 = , Browne–Pinter, Las Palmas 1982.

(m) 11 . . . Qa5 12 d5 exd5 13 exd5 Ne7 14 0–0 is better for White, Browne–D. Gurevich, US Chp. 1983.

(n) If 13 . . . b4 14 d5 Ftáčnik–Paulsen, Dortmund 1981, is bad for Black. In the column after 14 0–0 0–0 15 Rxa4 (Martz–Bisguier US Chp. 1973), White is slightly better.

QUEEN'S GAMBIT DECLINED

Semi-Tarrasch Defense

1 d4 d5 2 c4 e6 3 Nc3 Nf6 4 Nf3 c5

	91	92	93	94	95	96
5	(cxd5).............................e3......................Bg5					
	(Nxd5)			Nc6		cxd4
6	g3			a3		Nxd4(m)
	Nc6			Ne4........cxd4		e5
7	Bg2			Bd3(i)	exd4	Nf3
	Be7(a)			Nxc3	Be7	d4
8	0–0			bxc3	c5(j)	Nd5
	0–0			Be7	Ne4	Be7(n)
9	Nxd5...................e4			0–0	Qc2	Bxf6
	exd5		Ndb4(f)	dxc4	Nxc3	Bxf6
10	dxc5		d5(g)	Bxc4	Qxc3	e4
	Bxc5		exd5	0–0	a5(k)	dxe3
11	Qc2........Bg5		exd5	Qe2	Bb5	Nxe3
	Bb6	Qb6(d)	Nd4	Bd7	0–0	Qxd1†
12	Ng5(b)	Qxd5	a3	Bb2	b3	Rxd1
	g6(c)	Be6(e)	Nxd5(h)	Rc8 ±	Bd7(l)	e4(o)

(a) If 7 ... Nxc3 8 bxc3 cxd4 9 cxd4 Bb4† 10 Bd2 Be7 11 0–0 ±, Petrosian–Spassky, World Chp. 1966.

(b) 12 Bf4 Qf6 13 Bg5 Bf5 =, Hübner–Tukmakov, Tilburg 1984.

(c) Smyslov–Alburt, Subotica 1987, continued 13 Qd2 Nd4 14 Nf3 Qf6 15 Rd1 Nxf3† 16 Bxf3 Be6, with a small plus for White.

(d) 11 ... f6 12 Bd2 Qe7 13 Bc3 Rd8 14 e3 led to a small White advantage in Agdestein–Alburt, Taxco 1985.

(e) After 13 Qd2 h6 14 Bf4 Rfd8 15 Qc3 Rae8 Black has play for the pawn, (Parma).

(f) 9 ... Nb6 10 d5 exd5 11 exd5 Nb4 12 Ne1 Bf6 13 Be3 ± (Ftáčnik).

(g) 10 a3 cxd4 11 axb4 dxc3 12 bxc3 b6 is equal, Polugaevsky–Radulov, Skara 1980.

(h) 13 Nxd4 Nxc3 14 bxc3 cxd4 15 cxd4 Rb8 =, Ribli–Lukacs, Baile Herculaine 1982.

(i) 7 Nxe4 dxe4 8 Ne5 Nxe5 19 dxe5 Qg5 ∓, Solmundarsson–Smyslov, Reykjavik 1974.

(j) 8 Bd3 dxc4 9 Bxc4 0–0 leads to typical isolated queen-pawn positions.

(k) Better than 10 ... 0–0 11 b4 a6 12 Bf4 ±, Petrosian–F. Olafsson, Los Angeles 1963.

(l) Ivkov–Suba, Sochi 1983. Black has achieved equality; yet best in the column may be 9 ... 0–0 10 Bb2 Na5 11 Nd2 dxc4 12 Nxc4 Nxc4 13 Bxc4 Qc7 14 Qe2 Bd7 =, Uhlmann–Portisch, Thessaloniki 1988.

(m) 6 Qxd4 Be7 (6 . . . Nc6 7 Bxf6 leads to Pillsbury–Lasker, Cambridge Springs 1904) 7 cxd5 exd5 8 e3 Nc6 9 Qa4 0–0 =, Barczay–Dely, Budapest 1955.

(n) 8 . . . Nc6 9 e4 Be7 10 Bxf6 Bxf6 11 b4 ±, Euwe–Alekhine, World Chp. 1937, but 8 . . . Qa5† 9 Bd2 Qd8 might repeat the position.

(o) 13 Nd4 Nc6 14 Nb5 0–0 with equality (Filip).

QUEEN'S GAMBIT DECLINED

Tarrasch Defense

1 d4 d5 2 c4 e6 3 Nc3 c5 4 cxd5 exd5 5 Nf3 Nc6 6 g3 Nf6 7 Bg2 Be7 8 0–0 0–0 9 Bg5

	97	98	99	100	101	102
	cxd4..c4					
10	Nxd4					Ne5
	h6					Be6
11	Be3					Nxc6
	Re8 ....Bg4					bxc6
12	Rc1........Qc2.........Qa4.........Qb3				Qa4	b3
	Bg4	Bg4	Bd7(g)	Na5	Qd7(m)	Qa5
13	h3	Rfd1(d)	Rad1	Qc2	Rfd1(n)	Na4
	Be6(a)	Qd7(e)	Nb4	Bg4	Bh3	Rfd8
14	Qc2(b)	Nb3	Qb3	h3(j)	Nf3(o)	e3(p)
	Qd7	Rad8	a5	Bd7(k)	Bxg2	c5
15	Nxe6	Rac1	a4(h)	Rad1	Kxg2	Nxc5
	fxe6(c)	Be6(f)	Rc8(i)	Qc8(l)	Rfd8 $\pm$	Bxc5(q)

(a) 13 ... Bc8 14 Na4 Bd6 15 Nxc6 bxc6 16 Rxc6 Bxg3 17 Rxf6 gxf6 18 Qxd5 Qxd5 19 Bxd5 $\pm$, Shestoperov–Malevinsky, USSR 1986.

(b) 14 Nxe6 fxe6 15 f4 Qd7 16 Bf2 Red8 and the position is all right for Black, Spassky–Xu Jun, Dubai 1986.

(c) After 16 Rfd1 Rac8 17 f4 with the plan of Bf2 and e4, White is somewhat better, Marin–Petursson, match Politechnica–Taflfelag 1987.

(d) 13 h3 Be7 14 Rad1 Rc8 15 Kh2 Bb4 = , Adorjan–Tarjan, Indonesia 1984.

(e) 13 ... Bf8 14 Rac1 Rc8 15 Qa4 Na5 16 Nb3 Nc4 17 Nxd5 is better for White (Kasparov).

(f) 16 Nc5 Bxc5 17 Bxc4 d4 18 Nb5 Nb4 = , Sandstrom–Brojtigem, Berlin 1985.

(g) 12 ... Na5 13 Rad1 Nc4 14 Bc1 Bd7 is also quite playable, Kirov–Makropoulos, Pernik 1981.

(h) (A) 15 Nxd5 is bad: 15 ... Nxd5 16 Bxd5 Nxd5 17 Qxd5 Bh3 $\mp$, Vaganian–Ivkov, USSR–Yugoslavia 1975. (B) 15 Rd2 a4 16 Qd1 a3, Beliavsky–Kasparov match, Moscow 1983 is unclear.

(i) The position after 16 Ndb6 Bc6 17 Bd4 Be5 18 Bxc5 Rxc5 is equal, Yusupov–Illescas, Linares 1988.

(j) 14 Rfd1 Nc4 15 Bf4 Rc8 16 h3 (Petran–Honfi, Hungary 1984) 16 ... Bd7 = .

(k) 14 ... Be7 is possible. After 15 Rad1 Qd7 16 Nxe6 fxe6 White has the interesting sacrifice noted by Kasparov: 17 Bxh6.

(l) After 16 Kh2 Nc6 17 Nxd5 Nxd5 18 Bxd5 Bxh3, Play is equal, Vukić–Novoselski, Yugoslavia 1984.

(m) 12 . . . Na5 13 Rad1 Nc4 14 Bc1 Qc8 15 Qb5 Nb6 16 Bf4 and according to Spassky, White is somewhat better.

(n) 13 Bxd5 Nxd5 14 Nxd5 Bd8 (Farago–Marjanović, Belgrade 1982) and now Kasparov claims 15 Nxc6 bxc6 16 Nc3 is very good for White. Nevertheless, Marjanović still plays the line.

(o) 14 Nb3 Bxg2 15 Kxg2 Rfd8 16 Rd2 Bb4 =, Kouatly–Marjanović, Kolhapur, 1987.

(p) 14 Qc2 Rac8 15 Bxf6 Bxf6 16 Nc5 Bxd4 =, Portisch–Spassky, match 1977.

(q) After 16 dxc5 Qxc5 17 Bxf6 gxf6 Chernin tried 18 bxc4 against Marjanović in Subotica 1987, and after 18 . . . dxc4 19 Bxa8 Rxd1 20 Rfxd1 he scored a fine victory.

QUEEN'S GAMBIT DECLINED
Tarrasch Defense

1 d4 d5 2 c4 e6 3 Nc3 c5 4 cxd5 exd5 5 Nf3 Nc6 6 g3 Nf6 7 Bg2 Be7 8 0–0 0–0

	103	104	105	106	107	108
9	dxc5				b3	Be3
	Bxc5			d4	Ne4	Ng4
10	Bg5		Na4	Na4	Bb2	Bf4
	d4		Be7(f)	Bf5	Bf6	Be6
11	Bxf6		Be3	Ne1(i)	Na4	dxc5
	Qxf6		Bg4	Qd7	Re8(l)	Bxc5
12	Nd5		Nd4	Nd3(j)	Rc1	Na4(o)
	Qd8		Qd7(g)	Rad8	b6(m)	Be7
13	Nd2		Nxc6	Bd2	dxc5	Nd4
	Re8(a)		bxc6	Bh3	Bxb2	Nxd4
14	Re1	Rc1	Rc1	b4	Nxb2	Qxd4
	a6(b)	Bb6(d)	Bh3	Rfe8	bxc5	Qa5
15	Rc1	Nb3	Bd4	Nab2	Nd2(n)	Rac1
	Ba7(c)	Be6(e)	Bxg2(h)	Bxg2(k)	Qf6 ∞	Rac8(p)

(a) 13 ... a6 14 Rc1 Ba7 15 Nb3 Qd6 16 Qd2 Re8 17 Nf4 Bf5 18 Na5 was somewhat better for White in Plachetka–Nunn, Skara 1980.

(b) 14 ... Bg4 is equally reasonable. If then 15 Nb3 Bb6 16 Rc1 Ba5 17 Nxa5 Qxa5 18 b4 Nxb4 19 Qd2 Nc6 20 Qxa5 Nxa5 21 Nc7 d3 is equal, Spraggett–Leski, San Francisco 1987.

(c) After 16 Qb3 Rb8 17 Nf4 Re5 the position is even, Miles–Hjorth, London 1984.

(d) 14 ... Bf8 is also good. Grooten–Vladimirov, Antwerp 1986, continued 15 Nb3 Bf5 16 Nf4 Be4 = .

(e) 16 Nxb6 Qxb6 17 Nc5 Bg4 = , Palatnik–Legky, USSR 1981.

(f) If 10 ... Bb6 11 Nxb6 axb6 12 Be3 Re8 13 Nd4 Ng4 14 Bf4 Nxd4 15 Qxd4 Rxe2 16 Rac1 White has an advantage (Kasparov).

(g) 12 ... Ne5 and 12 ... Re8 are also to be considered (Kasparov).

(h) Chances are equal, Tatai–Rajković, Italy 1972.

(i) Many moves are possible here. If 11 b4 d3 12 e3 Nxb4 = , or 11 Nh4 Bg4 12 a3 Nd5 13 Qb3 Be6 14 Nf5 Nb6 $\mp$, Fine–Vidmar, Hastings 1938. 11 a3 and 11 Bf4 also fail to give White any advantage.

(j) 12 Bg5 Rfe8 13 Nd3 Ng4 14 Bxe7 Rxe7 Black has enough compensation for his pawn, Cappelo–Zichichi, Reggio Emilia 1978–79.

(k) Black has play for his pawn, Vaisman–Urzica, Romania 1974.

(l) (A) 11 . . . Bg4 12 Ne5 Bh5 13 Nxc6 bxc6 14 f3 Nd6 15 g4 ±, Jadoul–Torre, Brussels 1986. (B) 11 . . . b5 12 Nxc5 Nxc5 13 Rc1 Nb4 14 Rxc5 ±, Szabo–Padevsky, Kapfenberg 1976.

(m) 12 . . . cxd4 13 Nxd4 Bd7 14 Nc5 is better for White (Larsen).

(n) (A) 15 Nd3 Ba6 16 Nf4 d4!?. (B) 15 Na4 Ba6 16 Re1 c4 17 Nd2 Qf6 18 Nxe4 dxe4 19 bxc4 Rad8 20 Qb3 e3 is unclear, Novikov–Sturua, USSR 1984. The column is a line of Kasparov's that is worth a try.

(o) Other moves are 12 Ne1, 12 Rc1, 12 e3, 12 Qc2, and 12 Ng5. None seem to lead to White's advantage.

(p) After 16 Nc3 Bc5 17 Qd2 Qb6 the position is equal, Agdestein–Petursson, Gausdal 1985.

QUEEN'S GAMBIT DECLINED

Tarrasch Defense

1 d4 d5 2 c4 e6 3 Nc3 c5 4 cxd5

	109	110	111	112	113	114
					(Marshall	
	(exd5)	....	....	....	Gambit)	....cxd4
5	(Nf3)......	....	....	dxc5........	e4	Qxd4(l)
	(Nc6)			d4	dxe4	Nc6
6	(g3)......	....	Bg5	Na4	d5	Qd1
	c4 (Swedish Variation)		Be7	b5(g)	f5(j)	exd5
7	Bg2		Bxe7	cxb6	Bf4	Qxd5
	Bb4		Ngxe7	axb6	Bd6	Bd7(m)
8	0–0		e3(d)	b3	Bb5†	Nf3
	Nge7		cxd4	Nf6	Kf7	Nf6
9	e4	a3	Nxd4	e3	Nh3	Qd1
	0–0(a)	Ba5	Qb6(e)	Bd7(h)	Nf6	Bc5
10	exd5	e4	Nb3	Qxd4	Bc4	e3
	Nxd5	0–0	Be6	Nc6	a6	Qe7
11	Bg5	exd5	Bd3	Qb2	a4	a3
	Qa5(b)	Nxd5(c)	0–0(f)	Ne4(i)	h6(k)	0–0–0(n)

(a) 9 ... dxe4 10 Nxe4 0–0 11 Qc2 Qd5 12 Be3 Ng6 13 Nh4 Qb5 14 Nxg6 hxg6 is bad after 15 a3 Be7 16 d5 Na5 17 d6 ±, Reshevsky–Stahlberg, Zürich 1953.

(b) 12 Nxd5 Qxd5 13 Ne5 Qxd4 14 Nxc6 Qxd1 (Kasparov). Black can probably hold his own in the ending.

(c) After 12 Nxd5 Qxd5 13 Ne5, the previous line (13 ... Qxd4 14 Nxc6) is unplayable for Black because of Ne7†, so Black must play 13 ... Qb5 14 a4 Qa6 when White is slightly better (Samarian).

(d) 8 dxc5 d4 9 Ne4 0–0 10 g3 Bf5 =, Nimzowitsch–Spielmann, Carlsbad 1907.

(e) 9 ... 0–0 10 Nxc6 bxc6 11 Be2 Be6 12 0–0 ±, P. Nikolić–Kotronias, Kavala 1985.

(f) 12 0–0 Rfd8 13 Qe2 d4 resulted in equality in Aronson–Polugaevsky, USSR 1957.

(g) 6 ... Bxc5 7 Nxc5 Qa5† 8 Bd2 Qxc5 9 Rc1 is better for White, Burn–Tarrasch, Breslau 1889.

(h) 9 ... Nc6 10 Nf3 b5 fails to 11 Bxb5 Qa5† 12 Nc3 Qxc3† 13 Bd2 Qc5 14 Nxd4 ±.

(i) The position is unclear. After 12 a3 b5 13 Bd3 f5 Black has compensation for his lost material (Kasparov).

(j) 6 ... Nf6 is equal after 7 Bg5 Be7 8 Bb5† Kf8 9 Nge2 a6 10 Ba4 b5 11 Bc2 Bb7, Bronstein–Aronin, Moscow 1962.

(k) White doesn't have quite enough for the pawn, Bronstein–Marjanović, Kirovakan 1978, though attacking players may like White's position anyway.

(l) With best play 5 Qa4† transposes back to this line. 4 . . . cxd4 is the von Hennig–Schara Gambit.

(m) 7 . . . Be6 is not sufficient after 8 Qxd8† Rxd8 9 e3 Nb4 10 Bb5† Ke7 11 Kf1 ±.

(n) After 12 Qc2 Kb8 the position is somewhat better for White. If 12 . . . g5 then 13 b4 g4 14 bxc5 gxf3 15 Nb5 ±, Korchnoi–O. Rodriguez, Rome 1981.

QUEEN'S GAMBIT DECLINED

1 d4 d5 2 c4 e6

	115	116	117	118	119	120
3	(Nc3) Nf3					
	Be7 . . . . .a6(j)				Nf6	
4	cxd5			cxd5(k)	Bg5 . . . . .e3	
	exd5			exd5	h6(m)	c5
5	Bf4			Bf4	Bxf6	dxc5(p)
	c6			Nf6	Qxf6	Bxc5
6	e3 . . . . .Qc2			e3	Nc3	a3
	Bf5		g6	Bd6	Qd8(n)	0–0
7	g4		e3(g)	Bxd6	a3	b4
	Be6(a)		Bf5	Qxd6	Be7	Be7(q)
8	h3 . . . . .h4		Qd2	Bd3	e4	Bb2
	Nf6	Nd7(d)	Nf6	Nc6	dxe4	dxc4
9	Bd3	h5	f3	Nge2	Nxe4	Qxd8
	c5(b)	Qb6(e)	c5(h)	0–0	Nd7	Rxd8
10	Nf3	Rb1	Bb5†	a3	Bd3	Bxc4
	Nc6(c)	Ngf6(f)	Nc6(i)	Ne7(l)	c5(o)	Bd7(r)

(a) 7 . . . Bg6 8 h4 h5 (8 . . . Bxh4 9 Qb3 b6 10 Nf3 Be7 11 Ne5 ±) 9 g5 Bd6 10 Nge2 Ne7 11 Bxd6 Qxd6 12 Nf4 is better for White (Miles).

(b) After 9 . . . Bd6 10 Nge2 h6 11 Qb3 Bc8 White had a large space advantage, Taimanov–Rukavina, Leningrad 1973. 9 . . . 0–0 is a better try.

(c) 11 Kf1 0–0 12 Kg2 cxd4 13 Nxd4 Nxd4 with an approximately equal position.

(d) Again 8 . . . Bxh4 is disadvantageous after 9 Qb3 g5 10 Bh2, but 8 . . . Qb6 9 a3 Nd7 10 Na4 Qd8 is balanced, Timman–Csom, Bad Lauterberg 1977.

(e) 9 . . . h6 10 Be2 Nb6 11 Rc1 Nc4 =.

(f) 11 f3 0–0 12 Bd3 c5 is double-edged but about equal (Larsen).

(g) 7 e4 Be6 8 e5 Bf5 9 Qd2 Nd7 =, Garcia Palermo–Portisch, Reggio Emilia 1984–85.

(h) 9 . . . h5 10 Bd3 Bxd3 11 Qxd3 Nbd7 12 Nge2 0–0 13 e4 dxe4 14 fxe4 Nc5 15 Qf3 with an advantage in space, M. Gurevich–Geller, Moscow 1987.

(i) 11 dxc5 Bxc5 12 Na4 Be7 left it equal in Petrosian–Beliavsky, USSR 1982.

(j) (A) 3 . . . c6 transposes to the Slav-Semi-Slav Defense. (B) 3 . . . b6 4 Nf3 Bb7 5 cxd5 exd5 6 e4 dxe4 7 Ne5 Bd6 8 Qg4 Kf8 9 Bc4 Bxe5 10 dxe5 Qxd4 11 Bd5 gave White a crushing attack in Pillsbury–Swiderski, Hanover 1902.

(k) If 4 c5, Pachman recommends 4 . . . e5.

(l) After 11 Qc2 Ng6 (not 11 . . . b6 12 e4 ±, Euwe–Alekhine, Zürich 1934) leaves White somewhat better (Alekhine).

(m) (A) 4 . . . Bb4† 5 Nc3 (also known as the Vienna Variation), transposing to cols. 73–75; or (B) 4 . . . dxc4.

(n) 6 . . . c6 is treated under the Semi-Slav, col. 37.

(o) After 11 dxc5 Nxc5 12 Nxc5 Bxc5 White's position is preferable, Christiansen–Lombardy, Grindavik 1984.

(p) White attempts to play the Queen's Gambit Accepted with colors reversed and an extra tempo.

(q) 7 . . . Bd6 8 Bb2 Nc6 9 Nbd2 b6 was adequate for Black in Delander–Hess, West Germany 1967.

(r) The position is balanced, but without much life, Gurgenidze–Spassky, USSR 1975.

QUEEN'S GAMBIT DECLINED

Chigorin's Defense

1 d4 d5 2 c4 Nc6

	121	122	123	124	125	126
3	Nf3			Nc3		cxd5
	Bg4			dxc4	Nf6	Qxd5
4	cxd5		Qa4	Nf3(j)	Nf3	Nf3
	Bxf3		Bxf3	Nf6	Bg4(l)	e5!
5	gxf3	dxc6	gxf3(h)	e4	cxd5	Nc3
	Qxd5	Bxc6	Nf6	Bg4	Nxd4	Bb4
6	e3	Nc3	Nc3	Be3	e4	Bd2(o)
	e6(a)	Nf6(d)	e6	Bxf3	Nxc3	Bxc3
7	Nc3	f3(e)	Bg5	gxf3	bxc3	Bxc3
	Qh5(b)	e5!	dxc4	e5	e5	e4!
8	f4	dxe5	0–0–0	d5	d5	Nd2
	Qxd1†	Nd7	Be7	Ne7	Nb8(m)	Nf6
9	Kxd1	e4(f)	Qxc4	Qa4†	Qa4†	e3
	0–0–0(c)	Bb4(g)	Nd5!(i)	Nd7(k)	Nd7(n)	0–0 =

(a) 6 . . . e5 is sharper but leads to trouble: 7 Nc3 Bb4 8 Bd2 Bxc3 9 bxc3 Qd6 10 Rb1 b6 11 f4! exf4 12 e4 Nge7 13 Qf3 0–0 14 Bxf4 and White's bishops become dangerous, Kasparov–Smyslov, match 1984.

(b) 7 . . . Bb4 8 Bd2 Qh5 9 Bg2 Nge7 10 f4 $\pm$, Polugaevsky–Ye, Lucerne 1985.

(c) 10 Bd2 Nf6 11 Bb5 Ne7 12 Ke2 Nf5 13 Rac1 Be7 14 Bd3 Kb8 15 Rhg1 g6 16 Na4 with an endgame advantage, Karpov–Miles, Bugojno 1986.

(d) 6 . . . e6 7 e4 Bb4 8 f3 f5 9 Bc4! is strong. If 8 . . . Qh4† 9 g3 Qf6 10 Be3 0–0–0 11 Bd3 Ba5 12 0–0 Bb6 13 e5 Qe7 14 Be4 $\pm$, Bass–Chow, Chicago 1983.

(e) Safer is 7 Bg5 Qd6 8 Qd2 (8 Qd3 0–0–0 =) 8 . . . Nd5 ∞.

(f) 9 Qd4?! Bc5 10 Qg4 Nxe5! 11 Qxg7 Bf2†! 12 Kxf2 Qd4† 13 Kg3 0–0–0 14 Bg5 Rhg8 15 Qf6 Nxf3! 16 Qxd4 Nxd4 17 Kh4 f6 should win, Markov–V. Ivanov, USSR 1985.

(g) 10 Qb3 Qh4† 11 g3 Qe7 12 Be2 (Henley–Miles, Indonesia 1982); now 12 . . . 0–0–0 gives Black a pull, according to Henley.

(h) 5 exf3 e6! 6 Nc3 Ne7 7 cxd5 exd5 8 Bb5 a6 9 Bxc6† Nxc6 10 0–0 Be7 (Soltis) 11 Qb3 $\pm$ (ECO).

(i) 10 Bxe7 Ncxe7 11 Kb1 Nxc3† 12 Qxc3 Nd5 13 Qc1 Qe7 =, Portisch–Smyslov, match 1971.

(j) 4 d5 Ne5 5 5 Bf4 (5 f4 Ng4 6 h3 N5f6 =) 5 . . . Ng6 6 Bg3 e5 7 dxe6 Bxe6 8 Nf3 Nc6 9 Nd4 Bd7 10 e3 Bb4 11 Bxc4 0–0 is equal, Gligorić–Smyslov, Amsterdam 1971.

(k) 10 d6! cxd6 11 Bxc4 d5 (12 Qb3 is threatened) 12 Nxd5 Nc6 13 Rg1 Rc8 14 Rd1 Qa5† 15 Qxa5 Nxa5 16 Bf1 and White is much better, Ligterink–Halldorsson, Reykjavik 1986.

(l) 4 . . . Bf5 5 cxd5 Nxd5 6 Qb3 e6 7 e4 Nxc3 8 exf5 Nd5 9 a3! ±, Furman–Shamaev, USSR 1954.

(m) Black's best is probably 8 . . . Bxf3 9 Qxf3 Nb8, planning . . . Nd7 and . . . Bc5, although he is still worse.

(n) 10 Nxe5! Qf6 11 Be2! Bd6? (11 . . . Qxe5 12 Bxg4 Rd8 13 0–0 ±, or 12 . . . Qxc3† 13 Bd2 Qxa1† 14 Ke2 wins—P. Cramling) 12 Bxg4 Qxe5 13 Bxd7† Kd8 14 Bd2 Resigns, Cramling–Landenbergue, Biel 1987.

(o) 6 e3 exd4 7 exd4 Bg4 8 Be2 Bxf3 9 Bxf3 Qc4 =. The column is Petrov–Ravinsky, USSR 1940.

QUEEN'S GAMBIT ACCEPTED

1 d4 d5 2 c4 dxc4

Diagram 55

ESPITE ITS NAME, the Queen's Gambit Accepted (QGA) is not an attempt to win a pawn. The difficulty Black encounters trying to hold on to his booty is almost always too great, and that materialistic strategy gave the opening a poor reputation in early centuries (it dates back to Damiano in 1512). The modern concept behind 2 ... dxc4 is instead to play for free development and to saddle White with an isolated d-pawn. Black's "problem child" in the Queen's Gambit Declined—his light-squared bishop—always finds an active post at g4 or b7 in the QGA.

The disadvantage of 2 ... dxc4 is that Black gives up the center. White obtains active pieces and good attacking chances, as his isolated d-pawn may threaten to advance, opening lines of attack. Yet this advance can also lead to wholesale exchanges, producing sterile equality. For this reason the QGA is considered a rather safe opening.

Diagram 56

The main line is 3 Nf3 Nf6 4 e3 e6 5 Bxc4 c5 6 0-0 a6 (see diagram) 7 Qe2 (columns 1–6). White plays aggressively, preparing Rd1, Nc3 and e4 with an attack in the center. If Black exchanges with . . . cxd4, White gets an isolated d-pawn, but with it freedom of action for his pieces. 7 . . . b5 (cols. 1–4) gains queenside space and allows the queen's bishop to move to b7. Positionally Black is in good shape, though his kingside development lags. 7 . . . Nc6 (cols. 5–6) also fails to equalize if White avoids 8 dxc5 (col. 6).

White stops Black on the queenside in columns 7–8 with 7 a4. Although black is slightly cramped, the hole created by a4 allows him to equalize. 6 . . . Nc6 (col. 9) is an unambitious if safe continuation that concedes White the initiative.

In columns 10–12 Black plays 4 . . . Bg4, giving the game a different character. Both sides develop without trouble, and the play is less sharp. White maintains a spatial advantage, but that is all.

With 4 Nc3 (cols. 13–14) White makes a true gambit out of the opening. Although it is difficult to play, this line is as promising as 4 e3.

Black has two unusual continuations that may be as good as the main variations. 3 . . . c5 (cols. 15–16) leads to different pawn structures after 4 d5 and . . . e6. 3 . . . a6 (cols. 17–18) is similar to the 4 Nc3 line after 4 e4 (col. 17) or to the 4 . . . Bg4 variation after 4 e3 (col. 18).

QUEEN'S GAMBIT ACCEPTED

1 d4 d5 2 c4 dxc4 3 Nf3 Nf6 4 e3 e6 5 Bxc4 c5 6 0-0 a6 7 Qe2

	1	2	3	4	5	6
.	b5 ....Nc6					
8	Bb3 ....Bd3			Nc3(o)......dxc5		
	Bb7			cxd4	b5(p)	Bxc5
9	Rd1(a)			exd4	Bb3	e4
	Nbd7(b)			Be7(l)	Bb7	Ng4(r)
10	Nc3(c)			a4	Rd1	Bf4
	Qb8 ....Qc7........Bd6(i)			bxa4	Qc7	e5
11	d5(d)	e4	e4	Rxa4	d5	Bd2
	Nxd5(e)	cxd4	cxd4	0-0	exd5	0-0
12	Nxd5	Nxd4	Rxd4	Nc3	e4!	h3
	Bxd5	Bc5(g)	Bc5	Bb7	d4	Nf6
13	Bxd5	a3	Rd3	Rd1	Nd5	Nc3
	exd5	0-0	Ng4(j)	a5	Qd8	Be6
14	Rxd5	Be3	Bg5!	Ne5(m)	Bf4	Bg5
	Be7(f)	Rad8(h)	Qb6(k)	Nc6(n)	Rc8(q)	h6(s)

(a) On (A) 9 a4 Black can play either 9 . . . b4 10 Nbd2 cxd4 11 exd4 Nc6 =, or 9 . . . Nbd7 10 axb5 axb5 11 Rxa8 Qxa8 12 Nc3 b4 13 Nb5 Bxf3 14 gxf3 Qb8 15 Bd2 Draw, Miles–Seirawan, Dubai 1986. (B) 9 Nc3 Nbd7 10 Rd1 transposes back to the column.

(b) (A) 9 . . . Nc6 tranposes into col. 5. (B) 9 . . . Be7 10 Nc3 0-0 11 e4 b4 (11 . . . cxd4 12 Nxd4 Qc7 13 Bg5 ±) 12 d5! bxc3 13 dxe6 Qc7 14 exf7† Kh8 15 e5 favors White, Vaiser–Donchev, Vrnjačka Banja 1984.

(c) 10 e4!? Bxe4 11 d5 (Gorelov's imaginative 11 Ng5 Bg6 12 d5 e5 13 Ne6 Qb6 is simply better for Black) 11 . . . e5 12 d6 c4 13 Nxe5 Nxe5 14 Nc3 Bxd6 15 Nxe4 Nxe4 16 Qxe4 0-0 17 Bc2 g6 18 a4 Rc8 =, Khasanov–Korunsky, USSR 1984. Also 10 . . . cxd4 11 e5 Bxf3 12 gxf3 Nh5 13 f4 Qh4 14 Rxd4 Bc5 is allright for Black, Salov–Kupreichik, USSR Chp. 1987.

(d) 11 e4 cxd4 12 Nxd4 Bd6 13 h3 0-0 14 a3 Rd8 =, Reshevsky–Portisch, Amsterdam 1964.

(e) 11 . . . exd5 12 Nxd5 c4? 13 d4! threatens the devastating 14 Bf4. Black's best is then 13 . . . Bd6 14 Bc2 0-0 15 Nxf6† Nxf6 16 Bg5, but he still has many problems (Mirković).

(f) 15 e4 Qb7 (15 . . . Nb6 16 Rh5 ±) 16 Bg5 Nb6 17 Rd2 ±, as White will double rooks on the d-file.

(g) (A) 12 . . . b4?! 13 Na4 Nxe4?! 14 Bxe6! fxe6 15 Nxe6 is strong (Gufeld). (B) 12 . . . Be7 13 Bg5 b4 14 Na4 Qe5 15 Bxf6 Nxf6 16 Nb6 Rd8 17 Ba4† ±, Smyslov–Keres, Candidates, Budapest, 1950.

(h) Not 14 . . . Nxe4? 15 Nxe4 Bxe4 16 Nxe6 fxe6 17 Bxe6† +. After 14 . . . Rad8 15 f3 White is somewhat better, Kakageldiev–Suetin, Tallinn 1980.

(i) 10 . . . Qb6 11 d5 exd5 12 Nxd5 Nxd5 13 Bxd5 Bxd5 14 Rxd5 Be7 15 e4 Qb7 tranposes to col. 1.

(j) 13 . . . 0-0 14 Bf4 b4 15 Na4 Qa5 16 Nd2 allows White a simple plus, Tal–Georgadze, USSR 1970.

(k) 15 Nd5! exd5 (15 . . . Bxd5 16 exd5 Nxf2 17 dxe6 Nxd3† 18 Kf1 fxe6 19 Qxd3 also lets White have an attack, Klovans–Koblents, USSR 1962) 16 exd5† Kf8 17 d6 is strong, since 17 . . . Re8 18 Be7† Kg8 19 Qe6! wins (Ribli).

(l) 9 . . . Nc6 10 a4 bxa4 11 Rxa4 Nb4 12 Bc4 Be7 13 Bg5 a5 14 Bb5† Bd7 (Portisch–Seirawan, Dubai 1986) 15 Nc3 0-0 16 Bxd7 leaves Black's a-pawn in need of attention.

(m) 14 Bg5 Bc6 15 Raa1 Nbd7 16 Ne5 Nxe5 Draw, Reshevsky–Portisch, Santa Monica 1966.

(n) 15 Bg5 Nb4 16 Bxf6 Bxf6 17 Be4 Bxe4 18 Nxe4 Be7 = , Nogueiras–Ehlvest, Zagreb 1987.

(o) 8 Rd1 b5 9 dxc5 (9 Bb3 c4 10 Bc2 Nb4 =) 9 . . . Qc7 10 Bd3 Nb4! 11 a4 bxa4 12 Rxa4 Rb8 13 Nc3 Bxc3 = (Ribli).

(p) (A) 8 . . . cxd4 9 Rd1 regains the pawn with a favorable opening of the position. (B) 8 . . . Qc7?! 9 Bd3 Be7 10 dxc5 Bxc5 11 Ne4 Be7 12 b3 and White is well ahead in development, Timman–Miles, Tilburg 1986.

(q) 15 a4 with a big advantage. On 15 . . . c4 Neistadt analyses the fantastic variation 16 axb5 d3 17 dxc6! dxe2 18 cxb7 exd1 (Q)† 19 Rxd1 cxb3 20 Nc7† Ke7 21 Bd6† Qxd6 22 bxc8 (N)† Kd7 23 Nxd6 with a winning endgame.

(r) (A) 9 . . . Qc7 10 e5 Ng4 11 Bf4 f6 12 Nbd2 $\pm$, Nogueiras–Seirawan, Montpellier 1985. (B) 9 . . . e5? 10 Bxf7† Kxf7 11 Qc4† ± (C) 9 . . . b5 10 Bb3 e5 11 Be3 Qb6 12 Nc3 Bxe3 13 fxe3 is also good for White, Nogueiras–Spraggett, Szirak 1986.

(s) 15 Rad1 Nd4 16 Nxd4 Bxd4 with even chances, Fedorowicz–Chandler, London 1982.

QUEEN'S GAMBIT ACCEPTED

1 d4 d5 2 c4 dxc4 3 Nf3 Nf6 4 e3

	7	8	9	10	11	12
	(e6)			Bg4		
5	(Bxc4)			Bxc4(j)		
	(c5)			e6		
6	(0-0)(a)			h3		
	(a6).....................		Nc6	Bh5		
7	a4		Qe2	0-0(k)		
	Nc6(b)		cxd4	Nbd7		a6
8	Qe2		Rd1	Nc3		Nc3
	cxd4	Qc7	Be7(g)	Bd6(l)		Nc6
9	Rd1	Nc3	exd4	e4		Be2
	Be7	Be7(e)	0-0	e5		Bd6
10	exd4	Rd1	Nc3	g4!	Be2	b3
	0-0	0-0	Na5(h)	Bg6	0-0	0-0
11	Nc3	b3	Bd3	dxe5	dxe5(n)	Bb2
	Nb4(c)	Rd8	b6	Nxe5	Nxe5	Qe7
12	Ne5	Bb2	Bg5	Nxe5	Nd4	Rc1(p)
	Bd7(d)	Nb4(f)	Bb7(i)	Bxe5(m)	Bc5!(o)	Rfd8(q)

(a) An independent line is (A) 6 Qe2 a6 7 dxc5 Bxc5 8 0-0 Qc7 9 Nbd2, but this is too sterile to gain a plus, e.g. 9 . . . 0-0 10 a3 b5 11 Bd3 Bd6 12 b4 Bb7 13 Bb2 Nbd7 14 Rac1 Qb8 =, Christiansen–Dlugy, US Chp. 1985. Even more insipid is (B) 6 Nc3 a6 7 0-0 b5 8 Be2 Bb7 9 dxc5 Bxc5 10 Qxd8† Kxd8 11 a3 Ke7 12 b4 Bd6 13 Bb2 Nbd7 =, Capablanca–Rubinstein, Moscow 1925.

(b) It is poor to exchange on d4 before White moves any more pieces: 7 . . . cxd4 8 exd4 Nc6 9 Nc3 Be7 10 Re1 0-0 11 Bg5 Nd5 12 Bxe7 Ncxe7 13 Qb3 Nf6 14 Rad1 with the initiative, Timoshchenko–Anikaev, USSR 1981.

(c) 11 . . . Nd5 12 Ne5 Ncb4 (12 . . . Nxc3 13 bxc3 Nxe5 14 dxe5 Qc7 15 Bd3 ±) 13 Qg4 Kh8 14 Qf3 Kg8 15 a5 ±, Kouatly–Marjanović, Marseilles 1986.

(d) 13 Bg5 Rc8 14 Bb3 Bc6 15 Nxc6 Rxc6 16 Bxf6 Bxf6 17 d5 exd5 18 Nxd5 Nxd5 19 Bxd5 Rd6 20 Bxb7 a5 and White's extra pawn has little meaning, Ivkov–Gheorghiu, Hamburg 1965.

(e) 9 . . . Bd6 10 Rd1 0-0 11 h3 Re8 12 dxc5 Bxc5 13 e4 Nd7 14 Ba2 b6 15 e5! Ndxe5 16 Bf4 f6 17 Rac1 Bb7 18 Nxe5 fxe5 19 Bg3 ±, Lputian–Hübner, Rotterdam 1988.

(f) 13 dxc5 Bd7 14 e4 Bc6 15 Rd6!? (15 Nd4 =) 15 . . . Nd7 16 Nd5?! exd5 17 exd5 Bxd6 18 cxd6 Qxd6 19 dxc6 bxc6 ∓, Benjamin–Dlugy, US Chp. 1986.

(g) 8 . . . d3 is dubious; 9 Bxd3 Qc7 10 Nc3 a6 11 e4 Be7 12 e5 ±, Yudovich–Klidzeis, Ventspils 1976.

(h) Now 10 . . . Nb4 is not so strong since there is no hole at b4 as in col. 7; 11 Bg5 Nd5 12 Rac1 ±.

408

(i) 13 Rac1 Nd5 14 Qe4 g6 15 Qh4 f6 16 Bh6 Nxc3 17 bxc3 Bxf3 18 gxf3 $\pm$, Vukić–Marjanović, Ni 1979.

(j) 5 h3 Bh5 6 g4!? Bg6 7 Ne5 e6 8 Bg2 Be4 9 f3 Bxb1 10 Rxb1 Nd5 ∞, Nogueiras–Hort, Lugano 1987.

(k) (A) 7 Qb3 Bxf3 8 gxf3 Nbd7! 9 Qxb7 c5 10 Nc3 cxd4 11 exd4 Bd6 with good play for the pawn, Toth–Sapi, Hungary 1966. (B) 7 Nc3 Nbd7 8 0-0 transposes into the column, but not 7 Nc3 Nc6?! 8 Bb5 $\pm$.

(l) 8 . . . Be7 is passive, allowing White to control the center after 9 Be2 0-0 10 e4 Nb6 11 Be3 Bb4 12 Nd2, Cuartas–Mestrović, Rio de Janeiro 1979.

(m) 13 f4 Qd4† 14 Qxd4 Bd4† 15 Kh2 Bxc3 16 bxc3 Bxe4 17 g5 Bd5 18 Re1† Kf8 (Ftáčnik–Matulović, Vrsać 1981) 19 gxf6! Bxc4 20 f5!, threatening 21 Rg1 and 22 Ba3†, creates a strong attack (G. Hillyard).

(n) 11 Bg5 may be stronger, e.g. 11 . . . Bxf3 12 Bxf3 exd4 13 Qxd4 Ne5 14 Rad1! h6 15 Be3 $\pm$, Mikhalchishin–Henley, Mexico City 1980.

(o) Not 12 . . . Bxe2?! 13 Qxe2 $\pm$. After 12 . . . Bc5! 13 Nb3 Qxd1 14 Bxd1 Bb6 15 a4 Bxd1 16 Rxd1 a5 17 Bg5 c6! the game is level, U. Andersson–Miles, Wijk aan Zee 1979.

(p) 12 e4 Bxf3 13 Bxf3 Rfd8! 14 Ne2 e5 =, Suarez–Lebredo, Cienfuegos 1981.

(q) 13 Ne5! Bxe2 14 Nxc6 Bxd1 15 Nxe7† Bxe7 16 Rfxd1 with an endgame advantage (Taimanov).

QUEEN'S GAMBIT ACCEPTED

1 d4 d5 2 c4 dxc4 3 Nf3

	13	14	15	16	17	18
.	(Nf6) . . . . c5 . . . . a6					
4	Nc3		d5(h)		e4 . . . . e3(p)	
	a6		Nf6 . . . . e6		b5	Bg4(q)
5	e4(a)		Nc3	Nc3	a4	Bxc4
	b5		e6	Ne7(l)	Bb7	e6
6	e5		e4	e4	axb5	Qb3(r)
	Nd5		exd5	exd5	axb5	Bxf3
7	a4 . . . . Ng5		e5(i)	exd5	Rxa8	gxf3
	Nxc3(b)	e6	Nfd7	Nf5	Bxa8	b5
8	bxc3	Qh5	Bg5(j)	Bxc4	Nc3	Be2
	Qd5(c)	Qd7	Be7	Nd6	e6(n)	Nd7
9	g3	Be2(f)	Bxe7	0-0!	Nxb5	a4
	Bb7(d)	Bb7	Qxe7	Be7	Bxe4	b4
10	Bg2	0-0	Nxd5	Bb3	Bxc4	Nd2 $\pm$
	Qd7(e)	g6(g)	Qd8(k)	0-0(m)	c6(o)	

(a) Preventing 5 . . . b5 is safe but unpromising: 5 a4 Nc6! 6 e4 (6 d5 Nb4 7 e4 e6 =) 6 . . . Bg4 7 Be3 e5 8 dxe5 Nd7! 9 Bxc4 Ndxe5 = (Taimanov).

(b) (A) 7 . . . c6 8 axb5 Nxc3 9 bxc3 cxb5 10 Ng5 f6 11 Qf3 Ra7 12 e6! Bb7 13 d5! Qxd5 14 Qxd5 Bxd5 15 Be3 fxg5 (15 . . . Rb7 16 0-0-0 is worse) 16 Bxa7 Nc6 17 Rxa6 with an endgame plus (Vaiser). (B) 7 . . . Nb4!? is complicated but suspect: 8 Be2 Bf5 9 0-0 Nc2 10 Ra2 Nb4 11 Ra3 Nc2 12 Nh4!? Bd3 13 Bxd3 cxd3 14 e6 fxe6 15 Qh5† g6 16 Nxg6 hxg6 17 Qxh8 b4 18 Qg8 bxc3 19 Qxg6† Kd7 20 Qxd3 $\pm$, Zlochevsky–Baryshev, USSR 1986.

(c) On 8 . . . Bb7?! 9 e6! is strong. If (A) 9 . . . fxe6 10 Ng5 Qd5 11 Be2 Qxg2 12 Rf1 Bd5 13 axb5 and Black is in difficulties (Gufeld). (B) 9 . . . f6 10 Be2! Qd5 11 0-0 Qxe6 12 Re1 Qd7 13 Nh4 g6 14 Bg4 f5 15 Bf3 Nc6 16 Bg5 h6 17 d5! with a winning position (Beliavsky–Dlugy, Tunis 1985), since 17 . . . hxg5 18 Nxg6 Na5 19 Ne5! Qc8 20 Bh5† is crushing. The game continued 17 . . . Ne5 18 Rxe5 hxg5 19 Nxg6 Qd6 20 Nxh8 Qxe5 21 d6! Rd8 22 Bh5† Resigns.

(d) 9 . . . Be6 10 Bg2 Qb7 11 0-0 Bd5 is too slow: 12 e6! Bxe6 13 Ne5 Bd5 14 Bxd5 Qxd5 15 axb5 axb5 16 Rxa8 Qxa8 17 Qg4 e6 18 Qg5 g6 19 Nxg6! wins, since 19 . . . fxg6 20 Qe5 Rg8 21 Qxe6† wins the rook, Vaganian–P. Nikolić, Naestved 1985.

(e) 11 Ba3 Bd5 12 0-0 Nc6 13 Re1 with more than enough initiative for the pawn, van der Sterren–Hort, Amsterdam 1982.

(f) 9 Nxd5 exd5 10 a3 Nc6 11 Be3 Nd8 12 Be2 Qf5 and Black has at least equality, Bogolyubov–Alekhine, World Chp. 1934.

(g) 11 Qg4 h5 12 Qh3 Nc6 13 Rd1 Ncb4 14 Nce4 0-0-0 with roughly level chances, Grigorian–Mariasin, Beltsi 1979.

(h) (A) 4 e3 cxd4 5 Bxc4 (5 exd4 Qc7 =) 5 ... Qc7 6 Na3 (6 Qb3 e6 7 exd4 Nc6 =) 6 ... e6 7 Qa4† Bd7 8 Nb5 Qd8 9 0-0 a6 10 Be2 Nf6 11 Ne5 d3 12 Bxd3 Nc6 =, Christiansen—de la Villa Garcia, Szirak 1987. (B) 4 Nc3 cxd4 5 Qxd4 Qxd4 6 Nxd4 Bd7 7 Ndb5 Na6 8 e4 Nf6 =, Kasparov—Seirawan, Thessaloniki 1988.

(i) 7 exd5 Bd6 8 Bxc4 0-0 9 0-0 Bg4 10 h3 Bxf3 11 Qxf3 Nbd7 is fully equal, I. Ivanov— Spraggett, Montreal 1986.

(j) 8 Qxd5 Nb6! 9 Qxd8† Kxd8 10 Bg5† Be7 11 0-0-0† Ke8 12 Nb5 Na6 13 Bxe7 Kxe7 =, Torre—Seirawan, London 1984.

(k) 11 Bxc4 Nc6 12 Qa4 0-0 13 0-0-0 Nd4 14 Rhe1 Nb6 15 Nxb6 ±, Cvitan—Ehlvest, Vrsać 1987.

(l) 5 ... exd5 6 Qxd5 Qxd5 7 Nxd5 Bd6 8 Nd2 Ne7 9 Nxc4 Nxd5 10 Nxd6† Ke7 11 Nxc8† Rxc8 12 Bg5† f6 13 0-0-0 with a pull in the endgame, Ribli—Seirawan, Montpellier 1985.

(m) 11 h3 Bf5 12 Bf4 Nd7 13 Re1 ±, as White has better control of the center, Farago— Karolyi, Balatonbereny 1985.

(n) (A) 8 ... b4? 9 Qa4† wins. (B) 8 ... c6 9 Bg5 h6 10 Bh4 Qb6 11 Be2 e6 12 0-0 Be7 13 b3 ±, Knaak—Chekhov, Leipzig 1986.

(o) If 10 ... Bxf3?! 11 Qxf3 c6 12 0-0! (Lputian—Kraidonov, Irkutsk 1983) when 12 ... cxb5 13 Bxb5† Nd7 14 d5 gives White a dangerous attack. After 10 ... c6 11 Ne5! Nf6 12 0-0 Be7 13 Nc3 White is better (Lputian).

(p) 4 a4?! Nf6 5 e3 Bg4 6 Bxc4 e6 7 0-0 Nc6 8 Nc3 Bd6, planning ... 0-0 and ... e5, is completely equal.

(q) Black cannot hold the c-pawn. If 3 ... b5 4 b3 wins the pawn back with advantage.

(r) 6 h3 Bh5 7 0-0 Nf6 transposes to column 12. The column is Botvinnik—Smyslov, World Chp. 1954.

QUEEN'S GAMBIT ACCEPTED

1 d4 d5 2 c4 dxc4

	19	20	21	22	23	24
3	(Nf3)		.e4			.e3
	(Nf6)		e5	Nf6	c5(n)	e5(q)
4	e3	Qa4†	Nf3	e5(j)	d5	Bxc4
	g6	c6(d)	exd4(g)	Nd5	Nf6	exd4
5	Bxc4	Qxc4	Bxc4	Bxc4	Nc3	exd4
	Bg7	Bf5	Bb4†	Nb6	e6	Nf6
6	0-0	Nc3	Nbd2(h)	Bb3(k)	Bxc4	Nf3(n)
	0-0	e6	Nc6	Nc6	exd5	Be7
7	Nc3	g3	0-0	Nf3	Nxd5!	0-0
	Nfd7(a)	Nbd7	Nf6	Bg4	Nxd5	0-0
8	h3(b)	Bg2	e5	Bxf7†(l)	Bxd5	Nc3
	Nb6	Be7	Nd5	Kxf7	Bd6(o)	Bg4(s)
9	Be2	0-0	Nb3	Ng5†	Nf3	h3
	Nc6	0-0(e)	Nb6	Ke8	0-0	Bh5
10	b3	Bg5	Bb5	Qxg4	0-0	g4
	a5(c)	Ne4(f)	Qd5!(i)	Qxd4(m)	Qc7(p)	Bg6(t)

(a) This Grünfeld-type move is best. If (A) 7 ... c5 8 d5 Bg4 9 e4 Nbd7 10 Be2 Bxf3 11 Bxf3 a6 12 Re1 ±, Taimanov–Portisch, Leningrad vs. Budapest 1959. (B) 7 ... Nc6 8 d5 Na5 9 Be2 c6 10 dxc6 Nxc6 11 Qa4 followed by Rd1 is good (Gufeld).

(b) 8 e4 Nb6 9 Be2 Bg4 10 Be3 Nc6 11 d5 Bxf3 12 Bxf3 Ne5 13 Be2 Nec4 14 Bc1 c6 =, Evans–Smyslov, Helsinki 1952.

(c) 11 Ba3 Re8 12 Rc1 Nb4 13 Bb2 N6d5 14 Qd2 b6 15 Nxd5 Nxd5 16 e4 ±, Lukacs–Velikov, Vrnjačka Banja 1985.

(d) (A) 4 ... Nc6 5 Nc3 Nd5 6 e4! Nb6 7 Qd1 Bg4 8 d5 Ne5 9 Bf4 Ng6 10 Bg3 leaves White somewhat better, Alburt–Dlugy, US Chp. 1984. (B) 4 ... Nbd7 5 Nc3 (5 g3, like the Catalan, is also possible) 5 ... e6 6 e4 ±.

(e) 9 ... Bc2 threatens to trap the queen with 10 ... Nb6, but after 10 e3 0-0 11 a3 a5 12 Qe2 White is better, Bogolyubov–Alekhine, World Chp. 1934.

(f) 11 Bxe7 Qxe7 12 Rfd1 Nxc3 13 Qxc3 Be4 14 Rd2 Rfd8 15 Rad1 h6 16 a3 Nf6 =, M. Gurevich–Kallai, Baku 1986.

(g) 4 ... Bb4† 5 Nc3 exd4 6 Qxd4 Qxd4 7 Nxd4 Nf6 8 f3 a6 9 Bxc4 leaves White with the better ending, Skembris–Grivas, Greece 1983, but more active is 8 ... Bc5! 9 Be3 Nc6 10 Nc2 Bxe3 11 Nxe3 Be6 12 0-0-0 0-0 =, Albert–Leverett, New York 1989.

(h) 6 Bd2 Bxd2† 7 Nbxd2 Nc6 8 0-0 Qf6 9 e5 Qg6 10 Qb3 Nge7 11 Rfe1 0-0 ∞, Bagirov–Romanishin, USSR 1978.

(i) 10 ... 0-0?! 11 Bxc6 bxc6 12 Nbxd4 ±. After 10 ... Qd5 11 Nbxd4 Bd7 12 Nxc6 Qxb5 13 Nfd4 Qc5, the game is equal, P. Nikolić–Matulović, Yugoslavia 1984.

(j) 4 Nc3 is met by 4 . . . e5 5 Nf3 exd4 6 Qxd4 Qxd4 7 Nxd4 Bc5 8 Ndb5 Na6 =, Azmayparashvili–Petrosian, USSR Chp. 1983.

(k) 6 Bd3 Nc6 7 Be3 Nb4 8 Be4 c6 9 Nc3 Be6 10 Nge2 N4d5 11 0-0 Qd7 12 Ng3 f5! 13 exf6 exf6 14 Re1 0-0-0 and Black is well placed, Beliavsky–Yakovich, Sochi 1986.

(l) 8 Ng5 Bxd1 9 Bxf7† Kd7 10 Be6† Ke8 11 Bf7† is a draw.

(m) 11 Qe2 Qxe5 12 Be3 Nd5 13 Nf3 Qf5 14 0-0 e6 15 Nc3 Rd8 16 Rfe1 Be7 17 Bd2 Nxc3 18 Bxc3 with just a small pull for White, Alburt–Gulko, Somerset 1986. The game continued 18 . . . Kf7 19 Qc4 Bf6 20 Re3 Bxc3? (after 20 . . . Rhe8 21 Rae1 White has good play for the pawn) 21 Ng5†! Kg6 (21 . . . Qxg5 22 Qxe6† Kf8 23 bxc3 with a winning attack) 22 Qxc3 Rhf8 23 Rf3 Qd5?! (23 . . . Nd4 24 Rxf5 Ne2† 25 Kf1 Nxc3 26 Rxf8 Rxf8 27 Nxe6 Re8 28 Nxc7 with a pawn-up endgame—Alburt—but this is the lesser evil) 24 Rg3 Qd1† 25 Qe1 Qxe1† 26 Rxe1 Rfe8 27 Nxe6† Kf6 28 Rf3† Kg6 29 Rfe3 Rc8 30 h4 (even in the endgame White's attack is strong) 30 . . . Re7 31 h5† Kxh5 32 Rg3 Rf8 33 Re4 Resigns, since 34 Rg5† (or 34 Nxg7†) 34 . . . Kh6 35 Rh4 with mate coming.

(n) Another legitimate choice, recently developed, is 3 . . . Nc6 4 Be3 Nf6 (A) 5 Nc3 e5 6 d5 Ne7 7 Bxc4 Ng6 8 h4 Bd6 9 g3 Ng4 10 Bb5† Kf8 ∞, Wilder–Ronggunang, Belgrade 1988. (B) 5 f3 e5 6 d5 Nxd4 7 Bxd4 exd4 8 Qxd4 c6 9 Bxc4 (or 9 Nc3 cxd5 10 0-0-0 Bb4 =) 9 . . . cxd5 10 exd5 Bd6 =, Timoshchenko–Balashov, Sverdlovsk 1987.

(o) 8 . . . Be7 9 Nf3 0-0 10 0-0 Qb6 (Bukić–Kovaćević, Tuzla 1981) 11 Ne5 ±.

(p) Beliavsky–de la Villa Garcia, Szirak 1987; now 11 Be3 Bg4 12 h3 Bh5 13 Rc1 Nd7 14 b4 is much better for White (Beliavsky).

(q) Black can transpose into the main lines with (A) 3 . . . Nf6 4 Bxc4 e6 5 Nf3 c5. (B) Holding the pawn with 3 . . . b5? 4 a4 c6 5 axb5 cxb5 6 Qf3! would lose a piece.

(r) 6 Qb3 Qe7† 7 Ne2 Qb4† 8 Nc3 Qxb3 9 Bxb3 Bd6 is roughly even, Wirthensohn–Miles, Biel 1977.

(s) 8 . . . Nc6 9 h3 leaves White more active.

(t) 11 Ne5 c5 12 Be3 cxd4 13 Qxd4 ±, as White will gain the two bishops.

QUEEN'S GAMBIT—SLAV AND SEMI-SLAV DEFENSE

1 d4 d5 2 c4 c6

Diagram 57

T HE SLAV GENEALOGY is the largest on the Queen's Gambit tree. It was originated by Alapin, widely adopted in this century, and became prominent during and after the 1935–37 world title matches between Alekhine and Euwe. Featuring the solid 2 . . . c6, the Slav aims at bolstering Black's queen-pawn without hemming in his perennial "problem child" (the queen's bishop), which is free to develop at f5 or g4. The Semi-Slav is identified by an early . . . e6, creating a phalanx-like formation of Black's center pawns. With the Meran Variation and the Anti-Meran in this family, the Semi-Slav can often lead to wild play.

For reference, variations are broken down into: (A) Semi-Slav—Meran Variation, (B) Semi-Slav—Various, (C) Semi-Slav—Anti-Meran, (D) Slav Proper, (E) Sundry lines and Slav Exchange Variation.

Diagram 58

(A) SEMI-SLAV—MERAN VARIATION (cols. 1–30) is 3 Nf3 Nf6 4 Nc3 e6 (see diagram) 5 e3 Nbd7 6 Bd3 dxc4 7 Bxc4 b5. Black shuts in his queen's bishop temporarily, but this is balanced by the rapid grouping of his pieces on the queen's wing and the liberating move . . . c5. White must seize the opportunity to act in the center or renounce his chance of gaining the initiative. After enjoying great popularity in the 1940s and 1950s, the Meran slipped out of favor for twenty years. Recently, due to the efforts of some grandmasters, especially Ribli and Kasparov, the Meran has once again come to center stage. Especially critical for this defense are the lines arising from 10 e5 (cols. 1–12). 10 d5 (cols. 13–18) is the *Reynolds Variation* analyzed by him in *Chess*, England, 1939.

(B) SEMI-SLAV—VARIOUS (cols. 31–36) offers a rich mixture of developing patterns for White and Black after the distinguishing move 5 e3. These lines are usually employed by those who wish to avoid the Meran and its large body of theory. The *Romih Variation*, 6 . . . Bb4 (col. 31), was used by Larry Evans in the 1950s and 1960s, and lately by Robert Hübner. White gains a small advantage. Similar play evolves from Chigorin's 6 . . . Bd6 (col. 32), a longtime favorite of Bisguier's. Columns 33–36 represent different interpretations of Gösta Stoltz's 6 Qc2. Black obtains comfortable play in all variations.

(C) SEMI-SLAV—ANTI-MERAN, 5 Bg5 dxc4 6 e4 b5 7 e5 h6 8 Bh4 g5 (cols. 41–48), is a very complex variation—the queenside equivalent of the Najdorf Sicilian's labyrinthine poison-pawn lines. It was popularized by Botvinnik's famous game against Denker in the USSR–USA radio match of 1945, but theory has been changing. For those who want a quieter reply to 5 Bg5 than 5 . . . dxc4, column 37 may be the answer, gaining Black the bishop pair and a solid position at the cost of some space.

Diagram 59

(D) The SLAV-PROPER (cols. 49–60) is characterized by 4 . . . dxc4 (see diagram). It has been a Smyslov favorite throughout his career. Cols. 49–51 deal with attempts by White to avoid a4, but lead to no advantage for the first player. After 5 a4 Black has three playable alternatives, which players will select according to temperament. With 5 . . . Na6 (col. 52), intending to post the knight in the hole on b4, play is less forced and more positional. A more combative choice is the aggressive 5 . . . Bg4 (col. 53–54) which often leads to very sharp play. The main lines commencing with 5 . . . Bf5 (cols. 55–60) lead to technical play. Having given up the center with . . . dxc4, Black capitalizes on White's delayed development to strike back with . . . e5, but White may stop this by playing e5 himself. The resulting pawn structures often resemble those of the French Defense.

(E) Sundry lines and the SLAV EXCHANGE VARIATION are covered in columns 61-66.

The earmark of col. 61 is Black's developing the bishop to f5 before playing e6. The *Marshall Gambit* is 3 Nc3 e6 4 e4 (col. 62), which Black does best to accept with 4 . . . dxe4 5 Nxe4 Bb4† 6 Bd2 Qxd4, later returning the pawn to complete development. The complicated *Abrahams–Noteboom Variation* (col. 63) gives Black two connected, passed queenside pawns against White's central pawn roller. These two variations plus the Meran or cols. 31 or 32 make a complete repertoire to 1 d4. The SLAV EXCHANGE VARIATION (cols. 64-66) contains a drop of poison after 4 cxd5 cxd5. Previously labeled variously as anything from a refutation to a dead draw, it has been endorsed by Seirawan and U. Andersson, yet now seems to lead to equality. Players seeking to win with Black should avoid this line at all cost by playing the move order 2 . . . e6 and then 3 . . . c6 so that cxd5 can be met by the asymmetrical capture . . . exd5.

QUEEN'S GAMBIT

Semi-Slav Defense

1 d4 d5 2 c4 c6 3 Nf3 Nf6 4 Nc3 e6 5 e3 Nbd7 6 Bd3 dxc4 7 Bxc4 b5 8 Bd3 a6 9 e4 c5 10 e5 cxd4 11 Nxb5

	1	2	3	4	5	6
	axb5		Ng4		Nxe5	
12	exf6		Nbxd4	Qa4!	Nxe5	
	Qb6	Bb7	Bb4†	Ngxe5(g)	axb5	
13	0-0	0-0	Bd2	Nxe5	Qf3(k)	
	gxf6	gxf6(c)	Bxd2†	Nxe5	Bb4†	Qa5†
14	Be4	Nxd4	Qxd2	Nd6†(h)	Ke2(l)	Ke2
	Bb7	Rg8	Bb7	Ke7	Rb8	Bd6
15	Bxb7	f3	Rd1(e)	Nxc8†	Qg3(m)	Qc6†(o)
	Qxb7	Bc5	0-0	Rxc8(i)	Qd6	Ke7
16	Nxd4	Be3	0-0	Bxa6	Nf3	Bd2
	Rg8	Qb6	Ngxe5	Ra8	Qxg3	b4
17	f3	Bxb5	Be2	Qb5	hxg3	Qd6†
	Rd8(a)	Rd8	Qb6	Qd5	Bd6	Kxd6
18	Qe2	Qb3	b3	Qxd5	Bf4	Nc4†
	Bc5(b)	Rg5(d)	Nxf3†(f)	exd5(j)	Bxf4(n)	Kd7(p)

(a) 17 . . . Bc5 18 Kh1 Ne5 19 Nb3 Ba7 20 Qe2 Ke7 21 Bd2 b4 22 a3! ±, Trifunović–Fuderer, Yugoslav Chp. 1949.

(b) 19 Be3 Ne5 20 Nc2 ±, White's pawn structure and king position are better.

(c) 13 . . . Qb6 14 Qe2 Bc6 15 Be4 Bxe4 16 Qxe4 Rd8 17 fxg7 Bxg7 18 Bg5 f6 19 Bd2 Nc5 20 Qh4 ±, Fernandez–Rivas, Cienfuegos 1983.

(d) 19 Ba4 Qxb3 20 axb3 (20 Bxb3 Nb6 gives Black counterplay) 20 . . . Ke7 (threatening . . . Nb6, . . . Ne5) 21 Rac1 ±. If 21 . . . Nb6? 22 Nc6† Bxc6 23 Bxc5† winning.

(e) On 15 Be2 Black equalized in Seirawan–Chernin, Montpellier 1985, with 15 . . . Ndxe5 16 h3 Nxf3† 17 Bxf3 Bxf3 18 Nxf3 Qxd2† 19 Nxd2 Nf6 20 Ke2 Ke7.

(f) 19 Bxf3 Nf6 20 Bxb7 Qxb7 21 Nc2 a5 22 Ne3 Rfb8 23 Qb2 Qc7 Draw, Miles–Kasparov, match 1986.

(g) 12 . . . Rb8 13 Nd6† Bxd6 14 exd6 Qb6 15 h3 Ngf6 16 Qxd4 Qxd4 17 Nxd4 Rb6 18 Nb3 Rxd6 19 Be2 0-0 20 0-0 Nd5 21 Bd2 Ne5 22 Rfd1 ±, Tukmakov–J. Horvath, Sochi 1987.

(h) 14 Nc7† Ke7 15 Nxa8 Nxd3† 16 Ke2 Bd7! 17 Qxd4 Nxc1† 18 Raxc1 Qxa8 19 Rc7 Qd8 20 Rhc1 Ke8 21 Ra7 Be7 22 Rcc7 Bb5† 23 Ke3 Bd6! 24 Rxf7 e5 25 Qd5 Bc5† 26 Ke4 Qxd5† 27 Kxd5 Bxa7 28 Rxa7 Rf8 and Black stands well (Christiansen).

(i) 15 . . . Kf6?! is Kasparov's interesting attempt to breathe life into 11 . . . Ng4, but it just falls short after 16 Bxa6! Nd3† 17 Kf1! Nb4 18 Qb3 d3 19 Qc4 Qd5 20 Nb6 + (analysis by Veličković).

(j) 19 Bb5 Kf6 20 0-0 Bb4 21 Bf4 ±, Speelman–Ribli, Subotica 1987. White's bishop pair and better pawn structure give him a clear edge.

(k) 13 Qb3?! Qa5† 14 Bd2 b4 15 f4 Bb7 16 0-0 Be7 17 Bc4 0-0! 18 Bxe6 Nd5 19 Bh3 Ne3 20 Rfc1 Qd5 21 Qxd5 Bxd5 22 Nc6 Bxc6 23 Rxc6 f5 ∓, Vaganian–Dolmatov, USSR Chp. 1979.

(l) 14 Kd1 (14 Kf1 Rb8 15 Qg3 Qc7! 16 Nc6?! Bd6 17 Qxg7 Rg8 18 Qxf6 Qxc6 ∓, Kramer–Bisguier, New York 1955) 14 . . . Bd7 15 Nc6 Bxc6 16 Qxc6† Ke7 17 Qxb5 Rb8 18 Qg5 h6! 19 Qxg7 Qd5 20 Qg3 Rhg8 ∓, Ree–Torre, Wijk aan Zee 1984.

(m) 15 Nc6 was played in Bronstein–Botvinnik, World Chp. 1951. This game is an excellent illustration of a typical Meran ending, i.e., White's queenside passed pawns versus Black's central majority. It continued 15 . . . Bb7 16 Bf4 Bd6 17 Nxd8 Bxf3† 18 Kxf3 Rxd8 19 Bxb5† Ke7 20 Bd2 Rb8! 21 a4 Nd5 22 b3 f5 23 Rfc1 e5 24 Ke2 e4 25 Rc6 Rhc8 26 Rac1 Rxc6 27 Rxc6 Rb6 28 Rxb6 Nxb6 29 a5 Nd5 30 a6 Bc5 31 b4 Ra7 32 Bc6 Kd6 33 Bb7 h6 34 h4 g5 35 hxg5 hxg5 36 Bxg5 Nxb4 37 Bc8 Ke5 38 Bd2 Nd5 39 Bb7 Nc3† 40 Bxc3 dxc3 41 g3 Draw.

(n) 19 gxf4 Bd7 20 Nxd4 Ke7 21 Rac1 Rhc8 =, Szabo–Stahlberg, Saltsjöbaden 1948.

(o) Less analyzed but possibly more dangerous is 15 Bd2 Qa6 (on 15 . . . Qa4 16 b3 Qa6 17 a4 0-0 18 axb5 Qxa1 19 Rxa1 Rxa1 20 Ng4 Nd5?—20 . . . Nxg4 was necessary though unclear—21 Nh6†! +, Lalić–Mnatsakanian, Varna 1986) 16 a4 0-0 17 Bxb5 Bxe5 18 Bxa6 Bxa6† 19 Kd1 (± Korchnoi, ∓ Pachman!). One possible line is 19 . . . Rfb8 20 Re1 Bb7 21 Qd3 Ng4 22 Qe2 h5 23 h3 Ba6 24 Qf3 Bb7 25 Qe2 Ba6 = (Donaldson).

(p) 19 Nxa5 Rxa5 20 Rhc1 (20 Bxb4 Re5† 21 Kf1 Bb7 22 f3 Bc6 23 Rd1?! Rb8 24 Ba3 Nd5 ∓, Agzamov–Vera, Sochi 1985) 20 . . . Ba6 21 Bxa6 Rxa6 22 Rc4 Nd5 23 Rxd4 Rb8 24 Kd3 =, Reshevsky–Botvinnik, Moscow 1955.

QUEEN'S GAMBIT

Semi-Slav Defense

1 d4 d5 2 c4 c6 3 Nf3 Nf6 4 Nc3 e6 5 e3 Nbd7 6 Bd3 dxc4 7 Bxc4 b5 8 Bd3 a6 9 e4 c5 10 e5 cxd4 11 Nxb5 Nxe5 12 Nxe5 axb5

	7	8	9	10	11	12
13	0-0					Bxb5†
	Qd5					Bd7
14	Qe2					Nxd7(l)
	Rb8(a) Ba6					Qa5†
15	Bg5(b)	Bg5(d)				Bd2
	Bd6	Be7(e)				Qxb5
16	f4	f4(f)				Nxf8(m)
	h6	0-0				Kxf8
17	Bh4	Rf3				a4
	g5	Bb7				Qxb2
18	Bg3	Rh3........Re1.........Qf2.........Rg3				0-0(n)
	gxf4	g6	g6	Rxa2!	Rxa2!(j)	h5!?(o)
19	Bxf4	b3	Qf2?!	Rf1	Rxa2	Rb1
	Rg8(c)	Rfc8(g)	Rxa2(h)	Rfa8(i)	Qxa2(k)	Qa2(p)

(a) 14 ... Ra5?! 15 f4 Bd6 16 Bd2 b4 17 a3 Bxe5 18 fxe5 Qxe5 19 Qf3 Qd5 20 Qg3 Ra7 21 Rxf6 gxf6 22 Qg7 Rf8 23 Bxb4 Re7 24 Rc1 Bb7 25 Rc5 Resigns, Botvinnik–Belavenets, Leningrad 1934.

(b) 15 f4?! Be7 16 Rf3 0-0 17 Bd2 Bb7 18 Rh3 g6 19 Bxb5 Qxg2†! 20 Qxg2 Bxg2 21 Kxg2 Rxb5 ±, Kouatly–M. Raicević, Trnava 1986.

(c) Toshkov–Bagirov, Baku 1983, continued 20 Rac1 Bb7 21 Bxb5† Kf8 22 Rf3 d3 23 Bxd3 Qd4† 24 Qe3 Bxe5 25 Bxe5 Rxg2† 26 Kf1 Qxe3 27 Rxe3 Ng4 =. A possible improvement is Christiansen's 20 Ng6!? Nd7 21 Qf2.

(d) The attempt to regain the sacrificed pawn immediately is a mistake, e.g., 15 a4?! Bd6! 16 axb5 Bb7 17 Rxa8† Bxa8 18 Nc6 Bxc6 19 bxc6 Ke7 20 Bc4 Qxc6 ∓, Lilienthal–Botvinnik, Moscow 1941.

(e) Bronstein's idea of 15 ... h6?! is refuted by 16 Bh4 Bd6 17 f4 Rc8 18 a4 Bxe5 19 fxe5 Nd7 20 Rae1 ±, Seirawan–Younglove, US Open 1985.

(f) Alternatives offer White nothing: (A) 16 a4 0-0 17 axb5 Bb7 18 f4 h6 19 Bh4 Rxa1 20 Rxa1 Ra8 ∓, Alekhine–Bogolyubov, World Chp. 1934. (B) 16 Rac1 0-0 17 f4 Rac8 18 a4 Rxc1 19 Rxc1 Rc8 20 Rxc8† Bxc8 21 axb5 Bb7 22 Qc2?! Bd6! ∓, Toshkov–Dolmatov, Sofia 1984.

(g) 20 Bxb5 d3 21 Rxd3 Qc5† 22 Kh1 Ne4 (22 ... Qxb5!? 23 Rd8† Rxd8 24 Qxb5 Rxa2 25 Rg1 Ne4 26 h3 Bxg5 27 fxg5 Bd5 ∓) 23 Bxe7 Nf2† 24 Kg1 Nh3† 25 Kh1 Draw (analysis by Bogolyubov).

(h) Black's counterattack takes over before White's attack gets rolling: 20 Bb1 Ra1 21 Qh4 d3 22 Bxf6 Bxf6 23 Qxf6 d2 24 Rd1 Rxb1 25 Rxb1 d1(Q)† 26 Rxd1 Qxd1† ∓, Miles–Yusupov, Bugojno 1986.

419

(i) Bronstein's idea (18 Qf2) falls short: 20 Qh4 Ra1 21 Bxf6 Rxf1† 22 Kxf1 Bxf6 23 Qxh7†
Kf8 24 Qh5 Bxe5 25 fxe5 f5 ∓ (Donaldson).

(j) 18 . . . g6 19 h4 Kg7 20 h5 Ng8 21 hxg6 fxg6 22 Bxg6 hxg6 23 Bh6† (23 Bh4 wins) Nxh6
24 Rxg6† Kh7 25 Qh5 Bg5! 26 Rxh6† Bxh6 27 Qg6† Kh8 28 Qh6† Kg8 29 Qg6† Draw,
Donaldson–O'Donnell, Bellingham 1987. The move 18 . . . Rxa2 and the whole line with
18 Rg3 seem state-of-the-art, but it was in fact all seen in Gereben–Honfi, Hungarian
Chp. 1952, which went 18 Rg3 Rxa2 19 Re1 g6 20 h4 Qb3 21 Bxf6 Bxf6 22 Qg4 Bxe5 23
Bxg6 Qxg3 24 Qxg3 hxg6 ∓.

(k) 20 Bxf6 (on 20 Bh6 Black can choose between 20 . . . Qa1† 21 Kf2 g6 22 Bxf8 Bxf8
intending . . . Bh6 and . . . Nd5 with excellent compensation, and 20 . . . g6 21 h4 Rc8
22 f5 exf5 23 Bxf5—Maciejewski–Pinkas, Polish Chp. 1987—23 . . . d3! 24 Nxd3 Re8!
[analysis by Dobosz]) 20 . . . Bxf6 21 Nd7 Be7 22 Bxh7† (22 Nxf8?! Bxf8 23 Bxb5 Qb1†
24 Kf2 Qc1 ∓, Cichocki–Bany, Polish Chp. 1987) 22 . . . Kxh7 23 Rxg7† Draw,
Staniszewski–Kuczynski, Polish Chp. 1987.

(l) This is more challenging than 14 Bxd7†, when Black stands well after 14 . . . Nxd7
against: (A) 15 Nxd7 Bb4† 16 Bd2 Qa5 17 a3 Bxd2† 18 Qxd2 Kxd7 19 Qxa5 Rxa5 ∓,
Pokorný–Šulc, Trenčianské Teplice 1925. Black's central majority and queenside pressure give him the edge. (B) 15 Nd3 Qa5† 16 Bd2 Qd5 (16 . . . Qf5!) 17 0-0 Bd6 18 Qg4
Nf6! 19 Qg5 Qxg5 20 Bxg5 Nd5 21 Rfe1 Kd7 =, Karasev–Panchenko, USSR 1974.

(m) White gains nothing better by 16 Nxf6†, e.g. 16 . . . gxf6 17 Qe2 (17 Qf3 Qe5† 18 Kd1 Rc8
19 Re1 Qd6 20 Qxf6 Rg8 gives Black good counterplay) 17 . . . Qxe2† 18 Kxe2 Kd7 19
Rhb1 Rg8 20 g3 Ra4 =, Trifunović–Schmid, Oberhausen 1961.

(n) Karpov's novelty, prepared for his 1986 match against Kasparov, but first utilized in
Vaganian–Kuczynski, Dubai 1986. Not so good is 17 a4, e.g. 17 . . . Qxb2 18 Rb1 Qa2 19
0-0 h6 20 Rb4 Rd8 21 Bf4 Qd5 =, Smyslov–Torre, Bugojno 1984.

(o) Other possibilities are: (A) 18 . . . Kg8?! 19 Bf4 h6 20 Be5 Rd8 21 Qd3 Ng4 22 Bc7 Rc8
23 Rac1 ±, Ftáčnik–Pinter, Warsaw 1987. (B) 18 . . . Nd5 19 Rb1 Qa3 20 Qh5! Kg8 21
Rb7 Rf8 22 Qe2! ±, Staniszewski–Bany, Polish Chp. 1987. With 18 . . . h5 Black keeps
White's queen away from h5 and prepares to develop his rook via . . . h4 and . . . Rh5.

(p) 20 Bf4 Kg8 (interesting is 20 . . . Qd5 centralizing the queen) 21 Rb4 Nd5 22 Rxd4 Nxf4
23 Rxf4 e5 24 Re4 Rh6! 25 h3 Rha6 26 Qxg5 Rxa4 27 Rxe5 ±, Vilela–Kuczynski,
Camaguey 1987.

QUEEN'S GAMBIT

Semi-Slav Defense

1 d4 d5 2 c4 c6 3 Nf3 Nf6 4 Nc3 e6 5 e3 Nbd7 6 Bd3 dxc4 7 Bxc4 b5 8 Bd3 a6 9 e4 c5 10 d5 (Reynolds Variation)

	13	14	15	16	17	18
10	e5(a)			c4		
11	b3			dxe6(l)		
	Bd6		c4!?	cxd3		
12	0-0		bxc4	exd7†		
	0-0		Bb4(i)	Qxd7		
13	a4	Re1	Bd2	Ne5(m)	0-0	
	c4!?	Rb8(e)	bxc4	Qe7	Bb7	
14	bxc4	Bf1!(f)	Bc2	Bf4(n)	Bg5(p)	Re1
	b4	Re8(g)	Qa5(j)	Nxe4!	Be7	Be7(t)
15	Ne2	a4	Ne2	0-0	e5(q)	e5(u)
	Nc5	b4	Nxe4	Nxc3	Ne4	Nd5
16	Ng3	Nb1	Bxe4	bxc3	Bxe7	Ne4(v)
	Qc7(c)	Nb6	c3	Qb7	Kxe7	0-0
17	Be3	Nbd2	Nxc3	Re1	Nxe4(r)	Qxd3
	a5(d)	Re7(h)	Bxc3(k)	Be7(o)	Bxe4(s)	Qg4(w)

(a) With this move Black resolves the situation in the center. White has a protected passed d-pawn while Black has a queenside majority. Black will try to mobilize this majority while White is trying to undermine it with a2-a4. Three inferior tries for Black on move 10 are: (A) 10 . . . exd5 11 e5 Ng4 12 Bg5 f6 13 exf6 Ndxf6 14 h3 Nh6 15 0-0! Bb7 16 Re1† Be7 17 Bxf6 gxf6 18 Qd2 Nf7 19 Qf4 ± (Trifunović). (B) 10 . . . Bb7 11 0-0 Be7 12 Bf4 Nh5? 13 Be3 e5 14 a4! b4 15 Nb1 0-0 16 Nbd2 ±, Ribli–Smyslov, London 1983. (C) 10 . . . Nb6 11 dxe6 Bxe6 12 Qe2 Be7 13 0-0 b4 14 Nd1 c4 15 Bc2 Bc5 16 Ne3 Qc7 17 Bd2 h6 18 Rfc1 0-0 19 e5 Nd5 20 Nf5 ±, Suvalić–Trifunović, Yugoslav Chp. 1961.

(b) This pawn sacrifice of Simagin's is the best practical chance. Black gains c5 for his pieces while denying c4 to White. On 13 . . . b4 White gets a clear edge by 14 Ne2 Nh5 15 Nd2 Nf4 16 Nc4 Nb6 17 Nxf4 Nxc4 18 Ne6! fxe6 19 Bxc4 Qe7 20 dxe6 Bxe6 21 Bg5 Qd7 22 Qd3 Bxc4 23 Qxc4† Qf7 24 Rac1 Qxc4 25 Rxc4 ±, Agzamov–Rajković, Vršac 1983.

(c) 16 . . . a5 17 h3 Qc7 18 Nh4 g6 19 Bh6 Ne8 20 Re1 (20 Bxf8?! Bxf8 intending . . . Nd6 with strong counterplay on the dark squares) 20 . . . Ng7 21 Re3 ±, Boleslavsky–Botvinnik, USSR 1952.

(d) 18 Bxc5 Bxc5 19 Nd2 g6 20 Nb3 Nd7 21 Qd2 Bd6 22 Ne2 Nc5 23 Nc5 Bxc5 24 Nc1 f5 25 exf5 Bxf5 26 Bxf5 Rxf5 27 Nb3 Raf8 =, van der Sterren–Bagirov, Baku 1986. Black's activity just compensates for the material deficit.

(e) (A) Now 13 . . . c4 is inappropriate in view of 14 bxc4 b4 15 Na4!. (B) On 13 . . . Nb6 White obtains a clear edge via 14 Bf1 Qc7 15 Bg5 Ne8 16 a4! b4 17 Nb1 a5 18 Nbd2 Bb7 19 Rc1 as in Portisch–E. Kristiansen, Skopje 1972.

(f) The bishop steps out of the way of . . . c4 as the final preparation for a4.

(g) On 14 . . . Ne8 White has 15 a4 Nc7 16 axb5 axb5 17 Bg5 f6 18 Be3 intending Nh4, g3, and f4 with a clear advantage.

(h) 18 Bb2 Ne8 19 Rc1 f6 20 a5 Na8 21 Nc4 Rc7 22 Nfd2 Bd7 23 f4! ±, Polugaevsky–Biyiasas, Petropolis 1973.

(i) Here 12 . . . bxc4 13 Bc2 Bb4 14 Bd2 transposes back to the column.

(j) Black has to play sharply. On 14 . . . 0-0 White had time to consolidate his positional advantage in Flear–Haugli, Gausdal 1987, by 15 0-0 a5 16 a3 Bc5 17 Qe2 Ba6 18 a4 Qc7 19 Rab1 Bb4 20 Rfc1 Rfc8 21 Qe3 Nc5 22 Na2 Bxd2 23 Nxd2 Rab8 24 Rxb8 Rxb8 25 Qc3.

(k) 18 0-0 Bxd2 19 Nxd2 0-0 20 Nc4 Qb4 21 d6! Ra7 22 Bd5 Rd8 23 Re1 ±, Honfi–Kempe, corr. 1978–79.

(l) 11 Bc2 and now: (A) 11 . . . Nc5?! 12 Bg5 b4 13 Na4! exd5 14 e5 h6 15 Nxc5 Bxc5 16 exf6 hxg5 17 fxg7 Rg8 18 Ba4† Bb5 19 0-0 ±, Brglez–Archangelsky, corr. 1985–87. (B) 11 . . . Qc7 12 0-0 Bc5 13 Qe2 (better might be 13 dxe6, transposing to col. 21) 13 . . . e5! 14 Nh4 0-0 15 Kh1 Bd4 ∓, Kharitonov–Ivanchuk, USSR Chp. 1988.

(m) (A) 13 e5 Nd5 14 Qxd3 Nxc3 15 Qxc3 (15 Qxd7† Bxd7 16 bxc3 Rc8 17 Bd2 Ba3 =) 15 . . . Bb7 16 0-0 Rc8 17 Qd4 (17 Qb3 Be7 18 Bf4 Qf5! 19 Bg3 h5! 20 e6 fxe6 21 Rfe1 Bd5 22 Qe3 h4 23 Be5 0-0 ∓, Scheeren–R. Kuijf, Hilversum 1986) 17 . . . Bxf3 18 Qxd7† Kxd7 19 gxf3 Ke6 20 Bf4 Rc4! ∓, Ivanov–Sakharov, Kislovodsk 1976. (B) 13 Bg5 Be7 14 Bxf6 Bxf6 15 Nd5 Bb7! 16 Nxf6† gxf6 17 0-0 0-0 18 Re1 Re8 19 Nd2 f5 =, Vaganian–Drago Cirić, San Feliu de Guixols 1975.

(n) Black has an easy game after 14 Nxd3, e.g. 14 . . . b4 15 Ne2 Qxe4 16 0-0 Be7 17 Ng3 (17 Re1 Qb7, Portisch–Trifunović, Sarajevo 1962) 17 . . . Qb7 18 Bg5 0-0 19 Nh5 Nxh5 20 Bxe7 Qxe7 21 Qxh5 Qxe4 =, Gligorić–Torre, Bugojno 1984.

(o) 18 Qxd3 0-0 19 Nd7 Qxd7 20 Qxd7 Bxd7 21 Rxe7 Be6 Draw, Chekhov–Alexandria, Halle 1981.

(p) (A) 14 Ne5 (played if White is satisfied with a draw) 14 . . . Qd4 15 Nf3 (15 Nxd3 is strongly met by 15 . . . 0-0-0) 15 . . . Qd7 16 Ne5 Qd4 17 Nf3 Qd7 Draw, Suba–Chernin, Tunis 1985. (B) 14 e5 Nd5 15 Qxd3 (not 15 Ne4? Qg4! 16 Qxd3? Nb4 wins) 15 . . . Nxc3 16 Qxc3 is a transposition to note (m).

(q) Two other options for White are: (A) 15 Ne5 Qd4 16 Nxd3 Rd8 17 Bxf6 Bxf6 18 Nf4 0-0 when Black's bishop-pair gives him good compensation for the pawn. (B) 15 Re1 Rd8 (15 . . . 0-0 16 e5 Ng4 17 Bxe7 Qxe7 18 Qxd3 Bxf3 19 Qxf3 Nxe5 20 Qg3 Rae8 21 Rad1 f6 =, Korchnoi–Flear, Wijk aan Zee 1987) 16 e5 Ng4 17 Ne4 (17 Bf4?! Qf5 18 Bg3 h5! 19 h3 h4 20 hxg4 Qxg4 21 Nxh4 Rxh4 22 Qxg4 Rxg4 23 Red1 Bg5 24 a3 f5 +, L. Popov–Bojković, Novi Sad 1980; or 17 Bxe7 Qxe7 18 h3 d2! 19 Nxd2 Nxf2 20 Kxf2 Qh4† 21 Kg1 Qd4† 22 Kh1 Qxd2 ∓, van der Sterren–R. Kuijf, Dutch Chp. 1986) 17 . . . 0-0 18 Qd2 (18 h3? Bxe4 19 Rxe4 Nxf2!, Gligorić–Ljubojević, Belgrade 1979) 18 . . . Bxg5 19 Qxg5 Bxe4 20 Rxe4 f6 21 exf6 Nxf6 ∓, Nenashev–Kajdanov, Pinsk 1986.

(r) (A) 17 Re1 Nxc3 18 bxc3 Qg4! 19 h3 Bxf3 20 hxg4 Bxd1 21 Raxd1 Rhd8 22 Re3 d2 ∓, Gavrikov–Chernin, USSR Chp. 1987. (B) 17 Qb3 Nxc3 18 Qxc3 Rhc8! 19 e6?! Rxc3 20 exd7 Bxf3 21 bxc3 Be2 ∓, Farago–Tukmakov, Dortmund 1987.

(s) 18 Re1 Qd5 19 Nd2 Bg6 20 Qg4 Rhc8 21 h4 h5 22 Qb4 Ke8 23 a4 a5 24 Qf4 ±, Tukmakov–Nogueiras, Leningrad 1987.

(t) 14 . . . Bb4 15 Ne5 Qe6 16 Nxd3 Bxc3 17 Nf4 Qd7 18 bxc3 Nxe4 19 Qxd7† Kxd7 20 Ba3 with a big advantage for White, Karpov–Tal, Bugojno 1980.

(u) 15 Bg5 transposes to note (q).

(v) 16 Qxd3 Nxc3 17 Qxc3 0-0 18 Bg5 Rac8 19 Qe3 Bxg5 20 Qxg5 Bxf3 21 gxf3 Rc6 =, Portisch–Yusupov, Montpellier 1985.

(w) 18 Ng3 Nb4 19 Qf5 Qg6 20 Rd1 Rad8 21 Rxd8 Rxd8 22 Bg5 Qxf5 23 Nxf5 Bxg5 24 Nxg5 Nxa2 25 Nd6 Bd5 = (Donaldson).

QUEEN'S GAMBIT

Semi-Slav Defense

1 d4 d5 2 c4 c6 3 Nf3 Nf6 4 Nc3 e6 5 e3 Nbd7 6 Bd3 dxc4 (Meran Variation) 7 Bxc4 b5 8 Bd3 a6 9 e4 c5 10 d5 c4 11 dxe6 fxe6 12 Bc2

	19	20	21	22	23	24
	Qc7(a) Bb7				
13	Ng5 0-0				0-0(o)	
	Nc5	Bd6 . . . . Bc5!?			Qc7	
14	f4	Nd4(d)	e5(h) Qe2		Ng5 . . . . Qe2	
	Bb7(b)	Nb6	Nxe5	Ne5	Nc5	Bd6(r)
15	e5	Kh1(e)	Bf4	Nxe5(k)	f4	Ng5(s)
	Rd8	Bd7	Bd6	Qxe5	h6!?	Nc5
16	Bd2	f4	Bxe5(i)	Be3(l)	e5?!	f4
	Nd5	e5	Bxe5	Bxe3	Nd3	e5
17	Qh5†	Nf3	Nxe5	Qxe3	Bxd3(p)	a4!
	g6	Bg4	Qxe5	0-0(m)	0-0-0!	b4
18	Bxg6†	a4	Re1	Rad1	Nf3	Nd5
	hxg6	b4!?(f)	Qc5	Ng4	Rxd3	Nxd5
19	Qxh8	a5	Ne4	Qg3	Qe2	exd5
	Nxf4(c)	Bxf3(g)	Nxe4(j)	Qxg3(n)	Bc5†(q)	0-0-0(t)

(a) (A) 12 . . . Nc5 13 Qxd8† Kxd8 14 0-0 Bb7 15 Ng5 Ke7 16 e5 Nfd7 17 f4 b4 18 Nce4 h6 19 Be3! ±, Forintos–Ciric, Sarajevo 1965. (B) 12 . . . Qb6 13 0-0 Bb7 14 Qe2 0-0-0 15 a4 b4 16 a5 Qc7 17 Na4 b3 18 Bb1 Bb4 19 Bf4! ±, Christiansen–Nikolac, Wijk aan Zee 1976.

(b) An interesting alternative is 14 . . . h6, e.g. 15 e5 hxg5 16 exf6 gxf6 17 Bg6† Ke7 18 Qd4 Rg8 19 Bh7 Rg7 20 Be4 Qa7 21 Be3 (Guseinov–Ziatdinov, Tashkent 1985) 21 . . . Nxe4 22 Nxe4 Qxd4 23 Bxd4 Rg6 24 fxg5 f5 $\overline{\overline{=}}$.

(c) 20 0-0-0 Qxe5 21 Qxe5 Nfd3† 22 Kc2 Nxe5 23 Be3! ±, Farago–Chandler, Belgrade 1982.

(d) The most energetic choice. With this move White attacks e6, prepares f2-f4, and sets up possibilities of Nxb5. Other moves are not nearly so effective, e.g. 14 Ne2?! Nc5 15 Qd4?! e5 16 Qe3 Ne6 17 b3 0-0 18 Bb2 Ng4! 19 Qd2 Nd4 20 Nexd4 exd4 21 Qxd4 Bxh2† 22 Kh1 Bb7 23 e5 Rf4 24 Qd6 Qxd6 25 exd6 Rxf3 26 Bd1 Raf8 27 d7 Nxf2† $\overline{\overline{=}}$, Peev–Kupreichik, Plovdiv 1980.

(e) 15 f4?! e5 16 Nf3 Bg4 17 h3 0-0-0 18 Kh1 Bxf3 19 Qxf3 exf4, $\overline{\overline{=}}$, Farago–Radulov, Baile Herculaine 1982. White's best is probably 15 a4! b4 16 a5 bxc3 17 axb6 cxb2 18 Bxb2 Qxb6 19 Rb1 ±.

(f) 18 . . . exf4 19 axb5 a5 20 Qe1 Bxf3 21 Rxf3 0-0 22 Qh4 $\pm$, Furman–Bronstein, USSR Chp. 1975.

(g) 20 Rxf3 Nbd7 21 Nd5 Nxd5 22 Qxd5 0-0-0! =, Browne–Stoliarov, Berkeley 1978.

(h) (A) 14 b3?! 0-0 15 h3 Ne5 16 bxc4 Nfg4! 17 Nxe5 Nxf2 18 Qh5 g6 19 Qe2 Nh3† 20 Kh2 Qxe5† 21 Kh3 Qxc3† 22 Resigns, Vaganian–Panchenko, Moscow 1981. (B) 14 Ng5?!

424

Ne5! 15 Bf4 0-0 16 Bg3 h6 17 Nh3 Bb7 18 Qe2 Bd4 19 Rad1 Rad8 20 Nf4 Qb6 21 h3 b4 22 Na4 Qc6 $\mp$, Georgadze–Yusupov, USSR Chp. 1980–81.

(i) Black has good compensation for the exchange after 16 Re1 Nxf3† 17 Qxf3 Bxf4 18 Qxa8 Bxh2† 19 Kh1 0-0 20 Qf3 g6, Loginov–Bagirov, Yaroslavl' 1980.

(j) 20 Bxe4 Ra7 21 b4!? Qg5 22 Bc6† Kf7 23 a4 Rd8 24 Qf3† Kg8 25 axb5 Rf7 =, Korchnoi–Torre, Brussels 1987.

(k) 15 Bf4 Nxf3† 16 Qxf3 e5 17 Bg5 0-0 18 Bxf6 gxf6 19 Nd5 Qg7 ∞, Suba–Vera, Timisoara 1987.

(l) Black's bishops become very strong if White plays for f4 without first Be3: 16 Kh1 Bb7 17 f4 Qh5 18 Qxh5 Nxh5 19 e5 0-0-0 20 f5 Rd4 21 Re1 Rh4 $\mp$, Lukacs–Vera, Cienfuegos 1983.

(m) Also quite good is 17 . . . Ng4, e.g. 18 Qh3 h5 19 Rad1 0-0 20 Rd2 Qg5 21 f4 Qc5† 22 Kh1 Qe3 23 Qxe3 Nxe3 24 Rff2 Nxc2 25 Rxc2 Bb7 26 a3 Rhd8 27 Kg1 Rd4 28 Rcd2 Rfd8 29 Rxd4 Rxd4 $\mp$, Tarjan–Remlinger, Los Angeles 1981. The d-file, bishop vs. knight, and 3 vs. 2 pawns on the queenside eventually proved to be too much for White.

(n) 20 hxg3 Ra7 21 Rd2 b4 22 Na4 Rc7 23 Rfd1 a5 24 Rd8 Rxd8 25 Rxd8† Kf7 26 Nb6 Bb7 27 Rd1 Ke7 $\mp$, Hort–Sehner, German Bundesliga 1985–86.

(o) 13 Ng5!? Qb6 14 Qf3 Bc5 15 0-0 $\pm$ is an interesting try.

(p) Black has good play after 17 Nxe6 Qb6† 18 Kh1 Qxe6 19 exf6 0-0-0 or 17 exf6 hxg5 18 f7† Qxf7 19 Bxd3 0-0-0 (Yusupov).

(q) 20 Kh1 Nd5 21 Ne4 Rf8! 22 Ne1 Rd4 23 Nxc5 Qxc5 24 Qg4 Qe7 25 Nf3 Rdxf4 26 Bxf4 Rxf4 27 Qg3 g5 28 Rael Qb4! 29 Rf2 Ne7! was good for Black in Gligorić–Yusupov, Vrbas 1980.

(r) 14 . . . Bc5 15 e5 Ng4 16 Be4! 0-0 17 Bxh7† Kxh7 18 Ng5† Kg8 19 Qxg4 Qxe5 20 Qxe6† $\pm$, Portisch–Inkiov, Lucerne 1982.

(s) 15 Re1!? Ne5 16 Ng5 Qe7 17 f4 Bc5† 18 Kh1 Nd3 19 Bxd3 cxd3 20 Qxd3 Ng4 21 Nh3 0-0 22 Qg3 h5 23 Nd1 Rad8, Torre–A. Mikhalchishin, Baku 1980. Black has full compensation for the pawn.

(t) 20 Qxc4 exf4 21 Bxf4 Bxf4 22 Rxf4 Rxd5 23 Rf7 Rd7 24 Rxd7 Nxd7 25 Qxc7† Kxc7 26 Ne6† Kd6 27 Nxg7 Nc5 =, Black's active pieces compensate for the pawn.

QUEEN'S GAMBIT

Semi-Slav Defense

1 d4 d5 2 c4 c6 3 Nf3 Nf6 4 Nc3 e6 5 e3 Nbd7 6 Bd3 dxc4 7 Bxc4 b5

	25	26	27	28	29	30
8	(Bd3)...Bb3........Be2					
	Bb7 ....b4			Be7	Bb7	
9	e4 0-0		Ne4		0-0	0-0(o)
	b4	b4	Be7........Nxe4		0-0	Be7(p)
10	Na4	Ne4	Nxf6†	Bxe4	Re1(l)	e4
	c5	Be7(c)	Nxf6	Bb7	Bb7	b4
11	e5	Nxf6†	e4	Qa4(i)	e4	e5
	Nd5	Nxf6	Bb7	Qb6	b4	bxc3
12	0-0	e4	Qe2(f)	Nd2	Na4	exf6
	cxd4	0-0	Qb6(g)	Rc8	c5	Nxf6(q)
13	Nxd4	e5	0-0	a3	d5(m)	bxc3
	a6(a)	Nd7(d)	Rc8	bxa3	exd5	0-0
14	Nxe6	Be4	Bg5	b3(j)	e5	Rb1
	fxe6(b)	Qb6(e)	h6(h)	Ba6(k)	Ne8(n)	Qc7(r)

(a) (A) 13 . . . g6 14 Qg4 Bg7 15 Bg5 Nxe5 16 Nxe6! ±, Razuvaev–Bagirov, USSR 1987. (B) 13 . . . Nxe5 14 Bb5† Nd7 15 Re1 Rc8 (15 . . . a6 16 Bc6 Qc7 17 Nxe6 fxe6 18 Qxd5 ±, Ftáčnik) 16 Qh5 g6 17 Qe5 Qf6 18 Qxf6 Nxf6 19 Bg5 Bg7 with good prospects for Black, Ftáčnik–Tukmakov, Biel 1988.

(b) 15 Qh5† Ke7 16 Bg5† N5f6 17 exf6† gxf6 18 Bh4 Qe8 19 Qg4 Kf7 20 Rfe1 Bd6 21 Rxe6 Rg8 22 Qh5† Kxe6 23 Bc4† Ke7 24 Qxh7† Kd8 25 Qxg8 wins, Simagin–Sveshnikov, Sochi 1987.

(c) 10 . . . Nxe4 transposes to column 28.

(d) If 13 . . . Nd5?! 14 Qc2 g6 15 Bh6 Re8 16 Nd2 intending 17 Nb3 or 17 Ne4 controlling c5 ± (Mednis).

(e) 15 Bg5 Rfe8 (15 . . . Bxg5 16 Bxh7† Kxh7 17 Ng5† Kg6 18 Qg4—or 18 h4!?—18 . . . f5 19 Qg3 c5 20 Nxe6† Kf7 21 Nxf8 Rxf8 22 dxc5 Nxc5 23 Rad1 Kg8 24 Rd6 Qb5 25 Rfd1 f4 26 Qg4, intending 27 Rf6 or 27 Rd8 ±, analysis by Donaldson and Silman) 16 Bxe7 Rxe7 17 Qc2 h6 18 a3! b3 19 Qc3 c5 20 Bxb7 Qxb7 21 dxc5 Rc8 22 Qb4! Nxc5 23 Rac1 Qc6 (Polugaevsky–Mednis, Riga 1979) 24 Rc4 Rec7 25 Rfc1 Qd5 26 Qb5! ±.

(f) 12 0-0 = is column 26.

(g) 12 . . . Nd7?! 13 0-0 0-0 14 Rd1 Qa5 15 a3 c5 16 Bd2 cxd4 17 Nxd4 Qb6 18 be3 ±, Tarjan–Paoli, Odessa 1976.

(h) 15 Bh4 c5 16 Bxf6 Bxf6 17 d5 ± (Korchnoi).

(i) While present theory considers 12 Qa4 to be a refutation of 8 . . . b4, it fails to take into account analysis given below. So White does better with 11 0-0 Be7 12 Nd2 Qc7 13 b3 0-0 14 Bb2 f5 15 Bf3 e5 16 Nc4 e4 17 Be2 c5 18 Rc1 Rad8 19 Qc2 ±, Tukmakov–A. Mikhalchishin, Frunze 1979.

(j) 14 Nc4 Qa6 15 Qb3 Rb8 16 0-0 c5 17 Bxb7 Qxb7 18 Qxa3 cxd4 19 Nd6† Bxd6 20 Qxd6 Qb6 21 Qa3 Qc5 22 Qxa7 Qxa7 23 Rxa7 Nf6 24 exd4 0-0 25 Rc7 Nd5 26 Rc4 h6 27 Rd1 Rc8 28 Rxc8 Draw, Tukmakov–Ornstein, Vrnjačká Banja 1979. Black has full compensation for the pawn.

(k) 15 Nc4 Qb4† (15 . . . Qb5?! 16 Rxa3! Bxa3 17 Qxa3 Kd8 18 0-0 Rc7 19 Bd2 Nb6 20 Bd3 Rc8 21 Nxb6† Qxb6 22 Ba5 Qd8 23 Qd6† Bd7 24 Ba6! Re8 25 Rc1 Resigns, Tarjan–Silva, Odessa 1976) 16 Qxb4 Bxb4† 17 Bd2 Bxc4 18 Bxb4 Bxb3 19 Rxa3 Bd5 20 Bxd5 cxd5 21 Rxa7 ± (Kondratiev) 21 . . . Nb8! = (an idea of Cincinnati master J. Ginsburg) 22 Re7† (22 Ra8 Kd7 23 Kd2 Nc6 =; or 22 Bc5 Nc6 23 Rb7 Rb8 =; or 22 Rb7 Nc6 23 Bc5 Rb8 =) 22 . . . Kd8 23 Rb7 Nc6 24 Bd6 (24 Bc5 Rb8) 24 . . . Na5 =.

(l) 10 e4 b4 11 e5 bxc3 12 exf6 Nxf6 13 bxc3 Bb7 14 Rb1 c5! =, Fairhurst–Reshevsky, Margate 1935.

(m) 13 e5 Nd5 14 Qd3 Rc8 15 Nxc5 Nxc5 16 dxc5 Rxc5 17 Bc2 g6 18 Bh6 Re8 19 Ba4 Nb6! with an edge for Black, Korchnoi–Ribli, Montpellier 1985.

(n) 15 Bxd5 Bxd5 16 Qxd5 Nb6 =, Tatai–Pinter, Rome 1984.

(o) (A) 9 a3 b4! 10 Na4 bxa3 11 bxa3 Be7 12 0-0 0-0 13 Bb2 c5 Draw, Karpov–Kasparov, World Chp. 1984-85. (B) 9 e4 b4 10 e5 bxc3 11 exf6 cxb2 12 fxg7 bxa1 (Q) 13 gxh8 (Q) Qa5† 14 Bd2 Qxd1† 15 Bxd1 Qf5 16 0-0 0-0-0 17 Qg8 Be7 18 Qg7 Qg6 =, Chekhover–Suetin, USSR 1951.

(p) 9 . . . a6 10 e4 c5 11 e5 Nd5 12 a4 Nxc3 13 bxc3 c4 14 Ng5! Be7 15 Bf3 Bxf3 16 Qxf3 0-0 17 Qg4! Nb6 18 axb5 axb5 19 Rxa8 Nxa8 20 Ne4 Kh8 21 Re1 b4 22 Re3 bxc3 23 Rh3 g6 24 Qf4 g5?! 25 Nf6 Resigns, Christiansen–Flear, Szirak 1987.

(q) 12 . . . Bxf6 13 bxc3 c5 14 dxc5 0-0 15 Ba3 Be7 16 Qd4 Bd5 17 c4 Bc6 18 Rab1 with a pull for White, Seirawan–Petursson, New York 1987.

(r) 15 Bf4 Qxf4 16 Rxb7 Bd6 17 g3 Qf5 18 Qa4 Ne4 19 Rc1 c5 20 Qc2 Qd5 Draw, Portisch–Chernin, Reggio Emilia 1986-87.

QUEEN'S GAMBIT

Semi-Slav Defense

1 d4 d5 2 c4 c6 3 Nf3 Nf6 4 Nc3 e6 5 e3 Nbd7

	31	32	33	34	35	36
6	(Bd3) Qc2					
	Bb4 . . . . .Bd6(d)		Bd6			
7	a3	e4!(e)	Be2 . . . . .b3 . . . . .e4 . . . . .Bd2			
	Ba5(a)	dxe4(f)	0-0	0-0	dxe4	0-0
8	0-0	Nxe4	0-0	Be2	Nxe4	0-0-0
	0-0	Nxe4	dxc4	Re8(k)	Nxe4	b5(q)
9	Qc2	Bxe4	Bxc4	0-0	Qxe4	cxb5
	dxc4(b)	0-0	b5	dxc4	e5(n)	c5
10	Bxc4	0-0	Bd3	bxc4	dxe5	e4
	Bc7	h6(g)	Bb7	e5	0-0	Bb7
11	Ba2!	Bc2	e4	Bb2	exd6(o)	exd5
	e5	e5	e5	e4	Re8	Nxd5
12	h3	b3(h)	dxe5	Nd2(l)	Qxe8†	Ng5(r)
	h6(c)	f5(i)	Nxe5(j)	Qe7(m)	Qxe8†(p)	g6(s)

(a) 7 . . . Bd6 8 e4 dxe4 9 Nxe4 Nxe4 10 Bxe4 e5 11 0-0 0-0 12 Bc2 (White could win a pawn by 12 dxe5 Nxe5 13 Nxe5 Bxe5 14 Bxh7† Kxh7 15 Qh5† Kg8 16 Qxe5, but after 16 . . . Qd3! White is forced to play 17 b3, and the position after 17 . . . Be6 intending . . . Bd5 is very drawish despite the extra pawn. Compare this to column 32 where the White pawn stands on a2 and the sacrifice would be unsound) 12 . . . Re8 13 Re1 exd4 14 Rxe8 Qxe8 15 Qxd4 Be7 16 Bg5! ±, Kasparov–Hübner, Brussels 1986.

(b) 9 . . . Qe7 10 Bd2 dxc4 11 Bxc4 e5 12 Ba2! Bxc3 13 Bxc3 exd4 14 Nxd4 ±, Rogoff–Lombardy, US Chp. 1978.

(c) 13 e4 Re8 14 Be3 Nh5?! 15 Rad1 exd4 16 Bxd4! Qe7 17 e5! Nf8? 18 Nb5! Ne6 19 Bxe6 fxe6 20 Nxc7 Qxc7 21 Qg6 Qf7 22 Qxf7† Kxf7 23 Be3 Rf8 24 Rd4 Kg8 25 Rfd1 b6 26 Rh4 Rf5 27 Nd4 Resigns, Kasparov–van der Wiel, Brussels 1987.

(d) 6 . . . Be7 7 b3 0-0 8 0-0 b6 9 Bb2 Bb7 10 Qe2 Rc8 11 e4 dxe4 12 Nxe4 c5 13 Rad1 Qc7 14 dxc5 bxc5 15 Rfe1! Rfd8 16 Neg5 ±, Chernin–Utasi, Starý Smokovec 1984.

(e) Timing is critical. If White delays for one move, Black will be all right, e.g. 7 0-0 0-0 8 e4 dxc4 9 Bxc4 e5 10 Bg5 h6 11 Bh4 Qe7.

(f) Forced, as 7 . . . dxc4 8 Bxc4 e5 9 dxe5 Nxe5 10 Nxe5 Bxe5 11 Qxd8† Kxd8 12 Bxf7 is good for White.

(g) To prepare . . . e5, which if played immediately drops a pawn to 11 dxe5 Nxe5 12 Nxe5 Bxe5 13 Bxh7† Kxh7 14 Qh5† Kg8 15 Qxe5. On 10 . . . c5 White keeps the edge with 11 Bc2 b6 12 Qd3 g6 13 Bh6 Re8 14 Rad1 Bf8 15 dxc5 Bxh6 16 c6, Rubinstein–Bogolyubov, Triberg 1921.

(h) On 12 Re1 Black has two paths to equality: (A) 12 . . . Bb4 13 Bd2 Bxd2 14 Qxd2 exd4 15 Nxd4 Nf6 16 Rad1 Qc7 =, Bagirov–Chernikov, USSR 1975. (B) 12 . . . exd4 13 Qxd4

Bc5 14 Qf4 Nf6 15 h3 Bd6 (15 . . . Be6 16 b3 Bd6 17 Qh4 Nd7? 18 Bg5 ±, F. Olafsson–O'Kelly, Varna 1962; correct was 17 . . . Nh7) 16 Qh4 (threatening 17 Bxh6) 16 . . . Nh7! =, Donaldson–Bisguier, Philadelphia 1987.

(i) 12 . . . f5 (12 . . . exd4 13 Qxd4 Bc5 14 Qf4 ±; or 12 . . . Re8 13 Re1 exd4 14 Rxe8 Qxe8 15 Qxd4 Bc5 16 Qd3 Nf8 17 Bb2 Be6 ±) 13 dxe5 Nxe5 14 Bb2 Qc7 15 h3 Nxf3† 16 Qxf3 Be6 17 Rfe1 Rae8 18 Re2! Bc8 19 Rae1 Qf7? (19 . . . Rxe2 20 Rxe2 b6 ±) 20 c5! ± Bb8 21 b4 Rxe2 22 Rxe2 Kh7 23 Bb3 Rd8 24 Qe3! Qg6 25 Qe7 Rh8 26 h4! h5 27 Bf7 Qh6 28 Re6! Resigns, Tukmakov–Bareyev, USSR Chp. 1987.

(j) 13 Nxe5 Bxe5 14 h3 (on 14 f4 Black has . . . Bd4† and . . . Ng4) 14 . . . Re8 15 Be3 (as 15 f4 is still answered by . . . Bd4† and . . . Ng4) 15 . . . Qe7 16 Rae1 a6 17 Ne2 (with the threat of e4) 17 . . . c5! 18 Bxc5 (18 f4 c5) 18 . . . Qc7 19 Bd4 draw, Portisch–Tukmakov, Reggio Emilia 1987-88.

(k) 8 . . . e5 9 cxd5 Nxd5 10 Nxd5 cxd5 11 dxe5 Nxe6 12 Bb2 (12 0-0? Nxf3† 13 Bxf3 Qh4 14 g3 Qf6 15 Bxd5 Bf5! 16 e4 Bh3 17 Rd1 Be5! 18 Resigns, Teichmann–de Carbonnel, corr. 1960) 12 . . . Bb4† 13 Kf1 (13 Bc3 Bf5 14 Qd2 Nxf3† 15 Bxf3 Bxc3 16 Qxc3 Be4 =) 13 . . . Nxf3† 14 Bxf3 Be6 15 Qd3 Be7 16 Ke2 Qa5 17 Rhc1 Rac8 18 a3 h6 19 Kf1 Qb6 20 Kg1 Qd6 21 Bd1 ±, Portisch–Hübner, Brussels 1986.

(l) 12 Ng5 (hoping for 12 . . . Qe7? 13 c5 Bc7 14 Bc4) 12 . . . Ng4! 13 Bxg4 Qxg5 =.

(m) 13 Rfe1 (13 Rae1 Nf8 14 Bd1 Bc7 15 f3 exf3 16 Nxf3 Be6! 17 Be2 Bg4 18 Bd3 Rad8 19 Kh1 Ng6 =, Co. Ionescu–Chernin, Sochi 1986) 13 . . . Nf8 14 f3 exf3 15 Bxf3 Ng4 16 Nf1 Qh4 17 g3 (if 17 h3 Nf6 18 e4 Ne6 intending . . . Ng5 with good attacking chances) 17 . . . Qg5 18 Ne4?! Qg6 19 Qg2 Bb4 20 Re2 Bf5 ∓, Taimanov–Barbero, Montpellier 1986. Black has good play against White's ponderous center and weakened kingside.

(n) (A) 9 . . . c5 10 Bd2 Nf6 11 Qc2 cxd4 12 Nxd4 Bc5 13 Nb3 Be7 14 Be2 Qc7 15 0-0 Bd7 16 Rac1 Rc8 17 Nd4 0-0 =, Smyslov–Chernin, Subotica 1987. (B) 9 . . . Bb4† 10 Bd2 Bxd2† 11 Nxd2 0-0 12 0-0-0! Stoltz–0. Bernstein, Groningen 1946.

(o) Pretty much forced, as alternatives favor Black, e.g. (A) 11 Ng5?! Nf6!; (B) 11 Bd3?! f5!; (C) 11 Be2 Nxe5 12 Nxe5 Qa5† ∓; (D) 11 Bf4 Bb4† 12 Ke2 Nc5 13 Qe3 Ne6 and . . . f6 ∓.

(p) 13 Be3 Nf6 14 0-0-0 Bf5 (14 . . . Be6 15 Bd3 b5 16 c5 Bxa2 17 Rhe1 Bb3 18 Bg5 Qd8 19 Nd4! ±) 15 Bd3 Bxd3 16 Rxd3 Qe6 17 b3 a5 18 Rhd1 a4 (18 . . . Nd7!?) 19 d7 Rd8 20 Bg5 Rxd7 21 Rxd7 Nxd7 22 Re1 Qg4 23 Re8† Nf8 24 Be7 h6 25 Rxf8† Kh7 26 Bc5 f6 27 Kd2 (27 Be3? Qxg2 28 Nd4 Qxh2 29 Rf7? Qe5! 30 Rxb7 h5! ∓, Schneider–Chekhov, USSR 1982) 27 . . . Qxg2 28 Ke2 Qg6 is unclear.

(q) 8 . . . e6 9 cxd5 cxd5 10 Nb5 Bb8 11 dxe5 (11 Bb4 Re8 12 Nd6 Bxd6 13 Bxd6 e4 14 Bc7 Qe7 15 Ne5 Nxe5 16 dxe5 Ng4 17 Bd6 Qe6 ∓, Petrosian–Korchnoi, USSR Chp. 1955) 11 . . . Nxe5 12 Bc3 Qe7 13 Bd4 Rd8 14 Nc3 g6 15 Nxe5 Bxe5 16 Bxe5 Qxe5 17 Rd4 Be6 18 Bd3 a6 19 Qd2 b5 =, Akesson–Dlugy, Gausdal 1982. Black's play on the queenside provides full compensation for the isolated pawn.

(r) 12 Ne4 (12 Nxd5 Bxd5 13 Bc4 Bxf3 14 gxf3 cxd4 ∓—Kupreichik) 12 . . . Be7 13 dxc5 Nxc5 14 Nxc5 Bxc5 15 Ng5 g6 16 Ne4 Bd4! 17 Kb1 Rc8 18 Qd3 Nf6! 19 f3 Nxe4 20 fxe4 Qf6 21 Bc1 Rfd8 22 Qf3 Qe5 23 Bd3 Rxc1† 24 Rxc1 Bxb2 25 Rc2 Ba3 26 Rf1 f5 27 Qe2 Rd4 28 Resigns, Marović–Kupreichik, Medina del Campo 1980.

(s) 13 Nge4 Be7 14 dxc5 Nxc5 15 Nxc5 Bxc5 16 Bh6 Re8 =. Black's active pieces and pressure along the c-file yield adequate play for the pawn.

QUEEN'S GAMBIT

Semi-Slav Defense

1 d4 d5 2 c4 c6 3 Nf3 Nf6 4 Nc3 e6 5 Bg5(a)

	37	38	39	40	41	42
	h6................dxc4					
6	Bxf6(b)		e4(h)			
	Qxf6		b5			
7	e3 ....g3(f)		a4 ....e5			
	Nd7	Nd7	Bb7		h6	
8	Bd3	Bg2	e5(i)		Bh4	
	Bd6(c)	dxc4	h6		g5	
9	0-0	0-0	Bh4........Bxf6(m)		exf6	
	Qe7	Be7	g5	gxf6	gxh4	
10	c5(d)	e3	exf6(j)	axb5	Ne5	
	Bc7	0-0	gxh4	cxb5	Qxf6	
11	e4	Qe2	axb5(k)	Nxb5	a4 ....Be2(t)	
	dxe4	e5	cxb5	Qb6!(n)	Bb7(q)	Nd7
12	Bxe4	Qxc4	Nxb5	Qa4(o)	Be2(r)	0-0(u)
	0-0(e)	exd4(g)	Bb4†(l)	Nc6(p)	c5(s)	Nxe5(v)

(a) (A) 5 Qb3 dxc4 6 Qxc4 b5 7 Qb3 Nbd7 8 g3 a6 9 Bg2 Bb7 10 0-0 c5 11 Bg4 cxd4 12 Nxd4 Bxg2 13 Kxg2 Qb6 14 Rad1 Bc5 15 Nf3 0-0 16 Nd2 h6 17 Bxf6 Nxf6 =, Radulov–S. Grunberg, Sofia 1986. (B) 5 g3 dxc4 6 Bg2 Nbd7 7 0-0 Be7 8 e4 0-0 9 a4 b6 10 Qe2 Ba6 11 Rd1 Rc8 12 Bf4 Re8 13 h3 Bb4 14 g4 Bxc3 15 bxc3 Qe7 16 Bg5 h6 17 Bc1 Nh7 ∓, Kopec–Bisguier, US Open 1987.

(b) 6 Bh4 dxc4 7 e4 g5 (7 . . . b5 transposes into columns 39-42) 8 Bg3 Bb4 9 Bxc4 (9 Be5 Nbd7 10 Bxc4 Nxe5 11 Nxe5 Nxe4 12 Qf3 Nd6 13 0-0-0 g4 14 Qxg4 Qxg5† 15 Qxg5 hxg5 =, Pytel–Minev, Albania 1973) 9 . . . Nxe4 10 0-0 Nxg3 11 fxg3 Nd7 12 Qb3 Be7 13 Rae1 Nb6 14 Bd3 0-0 =, Lputian–Sveshnikov, USSR Chp. 1985.

(c) 8 . . . Qd8 9 0-0 Be7 10 Rc1 0-0 11 e4 dxc4 12 Bxc4 b5 13 Bd3 Bb7 14 e5 Qb6 15 Be4 Rfd8 16 Qe2 ±, Rastenis–Chernin, USSR 1985.

(d) Preparing for e4 while preventing Black's answer . . . dxc4 and . . . e5. Tamer is 10 e4 dxc4 11 Bxc4 e5 12 d5 Nb6 13 dxc6 bxc6 14 Bb3 Bg4 15 h3 Bh5 16 Rc1 0-0 17 g4 Bg6 18 Nh4 Rfd8 19 Nxg6 Qf6 20 Ne2 Rac8 21 Ng3 Qg6 =, Beliavsky–Bagirov, USSR 1982.

(e) 13 b4 Rd8 14 Re1 Nf6 15 Bc2 b6 16 Ba4! Bb7 17 Qe2 a5 18 a3 ±, Polugaevsky–Mecking, match 1977.

(f) Alternatives are (A) 7 Qc2 Nd7 8 e4 dxe4 9 Qxe4 Bb4! 10 Bd3 Qe7 11 0-0 Nf6 12 Qh4 c5 =, Murey–Mednis, Amsterdam 1986. (B) 7 a3 dxc4 8 Ne5 c5 9 Nxc4 cxd4 10 Nb5 Qd8 11 Qxd4 Qxd4 12 Nxd4 Bd7 13 g3 Bc5 14 Nb3 Be7 15 Nca5 Bc6 16 Nxc6 Nxc6 17 Bg2 Rc8 =, Kasparov–Sveshnikov, USSR Chp. 1981. (C) 7 e4!? dxe4 8 Nxe4 Bb4† 9 Ke2 Qf4 10 Qd3 0-0 11 g3 Qc7 12 Bg2 Be7 13 Rhe1 Nd7 14 Kf1 e5 ∓. (D) 7 Qb3 a5 8 a3 a4 9 Nxa4 dxc4 10 Qc2 Qd8 11 Nc3 b5 =.

430

(g) 13 Nxd4 Ne5 14 Qb3 Rd8 15 f4 Ng4 16 Ne4 Qg6 17 f5 Qh7 18 h3 Nf6 =, Tukmakov–Sveshnikov, Kuybyshev 1986.

(h) (A) 6 a4 Bb4 7 e4 Bxc3† 8 bxc3 Qa5 9 e5 Ne4 10 Bd2 Qd5 11 Be2 c5! $\mp$, Cebalo–Pinter, Gosa-Honved 1987. (B) 6 e3 b5 7 a4 Bb4 8 Nd2 a6 9 axb5 cxb5 10 Nxb5 axb5! 11 Rxa8 Bb7 12 Bxf6 gxf6 13 Ra1 e5 ∞, Koerholz–Karsa, Luxembourg 1986.

(i) 8 axb5 cxb5 9 Nxb5 Bxe4 10 Bxc4 Bb4† 11 Nc3 Nbd7 12 0-0 Bxc3 13 bxc3 0-0 14 Bd3 Qc7 =, Ribli–Inkiov, Dubai 1986.

(j) 10 Nxg5 hxg5 11 Bxg5 Nbd7 12 g3 (12 axb5 cxb5 13 Nxb5 Qb6 +) 12 . . . c5! $\mp$, Black is in a main-line Anti-Meran in which he has played the useful . . . Bb7 compared with White's a2–a4.

(k) 11 Ne5 Nd7 12 Be2 Nxe5 13 dxe5 Qc7 14 Qd4 h3 15 0-0-0 hxg2 16 Rhg1 bxa4 17 Bc4 a3 $\mp$, Kohlweyer–Ribli, Dortmund 1986.

(l) 13 Nc3 Qf6?! (13 . . . 0-0! 14 Bxc4 Qxf6 $\mp$) 14 Qa4† Nc6 15 Ne5 Qf4 16 Nxc6 Bxc3† 17 bxc3 Qe4† 18 Be2 Bc6 19 f3 =, Kir. Georgiev–Nogueiras, Sarajevo 1985.

(m) 9 exf6 hxg5 10 fxg7 Bxg7 11 Ne4 c5 12 Nxc5 Bxf3 13 Qxf3 Qxd4 14 Qxa8 0-0 15 Ne4 (15 Be2 Qxc5 16 0-0 Nc6 $\mp$) 15 . . . Qxb2 16 Rd1 Bc3† 17 Nxc3 Qxc3† = (Lukacs).

(n) 11 . . . Bb4† 12 Nc3 fxe5 13 Nxe5 Nc6 14 Nxc6 Bxc6 15 Bxc4 Rg8 16 Rg1 Qh4 $\mp$.

(o) 12 Bxc4 a6 13 Nc3 Qxb2 14 Rc1 Bxf3 15 gxf3 Bb4 16 Qd2 Qxd2† 17 Kxd2 Nc6 $\mp$.

(p) 13 Bxc4 a6 14 Na3? (14 Nc3 $\mp$) 14 . . . Rg8 15 0-0 0-0-0 16 Rfc1 Kb8 17 d5 Nxe5! 18 Nxe5 fxe5 19 Rc3 exd5 20 Rb3 Rxg2† 21 Kh1 Rxh2†! 22 Kxh2 Qxf2† 23 Kh1 dxc4† 24 Rxb7† Kxb7 25 Nxc4 Qf3† 26 Kh2 Qh5† 27 Kg2 Qg6† 28 Kf1 Bc5 29 Na5† Kc7 30 Resigns, D. Ilić–Lukacs, Vrnjačka Banja 1987.

(q) (A) 11 . . . c5!? 12 Ng4 Qe7 13 Be2 Bg7 14 dxc5 b4 15 Nb5 0-0 =, Epishin–Dzhandzhava, Vilnius 1988. (B) 11 . . . Bb4 12 Be2 c5 13 0-0 Bxc3 14 bxc3 Bb7 15 Qb1 $\pm$, Pein–Iclicki, Brussels 1987.

(r) 12 axb5 c5! 13 b6 cxd4 14 Qa4† (14 Qxd4 axb6!) 14 . . . Kd8 15 Qa5 Bd6! 16 bxa7† Ke7 wins.

(s) (A) 13 Bh5!? Rh7 14 axb5! h3 15 Bf3 Bxf3 16 gxf3 Qd8 17 dxc5 Bxc5 18 Qxd8 $\pm$, Piskov–S. Ivanov, USSR 1986. (B) 13 Nb5 Na6 14 0-0! Rg8 15 Bf3 Bxf3 16 Nxf3 cxd4 17 Rc1 Rc8 18 Nfxd4 Rc5 19 f4! $\pm$, Seirawan–Pinter, Zagreb 1987.

(t) 11 g3 Nd7 12 Qe2 c5 13 Bg2 cxd4 14 Nxd7 Bxd7 15 Nd5 Qg7 16 Nc7† Kd8 17 Nxa8 Bb4† 18 Kf1 d3 19 Qd1 Qxb2 20 Rb1 Qd2 21 f4 Qxd1† 22 Rxd1 Ke7 23 Rb1 Ba3 24 Ke1 c3 25 Rb3 b4 $\mp$, Murshed–Ivanchuk, Sharya 1985.

(u) 12 Nxc6 Bb7 13 Bf3 a6 14 0-0 Bg7 15 a4 b4 16 Ne4 Qf4 17 Qc1 Qc7 18 Qxc4 Bxc6 19 Rac1 0-0 20 Qxc6 Qxc6 21 Rxc6 (Barlov–Karaklájić, Yugoslavia 1987) 21 . . . Ra7 =.

(v) 13 dxe5 Qxe5 14 Bf3 Bb7 15 Re1 Qd6 16 Nxb5 Qxd1† 17 Rexd1 cxb5 18 Bxb7 Rb8 19 Bc6† Ke7 20 a4 b4! 21 Rd7 Kf6 22 Rc1 c3 $\mp$, Amos–R. Morrison, Canada 1985.

QUEEN'S GAMBIT
Semi-Slav Defense

1 d4 d5 2 c4 c6 3 Nf3 Nf6 4 Nc3 e6 5 Bg5 dxc4 6 e4 b5 7 e5 h6 8 Bh4 g5 9 Nxg5 (Anti-Meran Gambit)

	43	44	45	46	47	48
	Nd5	.... hxg5				
10	Nxf7(a)	Bxg5				
	Qxh4	Nbd7	....			Be7
11	Nxh8	g3(c)	....	exf6		exf6
	Bb4	Qa5	.... Rg8(f)	Bb7		Bxf6
12	Rc1	exf6	Bxf6	g3(h)		Be3
	Qe4†	b4	Nxf6	c5		Bb7(l)
13	Be2	Ne4	exf6	d5		a4
	Nf4	Ba6	Qxf6	Nb6	.... Qb6(j)	b4
14	a3	Qf3(d)	Bg2	dxe6	Bg2	Ne4
	Nxg2†	0-0-0	Bb7	Bxh1	0-0-0	c5
15	Kf1	Be2	a4	e7	0-0	Nxc5
	Nxe3†(b)	Bb7(e)	0-0-0(g)	Qd7(i)	b4(k)	Bd5(m)

(a) 10 Nf3 Qa5 11 Rc1 Bb4 12 Qd2 Nd7 13 Be2 Bb7 14 0-0 c5 15 Rfd1 Rc8 16 Kf1 Bxc3 17 bxc3 b4 18 dxc5 bxc3 19 Qd4 Qxc5 20 Qg4 Qf8 21 Qd4 Qc5 =, Gavrikov–Nogueiras, Tbilisi 1983.

(b) 16 fxe3 Qxh1† 17 Kf2 Qxh2† 18 Ke1 Be7 19 Kd2 ±, Timman–Ljubojević, Buenos Aires 1980.

(c) 11 Qf3 Bb7 12 Be2 Bh6! 13 Bxf6 Nxf6 14 Qxf6 Qxf6 15 exf6 0-0-0 16 Rd1 b4 17 Na4 c5 18 Bxc4 Bxg2 19 Rg1 Bf3 20 Be2 Bxe2 21 Kxe2 cxd4 ±, Hartoch–Zuidema, Wijk aan Zee 1973.

(d) (A) 14 Bg2 c3 15 bxc3 16 Qc2 Rb8 17 a3 Rb2 18 Qxc3 Bb4 19 Qxb4 Rxb4 20 Bd2 Qh5 +, Kramer–Berliner, US 1945. (B) 14 b3 Nb6 15 Be2 0-0-0 16 0-0 Qf5 17 f3 c5 18 Qc2 Bb7 19 h4 Rxd4 20 bxc4 Qh3 21 Qb3 Bxe4 22 fxe4 Bd6 23 Rf3 Be5 ∞, Spassov–Torre, Sochi 1980.

(e) 16 0-0 Qd5 17 Be3 Rg8 18 Rfc1 c5 19 Nd2 cxd4 = (Flohr).

(f) 11 ... b4 12 Ne4 Nxe4 13 Bxd8 Kxd8 14 Bg2 f5 15 exf6 Nexf6 (15 ... Ndxf6? 16 Bxe4 Nxe4 17 Qf3 +, P. Nikolić–Bagirov, Sarajevo 1980) 16 Qe2 Nd5 17 Qxc4 ±, Lipiridi–Lutovinov, corr. 1984.

(g) 16 axb5 cxb5 17 Bxb7† Kxb7 18 Nxb5 Bb4† 19 Nc3 Rxd4 20 Qe2 Qf5 21 0-0 Rgd8 22 Nd1! ±, Rogers–M. Kuijf, Wijk aan Zee II 1987. White's pressure against c4 and the Black king count for more than Black's control of the d-file. In the column, better is 12 h4!? Rxg5 13 hxg5 Nd5 14 g6 fxg6 15 Qg4 Qa5 16 Qxe6† Kd8 17 Bg2 ± (Knaak).

(h) 12 Be2 Qb6 13 0-0 0-0-0 14 a4 b4 15 Ne4 c5 16 Qb1 Qc7 17 Ng3 cxd4 18 Bxc4 Qc6 19 f3 d3 ∓, Denker–Botvinnik, USA–USSR radio match 1945.

(i) 16 Qxd7† (16 f3?! Bxe7 17 fxe7 f6! 18 Bxf6 Rxh2 =, Bareyev–Lukacs, Vrnjačka Banja 1987) 16 . . . Nxd7! 17 Nxb5 Bxe7 18 fxe7 f6 19 Nc7† Kxe7 20 Nxa8 fxg5 21 Nc7 Ne5 22 h3 Nf3† = (Sapis). Black's threats against b2 and the offside knight provide full compensation for the pawn.

(j) 13 . . . Nf6 14 Bg2 Be7 15 0-0 Nxd5 16 Bxe7 Kxe7 17 Nxb5 Qb6! 18 Na3 c3 19 Nc4 Qc7 =, E. Vladimirov–Dzhandzhava, Pavlodar 1987.

(k) 16 Na4 Qb5 17 a3 Nb8 18 axb4 cxb4 19 Qg4 Bd5 20 Rfc1 Nc6 21 Bxd5 Rxd5 22 Rxc4 Rxg5 23 Qd4 Kb8 24 Rxc6 Rxg3?! 25 fxg3 Qxc6 26 Rd1 Bh6 27 Nc5 Ka8 28 Qe4 =, Yusupov–Tukmakov, Leningrad 1987.

(l) 12 . . . Bg5 13 g3 Bb7 14 Bg2 Bxe3 15 fxe3 Qc7 16 Qf3 ±, Georgadze–Landero, Seville 1985.

(m) 16 Rc1 Rg8 17 Bxc4 Rxg2 18 Qh5 ±, Nogueiras–Rogers, Dubai 1986.

QUEEN'S GAMBIT

Slav Defense

1 d4 d5 2 c4 c6 3 Nf3 Nf6 4 Nc3 dxc4

	49	50	51	52	53	54
5	e3(a).......e4......................a4					
	b5	b5		Na6........Bg4		
6	a4	e5		e4(m)	Ne5	
	b4	Nd5		Bg4	Bh5	
7	Nb1(b)	a4(g)		Bxc4	f3..........g3	
	Ba6	e6		e6	Nfd7	e6
8	Qc2(c)	axb5........Ng5		Be3	Nxc4	Bg2
	b3(d)	Nxc3	h6(j)	Be7(n)	e5	Bb4
9	Qd1	bxc3	Nge4	0-0	Ne4	0-0
	e6	cxb5	b4	Nb4	Bb4†	Nd5
10	Nbd2(e)	Ng5	Nb1	Be2	Bd2	Bd2
	Qd5	Bb7	Ba6(k)	0-0	Qe7	0-0
11	Be2	Qh5(h)	Nbd2	h3	Bxb4(p)	g4
	Nbd7(f)	g6(i)	c3(l)	Bh5(o)	Qxb4†(q)	Bg6(r)

(a) 5 Ne5 b5 6 g3 Bb7 7 Bg2 a6 8 a4 (8 0-0 e6 9 Bg5 h6 10 Bxf6 gxf6 11 Ng4 h5 12 Ne3 Nd7 13 a4 Qxb6 14 b3 cxb3 15 Qxb3 Be7 16 Rfd1 h4 ∓, J. Whitehead–Donaldson, San Jose 1987) 8 . . . e6 9 Bg5 Qb6 10 0-0 Be7 11 e3 h6 12 f4 hxg5 13 fxg5 Rf8! 14 gxf6 gxf6 15 Nf3 Nd7 ∞ (Portisch).

(b) 7 Na2 e6 8 Bxc4 Bb7 (8 . . . Nbd7 9 a5!? Qxa5 10 Bd2 Qb6 11 Qa4 Rb8 12 Nc1 a6 13 Nb3 Bb7 14 Na5 Bc8 15 Bd3 Be7 16 e4 0-0 17 e5 Nd7 18 Qc2 g6 19 Nc4 Qc7 20 h4 ±, Wilder–Belopolsky, Columbus 1986) 9 0-0 Be7 10 Qe2 0-0 11 Rd1 a5 12 Bd2 Nbd7 13 Nc1 Qb6 14 Nb3 c5 15 Be1 Rfd8 =, Reshevsky–Smyslov, USA–USSR radio match 1945.

(c) 8 Nbd2 c3 9 bxc3 bxc3 10 Nb1 Bxf1 11 Kxf1 e6 =, Pfliester–A. Martin, Andorra 1986.

(d) 8 . . . e6 9 Bxc4 Bxc4 10 Qxc4 Qd5 11 Nbd2 Nbd7 12 Qe2 Ne4 =, Stahlberg–Euwe, Stockholm 1937.

(e) 10 Ne5!? c5 11 Be2 cxd4 12 exd4 Bb4† 13 Bd2 Bxd2† 14 Qxd2 0-0 15 0-0 Qc7 16 Rc1 Rc8 17 Na3 Nc6 18 Bf3 Nd5 =, Gelpke–Ree, Dutch Chp. 1983.

(f) 12 0-0 Rb8! 13 Nb1 Ne4 ∓, Adorjan–Torre, Toluca 1982.

(g) 7 Ng5 f6 (7 . . . h6 8 Nge4 Bf5 9 g4 Bxe4 10 Nxe4 e6 11 Bg2 Bb4 12 Bd2 =, Glek–Bagirov, Minsk 1983; or 7 . . . e6 8 Qh5 Qc7 9 Be2 h6 10 0-0 g6 11 Qh3 Nd7 12 a4 N7b6 13 Nge4 a6 14 b3 Nxc3 15 Nf6† Kd8 16 Qxc3 b4 17 Qf3 c3 18 a5 Nd5 19 Nxd5 Resigns, Grefe–Pollard, Berkeley 1988) 8 Nge4 f5! 9 Ng5 e6 10 h4 Na6 11 Be2 Be7 12 Bh5† g6 13 Be2 Nab4 14 Nf3 Nxc3 15 bxc3 Nd5 ∓, Wockenfuss–Wiemer, German Bundesliga 1983-84.

(h) 11 Qg4 Bd5 12 Be2 (12 Ne4 h5 13 Qf4 ∞, Miralles–Drasko, Vrnjačka Banja 1987) 12 . . . Nc6 13 0-0 a5 14 Ne4 h5 15 Qf4 Be7 =, R. Rodriguez–Thipsay, Bangalore 1981.

(i) Black has two ways to counter the threat to f7, the solid 11 . . . Qd7 and the dynamic 11 . . . g6: (A) 11 . . . Qd7 12 Be2 Bd5 13 Nxh7 Nc6 14 Nxf8 Rxf8 15 Qg5 a5 = . Black's queenside play counterbalances White's kingside pressure. (B) 11 . . . g6 (weakening f6 but gaining critical time) 12 Qg4 (12 Qh3 Be7 13 Qh6 Bf8 14 Qh3 Nd7 15 Be2 Be7 16 Bf3 Qc7 17 0-0 Nb6 18 Ne4 Bxe4 19 Bxe4 0-0 ∞, Petrosian–Smyslov, Moscow 1952) 12 . . . Be7 13 Be2 Bd5 14 Bf3 h5 15 Qg3 b4 16 Ne4 Nc6 17 0-0 Rb8 18 Bg5 Bxe4 (18 . . . Bxg5!?) 19 Bxe4 Nxd4 20 cxd4 Bxg5 21 d5! exd5 22 Rfd1 (22 e6 h4 23 Qf3 Qf6 24 exf7† Kf8 25 Bxd5 Qxf3 26 gxf3 c3 ∓, I. Zaitsev–Bagirov, Alma Ata 1963) 22 . . . h4 23 Qg4 dxe4 24 Rxd8† Bxd8 25 Qxe4 0-0 26 Qxc4 a5 Draw, Shaposhnikov–Sadomski, corr. 1958.

(j) 8 . . . Be7!? 9 Nge4 b4 10 Nb1 Ba6 (or 10 . . . f5!) 11 Qg4 Kf8 12 Be2 Nd7 =, Sosonko–Hübner, Brussels (blitz) 1987.

(k) 10 . . . Qh4 11 Qf3 f5 12 exf6 Nxf6 13 Nbd2 (13 Nxf6† Qxf6 14 Qe4! ±) 13 . . . c3 14 bxc3 bxc3 15 Nxf6† Qxf6 16 Qxc3 a5! 17 Ba3 Bxa3 18 Rxa3 0-0 19 Qe3 Ba6 = (Donaldson).

(l) Suspect is 11 . . . Nf4?! 12 Qg4! Nd3† 13 Bxd3 cxd3 14 Nd6† Bxd6 15 Qxg7 ±. After 11 . . . c3 12 Nc4 cxb2 13 Bxb2 Bxc4 14 Bxc4 Be7 15 0-0 Nd7 (15 . . . 0-0 16 Qg4 Nd7 17 Rae1 Qc8 18 Ng3 ±) 16 Qg4 g6 17 Rfd1 h5 18 Qg3 a5 19 Rac1 Kf8 20 Rd3 h4! 21 Qg4 Rh5, reaching a position with chances for both sides, Rajković–Tischbierek, Budapest 1987.

(m) 6 Ne5 (6 e3 Bg4 7 Bxc4 e6 8 h3 Bh5 9 0-0 Nb4 10 Qe2 Be7 11 Rd1 0-0 =) 6 . . . Ng4 7 Nxc4 e5 8 Nxe5 Nxe5 9 dxe5 Qxd1† 10 Kxd1 Be6 11 Bg5 h6 12 Bh4 g5 13 Bg3 0-0-0† ∞, Whiteley–Speelman, London 1982.

(n) 8 . . . Nb5 9 Be2 a5 10 0-0 Be7 11 Ne5 Bxe2 12 Qxe2 0-0 13 Rad1 Nd7 14 f4 f6 15 Nc4 ±, Wilder–Christiansen, US Chp. 1987.

(o) 12 Ne5 Bxe2 13 Qxe2 Nd7 14 Nc4 Qc7 15 Rac1 Rad8 16 Rfd1 ±, Razuvaev–Plachetka, Keszthely 1981.

(p) 11 dxe5 0-0 12 Rc1 b5 13 Bxb4 Qxb4† 14 Qd2 Qxa4 15 Qa5 Qxa5 16 Nxa5 Bg6 17 Nd6 =, Dohosian–Bareyev, Irkutsk 1986.

(q) 12 Qd2 Qxd2† 13 Kxd2 exd4 14 Ned6† Ke7 15 Nxb7 Na6 16 e3 Ndc5 17 Nxc5 Nxc5 18 Na5 ±, Adorjan–Flear, Szirak 1986.

(r) 12 e4 Nb6 13 a5 Nc8 14 Qa4 Na6 15 Be3 ±, Miralles–Flear, Clichy 1987-88. This line is a good choice if White wants to avoid complications.

QUEEN'S GAMBIT

Slav Defense

1 d4 d5 2 c4 c6 3 Nf3 Nf6 4 Nc3 dxc4 5 a4 Bf5

	55	56	57	58	59	60
6	Ne5			e3		
	e6(a)			e6		
7	f3			Bxc4		
	Bb4			Bb4		
8	Nxc4	h4(c)	Bg5(g)	0-0		
	0-0	c5(d)	h6	Nbd7(j) 0-0		
9	Bg5	dxc5(e)	Bh4	Qe2	Nh4(m)	Nh4(p)
	h6	Qc7	c5	0-0(k)	Bg4	Bg6
10	Bh4	Qd6	dxc5	e4	f3(n)	f3
	c5	Qxd6	Qxd1†	Bg6	Bh5	Nbd7
11	dxc5	cxd6	Kxd1(h)	Bd3	g4	Nxg6
	Qxd1†(b)	Bxd6(f)	Nbd7(i)	Bh5(l)	Nd5(o)	hxg6(q)

(a) 6 . . . Nbd7 7 Nxc4 Qc7 8 g3 e5 9 dxe5 Nxe5 10 Bf4 Rd8 (10 . . . Nfd7 11 Bg2 f6 12 0-0 Be6 13 Nxe5 fxe5 14 Be3 Bc5 15 Ne4 [15 Qc1 $\pm$] 15 . . . Bxe3 16 fxe3 0-0-0 17 Ng5 Nf6 18 Qc2 Bg8 =, Capablanca–Dake, New York 1931) 11 Qc1 Bd6 12 Nxd6† Qxd6 13 Bg2 a5 14 0-0 0-0 15 Qe3 Nfg4 16 Qb6 Qb4 17 Qxb4 axb4 18 Na2 Ng6 19 Bc1 b3 20 Nc3 Bc2 21 a5 $\pm$, Browne–Miles, Indonesia 1982.

(b) 12 Kxd1 (12 Rxd1 Bc2 13 Rc1 Bxa4 14 Bxf6 gxf6 15 Ra1 Bb3 16 Nb6 Nc6 17 Nxa8 Rxa8 18 e3 Bxc5 $\mp$, Bareyev–Ehlvest, USSR 1986; the extra pawn, two bishops, and more harmonious development easily compensate for the sacrificed exchange) 12 . . . Rd8† 13 Kc1 Nbd7 14 e4 Bh7 15 Kc2 Nc5 16 Be2 is given as unclear by Tukmakov. Black should consider 16 . . . g5 17 Bg3 Nd5 with . . . f5 to follow. Again the problem for Black is how to liberate the bishop on h7.

(c) A new and dangerous try which has two points: to trap the bishop on f5, and, in certain lines, to deny Black's queen the square h4.

(d) 8 . . . h6 9 Nxc4 c5 10 dxc5 Qxd1† 11 Kxd1 Bxc5 12 e4 Bg6 13 Nb5 $\pm$, Ftáčnik–Westerinen, Altensteig 1987.

(e) 9 . . . Qd5 (9 . . . Qxd1† 10 Kxd1 Nbd7 11 Nxd7 0-0-0 12 e4 Rxd7† 13 Kc2 $\pm$, Ftáčnik) 10 Bf4 Na6? (10 . . . Nbd7!) 11 e4! Bxe4 12 Bxc4 Qxd1† 13 Rxd1 Bd5 14 Bb5† Ke7 15 Nd3 $\pm$, Ftáčnik–Drasko, Belgrade 1987.

(f) 12 Nxc4 Bg3† 13 Kd1 Nc6 (13 . . . Nh5 14 e4 Bg6 with the idea of . . . Nc6, . . . 0-0-0, and . . . f5 is also worth a try) 14 e4 Rd8 15 Bd2 ∞ (Ftáčnik).

(g) 8 e4 Bxe4 9 fxe4 Nxe4 10 Qf3 (10 Bd2 Qxd4 11 Nxe4 Qxe4† 12 Qe2 Bxd2† 13 Kxd2 Qd5† 14 Kc2 Na6 15 Nxc4 0-0-0 [15 . . . Rd8! 16 Qe5 0-0 =] 16 Qe5 f6 17 Qe3! c5 18 Kb3 Nb4 19 Rc1 Nc6 20 Ka3 $\pm$, Karpov–Hjartarson, Tilburg 1988) 10 . . . Qxd4 11 Qxf7† Kd8 12 Bg5† Nxg5 13 Qxg7 Qe3† (13 . . . Bxc3† 14 bxc3 Qxc3† 15 Ke2 Qc2† 16 Ke1 Qc3† =) 14 Kd1 Rf8 15 Nxc4 Qf4 16 Qxb7 Bxc3 17 bxc3 Ne4 18 Qxa8 Rf7! 19 Kc2 Qf2† 20 Kb3 Rb7† 21 Qxb7 Nc5† 22 Ka3 Nxb7 and a draw was agreed in Euwe–Alekhine, Amsterdam exhibition game played with living pieces. Black seems all right; his king is safe and he threatens . . . Qc2.

(h) 11 Rxd1 Bc2 12 Rd4 Nc6 13 Rxc4 a5 14 Nxc6 bxc6 =.

(i) 12 Nxd7 0-0-0 13 e4 Rxd7† 14 Kc2 Bh7 15 c6 bxc6 16 Bxc4 Bd7 17 Bd3 Nh5 (heading for f4 and preparing the liberating . . . f5 to bring the bishop on h7 back into the game—a typical motif in the lines arising from 6 Ne5 and e6) 18 Ne2 g5 19 Bf2 f5 20 Rad1 fxe4 21 Bxe4 Bxe4 22 fxe4 Rhd8 23 h3 Draw, Gulko–Anikayev, Volgodonsk 1981. After 23 . . . Nf6 24 Nc3 Be5 the game would be quite even.

(j) Black's major decision in this variation is whether to delay . . . 0-0 for one move. Both 8 . . . 0-0 and 8 . . . Nbd7 have their advantages: the former leaves Black better placed to meet 9 Qb3, the latter to meet 9 Nh4. See note (k).

(k) Besides castling queenside, Black's other option through the move order 8 . . . Nbd7 is 9 . . . Bg6. This forces White to sacrifice a pawn if he wants to achieve e4, the most serious try for advantage. Play is very sharp after 9 . . . Bg6 10 e4, e.g. 10 . . . Bxc3 11 bxc3 Nxe4 12 Ba3 Qc7 13 Rfc1 0-0-0 (13 . . . Nd6 14 Bxe6 0-0 15 Bb3 is unclear) 14 a5 Rhe8 15 Qb2 Kb8 16 Rcb1 Ka8 17 Bf1, with the intention of g3 and Bg2, giving White a slight advantage, Gligorić–Beliavsky, Belgrade 1987.

(l) (A) 12 e5 Nd5 13 Nxd5 cxd5 14 Qe3 Be7 15 Bd2 (15 Ne1 Bg6 16 f4 Rc8 17 g4 Bxd3 18 Nxd3 Rc4! 19 Bd2 Qb6 20 Bc3 f5 =, Gligorić–Donaldson, Lone Pine 1981) 15 . . . Bg6 16 Rfc1 Nb8 17 Bxg6 fxg6 18 b4 Nc6 19 Rab1 (19 b5 Na5 20 Bxa5 Qxa5 21 Qc3 Qxc3 22 Rxc3 Rfc8 23 Rac1 Rxc3 24 Rxc3 Kf8 25 Rc7 Rb8 =, with . . . Ke8 and . . . Kd8 to follow) 19 . . . a6 followed by . . . Qd7 and . . . Rfc8. White's edge is minimal at best. (B) 12 Bf4 Re8 13 e5 (the only way to stop . . . e5) 13 . . . Nd5 14 Nxd5 cxd5 15 h3 a6 16 Rfc1 Bg6 17 Qe3 (17 Bg5 Qa5 18 Bxg6 fxg6 19 Bd2 Rac8 =) 17 . . . Nb8 18 Bxg6 fxg6 19 Qb3 a5 =, van der Sterren–Torre, Adelaide 1986-87.

(m) 9 Qb3 a5 10 Na2 Be7 11 Nh4 (11 Qxb7 Rb8 12 Qa6 Ra8 13 Qc6 Rc8 =) 11 . . . Be4 12 Nc3 Nb6 13 Be2 0-0 14 Nxe4 Nxe4 15 Nf3 Nd5 =, Kasparov–Kupreichik, USSR Chp. 1981.

(n) 10 Qb3 a5 11 f3 Bh5 12 g3 0-0 13 e4 Nb6 14 Be3 Nxc4 15 Qxc4 Nd7 16 Ng2 e5 17 Rad1 Qe7 18 Nh4 Bg6 =, Cebalo–Portisch, Reggio Emilia 1985-86.

(o) 12 Ng2 Bg6 13 Na2 Be7 14 e4 N5b6 15 Bb3 a5 16 Nc3 h5 17 Nf4 Nf8 18 gxh5 Bxh5 19 Be3 Bd6 20 Qd2 g5!? (20 . . . Ng6!?, 20 . . . Qh4!?) 21 Nd3 Be7 22 f4 Ng6 23 fxg5 Nh4 24 Ne5 Bg5! 25 Bd1! Bxe3† 26 Qxe3 Nd7, Tukmakov–Ehlvest, Kuybyshev 1986. In this very complicated position chances are equal.

(p) 9 Qb3 Qe7 10 a5 c5 11 Ne5 cxd4 12 exd4 Nc6 13 Nxc6 bxc6 14 Bg5 Rab8 =.

(q) 12 Qc2 Qa5 13 Na2 Be7 14 b4 Qc7 15 Bd2 Rfd8 16 Rab1 ±, Yusupov–Smyslov, Montpellier 1985. If Black had played 9 . . . Bg4 in this line, White would obtain the advantage by advancing his kingside pawns since Black does not have the option of queenside castling.

QUEEN'S GAMBIT
Semi-Slav and Slav Defense

1 d4 d5 2 c4 c6

	61	62	63	64	65	66
3	(Nf3)	Nc3				
	(Nf6)	e6		Nf6(l)		
4	e3	e4(e).......	Nf3	cxd5 (Slav Exchange Variation)		
	Bf5	dxe4	dxc4	cxd5		
5	Nc3(a)	Nxe4	a4(j)	Bf4		
	e6	Bb4†	Bb4	Nc6		
6	Nh4(b)	Bd2(f)	e3	e3		
	Be4	Qxd4	b5	Bf5		e6
7	Qb3	Bxb4	Bd2	Nf3		e3
	Qb6(c)	Qxe4†	a5	e6		Be7(s)
8	Qxb6	Be2	axb5	Bb5(m)	Ne5	Bd3
	axb6	Na6(g)	Bxc3	Nd7	Nxe5	0-0
9	Bd2	Bd6(h)	Bxc3	Qa4(n)	Bxe5	h3(t)
	h6	e5	cxb5	Rc8(o)	Nd7	Bd7
10	cxd5	Nf3	b3	0-0	Qb3(q)	0-0
	cxd5(d)	Bg4(i)	Bb7(k)	a6(p)	Nxe5(r)	Qb6(u)

(a) 5 cxd5 cxd5 6 Nc3 Nc6! (6 . . . e6 7 Qb3 Qb6 8 Bb5 Nc6 9 Na4 Qc7 10 Bd2 ±, Strauss) 7 Qb3 Rb8 8 Be2 (8 Bb5 e6 9 Ne5 Bd6! 10 Nxc6 bxc6 11 Bxc6† Ke7 12 Qa4 Qb6 ∓, as . . . Rhc8 and . . . Ne4 are soon to follow) 8 . . . e6 9 0-0 Bd6 10 Bd2 0-0 11 Rfc1 Re8 12 h3 a6 =, I. Ivanov–Strauss, Los Angeles 1981.

(b) 6 Bd3 Bxd3 7 Qxd3 Nbd7 8 0—0 Be7 9 e4 dxe4 10 Nxe4 Nxe4 11 Qxe4 Nf6 12 Qe2 0-0 13 Rd1 Qc7 14 g3 b6 15 Bf4 Qb7 16 Ne5 c5 =, Romanishin–Vaganian, USSR Chp. 1980-81.

(c) 7 . . . Qc7 8 f3 Bg6 9 Bd2 Nbd7 10 Rc1 Rc8 11 g3! Qb8 12 Kf2 Be7 13 cxd5 exd5 14 Bh3 ±, Smyslov–Chernin, Montpellier 1985.

(d) 11 f3 Bh7 12 g4 b5 13 Nf5 h5 14 h3 g6 15 Ng3 h4 =, P. Nikolić–Beliavsky, Sarajevo 1982.

(e) 4 Bf4 dxc4 5 e3 b5 6 a4 Qb6! 7 Qf3? bxa4! 8 Ra2 Qb3 9 Bxb8 Rxb8 10 Qxc6† Bd7 11 Qxc4 a3 ∓, Epishin–Boiman, Krasnodar 1982. The absence of White's bishop from the queen-side is clearly felt. The column is the Marshall Gambit.

(f) 6 Nc3 c5 7 a3 Ba5 8 Be3 Nf6 9 Nf3 Nc6 10 dxc5 Qxd1† 11 Rxd1 Ne4 12 Rc1 Nxc3 13 bxc3 e5 14 Nd2 Bf5 =, Lerner–Lukacs, Polanica Zdroj 1986.

(g) The most logical move, concentrating on development. The immediate capture on g2 is very risky, but the alternative capture 8 . . . c5 9 Bxc5 Qxg2 is sometimes tried. In Vladimirov–Monin, USSR 1980, White obtained a strong attack with 10 Bf3 Qg5 11 Bd6 Ne7 12 Nh3 Nf5 13 Rg1 Qf6 14 Ba3 Qe5† 15 Kf1 Nc6 16 Qd3 Qd4 17 Bxc6† bxc6 18 Qe2 Qh4 19 Ng5 Qxh2 20 Rd1.

438

(h) Alternatives are less dangerous, e.g. 9 Ba5 Bd7 (the idea of 9 Ba5 to weaken c6 is realized after 9 . . . b6 10 Bc3 Nf6 11 Qd6) 10 Nf3 Nf6 11 Qd6 Qf5 12 Ne5 (12 Bc3 Ne4 13 Qd4 f6 14 Nh4 e5!) 12 . . . Qxf2† 13 Kxf2 Ne4† 14 Kf3 Nxd6 15 Rad1 Ke7 16 Rxd6 Kxd6 17 Nxf7† Ke7 18 Nxh8 Rxh8 19 Bc3 and White's bishops and better pawn structure barely compensate for the pawn.

(i) 11 0-0 0-0-0 12 Bd3 Qf4 13 Bxe5 Qxe5 14 Nxe5 Bxd1 15 Bf5† Kc7 16 Nxf7 (Tal–Dorfman, USSR 1978). According to Tal, Black could now have equalized with 16 . . . Nh6! 17 Nxh6 (17 Nxh8 Nxf5 18 Nf7 Rd7 19 Ne5 Be2!; 17 Nxd8 Rxd8 18 Bxh7 Be2 =) 17 . . . Bh5! 18 Bg4 Bxg4 19 Nxg4 Rd2.

(j) (A) A recent try is 5 Bg5, when Black can choose between 5 . . . f6 and 5 . . . Qa5 or can transpose to the Anti-Meran (columns 43–48) with 5 . . . Nf6. (B) 5 e3 b5 6 a4 b4 7 Ne4 Ba6 8 Qc2 Qd5 9 Ned2 c3 equalizes.

(k) A key position of the Abrahams–Noteboom Variation. White must choose between the sharp 11 d5 and the more restrained 11 bxc4: (A) 11 d5 Nf6 12 bxc4 b4 13 Bxf6 Qxf6 (13 . . . gxf6 14 Nd4! exd5 15 c5 ±) 14 Qa4† Nd7 15 Nd4 e5 (15 . . . Qe7!?) 16 Nb3 Ke7 17 Qb5 Ba6 18 Qxa5 Rhb8 19 d6†?! Ke8! ∓, Ionov–Moroz, USSR 1984. Correct is 19 Qc7 Rc8 =. (B) 11 bxc4 b4 (creating the typical imbalance of the Abrahams–Noteboom. White will strive to mobilize his center pawns while Black will seek to blockade them with a timely . . . e5 and then crash through with his queenside runners) 12 Bb2 Nf6 13 Bd3 Nbd7 (13 . . . Be4 14 Bxe4 Nxe4 15 Qc2 Nf6 16 e4 ±) 14 Qc2 0-0 15 e4 e5 16 0-0 Qc7 17 Rfe1 Rfe8 18 c5 exd4 19 Bxd4 Ng4 20 Bc4 Nde5 21 Nxe5 Nxe5 22 Bd5 Bc6 23 Qb3 Ng4 24 Qh3 Bxd5 25 Qxg4 f5 26 Qxf5 Be6 27 Qg5 a4 =, Kan–Simagin, Moscow 1949. In this complicated position Black's queenside pawns provide enough counterplay to compensate for the pawn.

(l) 3 . . . dxc4! 4 e4 b5 (4 . . . e5 5 Nf3 exd4 6 Qxd4! Qxd4 7 Nxd4 Nf6 8 f3 ±) 5 a4 e5 6 Nf3 exd4 7 Qxd4 Qxd4 8 Nxd4 b4 9 Nd1 Ba6 10 Bf4 Nf6 and now either 11 f3 Bc5 as in Kasparov–Hübner, Belfort 1989 with a good game for Black, or the sacrificial 11 Rc1! Nxe4 (11 . . . Bc5 12 Nb3!) 12 Bxc4 Bxc4 13 Rxc4 Nd6 14 Rc2 ±, Smejkal—Chandler, German Bundesliga 1989.

(m) 8 Qb3 Bb4 9 Bb5 (9 a3 Bxc3† 10 bxc3 0-0 11 Qxb7 Qa5 12 Qb2 Rab8 13 Bxb8 Rxb8 14 Qc1 Rb3 15 Nd2 Rxc3 16 Qd1 Rc2 17 Rc1 Qc3 18 Rxc2 Bxc2 ∓, Dolgitser–Shipman, Philadelphia 1987) 9 . . . 0-0 10 0-0 Bxc3 11 Qxc3 Rc8 12 Rfc1 Qb6 13 Qc5 Nxd4 14 Qxb6 Nxf3† 15 gxf3 axb6 16 Bd6 Rxc1 17 Rxc1 Ra8 18 a3 (Seirawan–Yusupov, Indonesia 1983) 18 . . . Ne8! =.

(n) 9 0-0 Be7 10 Bxc6† bxc6 11 Rc1 Rc8 12 Na4 g5 13 Bg3 h5 14 h3 g4 15 hxg4 hxg4 16 Ne5 Nxe5 17 Bxe5 f6 18 Bg3 Kf7 19 Re1 Rh5 20 Qd2 Be4 21 Kf1 Bf3! 22 Resigns, Seirawan–Beliavsky, Brussels 1988.

(o) 9 . . . Qb6 10 Ng4 Be4 11 0-0-0 Rc8 12 f3 Bg6 13 Nxg6 hxg6 14 Kb1 a6 15 Be2 Bb4 16 Rc1 0-0 17 a3 Bxc3 18 Rxc3 e5 19 dxe5 Ncxe5 20 Rhc1 ±, Mordasov–Veksenkov, USSR 1980.

(p) 11 Bxc6 Rxc6 12 Rfc1 Be7 13 Ne2 (13 Nd1 b5 14 Qb3 Rc4 15 Nd2 Qa5 16 Nc3 Rb4 17 Nxd5 Rxb3 18 Rc8† Bd8 19 Bc7 0-0 20 Ba5 Rb2 =) 13 . . . Qb6 14 Rxc6 bxc6 15 Rc1 Bd3 16 Qd1 Bxe2 17 Qxe2 0-0 18 Be5 Bxe5 19 Bxe5 Rc8 =, Rashkovsky–Dolmatov, USSR Chp. 1980-81.

(q) (A) 10 Bb5 a6 11 Bxd7† Qxd7 12 0-0 Rc8 13 Rc1 f6 14 Bg3 Be7 15 f3 Bg6 16 Ne2 Kf7! ∓, Lerner–Simagin, USSR Chp. 1985. (B) 10 Bg3 a6 11 Bd3 Bxd3 12 Qxd3 Be7 13 0-0 0-0 =, Spraggett–Yusupov. Montpellier 1985.

(r) 11 dxe5 Be7 12 Bb5† Kf8 13 0-0 Qb6 14 Na4 Qc7 15 f4 Rc8 16 Bd3 Bxd3 17 Qxd3 g6 =.

(s) 7 . . . Nh5 8 Bg5 Qb6 9 Bb5 h6 10 Bh4 g5 11 Ne5 Ng7 12 Bg3 Nf5 13 Qa4 Nxg3 14 hxg3 Bd7 15 Nxd7 Kxd7 16 e4! a6 17 exd5 exd5 18 0-0! ±, Smejkal–P. Nikolić, Novi Sad 1982.

(t) White needs to preserve his queen bishop to keep an edge. On 9 0-0 Black has 9 . . . Nh5 10 Be5 f5 11 Rc1 Nf6 12 Bxf6 gxf6 13 Nh4 Kh8 14 f4 Rg8 with equality, Capablanca–Lasker, New York 1924.

(u) 11 a3 Na5 12 b4 Nc4 13 Ne5! Rac8 14 Bxc4 dxc4 15 Bg5 Qd8 16 Qf3 $\pm$, Portisch–Petrosian, match 1974.

QUEEN'S PAWN GAMES

1 d4

THIS IS A COMPREHENSIVE HEADING for all openings that begin with 1 d4 except the Queen's Gambit and Indian Systems, and those that are played too infrequently to merit chapters of their own. Many of these openings are reached by transposition, but this section deals mainly with lines that flow in unique channels.

The first sections deal with variations after 1 d4 without White's c4.

The BLACKMAR–DIEMER GAMBIT, 1 . . . d5 2 e4 (cols. 1–3), is a brash sacrifice that immediately opens the game. Instead of having to deal with a closed strategical position, White immediately begins tactical play. The gambit is not necessarily good, but is dangerous against an unwary opponent.

Somewhat interrelated are the RICHTER–VERESOV Attack (col. 4), the QUEEN'S BISHOP ATTACK (col. 5), the TORRE ATTACK (cols. 12–15), and the RUTH–TROMPOWSKI ATTACK (cols. 16–17). They share the characteristics of White's thrust Bg5 at various stages.

Diagram 60

The Trompowski Attack was co-authored by Opočenský (along with Trompowski) in the 1930s, but long before them it was consistently propagated by the American W. A. Ruth. The STONEWALL VARIATION (col. 6) is a somewhat stultified version of the COLLE SYSTEM, 1 . . . d5 2 e3 Nf6 3 Nf3 e6 4 Bd3 c5 (cols. 7–11), which reins in White's queen's bishop temporarily while aiming at a liberating breakthrough in the center (see diagram). Historically, the system originated with J. H. Zukertort over a century ago, was forged into a system by Edgar Colle in the 1930s, then was further developed and popularized by George Koltanowski.

The KING'S FIANCHETTO DEFENSE, 1 . . . g6 (col. 18), is explained under note (s).

The POLISH DEFENSE (cols. 19–22) was, in this century, first used and analyzed in 1913–14 by Alexander Wagner of Poland. It may also be reached via the Reti Opening and has on occasion been used by prominent masters, such as Karpov, Larsen, Miles, and Spassky. For variations without d4 see Flank Openings.

The QUEEN'S KNIGHT DEFENSE (cols. 23–24) is a more functional heading chosen to replace a variety of names attributed to different proponents of similar systems. Col. 23, often traced to the Lithuanian master Mikenas, shows his idea of an early . . . e5, which he employed in a number of international tournaments. Col. 24 used to be called the *Kevitz–Trajković Defense*. It is a kind of Alekhine Defense against the queen's pawn, with the same concept: inviting White to establish a far-flung center that later may be undermined. The American Alexander Kevitz was a virtuoso in handling the intricacies of this system.

The next section deals with openings that include an early c4, namely the ALBIN COUNTER GAMBIT, 1 d4 d5 2 c4 e5 (cols. 25–27) and the BLUMENFELD COUNTER GAMBIT (cols. 28–30). The Albin Counter Gambit is a romantic defense named after the Austrian master Adolf Albin, who practiced it successfully in the latter nineteenth century. While it falls into the category of the Queen's Gambit Declined, it is considered dubious and is rarely seen, as Black obtains less than full value for the pawn. However, Black has practical chances and there is considerable scope for original play. White has several choices after 3 dxe5 d4 4 Nf3 Nc6; best seems to be 5 Nbd2 Bg4 6 g3 (col. 26), where White develops a counterattack.

The Blumenfeld Counter Gambit, 1 d4 Nf6 2 c4 e6 3 Nf3 c5 4 d5 b5, is positionally well motivated: Black sacrifices a wing pawn to obtain control of the center. Black has good chances if White takes the pawn (col. 28), but the problem is 5 Bg5! (cols. 29–30), pinning the knight to control e4 and d5. Black's most interesting try is col. 29 where he plays 8 . . . Kd8!?, mixing up the position.

QUEEN'S PAWN GAMES

1 d4 d5

	Blackmar–Diemer Gambit			Richter–Veresov Attack	Queen's Bishop Attack	Stonewall Variation
	1	2	3	4	5	6
2	e4(a) dxe4			Nc3 .... Nf6	Bg5 .... h6!(p)	e3(s) Nf6
3	Nc3(b) Nf6(c)			Bg5 ╱ Nbd7(l)	Bh4 c5(q)	Bd3 c5(t)
4	f3(d) exf3(e)			f3 h6(m)	Nc3 Nc6	c3 Nc6
5	Nxf3 .... Bf5 .... Bg4(h)		Qxf3 g6(j)	Bh4 e6(n)	e3 Qa5	f4 Bg4(u)
6	Ne5 e6	h3 Bxf3	Be3 c6	e4 g5	Nf3 Bg4	Nf3 e6
7	g4 Bg6(f)	Qxf3 c6	Bc4 Bg7	Bg3 Nxe4	Be2 Bxf3	0-0 Bd6
8	Qf3 c6(g)	Be3 e6(i)	Nge2 Nbd7(k)	Nxe4 dxe4(o)	Bxf3 cxd4(r)	Qe1 0-0(v)

(a) (A) 2 f3 d5 3 e4 dxe4 4 Nc3 leads to the main line, but Black can bypass the gambit with 2 ... b6 followed by ... e6. If (B) 2 Nc3 Nf6 3 e4 Nxe4 4 Nxe4 dxe4 5 Bc4 (5 f3 e5!) 5 ... Bf5 6 f3 e5 7 Be3 Nc6 $\overline{\mp}$ (Korn).

(b) Blackmar's original 3 f3 is refuted by 3 ... e5! 4 dxe5 Qxd1† 5 Kxd1 Nc6 6 Bf4 Nge7 $\mp$.

(c) Popiel's idea 3 ... e5 (the Lemberg Counter Gambit) is met by 4 Be3 exd4 5 Bxd4! Nc6 6 Bb5 Bd7 7 Nge2 Nxd4 8 Qxd4 c6 9 Bc4 Nf6 10 0-0-0 Be7 11 Rhe1 0-0 12 Ng3 $\pm$ (Friedl).

(d) The German player Diemer's move, introduced in 1932 and replacing Popiel's "Polish Gambit" 4 Bg5 (... e6 =).

(e) 4 ... Bf5 5 fxe4! (5 g4 Bg6 6 h4 h6 ∞—*ECO*) 5 ... Nxe4 6 Qf3 Nd6 7 Bf4 e6 8 0-0-0 c6 (A) 9 d5? cxd5 10 Nxd5 Be4 (10 ... exd5 11 Bxd6 $\pm$) 11 Qe3 exd5 12 Rxd5 f5 13 Bb5† Nc6 14 Nf3 Be7 15 Rxd6 Bxd6 16 Rd1 0–0 ∞. (B) 9 g4 Bg6 10 Qe3 Be7 11 Nf3 Nd7 12 d5 cxd5 13 Nxd5 exd5 14 Bxd6 Rc8 15 Rxd5 Bxc2 16 Kd2 $\pm$ (Weber in *Europa–Rochade*).

(f) 7 ... Be4 8 Nxe4 (8 Rg1 Bb4 9 d3 Nc6 10 Be3 Nxe5 11 dxe5 Bxd3 =) 8 ... Nxe4 9 Qf3 Qxd4! 10 Qxf7† Kd8 11 Qf4 Bb4† (11 ... g5? 12 c3 Qd5 13 Nf7† Ke8 14 Qf3 Rg8 15 Bg2 $\pm$) 12 c3 Bxc3 (12 ... g5 13 Qe3) 13 bxc3 Qxc3† 14 Kd1 $\pm$ (from analyses by Jürgen Gegner in *Europa-Rochade* 1986-88).

(g) 9 g5 Ng8 10 Bd3 Qxd4 11 Nxg6 hxg6 12 Bf4 c5 13 Rf1 e5 14 Qe2 Ne7 15 Bxe5 Qe3 16 Qxe3?! (16 Ne4!) 16 ... Bxe3 ∞, Stader–Altrock, corr. 1981-84.

(h) Other defenses are: (A) 5 ... e6 6 Bg5 h6 (or 6 ... c5) 7 Bxf6 Qxf6 8 Bc4 Bd6 9 0-0 Qd8 10 Qe2 $\pm$; or (B) 5 ... g6 6 Be4 Bg7 7 Ne5 0-0 8 Bg5 Nd7 (8 ... Nc6 9 Nxc6 bxc6 10 0-0-0 $\pm$) 9 0-0 c6 10 Kh1 Nb6 11 Nb3 a5 =, Heil–Bogolyubov, Wangen 1952.

(i) (A) 9 Bd3 Be7 10 g4 Nd5 11 Rf1 0-0 12 Ne4 Nd7 = (Gegner); or (B) 9 Bd3 Nbd7 10 0-0 Be7 11 Rf2 Qa5 12 g4 0-0 =, Callahan–Bisguier, Washington 1986. In the column, 8 Bf4 e6 9 0–0–0 Bb4 10 Bd2 Nbd7 11 Bd3 Nb6 12 Qg3 Qe7 = is Velimirović–Bellon, Metz 1988.

(j) 5 . . . Qxd4 is double-edged and not yet fully explored, e.g. 6 Be3 (6 Nb5 Qe5† 7 Be2 Na6 ±) 6 . . . Qb4 7 a3 Qb6 8 Bc4 Bg4 9 Qg3 Nxc6 ∞ (Korn).

(k) 9 0-0-0 Nb6 10 Bb3 a5 11 a3 Bg4 ∓.

(l) (A) 3 . . . c6 4 Bxf6 exf6 5 e3 (1) 5 . . . Qb6 6 Rb1 Bb4 7 Qd2 f5 8 Bd3 Be6 9 a3 Bd6 10 Nf3 Nd7 11 0-0 Qc7 12 Ne2 Nf6 =, van der Vliet–Liegterink, Amsterdam 1982. (2) 5 . . . f5 6 Bd3 g6 7 Nce2 Nd7 8 Nf3 Bd6 9 c4 dxc4 10 Bc4 Qe7 11 0-0 Nb6 12 Bb3 Be6 13 Nc3 Rd8 14 Qc2 0-0 =, K. Burger–Henley, New York 1983. (B) 3 . . . Bf5 4 Bxf6 exf6 5 e3 c6 6 Bd3 Bxd3 ∞.

(m) (A) 4 . . . g6 5 e3 Bg7 6 Bd3 0-0 7 0-0 c5 8 Re1 b6 9 e4 dxe4 10 Nxe4 Bb7 11 c3 cxd4 12 Nxd4 Nxe4 13 Bxe4 Bxe4 14 Rxe4 Nf6 15 Re1 Qd5 16 Nf3 Qb7 =, Plaskett–Hazai, Maribor 1985. (B) 4 . . . c6 5 Qd2 b5 6 a3 h6 7 Bh4 e5 8 dxe5 Nxe5 9 e4 Nxe4 10 fxe4 Qxh4† 11 g3 Qg5 ∓ Lakdawa–Browne, USA 1988. (C) 4 . . . c5 5 e4 dxe4 6 d5 (or 6 dxc5) 6 . . . exf3 7 Nxf3 h6 = (Shirazi).

(n) 5 . . . c6 6 Be3 e6 7 d3 Be7 8 0-0 0-0 9 Re1 c5 10 Bg3 Nh5 11 Ne5 Nxe5 12 dxe5 g6 13 Qd2 Kh7 =, Veresov–Boleslavsky, USSR 1971.

(o) 9 Nd2 Bg7 10 h4 Bxd4 11 c3 gxh4 12 Rxh4 Bg7 13 Nxe4 Qe7 14 Qh5 Nf6 ∞, Tischbierek–Uhlmann, Leipzig 1983. White's open lines are a strong asset.

(p) For 2 . . . Nf6 3 Bxf6 refer to the Trompowski Attack, and 3 Nd2 c6 4 e3 g6 5 Bxf6 exf6 6 Bd3 Bd6 7 Ne2 (7 Qf3 f5 8 Ne2 is more aggressive) 7 . . . f5 8 h4 Nd7 9 h5 Nf6 10 Nxg6 fxg6 11 Nf4 Kf7 = is Rogers–Psakhis, Szirak 1986.

(q) 3 . . . c6 4 Nf3! (4 e3? Qb6 5 b3 e5! ∓, a move found by Hans Berliner's HITECH computer program, Columbus Open 1988; if 5 . . . dxe5 6 Qb4† +) 4 . . . Qb6 5 b3 Bf4 6 e3 e6 7 Bd3 Bxd3 8 Qxd3 Nd7 9 Ndb2 Ngf6 10 0-0 Bd6 =, Přibyl–Lengyel, Trnava 1979.

(r) 9 exd4 e6 10 0-0 g5 11 Bg3 Bg7 (Kupreichik–Marjanović, USSR vs. Yugoslavia 1979) 12 Re1 Nge7 13 Be5 Nxe5 14 dxe5 Nc6 ∓.

(s) 2 Bf4 Nf6 3 e3 e6 4 Nd2 c5 5 c3 Nc6 6 Bd3 Bd6 7 Bxd6 Qxd6 8 f4 Bd7 9 Nh3 Ne7 10 Qb6 =, Kovačević–Rajković, Yugoslav Chp. 1983, is a Stonewall deferred. The formations of the Stonewall are similar to those of the Colle–Zukertort System except that here White moves the queen's bishop out before playing e3.

(t) 3 . . . e6 4 Nd2 b6 5 f4 Nbd7 6 Ngf3 Bd6 7 0-0 c5 8 c3 Qc7 9 Ne5 Nc6 10 Ndf3 Bb7 11 Bd2 Nd7 12 Qe2 f6! 13 Nxd7 Kxd7 illustrates Black's strategy against a rigid stonewall; namely, to enforce . . . e5 and . . . Rae8, saddling White with a restrictive backward pawn on e3.

(u) 5 . . . cxd4 6 exd4 g6 followed by . . . Bf5 may also be recommended.

(v) 9 Ne5 Bf5 10 Qe2 (10 Bxf5 leaves White with the same, self-blocking pawn on e3) 10 . . . Bxd3 11 Qxd3 Nd7 12 Nd2 Qc7 13 Rf3 f6 14 Ng4 g6 ∓, E. Richter–Korn, Prague 1936.

444

QUEEN'S PAWN GAMES

1 d4

	Colle System					Torre Attack
	7	8	9	10	11	12
	(d5)..Nf6					
2	(e3) (Nf6)				Nf3 e6	
3	Nf3 e6(a)				e3 ....Bg5 c5	c5(k)
4	Bd3 c5				Bd3 b6	e3(l) d5
5	b3 ....c3 Nbd7 ....Qa5† Nc6			Nbd7(g)	0-0 Bb7	Nbd2 Qb6
6	Bb2 b6	Nbd2(c) cxd4!	0-0 Be7!(e)	Nbd2 Bd6	b3(i) Nc6	Bxf6 gxf6
7	0-0 Bb7	exd4 Bb4	Bb2 0-0	0-0 0-0	Bb2 Be7	c4 cxd4
8	Nbd2(b)	0-0! Bxc3(d)	Nbd2 b6(f)	Re1 b6(h)	Nbd2 cxd4(j)	exd4 Nc6(m)

(a) This position arises also after 1 d4 Nf6 2 Nf3 e6 or 1 Nf3 d5 2 d4 e6 3 e3. In the "Indian" style is 3 . . . g6 4 Bd3 (for 4 c4 Bb7 5 Nc3 see Grünfeld Defense) 4 . . . Bg7 5 Nbd2 Nbd7 6 0-0 and now (A) 6 . . . Bf5 7 Qe2 Nbd7 8 e4 dxe4 9 Nxe4 Nxe4 10 Bxe4 Bxe4 11 Qxe4 c6 12 Bg5 Nf6 =, Pedersen–Cobo, Helsinki 1952. (B) 6 . . . c6 7 e4 (7 Re1 Qc7 8 b3 0-0 9 Bb2 Re8 10 e4 dxe4 11 Nxe4 Nxe4 12 Bxe4 e5! 13 c4 exd4 exd4 14 Bxd4 Bxd4 15 Nxd4 Nf6 =, Korn) 7 . . . dxe4 8 Nxe4 Nxe4 9 Bxe4 Bg4 =. (C) 6 . . . c5 7 c3 0-0 8 Qe2 (8 b4 c4! 9 Bc2 Re8—Kovačević) 8 . . . Qc7 (Koltanowski) 9 e4 dxe4 10 Nxe4 cxd4 11 Nxf6† Nxf6 12 Nxd4 e5 ∞. Both sides ultimately achieve their center thrusts but neither side has a clear advantage.

(b) (A) 8 . . . Be7 9 Ne5 0-0 10 Qf3 Rc8 11 Qh3 Nxe5 12 dxe5 Ne4 13 Rad1 Ng5 14 Qh5 g6 15 Qe2 Qc7 16 c4 f5 17 f4 Ne4 =, Hartston–Upton, London 1984. (B) 8 . . . a6 9 Ne5 b5 10 Nxd7 Qxd7 11 dxc5 Bxc5 12 Qf3 Be7 13 Qg3 0-0 14 Nf3 (Yusupov–Scheeren, Plovdid 1983) 14 . . . Nh5! 15 Qh3 g6 16 Ne5 Qd6 = (Korn).

(c) Solid is 6 c3 Nc6 7 0-0 Qc7 (trying for . . . e5) 8 c4! dxc4 9 bxc4 Be7 10 Bb2 0-0 11 Nc3 Rad8 12 Rc1 Bb7 (12 . . . Nb4 13 Bb1 b6 14 Qe2 Bb7 15 Rfd1 ∓) 13 Qe2 Rd7 14 Rfd1 Rfd8 15 Bb1 Rf8 =.

(d) 9 b4! Qc7! (both 9 . . . Bxb4 10 c4! and 9 . . . Qxb4 10 Rb1 Qe7 11 Rb3 Bb4 12 Ne5 are risky) 10 Rb1 Nc6 11 Bb5 a5! (Hall/Smith prefer 11 . . . 0-0 12 Bxc6 Qxc6 =) 12 bxa5 0-0 13 Ba3 Rd8 14 Bc5 Nd7 15 Rb3 Bxa5 16 Ba3 Nf6 (16 . . . Bb6 ∓, ECO) 17 c3 Ne7! ∓.

(e) 6 . . . Bd6 7 Bb2 0-0 8 Nbd2 Qe7 9 Ne5 cxd4 10 exd4 Ba3 11 Bxa3 Qxa3 12 c3! Bd7 13 f4 ±, Hulak–Spiridonov, Opatja 1985.

445

(f) 9 Ne5 Nb4 10 Be2 Bb7 11 f4 Ne4 12 Nxe4 dxe4 13 a3 Nd5 =, Yusupov–Spiridonov, Plovdiv 1983.

(g) 5 . . . Nc6 6 Nbd2 Bd6 7 0-0 0-0 (7 . . . b6 8 dxc5 bxc5—Korn) 8 dxc5 Bxc5 9 Qe2 e5 10 e4 Be6 11 b4 Bd6 12 Ng5 d4 13 Nxe6 fxe6 14 b5 ±, Kovačević–Abramović, Yugoslav Chp. 1984.

(h) 9 e4 dxe4 10 Nxe4 Be7 11 Qe2 cxd4 12 Nxd4 Bb7 13 Bg5 Nxe4 14 Bxe4 Bxe4 15 Bxe7 Qxe7 16 Qxe4 Nf6 = (Bagirov).

(i) The position reached is a Colle without . . . d5. Possible continuations are: (A) 6 c3 Be7 7 Nbd2 Nc6 8 Qe2 0-0 9 a3 Rc8 10 e4 cxd4 11 cxd4 d6 12 b4 Nh5 =, Koltanowski–Flohr, Antwerp 1932. (B) 6 Nbd2 Be7 7 e4!? d6 =, (7 . . . cxd4 8 e5 ±; if 7 . . . d5 as in Yusupov–Timman, match 1986, then 8 e5 Nfd7 9 Re1 ±.)

(j) 9 exd4 0-0 10 a3 Rc8 11 Rc1 Re8 12 Re1 d5 (Yusupov–Gentes, Winnipeg 1986) 13 c4 ± (Bagirov). In the column, 3 . . . Ne4 is the Döry Defense, but see col. 28 (m).

(k) Wasted is the push 3 . . . h6 4 Bxf6 Qxf6 5 Nbd2 (or 5 e4) 5 . . . d6 6 c3 Nd7 7 a4 g5 8 g3 Bg7 9 Bg2 0-0 10 a5 Rb8 11 0-0 e5 12 e3 Qe7 13 e4 ±, Vaganian–Plaskett, Hastings 1982-83. The attack was named after its proponent, the late Mexican grandmaster Carlos Torre.

(l) (A) 4 c3 cxd4 5 cxd4 Qb6 6 Qc2 Nc6 7 Bxf6 gxf6 8 e3 d5 9 Nc3 Bd7 10 Be2 allows White slightly more flexibility. (B) 4 e4!? is the Heinrich Wagner Gambit.

(m) 9 cxd5 exd5 10 Bd3 Be6 11 0-0 Bd6 12 Rc1 0-0-0 =, Harding–Hardicsay, Stary Smokovec 1982. In the column, 3 g3 b5 leads into cols. 21–22.

QUEEN'S PAWN GAMES

1 d4

	Torre Attack		Ruth Opening (Trompowski Attack)			
	13	**14**	**15**	**16**	**17**	**18**
	(Nf6)					g6(s)
2	(Nf3)		Bg5			Nf3(t)
	(e6)........g6		c5 ....Ne4(k)			Bg7
3	(Bg5)	Bg5	Bxf6(g)	Bf4(l)......b4		g3(u)
	(c5)	Bg7(c)	gxf6	d5(m)	c5(q)	c5
4	(e3)	Nbd2	d5(h)	f3(n)	f3	c3
	cxd4(a)	d5!(d)	Qb6	Nf6	g5	Qb6
5	exd4	e3	Qc1	Nc3(o)	fxe4	Qb3
	Be7	0-0(e)	f5	e6	gxh4	Nf6
6	Nbd2	c3	c3(i)	e4	e3	Qxb6
	d6	b6	Bg7	c5	Bh6	axb6
7	c3	b4	c3	Nb5	Kf2	Na3
	Nbd7	Bb7	e6	Na6	cxd4	d6
8	Bd3	Be2	Nh3	e5	exd4	Bg2
	b6(b)	Nbd7(f)	Qd6(j)	Nd7(p)	d5(r)	Nc6 =

(a) Chancy is 4 ... Qb6 5 Nbd2 Qxb2 6 Rb1 Qxa2 (6 ... Qc3 7 Rb3 Qa5 8 Rb5, Kopec–de Firmian, US 1985-86, 8 ... Qd8 ∞) 7 Bc4 Qa5 8 Bxf6 gxf6 9 Rb5 with pressure, but not necessarily compensating for the lost pawn (Korn).

(b) 9 0-0 (9 Qe2 retains the option of castling kingside or queenside) 9 ... Bb7 10 Re1 (10 Qe2 Qc7 11 Ne4 0-0 12 Rfe1 Rfe8 13 Rad1 Nf8 14 Bc1 ±, Torre–Lasker, Moscow 1925) 10 ... 0-0 11 a4 a6 12 Nf1 Re8 13 Ng3 Nf8 14 Bd2 Qd7 15 Nf5 h6 16 Nh3 Qc6 17 f3 N8d7 18 Nf2 Bf8 19 Nfe4 Qc7 20 Qe2 Nh7 =, Spassky–Portisch, Reggio Emilia 1986-87.

(c) 3 ... Ne4 (A) 4 Bh4 d5 5 e3 Bg7 6 Nbd2 c5 7 c3 cxd4 8 cxd4 ±, or (B) 4 Bf4 d5 5 e3 Bg7 6 Nbd2 c5 7 c3 0-0 8 Nxe4 dxe4 9 Nd2 cxd4 10 exd4 f5 11 f3 with an active game in Rodriguez–Westerinen, Alicante 1980.

(d) 4 ... c5 5 c3 cxd4 6 cxd4 Nc6 or 6 ... d5 transposes to the column.

(e) (A) 5 ... Bg4 6 Bd3 Nbd7 7 c3 c6 8 Qc2 0-0 9 h3 Bxf3 10 Nxf3 a5 =, Danielson–J. Nielsen, Danish Jr. Chp. 1984. (B) 5 ... Nbd7 6 c3 0-0 7 b4 c6 8 Be2 Re8 9 0-0 e5 =, Torre–Kasparov, Thessaloniki 1988.

(f) 9 0-0 Qe8 =, (or 9 ... Re8, or 9 ... Ne4 =), Kavalek–Browne, US Chp. 1986. In the column, if 2 ... b5, see Polish Defense.

(g) Probably the best choice. Others are: (A) 3 Nc3 cxd4 4 Qxd4 Nc6 5 Qh4 e6 (5 ... d6!?) 6 e4 Be7 7 0-0-0 (7 f4 b5! 8 e5 b4 ∞) 7 ... a6 8 f4 b5 =. (B) 3 d5 Ne4! (3 ... Qb6 4 Nc3 Qxb2—burning his bridges—5 Bd2 Qb6 6 e4 d6 [or 6 ... e6] 7 f4 e6 8 Rb1 Qd8 9 dxe6 fxe6 10 e5 dxe5 11 fxe5 Nd5—Golubenko) 4 Bf4 Qb6 5 Bc1 e6 6 f3 Qa5† 7 c3 Nf6 8 e4 d6 9 Bd2 Qb6 10 c4 Qxb2 11 Nc3 Qb6 12 f4 Nbd7 13 Nf3 e5 =, Vyzhmanavin–Ehlvest, USSR Chp. 1984.

(h) 4 c3 Qb6 5 Qc2 d5 6 e3 Nc6 7 Nf3 e5 8 Be2 Bg7 9 0-0 0-0 10 Nbd2 cxd4 11 cxd4 e4 12 Nh4 f5 13 g3 f4! 14 gxf4 Bh3 15 Rf31! Nd4! 16 exd4 Bxd4 17 Kh1 Qf6! $\mp$, Meduna–Mokrý, Namestovo 1987.

(i) 6 g3 Bg7 7 c3 Qd6!? 8 Bg2 b5 9 a4 Bb7 10 Na3 a6 11 Qg5 Qf6 12 Qxf6 Bxf6 =, Sariego–Lugo, Cuban Chp. 1987.

(j) 9 Qd2 Na6 10 Na3 Qxd5 11 Qxd5 exd5 12 0-0-0 Nc7 13 Nf4 d4! 14 Nh5 Bh6 15 cxd4 cxd4 16 Rxd4 Ne6 17 Rd5 f4 18 Nc4 0-0 19 Nd6 $\pm$, Bellon Lopez–Kouatly, Brussels 1987.

(k) The text challenges White to disclose his intentions before Black has committed himself to a particular pawn structure. Black also has (A) 2 . . . e6 3 e4 (3 Nf3 becomes a Torre Attack) 3 . . . h6 4 Bxf6 Qxf6 5 Nf3 (again see Torre Attack) 5 . . . b6 6 Bd3 (1) 6 . . . Ba6 7 Bxa6 Nxa6 8 0-0 Be7 9 Ke2 Nb8 10 Nc3 0-0 11 Rad1 c6 12 e5 Qg6 13 Ne4 $\pm$, Ekstrom–Taimanov, Plovdiv 1984; (2) 6 . . . g6 7 Qd2 Bg7 8 0-0-0 a6 9 h4 b5 ∞. (B) 2 . . . d5 3 Bxf6 exf6 (3 . . . gxf6 is experimental) 4 e3 Bd6 5 Bd3 0-0 6 Qf3 Be6 7 Ne2 c5! 8 c3 Nc6 9 Nd2 Qd7 10 h3 c4 11 Bc2 b5 +, Bellon Lopez–Mikhalchishin, Hastings 1985-86.

(l) Another, legitimate, try is 3 Bh4: (A) 3 . . . c5 4 f3 g5 5 fxe4 gxh4 6 e3 (1) 6 . . . Qb6!? 7 Bc4 Qxb2 8 Bxf7† Kd8 9 Nd2 Qc3 ∞, or 7 Nc3 Nc6 8 Nd5 Qa5 9 c3 e6 10 Nf6 Ke7 11 Ng4 h5 ∞, Dezelin–Cvitan, Yugoslavia 1988; (2) 6 . . . Nc6 7 Bc4 e6 8 Nf3 Qb6 9 0-0 cxd4 10 exd4 Bg7 ∞—Golubenko. (B) 3 . . . g5 4 f3 gxh4 5 fxe4 e5!? (because of the transposition of moves, this is now playable instead of 5 . . . c5, but it is not necessarily better, notwithstanding this outcome) 6 Nf3 (6 d5!?) 6 . . . Bh6 7 g3 0-0 8 dxe5 Nc6 9 c3 d6 10 exd6 cxd6 11 Nbd2 Be6 12 Nb3 Qb6 13 gxh4 Be3 14 Qd3 Ne5 15 Nxe5? dxe5 and White resigned, having overlooked . . . Bf2† followed by . . . Bxb3 and . . . Rfd8 winning, Bellon–W. Watson, Gijon 1988.

(m) Livelier is 3 . . . c5 4 f3 Qa5† 5 c3 Nf6 6 d5 e6 (or 6 . . . d6 7 e4 g6 8 Na3 Bg7 9 Qd2 0-0 =) 7 e4 exd5 8 exd5 d6 9 Qe2† Be7 10 Bd6 Nd5 11 Qe4 Nc6 12 Qxd5 Be6 13 Qxc5 Qxc5 14 Bxc5 Bxc5 15 Nd2 0-0-0 wins, Kogan–Wilder, US Chp. 1986.

(n) 4 Nd2 Nxd2 5 Qxd2 Bf5 6 Nf3 e6 =, Pachman.

(o) Bypassing the immediate gambit 5 e4 dxe4 6 Nc3 (compare Blackmar–Diemer Gambit) 6 . . . exf3 7 Nxf3 e6 8 Bc4 c6 9 Qe2 Nbd7 10 0-0-0 Nb6 11 d5 Nbxd5 12 Bxd5 $\pm$, (Jansa).

(p) 9 c3 Be7 10 dxc5 Naxc5 11 b4 Na6 12 Bd3 Nab8! =, Yudasin–Uhlmann, Leipzig 1986.

(q) 3 . . . d5 4 Nd2 Nxg5 5 hxg5 Bf5 6 e3 e6 7 g4 Bg6 8 f4 c5 9 Ngf3 Nc6 10 c3 Qb6 =, Hodgson–Gufeld, Hastings 1986-87.

(r) 9 exd5 Qxd5 10 Nf3 Nc6 11 Nc3 Qa5 12 Bb5† Bd7 13 Re1 0-0-0 14 Ne5 Qb6 15 Bxc6 Bxc6 16 Nxc6 Qxc6 17 Qg4 e6 18 Rad1 Rhg8 =, Bellon Lopez–Hjartarson, Hastings 1985-86.

(s) This King's Fianchetto Defense deals with some of the rarer lines without c4 which might not arise from the Reti and other Flank Openings; the move . . . g6 usually occurs in conjunction with . . . d6. 1 . . . e6 2 c4 Bb4† is the *Franco-Indian Defense*. It transposes to the Nimzo-Indian Defense after 3 Nc3 Nf6, but takes on independent significance after 3 . . . c5 4 dxc5 Bxc3† 5 bxc3 Qa5 6 Nf3 Nf6 7 e3 0-0 8 Nd4 Ne4 9 Bb2 Nxc5 10 Nb3 Qc7 11 Nxc5 Qxc5 12 a4! when Black stands worse. 1 . . . e6 2 c4 b6, followed by . . . f5 is the English Defense.

(t) For 2 e4 see Pirc Defense and Robatsch Defense and the English Opening, col. 123(h).

(u) Innocuous are (A) 3 Bf4 d6 4 e3 Nd7 5 h3 e5 6 Bh2 e4 7 Nfd2 f5 8 f4 Nh6 9 gxf5 Nxf5 10 Nxe4 0-0 11 Nbc3 Nh4 12 Be2 b5 = (*ECO*). (B) 3 c3 d6 4 e4 Nd7 5 Bd3 e5 6 0-0 Ngf6 7 a4 c6 8 Na3 Qc7 9 Qd2 0-0 10 Nc2 Re8 11 Rfe1 Nf8 12 h3 Bd7 =. *Comments.* The column is Pomar–Uhlmann, Madrid 1973.

QUEEN'S PAWN GAMES

1 d4

	19	20	21	22	23	24
		Polish Defense			Queen's Knight Defense	
	b5				Nc6(k)	
2	e4	a4	Nf3		c4(l)	
	Bb7(a)	b4	Bb7	Nf6	e5	Nf6
3	f3(b)	e4	e3	g3(g)	d5(m)	Nc3(p)
	a6	Bb7	a6	e6	Nce7	d6(q)
4	Be3	Bd3	c4	Bg2(h)	e4	Nf3
	e6	f5(d)	bxc4	Bb7	Ng6(n)	e5
5	Nd2	exf5	Bxc4	0-0(i)	Be3	d5
	a5	Bg2	e6	c5	Bb4†	Ne7
6	Bd3	Qh5†	Nc3	c3	Nd2	e4
	Nf6	g6	Nf6	cxd4	Nf6	Ng6
7	e5	fxg6	0-0	cxd4	f3	Be2
	Nfd7	Bg7	d5	Be7	Qe7	Be7
8	f4	gxh7†	Be2	Bg5	Nh3	h4
	c5(c)	Kf8(e)	c5(f)	a6(j)	Bc5(o)	h6(r)

(a) For 2 . . . a6 3 Nf3 or 3 Bd3 see Baker's Defense col. 1.

(b) (A) 3 Bd3 e6 again leads to Baker's Defense. (B) 3 Nd2 Nf6 4 e5 Nd5 5 Ngf3 a6 6 a4 b4 7 Bd3 e6 8 Ne4 Be7 9 Nfg5 h6 10 Nh3 d6 11 f4 ±, Knežević–Klarić, Belgrade 1981. (C) 3 Bxb5 Bxe4 (3 . . . f5!? 4 exf5 Bxg2 5 Qh5† g6 6 fxg6 Bg7 is similar to col. 2) 4 Nf3 e6 5 0-0 Nf6 6 Be2 (6 c4 c5! =) 6 . . . Be7 7 c4 Bb7 8 Nc3 0-0 9 h3 d6 =.

(c) 9 c3 Nc6 10 Ndf3 Be7 11 Ne2 Qc7 12 0-0 c4! = (Kapitaniak).

(d) 4 . . . Nf6 safely avoids complications but forgoes the gambitlike flavor of the opening.

(e) 9 Nf3! Nf6 10 Qg6 Bxf3 11 Rg1 Rxh7 12 Qg3 Be4 13 Bxe4 Nxe4 14 Qf3† Kg8 15 Qxe4 d5 16 Qe6† Kh8 and 17 . . . Qd7 = (Kapitaniak).

(f) 9 b3 (9 Qb3! with a small plus for White—Miles) 9 . . . cxd4 10 exd4 Nbd7 11 a3 Bd6 12 b4 Ne4 13 Na4 Bc6 14 Bb2 0-0 15 Nc5 Qb6! 16 Rb1 a5! =, Anderson–Miles, Tilburg 1984.

(g) 3 e3 a6 4 Bd3 Bb7 5 0-0 d6 6 b3 Nbd7 7 Bb2 c5 8 Nbd2 e6 9 Qe2 Be7 10 c4 b4 11 0-0 =, Kopley–Benjamin, Pasedena 1983. This, and the column, may arise after the frequent order of moves 1 d4 Nf6 2 Nf3 b5, or 2 . . . e6 3 g3 b5.

(h) Other ideas are: (A) 4 Qd3 Ba6 5 Bg2 d5 6 0-0 c5 7 Bg5 Be7 8 Nbd2 b4 9 Qb3 Bxe2 10 Bxf6 Bxf6 11 Re1 Bxf3 12 Nxf3 0-0 13 dxc5 Nc6 = (Okhotnik). (B) 4 a4 b4 5 c4 bxc3 6 bxc3 c5 7 Bg2 Bb7 8 0-0 Be7 9 Nbd2 0-0 =, Simić–de Firmian, Stara Pazova 1983.

(i) 5 Bg5 c5 6 c3 cxd4 7 Bxf6 gxf6 8 cxd4 d5 9 0-0 Nd7 10 Qd3 Qb6 11 Nbd2 Be7 12 e4 dxe4 13 Nxe4 0-0 =, Speelman–Karpov. London 1984.

(j) 9 Nc3 0-0 10 Qd3 d5 11 Ne5 Nc6 12 f4 Rc8 13 Kh1 ±.

(k) The Englund Gambit, 1 . . . e5 2 dxe5, is risky, e.g. (A) 2 . . . d6 3 exd6 Bxd6 4 Nf3 Nc6 5 e4 (or, more positionally, 5 b3 or e3 or g3) 5 . . . Bg4 6 Be2 Qe7 7 Nc3 h6 (7 . . . Nf6 8 Bg5 0-0-0 9 0-0 ±) 8 Be3 Nf6 9 Nd2 Be6 10 f3 ∞ (Korn). (B) 2 . . . Nc6? 3 Nf3 Qe7 4 Nc3 Nxe5 5 Nd5 Nxf3† 6 gxf3 Qd8 7 Qd4! d6 8 Bg5 ± (Korchnoi).

(l) (A) 2 d5?! Ne5 3 e4 e6 4 dxe6 dxe6 5 Qxd8† Kxd8 6 f4 Nc6 7 Nf3 Nf6 8 Bd3 Bc5 9 c3 with some advantage to White, Miles–Mestrović, Lone Pine 1978 (B) For 2 e4 see the Nimzowitsch Defense. (C) 2 Nf3 d6 3 e4 Nf6 4 Nc3 Bg4 5 Be3 e5 or 5 . . . g6 =.

(m) (A) The early 2 . . . e5 was developed into a system by Mikenas; if here (A) 3 e3 exd4 4 exd4 5 Nf3 Bg4 (now a French Exchange Variation by transposition) 6 Be2 dxc4 7 0-0 Bd6 8 Bxc4 Qf6! 9 Qe1† Kf8 ∓, Stahlberg–Mikenas, Munich 1936. Or (B) 3 dxe5 Nxe5 4 e3 Nf6 5 Nc3 Bb4 6 Bd2 0-0 7 Be2 d6 8 Nf3 Be6 9 b3 c6 ∞.

(n) Or first 4 . . . Nf6 5 Nc3 Ng6 6 Nf3 Bc5 7 Be2 d6 ∞. Compare English Opening, col. 126.

(o) 9 Qb3 d6 10 Bxc5 dxc5 11 Nf2 0-0 12 g3 Ne8 13 h4 b6 14 h5 Nh8 15 Qe3 Nd6 16 0-0-0 Draw, Spassov–Z. Nikolić, Vrnjačka Banja 1984.

(p) (A) 3 d5 Ne5 4 e4 d6 (or 4 . . . e6 5 f4 Ng6 6 Bd3 exd5 7 exd5 Bb4† 8 Bd2 Qe7† 9 Kf1 Bxd2 10 Qxd2 Ne4 = [Orlov in Inside Chess, 1989, No. 19–20]) 5 f4 Ng6 6 Nc3 e5!? ∞. (B) 3 Nf3 d6 4 d5 Ne5 5 Nc3 Nxf3† 6 exf3 e5 7 Bd3 Be7 8 Qc2 0-0 9 Be3 c6 10 g4 cxd5 11 cxd5 Qa5 12 0-0-0 Kh8 13 Qb3 Rb8 =, Nedeljković–Trajković, Belgrade 1952. (C) For 3 . . . e6 4 Nc3 Bb4 see Nimzo-Indian Defense, and 4 g3 Bb4† is a Bogo-Indian Defense.

(q) (A) For 3 . . . d5 see Queen's Gambit, Chigorin Defense. (B) 3 . . . e5 4 d5 Ne7 5 e4 (or 5 d6!?) 5 . . . d6 6 g3 g6 ∞, Vanno–Kevitz, Manhattan C.C. 1954.

(r) 9 h5 Nf8 10 Ng1 Nfd7 11 Bf3 c6 12 Nge2 a4 =, Trapl–Lutikov, Warsaw 1969. Compare English Opening, col. 126.

QUEEN'S PAWN GAMES

1 d4

	Albin Counter Gambit			Blumenfeld Counter Gambit		
	25	26	27	28	29	30
	d5................................Nf6					
2	c4			c4		
	e5			e6		
3	dxe5(a)			Nf3		
	d4			c5(m)		
4	Nf3(b)			d5		
	Nc6			b5		
5	Nbd2...................a3(j)			dxe6.......Bg5		
	Bg4(c)		Be6(k)	fxe6	h6.........exd5	
6	a3(d).......g3		e3	cxb5	Bxf6	cxd5
	Qe7	Qd7	dxe3	d5	Qxf6	Qa5†(r)
7	h3	Bg2	Qxd8†	e3(n)	Nc3	Nc3
	Bxf3(e)	0-0-0(g)	Rxd8	Bd6	b4	Ne4
8	Nxf3	h3(h)	Bxe3	Nc3	Nb5	Bd2
	0-0-0	Bf5	Nge7	Bb7!(o)	Kd8!?	Nxd2
9	Qd3	a3	Bf4	Be2	e4	Nxd2
	Nxe5(f)	f6(i)	Ng6(l)	0-0(p)	g5(q)	b4(s)

(a) (A) 3 e3 exd4 4 exd4 Nf6 5 Nc3 Be7 6 Nf3 0-0 =. (B) 3 Nc3 exd4 4 Qxd4 Nc6! 5 Qxd5 Be6 6 Qb5 a6 7 Qa4 Bb4 and Black's development gives him the advantage, Marshall–Duras, Carlsbad 1907.

(b) (A) 4 e3? Bb4† 5 Bd2 dxe3! 6 fxe3 (worse are 6 Qa4† Nc6 7 Bxb4 exf2† 8 Kxf2 Qh4† ∓, Linse–Kjelberg, Malmö 1917, and 6 Bxb4? exf2† 7 Ke2 fxg1 (N)! 8 Resigns, Korody–Balogh, 1933) 6 . . . Qh4† 7 g3 Qe4 leaves Black on top. (B) 4 e4?! Nc6 5 f4 f6! 6 exf6 Nxf6 7 Bd3 Bb4† 8 Nd2 Ng4 is troublesome for White, Osipov–Zhuravlev, Latvia 1972.

(c) (A) 5 . . . f6 6 exf6 Qxf6 7 g3 Bg4 8 Bg2 0-0-0 9 h3 Bh5 10 0-0 d3 11 exd8 Rxd3 12 g4 ±, Grünfeld-Schoenmann, corr. 1918-19. (B) 5 . . . Nge7 6 Nb3 Nf5 7 e4 dxe3 8 Qxd8† Kxd8 9 fxe3 Bb4 10 Kf2 Nh6 ∞ (Lamford and J. Shipman).

(d) On the immediate 6 h3, Black has 6 . . . Bxf3 7 Bxf3 Bb4† 8 Bd2 Qe7 with even chances, Szabo–Krenosz, Budapest 1939.

(e) 7 . . . Bh5 8 Qa4 0-0-0 9 g4 Bg6 10 Bg2 h5 11 b4 hxg4 12 hxg4 Rxh1† 13 Bxh1 ±, Suetin–Mosionzhik, USSR 1962.

(f) 10 Qf5† Nd7 11 Nxd4 g6 12 Qc2 Bg7 13 Nf3 Nc5 14 e3 and Black's initiative is worth less than the pawn.

(g) 7 . . . Bh3 8 0-0 0-0-0 9 Nb3 Bxg2 10 Kxg2 Qe6 11 Qd3 Nxe5 12 Nbxd4! with a clear plus, Korchnoi–Mosionzhik, USSR 1969.

(h) If 8 0-0 h5! starts kingside play; after 9 h4 Nge7 10 Qa4 Ng6 11 Nb3 Kb8 12 Na5 Nxa5 13 Qxa5 Qf5 14 Re1 f6, both sides have chances, Browne–Mestel, Las Palmas 1982.

(i) 10 exf6 Nxf6 11 b4 Re8 12 Bb2! Bd3 13 0-0 Bxe2 14 Qa4 Bxf1 15 Rxf1 Kb8 16 b5 Nd8 17 Nxd4 with excellent compensation for the exchange, Bondarevsky–Mikenas, USSR Chp. 1950.

(j) On (A) 5 g3 Bg4 White can transpose to col. 2 with 6 Nbd2 or play 6 Bg2 Qd7 7 0-0 h5 ∞. (B) 5 Bg5 Be7 6 Bxe7 Ngxe7 (6 . . . dxe7! 7 g3 c5 ∞) 7 Nbd2 0-0 8 Nb3 Nf5 9 Qd2 Qe7 10 Nbxd4 Nfxd4 11 Nxd4 Nxe5 is roughly equal.

(k) (A) 5 . . . Bg4 6 Nbd2 transposes to col. 1. (B) For 5 . . . Nge7 6 Nbd2 see note (c)(B).

(l) 10 Bg3 h5 (Simonson–Opočensky, Folkestone 1933) 11 h3 h4 12 Bh2 Rh5 13 Be2 Rf5 regains the pawn with a good position (Lamford).

(m) (A) 3 . . . a6 (Dzindzihasvili) 4 Nc3 c5 is suspect after 5 d5 b5 6 Bg5 b4 7 Ne4 d6 8 Nxf6† gxf6 9 Bd2 f5 10 a3! bxa3 11 Rxa8 ±, Chernin–Alburt, Subotica 1987. (B) 3 . . . Ne4!? (the Döry Defense) 4 e3 b6 5 Bd3 Bb4† 6 Nbd2 Bb7 7 a3 ±.

(n) 7 Bf4 Bd6 8 Bxd6 Qxd6 9 Nbd2 0-0 10 g3 a6! 11 bxa6 Bxa6 allows Black excellent play for the pawn, P. Nikolić–Barlov, Yugoslav Chp. 1982.

(o) 8 . . . 0-0 9 e4! dxe4 10 Ng5 is very good for White.

(p) 10 b3 Nbd7 11 Bb2 Qe7 with a strong center and attacking chances for the pawn, Tarrasch–Alekhine, Pistyan 1922.

(q) (A) 10 Bd3 Bb7 11 e5 Qg7 12 Qa4 a5 13 0-0 g4 ∞, Portisch–Rodgers, Reggio Emilia 1984-85; Rodgers suggests 11 Qa4 a5 12 Qc2 is better for White.

(r) 6 . . . d6 7 e4 a6 8 a4 Be7 9 Bxf6 Bxf6 10 axb5 Bxb2 11 Ra2 Bf6 12 Nbd2 ±, Vaganian–Grigorian, USSR Chp. 1971.

(s) Petrosian–Sax, Niksić 1983; now 10 Nce4 Ba6 11 g3 is pleasant for White.

BUDAPEST DEFENSE

1 d4 Nf6 2 c4 e5

Diagram 61

THIS USED TO BE KNOWN as the Budapest (Counter) Gambit—properly so, since Black can turn it into a true gambit—but "Defense" has been adopted here as the broader term, covering as well variations that are not gambits. It is played enough to merit an individual chapter.

The Budapest Defense is another example of an idea which developed as a regional favorite—in this case in Hungary, where it made its tournament debut in Esser–Breyer, Budapest 1916. But it had been essayed even earlier, by S. R. Barrett of Philadelphia in 1883, and the U.S. Open Champion Stasch Mlotkowski published a competent analysis of it in *The British Chess Magazine* for January 1919.

Precise handling generally leaves White in a better strategic position, and the defensive possibilities are too narrow to interest grandmasters for long. Yet it serves as a serious weapon in the hands of the daring versus the timid soul.

After 3 dxe5 Ng4, the move 4 Nf3 (cols. 1–2) has regained status over Rubinstein's solid 4 Bf4 (col. 3) with its aim of developing the bishop before playing e3; 11 g3 (note 1) has recently been revived.

4 e4 (col. 4) was Alekhine's preference and still contains some venom if not answered carefully.

The *Fajarowicz Variation* is entered with 3 . . . Ne4 (cols. 5–6), which seems inconspicuous but can turn vitriolic, especially in "blitz."

BUDAPEST DEFENSE

1 d4 Nf6 2 c4 e5 3 dxe5(a)

	1	2	3	4	5	6
	Ng4......................................Ne4					
4	Nf3.....................Bf4.........e4(m)			Qc2.........Nf3(t)		
	Nc6........Bc5		Nc6(j)	Nxe5(n)	Bb4†(q)	Nc6(u)
5	e3(b)	e3	Nf3	f4	Nc3(r)	a3!(v)
	Bb4†(c)	Nc6	Bb4†	Nec6(o)	d5	d6(u)
6	Bd2(d)	a3(f)	Nc3(k)	Be3	exd6	Qc2
	Bxd2†	a5	Bxc3†	Bb4†	Bf5	Bf5
7	Qxd2	b3	bxc3	Nc3	Bd2	Nc3
	0-0	0-0	Qe7	Qh4†	Nxd6	Nxf2
8	Be2	Bb2	Qd5	g3	e4	Qxf5
	Ncxe5	Re8	f6?!	Bxc3†	Bxc3	Nxh1
9	Nxe5	Nc3(g)	exf6	bxc3	Bxc3	e6
	Nxe5	Ngxe5(h)	Nxf6	Qe7	Bxe4	fxe6
10	0-0	Nxe5	Qd3	Bd3	Qd2	Qxe6†
	d6(e)	Nxe5(i)	d6(l)	Na6(p)	0-0(s)	Qe7(w)

(a) Declining the sacrifice gives Black an easy game, e.g. 3 d5 Bc5 4 Nc3 d6; or 3 e3 exd4 4 exd4 d5 5 Nc3 Be7 6 cxd5 Nxd5.

(b) (A) 5 Bg5 Be7 6 Bxe7 Qxe7 7 Nc3! Qc5! 8 e3 0-0 (or 8 . . . Ngxe5 9 Qd5 Qe7 10 Qd2 d6 11 Nd5 Qd8 12 0-0 0-0 13 Be2 Be6 =) 9 Qd5 Qb4 10 Qb5 Re8 11 Nd4 Qe7 with lively prospects for both sides (Kaposztas). (B) 5 Bf4 may transpose to col. 3.

(c) (A) 5 . . . Bc5 6 Nc3 Ngxe5 (6 . . . Ncxe5? 7 h3! Nxf3† 8 Qxf3 Ne5 9 Qg3 ±, Nikolic–Barbero, Mexico 1979) 7 Qd5 or 7 Be2 may transpose to note (f). (B) 5 . . . Ngxe5 6 Be2 (6 b3 or 6 Nc3 safely transposes to the main lines) 6 . . . g6?! 7 Nc3 Nxf3† 8 Bxf3 Bg7 9 Qd2 d6 10 b3 Ne5! 11 Bb2! Nxf3† 12 gxf3 0-0 13 0-0-0 Bh3 =, Sosonko–Ree, Amsterdam 1982. The game continued 14 Rhg1 Be6 15 Ne4 f5 16 Ng5 Bxb2† 17 Qxb2 Qf6 18 f4 Qxb2† 19 Kxb2 Bf7 20 c5! dxc5 21 Rd7 Rad8! 22 Rgd1 Rxd7 23 Rxd7 h6 24 Nf3 Rc8 25 Ne5 Be8 26 Re7 Kf8 27 Rh7 Kg8 28 Re7 Kf8 29 Rh7 Kg8 Draw.

(d) (A) 6 Nc3 Bxc3†! 7 bxc3 Qe7! (preventing an immediate c5 or Ba3) 8 a4 Ngxe5 9 Ba3 d6 10 c5 Nxf3† 11 gxf3 Qe5 12 Qd2 dxc5 13 Bb5 Bd7 14 0-0 0-0-0 with an excellent game for Black. (B) 6 Nbd2 looks solid, but Black may free himself by 6 . . . Ngxe5 7 Nxe5 Nxe5 8 Be2 d5! 9 cxd5 Qxd5 10 Qa4† Nc6 11 Bf3 Qd6 12 0-0 0-0 13 Rd1 Qe7, and if 14 Bxc6 bxc6 15 Qxc6 Rb8 ∓, and Black's open lines are dangerous for White (Trajković).

(e) 11 Nc3 Bg4 12 f3 Be6 13 b3 Qh4 14 f4 (14 Nd5? c6 =) 14 . . . Ng4 15 Bxg4 Qxg4 16 Nb5 Rfc8 =, Gutman–Shvidler, Beer-Sheba 1982.

(f) (A) 6 Qd5 (this aggressive sortie exposes the queen to later attack but that remains for Black to prove) 6 . . . Qe7 7 a3! (7 Nc3 Ngxe5 8 Be2 d6 9 Ne4 Be6 10 Qd1 Bb4† 11 Bd2 0-0-0 12 Bxb4 Nxb4 13 Qb3 Nxf3† 14 Bxf3 d5 ∓ is as old as Adler–Maroczy, Budapest 1896) 7 . . . a5 8 Nc3 0-0! 9 Ne4 b6 10 Nxc5 bxc5 11 Be2 Bb7 12 0-0 Rfb8 13 Qd1 Ncxe5

= (Borik). (B) 6 Be2 Ngxe5 7 0-0 0-0 8 Nxe5 Nxe5 9 b3 Re8 10 Nc3 d6 (10 . . . a5!? 11 Bb2 Ra6 12 Qd5 Ba7 13 Ne4 Rae6 14 Ng3—Korn) 11 Bb2 Re6 12 g3 Qd7 =, or 11 Na4 Bb6 =.

(g) (A) 9 Bd3!? d6! 10 exd6 Nxf2 11 Kxf2 Rxe3 12 Kf1 Bg4 13 Be2 Bxf3 14 Bxf3 Qh4 15 Ra2 Rae8 16 Bc3 cxd6 17 g3 Qh3† 18 Bg2 Qf5† 19 Rf2 Qxf2† 20 Kxf2 Rd3† 21 Resigns, Yrjola–Liew, Dubai 1986. (B) 9 Qd5 Qe7 10 Be2 Ngxe5 11 0-0 d6 and 12 . . . Be6 ∓.

(h) If now 9 . . . d6? 10 Na4 Ba7 (10 . . . Bb6 11 c5!) 11 exd6 ± (11 . . . Nxf2? 12 Kxf2 Bxe3† 13 Kg3, Korn).

(i) 11 Be2 d6 (11 . . . Ra6, Akesson) 12 0-0 Re6! (Staker's suggestion) 13 g3 Rh6 =, or 13 Na4 b6 =.

(j) Impetuous is Balogh's 4 . . . g5 5 Bd2 Nxe5 6 Bc3! (6 Nf3 Bg7 7 Nxe5 Bxe5 8 Qc1 h6 9 Nc3 d6 10 h4 g4 11 g3 Nc6 12 Bg2 Be6 =, Tartakower–Korn, Mandrake Club, London 1949) 6 . . . Bg7 7 e3 g4 8 Ne2 d6 9 Nf4 h5 10 Qc2 Qg5 11 Nd2 Bf5 12 Qb3 b6 13 c5 ± (Borik).

(k) 6 Nbd2—see also note (d)(B)—6 . . . Qe7 7 a3 Ngxe5 (7 . . . Ncxe5?! 8 axb4? Nd3 mate!) 8 Nxe5 Nxe5 9 e3 Bxd2† 10 Qxd2 d6 11 Be2 0-0 12 0-0 b6 13 b4 Bb7 14 c5 Rfd8 15 Qc3 Bd5 = (Schüssler and Wedberg).

(l) (A) 11 g3 and now: (1) 11 . . . 0-0 12 Bg2 Ne4 (12 . . . Re8 13 0-0 Qe2 14 Qxe2 Rxe2 15 Nd4 Nxd4 16 exd4 with the better ending, Donaldson–Dubisch, Seattle 1987) 13 0-0 Nc5 14 Qe3 Be6 15 Nd4 Bxc4 16 Nxc6 Qxe3 17 Bxe3 bxc6 18 Bxc6 Rab8 19 Rfb1 with an active game, Seirawan–Schulien, Columbus 1987; (2) 11 . . . Ne4 12 Bg2 Nc5 13 Qe3 Ne6 14 Ng5 Nxf4 15 Qxf4 ± (Donaldson). (B) 11 e3 0-0 12 Be2 Ne4 13 Rc1 Bg4 14 0-0 Kh8 =, Campos–Akesson, Valjevo 1984.

(m) Of surprise value is 4 e6: (A) 4 . . . fxe6 5 e4 Ne5 6 f4 Nf7 7 Be3 Bb4† 8 Nd2 0-0 9 a3 Be7 10 Ngf3 (Koltanowski–Neikirch, Belgian Chp. 1926) 10 . . . d5 11 cxd5 exd5 12 e5 c5 =. (B) 4 . . . Bb4† 5 Bd2 Qf6! 6 exf7† Kxf7 7 Nf3 Qxb2 8 Bxb4 Qxb4† 9 Nd2 Re8 10 e3 Qe7 11 h3 (Khasin–A. Ivanov, USSR 1979) 11 . . . Nf6 =.

(n) 4 . . . d6 5 Be2 (this is more conservative than 5 exd6 Bxd6 6 Be2 f5 7 exf5 Qe7 8 c5! Bxc5 9 Qa4† Nc6 10 Qxg4 0-0! 11 Qc4† Kh8 12 Nf3 Rxf5 13 0-0 b5 14 Qxb5 Nb4—Balogh—15 Nc3 Ba6 16 Qxa6 Nxa6 17 Bxa6 ±, Borik) 5 . . . Nxe5 6 f4 Ng4 (Myers) 7 Nf3 Be7 8 Nc3 0-0 9 0-0 Nc6 10 h3 ±.

(o) 5 . . . Ng6 6 Be3 Qb4† 7 Nc3 (7 Nd2 Qe7 8 Bd3 f5—better is 8 . . . Qd6!—9 Qc2 fxe4 10 Bxe4 d5!? 11 Bxg6† hxg6 12 Qxg6† ±, Alburt–McClintock, Las Vegas 1987) 7 . . . Bxc3† 8 bxc3 Qe2 (8 . . . b6!?) 9 Bd3 f5 10 Qc2 fxe5 11 Bxe4 Nxf4 12 Bxf4 d5 13 cxd5 Bxf5 ∞.

(p) 11 Bc2! b6 12 Nf3 Nc5 13 0-0 Bb7 14 e5 0-0-0 15 Nd4 (Keres–Gilg, Prague 1937) 15 . . . g6 =.

(q) Many complications follow 4 . . . d5?! 5 exd6 Bf5 6 Nc3 Nxd6 7 e4 Nxe4 8 Bd3 Nxf2 9 Bxf5 Nxh1 10 Nf3 g6 11 Be4 c6 12 Be3 f5 (Borik).

(r) 5 Nd2 d5 6 exd5 Bf5 7 a3 Bxd2† 8 Bxd2 Qxd6 9 g4 Qxd2† 10 Qxd2 Nxd2 =.

(s) 11 0-0-0 Nd7 12 f3 Bg6 13 h4 h6 14 Ne2 Nc5 15 Nf4 Bh7 = (Borik).

(t) 4 a3! Qh4 5 g3 (5 Be3 Bc5 6 Bxc5 Nxc5 7 Nf3 ±, Benjamin) 5 . . . Qh5 6 Nd2 Nxd2 7 Qxd2 Nc6 (or 7 . . . Qxe5) 8 Nf3 Nc6 =.

(u) On 4 . . . Bb5† (A) 5 Bd2 Nxd2 6 Nbxd2 Nc6 7 a3 Bxd2† 8 Qxd2 Qe7 9 Qc3 (Smyslov–H. Steiner, Groningen 1946) 9 . . . b6! 10 e3 Bb7 11 Be2 0-0-0 12 0-0-0 Rde8 13 Rd5 g5!. (B) 5 Nbd2! Nc6 6 a3 Nxd2 7 Nxd2 (7 Bxd2 Bxd2† 8 Qxd2 Qe7 9 Nc3 b6 leads to [A]) 7 . . . Bf8!? 8 Nf3 Qe7 9 Bg5 Qe6 ∞ (Borik).

(v) 5 Nbd2 Nc5 6 g3 d6 7 exd6 Qxd6 8 Bg2 Bf5 9 0-0 (or 9 a3 a5 10 0-0 0-0-0 =) 9 . . . 0-0-0 10 a3 Qf6! 11 Ra2 Bb1 (or 11 . . . Ne4 =) 12 Ra1 Bf5 = (Korn).

(w) 11 Qd5 h6 12 g3 g5 13 Bg2 ±, Reshevsky–Bisguier, New York 1955.

DUTCH DEFENSE

1 d4 f5

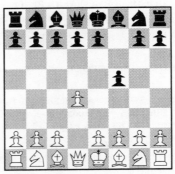

Diagram 62

THIS DEFENSE WAS FIRST ANALYZED by the Dutch player Elias Stein in his book "Nouvel essai sur le jeu des échecs" (1789), linking chess and military strategy. It was occasionally played by Morphy in the 1850s and later by Chigorin and Pillsbury before World War I, but the opening really blossomed in the 1920s and 1930s when Alekhine and then Botvinnik used it successfully. Yet for several decades now, no world-class player has used it on a regular basis. This is not just a matter of fashion, but a distrust of the underlying strategy behind the Dutch. Most grandmasters consider that the early advance of the f-pawn weakens the kingside. Nonetheless, a group of young Russians, headed by Yusupov and Beliavsky, have been using the Dutch as a surprise weapon and may change the current view.

The idea of 1 . . . f5 is to control the e4-square while unbalancing the position. If White plays e4 then the exchange of pawns allows Black play on the open f-file. If not, Black can advance his kingside pawns, gaining space and beginning an attack. The best plan for White usually involves g3 and Bg2, controlling the important long diagonal. White can advance either on the queenside or in the center with d5 or e4. As the two sides have different strategies, games become sharp and lively.

Diagram 63

The LENINGRAD VARIATION is 2 c4 Nf6 3 g3 g6 4 Bg2 Bg7 (see diagram) (cols. 1-6). Black's fianchettoed bishop eyes the center and helps protect the kingside, as in the King's Indian Defense. This modern strategy may be Black's best line in the Dutch as it has a sounder positional basis than the older variations.

The STONEWALL FORMATION (cols. 7–9 and 11) is characterized by the Black pawn chain . . . c6, . . . d5, . . . e6 and . . . f5, by which Black seeks to prevent any central action so that he can calmly proceed on the kingside. Though this is a tough nut to crack, White has the edge because of the weakness at e5.

The CLASSICAL (or Ilyin-Genevsky) SYSTEM is 2 g3 Nf6 3 Bg2 e6 4 c4 Be7 (cols. 13–16). Black places his pawns on e6 and d6 to protect the center, then develops the minor pieces and brings the queen to the kingside to begin operations there. Yet White can maintain some initiative by taking action in the center.

Columns 17, 18, and 20 cover unusual choices by Black. These lines do not equalize if White responds correctly. In col. 19 White plays Nc3, allowing . . . Bb4!, a hybrid Dutch–Nimzo-Indian.

The STAUNTON GAMBIT, 2 e4 (cols. 21–22) seeks to take immediate advantage of the weakening caused by . . . f5, but Black can obtain equal chances by keeping the pawn or allowing White to recapture it.

Cols. 23 and 24 examine 2 Nc3 and 2 Bg5. These are simpler lines that, though they gain no theoretical advantage, require accurate play by Black.

DUTCH DEFENSE

Leningrad Variation

1 d4 f5 2 c4 Nf6 3 g3 g6 4 Bg2 Bg7

	1	2	3	4	5	6
5	Nf3 .... Nh3					
	0-0					0-0
6	0-0					Nc3
	d6					d6
7	Nc3					d5(p)
	Nc6 .... c6 .... Qe8					c6
8	d5		d5(f)		d5(m)	0-0
	Ne5 .... Na5		e5(g)		Na6	Bd7
9	Nxe5(a)	Nd2	dxe6		Rb1	Qb3(q)
	dxe5	c5	Bxe6		Bd7	Qb6
10	Qb3(b)	Qc2	b3 .... Qd3		b4	Be3
	h6(c)	e5(d)	Na6(h)	Na6(k)	c6(n)	Qxb3
11	Be3	dxe6	Bb2	Ng5	Qd3	axb3
	Kh8	Bxe6	Nc5(i)	Bc8	Ne4	c5
12	Rad1	Rd1	Qc2	Bf4	Nd1	Nf4
	g5 =	Nc6(e)	Qe7(j)	Nh5(l)	Nc7(o)	Na6 =

(a) 9 Qb3 Nxf3† (or 9 . . . Nf7 10 Be3 Ng4 11 Bd4 Nge5 ∞, Koshnitsky–Ozols, Australia 1963) 10 exf3 (10 Bxf3 e5 11 dxe6 c6 is equal, Kochiev–Ftáčnik, Groningen 1975) 10 . . . e5 11 dxe6 Bxe6 12 Re1 Qd7 =, Pilnik–Tartakower, Paris 1954.

(b) Interesting is 10 e4 f4 11 gxf4 (11 b4 g5 12 Re1 a6 is about equal, Farago–Putianen, Budapest 1975) 11 . . . exf4 12 Ne2 with a complicated position that may favor White.

(c) 10 . . . e6 11 Rd1 exd5 12 Nxd5 c6 13 Bg5 cxd5 14 Bxd5† Kh8 15 Bxb7 Qxd1† 16 Rxd1 Rb8 17 Qa3 ±, Ribli–Barber, Lugano 1985. The column is Magerramov–Arsalumov, USSR 1987.

(d) 10 . . . a6 11 b3 Bd7 12 Bb2 b5 13 Rab1 ±, Averbakh–Spassky, USSR 1958.

(e) After 13 Nb3 Qe7 14 Bf4, White has the edge, Browne–Cripe, US 1987.

(f) Alternatives are: (A) 8 Rc1 Qc7 9 e4 fxe4 10 Nxe4 Nxe4 11 Rxe4 e5 =, Bondarevsky–Lievert, Rostov 1961; (B) 8 b3 a5 9 Bb2 Na6 10 Qc2 Qc7 11 Rad1 Kh8 =, Kovacs–Knaak, Polanica Zdroj 1975.

(g) (A) 8 . . . Qa5 9 Nd4 Qc5 10 Bg5 ± (Jansa). (B) On 8 . . . Bd7, both 9 Nd4 Qb6 10 e3 Na6 11 Rb1, Palatnik–Gulko, Kiev 1973, and 9 Rb1 Na6 10 b3 Nc5 11 Bb2, Ribli–Mestl, London 1986, give White a pull.

(h) 10 . . . Ne4 11 Nxe4 Bxa1 12 Qxd6 Qxd6 13 Nxd6 is much better for White.

(i) 11 . . . Qe7 12 Nd4 Bd7 13 e3 ± (Georgiev).

(j) 13 Ng5 Bd7 14 Rad1 Rad8 with even chances, Uhlmann–Lutikov, Leipzig 1977.

(k) (A) 10 . . . Nbd7 11 Bf4 Nb6 12 b3 Ne4 13 Nd4 ±, Uhlmann–Zweig, Halle 1967. (B) 10 . . . Ne4 11 Nd4 Bf7 12 Bxe4 fxe4 13 Nxe4 ±.

(l) 13 Qxd6 Nxf4 14 Qxf4 h6 and Black has play for the pawn, Simagin–Khasin, USSR 1956.

(m) (A) 8 Nd5 Nxd5 9 cxd5 h6 (or the risky 9 . . . Qb5) 10 Bd2 Kh7 11 Re1 c6 =, Pugach–Pelikan, Buenos Aires 1959. (B) 8 Re1 Qf7 9 Ng5 Qxc4 10 Bf1 Qb4 (10 . . . Qc6 11 Qb3 d5 12 Bf4, Scoones) 11 a3 Qb6 12 e4 fxe4 13 Bc4† Kh8 14 Nf7† Rxf7 15 Bxf7 Bg4 (Kharitonov and Vyzhmanagin). (C) 8 b3 Na6 9 Ba3 c6 10 Qd3 Bd7 11 Rfe1 ±, Karpov–Malanyuk, USSR Chp. 1988.

(n) 10 . . . e5 11 dxe6 Bxe6 12 Nd4 ±, Rukavina–Cvitan, Yugoslavia 1986.

(o) 13 Bb2 Qf7 14 Bxg7 Kxg7 15 dxc6 ±, Vogt-Casper, East Germany 1987. 7 . . . Qe8 is Chermin's idea.

(p) The alternatives are: (A) 7 Bf4 Nc6 8 h4 e5 9 dxe5 dxe5 10 Nfd5 Nd4 is roughly equal, Bannik–Savon, USSR 1962. (B) 7 0-0 e5 8 dxe5 dxe5 9 Qxd8 Rxd8 10 Nd5 Rd7 11 Bg5 Kf7 and Black will equalize, R. Byrne–Pelikan, Mar del Plata 1961.

(q) 9 Re1 Na6 10 e4 fxe4 11 Nxe4 Nxe4 12 Rxe4 ± (Dolmatov). The column is Zaichik–Dolmatov, Kharkov 1985.

DUTCH DEFENSE

1 d4 f5 2 c4 Nf6 3 g3 e6 4 Bg2

	7	8	9	10	11	12
	Be7				d5	Bb4†
5	Nf3			Nh3	Nf3	Bd2(p)
	0-0			d6(k)	c6	Be7(g)
6	0-0			Nc3	0-0	Nf3(r)
	d5 (Stonewall Formation)			0-0	Bd6	d6
7	Nc3 .... b3		Nbd2	0-0	Nc3(n)	0-0
	c6	c6	c6	Qe8(l)	Nbd7	0-0
8	Bg5(a)	Ba3(e)	Qc2	e4	Qc2	Nc3
	Nbd7(b)	Nbd7(f)	Qe8(h)	fxe4	0-0	Qe8
9	cxd5	Bxe7	Ne5	Nf4	cxd5(o)	Qc2
	exd5	Qxe7	Nbd7(i)	c6	cxd5	Qh5
10	Rb1(c)	Qc2	Nd3	Nxe4	Nb5	e4
	Ne4	Ne4	Kh8	Nxe4	Bb8	e5
11	Bxe7	Nc3	Nf3	Bxe4	Bf4	dxe5
	Qxe7	Nd6	Ne4	e5	Bxf4	dxe5
12	e3	Na4	Rb1	Ng2	gxf4	Nd5
	Rf6(d)	b6(g)	g5(j)	Nd7(m)	Nb6 ±	Nxd5(s)

(a) Other tries are: (A) 8 Ne5 Nbd7 9 Qb3 Ne4 10 cxd5 Nxe5 11 Nxe4 cxd5 12 dxe5 fxe4 =, Filip–Szabo, Göteborg 1955. (B) 8 Rb1 Qe8 9 c5 Qh5 10 b4 Ne4 ∞, Reshevsky–Botvinnik, Nottingham 1936.

(b) (A) 8 ... Ne4 is recommended by Taimanov. (B) 8 ... Qe8, (C) 8 ... Bd7 and (D) 8 ... Na6 have been tried, but all leave White with the upper hand.

(c) Also good is 10 e3 h6 11 Bxf6 Nxf6 12 Rb1 ±, Najdorf–Gligorić, Saltsjöbaden 1948.

(d) After 13 Qc2 Rh6 14 b4 g5 15 Ne2 White is better, Maderna–Castillo, Mar del Plata 1948.

(e) 8 Nbd2, 8 Bb2, and 8 Qc2 are also playable.

(f) (A) 8 ... Bxa3 9 Nxa3 Qe7 10 Qc1 Nbd7 11 Qb2 ±, Petrosian–Hoen, Havana 1966. (B) 8 ... Ne4 9 Bxe7 Qxe7 10 Nbd2 Qf6 11 e3 ±, Hort–Bertok, Vinkovči 1970.

(g) 13 cxd5 cxd5 14 Rfc1 Ba6 =, Gligorić–Mariotti, Nice 1974.

(h) 8 ... Ne4 9 Ne5 Nd7 10 Nd3 Nb6 11 c5 Nxd2, Averbakh–Lisitsin, USSR 1954 may be a better try for Black, although White maintains a pull.

(i) 9 ... Qh5 10 Ndf3 Ne4 11 Nd3 ±, Rozma–Tepper, Czechoslovakia 1956.

(j) 13 b4 and White's play on the queenside is more meaningful than Black's on the kingside, Reshevsky–Guimard, Buenos Aires 1960.

(k) 5 ... d5 6 0-0 0-0 7 Nc3 c6 8 Qb3 Qe8 9 Nf4 Kh8 10 Nd3 gives White an edge (Petrosian).

(l) 7 . . . c6 turns out poorly: 8 b3 a5 9 e4 fxe4 10 Nxe4 a4 11 Bb2 e5 12 dxe5 dxe5 13 Nhg5 ±, Uhlmann–Johansson, Halle 1963.

(m) 13 Ne3 exd4 with even chances, Reshevsky–Botvinnik, Hague and Moscow 1948.

(n) (A) 7 b3 Qe7 (1) 8 Bf4 Bxf4 9 gxf4 0-0 =, Yrjola–Yusupov, Mendoza 1985. (2) 8 a4 0-0 9 Ba3 Bxa3 10 Nxa3 a5 11 Nc2 b6 12 Nce1 Bb7 13 Nd3 Na6 =, Atali–Bany, Istanbul 1988. (B) 7 Bf4 0-0 8 Nbd2 Bxf4 9 gxf4 Nbd7 10 e3 Ne4 is about equal, Rashkovsky–Bareyev, USSR 1986.

(o) 9 b3 Ne4 10 Bb2 Qe8 11 Nd1 Qh5 12 Ne5 Rf6 =, Germek–Ivkov, Yugoslavia 1949. The column is Bogolyubov–Tartakower, New York 1924.

(p) 5 Nd2 0-0 6 Nf3 d5 (6 . . . a5 7 0-0 b6 8 Ne5 Ra7 9 Nb1 Be7 10 Nc3 Bb7 11 d5 ±, Gelfand–Knaak, Halle 1987) 7 0-0 c6 8 Qc2 Nbd7 =, Goldberg–Ragozin, USSR 1945.

(q) (A) 5 . . . Bxd2† 6 Qxd2 0-0 7 Nc3 d6 8 Nf3 ±, Stoltz–Spielmann, Bled 1931. (B) 5 . . . Qe7 6 Nf3 0-0 7 0-0 Bxd2 8 Qxd2 Ne4 9 Qc2 ±, Malich–Fabian, Marianské Lázně 1959.

(r) (A) 6 Nc3 0-0 7 Qb3 c6 8 d5 d6 9 dxe6 ±, M. Gurević–Dolmatov, USSR 1987. (B) 6 Qb3 c6 7 d5 cxd5 8 cxd5 e5 9 Nc6 d6 produced an unclear position in Sosonko-Abramović, New York 1986. The game continued 10 Nf3 Nbd7 11 0-0 0-0 12 Ng5 Nc5 13 Qc4 h6 14 b4 Ncd7! 15 Ne6 Nb6 16 Qb3 Bxe6 17 dxe6 d5 18 Rfd1 Qd6 19 Nb5 Qc6 20 a4 Nc4 21 Be3 a6 22 Nc3 Nxe3 23 fxe3 e4 24 Nxd5 Nxd5 25 Qxd5 Qxd5 26 Rxd5 h5! 27 Rc1? (White, believing he has the advantage, is unaware that his bishop is in danger of being imprisoned unless he quickly plays h3 and g4) 27 . . . Rad8 28 Rxd8 Rxd8 29 Kf2? Bd6 30 h3 (now it is too late) 30 . . . g6 31 g4 h4! 32 b5 axb5 33 axb5 Kf8 34 Rc4 Ke7 35 gxf5 gxf5 36 Bxe4 (in any case Black will be able to win the b-pawn and promote it to a queen) 36 . . . fxe6 37 Rxe4 and resigns.

(s) 13 cxd5 Bf6 14 Bc3 with advantage to White, Szabo–Bronstein, Budapest 1950.

DUTCH DEFENSE

1 d4 f5 2 g3 Nf6 3 Bg2

	13	14	15	16	17	18
	e6 (Classical System)...................................d6					
4	c4...Nf3					c4
	Be7				c5	c6
5	Nf3				c4(n)	Nf3
	0-0				cxd4	Qc7
6	0-0				Nxd4	Nc3
	d6				Bb4†	e5
7	Nc3................................b3			Qe8	Bd2	0-0(g)
	Qe8			Qe8	Qb6	e4(r)
8	b3 ....Qc2.........Re1			Bb2	Bxb4	Ne1
	Qh5(a)	Qh5(d)	Qg6(h)	a5(k)	Qxb4†	Be7
9	Bb2	Bg5(e)	e4	Nbd2	Qd2	f3
	Nbd7(b)	Nc6(f)	fxe4	Nc6(l)	Qxd2†(o)	exf3
10	Qc2	Rad1	Nxe4	a3	Nxd2	exf3
	Ng4	e5	Nxe4(i)	Bd8	Nc6	0-0
11	h3	dxe5	Rxe4	Ne1	Nb5	Nd3
	Nh6(c)	Nxe5(g)	Nc6(j)	e5(m)	Ke7(p)	Be6 ±

(a) (A) 8 ... Nc6 9 d5 Nd8 10 Nb5 Nxd5 11 Nxd6 cxd6 12 cxd5 e5 13 Ba3 ±, van Scheltinga–Enevoldsen, Amsterdam 1964. (B) 8 ... a5 9 Re1 Qg6 10 Ba3 Na6 11 e3 ±, Csom–Szabolcsi, Hungary 1972.

(b) 9 ... c6 10 Re1 d5 11 Ne5 Nbd7 12 e3 Qxd1 also is adequate for Black, Kholmov–Zhurakhov, USSR 1956.

(c) After 12 e3 g5 13 Ne2 c6 14 Rfd1 Nf6 an unclear but about even position was reached in Grünfeld–Bogolyubov, Zandvoort 1936.

(d) 8 ... Nc6 9 d5 Nb4 10 Qb3 Na6 11 dxe6 Nc5 12 Qc2 ±, Sämisch–Sanz, Madrid 1943.

(e) 9 e4 fxe4 10 Nxe4 e5 11 dxe5 dxe5 12 Nxf6† Bxf6 =, Mastichiades–Ojanen, Helsinki 1952.

(f) (A) 9 ... h6 10 Bxf6 Bxf6 11 e4 Nc6 12 Nb5 ±, Olafsson–Kan, Nice 1974. (B) 9 ... Nbd7 and (C) 9 ... e5 also leave White the advantage.

(g) 12 Bxf6 Bxf6 13 c5 dxc5 14 Nd5 Qf7 15 Qxc5 with a small plus, Savitsky–Ryumin, USSR 1933.

(h) (A) 8 ... Ne4 9 Qc2 Qg6 10 Be3 Nxc3 11 Qxc3 Nd7 12 c5 ±, Averbakh–Ragozin, USSR 1954. (B) 8 ... Qh5 9 e4 fxe4 10 Nxe4 Nxe4 11 Rxe4 Nc6 12 Bf4 ±, Keres–Simagin, USSR 1951.

(i) 10 ... Nc6 11 Nxf6† Bxf6 12 Bf4 Qf5 13 Qd2 ±, Krogius–A. Zaitsev, USSR 1961.

(j) 12 Re1 e5 13 dxe5 Bg4 14 exd6 Bxd6 15 Be3 Qf6 16 Qd5† Kh8 Black has sufficient play for the sacrificed pawn, H. Kramer–Cortlever, Amsterdam 1954. If 11 . . . Qxe4 12 Nh5 wins the queen.

(k) 8 . . . Qh5 9 Nbd2 Nc6 10 e3 g5 11 Ne1 Qh6 12 Nd3 Bd7 13 Re1 ±, Eliskases–Pelikan, Mar del Plata 1958.

(l) 9 . . . Nbd7 10 a3 Qh5 11 Re1 Ne4 12 e3 Nfd6 =, Eliskases–Larsen, Mar del Plata 1958.

(m) 12 e3 Bd7 13 Nc2 exd4 14 Nxd4 Nxd4 15 Bxd4 Bc6 with even chances, Averbakh–Boleslavsky, Zürich 1953.

(n) 6 0-0 Nc6 7 c4 cxd4 8 Nxd4 Bd5 9 e3 ±, Rubinstein–Tarrasch, Hastings 1922.

(o) If 9 . . . Qxc4?! 10 Na3 followed by Ndb5 is strong (Uhlmann).

(p) After 12 0-0 a6 13 Nc3 d6 14 e4 g6 15 Rfe1 White has the more harmonious position, Liebert-Pedersen, Kapfenberg 1970.

(q) 7 dxe5 dxe5 8 e4 Bb4 9 exf5 Bxf5 10 Qb3 Na6 11 0-0 ±, if 11 . . . 0-0-0?! 12 Be3 Bc5 13 Bxc5 Nxc5 14 Qa3 Na6 15 Nb5 ±, Farago–Bokov, Hungary 1967.

(r) 7 . . . Be6 8 d5 Bd7 9 e4 fxe4 10 Ng5 ±, Kozma-Marszalet, Czechoslovakia 1962. The column is Udovčíc–Antoshin, Yugoslavia vs. USSR 1964.

DUTCH DEFENSE

1 d4 f5

	19	20	21	22	23	24
2	c4		e4 (Staunton Gambit)		. . . Nc3	Bg5
	Nf6		fxe4(f)		Nf6(o)	h6(r)
3	Nf3		Nc3		Bg5	Bh4
	e6		Nf6(g)		d5	g5
4	Nc3	g3	Bg5	f3	Bxf6	Bg3
	Bb4	b6	Nc6(h)	d5(l)	exf6	Nf6(s)
5	Qb3(a)	Bg2	d5	fxe4	e3	e3
	Qe7(b)	Bb7	Ne5	dxe4	c6	Bg7
6	e3	0-0	Qd4	Bg5	Bd3	Nd2(t)
	b6	Be7	Nf7	Bf5	g6	d6
7	Be2	Nc3(d)	Bxf6(i)	Bc4(m)	Qf3	h4
	Bxc3†	0-0	exf6	Nc6	Bd6(p)	g4
8	Qxc3	d5	Nxe4	Nge2	h4(q)	h5
	d6	Bb4	Be7(j)	Qd7	h5	Nc6
9	b4	Bd2	0-0-0	0-0	Nge2	Bb5
	Ne4(c)	Na6(e)	0-0(k)	e6(n)	Be6 =	Bd7 =

(a) Alternatives are: (A) 5 Qc2 0-0 6 g3 b6 7 Bg2 Bb7 8 0-0 Bxc3 9 Qxc3 Qe8 =, Kestler–Besser, West Germany 1965. (B) 5 Bd2 0-0 6 e3 b6 7 Bd3 Bb7 8 Qc2 Bxc3† 9 Qxc3 Be4 =, Wotkowsky–O'Kelly, Heidelberg 1949.

(b) 5 . . . Bxc3† 6 Qxc3 d6 7 g3 0-0 8 Bg2 Qe7 9 0-0 Nbd7 10 b3 slightly favors White, Benjamin–Dolmatov, Moscow 1987.

(c) After 10 Qc2 Bb7 11 0-0 0-0 the game is equal, Ribli–Putianen, Budapest 1975.

(d) If 7 d5, not 7 . . . exd5? 8 Nd4 g6 9 Nc3 ± (Grünfeld–Opočenský, Meran 1924), but 7 . . . 0-0 8 Nd4 Qc8 with chances for both sides.

(e) 10 Nd4 Qe8 11 Rc1 Bc5 12 Bg5 and White is somewhat better, Cebalo–Djurić, Yugoslavia 1984.

(f) 2 . . . d6 (Balogh's defense) 3 exf5 Bxf5 4 Qf3 Qc8 5 Bd3 Bxd3 6 Qxd3 Nc6 7 Nf3 ±, Euwe–Weenink, Amsterdam 1923.

(g) 3 . . . g6 is worthy of attention: after 4 Nxe4 d5 5 Ng5 c5 6 N1f3 Nc6 7 Bd3 c4 8 Be2 Bg7 chances are balanced, Luckis–Engels, Buenos Aires 1939; also 5 Ng3 Bg7 6 h4 Nc6 7 Bb5 Qd6 is equal, Fuderer–Alexander, Belgrade 1952.

(h) 4 . . . b6, 4 . . . c6, 4 . . . e6 and 4 . . . g6 are all acceptable moves, but the column is the steadiest path to equality.

(i) 7 h4 c6 8 0-0-0 Qb6 9 Bxf6 gxf6 10 Qxe4 ±, Yudinchev–Martinov, corr. 1964.

(j) 8 . . . f5 9 Ng3 g6 10 0-0-0 Bh6† 11 f4 0-0 =, Sumichev–Shaposhnikov, corr. 1969.

(k) 10 Nf3 d6 11 Kb1 c5 with equality, Schuster–Johannessen, Bergendaal 1960.

(l) 4 . . . exf3 5 Nf3 g6 6 Bf4 Bg7 7 Qd2 0-0 8 Bh6 d5 ∞, Bronstein–Alexander, Hastings 1953.

(m) Suspect is 7 Nge2?! e6 8 Ng3 Bb4 9 Bc4 Nc6 ∓, Martinez–R. Byrne, Nice 1974.

(n) 10 Qe1 0-0-0 11 Rd1 Na5 12 Bb5 c6 with an equal game, Schultz–Wille, West Germany 1957.

(o) 2 . . . d5 is the alternative. (A) 3 e4 dxe4 transposes to the Blackmar–Diemer Gambit. After (B) 3 f3 c5 4 e4 e5 the position is sharp and unclear, Pomar–Larsen, Spain 1975.

(p) (A) 7 . . . Be6 8 Nge2 Nd7 9 h3 ±, Korchnoi–Rostjozin, Havana 1966. (B) 7 . . . Bb4! 8 Ne2 Nd7 9 h3 Ne5! ∓, Maksimović–Akhmilovskaya, Sochi 1987.

(q) 8 h3, 8 Nge2, and 8 Nh3 are plausible alternatives that deserve testing. The column is Visier–Zweig, Costa Brava 1976.

(r) 2 . . . g6 3 Nc3 Bg7 4 e4 fxe4 is similar to the Staunton Gambit line in note (g).

(s) Of course 4 . . . f4? 5 e3 wins a pawn due to the threat of 6 Qh5 mate. Interesting is 4 . . . d6 5 e3 Nf6 6 h4 Rg8 7 hxg5 hxg5 8 Bc4 e6 = (Bareyev).

(t) 6 Bd3 c6 7 Ne2 d6 8 f3 Qc7, B. Damjanović–M. Gurevich, 1986, is probably a balanced position. The column is Magerramov–Avsalumov, USSR 1987.

IV
INDIAN
DEFENSE SYSTEMS

QUEEN'S INDIAN DEFENSE

1 d4 Nf6 2 c4 e6 3 Nf3 b6 (diagram)
or 1 d4 Nf6 2 Nf3 b6

Diagram 64

THE QUEEN'S INDIAN DEFENSE, a close relative of other Indian defenses, was popularized by Nimzowitsch and other hypermoderns. Black's chief idea is to find good squares for his pieces in the fight for the central squares—especially the square e4, since White frequently comes out on top when he can play e4. Black sets out to control the center first with pieces and only then deploys his central pawns. In this way Black usually achieves a position both sound and active, avoiding the static lines characteristic of the double queen-pawn openings (1 d4 d5) and the adventures of the King's Indian and Modern Benoni defenses.

For many years the Queen's Indian was considered hard to beat and also somewhat dull and drawish. Consequently it was neglected while the Nimzo-Indian flourished. Black's considerable success in the 1970s with the Hübner Variation of the Rubinstein Nimzo-Indian spurred players in search of effective new weapons for White to take another look at the Queen's Indian. This resulted in the discovery of many dynamic new ideas for both sides, bringing about the current renaissance. It is no longer an opening players venture on occasion because they are bored with the Nimzo-Indian—it is now something they play with gusto.

Diagram 65

The Petrosian System, 4 a3 (cols. 1–24) was the most popular line for White in the eighties (see diagram). It was the reason many masters switched from 3 Nc3 to 3 Nf3, to play the exciting attacking positions that frequently arise from the latter. The late Tigran Petrosian pioneered this line, but it was Gary Kasparov's brilliant attacking games that forged it into a cohesive system. This system was covered briefly in the previous edition of *MCO*, but it has now become important enough to command 24 columns.

The sharpest way for Black to play is shown in cols. 1–4. White has a mobile pawn center, which offers him good chances for a kingside attack, but Black, with queenside play, is not without resources. Decisive results are the rule rather than the exception, even for cautious grandmasters.

Black plays 6 . . . Nxd5 also in cols. 5–12, but his strategy against the pawn center is somewhat different than that of cols. 1–4.

With 7 Qc2 (cols. 10–12) White hopes to achieve the thrust e4 in one move, but his queen proves vulnerable on c2.

6 . . . exd5 (cols. 13–17) is a solid reply, with play resembling the Queen's Gambit or the 4 g3 lines of the Queen's Indian.

Benoni-type play may result from 4 . . . c5 (cols. 19–21). In cols. 22–24 (4 . . . Ba6) Black tries to find play by threatening White's c-pawn.

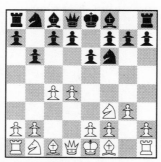

Diagram 66

The classical way to meet the Queen's Indian is 4 g3 (see diagram). White places his king's bishop on the long diagonal to take part in the battle for the central light squares. Play tends to be of a positional rather than attacking nature.

The old "main line" is 8 Qc2 (cols. 25–28). White achieves a small space advantage without any weaknesses; logical development by Black leads to equality. The sequence 6 Nc3 Ne4 7 Bd2 is also known as the anti-Queen's Indian System.

More interesting is 8 Bd2 (cols. 29 and 30). White is willing to give up the bishop pair for greater control in the center. This plan is effective if Black's bishops don't become active.

Less common lines are seen in cols. 31–36. Noteworthy is 7 d5!? (col. 33). This sharp pawn sacrifice must be met precisely by Black or he will come under heavy attack. The position after 4 . . . Bb7 may be arrived at by the transposition 1 Nf3 Nf6 2 c4 b6 3 g3 Bb7 4 d4 e6, thus avoiding Nimzowitsch's . . . Ba6, shown next.

Nimzowitsch's idea of drumming up counterplay by attacking White's c-pawn with 4 . . . Ba6 is the subject of cols. 37–45. Black seeks to profit by the absence of White's bishop from its normal diagonal. This "exaggerated fianchetto" gives Black the opportunity to wage a hard fight instead of having to play sterile positions that arise out of the old main line.

Blocking the a6-f1 diagonal by supporting the c-pawn with 5 b3 (cols. 37–41) is the most common reply, by defending c4 with the queen or knight (cols. 42–45) seems just as promising. The pawn structure in these variations is flexible, so there is much room for originality.

Not often seen, but playable, is . . . Bb4† for Black on move 4 or 5 (cols. 46–48).

Straightforward development with 4 e3 or 4 Nc3 (cols. 49–53) is certainly reasonable for White and can lead to promising attacks, but Black has equalizing methods against these moves.

Col. 54 is an accelerated fianchetto, an earlier version of the Queen's Indian. It is solid but now rarely seen.

QUEEN'S INDIAN DEFENSE
Petrosian System

1 d4 Nf6 2 c4 e6 3 Nf3 b6 4 a3 Bb7 5 Nc3 d5 6 cxd5 Nxd5 7 e3 Be7 8 Bb5† c6 9 Bd3

	1	2	3	4	5	6
	Nxc3...				0-0	Nd7
10	bxc3				e4(n)	e4
	c5				Nxc3	Nxc3
11	0-0(a)				bxc3	bxc3
	Nc6(b)				c5	c5
12	e4....................................			Qe2	Qe2(o)	0-0(p)
	0-0		Rc8	0-0	cxd4	0-0
13	Be3........	Bb2(h)	Bb2	Bb2	cxd4	Qe2
	cxd4	cxd4	Bf6(i)	Rc8	Qc8	Rc8
14	cxd4	cxd4	d5!	Rad1	Bb2	Bb2
	Rc8(c)	Rc8	exd5	cxd4	Ba6	Qc7
15	Qe2	Qe2	exd5	exd4(k)	0-0	Nd2
	Na5(d)	Na5	Qxd5	Bf6(l)	Bxd3	Bg5
16	Rfd1(e)	Rad1	Re1†	c4	Qxd3	a4
	Rc3(f)	Bf6	Kf8	Na5	Nd7	Rfd8
17	a4	Rfe1	Qc2	Ne5	Rfe1	Rfd1
	Nb3(g)	Re8 =	Ne5(j)	Bxe5!(m)	Rd8 =	g6(q)

(a) 11 Qe2!? Nc6 12 Bb2 0-0 13 Rd1 Qc7 14 e4 Na5 15 0-0 Rac8 16 Rfe1 Rfd8 17 d5! brought White the initiative in Henley–Sosonko, Lone Pine 1981.

(b) 11 . . . 0-0 is suspect because of 12 Qc2! g6 13 e4 Qc7 14 Qe2 Rd8 15 h4! Nc6 16 Be3 Bf6 17 e5 Bg7 18 h5 with good attacking prospects for White, Polugaevsky–Petrosian, Moscow 1981.

(c) 14 . . . Kh8 15 Qe2 f5 16 Rad1? f4 17 Bc1 Nxd4 ∓, Vaganian–Razuvaev, Yaroslav 1982. Correct is 16 exf5.

(d) 15 . . . Qd6 16 Rfd1 Rfd8 17 d5 Ne5 18 Nxe5 Qxe5 19 f4 Qc3 20 Rac1 Qb3 = , Psakhis–Didishko, Minsk 1982.

(e) 16 Rfe1 Kh8 17 h4 Bxh4 18 Rad1 Be7 19 d5 Bc5 20 Bf4 f6 21 dxe6 Qe7 = , Kasparov–Groszpeter, Graz 1981.

(f) 16 . . . Kh8 17 a4 f5 18 exf5 exf5 19 Rab1 Bd6 20 Ne5 Qe8 21 Bf4 ±, Van der Sterren–Ligterink, Wijk aan Zee 1982.

(g) 18 Rab1 Qa8 19 Bf4 Rfc8 ∞, Shapiro–K. Burger, US 1981.

(h) 13 d5 exd5 14 exd5 Na5 15 c4 b5 16 Qc2 (16 Rb1 bxc4 17 Bxc4 Nxc4 18 Rxb7 Nd6 =) 16 . . . h6! = .

472

(i) 13 . . . 0-0 14 d5!? exd5 14 exd5 Na5 16 c4 b5 17 Qc2 is interesting.

(j) 18 Be4 Nxf3† 19 Bxf3 Qd7 20 Rad1 gave White a strong game for the pawn in Kasparov–Ivkov, Bugojno 1982.

(k) 15 cxd4 Bf6 16 h4 Bxh4 17 e4 Na5 18 d5 exd5 19 e5 Nc4 20 Bd4 with a complicated fight, Yusupov–A. Sokolov, Riga 1986.

(l) 15 . . . Na5?! 16 Ne5 Bf6 17 f4 g6 18 c4 Bg7? 19 d5! exd5 20 f5! d4 21 fxg6 fxg6 22 Nxg6! Re8 23 Qh5 Be4 24 Bxe4 Rxe4 25 Qf5 Resigns, Browne–Ribli, Indonesia 1982.

(m) 18 dxe5 Qc7 19 Qh5 g6 20 Qh6 Qc6 21 f3 Qc5† 22 Kh1 Nxc4 23 Bd4 Qxa3 led to double-edged play in Kasparov–Tukmakov, USSR 1982.

(n) Better may be 10 0-0 c5 11 Nxd5 Qxd5 12 e4 Qh5 13 dxc5 Qxc5 14 Bf4 Nc6 15 Rc1 with advantage, Malich–Augustin, Halle 1976.

(o) 12 h4 is risky: 12 . . . cxd4 13 cxd4 Ba6! 14 Bb1 Nc6 15 e5 g6 16 Bh6 Qd5! $\overline{\overline{\mp}}$, Lputian–Georgadze, USSR 1980–81. The column is Browne–Portisch, Mar del Plata 1981.

(p) Also good for White is 12 e5 0-0 13 0-0 Qc7 14 Ng5! Bxg5 15 Bxg5 Re8 16 Re1 Nf8 17 Re3, Winslow–Morris, St. Louis 1980.

(q) 18 a5 with advantage, Browne–Gheorghiu, Novi Sad 1979.

QUEEN'S INDIAN DEFENSE

Petrosian System

1 d4 Nf6 2 c4 e6 3 Nf3 b6 4 a3 Bb7 5 Nc3 d5 6 cxd5 Nxd5

	7	8	9	10	11	12
7	(e3)......................Bd2(g)......Qc2					
	g6 ....Nd7(d)		Nd7	c5 ....Nxc3(n)		
8	Bb5†(a)	Bd3	Qc2	e4 ....dxc5		Qxc3(o)
	c6	c5	c5	Nxc3	Bxc5	h6
9	Bd3(b)	e4	e4	bxc3	Bg5	e3
	Bg7	N5f6	Nxc3	Nd7(h)	Qc8(l)	Be7
10	e4	Bf4	Bxc3	Bf4(i)	Rc1	Bb5†
	Nxc3	a6(e)	cxd4	cxd4	h6	c6
11	bxc3	d5	Nxd4	cxd4	Nxd5	Ba4
	c5	exd5	a6	Rc8	hxg5	0-0
12	Bg5	exd5	g3	Qb3	b4	0-0
	Qd6	Nxd5	Be7	Be7(j)	g4	Nd7
13	e5	Nxd5	Bg2	Bd3	Ne5	Rd1
	Qd7(c)	Bxd5(f)	0-0 =	Nf6(k)	Rh5(m)	Rc8 =

(a) 8 Nxd5 exd5 9 Bd2 Nd7 10 Qa4 a6 11 Rc1 Bg7 12 Bb4 Rc8 13 Bd3 a5 14 Bd2 0-0 15 Bb5 Nb8 =, Portisch–Sosonko, Tunis 1985.

(b) Worth a try is 9 Ba4 Bg7 10 0-0 Nxc3 11 bxc3 0-0 12 e4 c5 13 Bg5 Qd6 14 e5 Qc7 15 Nd2 Nc6 16 Qg4 ±, Kupreichik–Makarichev, USSR 1984.

(c) 14 dxc5?! 0-0 15 cxb6 axb6 16 0-0 Qc7 with advantage to Black, Kasparov–Korchnoi, match 1983. Correct is 14 0-0 0-0 15 Qd2 cxd4 16 cxd4 Nc6 17 Qf4 with an equal position.

(d) 7 . . . Nxc3 8 bxc3 g6 9 a4 (9 Bb5† is more sensible) 9 . . . Bg7 10 Ba3 Nd7 11 a5 c5 12 Bb5 0-0 13 a6 Bd5 14 c4 Bxf3 15 Qxf3 cxd4 16 Bxf8 Ne5 17 Qe2 d3! 18 Bxg7 dxe2 19 Bxe5 Qd3 with at least equality for Black, Thorsteins–Petursson, Akureyri 1988.

(e) 10 . . . Nh5 11 Be3 cxd4 12 Nxd4 Nhf6 13 0-0 Bc5 14 b4 ±, S. Agdestein–Olafsson, Gjovik 1985.

(f) 14 Qc2 Nf6 15 0-0 Bd6 16 Qe2† Kf8 17 Ne5 with advantage, Portisch–Miles, Thessaloniki 1984.

(g) 7 e4!? Nxc3 8 bxc3 Bxe4 9 Ne5 Qh4! 10 Qa4† c6 11 d5 Bd6! 12 Nxf7 Kxf7 13 dxe6† Kxe6 left Black clearly on top, Nogueiras–Beliavsky, Thessaloniki 1984.

(h) 9 . . . Nc6 10 Bb2 and now (A) 10 . . . Rc8 11 d5! exd5 12 exd5 Qxd5 13 Bd3 Ne5 14 0-0-0 ±, S. Agdestein–Lau, Dortmund 1987. (B) 10 . . . Be7 11 d5 exd5 12 Rd1 Qd6 13 exd5 Ne5 14 Bb5† Kf8 =, Kayarov–Aseyev, USSR 1987.

(i) 10 Bd3 Qc7 11 Qb1 g6 12 0-0 Bg7 13 Ra2 0-0 14 Re2 Rac8 is equal, Hort–Miles, Lucerne 1982.

(j) After 12 . . . Qf6 13 Qe3 Qg6 14 Bd3 Be7 15 0-0 0-0 16 e5 Qh5 17 Be4 White was on top, Gelfand–Mikhalchishin, Minsk 1986.

(k) 14 Qb5† Qd7 15 Ne5 Qxb5 16 Bxb5† Kf8 17 f3 Ne8 =, Browne–Miles, New York 1987.

(l) 9 . . . f6 10 Bd2 Nd7 11 e4 Nxc3 12 Bxc3 Qc8 13 0-0-0 0-0 14 b4 Be7 15 Qb3 Rf7! ∞, Plaskett–Short, Plovdiv 1984.

(m) 14 Qb2 Rxe5 15 Qxe5 Bxb4† 16 Kd1 Nc6 17 Rxc6 Qxc6 18 Nxb4 0-0-0† 19 Nd3 f6 with chances for both sides, Dreyev–Gelfand, Minsk 1986.

(n) 7 . . . Nd7 8 Nxd5 exd5 9 Bg5 Qc8 10 g3 Bd6 11 Bh3 0-0 12 0-0 c5 13 Qf5 Nb8 14 Qxc8 Bxc8 15 Bxc8 Rxc8 =, Ftáčnik–Gheorghiu, Prague 1985.

(o) 8 bxc3 g6 9 Bg5 Qd5 10 Bf6 Rg8 11 e3 Qf5 12 Qxf5 gxf5 13 Ne5 Nd7 14 Nxd7 Kxd7 and Black stands better, J. Whitehead–Sax, Philadelphia 1986.

QUEEN'S INDIAN DEFENSE
Petrosian System

1 d4 Nf6 2 c4 e6 3 Nf3 b6 4 a3 Bb7 5 Nc3

	13	14	15	16	17	18
	(d5)..Ne4(j)					
6	(cxd5)					Nxe4
	exd5					Bxe4
7	Bf4.........g3(b)					Nd2
	Bd6(a)	Be7(c)..............................Bd6				Bb7(k)
8	Bxd6	Qa4†...................Bg2		Bg2		e4
	Qxd6	c6..........Nbd7		0-0	0-0	g6(l)
9	Rc1	Bg2(d)	Ne5	0-0	0-0	Bd3
	a6	0-0	c5	Na6(h)	Re8	Bg7
10	g3	0-0	Nc6(f)	Bf4	Ne1	Nf3
	0-0	Nbd7	Bxc6	c5	Nbd7	d6
11	Bg2	Bf4	Qxc6	Qc2	Nd3	0-0
	Nbd7	Nh5	cxd4	Nc7	Qe7	0-0
12	0-0	Rad1	Nxd5	Rfd1	Bf4	Bg5
	c5 =	Nxf4(e)	Rc8(g)	Ne6(i)	Ne4 =	Qd7(m)

(a) 7 ... Be7 8 e3 0-0 9 Bd3 c5 10 0-0 Nc6 11 Ne5 cxd4 12 Nxc6 Bxc6 13 exd4 Bd6 14 Bg5 h6 15 Bh4 Re8 16 Bc2 ±, Portisch–P. Nikolić, Portorož 1985.

(b) Or White can exchange his "bad" bishop with: (A) 7 Bg5 Be7 8 Bxf6 Bxf6 9 g3 0-0 10 Bg2 Re8 11 0-0 Na6 12 b4 ±, or (B) 7 Qa4† Nbd7 (7 ... Qd7 8 Qxd7† Nbxd7 9 Nb5 Bd6 can be played) 8 Bg5 Be7 9 Bxf6 Bxf6 10 g3 c5 11 Bh3 cxd4?! 12 Nxd4 0-0 13 Bxd7 Bxd4 14 Qxd4 Qxd7 15 0-0 ±, Browne–Chandler, Naestved 1985.

(c) 7 ... c5 8 Ne5 Nbd7 9 Bg2 cxd4 10 Qxd4 Nxe5 11 Qxe5† Be7 12 0-0 0-0 13 Bf4 Qd7 14 Rad1 Rad8 15 Qc7 ±, Portisch–Tukmakov, Tilburg 1984.

(d) 9 Bh3 0-0 10 0-0 c5 11 Rd1 Nc6 12 Bg5 Re8! 13 dxc5 bxc5 14 Bxf6 Bxf6 15 Nxd5 Rxe2 16 Nf4 Nd4 17 Nxd4 cxd4 18 Nxe2 Qd5 19 Kf1 g5! 20 Rac1 g4 21 Bxg4 Qh1† 22 Ng1 Qg2† 23 Ke2 Qe4† 24 Kf1 Qg2† 25 Ke1? (White should take a draw with 25 Ke2) 25 ... Qxg1† 26 Ke2 d3†! 27 Kxd3 Qxf2 28 Rc7 Qxb2 29 Rd2 Qb6 30 Rxb7 Qxb7 31 Qb4 Qc6 32 Ke2 Bc3 33 Resigns, Yusupov–Ljubojević, Bugojno 1986.

(e) 13 gxf4 Nf6 14 Ne5 Qd6 15 Kh1 Nh5 16 e3 f6 17 Nd3 and White has the edge, Yusupov–Short, Dubai 1986.

(f) 10 dxc5 0-0!? 11 c6 Nc5 12 Qd1 Ba6 13 b4 Nce4 ∞.

(g) 13 Nxf6† Bxf6 14 Qe4† Qe7 15 Qxe7† Kxe7 16 Bh3 Rc2 =, Razuvaev–Polugaevsky, USSR 1981.

(h) 9 ... c5 10 Qc2 Nbd7 11 Rd1 Rc8 12 Qf5 g6 13 Qh3 Re8 14 dxc5 bxc5 15 Ng5 ±, Kharitonov–Vladimirov, Irkutsk 1983.

476

(i) 13 Be5 Ng4 14 dxc5 Bxc5 15 e3 and White has a pull, P. Nikolić–Adianto, Dubai 1986.

(j) Christiansen's 5 . . . g6 6 d5 Bg7 7 g3 Na6 8 Bg2 Nc5 merits attention.

(k) 7 . . . Bg6?! 8 g3 Nc6 9 e3 a6 10 b4 b5 11 cxb5 axb5 12 Bb2 (12 Bxb5? Nxb4) 12 . . . Na7 13 h4 h6 14 d5! exd5 15 Bg2 c6 16 0-0 ±, Kasparov–Andersson, Tilburg 1981. White has excellent attacking chances due to his active pieces and kingside pressure. The game continued 16 . . . f6 17 Re1 Be7 18 Qg4 Kf7 19 h5 Bh7 20 e4 dxe4 21 Bxe4 Bxe4 22 Nxe4 Nc8 23 Rad1 Ra7 24 Nxf6! gxf6 25 Qg6† Kf8 26 Bc1 d5 27 Rd4! (better than the immediate 27 Bxh6†) 27 . . . Nd6 28 Rg4 Nf7 29 Bxh6†! Ke8 30 Bg7 Resigns; a brilliant game.

(l) 8 . . . Qf6 9 d5 Na6 10 Bd3 Nc5 11 Bc2 exd5 12 exd5 Qe5† 13 Kf1 Ba6 14 Rb1 Qxd5 15 b4 Bxc4† 16 Kg1 Bd3 17 bxc5 and the piece is worth somewhat more than Black's pawns, Lobron–Korchnoi, Wijk aan Zee 1985.

(m) 13 Qd2 Nc6 14 d5 ±, Polugaevsky–Christiansen, Thessaloniki 1984.

QUEEN'S INDIAN DEFENSE

Petrosian System

1 d4 Nf6 2 c4 e6 3 Nf3 b6 4 a3

	19	20	21	22	23	24
	c5(a) Ba6					
5	d5			Qc2(j)		
	exd5 . . . . . . .Ba6			Bb7		
6	cxd5	Qc2		Nc3		
	g6	exd5(e)		c5		
7	Nc3(b)	cxd5		e4 . . . . .dxc5(m)		
	Bg7	Bb7 . . . . .g6		cxd4		bxc5
8	e4(c)	e4(f)	Nc3(h)	Nxd4		Bg5
	0-0	Qe7	Bg7	Bc5 . . . . .Nc6(l)		Be7
9	h3	Nc3	g3	Nb3	Nxc6	e3
	d6	Nxd5	0-0	Nc6	Bxc6	0-0
10	Bd3	Nb5	Bg2	Nxc5	Be2	Be2
	Qe7	a6	d6	bxc5	Qb8	Nc6
11	0-0	Bg5	0-0	Bd3	Be3	0-0
	Ba6(d)	f6(g)	Re8(i)	d6(k)	Bc5 =	Qb6 =

(a) 4 . . . Ne4 5 Nfd2 d5 6 e3 Bb7 7 cxd5 exd5 8 Nxe4 dxe4 9 Nc3 Bd6 10 Bb5† Kf8 11 Qc2 ±, Glek–Rosentalis, Vilnius 1984.

(b) Sharper is 7 e4 Nxe4?! (7 . . . d6 is better) 8 Bd3 Nf6 9 0-0 Bg7 10 Re1† Kf8 11 d6! Bb7 12 Nc3 Bxf3 13 Qxf3 Nc6 14 Nb5 with tremendous compensation for the pawn, Benjamin–de Firmian, US Chp. 1986.

(c) 8 Bg5 0-0 9 e4 d6 10 Nd2 a6 11 a4 Nbd7 12 Be2 Re8 13 0-0 h6 14 Bh4 g5 15 Bg3 ±, Ftáčnik–Vadasz, Trnava 1979.

(d) 12 Bxa6 Nxa6 13 Re1 Qb7 14 Bf4 ±, Epishin–Yudasin, USSR 1987. Black does better to play 10 . . . a6 and 11 . . . Nbd7, as in the Benoni.

(e) 6 . . . Qe7 is dubious. Miles–Kudrin, London 1982, continued 7 Nc3 Bxc4 8 Bg5 exd5 9 e4! h6 10 Bxf6 Qxf6 11 exd5 Bxf1 12 Kxf1 d6 13 Re1† Be7 14 Qa4† Kf8 15 Qg4 Na6 16 Qd7 +.

(f) 8 Nc3!? Nxd5 9 Bg5 f6 10 Nxd5 Bxd5 11 Bf4 Qe7 12 e3 g5 13 Bg3 Qf7 14 0-0-0 Be6 15 Nd4 brought about an unclear position in Lputian–Sturua, Odessa 1982.

(g) 12 0-0-0! Nb4 13 Nc7† Kd8 14 axb4 Kxc7 15 Bf4† Kd8 16 e5 with good play for White, Miles–van der Vliet, Amsterdam 1982.

(h) 8 Bf4 d6 9 Nc3 Bg7 10 Qa4† Qd7 11 Bxd6 Qxa4 12 Nxa4 Nxd5 13 0-0-0 Ne7 14 e4 Bxf1 15 Rhxf1 Nbc6 16 Nc3 Bxc3! =, Browne–Timman, Las Palmas 1982.

(i) 12 Re1 Nbd7 13 h3 Ne5 14 Nxe5 Rxe5 15 e4 Re8 16 Be3 Nd7 17 f4 with advantage, Yusupov–Timman, match 1985.

(j) 5 Nbd2 Bb7 6 b4 d6 7 e3 Nbd7 8 Bb2 c5 9 Bd3 Be7 10 0-0 0-0 11 Qe2 is slightly more comfortable for White, Rohde–Seirawan, US Chp. 1987.

(k) 12 0-0 0-0 13 Bg5 h6 14 Bh4 g5 15 Bg3 e5 =, Vyzhmanavin–Salov, Irkutsk 1986.

(l) 8 ... d6 9 Bg5 a6 10 Rd1 Nbd7 11 f4 Be7 12 f5 0-0 13 fxe6 Nc5 14 Nf5 fxe6 =, A. Petrosian–A. Sokolov, USSR 1985.

(m) 7 e3 cxd4 8 exd4 Be7 9 Bd3 Bxf3 10 gxf3 Nc6 11 Be3 Rc8 12 0-0 0-0 13 Rad1 Na5 14 d5 leads to an unbalanced position with no advantage for White, Plaskett–Polugaevsky, Lucerne 1985. The column is Christiansen–Schüssler, New York 1985.

QUEEN'S INDIAN DEFENSE

1 d4 Nf6 2 c4 e6 3 Nf3 b6 4 g3 Bb7 5 Bg2 Be7 6 0-0 0-0 7 Nc3 Ne4

	25	26	27	28	29	30
8	Qc2..Bd2					
	Nxc3				Bf6(g)	
9	Qxc3				Rc1........Qc2	
	c5 ....f5 ....Be4				c5(h)	Nxd2
10	Rd1(a)	b3(b) Be3		Bf4(f)	d5(i)	Qxd2
	d6	Bf6	Bf6	Nc6	exd5	d6
11	b3	Bb2	Qd2	Rfd1	cxd5	Rad1(k)
	Bf6	a5(c)	d6	d5	Nxd2	Nd7
12	Bb2	Qd2	Rfd1	Ne5	Nxd2	d5
	Qe7	Na6	Qe8	Nxe5	d6	Bxc3
13	Qd2	Rad1	Rac1	Bxe5	Nde4	Qxc3
	Rd8	Qe8	Be4	Bxg2	Be7	e5
14	Ne1	Ne1	Ne1	Kxg2	f4	e4
	Bxg2 =	Bxg2(d)	Bxg2(e)	c6 =	Nd7(j)	Qe7(l)

(a) 10 dxc5 bxc5 11 Rd1 d6 12 b3 Nc6 13 Bb2 Bf6 14 Qd2 Bxb2 15 Qxb2 Qe7 = , Najdorf–Gheorghiu, Buenos Aires 1970.

(b) 10 Ne5 Qc8 11 h4 d6 12 Nd3 Bxg2 13 Kxg2 Bf6 14 Bg5 Qb7† is roughly equal, P. Nikolić–Hjartarson, Belgrade 1987. Some players are satisfied to play unambitiously with the White pieces, reaching an equal position and waiting for their opponents' errors. While this approach sometimes has practical value, it is usually unsuccessful against an experienced opponent. In this game, however, it works: 15 f3 Nd7 16 b4 a5 17 b5 Rae8 18 Rae1 h6 19 Bxf6 Nxf6 20 a4 c6? (Black is too eager to play actively and initiates an unfavorable battle. Simply adjusting his piece placement with 20 . . . Rf7 or 20 . . . Qa8, to be better organized for an eventual break, leaves the game balanced) 21 Rb1! Nh5?! 22 c5! (just where he began the battle, Black loses it) 22 . . . dxc5 23 dxc5 Rc8 24 Qe5 Kh8 25 Rfc1 Nf6 26 cxb6 cxb5 27 Rxc8 Rxc8 28 Rxb5 Resigns.

(c) 11 . . . d6 12 Rad1 Qe7 13 Ne1 Bxg2 14 Nxg2 Nc6 15 Qf3 Qd7 16 Nf4 Rae8 17 d5 Nd8 Draw, Tal–Botvinnik, World Chp. 1960.

(d) 15 Nxg2 g5 16 Rfe1 Qg6 with equal chances, Petrosian–Bronstein, USSR Chp. 1951.

(e) 15 Nxg2 Nd7 16 Qc2 a5 = , Flohr–Averbakh, USSR Chp. 1951.

(f) 10 Rd1 f5 11 Qb3 Nc6 12 d5 Na5 13 Qa4 exd5 14 cxd5 Bf6 = , Guimard–Stahlberg, Buenos Aires 1943. It is difficult for White to get an advantage with 8 Qc2.

(g) 8 . . . d5 9 cxd5 exd5 10 Rc1 Nd7 11 Qb3 is better for White.

(h) (A) 9 . . . d6 10 Qc2 Nxd2 11 Qxd2 Nd7 12 Rfd1 Qe7 13 Ne1 Bxg2 14 Kxg2 Rfd8 15 Nf3 ± , Andersson–Sanguinetti, Biel 1972. (B) 9 . . . Nxf2 10 Qxd2 d6. (C) 9 . . . d5 10 cxd5 exd5 11 Be3 Na6 12 Qa4 c5 13 Rfd1 Qe8 14 Qa3 ± , Karpov–von der Wiel, Amsterdam 1988.

480

(i) Nothing comes of 10 Nxe4 Bxe4 11 Bc3 Nc6 12 e3 cxd4 13 Nxd4 Bxg2 14 Kxg2 Bxd4 15 Bxd4 d5 16 b3 e5 17 Bb2 d4 = , Petrosian–Portisch, Palma de Mallorca 1974.

(j) 15 g4 with an advantage in space, van der Sterren–de Firmian, Wijk aan Zee 1986. Black's bishop pair is no asset because the bishops cannot find active diagonals.

(k) Or 11 e4 Nd7 12 d5 Qe7 13 Rfe1 Bxc3 14 Qxc3 e5 = , Petrosian–Karpov, Milan 1975.

(l) 15 Ne1 c6 16 dxc6 Bxc6 Draw, Damjanović–Smyslov, Hastings 1976–77.

QUEEN'S INDIAN DEFENSE

1 d4 Nf6 2 c4 e6 3 Nf3 b6 4 g3 Bb7 5 Bg2 Be7

	31	32	33	34	35	36
6	(0-0)					Nc3
	(0-0)					Ne4(k)
7	(Nc3)		d5	b3	Qc2	Bd2
	(Ne4) d5		exd5	d5	c5	f5(l)
8	Nxe4	Ne5	Nh4	cxd5(h)	dxc5	d5
	Bxe4	Nbd7(c)	c6	exd5	bxc5	Bf6
9	Ne1	cxd5	cxd5	Bb2	Nc3	Qc2
	Bxg2(a)	exd5	Nxd5(e)	Nbd7	d6	Nd6
10	Nxg2	Qa4!	Nf5	Nc3	Rd1	b3
	d5	Nxe5	Nc7(f)	a6	Qb6	Na6
11	Qa4	dxe5	Nc3	Rc1	b3	Rad1
	Qd7	Ne8	d5	Bd6	Nc6	Qe7
12	Qxd7	Nxd5!	e4	e3	Bb2	0-0
	Nxd7(b)	Bxd5(d)	Bf6(g)	Re8(i)	h6(j)	0-0(m)

(a) 9 ... d5 10 cxd5 Bxg2 11 Kxg2 Qxd5† 12 Nf3 Qb7 13 Be3 Rd8 =, Benko–Smyslov, Venice 1974.

(b) 13 cxd5 exd5 14 Bf4 c5 =. This line has led to many a "grandmaster draw."

(c) Although it doesn't fully equalize, 8 ... Na6 is probably better, e.g., 9 b3 c5 10 Bb2 Rb8 11 cxd4 exd5 12 Rc1 Nc7 13 e3 Ne6 14 Qd3 Bd6 15 Bfd1 ±.

(d) 13 Rd1 c6 14 e4 with a big plus, Najdorf–Wexler, Buenos Aires 1965.

(e) 9 ... cxd5 10 Nc3 Na6 11 Nf5 Nc7 12 Bf4 Ne6 13 Be5 d6 14 Bxf6 Bxf6 15 Nxd5 Rb8 16 Qd2 and Black's isolated d-pawn makes him somewhat worse, Pachenko–Inkiov, 1982.

(f) 10 ... Nf6 11 e4 d5 12 Nc3 dxe4 13 Bg5 h6 14 Bf4 Bb4 15 Qb3 Bxc3 16 Qxc3 Qd3 17 Qcl with threats, Pelitov–Padevsky, Bulgaria 1964.

(g) Kasparov–Karpov, game 2 of the World Chp. 1984–85, continued 13 Bf4 Bc8 14 g4 Nba6 15 Rc1 Bd7 (15 ... Bxf5! 16 gxf5 Bg5 =, Sosonko–Tukmakov, Tilburg 1984) 16 Qd2 Nc5 17 e5 (Kasparov later recommended 17 Bxc7 Qxc7 18 exd5 Bxf5 19 gxf5 Rad8 20 b4 Nb7 21 Ne4 ±) 17 ... Be7 18 Nxe7†?! Qxe7 19 Bg5 Qe6 20 h3 Qg6 21 f4 f6 22 exf6 gxf6 23 Bh4 f5 24 b4? fxg4! 25 hxg4 Nd3 26 Rf3!? (White is in trouble—if 26 f5 then Qxg4 attacks the bishop on h4—so Kasparov plays creatively out of desperation) 26 ... Nxc1 27 f5 Qg7 28 Qxc1 Rae8 29 Qd2 d4 30 Ne2 Nd5 31 Nxd4 Kh8 32 g5 Re4 33 Bf2 Qe2 34 Rg3 Rf4 35 f6 Be8 36 b5 c5 37 Nc6 Qa1† 38 Bf1 Rf5 39 g6 Bxg6 40 Rxg6 R5xf6? (not 40 ... hxg6?? 41 Qh6†, but 40 ... Rxf2 41 Kxf2 Nxf6 wins immediately; now White can draw) 41 Rxf6 Qxf6 42 Qe1 Rg8† 43 Kh2 Qf4† 44 Bg3 Rxg3 45 Qxg3 Qxf1 46 Qb8† with perpetual check.

(h) 8 Ne5 Qc8 9 cxd5 Bxd5 10 Bxd5 Nxd5 11 Bb2 c5! =, Vidmar–Yanofsky, Groningen 1946.

(i) 13 Ne2 Ne4 14 Qc2 c5 is equal, U. Andersson–Matanović, Biel 1976.

(j) 13 e3 Rfe8 14 Rac1 a6 15 Qe2 Qc7 =, Grünfeld–Eliskases, Vienna 1935.

(k) 6 . . . 0-0?! 7 Qc2 takes away Black's option of . . . Ne4.

(l) Best is 7 . . . Bf6! 8 0-0 0-0 transposing to cols. 29 and 30.

(m) 13 Be3 e5 14 Na4 Qf7 15 c5 with the initiative, D. Gurevich–Rey, San Francisco 1987.

QUEEN'S INDIAN DEFENSE

1 d4 Nf6 2 c4 e6 3 Nf3 b6 4 g3 Ba6

	37	38	39	40	41	42
5	b3					Qa4
	Bb7(a)	Bb4†				Bb7
6	Bg2	Bd2				Bg2
	Bb4†	Be7(d)				c5
7	Bd2	Nc3		Bg2		dxc5
	a5	0-0	d5(g)	c6	d5(l)	Bxc5(o)
8	0-0	e4	cxd5	Bc3	Ne5	0-0
	0-0	d5(e)	Nxd5	d5	Bb7(m)	0-0
9	Bc3(b)	cxd5	Bg2(h)	Nbd2(j)	0-0	Nc3
	Ne4	Bxf1	0-0	Nbd7	Nbd7	Be7
10	Bb2	Kxf1	Nxd5	0-0	Nc3	Bf4
	d5	exd5	exd5	0-0	c5	Na6
11	c5	e5	0-0	Re1	Bf4	Rad1
	Qf6	Ne4	Nd7	c5	0-0	Nc5
12	Ne5	Qe2	Rc1	e4	cxd5	Qc2
	bxc5(c)	Nxc3(f)	Re8(i)	dxe4(k)	Nxe5(n)	Qc8(p)

(a) Attacking the pawn chain leaves White on top: (A) 5 . . . b5 6 cxb5 Bxb5 7 Bg2 Be7 8 0-0 0-0 9 Nc3 Ba6 10 Bb2 Bb7 11 Qc2 Na6 12 a3 c5 13 dxc5 Nxc5 14 b4 Na6 15 e4 Nc7 16 Rfd1 ±, Mikhalchishin–Aseyev, USSR 1984. (B) 5 . . . d5 6 Bg2 dxc4 7 Ne5 Bb4† 8 Kf1 Nfd7 9 Nxc4 c6 10 Qc2 0-0 11 Bf3 ±, Chernin–Sax, Subotica 1987.

(b) 9 Bg5 Be7 10 Nc3 Ne4 11 Bxe7 Qxe7 12 Qc2 Nxc3 13 Qxc3 d6 14 Ne1 Bxg2 is equal, Kasparov–Hübner, match 1985.

(c) 13 a3 cxd4 14 Ng4 Qg5 15 axb4 Nc3 16 Nxc3 dxc3 17 Bxc3 Qxg4 18 bxa5 with a slight edge, D. Gurevich–Browne, San Francisco 1987.

(d) (A) 6 . . . Bxd2† 7 Qxd2 transposes to col. 46. (B) 6 . . . c5 7 Bxb4 cxb4 8 a3 Na6 9 axb4 Nxb4 ∞ is Yusupov–Benjamin, Saint John 1988.

(e) 8 . . . Bb7 9 Bd3 d5 10 cxd5 exd5 11 e5 Ne4 12 0-0 c5 13 Rc1 Na6 14 Re1 Nb4 15 Bb1 ±, Pinter–Adorjan, Prague 1985.

(f) 13 Bxc3 Qd7 14 Kg2 Nc6 15 Rhe1 Nd8 16 Ng1!? c5 17 f4 with an edge due to the strong pawn chain, Karpov–A. Sokolov, match 1987.

(g) 7 . . . c6 8 e4 d5 9 e5 Ne4 10 Bd3 Nxc3 11 Bxc3 Bb7 12 Qe2 c5 13 dxc5 bxc5 14 0-0 0-0 15 Rad1 d4 16 Bd2 Nd7 17 Be4 with a plus, Kavalek–Portisch, Thessaloniki 1984.

(h) 9 e4 Nxc3 10 Bxc3 Bb7 11 Bb5† c6 12 Bd3 0-0 13 0-0 Nd7 14 Qe2 c5 15 Rfd1 Qc7 16 Rac1 ±, Tarjan–Ljubojevic, Indonesia 1983.

(i) 13 Re1 c5 14 Be3 Bb7 15 Bh3 cxd4 16 Bxd4 Nf6 17 Rc2 Bb4 18 Rf1 Ba6, Karpov–A. Sokolov, match 1986. White is a little better.

(j) 9 Ne5 Bb7 10 Nd2 Nbd7 11 0-0 c5 12 Nxd7 Qxd7 13 dxc5 bxc5 14 cxd5 exd5 15 Bxf6 Bxf6 16 Rc1 Rc8 17 e4 dxe4 18 Nxe4 Bxe4 19 Bxe4 gave White a pull in Yusupov–A. Sokolov, match 1986.

(k) 13 Nxe4 Bb7 14 Nfg5 cxd4 15 Bxd4 Qc7 16 Nxf6† Bxf6 =, Eingorn–Lerner, USSR Chp. 1986.

(l) 7 . . . Bb7 8 Nc3 0-0 9 0-0 d5 10 cxd5 exd5 11 Bf4 turned out slightly better for White in Mikhalchishin–Psakhis, USSR 1984.

(m) 8 . . . 0-0 9 0-0 c6 10 Bc3 Nfd7 11 Nxd7 Nxd7 12 Nd2 Rc8 13 e4 b5 14 Re1 dxc4 15 bxc4 ±, Kasparov–Karpov, World Chp. 1984.

(n) 13 Bxe5 Nxd5 14 Nxd5 Bxd5 15 e4 Bb7 16 Qg4 f6 17 Qxe6† Kh8 18 Bf4 cxd4 with chances for both sides, Yusupov–A. Sokolov, match 1986.

(o) 7 . . . bxc5 8 0-0 Be7 9 Nc3 0-0 10 Bf4 d6 11 Rfd1 Qb6 12 Rd2 Rd8 13 Rad1 with pressure, Dlugy–Sigurjonsson, Dubai 1986.

(p) 13 Nb5 Nce4 14 Nfd4 a6 15 Nc7 Ra7 with a very complicated game, Dlugy–Adorjan, New York 1987.

485

QUEEN'S INDIAN DEFENSE

1 d4 Nf6 2 c4 e6 3 Nf3 b6 4 g3

	43	44	45	46	47	48
	(Ba6).................			.Bb4†...................		.Bb7
5	Nbd2.................		Qb3(i)	Bd2........	Nbd2	Bg2
	Bb7(a)		Nc6(j)	Bxd2†	Ba6	Bb4†
6	Bg2		Nbd2	Qxd2	Qc2	Bd2(n)
	Be7........	c5(f)	Na5	Ba6	Bb7	Bxd2†
7	e4	e4	Qa4	b3(l)	Bg2	Qxd2
	Nxe4(b)	cxd4	Bb7	c6	Be4	0-0
8	Ne5	e5	Bg2	Qb2	Qb3	Nc3
	Bb4(c)	Ne4(g)	c5	d5	Bxd2†	d6
9	Qe2(d)	0-0	dxc5	Nbd2	Bxd2	Qc2
	d5	Nxd2	bxc5	Nbd7	0-0	Qe7
10	cxd5	Bxd2	0-0	Bg2	0-0	0-0
	Qxd5	Bxf3	Be7	0-0	d6	Nbd7
11	Nd3	Bxf3	Ne5	0-0	Qa3	e4
	Bxd2†(e)	Nc6(h)	Bxg2(k)	c5 =	Nbd7(m)	Rac8(o)

(a) A good try to unbalance the game is 5 . . . c5 6 e4 cxd4 7 e5 Ng4.

(b) 7 . . . d5 8 cxd5 exd5 9 e5 Ne4 10 0-0 0-0 11 Nxe4 dxe4 12 Nd2 Qxd4 13 Nxe4 Nc6 14 Nc3 Qxe5 15 Bf4 with good play for the pawn, Romanishin–Timman, Tilburg 1985.

(c) Not 8 . . . Nc3? 9 Qh5 g6 10 Qh3 winning.

(d) 9 Qg4 0-0 10 Bxe4 f5 11 Bxb7 fxg4 12 Bxa8 is unclear.

(e) 12 Bxd2 Nd7 13 Rc1 0-0-0 14 Bf4, Timman–A. Sokolov, Montpellier 1985. White has a strong position.

(f) 6 . . . d5 7 cxd5 Bxd5 8 0-0 Nbd7 9 Re1 Be7 10 e4 Bb7 11 e5 Nd5 12 Ne4 0-0 13 Bg5 $\pm$, Korchnoi–Polugaevsky, Tilburg 1985.

(g) 8 . . . Ng4 9 0-0 Qc7 10 Re1 Bc5?! (10 . . . f6 is better) 11 Ne4 d3 12 Nfg5! Nxe5 13 Bf4 d6 14 Qh5 Kf8? 15 Nxc5 bxc5 16 Rxe5! dxe5 17 Bxe5 Qd7 18 Bxb7 Qxb7 19 Nxe6†! Kg8 20 Nxg7 Nc6 21 Nf5 Nxe5 22 Qg5† Ng6 23 Qf6 Resigns, Adorjan–Kudrin, New York 1987.

(h) 12 Re1 Be7 13 b4?! Nxb4 14 Bxa8 Qxa8 15 Qg4 g6 16 Bxb4 Bxb4 17 Re4 0-0 $\mp$, Petursson–Adorjan, Thessaloniki 1984.

(i) (A) 5 Qc2 c5 6 Bg2 Nc6 7 dxc5 Bxc5 8 a3 Rc8 9 Qa4 Bb7 (9 . . . Nb8!?) 10 0-0 0-0 11 Nc3 Be7 12 Bg5 Na5 13 Nd2 Bxg2 14 Kxg2 Qc7 15 Rfd1! is better for White, Skembris–P. Nikolić, Dubai 1986, but 15 . . . Qc6 might hold Black's game. (B) 5 Qa4 c6 6 Nc3 b5 7 cxb5 cxb5 8 Nxb5 Qb6 9 e3 Bb7 10 Be2 Bc6 11 Qc4 Qb7 12 0-0 a6 13 Nc3 Bxf3 14 Bxf3 Qxf3 15 Qc8† Ke7 16 e4 h5 ∞, Dlugy–Wilder, US Chp. 1987.

(j) 5 . . . d5 6 cxd5 Qxd5 7 Qc2 Bb4† 8 Nc3 Bxc3† 9 bxc3 Qe4 10 Qb2 Bc4 11 Bg2 Qb7 12 Qb4 Bd5 13 c4 $\pm$, Torre–van der Wiel, Brussels 1986.

(k) 12 Kxg2 Qd6 13 Ndf3 Qb4 14 Qc2 Qb7 15 Rd1 and White is somewhat better, Ftáčnik–Farago, Warsaw 1987.

(l) 7 Qc2 c5 8 Bg2 Nc6 9 dxc5 bxc5 10 0-0 0-0 11 Rd1 Rb8 = , Cobo–Szabó, Varna 1962.

(m) 12 Rac1 favors White, Romanishin–Timman, Taxco 1985.

(n) 6 Nbd2 0-0 7 0-0 d5 8 a3 Be7 9 b4 c5 = , Rubinstein–Alekhine, Semmering 1926.

(o) 12 Rfe1 e5 13 Rad1 c6 14 Qc7 with a slight pull, Reshevsky–Keres, Semmering 1937.

QUEEN'S INDIAN DEFENSE

1 d4 Nf6

	49	50	51	52	53	54
2	(c4)					Nf3
	(e6)					b6
3	(Nf3)					g3(l)
	(b6)					g6(m)
4	e3			Nc3(g)		Bg2
	Bb7		c5	Bb7(h)		Bb7
5	Bd3		Bd3	Bg5		c4
	Be7	Bb4†(c)	d6	h6	Be7	Bg7
6	Nc3(a)	Nbd2(d)	0-0	Bh4	Qc2	0-0
	d5	0-0	Nbd7	Be7(i)	d5	0-0
7	0-0	0-0	b3	e3	Bxf6	Nc3
	0-0	d5	Be7	c5	Bxf6	Ne4
8	b3	a3	Bb2	Be2	cxd5	Nxe4
	c5	Be7	0-0	cxd4	exd5	Bxe4
9	Bb2	b4	Nc3	Nxd4	g3	Bf4
	Nc6(b)	c5(e)	g6(f)	0-0(j)	0-0(k)	d6(n)

(a) 6 0-0 c5 7 b3 0-0 8 Bb2 cxd4 8 exd4 d5 10 Nbd2 Nc6 11 Qe2 Re8 12 Rac1 Rc8 13 Rfd1 Bf8 14 Nf1 g6 15 Ne3 (Hort–Langeweg, Beverwijk 1968) 15 ... Nh5 = .

(b) 10 Rc1 cxd4 11 exd4 Rc8 (11 ... dxc4?! 12 bxc4 gives White too much mobility in the center) 12 Qe2 Re8 13 Rfd1 Bf8 reaches a classic position where both sides have developed their pieces to good squares. Chances are about even.

(c) 5 ... d5 6 b3 Bd6 7 0-0 0-0 8 Bb2 Nbd7 9 Nbd2 Ne4 10 Qc2 f5 is equal, but Dižarević–Miles, Biel Open 1985, concluded 11 Rad1? Nxd2! 12 Nxd2 (12 Qxd2 loses to 12 ... Bxf3 13 gxf3 Bxh2† 14 Kxh2 Qh4† 15 Kg2 Qg5† 16 Kh2 Rf6 and 17 ... Rh6 mate!) 12 ... dxc4 13 Nxc4 Bxh2†! 14 Kxh2 Qh4† 15 Kg1 Bf3! (A fine move! The immediate 15 ... Bxg2 allows some defense with 16 f3) 16 Nd2 Bxg2! 17 f3 Rf6 18 Nc4 Bh3 19 Resigns.

(d) 6 Bd2 Bxd2† equalizes. 6 Nc3 is the Nimzo-Indian Defense.

(e) 10 bxc5 bxc5 11 cxd5 cxd4 12 e4! exd5 13 e5 with an edge, Keres–Beliavsky, USSR 1973.

(f) 10 Qe2 a6 11 Rad1 Bb7, Ivkov–Romanishin, Moscow 1985. Black has equalized and retains a very flexible position.

(g) 4 Bf4 Bb7 5 e3 Be7 6 h3 0-0 7 Nc3 d5 8 cxd5 exd5 9 Bd3 c5 10 0-0 Nc6 11 Ne5 a6 = , Miles–Spassky, Buenos Aires 1978.

(h) 4 ... Bb4 now or on the next two moves transposes to col. 92 of the Nimzo-Indian Defense.

(i) 6 ... g5 7 Bg3 Nh5 8 Qc2 Nc6 9 0-0-0 Nxg3 10 hxg3 g4 11 Ne1 Qg5†! 12 e3 0-0-0 = , Uhlmann–Taimanov, Havana 1964.

(j) 10 0-0 Nc6 11 Rc1 Nxd4 12 Qxd4 Ne4! 13 Bxe7 Nxc3 14 Rxc3 Qxe7 =, Spassky–Keres, USSR 1965.

(k) 10 Bg2 c5 11 Rd1 Nc6 12 dxc5 d4! ∞, Seirawan–Christiansen, Santa Monica 1985.

(l) 3 e3 c5 4 Nbd2 e6 5 Bd3 Bd7 6 0-0 Nc6 7 c3 Be7 = is solid. The column is the Marienbad System.

(m) Black can also contest the center normally, e.g. 3 . . . Bb7 4 Bg2 c5! 5 dxc5 bxc5 =, Tartakover–Balogh, Prague 1931.

(n) 10 Qd2 Nd7 11 Bh6 e6 12 Bxg7 Kxg7 =, Guimard–Euwe, Groningen 1946.

BOGOLYUBOV (OR BOGO-) INDIAN DEFENSE

1 d4 Nf6 2 c4 e6 3 Nf3 Bb4†

Diagram 67

THIS DEFENSE, a close cousin to the Queen's Indian and Nimzo-Indian, is named after the world title contender of the 1930s, Yefim Bogolyubov. As in all of the "hypermodern" openings, Black deploys his pieces first so that he has flexibility in placing his pawns. The Bogo-Indian is a safe opening—even safer than the Queen's Indian—and for this reason it has been played less often than its merits warrant.

The trend is changing, however, and the Bogo is coming to the fore of opening theory. The large choice of plans offers something for everyone.

White has three responses to the check: 4 Nc3, transposing to the Nimzo-Indian; 4 Bd2; and 4 Nbd2.

4 Bd2 (cols. 1–6) "puts the question" to the bishop, but nonetheless allows Black an array of replies. With 4 . . . Qe7 (cols. 1–2) Black tries to counter White's fianchetto, followed by e4, by forcing a more passive recapture on d2. 4 . . . a5 (cols. 3–4) fits in well with the strategy of playing for . . . d6 and . . . e5; after White's d5, Black's a-pawn stops White's move b4. 4 . . . Bxd2† (col. 5) is the most humble of the alternatives, favored by Ulf Andersson, with which Black returns to a Queen's Gambit formation. 4 . . . c5!? (col. 6), on the other hand, is a favorite of Korchnoi's. The bizarre pawn structure that results is very difficult to take advantage of directly, so White will have to proceed at a moderate pace.

4 Nbd2 (cols. 7–12) seems to limit Black's choices by not threatening the bishop. 4 . . . b6 (cols. 7–8) plays a Queen's Indian formation with . . . d6 and . . . Ndb7. 4 . . . c5 (col. 11) slips into a Hedgehog. 4 . . . d5 (col. 12) has similarities with the Ragozin Queen's Gambit. And 4 . . . 0-0 (cols. 9–10) postpones these decisions for one move.

490

BOGOLYUBOV INDIAN DEFENSE

1 d4 Nf6 2 c4 e6 3 Nf3 Bb4† 4 Bd2

	1	2	3	4	5	6
	Qe7 . . . . .a5 . . . . .Bxd2† . . . . . .c5(n)					
5	g3(a)		Nc3 . . . . .g3		Qxd2(k)	Bxb4
	Nc6(b)		b6	d6(i)	0-0	cxb4
6	Nc3 . . . . .Bg2		e3	Bg2	Nc3	g3(o)
	d5(c)	Bxd2†	Bb7	Nbd7	d5	0-0
7	cxd5	Nbxd2(e)	Bd3	0-0	e3	Bg2
	exd5	d6	d6	e5	Qe7(l)	d6
8	Bg2	e4	Qc2	Bg5	Rc1	0-0
	0-0	e5	Nbd7	exd4	Rd8	a5
9	0-0	d5	e4	Nxd4	Qc2	Qd3
	Re8	Nb8	e5	h6	dxc4	Nbd7
10	e3	0-0	Nd5	Bf4	Bxc4	Nbd2
	Bg4	0-0(f)	Bxd2†	0-0	c5	e5
11	Qc2	b4	Qxd2	Qc2	0-0	Rfe1
	Qd7(d)	a5(g)	exd4(h)	Ne5(j)	cxd4(m)	Re8(p)

(a) 5 e3 Bxd2† 6 Qxd2 0-0 7 Nc3 d6 8 Be2 e5 9 d5 a5 10 0-0 Na6 = , Tukmakov–Polugaevsky, USSR Chp. 1969. 5 g3 easily leads into the Catalan Opening.

(b) 5 . . . 0-0 6 Bg2 Bxd2† 7 Nbxd2 is similar to column 2, but . . . Nc6 is more flexible than . . . 0-0.

(c) 6 . . . Bxc3 7 Bxc3 Ne4 8 Rc1 0-0 9 Bg2 a5 10 0-0 d6 11 Nh4 f5 12 d5 Nb4 13 Be1! ± , Rohde–Miles, San Francisco 1987.

(d) 12 Rfc1 Re7 13 a3 Bxc3 14 Bxc3 Ne4 15 b4 ± , Gligorić–A. Rodriguez, Lucerne 1982.

(e) 7 Qxd2?! Ne4 8 Qc2 Qb4† 9 Nc3 Nxc3 gives White doubled pawns.

(f) 10 . . . a5 11 c5! 0-0 (11 . . . dxc5?! 12 Nc4 threatening 13 Nxe5 and 13 d6!) 12 cxd6 cxd6 13 a3 a4 14 Ne1 Bd7 15 Nd3 ± , Beliavsky–Rashkovsky, Lvov 1981.

(g) 12 a3 Na6 13 Qb3 Bg4 (Psakhis–Petrosian, USSR 1982); now Petrosian's 14 Nh4 maintains White's edge.

(h) 12 Nxd4 Nc5 13 0-0 0-0 14 Rfe1 ± , Kasparov–Tal, Nikšić 1983.

(i) 5 . . . 0-0 6 Bg2 d5 7 Qc2 Ne4 8 0-0 Nxd2 9 Nbxd2 Nc6 10 Rfd1 f5 11 e3 Bd7 12 Ne1 Ne7 13 Nd3 is pleasant for White, Benko–Damjanović, Monte Carlo 1968.

(j) 12 Rd1 Ng6 13 Bc1 Re8 14 Nc3 c6 15 b3 Bg4 16 Bb2 Qc8 = , Wilder–Smyslov, New York 1987.

(k) 5 Nbxd2 d6 6 e4 0-0 7 Bd3 e5 8 dxe5 dxe5 9 Nxe5 Nc6 10 Nxc6 Qxd3 = (Gipslis).

(l) 7 . . . Nbd7 8 Bd3 c6 9 0-0 (9 e4 dxe4 10 Nxe4 Nxe4 11 Bxe4 Qc7 12 0-0 b6 = , Korn) 9 . . . dxc4 10 Bxc4 e5 11 Bb3 Qe7 (better 11 . . . exd4 12 Qxd4 Qb6 13 Qf4 Nc5 = ,

491

Comments) 12 e4 exd4 13 Nxd4 Nc5 14 Bc2 Rd8 15 Rad1 ± is Alekhine–Bogolyubov, Budapest 1921. In the column, if 6 g3!? b6! 7 Bg2 Bb7 8 0-0 Na6 = (Korn).

(m) 12 Nxd4 Bd7 13 Rfd1 Nc6 with only a minimal edge for White, Chernin–Spassky, Reggio Emilia 1986–87.

(n) 4 . . . Be7 5 g3 d5 6 Bg2 0-0 7 0-0 c6 8 Qc2 Nbd7 9 Rd1 b6 10 a4 Ba6 11 b3 c5 12 Na3 Bb7, practically with equality, Beliavsky–Yusupov, USSR Chp. 1988.

(o) The simplest plan for White is 6 a3 bxa3 7 Rxa3 d6 8 e3 0-0 9 Be2 b6 10 0-0 with a small plus, Beliavsky–Seirawan, Montpellier 1985.

(p) 12 Ng5 Ra6 13 Rad1 h6 14 Nge4 Nxe4 15 Bxe4 Nf6 16 Bg2 Qe7 17 e4 ±, Pinter–P. Nikolić, Reggio Emilia 1987–88.

BOGOLYUBOV INDIAN DEFENSE

1 d4 Nf6 2 c4 e6 3 Nf3 Bb4† 4 Nbd2

	7	8	9	10	11	12
	b6............................0-0............................c5..........d5					
5	a3..........e3		a3..........e3(j)		a3	Qa4†
	Bxd2†	Bb7	Be7(g)	d6(k)	Bxd2†	Nc6
6	Bxd2(a)	Bd3	e4	Be2	Bxd2(m)	a3(o)
	Bb7(b)	c5(d)	d5	Qe7	cxd4	Be7(p)
7	Bg5	a3(e)	e5	0-0	Nxd4	e3
	d6	Bxd2†	Nfd7	Bxd2	Ne4	0-0
8	e3	Bxd2	cxd5	Nxd2	Be3	Qc2
	Nbd7	d6	exd5	e5	0-0	a5
9	Bd3	dxc5	Bd3	b3	g3	b3
	h6	bxc5	c5	Re8!	b6	Bd7
10	Bh4	0-0	0-0	d5(l)	Bg2	Bb2
	g5	a5	Nc6	Nbd7	Bb7	Na7?!
11	Bg3	b3	Re1	Bb2	0-0	Bd3
	Qe7	Nbd7	a5	Nf8	Nd6	h6
12	Qc2	Qc2	h3(h)	Qc2	Bxb7	Rg1
	h5(c) ⟋	Qc7(f) ⟍	Re8(i) ±	Ng6 =	Nxb7(n) ⟋	c5(q) ×

(a) 6 Qxd2 Bb7 7 e3 0-0 8 Be2 d6 9 b4 a5 10 Bb2 Ne4 11 Qd3 f5 12 0-0 Nd7 13 d5 e5 14 Nd2 Nxd2 15 Qxd2 Qe7 16 f4! exf4 17 exf4 also gives White a small advantage, Timman–Andersson, Tilburg 1984.

(b) 6 . . . Ne4 7 Bf4 Bb7 8 e3 d6 9 Bd3 Nd7 10 0-0 0-0 11 b4 a5 12 Qc2 ±, Lputian–Agzamov, Sochi 1985.

(c) 13 h3 h4 14 Bh2 g4 15 hxg4 h3 16 Bg1! ±, P. Nikolić–Seirawan, Wijk aan Zee 1986.

(d) 6 . . . d5 is also reasonable, and if 7 a3 Be7 =.

(e) 7 0-0 cxd4 8 exd4 0-0 9 a3 Be7 10 Re1 d5 11 cxd5 Nxd5 12 Ne4 Nc6 is equal, Lputian–Psakhis, USSR 1979.

(f) 13 Bc3 Bxf3 14 gxf3 Ne5! 15 Bxe5 dxe5 =, Miles–Andersson, Nikšić 1983.

(g) 5 . . . Bxd2† 6 Bxd2 d6 7 Bg5 Nbd7 8 e3 e5 9 Be2 b6 10 0-0 and White's two bishops are well placed, giving him the edge, Lputian–Larsen, Hastings 1986–87.

(h) 12 Qc2 h6 13 Nf1 cxd4 14 Ng3 Nc5 with even chances, Browne–Makarychev, Saint John 1988.

(i) 13 Nf1 cxd4 14 Ng3 Nf8 15 b3 Bd7 16 Ra2 f6 17 Rae2, Yusupov–Kindermann, Munich 1988; White is fully developed and has attacking chances.

(j) 5 g3 d5 6 Bg2 dxc4 transposes to the Catalan Opening, or 5 . . . Nc6 6 Bg2 d5 7 a3 Be7 ∞. Also compare Queen's Knight's Defense.

(k) 5 . . . d5 6 Bd3 dxc4! 7 Bxc4 Nc6 8 0-0 Qe7 9 a3 Bd6 = is a good alternative.

(l) 10 Bb2 exd4 11 Bxd4 Nc6 12 Bb2 Bf5 with full equality as all of Black's pieces are on good squares. The column is Alster–Augustin, Czechoslovakia 1965.

(m) 6 Qxd2 cxd4 7 Nxd4 Nc6 8 e3 d5 9 cxd5 exd5 10 Nxc6 bxc6 is equal as Black's development compensates for the two bishops, Browne–Djurić, New York 1986.

(n) 13 Qc2 Qc8 14 Rfd1 Nc6 15 Rac1 Ne5 16 h3 ±, Cebalo–Djurić, Yugoslav Chp. 1986.

(o) 6 Ne5 Bd7 7 Nxc6 Bxd2† 8 Bxd2 Bxc6 9 Qc2 Ne4 is completely equal.

(p) 6 . . . Bxd2† 7 Bxd2 Ne4 8 Qc2 e5!? 9 dxe5 Bf5 10 Rd1! 0-0 (10 . . . Ng3?! 11 Qb3 Nxh1 12 cxd4 Ne7 13 e4 is strong—Goldin) 11 Qc1 d4 (Chekhov–Goldin, USSR 1987); now 12 Bc3 is better for White.

(q) 13 dxc5 Bxc5 14 g4 dxc4 15 Bxc4 Rc8 16 g5 hxg5 17 Nxg5 Re8 18 Nxf7! Qe7 19 Ne4 Kxf7 20 Nf6! Resigns, Wilder–Kogan, US Chp. 1987.

NIMZO-INDIAN DEFENSE

1 d4 Nf6 2 c4 e6 3 Nc3 Bb4

Diagram 68

THE NAME ARON NIMZOWITSCH has become attached to one of Black's most active and soundest defenses. With a slight inversion of moves it was introduced in the game Steinitz–Englisch, Vienna 1882, but the inventive Nimzowitsch realized the hidden possibilities of Black's early development of the king's bishop. When Tarrasch charged that Nimzowitsch's moves were ugly, he replied: "The beauty of a chess move lies not in its appearance, but in the thought behind it."

The Nimzo-Indian, as it became known despite its having no "Indian" structure (it involves no fianchetto), is one of the turning points of modern opening theory. Characterized by the pinning sortie 3 ... Bb4, which exerts pressure on the queenside and on the center, it reduces White's influence on the e4 and d5 squares. Black must often exchange his pinning bishop for the pinned knight, but as compensation he will achieve rapid development or the doubling of White's c-pawns or both. Thus, instead of trying merely to neutralize White's advantage, Black seeks to equalize with compensating strengths, with an eye on winning chances. As the defense is also eminently sound, it has become a standard fixture of the opening repertoire. It is hard to think of any modern master who at one time or another has not resorted to it.

Diagram 69

The Classical Variation 4 Qc2 (cols. 1–18), is the safest approach for White (see diagram). It leads to clear play, neither side having noticeable weaknesses. White intends to win the bishop pair without doubling his pawns, though at the cost of a tempo. The well-tested response 4 . . . d5 (cols. 1–6) still offers White some chances for advantage. Probably the sharpest line for Black is 4 . . . c5 (cols. 7–9), which hits at the now unprotected square d4. The *Milner–Barry Variation,* 4 . . . Nc6 (cols. 10–12), though playable, is not currently fashionable. Other methods often leave White slightly freer at best.

Diagram 70

The Rubinstein Variation, 4 e3 (cols. 19–66), has for many years been White's favored reply to the Nimzo-Indian (see diagram). Though this move temporarily locks in White's queen bishop, it strengthens the center, allows the developing moves 5 Bd3 and 5 Nge2, and retains White's flexibility. Cols. 19–24, the most deeply explored variation of the Nimzo-Indian, is the main line of the Rubinstein. White undoubles his pawns, but Black equalizes in space and develops his pieces to good squares. Currently 11 Ba2 seems promising for White. Black has many equally promising ways of avoiding the main line after he has played the standard moves 4 ... 0-0, 5 ... d5, and 6 ... c5 (in any order). Players with a preference for bishops should look at Ba5 for Black on move 8 or 9 (cols. 27–31), or at retreating the bishop to e7 (cols. 33–36).

Cols. 37–47 constitute the *Gligorić Variation*; we have so dubbed it on account of the Yugoslav grandmaster's extensive practice against the lines 7 ... dxc4 and 7 ... Nbd7. Gligorić scored many victories here for White and added valuable analysis to the theory of this line.

If Black wants to play someting less thoroughy analyzed, 4 ... b6, the *Fischer Variation,* is recommended (cols. 55–60) for its flexibility—Black doesn't commit his center pawns immediately.

Noteworthy are columns 63 and 64, the *Hübner System*, which has proved so strong that White now regularly answers 4 ... c5 with 5 Ne2, blocking the bishop but avoiding the doubled pawns.

Diagram 71

The Sämisch Variation, 4 a3 Bxc3† 5 bxc3 (cols. 67–84), is White's sharpest answer to the Nimzo (see diagram). White spends a move to force Black to carry out his strategy! The resulting doubled pawns, though a weakness, also give White a strong center. This, combined with the bishop pair, makes White's course clear—he must attack!

Black's most respected response is 5 ... c5 (cols. 67–72), which is usually followed by ... Nc6, ... b6, ... Ba6, and ... Na5 in some order, attacking c4 with good counterplay.

Also reasonable is 5 ... d5 (cols. 73–78), but then at least White will not have to worry about losing the weak c4 pawn.

Black's other replies (cols. 79–83), though not as common, are perfectly reasonable.

The Leningrad Variation, 4 Bg5 (cols. 85–88), was a favorite weapon of Spassky's for many years. White counters Black's pin with a pin of his own. However, after 4 ... h6 5 Bh4 c5 the white bishop may be missed on the queenside.

The *Spielmann Variation,* 4 Qb3 (cols. 89–90), was popularized by its namesake at Carlsbad 1929, but despite its soundness it has fallen from favor as too lackluster.

Of recent interest is Kasparov's favorite 4 Nf3 (cols. 91–93, and often cols. 94–95 by transposition). This flexible move allows White to wait for Black's reply before committing himself to a particular strategy. Col. 94 may also transpose to the Catalan Opening.

NIMZO-INDIAN DEFENSE

Classical Variation

1 d4 Nf6 2 c4 e6 3 Nc3 Bb4 4 Qc2 d5

	1	2	3	4	5	6
5	a3...............................cxd5(i)					
	Bxc3†			Qxd5......exd5		
6	Qxc3			Nf3(j)	Bg5(m)	
	Nc6........Ne4			c5	h6.........Be6	
7	Nf3(a)	Qc2		Bd2	Bxf6	e3
	Ne4	Nc6........c5		Bxc3	Qxf6	Nbd7
8	Qb3(b)	e3(d)	dxc5	Bxc3	a3	f4!?
	Na5	e5	Nc6	cxd4	Bxc3†	h6
9	Qa4†	cxd5	cxd5(f)	Rd1!	Qxc3	Bxf6
	c6	Qxd5	exd5	Nc6(k)	0-0	Qxf6
10	cxd5	Bc4	Nf3	Nxd4	e3	Bd3
	exd5	Qa5†	Bf5	0-0	c6(n)	Nb6
11	e3	b4	b4	f3	Nf3	Nf3
	Bf5	Nxb4	0-0(g)	Qxa2	Bf5	0-0
12	Bd2	Qxe4	Bb2	e4	Ne5	0-0
	Nxd2(c)	Nc2†(e)	b6!(h)	Nxd4(l)	Nd7 ±	Rac8(o)

(a) 7 e3 e5 8 dxe5 Ne4 (8 . . . d4 9 Qd3 Ng4 10 Nf3 dxe3 11 Qxd8† Kxd8 =) 9 Qd3 Nc5 10 Qc2 dxc4 11 Bxc4 Nxe5 12 Bb5† c6 13 Qxc5 Qa5† =, Kotov–Szabo, Budapest 1950.

(b) 8 Qc2 e5 is column 2, note (d).

(c) 13 Nxd2 0-0 14 Be2 b5 15 Qb4 Nc4 16 b3 a5 17 Qc5 Nxd2 18 Kxd2 ± (Boleslavsky). White's king is safe while Black's queenside is weak.

(d) 8 Nf3 e5 9 e3 Bf5 10 Bd3 exd4 allows Black's pieces to jump into the game effectively.

(e) 13 Ke2 Qe1† 14 Kf3 Nxa1 15 Bb2 (15 Qxe5† Be6 16 Bxe6 0-0!) 15 . . . 0-0 16 Kg3 Bd7 17 Nf3 Qxh1 18 Ng5 g6 19 Qxe5! Rae8 20 Qf6 Rxe3† 21 fxe3 Qe1† 22 Qf2 Nc2! 23 Qxe1 Nxe1 24 Kf2 b5 25 Be2 Nc2 26 Bd1 Nxa3 27 Bxa3 Ra8 28 Bb3 Be8 =. *Comments.*

(f) 9 e3 Qa5† 10 Bd2 Nxd2 11 Qxd2 dxc4 12 Qxa5 Nxa5 13 Rc1 b5! 14 cxb6 Bb7 15 Nf3 Ke7! gives Black good play, Tolush–Sokolsky, Leningrad 1934.

(g) 11 . . . Ng3 12 Qb2 Nxh1 13 Qxg7 Rf8 14 Bh6 Qe7 15 Qxf8† Qxf8 16 Bxf8 Kxf8 17 g3 Be4 18 Bg2 a5 is unclear.

(h) 13 b5 bxc5 14 bxc6 Qa5† 15 Nd2 Rab8 gives Black sufficient play for the piece.

(i) 5 e3 0-0 6 a3 Be7 7 Nf3 c5 8 dxc5 Bxc5 9 Be2 Nc6 =.

(j) 6 e3 c5 7 a3 Bxc3† 8 bxc3 Nc6 9 Nf3 0-0 10 c4 Qd6 11 Bb2 cxd4 12 exd4 b6 =, Alekhine–Euwe, World Chp. 1937.

(k) (A) 9 . . . e5 10 Bxd4! ±. (B) 9 . . . Qxa2 10 Rxd4 Nc6 11 Ra4 ±.

(l) 13 Rxd4 Bd7 14 Bc4 Qa1† 15 Rd1 gives White good compensation for the pawn, Glek–Gulko, Tashkent 1984.

(m) (A) 6 a3 Bxc3† 7 bxc3 c5 =. (B) 6 Nf3 c5 7 Bg5 h6 =.

(n) More recently tested is 10 . . . Bf5 11 Ne2! (11 Nf3 Nd7 12 Rc1 Rfc8 13 b4 a5 ∞, Nogueiras–A. Sokolov, Leningrad 1987) (A) 11 . . . Re8 12 Ng3 ±, Seirawan–Tal, Nikšić 1983, or (B) 11 . . . Rc8 12 Rc1 Nd7 13 b4 a5 14 Ng3 axb4 15 axb4 Bg6 16 Be2 ±, Beliavsky–Portisch, Reykjavik 1988.

(o) 13 Na4! ±, Ragozin–Botvinnik, match 1940. White has play on the queenside and in the center.

Classical Variation

1 d4 Nf6 2 c4 e6 3 Nc3 Bb4 4 Qc2

	7	8	9	10	11	12
	c5!.................................Nc6 (Milner–Barry Variation)					
5	dxc5			Nf3		
	0-0(a)..................Nc6			d6......................0-0		
6	Bg5(b) Nf3		Nf3	a3 ....Bd2		Bg5(k)
	Na6	Na6!	Bxc5	Bxc3†	0-0(i)	h6
7	a3	e3(d)	Bg5	Qxc3	a3	Bh4
	Bxc3†	Nxc5	b6	a5(f)	Bxc3	d6
8	Qxc3	Bd2	e3	b3	Bxc3	e3
	Nxc5	b6	Bb7	0-0	Qe7(j)	Qe7
9	Bxf6(c)	Be2	Be2	Bb2(g)	b4	Be2
	Qxf6	Ba6	Rc8	Re8	e5	e5
10	Qxf6	a3	0-0	Rd1	dxe5	d5
	gxf6	Bxc3	Be7	Qe7	Nxe5	Nb8
11	f3	Bxc3	Rad1	d5	e3	Nd2
	a5	Nce4	d6	Nb8	Bg4	Nbd7
12	e4	Bxf6	Rd2	dxe6	Nxe5	0-0
	b6 =	Nxf6 =	a6(e)	fxe6(h)	dxe5 ±	a5(l)

(a) 5 . . . Qc7?! 6 Nf3 Bxc5 7 Bg5! Be7 8 e4 d6 9 Nb5 Qc6 10 0-0-0 Nbd7 11 c5! dxc5 (on 11 . . . Nxc5 12 e5 dxe5 13 Nxe5 is strong) 12 e5 Nd5 13 Bxe7 Kxe7 14 Qe4 N7b6 15 Qh4† f6 16 Bc4 Nxc4 17 Qxc4 Bd7 18 Nc3 Nxc3 19 bxc3 (Black has an extra pawn, but he is defenseless against the invasion of the White rooks on the d-file) 19 . . . Rae8 20 Rd6 Qc7 21 Rhd1 Bc8 22 Nd4! Kf7 23 Nb5 Qa5 24 R6d3 Rd8 25 Nd6† Rxd6 (25 . . . Ke7 26 Nxc8† Rxc8 27 Rd7† is a faster way to lose) 26 Rxd6 fxe5 27 Rd7!† Bxd7 28 Rxd7† Kf8 29 f4 e4 30 Rxb7 g6 31 Kb2 Qd8 32 Qxc5† Kg8 33 Kc1 e3 34 Qxe3 Qd5 35 Rb8† Kg7 36 Qxa7† Resigns, Seirawan–Portisch, Indonesia 1983.

(b) (A) 6 Bf4 Na6 7 Bd6 Re8 8 a3 Qa5 9 Rc1 Bxc3† 10 Qxc3 Qxc3 11 Rxc3 Ne4 =, Donner–Karpov, Amsterdam 1981. (B) 6 a3 Bxc5 7 Nf3 Nc6 8 Bg5! (8 Bf4 d5 9 Qc2 transposes to the Queens Gambit Declined, col. 88) 8 . . . Nd4?! 9 Nxd4 Bxd4 10 e3 Qa5 11 exd4 Qxg5 12 Qd2! ±, Seirawan–Kudrin, US Chp. 1986. This game is a good advertisement for 8 a3, but Black could try 8 . . . Be7 instead.

(c) 9 f3 Nfe4! 10 Bxd8 Nxc3 11 Be7 Nb3 12 Bxf8 Kxf8 ∓. The column is Kotov–Averbakh, USSR Chp. 1951.

(d) (A) 7 g3 Nxc5 8 Bg2 (8 a3 Bxc3† 9 Qxc3 Nce4 10 Qc2 b5! 11 cxb5 Qa5† 12 b4 Qxb5 13 Bg2 Ba6 ±, P. Nikolić–Yusupov, Tilburg 1987) 8 . . . Nce4 9 0-0 Nxc3 10 bxc3 Be7 11 Rd1 Qc7 12 Qd3 Rd8 =, Wilder–Pinter, Dortmund 1988. (B) 7 a3 Bxc3 8 Qxc3 Nxc5 9 e3 a5 =, Kogan–Seirawan, US Chp. 1981. The column is Knezevic–Romanishin, Yugoslavia vs. USSR 1979.

(e) 13 Rfd1 0-0 14 Bf4 Ne8 $\pm$, Rubinstein–Sämisch, Berlin 1926. Black is solid but under pressure.

(f) 7 . . . 0-0 8 b4 e5 9 dxe5 Ne4! 10 Qe3 f5 11 Bb2 Be6 12 Rc1 Qe7 13 exd6 Qxd6 14 g3 Rad8 gives Black enough play for the pawn, Gadalinski–Szabo, Špindlerovy Mlýny 1948.

(g) 9 g3 Qe7 10 Bg2 Ne4 11 Qc2 f5 12 0-0 e5 13 d5 Nb8 14 Bb2 Qf7! =. *Comments.*

(h) 13 g3 b6 =, Donner–Reshevsky, Amsterdam 1950.

(i) 6 . . . e5 7 dxe5 dxe5 8 0-0-0! Bxc3 9 Bxc3 Qe7 10 e3 Bg4 11 h3 Bh4 12 Qb3 Rb8 13 g4 Bg6 14 Nh4 $\pm$, Ragozin–Lisitsin, USSR Chp. 1944.

(j) 8 . . . Re8 9 b4! e5 10 dxe5 Nxe5 11 e3 Bg4 12 Nxe5 dxe5 13 f3 Bh5 14 Be2 Bg6 15 Qb2 Nd7 16 0-0 f6 17 c5 $\pm$, Euwe–Kramer, Dutch Chp. 1952.

(k) 6 e4 Bxc3 7 bxc3 e5 8 Ba3 Re8 9 d5 Nb8 10 c5 is as good as the column and also gives White some advantage.

(l) 13 Rae1 Re8 14 f4 $\pm$, Keres–Euwe, match 1940. One of the variation's stem games went 6 Bg5 (6 Bd2!) 6 . . . h6 (6 . . . d5) 7 Bxf6! Qxf6 8 e3 d6 9 Bd3 e5 10 d5 Ne7 11 0-0 Bxc3 12 Qxc3 Bf5 =, Aloni–Milner–Barry, Helsinki 1952. Also compare Queen's Knight's Defense.

NIMZO-INDIAN DEFENSE

Classical Variation

1 d4 Nf6 2 c4 e6 3 Nc3 Bb4 4 Qc2

	13	14	15	16	17	18
	d6.................................			.0-0(g)....................		.b6?!
5	Nf3........	.Bg5........	.a3	a3	.e4	e4
	Nbd7	0-0(c)	Bxc3†	Bxc3	d5(k)	Bxc3†
r	g3(a)	e3(d)	Qxc3	Qxc3	e5	bxc3
	b6	e5	0-0	b6	Ne4	Nc6
7	Bg2	Ne2	Nf3(e)	Nf3(h)	Bd3	e5
	Bb7	Qe7	Nbd7	Bb7	c5	Ng8
8	0-0	dxe5	e3(f)	e3	dxc5	Nf3
	Bxc3	dxe5	b6	d6	Nc6	Ba6
9	Qxc3	a3	b4	b4(i)	Bxe4	Bd3
	0-0	Bxc3†	Bb7	Nbd7	dxe4	Na5
10	b3(b)	Nxc3	Bb2	Bb2	Qxe4	Bxh7
	Qe7	c6 =	Qe7	a5!	Bxc3†	Ne7
11	Bb2		Be2	Be2	bxc3	Bd3
	Ne4		Ne4	Ne4	Qa5	d5
12	Qc2		Qc2	Qc2	Ne2	cxd5
	f5 =		f5 =	c5(j)	Qxc5 $\overline{\overline{\mp}}$	Bxd3(l)

(a) 6 Bd2 b6 7 e4 Bb7 8 Bd3 e5 9 0-0-0 0-0 10 d5 Nc5 11 a3 Bxc3 12 Bxc3 c6 13 Nd2 cxd5 14 cxd5 Qd7 =, Petrosian–Bronstein, USSR Chp. 1949.

(b) Too aggressive is 10 b4 c5 11 a3 Ne4 12 Qc2 Qc7 13 dxc5 bxc5 14 Be3 Rfc8 $\overline{\overline{\mp}}$, Schwarzman–Luckis, Buenos Aires 1944. The column is Makagonov–Kan, USSR 1939.

(c) 5 . . . Nbd7 6 Nf3 Qe7 7 e3 b6 8 Be2 Bb7 9 0-0 Bxc3 10 bxc3 (10 Qxc3 Ne4) 10 . . . h6 11 Bxf6 Nxf6 = (Taimanov).

(d) 6 Nf3 Nbd7 7 a3 Bxc3† 8 Qxc3 Re8 = (Suetin). The column is Comments.

(e) 7 Bg5 b6 8 e3 Bb7 9 f3 Nbd7 10 Bd3 c5 11 Nge2 Rac8 12 0-0 d5 =.

(f) 8 g3 b6 9 Bg2 Bb7 10 0-0 Qe7 11 b4 c5 12 Bb2 cxd4 13 Qxd4 e5 14 Qd2 Rac8 =, Porath–Portisch, Tel Aviv 1964. The column is Miles–Andersson, Wijk aan Zee 1981.

(g) Note that 4 . . . 0-0 and 4 . . . d6 can lead to the same line by transposition.

(h) 7 Bg5 Bb7 8 e3 (worthy of investigation is 8 f3!? c5 9 dxc5 bxc5 10 e3 Nc6 ∞, Hjartarson) 8 . . . d6 9 f3 Nbd7 10 Bd3 c5 11 Ne2 Rc8 12 Qd2 (12 0-0 d5 =) 12 . . . h6 13 Bh4 cxd4 14 exd4 Ba6 15 Rc1 d5 16 b3 dxc4 17 bxc4 e5 =, Pr. Nikolić–Short, Tilburg 1988.

(i) 9 Be2 Ne4 10 Qc2 Ng5 (Petrosian–Larsen, Nikšić 1983) is an active maneuver for Black.

(j) 13 dxc5 bxc5 14 b5 f5 15 0-0 e5, Gudmundsson–Arnasson, Grindavik 1984. The position is unbalanced, but the chances are probably equal.

(k) Less enterprising is 5 . . . d6 6 Bd3 Nc6 7 Ne2 e5 8 d5 Ne7 =. The column is analysis by Pachman.

(l) 13 Qxd3 Qxd5 14 Bg5 ±, Bronstein–Bisguier, Tallinn 1971. This is a good example of a normally logical move (4 . . . b6) not meeting the needs of the position.

NIMZO-INDIAN DEFENSE
Rubinstein Variation

1 d4 Nf6 2 c4 e6 3 Nc3 Bb4 4 e3 0-0 5 Bd3 d5 6 Nf3 c5 7 0-0 Nc6 8 a3 Bxc3 9 bxc3 dxc4 10 Bxc4 Qc7

	19	20	21	22	23	24
11	a4	Re1	Bb5	Ba2	Bb2	Qc2(j)
	e5(a)	e5	Bd7(c)	e5	e5	e5
12	Ba3	d5(c)	a4	h3	h3(h)	Bd3
	e4	Na5	Na5	e4	Bf5	Re8
13	Nd2	d6	Ba3	Nh2	Bb5	e4(k)
	b6	Qb6	b6	Bf5	e4	c4
14	Qc2(b)	Nxe5	Bd3	Ng4	Ng4	Bxc4
	Na5	Nxc4	Bc6	Nxg4(e)	Bd7	exd4
15	Be2	Nxc4	Ne5	hxg4	c4	cxd4
	Re8	Qa6	Be4	Bg6	cxd4	Na5
16	dxc5	Qd3	Be2	a4	exd4	Bd3
	bxc5	Rd8	Rfd8	Rfd8(f)	Qf4	Qxc2
17	c4	e4	Rc1	Qe2	g3	Bxc2
	Bg4 =	Be6 =	Rac8 =	b6(g)	Qd6(i)	Nxe4 =

(a) Also 11 . . . Rd8 12 Ba3 b6 13 Re1 Bb7 14 Ba2 Ne4 15 Qc2 Na5 = (Taimanov).

(b) 14 dxc5 Rd8 15 cxb6 axb6 16 Qc2 Ng4 17 g3 Nce5 18 Be2 Bf5 (Taimanov) gives Black strong play for the pawn. The column is Panno–Ivkov, Copenhagen 1953.

(c) 12 Qc2 e4 13 Nd2 Re8 14 Bb2 Na5 15 Ba2 c4 =, Kholmov–Chuvaev, USSR 1955. The column is Kluger–O'Kelly, Bucharest 1954.

(d) 11 . . . Rd8 and 11 . . . a6 are also satisfactory.

(e) 14 . . . Bxg4 15 hxg4 h6 16 Rb1 ± (Taimanov).

(f) 16 . . . Rad8 17 Qe2 Rfe8 18 Ba3 b6 19 Bc4! Na5 20 Ba6 ±, Knaak–Kir. Georgiev, East Germany vs. Bulgaria 1986.

(g) 18 Ba3 Kh8 19 Rad1 cxd4 20 cxd4 ±. In this line both white bishops are working while the black bishop on g6 does little.

(h) 12 Be2 Rd8 13 Qc2 Bg4 14 dxe5 Nxe5 15 c4 Nxf3+ 16 gxf3 Bh5! =, Korchnoi–Drashko, Sarajevo 1984. Play continued 17 Rad1 Bg6 18 Qb3 Nd7 19 Kh1 (there is little point to this move; doubling on the d-file immediately is more logical) 19 . . . f6 20 Rd2 Nb6 21 Bc3 Rxd2 22 Bxd2 Rd8 23 Ba5 Rd6 24 Rd1 Qd7 25 Rxd6 Qxd6 (Black has a modest plus because of White's marred pawn structure) 26 Kg2 Kf8 27 Bxb6 axb6 28 Qc3 Ke7 29 f4 Be4+ 30 f3 Bg6 31 Kf2 Kd7 32 Ke1 Kc7 33 Qd2 Qxd2+ 34 Kxd2 Be8 35 Bd3 h6 36 Kc3 37 Be2 Kd6 (Black now has only an apparent advantage—there is no way to make progress) 38 Kd2 Kc7 39 f5 Kd6 40 f4 Be4 41 Bd3 Bc6 42 Kc3 Kc7 43 Kb3 Kd6 44 a4 Kc7 45 Bc2 Kd6 46 Kc3 Kc7 47 Kd2 Kd6 48 Ke2 Draw.

(i) 18 d5 Ne5 19 Bxd7 Nfxd7 20 Qd4 f5 21 f4 exf3 22 Nxf3 Qg6! =, Uhlmann–Szabó, Wageningen 1957.

(j) Also possible are (A) 11 Be2 e5 12 Qc2 Bg4 13 d5!?, Knaak–Prandstetter, Bratislava 1983, and (B) 11 Qe2 e5 12 d5 e4 13 dxc6 Bg4 14 cxb7 Qxb7 15 Qb2 Qxb2 16 Bxb2 exf3 17 h3 Bh5 18 Bb5 fxg2 with an endgame advantage, Hübner–Chandler, Biel 1987.

(k) 13 Nxe5 Nxe5 14 dxe5 Qxe5 15 f3 Bd7! 16 a4 (16 Rd1 Rad8 17 e4 Bc6 18 Bb2 Rd7 =, Evans–Rossolimo, US Chp. 1963) 16 . . . Rac8!? (16 . . . Rad8 led to trouble after 17 e4 Bc6 18 Bc4 Rd7 19 Re1, Beliavsky–Korchnoi, Wijk aan Zee 1984) 17 Re1 c4 18 Bf1 Nd5 19 Bd2 a6 ∞, Flear–Romanishin, Szirak 1986. This is at least more interesting than the rather sterile play that results from the column.

NIMZO-INDIAN DEFENSE
Rubinstein Variation

1 d4 Nf6 2 c4 e6 3 Nc3 Bb4 4 e3 0-0 5 Bd3 d5 6 Nf3 c5 7 0-0 Nc6 8 a3

	25	26	27	28	29	30
	(Bxc3)............		Ba5............		dxc4	
9	(bxc3)		cxd5(h)		Bxc4	
	Qc7........	b6	exd5		Ba5	
10	cxd5(a)	cxd5(e)	dxc5		Bd3(l)	Qd3
	exd5	exd5	Bxc3		cxd4	a6
11	Nh4!	Nd2(f)	bxc3		exd4	Rd1
	Ne7(b)	Be6	Bg4........	Qa5?!	Bb6	b5
12	g3(c)	Bb2	c4	Qc2	Be3	Ba2
	Bh3(d)	c4	Ne5	Qxc5	Nd5	c4(n)
13	Re1	Bc2	Bb2(i)	a4	Nxd5	Qe2
	Ng6	b5	Nxf3+	Re8	exd5	Qe8
14	Ng2	f3	gxf3	Rb1(k)	h3	e4
	c4	a5	Bh3	Bg4	Ne7	e5
15	Bc2	e4	cxd5!	Rb5 ±	Bg5	d5
	Ne4 ±	Qb6(g)	Qxd5(j)		f6(m)	Nd4(o)

(a) (A) 10 Bb2 dxc4 11 Bxc4 e5, see col. 23. (B) 10 Qc2 Na5! 11 cxd5 c4 =, Geller–Petrosian, Amsterdam 1956.

(b) 11 ... Qa5 12 Bb2 Re8 13 Qe1! Qd8 14 Rd1 cxd4 15 cxd4 Ne4 16 f3 also gave Black slightly the worst of it in Vaiser–Makarychev, USSr 1982.

(c) 12 Ra2 Ng6 13 Nxg6 hxg6 14 f3 Bf5 15 Be2 Rac8 ∞, Yusupov–A. Sokolov, match 1986.

(d) 12 ... c4 13 Bc2 Ng6 14 Ng2 Ne4 15 Bb2 ±, Portisch–Rubinetti, Palma de Mallorca 1970. The column is Gligorić–Averbakh, Yugoslavia vs. USSR 1963.

(e) 10 Bb2 Ba6 11 xcd5 Bxd3 12 Qxd3 Qxd5 =.

(f) Other promising continuations are (A) 11 Bb2 c4 12 Bc2 Bg4 13 Qe1! Bxf3 14 gxf3 Qd7 15 Kg2 Rae8 16 Rg1 ±, and (B) 11 Ne5 Qc7 12 Nxc6 Qxc6 13 f3 Be6 14 Qe1 Nd7 15 Ra2 ±.

(g) 16 Kh1 b4 17 e5 Nd7 18 f4 f5 19 g4 ± (Taimanov).

(h) 9 Na4 cxd4 10 exd4 dxc4 11 Bxc4 h6 12 b4 Bc7 13 Bb2 b6 =, Reshevsky–Levenfish, Moscow 1939.

(i) 13 cxd5 Bxf3 14 gxf3 Qxd5 15 Be2 Qxc5 16 Bb2 ±.

(j) 16 Bxf6 gxf6 17 Kh1 (17 Bxh7+ Kxh7 18 Qxd5 Rg8+ ∓) 17 ... Rfd8 18 Rg1+ Kh8 19 Be4! Bg2+ 20 Kxg2 Qg5+ 21 Kh1 Rxd1 22 Raxd1 ±, Beliavsky–Tal, USSR 1975.

(k) *Comments* to Flohr–Landau, Bournemouth 1939.

(l) Other tries: (A) 10 dxc5?! Bxc3 11 bxc3 Qxd1 12 Rxd1 Ne4 13 a4 Na5 14 Ba2 Nxc3 ∓, Ilivitsky–Bisguier, Göteborg 1955. (B) 10 Ne2 cxd4 11 exd4 h6 =. (C) 10 Ba2 a6 11 Bb1

507

Bb6 12 Qc2 g6 13 dxc5 Bxc5 14 b4 Be7 15 Bb2 $\pm$, Polugayevsky–Karpov, match 1974.

(m) 16 Bd2 Bf5 17 Bb4 Bxd3 18 Qxd3 Re8 =, Gligorić–Karpov, Hastings 1971–72.

(n) 12 . . . Bb6 13 h3 Bb7 14 dxc5 Qxd3 15 Rxd3 Bxc5 16 b4 Be7 =, Korchnoi–Polugaevsky, USSR Ch. 1973.

(o) 16 Nxd4 exd4 17 Rxd4 Qe5 18 Be3 Ng4 19 f4 Qb8 20 Rad1 Nxe3 21 Qxe3 Bb6. White has an attack for his lost material, Gligorić–Gheorghiu, Skopje 1968.

NIMZO-INDIAN DEFENSE

Rubinstein Variation

1 d4 Nf6 2 c4 e6 3 Nc3 Bb4 4 e3 0-0 5 Bd3 d5 6 Nf3 c5 7 0-0 Nc6 8 a3 dxc4 9 Bxc4

	31	32	33	34	35	36
	(Ba5)	cxd4				
10	(Qd3)	axb4........	exd4			
	(a6)	dxc3	Be7(e)			
11	Ne4	bxc3(c)	Re1........	Qd3		Bf4(l)
	b5	Qc7	b6(f)	a6	b6	a6
12	Nxf6†	Qb3	Bd3	Bg5	Bg5	Ba2
	Qxf6(a)	b6	Bb7	b5	Bb7	b5
13	Qe4	Be2	Bc2	Ba2	Rfe1(j)	d5
	Bb7	Bb7	Re8	Bb7(h)	Nd5	exd5
14	Bd3	Rd1	Qd3	Rad1	Bxd5	Nxd5
	g6	Rfd8	g6	Rc8	exd5	Nxd5
15	dxc5	Bb2	Bh6	Rfe1	Bxe7	Bxd5
	Nb4!(b)	Rxd1†(d)	Rc8(g)	Nd5(i)	Nxe7(k)	Bb7 =

(a) 12 ... gxf6?! 13 Qe4 Bb7 14 Bd3 f5 15 Qf4 c4 is unclear according to Larsen, but the weakening of the pawn structure is suspect.

(b) 16 Qe5 Qxe5 17 Nxe5 Nxd3 18 Nxd3 Rfd8 19 Ne5 Bc7 20 Nf3 Bxf3 21 gxf3 a5! 22 Rb1 b4 =, Timman–Tal, Hastings 1973–74.

(c) 11 Qxd8 Rxd8 12 bxc3 b6 13 Bb2 Bb7 14 Be2 gives White a small pull in the endgame. Black can avoid this by the move order 8 . . . cxd4 9 axb4 dxc3 10 bxc3 dxc4 11 Bxc4 Qc7.

(d) 16 Rxd1 Rd8 17 Rxd8† Qxd8 18 c4 $\pm$, Stein–Ivkov, USSR–Yugoslavia 1963.

(e) 10 . . . Bxc3 11 bxc3 Qc7 12 Qe2 Na5 13 Bd3 Qxc3? 14 Bd2 Qc7 15 Qe5! wins.

(f) 11 . . . a6 12 Ba2 b5 13 d5! exd5 14 Nxd5 Nxd5 15 Qxd5 Bb7 16 Qh5 $\pm$, Benjamin–Dlugy, US Chp. 1985.

(g) 16 Rad1 Bf8 17 Bg5 Be7 18 Ba4 $\pm$, Tarjan–Browne, US 1977.

(h) 13 . . . Ra7 14 Rad1 Rd7 15 Bb1 g6 16 Rfe1 b4 17 axb4 Nxb4 18 Qd2 was also bad for Black in Fedorowicz–Dlugy, match 1984. White quickly achieved a dominating position: 18 . . . Nc6 19 Bh6 Re8 20 Bc2! (maneuvering the bishop to the a4-e8 diagonal gives White the extra pressure needed for a breakthrough) 20 . . . Bb7 21 Ba4 Qb6 22 d5! exd5 (22 . . . Nxd5 23 Nxd5 Rxd5 24 Qc3 f6 25 Rxd5 exd5 26 Nd4 +, Fedorowicz) 23 Bg5 Qd8 24 Bxf6? (24 Nd4, using the pin, would have won; White overlooked Black's 26th move) 24 . . . Bxf6 25 Rxe8† Qxe8 26 Nxd5 Kf8! (the only defense) 27 Qc1 Qe6 28 Nxf6 Draw.

(i) 16 Nxd5 Bxg5 17 Nb6 $\pm$, Bondarevsky–Sokolsky, USSR Chp. 1950.

(j) 13 Rac1 Rc8 14 Rfd1 Nd5 15 Bxd5 Bxg5 16 Nxg5 Qxg5 =, Portisch–Karpov, Milan 1975.

(k) 16 Ng5 Ng6 17 h4 $\pm$ (Averbakh).

(l) 11 Bg5 Nd5 12 Bxe7 Ncxe7 is quick equality for Black. The column is Bronstein–Boleslavsky, match 1950.

NIMZO-INDIAN DEFENSE

Rubinstein Variation

1 d4 Nf6 2 c4 e6 3 Nc3 Bb4 4 e3 0-0 5 Bd3 d5 6 Nf3 c5 7 0-0 dxc4 8 Bxc4 (Gligorić Variation)

	37	38	39	40	41	42
	Nbd7					Qe7
9	Qe2		a3	Bd3(i)	a3!	
	b6	a6?!	cxd4	b6	Ba5	
10	d5(a)	a3(d)	exd4(g)	a3	Qc2	Qd3(m)
	Bxc3	Ba5	Bxc3	cxd4	Bd7	Nbd7
11	dxe6	Bd3(e)	bxc3	exd4(j)	Ba2	Ne4
	Ne5(b)	b5	Qc7	Bxc3	Rc8	Bc7
12	exf7†	b4!	Qe2	bxc3	Bd2	b4
	Kh8	cxb4	Nb6	Bb7	cxd4	Nxe4
13	bxc3	axb4	Bd3	Re1	exd4	Qxe4
	Bg4	Bxb4	Nbd5(h)	Qc7	h6(k)	Nf6
14	e4(c)	Nxb5	c4	Bd2	Rfe1	Qh4
		Bb7(f)	Nf4 =	Rad8 =	Qd8(l)	cxd4(n)

(a) 10 Rd1 cxd4 11 exd4 Bb7 and now: (A) 12 d5 Bxc3 13 dxe6 Bxf3 14 gxf3 fxe6 15 bxc3 Qc7 16 Bxe6† Kh8 17 Be3 Nc5 =, Gligorić–Unzicker, Leipzig 1960. (B) 12 Bg5!? Bxc3! (12 ... Qc7? 13 Nb5!) 13 bxc3 Qc7 14 Bd3 Qxc3 15 Ne5 Qa5! 16 Qe3! with compensation for the pawn, Azmayparashvili–Farago, Albania 1984.

(b) 11 ... Ba5 12 exd7 Qxd7 13 Rd1 ±, Gligorić–Matanović, Titograd 1965. Black's bishop on a5 is badly misplaced.

(c) (A) 14 ... Qe7 and now: 15 Re1 b5! 16 Bxb5 Nh5 17 Bg5 Qe6 18 Qe3 Bxf3 19 gxf3 Qxf7. Chances are equal in this sharp position. (B) 14 ... Nh5 15 Bd5 Bxf3 16 gxf3 Qh4 17 f4! Nxf4 18 Bxf4 Qxf4 19 Qe3! ±, Knaak–Sax, Thessaloniki 1988.

(d) 10 a4 Qc7 11 Na2 b5 12 Bd3 Ba5 13 b4! cxb4 14 axb5 b3 15 Ba3 bxa2 16 Bxf8 also worked out well for White in Azmayparashvili–A. Sokolov, USSR 1984.

(e) (A) 11 dxc5?! Bxc3. (B) 11 Rd1 b5 12 Bd3 Bb7 =.

(f) 15 Ba3 Bxa3 16 Nxa3 ±, Taimanov–Kuzmin, USSR 1973.

(g) 10 axb4 dxc3 11 bxc3 Qc7 12 Qb3 Nb6 13 Be2 e5 14 c4 Be6 =, Timman–Keene, Reykjavik 1976.

(h) 13 ... Qxc3 14 Bg5 Nbd5 15 Rfc1 Qa5 16 Qe5 (Euwe) gives White more than enough for the pawn. The column is Gligorić–Filip, Amsterdam 1954.

(i) 9 Qd3 a6 10 a4 b6 11 Na2 b5! 12 axb5 axb5 13 Bxb5 Bb7 14 b3 cxd4 15 Bb2 Bd6 16 Qxd4 Nc5 (as played by Gligorić) with good compensation for the pawn.

(j) 11 axb4 dxc3 12 bxc3 Bb7 13 Qe2 Bxf3 14 gxf3 Ne5 15 Ba6 Qd5! with no problems for Black, Larsen–Sax, Linares 1983.

(k) 13 ... Bc6 14 d5! Bxc3 (14 ... exd5 15 Nxd5 Nxd5 16 Bxa5 ±) 15 dxc6 Bxd2 16 cxb7 Qxb7 17 Qxd2 ±, Portisch–Gheorghiu, Skopje 1968.

(l) 15 Qd3 Nc6 16 Rad1 Be8 ± (Taimanov).

(m) Alternatives are (A) 10 Bd3 Nbd7 11 Ne4 Nxe4 12 Bxe4 Bb6 13 Bc2 Rd8 14 Qe2 Nf8 15 dxc5 Qxc5 16 b4 Qh5 =, Gligorić–Smyslov, Moscow 1967. (B) 10 Qe2 Nc6 11 Rd1 Rd8 12 Rb1 Bd7 13 Bd2 Bb6 14 dxc5 Bxc5 =, Liberzon–Smyslov, Moscow 1963.

(n) 15 exd4 Nd5 with equal chances, Knaak–Smyslov, Berlin 1979.

NIMZO-INDIAN DEFENSE

Rubinstein Variation

1 d4 Nf6 2 c4 e6 3 Nc3 Bb4 4 e3 0-0 5 Bd3 d5 6 Nf3 c5 7 0-0 (Gligorić Variation)

	43	44	45	46	47	48
	(dxc4)............................Nbd7...................b6					
8	(Bxc4)			a3	cxd5	cxd5
	Bd7.........b6(c)			Ba5	exd5	exd5
9	Qe2(a)	Qe2........a3		Bd2(h)	a3	dxc5
	Bc6	Bb7	cxd4	dxc4	Ba5(j)	bxc5
10	Rd1	Rd1	axb4	Bxc4	b4!	Ne2
	Qe7	cxd4(d)	dxc3	cxd4	cxb4	Bb7(l)
11	a3	exd4(e)	Qxd8	exd4	Nb5	b3
	Bxc3	Bxc3	Rxd8	a6	Nb8(k)	Nbd7
12	bxc3	bxc3	bxc3	a4	axb4	Bb2
	Nbd7	Qc7	Ne4	b6	Bxb4	Ba5
13	a4	Bd3!?	Bb2	Qe2	Rxa7 ±	Ng3
	Rfc8(b)	Qxc3(f)	Bb7(g)	Bb7(i)		g6 ±

(a) Only equalizing are (A) 9 Bd3 Bc6 10 a3 cxd4 11 exd4 Be7 12 Re1 Nbd7 13 Bc2 a6 14 Qd3 Re8 15 Bg5 g6 =, Gligorić–Najdorf, Los Angeles 1963; and (B) 9 a3 Bxc3 10 bxc3 Bc6 11 Ne5 Bd5 12 Be2 cxd4 13 cxd4 Nc6 =, Taimanov–Wade, Buenos Aires 1960.

(b) 14 Bb3 Qe8 15 c4 cxd4 16 exd4 Nb6 17 a5 Bxf3 18 gxf3 Nbd7 ±. Black's play in this column is a speculative idea of Taimanov's.

(c) 8 ... cxd4 9 exd4 b6 10 Bg5 (10 Qe2 Bb7 11 Rd1 transposes to the column) 10 ... Bb7 11 Rc1 Nbd7 12 Bg4 Rc8 13 Bd3 Be7 14 Qe2 Nh5 15 Bxe7 Qxe7 16 Be4 Nf4 17 Qe3 Bxe4 18 Qxe4 Ng6 19 Qb7 Nb8 20 Qxe7 Draw, Beliavsky–Polugaevsky, USSR Chp. 1983.

(d) Safer is 10 ... Qc8 11 Bd2 cxd4 12 Nxd4 Nc6 13 Nf3 Qb8 =, Bilek–Geller, Havana 1965.

(e) 11 Nxd4 Qe7 12 Bd2 Nc6! 13 Nxc6 Bxc6 14 a3 Bc5 15 e4 e5 =, Korchnoi–Kindermann, Zürich 1984.

(f) 14 Bb2 Qc7 15 d5 with a sharp attacking position for the pawn, Beliavsky–Kasparov, match 1983.

(g) 14 Rfd1 Nc6 15 Rxd8† Rxd8 16 Nd4 a5 17 f3 Nd6 18 Nxc6 Bxc6 19 Bf1 ±, Gligorić–Filip, Varna 1962. White has the bishop pair in the endgame.

(h) (A) 9 Qc2 dxc4 10 Bxc4 cxd4 11 exd4 Bxc3! 12 Qxc3 b6 13 Bf4 Bb7 14 Qd3 Nd5 = (Taimanov). (B) 9 Qe2 a6 10 a4 Qe7 11 Rd1 dxc4 12 Bxc4 e5 =.

(i) 14 Rfd1 Re8 15 Ne5 Bxc3 16 Bxc3 Nd5 =, Gligorić–Averbakh, Titovo Užice 1966.

(j) 9 ... Bxc3 10 bxc3 c4 11 Bc2 Re8 12 Nd2 Qa5 13 Bb2 b5 14 Re1 Bb7 15 f3 ±, F. Olafsson–Barcza, Prague 1954.

(k) 11 . . . bxa3? 12 Bxa3 Re8 13 Nd6 Re6 14 Ng5 is winning. The column is Tukmakov–Tal, USSR 1970.

(l) On 10 . . . Bg4 Euwe gives 11 b3 Nc6 12 Bb2 d4 13 exd4 Bxf3 14 gxf3 Nxd4 15 Nxd4 cxd4 16 Bxd4 Nh5 17 Kh1 Qh4 18 Rg1 Rad8 19 Rg4 ±. The column is Gligorić–Szabó, Moscow 1956.

NIMZO-INDIAN DEFENSE

Rubinstein Variation

1 d4 Nf6 2 c4 e6 3 Nc3 Bb4 4 e3 0-0

	49	50	51	52	53	54
5	(Bd3)				Ne2	
	(d5)				d5	Re8
6	(Nf3)		a3(g)		a3(l)	a3
	b6(a)		Bxc3(h)		Be7(m)	Bf8
7	0-0		bxc3		cxd5(n)	d5(s)
	Bb7		c5	dxc4!	exd5(o)	exd5
8	a3	cxd5	cxd5	Bxc4	g3(p)	cxd5
	Bd6(b)	exd5	exd5	c5	c6	c5
9	b4	Bd2(d)	Ne2	Ne2(k)	Bg2	Ng3
	dxc4	Bd6(e)	b6(i)	Nc6	a5(q)	d6
10	Bxc4	Nb5	0-0	a4	0-0	Bd3
	Nbd7	Be7	Ba6	Qc7	Na6	Nbd7
11	Bb2	Rc1	Bxa6	Ba3	Qd3	0-0
	a5(c)	c6(f)	Nxa6(j)	b6 =	Nc7(r)	a6(t)

(a) There are transpositional possibilities: 6 . . . c6 transposes to the Semi-Slav Defense, Romih Variation; 6 . . . Nc6 to the Queen's Gambit, Ragozin Variation.

(b) (A) 8 . . . Bxc3 9 bxc3 dxc4 10 Bxc4 Nc6 11 Re1 Na5 12 Bd3 Be4 is also a good try for Black. (B) 8 . . . Be7 transposes to col. 65 note (o).

(c) (A) 11 . . . Qe7?! 12 Nb5 wins the bishop for a knight. (B) 11 . . . a5 12 b5 Qe7 and Black is equal (planning . . . e5), F. Olafsson–Bisguier, Stockholm 1962.

(d) 9 Ne5 Bd6 10 f4 c5 11 Rf3 g6! 12 Bd2 Nc6 13 Rh3 cxd4 =, Knaak–Petrosian, Tallinn, 1979.

(e) 9 . . . Nbd7 10 Rc1 a6 11 Na4 Bd6 12 b4 Ne4 =, Kuzmin–Gulko, USSR 1975.

(f) 12 Nc3 c5 13 Ne5 Nc6 14 Qa4 Nxe5 15 dxe5 Ne4 with a balanced position, Ivkov–Filip, Palma de Mallorca 1970.

(g) The Botvinnik Variation. If 6 Nge2 dxc4 7 Bxc4 e5 8 0-0 Nc6 9 d5 Ne7 10 e4 Ng6 11 a3 Bc5 12 b4 Bb6 13 Bg5 Bd7 14 Qd2 h6 15 Be3 Nh5 is unclear, Groszpeter–Rohde, New York 1988.

(h) A good alternative is (A) 6 . . . dxc4 7 Bxc4 Bd6 8 Qc2 Nbd7 9 Nf3 when 9 . . . c5 and 9 . . . a6 were both used successfully in the 1986 match Vaganian–A. Sokolov. (B) 6 . . . Be7 transposes into column 65.

(i) 9 . . . Nc6 10 0-0 Re8 11 f3 Bd7 12 Ng3 Qc7 13 Ra2 ±, Rubinetti–Najdorf, Mar del Plata 1971.

(j) 12 f3 Nc7 13 Ng3 Re8 14 Re1 Qd7 15 e4 ±, Vaganian–Antoshin, USSR Chp. 1970.

(k) 9 Nf3 transposes into columns 19–30. The column is Botvinnik–Reshevsky, US–USSR match 1946.

(l) 6 cxd5 exd5 7 g3 Nc6!? 8 Bg2 Ne7 9 0-0 Bd6 results in equality, D. Gurevich–Browne, New York 1987.

(m) 6 . . . Bd6?! 7 c5 Be7 8 b4 b6 9 Nf4 bxc5 10 bxc5 Ba6 11 Bxa6 Nxa6 12 0-0 Nb8 13 Bd2 Nc6 14 Qa4 Qd7 15 Nd3 ±, Saidy–Fischer, US Chp. 1961.

(n) 7 Nf4 dxc4 8 Bxc4 c5 9 d5 e5 10 Nfe2 Ne8 11 Ng3 Nd6 =, Lavdansky–Estrin, USSR 1962.

(o) 7 . . . Nxd5 8 Qc2 Nd7 9 g3 (9 Ng3 c5 10 Bd3 N5f6 11 0-0 b6 12 dxc5 Nxc5 =, Spassky–Smyslov, Amsterdam 1956) 9 . . . Nxc3 10 Nxc3 c5 11 dxc5 Nxc5 12 b4 Nd7 13 Bg2 a5! =, D. Gurevich–Korchnoi, Beersheva 1987.

(p) White has other tries here, but Black seems safe in all lines: (A) 8 Ng3 c5! 9 dxc5 Bxc5 =. (B) 8 b4 c6 9 Bb2 Nbd7 10 Ng3 Nb6 11 Bd3 Re8 =, Kholmov–Smyslov, USSR 1969. (C) 8 Nf4 c6 9 Bd3 a5 10 0-0 Na6 =.

(q) 9 . . . Na6 10 0-0 Nc7 (Christiansen–Kavalek, match 1987) 11 f3!? (Christiansen).

(r) 12 f3 c5! 13 Rd1 Ne6 =, Bukhman–Tal, USSR Chp. 1967.

(s) 7 e4 d5 8 e5 Nfd7 9 cxd5 exd5 10 Be3 c5 11 f4 Nc6 12 dxc5 Bxc5 13 Bxc5 Nxc5 14 b4 Ne6 15 Nxd5 Ned4! with even chances, Nemet–Dizdar, Liechtenstein 1988.

(t) 12 a4 Qc7 13 e4 (Marin-Benjamin, Szirak 1987); now 13 . . . g6, playing as in a Benoni Defense, would maintain equality.

NIMZO-INDIAN DEFENSE

Rubinstein Variation

1 d4 Nf6 2 c4 e6 3 Nc3 Bb4 4 e3 b6 (Fischer Variation)

	55	56	57	58	59	60
5	Ne2..Bd3					
	Ba6....................		Bb7........	Ne4	Bb7	
6	a3	Ng3	a3	Qc2(i)	Nf3	
	Bxc3†(a)	Bxc3†(d)	Bxc3†(g)	Bb7	Ne4........	0-0
7	Nxc3	bxc3	Nxc3	a3	0-0!	0-0
	d5	d5	d5(h)	Bxc3†	Bxc3(k)	c5(n)
8	b3(b)	Ba3(e)	cxd5	Nxc3	bxc3	Na4
	0-0	Bxc4	exd5	f5(j)	f5(l)	cxd4
9	Be2	Bxc4	b4	d5	Ne1	exd4
	Nc6	dxc4	0-0	Nxc3	0-0	Be7
10	a4	0-0	Bd3	Qxc3	f3	Re1
	dxc4	Qd5	Nbd7	Qe7	Nf6	d6
11	Ba3	e4	0-0	Be2	Nc2	b4
	Re8	Qb5	c5	0-0	c5	Nbd7
12	b4	Qf3	bxc5	0-0 ±	Bd2	Bb2
	Ne7(c)	Nbd7(f)	bxc5 ±		Qe7(m)	a5(o)

(a) 6 ... Be7 7 Nf4 d5 8 cxd5 Bxf1 9 Kxf1 Nxd5 (9 ... exd5 10 g4 ±) 10 Ncxd5 exd5 11 Qh5 c6 12 Ne6 g6 13 Qe5 Bf6 14 Nxd8† Bxe5 15 Nxc6 16 dxe5 ±, Ruderfer–Veselovsky, USSR 1980.

(b) 8 Qf3 0-0 9 Be2 c5 10 dxc5 Nbd7! =, Taimanov–Spassky, USSR Chp. 1961.

(c) 13 b5 Bb7 14 0-0 with a small pull for White (Fischer).

(d) (A) 6 ... 0-0 7 e4 d5 (7 ... Nc6 8 Bd3 9 d5 Bxc3† 10 bxc3 Ne7 11 Bg5 Ne8 12 h4!, Knaak) 8 cxd5 Bxc3† 9 bxc3 Bxf1 10 Kxf1 exd5 11 e5 ±. (B) 6 ... h5 7 h4 Bb7 8 Qd3 d5 9 cxd5 exd5 10 Qc2 c5 11 a3 cxd4 12 axb4 dxc3 13 bxc3 Nbd7 14 Nf5 0-0 15 Bb2 Ne5 16 c4! ±, Knaak–Bronstein, Tallinn 1979.

(e) 8 Qf3 0-0 9 e4?! dxe4 10 Nxe4 Nxe4 11 Qxe4 Qd7! 12 Ba3 Re8 13 Bd3 f5 14 Qxa8 Nc6 15 Qxe8† Qxe8 16 0-0 Na5 17 Rae1 Bxc4 18 Bxc4 Nxc4 19 Bc1 c5 20 dxc5 bxc5 21 Bf4 h6 22 Re2 g5 23 Be5 Qd8 24 Rfe1 Kf7 25 h3 f4 26 Kh2 a6 27 Re4 Qd5 28 h4? Ne3! 29 R1xe3 fxe3 30 Rxe3 Qxa2 31 Rf3† Ke8 32 Bg7 Qc4 33 hxg5 hxg5 34 Rf8† Kd7 35 Ra8 Kc6 36 Resigns, Portisch–Fischer, Santa Monica 1966.

(f) 13 Rfe1 ± (Christiansen).

(g) 6 ... Be7 7 d5 0-0 8 e4 Re8 9 Ng3 exd5 10 cxd5 ±.

(h) 7 ... 0-0 8 Bd3! c5 (8 ... Bxg2 9 Rg1 Bb7 10 e4 ±) 9 d5 exd5 10 cxd5 16 11 e4 d6 12 0-0 ±, Bronstein–Trifunović, Amsterdam 1954. The column is Gligorić–Andersson, Wijk aan Zee 1971.

(i) 6 Bd2 Nxd2 7 Qxd2 Bb7 8 a3 Be7 9 d5 exd5, D. Gurevich–de Firmian, US Chp. 1986, and now 10 Nxd5 is slightly better for White.

(j) 8 . . . Nxc3 9 Qxc3 0-0 10 b4 $\pm$. The column is a recommendation of Smyslov's.

(k) 7 . . . Nxc3 8 bxc3 Bxc3 9 Rb1 Nc6 10 Rb3 Ba5 11 e4 makes life dangerous for Black, Gligorić–Larsen, Lugano 1970.

(l) 8 . . . Nxc3 9 Qc2 Bxf3 10 gxf3 Qg5† 11 Kh1 Qh5 12 Rg1 Qxf3† 13 Rg2 f5 14 Ba3! Ne4 15 Rf1 Rg8 16 Be2 Qh3 17 f3 Nf5 18 d5! $\pm$ Keres–Spassky, match 1965.

(m) 13 Qe2 d6 14 e4 $\pm$, Gligorić–Kuzmin, Bled 1979.

(n) (A) 7 . . . Bxc3 8 bxc3 Be4 9 Be2 c5 10 Nd2 Bg6 11 Nb3 $\pm$, Gligorić–Bisguier, US 1972. (B) 7 . . . d5 transposes to columns 49 and 50.

(o) 13 a3 (or 13 b5 d5 =) 13 . . . axb4 14 axb4 b5! 15 cxb5 Nb6 =, Kane–Kaplan, US 1970.

NIMZO-INDIAN DEFENSE

Rubinstein Variation

1 d4 Nf6 2 c4 e6 3 Nc3 Bb4 4 e3

	61	62	63	64	65	66
	c5..d5..........Nc6					
5	Ne2 ....Bd3 cxd4........d5(d)		Nc6		a3 Be7(l)	Ne2(p) d5
6	exd4 d5(a)	a3 Bxc3†	Nf3(f) Bxc3†(g)	(Hübner System)	Nf3 0-0	a3 Be7
7	c5(b) Ne4	Nxc3 cxd4	bxc3 d6		Bd3(m) b6(n)	cxd5 exd5
8	Bd2 Nxd2	exd4 dxc4	e4 ....0-0(j) e5	e5	0-0(o) c5	Nf4 0-0(q)
9	Qxd2 a5	Bxc4 Nc6	d5 Ne7	Ng5 0-0	b3 Nc6	Be2 Bf5
10	a3 Bxc3	Be3 0-0	Nh4(h) h6	f4 exd4	Bb2 cxd4	g4 Be6
11	Nxc3 a4(c)	0-0 b6(e)	f4 Ng6(i)	cxd4 cxd4(k)	exd4 Ba6 =	g5 Nd7 ±

(a) The modern line is 6 . . . 0-0 7 a3 Be7 8 d5 exd5 9 cxd5 Re8 (9 . . . Bc5 10 b4 Bb6 11 Na4 d6 12 Nxb6 axb6 13 Ng3 ±, Torre–Karpov, London 1984) and now: (A) 10 g3 Bc5 11 Bg2 d6 12 h3 Bf5 13 0-0 (Kasparov–Csom, Baku 1980) 13 . . . Ne4! =. (B) 10 Be3 Ng4 11 Bd4 Nh6! ∞ (Adorjan). (C) 10 d6 Bf8 11 g3 b6 12 Bg2 Nc6 13 Nb5 Ba6 14 a4 Ne4 ∞, D. Gurevich–Adorjan, New York 1984.

(b) 7 a3 Be7 8 c5 0-0 9 g3 b6 10 b4 bxc5 11 dxc5 a5 12 Rb1 Nc6 13 Bg2 Rb8! 14 Bf4?! axb4 15 Bxb8 bxc3 ∓, Salov–M. Gurevich, Leningrad 1987.

(c) 12 Bd3 b6 13 0-0 bxc5 14 dxc5 Qa5 =, Gligorić–Gheorghiu, Baden 1980.

(d) Less respected moves are (A) 5 . . . d6 6 a3 Ba5 7 Rb1 Nc6 8 b4! Bc7 ±, Evans–Keres, San Antonio 1972. (B) 5 . . . b6 6 a3 Ba5 7 Qa4 Nc6 8 g3 ± (Romanishin).

(e) White is slightly more active, Korchnoi–Karpov, World Chp. 1978.

(f) (A) Interesting is 6 Nge2 cxd4 7 exd4 d5 8 cxd5 dxd5 (8 . . . Nxd5 9 a3 Bd6 10 Ne4 Be7 11 0-0 0-0 12 Bb1 Re8 is reasonable, Marin–Beliavsky, Thessaloniki 1988) 9 0-0 Qd8 10 Bc2 Be7 11 a3 with chances for an initiative, Timman–Kir. Georgiev, Linares 1988. (B) 6 a3 transposes to column 51 or into the Sämisch Variation, cols. 67–84.

(g) The Hübner System, now regarded as Black's most solid defense to the Rubinstein Variation, consists of 4 . . . c5, 5 . . . Nc6 and 6 . . . Bxc3. If 6 . . . d6 7 Qc2 e5 8 dxe5 dxe5 9 Nd2 Bxc3 10 Qxc3 ±, Petrosian–Romanishin, USSR 1976. Also see note (i).

(h) 10 Nd2 Bd7 11 Nf1 Qc7 12 Ng3 0-0-0 =, Gligorić–Andersson, Tilburg 1978.

(i) 12 Nxg6 fxg6 13 0-0 (13 fxe5? leaves the position too blocked for White's bishops, Spassky–Fischer, World Chp. 1972) 13 . . . 0-0 14 f5 b5 15 g4 Qa5 =. 11 g3 g5 12 Ng5

Qa5 13 Qb3 Bh3, Najdorf–Hübner, Wijk aan Zee 1971, was one of the stem-games of this variation.

(j) 8 Nd2 e5 9 Nb3 0-0 10 0-0 Qe7 =, Portisch–Seirawan, Toluca 1982.

(k) 12 exd4 Nxd4 13 Bb2?! (13 Nxh7 Nxh7 14 Bxh7† Kxh7 15 Qxd4 Qb6 =, Christiansen–de Firmian, US Chp. 1984) 13 . . . Nf5 14 Qc2 Ne3 15 Bxh7† Kh8 16 Qd3 Nxf1 17 Rxf1 Bg4! ∓, C. Hansen–Hjartarson, Gausdal 1985.

(l) 5 . . . Bxc3† transposes to the Sämisch Variation or to column 51.

(m) 7 b4 Nbd7 8 Bb2 c6 9 Qc2 dxc4 10 Bxc4 a5 11 b5 Nb6 12 Bd3 cxb5 13 Bxb5 Bd7 =, Korchnoi–Reshevsky, Sousse 1967.

(n) 7 . . . dxc4?! 8 Bxc4 c5 9 dxc5 ±.

(o) 8 cxd5! exd5 9 b4 Bb7 10 0-0 is the same as column 50 but with the black bishop on e7 instead of d6 where it is more active. The column is Szabo–Keres, Budapest 1952.

(p) 5 Bd3 e5 6 Ne2 d5 7 cxd5 Nxd5 ∞.

(q) 8 . . . Bf5 9 Qb3 Na5 10 Qa4† Nc6 (10 . . . c6?! 11 Bd2, eyeing a5) 11 Ba6 bxa6 12 Qxc6† Bd7 13 Qxa6 Bd6 ∞, Mohrlok–Hecht, Büsum 1968, is a more interesting (if speculative) way to play. The column is Golenishchev–Aleshin, USSR 1952.

NIMZO-INDIAN DEFENSE
Sämisch Variation

1 d4 Nf6 2 c4 e6 3 Nc3 Bb4 4 a3 Bxc3† 5 bxc3 c5 6 e3

	67	68	69	70	71	72
	0-0...b6 ....Nc6(q)					
7	Bd3				Bd3(n)	Bd3
	Nc6(a) b6				Bb7	e5
8	Ne2(b)			e4	f3	Ne2
	b6......................d6(i)			Bb7	Nc6	e4
9	e4(c)		e4(j)	Bg5	Ne2	Bb1
	Ne8		e5	h6	0-0(o)	b6
10	0-0 ....Be3(f)		0-0(k)	h4!	e4	Ng3
	Ba6	Ba6!	Nh5	d6	Ne8	Ba6
11	Qa4(d)	Ng3(g)	Be3	e5	0-0	f3(r)
	Qc8	Na5	Qe7	dxe5	Rc8	Bxc4
12	Be3	Qe2	f4	dxe5	Be3	Nf5
	Na5	Rc8	Nxf4	Be4	Na5	0-0
13	dxc5	Rc1	Nxf4	Rh3	dxc5	Nd6
	d6!(e)	Nd6(h)	exf4(l)	Bxd3(m)	bxc5(p)	Bd3 =

(a) This position may also be reached by 6 . . . Nc6 7 Bd3 0-0 or 5 . . . 0-0 6 e3 c5 7 Bd3 Nc6, as well as by 4 e3 0-0 5 a3, etc., or 4 e3 c5 5 a3, etc.

(b) (A) 8 e4 cxd4 9 cxd4 Nxd4 10 e5 Qa5† 11 Kf1 Ne8 (11 . . . Qxe5? 12 Bb2) 12 Bd2 Qd8 13 Bb4 d6 14 Bxh7† Kxh7 15 Qxd4 a5 16 Bxd6 Nxd6 17 exd6 Bd7 18 Nf3 f6 = (Euwe). (B) 8 Nf3?! d6 9 e4 e5 and Black is a tempo ahead in a Hübner System (cols. 63–64), since White has played a3, a useless move here.

(c) 9 Ng3 Ba6 10 0-0 Na5 11 Qe2 Rc8 12 d5 exd5 13 cxd5 Bxd3 14 Qxd3 Nb3 15 Rb1 c4 = (Taimanov).

(d) 11 f4 Na5 12 f5 f6 13 Nf4 cxd4 =, Timman–Polugaevsky, Tilburg 1983.

(e) 14 Ng3 dxc5 15 e5 f5 =, Szabó–Portisch, Hungary 1959.

(f) 10 e5 f5 11 exf6 Qxf6 12 Be3 cxd4 13 cxd4 Ba6 14 Qc2 g6 15 0-0 ±, Averbakh–Taimanov, USSR Chp. 1948. But 10 . . . Ba6, delaying . . . f5, looks better.

(g) 11 dxc5 Ne5 12 Bd4 Nxd3 13 Qd3 bxc5 14 Bxc5 d6 15 Bb4 Rc8 wins back the pawn with advantage for Black, Zilber–Koblents, USSR 1964.

(h) 14 e5 cxd4 15 Bxd4 Nf5 16 Bxf5 exf5 17 Bxf5 Qg5 18 Ne3 Nxc4 ∓ (Taimanov).

(i) (A) 8 . . . d5 transposes to the Rubinstein Variation, col. 51. (B) 8 . . . e5!? 9 e4 cxd4 10 cxd4 11 0-0 Ng4 12 Nxd4 Nxd4 13 Qxg4 d5 14 Qh5 dxc4 15 Bxc4 Be6 and White has only a minimal advantage, Hübner–P. Nikolić, Tilburg 1987.

(j) 9 0-0 e5 10 f3 b6 11 d5 Na5 12 Ng3 Ba6 13 Qe2 e4! 14 Nxe4 Nxe4 15 fxe4 Nb3 =.

(k) 10 d5 Ne7 11 f3 Ne8 12 g4 Ng6 13 Be3 Nh4 14 0-0 ±, Barczay–Kovacs, Budapest 1970.

(l) 14 Rxf4 f5 (Balashov–Antoshin, USSR 1969) 15 Qf3 g5 16 Rxf5 Bxf5 17 exf5 ±.

(m) 14 Rxd3 Qc7 15 Bxf6 ±, Keres–Reshevsky, Zürich 1953.

(n) 7 Ne2 Bb7 8 Ng3 0-0 9 Bd3 Bxg2 10 Rg1 Bb7 ∞.

(o) 9 . . . Rc8 10 e4 Na5 11 e5 Ng8 12 0-0 f5 13 d5 Ne7 14 d6 Ng6 15 f4 ±, Beni–O'Kelly, Amsterdam 1954.

(p) 14 Ng3 Nd6 15 Qe2 f6 16 f4 f5 17 e5 Ne8 =, Barbero–Panno, Buenos Aires 1980.

(q) 6 . . . Qa5 7 Bd2 Ne4 8 Bd3 Nxd2 9 Qxd2 ±.

(r) 11 Nxe4 Nxe4 12 Bxe4 Bxc4 13 dxc5 bxc5 14 Bxc6 dxc6 = (Taimanov). The column is Spassky–Tal, USSR Chp. 1958.

NIMZO-INDIAN DEFENSE

Sämisch Variation

1 d4 Nf6 2 c4 e6 3 Nc3 Bb4 4 a3 Bxc3† 5 bxc3 d5

	73	74	75	76	77	78
6	f3..Bg5(n)					
	c5(a)..0-0(k)					c5
7	cxd5				cxd5	cxd5
	Nxd5(b)				exd5	exd5
8	dxc5 ....Qd2 ....Qd3			e3	e3
	f5...........Qa5	Qa5(h)	cxd4(j)	Bf5(l)	Qa5
9	Nh3(c)	e4!	Bb2(i)	cxd4	Ne2	Ne2
	0-0	Nf6(f)	Nc6	Nc6	Nbd7	Ne4
10	c4	Be3	e4	e4	Ng3	Bf4
	Qh4†	0-0	Nb6	Nb6	Bg6	cxd4
11	Nf2(d)	Qb3	a4	Be3	Bd3	exd4
	Nf6	Nc6	0-0	0-0	c5	0-0 =
12	e3	Bb5	Bd3	Rd1	0-0	
	Nc6(e)	Bd7(g)	Rd8 =	f5 =	Re8(m)	

(a) This may commonly be reached also by 5 . . . c5 6 f3 d5.

(b) 7 . . . exd5 8 e3 0-0 9 Bd3 b6 10 Ne2 $\pm$ is similar to column 51.

(c) (A) 9 e4 fxe4 10 Qc2 e3 11 Bd3 Nd7 12 c4 Qa5† 13 Kf1 Nf4 14 Bxe3 Nxd3 15 Qxd3 0-0 = (Polugaevsky). (B) 9 c4 Qf6 10 Bd2 Nc3 11 Qc1 Na4 = (Pachman).

(d) 11 g3 Qxc4 12 e4 Qc3† 13 Bd2 Qe5 $\overline{\overline{\mp}}$ (Taimanov). The point of 11 Nf2 is that in this line (11 . . . Qxc4, etc.) 14 Nd3 wins.

(e) 13 Be2 e5 14 0-0 Be6 15 Rb1 Rf7 ∞, Gutman–Dzanoev, USSR 1972.

(f) (A) 9 . . . Nxc3 10 Qd2 Nc6 11 Bb2 Na4 12 Bxg7 $\pm$, Polugaevsky–Shaposhnikov, USSR 1958. (B) 9 . . . Qxc3† 10 Bd2 Qe5 11 Ne2 Nf6 12 Rc1 $\pm$ (Taimanov). (C) 9 . . . Ne7 10 Be3 Qxc3† 11 Kf2 0-0 12 Ne2 Qa5 13 h4 e5 14 Qc1 Be6 15 h5 $\pm$, Přibyl–Timoshchenko, Czechoslovakia 1973.

(g) 13 Bxc6! Bxc6 14 Ne2 $\pm$ (Taimanov).

(h) Also good is 8 . . . cxd4 9 cxd4 f5 10 e3 Nc6 11 Bd3 0-0 12 Ne2 Qh4† 13 g3 Qh3 14 Bb2 Bd7 =, Portisch–Padevsky, Budapest 1959.

(i) 9 e4 Qxc3 10 Bb2 Qxd2† 11 Kxd2 Ne7 12 dxc5 0-0 13 Rc1 Nec6 14 Ke3 Bd7 15 Bd3 Rc8 16 Ne2 Be8 17 f4 Nd7 =, R. Weinstein–Sherwin, US Chp. 1961. The column is Tal–Barstatis, Riga 1961.

(j) 8 . . . b6 9 e4 Ba6 10 Qc2 Bxf1 11 Kxf1 Ne7 12 Ne2 0-0 =, Keller–Unzicker, Lenzerheide 1964. The column is Darga–Zuidema, Krefeld 1967.

(k) 6 . . . b6 7 Bg5 Ba6 8 e4 Bxc4 9 Bxc4 dxc4 10 Qa4† Qd7 11 Qxc4 $\pm$, Veresov–Yudovich, USSR 1934.

(l) 8 . . . Nh5 9 g3 b6 10 Bd3 f5 11 Ne2 Ba6 12 Bxa6 Nxa6 13 Qd3 Qc8 14 c4 c6 15 0-0 $\pm$, Gheorghiu–Averbakh, Mar del Plata 1965.

(m) 13 Re1 Qc7 14 Bxg6 hxg6 15 e4 $\pm$, Botvinnik–Tal, World Chp. 1960.

(n) 6 e3 c5 7 cxd5 Nxd5 (7 . . . exd5 8 Bd3 0-0 is col. 51) 8 Bd2 Nc6 ∞. The column is analysis by Taimanov.

NIMZO-INDIAN DEFENSE

Sämisch Variation

1 d4 Nf6 2 c4 e6 3 Nc3 Bb4 4 a3 Bxc3† 5 bxc3

	79	80	81	82	83	84
	0-0.....................b6.......................d6.........Ne4					
6	f3 Ne8(a)	e3(c) Re8!?	f3 Ba6		f3 Nfd7!?(i)	e3(j) 0-0(k)
7	e4 b6	Bd3 e5	e4 Nc6........d5?!		e4 Nc6	Ne2 b6
8	Nh3(b) Ba6	Ne2 e4	e5(e) Ng8	Bg5! h6	f4 Qh4†	f3 Nd6
9	e5 Nc6	Bb1 b6	Nh3 Na5	Bh4 Bxc4(h)	g3 Qe7	Ng3 Ba6
10	Bg5 f6	Ng3 Ba6	Qa4 h6(f)	Bxc4 dxc4	Nf3 b6	e4 Bxc4
11	exf6 Nxf6	f3 Bxc4	Nf2 Ne7	Qa4† Qd7	Bd3 Na5	Bxc4 Nxc4
12	Bd3 e5 ±	fxe4 d6(d)	Ne4 0-0(g)	Qxc4 Qc6 ±	0-0 Ba6 ∞	Qd3 d5(l)

(a) 6 ... Nh5 7 Nh3 f5 8 e3 d6 9 Bd3 Nc6 10 0-0 Qe8 11 g4 ±, Karaklajić–O'Kelly, Tunis 1964.

(b) 8 Bd3 Ba6 9 a4 Nc6 10 Ba3 d6 11 f4 Na5 12 Qe2 f5 13 Nf3 dxe4 14 Qxe4 Nf6 15 Qxe6† Kh8 16 0-0 Qe8 ∓ (Taimanov). The column is Dittman–Pachman, Marianské Lázně 1960.

(c) 6 Bg5 c5 7 d5 d6 8 f3 exd5 9 cxd5 Re8 ∓ (Botvinnik and Abramov).

(d) 13 Qf3 Nbd7 =, Spassky–Uusi, USSR 1958.

(e) 8 Bd3 Na5 and now: (A) 9 Qe2 d6 10 Bg5 h6 11 Bh4 Qd7 12 f4 Qa4 13 e5 dxe5 14 fxe5 Nd7 15 Nf3 Bxc4 16 Nd2 Bxd3 17 Qxd3 g5! 18 Bg3 0-0-0 19 0-0 Rhf8 20 Rab1 Qc6 21 c4 Nc5 22 Qe3 Qd7 23 Bf2 Ncb7 24 Ne4 Nxc4 25 Qc3 Qc6 26 Qf3 Qd5 27 Rfc1 Kb8? (Black wins with 27 ... f5! 28 exf6 Nbd6 according to Browne; now the tide turns) 28 Qe2 Nba5 29 Nf6 Qc6 30 Rb4 b5 31 a4 a6 32 axb5 axb5 33 Ne4 Rd5 34 Nc3 Rfd8 35 Nxd5 Rxd5 36 Qh5 Qa6 37 Qxf7 Nc6 38 Rbb1 b4 39 Qxe6 Qb5 40 Qe8† Rd8? 41 Rxb4! Resigns, Zsu. Polgar–Browne, New York 1986. (B) 9 e5 Ng8 10 Ne2 (10 Qa4 is also good—Korn) 10 ... Bxc4 11 Bxc4 Nxc4 12 Qa4 Na5 13 0-0 Qc8 14 Qb5! Qb7 15 Bg5 Qc6 16 Qd3 f6 17 exf6 Nxf6 18 Bxf6 gxf6 19 Rac1 Nc4 20 Nf4! 0-0-0 21 a4 a5 22 d5 Qc5† 23 Kh1 Ne3 24 Rfe1 Nxd5 25 Qa6† Kb8 26 Nd3! with a very aggressive game, Pafnutieff–J. Whitehead, Santa Clara 1986.

(f) 10 ... Ne7 11 Bd3 0-0 12 Bg5! ±, Kotov–Keres, Budapest 1950.

(g) 13 Bf4! and White is better (Gutman).

(h) 9 ... g5 10 Bg3 dxe4 11 fxe4 Nxe4 12 Be5 ±. The column is Lilienthal–Capablanca, Hastings 1934–35.

(i) 6 . . . Qe7 7 e4 e5 8 Bd3 c5 9 Ne2 Nc6 10 0-0 Nd7 11 f4 ±, Enevoldsen–Zimmerman, Amsterdam 1954. The column is Gutman–Taimanov, USSR 1977.

(j) 6 Qc2 f5 7 f3 Qh4† 8 g3 Nxg3 9 hxg3 Qxh1 10 Nh3 d6 11 Kf2 e5 12 Bg2 Qh2 13 Bf4 exf4 14 gxf4 Nc6 15 Rh1 Qxh1 ∓ (Taimanov).

(k) 6 . . . f5 7 Qh5† g6 8 Qh6 d6 9 f3 Nf6 10 e4 e5 11 Bg5 Qe7 12 Bd3 Rf8 (Botvinnik–Tal, World Chp. 1960) 13 Qh4 ±.

(l) 13 0-0 Qd7 14 e5 f5 15 exf6 Rxf6 16 Re1 Qf7 17 Ra2 Nc6 18 Rae2 with a very obscure position, Vaganian–Rashkovsky, USSR 1977.

NIMZO-INDIAN DEFENSE

1 d4 Nf6 2 c4 e6 3 Nc3 Bb4

	85	86	87	88	89	90
4	Bg5 (Leningrad Variation)..................Qb3					
	h6				c6 ....Nc6(r)	
5	Bh4				dxc5	Nf3
	c5				Nc6	d5
6	d5(a)				Nf3(o)	e3(s)
	d6.....................exd5.......b5(k)				Ne4	0-0
7	e3		cxd5	dxe6(l)	Bd2	a3
	Bxc3†(b)		d6	fxe6	Nxc5(p)	dxc4
8	bxc3		e3	cxb5	Qc2	Bxc4
	e5(c)		Nbd7	d5	0-0	Bd6
9	f3..........Qc2(g)		Bd3	e3	a3	Nb5
	Bf5(d)	Nbd7	0-0(i)	0-0	Bxc3	e5
10	Bd3(e)	Bd3	Ne2	Bd3(m)	Bxc3	Nxd6
	Bxd3	Qe7	Ne5	d4	a5	cxd6
11	Qxd3	f3	0-0	exd4	g3	dxe5
	Nbd7(f)	Kd8(h)	Ng6(j)	cxd4(n)	f5(q)	dxe5 =

(a) 6 e3 cxd4 7 exd4 Qa5 8 Qc2 Ne4 $\mp$, Boleslavsky–Taimanov, Leningrad 1945.

(b) 7 ... g5 8 Bg3 Ne4 9 Qc2 Qf6 10 Ne2 exd5 11 0-0-0! Bxc3 12 Nxc3 Nxc3 13 Qxc3 Qxc3 14 bxc3 and White wins his pawn back with great advantage, Timman–Winants, Brussels 1988.

(c) 8 ... Qe7!? 9 Bd3 Nbd7 10 Nf3 e5 11 Nd2 Nf8 (11 ... g5!?) 12 Bxf6 Qxf6 13 0-0 Qe7 14 Qc2 Nd7 15 f4 Nf6 16 Rae1 0-0 17 f5 $\pm$, Timman–Romanishin, Tilburg 1985.

(d) (A) 9 ... g5 10 Bg3 Qe7 11 Qc2 h5 12 h4 g4 13 Bd3 Rg8 14 Ne2 Nbd7 15 a4 Nf8 16 Kd2 Kd8 is roughly equal, Pekarek–Pinter, Warsaw 1987. (B) 9 ... Nbd7 10 Bd3 g5 11 Bg3 h5 ∞, Ree–Rashkovsky, Sochi 1976.

(e) (A) 10 Qb3?! b6 11 h3 Nbd7 12 g4 Bb7 13 Ne2 g5 $\mp$, Timman–Dzindzichashvili, Geneva 1977. (B) 10 e4 Bh7 ∞.

(f) 12 e4 Nf8 13 Rb1 b6 14 Qc2 Ng6 15 Bxf6 Qxf6 16 Qa4† Ke7 =, Böhm–Szabo, Amsterdam 1975.

(g) 9 Bd3 e4 10 Bc2 Nbd7 11 Ne2 Qe7 12 Qb1 0-0 13 Bxf6 =.

(h) 12 Ne2 g5 13 Bg3 Kc7 14 h4 Rg8 15 hxg5 16 Rh6 Qf8 =, Timman–Andersson, Tilburg 1977.

(i) 9 ... Qa5 10 Ne2 Nxd5 11 0-0 Nxc3 12 bxc3 Bxc3 13 Nxc3 Qxc3 14 Be2 0-0 15 Qxd6 $\pm$, Portisch–Donner, Madrid 1960.

(j) 12 Bg3 Nh5 13 f4 Bg4 14 Qc2 Bxe2 15 Nxe2 $\pm$, Planinc–Parma, Yugoslavia 1968.

(k) (A) 6 . . . Bxc3† 7 bxc3 e5 8 d6!? Nc6 9 Qc2 g5 10 Bg3 Nh5 11 e3 Qf6 12 Rd1 b6 13 Be2 Nxg3 14 fxg3 Bb7 15 Bf3 0-0-0 16 Ne2 Na5 17 0-0 Qe6 ∞ (Taimanov). (B) 6 . . . Qa5?! 7 Bxf6 gxf6 8 Qc2 ±.

(l) Declining the gambit gives no advantage: 7 e4 g5 8 Bg3 Nxe4 9 Be5 0-0 10 Qh5 d6 11 Bd3 Nxc3 12 Qxh6 Ne4† 13 Kf1 dxe5 14 Bxe4 f5 15 Qg6† Kh8 16 Qh6† Draw, Penrose–Unzicker, Clare Benedict Tournament (West Germany) 1961.

(m) 10 Nf3?! Qa5 11 Bxf6 Rxf6 12 Qd2 a6 13 bxa6 Nc6 ∓, Spassky–Tal, Tallinn 1973.

(n) 12 a3 Ba5 13 b4 dxc3 14 bxa5 Bb7 15 Ne2! Bxg2 16 Rg1 ±, Cooper–Adamski, Nice 1984.

(o) 6 Bd2 Bxc5 7 e3 0-0 8 Nf3 d5 9 Be2 dxc4 10 Qxc4 Qe7 11 0-0 b6 = (Levenfish).

(p) Also 7 . . . Nxd2 8 Nxd2 f5 9 e3 0-0 10 Be2 Bxc5 11 0-0 b6 12 Nf3 Bb7 =, Stahlberg–Lovcki, Yurata 1937.

(q) 12 Bg2 Qc7 13 0-0 a4 14 Nd2 b6 15 f4 Ba6 =, Euwe–Evans, Hastings 1949–50.

(r) 4 . . . Qe7 5 a3 Bxc3† 6 Qxc3 b6 7 f3 d5 8 cxd5 Nxd5 9 Qc2 Qh4† 10 g3 Qxd4 11 e4 Ne7 12 Bf4 ±. Comments.

(s) 6 Bg5 h6 7 Bxf6 Qxf6 8 e3 dxc4 9 Bxc4 0-0 =. The column is Trifunović–Barcza, Špindlerovy Mlýny 1947.

NIMZO-INDIAN DEFENSE

1 d4 Nf6 2 c4 e6 3 Nc3 Bb4

	91	92	93	94	95	96
4	Nf3			g3		.f3
	b6(a)			c5	d5	d5(p)
5	Qb3	Bg5		Nf3	Bg2	a3
	c5(b)	h6		Ne4(k)	0-0	Be7
6	a3	Bh4		Qd3	Nf3	e4
	Ba5	Bb7		Qa5	dxc4	dxe4
7	Bf4	e3(d)		Qxe4	0-0	fxe4
	Bb7	g5	Bxc3†	Bxc3†	Nc6	e5
8	Rd1(c)	Bg3	bxc3	Bd2	Re1(n)	d5
	0-0	Ne4	d6	Bxd2†	Nd5(o)	Bc5
9	e3	Qc2(e)	Nd2	Nxd2	Qc2	Bg5
	cxd4	Bxc3†	Nbd7(h)*	Nc6(l)	Be7	h6
10	Nxd4	bxc3	f3	d5	Ne4	Bh4
	Ne4	d6(f)	Qe7	Nd4	b5	Bd4
11	Qc2	Bd3	e4(i)	Bg2	Neg5	Bd3
	Bxc3† =	Nxg3(g)	e5(j)	Nb3(m)	g6 =	c6(q)

(a) (A) 4 ... c5 5 d5 (5 e3 is back in the Rubinstein Variation, while 5 g3 is column 94 without allowing 4 ... d5) 5 ... Ne4 6 Bd2 Bxc3 7 bxc3 d6 8 Qc2 Nxd2 9 Nxd2 e5 =. (B) 4 ... 0-0 5 Bg5 h6 6 Bh4 c5 7 e3 cxd4 8 exd4 Be7 9 Bd3 b6 10 0-0 Bb7 11 Re1 ±, Pachman–Zuidema, Vrnjačka Banja 1967. (C) For 4 ... d5 see the Queen's Gambit Declined, Ragozin Variation.

(b) 5 ... a5 6 g3 Nc6 7 Bg2 a4 8 Qc2 Ba6 9 0-0 Bxc4 10 Ne5 Nxe5 11 dxe5 Nd5 12 Nxa4 ±, T. Georgadze–Gomez, Seville 1985.

(c) 8 dxc5 Ne4 9 cxb6 Qxb6 10 Qxb6 Bxc3† 11 bxc3 axb6 ∓. The column is Portisch–Polugaevsky, Linares 1985.

(d) 7 Qc2 g5 8 Bg3 Ne4 9 Be5 f6 10 d5 exc5 11 cxd5 Bxc3† 12 Bxc3 Nxc3 13 Qxc3 Bxd5 14 0-0-0 Be6 15 h4 g4 16 Nd4 Qe7 =.

(e) 9 Nd2?! Nxc3 10 bxc3 Bxc3 11 Rc1 Bxd2† 12 Qxd2 d6 leaves White with too little for the pawn.

(f) 10 ... Nxg3 11 fxg3 g4 12 Nh4 Qg5 13 Qd2 Nc6 14 Bd3 f5 15 0-0 Ne7 16 a4 a5 (Salov–Timman, Brussels 1988); now 17 Rb1 threatening 18 c5 is strong.

(g) 12 fxg3!? Nd7 13 0-0 Qe7 14 Rf2 0-0-0 15 Be4 f5 16 Bxb7† Kxb7 17 e4 ±, Timman–Miles, Tilburg 1985. The variation with 11 ... f5?! is suspect: 12 d5 Nc5 13 h4 g4 14 Nd4 Qf6 15 0-0 Nxd3 16 Qxd3 e5 17 Nxf5 Bc8 18 f4! Qxf5 19 e4 Qh5 20 fxe5 dxe5 21 c5! Kd8 22 d6 Qe8 23 dxc7† Kxc7 24 Qd5 Nc6 25 Rf7† Bd7 26 Raf1 Rd8 27 R1f6 Kc8 28 cxb6 axb6 29 Qb5 Resigns, Miles–Beliavsky, Tilburg 1986.

(h) 9 ... g5 10 Bg3 Qe7 11 h4 Rg8 12 hxg5 hxg5 13 a4 Nc6! should equalize, J. Piket–Lerner, Amsterdam 1988.

(i) A good alternative is 11 Bd3 g5 12 Bf2 0-0-0 13 Qa4 Kb8 14 0-0-0 c5 15 e4 Nh5 16 Rhe1 Nf4 17 Bf1 $\pm$, Gligorić–Hjartarson, Belgrade 1987.

(j) 12 Bd3 g5 13 Bf2 Nh5 14 Nf1 Nf4 15 Ne3 g4 ∞, Razuvaev–Stoica, Nikea 1986.

(k) 5 . . . 0-0 6 Bg2 cxd4 7 Nxd4 d5 8 cxd5 Nxd5 9 Qb3 Bxc3† 10 bxc3 bxc4 11 Qa3 ∞, Karpov–Portisch, Lucerne 1985.

(l) 9 . . . cxd4 10 Qxd4 Nc6 11 Qe3 leaves White more active.

(m) 12 Rd1 Qxa2 13 Qe5 0-0 14 Qc3 and according to Romanishin White has good compensation for the pawn.

(n) 8 a3 Be7 9 e4 Na5 10 Bf4 c6 11 Qe2 b5 12 Rad1 worked out well for White in Gulko–Popovich, Clichy 1986–87, but 8 . . . Bxc3 is more logical.

(o) 8 . . . Rb8 9 a3 Be7 10 e4 b5 11 d5 gives White spatial compensation for the pawn (Taimanov). The column is Bradford–Peters, US Chp. 1980, with 11 . . . g6 instead of Peter's 11 . . . f5?!

(p) 4 . . . c5 5 d5 Nh5 6 g3 f5 7 Bd2 0-0 8 e3 d6 = .

(q) 12 Nge2 Bg4 13 Qc2 Bxd2 14 Nxe2 Be3 15 Ng3 g6 16 Nf1 Bd4 17 0-0-0 Nbd7 = , Gheorghiu–Keres, Hastings 1964–65.

CATALAN OPENING

1 d4 Nf6 2 c4 e6 3 g3

Diagram 72

THE CATALAN FIRST SAW THE LIGHT OF DAY during a tournament in Barcelona, Spain, in 1929. It was named "Catalan" by Tartakower in honor of the province of Catalonia, of which Barcelona is the capital. The modern form of the opening, 1 d4 Nf6 2 c4 e6 3 g3, which began to be played in the late 1930s, has been employed by Alekhine, Botvinnik, Reshevsky, Keres, Symslov, Petrosian, Kasparov, and a great number of other ranking masters. It should be noted that the order of moves 1 d4 d5 2 c4 e6 3 Nf3 Nf6 4 g3 is a common path to both the Open and the Closed variations of the Catalan. Much of the modern Catalan opening classification owes its existence to Yakov Neishtadt, who wrote the first systematic treatise on the opening in 1969. In recent times the Catalan has seen an enormous resurgence; it is seen in the strongest international tournaments as well as in World Championship matches.

Typical Catalan positions frequently arise from other openings, such as the Reti, Slav, Queen's Gambit, English or Bogo-Indian. To this day there exist difficulties in clearly distinguishing certain lines of the English opening (1 c4 c5 2 Nf3 Nf6 3 d4 cxd4 4 Nxd4 e6 5 g3 d5 6 Bg2), the Bogo-Indian (1 d4 Nf6 2 c4 e6 3 Nf3 Bb4†, e.g. 4 Nbd2 Qe7 5 g3), the Nimzo-Indian (1 d4 Nf6 2 c4 e6 3 Nc3 Bb4 4 g3), and the Catalan. The fianchetto of White's king bishop combined with an early d4 and c4 is the essential element of the Catalan. The "Catalan bishop" inhibits the development of Black's queenside and thus avoids the Queen's Indian Defense; the last development of White's queen knight prevents the Nimzo Indian Defense.

Diagram 73

Currently the most popular variation of the Catalan by far is the OPEN
VARIATION (cols. 1–36), characterized by the moves 1 d4 Nf6 2 c4 e6 3 g3 d5
Bg2 dxc4 (see diagram). At this juncture, White has to decide whether to
develop with 5 Nf3 (cols. 1–30), or to recapture the pawn immediately
with 5 Qa4† (cols. 34–36). If White chooses to develop and Black plays the
Classical Line (cols. 1–12), White can either play against Black's planned
queenside expansion with 8 a4 (cols. 1–6) or restore material equality by
following 7 Qc2 with the natural 8 Qxc4 (cols. 7–12). After White's 5 Nf3
Black has two other main continuations: he can choose either to counterattack against d4 with 5 . . . c5 (cols. 13–18) or to attempt to secure the
pawn at c4 with 5 . . . a6 (cols. 19–24). Other fifth moves for Black are 5
. . . Bd7 (cols. 25–26), which is designed to reduce White's domination of
the "Catalan diagonal" by transferring Black's queen bishop as quickly as
possible to c6, and 5 . . . Nbd7 (col. 27), 5 . . . b5 (col. 28), and 5 . . . Nc6
(col. 30), all of which are attempts to hold on to the gambit pawn.

Columns 31–33 present a Catalan with an "English" flavor. As always, White's intention is to apply significant pressure against Black's
queenside. Black has many fifth-move alternatives, but only 5 . . . d5 is
classified as a Catalan, all others belonging to the English Opening.

The immediate recapture of the pawn by 5 Qa4† (cols. 34–36) involves a loss of time by White and has the additional disadvantage of
allowing Black counterplay and rapid queenside development.

Diagram 74

The CLOSED VARIATION, 1 d4 Nf6 2 c4 e6 3 g3 d5 4 Bg2 Be7 5 Nf3 0-0 6 0-0 (see diagram) is treated in columns 37–48.

After Black's most common response, 6 . . . Nbd7, White has a spatial superiority and pressure both in the center and on the queenside. By playing 7 Qc2 together with a subsequent Nbd2 (or Nc3), White prepares for the central thrust e4 and appears to retain a slight but permanent edge.

CATALAN OPENING

Open Variation

1 d4 Nf6 2 c4 e6 3 g3 d5 4 Bg2 dxc4 5 Nf3 Be7 (Classical Line) 6 0-0 0-0 7 Qc2 a6 8 a4

	1	2	3	4	5	6
	Nbd7 . . . . Bd7(b)					
9	Nbd2	Rd1 . . . . Qxc4				
	c5	Bc6		Bc6		
10	dxc5	Nc3		Bf4 . . . . Bg5(k)		
	Nxc5	Bb4 . . . . Bxf3		Nbd7 . . . . a5(h)		a5
11	Ne5	Bg5	Bxf3	Nc3	Nc3	Nc3
	c3	Bxc3	Nc6	Nb6	Na6	Na6
12	Qxc3	Bxf6	Bxc6(d)	Qb3(f)	Rfe1	Rac1
	Nd5	Qxf6	bxc6	a5	Bd5	Bxf3(l)
13	Qc2	Qxc3	a5	Rfd1	Nxd5	Bxf3
	Qc7	Qe7	Qb8	Ra6	exd5	c6
14	Ndf3	Qxc4	Qa4	Qc2	Qb5	e4
	f6	Nd7	c5	Nbd5	Qc8	Nd7
15	Nd3	Rac1	Qxc4	Bd2	Qb3(i)	Be3
	Nxd3(a)	Rfd8(c)	cxd4(e)	Nxc3(g)	c6(j)	Bg5(m)

(a) 16 Qxd3 Bd7 17 Bd2 Rfc8 18 Rac1 Qd8 19 b3 Rxc1 20 Rxc1 Rc8 =, Gorelov–Rozentalis, USSR Chp. 1984. In the heading, White may also try 7 Ne5 Nc6! 8 Bxc6 (8 Nxc6 bxc6 9 Bxc6 Rb8 =) 8 . . . bxc6 9 Nxc6 Qe8 10 Nxe7† Qxe7 11 Qa4 a5 12 Qxc4 Ba6 13 Qc2 e5 14 dxe5 Qxe5 15 Nc3 Rfe8 16 Re1 Rb7 with good play for the pawn, C. Hansen–Vaganian, Esbjerg 1988.

(b) The two other moves are played less frequently: (A) 8 . . . c5 9 dxc5 (9 Rd1 Nd5 10 Qxc4 Nc6 11 dxc5 Ne3! 12 Rxd8 Nxc4 =) 9 . . . Nc6! 10 Qxc4 e5 11 Be3 Be6 12 Qc1 Rc8 13 Rd1 Qa5 14 Ng5 Bg4 15 Nc3 Bxc5 16 Bxc5 Qxc5 =, P. Nikolic–Gligorić, Yugoslavia 1988. (B) 8 . . . Nc6 9 Qxc4 Qd5 10 Qd3 Rd8 11 Nc3 Qh5 12 Qc4 Nd5 13 a5 Bd7 14 e4 Nxc3 15 bxc3 Nxa5 16 Qxc7 Nb3 17 Ba3 ± (Neishtadt).

(c) The column is Azmayparashvili–Novopashin, USSR Chp. 1981; Neishstadt's 16 Ne1 Bxg2 17 Nxg2 c6 18 Qb3 Nf6 19 Ne3 Nd5 20 Nc4 gives White a pull.

(d) 12 e3 Nd5 13 Qe2 Na5 14 Rb1 c6 15 e4 Nb4 16 d5 Nd3 17 Be3 Nb3 Draw, Romanishin–Geller, USSR Chp. 1980–81.

(e) 16 Rxd4 c5 17 Rd1 Qb4 18 Ra4 Draw, Razuvaev–Geller, Moscow 1982.

(f) 12 Qd3 Nbd5 13 Bg5 Nxc3 14 bxc3 Be4 15 Qe3 Bc6 (15 . . . Bd5 is recommended by Alburt as simpler) 16 a5! h6 17 Bxf6 Bxf6 18 Rfb1 b5! 19 axb6 cxb6 20 Qd3 Qc7! =, Alburt–Prandstetter, Taxco 1985.

(g) 16 bxc3 Be4 17 Qb2 c5 18 Bg5 Nd5 =, Petrosian–Ivanović, Vrbaś 1980.

(h) (A) 10 . . . Bd6 11 Nc3 Bxf4 12 gxf4 Qd6 13 e3 Nbd7 14 Rfc1 Rac8 15 b4 Nb6 16 Qc5! ±, Vadasz–Plachetka, Trnava 1979. (B) 10 . . . Nd5 11 Nc3 Nxf4 12 gxf4 Nd7 13 Qd3 Nf6 14

Rfd1 Qd6 15 e3 Rfd8 16 Qc2 Rac8 17 h3 Qb4 18 Rde1 Qa5 19 Ne5 Bxg2 20 Kxg2 c5 21 Ne4 ±, Vukić–Cebalo, Yugoslav Chp. 1979.

(i) 15 Qxa5? Nc5 traps the Queen.

(j) 16 Ne5 Bb4 17 Red1 Qe6 with equality, Donchenko–Geller, USSR 1979.

(k) 10 Nc3 b5! 11 Qd3 b4 12 Nb1 (not 12 Nd1? Be4 13 Qd2? Nc6 14 e3 Na5 wins, Poldauf–Tischbierek, East Germany 1979) 12 . . . Be4 13 Qd1 c5 14 Nbd2 Bd5 15 dxc5 Nbd7 $\overline{\mp}$, S. Garcia–Ubilava, Tbilisi 1980.

(l) (A) 12 . . . Qd6 13 Ne5 Bxg2 14 Kxg2 c6 (14 . . . Qb4!?) 15 Bxf6 gxf6 16 Nf3 ±, Kasparov–Karpov, World Chp. Moscow 1984–85. (B) 12 . . . Bd5 13 Nxd5 exd5 14 Qb5 Nb4! 15 Qxb7 Bd6 16 Be5 Rb8 17 Qa7 Draw, Hübner–Karpov, Montreal 1979.

(m) 16 Qb5! and White stood better in Vlada–Plachetka, Trnava 1979.

CATALAN OPENING
Open Variation—Classical Line

1 d4 Nf6 2 c4 e6 3 g3 d5 4 Bg2 dxc4 5 Nf3 Be7 6 0-0 0-0 7 Qc2 a6(a) 8 Qxc4 b5 9 Qc2 Bb7

	7✓	8	9	10	11✓	12
10	Bf4			Bd2.....		......Bg5(m)
	Nc6........	Nd5	Bd6........	Be4(j)		Nbd7
11	Rd1	Nc3	Nbd2(h)	Qc1		Bxf6
	Nb4	Nxf4	Nbd7	Nc6........	Bb7	Nxf6
12	Qc1	gxf4	Nb3	Be3	Be3	Nbd2
	Qc8(b)✓	Nc6(f)	Be4	Nb4	Nd5	Rc8
13	Bg5(c)	Rfd1	Qc1	Nbd2	Nc3	Nb3
	c5	Nb4	Rc1	Bb7	Nd7	c5(n)
14	Bxf6	Qc1	a4	Bg5	Rd1	dxc5
	gxf6	Qb8	Qe7	Rc8	Rc8	Bd5
15	a3(d)	a3	axb5	a3	Nxd5	Rfd1(o)
	Nd5(e)	Nd5(g)	axb5(i)	Nbd5(k)	Bxd5(l)	Bxd3(p)

(a) Other possible moves are: (A) 7 ... c5 8 dxc5 Qc7 9 Qxc4 Qxc5 10 Qxc5 Bxc5 11 Ne5 Nbd712 Nc4 Nd5 13 Rd1 N7f6 14 Nc3 ±, Korchnoi–Khanov, Frunze 1956. (B) 7 ... Nbd7 8 Nbd2 c5 9 Nxc4 cxd4 10 Rd1 Nb6 11 Rxd4 Qc7 12 Bf4 Qc5 13 a3 Nbd5 14 b4 Qb5 15 Bd2 ±, Pelikan–Najdorf, Buenos Aires 1939. (C) 7 ... b5? 8 a4! c6 9 axb5 cxb5 10 Ng5 wins.

(b) (A) 12 ... Rc8 13 Nc3 Nbd5 14 Nxd5 =, Ftáčník–Speelman, Hastings 1980–81. (B) 12 ... Nbd5 13 Nc3 Nf4 14 Qf4 Bd6 15 Ne5 Bxg2 16 Kxg2 Qb8 17 Qf3 c5 18 Nc6 Qb6 19 dxc5 Bxc5 20 a4 ±, Andersson–Braga, Mar del Plata 1982.

(c) (A) 13 Bxc7?! Nfd5! 14 a3 Qxc7 ∓ (Neishtadt). (B) 13 Nbd2 c5 14 dxc5 Bxc5 15 Nb3 Be7 16 Na5 Bd5 17 Nd4 Qe8 18 a3 Rc8 19 Qd2 Bxg2 20 Kxg2 Nbd5 21 Rac1 Rxc1 =, Andersson–Karpov, Tilburg 1982.

(d) Agzamov–Karpov, USSR 1983, the stem-game of the 12 ... Qc8 variation, continued: 15 Nc3 Rd8 16 a3 Nd5 17 Nxd5 Bxd5 18 dxc5 Qxc5 19 Qxc5 Bxc5 20 Ne1 Bxg2 21 Kxg2 f5 22 Rxd8† Rxd8 23 Nd3 Be7 24 a4 (Agzamov suggested 24 Rc1 as an improvement) 24 ... bxa4 25 Rxa4 Rd6 =.

(e) 16 e4 Nb6 17 d5 (17 Qf4 cxd4 18 Nxd4 e5 19 Nf5 exf4 20 Nxe7† Kg7 21 Nxc8 Raxc8 ∞) 17 ... exd5 18 Qf4 dxe4 19 Nh4 Rd8 20 Rd8† Qxd8 21 Nc3 with a dangerous attack for the pawns (Kholmov).

(f) 12 ... Nd7 13 Rfd1 Qc8 14 Ne4! c5 15 Nxc5 Nxc5 16 dxc5 Qxc5 17 Qxc5 Bxc5 18 Rac1 Rfc8 19 Ne5! Bxg2 20 Kxg2 ±, Ribli–Karpov, Amsterdam 1980.

(g) The column through 14 ... Qb8 is Ribli–Gruenfeld, European Team Chp. 1980: 16 Nxd5 Bxd5 17 Ne5 ± (Neishtadt).

(h) (A) 11 Rd1 Qe7 12 Nbd2 Nbd7 13 Nb3 Be4 14 Qd2 Rac8 15 Ne5 Bb4 (Kirov–Prandstetter, Prague 1983) 16 Qe3 Bxg2 17 Kxg2 Nd5 18 Qf3 Nf4 19 Qxf4 Nxe5 20 dxe5 Bc5 21 Na5

$\pm$ (Neishtadt). (B) 11 Bxd6 cxd6 12 Nbd2 Nbd7 13 Rfc1 Rc8 14 Qd1 Qb6 =, Trifunović–Parma, Yugoslav Chp. 1964.

(i) 16 Ra7 Bxf4 17 Qxf4 Qb4! 18 Nbd2 Bf3 19 Bxf3 c5 20 dxc5 Qxc5 =, Smyslov–Gligorić, Warsaw 1947.

(j) Beliavsky–Karpov, Brussels 1988, continued 10 . . . Nc6 11 e3 Nb4 12 Bxb4 Bxb4 13 a3 Bd6 14 Nbd2 Rc8 15 b4 a5 16 e4 Be7 17 Rab1 axb4 18 axb4 Ra8 19 Rfe1 Ra4 20 Qc3 Qa8 21 Ne5 Rd8 22 Qxc7 Kf8 23 d5 Qb8 24 Qxb8 Rxb8 25 Nb3 Bxb4 26 Rec1 exd5 27 exd5 Ba3 28 Rd1 Bd6 29 Nc6 Bxc6 30 dxc6 Ne8 31 Nd4 b4 32 Nf5 Bc5 33 Rd7 Ra7 34 Rb7 Rd8 35 Rc1 Ra5 36 Bh3 g6 37 Nh6 Nd6 38 Nxf7 Nxf7 39 c7 Re8 40 c8(Q) Rxc8 41 Bxc8 Nd6 42 Rb8 Ke7 43 Re1† Kf6 44 Be6 Ra3 45 Kg2 Ra7 46 Bd5 Nf5 47 Re6† Kg7 48 Rc6 Be7 49 h4 Ra5 50 Bc4 Ra7 51 h5 Nd6 52 hxg6 hxg6 53 Rxb4 Ra1 54 Bd3 g5 55 Rd4 Nf7 56 Rd7 Re1 57 Bc4 Kf8 58 Bxf7 Kxf7 59 Kf3 Ke8 60 Ra7 Resigns.

(k) 16 Nb3 b6 17 Na5 Ba8 18 Nc6 Bxc6 19 Bxf6 Bb7 20 Bxe7 Qxe7 $\pm$, Korchnoi–Kasparov, London 1983.

(l) 16 Ne1 c6 17 Nd3 Qb6 18 Qc3 b4 19 Qd2 a5 =, Kasparov–Karpov, World Chp. 1984–85.

(m) Other moves that have been tried: (A) 10 Nbd2 Nbd7 11 e4 c5 12 e5 Nd5 13 Qe4 Qb6 14 dxc5 Nxc5 15 Qg4 Rac8 $\pm$, Reshevsky–Rogoff, Lone Pine 1978. (B) 10 a4 Nc6 11 Bf4 Nb4 12 Qc1 c5 13 dxc5 Rc8 14 Rd1 Rxc5 15 Nc3 Nbd5 =. Uhlmann–Drimer, Leipzig 1960

(n) 13 . . . Be4 14 Qc3 (14 Qc1 c5 15 dxc5 Qc7 16 Qf4 Qxf4 17 gxf4 Bxc5 18 Ne5 Bxg2 19 Kxg2 Bd6 20 Nd3 Nd5 21 e3 Nb6 =, Razuvaev–Hübner, USSR vs. World 1984) 14 . . . Nd5 15 Qd2 c5 16 Nxc5 Bxc5 17 dxc5 Rxc5 18 Rac1 Rxc1 19 Rxc1 Nf6 20 Qd8 Rxd8 21 Ne5 Bxg2 22 Kxg2 $\pm$, Larsen–Tal, Naestved 1985.

(o) 15 Ne1!, played in Huzman–Timoshchenko, Tashkent 1987, deserves attention, e.g., 15 . . . Bxb3 16 Qxb3 Bxc5 17 Nd3 18 a4 Bd6 19 axb5 axb5 20 Qa2 Rb8 21 Rfc1 Rfc8 22 Rxc8 Rxc8 23 Qa6 $\pm$.

(p) The column is Kasparov–Karpov, World Chp. 1986. The game continued 16 Qxb3 Qc7 17 a4 Qxc5 18 axb5 axb5 19 Nd4 b4 20 e3 Rfd8 21 Rd2 Qb6 Draw.

CATALAN OPENING

Open Variation

1 d4 Nf6 2 c4 e6 3 g3 d5 4 Bg2 dxc4 5 Nf3 c5 6 0–0(a) Nc6(b)

	13	14	15	16	17	18
7	Qa4			Ne5		
	Bd7 .... cxd4			Bd7		
8	Qxc4	Nxd4		Nxc6 .... Na3 .... Nxc4		
	b5	Qxd4		Bxc6	cxd4	cxd4
9	Qd3(c)	Bxc6†		Bxc6†	Naxc4	Bf4
	Rc8	Bd7		bxc6	Rc8(j)	Be7
10	dxc5	Rd1 .... Be3		Qa4	Qb3	Nd6†
	Bxc5	Qxd1†	Bc6	cxd4	Nxe5	Kf8
11	Nc3	Qxd1	Qc6	Qxc6†	Nxe5	Nxb7
	b4	Bxc6	Qd7	Nd7	Bc6	Qb6
12	Nb5	Nd2	Qc4(f)	Qxc4	Nc6	Nd6
	0-0	b5	Be7	Bc5(h)	bxc6	Nd5
13	Be3	a4	Nc3	Nd2	Rd1	Nc4
	Bxe3(d)	Be7(e)	0-0(g)	0-0(i)	c5(k)	Qc5(l)

(a) Also good is 6 Qa4† (for 6 . . . Nbd7 see 5 Qa4† Nbd7) 6 . . . Bd7 7 Qxc4 Bc6 8 dxc5 Nbd7 9 Be3 Bd5 10 Qb4! Qc8 11 Nc3 Bxc5 12 Bxc5 Qxc5 13 Nxd5! Nxd5 14 Qd2 Rc8 15 0-0 0-0 16 Rac1 Qb6 17 Qd4 Rfd8 18 Rfd1 Qxd4 19 Nxd4 ±, Korchnoi–Kasparov, London 1983.

(b) 6 . . . cxd4 is playable; Korchnoi–Miles, London 1984, continued 7 Qa4† Bd7 8 Qxc4 Na6 9 Qxd4 Bc6 10 Nc3 Qxd4 (Miles suggests 10 . . . Nc5 as an improvement) 11 Nxd4 Bxg2 12 Kxg2 Bc5 13 Ndb5 0-0 14 a3 ±.

(c) 9 Qxb5? Nxd4 followed by 10 . . . Bb5 wins.

(d) 14 Qxe3 Ne7! 15 Rfd1 Ned5 16 Qd3 Qb6 17 Nbd4 h6! 18 e4 Ne7 19 e5 Nfd5 =, Yusupov–Sokolov, Riga 1986.

(e) 14 axb5 Bxb5 15 Nc4 0-0 16 b3 ±, Kasparov–Andersson, Nikšić 1983.

(f) 12 Qxd7 Nxd7 13 Nd2 Bc5 is equal according to Gulko.

(g) 14 Rfd1 Qc8 15 Qb5 a6 16 Qb6 Bd8 17 Qb4 b5 18 Rd3 Re8 19 Rc1 Be7 20 Qb3 Qb8 21 Bd4 Rd8 22 Rcd1 Qc7 23 a4 bxa4 24 Qxa4 e5 25 Be3 Rxd3 26 Rxd3 Qb7 27 Rd2 Bb4! 28 Bg5 Bxc3 29 bxc3, Gulko–Zhu. Polgar, Biel 1987; here Gulko suggests 29 . . . Ne4 30 Rd8 =, or 29 . . . Qb1 30 Rd1 Qb5 =.

(h) 12 . . . Nb6 is also quite playable: (A) 13 Qc6 Qd7 14 Qxd7† Nxd7 15 Nd2 Rc8 16 Nb3 e5 17 Bd2 Bd6 18 Rac1 =. (B) 13 Qd3 Qd7 (or 13 . . . Rc8) 14 e3 dxe3 15 Qxd7 Nxd7 16 Bxe3 =, Jansson–Ivkov, Stockholm 1971.

(i) 14 Ne4 Bb6 15 Bg5 and now White has only a minimally more active position.

(j) Tal–Sokolov, Brussels 1988, continued 9 . . . Bc5 10 Qb3 0-0 11 Bf4 Qc8 12 Rfd1 Rd8 13 Rac1 Nd5 14 Nxf7 Kxf7 15 Ne5† Nxe5 16 Bxe5 b6 17 Qf3† Kg8 18 Qg4 g6 19 Be4 Be8

537

20 b4 Nxb4 21 Bxa8 Qxa8 22 Qxe6† Bf7 23 Qf6 Kf8 24 Qh8† Ke7 25 Bf6† Kd7 26 Bxd8 Nc6 27 Bf6 Qxh8 28 Bxh8 Bxa2 29 e3 a5 30 Bxd4 Nxd4 31 exd4 Bd6 32 d5 a4 33 Rc6 Bc5 34 Rc1 Bd4 35 R6c4 Bxc4 36 Rxc4 b5 37 Rxd4 a3 38 Rd1 b4 39 Ra1 Kd6 40 Kf1 Kxd5 41 Ke2, Resigns.

(k) The column is Kasparov–Andersson, Belgrade 1985. 8 Na3 has been adopted by a number of Catalan enthusiasts since its introduction by Kasparov and could become a fixture in the White repertoire. The game continued: 14 e3 Bd6 15 exd4 c4 16 Qb5† Qd7 17 a4 0-0 18 Be3 Rc7 19 d5 e5 20 Rdc1 Rfc8 21 Bf1 g6 22 Bxc4 Qxb5 23 Bxb5 Nxd5 24 Ba6 Rxc1† 25 Rxc1 Rxc1† 26 Bxc1 $\pm$, although the game ended in a draw.

(l) 14 Ne5 Rd8 15 Nd3 Qb5 16 a4 Qa6 is Rogers–Varnusz, Balatonbereny 1983; now 17 Bxd5 exd5 18 b4! would have given White the advantage (Rogers).

CATALAN OPENING

Open Variation

1 d4 Nf6 2 c4 e6 3 g3 d5 4 Bg2 dxc4 5 Nf3 a6

	19	20	21	22	23	24
6	0-0(a) Ne5					
	b5 . . . . Nc6			c5		
7	Ne5		e3(g)	Be3. Na3		
	Nd5(b)		Bd7	Nd5		cxd4
8	Nc3(c)		Nc3	dxc5		Naxc4
	Bb7		Bd6	Nd7(j)		Ra7
9	Nxd5		Qe2	Nxc4 . . . . Bd4		Bd2
	exd5		b5	Nxe3	Nxe5	b6
10	e4 . . . . b3	Rd1	Nxe3	Bxe5	Qb3
	dxe4	cxb3	0-0	Bxc5	f6	Bb7
11	Qh5	e4	e4	Nc4	Bd4	Bxb7
	g6(d)	dxe4	e5(h)	0-0	Bxc5	Rxb7
12	Nxg6	Qh5	dxe5	0-0	Bxc5	Na5
	fxg6	g6	Nxe5	Qc7	Qa5†	Re7(m)
13	Qe5†	Nxg6	Nxe5	Qb3	Nd2	Nac6
	Qe7(e)	fxg6(f)	Bxe5(i)	Rb8(k)	Qxc5(l)	Nxc6(n)

(a) 6 a4 is another possibility that seems to lead only to equality: 6 . . . Nc6 7 0-0 Na5 8 Nbd2 c5 9 dxc5 Bxc5 10 Ne5 c3 11 bxc3 0-0 12 Nec4 Be7 13 Nxa5 Qxa5, Gulko–Bronstein, Vilnius 1975.

(b) 7 . . . c6 has been tried a number of times; Flear–Andersson, Wijk aan Zee 1987, continued 8 b3 (8 Nxc6 Qb6 9 Ne5 Bb7 10 a4 Bxg2 11 Kxg2 Qb7† 12 Kg1 Nc6 13 Nxc6 Qxc6 favors White) 8 . . . cxb3 9 Nc6 Qb6 10 Na5 Ra7 11 Nb3 Rd7 12 Bg5 Be7 13 N1d2 h6 14 Bxf6 Bxf6 15 e3 0-0 with even chances.

(c) 8 a4 Bb7 9 b3 (9 e4 Nf6 10 axb5 axb5 11 Rxa8 Bxa8 12 Nc3 c6 13 Bg5 Bb7 14 Nxf7, Khalifman–Novikov, Lvov 1985, is unclear) 9 . . . cxb3 10 Qb3 Nc6 ∞ (Timman).

(d) 11 . . . Qd5? 12 Bxe4 wins.

(e) Black's compensation for the exchange seems to be adequate. Beliavsky–Sveshnikov, USSR Chp. 1981, continued 14 Qxh8 Nd7 15 Bh3 Nf6 16 Bg5 Kf7 17 Bxf6 Qxf6 18 Qxf6† Kxf6 19 a4 Ke7 20 axb5 axb5 21 Rxa8 Bxa8 22 Ra1 Bc6 23 Ra6 Kd6 = .

(f) 14 Qe5† Qe7 15 Qxh8 Nd7 16 Bh3 Nf6 17 Ba3 Qxa3 with chances for both sides; Black's excellent position appears to compensate for the exchange. The move 10 b3 was originated by Gulko in 1982; the column is Bandza–Smirin, Kiev, 1983.

(g) 7 Ne3 leads to approximate equality: 7 . . . Rb8 8 e4 b5 9 d5 Nb4 10 Ne5 Bd6 11 f4 exd5 12 a3 Nd3 13 Nxd3 cxd3 (Vukić–Marjanović, Yugoslav Chp. 1980) 14 Nxd5 Nxd5 15 exd5 0-0 16 Qxd3 c6 = .

(h) 11 . . . Be7 12 Bg5 Rb8 13 d5 exd5 14 Nxd5 ±, Azmayparashvili–A. Petrosian, USSR 1983.

(i) 14 Bg6 c6 15 Bxf6 gxf6 16 f4 Bxc3 17 bxc3 Qe7; In this position it is not clear whether Black's broken-up kingside is sufficient compensation for the pawn. The column is Razuvaev–A. Petrosian, Tashkent 1984.

(j) 8 . . . Qc7 9 Bd4 Bxc5 10 Nxc4 0-0 11 0-0 Bxd4 12 Qxd4 Nc6 13 Qc5 $\pm$ (Neishtadt).

(k) The chances are equal; the column is Langeweg–Ree, Dutch Chp. 1981.

(l) Ivanchuk–Kuporosov, USSR 1986; 14 Rc1 b5 15 b3 Bb7 16 0-0 Ne3 17 fxe3 Qxe3† 18 Rf2 Bxg2 19 Kxg2 Rd8 and Black appears to hold his own in this complicated position.

(m) 12 . . . Rc7 13 Qxb6 Bc5 14 Qb3 0-0 15 0-0 Qd5 16 Nf3 Nbd7 17 Qxd5 Nxd5 18 Rfc1 Rfc8 19 Nb3 e5 20 Nxc5 Rxc5 = , Sveshnikov–Chernin, USSR Chp. 1981.

(n) 14 Nxc6 Qa8 15 Rc1 Rc7 16 Qxb6 Nd5 17 Qb8† Qxb8 18 Nxb8 Rxc1† 19 Bxc1 Bd6 = . Rashkovsky–A. Petrosian, Erevan 1984.

CATALAN OPENING

Open Variation

1 d4 Nf6 2 c4 e6 3 g3 d5 4 Bg2 dxc4 5 Nf3

	25	26	27	28	29	30
	Bd7....................		Nbd7........	b5..........	Bb4†........	Nc6
6	Ne5(a)		0-0	a4	Bd2	Qa4(m)
	Bc6		c5	c6	Be7	Nd7
7	Nxc6		Na3	axb5	Qc2	Qxc4
	Nxc6		Nb6	cxb5	Bd7(j)	Nb6
8	e3	Qa4(c)	Nxc4	Ne5	Qxc4	Qd3
	Nd5	Qd7	Nxc4	Nd5	Bc6	e5
9	0-0	Qxc4	Qa4†	Nc3	Nc3	Ne5
	Be7	Nxd4	Bd7	Bb4	Ne4	Nb4
10	Qe2	0-0	Qxc4	0-0	Rd1(k)	Qc3
	Nb6	c5	b5	Bxc3	Nc3	Qd4
11	Rd1	Nc3	Qc2	e4(g)	Bxc3	0-0
	0-0	Rd8	Rc8	Bxd4(h)	Nd7	Qc3
12	Nd2	Bg5	Bg5(e)	Qxd4	0-0	Nc3
	Na5(b)	b5(d)	cxd4(f)	Qb6(i)	0-0(l)	g6(n)

(a) Two other moves are possible here: (A) 6 Qc2 c5 (for 7 Qxc4 Bc6 or 7 0-0 Bc6 8 Qxc4 see 5 ... c5 6 Qa4† Bd7, col. 13 note a) 7 Ne5 cxd4 8 Ncb7 Qa5† 9 Kf1 Qxe5 10 Bxa8 Qc7 11 Nd2 Bb5 is not clear, according to Kasparov. (B) 6 Nbd2 Bb4 7 Ne5 Nc6 8 0-0 (Sosonko–Korchnoi, Zürich 1984) 8 ... Bxd2! 9 Qxd2 Nd5 = (Matanović).

(b) Beliavsky–Portisch, Linares 1988, continued 13 Nf3 Qc8 14 Bd2 Nc6 15 Bc3 Nb4 16 Ne5 N4d5 17 Be1 c5 18 Rac1 cxd4 19 Nxc4 Qe8 20 Rxd4 Rc8 21 b3 Qb5 22 Qd1 Bc5 23 Rd3 Bb4 24 a4 Qa6 25 Bxb4 Nxb4 26 Rd6 Nc6 27 Ne5 Qa5 28 Nxc6 bxc6 29 Rcxc6 Rxc6 30 Bxc6 Qc5 31 Bf3 Qg5 32 Qd2 Qe7 33 Rd4 e5 34 Rd6 e4 35 Be2 h6 36 a5 Resigns.

(c) 8 0-0 Qd7 9 e3 Rb8 10 Qc2 b5 11 b3 Nb4 12 Qe2 cxb3 13 axb3 c6 14 Bd2 Be7 15 Bxb4 Bxb4 16 Ra6 Nd5 17 Rc1 Rc8 18 Nd2 with good compensation for the pawn, Gulko–Christiansen, Philadelphia 1987.

(d) 13 Qd3 c4 (13 ... Be7 14 Bxf6 gxf6 15 a4 b4 16 Nb5 0-0 favors Black, according to Lucacs, but this needs testing) 14 Qd1 b4 15 Bxf6 ±, Sosonko–Lukacs, club match Volmac–Spartacus 1987.

(e) 12 dxc5 Bxc5 13 Qb3 0-0 14 Ne5 Qb6 15 Bg5 Rfd8 16 Qf3 Be7 17 Nxd7 Rxd7 18 Rac1 (18 Rfc1!? Rcd8 19 e4 Rd3 20 Qe2 h6 21 Be3 Qb8 22 Rd1 Rxd1† 23 Rxd1 gives White the advantage—Kasparov) 18 ... Rcd8 19 Qc6 Qa5 20 a3 b4 21 Bf4 Nd5 Draw, Kasparov–Korchnoi, match 1983.

(f) 13 Qd3 Bc5 14 Nxd4 b4 15 Nb3 Be7 16 Rfd1 with advantage to White, Shipman–Shapiro, New York 1983.

(g) 11 bxc3? Nxc3 and White has insufficient compensation for the material.

(h) A most interesting continuation occurred in Chernin–Yudasin, USSR Chp. 1984: 11 . . .
Bxb2 12 exd5 (12 Bxb2 Ne7 13 d5 0-0 14 Ba3 f6 15 d6 Nec6 16 Nxc6 Nxc6 17 d7 b4! 18
dxc8 (Q) Rxc8 when Black has three passed pawns for the piece) 12 . . . Bxa1 13 Ba3 a5
14 Qg4 and now if 14 . . . Qf6 15 Rxa1 Ra6 16 Bc5 Nd7 17 Nxd7 Bxd7 18 Qe4 (Chernin)
is complicated; or 14 . . . Bxd4 15 Qxg7 Bxe5 16 Qxe5 Rg8 17 dxe6 Bxe6 18 Bxa8 b4 19
Bc1 and White has compensation for the pawns.

(i) 13 Nf3 Qxd4 14 Nxd4 Ne7 15 e5 Nd5 16 Nxb5 with advantage to White (Neishtadt).

(j) 7 . . . a6 8 a4 Nc6 9 Qxc4 Bd6 10 Nc3 h6 11 0-0 0-0 12 e4 e5 13 dxe5 Nxe5 14 Nxe5 Bxe5
15 Be3 $\pm$.

(k) Kovačević suggests 10 0-0 Nxd2 11 Nxd2 Bxg2 12 Kxg2 with a pull for White.

(l) The column is Beliavsky–Kovačević, Sarajevo 1982, which continued 16 e4 c5 17 Qa4
a6 =.

(m) 6 0-0 is less good, e.g. 6 . . . Rb8 7 Nc3 Bb4 8 Bg5 0-0 9 Rc1 h6 10 Bxf6 Qxf6 11 Ne4 Qf5
12 Ned2 Qa5 13 a3 Bxd2 14 Nxd2 Qb6 15 Nxc4 Qxd4 16 Bxc6 Qxd1 17 Rfxd1 bxc6 =,
Taimanov–Knaak, Bucharest 1973.

(n) 13 Nb5 Na6 14 Bf4 $\pm$, Tukmakov–Gelfand, Sverdlovsk 1987.

CATALAN OPENING

Open Variation

1 d4 Nf6 2 c4 e6 3 g3

	31	32	33	34	35	36
	d5			c5(f)		
4	Bg2			Nf3(g)		
	dxc4			cxd4		
5	Qa4†			Nxd4		
	Nbd7			d5		
6	Nf3	Nd2	Qxc4	Bg2		
	a6	c6	b5(d)	e5		
7	Nc3	Qxc4	Qc6	Nf3		
	Rb8	e5	Rb8	d4		
8	Qxc4	dxe5(b)	Nf3	0-0		
	b5	Nxe5	Q6	Nc6		
9	Qd3	Qc3	Bf4	e3		
	Bb7	Bd6	Nd5	Bc5	Be7	d3(j)
10	0-0	Ngf3	Bg5	exd4	exd4	Nc3
	c5	Qe7	Be7	exd4	exd4	Bb4(k)
11	dxc5	0-0	Bxe7	Re1†	Bf4	Nxe5
	Bxc5(a)	0-0(c)	Qxe7(e)	Be6(h)	0-0(i)	Nxe5(l)

(a) 12 Bf4 Rc8 13 Rad1 0-0 14 Ne5 Bxg2 15 Kxg2 Nxe5 16 Bxe5 Qxd3 17 Rxd3 Rfd8 18 Rxd8 Rxd8 19 Bxf6 gxf6 20 Rd1 Rxd1 =, Andersson–Karpov, Wijk aan Zee 1988.

(b) 8 Ngf3 Nb6 9 Qd3 exd4 10 Nxd4 Be7 11 0-0 0-0 12 N2b3 Re8 13 Qc2 Nbd5 14 a3 Qb6 =, Mikenas–Averbakh, Moscow, 1953.

(c) 12 Nxe5 Bxe5 13 Qc2 Bc7 14 e4 Re8 15 b3 Bg4 16 Nc4 Rad8 17 Ba3 Qe6 18 f3 Bh3 =, Smyslov–Keres, USSR Champ. 1950

(d) 6 . . . a6 7 Qc2 (7 Qd3 or 7 Nf3 or 7 Nd2 lead, at best, to equality) 7 . . . c5 8 Nf3 cxd4 9 Nxd4 Bc5 10 Nb3 Bd6 11 0-0 0-0 12 Nc3 Rb8 13 Rd1 Qc7 14 Bg5 h6 15 Qd2 with an edge for White (Neishtadt).

(e) 12 0-0 Bb7 13 Qc2 c5 14 dxc5 Qxc5 15 Qxc5 Nxc5 16 Rc1 Rc8 17 Ne1 Ke7 =, Kavalek–Ljubojević, Torino 1982.

(f) The move order of the column is the one most often adopted, or 1 d4 Nf6 2 c4 e6 3 g3 d5 4 Bg2 c5 5 Nf3 cxd4 6 Nxd4. If 4 Nf3 Bb4† 5 Bd2 it is a Bogo-Indian Defense and 4 Nc3 Bb4 is a Nimzo-Indian.

(g) For 4 d5 see Benoni Defense; for 4 Nf3 cxd4 5 Nxd4 see English Opening.

(h) 12 Ng5 0-0 13 Nxe6 fxe6 14 Nd2 (White does better not to accept the sacrifice with 14 Rxe6?! d3 15 Bxc6 bxc6 16 Be3 Bd4 17 Nc3 Qd7 18 Qxd3 Qxe6 ∓) 14 . . . d3 15 Nb3 Bd4 and now: (A) 16 Be3 Bxb2 17 Rb1 Bc3 18 Rf1 Bb4 19 Bxc6 bxc6 20 Nc1 d2 21 Rb4 dxc1

(Q) 22 Qxc1 $\pm$, Pergericht–Sax, Brussels 1985. (B) 16 Nxd4 Qxd4 17 Bxc6 bxc6 18 Be3 Qxc4 19 b3 Qb5 = (Sax).

(i)   12 Ne5 Nxe5 13 Bxe5 Bc5 14 Nd2 Re8 (14 . . . Ng4 15 Bf4 Re8 16 Re1 Rxe1 17 Qxe1 d3 is unclear—Nogueiras) 15 Re1 Ng4 16 Bf4 $\pm$, Alburt–Furman, USSR Chp. 1975.

(j)   9 . . . Bg4 10 h3 Bxf3 11 Bxf3 (11 Qxf3 Bc5 12 exd4 Nxd4 13 Qd3 0-0 is equal, Rashkovsky–Tal, Lvov 1981) 11. . . Be7 12 exd4 exd4 13 Bf4 0-0 14 Nd2 h6 15 Re1 Bd6 16 Bxd6 Qxd6 17 Nb3 Rad8 18 c5 Qe7 19 Rc1 $\pm$, Karpov–Quinteros, Linares 1981.

(k) 10 . . . Be6, (Khalifman–Oll, Kiev 1984,) led to a position favoring White, e.g. 11 Ng5 Bg4 12 Qb3 Qd7 13 Nd5 Nxd5 14 Bxd5 f6 15 f3 Bf5 16 Nf7 Rg8 17 Nd6† Bxd6 18 Bxg8 Bb4 19 Bd5 d2 20 Bxd2 Bxd2 21 Rad1 Ba5 22 Be4 Qc8 23 Bxf5 Qxf5 24 Qxb7 $\pm$.

(l)   12 Qa4† Nc6 13 Bxc6† bxc6 14 Qxb4 Bh3 15 Bd2 Bxf1 16 Rxf1 Qe7 17 Na4 Qb4 ∞, Pelts–B. Hartman, Canadian Chp. 1984.

CATALAN OPENING

Closed Variation

1 d4 Nf6 2 c4 e6 3 g3 d5 4 Bg2 Be7 5 Nf3 0-0 6 0-0 Nbd7 7 Qc2 c6

	37	38	39	40	41	42
8	Nbd2				b3	Bf4
	b6				b5	b6(l)
9	e4			b3	Nbd2(i)	Nbd2
	Bb7	Ba6	dxe4?!	Bb7	bxc4	Bb7
10	b3	b3	Nxe4	Bb2	bxc4	e4
	Rc8	Rc8	Bb7	Rc8	Ba6	Rc8
11	Bb2	Bb2	Rd1	Rac1	Bb2	e5
	c5(a)	c5	Nxe4	c5	Rb8(j)	Ne8
12	exd5	exd5	Qxe4	Qb1(f)	Rab1	h4
	exd5	exd5	Re8	dxc4	Qa5	b6
13	dxc5	Qf5	Bf4	Nxc4	Bc3	cxd5
	dxc4(b)	g6	Rc8	b5	Bb4	cxd5
14	Nxc4	Qh3	Rac1	Ncd2(g)	Rxb4	Qb3
	b5	cxd4	Ba8	a6	Rxb4	Qc7
15	Nce5	Nxd4	Qc2(e)	dxc5	Rc1	Rfd1
	Rxc5(c)	Nc5(d)		Bxc5(h)	Qa4(k)	Nb8 =

(a) 11 ... dxe4 12 Nxe4 c5 13 Nxf6† Bxf6 14 Ng5 Bxg5 15 Bxb7 Rc7 16 Be4 g6 17 d5 exd5 18 cxd5 Bf6 19 d6 and White stood much better in Padevsky–Janošević, Örense 1973.

(b) 13 ... Bxc5 is also possible; Shamkovich–Moiseyev, USSR 1951, continued 14 Qf5 Re8 15 Rad1 Qc7 16 Rc1 dxc4 17 Nxc4 Be4 18 Qh3 when 18 ... Qb7 gives equal chances.

(c) The column is Smyslov–Benko, Monte Carlo 1968, which continued: 16 Qe2 Nxe5 17 Nxe5 Bxg2 18 Kxg2 Qd5† 19 Kg1 Re8 20 Ng4 Draw.

(d) 16 Rad1 h5 17 N2f3 Nce4 18 Ne5 Qe8 19 Bxe4 dxe4 20 Nf5 gxf5 21 Qxf5 Re5 22 Qg5† Kh7 23 Qf5† Kg8 24 b4 Rc7 25 Qg5† Kh7 26 Qf5† Kg8 27 Qg5† Kh7 28 Qf5†Kg8 29 Rd6 Bc8 30 Qg5† Kh7 31 Nd7 Qxd7 32 Rxd7 Bxd7 33 Bxf6 Bxf6 34 Qxf6 Rxc4 35 Qe7 Resigns, Razuvayev–Lputian, USSR Chp. 1979.

(e) The column is Smyslov–O'Kelly, Havana 1967, which illustrates that the exchange starting with 9 ... dxe4 is not favorable for Black prior to the completion of his Queen-side development: White has a great advantage.

(f) 12 Ne5 cxd4 13 Bxd4 Nxe5 14 Bxe5 Ba3 15 Bb2 Qe7 16 Qb1 $\pm$, Rashkovsky–Beliavsky, USSR Chp. 1976.

(g) 14 Ne3 Qb6 15 Rfd1 Be4 =, Barcza–Sandor, Hungarian Chp. 1958.

(h) 16 b4 Bb6 17 Rxc8 Qxc8 18 Rc1 Qa8 19 Nb3 Rd8 is equal, Averkin–Kholmov, USSR Chp. 1969.

(i) 9 c5 Ne4 10 Nbd2 f5 11 Bb2 b4 12 Nxe4 fxe4 13 Ne5 Nxe5 14 dxe5 Bd7 15 Bd4 a5 16 a3 Qc7 17 Ra2 Rfb8 =, Sigurjonson–Hoi, Reykjavik 1981.

(j) 11 . . . Qa5 12 Bc3 Bb4 13 Bxb4 Qxb4 14 Rfb1 Qa5 15 e3 Rab8 = , Barcza–Bouwmeester, Lugano 1968.

(k) 16 Bxb4 Qxb4 17 e3 Rc8 18 Qb3 Qa5 = , Geller–Larsen, Copenhagen 1966.

(l) 8 . . . Ne4 9 Nc3 f5 10 Rab1 a5 11 Rfd1 Qe8 12 Ne1 g5 13 Bc1 Qh5 14 Nxe4 fxe4 15 f3 Nf6 16 Qd2 h6 17 b3 Bd6 with roughly equal chances, Lengyel–Pogacs, Hungarian Chp. 1964. The column is Averbakh–Smyslov, USSR Chp. 1961.

CATALAN OPENING

Closed Variation

1 d4 Nf6 2 c4 e6 3 g3 d5 4 Bg2 Be7 5 Nf3 0-0 6 0-0

	43	44	45	46	47	48
	(Nbd7)...c5					
7	Nc3					cxd5(h)
	dxc4........c6					Nxd5
8	e4	b3				e4(i)
	c5(a)	b6				Nf6
9	d5	Bb2 ....Qc2				Nc3
	exd5	Bb7........Ba6		Bb7		cxd4
10	exd5	Qc2	Nd2	Rd1		Nxd4
	Nb6	Rc8	b5	Rc8........b5		Nc6
11	Ne5	Rad1	c5	e4	c5	Nxc6
	Bd6	Qc7	b4	dxe4	b4	bxc6
12	f4	e4	Na4	Nxe4	Na4	Qc2
	Re8	dxe4	Qc7(d)	c5	a5	Ba6
13	a4	Nxe4	Re1	Nxf6+	Nb2	Rad1
	Bxe5	Nxe4	Rfb8	Bxf6	Ba6	Qa5
14	fxe5(b)	Qxe4(c)	e4(e)	Ng5(f)	Nd3(g)	Bd2 ±

(a) 8 . . . c6 9 a4 b6 10 Qe2 Ba6 11 Rd1 Qc8 12 d5 exd5 13 exd5 Re8 14 dxc6 Nc5 with a double-edged position, Zaitsev–Lukacs, Dubna 1979.

(b) 14 . . . Rxe5 15 Bf4 Re8 16 a5 and the position favors White (Neishtadt).

(c) 14 . . . c5 15 d5 and here two moves have been tried: (A) 15 . . . Nf6 16 Qc2 exd5 17 Be5 Qd8 18 Ng6 g6 19 h4 Bd6 20 Ba1 Re8 21 cxd5 Be5 22 Ne6 Qd6 23 Bxe5 Qxe5 24 Rfe1 Qf5 25 Qxf5 gxf5 26 Nf4 and White stood clearly better in Geller–Lutikov, USSR 1966. (B) 15 . . . Bf6 16 Qc2 exd5 17 cxd5 Bxb2 18 Qxb2 Rcd8 19 d6 Qb8 20 Rfe1 Nf6 21 Re7 Rxd6 22 Rxd6 Qxd6 23 Rxb7 Qd1† 24 Bf1 Qxf3 25 Rxa7 Re8 26 Qd2 Ne4 27 Qe3 Qxe3 28 fxe3 g6 = , Geller–Nei, USSR Chp. 1967.

(d) 12 . . . Bb5 13 Re1 Re8 is approximately equal.

(e) 14 . . . dxe4 15 Nxe4 Nxe4 16 Bxe4 Nf6 17 Bg2 is Pytel–Benko, Skopje 1972: 17 . . . Rd8 provides chances for both sides.

(f) 14 . . . Bxg5 15 Bxb7 Rc7 16 Be4 h6 17 dxe5 bxc5 18 Bb2 Bf6 19 Rd6 Bxb2 20 Qxb2 Qf6 21 Qxf6 Nxf6 22 Bf3 Rfc8 23 Rad1 Kf8 24 Ra6 Ke7 25 Rdd6 Ne8 26 Rdc6 Kd7 27 Rxc7† Rxc7 28 Kf1, Bronstein–Čirić, Sarajevo 1971, is approximately equal.

(g) White stands clearly better. Razuvaev–Lputian, USSR Chp. 1980–81, continued 14 . . . Bxd3 15 exd3 Ne8 16 a3 Nc7 17 axb4 axb4 18 Bd2 ± .

(h) 7 Qc2 cxd4 8 Nxd4 Nc6 9 Nxc6 bxc6 10 b3 Ba6 11 Bb2 Rc8 = , Gulko–Karpov, Thessaloniki 1988.

(i) 8 dxc5 Bxc5 9 Qc2 Qe7 10 a3 Nc6 11 b4 Bb6 12 Bb2 Bd7 13 e4 Nc7 14 Nc3 ± . Eliskases–Weil, Bad Oeynhausen 1938. The column is Keres–Stahlberg, Stockholm 1938.

GRÜNFELD DEFENSE

1 d4 Nf6 2 c4 g6 3 Nc3 d5

Diagram 75

I NVENTED BY THE AUSTRIAN MASTER Ernst Grünfeld in 1922, this defense is a child of the hypermodern revolution. Following the upheaval of World War I, new and revolutionary ideas were brought forth in literature and the arts, including chess. A group of young players in the 1920s, led by Nimzowitsch and Reti, questioned the dogmatism of the reigning classical school of chess, especially the concept that it is necessary to occupy the center.

The Grünfeld is the most dramatic antithesis of the old belief. Black allows White to establish a classical pawn center, which would be deadly in an open game. But by sidestepping the pawn steamroller and attacking the central squares instead of occupying them, Black is able to generate counterplay. Notable exponents of this opening have included Alekhine, Smyslov, Fischer, and, more recently, Kasparov.

Diagram 76

The most direct challenge to the Grünfeld is the EXCHANGE VARIATION, 4 cxd5 Nxd5 5 e4 (cols. 1–18). White immediately obtains the classical pawn center with its attacking prospects. After the usual 5 . . . Nxc3 6 bxc3 Bg7 (see diagram) the main line is 7 Bc4 0-0 8 Ne2 c5 9 0-0 Nc6 10 Be3 cxd4 11 cxd4 Bg4 12 f3 Na5 (cols. 1–5). White gains a strong initiative with the sacrifice 13 Bd3 Be6 14 d5 Bxa1 15 Qxa1 (cols. 1–3); he has clearly sufficient compensation for the exchange, but it is difficult to show more than this. Of White's other tries, the most promising is the pawn sacrifice 14 Rc1 (col. 4).

Columns 6–12 cover deviations from the above lines. Except for col. 7, these are all options for Black which take the game into less examined territory. These lines are riskier because they are less forceful and hence give White a freer hand. Nonetheless, they are difficult to refute. Col. 7 covers the bold pawn snatch by White, 10 . . . Bg4 11 f3 Na5 12 Bxf7†. Karpov has used it, but Black seems to have had little difficulty equalizing.

7 Nf3 (cols. 13–18) is a modern approach in the Exchange Variation, in vogue in the early 1980s. White places the knight on its best square without fearing the pin . . . Bg4, but Black seems to have sufficient play. 7 . . . c5 8 Rb1 (cols. 13–16) is still an interesting line.

4 Bf4 (cols. 19–24) is a safe way to play for the initiative. White eschews a big pawn center and simply develops, intending queenside operations. This line is too slow to gain an advantage against accurate play.

Diagram 77

The system 4 Nf3 Bg7 5 Qb3 dxc4 6 Qxc4 0-0 7 e4 (cols. 25–36) is considered the CLASSICAL LINE against the Grünfeld (see diagram). It is safer than the Exchange Variation but more aggressive than 4 Bf4. The *Smyslov Variation* 7 . . . Bg4 (cols. 25–30) is the most frequently tested response, meeting 8 Be3 with 8 . . . Nfd7! (cols. 25–29), uncovering the bishop to attack d4. Black's minor pieces become active, yet White's spatial advantage may still tell.

Other seventh moves for Black are covered in cols. 30–36. Notable is the *Prins Variation*, 7 . . . Na6 (cols. 31–32), which prepares the central attack 8 . . . c5. This has been Kasparov's favorite choice in his World

Championship matches with Karpov. Another reasonable line for Black is 7 . . . a6 8 Qb3 b5 (col. 33), gaining queenside space. Black's remaining options (8 . . . c5, 7 . . . Nc6, and 7 . . . c6) (cols. 34–36) are playable, but probably inferior.

5 Bg5 (cols. 37–39) is a positional continuation used by Seirawan. 5 . . . Ne4 6 Bh4 c5 (col. 37) allows Black active play. 5 cxd5 Nxg5 6 Nxg5 (cols. 37–38) gains White some initiative at the cost of the bishop-pair.

5 e3 (cols. 40–42) develops the kingside quickly and prepares for central action, but it is too passive to achieve anything if Black reacts calmly.

Less frequently played alternatives for White are 4 Nf3 Bg7 5 Qa4† (col. 43), 5 cxd5 (cols. 44–45), 4 Bg5 (cols. 46–47), and 4 Qb3 (col. 48). Though none of these are very threatening, and Black often gains the advantage, they contain elements of surprise.

Diagram 78

In the NEO-GRÜNFELD DEFENSE, 1 d4 Nf6 2 c4 g6 3 g3 Bg7 4 Bg2 d5 (see diagram) (cols. 49–60), the pawn-push . . . d5 is employed despite the fact that instead of 3 Nc3, White embarked on the Catalan setup with 3 g3. Black's system underwent its first test in Alekhine vs. Mikenas, Kemeri 1937, in step with the first ten moves of column 54; but 8 dxc5 (col. 53) seems better. The defense has since been well analyzed, and, though played occasionally (see col. 52), Black usually shifts into the King's Indian or the English Defense with . . . d6 and possibly . . . c5.

GRÜNFELD DEFENSE

Exchange Variation

**1 d4 Nf6 2 c4 g6 3 Nc3 d5 4 cxd5 Nxd5 5 e4 Nxc3 6 bxc3 Bg7 7 Bc4
0-0 8 Ne2 c5 9 0-0 Nc6 10 Be3 cxd4 11 cxd4 Bg4 12 f3**

	1	2	3	4	5	6
	Na5..Bd7					
13	Bd3..Bd5(l)				Bd5(l)	Rb1
	Be6				Bd7	e6
14	d5.................................Rc1			Rc1	Rb1	Qd2(o)
	Bxa1			Bxa2	a6	Na5
15	Qxa1			Qa4(i)	Bxb7(m)	Bd3
	f6			Be6	Ra7	a6
16	Rb1 ....Bh6(f)		Bh6(f)	d5	Bd5	Bg5
	Bd7(a)......Re8	Re8	Re8	Bd7	Bb5	f6
17	Bh6(b)	Qc3(e)	Nf4(g)	Qb4	a4	Bh6(p)
	Rf7(c)	Bd7	Bf7	e6(j)	Bxe2	Rc8
18	e5	Bd2	Re1	Nc3	Qxe2	Rfc1
	e6(d)	b6 =	Qb6†(h)	b6(k)	e6(n)	b5 =

(a) 16 . . . Bf7 is playable; after 17 Bh6 Re8 18 Bb5 Qd6 19 Bxe8 Bxe8 20 Qc3 b6 21 Rc7 Nb7 Black had near equality in Pinter–Přibyl, Sochi 1981.

(b) 17 e5 fxe5 (17 . . . Bf5 18 Bxf5 gxf5 19 exf6 is sharp, Knaak–Ganglitz, Dresden 1985) 18 Qxe5 Qb8 19 Qd4 (19 Qxe7 Re8 ∞, Miles–Bor, Utrecht 1986) 19 . . . Qd6 20 Bd2 b6 21 Nc3 Qf6 22 Qe3 Qd6 23 Qd4, Draw, Lukacs–Wl. Schmidt, Trnava 1986.

(c) 17 . . . Re8 18 e5 Rc8 19 Nd4 leaves White with good compensation for the exchange (Timman).

(d) if 18 . . . fxe5 19 Qxe5 gives White the edge, Kavalek–Timman, Wijk aan Zee 1978. After 18 . . . e6 19 Nf4 fxe5 20 Nxe6 Bxe6 the game is even, Polugaevsky–Chandler, Amsterdam 1984.

(e) 17 Nf4 Bf7 18 Rb5 a6 19 Rb6 Rc8 is slightly better for Black, W. Garcia–Alonso, Varadero 1987.

(f) Other tries are 16 Qd4, 16 Qb1, and 16 Bd2, but Black maintains equal chances in any case.

(g) (A) 17 Nd4 Bd7 18 e5 e6 19 exf6 Qxf6 leaves Black on top, Padevsky–Minev, Bulgaria 1955. (B) 17 Rb1 a6 18 Qd4 Bf7 $\mp$.

(h) After 19 Kf1 Red8 the position is unclear, but perferable to 19 Kh1?! Qf2 20 Ne2 Rac8 $\mp$.

(i) 15 d5 Bb3 16 Qe1 e6 17 Qb4 exd5 18 Rc5 Bc4 and now both (A) 19 Bxc4 Nxc4 20 Rxd5 Qxd5! and (B) 19 Rxa5 Bxd3 20 Rxd5 Bxe2 gives Black adequate compensation for the queen.

(j) 17 ... b6 18 f4 Rc8 19 Ba6 Rxc1 20 Rxc1 e6 21 d6 Nc6 =, Dolmatov–Gavrikov, USSR 1987.

(k) (A) 18 ... exd5 19 exd5 Re8 20 Bf2 Bf8! 21 Qb2 Bg7 22 Qb4 Bf8 23 Qb2, Draw, Beliavsky–Kasparov, USSR Chp. 1988. (B) After 18 ... b6 19 Ba6 Qf6 20 f4 exd5 the game is even, Spassky–Düball, Dortmund 1973.

(l) 13 Bxf7† is probably harmless, although Karpov has played it without the exchange 10 ... cxd4 11 cxd4; see col. 7.

(m) 15 a4 e6 16 Ba2 b5 17 d5 Nc4 $\overline{\mp}$, Browne–Mecking, Manila 1976.

(n) Now (A) 19 Bc4 Bxd4 is completely equal, while the sacrifice (B) 19 Bxe6?! fxe6 20 d5 Ra8 proved unsound in Spassky–Beliavsky, Riga 1975.

(o) 14 Rab7 Na5 15 Rb4 Nxc4 16 Rxc4 Bb5 17 Rb4 Qa5 and Black's initiative is worth the pawn.

(p) (A) 17 Bf4 e5 18 dxe5 fxe5 =, Spassky–Milev, Bucharest 1953; Botvinnik regards (B) 17 Bh6 and (C) 17 Be3 as better for White. The column is analysis by Mikhalchishin.

GRÜNFELD DEFENSE

Exchange Variation

1 d4 Nf6 2 c4 g6 3 Nc3 d5 4 cxd5 Nxd5 5 e4 Nxc3 6 bxc3 Bg7 7 Bc4

	7	8	9	10	11	12
	(0-0)					b6
8	(Ne2)					Qf3
	(c5)			Nc6	b6	0-0
9	(0-0)(a)			Bg5(k)	h4(m)	e5(o)
	(Nc6)			Na5(l)	Nc6	Ba6
10	(Be3)			Bb3	Bd5(n)	Bd5(p)
	Bg4	Qc7		Nxb3	Qd7	c6
11	f3	Rc1		axb3	h5	Bb3
	Na5	Rd8		b6	e6	Qd7
12	Bxf7†	Qd2(d)	Bf4(h)	0-0	Bb3	Ne2
	Rxf7	a6(e)	Qd7	Bb7	Na5	e6
13	fxg4	f4(f)	d5(i)	Qd3	hxg6	0-0
	Rxf1†	b5	Na5	Qd7	fxg6	c5
14	Kxf1	Bd3	Bd3	Rad1	Be3	Rd1
	Qd6	f5	e5	a5	Qb5	Nc6
15	e5(b)	Ng3	Be3	f4	0-0	Bg5
	Qd5(c)	e6(g)	b6(j)	e6 =	c5 =	cxd4 ±

(a) Interesting is 9 Be3 Nc6 10 Rc1!? cxd4 11 cxd4 Qa5† 12 Kf1 Bd7 13 h4 Rac8 14 h5 with attacking chances, Polugaevsky–Kudrin, New York Open 1989.

(b) 15 Kg1 Qe6 16 Qd3 Qc4 17 Qxc4 Nxc4 (A) 18 Bf2 cxd4 19 cxd4 e5 and Black has compensation for the pawn, Karpov–Kasparov, World Chp. (game 11) 1987. (B) 18 Bg5 cxd4 19 cxd4 e5 is also roughly equal, Seirawan–Hort, Lugano 1988.

(c) 16 Bf2 Rd8 17 Qa4 b6 18 Qc2 (A) 18 . . . Rf8 19 Kg1 Qc4 20 Qd2 Qe6 21 h3 ±, Karpov–Kasparov, Belfort 1988. (B) 18 . . . Rc8 19 Qd1 Rd8! =, Lputian–Dzhandzhava, Simferopol 1988.

(d) (A) 12 Qe1 Qa5! 13 Rd1 cxd4 14 cxd4 Qxe1 15 Rfxe1 b6 with an equal endgame, Pachman–Smejkal, Czechoslovakia 1968. (B) 12 h3 b6 13 f4 e6 14 Qe1 Na5 15 Bd3 f5 16 g4 was played in the great encounter Spassky–Fischer, Siegen 1970; now 16 . . . Bb7 is better for Black, but the game continued instead 16 . . . fxe4 17 Bxe4 Bb7 18 Ng3 Nc4 19 Bxb7 Qxb7 20 Bf2 Qc6 21 Qe2 cxd4 22 cxd4 b5 23 Ne4 Bxd4 24 Ng5 Bxf2†?! (24 . . . Bb6 is preferable, with a balanced game) 25 Rxf2 Rd6 26 Re1 Qb6 27 Ne4 Rd4 28 Nf6† Kh8 29 Qxe6! Rd6 (it looks as if 29 . . . Rd1 wins, as 30 Qxb6 loses to 30 . . . Rxe1†, but White plays 30 Qf7! Rxe1† 31 Kg2 when the threat of Qxh7 mate is deadly) 30 Qe4 Rf8 31 g5 Rd2 32 Ref1 Qc7?! (it is illogical to give up the pin; 32 . . . Rxf2 is better, but White is still clearly ahead because of the dominating position of the knight on f6) 33 Rxd2 Nxd2 34 Qd4! Rd8 35 Nd5† Kg8 36 Rf2 Nc4 37 Re2 Rd6 38 Re8† Kf7 39 Rf8†! Resigns.

(e) 12 ... Ne5 13 Bb3 Ng4 14 Bf4 e5 15 Bg3 Qe7 (not 15 ... Bh6? 16 Bxe5 Qxe5 17 Qxh6 Qxe4 18 Bxf7†, Muratov–Kremenetsky, Moscow 1974) 16 f3 with a plus, Razuraev–Malanchek, USSR 1978.

(f) If 13 Bh6 b5 14 Bd3 Qd7 with good play against the d-pawn (Adorjan).

(g) 16 d5 fxe4 17 Nxe4 Rxd5 18 Bxc5 Qd7 with balanced chances.

(h) 12 f4 is best met by 12 ... e6, when 13 f5 exf5 14 Bg5 Rf8 15 exf5 Bxf5 16 Ng3 cxd4 17 Rxf5 gxf5 18 Nxf5 Qe5 results in even chances, Antoshin–Haag, Zinnowitz 1966.

(i) 13 dxc5 Ne5 14 Bxe5 Bxe5 15 Qxd7 Bxd7 16 f4 Bg7 17 Bd5 Bb5 =, Knaak–Malich, West Germany, 1974.

(j) 16 f4 exf4 17 Bxf4 Qe7 18 Qd2 Bg4 with only a minimal edge for White, Polugaevsky–Tukmakov, Moscow 1985.

(k) The violent (A) 9 h4 allows Black good play: 9 ... Na5 10 Bb3 c5 11 h5 Nxb3 12 axb3 cxd4 ∓, Spassky–Stein, USSR 1964. (B) 9 0-0 b6 10 Be3 Bb7 11 Rc1 Qd6 12 f4 e6 13 f5 Na5 is equal, Najdorf–Sanguinetti, Argentina 1973.

(l) 9 ... Qd7 10 Qd2 e5 11 Rd1 exd4 12 cxd4 Qg4 with a complex position, Beliavsky–Milos, Szirak 1987. The column is Ovchinin–Dubinin, corr. 1960.

(m) 9 0-0 Bb7 10 f3 c5 11 Be3 cxd4 12 cxd4 Nc6 =, Uhlmann–Pachman, Czechoslovakia 1954.

(n) After 10 h5 Na5 11 Bd3 e5 12 hxg6 fxg6 13 Be3 Qe7 Black has sufficient counterplay, Tarjan–Adorjan, Hastings 1976. The column is van der Sterren–Raynor, London 1979.

(o) 9 Ne2 Nc6 10 h4 Na5 11 Bd3 e5 12 Ba3 Re8 13 h5 Qd7 14 Rd1 (Yusupov–Timman, Tilburg 1986); now 14 ... Qg4 is the best chance as 14 ... Qa4 15 Bc1 c5 16 d5 is somewhat better for White.

(p) 10 Qxa8 Bxc4 11 Qf3 f6 gives Black good play, Kane–Benko, US 1973. The column is Yusupov–Timman, Bugojno 1986.

GRÜNFELD DEFENSE

Exchange Variation

1 d4 Nf6 2 c4 g6 3 Nc3 d5 4 cxd5 Nxd5 5 e4 Nxc3(a) 6 bxc3 Bg7 7 Nf3 c5

	13	14	15	16	17	18
8	Rb1				Be3	
	0-0(b)				Qa5	Bg4
9	Be2				Qd2	Rc1(s)
	cxd4	Nc6	Qa5	Bg4	0-0(p)	Qa5
10	cxd4	d5	0-0(j)	0-0(m)	Rc1	Qd2
	Qa5†	Ne5(g)	Qxa2(k)	Bxf3	cxd4	Bxf3(t)
11	Qd2(c)	Nxe5	Bg5	Bxf3	cxd4	gxf3
	Qxd2†	Bxe5	Qe6	cxd4	Qxd2†	e6
12	Bxd2	Qd2	e5	cxd4	Nxd2(q)	Rb1
	e6(d)	e6	Rd8	Bxd4(n)	Nc6	cxd4
13	0-0	f4	Qa4	Rxb7	Nb3	cxd4
	b6	Bg7(h)	Qc6	Nc6	Rd8	Qxd2†
14	Rbc1(e)	c4	Qb3	Bh6	d5	Kxd2
	Bb7	exd5	Be6	Re8	Nb4	0-0
15	Bb4	cxd5	c4	Qa4	a3	e5
	Rd8(f)	Bd4(i)	cxd4(l)	Rc8(o)	Na2(r)	Nc6(u)

(a) 5 . . . Nb6 6 h3 Bg7 7 Nf3 0-0 8 Be2 Be6 9 0-0 ±, Polugaevsky–Dorfman, USSR 1978; 8 . . . Nc6 and 8 . . . c5 have been tried, but this line still seems better for White.

(b) Alternatives are: (A) 8 . . . Qa5 9 Rb5 Qxc3† 10 Bd2 Qa3 11 Qc2 c4 (11 . . . Nc6? 12 Rb3 Resigns, Polevodin–Maslov, USSR 1984) 12 Bxc4 ±, Gaprindashvili–J. Khadilkar, Lucerne 1982; (B) 8 . . . Nc6 9 d5 Bxc3† 10 Bd2 Bxd2† 11 Qxd2 Nd4 12 Nxd4 +, Ksieski–Szitkey, Trnava 1986; (C) 8 . . . Bg4 is possible but also fails to equalize.

(c) 11 Bd2 Qxa2 12 0-0 b6 (12 . . . Qe6?! 13 Qc2 Qd7 14 d5 ±, Conquest–Korchnoi, Lugano 1986) 13 Qc1 Qe6 is unclear, Petursson–Ftáčnik, Tallinn 1981.

(d) 12 . . . b6 13 0-0 (13 Rc1 Bb7 14 Bd3 Na6 =, de Boer–Mikhalchishin, Cascais 1986) 13 . . . Bb7 14 d5 Ba6 15 Bxa6 Nxa6 16 Be3 f5 with equal chances, Gaprindashvili–Levitina, Smederevska Palanka 1987.

(e) 14 Rfd1 Bb7 15 d5 exd5 16 exd5 Nd7 17 Bb4 Rfc8 18 Be7 Bf6 is roughly equal, Karpov–Kasparov, World Chp. 1987.

(f) 16 Bb5 Bf8 (16 . . . Na6 17 Be7 Rdc8 18 d5 ±, A. Ivanov–Baikor, USSR 1986) 17 Bxf8 Rxf8 ±.

(g) 10 . . . Bxc3† 11 Bd2 Bxd2† 12 Qd2 Na5 (12 . . . Nd4 is bad: 13 Nxd4 cxd4 14 Qxd4 ±, Kasparov–Natsis, Malta 1980) 13 h4 Bg4 14 h5 Bxf3 15 gxf3 e5 with an imbalance.

(h) 13 . . . Bh8 14 c4 Re8 15 e5 f6 16 f5! is very strong for White, McCambridge–Hjartarson, Grindavik 1984.

(i) After 16 Bb2 Qb6 17 Bd3 c4 18 Bxc4 (18 Bxd4 Qxd4 19 Bc2 Qc5 20 Qf2 Qa5† 21 Qd2 Qc5, Draw, Schüssler–Helmers, Gjovik 1985) 18 . . . Re8 19 e5 Bf5 20 Qxd4 Bxb1 the position is unclear.

(j) (A) 10 Rb5 Qxc3† 11 Bd2 Qa3 12 Ra5 Qb2 13 Rc5 Qa2 14 0-0 Bg4 is sharp but about equal, Groszpeter–Parlov, Thessaloniki 1981. (B) 10 Qd2 a6 11 0-0 Nc6 12 Qe3 Qxa2 with good play, Przewoznik–Soltau, corr. 1986.

(k) 10 . . . Qxc3 11 Bd2 Qa3 12 Qc2 Bd7 13 dxc5 Bc6 14 Bb5 Na6 15 Rfc1 Nc7 16 Rb3 Qxb3 ∞, Beliavsky–Tukmakov, USSR 1983.

(l) 16 Bxe7 Rc8 17 Nxd4 Bxc4 18 Nxc6 Bxb3 19 Nxb8 Be6 20 Bd6 Bf8 21 Bf3 Bxd6 22 Bxb7 Bxb8 23 Bxe8 Bxe5 =, B. Damljanović–W. Schmidt, Athens 1984.

(m) 10 Rb7 Nc6 11 dxc5 Bxf3 12 Bxf3 Bxc3† 13 Bd2 Qa5 with equal chances, Kostić–Grünfeld, Teplice Šanov 1922.

(n) 12 . . . Qxd4 13 Rxb7 Nc6 14 Qxd4 Bxd4 15 Ba3 ±, Polovodin–Semenjuk, USSR 1982.

(o) After 16 Be2 Qa5 17 Bb5 Qxa4 18 Bxa4 Na5 the game is level, Commons–Tarjan, US 1978.

(p) Equally playable is 9 . . . Nc6 10 Rc1 cxd4 11 cxd4 Qxd2† 12 Kxd2 0-0 13 d5 Rd8 14 Ke1 Na5 =, Kaminsky–Dvojris, USSR 1982.

(q) 12 Kxd2 can be met by 12 . . . Nc6 13 d5 Rd8 14 Ke1 Nb4 with good play (Adorjan).

(r) 16 Rc2 Nc3 17 Bd3 e6 18 Bg5, Portisch–Adorjan, Hungary 1981, when 18 . . . Rd6 is equal (Adorjan). 8 Be3, as in the column, may also be played earlier, e.g., 7 Be3 c5 8 Qd2 Qa5 9 Nf3 Nc6 =.

(s) 9 Qa4† Nc6 10 Ne5 Bxe5 11 dxe5 Qc7 12 f4 0-0 ∞, Kolder–Lukin, Naleczow 1981.

(t) After 10 . . . Nd7 11 Ng5 Nb6 12 h3 Rc8 13 dxc5 Na4 an obscure position arose in Pasman–Gutman, Beer-Sheva 1982.

(u) 16 f4 Rad8 17 Kc3 Rd7 18 Bb5 Rc8 =, Sande–Nesis, corr. 1985.

GRÜNFELD DEFENSE

1 d4 Nf6 2 c4 g6 3 Nc3 d5 4 Bf4 Bg7

	19	20	21	22	23	24
5	e3(a)			Nf3		
	c5		0-0	c5	0-0	
6	dxc5		cxd5(f)	dxc5	Rc1	e3
	Qa5		Nxd5	Qa5	c5	c6
7	Rc1(b)		Nxd5	Rc1(k)	dxc5	Rc1(p)
	Ne4		Qxd5	dxc4	Be6(m)	Bg4
8	cxd5		Bxc7	e3	Nd4	h3
	Nxc3		Na6(g)	Qxc5	Nc6	Bxf3
9	Qd2		Bxa6	Qa4†	Nxe6(n)	Qxf3
	Qxa2		bxa6(h)	Nc6	fxe6	Qa5(q)
10	bxc3		Nf3	Bxc4	e3	Bd3
	Qxd2†	Qa5	Bf5(i)	0-0	Qa5	Nbd7
11	Kxd2	Bc4	Qb3	0-0	Be2	0-0(r)
	Nd7	Nd7	Qxb3	Bd7	e5	dxc4
12	Bb5	Nf3(d)	axb3	Qb5	cxd5	Bxc4
	0-0(c)	Nxc5(e)	Rfc8(j)	Qxb5(l)	exf4(o)	e5(s)

(a) 5 Rc1 dxc4 6 e4 c5 7 dxc5 Qa5 8 Bc4 0-0 9 e5 Nfd7 10 Nf3 Nc6 (not 10 ... Nxc5? 11 0-0 Nc6 12 Nd5 ±, Portisch–Nunn, Budapest 1987), when 11 e6 leads to very unclear complications.

(b) Other tries: (A) 7 cxd5 Nxd5 8 Qxd5 Bxc3† 9 bxc3 Qc3† is fine for Black. (B) 7 Qa4† Qxa4 8 Nxa4 Ne4 9 f3 (if 9 Bxb8 Bd7 10 f3 Bxa4 11 fxe4 dxc4 is strong, Böhm–Timman, Holland 1983) 9 ... Bd7 10 fxe4 Bxa4 11 cxd5 Bxb2 =, van der Heijden–van Mil, Holland 1986. (C) 7 Qb3 Nc6 8 Qb5 Be6 ∞, Tal–Mikhalchishin, Lvov 1984.

(c) 13 Bxd7 Bxd7 14 e4 (14 Rb1 e5 =) 14 ... f5 15 e5 e6 (is 15 ... Rac8 16 c4 Rxc5 17 Be3 ±, Karpov) 16 c4 Rfc8 17 c6 bxc6 18 d6 (Karpov–Kasparov, World Chp. 1986); now 18 ... g5 19 Bxg5 Bxe5 20 c5 Rcb8 gives Black counterplay, but he is still worse.

(d) 12 Ne2 Nxc5 13 0-0 Ne4 14 Qd3 Nd6 is roughly equal, Farago–Tseshkovsky, Banja Luka 1981.

(e) 13 0-0 0-0 14 Be5 Bxe5 15 Nxe5 f6 16 d6† Kg7 17 dxe7 Re8 18 Qd5! Be6 19 Qd6 ±, Petursson–Thorsteins, Icelandic Chp. 1988.

(f) Alternatives are: (A) 6 Qb3 dxc4 7 Bxc4 Nc6 8 Be2 a5 9 Nf3 Nb4 10 0-0 Be6 =, Mecking–Hort, Palma 1970, (B) 6 Rc1 c5 7 dxc5 Be6 8 Nge2 Nc6 9 cxd5 Nxd5 10 Nxd5 Qxd5 =, D. Paunović–Ghinda, Nikea 1986.

(g) (A) 8 ... Nc6 is dubious, since 9 Ne2 Bg4 10 f3 Rac8 11 Nc3 Qe6 12 Bf4 Bxd4 13 fxg4 is strong. (B) 8 ... Bf5 9 Ne2 Rc8 10 Nc3 Qc6 11 Bg3 Na6 ∞, Tamme–Gulko, USSR 1977. (C) 8 ... b6 9 Be2 Nc6 10 Nf3 Qa5† 11 Qd2 ± (Botvinnik).

(h) 9 ... Qxg2 10 Qf3 Qxf3 11 Nxf3 bxa6 12 Rc1 f6, Lengyel–Gligorić, Enschede 1963; Black is solid but passive.

(i) (A) 10 . . . Bb7 11 0-0 Rac8 12 Bg3 Rc4 13 b3 Rc3 14 Qd2 leaves White on top, Gastonyi–Sallay, Budapest 1964. (B) 10 . . . Qb7 11 Bg3 Qxb2 12 0-0 Be6 13 Qc1 ±, Ivkov–Lengyel, Belgrade 1962.

(j) 13 Rc1 Rab8 14 Rc3 Rb7 15 Ba5 Rxc3 16 Bxc3 Rxb3 17 Kd2 Be4 18 Ra1 ±, Riskin–Malisauskas, USSR 1986.

(k) 7 cxd5 Nxd5 8 Qxd5 Bxc3† 9 Bd2 Be6 with: (A) 10 Qxb7 Bxd2† 11 Nxd2 0-0 12 b4 Qa4 and Black has good chances, Tseshkovsky–Grigorian, USSR 1977. (B) 10 Bxc3 Qxc3†! equalizes easily.

(l) 13 Bxb5 Rac8 14 Rfd1 Rfd8 15 h3 h6 16 Kf1 a6 17 Be2 Be6 18 Rxd8† Rxd8 19 Ne5 Nxe5 20 Bxe5 Rd2, Draw, Karpov–Kasparov, London 1986.

(m) 7 . . . dxc4 8 Qxd8 Rxd8 9 e3 Na6 10 c6 bxc6 11 Bxc4 Nd5 gives Black sufficient play, Korchnoi–Stein, USSR 1963.

(n) 9 e3 Nxd4 10 exd4 dxc4 11 Be2 Rc8 12 0-0 b6 =, D. Gurevich–Henley, Hastings 1982.

(o) 13 dxc6 bxc6 14 exf4 Ne4 15 0-0 Nxc3 =, Veksler–Chudinovsky, USSR 1967.

(p) White has several choices here: (A) 7 Qb3 is best met by 7 . . . Qa5 8 Nd2 Nbd7 9 Be2 Nh5 10 Bxh5 dxc4 11 Qd1 Qxh5 =, Kotov–Novotelnov, Moscow 1947. (B) 7 Be2 dxc4 8 Bxc4 Bg4 9 h3 Bxf3 10 Qxf3 Qa5 and Black is all right. (C) 7 Qc2 Bf5 8 Qb3 Qb6 9 c5 Qxb3 =, Miles–S. Agdestein, Oslo 1984.

(q) 9 . . . e6 10 Bd3 Nbd7 11 0-0 Re8 with a solid position, Hausner–Lechtinský, Hradec Králové 1981.

(r) 11 Qe2 e5 12 dxe5 dxc4 13 Bxg6 hxg6 14 exf6 Nxf6 15 Qxc4 b5 16 Qb3 Nd5 gives Black compensation for the pawn, Bukhman–Tseitlin, USSR 1975.

(s) 13 dxe5 Nxe5 14 Bxe5 Qxe5 is completely equal, Najdorf–Flohr, Budapest 1950.

GRÜNFELD DEFENSE
Classical Line (Smyslov Variation)

1 d4 Nf6 2 c4 g6 3 Nc3 d5 4 Nf3 Bg7 5 Qb3 dxc4 6 Qxc4 0-0 7 e4 Bg4

	25	26	27	28	29	30
8	Be3..Be2(q)					
	Nfd7					Nc6
9	Qb3.................................			Rd1.........	0-0-0(n)	d5
	Nb6(a)			Nc6	Nb6	Bxf3(r)
10	Rd1			Be2	Qc5	gxf3
	Nc6		e6	Nb6(j)	e6(o)	Na5
11	d5		Be2(g)	Qc5	h3	Qd3
	Ne5		Nc6	Qd6	Bxf3	c5
12	Be2		e5(h)	h3(k)	gxf3	f4
	Nxf3†		Ne7	Bxf3	N8d7	c4
13	gxf3		0-0	gxf3	Qa3	Qf3
	Bh5(b)		c6	Rfd8	Qh4	e6
14	Rg1.........f4(e)		h3	d5(l)	Kb1	dxe6
	Qd7(c)	Bxe2	Bxf3	Ne5	Bh6	fxe6
15	Rg3	Nxe2	Bxf3	Nb5	Bxh6	Qh3
	c6(d)	Qd7(f)	Nf5(i)	Qf6(m)	Qxh6(p)	Qe7 =

(a) (A) 9 . . . c5 10 d5 Na6 11 Be2 Qa5 12 0-0 Rab8 13 Bf4 $\pm$, Sturua–Henley, Tbilisi 1983. (B) 9 . . . Nc6 10 Qxb7 Na5 11 Qa6 c5 is unclear, Polugaevsky–Simagin, USSR 1960.

(b) If 13 . . . Bh3 14 Rg1 Qc8 15 f4 Bd7 16 f5 Kh8 17 fxg6 fxg6 18 h4 Qe8 19 h5 with excellent chances for White (Hübner).

(c) 14 . . . Qc8 15 Rg3 c6 16 a4 Qc7 (the more recent tries, 16 . . . Kh8 and 16 . . . Be5 are even worse for Black) 17 a5 $\pm$, van den Berg–Božić, Holland vs. Yugoslavia 1949.

(d) 16 dxc6 Qxc6 17 Nb5 Rfc8 18 Nxa7 Rxa7 19 Bxb6 Raa8 20 Rg5 Qf6 21 Rc5 Qxb2 (Cebalo's 20 . . . Qf4 may be better) 22 Qxb2 Bxb2 23 Rxc8† Rxc8 24 Rd7 $\pm$, Dlugy–Peelen, Amsterdam 1987.

(e) 14 h4 Qd7 15 a4 a5 16 Nb5 Nc8 17 f4 Bxe2 18 Kxe2 Nd6 =.

(f) (A) 16 Bd4 Bxd4 17 Rxd4 c6 18 dxc6 =, Averbakh–Petrosian, Moscow 1966. (B) 16 h4 c6 17 h5 cxd5 18 hxg6 hxg6 =, Daja–Gligorić, Yugoslavia 1948.

(g) 11 Bg5 Bxf3 12 gxf3 Qh4 13 a4 a6 $\overline{\mp}$, Suba–Ftáčnik, Dortmund 1981.

(h) 12 Ng1 Bxe2 13 Ngxe2 Qe7 14 0-0 Rfd8 15 a3 Na5 16 Qb5 Nac4 is about even, Gligorić–Smejkal, Novi Sad 1982.

(i) 16 Ne4 Nd5 17 Bg5 Qb6 18 Qxb6 axb6 19 g4 Nxd4 20 Rxd4 Bxe5, results in a balanced but complicated position, Vaganian–Hübner, Rio de Janeiro 1979.

(j) 10 . . . Bxf3 11 gxf3 e5 12 dxe5 Ncxd4 13 Qa4 Qc8 14 f4 Nb6 15 Qb3 Nc6 16 e5 Rd8 17 0-0 $\pm$, Donner–Scholl, Holland 1974.

(k) If (A) 12 Nb5 Qxc5 13 dxc5 Na4 =. (B) 12 d5 Ne5 13 Nb5 Qxc5 14 Bxc5 c6 = (Hübner). (C) 12 e5 Qxc5 13 dxc5 Nc8 14 h3 Bxf3 15 Bxf3 Bxe5 leads to a drawn endgame, Karpov–Timman, Tilburg 1986.

(l) 14 e5 Qxc5 15 dxc5 Rxd1† 16 Kxd1 Nd7 17 f4 g5 18 fxg5 Bxe5 is equal (Fischer).

(m) 16 f4 Ned7 17 e5 Qxf4 18 Bxf4 Nxc5 19 Nxc7 Rac8 20 d6 exd6 21 exd6 Bxb2 with even chances, Botvinnik–Fischer, Varna 1962.

(n) 9 Be2 Nc6 10 0-0-0 Nb6 11 Qc5 Qd6 12 h3 Bxf3 13 gxf3 f5 (13 . . . Rfd8?! 14 e5 Qxc5 15 dxc5 Nd7 16 f4 ±, Reshevsky–Evans, US 1965) 14 e5 Qxc5 15 dxc5 f4 =.

(o) 10 . . . e5 11 d5 N8d7 12 Qa3 Bxf3 13 gxf3 Qf6 14 h4 Qxf3 15 Be2 Qf6 is unclear, Sosonko–Timman, Wijk aan Zee 1979.

(p) After 16 h4 Nf6 17 Nb5, the players agreed to a draw in Sosonko–Smejkal, Amsterdam 1979; the position is difficult to assess.

(q) 8 Ne5 Be6 9 d5 Bc8 10 Be2 c6 11 Bf4 exd5 12 exd5 Ne8 =, Kotov–Lilienthal, Parnu 1947.

(r) If 9 . . . Na5 10 Qb4 Bxf3 11 Bxf3 c6 12 Be3 cxd5 13 exd5 leaves White with a spatial advantage, M. Gurevich–Sideifzade, Baku 1986. The column is Lilienthal–Smyslov, USSR 1946.

GRÜNFELD DEFENSE
Classical Line

1 d4 Nf6 2 c4 g6 3 Nc3 d5 4 Nf3 Bg7 5 Qb3 dxc4(a) 6 Qxc4 0-0 7 e4

	31	32	33	34	35	36
	Na6 (Prins Variation)		...a6		Nc6	c6
8	Be2	Bg5(e)	Qb3(i)		h3	Qb3(s)
	c5	h6	b5	c5	Nd7	e5
9	d5	Bh4	e5	dxc5	Be3	dxe5
	e6	c5	Ng4(j)	Qa5(m)	Nb6	Ng4
10	0-0(b)	d5(f)	h3	Qb6	Qc5(p)	Be2
	exd5	b5	Nh6	Qxb6	f5(q)	Qb6
11	exd5	Nb5(g)	Bf4	cxb6	Rd1	0-0
	Bf5	Qa5†	c5	Nbd7	fxe4	Re8(t)
12	Rd1	Nd2	Rd1(k)	e5(n)	Ne5	Bf4
	Re8	Rb8	cxd4	Ng4	Qd6	Nxe5
13	d6(c)	Bg3	Nxd4	e6	Nxc6	Nxe5
	h6	Ne4	Qa5	Nxb6	bxc6	Bxe5
14	Bf4	Qxe4	Qd5	exf7†	Nxe4	Bxe5
	Nd7	Rxb5	Ra7	Rxf7	Qd5	Rxe5
15	Rd2	Bxb5	Nb3	h3	Nc3	Qc2
	Nb4(d)	Qxb5(h)	Qc7(l)	Ne5(o)	Qxc5(r)	Re8 ±

(a) 5 . . . c6 is playable: after (A) 6 cxd5 cxd5 7 Bg5 e6 8 e3 0-0 9 Be2 Nc6 10 h3 h6 Black has near equality, Sosonko–Romanishin, Amsterdam 1973. (B) 6 Bf4 dxc4 7 Qxc4 Be6 8 Qd3 Nd5 = , Euwe–Botvinnik, AVRO 1938.

(b) 10 Bg5 h6 11 Bxf6 Bxf6 12 e5 Bg7 13 Rd1 exd5 14 Nxd5 Be6 is equal, Sosonko–Smejkal, Amsterdam 1975. Also 10 . . . exd5 11 Nxd5 Qa5† 12 Bd2 Qd8 13 Nxf6† Bxf6 14 e5 Bg7 15 0–0 Be6 = (Gutman).

(c) The older move is 13 Bg5, but after 13 . . . h6 14 Bxf6 Bxf6 15 a3 Qb6, Black gained the advantage in Adamski–Timoshchenko, Slupsk 1979.

(d) 16 Qb3 Be6 17 Bc4 Nb6 with chances for both sides, Karpov–Kasparov, World Chp. 1987. The game continued 18 Bxe6 Rxe6 19 a3?! (overlooking Black's reply; better is 19 Bg3 Qd7 20 a3 Nc6 21 Qb5 Rc8 22 Nd5 Nxd5 ∞) 19 . . . Nd3! 20 Bg3 c4 ∓ 21 Qc2 Rc8 22 Rad1 Qd7 23 h3 f5?! (this threatens a kingside pawn advance, but weakens Black's kingside; 23 . . . Qe8 or 23 . . . Qc6 would keep White in a bind as the exchange sacrifice would then be unsound) 24 Rxd3! cxd3 25 Qxd3 Nc4 26 Qd5 Nb6 (White has enough play for the exchange, so Black repeats the position; if 26 . . . Nxb2 27 Re1 Rce8 28 Rxe6 Rxe6 29 Nb5 Kh7 30 Ne5 is stong—Karpov) 27 Qd3 Nc4 28 Qd5 Nb6, Draw. Gutman suggests 14 b3! Nd7 15 Qa2 ∞.

(e) Alternatives are: (A) 8 Bf4 c5 9 Rd1 cxd4 10 Rxd4 Qb6 = . (B) 8 Qa4 c5 9 d5 Qb6 10 Bxa6 bxa6 11 0-0 e6 =. (C) 8 Qb3 c5 9 d5 e6 10 Bxa6 bxa6 11 0-0 exd5 12 exd5 Re8 = .

561

(f) 10 0-0-0 b5 11 Qxb5 Rb8 12 dxc5 Qc7 13 Bg3 Rxb5 14 Bxc7 Rxc5 15 Bd8 Re8 16 Bb5, draw, Vladimirov–Faibisovich, USSR 1968.

(g) 11 Qxb5 fails to 11 . . . Rb8 12 Qe2 Rxb2! 13 Qxb2 Nxe4 14 Rc1 Qa5 with clear advantage to Black.

(h) 16 Qe2 Qb7 17 0-0 Nb4 with an unclear position.

(i) (A) 8 Be2 b5 9 Qb3 c5 10 dxc5 Nbd7 11 e5 Nxc5 =, Ree–Mecking, Wijk aan Zee 1978. (B) 8 Bf4 b5 9 Qxc7 Qxc7 10 Bxc7 Bb7 leads to an equal game. (C) 8 a4 b5 9 Qb3 c5 is poor for White.

(j) 9 . . . Nfd7 is a good alternative, if 10 Be3 Nb6 11 Rd1 c6 =, or 10 h4 Nb6 11 h5 Nc6 ∞.

(k) If 12 dxc5 Nc6 13 Be2 Be6 14 Qd1 Nf5 gives Black good play (Adorjan).

(l) 16 Qd2, Draw, Ivkov–Sax, Osjek 1978; 16 . . . Nf5 17 Nd5 Qc6 would leave Black with good chances.

(m) 9 . . . Nbd7 is also often played, when White has a choice of: (A) 10 c6 bxc6 11 Be2 Qc7 12 0-0 Rb8 =, Baragar–Vaganian, Mexico 1987. (B) 10 Qa3 Qc7 11 Be3 Ng4 with sufficient play, Tukmakov–Tseitlin, USSR 1979. (C) 10 Qb4 Qc7 11 Na4 a5 12 Qc4 now either 12 . . . b5 or 12 . . . Rb8 produces an unbalanced game.

(n) 12 Be2 Nxb6 13 Be3 Nbd7 led to a quick draw in Timoshchenko–Yermolinsky, Sverdlovsk 1987.

(o) 15 . . . Nf6 led to White's advantage in Naumkin–Plachetka, Namestoro 1987, but after 15 . . . Ne5 16 Nxe5 Bxe5 17 Be3 Rf6 the position is equal (Naumkin).

(p) 10 Qd3 f5 11 Rd1 Nb4 =, Uhlmann–Jimenez, Tel Aviv 1964.

(q) If 10 . . . Qd6 11 0-0-0 f5 12 e5 Qxc5 13 dxc5 f4 14 Bd2 White has an edge (Smyslov).

(r) 16 dxc5 Nd5 17 Nxd5 cxd5 18 Rxd5 Be6 with even chances, Lputian–Balashov, USSR 1981.

(s) Alternatives are: (A) 8 Be2 b5 9 Qb3 Qa5 10 Bd2 b4 11 Na4 Nxe4 12 Bxb4 Qc7 13 0-0 Be6 =, Antoshin–Suetin, Havana 1964. (B) 8 Bf4 b5 9 Qb3 and now in place of the 9 . . . Qa5?! played in Miles–Kasparov, match 1986, Kasparov suggests 9 . . . Be6 10 Qd2 Qa5, which may equalize.

(t) 11 . . . Nxe5 12 Nxe5 Bxe5 13 Be3 Qxb3 14 axb3 a6 15 f4 ±.

GRÜNFELD DEFENSE

1 d4 Nf6 2 c4 g6 3 Nc3 d5 4 Nf3 Bg7

	37	38	39	40	41	42
5	Bg5			e3		
	Ne4(a)			0-0		
6	Bh4(b)	......cxd5		cxd5(l)	....Be2(o)	.....Qb3
	c5(c)	Nxg5(e)		Nxd5	c5	e6(q)
7	cxd5	Nxg5		Bc4	0-0(p)	Bd2
	Nxc3	e6(f)		Nxc3	cxd4	b6
8	bxc3	Qd2	........Nf3	bxc3	exd4	Be2
	Qxd5	exd5(g)	exd5	c5	Nc6	Bb7
9	e3	Qe3†	e3	0-0	h3	0-0
	Nc6	Kf8	0-0	Qc7	Be6	Nbd7
10	Be2	Qf4	b4(i)	Qe2(m)	c5	cxd5
	cxd4	Bf6	c6(j)	Bg4	Ne4	exd5
11	cxd4	h4	Be2	Ba3	Bf4	Rfd1
	0-0	h6	Be6	Nd7	Nxc3	Re8
12	0-0	Nf3	0-0	Rac1	bxc3	Be1
	e5(d)	c6(h)	Nd7(k)	Qa5(n)	b6 =	c6(r)

(a) 5 . . . dxc4 6 e4 0-0 (6 . . . c5 7 Bxc4 Qa5 8 e5 Ng4 9 0-0 cxd4 10 Nd5 ±, Browne–Strauss, Lone Pine 1973) 7 Bxc4 Bg4 8 Be2 Nfd7 9 0-0 Nb6 10 d5 h6 11 Be3 ±, Pytel–Ghinda, Zabrze 1977.

(b) 6 Qc1, Zaitsev's method, can be met by 6 . . . h6 7 Bf4 Nxc3 8 bxc3 c5 9 cxd5 Qxd5 10 e3 Nc6 =, I. Zaitsev–Tukmakov, Erevan 1982.

(c) 6 . . . Nxc3 7 bxc3 dxc4 is also reasonable, e.g. 8 Qa4† Qd7 9 Qxc4 b6 =, or 8 e3 b5 9 a4 c6 10 Be2 a6 ∞. Zaichik–Lechtinský, Prague 1985.

(d) After 13 dxc5 Qa5, both 14 Bf6 Bxf6 15 exf6 Qf5, Rashkovsky–Adorjan, Sochi 1977, and 14 Qb3 Nxe5 15 Nd4 Nc6, Ftáčnik–Adorjan, Sochi 1977, are equal.

(e) 6 . . . Nxc3 7 bxc3 Qxd5 8 e3 c5 9 Be2 Nc6 10 0-0 ±, Rogoff–Zaltsman, Lone Pine 1978.

(f) 7 . . . c6 is an interesting sacrifice; after 8 dxc6 Nxc6 9 e3 0-0 (9 . . . e5 10 d5 Qxg5 11 dxc6 0-0 12 h4 ±, Hübner–Ftáčnik, Biel 1984) 10 Nf3 e5 Adorjan thought that Black had good compensation, but that was optimistic.

(g) 8 . . . h6 9 Nh3 exd5 10 Nf4 0-0 11 e3 c5 =, Pytel–Adorjan, Polanica Zdroj 1971.

(h) 13 e3 Be6 14 Bd3 Nd7 15 0-0-0 Qb8 16 Qxb8 Rxb8 =, Bisguier–Korchnoi, Lone Pine 1979.

(i) (A) 10 Be2 c6 11 0-0 Qe7 12 a3 Nd7 is roughly equal, Aronin–Korchnoi, USSR 1957. (B) 10 Bd3 c6 11 0-0 Bg4 12 h3 Bxf3 13 Qxf3 Qd6 =, Mista–Cibulka, Czechoslovakia 1966.

(j) (A) 10 . . . Be6 11 Be2 Nd7 12 0-0 f5 13 Re1 g5 with even chances, Ivkov–Jansa, Bor 1984. (B) 10 . . . Nc6 11 b5 Ne7 12 Be2 a6 13 a4 c5 14 bxc6 bxc6 15 Qd2 ±, Petrosian–Gligorić, Moscow 1977.

(k) 14 b5 f4 15 bxc6 bxc6 16 Qa4 fxe3 17 Qxc6 exf2† 18 Rxf2 Qb6 =, Kuskmaa–Klovans, corr. 1971.

(l) (A) 6 Bd2—the Opočenský system—can be met by 6 . . . c5 7 dxc5 Na6 8 cxd5 Nxc5 9 Bc4 a6 10 a4 Bf5 or 10 . . . b6 with an active game for Black. (B) 6 b4 (Makagonov) b6 7 Bb2 c5 8 bxc5 bxc5 9 Rc1 cxd4 10 Nxd4 Bb7 11 Qb3 Qb6 is equal, Schneider–Adorjan, Hungary 1977.

(m) 10 Be2 b6 11 a4 Nc6 12 Nd2 Rd8 13 Nc4 Ba6 and Black has at least equality, Plachetka–Tukmakov, Děčín 1977.

(n) 13 Bb2 Rac8 14 a3 cxd4 15 cxd4 Nb6 =, Najdorf–Korchnoi, Hastings 1971.

(o) If 6 Bd3 Black can play 6 . . . c5 as in the column or opt for a Slav–Grünfeld formation with 6 . . . c6 7 0-0, when 7 . . . e6, 7 . . . Bg4, 7 . . . dxc4 and 7 . . . Be6 are all reasonable moves. Usually Black maintains a solid position, but concedes either the two bishops or a spatial advantage.

(p) 7 dxc5 dxc4 8 Qxd8 Rxd8 9 Bxc4 Nc6 10 a3 Bg4 =, A. Zaitsev–Zhilinsky, USSR 1974. The column is Sturua–Gavrikov, Tbilisi 1983. This variation is like the Tarrasch Defense with colors reversed.

(q) Also good is 6 . . . c6 7 Bd2 e6 8 Bd3 Nbd7 9 0-0 b6 10 cxd5 exd5 11 e4 c5 with an even game, Bondarevsky–Lilienthal, USSR 1939.

(r) 13 Qc2 Qe7 14 a4 a5 15 Na2 Ne4 with a good game for Black, Smyslov–Balashov, USSR 1971.

GRÜNFELD DEFENSE

1 d4 Nf6 2 c4 g6 3 Nc3(a) d5

	43	44	45	46	47	48
4	Nf3 .... Bg7			Bg5 .... Ne4		Qb3 dxc4
5	Qa4† cxd5 Bd7	Nxd5		Bh4(k) Nxc3		Qxc4 Be6
6	Qb3 dxc4	Qb3 .... Bd2 Nxc3(e)	0-0(h)	bxc3 c5(l) Bg7		Qb5† Bd7
7	Qxc4(b) 0-0	bxc3 0-0	Rc1 Nb6(i)	cxd5 Qxd5	e3 c5	Qb3(p) Nc6
8	e4 b5	e3 c5	Bg5 h6	e3 cxd4	cxd5 Qxd5	Nf3 Bg7
9	Nxb5(c) Nxe4	Be2 b6	Bh4 g5	Qxd4 Qxd4	Qf3 Qd8(n)	e4 0-0
10	Nxc7 Nc6	0-0 Nc6	Bg3 c5	cxd4 e6	Bb5† Nd7	h3(q) Rb8
11	Nxa8 Qa5†(d)	Ba3(f) Na5(g)	e3 Nc6(j)	Bb5† Bd7(m)	Ne2 cxd4(o)	Be3 b5(r)

(a) 3 f3 d5 4 cxd5 Nxd5 5 e4 Nb6 6 Nc3 Bg7 7 Be3 0-0 8 f4 (8 Qd2 Nc6 9 0-0-0 e5 10 d5 Nd4 =, Padevsky–Pachman, Moscow 1956) 8 . . . Nc6 9 d5 Na5 10 Bd4 Bg4 11 Qd3 e5 results in an even game, Gheorghiu–Korchnoi, Zürich 1984.

(b) Not 7 Qxb7? Nc6 8 Bf4 Rb8 9 Qxc7 Qxc7 10 Bxc7 Rxb2 ∓, Kovacs–Paoli, Vienna 1949.

(c) The text is undesirable, but it is better than 9 Qb3 c5 10 e5 Ng4 11 Bxb5 cxd4 12 Nxd4 Bxb5 13 Ndxb5 a6 14 Na3 Qd4 ∓, Hübner–Kasparov, Brussels 1986.

(d) 12 Bd2 Nxd2 13 Nxd2 Nd4 14 Qc7 Qxc7 15 Nxc7 Nc2† 16 Kd1 Nxa1 with an edge for Black, Bonsch–Jasnikowski, Harkamy 1985.

(e) Also playable is 6 . . . Nb6 7 Bg5 h6 8 Bh4 Be6 9 Qc2 Nc6 10 Rd1 Nb4 11 Qb1 0-0 =, Tisdall–Jansa, Aarhus 1983.

(f) 11 a4 Na5 12 Qa3 Qc7 ∓, Goglidze–Botvinnik, USSR 1935.

(g) Smejkal–Ribli, Budapest 1975, continued 12 Qc2 Qc7 13 Rac1 Bb7 14 dxc5 bxc5 with at least equality for Black.

(h) 6 . . . c5 7 Rc1 Nxc3 8 Bxc3 cxd4 9 Nxd4 0-0 10 e3 Nd7 with even chances, F. Olafsson–Hort, Las Palmas 1975.

(i) 7 . . . Nc6 8 e3 e5 9 Nxd5 Qxd5 10 Bc4 Qd6 11 d5 Ne7 is also equal, Kholmov–Platonov, USSR 1970.

(j) 12 d5 Bxc3† 13 Rxc3 Qxd5 14 Qxd5 Nxd5 15 Rxc5 Be6 =, Bukić–Ribli, Bucharest 1971.

(k) Black gets the upper hand after either (A) 5 Nxe4 dxe4 6 Qd2 Bg7 7 0-0-0 c5, Kuntsovich–Kutianin, Moscow 1955, or (B) 5 cxd5 Nxg5 6 h4 Ne4 7 Nxe4 Qxd5 8 Nc3 Qa5, Canal–Gligorić, Dubrovnik 1956.

(l) 6 . . . dxc4 7 e3 Qd5 (or 7 . . . Be6 8 Rb1 b6 9 Be2—Taimanov–Fischer, match 1971—9 . . . Bd5 10 Nf3 Bg7 =) 8 Qa4† b5 9 Qa5 c6 10 a4 Bg7 is unclear, Alburt–Faibisovich, USSR 1971.

(m) 12 Rb1 Be7 13 Bxe7 Kxe7 14 Bxd7 Nxd7 =, Zhuravlev–Gipslis, USSR 1975.

(n) (A) 9 . . . Qxf3 10 Nxf3 Nc6 11 Bb5 Bd7 12 0-0 Rc8 13 Rab1 allows White queenside pressure, Taimanov–Savon, USSR 1969. (B) 9 . . . Qd7 10 Bc4 0-0 11 Ne2 cxd4 12 exd4 Nc6 is about even, Vilela–Popović, Polanica Zdroj 1982.

(o) 12 exd4 0-0 13 0-0 a6 14 Bd3 Qc7 15 Rab1 e5 16 Be4 Ra7 17 Bd5 Nb6 18 Rxb6 Qxb6 19 Bxe7 Be6 =, Gipslis.

(p) 7 Qxb7?! Nc6 8 e3 Rb8 9 Qa6 Nb4 10 Qe2 c5 is risky for White.

(q) 11 Qxb7 Nxd4 12 Nxd4 Bxd4 hands Black the initiative.

(r) After either (A) 12 Bd3 Ne8 13 0-0 Nd6 or (B) 12 e5 Ne8 13 Qd1 b4, the position is involved, but roughly equal.

GRÜNFELD DEFENSE

Neo-Grünfeld

1 d4 Nf6 2 c4 g6 3 g3 Bg7 4 Bg2 d5 5 cxd5 Nxd5 6 Nf3 0-0 7 0-0

	49	50	51	52	53	54
	Nb6..c5					
8	Nc3				dxc5........	e4
	Nc6				Na6	Nf6
9	e3				Ng5	e5
	e5 .... a5 .... Re8				Nbd4	Nd5
10	d5		d5	Ne1	Nc3	dxc5
	Ne7........ Na5		Nb4	e5	Qxd1	Na6
11	e4	e4	e4	d5	Rxd1	Qe2
	Bg4	c6	c6	Na5	Nxc5	Nxc5
12	h3	Bg5	a3	e4	Be3	Rd1
	Bxf3	f6	Na6	c6	Ne6	e6
13	Qxf3(a)	Be3	dxc6	Nc2(g)	Rac1	Be3
	c6	cxd5	bxc6	cxd5	Nc6	Qe7
14	Rd1	exd5	Qc2	exd5	Nxe6	Bd4
	cxd5	Nac4(c)	Qc7(e)	Nac4	Bxe6	b6
15	Nxd5	Bc5	Rd1	b3	b3	Nc3
	Nexd5(b)	Rf7(d)	Rb8(f)	Nd6(h)	Rad8(i)	Bb7(j)

(a) 13 Bxf3 c6 14 a4 cxd5 15 exd5 Nf5 16 a5 Nc4 17 a6 Rb8 18 Nc4 Ncd6 19 axb7 Rxb7 20 Ra6 Nxe4 21 Bxe4 Nd4 =, Veremechich–Mochalov, USSR 1975.

(b) 16 exd5 Qd6 17 Qb3 Rfc8 18 Bd2 Bf8 19 Rac1 Rxc1 20 Rxc1 Qd7 21 Be3 Bd6 22 a3 Rc8 =, Tukmakov–Mikhalchishin, USSR 1981.

(c) 14 ... Bg4 15 Rc1 Nac4 16 Bc5 Nd6 17 h3 Bxf3 18 Bxf3 Nbc8 = (Botvinnik).

(d) 16 Nd2 Bf8 17 Bxf8 Qxf8 18 b3 Nd6 19 a4 Bf5 20 a5 Nd7 21 b4 Bd3 22 Re1 f5 is unclear, Gligorić–Savon, Skopje 1968.

(e) 14 ... Bg4 15 h3 Bd7 16 Rd1 Qc8 17 Kh2 c5 18 Be3 ±, Keene–Smyslov, Moscow 1975.

(f) 16 Rb1 Nc5 17 Be3 Ne6 18 Bf1 ±, Olafsson–Sigurjonsson, Reykjavik 1966.

(g) 13 Bg5 f6 14 Be3 Nac4 15 dxc6 Nxe3 16 Qxd8 Rxd8 17 cxb7 Bxb7 18 Rxe3 Bh6 19 Ree1 Nc4 20 Rad1 Kf8! with compensation for the sacrificed pawn, Karpov–Kasparov, Amsterdam 1988.

(h) 16 Be3 ± (Vaganian).

(i) 16 Nd5 Bb2 17 Re2 Be5 18 Rcd2 Kg7 19 Nf4 Bxf4 20 Bxf4 Rxd2 21 Bxd2 f6 22 Be3 ±, Darga–Robatsch, Havana 1963.

(j) 16 Nd2 Nxc3 17 Bxc3 Rad8 =, Germek–Gligorić, Yugoslav Chp. 1949.

GRÜNFELD DEFENSE

Neo-Grünfeld

1 d4 Nf6 2 c4 g6 3 g3 Bg7 4 Bg2 d5

	55	56	57	58	59	60
5	(cxd5)........................Nf3					
	(Nxd5)			0-0		
6	e4.....................Nc3			0-0		
	Nb6 ....Nb4		Nxc3	dxc4........c6		
7	Ne2	d5	bxc3	Na3	Nbd2 ....cxd5(l)	
	0-0	0-0	c5	c3(g)	Bf5(i)	cxd5
8	0-0	a3	e3	bxc3	b3	Ne5
	e5	N4a6	Nc6	c5	Ne4	e6
9	d5	Ne2	Ne2	Ne5	Bb2	Nc3
	Nc4	c6	Bd7	Nc6	a5(j)	Nfd7
10	b3	0-0	0-0	Nac4	Nh4	f4
	Nd6	e6(b)	Rc8	Nd5	Nxd2	Nc6(m)
11	Bb2	Nbc3	a4(e)	Bb2	Qxd2	Qe3
	Re8	cxd5	Na5	Be6	Bc8	Nb6
12	Nd2	exd5	e4	Nxc6	e4	Bf2
	Na6	exd5	0-0	bxc6	dxe4	Ne7
13	f4	Nxd5(c)	d5	Ne5	Bxe4	a4
	Bd7(a)	Nc6(d)	e6(f)	Qc7(h)	Bh3(k)	a5(n)

(a) 14 Bxe5 Bxe5 15 fxe5 Rxe5 16 Nc3 Qe7 =, Donner–Hort, Wijk aan Zee 1971.

(b) 10 . . . Nd7 11 Nbe3 Nb6 12 dxc6 bxc6 13 Bg5 Be6 14 Qxd8 Rfxd8 15 Bxe7 Rd2 16 Rfd1 Rb2 =, Smyslov–Bronstein, Moscow 1952.

(c) 13 Qxd5 Nc6 14 Bg5 Qxd5 15 Bxd5 Nc7 16 Be4 Be6 =, Böök–Filip, Helsinki 1952.

(d) 14 Nec3 Nc7 15 Nxc7 Qxc7 16 Nd5 Qd8 17 Bf4 Bf5 18 Qd2 Qd7 19 Bh6 f6 20 Rfe1 Rae8 =, Averbakh–Ilivitsky, USSR Chp. 1954.

(e) 11 Rb1 b6 12 dxc5 bxc5 13 c4 Na5 14 Qc2 0-0 15 Bb2 Bf5 16 Be4 Be6 =, Kirilov–Suetin, USSR 1961.

(f) 14 Re2 exd5 15 exd5 Re8 =, Gligorić–Korchnoi, Yugoslavia vs. USSR 1967.

(g) 7 . . . Nc6 8 Nxc4 Be6 9 b3 a5 10 Bb2 a4 11 Ng5 Bd5 12 e4 Bxc4 13 bxc4 h6 14 Nh3 a3 15 Bc3 Nd7 16 e5 Nb6 17 Rb1 Na4 is not clear, Ilievski–Fischer, Skopje 1967.

(h) 14 Nd3 Rab8 15 Qc1 cxd4 16 cxd4 Nb4 17 Nc5 ±, Florian–Honfi, Magyarorszag 1965.

(i) An alternative is 7 . . . a5 8 b3 Ne4 9 Bb2 a4 10 bxa4 Nc5 11 a5 Qxa5 12 Nb3 Qb4 13 Nc5 Qb2 14 cxd5 cxd5 15 a4 Bf5 16 e3 b6 17 Nd3 Qc3 18 Nf4 e6 19 Qe2 Rfc8 20 Qb5 Qa5 21 Rfc1 Na6 =, Kavalek–Cooper, Thessaloniki 1986.

(j) Also possible are: (A) 9 . . . Nd7 10 Nh4 Nxd2 11 Qxd2 Be6 12 e4 dxe4 13 Bxe4 Bh3 14 Rfe1 Re8 15 Bh1 Qc7 =, Vukić–Pietzsch, Sarajevo 1967. (B) 9 . . . Nxd2 10 Qxd2 Nd7 11

Rac1 Be4 12 cxd5 cxd5 13 Rc3 Qb6 14 Rfc1 Bxf3 15 Rxf3 e6 =, Portisch–Smyslov, Burevestnik 1978.

(k) 14 Rfe1 Nd7 15 Bh1 Re8 16 Nf3 h6 17 d5 e5 =, Spassky–Najdorf, Santa Monica 1966.

(l) Other moves: (A) 7 Qb3 dxc4 8 Qxc4 Be6 9 Qa4 Nbd7 10 Nc3 Bf5 11 Nh4 Nb6 12 Qd1 Bg4 13 h3 Be6 14 Nf3 Bd5 15 Nxd5 cxd5 =, Lombardy–Gligorić, Manila 1973. (B) 7 Qa4 Bg4 8 Nc3 dxc4 9 Qxc4 Nbd7 10 Rd1 Qa5 11 Qb3 Nb6 12 Bf4 Nfd7 13 h3 Bxf3 14 Bxf3 e5 15 Be3 exd4 =, Csom–Jacobsen, Esbjerg 1984.

(m) 10 . . . f6 11 Nf3 Nc6 12 e4 dxe4 13 Nxe4 Nb6 14 Be3 Nd5 15 Bf2 is unclear (Kasparov).

(n) 14 Qb3 Bd7 15 Rfc1 Bc6 16 Nb5 Nbc8 17 e3 Nd6 18 Nxd6 Qxd6 19 Be1 Rfb8 =, Karpov–Kasparov, World Chp. 1987.

KING'S INDIAN DEFENSE

1 d4 Nf6 2 c4 g6 (Including the Old Indian: 1 d4 Nf6 2 c4 d6)

Diagram 79

THE KING'S INDIAN is a "hypermodern" defense renowned for its fighting, complex character. Black cedes his opponent the center but only to attack it after mobilizing his pieces. This is a risky strategy, of course, since Black may suffocate from lack of space if he is unable to counter the force of White's pawn center.

Though developed in the hypermodern era of the 1920s, the opening was little appreciated until Bronstein and Boleslavsky scored brilliant victories with it in the 1940s. It then became one of the most popular tournament openings in the 1950s through the '70s, with a strong following of grandmasters, most notably Fischer. In recent years England's John Nunn has found promising new plans for Black.

Although many years of practice have confirmed the correctness of Black's hypermodern approach to the center, he must not equivocate when the time comes to throw his own pawns into the central battle. If White is allowed time to consolidate his central pawn mass, it will become a formidable front. Black has two central pawn breaks—... e5 and ... c5—although he should generally choose only one of these. If White responds with d5, the resulting blocked center necessitates play on the wings that often leads to fierce struggles with Black attacking on one side and White on the other.

Diagram 80

The CLASSICAL VARIATION, 3 Nc3 Bg7 4 e4 d6 5 Nf3 0–0 6 Be2 (cols. 1–24), features direct, no-nonsense development of White's kingside once he has set up the familiar three-pawn center (see diagram). The line 6 . . . e5 7 0–0 Nc6 (cols. 1–6) has been analyzed to great depth but still presents many unsolved problems. Attempts by White to maintain the central tension can be found in columns 11–14 and column 16, while the moderate queen exchange (cols. 17–18) dilutes Black's attempts to complicate. Black may also develop his queen knight to d7 (cols. 13–14). Columns 19–24 see both sides promoting less orthodox schemes of development, avoiding the Classical proper. In the lines with . . . c5 (cols. 22–24), White avoids transposition to the Benoni Defense by not capturing on d5 with the c-pawn.

Diagram 81

The SÄMISCH ATTACK (cols. 25–42) 5 f3 (see diagram), permits White to pursue a ready-made kingside attack with Be3-Qd2-Bh6 and g4-h4-h5. However, the blocking of f3 with a pawn frequently forces the king's knight to be developed to e2 to defend d4, which blocks the king bishop. Thus lengthy maneuvering is often required just to complete development. Black can choose to occupy the center immediately with 5 . . . 0–0 6 Be3 e5 (the *Orthodox Variation*, cols. 25–30), or develop behind the scenes with the *Panno Variation*, 6 . . . Nc6 (cols. 31–36), being ready to react with . . . e5 when White deploys his Ne2, or play one of a number of systems involving . . . c5 (cols. 37 and 39–41). Worthy of attention is col. 29, in which Black sacrifices his queen for two pieces and positional compensation.

Diagram 82

The FIANCHETTO SYSTEM, 3 g3 Bg7 4 Bg2 0–0 5 Nc3 (or 5 Nf3) d6 6 Nf3 (or 6 Nc3) (cols. 43–60), features a positional approach, adding the bishop's weight to control of the center and defense of the king (see diagram). Black may choose the Fianchetto's Classical Variation, 6 . . . Nbd7 7 0-0 e5 (cols. 43–48), to achieve a central clarification through blockade or exchange; the variation with 6 . . . Nc6 7 0-0 a6 (cols. 49–52), highlighting the weakness of White's system by going for . . . b5; the Yugoslav line 6 . . . c5 (cols. 55–57) with possible transposition into the Benoni, or less strategically clear variants (cols. 58–60).

The AVERBAKH VARIATION, 5 Be2 0-0 6 Bg5 (cols. 61–66), attempts to restrict Black in space and to worry him with the veiled pin on the king's knight. The most common response is 6 . . . c5 (cols. 61–63), when after 7 d5 Black can sacrifice a pawn two ways for active play.

In the FOUR PAWNS ATTACK, 5 f4 0-0 6 Nf3 (cols. 67–72), White obtains an enormous center but Black is able to control it with 6 . . . c5; then 7 d5 (cols. 67–68) can lead to the sharp Benoni Four Pawns Attack—see note (c)—or the exclusively King's Indian lines considered here. 7 Be2 (cols. 69–70) and 7 dxc5 (col. 71) allow Black clear equality with accurate play.

Several minor methods for White are covered in columns 73–78. These include 3 Nc3 Bg7 4 e4 d6 5 h3, 5 g3, 4 Bg5, and 4 Bf4. These systems can be effective against an unwary opponent but gain no advantage against proper play.

Diagram 83

The OLD INDIAN DEFENSE, 1 d4 Nf6 2 c4 d6 (cols. 79–84), is a flexible opening in which Black can place his pieces and pawns in many different configurations (see diagram). The feature that distinguishes it from the King's Indian is the dark-squared bishop's development to e7 (after . . . e5). This placement is passive, though solid, and White has a number of ways to obtain an edge.

KING'S INDIAN DEFENSE

Classical Variation

1 d4 Nf6 2 c4 g6 3 Nc3 Bg7 4 e4 d6 5 Nf3 0-0 6 Be2 e5 7 0-0 Nc6 8 d5 Ne7 9 Ne1 Nd7(a)

	1	2	3	4	5	6
10	Nd3			f3		
	f5			f5		
11	Bd2		f3	g4(h)		Be3
	Nf6(b)		f4	Nf6	Kh8	f4
12	f3		Bd2	Nd3	Be3	Bf2
	f4		g5	c6	Ng8	g5
13	c5		g4	Nf2	Qd2	Nb5!(j)
	g5		fxg3	Kh8	Ndf6(i)	Nf6(k)
14	Rc1	cxd6	Bxg5	Bd2	h3	Nxa7
	Ng6	cxd6	gxh2†	a5	h5	Bd7
15	cxd6	Nf2	Kh1	a3	Kg2	c5
	cxd6	h5(e)	h6	Bd7	Nh7	Rxa7
16	Nb5(c)	h3	Bh4	Rb1	Nd3	cxd6
	Rf7	Ng6	Bf6	Qb8	hxg4	Nc8
17	Qc2	Qc2	Bxf6	b3	hxg4	dxc7
	Ne8(d)	Ne8(f)	Rxf6(g)	Rf7 =	Ngf6 ±	Qxc7(l)

(a) (A) 9 ... Ne8 is weaker because it fails to inhibit c4-c5: 10 f3 f5 11 Be3! f4 12 Bf2 g5 13 c5 Ng6 14 a4 Rf7 15 cxd6 cxd6 16 a5 ± . (B) 9 ... c5 is also suspect here due to 10 f4! exf4 11 Bxf4 Ne8 12 Nd3 f6 13 Qd2 Kh8 14 Rab1 Ng8 15 b4 b6 16 bxc5 bxc5 17 Nb5 ± , Korchnoi–Ciocaltea, Nice 1974.

(b) If Black wishes to avoid the do-or-die line of the column, he can bail out here with 11 ... fxe4 12 Nxe4 Nf6 13 f3 Nf5 14 Ndf2 c5 with reasonable play, or try 11 ... c5 12 f4 a6 13 a4 exf4 14 Bxf4 Bxc3!? 15 bxc3 fxe4 16 Ne1 Nf5 17 g4 Ng7 18 Bxd6 Rxf1† 19 Bxf1 Nf6 with a double-edged position.

(c) 16 Nf2 a6! 17 Qb3 h5 18 h3 Nh4 19 Rc2 Rf7 20 Rfc1 Bf8 21 Na4 b5 22 Nb6 Qxb6 and Black holds his own, Furman–Browne, Wijk aan Zee 1975.

(d) 18 a4 h5 19 Nf2 Bf8 20 h3 (20 Nxa7 Rc7 21 Ba5 Rxc2 22 Bxd8 Rxe2 23 Nxc8 Rxa4 =) 20 ... Rg7 21 a5 Nh4 22 Be1 Kh8 23 Qc3 Bd7 24 Qb3 Nf6 25 Qd1 g4 with complications typical of the whole variation, Torre–A. Rodriguez, Toluca 1982.

(e) 15 ... Kh8 is too slow: 16 Qb3 h5 17 h3 Neg8 18 Rfc1 Nh6 19 Nb5 Rf7 20 Qa3 Bf8 21 Ba5 b6 22 Bb4 ± , Averkin–Kalinichenko, USSR 1975.

(f) Karpov–van der Wiel, Brussels 1987, which continued 18 a4! Bf6 19 Ra3 Qc7 20 Rc1 Bd8 21 Nb5 Qb8 22 a5 a6 23 Nc3 b6 24 Ncd1 Rf7 25 Qb3 with a small plus for White.

(g) 18 f4 exf4 19 Nxf4 Ne5 20 Qd2 ± , Barlov–Mortensen, Budapest 1987.

(h) Benko's idea: White plans to lock up the kingside. The column is Taimanov–Kavalek, Montilla 1977.

(i) 13 . . . a6 14 Ng2 f4 15 Bf2 h5 (Pinter–Nunn, Dubai 1986); now 16 h3 Bf6 17 Kh2 Rf7 18 Rh1 Rh7 19 Kg1 would bring White a small plus.

(j) Alternatives are: (A) 13 Nd3?! Nf6 14 c5 Ng6 15 a4 h5 16 cxd6 cxd6 17 a5 g4 18 Nb5 g3! 19 Bxa7 Nh7 20 h3 Qh4 with a classic attack, Larsen–Torre, Bauang 1973. (B) 13 b4 Ng6 14 c5 Nf6 15 Rc1 Rf7 16 cxd6 cxd6 17 a4 b6 (17 . . . h5 18 a5 g4?! 19 Nb5 g3 20 Bxa7 Nh7 21 Kh1! Rxa7 22 Rxc8! ±, Bass–Spraggett, New York 1983, but 18 . . . Bd7! 19 Nb5 Bxb5! 20 Bxb5 g4 21 Kh1?! g3! 22 Bg1 gxh2 23 Bf2 h4 Black succeeded in D. Gurevich–Wl. Schmidt, Beersheba 1986) 18 a5! bxa5 19 bxa5 h3 ∞, Quinteros–Kavalek, Montilla 1974.

(k) 13 . . . a6 14 Na7 Rxa7 15 Bxa7 b6 16 b4 Bb7 17 c5 dxc5 18 Rc1 with a big plus for White, Hulak–Korchnoi, Zagreb 1987.

(l) White stands much better, Benjamin—Nunn, Hastings 1987–88.

KING'S INDIAN DEFENSE

Classical Variation

1 d4 Nf6 2 c4 g6 3 Nc3 Bg7 4 e4 d6 5 Nf3 0-0 6 Be2 e5 7 0-0 Nc6

	7	8	9	10	11	12
8	(d5)...Be3(j)					
	(Ne7)				Ng4........Re8	
9	Nd2....................		b4..........	Bd2	Bg5	dxe5
	c5(a).......a5		Nh5	Ne8	f6	dxe5
10	Rb1(b)	b3(e)	c5(g)	Rc1	Bh4(k)	Qxd8
	Ne8	c5	Nf4	f5	Kh8(l)	Nxc8
11	b4	a3	Bxf4	Qb3	dxe5	Nb5
	b6	Ne8	exf4	b6	dxe5	Ne6
12	bxc5	Rb1	Rc1	exf5	c5	Ng5
	bxc5	f5	h6	gxf5	Be6(m)	Re7
13	Nb3	b4	h3	Ng5	Qa4	Rfd1
	f5	axb4	g5	Nf6	Qe8	b6
14	Bg5	axb4	a4	f4	Rfd1	c5
	Kh8(c)	b6	Ng6	h6	Nh6	Nxc5
15	exf5	Qb3	a5	fxe5	h3	Rd8†
	gxf5(d)	Nf6(f)	Re8(h)	dxe5(i)	f5(n)	Bf8(o)

(a) 9 ... Nd7 10 b4 f5 11 f3 Nf6 12 c5 f4 13 Nc4 g5 14 a4 Ng6 15 Ba3 Rf7 16 b5 Bf8 17 a5 gives White a dangerous initiative, Bukić–Marjanović, Yugoslavia 1970.

(b) Opening the center with 10 dxc6 bxc6 11 b4 d5! 12 Ba3 a6 13 Re1 Be6 14 Bf1 Re1 promises White little, Keene–Quinteros, Haifa 1976.

(c) 14 ... h6 is interesting. Pekarak–Sznapik, Warsaw 1987, went 15 Bxe7 Qxe7 16 Na5 Nf6 17 Nc6 Qd7 18 exf5! gxf5 19 Rb3 e4 20 Qc1 Bb7 21 Qf4 Bxc6 22 dxc6 Qxc6 23 Nb6 Nh7 24 Nxd6 Qd7 25 Rd1 Qe6 26 Rd5 Rad8! 27 Rg3 Kh8 28 Bh5 Rd7 29 Rg6? (29 Bg6!) 29 ... Rf6! 30 Rxg7 Rxg7 31 Ne8 Rb7! 32 h4 Rf8 33 Nd6 Rd7 34 Qd2 Qf6! 35 Ne8 Qa1† and Black wins.

(d) 16 Nxc5 dxc5 17 d6 Nxd6 18 Nd5 Re8 19 Nxe7 Nxe7 20 Qd5 Bb7 21 Rxb7 Nxb7 22 Qxd8 Rxd8 =, Farago–W. Watson, Beersheba 1987.

(e) 10 a3 Nd7 11 Rb1 f5 12 b4 Kh8 13 Qc2 b6 14 Nb3 axb4 15 axb4 fxe4 16 Nxe4 Nf6 17 Bd3 Nxe4 18 Bxe4 Nf5 19 Qd3 Qh4 is equal, Gavrikov–Kasparov, USSR Chp. 1988.

(f) 16 Bd3 Bh6 17 Rb2 Ra1 with approximate equality, Karpov–Kasparov, World Chp. 1987.

(g) 10 g3 f5 11 Ng5 Nf6 12 f3 f4 13 b5 h6 14 Ne6 Bxe6 15 dxe6 fxg3! 16 hxg3 Qc8 17 Nd5 Qxe6 18 Nxc7 Qh3 with a quick draw, Pachman–Taimanov, Havana 1967.

(h) 16 Nd2 Nxc3!? 17 Rxc3 ±, Malich–Bukić, Yugoslavia 1972. In the column, if 12 Qd2 f5 13 Rad1 Bxc3 14 Qxc3 fxe4 ∞.

(i) 16 c5 Nfxd5 17 Nxd5 Nxd5 18 cxb6 axb6 19 Rc6 Kh8! 20 Nf3? Bb7 21 Rg6 Nf4! 22 Bxf4 exf4 23 Rd1 Qe7 ∓, Taimanov–Fischer, match 1971. Correct is 20 Qh3 Rf6 21 Bc4 f4 22 Qh5 Bb7 23 Re6 Qf8! =.

(j) This attempt to maintain the central tension can lead to some intricate maneuvering by White's minor pieces.

(k) 9 Bc1 Kh8 10 d5 Ne7 11 Ne1 f5 12 Bxg4 fxg4 13 f3 gxf3 14 Nxf3 h6 =, Reshevsky–Najdorf, 1953.

(l) 10 ... Nh6 11 dxe5 dxe5 12 Qb3 Kh8 13 Rad1 Qe8 14 Nd5 Rf7 15 h3 f5 16 Rfe1 fxe4! 17 Ng5 Nf5 ∞, Speelman–Gallagher, England 1987.

(m) 12 ... Nh6 13 h3! Be6 14 Qa4 Qe8 15 Rad1 f5 16 Bb5 a6 17 Bxe6 bxc6 18 exf5 ±, Suba–W. Watson, New York 1987.

(n) 16 Nd5 fxe4?! (16 ... Nd4 17 Rxd4 exd4 18 Qxe8 Raxe8 19 Nxc7 exf3 20 Bb5!, Suba) 17 Nxc7 exf3 18 Nxe8 fxe2 19 Nc7! exd1(Q)† 20 Rxd1 ±, Suba– Spraggett, Dubai 1986.

(o) 16 Nxa7 Rxa7 17 Rxc8 (Larsen–Fischer, Monte Carlo 1968), and now 17 ... h6 18 Nf3 Kg7 is equal (Fischer).

KING'S INDIAN DEFENSE
Classical Variation

1 d4 Nf6 2 c4 g6 3 Nc3 Bg7 4 e4 d6 5 Nf3 0-0 6 Be2 e5

	13	14	15	16	17	18
7	(0-0).....................d5.........Be3.........dxe5					
	Nbd7(a)		Nbd7(g)	Ng4(k)	dxe5	
8	Qc2........Re1		Bg5	Bg5	Qxd8	
	c6	c6	h6	f6	Rxd8	
9	Be3(b)	Bf1	Bh4	Bh4	Bg5.........Nd5	
	Ng4	exd4(d)	g5	Nc6	c6(n)	Rd7
10	Bg5	Nxd4	Bg3	d5	Nxe5	Nxf6+
	f6	Ng4	Nh5	Ne7	Re8	Bxf6
11	Bd2	h3(e)	h4(h)	Nd2	Bf4	c5
	f5	Qb6	g4	f5(l)	Na6	Nc6
12	dxe5	hxg4	Nd2(i)	c5	0-0-0	Bb5
	Ndxe5	Qxd4	f5	Bf6	Nc5	Rd8
13	Nxe5	Be3	exf5	Bg3	f3	Bxc6
	Bxe5	Qe5	Ndf6	h5	Nh5	bxc6
14	Bxg4	Qd2	Bxg4	h3	Be3	0-0
	fxg4(c)	Qe7(f)	Nxg3(j)	Nh6(m)	Nxe4(o)	Bg4(p)

(a) 7 . . . exd4 8 Nxd4 Re8 9 f3 c6 10 Kh1 Nbd7 11 Bg5 Qa5 12 Bd2 Qd8 13 Nb3 Nb6 14 Rc1 Be6 Na5 $\pm$, R. Hernandez–Schlosser, Thessaloniki 1988.

(b) 9 Rd1 Qe7 10 Rb1 Re8 11 d5 c5 12 Ne1 Nh5 13 Bxh5 (13 g3 may be stronger) 13 . . . gxh5 14 Nf3 Nf8 15 Re1 Ng6 is roughly equal, van Seters–Pilnik, Beverwijk 1951.

(c) 15 Ne2 Be6 16 Rad1 Qh4 =, Uhlmann–Knaak, Leipzig 1986.

(d) 9 . . . Re8 10 d5 c5 11 g3 Nf8 12 a3 Ng4 13 Nh4 a6 14 Bd2 h5 15 h3 Nf6 16 b4 $\pm$, Taimanov–Geller, Candidates, Zürich 1953.

(e) 11 Qxg4 Bxd4 12 Be3 Nc5 13 Qd1 Be5 14 Qd2 Re8 15 f3 a5 =, Lalev–Ivanchuk, Lvov 1988.

(f) 15 Rad1 Ne5 16 f3 Be6 17 b3 Rad8 (Vilela–Zapata, Cienfuegos 1980); now 18 Ne2 gives White a pull.

(g) 7 . . . a5 8 Bg5 h6 9 Bh4 Na6 10 0-0 Qe8 11 Nd2 Nh7 12 b3 Bd7 13 a3 h5 14 f3 Bh6 15 Rb1 Be3+ 16 Kh1 f5 =, Naumkin–A. Kuzmin, Moscow 1987.

(h) 11 0-0 Nf4 12 Nd2 f5 13 exf5 Nxe2+! 14 Qxe2 Nf6 15 c5 Bxf5 16 Rac1 Rf7 17 Nc4 Bf8 =, Wexler–Reshevsky, Mar del Plata 1960.

(i) 12 Nh2 f5 13 exf5 Nxg3 14 fxg3 Nc5 15 Nxg4 (15 Bxg4 Bxf5 16 0-0 Bd3 17 Rxf8+ Qxf8 18 b4 e4!) 15 . . . Bxf5 16 0-0 Qe7 17 Qd2 Bxg4 18 Bxg4 e4 with play for the pawn.

(j) 15 fxg3 Nxg4 16 Qxg4 Bxf5 17 Qe2 e4 18 0-0 Qd7 =.

(k) (A) A better defense is offered by 7 . . . Qe7 8 d5 Ng4 9 Bg5 f6 10 Bh4 Nh6 11 Nd2 a5 12 a3 Bd7 ∞, Ivanchuk–Ehlvest, USSR Chp. 1988. (B) Nunn's specialty was 7 . . . h6 (to forestall Bg5) 8 0-0 Ng4 9 Bc1 Nc6 10 d5 Ne7 ∞.

(l) 11 . . . Nh6 12 g4 Nf7 13 Qd2 c5 14 Nf1 h5 15 gxh5 g5 16 Bg3 f5 17 f3 f4 18 Bf2 Bh3 19 Nd2 a6 20 Bf1 ±, Renet–Zhu. Polgar, Paris 1987.

(m) 15 cxd6 cxd6 16 f3 ±, Speelman–Kr. Georgiev, Dubai 1986.

(n) 9 . . . Re8 10 Nd5 Nxd5 11 cxd5 c6 12 Bc4 cxd5 13 Bxd5 Nd7! 14 Nd2 Nc5 15 0–0–0 Ne6 16 Be3 Nf4 =, Andersson–Zhu. Polgar, Bilbao 1987.

(o) 15 Nxe4 Bxe5 16 Bd4 Bf5 17 Bxe5 Rxe5 18 Nc3 Nf4 ∓, Bouaziz–Nunn, Szirak 1987.

(p) 15 Be3 Rab8 =, Ivkov–Tal, Bled 1961.

KING'S INDIAN DEFENSE

1 d4 Nf6 2 c4 g6 3 Nc3 Bg7 4 e4 d6 5 Nf3

	19	20	21	22	23	24
5	(0-0) c5					
6	(Be2) . . . . . . .Be3 . . . . .h3(i)				d5(n)	
	Bg4(a)	e5	e5 . . . . .c5		0-0	
7	Be3(b)	dxe5	d5	d5	Be2 . . . . .Bd3	
	Nfd7(c)	dxe5	Na6(j)	e6	e6	e6
8	Ng1	Qxd8	Be3	Bd3	0-0	0-0(q)
	Bxe2	Rxd8	Nh5	exd5	Re8(o)	exd5
9	Ngxe2	Nd5	Nh2	exd5	dxe6	exd5
	Nb6(d)	Rd7!(f)	Qe8	Re8†	Bxe6	Bg4
10	b3	Nxf6†(g)	Be2	Be3	Bf4	h3
	e6	Bxf6	Nf4	Nd7(l)	Qb6	Bxf3
11	0-0	c5	Bf3	0-0	Qc2	Qxf3
	d5	Nc6	f5	Nh5	Nc6	Nfd7(r)
12	cxd5	Bb5	0-0	Bg5	Rad1	Qd1
	exd5(e)	Rd8(h)	b6(k)	f6(m)	Nxe4!(p)	Ne5(s)

(a) 6 . . . Nbd7 7 0-0 e5 transposes into col. 13.

(b) 7 0-0 Nfd7 8 Be3 Nc6 9 d5 Bxf3 10 Bxf3 Na5 11 Be2 Bxc3 12 bxc3 e5 is roughly equal, Cuellar–Tal, Leningrad 1973.

(c) 7 . . . Nc6 8 d5 Bxf3 9 Bxf3 Ne5 10 Be2 c6 11 0-0 Qc7 12 Rc1 Rfe8 13 h3 Ned7 14 Re1 ±, Larsen–Spassky, Linares 1983.

(d) (A) 9 . . . e5 10 Qd2 ±. (B) 9 . . . c5 10 0-0 Nc6 11 d5 Na5 12 b3 a6 13 Rb1 ±, Ivkov–Szabo, Amsterdam 1972.

(e) 13 e5 c6 14 Qd2 f6 15 f4 f5 16 g4! fxg4 17 f5 gxf5 18 Ng3 Qd7 19 Rae1 Na6 20 Bh6 with a strong attack for the pawns, Cebalo–Züger, San Bernardino 1986.

(f) 9 . . . Nxd5 10 cxd5 c6 11 Bc4 cxd5 12 Bxd5 Nc6 13 Bxc6 bxc6 14 Rc1 Be6 15 b3 a5 is equal (Grefe–de Firmian, Saratoga 1976), but 13 0-0-0 is stronger.

(g) 10 0-0-0 Nc6 11 Bd3 Ng4 12 Bc5 Nd4 was here agreed drawn in Tal–Gligorić, Belgrade 1968.

(h) 13 Bxc6 bxc6 14 0-0 Rb8 15 b3 Ba6 =, Renet–Zsu.Polgar, Brest–Paris 1987.

(i) 6 Bg5 h6 7 Bh4 g5 8 Bg3 Nh5 9 Be2 e6! 10 d5 f5 11 Nd4 Nxg3 12 hxg3 fxe4 13 Nxe6 Bxe6 14 dxe6 Bxc3! 15 bxc3 Qf6 =, Uhlmann–Fischer, Havana 1966.

(j) 7 . . . c6 8 Be3 a5 9 Nd2 Na6 10 Be2 Bd7 11 a3 with an edge for White, Benko–Schaufelberger, Skopje 1972.

(k) 13 h4 Nc5 14 Bxc5 bxc5 15 g3 Nh3† 16 Kg2 h5 (Korchnoi–Romanishin, Tilburg 1985); now 17 exf5 Rxf5 18 Be4 Rf6 19 Bd3 is good for White (Romanishin).

(l) (A) 10 . . . Bh6 11 0-0 Bxe3 12 fxe3 Nbd7 (12 . . . Rxe3?! 13 Qd2 accelerates White's attack) 13 Rf2 a6 14 a4 Qe7 15 Qc2 b6 16 Raf1 and White has pressure on the kingside, Tarjan–Lobron, Indonesia 1983. (B) 10 . . . Bf5!? 11 Bxf5 gxf5 12 0-0 Ne4 13 Ne2! b5 14 cxb5 Bxb2 15 Rb1 Bg7 16 Nd2 $\pm$, Lukacs–Veliković, Vrnjačka Banja 1985.

(m) 13 Bd2 f5 14 Ng5 Ne5 15 Be2 Nf6 16 Qc2 a6 17 a4 h6 with only a minimal edge for White, Pinter–Gheorghiu, Prague 1985.

(n) (A) 6 Be2 cxd4 (6 . . . 0-0 7 0-0 Nc6?! 8 d5 $\pm$) 7 Nxd4 0-0 8 0-0 Nc6 9 Be3 transposes to the Sicilian Defense, Maróczy Bind. (B) 6 dxc5 Qa5 7 Bd2 Qxc5 8 Be2 Bg4 9 0-0 0-0 is only minimally better for White, even though he is a tempo up in a line from the Averbakh Variation. Note that . . . c5 can be played earlier or later than the fifth move.

(o) 8 . . . exd5 9 exd5 Re8 10 h3 Ne4 11 Nxe4 Rxe4 12 Bd3 Re8 13 Bg5 gives White some initiative, Karpov–Rashkovsky, USSR Chp. 1973.

(p) 13 Nxe4 Bf5 14 Nfd2 Nd4 15 Qd3 Bxe4 16 Nxe4 Nxe2† 17 Qxe2 f5 18 Rxd6 Rxe4 =, Hulak–Gheorghiu, New York 1986.

(q) 8 h3 transposes to col. 22.

(r) 11 . . . Nbd7?! 12 Qd1 $\pm$, Winslow–G. Rey, San Francisco 1986.

(s) 13 Be2 f5 14 f4 Nf7 15 Be3 Nd7 16 Bf3 a6 17 a4 $\pm$, Seirawan–de Firmian, Los Angeles 1987.

KING'S INDIAN DEFENSE
Sämisch Attack, Orthodox Variation
1 d4 Nf6 2 c4 g6 3 Nc3 Bg7 4 e4 d6 5 f3 0-0 6 Be3 e5

	25	26	27	28	29	30
7	d5					Nge2
	c6			Nh5		c6
8	Bd3	Qd2		Qd2(k)		Qd2
	cxd5 ....b5!?		cxd5	f5	Qh4†!?	Nbd7(q)
9	cxd5	Nge2(d)	cxd5	0-0-0	g3(n)	0-0-0
	Na6(a)	bxc4(e)	a6(g)	Nd7	Nxg3	a6
10	Nge2	Bxc4	Nge2(h)	exf5	Qf2	Kb1
	Nc5	c5	Nbd7	gxf5	Nxf1	b5
11	Bc2	0-0	g4	Bd3	Qxg4	Nc1
	a5	Nbd7	h5!	Ndf6	Nxe3	exd4!?(r)
12	0-0	a3	g5(i)	Nge2	Ke2!	Bxd4
	Bd7	Rb8	Nh7	Kh8	Nc4	Re8
13	a3	b4!?	h4	Bg5(l)	Rc1(o)	Bf2
	Nh5	cxb4	f6	Qe8	Na6	Bf8
14	Bxc5!(b)	Nb5	gxf6	Rde1	Nd1!	Bg3(s)
	dxc5	Nb6	Rxf6	Qf7	Nb6	Re6
15	Ba4	Bd3	Bg2	Ng3	Nh3	N3e2
	Bh6(c)	a5(f)	b5(j)	Ng8(m)	f6(p)	Qb6 =

(a) Other moves: (A) 9 . . . Nh5 10 Nge2 f5 11 exf5 gxf5 12 0-0 Nd7 13 Kh1! (avoiding . . . Qb6† after lines with f4) 13 . . . Kh8 14 Rc1 Ndf6 15 Qb3 e4 16 Bb1! exf3 17 gxf3! with play on the g-file, Furman–Gligorić, Bad Lauterberg 1977. (B) 9 . . . Ne8 10 Qd2 (10 Nge2 Bh6!) 10 . . . f5 11 exf5 gxf5 12 Nge2 Nd7 13 0-0 Ndf6!? 14 Rac1 Qe7 15 Bg5 Qf7 16 Ng3 f4 17 Nge4 Kh8 with play on the g-file, Gheorghiu–Sznapik, Warsaw 1979.

(b) On 14 Rb1 b5!? 15 b4 axb4 16 axb4 Na4 17 Bxa4 bxa4 18 b5 Qa5 ∞, Knaak–Uhlmann, East Germany 1984.

(c) 16 Qd3 and White has the queenside under control while Black has insufficient counterplay on the other side, Rozentalis–Yrjola, Voronezh 1987.

(d) 9 cxb5 cxd5 10 exd5 e4!? 11 Nxe4 Nxd5 12 Bg5 Qa5† 13 Qd2 Qxd2† 14 Bxd2 Bxb2 15 Rb1 Bg7 16 Ne2 Nd7 17 Nxd6 Nc5 18 Bc2 Be6 with an initiative, Timman–Kasparov, Reykjavik 1988.

(e) 9 . . . b4?! 10 Na4 c5 11 a3 a5 12 0-0 Ne8 13 Qd2 f5 (Christiansen–Zhu. Polgar, New York Open 1987); now with 14 axb4 axb4 15 Nxc5! Rxa1 16 Rxa1 dxc5 17 Bxc5 White could have mobilized his pawns on the queenside.

(f) After 16 axb4 axb4 17 Qb3 Bd7, draw, Ligterink–Spraggett, Wijk aan Zee 1985.

(g) 9 . . . Ne8 10 g4! f5 11 gxf5 gxf5 12 0-0-0 White played for the attack, Larsen–Donner, the Hague 1958.

(h) 10 0-0-0 Nbd7 11 Kb1 (11 Nge2? b5! leaves White unready to deal with . . . Nb6 and . . . b4) 11 . . .b5 12 g4 Nc5 (12 . . . h5 13 h3 Qa5 14 Rc1 Bb7 with threats of . . . b4 and . . . Nxd5) 13 Rc1 Ne8 14 h4 f5 with a balanced position, Perez–Najdorf, Havana 1962.

(i) (A) 12 h3 Nh7! 13 0-0-0 (13 h4 hxg4 14 fxg4 Ndf6! 15 g5 Nh5 $\pm$, Karaklajić–Bertok, Yugoslav Chp. 1961) 13 . . . h4 14 Kb1 Bf6 15 Nc1 Ng5 16 Nd3 (Radev–Stefanov, Bulgarian Chp. 1959) 16 . . . Nb6 17 b3 Bd7 18 Rc1 Rc8 19 f4 exf4 and 20 . . . Re8 = (Lilienthal). (B) 12 Bg5 hxg4 13 fxg4 Nc5 14 Ng3 (14 h3 Ncxe4! gives Black the better endgame) 14 . . . Bxg4 15 h3 Bf3! 16 Rg1 Ncxe4! 17 Ngxe4 Nxe4 18 Nxe4 f6 recovering the piece with a good game.

(j) 16 Nd1 Nc5 17 Nf2 Rf7! (hindering Nh3-g5) 18 Nd3 Nxd3 19 Qxd3 Bf6 20 Bf2 Nf8! (heading for c5), Spassky–A. Rodriguez, Toluca 1982. Black has full equality.

(k) 8 Nge2 f5 9 Qd2 Nd7 10 0-0-0, Seirawan–Adriansyah, Dubai 1986; now, instead of 10 . . . Nhf6 11 h3! fxe4?! 12 fxe4 a6 13 g4 and 14 Ng3 $\pm$, Black could play 10 . . . Ndf6 controlling g3 with a reasonable game.

(l) 13 Kb1 a6 14 g3 Bd7 15 Bh6 Qe8 16 h3 b5 17 Rde1 bxc4! 18 Bxc4 Bxh6 19 Qxh6 Qf7 20 g4 Ng7 with counterplay on the b-file, Ostermeyer–Zapata, Dortmund 1984.

(m) 16 Nxh5 Qxh5 17 Be3 a6 18 Reg1 $\pm$, Liberzon–Pietzsch, Zinnowitz 1967.

(n) Avoidance of the queen sacrifice by 9 Bf2 is best met by 9 . . . Qe7 (9 . . . Qf4 encourages a draw by 10 Be3 Qh4† 11 Bf2, but White can just play 10 Qc2 or 10 Qe2) 10 0-0-0 f5 11 Kb1 Nd7 12 Nh3!? e4!? with complications, Miles–van der Wiel, Wijk aan Zee 1987.

(o) 13 Nb5?! Na6 14 Rc1 permits Black the option of 14 . . . Bd7! 15 Nxc7 Nxc7 16 b3 f5 (Holzl–Duriga, Vienna 1986) as well as the much older 14 . . . Nxb2 15 Nxc7 Nxc7 16 Rxc7 b6 (Kikiani–Goldin, USSR 1963).

(p) 16 Rg1 Bd7 17 Ne3 Rae8! (17 . . . Rad8?! 18 b3 c6 19 dxc6 bxc6 20 Nf5! gxf5 21 Rxg7†! with a lasting attack, Karpov–Velimirović, Skopje 1976) 18 Rg2 Re7!! =; with his defense secure, Black is ready for some sort of pawn break, Spycher–J. Piket, Groningen 1986–87.

(q) 8 . . . exd4 9 Bxd4! Be6 10 Nf4 c5 11 Be3 Nc6 12 0-0-0 Nd4 13 h4 $\pm$, Sliwa–Boleslavsky, Poland–Byelorussia 1954.

(r) 11 . . . bxc4?! 12 dxe5 Nxe5 13 Qxd6 Qxd6 14 Rxd6 with an edge, Pachman–Uhlmann, Marianské Lázně 1965.

(s) 14 Nb3?! b4 15 Na4?! c5 16 Bg3 Re6 17 Nc1 Bb7 18 b3 Bc6 19 Nb2 a5 with a strong attack, Meshkov–Petrushin, Kazan 1980. The column is Pismeni's suggestion.

KING'S INDIAN DEFENSE
Sämisch Attack, Panno Variation

1 d4 Nf6 2 c4 g6 3 Nc3 Bg7 4 e4 d6 5 f3 0-0 6 Be3 Nc6

	31	32	33	34	35	36
7	Nge2					Qd2
	a6...				Rb8	a6
8	Qd3.................................			a3(l)	Qd2	0-0-0
	Rb8			Bd7	Re8	b5!?
9	h4......................		Nc1(g)	b4	Rd1(o)	cxb5?!(r)
	h5(a)		e5	Qb8!	a6	axb5
10	0-0-0(b)		d5(h)	Nc1	Nc1	Bxb5
	b5		Nd4	e5(m)	e5	Na5!
11	Bh6.........Nf4(e)		N1e2(i)	d5	d5(p)	Kb1(s)
	e5!	bxc4!	e5	Nd4	Nd4	Ba6
12	Bxg7	Bxc4	dxc6	Nb3	N1e2	Bxa6
	Kxg7	e5!	Nxc6!	Nxb3	c5!	Rxa6
13	d5(c)	dxe5	Rd1(j)	Qxb3	dxc6	Qd3
	Na5	Nxe5	Be6	Nh5!	bxc6	Qa8 $\overline{\mp}$
14	cxb5	Bb3	Nd5	g3!(n)	Nxd4	
	axb5	Qe8!	b5!	f5	exd4	
15	Ng3	Kb1	cxb5	Be2 $\pm$	Bxd4	
	b4(d)	a5(f)	axb5(k)		d5!(q)	

(a) Other moves are (A) 9 . . . e5 10 d5 Na5 11 Ng3 c5 12 h5 Bd7 13 0-0-0 b5 14 Kb1!. (B) 9 . . . b5 10 h5 Na5!? 11 Nf4 c6 12 cxb5 axb5 gives Black good play, e.g. Gligorić–Djurić, Yugoslavia Chp. 1986: 13 hxg6 fxg6 14 e5 b4! 15 exf6 bxc3 16 Qxc3 Rf8 =. (C) 9 . . . Re8 10 Bh6 Bh8 11 h5 e5 12 d5!? Nd4 13 hxg6 fxg6 14 Be3 c5 15 dxc6 Nxc6 16 Nd5 $\pm$, Murey–W. Watson, Montpellier 1985.

(b) (A) 10 Nc1!? e5 11 d5 Nd4 12 Nb3 Nxb3 13 axb3 c5 14 Be2 Bd7 15 Nd1 Qb6 16 Nf2 Qxb3 17 Nd3 Rfc8 18 0-0 Be8 19 Ra3 Qb6 20 b4 $\pm$, Christiansen–Nunn, Cologne 1988. (B) 10 Nd5 can be met by 10 . . . Nh7!? 11 g4 hxg4 12 h5 e6! $\overline{\mp}$, Petursson–Westerinen, Gausdal 1985. (C) 10 Bh6 b5 11 g4?! e5! 12 d5 Nd4 13 Nxd4 Bxh6 14 Qxh6 exd4 15 Ne2 bxc4 16 Nxd4 Rxb2 17 Bxc4 Qe8 18 0-0-0 Rb4 19 Bb3 (Kraidman–Westerinen, Ramat Hasharon 1982) and now 19 . . . Bd7 gives Black a clear advantage (Liberzon).

(c) (A) 13 dxe5 dxe5! 14 Qg5 Qe7 15 Nd5 Nxd5 16 exd5 f6 17 Qd2 Rd8! and Black has the initiative, Mestel–Gufeld, Hastings 1986–87. (B) 13 cxb5 axb5 14 dxc5 Nxe5 15 Nf4 b4 16 Ncd5 c5! 17 Nxf6† Qxf6 18 Nd5 Qe6 $\overline{\mp}$, Miralles–Züger, Arandelovac 1985.

(d) 16 Nb5! Bd7 and White can take one pawn with 17 Qxb4 or two with 17 . . . c6 18 dxc6 Nxc6 19 Qxd6, but 19 . . . Qa5 leads to an attack.

(e) 11 Nd5 bxc4 12 Nxf6† Bxf6 13 g4 Nb4 14 Nc3 c5!? 15 Bxc4!? cxd4 16 Bxd4 Qc7 17 Bb3 Bxd4! 18 Qxd4 Be6! leads to complications, W. Schmidt–Sznapik, Prague 1985.

584

(f) The game Didishko–Gelfand, Minsk 1986, continued 16 Bd4 Nfd7 17 Nfd5 c6 18 Ne3 Ba6! 19 Bxe5 (else 19 . . . Nd3) 19 . . . Bxe5 20 g4 d5! opening the center to Black's advantage.

(g) White has tried many moves here—9 Rb1, 9 Rc1, 9 Rd1, 9 a3, 9 a4, 9 Bh6, 9 g3, 9 g4, and 9 0-0-0—but 9 h4 and 9 Nc1 are the most promising.

(h) A calm approach is 10 Nb3 exd4 (11 d5 was threatened) 11 Nxd4 Nxd4 12 Bxd4 Be6 13 Be2 c5 14 Be3 b5!? 15 cxb5 axb5 16 0-0 (16 Nxb5 d5 ∞) 16 . . . c4 =, Ledić–Chiburdanidze, Vinkovči 1982.

(i) 11 Nb3 Nxb3 (now 11 . . . c5 12 dxc6 Nxc6 would not leave White's development compromised, but 12 . . . bxc6!? 13 Nxd4 exd4 14 Bxd4 transposes to 8 Nc1, note 1) 12 axb3 c5 13 g4 h5 14 h3 Nh7! 15 gxh5 Qh4† 16 Qf2 (Ivkov–Sofrevsky, Yugoslav Chp. 1965) 16 . . . Qxf2†! 17 Kxf2 gxh5 with equality.

(j) 13 Nc1 b5!? 14 cxb5 axb5 15 Bxb5 Nd4 16 Bd3 Qb6 17 b3 d5! with more than enough compensation, Brenninkmeier–Reimersma, Wijk aan Zee 1987. After 18 exd5 e4! 19 Bb1!? exf3! 20 Bxd4 Re8† 21 N1e2 Nxd5! Black launched a strong sacrificial attack.

(k) 16 Nxf6 Bxf6 (not 16 . . . Qxf6? 17 Bg5) 17 g3 Bxa2 18 Qxd6 Bb3! and Black stands somewhat better, Zsu. Polgar–Gufeld, Wellington, 1988.

(l) (A) 8 Nc1 e5 9 d5 Nd4 10 Nb3 c5 11 dxc6 bxc6!? 12 Nxd4 exd4 13 Bxd4 Rb8!? 14 Qd2 Qa5! (Black threatens 15 . . . c5 16 Be3 Rxb2! 17 Qxb2 Nxe4) 15 Rc1 Rd8 16 Be2 Be6 17 0-0 Qb4! 18 b3 d5 with good play, A. Rodriguez–Kuzmin, Minsk 1982. (B) 8 d5 Ne5 9 Ng3 c6 10 a4 cxd5 11 cxd5 e6 12 Be2 exd5 13 exd5 Re8 14 Qd2 (Seirawan–Nunn, Brussels 1988) and now 14 . . . Qc7! is equal according to Nunn.

(m) On 10 . . . b5 11 cxb5 axb5 12 Nb3 e5 13 d5 Ne7 the passive position of this knight assures White some advantage, Gheorghiu–Messa, Rome 1983.

(n) The column is Van der Tak's improvement on the game Soulder–Simon, which went 14 Be2 Nf4 15 0-0 h5! 16 c5 Bh6 17 Bf2 Qd8! 18 Kh1 h4 19 a4 Qg5 with storm clouds growing over White's king.

(o) (A) 9 h4!? is worthy of attention, transposing to note (a–C). (B) 9 Nc1 e5 10 d5 Nd4 11 Nb3 c5 12 dxc6 bxc6 13 Nxd4 exd4 14 Bxd4 d5! 15 cxd5 cxd5 16 e5 (16 Bb5 Rxb5! 17 Nxb5 Nxe4! leads to at least a draw, Draidman–Westerinen, Lugano 1968) 16 . . . Nh5 17 0-0-0 (Bokor–F. Portisch, Hungary 1970) 17 . . . Qa5!? ∞ (Barden).

(p) (A) 11 Nb3 exd4 12 Nxd4 allows 12 . . . d5!. (B) 11 dxe5 Nxe5 12 b3 (12 c5 lets Black try 12 . . . d5 13 Nxd5 Nxe4!?; 12 Be2 b5! 13 cxb5 axb5 14 Bxb5 Nxe4! 15 fxe4 Rxb5 16 Nxb5 Nc4, Gheorghiu–Kavalek, Amsterdam 1969) 12 . . . Bd7 13 a4 Nh5 14 Be2 Qh4† 15 Bf2 Qf4 =, Kraidman–Richter, Netanya 1971.

(q) 16 cxd5 cxd5 17 e5 Nh5 18 Be2 Qh4† 19 Bf2 Qb4! 20 Nxd5 Qxb2! (20 . . . Qxd2† 21 Rxd2 Nxe5 22 0-0!, Browne–Hammie, Saratoga 1976) 21 0-0 (Petursson–J. Watson, New York 1980); now 21 . . . Bxe5 22 Ne7† Kg7 23 Nc6 Bc3! keeps the game equal (Watson).

(r) Better is 9 h4 h5 10 Bh6 e5 11 Nge2, Dolmatov–Thorsteins, Polanica Zdroj 1987, when instead of 11 . . . bxc4 Black should transpose to col. 31 with 11 . . . Rb8.

(s) 11 Bh6 c6 12 Bxg7 Kxg7 13 Bd3 Qb6 intending . . . Ba6 is good for Black, according to Hjartarson. The column is Petursson–Gufeld, Hastings 1986–87.

585

KING'S INDIAN DEFENSE
Sämisch Attack

1 d4 Nf6 2 c4 g6 3 Nc3 Bg7 4 e4 d6(a) 5 f3 0-0(b)

	37	38	39	40	41	42
6	(Be3)					Bg5(u)
	b6	c6	Nbd7!?	c5!?	a6!?	Nc6(v)
7	Bd3(c)	Bd3(g)	Qd2(j)	dxc5(n)	Bd3(r)	Nge2
	a6(d)	a6	c5	dxc5	· c5	a6
8	Nge2	a4(h)	d5	Qxd8	dxc5	Qd2
	c5	a5	Ne5	Rxd8	dxc5	Rb8
9	e5	Qd2	Bg5!(k)	Bxc5	e5!(s)	d5!?(w)
	Nfd7!(e)	e5	Nh5!?(l)	Nc6	Nfd7	Ne5
10	exd6	Nge2	g4	Ba3(o)	f4	Ng3
	cxd4!	Na6	Nf6	a5!(p)	Nc6	c6
11	Nxd4	Rd1	h3	Rd1	Nf3	Be2
	Nc5	Nb4	a6	Be6!(q)	f6(t)	b5
12	Nb3(f)	Bb1	f4	Nd5	e6	cxb5
	exd6	Qe7(i)	Ned7	Bxd5	Nb6	cxd5
13	0-0	0-0	Nf3	cxd5	Bxc5	Bxf6
	Nc6	exd4	b5	Nb4	Bxe6	Bxf6
14	Nxc5	Nxd4	cxb5	Bb5!?	Qe2	Nd5 ±
	dxc5 =	Re8 ±	Nb6(m)	Nc2† =	Bg4!∞	

(a) Occasionally seen is 4 ... 0-0, to answer 5 f3 with 5 ... c5!? 6 dxc5 b6 ∞. White can avoid this with 5 Be3 d6 6 f3.

(b) (A) 5 ... e5 was popular in the 1950s; however, 6 d5 Nfd7 7 g3! crudely prevents 7 ... Bh6; after 7 ... a5 8 Be3 Na6 9 Qd2 0-0 10 h4 f5 11 h5 f4 12 gxf4 Qf6 13 h6 Bh8 14 Bh3 Nb6 15 Bxb6 Black's position was a shambles in Miles–Pickles, Adelaide 1986–87. (B) 5 ... c6 6 Be3 a6 7 a4!? (this positional approach has superseded 7 Bd3 and 7 Qd2 b5 8 0-0-0) 7 ... a5 8 Bd3 e5 9 Nge2 Nh5 10 Qd2 f5 11 exf5 gxf5 12 dxe5! dxe5 13 0-0-0 Qe7 (13 ... 0-0 14 g4 fxg4? 15 Bxh7†) 14 Ng3!Nxg3 15 hxg3 Na6 16 g4! ±, Browne–Byrne, Philadelphia 1988. Perhaps 9 ... exd4 10 Nxd4 Na6 11 Rc1 Qc7 holds up better (Korn).

(c) 7 Qd2 c5 (7 ... a6 transposes into note r) 8 Nge2 Nc6 9 d5 e6 with counterplay.

(d) (A) 7 ... Nfd7!? is interesting: 8 Nge2 c5 9 Bc2 Nc6 (Black intends ... e5 gaining control of d4) 10 d5 Nb4 11 Bb3!? Rb8!? 12 Qd2 Ne5 13 f4!? Ng4 14 Bg1 Na6 15 h3 Nf6 16 Bc2!, and White consolidates his space advantage, although Black is not without chances, Timman–Cvitan, Zagreb/Rijeka 1985. (B) 7 ... Bb7?! 8 Nge2 c5 9 d5 e6 10 0-0 exd5 11 cxd5 leads to an unshakable space advantage for White.

(e) 9 ... Ne8 10 Be4 Ra7 11 dxc5 bxc5 12 Bxc5 Rd7 13 Be3 Bb7 (14 Qb3 was threatened) 14 e6! fxe6 15 Nd4 Bxd4 16 Bxd4 d5 17 cxd5 exd5 18 Bc2 ± (Black's center is shaky), Kir. Georgiev–Cvitan, San Bernadino 1987.

(f) 12 dxe7 Qxe7 13 Nd5 Qe5 14 f4 Qd6 15 0-0 Re8! 16 Bf2 Bb7 17 Rc1 Nbd7 18 b4 Nxd3 19 Qxd3 b5! ∓, Dorfman–Rashkovsky, USSR Chp. 1981. The column is Camriuk–Rashkovsky, USSR 1981.

(g) 7 Qd2 a6 8 0-0-0 b5 (perhaps better is 9 . . . Qa5 10 Bxg7 Kxg7 11 Kb1) 9 Bh6 Nbd7 10 Bxg7 Kxg7 11 e5! Ne8 12 h4 h5 13 g4! dxe5 14 gxh5 Ndf6 15 hxg6 Qxd4 Bd3 ±. Gheorghiu–Kir. Georgiev, Prague 1985.

(h) 8 Nge2 b5 allows White a variety of plans, all leading to a slightly freer position: (A) 9 Qd2 Nbd7 10 Rc1 Bb7 11 0-0 e5 12 cxb5 axb5 13 b3 Qa5 14 dxe5 drawn, Fedorowicz–Byrne, US Chp. 1985; (B) 9 0-0 Nbd7 10 Qd2 bxc4 11 Bxc4 Nb6 12 Bb3 a5 13 Na4 ±, Saidy–Bednarsky, Tel Aviv 1964.

(i) Here or next move, 12 . . . Nd7 is another try, when White should play for f4. The column is Gheorghiu–Werner, Bad Aibling 1982.

(j) (A) 7 Bd3 c5 8 Nge2 cxd4 9 Nxd4 e6 10 0-0 d5 11 exd5! exd5 12 Qd2 ±, Lerner–Sznapik, Polanica Zdroj 1985. (B) 7 Nge2 c5 8 d5 a6 9 Ng3 Qa5 10 a4 Ne5 11 Ra3 e6 12 Be2 h5 ∞, Seirawan–Nunn, Lugano 1986. (C) 7 Nh3 e5 8 d5 Nh5 9 g4!? Nf4 10 Nxf4 exf4 11 Bxf4 Ne5 12 Be2 f5 13 gxf5 gxf5 14 Qd2 fxe4!? (better than 14 . . . Qh4†?! 15 Bg3 Qh5 16 f4!, Seirawan–Wilder, US Chp. 1986) 15 Nxe4 Qh4† 16 Bg3 Qh5 17 Ng5 Nxf3†! =, Seirawan–Nunn, Lugano 1987.

(k) 9 h3?! Nh5 10 Bf2 f5! 11 exf5 (11 f4 Bh6 12 g3 fxe4 13 Nxe4 Nxf4 14 Be3 Ng2†! is unclear, Karolyi–Weindl, London 1986) 11 . . . Rxf5! 12 g4 Rxf3! when Black had a raging attack, Beliavsky–Nunn, Wijk aan Zee 1985: 13 gxh5 Qf8! 14 Ne4! Bh6 15 Qc2 Qf4! 16 Ne2 Rxf2! 17 Nxf2 Nf3† 18 Kd1 Qh4! 19 Nd3 Bf5 20 Nec1 Nd2! 21 hxg6 hxg6 22 Bg2 Nxc4 23 Qf2 Ne3† 24 Ke2 Qc4 25 Bf3 Rf8 26 Rg1 Nc2 27 Kd1 Bxd3 28 Resigns.

(l) 9 . . . a6 10 f4 Ned7 11 Nf3 b5 12 cxb5 Qa5! 13 e5 dxe5 14 fxe5 Ng4 15 Bxe7 Re8 16 d6 Bh6 is in Black's favor, Kriničny–Sirota, corr. 1988.

(m) 15 a4 (Dlugy–Rohde, Philadelphia 1985); now 15 . . . Bb7 is equal.

(n) 7 Nge2 Nc6 8 d5 Ne5 9 Ng3 a6 10 f4 Neg4 11 Bd2 e5 12 dxe6! fxe6 13 h3 Nh6 14 Be3 ±, Dlugy–Zsu. Polgar, New York 1985.

(o) (A) 10 Nd5 Nd7! 11 Nxe7† (11 Bxe7 Nxe7 12 Nxe7† Kf8 followed by 13 . . . Bxb2 gives Black a dangerous lead in development, while 11 Ba3 is now effectively answered by 11 . . . e6 12 Nc7 Rb8 13 0-0-0 b6!, Petursson–Sax, Biel 1985) 11 . . . Nxe7 12 Bxe7 Bxb2 13 Rb1 Bc3† 14 Kf2 Bd4† 15 Kg3 (15 Ke1 Re8 and 16 . . . f5) 15 . . . Re8 16 Bg5 Nf6 17 Nh3 Nh5 18 Kh4 Kg7! with excellent winning chances, Gil–Howell, Gausdal 1986. (B) 10 Rd1 Nd7 11 Ba3 b6 12 Nge2 Bb7 13 Nd5 Nde5 14 Nc1 e6 15 Ne7† Nxe7 16 Bxe6 Rxd1† 17 Kxd1 Re8 18 Bg5 f5 19 exf5 Nxf3! ∓, Arlandi–Khalifman, Groningen 1985–86. (C) 10 Be2!? Nd7 11 Ba3 Bxc3† 12 bxc3 Nde5?! (12 . . . b6) 13 Rd1 Be6 14 Rd5! Kf8 15 f4 ±, Christiansen–Wilder, US Chp. 1986.

(p) (A) 10 . . . Nd7 11 0-0-0 b6 (11 . . . Bxc3?! 12 bxc3 b6 13 Ne2! e5 14 Kc2 Ba6 15 Nc1 ±, Knaak–Vogt, East German Chp. 1986) 12 Nd5 e6 13 Ne7† Nxe7 14 Bxe7 Re8 15 Ba3 f5 16 exf5 exf5 17 Ne2 Nc5 with adequate compensation, Grigorian–Yermolinsky, Pinsk 1986. (B) 10 . . . b6 11 Be2 Bb7 12 Nh3 Nd7 13 0-0-0 Bxc3 14 bxc3 Ba6 15 Nf4 e6 16 c5 Bxe2 17 Nxe2 Nxc5 18 Bxc5 =, Knaak–Hazai, Camaguey 1987.

(q) 11 . . . Rxd1† 12 Kxd1 Nb4 13 Ng2 Be6 14 Nf4! Rd8† 15 Ncd5 ±, V. Kozlov–Kuzmin, USSR 1986. The column is Andrianov–Glek, corr. 1987.

(r) 7 Qd2 b6!? 8 0-0-0 c5 9 dxc5 (9 d5 b5 10 Bh6 Bxh6 11 Qxh6 Qa5 12 h4!? b4 13 Nb1 Qxa2 14 h5 Nbd7 15 Nh3, Miles–Fedorowicz, Dortmund 1986; now 15 . . . Re8! 16 Ng5 Nf8 17 Bd3 e5 favors Black, according to van der Sterren) 9 . . . bxc5 10 e5 Ne8 11 Bh6 Bxe5! 12 Bxf8 Kxf8 ±, Gheorghiu–Sax, Teesside 1975.

(s) 9 Bxc5 Nc6 10 Be3 (10 Nge2? Nd7! 11 Bf2 Nde5 12 Nc1 Bh6! 13 Nd5 e6 14 Bb6 Qg5! 15 0-0! exd5! 16 f4 Qh4 17 fxe5 d4! ∓, Beliavsky–Kasparov, match 1983) 10 . . . Nd7 11 Rc1

587

(Kasparov suggests 11 f4) 11 . . . Qa5 12 Ne2 Nc5 with equal chances, Bobotsov–Timman, Amsterdam 1971.

(t) 11 . . . Nd4?! 12 0-0! (not 12 Nxd4? Nxe5!) 12 . . . f6 13 e6! Nb6 14 f5! ±, Christiansen–I. Ivanov, Los Angeles 1985, which concluded 14 . . . Nxf5 15 Bxf5 gxf5 16 Bxc5 Nxc4 17 Qd5 Ne5 18 Nxe5 fxe5 19 Rxf5 Bf6? 20 Rxf6! Resigns. The column is Christiansen–Ree, Reykjavik 1984.

(u) 6 Nge2 is best met by 6 . . . c5 7 d5 e6 with a likely transposition to the Benoni Defense.

(v) 6 . . . c5 7 d5 e6 8 Qd2 exd5 9 cxd5 transposes to the Benoni Defense; on 9 Nxd5 Be6 10 Ne2 Bxd5 11 cxd5 Nbd7 12 Nc3 a6 13 a4 Qa5 14 Be2 Rfe8! =, Davidović–Veličković, Yugoslavia 1986.

(w) On 9 h4 h5 10 0-0-0 b5 11 Nd5 (11 Bh6 is covered in the Panno lines) 11 . . . bxc4 12 g4? Nxd5 13 exd5 Nb4 14 Nc3 c5! ∓, Vegh–Vogt, Eger 1984. The column is Polugaevsky–Nunn, Plovdiv 1983.

KING'S INDIAN DEFENSE
Fianchetto System, Classical Variation

1 d4 Nf6 2 c4 g6 3 g3 Bg7 4 Bg2 0-0 5 Nc3 d6 6 Nf3 Nbd7 7 0-0 e5

	43	44	45	46	47	48
8	e4					Qc2(u)
	c6			exd4	a6	c6(v)
9	h3(a)			Nxd4	Qc2(q)	Rd1
	Qb6		Qa5(i)	Re8	exd4	Qe7
10	Re1(b)		Re1(j)	h3	Nxd4	e4
	Re8	exd4(d)	exd4(k)	Nc5	Ne5	Re8(w)
11	d5	Nxd4	Nxd4	Re1	b3	b3
	Nc5(c)	Ne8(e)	Ne5	a5	c5	exd4
12	Rb1	Nf3!(f)	Bf1	Qc2(m)	Nde2	Nxd4
	a5	Nc5(g)	Re8	c6	Rb8	Nc5
13	Be3	Qe2	Be3	Be3	Be3(r)	f3
	Qc7	a5	Be6	a4	b5	a5
14	Nd2	Bg5!(h)	Nxe6	Rad1(n)	Rad1	Be3!
	Bd7	±	Rxe6	Nfd7	bxc4(s)	Nfd7!?(x)
15	Bf1		Kg2(l)	Re2(o)	Bxc5	
	Rab8		Rae8	Qa5	cxb3	
16	a3 ±		Qd2 ±	Red2	axb3	
				Qb4(p)	Be6(t)	

(a) There are two moves designed to anticipate . . . Qb6 by guarding b2 (so as to play Be3): (A) 9 Rb1 exd4 10 Nxd4 Re8 (Donner–Geller, Wijk aan Zee 1969) 11 h3! with play similar to col. 46. (B) 9 b3 exd4 10 Nxd4 Nc5 11 h3! Re8 12 Re1 a5 13 Rb1 Bd7 14 Bf4 Qb6! 15 Be3! Qc7 16 Qc2 ±, Smejkal–Uhlmann, Sarajevo 1982. If (C) 9 Re1?! exd4 10 Nxd4 Ng4! 11 h3 Qf6! ∓, Larsen–Tal, match 1969; (D) 9 Be3 Ng4 10 Bg5 Qb6 11 h3 exd4 12 Na4 Qa6 13 hxg4 b5 ∞, Botvinnik–Smyslov, match 1954. (E) 9 Qc2 transposes to col. 48.

(b) (A) 10 d5 Nc5 11 Ne1 cxd5 12 cxd5 Bd7 13 Nd3 Nxd3 14 Qxd3 Rfc8 15 Rb1 Nh5 16 Be3 Qb4 17 Qe2 Rc4 was fine for Black in Botvinnik–Tal, World Chp. 1960. The game continued 18 Rfc1 Rac8 19 Kh2 f5! 20 exf5 Bxf5 21 Ra1 Nf4! 22 gxf4 exf4 23 Bd2 Qxb2? (23 . . . Be5!) 24 Rab1 f3 25 Rxb2? (25 Bxf3 Bxb1 26 Rxb1 Qc2 27 Be4! Rxe4 28 Nxe4! ±) 25 . . . fxe2 26 Rb3 Rd4! winning for Black. (B) 10 dxe5 dxe5 (10 . . . Nxe5?! 11 b3! Nxf3+ 12 Qxf3 Nxe4 13 Nxe4! Bxa1 14 Bh6! ±, Chandler–W. Watson, London 1985) 11 Qe2 Ne8 12 Be3 Qb4 13 c5 b6 14 a3 Qb3 15 Nd2 Qe6 16 Rfd1 Nc7 17 cxb6 Ba6 =, Najdorf–Bronstein, Moscow 1956.

(c) 11 . . . c5 12 Be3 a6 13 Qd2 Rf8 14 Nh2 Qc7 15 a4 Nh5 16 Qe2 ±, Ribli–Biyiasas, Manila 1976. The column is Najdorf–Tal, Belgrade 1970.

(d) On the immediate 10 . . . Ne8?! 11 Na4! Qd8 (11 . . . Qb4?! 12 Bf1 threatens 13 Bd2; 11 . . . Qa6 12 dxe5 followed by 13 b3 ±) 12 Bg5! f6 13 Be3 ±, I. Ivanov–A. Rodriguez, Toluca 1982.

(e) The older 11 . . . Re8 is still playable, e.g. 12 Re2 Qb4 (12 . . . Ng4 13 Nc2 Ng5 14 Ne3 Nc5, Botvinnik–Geller, Belgrade 1969, and now 15 Rd2 Bf8 16 Rb1 ± would have been better than 15 b3? Bxh3!) 13 Rc2 Nc5 14 Bd2 Qb6 15 Be3 Qc7 16 f3 a5 17 Bf2 ±, Osnos–Nikitin, USSR Chp. 1969.

(f) (A) 12 Nb3 a5! 13 Be3 Qb4 14 a3 Qxc4 15 Nd4 Bxd4! ∓, Beil–Hausner, Czechoslovakia 1981. (B) 12 Nc2 Nc5 13 Qd2 a5 14 b3 f5!, Bukal–Hulak, Zagreb–Rijeka 1985. (C) 12 Nce2 Qa6!? 13 b3 c5 14 Nc2 Bxa1 ∞, Tomaszewski–Kuligowski, Poland 1981.

(g) 12 . . . Ne5 13 Nxe5 dxe5 14 Qa4 Nc7 15 Be3 Qa6 16 Qb4 Ne6 17 c5 (Pigusov–Tukmakov, USSR 1981); now 17 . . . b6! 18 cxb6 Nd4 was necessary.

(h) 14 Be3 a4 15 Bd4 is too slow to obtain an opening advantage, Naumkin–Zagrebelny, USSR 1987.

(i) Other moves, such as 9 . . . a5 10 Re1 exd4 11 Nxd4 Re8, 9 . . . Re8 10 Be3 exd4 11 Ncd4, and 9 . . . exd4 10 Nxd4 Re8 11 Be3 Nc5 12 Qc2 Qe7 13 Rfe1, frequently transpose to col. 46.

(j) 10 Be3 Nb6! 11 Qd3 (or 11 Nd2 exd4 12 Bxd4 Be6 =, Ilivitsky–Yukhtman, USSR 1957) 11 . . . exd4 12 Nxd4 Qa6 13 b3 d5! 14 Qc2! c5! 15 exd5 Nfxd5! 16 Ndb5! Nxe3! 17 fxe5 Bf5 = (analysis by Hübner, Keene, and Whiteley in Chessman Quarterly).

(k) 10 . . . Re8?! 11 Bd2 Qa6 12 d5! ±, Stefanov–Zorić, Križevci 1985.

(l) (A) 15 Kh1 Rae8 16 a3 Ned7 17 Bg2 Nb6 18 Qa6 ±, Nikitin–Polugaevsky, USSR Chp. 1967. (B) 15 f4 Ned7 16 Qc2 Rae8 17 Bf2 Nc5 18 Bg2 Nh5! 19 Rac1 Bxc3! =, Jukić–M. Vukić, Bogojno 1987. The column is Borisenko–Peterson, USSR Chp. 1965.

(m) (A) 12 Ndb5 Nfd7! 13 Be3 Ne5 14 Bxc5 dxc5 15 Qxd8 Rxd8 16 Nxc7 Rb8 17 Red1 Be6 18 Nxe6 fxe6 with compensation (Boleslavsky). (B) 12 Nb3 Nfd7 13 Be3 a4!? 14 Nxc5 Nxc5 15 Bxc5 dxc5 16 Qxd8 Rxd8 17 e5 c6! ∞ (Bukić). (C) 12 Rb1 a4 13 Ndb5 Nfd7 14 Be3 Ne5 is similar to 12 Ndb5 above, but Black has the added option of . . . Ra5. (D) 12 b3 c6 13 Rb1 h6 14 Bf4! Nh5 (14 . . . Ne6 15 Nxe6 Bxe6 16 Qd2 and 17 Rbd1 ±) 15 Be3 Nf6 16 Qc2 ± is a stock maneuver.

(n) On (A) 14 Rab1 simplest is 14 . . . Qa5 15 b4 axb3 16 axb3 Ne6 17 b4 Qc7 18 Rbd1 Nxd4 19 Bxd4 Be6 20 Bf1 Nd7 =, Bagirov–Dely, Vrnjačka Banja 1974. But (B) 14 Rad1 Qa5?! 15 Bf4! Bf8 16 Nf3! Be6 17 Bxd6 Bxc4 18 Bxf8 Kxf8 19 e5 with play on the dark squares, Reshevsky–Najdorf, match 1952.

(o) 15 f4 Qa5 16 Bf2 Qb4!? 17 b3 (17 a3?! Qa5! compromises White's queenside: 18 Nde2 Bf8 19 Nc1?! Nb6 20 N3a2 Be6 21 Bf1 f5! ∓, Saeed–Kir. Georgiev, Dubai 1986) 17 . . . axb3 18 axb3 Ra3 ∞ (Pfleger).

(p) 17 Nb1 Nf6!? (17 . . . Nb6 18 Na3 Bd7 19 Ne2 f5?! 20 Rxd6 Nxe4 21 Bxe4 Rxe4 22 Bxb6 Qxb6 23 Nc3! Bxc3 24 Qxc3 Be8 25 Rd7 Bf7 26 Qf6 ±, Averbakh–Dittmann, Dresden 1956) 18 f3! is strong since 18 . . . d5 fails to 19 cxd5 cxd5 20 Nf5!

(q) Other tries are (A) 9 Re1 exd4 10 Nxd4 Ng4 ∞, M. Vukić–Kočiev, Pula 1988. (B) 9 d5 Ne8! 10 Bd2 c5! (10 . . . h6, playing for f5, comes under pressure after 11 Qc1! Kh7 12 Qc2!, Ribli–Kindermann, Dortmund 1986) 11 dxc6 bxc6 12 b4 Nb6! 13 c5 Nc4 ∓, Yusupov–Reyes, Dubai 1986.

(r) 13 Bb2?! b5 14 cxb5 axb5 15 f4?! Nc6 16 Rad1 c4! 17 bxc4 (the threat is 17 . . . b4) 17 . . . bxc4 18 Ba3 Nb4 with good play for Black, Tukmakov–Knaak, Szirak 1985.

(s) In Bany–Sznapik, Polish Chp. 1988, Black played 14 . . . Qb6?! 15 cxb5 axb5 16 h3 h4, when 17 Na4 Qc7 18 f4 Ned7 19 Rd2 Re8 20 Rfd1 Bf8 21 g4 would have pushed him back.

(t) After 17 Bxd6 Bxb3 18 Bxb8 Qxb8 19 Qd2 Bxd1 20 Rxd1 White has an edge, since he can play for h3, f4 and e5.

(u) (A) 8 e3 Re8 9 b3 c6 10 Bb2 e4 11 Nd2 d5 $\mp$; better is 10 Qc2! exd4 11 Nxd4 a5 12 Ba3 Nc5 13 Rad1 Qe7 ∞, Andersson–Kavalek, match 1978. (B) 8 b3 Re8 9 Qc2 c6 10 Rd1 exd4 11 Nxd4 Qe7 12 e4 transposes to the column.

(v) 8 . . . exd4 9 Nxd4 Nb6 10 Rd1! Nxc4 11 Ncb5 a6 12 Qxc4 axb5 13 Nxb5 Ne8 14 Nc3 c6 (Tal–Lehmann, Palma de Mallorca 1966) 15 Be3 $\pm$.

(w) 10 . . . Nb6 11 b3 Bg4 12 dxe5 dxe5 13 a4! Rfd8 14 Ba3 Rxd1† 15 Nxd1 Qc7 16 Ne3 Bxf3 17 Bxf3 Rd8 18 c5 Nbd7 19 Nc4 with the better position, Agzamov–Soltis, Calcutta 1986.

(x) The radical 14 . . . d5!? 15 cxd5 Nxd5! (15 . . . cxd5 16 Bg5! dxe4 17 Nd5 leads to a big advantage for White) 16 Nxc6! bxc6 17 Nxd5 cxd5 18 Bxc5 Qc7 19 Rac1 dxe4 20 fxe4 Bh6 21 Bf2! gives White a weak but extra pawn, Bergreen–Judović, corr. 1981. After 14 . . . Nfd7 15 Bf2 Ne5 16 h3 a4 17 Rab1 (17 f4? axb3 18 axb3 Rxa1 19 Rxa1 Ned3 20 Be3 f5!) 17 . . . axb3 18 axb3 Na6! 19 Na2 (Kir. Georgiev–Knaak, Bulgaria–East Germany 1986) 19 . . . Nc5! would lead to a draw by perpetual check as 20 b4?! Ncd3 21 Be3 c5 22 bxc5 dxc5 is very good for Black (Kir. Georgiev).

KING'S INDIAN DEFENSE
Fianchetto System

1 d4 Nf6 2 c4 g6 3 g3 Bg7 4 Bg2 0-0 5 Nc3 d6 6 Nf3 Nc6

	49	50	51	52	53	54
7	0-0					
	a6...				e5	Bf5(p)
8	d5......................	h3			d5	Re1(q)
	Na5		Rb8		Ne7	e5(r)
9	Nd2		Be3........	e4	e4(n)	d5
	c5		b5	b5	Nd7	Ne7
10	Qc2(a)		Nd2	e5	b4	c5!?
	Rb8		Bd7(h)	Nd7(k)	a5	Ne4
11	b3		Rc1	e6(l)	Ba3	cxd6
	b5		Na5(i)	fxe6	axb4	cxd6
12	Bb2		cxb5	d5	Bxb4	Nd2!
	bxc4........	e5(e)	axb5	exd5	Bh6	Nxc3
13	bxc4	dxe6(f)	b4	cxd5	a4	bxc3
	Bh6	fxe6	Nc4	Na5(m)	b6(o)	e4
14	f4(b)	cxb5	Nxc4	Nd4	a5	Nxe4
	e5	axb5	bxc4	Ne5	Ba6	Bxe4
15	dxe6(c)	Nce4	b5	Nce2! ±	Qe2 ±	Bxe4 ∞
	Bxe6(d)	Nxe4(g)	d5(j)			

(a) 10 Rb1 Rb8 (Vaganian suggests 10 . . . e5!? 11 dxe6 Bxe6 12 Nde4 Nxe4 13 Nxe4 Nxc4 14 b3 Qb6!) 11 b3 b5 12 Bb2 h5!? 13 Qc2 h4 ∞, Gauglitz–Hába, Halle 1987.

(b) 14 Ncb1 e5 15 Bc3 Bd7 16 Na3 Rb4!? 17 Bxb4 cxb4 18 Nab1 Qc7! 19 c5!? (19 e3 Bf5 20 Ne4 Bxe4 21 Bxe4, Timman–Kasparov, Tilburg 1981; now 21 . . . Nxe4! 22 Qxe4 f5 23 Qc2 Qxc4 gives Black good play for the exchange, Lotti) 19 . . . Qxc5! =, Kurajica–Filipović, Banjaluka 1983.

(c) 15 Rae1 exf4 16 gxf4 Nh5 17 e3 Bg7 18 Nd1 Bf5 19 Be4 Bxe4 20 Nxe4 Bxb2 21 Nxb2 Re8 =, Ree–Sax, Amsterdam 1976.

(d) 16 Nd5 Rxb2! 17 Qxb2 Bg7 and now: (A) 18 Qc2 Nxd5 19 cxd5 Bxa1 20 Bxa1 Qf6 21 Rd1 Qd4† 22 Kh1 Bf5! =, Kir. Georgiev–J. Piket, Amsterdam 1985. (B) 18 Qa3 Nxc4 19 Nxc4 Nxd5 20 Rac1 Nb4 21 Rfd1 d5 22 Kh1 dxc4!? 23 Rxd8 Rxd8 24 Qa5 Rd2 with compensation for the queen, Van Oirschot–Hendriks, corr. 1985.

(e) 12 . . . e6 13 dxe6 is the same, or White can vary with 13 Rab1 or 13 Rad1, with an edge in either case.

(f) 13 Rae1 Nh5 14 e3 with advantage, Ribli–Sznapik, Warsaw 1979.

(g) 16 Bxe4 Bxb2 17 Qxb2 Bb7 18 Rad1 Bxe4 19 Bxe4 d5 20 Bg2 Nc6 21 e4 d4 22 Qd2 Qb6 23 Rc1 Nb4 24 Qxc5 Nxa2 25 Qxb6 Rxb6 =, Ftáčnik–W. Schmidt, Prague 1985.

(h) (A) 10 . . . Na5?! 11 cxb5 axb5 12 b4 Nc4 13 Nxc4 bxc4 14 b5 d5 15 a4 Bf5 16 a5 with a plus, Hjartarson–Ernst, Gausdal 1987. (B) 10 . . . Bb7 11 cxb5 axb5 12 Nxb5 Na5 13 Qa4! Bxg2 14 Kxg2 Qd7! 15 Nc3 Qxa4 16 Nxa4 Nd5 (Greenfeld–Nunn, Biel 1986); now 17 Rad1! Rb4 18 b3 Bxd4 19 Bxd4 Rxd4 20 Nc4 Rxd1 21 Rxd1 Nxc4 22 Rxd5 c6 23 Rd4 with an endgame advantage (Nunn).

(i) 11 . . . e5 12 dxe5 Nxe5 13 cxb5 axb5 14 b3 Re8 15 Nde4 with somewhat better chances, A. Mikhalchishin–Gleizerov, Pavlodar 1987.

(j) 16 a4! e6 17 Rb1 c6 18 Bf4 Rb7 19 Bd6 Re8 20 Qd2 Bf8 21 Bxf8 Rxf8 22 Rb4 cxb5 23 axb5 ±, Beil–W. Schmidt, Sofia 1985.

(k) 10 . . . dxe5 11 dxe5 Qxd1 12 Rxd1 Nd7 13 e6 fxe6 14 cxb5 axb5 15 Be3 (15 Bf4 Nde5 16 Nxe5 Nxe5 17 Rac1 c5 18 Ne4! c4 19 Nc5 Rb6 20 b3 cxb3 21 axb3 Rd6 =, Goldin–Gleizerov, USSR 1986) 15 . . . b4!? 16 Na4 Nce5 17 Nd4 Nb6 18 Nxb6 (18 Nc5 Kf7!) 18 . . . Rxb6 19 Rac1 Rd6 20 Rxc7 Ba6 with counterplay, P. Nikolić–Zapata, Tunis 1985.

(l) 11 cxb5 axb5 12 Ng5 dxe5 (or 12 . . . Nxd4!? 13 Qxd4 Nxe5 14 Qh4 h6 15 Nf3 Nxf3† 16 Bxf3 g5 17 Qh5 b4 with an unclear game, Thorsteins–van der Wiel, Reykjavik 1985) 13 Bxc6 exd4 14 Nb5 Rb6 15 Nd4 (also 15 Na7 is best met by 15 . . . Nb8!, Thorsteins–Hellers, Groningen 1984–85) 15 . . . Nb8! breaking the bind and regaining the material, Salov–Kuzmin, USSR 1981.

(m) 13 . . . Na7 14 Be3 Nb6 (14 . . . c5!? 15 dxc6 Nxc6 frees Black's game further; 16 Qd5† Kh8 17 Qxc6? Bb7 +) 15 Ng5 c5 16 dxc6 e6 17 Rc1 ±, Kanko–Teimann, corr. 1985. The column is Portisch–Vegh, Hungary 1986.

(n) 9 c5 Ne8 10 cxd6 cxd6 11 Qb3 h6 12 e4 f5 13 exf5 gxf5 14 Nd2 Ng6 15 Nc4 Rf7 16 a4 ±, Vaganian–Stein, USSR Chp. 170.

(o) 13 . . . f5 14 a5 Kh8 15 Nd2 Ng8 (Kharitonov–Loginov, Sverdlovsk 1987) 16 exf5!? gxf5 17 Na4 and White's breakthrough with c5 is more significant. The text is a suggestion by Kharitonov and Vyzhmanavin.

(p) 7 . . . Bg4 has fallen on hard times: 8 d5 Na5 9 Qd3! c5 10 Nd2 e5 11 dxe6 Bxd6 12 b3! ±, P. Nikolić–J. Piket, Wijk aan Zee 1988.

(q) 8 Be1 Qc8 9 e4 Bh3 10 Nc2 Bxg2 11 Kxg2 e5 12 d5 Ne7 13 Ne1! ±, Portisch–Korchnoi, Brussels 1986.

(r) 8 . . . Ne4 9 Nxe4! Bxe4 10 d5 Nb4 11 Ng5 Bxg2 12 Kxg2 a5 13 h4! ± (Gutman). The column is Gutman–Murey, Luxembourg 1986.

KING'S INDIAN DEFENSE

Fianchetto System

1 d4 Nf6 2 c4 g6 3 g3 Bg7 4 Bg2 0-0 5 Nc3(a) d6

	55	56	57	58	59	60
6	(Nf3) e3					
	c5 . . . . .c6					Nbd7
7	0-0 .d5		0-0			Nge2
	Nc6		Na6(i)	Qa5(k)		e5
8	d5 . . . . .dxc5		0-0	e4 . . . . .h3(n)		b3
	Na5	dxc5	Nc7	Bg4(l)	Be6(o)	Re8
9	Nd2	Be3(f)	a4	h3	Qd3(p)	a4(q)
	e5(b)	Be6(g)	Rb8	Bxf3	Qa6	c6
10	e4(c)	Qa4	Bf4	Bxf3	b3	Ba3
	Ng4	Nd4	a6	Nfd7	d5	exd4
11	b3	Rad1	a5	Be3	Ne5	exd4
	f5	Bd7	b5	a6	Nbd7	d5
12	exf5	Qa3	axb6	a3	cxd5	cxd5
	gxf5(d)	Nc2	Rxb6	c5	Qxd3	Nxd5
13	h3	Qxc5	Ra2	b4	Nxd3	Nxd5
	Nh6	b6	Re8	Qd8	Nxd5	cxd5
14	Bb2	Qg5	b3	Rc1	Bb2 $\pm$	0-0
	Bd7(e)	h6(h)	e5(j)	cxd4(m)		Nf6 =

(a) White can vary the order of his moves, interchanging g3, Bg2, Nc3, Nf3, and 0-0.

(b) 9 . . . a6 transposes into the Panno Variation, col. 25.

(c) 10 a3 b6 11 b4 Nb7 12 Nb3 Ne8 13 e4 f5 14 exf5 gxf5 15 Bd2 Bd7 16 Qe2 Nf6 17 b5 Be8 =, Hübner–Gligorić, Wijk aan Zee 1971.

(d) 12 . . . e4?! 13 f6! Nxf6 14 Ndxe4! Nxe4 15 Nxe4 Bxa1 16 Bg5 Bf6 17 Nxf6† Rxf6 18 Qa1 Kf7 19 Re1 Rb8 20 Re3 b6 21 Rf3 Bf4 22 g4 Qh8 23 Bxf6 Qxf6 24 Qxf6† Kxf6 25 gxf5 gxf5 26 Re3 with great advantage in the ending, Geller–Velimirović, Havana 1971.

(e) 15 Qc2 Qe7 16 Rae1 Rae8 17 Ne2 Qd8 18 f4 $\pm$, Bareyev–M. Gurevich, USSR Chp. 1986.

(f) 9 Bf4 Nh5 10 Be3 Nd4 11 Nd2 Rb8 12 Nb3 b6 13 Bxd4 cxd4 14 Nb5 Bb7 15 N5xd4 Bxg2 16 Kxg2 Rc8, Draw, Adorjan–Gufeld, Hastings 1987–88.

(g) Also reasonable is 9 . . . Qa5 10 Qb3 Ng4 11 Bd2 Nd4 12 Nxd4 cxd4 13 Qb5 Qd8 14 Nd5 e6 with equal chances, Ojanen–Rosetto, Mar del Plata 1953.

(h) 15 Qf4 g5 16 Qe5 Rc8 17 Nd5 Nxd5 18 Qxd5 Be6 19 Qb7 Qc7 20 Qxc7 Rxc7 21 b3, Draw (as 21 . . . Nxe3 is equal), Grigorian–Kasparov, USSR 1981.

(i) If 7 . . . e5 White should be happy with a slight structural advantage after 8 0-0 and 9 e4, and should avoid 8 dxe6 Bxe6 9 Ng5 Bxc4! 10 Bxb7 Nbd7 11 Bxa8 Qxa8 12 0-0 d5 when

Black has good compensation for the exchange, Korchnoi–Sherbakov, Spartakiad 1956.

(j) 15 dxe6 Nxe6 16 Na4 Nxf4 17 Nxb6 Qxb6 18 gxf4 Ne4 with sufficient play for the exchange, Korchnoi–Gligorić, Buenos Aires 1960.

(k) (A) 7 ... Bf5 is a good alternative, e.g. 8 b3 Ne4 9 Bb2 Nxc3 10 Bxc3 Be4 11 Qd2 Nd7 12 Rac1 Nf6 13 Rfd1 e6 =, Salov–Christiansen, Szirak 1987. (B) 7 ... a6?! 8 d5 cxd5 9 cxd5 b5 10 a3 Nbd7 11 Nd4 Nb6 12 b3 Bb7 13 e4 Rc8 14 Bb2 is very pleasant for White, Kozma–Mista, Luhačovice 1969.

(l) (A) 8 ... e5 9 d5 cxd5 10 cxd5 b5 11 Nd2 b4 12 Nb3 Qa6 13 Ne2 Bd7 14 Bd2 Bb5 15 Re1 ±, Savon–Kavalek, Sarajevo 1987. (B) 8 ... Qh5 9 e5 dxe5 10 Nxe5 Ng4 11 Nf3 ±, Pigusov–Zaichik, Moscow 1987.

(m) 15 Bxd4 Bxd4 16 Qd4 Nc6 17 Qd2 with a small edge, Pigusov–J. Piket, Dordrecht 1988.

(n) 8 d5 Qb4 9 Nd2 Bd7 10 e4 a5 11 Re1 Na6 12 a3 Qb6 13 Nf3 Nc5 14 Be3 cxd5 15 cxd5 a4 16 Rb1 Rfc8 = (Boleslavsky).

(o) 8 ... Qa6!? 9 b3 b5 10 Nd2 bxc4 11 Nxc4 Be6 12 Qd3 Nbd7 13 Bg5 Rac8 ∞, Vaganian–Romero, Dubai 1986.

(p) 9 d5 cxd5 10 Nd4 dxc4! 11 Nxe6 fxe6 12 Bxb7 Nbd7 13 Bxa8 Rxa8 14 Qa4 Qxa4 15 Nxa4 Ne4 is equal, Csom–Mortensen, Esbjerg 1984. The column is Karpov–Van der Wiel, Amsterdam 1988.

(q) 9 Ba3 h5 10 h3 a6 11 dxe5 is equal, Botvinnik–Smyslov, World Chp. 1954. The column is J. Watson–Winslow, Vancouver 1976.

KING'S INDIAN DEFENSE
Averbakh Variation

1 d4 Nf6 2 c4 g6 3 Nc3 Bg7 4 e4 d6 5 Be2 0-0 6 Bg5

	61	62	63	64	65	66
	c5............................Nbd7...................h6					
7	d5(a)			Qd2		Be3
	h6..........b5..........e6			c6..........e5		c5(p)
8	Bf4(b)	cxb5	Qd2(i)	Nf3(l)	d5	e5
	e5	a6	exd5	d5(m)	Nc5	dxe5
9	dxe6	a4(g)	exd5	exd5	f3	dxe5
	Bxe6	Qa5	Re8(j)	cxd5	a5	Qxd1†
10	Bxd6(c)	Bd2	Nf3	0-0	g4!	Rxd1
	Re8	axb5	Bg4	Ne4	c6	Ng4
11	Nf3(d)	Bxb5	0-0	Nxe4	h4	Bxc5
	Qb6(e)	Na6	Nbd7	dxe4	a4	Nxe5
12	Bxb8!	Nge2	h3	Ne1	h5	Nd5
	Raxb8	Nb4	Bxf3	f6	Qa5	Nbc6
13	Qc2	0-0	Bxf3	Bh6	Nh3	f4
	Nh5(f)	Ba6(h)	a6(k)	Bxh6(n)	cxd5(o)	Ng4(q)

(a) 7 dxc5 Qa5 8 Bd2 Qxc5 9 Nf3 Bg4 10 0-0 Bxf3! 11 Bxf3 Nc6 (11 . . . Qxc4? allows 12 e5 and 13 Bxb7) 12 Be2 Nd7 13 Rc1 a6 is equal as Black has play on the dark squares, Fuller–Evans, Haifa 1976.

(b) 8 Be3 e6 9 dxe6 (9 Qd2 exd5 10 exd5 Kh7 =) 9 . . . Bxe6 10 Qd2 Kh7 11 h3 Nc6 12 Nf3 Qa5 13 Rd1 Nd7 14 Qxd6 Rad8 15 0-0 Qb4 =, Portisch–Nunn, Brussels 1988.

(c) 10 Qd2 Qb6 11 Bxh6 Bxh6 12 Qxh6 Qxb2 13 Rc1 Nc6 14 h4 Ne5 15 Nh3 Bxh3 16 Bxh3 Nfg4 17 Qf4 f5 with even chances, Yakovich–Uhlmann, Leipzig 1986.

(d) It is dangerous to grab the second pawn: 11 Bxc5?! Qa5 12 b4 Qa6 ∓, and if 13 Nb5?! Nxe4.

(e) Also possible is 11 . . . Nc6 12 0-0 Nd4 13 e5 Nd7 14 Nxd4 cxd4 15 Qxd4 Nxe5 16 Bxe5 Qxd4 17 Bxd4 Bxd4 18 Rac1 Rad8 19 b3 Bxc3 20 Rxc3 Rd2 21 Bf3 Rxa2 22 Bxb7 Rb8 23 Bf3 Ra3 24 Bd5 a5 25 Re3 when White is better, but best play should lead to a draw, Barlov–Ramayrat, New York 1986.

(f) 14 g3 Bh3 15 Nd2 Bd4 16 Bxh5 gxh5 17 0-0-0 ±, Gelfand–Akopian, Vilnius 1988.

(g) 9 bxa6 Bxa6 10 Nf3 Qb6 11 Rb1 Nbd7 12 0-0 Rfb8 with good play for the pawn, Calvo–Benko, Palma de Mallorca 1968. This line is similar to the Benko Gambit.

(h) 14 h3 Qb6 15 Ra3 Ne8 16 Bg5 f6 17 Be3 Nc7 ∞, Kormanyos–Szell, Hungary 1986.

(i) 8 Nf3 allows 8 . . . h6! 9 Bh4 exd5 10 exd5 g5 11 Bg3 Nh5 12 Nd2 Nxg3 =.

(j) 9 . . . Qb6 10 Nf3 Bf5 11 Nh4! Ne4 12 Nxe4 Bxe4 13 f3 Qxb2 14 Rc1 Qxd2† 15 Kxd2 Bxd5 16 cxd5 Re8 17 Bf4 Bf6 18 g3 g5 19 Bxd6 gxh4 20 Bc7 ±, Grivas–Kotronias, Athens 1986.

(k) 14 a4 Qa5 (14 . . . Qe7 15 Rae1 Qf8 16 Bd1 h6 17 Bf4 Nh7 18 Bc2 $\pm$, Yusupov–Zapata, St. John 1988) 15 Qc2 Re7 16 Bd2 Qc7 17 Rae1 Rae8 18 Rxe7 Rxe7 19 Re1 $\pm$, Mochalov–Vaganian, USSR 1973.

(l) 8 f3 a6 9 Nh3 b5 10 Nf2 bxc4 11 Bxc4 d5! 12 Bb3 dxe4 13 fxe4 c5 14 e5 cxd4 15 Qxd4 Nh5 16 Qe4 Rb8 is a sharp position but roughly equal, Benjamin–Nunn, Szirak 1987.

(m) 8 . . . e5 9 0-0 exd4 10 Nxd4 Nc5 11 Qf4 Qe7 12 Rad1! Re8 (12 . . . Ncxe4 13 Nxe4 Qxe4 14 Qxd6 $\pm$, Polugaevsky–Geller, Amsterdam 1970) 13 Rfe1 $\pm$, Uhlmann–Planinć, Madrid 1973. However, 10 . . . Re8 11 Rad1 a5!? 12 Qf4 a4 13 Qxd6 Qb6 14 Rd2 Nxe4 ∞ merits attention (Podgaets).

(n) 14 Qxh6 e5 15 Qd2 f5 16 d5 Nf6 17 d6 f4 18 c5 Be6 19 Qc3 f3! =, Gelfand–Glek, USSR 1985.

(o) 14 cxd5 Bd7 15 Nf2 b5 16 Ncd1 Rfc8 17 Qxa5 Rxa5 18 Bd2 with a distinct advantage in the endgame, Fedorowicz–Kr. Georgiev, Dubai 1986.

(p) 7 . . . e5 8 d5 c6 9 Qd2 cxd5 10 cxd5 h5 11 f3 Na6 12 Nb5!? Nc5 13 Qc2 b6 14 b4 Na6 15 a3 is better for White, Alburt–Trapl, Děčín 1976.

(q) 14 h3 Nf6 15 Bf3 Bf5 16 g4 Bc2 is equal (Rashkovsky), as on 17 Rd2 Black has 17 . . . Ne4!

KING'S INDIAN DEFENSE

Four Pawns Attack

1 d4 Nf6 2 c4 g6 3 Nc3 Bg7 4 e4 d6 5 f4 0-0 6 Nf3

	67	68	69	70	71	72
	c5 . . . . .e5?!					
7	d5	.Be2			.dxc5	fxe5
	e6(a)		cxd4			Qa5	dxe5
8	Be2(b)		Nxd4			Bd3	d5(n)
	exd5		Nc6			Qxc5(l)	Nbd7
9	exd5(c) . . . . .e5?!		Be3(g)			Qe2	Bd3
	Re8(d)	Ne4!(f)	Ng4! Nd7			Bg4	Nc5
10	0-0	cxd5	Bxg4	0-0(j)		Be3	Bc2
	Bf5	Nxc3	Bxd4	Qb6		Qa5	a5
11	Bd3	bxc3	Bxd4	e5		0-0	0-0
	Qd7	Nd7	Bxg4	dxe5		Nc6	Qd6
12	h3	0-0	Qd2(h)	Nf5		Rac1	Qe1
	Na6	dxe5	Nxd4	Qxb2		Nd7	Bd7
13	a3	fxe5	Qxd4	Na4		Qf2	Qh4 ±
	Nc7(e)	Nxe5 ∓	e5!(i)	Qa3(k)		Bxf3(m)	

(a) 7 . . . b5 8 cxb5 a6 9 a4 e6 (9 . . . Qa5 10 Bd2 Qb4 11 Qc2 ±) 10 dxe6 Bxe6 11 Be2 axb5 12 Bxb5 Na6 13 0-0 Nb4 14 f5! is good for White, Lalić–Zakić, Yugoslavia 1986.

(b) 8 dxe6 fxe6 9 Bd3 Nc6 10 0-0 Nd4 11 Ng5 e5 12 f5 h6 13 Nh3 gxf5 14 exf5 b5! and Black takes a strong grip on the center, Hakki–Podzeliny, Gausdal 1980.

(c) More frequently played is 9 cxd5 which is covered in the Four Pawns Attack of the Benoni Defense.

(d) A good alternative is 9 . . . Nh5 10 0-0 Bxc3! 11 bxc3 f5 12 Bd3 Ng7 13 Bd2 Nd7 14 Be1 Nf6 =, Vladimirov–Gligorić, USSR–Yugoslavia, 1963.

(e) 14 g4 Bxg4 (14 . . . Bxd3 15 Qxd3 b5 ∞) 15 hxg4 Qxg4† 16 Kh2 b5 is at least equal for Black, Conquest–Mestel, Hastings 1986–87.

(f) (A) 9 . . . dxe5 10 fxe5 Ng4 11 Bg5 Qa5 12 0-0 Nc6 13 Nxd5 allows White some initiative. (B) 9 . . . Ng4 10 cxd5 dxe5 11 h3 e4 12 hxg4 exf3 13 exf3 Re8 14 f5 gxf5!? 15 Bh6 Bxc3† 16 bxc3 fxg4 ∞, Belin–Kalinen, USSR 1987. The column is Li Zunian–Gheorghiu, Dubai 1986.

(g) 9 Nc2 Be6 10 0-0 Rc8 11 Rb1 a6 12 b3 b5 13 cxb5 axb5 14 Bf3 Qa5 and Black has active play, Korn–Richter, corr. 1958.

(h) 12 Qxg4 Nxd4 13 Qd1 Nc6 14 0-0 Qb6† 15 Rf2 Qc5 16 b3 Rae8 17 Nd5 Nb4 =, Martz–Visier, Lanzarote 1974.

(i) 14 fxe5 Qh4† 15 Qf2 (15 g3 dxe5 16 Qxe5 Qh3 ∓, Uhlmann) 15 . . . Qxf2† 16 Kxf2 dxe5 =, Uhlmann–Fischer, Leipzig 1960.

(j) White can avoid the column continuation with 10 Qd2 Nc5 11 0-0, but this gives Black time to begin operations: 11 . . . Qa5 12 Rfd1 Nxd4 13 Bxd4 e5 14 Be3 exf4 15 Bxf4 Bxc3 16 Qxc3 Qxc3 17 bxc3 Nxe4 18 Bf3 f5 =, Malich–Gipslis, Pecs 1964.

(k) 14 Bc1 Qb4 15 Bd2 Qa3 16 Rf3 Qxf3 17 Bxf3 gxf5 with enough material for the queen, Trifunović–Vukcević, Yugoslav Chp. 1958.

(l) On 8 . . . Nfd7?! (intending 9 0-0 Nxc5) White gains the advantage by the spectacular 9 cxd6! Bxc3† 10 bxc3 Qxc3† 11 Qd2 Qxa1 12 dxe7 Re8 13 e5 with excellent compensation for the rook, Ljubojević–van der Wiel, Wijk aan Zee 1986. The game continued 13 . . . Nc6 14 0-0 Nd4 15 Bb2 Nxf3† 16 gxf3 Qxa2 17 f5 Nc5 18 f6 Bd7 (van der Wiel later preferred 18 . . . Bh3) 19 Be4 Kh8 20 Bd5 Be6 21 Ra1 Qb3 22 Ra3 Qb6 23 Kg2 Rac8 24 Bd4 Bxd5 25 cxd5 Qb1 26 Rc3 Nd3 (forced; if 26 . . . b6 27 e6 is decisive) 27 Qxd3 Qa2† 28 Kg1 Qxd5 29 Bxa7 Qe6 30 Rxc8 Qxc8 31 Kg2 h6 32 Be3 Kh7 33 Qb3 Kg8 34 Bxh6 Qc5 35 Qe3 Qxe3 36 Bxe3 b5 37 Bc5 Rc8 38 Kg3 g5 39 Kg4 Kh7 40 Kxg5 Rg8† 41 Kf5 Rb8 42 h4 Rc8 43 Bb4 Re8 44 h5 Ra8 45 f4 Rb8 46 Bd6 Resigns.

(m) 14 gxf3 Nc5 15 Bb1 Qb4! is equal (Spraggett). Black's queen is in some danger, but it gives him queenside play.

(n) 8 Nxe5?! c5! is good for Black, as 9 d5 is met by 9 . . . Nxe4. The column is Alekhine–Ed. Lasker, New York 1924.

KING'S INDIAN DEFENSE

1 d4 Nf6 2 c4 g6

	73	74	75	76	77	78
3	(Nc3) .... Nf3(n)					
	(Bg7)					Bg7
4	(e4)			Bg5	Bf4(k)	b3
	(d6)		0-0	d6	d6	0-0
5	h3	g3(d)	e5(f)	Nf3(i)	Nf3	Bb2
	0-0(a)	0-0	Ne8	h6	0-0	d6
6	Be3(b)	Bg2	f4(g)	Bh4	h3(l)	e3
	e5	c5(e)	d6	g5	c6	Nbd7
7	d5	d5	Be3	Bg3	e3	Be2
	Nbd7	e6	c5!	Nh5	a6	e5
8	g4(c)	Nge2	dxc5	e3	a4	dxe5
	Nc5	exd5	Nc6	Nd7	a5	Ng4
9	Qc2	exd5	cxd6?!	Nd2	Be2	0-0
	c6	Na6	exd6	Nxg3	Na6	Re8
10	Nge2	0-0	Ne4	hxg3	0-0	Nc3
	cxd5 =	Nc7 =	Bf5!(h)	Nf6(j)	Nd7(m)	dxe5(o)

(a) If 5 . . . c5, best is 6 d5 as in note (b), since 6 dxc5 Qa5 7 Bd3 Nfd7! 8 Bd2 Nxc5 9 Bc2 Nc6 10 Nf3 Nb4 allows Black a good position, Hess–Byrne, Philadelphia 1987.

(b) 6 Bg5 c5 (6 . . . Nbd7 and 7 . . . e5 is also possible) 7 d5 e6 8 Bd3 exd5 9 exd5 Nbd7 10 Nf3 Re8† 11 Kf1 h6 12 Bf4 Ne5 13 Nxe5 dxe5 14 Be3 b6 15 Qd2 h5 =, Suba–Nunn, Dubai 1986.

(c) 8 Nf3 transposes to col. 21. 8 Bd3 and 8 Ng2 are also played but give Black little trouble. The column is Bronstein–Gligorić, Zürich 1953; Black obtains chances on the queen-side.

(d) Other fifth moves: (A) 5 Nge2 c6 6 Ng3 Nbd7 7 Be2 h5 8 Bg5 a6 9 Qd2 b5 10 f3 0-0 11 Rd1 e5 =, Miles–Romanishin, Tilburg 1985. (B) 5 Be3 Ng4 =. (C) 5 Bd3 0-0 6 Nge2 c5 7 d5 e6 8 0-0 exd5 9 exd5 Ng4! 10 f4 Re8 =, Barczay–Suetin, Budapest 1970. (D) For 5 Bg5 see note (i).

(e) Also reasonable is 6 . . . e5 7 Nge2 Nc6 (7 . . . exd4 8 Nxd4 Nc6 ∞) 8 d5 Nd4 9 0-0 c5! 10 dxc6 bxc6 11 Nxd4 exd4 12 Qxd4 Ng4 13 Qd1 Ne5 with activity for the pawn (Bole-slavsky).

(f) The text is an attempt to punish Black for delaying . . . d6, but White does better to play any of the usual fifth moves and transpose into the major variations after 5 . . . d6.

(g) 6 Nf3 d6 7 Bf4 Bg4 8 Be2 Nc6 9 exd6 Nxd6 10 d5 Bxf3 11 Bxf3 Nd4 $\mp$, Eryomin–Polugaevsky, USSR 1969.

(h) 11 Ng3 Be6 12 Nf3 Qc7 13 cxd6 Nxd6 with a lead in development and excellent attacking chances for the pawn, Letelier–Fischer, Leipzig 1960. In the column, 9 Nf3 maintains even chances.

(i) On 5 e4 Black has (A) 5 . . . c5 6 d5 0-0 7 Qd2 (7 Be2 transposes to the Averbakh Variation) 7 . . . e6 8 Bd3 exd5 9 Nxd5 Be6 10 Ne2 Bxd5 11 cxd4 c4 12 Bc2 Nbd7 =, Christiansen–Rachels, Somerset 1986. (B) 5 . . . h6 6 Bh4 0-0 7 Bd3 e5 8 d5 Nbd7 9 Nge3 Nc5 10 Bc2 a5 11 f3 c6 with roughly equal chances, Sofrevsky–Minić, Yugoslav Chp. 1961.

(j) 11 Qc2 c6 12 Be2 Bd7 13 b4 Qc7 14 Nb3 0-0-0 =, Addison–R. Byrne, US Chp. 1963–64.

(k) 4 e3 is passive. Black can continue with (A) 4 . . . d6 5 Nf3 0-0 6 Be2 Nbd7 7 0-0 e5 =, or (B) 4 . . . c5 5 Nf3 0-0 6 Be2 d6 7 0-0 Bf5 =, Inkiov–Tal, Saint John 1988.

(l) 6 e3 Nbd7 7 Be2 Nh5 8 Bg5 h6 9 Bh5 g5 10 Nd2 hxg4 11 Bxh5 e5 =, Balcerowski–Jansa, Bad Liebenstein 1963.

(m) 11 Qd2 e5 12 Bh2 Qe7 13 Rfd1 Re8 14 Bf1 Nb4 15 Rac1 e4 =, Alburt–J. Kristiansen, Reykjavik 1986.

(n) 3 Nf3 and 3 g3 usually transpose into well-established systems after a later Nc3. The column instead considers White fianchettoing his queen's bishop.

(o) 11 h3 Nh6 12 e4 c6 13 Qc1 f6 with an equal game, Milić–Gligorić, Yugoslav Chp. 1955.

OLD INDIAN DEFENSE

1 d4 Nf6 2 c4 d6

	79	80	81	82	83	84
3	Nc3........				.....	Nf3
	Nbd7				.....e5(l)	Bg4(p)
4	Nf3				Nf3(m)	Qb3
	e5				e4(n)	Qc8(q)
5	e4		g3	Bg5	Ng5	g3
	Be7(a)		Be7	Be7	Bf5	Nbd7
6	Be2		Bg2	Qc2(i)	g4	Bg2
	0-0		c7	c6	Bxg4	c6
7	0-0		e4	0-0-0	Bg2	h3
	c6		0-0	Qc7(j)	Be7	Bxf3
8	Qc2........	Re1(e)	0-0	e3	Ngxe4	Bxf3
	Qc7(b)	a6	Re8(g)	a6	Nxe4	e5
9	Rd1	Bf1	h3	g4!	Bxe4	Be3
	a6	b5	Bf8	Qa5	c6	Be7
10	Bg5(c)	a3	Qc2	Bh4	Qd3	Nc3 $\pm$
	h6(d)	Bb7(f)	a6(h)	b5(k)	Bh5(o)	

(a) 5 . . . g6 6 Be2 Bg7 7 0-0 0-0 transposes to the Classical Variation of the King's Indian Defense.

(b) 8 . . . Re8 9 b3 Bf8 10 Bb2 Nh5 11 g3 g6 12 Rad1 $\pm$, Stahlberg–Kotov, Zürich 1953.

(c) 10 b3 b5 11 Bb2 Bb7 12 Rac1 Rac8 is equal, since 13 cxb5?! is met by 13 . . . cxb5 instead of 13 . . . axb5? 14 Nxb5.

(d) 11 Bh4 Re8 12 Rac1 Nf8 13 c5 exd4 14 cxd6 Bxd6 15 Rxd4 Ng4 16 Bg3 Bxg3 17 hxg3 Qe7 =, Beliavsky–Malanyuk, USSR Chp. 1986.

(e) White has other reasonable plans that give him a small plus: (A) 8 Rb1 Re8 9 b4 Qc7 10 h3 Nf8 11 Qc2 Ng6 12 Rd1 exd4 13 Nxd4 Bf8, Xu Jun–Ionescu, Timisoara 1987. (B) 8 h3 Re8 9 Be3 Qc7 10 Qc2 Bf8 11 Rad1 exd4 12 Bxd4 Ne5, Pomar–Kottnauer, Bad Aibling 1968. (C) 8 d5 Nc5 9 Qc2 a5 is only equal.

(f) 11 Bg5 Qb8 12 h3 Re8 13 Qc2 Bf8 14 Rad1 with an edge due to White's harmonious development, Marović–Kovačević, Zabreb 1971.

(g) 8 . . . a6 9 Re1 b5 10 c5! Bb7 (10 . . . exd4 11 cxd6 Bxd6 12 Nxd4 $\pm$) 11 h3 Qc7 12 cxd6 Bxd6 13 Bg5 $\pm$, Krogius–Peterson, USSR Chp. 1965.

(h) 11 a4 a5 12 Be3 cxd4 13 Bxd4 (or 13 Nxd4 $\pm$) 13 . . . Nb8 14 Rad1 Nfd7 (Baryev–Malanyuk, USSR Chp. 1986); now 15 e5 gives White excellent chances.

(i) White can achieve a small advantage with 6 e3 0-0 7 Qc2 c6 8 Bd3 Re8 9 0-0 Qc7 10 Rae1 a6 11 c5 h6 12 cxd6 Bxd6 13 Bxf6 Nxf6 14 Nxe5 $\pm$, Ornstein–Westerinen, Stockholm 1974–75. The column is sharper.

(j) 7 . . . Qa5 is stronger, limiting White to a small advantage.

(k) 11 g5 Nh5 12 dxe5 dxe5 13 Bh3 b4 14 Na4 Nc5 15 Bxc8 Rxc8 16 Nxc5 Qxc5 17 Bg3 Bd6
18 Nd2 Bc7 19 Ne4 Qa5 20 Kb1 (±) 0-0 21 Rd7 Rb8 22 Rhd1 Bd8 23 c5 Bc7 24 Qb3 Rbc8
25 Rxf7! Rxf7 26 Rd7 Rcd8 27 Rxf7 Rxf7 28 g6 Resigns, since 28 . . . hxg6 29 Ng5 and
30 Qxf7† follows, Christiansen–Blatný, Thessaloniki 1988.

(l) 3 . . . Bf5 is worthy of attention. On 4 f3 e5 5 e4 exd4 6 Qxd4 Nc6 7 Qd2 Be6 8 b3 a5
Black has good play.

(m) 4 dxe5 dxe5 5 Qxd8† Kxd8 6 Bg5 Be7 7 e3 c6 8 0-0-0† gives White just a small endgame
edge.

(n) 4 . . . Nbd7 transposes to col. 79. Also see English Opening, col. 33.

(o) 11 Qh3 Bg6 12 Bxg6 fxg6 13 Bf4 0-0 14 e3 Na6 15 0-0-0 ±, Kasparov–Speelman, Belfort
1988.

(p) (A) 3 . . . Nbd7 4 Nc3 transposes to col. 79. (B) 3 . . . Bf5 4 Nc3 c6 5 g3 g6 6 Bg2 Bg7 7
0-0 ±.

(q) 4 . . . Bxf3 5 exf3 Qc8 6 Be3 e6 7 Nc3 Be7 8 Be2 0-0 9 0-0 c6 10 d5 ±, M. Gurevich–
Marangunić, Zagreb 1987. The column is Smejkal–Andersson, Prague 1969.

BENONI DEFENSE

1 d4 Nf6 2 c4 c5 3 d5 e6 (diagram) (Including the Czech Benoni, 3 . . . e5, and the Old Benoni, 1 . . . c5 2 d5)

Diagram 84

THE BENONI IS A MODERN OPENING known for its aggressive, tactical, almost reckless nature. Black obtains active pieces and a queenside pawn majority at the cost of allowing White to expand in the center. If White is able to develop smoothly and consolidate his central space, Black's position can become critical. Black must use his activity to keep White off balance or to achieve a queenside advance. Failure to do so can lead to a quick defeat. An immediate 3 . . . d6 might ultimately lead to a precarious King's Indian Defense.

Due to the unstable situations Black often encounters, many masters consider the Benoni risky or even unsound. Older, conservative grandmasters would never dream of playing it. Yet it has quite a respectable following. It was Tal and then later Fischer who popularized the defense in the 1960s, and recently many other top players have been Benoni practitioners, notably Nunn and Kasparov.

Diagram 85

In cols. 1–22, White pursues classical development in the main line, 3 . . . e6 4 Nc3 exd5 5 cxd5 d6 6 Nf3 g6 (see diagram). After 7 e4 Bg7 8 Be2 0-0 9 0-0 (cols. 1–12), Black has three plans available: (A) 9 . . . Re8 10 Nd2 Nbd7 (cols. 2–5) seeks to gain play on the kingside from the strong post of the knight at e5, but to keep control of e5 usually requires the weakening move . . . g5. (B) 9 . . . Re8 10 Nd2 Na6 (cols. 7–9) guarantees Black queenside play but at the cost of placing the knight passively at c7. (C) 9 . . . a6 10 a4 Bg4 (cols. 10–12) allows Black to develop smoothly yet limits his aggressive options.

White has several options on move seven. He can pressure the square d6 and try to interfere with Black's development by 7 Bf4 (cols. 13–14). 7 g3 (cols. 15–17) is generally a positional choice, but it leads to unfathomable complications in col. 15. 7 Nd2 (cols. 18–19) is called the *Knight's Tour Variation*: White immediately maneuvers the knight to its best square at c4 before developing his other pieces. 7 Bg5 (cols. 20–22) seeks to provoke the weakening . . . h6 and . . . g5 at the price of trading bishop for knight. White can do this with 8 e3 or 8 e4, but both lines are satisfactory for Black.

In cols. 23 and 24, White places his king's knight elsewhere than f3. This leaves his f-pawn free to advance either to f3, protecting the center, or to f4, preparing an advance in the center. Both sides have considerable scope for original plans here.

The FOUR PAWNS ATTACK, 6 e4 g6 7 f4 Bg7 (cols. 25–29), is the most direct attempt to prove Black's strategy unsound. White immediately creates a broad pawn-center that is ready to advance. The drawback is that Black has counterplay against the center, and this balances the chances. Col. 27 (9 . . . Bg4) is Black's safest response. The immediate advance 8 e5 (col. 30) is the *Mikenas Attack*, in which accurate defense by Black gives him at least equality.

Taimanov's Variation, 8 Bb5† (cols. 31–33), is so feared by some players that they begin the game with 1 d4 Nf6 2 c4 e6 and only against 3 Nf3 will they play 3 . . . c5, which leads after 4 d5 to usual lines of the Benoni while avoiding the Taimanov. Yet Black has several tries to equalize and seems to have reasonable chances.

The CZECH BENONI, 3 . . . e5 (cols. 34–35), is more solid than the usual (or modern) Benoni, but Black lacks active chances. White has the better of it in a strategic, maneuvering game.

The OLD BENONI, 1 . . . c5 (col. 36), is rarely used. White gains the advantage by not playing c4.

BENONI DEFENSE

1 d4 Nf6 2 c4 c5 3 d5 e6 4 Nc3 exd5 5 cxd5 d6 6 Nf3 g6 7 e4 Bg7 8 Be2 0-0 9 0-0 Re8

	1	2	3	4	5	6
10	Qc2........Nd2					
	Na6(a)	Nbd7 ....a6				
11	Re1(b)	a4................................h3(q)				a4
	Bg4	Ne5(e)			g5	Nbd7
12	Bf4	Ra3........Qc2........Re1(n)			Nc4	Ra3(r)
	c4(c)	g5(f)	g5(j)	Nh5!(o)	Nxe4	Rb8
13	Bxc4	Re1(g)	b3(k)	Nf1	Nxe4	a5
	Bxf3	Ng6(h)	g4	f5	Rxe4	Qc7(s)
14	gxf3	Bb5	Bb2	exf5	Nxd6	h3
	Nh5	Re7	Nh5	Bxf5	Rd4	b5
15	Bg3	Nf1	g3	Be3	Qc2	axb6
	Be5	a6	f5(l)	Nf6	Rxd5	Rxb6
16	Bb5	Bc4	exf5	Ng3	Nxc8	Qc2 $\pm$
	Rf8(d)	h6(i)	Qg5(m)	Bd7(p)	Ne5! $=$	

(a) 10 . . . Nbd7 and 10 . . . Bg4 are playable alternatives, but the text is slightly better.

(b) 11 Bf4 Nb4 12 Qb1 Nh5 13 Bg5 f6 14 Be3 f5 15 a3 fxe4 16 Ng5 Nd3 17 Bxh5 gxh5 18 Ncxe4 c4 with at least equality, Ree–Tringov, Titovo Užice 1966.

(c) Now . . . Nh5 (with or without . . . Nb4) is not so accurate, e.g. 12 . . . Nh5 13 Bg5 f6 14 Bd2 Nb4 15 Qb1 f5 16 h3! fxe4 17 hxg4 exf3 18 Bxf3 with an edge, Filip–Janošević, Wijk aan Zee 1970.

(d) 17 Bxa6 bxa6 18 Bxe5 dxe5 19 Ne2 Rb8 with good play for the pawn, Reshevsky–Ničevski, Skopje 1976.

(e) (A) 11 . . . a6 transposes to column 6. (B) 11 . . . g5 12 Re1 Nf8 13 Bb5 Re7 14 a5! a6 15 Bd3 Ng6 16 Nc4 $\pm$, Pinter–Suba, Warsaw 1987.

(f) 12 . . . Bd7?! 13 Qc2 Rc8 14 f4! Neg4 15 Nc4 Qe7 16 h3 and Black is in serious trouble, T. Petrosian–Ljubojević, Milan 1975.

(g) 13 Qc2 a6 14 Nd1 b6 15 Ne3 Rb8 16 Re1 Ng6 17 f3 b5 $=$, Andruet–Renet, Marseille 1988.

(h) 13 . . . g4 14 Nf1 a6 15 Bg5! h6 16 Bh4 Bd7 17 Ng3 Qc8 18 Qd2 leaves Black somewhat loose, Browne–Nunn, London 1980.

(i) 17 Ng3 Bd7 18 Bd2 Qc7 19 Qc2 Rae8 with active play for Black, Stempin–Suba, Prague 1985.

(j) 12 . . . Nh5!? 13 Bxh5 gxh5 14 Nd1 Qh4 (14 . . . b6?! 15 Ra3 Ba6 16 Rh3! Bxf1 17 Nxf1 b5 18 Nde3 bxa4 19 Nf5 is tremendous compensation for the exchange, T. Petrosian–Rashkovsky, USSR Chp. 1976) 15 Ra3 Bd7 16 h3 b5?! (16 . . . Kh8 $\pm$) 17 axb5 Bxb5 18 Re1 f5 19 Ne3 $\pm$, Dlugy–Wedberg, New York 1986.

(k) (A) 13 Nxf3 Nxf3† 14 Bxf3 (Gligorić–Fischer, Palma de Mallorca 1970) 14 . . . Nd7 = . (B) 13 Nc4 Nxc4 14 Bxc4 Nh5 15 Ra3 Be5 16 Ne2 Qf6 = , F. Portisch–Donner, Reggio Emilia 1979–80. (C) 13 Ra3 transposes to note (g).

(l) 15 . . . Rf8 16 f4 exf3 17 Nxf3 is sharp, perhaps favoring White.

(m) 17 Nce4 Qxf5 18 f4 gxf3 19 Bxf3 ±, G. Garcia–Browne, Las Palmas 1979.

(n) (A) 12 Ndb1 h5! 13 h3 Nh7 14 f4?! Ng4! 15 Qe1 Bd4† 16 Kh1 Ngf6 17 Bf3 Bf5 is good for Black (Agapov). (B) 12 h3 g5 13 Nf3 Nxf3† 14 Bxf3 Re5! ∓.

(o) 12 . . . Nfg4 13 h3 Nxf2 14 Kxf2 Qh4† 15 Kg1 Bxh3 16 Nf1 and White is for choice.

(p) 17 Bg5 Nf7 18 Bxf6 Bxf6 19 Bb5 Bd4 = , Griffin–Hardicsay, Oberwart 1986.

(q) 11 Qc2 Nb6! = ; now if 12 a4?! Nfxd5 13 exd5 Bxc3 14 Bb5 Bxd2 15 Bxe8 Bxc1 is good for Black, Kapu–Bilek, Hungarian Chp. 1964.

(r) 12 Qc2 Ne5 13 Ra3 Qe7 14 a5 Bd7 15 Rb3 Rab8 16 Rb6 Bg4 ∞, Portisch–Velimirović, Portorož–Ljubljana 1975; 13 b3 is worth a try.

(s) Probably better is 13 . . . Ne5 14 h3 g5. The column is T. Petrosian–Quinteros, Lone Pine 1976.

BENONI DEFENSE

**1 d4 Nf6 2 c4 c5 3 d5 e6 4 Nc3 exd5 5 cxd5 d6 6 Nf3 g6
7 e4 Bg7 8 Be2 0-0 9 0-0**

	7	8	9	10	11	12
	(Re8)................a6(k)					
10	(Nd2)			a4		
	Na6			Bg4(l)		
11	f3(a)			Bf4.....................h3(s)		
	Nc7			Bxf3........Re8		Bxf3
12	a4			Bxf3	Nd2(p)	Bxf3
	b6......................Nd7			Qe7(m)	Bxe2	Nbd7
13	Nc4........Kh1		Kh1(h)	Re1(n)	Qxe2	Bf4
	Ba6	Rb8	b6	Nbd7	Nh5	Qe7
14	Bg5(b)	Nc4	Nc4	Qd2	Be3	Re1
	Qd7(c)	Ba6	Ne5	h5	Nd7	Rfe8
15	Qd2(d)	Bg5	Ne3	h3	a5	Qc2
	Bxc4	Qd7(f)	f5(i)	c4	Rc8	c4
16	Bxc4	b3	f4	Be7	g4(q)	Be2
	a6(e)	Nh5(g)	Nf7(j)	Rac8(o)	Nhf6(r)	Rac8 =

(a) (A) 11 Bxa6 bxa6 is at least equal, as Black's two bishops and open b-file provide good play. (B) 11 Re1 Nc7 12 a4 b6 13 Qc2 (13 h3 Rb8 14 Bb5?! Re7 15 Bc6 a6 ∓) 13 . . . Rb8 14 Nc4 Ba6 15 Bf4 Bxc4 16 Bxc4, Reshevsky–Tarjan, US Chp. 1977.

(b) (A) 14 Rb1 Bxc4 15 Bxc4 Nd7 16 Bd2 a6 17 b4 cxb4 18 Rxb4 Qe7 19 Kh1 Rec8 and Black has chances on the queenside, Adamski–Matulović, Lugano 1968. (B) 14 Bf4 Nh5! 15 Be3 (15 Bxd6 Bxc4 16 Bxc7 Bxe2 ∓) 15 . . . f5 16 Nd2 Bxc3! 17 bxc3 Nxd5 18 exd5 Bxe2 19 Qxe2 f4 =, Ekström–Hellers, match Sweden–Norway 1974.

(c) An important alternative is 14 . . . h6 15 Be3 Bxc4 16 Bxc4 a6 17 Qd2 Kh7 18 Rab1 Rb8 (18 . . . Qd7 19 b4 b5 20 Be2 c4 21 Rbe1 Qe7 22 Bd4 Rab8 23 a5 Qf8 24 Bd1 Qh8 25 f4 ±, C. Hansen–Paavilainen, Pohja 1985) and now: (A) 19 Qd3 b5 20 axb5 axb5 21 Nxb5 Nfxd5 22 Bxd5 Nxd5 23 Qxd5 Rxb5 24 Qxf7 (Matulović). (B) 19 b4 b5 20 Be2 c4 21 Bd4 Re7 22 a5 Qh8 23 Rbd1 Nce8 =, Ivanchuk–Mauer, Groningen 1986–87.

(d) 15 Rb1?! Bxc4 16 Bxc4 a6 17 b4 b5 18 Bd3 c4 19 Bc2 bxa4! 20 Bxa4 Nb5 =, Beliavsky–Portisch, Szirak 1987.

(e) 17 Qd3 Nh5 18 g4 (Dlugy–de Firmian, US Chp. 1988) 18 . . . Nf6 ∞.

(f) Also reasonable is 15 . . . h6 16 Bd2 Bxc4 17 Bxc4 a6 18 Qe2 Qc8 19 Bf4 Bf8 20 Rab1 (T. Petrosian–Schmid, Zürich 1961); now Nunn's 20 . . . Qb7 is fully equal.

(g) 17 Rc1 f6 18 Be3 f5 19 g4?! Bxc4 20 bxc4 fxg4 and Black is doing well, Polugaevsky–Nunn, London 1982.

(h) Equally good is 13 Nc4 Ne5 14 Ne4 f5 15 exf5 gxf5 16 f4 Ng6 17 Kh1 Qf6 18 Bd3 ±, Trois–Letelier, Mar del Plata 1973.

(i) 15 ... Rb8 16 Bd2 a6 17 Rb1 b5 18 b4 is slightly better for White (Adorjan).

(j) 17 exf5 gxf5 18 Bd3 Qf6 19 Qc2 Nh6 20 Bd2 Bd7 21 Rf3 Re7 22 Raf1 Kh8 23 Rg3 with pressure, Toth–Valenti, Italian Chp. 1977.

(k) The immediate 9 ... Bg4 is less accurate: 10 h3 Bxf3 11 Bxf3 a6 12 Bf4! Re8 (12 ... b5 13 e5 dxe5 14 d6 Ra7 15 Bxe5 $\pm$) 13 Re1 Nfd7 14 a4 (better than 14 Bxd6 Qb6) 14 ... Ne5 15 Be2 with advantage, Fridstein–Smilga, USSR 1957.

(l) (A) 10 ... b6 11 b4 Ra7 12 Nd2 Re7 13 Bf3 Ne8 14 Nc4 leaves Black under pressure, Smyslov–Ragozin, USSR 1953. (B) 10 ... Nbd7 11 Bg5 (White would not be able to develop this bishop if 10 ... Re8 11 Nd2 Nbd7, as in col. 6) 11 ... h6 12 Bh4 Qe7 13 Nd2 g5 14 Bg3 Ne5 15 Qc2 Nfd7 16 Nd1 Ng6 17 Bg4 Bd4 18 Nc4 $\pm$, Polugaevsky–Kapengut, USSR 1975.

(m) 12 ... Ne8 13 Be2 Nd7 14 Bg3 f5 15 exf5 gxf5 16 Bf4 Ne5 17 a5 $\pm$, Hjartarson–Lobron, Reykjavik 1984.

(n) 13 e5 dxe5 14 d6 Qe6 15 Re1 (15 Bg5 is safer) 15 ... Nbd7 16 Bxb7 Ra7 17 Bf3 Rb8! (threatening 18 ... Rb6) $\mp$, Browne–D. Gurevich, New York 1984.

(o) 17 a5 Rfe8 18 Bf1 Nh7 19 Ra4 f5 20 Rxc4 g5 ∞, van der Sterren–Psakhis, Tallinn 1987.

(p) 12 h3? Nxe4 13 Nxe4 (13 hxg4 Bxc3) 13 ... Rxe4 14 Bg5 Qe8 15 Bd3 Bxf3 16 Qxf3 Rb4 with an extra pawn, Uhlmann–Fischer, Palma de Mallorca 1970.

(q) The text is good, but White's best plan is 16 f4 Nhf6 17 Ra4 $\pm$.

(r) 17 f3 Ne5 18 Kh1 h6 19 g5 Nh5 20 f4 $\pm$, Browne–de Firmian, US Chp. 1985.

(s) (A) 11 Nd2 Bxe2 12 Qxe2 Nbd7 13 Nc4 Nb6 14 Ne3 Re8 15 a5 Nc8! =. (B) 11 Bg5 h6 12 Bh4 Bxf3 13 Bxf3 Nbd7 14 Qc2 Re8 15 Be2 Qa5 =.

BENONI DEFENSE

1 d4 Nf6 2 c4 c5 3 d5 e6 4 Nc3 exd5 5 cxd5 d6 6 Nf3 g6

	13	14	15	16	17	18
7	Bf4		g3			Nd2
	Bg7	a6	Bg7			Bg7(q)
8	Qa4†(a)	a4(e)	Bg2			Nc4(r)
	Bd7	Qe7!	0-0			0-0
9	Qb3	h3	0-0			Bg5
	Qc7(b)	Nbd7(f)	Nbd7		Na6(n)	Qe7(s)
10	e4	Nd2	Nd2	Re1(k)	Nd2(o)	e3
	0-0	Ne5	a6(g)	a6	Nc7	Nbd7
11	Nd2(c)	e4	a4	a4	Nc4	a4(t)
	Nh5	Bg7	Re8	Rb8(l)	Nfe8	Ne5
12	Be3	Be2	h3(h)	e4	a4	Na3
	f5	0-0	Rb8	b5	b6	h6
13	exf5	0-0	Nc4	axb5	Qc2	Bh4
	gxf5	Nfd7	Ne5(i)	axb5	f5	g5
14	Be2	Bh2	Na3	Bf1	Rb1	Bg3
	f4(d)	g5 =	Nh5(j)	Ng4!(m)	Ba6(p)	Nfd7 =

(a) 8 e4 0-0 9 Be2 a6 10 a4 Qe7 11 Nd2 Nbd7 12 0-0 Ne5 13 Re1 Rb8 =, Alterman–Kapengut, USSR 1975.

(b) 9 ... b5 10 Bxd6 Qb6 11 Be5 0-0 12 e3 c4 13 Qd1 Na6 (van der Sterren–Winants, Budel 1987); now simply 14 Be2 leaves White well ahead.

(c) 11 Be2 Nh5 12 Be3 Bg4 13 h3 Bxf3 14 Bxf3 Nd7 15 0-0 Nhf6 is roughly equal, Salov–Psakhis, Moscow 1986.

(d) 15 Bxc5! Na6 (15 ... f3 16 Bxf3 Rxf3 17 gxf3 Qxc5 18 Qxb7 ±, Korchnoi–Nunn, London 1984) 16 Ba3 Rae8 17 Nce4 Nf6 18 Bxd6 Qa5 19 Nc3 Rxe2† 20 Kxe2 and White's extra material decides, Schüssler–Fedorowicz, match Scandinavia–US 1986. If Black tries 14 ... Be8 instead, then 15 Nf3 f4 16 Bd2 Qe7 17 0-0! Bxc3 18 Bxc3 Qxe2 19 Qxb7 ±, Spraggett–Norwood, Toronto 1985.

(e) 8 e4 b5 9 Qe2 (9 e5 dxe5 10 Nxe5 Bd6 $\overline{\mp}$) 9 ... Be7 10 0-0-0 0-0 11 e5 Ng4 12 Ne4 dxe5 13 Nxe5 Nxe5 14 Bxe5 Nd7 15 Bf4 Re8 $\overline{\mp}$, Alburt–D. Gurevich, US Chp. 1986.

(f) The natural 9 ... Bg7?! fails to 10 Nd2! and 11 Nc4 ±. The column is Naumkin–Aseyev, USSR 1986.

(g) Black has a respectable alternative in 10 ... Nh5 11 Nde4 Ndf6 12 Bg5 h6 13 Nxf6† Nxf6 14 Bd2 Re8 15 h3 Bf5 =, Djurić–de Firmian, New York 1986.

(h) (A) 12 Nc4 Ne5 13 Na3 Nh5 14 h3 f5 15 f4 Nf7 16 Nc4 b6 =, Lein–Vasiukov, USSR Chp. 1969. (B) 12 Ra2?! Rb8 13 a5 b5 14 axb6 Nxb6 15 b3 h5 16 Nf3 Bb7 =, Shapiro–Fedorowicz, Somerset 1986.

(i) 13 ... Nb6 is equally viable: 14 Na3 Be7 15 Qc2 Nc8 16 Nc4 Bb5 17 Qb3 Bxc4 18 Qxc4 Nd7 19 Qd3 Ne5 is equal, Liberzon–Yusupov, Lone Pine 1981.

(j) 15 e4 Rf8 (15 . . . f5 16 exf5 Bxf5 17 g4 seems to favor White) 16 Kh2 f5 17 f4 b5! 18 axb5 axb5 19 Naxb5 fxe4 20 Bxe4 Bd7 with a wild position, Korchnoi–Kasparov, Lucerne 1982. The game continued 21 Qe2 Qb6 22 Na3 Rbe8 23 Bd2? (23 Kg2 ∞) 23 . . . Qxb2! 24 fxe5 (24 Rfb1 doesn't trap the queen because of 24 . . . Nf3†!) 24 . . . Bxe5 25 Nc4 Nxg3! 26 Rxf8† Rxf8 27 Qe1 Ne4† 28 Kg2 Qc2 29 Nxe5 Rf2† 30 Qxf2 Nxf2 31 Ra2 Qf5 32 Nxd7 Nd3 33 Bh6 Qxd7 34 Ra8† Kf7 35 Rh8?! (Kasparov's 35 Ne4 puts up stiffer resistance) 35 . . . Kf6 36 Kf3? Qxh3† 37 Resigns.

(k) 10 Bf4 Qe7 11 h3 a6 12 a4 h6 13 Re1 Rb8 14 e4 g5 (van Heste–Farago, Graz 1987) 15 Bd2 b5 16 axb5 axb5 17 Bf1 b4 =, Farago.

(l) After 11 . . . Re8 12 e4 c4 13 Bf1 Nc5 14 Nd2 Qc7 15 Bxc4 Bh3 Black has compensation for the pawn, Alburt–de Firmian, US Chp. 1987.

(m) If 14 . . . b4 15 Nb5 ±. After 14 . . . Ng4 there is: (A) 15 Nxb5 Nde5 16 Nxe5 Nxe5 17 Be2 Qb6 18 Nc3 Bh3 =, Scheeren–van der Wiel, Dutch Chp. 1986. (B) 15 Nd2 Nde5 16 h3 b4 17 Nb5 d4?! 18 Nxc4 Nxc4 19 Bxc4 Ne5 20 Bf1 Bxh3 21 Bxh3 Rxb5 =, Alburt–Sax, Subotica 1987.

(n) (A) 9 . . . Qe7 10 Re1 a6 11 a4 Nbd7 12 e4 Rb8 13 Bf1 Re8 14 h3 ±, Sosonko–Nunn, London 1980. (B) 9 . . . Re8 could transpose into col. 15 after 10 Nd2 a6 11 a4, or White can play 10 Bf4 Nh5 11 Bg5 Qb6 12 Qc1 (Alburt–D. Gurevich, US Chp. 1985) 12 . . . Nd7 ∞.

(o) 10 h3 Re8 11 Nd2 Nc7 12 Nc4 b5! 13 Nxd6 Qxd6 14 Bf4 Qb6 15 d6 Ne6 16 Bxa8 Nxf4 17 gxf4 Bh3 gives Black good compensation for his lost material, Kaidanov–Foisor, Moscow 1987.

(p) 15 Na2 Qd7 16 Rd1 Bxc4 17 Qxc4 a6 18 Qc2 b5 19 b4 c4 =, Draško–Suba, New York Open 1988.

(q) 7 . . . Nbd7 8 e4 Bg7 9 Nc4 (9 Be2 0-0 10 0-0 Re8 transposes to col. 2) 9 . . . Nb6 10 Ne3 0-0 11 Bd3 Bd7 12 0-0 a6 13 Bd2 Re8 14 a4 Qc7 =, Osnos–Ehlvest, Tallinn 1980.

(r) 8 e4 0-0 9 Be2 Na6 10 0-0 Ne8 (10 . . . Re8 transposes to col. 7) 11 Nc4 f5 12 exf5 Bxf5 13 Bf4 b5 ∞, Karolyi–Perenyi, Budapest 1988.

(s) 9 . . . h6 10 Bf4 b6 11 Bxd6 Re8 12 Bg3 Ne4 13 Nxe4 Rxe4 14 e3 b5 15 Nd2 Rb4 16 b3! ±, T. Petrosian–Nunn, Hastings 1977–78.

(t) 11 Nb5 a6 12 Nbxd6 b5 13 Nxc8 Raxc8 = (Dlugy). The column is Dlugy–Klinger, Sharjah 1985.

BENONI DEFENSE

1 d4 Nf6 2 c4 c5 3 d5 e6 4 Nc3 exd5 5 cxd5 d6

	19	20	21	22	23	24
6	(Nf3)..e4					
	(g6)				g6	
7	(Nd2)......Bg5				Bd3.........f3	
	(Bg7)	Bg7(d)			Bg7	Bg7
8	(Nc4)	e3 ....e4			Nge2	Bg5
	(0-0)	h6	h6		0-0	h6(o)
9	Bf4	Bh4	Bh4		0-0	Be3
	Ne8	g5(e)	g5 ....a6		a6(l)	0-0
10	Qd2	Bg3	Bg3	a4(j)	a4	Qd2
	b6(a)	Nh5	Nh5	g5	Nbd7	Re8(p)
11	e3(b)	Bd3(f)	Bb5†(h)	Bg3	h3	Be2(q)
	Ba6	Nxg3	Kf8	Nh5	Qc7	h5
12	a4	hxg3	e5	Be2	f4	a4
	f5	Nd7	Nxg3	0-0	Rb8	a6
13	Be2	Qc2	fxg3!	Nd2	Ng3(m)	a5
	Qf6(c)	Qe7(g)	a6(i)	Nxg3(k)	c4(n)	b5(r)

(a) Sharp and risky is 10 ... Bxc3!? 11 bxc3 (11 Qxc3 b5 and 12 ... b4) 11 ... b5 12 Nb2 Bb7 13 g3 Nd7 14 Bg2 f5 15 0-0 Ndf6 with almost even chances, Antoshin–Tal, USSR Chp. 1956.

(b) 11 Nb5 Ba6 12 Nbxd6? Nxd6 13 Nxd6 g5! 14 Bg3 f5 wins (Nunn).

(c) 14 Bg3 Bxc4 15 Bxc4 a6 16 0-0 Nd7 17 f4 Nc7 =, Osnos–Forintos, Leningrad–Budapest 1962.

(d) Black can also deal with the pin immediately: 7 ... h6 8 Bh4 g5 9 Bg3 Nh5 and now: (A) 10 e4 Nxg3 11 hxg3 Bg7 12 Nd2 0-0 13 Be2 a6 14 a4 Nd7 15 Nc4 Qe7 =, Najdorf–Uhlmann, Havana 1966. (B) 10 Qa4† Nd7 11 Qe4† Qe7 12 Bxd6 Qxe4 13 Nxe4 f5 14 Bxf8 fxe4 15 Bxh6 Rxh6 16 Nxg5 e3 ∓, Shadursky–Suetin, Vladimir 1962. (C) 10 e3 Nxg3 11 hxg3 Bg7 transposes to the column.

(e) 9 ... 0-0?! 10 Nd2 leaves White with a plus since Black will find it difficult to break the pin.

(f) (A) 11 Nd2 Nxg3 12 hxg3 Nd7 13 Nc4 Ne5 14 Nxe5 Bxe5 =, Bagirov–Savon, USSR 1973. (B) 11 Bb5† Kf8 12 Bd3 Nxg3 13 hxg3 Nd7 14 Qc2 Qe7 is fully equal, Desche–Velimirović, Sombor 1972.

(g) 14 0-0 a6 15 a4 0-0 16 Rab1 Ne5 =, Hartston–Nunn, match 1981.

(h) 11 Nd2 Nxg3 12 hxg3 transposes to note (d–A).

(i) 14 Be2 dxe5 15 0-0 Ra7 16 a4 b6 17 Qb3 f5 (Stean–Nunn, Birmingham 1976); now 18 Rad1 Kg8 19 Bd3 is much better for White (Nunn).

612

(j) 10 Nd2 b5 11 a4 (11 Be2 Nbd7 12 Qc2 Rb8! maintains an aggressive pawn-duo, as 13 a4 is met by 13 . . . c4) 11 . . . b4 12 Ncb1 0-0 13 Bd3 Re8 14 0-0 Nbd7 =, Alburt–Tukmakov, USSR Chp. 1978.

(k) 14 hxg3 Nd7! transposes into Najdorf–Uhlmann, note (d–A), or 14 . . . Re8 15 Nc4 Qc7 16 Ne3 Nd7 17 Nf5 Nf6 18 Nxh6† Kf8 ∞, Spassky–Stein, USSR 1971.

(l) (A) 9 . . . b6 10 a4 Na6 (10 . . . Ba6 11 Nb5! ±) 11 Bg5 Nb4 12 Bc4 a6 13 Qd2 Qe8 14 Ng3 leaves Black with little counterplay, Seirawan–Fedorowicz, US Chp. 1987. (B) 9 . . . Na6 10 f3 Nc7 11 Bg5 a6 (11 . . . b6! =) 12 a4 Bd7 13 a5 Rb8 14 Na4 ±, Miles–Arnason, Manchester 1981. (C) 9 . . . Ng4!? 10 h3 Ne5 11 Bc2 Na6 12 f4 Nc4 13 b3 Na5 14 Be3 b5 ∞, Nenashev–Shabolov, USSR 1987.

(m) 13 Be3 Re8 14 Ng3 c4 15 Bc2 Nc5 16 Qf3 b5 17 axb5 axb5 18 e5 dxe5 19 fxe5 Rxe5 20 Bd4 Rg5 21 Nge2 Bf5 ∞, Knaak–Postler, East German Chp. 1977.

(n) 14 Bc2 b5 15 axb5 axb5 16 Be3 b4 17 Ra7 Qd8 18 Na4 Rb5 =, Bertok–Portisch, Stockholm 1962.

(o) 8 . . . 0-0 9 Qd2 Re8 10 Be2 Na6 (10 . . . a6 11 a4 Qa5 12 Bf4 Qc7 13 a5 ±, Fedorowicz) 11 g4 Nc7 12 h4 b5 13 h5 b4 14 Nd1 Qe7 15 Nf2 with good chances on the kingside, Fedorowicz–Damjanović, New York 1987.

(p) 10 . . . a6 11 a4 Nbd7 allows 12 Nh3 Kh7 13 Nf2 and 14 Be2 ±, as White has found good squares for all his minor pieces.

(q) Not (A) 11 Bxh6?! Nxe4! 12 Nxe4 Qh4† 13 g3 Qxh6 ∓. (B) 11 Ng2 a6 12 a4 Nbd7 13 Nc1 (13 Ng3 h5 =) 13 . . . Ne5 =, Korchnoi–Ciocaltea, Bucharest 1966.

(r) 14 axb6 Qxb6 15 Bd1 Nbd7 16 Nge2 Ne5 17 b3 a5 18 0-0 Ba6 =, Christiansen–Marin, Szirak 1987.

BENONI DEFENSE

1 d4 Nf6 2 c4 c5 3 d5 e6 4 Nc3 exd5 5 cxd5 d6 6 e4 g6 7 f4 Bg7

	25	26	27	28	29	30
8	Nf3 (Four Pawns Attack)..e5(o)					
	0-0					Nfd7(p)
9	Be2...Bd3					Ne4
	Re8.....................Bg4.........b5?!			Bg4		dxe5
10	e5.........Nd2		0-0(i)	e5	0-0	Nd6†
	dxe5	Nbd7(e)	Nbd7	dxe5	Nbd7	Ke7
11	fxe5	0-0	a4(j)	fxe5	h3	Nxc8†
	Ng4	c4	Re8	Ng4	Bxf3	Qxc8
12	Bg5(a)	Kh1(f)	h3	Bg5(k)	Qxf3	Nf3(q)
	Qb6(b)	Nc5	Bxf3	Qb6	a6	Re8
13	0-0	e5	Bxf3	0-0	a4	Bc4(r)
	Nxe5	dxe5	c4	c4†	Rc8	Kf8
14	d6(c)	Nxc4(g)	Be3	Kh1	Kh1	0-0
	Qxb2	exf4	Qa5	Nd7(l)	c4	e4
15	Nd5	Bxf4	Bd4	e6	Bc2	Ng5
	Bf5(d)	Nce4(h)	Re7 =	fxe6(m)	Nc5(n)	h6 ∞

(a) 12 e6 fxe6 13 0-0 exd5 14 Nxd5 Be6 15 Bc4 Nc6 16 Bg5 Nf6 17 Ne5 Nxe5! 18 Bxf6 Nxc4 19 Bxd8 Rad8 20 Ne7† Kh8 ∓ (Petrosian).

(b) Black can play 12 . . . f6 13 exf6 Bxf6 14 Qd2 Bf5 15 0-0 Nd7 16 h3 Bxg5 17 Qxg5 Ne3 18 Qh6 Nxf1 19 Ng5 Qe7 20 d6 (Szabo–Timman, Amsterdam 1975); Szabo says now 20 . . . Qg7 21 Bc4† Kh8 22 Nf7† Kg8 draws, but White may be able to improve at some earlier point.

(c) 14 Nxe5 Bxe5 15 Bc4 Qb4 16 Nb5 (16 Qf3 Bf5 17 g4 [Szabo–Pietzsch, Salgotarjan 1967] 17 . . . Qxb2! wins) 16 . . . Nd7 17 a4 f6 18 a5 Qd8 =, Vaiser–Akopian, Uzgorod 1988.

(d) If 15 . . . Nxf3† 16 Bxf3 Qxa1 17 Qxa1 Bxa1 18 Rxa1 Nd7 19 Be7 Rb8 20 Nc7 is very strong, Vaiser–Hodos, USSR 1978. After 15 . . . Bf5! 16 Ne7† Rxe7 17 dxe7 Nbc6 the game is roughly equal, Peev–Makropoulos, match Bulgaria–Greece 1973.

(e) (A) 10 . . . Na6 is Black's best alternative to the text. After 11 0-0 Nc7 12 a4 a6 13 Bf3 Rb8 14 Nc4 (14 a5 Bd7 15 Nc4 Bb5 =) 14 . . . b5 15 axb5 axb5 16 Na5 Bd7 17 e5 dxe5 18 d6 e4! 19 dxc7 Qxc7 with fine play for the piece, Kolbaek–B. Andersen, Denmark 1967. (B) 10 . . . a6 11 a4 Nbd7 is similar to the column, but limits Black's options.

(f) (A) 12 Bxc4 Nc5 =. (B) 12 Bf3?! b5! 13 Kh1 a6 ∓, Pomar–Fischer, Havana 1966.

(g) 14 fxe5 Rxe5 15 Nxc4 Rf5 16 Bf4 g5 17 Be3 Nce4 ∞, Zöbisch–Hardicsay, Oberwart 1985.

(h) 16 Bf3 Nxc3 17 bxc3 Ne4 18 Qb3 b6 19 d6 Ba6 20 Bxe4 Rxe4 ∓, Dlugy–Vaiser, Havana 1985.

(i) 10 e5 Bxf3 11 Bxf3 dxe5 12 fxe5 Nfd7 13 e6 Ne5 14 exf7† Rxf7 is fully equal, Knežević–Gligorić, Yugoslavia 1970.

(j) The text is preferable to (A) 11 h3 Bxf3 12 Bxf3 a6 13 a4 (13 g4 h6 14 h4 h5!, Kouatly–Kindermann, Trnava 1987) 13 . . . c4 14 Be3 Qa5! 15 Qe2 Rac8 16 Kh1 Rfe8 17 Qf2 Nc5 when Black is active, Berkmortel–Gheorghiu, Bad Wörishofen 1988, and (B) 11 Nd2 Bxe2 12 Qxe2 Re8 leaves Black at least equal. The column is Peev–Velimirović, Sofia 1972.

(k) 12 Bf4 b4 13 Ne4 Nd7 14 e6 fxe6 15 dxe6 Rxf4 16 Qd5 Kh8 17 Qxa8 Nb6 18 Qc6 Ne3 is about equal, Martin–Botterill, Charlton 1978.

(l) (A) 14 . . . Nf2†?! 15 Rxf2 is tremendous play for the exchange. (B) 14 . . . Nxe5 15 Nxe5 Bxe5 16 Be7 Nd7 17 d6 Bb7 18 Bf3 ±, Cobo–Perez, Havana 1965.

(m) 16 dxe6 Ndf6 17 e7 Re8 18 Qd4 Bd7 (Kaidanov–Gleyzerov, USSR 1986); now 19 Qxb6 axb6 20 Nd4 h6 21 Bxf6 Nxf6 22 Ndxb5 Rxe7 23 Bxc4† is much better for White (Kaidanov).

(n) The position is equal, Platonov–Stolyarov, Ukrainian Chp. 1958.

(o) This aggressive system is the Mikenas Attack.

(p) 8 . . . dxe5?! 9 fxe5 Nfd7 10 e6 fxe6 11 dxe6 is unpleasant for Black, Mikenas–Kliukin, USSR 1971.

(q) 12 d6† Kf8 13 Nf3 e4 14 Ng5 h6 15 Nxf7 (15 Nxe4 Qe8 16 Qe2 Nc6 17 Kf2 Bd4† 18 Kg3 Kg7 19 Nc3 Qf8 ∓, Partos–Holm, Skopje 1972) 15 . . . Kxf7 16 Bc4† Kf8 17 f5 Bd4 18 fxg6 Ne5 19 Rf1† Kg7 is good for Black (Nunn).

(r) 13 fxe5 Nxe5 14 Bb5 Nbd7 15 Nxe5 Kf8! 16 0-0 Rxe5 17 Bf4 c4 18 Qd4 (18 Bxd7 Qc5† 19 Kh1 Rxd5 20 Qg4 f5 ∓, Sofman–Kapengut, USSR 1976, or 18 Bxe5 Nxe5 ∓) 18 . . . Rf5 =, Legky–Sveshnikov, USSR 1978. The column is Gigerl–Gruenfeld, Groningen 1974–75.

BENONI DEFENSE

1 d4

	31	32	33	34	35	36
	(Nf6) c5					
2	(c4) (c5)					d5 e5(q)
3	(d5)(a) (e6) ....e5 (Czech Benoni)					e4 d6
4	(Nc3) (exd5)			Nc3 d6		Nc3 Be7
5	(cxd5)(b) (d6)			e4 Be7		Nf3 Nf6
6	(e4) (g6)			Nf3.........g3(m) 0-0	0-0	Be2 0-0
7	(f4) (Bg7)			h3 Nbd7(j)	Bg2(n) Ne8	0-0 a6
8	Bb5† Nfd7	(Taimanov Variation) ....Nbd7?!		g4 a6	Nge2(o) Nd7	a4 Ne8
9	a4 ....Bd3(e) 0-0(c)	0-0(f)	e5 dxe5	a4 Rb8	0-0 a6	Nd2 Bg5
10	Nf3 Na6	Nf3 Na6	fxe5 Nh5	Bd3 Ne8(k)	a4 Rb8	Nc4 Bxc1
11	0-0 Rb8	0-0 Rb8	e6 Qh4†	Rg1 Nc7!?	Be3 b6	Qxc1 Nd7
12	Re1 Nc7(d)	Kh1(g) Nc7(h)	g3 Nxg3(i)	b3 Re8(l)	Nc1 Nc7(p)	a5 g6(r)

(a) (A) 3 dxc5 e6 4 Nf3 Bxc5 5 Nc3 d5 6 e3 0-0 =. (B) For 3 Nf3 see English Opening, col. 100. (C) 3 d5 Ne4 4 Qc2 Qa5† 5 Nd2 Nd6 (Bücker) 6 b3 ± (Schiller).

(b) 5 Nxd5 Nxd5 6 Qxd5 Nc6 7 Nf3 Be7 followed by . . . d6 and . . . Be6 results in active play for Black.

(c) (A) 9 . . . a6 10 Bd3 Qh4† 11 g3 Qd8 12 Nf3 0-0 13 0-0 Nf6 14 Qb3 Bh3 15 Re1 Ng4 16 Bf1 ± (Pigusov). (B) 9 . . . Na6 10 Nf3 Nb4 11 0-0 a6 12 Bxd7† Bxd7 13 f5! 0-0 14 Bg5 is very good for White. Kasparov–Nunn, Lucerne 1982, continued 14 . . . f6?! 15 Bf4 gxf5?! 16 Bxd6 Bxa4 17 Rxa4 Qxd6 18 Nh4 fxe4 19 Nf5 Qd7 20 Nxe4 Kh8 (20 . . . Rae8 21 Qg4 Kh8 22 Nxc5 wins—Kasparov) 21 Nxc5 Resigns, since Ne6 will win the exchange.

(d) 13 Bf1 Re8 14 Be3 Bxc3! 15 bxc3 Nf6 16 e5 Nfxd5 17 Bf2 dxe5 with chances for both sides, Petursson–Tisdall, Akuriyri 1988; 13 Bc4 may be an improvement.

616

(e) 9 Be2 0-0 10 Nf3 Na6 11 0-0 Nc7 12 a4 Rb8 13 Kh1 a6 14 a5 b5 15 axb6 Rxb6 with even chances, Hollis–Nunn, Oxford 1976.

(f) Two promising alternatives are: (A) 9 . . . Qh4† 10 g3 Qd8 (better than 10 . . . Qe7) 11 Nf3 0-0 12 0-0 Nf6 ∞. (B) 9 . . . a6 10 a4 Qc7!? 11 Nf3 c4 12 Bc2 Nc5 13 h3 0-0 14 0-0 Nbd7 15 Be3 Rb8 16 Bd4 b5 =, Ligterink–Lobron, Arnhem–Amsterdam 1983.

(g) Black is threatening 12 . . . b5 13 Nxb5 c4 14 Bxc4 Rxb5 15 Bxb5 Qb6† 16 Kh1 Qxb5 $\mp$.

(h) 13 a4 a6 14 f5 b5 15 axb5 (Spassky–Savon, Moscow 1971) 15 . . . axb5 16 Bg5 Bf6 17 Qd2 c4 is a sharp position where Black is no worse.

(i) 13 hxg3 Qxh1 14 Be3 Bxc3† (14 . . . 0-0 15 exd7 Bxd7 16 Bxd7 Rae8 17 Bxe8 Rxe8 18 Qe2 Bd4 19 0-0-0! ±, P. Littlewood–Norwood, Commonwealth Chp. 1985) 15 bxc3 Qe4 16 Qf3 Qxf3 17 Nxf3 fxe6 18 fxe6 0-0 19 exd7 Bxd7 20 Bxd7 Rxf3 (G. Nikolić–Lindemann, Harkany 1987); now 21 Bf4 maintains White's edge.

(j) 7 . . . Ne8 8 Bd3 a6 9 a4 Nd7 10 g4 g6 11 Qe2 Ndf6 12 Bh6 Ng7 13 Rg1 is better for White, and still better may be 12 Nd1 Bd7 13 Ne3 Ng7 14 Rg1 with advantage on both sides of the board, Balashov–Fedder, Graz 1972.

(k) 10 . . . Re8 11 Rg1 Nf8 12 g5 N6d7 13 h4 Ng6 14 Ne2 Bf8 15 Qc2 ±, Christiansen–Miles, New York 1987.

(l) 13 h4 b5 14 g5 Nf8 15 h5 with advantage in space, Kasparov–Miles, match 1986.

(m) (A) 6 Bd3 0-0 7 Nge2 Ne8 8 0-0 Bg5 9 a3 Nd7 10 g3 Bxc3 11 Nxc1 g6 12 Be2 Ng7 =, Hamann–Hort, Harrachow 1967. (B) 6 Be2 0-0 7 Nf3 Ne8 8 0-0 g6 9 Bh6 Ng7 10 Qd2 Nd7 11 Ng5 Bxg5 12 Qxg5 f6 with only a minimal edge for White, Bilek–Hort, Varna 1962.

(n) 7 Bh3 Bxh3 8 Nxh3 Qd7 9 Ng1 Na6 10 h3 Nc7 11 g4 b5 12 g5 Nfe8 13 cxb5 Nxb5 14 Qa4 Nec7 gave Black a queenside initiative in Verduga–Miles, San Francisco 1987.

(o) 8 Nf3 Nd7 9 0-0 a6 10 a4 g6 11 Bh6 Ng7 12 Qd2 Nf6 13 h3 $\pm$, Hort–Popov, Varna 1969.

(p) 13 Nd3 b5 14 cxb5 axb5 15 b4!, I. Sokolov–Miles, Sarajevo 1987; White is winning the battle on the queenside.

(q) (A) 2 . . . g6 3 Nc3 Nf6 4 e4 d6 5 Nf3 Bg7 6 Bb5† Bd7 7 a4 0-0 8 0-0 Na6 9 Re1 $\pm$, Kasparov–Beliavsky, match 1983. (B) 2 . . . e6 3 e4 exd5 4 exd5 d6 5 Nc3 Nf6 6 Nf3 Be7 7 Be2 0-0 8 0-0 Bg4 9 Bf4 $\pm$. In these two cases and in the column White benefits from not having played c4.

(r) 13 Na4 Qe7 (13 . . . f5 14 exf5 gxf5 15 f4 $\pm$) 14 Ra3 $\pm$. The column is Porath–Ciocaltea, Netanya 1965, through move 11.

BENKO GAMBIT

1 d4 Nf6 2 c4 c5 3 d5 b5

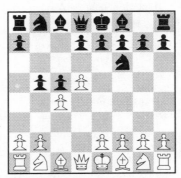

Diagram 86

T HIS GAMBIT bears the name of the American grandmaster Pal Benko, who brought it to world attention in the early 1970s. Since it is a young opening, many new ideas are still being found in it. Noteworthy explorers of Benko theory include Alburt and Fedorowicz of the United States and Vaganian of the Soviet Union.

Black's sacrifice is more positionally based than most gambits. For the pawn he obtains a slight lead in development, the better pawn structure, and pressure along the a- and b-files. Though White faces no immediate threats, he will find it difficult to make use of his extra pawn, even in the endgame.

White directly accepts the gambit in cols. 1–6 by 4 cxb5 a6 5 bxa6 Bxa6. The most explored position in the Benko is reached by 6 Nc3 g6 7 e4 Bxf1 8 Kxf1 d6 9 g3 (cols. 1–2); the verdict seems to be that Black obtains equality. 9 g4 (col. 3) and 7 f4 (col. 4) are new and risky plans that aim at attack. A safe and respected line is 6 g3 (cols. 5–6), which is White's best chance for an edge after 5 . . . Bxa6.

After 4 cxb5 a6, White can play for development instead of material by 5 e3 (cols. 7–8) or 5 Nc3 (col. 9). 5 e3 is particularly promising, as White obtains attacking chances. 4 Nf3 (cols. 10–11), ignoring the gambit, is currently fashionable. White wastes no time on cxb5, leaving the threat for later. Black's best response is 4 . . . b4 (col. 11), gaining queenside space. 4 Qc2 (col. 12) is played with similar ideas, but moving the queen early is less logical.

In its earliest origin (1946), the game was known as the Volga Gambit.

618

BENKO GAMBIT

1 d4 Nf6 2 c4 c5 3 d5 b5 4 cxb5 a6 5 bxa6 Bxa6(a)

	1	2	3	4	5	6
6	Nc3..g3				g3	
	g6				g6	
7	e4.................................f4(k)			f4(k)	Bg2(n)	
	Bxf1			d6	d6	
8	Kxf1			Nf3	Nc3........b3	b3
	d6			Bg7	Bg7	Bg7
9	g3(b)..................g4		g4	e4	Nf3	Bb2
	Bg7		Bg7	Bxf1	Nbd7	0-0
10	Kg2		Kg2(h)	Rxf1(l)	0-0	Nh3
	0-0		0-0?!(i)	Qb6	Nb6!(o)	Nbd7
11	Nf3........Nge2	Nge2	g5	e5	Re1(p)	0-0
	Nbd7	Qb6(f)	Nfd7	dxe5	0-0	Ra7(s)
12	Re1(c)	Rb1	h4	fxe5	Bf4(q)	Re1
	Ng4	Na6	Na6	Ng4	Nc4	Qa8
13	Re2(d)	a3	h5	Qe2	Qc1	e4
	Qa5(e)	Rab8(g)	Qc7(j)	Nd7(m)	Qa5(r)	Rb8(t)

(a) There is no harm in delaying the capture with 5 . . . g6 as 6 d6 exd6 is fine for Black. Delaying the capture gives Black the option of . . . Nxa6, which is good after 6 b3?! Bg7 7 Bb2 0-0, e.g. 8 g3 Nxa6 9 Bg2 Bb7 10 e4 Qa5† 11 Bc3 Nb4! 12 Ne2 (12 a3 Nh5 13 e5 Bxe5 wins) 12 . . . Qb5 $\mp$, Lputian–Bikhovsky, Irkutsk 1983. After 6 Nc3 there is little point to 6 . . . Nxa6, but Black can play 6 . . . Bxa6 transposing back to the main lines.

(b) White has also tried 10 h3 to make a place for his king, but then Black has more time to create play: 10 . . . 0-0 11 Kg1 Nbd7 12 Kh2 Qa5 13 Re1 Rfb8 14 Qc2 Ne8 15 Bd2 Qa6 16 a4 Rb4 with queenside pressure, Pytel–Peev, Lublin 1972.

(c) 12 h3 Ra7! 13 Re1 Qa8 14 Re2 Nb6 15 Qd3 Na4 allows Black at least equality, Rajković–Fedorowicz, Brussels 1987.

(d) 13 Qe2 Nge5 14 Nd2 Nb6 15 f4 Ned7 16 Nf3 Na4 17 Nd1 Ra7 18 Rb1 Qa8 19 Qc2 Nab6 20 a3 e6! 21 dxe6 fxe6 22 Nf2 d5 $\overline{\overline{\mp}}$, Hort–Ermenkov, Tunis 1985.

(e) 14 Bg5 Bxc3!? 15 bxc3 f6 16 Bd2 Qa4 17 Bf4 g5 and Black has enough compensation for the pawn, Gavrikov–Meshkov, USSR 1981.

(f) 11 . . . Nbd7 12 Rb1 Qa5 13 b3 Rfb8 14 a3 Ng4 15 Qc2 Qa6 16 Rd1 Nb6 =, Akhmilovskaya–Alekhina, USSR 1985.

(g) 14 b3 e6 15 Qd3 Nc7 16 dxe6 fxe6 17 Bf4 Rbd8 18 b4 Ng4 with good play for the pawn, Nowak–Sznapik, Poland 1986.

(h) 10 g5 Nh5 11 Nge2 Qc8 12 Kg2 h6! 13 gxh6 Bxh6 14 Bxh6 Rxh6 15 f3 Nd7 16 Qd2 Rh7 17 h3 c4 18 Nd1 Ne5 19 Nf2 g5 20 a4 f6 $\mp$, Seirawan–Alburt, US Chp. 1986.

(i) 10 . . . Nbd7, not yet defining the king's location, is an improvement.

(j) 14 Qg4 Rgb8 15 hxg6 hxg6 16 Qh4 with an attack, Seirawan–Belotti, Lugano 1988.

(k) 7 Nf3 d6 8 Nd2 Bg7 9 e4 Bxf1 10 Nxf1 0-0 11 Ne3 Nbd7 12 0-0 Qb6 13 Qe2 Rfb8 14 Re1 Ne8 15 Nc4 Qa6 16 Bd2 Nb6 is roughly equal, Ghitescu–Mikhalchishin, Reggio Emilia 1970–71.

(l) 10 Kxf1 0-0 11 e5 dxe5 12 fxe5 Ng4 13 Qe2 Nd7 14 Bf4 Qb8! 15 Re1 Qb4 16 Qd2 f6 17 e6 Nde5 ∞, Garakian–Kachian, USSR 1986.

(m) 14 e6 fxe6 15 dxe6 Nde5 16 Nxe5 Nxe5 (=) 17 Nd5?! Qd6 18 Qe4 0-0-0! 19 Ne7† Kc7 20 Bf4 Kb6! leaves White in difficulties, Christiansen–D. Gurevich, US Chp. 1986; but White managed to swindle his opponent after 21 Rf3! Nxf3† 22 Qxf3 Qxe6† 23 Kf1 Rhf8 (23 . . . Qxe7 24 Qb3† Kc6 25 Qa4† is a draw) 24 Re1 Qd6? 25 Bxd6 Rxf3† 26 gxf3 Kb5 (26 . . . Rxd6 27 Nc8†) 27 Be5 Bf8 28 Ng8 Resigns.

(n) 7 Nc3 d6 8 Nf3 Bg7 9 Bh3 (9 Bg2 is the column) 9 . . . Nbd7 10 0-0 0-0 11 Qc2 Bc4 12 Rd1 Ra7 13 e4 Qa8 14 a3 (14 b3 Bxb3 15 Qxb3 Nxe4 16 Nxe4 Bxa1 ∞) 14 . . . Rb8 15 Nd2 Ba6 =, Furman–Geller, USSR 1975.

(o) 10 . . . 0-0 is less precise as White can reach a better setup with 11 Qc2 Qa5 12 Bd2 Rfb8 13 Rab1 Nb6 14 b3 Qa3 15 Bc1 Qa5 16 Rd1 Ne8 17 Bb2 ±, Zaltsman–Benko, Lone Pine 1981.

(p) 11 Ne1 Nc4 12 Nd3 Nd7 13 Qc2 0-0 14 h4 Qa5 15 a3 Rab8 ∓, Ehlvest–Fedorovicz, New York 1989.

(q) 12 Nd2 Qc7 13 Nb3 Nc4 14 h3 Rfb8 15 Qc2 Qb6 16 Rb1 Nd7 17 Bf4 Nde5 ∓. Korchnoi–Greenfeld, Beersheba 1984.

(r) 14 Nd2 Rfb8 15 Nxc4 Bxc4 16 Bd2 Nd7 17 b3 Ba6 18 Na4 Qd8 19 Bc3 (P. Nikolić–Vaganian, Sarajevo 1987) 19 . . . Ra7 ∞.

(s) 11 . . . Qb8 12 Bc3 Rc8 13 Re1 Ra7 14 Nf4 Rb7 15 Na3 and White has achieved a harmonious setup, Portisch–Geller, Biel 1976.

(t) 14 Bc3 Ne8 15 Bxg7 Nxg7 16 Nd2 Ne5 17 Nf4 Bb5 =, Gheorghiu–Beliavsky, Moscow 1982.

BENKO GAMBIT

1 d4 Nf6 2 c4 c5 3 d5 b5

	7	8	9	10	11	12
4	(cxb5)................................			Nf3.....................		Qc2(q)
	(a6)			g6	b4(m)	bxc4
5	e3		Nc3(g)	cxb5(j)	a3(n)	e4
	Bb7.........	g6(d)	axb5	a6	g6(o)	e6(r)
6	Nc3	Nc3	e4	Nc3	axb4	Bxc4
	axb5	Bg7	b4	axb5	cxb4	exd5
7	Bxb5	Nf3	Nb5	d6	Nbd2	exd5
	Qa5	0-0	d6	Qa5	Bf7	d6
8	Ne2(a)	a4	Nf3	e3	e4	Nc3
	Nxd5(b)	Bb7(e)	g6(h)	Ba6(k)	0-0(p)	Be7
9	0-0	Ra3	Bf4	a4	Bd3	Nge2
	Nf6	e6	Bg7	Bg7	d6	0-0
10	e4!	dxe6	e5	Nd2	0-0	0-0
	Nxe4	fxe6	dxe5	c4	Bg4	Nbd7
11	Bf4	Qd6	Bxe5	Rb1	Qa4?!	a4
	Nf6(c)	Ne4(f)	0-0(i)	bxa4(l)	a5 $\mp$	Nb6 =

(a) 8 Bd2 Qb6 9 Qb3 e6 10 e4 Nxe4! 11 Nxe4 Bxd5 12 Qd3 f5 13 Ng3 (13 Ng5?! Bxg2 14 Qe2 Bxh1 15 f3 Ra6! $\mp$, Benjamin–Alburt, US Chp. 1984) 13 . . . Bxg2 14 a4 Be7 15 N1e2 Bxh1 16 Nxh1 0-0 is roughly equal, Conover–Alburt, US 1985; but 15 Nf3?! Bxh1 16 Nxh1 0-0 17 Ng3 d5 18 Kf1 may be better for White, I. Ivanov–Wolff, New York 1985.

(b) 8 . . . Bxd5 9 0-0 Bc6 10 a4 Bxb5 11 Nxb5 (Fedorowicz–Berg, Ostende 1987) is slightly better for White, but after 11 . . . d5? 12 e4 dxe4 13 b4! Qd8 14 Qc2 White was winning. (B) 10 . . . g6 11 Bd2 Qb6 12 e4 Bg7 13 Nf4 Nxe4 14 Nfd5 Bxd5 15 Nxd5 Qb7 16 Bf4 0-0 17 Nxe7† , Jonescu–Biriescu, Romanian Chp. 1988, likewise leaves White somewhat better.

(c) 12 Re1 Nc6 (Kouatly–Fedorowicz, Clichy 1986–87); now 13 Bxc6 Bxc6 14 Ng3 e6 15 Nf5 d5 16 Be5 puts White ahead (Fedorowicz).

(d) 5 . . . e6 6 Nc3 exd5 7 Nxd5 Bb7 8 Nxf6† Qxf6 9 Nf3 Be7 10 Bc4 ± (Bagirov).

(e) (A) 8 . . . e6 9 dxe6 fxe6 10 Qd6 ±. (B) 8 . . . d6 9 Ra3! Nbd7 10 e4 Ng4 11 Nd2 f5 12 Be1 axb5! 13 Nxb5 (Petursson–Manka Lugano 1989) 13 . . . Ngf6 14 exf4 gxf5 ∞ (Seirawan).

(f) Alternatives are: (A) 11 . . . axb5 12 Bxb5 Qc8 13 Be2 $\pm$. (B) 11 . . . Qc8 12 Be2 Ne8 13 Qg3 d5 14 0-0 Nf6 15 Qh3 Qe8 16 Rd1 Qe7 17 Ng5 ± , Tarjan–Benjamin, US Chp. 1983. After 11 . . . Ne4 12 Nxe4 Bxe4 13 Bd3 Bb7?! (13 . . . Bxd3 $\pm$) 14 Qxc5 axb5 15 axb5 White is clearly better, Flear–Fedorowicz, Brussels 1987.

(g) 5 f3 e6 6 e4 exd5 7 e5 Qe7 8 Qe2 Ng8 9 Nc3 Bb7 10 Nh3 Qd8 11 Nf4 Ne7 =, Timoshchenko–Yemolinsky, Tashkent 1987.

(h) 8 . . . Nxe4?! 9 Bc4 followed by 10 0-0 and 11 Re1 puts Black under pressure.

(i) 12 Bc4 Ba6 13 a4 bxa3 14 Rxa3 Bxb5! 15 Rxa8 Bxc4 16 Rxb8 Qa5† 17 Bc3 Qa6 with excellent compensation for the exchange, Rogers–Hodgson, Edinburgh 1985.

(j) 5 Qc2 Bg7 6 e4 bxc4 7 Bxc4 d6 8 0-0 0-0 9 h3 Nbd7 10 Nc3 Nb6 11 Be2 e6 12 dxe6 Bxe6 =, Anikaev–Gorelov, USSR 1981.

(k) 8 . . . exd6 9 Bxb5 d5 10 0-0 Bb7 11 e4! dxe4 (11 . . . d4 12 Nxd4! cxd4 13 Qxd4 Bg7 14 Bg5 Nh5 15 Qd6 is a winning attack—Gulko) 12 Ne5 Qc7 13 Bf4 Nh5 14 Nd5 Qd6 15 Nxd7 Nxf4 16 Nxc5† Bc6 17 Nxe4 Qe5 18 Bxc6† Nxc6 19 Ndf6† Resigns, Gulko–Renet, Somerset 1986.

(l) 12 Qxa4 Qxa4 13 Nxa4 Nd5 ∞, Psakhis–Hodgson, Tallinn 1987.

(m) (A) 4 . . . bxc4?! 5 Nc3 g6 6 e4 d6 7 e5! dxe5 8 Nxe5 Bg7 9 Bxc4 0-0 10 0-0 Bb7 11 Re1 ±, Browne–Wolff, US Chp. 1985. (B) 4 . . . Bb7 5 Nfd2 d6 6 e4 b4 7 a3 Na6 8 axb4 Nxb4 9 Be2 g6 10 0-0 Bg7 11 Nc3 0-0 12 Nb3 ±, S. Agdestein–Benjamin, match Scandinavia–US 1986.

(n) Safer is 5 Nbd2 g6 6 e4 d6 7 b3 Bg7 8 Bb2 0-0 with just a small pull for White.

(o) 5 . . . a5?! 6 Nbd2 g6 7 e4 d6 8 axb4 cxb4 9 c5! dxc5 10 Bb5† Bd7 11 Bc4 ±, Seirawan–D. Gurevich, US Chp. 1986.

(p) 8 . . . d6 9 Qa4† Nfd7! 10 Qxb4 Ba6 gives Black fine play for the pawn (Alburt). The column is Petursson–Alburt, New York 1988.

(q) (A) 4 Bg5 Ne4 5 Bf4 Qa5† 6 Nd2 bxc4 7 f3 Nf6 8 e4 Ba6 =, Plaskett–Hebden, Hastings 1982–83. (B) 4 a4?! b4 =.

(r) 5 . . . d6 6 Bxc4 g6 7 Nf3 Bg7 transposes into note (j) which is all right for Black, but the text is sharper. The column is S. Agdestein–Cramling, match 1986.

V
FLANK
OPENINGS

ENGLISH OPENING

1 c4

Diagram 87

T HE ENGLISH OPENING derives its name from its association with the Englishman Howard Staunton, who played it six times against St. Amant in their 1843 match, and also in the historic London tournament of 1851. Staunton and his contemporaries understood many of the strategies that today we call "hypermodern." But Morphy's disdain for this opening caused it to fall out of fashion, and it remained so for an entire century. A few daring explorers, such as Tartakower, Rubinstein, and Nimzowitsch, ventured it occasionally prior to World War II, but since then the English has become routine. It has been adopted by Botvinnik, Karpov, and Kasparov in their successful world championship matches, and Fischer's choice of it against Spassky in 1972 was a sensation that ended his hitherto unswerving devotion to the king's pawn.

English Opening strategy is characterized by fluid pawn formations and vigorous struggles for central control. Often White will follow his initial queenside thrust with a fianchetto of his king bishop and an attempt to establish a grip on the white squares. Black may counter this by taking the White side of a Sicilian Defense with colors reversed, or by attempting to transpose to one of several queen pawn openings, such as the Queen's Gambit Declined, the King's Indian, or the Dutch Defense. The independent alternative is the Symmetrical Variation, which is rich in possibilities ranging from countergambits and aggressive isolated queen-pawn formations to cramped but dynamic Hedgehog setups and the quiet, subtle maneuvering of the Ultra-Symmetrical Variation.

It is natural to treat the English as a *Sicilian Reversed*, but the results are often surprising—what is an obscure side variations of the Sicilian Defense corresponds to a main line of the English, and vice versa.

625

Diagram 88

The FOUR KNIGHTS' VARIATION, 1 . . . e5 2 Nc3 Nf6 3 Nf3 Nc6 (cols. 1–12), a direct and logical continuation, offers Black reliable defense with some flexibility for counterattack (see diagram). Black will usually follow a strategy like that of the Nimzo-Indian Defense, conceding his king bishop for a knight to get free development and an aggressive central posture. Cols. 7–8, in which Black departs from this safe strategy to play a genuine Dragon Sicilian with colors reversed, are important. It seems risky to enter a sharp variation with a tempo less, but healthy aggression brings Black nearly equal chances.

In CARLS' "BREMEN" SYSTEM (or the Accelerated Fianchetto) with 3 g3 (cols. 13–18), White tries to steal a march on Four Knights' lines, or at least to transpose to favorable subvariations, but he must contend with the *Keres Variation* (cols. 17–18), a formidable central bulwark.

Diagram 89

The CLOSED VARIATION, 2 . . . Nc6 3 g3 g6 4 Bg2 Bg7 (cols. 19–25), imitates the Closed Sicilian with colors reversed (see diagram). White can easily obtain complete domination of the queenside, but turning this to account while neutralizing Black's kingside chances is another matter.

Cols. 26–27 and 29–30 show the effects of an early . . . f5 by Black. The pawns on e5 and f5 present a strong front, but with careful play White can lure them forward to overextension. Col. 28 shows that Black should

626

not try to force transposition to the Closed Variation if White does not fianchetto.

The system 1 ... e5 2 Nc3 d6 d6 (cols. 31–36) is still somewhat off the beaten track, and a handy alternative to the usual defenses.

Of the miscellaneous variations in cols. 37–42, the most important are col. 38, an unrefuted attempt to accelerate the minor-piece trade that characterizes the Four Knights', and col. 39, a method for White to avoid that trade.

Black may choose to handle the English by playing his favorite defense to the queen's pawn against it. White in turn may play an early d4, transposing to Black's choice of opening, or he may postpone that move or avoid it altogether, leading to uniquely "English" lines. The results of the latter strategy are shown in cols. 43–46 (Nimzo-Indian English), 47–49 (Queen's Indian English), 50–54 (a hybrid variation with its own unique character), 55–60 (King's Indian English), 61–62 (Grünfeld English), and note (a) in col. 61 (Slav Defense English). Overall, White's loss of direct territorial control in delaying d4 is just balanced by gains in flexibility and tactical subtleties. If White delays development of his queen knight, Black may safely venture the Double Fianchetto Defense (cols. 63–65), featuring noteworthy quadruple fianchettoes in notes (m) and (q), or the impudent Romanishin Variation, favored by Korchnoi.

The SYMMETRICAL VARIATION (1 ... c5) is perhaps the most exciting defense to the English. In the main variations, one or both players will disrupt the center almost immediately by pushing the queen-pawn two squares, and an intense struggle for control of d4 and d5 will develop.

Diagram 90

The SYMMETRICAL FOUR KNIGHTS' VARIATION, 2 Nf3 Nf6 3 Nc3 Nc6 (cols. 66–78) epitomizes this type of game (see diagram). In the modern variations of cols. 67–72, it is often a question of whose pawn sacrifice comes first and most effectively, White's on c3 or Black's on d5. In the older fianchetto variation (cols. 73–78), Black cedes an advantage in central territory but can challenge the queenside by ... b5.

In cols. 79–81, Black energetically achieves ... d5 before White has played d4. The main variation (col. 81) is wild: White moves his king twice in the first eight moves, but sacrifices a pawn for a strong attack.

In cols. 82–84, Black chooses relief from the tactical melees of the previous columns with the popular 3 . . . e6. This is safer and less sharp than 3 . . . Nc6 and 3 . . . d5, but similar themes of central expansion and sacrifice on c3 and d5 recur.

The HEDGEHOG DEFENSE with 3 . . . e6 and 4 . . . b6 (cols. 85–90) is a development of the 1970s and '80s. As recently as the early 1970s, "hedgehog" was a generic term describing any setup that was cramped, defensive, and difficult to attack. Now it refers to a specific formation in which Black's c-pawn is exchanged for White's d-pawn and Black's minor pieces are developed as in a Queen's Indian. Black allows White a central bind with pawns on c4 and e4, but Black's chances to achieve . . . b5 or . . .d5 give his game dynamic potential. Other Hedgehog-related variations may be found in cols. 97–99 and in the Paulsen Variation of the Sicilian Defense.

Cols. 91–96 with 4 . . . d5 show another of the many inventions of the late Paul Keres. Black aims at a setup similar to the Tarrasch Defense to the Queen's Gambit Declined, but with his defense eased by the exchange of a pair of knights. White is not obliged to isolate Black's queen pawn, but may create his own advanced passed queen pawn, as in the Semi-Tarrasch Defense. Both strategies require alert handling by Black.

In col. 97, Black tries to enter a Hedgehog before White has committed his king bishop. This seems daring but is not clearly refuted.

In cols. 98–103, White plays d4 without the preparatory 3 Nc3. This pre-empts the counterattack of 3 Nc3 d5, but now White must reckon with the sharp countergambit 4 . . . e5 (col. 100), or transposition to a counterattacking variation of the Catalan (col. 102, note o).

In cols. 104–106, White lackadaisically fianchettoes his king bishop before enforcing d4. This plan is plausible, but the lifeless variations of col. 104, note (g) (B), are discouraging.

Cols. 107–108 are interesting sidelines. Theory condemns Black's move order of col. 108 but many strong grandmasters have given it a try.

When White plays 2 Nc3 instead of 2 Nf3, he is better prepared to prevent or meet Black's . . . d5 than to enforce his own d4.

When Black plays . . . d5 anyway, he may arrive at the RUBINSTEIN/ BOTVINNIK VARIATION (cols. 109–114), a sort of Maroczy Bind Sicilian with colors reversed. If Black can complete his development in spite of hair-raising white-square invasions or doubled isolated c-pawns, he can often look forward to good winning chances arising from his central spatial advantage.

The ULTRA-SYMMETRICAL VARIATION (cols. 115–121) arises when both players adopt the same negative strategy of preventing each other's d-pawn breaks. These lines require great patience, and the rewards for this patience are sometimes paltry. But connoisseurs such as Larsen and Andersson have shown that even here Black has no sure road to equality.

Cols. 122–126 are odds and ends. These unusual first and second moves will mostly transpose to other variations or other openings, but here are some exceptions that one must watch for.

ENGLISH OPENING

Four Knights' Variation

1 c4 e5 2 Nc3 Nf6 3 Nf3 Nc6 4 g3

	1	2	3	4	5	6
	Bb4..Bc5(p)					
5	Bg2				Nd5	Bg2(q)
	0-0				Nxd5(l)	d6
6	0-0(a)				cxd5	0-0
	e4.................................Re8				Nd4(m)	0-0
7	Ng5 ....Ne1		Nd5(i)	Nxd4	e3	
	Bxc3		Bxc3	e4(j)	exd4	Re8(r)
8	bxc3		dxc3	Ne1	Qc2	d4
	Re8		h6(g)	d6	Qe7	Bb6
9	d3.........f3		Nc2	d3	Bg2	h3
	exd3	exf3(d)	b6(h)	Bxe1	Bc5	h6
10	exd3	Nxf3	Ne3	Rxe1	b4(n)	a3
	d6(b)	d5(e)	Bb7	exd3	Bxb4	a5
11	Rb1	cxd5	Nd5	Bg5!(k)	Qxc7	b3
	h6	Qxd5	Ne5		0-0	Bf5
12	Ne4	Nd4	b3		Qc4	Bb2
	Nxe4(c)	Qh5(f)	Rfe8 =		Re8(o)	Qd7(s)

(a) 6 Nd5 e4 7 Nh4 Bc5 8 0-0 Re8 9 d3 cxd3 10 Qxd3 Ne5 11 Qc2 c6 $\overline{\mp}$, Smyslov–Mecking, Petropolis 1973.

(b) 10 ... h6 11 Ne4 b6 12 Bf4 $\pm$.

(c) 13 Bxe4 Ne5 14 f4! Nxc4 15 f5 =, Mecking–Tan, Petropolis 1973; White has just enough for the pawn.

(d) 9 ... e3!? 10 d3 d5 11 Qb3?! Na5! 12 Qa3 c5; White's game is disorganized, Kasparov–Karpov, World Chp. 1988 (game 2). White should try 11 cxd5 Nxd5 12 Ne4 ∞.

(e) 10 ... Qe7 11 e3 Ne5 12 Nd4! Nd3 (12 ... Nxc4 13 Nf5 Qe6 14 d3 with a dangerous attack) 13 Qe2 Nxc1 14 Raxc1 d6 15 Rf4 with pressure on the f-file, Kasparov–Karpov, World Chp. 1988 (game 4).

(f) 13 Nxc6 bxc6 14 e3 Bg4 15 Qa4 Re6 ∞, Sigurjonsson–Smyslov, Reykjavik 1974. The game continued 16 Rb1? Be2 17 Re1 Ng4! 18 h3 Qf5 19 Rxe2 Qxb1 20 Qxg4 Qxc1† 21 Kh2 Rd8 22 Qb4 h6 23 f4 Qd1 24 Rf2 Qe8 25 Resigns.

(g) 8 ... d6 9 Nc2 Re8 10 Bg5 h6 11 Bxf6 Qxf6 12 Ne3 Re5 (12 ... Bf5 13 f4!) 13 Qb3! Rb8 14 Rad1 b6 15 Qc2 Bf5 16 Rd5 Rbe8 17 Rfd1 $\pm$, as Black will lose a pawn, Uhlmann–Reshevsky, Skopje 1976.

(h) 9 ... d6 is also common: 10 Ne3 Re8 11 Qc2 Bd7 12 Bd2 a5 13 Rae1 a4 14 f4 $\pm$, Timman–Mestel, Las Palmas 1982. The column is Korchnoi–Karpov, World Chp. 1974.

(i) 7 d3 Bxc3 8 bxc3 e4 9 Nd4 h6 10 dxe4 Nxe4 11 Qc2 d5 12 cxd5 Qxd5, Kasparov–Karpov, World Chp. 1988 (game 16); now 13 Rd1 may give White an advantage.

(j) (A) 7 . . . Nxd5 8 cxd5 Nd4 9 Ne1 $\pm$. (B) 7 . . . Bf8 8 d3 h6 9 Bd2 $\pm$.

(k) White has a strong attack for the pawn, Smyslov–Mestel, Hastings 1972–73.

(l) The alternatives, 5 . . . Bc5 and 5 . . . e4, may be more reliable. Compare note (a) and col. 4.

(m) 6 . . . e4? 7 dxc6 exf3 8 Qb3 Resigns, Petrosian–Ree, Wijk aan Zee 1971.

(n) More forceful than 10 0-0 0-0 11 e3 Bb6 =, Korchnoi–Karpov, World Chp. 1978.

(o) 13 0-0 Bc5 14 Bb2 d6 15 e3! dxe3 16 fxe3 $\pm$, Hansen–H. Olafsson, Torshavn 1987.

(p) (A) 4 . . . d5 is col. 7–8. (B) 4 . . . g6 5 d4 exd4 6 Nxd4 Bg7 7 Bg2 0-0 8 0-0 Re8 9 Nxc6 bxc6 10 Bf4 $\pm$ (Uhlmann), (C) 4 . . . Nd4 is payable but lackluster: 5 Bg2 Nxf3† 6 Bxf3 Bb4 7 Qb3 Be7 8 0-0 $\pm$; but not 5 Nxe5? Qe7 6 f4 (6 . . . Nd3? 7 Nf3 mate) 6 . . . d6 7 Nd3 Bf5 $\pm$.

(q) 5 Nxe5 Bxf2† 6 Kxf2 Nxe5 7 e4 c5 8 d3 d6 9 h3 0-0 (better than 9 . . . h5 10 Be2 Nh7 11 Kg2! h4 12 g4 Ng5 13 Be3 $\pm$, Botvinnik–Keres, Moscow 1966) 10 Be2 Ne8 11 Kg2 Nc7 12 Be3 Ne6, Hickman–Camaratta, U.S. Corr. Chp. 1972–75; Black has nothing to fear.

(r) 7 . . . Bg4 8 h3 Bh5 9 d3 Qd7 10 g4 Bg6 11 Nh4 Rae8 12 b3 $\pm$. Uhlmann–Thormann, East German Chp. 1975.

(s) Black has a sound position, but White still holds more territory, Uhlmann–Knaak, Halle 1974.

ENGLISH OPENING

Four Knights' Variation

1 c4 e5 2 Nc3 Nf6 3 Nf3 Nc6

	7	8	9	10	11	12
4	(g3)................		e3................		d4(m)	
	d5		Bb4........	Be7	exd4.......	e4
5	cxd5		Qc2(h)	d4(k)	Nxd4	Nd2(o)
	Nxd5		Bxc3!(i)	exd4	Bb4	Bb4!?(p)
6	Bg2		Qxc3	Nxd4	Bg5	e3
	Nb6	Be6	Qe7	0-0	h6	0-0
7	0-0	0-0	a3	Be2	Bh4	Be2
	Be7	Be7	d5	d5	Bxc3†	Re8
8	d3(a)	d4(f)	d4(j)	Nxc6	bxc3	0-0
	0-0	exd4	exd4	bxc6	d6	Bxc3
9	a3(b)	Nxd4	Nxd4	0-0	f3(n)	bxc3
	Be6(c)	Nxc3	Nxd4	Bd6	Ne5	d6
10	b4	bxc3	Qxd4	b3	e4	f3
	a5(d)	Nxd4	0-0	Qe7	Ng6	Bf5
11	b5	cxd4	cxd5	Bb2	Bf2	fxe4
	Nd4(e)	c6(g)	Rd8 =	dxc4!(l)	0-0 =	Nxe4!(q)

(a) 8 a3 usually transposes. White may try 8 b3 or 8 a4!? a5 9 d3 ∞.

(b) 9 Be3 Be6 10 Qc1 (10 d4 leads only to equality after 10 . . . exd4 11 Nxd4 Nxd4 12 Bxd4 c6) 10 . . . f5 11 Rd1 Kh8 12 d4 e4 13 Ne5 Nb4 seems satisfactory for Black, Ivkov–Addison, Palma de Mallorca 1970.

(c) 9 . . . a5 (restraining White's queenside, weakening Black's) 10 Be3 Bg4 11 Rc1 Re8 12 Nd2 Qd7 13 Re1 Ra6 14 Bxb6!? cxb6!? 15 Qa4 ±, Petrosian–Psakhis, USSR Chp. 1983.

(d) (A) 10 . . . f6 is passive: 11 Ne4 Qd7 12 Bb2 ±, Miles–Timman, Tilburg 1984. (B) 10 . . . f5 11 Be3 Bf6 12 Rc1 Nd4 13 Nd2 c6 14 Bxd4 exd4 15 Na4 Bf7! is about equal.

(e) (A) 12 Nxd5? Bf6 13 f4 (13 Bf4 g5!) 13 . . . Nb3 14 Rb1 Qd4† +. (B) 12 Nd2 Qd7 13 Bxb7 Rab8 14 Bg2 Nxb5 15 Nxb5 Qxb5 16 a4 Qd7 17 Bb2 f6 18 Bc3 Bb4, Petrosian–Romanishin, USSR Chp. 1983; Black's aggressive development more than compensates for his difficult pawn structure. (C) Tarjan suggested 12 Nxd4 exd4 13 Na4 (if then 13 . . . Nd5 14 Bb2), or 12 Be3 or 12 Bb2 as better.

(f) 8 d3 0-0 9 Bd2 Qd7 =.

(g) (A) 12 Qc2 0-0 13 Rd1 f5 =, Dzindzihashvili–Formanek, Pennsylvania Chp. 1984. (B) 12 Rb1 Qd7 13 Qa4 0-0 14 d5!? ∞, Carls–Antze, Bremen 1933.

(h) 5 Nd5 e4 6 Ng1 0-0 7 a3 Bd6! 8 d3 exd3 9 Bxd3 Ne5 10 Be2 c6 11 Nc3 Nc7 =, Petrosian–Timman, Nikšić 1983.

(i) 5 . . . 0-0 6 Nd5 Re8 7 Qf5! leads to complications favoring White, e.g. 7 . . . d6 8 Nxf6†, gxf6 9 Qh5 d5 10 Bd3! (Watson).

(j) (A) 8 b4 d4!. (B) 8 cxd5 Nxd5 9 Qe2 e4 with good chances.

(k) More circumspect is 5 Qc2 0-0 6 a3 d6 7 Be2 Re8 8 0-0 Bf8 9 d4 Bg4 10 d5 $\pm$, Tartakower–Lasker, New York 1924.

(l) 12 bxc4 Rb8 13 Qc1 Ng4 14 g3 Re8 15 Nd1 Nxh2 $\pm$, Timman–Karpov, Montreal 1979. 10 cxd5 cxd5 11 b3 would avoid a disadvantage.

(m) (A) 4 d3 can lead to a setup akin to the Scheveningen Sicilian, e.g. 4 . . . Be7 5 e3 d5 6 cxd5 Nxd5 7 Be2 0-0 8 0-0 Be6 9 a3 a5 10 Qc2 Qd7, Spraggett–Sokolov, match 1988. Black may also play 4 . . . Bb4 as in cols. 1–5. (B) 4 e4 is more dangerous than it looks: (1) 4 . . . Bc5 5 Nxe5 Nxe5 6 d4 Bb4 7 dxe5 Nxe4 8 Qd4 Nxc3 (8 . . . f5 9 exf6 Bxc3† 10 bxc3 Nxf6 11 c5!, Watson) 9 bxc3 Ba5 10 Ba3 $\pm$, Korchnoi–Hübner, Solingen 1973. (2) 4 . . . Bb4 5 d3 d6 6 g3 0-0 7 Bg2 Ne8 (a6!?) 8 0-0 Bxc3 9 bxc3 f5 10 exf5 Bxf5 11 Nh4 Be6 12 f4 exf4 13 Qe2 Qd7 14 Bxf4 Nf6 15 Bg5 with a lasting initiative, Wrathall–Stopa, corr. 1984–87. (3) 4 . . . d6 5 d4 Bg4 ∞, Panno–Savon, Petropolis 1973. (C) 4 a3 (1) 4 . . . g6 5 g3 (5 d4 exd4 6 Nxd4 Bg7 7 g3 0-0 8 Nxc6 bxc6 9 Bg2 is col. 28 but White has played the useless move a3) 5 . . . Bg7 6 Bg2 0-0 7 0-0 d6 =, similar to cols. 63–66, but White has played a3. (2) 4 . . . e4!? 5 Ng5 Qe7 6 d3 exd3 7 Qxd3 g6 8 e3 Bg7 =, Friedgood–Leverett, Ramsgate 1981. (3) 4 . . . d5 5 cxd5 Nxd5 6 Qc2 Be7 7 e3 0-0 8 Nxd5 Qxd5 9 Bd3 $\pm$ (Vaganian).

(n) 9 Nxc6?! bxc6 10 f3 Qe7 11 e4? g5 12 Bf2 d5 $\pm$. The column is Botvinnik–Pirc, Moscow 1935.

(o) 5 Ng5 h6 6 Ngxe4 Nxe4 7 Nxe4 Qh4 8 Qd3? (8 Nc3 =) 8 . . . d5! 9 cxd5 Nb4 10 Qb1 Bf5 11 Nd6† cxd6 12 Qxf5 g6 13 Qb1 Rc8 + (Sudnitsin).

(p) 5 . . . Nxd4 is simplest: 6 Nde4 Ne4 7 Qd4 Nxc3 8 Qxc3 d5 9 e3 Be6 10 Bd2 Be7 =, Ragozin–Mikenas, Moscow 1944.

(q) 11 . . . Bxe4?! 12 Nxe4 Nxe4 13 Bd3 g6 14 Bxe4 Rxe4 15 Rxf7! (Botvinnik). The text is Lonoff–Frankle, Massachusetts 1974; Black easily maintains control of e4. If 12 Rxf5? Nxc3 13 Qf1 Nxe2† 14 Qxe2 Nxd4 wins.

ENGLISH OPENING

Carls' *"Bremen"* System

1 c4 e5 2 Nc3 Nf6 3 g3(a)

	13	14	15	16	17	18
	Bb4		d5		c6 (Keres variation)	
4	Nf3	Bg2(e)	cxd5		Nf3(o)	
	e4(b)	0-0	Nxd5		e4	
5	Nd4	e4(f)	Bg2		Nd4	
	0-0	Bxc3	Nb6	Ne7(k)	d5	Qb6(t)
6	Bg2	bxc3(g)	d3	Nf3	cxd5	Nb3(u)
	Bxc3(c)	c6	Be7	Nbc6	Qb6(p)	a5!?
7	dxc3	Ne2(h)	Be3(i)	0-0	Nb3	d3(v)
	h6	d5	0-0	g6(l)	cxd5	a4
8	Qc2	cxd5	Rc1	b4!	Bg2	Nd2
	Re8	cxd5	Kh8	a6	Bf5	e3
9	Bf4	exd5	Qd2	a4(m)	d3(q)	dxe3
	d6	Nxd5	Nc6	Bg7	Bb4(r)	Ng4
10	0-0-0!(d)	0-0	Bxc6	Ba3	0-0	Nde4
		Nc6 =	bxc6	0-0	Bxc3	Nxe3
11			Nf3	b5	bxc3	Qd2!(w)
			f6(j)	Nd4(n)	0-0(s)	

(a) Carl Carls of Bremen, Germany, initiated the early fianchetto, 3 g3, before World War I. 3 e3 is col. 37.

(b) 4 ... Qe7 (4 ... Nc6 is cols. 1–5; 4 ... d6 is also possible) 5 Bg2 c6 6 0-0 0-0 7 d3 Bxc3 8 bxc3 h6 9 e4, Portisch–Kavalek, Amsterdam 1981; Black's setup is interesting, but he has not equalized. If 9 ... d5? 10 cxd5 11 exd4 Nxd5 12 Qb3 +.

(c) 6 ... Re8 7 0-0 Nc6 8 Nc2 Bxc3 9 dxc3 h6 is similar to col. 3, and probably safer than the text.

(d) Kavalek–Fedorowicz, U.S. Chp., 1981. Each side will attack the other's king.

(e) 4 Qb3 Nc6 5 Nd5 Bc5 6 e3 0-0 7 Bg2 Nxd5 8 cxd5 Ne7 9 Ne2 d6 =, Korchnoi–Karpov, World Chp. 1978 (game 25).

(f) 5 Nf3 Re8 (5 ... Nc6 is cols. 1–5) 6 0-0 c6: (A) 7 Qb3 Bf8 =. (B) 7 d4!? e4 8 Ng5 d5 9 Qb3 Bf8 10 cxd5 cxd5 11 f3 h6 12 Nxf7! ±, Přibyl–Lutikov, Bucharest 1975.

(g) 6 dxc3 is less dynamic: 6 ... b6 7 Nh3 Bb7 8 Qc2 d6 9 0-0 Nbd7 =, Kavalek–Timman, Tilburg 1979.

(h) 7 Qb3 Na6 8 Ba3 d6 9 Ne2 Be6!? 10 d4 exd4 11 Nxd4 Nc5 12 Bxc5 dxc5 13 Nxe6 fxe6 14 0-0 Qc7 15 e5 Ng4 16 Bh3 Nxe5 17 f4 Nf7 18 Bxe6 Rae8 19 Rae1 ±, Hort–Symslov, Reggio Emilia 1986–87.

(i) 7 Nf3 Nc6 8 0-0 0-0 9 a3 Be6 10 b4 Nd4 11 Bb2 Nxf3! 12 Bxf3 c6 13 Ne4 Bd7 =, Kasparov–Salov, USSR Chp. 1988.

(j) 12 Qc2 (12 0-0 Nd5) 12 ... Bh3 13 Rg1 Bg4 14 Nd2 Nd5 15 Nd1, Shamkovich–Fedorowicz, US Chp. 1981; White stands slightly better, but his pressure on the c-file was not enough to win the game. In the column, 8 ... Re8 is better.

(k) 5 ... Nxc3!? 6 bxc3 Nc6 7 d3 Bc5 8 Nf3 0-0 9 0-0 Bg4 10 h3 Bh5 11 Qa4 Re8 is equal.

(l) 7 ... Nf5 is likewise met by 8 b4!.

(m) 9 Bb2 Bg7 10 a3 gives Black time to catch his breath: 10 ... 0-0 11 d3 h6 12 Rc1 Nd4 13 Nd2 Rb8 14 e3 Ndc6 15 Qc2 b6 =, Popov–Gheorghiu, Sofia 1982.

(n) 12 Ng5, Larsen–Lehmann, Palma de Mallorca 1967; White's active pieces will soon force important concessions.

(o) (A) 4 d4 exd4 5 Qxd4 d5 6 Nf3 (6 cxd5? cxd5 7 Nf3 Nc6 8 Qa4 d4 9 Nb5 Bc5 $\overline{\mp}$) 6 ... Be7 7 cxd5 (7 Bg2 c5 8 Qd3 d4 $\overline{\mp}$) 7 ... cxd5 8 Bg2 Nc6 9 Qa4 0-0 10 Be3 Ng4 11 Bd4 Nxd4 12 Nxd2 Nf6 =, Hort–Kavalek, Waddinxveen Quad 1979. (B) 4 Bg2 d5 5 cxd5 exd5 6 Qb3 Nc6 7 Nxd5 Nd4 8 Nxf6† gxf6 9 Qd3 Bf5 10 Be4 Bxe4 11 Qxe4 Qc7 12 Kf1 $\overline{\mp}$, Zamikhovsky–Zhurakhov, Kiev 1958.

(p) 6 ... cxd5 7 d3 Qb6 8 Nb3 Ng4!? 9 d4 Be6 10 f3 exf3 11 exf3 Nf6 12 Be3 Nc6 =, Korchnoi–Keres, Curaçao 1962. 9 e3 may be an improvement.

(q) 9 0-0 d4! 10 Nb1 (10 Na4 Qb4 11 ... Nc6 $\overline{\mp}$ (Watson).

(r) 9 ... exd3? 10 0-0! Nc6 11 Bg5 0-0-0 12 exd3 Be6 13 Rc1 Kb8 14 d4 Be7 15 Na4 Qc7 16 Nbc5 ±, Polugaevsky–Jongsma, Amsterdam 1970.

(s) 12 Be3 Qc7 13 Rc1 Nc6 14 c4 Rad8 =, Reshevsky–Keres, Los Angeles 1963; White's counterplay will neutralize Black's strong center.

(t) 5 ... Bc5 6 Nb3 d6 7 Bg2 Bf5 8 0-0 Nbd7 9 d3 exd3 10 exd3 0-0 11 Bf4 Re8 12 Qd2 with a pull, Smyslov–Bronstein, Monte Carlo 1969.

(u) 6 e3 d5 7 Qc2 Bd7 (7 ... Nbd7 8 cxd5 9 Ncb5 is strong, Taimanov) 8 a3 Be7?! 9 b4 0-0 10 Bb2 ±, Najdorf–Rossetto, Buenos Aires 1968.

(v) 7 d4 a4 8 c5 Qb4 9 Nd2 d5 (9 ... Qxd4 is also playable: 10 Ndxe4 Qxd1† 11 Kxd1 Nxe4 12 Ndxe4 d5! 13 cxd5 Bf5 =) 10 e3 g6 11 h3 Bg7 ∞, Bagirov–Tal, Moscow 1963.

(w) 11 ... Nxf1 12 Rxf1 Be7 13 c5! Qd8 14 Qf4 ±, Matera–Soltis, New York 1969.

ENGLISH OPENING

Closed Variation

1 c4 e5 2 Nc3 Nc6 3 g3 g6 4 Bg2 Bg7

	19	20	21	22	23	24
5	e3............			.......Rb1........	.d3.........	.e4
	d6			a5(f)	d6(i)	Nge7(m)
6	Nge2			a3	Rb1(j)	Nge2
	Nge7	Be6........	h5	f5(g)	f5(k)	d6
7	Rb1(a)	d4(d)	d4	b4	b4	d3
	a5(b)	Bxc4	h4	axb4	Nf6	f5
8	d3	d5	d5	axb4	b5	Nd5
	Be6	Bxe2	Nce7(e)	Nf6	Ne7	0-0
9	Nd5	Qxe2	e4	d3	Qb3	Be3
	Qd7	Nb8	h3	Qe7	h6	Be6
10	a3	Qb5†	Bf1	b5	e3	Qd2(n)
	0-0	Nd7	f5	Nd8	0-0	Qd7
11	0-0	Qxb7 ∞	Ng1	e3	Nge2	0-0
	Kh8		exf4	Ne6	Kh7	Rf7
12	Bd2	Nxe4	Nge2	a4	Rae1	
	f5(c)	Nf6 =	0-0(h)	Rb8(l)	Raf8(o)	

(a) 7 d3 0-0 8 0-0 Be6 9 Nd5 and now: (A) 9 . . . Rb8?! 10 e4 Qd7 11 Be3 b5 12 b3 Nd4 13 Nxd4 exd4 14 Bg5 f6 15 Bd2 ±, Portisch–Ljubojević, Tilburg 1981. (B) 9 . . . Qd7 10 Qd2!? Nf5?! 11 b3 Nd8 12 e4 Ne7 13 Bb2 Ndc6 14 d4 ±. In both variations White has achieved the central superiority denied him in col. 24.

(b) 7 . . . Be6 8 Nd5 0-0 9 d3 Bg4! ∞, Kagan–Spassky, Winnipeg 1967; Black aims to exchange the knight on d5.

(c) 13 f4 Bg8 14 Qa4 (threatening 15 Qb5) 14 . . . Nxd5 15 cxd5 Nb8 16 Qc2 ±, Gulko–Smyslov, USSR Chp. 1977.

(d) (A) 7 Nd5 Nce7! =. (B) 7 d3 Qd7 8 0-0 h5!? (8 . . . Nge7 is col. 19) 9 h4 Nh6 =, Janković–Hort, Czechoslovakia 1970. The column is Larsen–Suttles, Palma de Mallorca 1970.

(e) 8 . . . Nb8 9 e4 Bg4 10 Qa4† Kf8 11 Ng1 Na6 ∞, Portisch–Petrosian, Tilburg 1982.

(f) 5 . . . d6 6 b4 Bf5 7 d3 Qd7 8 b5 Nd8 9 Nd5 c6 10 bxc6 bxc6 11 Nc3 ±, Kasparov–Karpov, World Chp. 1987 (game 6); White has queenside pressure.

(g) 6 . . . Nh6!? 7 d3 0-0 8 Nf3 d6 9 h4 Ng4 10 h5 h6 11 hxg6 fxg6 12 Ne4 g5 13 b4 axb4 14 axb4 Ne7 15 b5 Be6 16 Bb2 Qd7 17 Ra1 c6 18 bxc6, Draw, Hort–Karpov, Amsterdam 1980

(h) 13 0-0 d6 =, Ivkov–P. Nikolić, Yugoslav Chp. 1983.

(i) 5 . . . f5 6 e3 Nf6 7 Nge2 d6 8 0-0 0-0 9 b3?! (9 f4 ∞) 9 . . . g5! 10 Bb2? (10 f4 is still best) 10 . . . f4! 11 exf4 gxf4 12 gxf4 exf4 13 Nxf4 (13 Nd5 $\overline{\mp}$) 13 . . . Ng4 14 Bd5† Kh8 15 Ng2

Qf6 16 Qd2 Qe5 17 f4 Qh5 18 h4 Ne5 19 Rae1 Nf5 20 Ne4? (20 Ne2 Nf6 21 Bf3 keeps White in the game) 20 . . . c6 21 Bxg7† Kxg7 22 Qb2† Kh6 23 Ng5 cxd5 24 Ne6 Rg8 25 Ng5 Bd7 26 cxd5 Rae8 27 Rxe8 Rxe8 28 Rf3 Qg6 and is this losing position White lost on time, J. Watson–Browne, Las Vegas 1984.

(j) (A) 6 f4 Nge7 7 Nf3 0-0 8 0-0 h6 9 e4 f5?! 10 Nd5 Nxd5 11 exd5 Nd4 12 f3 Nxf3† 13 Bxf3 ±, Alekhine–Tarrasch, Vienna 1922. (B) 6 Nh3 h5!? 7 f4 h4 8 Nf2 Nge7 9 Rb1 Be6 10 Nce4 Qc7 11 b4 ±, Stoyko–J. Watson, New York 1975.

(k) 6 . . . Be6 is also important: 7 b4 Qd7 8 b5 Nd8 9 e3 Nh6 10 a4 0-0 11 Qc2 Re8 12 Bd2 Kh8 13 h4 f6 14 Nge2 Nhf7 15 a5 with the better game, Seirawan–Suttles, Vancouver 1981.

(l) 13 Ba3 Be6 14 0-0 g5 15 d4 ±, Korchnoi–Seirawan, Lugano 1986.

(m) 5 . . . d6 6 d3 Nh6 7 Nge2 0-0 8 0-0 f5 9 Nd5 Be6 10 Rb1 g5 11 exf5 Nxf5 12 b4 Nfd4 with even chances, Larsen–Spassky, Tilburg 1981.

(n) More solid is 11 Rc1 Rf7 12 Qd2 Raf8 13 f3! Kh8 14 b3 ±, Csom–Gulko, Biel 1976; White consistently aims for exf5 and d4.

(o) 13 f4 fxe4 14 dxe4 Nc8! 15 c5 Bh3 16 b4 Bxg2 17 Kxg2 exf4 18 gxf4 Re8 19 Nge?! (19 Nec3 is safer) 19 . . . h5!, Benko–Botvinnik, Monte Carlo 1968; Black has a dangerous attack.

ENGLISH OPENING

1 c4 e5 2 Nc3 Nc6

	25	26	27	28	28	30
3	(g3)			Nf3		
	d6	f5		g6	f5	
4	Bg2	Bg2		d4	d4	
	Be6	Nf6		exd4	e4	
5	d3	d3	e3	Nxd4	Nd2	Ng5(o)
	Qd7	Bc5?!(e)	e4!?(h)	Bg7(j)	Nf6	Bb4
6	Nf3(a)	e3	d3	Nxc6	e3	Nh3
	Bh3	f4	Bb4	bxc6	g6(m)	Nf6
7	Bxh3	exf4	dxe4	g3	a3	Nf4
	Qxh3	0-0	Bxc3†	Ne7(k)	Bg7	0-0
8	Nd5	Nge2	bxc3	Bg2	b4	h4
	Qd7	Qe8	Nxe4	0-0	0-0	d6
9	e4(b)	0-0	Ne2	0-0	b5(n)	e3
	g6?!(c)	d6	d6	Rb8	Ne7	Bxc3†
10	h4!	Na4?!(f)	0-0	Qc2	a4	bxc3
	h5(d)	Bd4(g)	Be6(i)	d6(l)	d5 =	Ne7(p)

(a) 6 Rb1 Nge7 7 b4 d5 8 b5 Nd8 =.

(b) 9 0-0 Nd8 10 d4 e4 11 Nd2 c6 12 Ne3 d5 13 f3 f5 14 fxe4 fxe4 15 Nb1 Nf6 16 Nc3 dxc4! 17 Nxc4 Ne6 18 e3 Ng5 and Black has a powerful attack, Hübner–Ljubojević, Tilburg 1981.

(c) The text is weakening. 9 . . . Nge7, planning 10 . . . 0-0 and 11 . . . f5, gives prospects of a hard fight.

(d) 11 Bg5! Bg7 12 Qb3! f6 13 Be3 Nd8 14 d4 ±, Karlsson–Bellon, Metz 1983. By a series of alert moves, White forced serious weaknesses in Black's position.

(e) Not the best move but certainly the most famous! Instead, after 5 . . . Bb4 there may follow 6 Bd2 0-0 7 Nf3 d6 8 0-0 Bxc3 =.

(f) 10 Ne4! Nxe4 11 dxe4 Qh5 12 Kh1 should contain the attack.

(g) 11 Nxd4?! (11 fxe5 dxe5 12 Nxd4 ±, Bellon) 11 . . . exd4 with: (A) 12 h3 h5 13 a3 a5 14 b3 Qg6 with a strong attack, Saidy–Fischer, Metropolitan League, New York 1969. (B) 12 a3 a5 13 b3 Bf5 14 Nb2 Qg6 15 Qc2 Nd7 16 Rc1 Nc5 17 Bf1 Ra6! ∓, Karpov–Bellon, Madrid 1973.

(h) 5 . . . g6 6 Nge2 Bg7 7 d4 e4 8 0-0 d6 9 f3 exf3 10 Bxf3 ±, Tal–Klaput, Poland 1966.

(i) 11 Nd4 Qf6 12 Nxe6 Qxe6 =, Rizzitano–Johnson, Boston 1981.

(j) 5 . . . Nge7 is possible: 6 g3 Bg7 7 Nxc6 Nxc6 8 Bd2 d6 9 Bg2 0-0 10 0-0 Bg4 11 h3 Be6 12 b3 ±, Petrosian–Botvinnik, World Chp. 1963. Neither this variation nor that of note (k) avoids the main problem of this column, which is White's spatial advantage.

(k) 7 . . . Nf6 8 Bg2 0-0 9 0-0 Re8 10 Qa4! (threatening Qa5 and Bf4) 10 . . . a5 11 Rd1 Bd7 12 Rd3 ±, Uhlmann-Rajković, Hastings 1972–73.

(l) 11 b3 c5 12 Bb2 Bb7 13 Bxb7 Rxb7 14 Ne4! ±, Gheorghiu–Suba, Romanian Chp. 1977. White has a lasting advantage.

(m) 6 . . . Bb4 7 Nd5 0-0 8 Nxb4 Nxb4 9 a3 Nc6 10 b4 d5 11 b5 Ne7 12 a4 ± (Watson).

(n) 9 g3? d6 10 Nb3 Qe7 ∓, Korchnoi–Spassky, match 1968. The column is analysis by Korchnoi.

(o) (A) 5 d5 exf3 6 dxc6 fxg2 7 cxd7† Qxd7 8 Qxd7† Bxd7 9 Bxg2 0-0-0 (9 . . . c6?! 10 Be3 Nf6 11 Bd4 ±, Mikenas–Furman, Leningrad 1965) 10 Be3 Bb4 11 Rc1 Nf6 = (Taimanov). (B) 5 Bg5 Be7 6 Bxe7 Ncxe7! 7 Nd2 Nf6 8 e3 0-0 9 Be2 d6 = .

(p) 11 Ba3 Ng6 12 g3 Nxf4 13 gxf4 ∞, Timman–Sax, Linares 1983.

ENGLISH OPENING

1 c4 e5 2 Nc3 d6

	31	32	33	34	35	36
3	d4	Nf3			g3	
	exd4	f5	Nf6	Bg4	Be6	f5
4	Qxd4	d4(f)	d4	d4	Bg2	d4(r)
	Nc6	e4	e4	Bxf3(n)	c6	Be7(s)
5	Qd2	Ng5(g)	Ng5	gxf3	d3	dxe5
	Nf6(a)	Nf6(h)	Bf5(j)	exd4	Nf6(p)	dxe5
6	g3(b)	Nh3	g4(k)	Qxd4	Nf3	Qxd8+
	Be6!(c)	c6	Bxg4	Ne7	Be7	Bxd8
7	Nd5	e3	Bg2	b3	0-0	Bg2
	Ne5	Be7	Nc6	Nbc6	0-0	Nf6
8	b3	Be2	Ngxe4	Qd2	c5!?	b3
	Ne4	Na6	Be7(l)	Qd7(o)	h6	c6
9	Qe3	0-0	b3	Bb2	cxd6	Bb2
	Nc5	0-0	Nxe4	0-0-0 ±	Bxd6	Nbd7
10	Bb2(d)	f3	Nxe4		b3(q)	Nf3
	c6(e)	d5(i)	0-0(m)			0-0(t)

(a) 5 ... g6 6 b3 Bg7 7 Bb2 Nf6 8 g3 0-0 9 Nb3! Ne5 10 Bg2 ±, Robatsch–Korchnoi, Buenos Aires 1978.

(b) (A) 6 b3 g6 (6 ... Be6 7 e4 ±) 7 Bb2 Bg7 8 g3 transposes to note (a). (B) 6 e4 g6 7 b3 Bg7 8 Bb2 0-0 9 Bd3 (or 9 f3 Nh5!) 9 ... Ng4 gives Black good counterplay (Shamkovich).

(c) Again, 6 ... g6 transposes to note (a). But now if 7 b3 d5! is dangerous.

(d) Better is 10 Bg2 c6 11 Nc3 Be7 planning 12 ... a5 and 13 ... a4 (Kasparov).

(e) 11 Nf4? (11 Nc3 Qb6 12 Qd2 a5! ∓) 11 ... Ng4 12 Qd4 Ne4! ∓, Hübner–Kasparov, match 1985.

(f) 4 g3 c6 5 d3 Nf6 6 Bg2 Be7 7 0-0 a5 8 a3 0-0 9 Rb1 Kh8 10 b4 axb4 11 axb4 Be6 12 b5 Qc7 13 Qb3 Nbd7 =, Averbakh–Kotov, USSR 1953.

(g) (A) 5 Nd2 Nf6 6 e3 g6 7 Be2 Bg7 8 f3 exf3 9 Bxf3 0-0 10 0-0 Nc6 =, Ribli–Polugaevsky, Budapest 1975. This position can also be reached from col. 29, note (n). (B) 5 Bg6 Nf6 6 Nd2 Be7 7 e3 0-0 8 Be2 c6 9 0-0 Na6 10 f3 exf3 11 Bxf3 Nc7 =.

(h) 5 ... h6 6 Nh3 g5 7 Ng1! Bg7 8 h4 g4 (8 ... Nc6 9 e3 Nf6 10 hxg5 hxg5 11 Rxh8+ Bxh8 12 Nh3 ±, Farago–Ermenkov, Albania 1983) 9 e3 Nd7 10 Ng2 h5 11 Nf4 Nf8 12 Qa4+ ±, Portisch–Seirawan, Clarin 1982.

(i) 11 cxd5 cxd5 12 fxe4 fxe4 13 Nf4 Nc7 14 Bd2 Bd7 15 Be1 Bc6 16 Bg3 Qd7 17 Qb3 Kh8 18 a4, Uhlmann–Tseshkovsky, Leipzig 1975. White has a slight initiative, but Black's central grip is formidable.

(j) 5 . . . Qe7 6 Qc2 Bf5 7 g4 Bg6 8 Bg2 with two choices: (A) 8 . . . Nc6 9 d5 Ne5 10 Ngxe4 Nxe4 11 Nxe4 Nxg4 $\pm$. (B) 8 . . . e3 9 Qa4† c6 10 Bxe3 Nxg4 11 Bf4 Nf6 12 0-0-0 h6 13 Nh3 Qd8 ∞, Dlugy–Benjamin, Philadelphia 1983.

(k) 6 Qc2? h6 7 Ngxe4 Nxe4 8 Nxe4 Qh4 $\mp$, Boleslavsky–Bronstein, Budapest 1950.

(l) Better than 8 . . . Nxe4 9 Nxe4 Qd7? 10 h3 Bf5 11 Ng3 Bg6 12 h4! Schmidt–Westerinen, Helsinki 1966.

(m) 11 Bb2 f5 12 Ng3 f4 13 Ne4 d5 ∞, Benjamin–Ginsburg, Manhattan Club Chp. 1983. The column, a vivid variation, is often reached by transposition from the Old Indian: 1 d4 Nf6 2 c4 d6 3 Nc3 e5 4 Nf3.

(n) (A) 4 . . . Nc6 5 d5 Nce7 6 c5! Nf6 7 cxd6 cxd6 8 e4 Ng6 9 Bb5† Bd7 10 a4 $\pm$, Gorelov–Didishko, USSR Chp. Semi-Final 1982. (B) 4 . . . Nd7 5 g3 Bxf3 6 exf3 Nf6 7 Bg2 Be7 8 0-0 0-0 9 d5 $\pm$ (Watson).

(o) 8 . . . g6?! 9 Bb2 Bg7 10 h4 with a strong attack, Suba–Mititelu, Romania 1972.

(p) 5 . . . g5?! 6 f4 Nf6 7 Nf3 Nbd7 8 0-0 g6 9 Ng5 Bg8 10 e4, Hübner–Ljubojević, Tilburg 1978. Black's center and kingside are coming under fire.

(q) 10 . . . Qe7 11 Bb2 Nbd7 12 Qc2 $\pm$, Averbakh–Balashov, USSR 1973. Black's development is passive and not harmonious. 10 . . . Qd7 (planning 11 . . . c5 and 12 . . . Nc6, or 11 . . . Bh3) may be an improvement.

(r) 4 Bg2 Nf6 5 d3 Be7 (5 . . . c6 is note f in col. 32) 6 e3 0-0 7 Nge2 Qe8 8 0-0 Nc6 9 f4 Bd8 =, Karpov–Korchnoi, World Chp. 1978. The game continued 10 a3 Rb8 11 b4 Be6 12 Nd5 b5 13 Bb2 bxc4 14 dxc4 e4 15 Nxf6† Bxf6 16 Bxf6 Rxf6 17 Rc1 a5 18 b5 Nd8 19 Rf2 Nb7 20 Bf1 Nc5 21 Nc3 Bf7 22 Nd5 Bxd5 23 cxd5 Nd3 24 Bxd3 cxd3 25 Qxd3 Qxb5 26 Qxb5 Rxb5 27 Rxc7 Draw.

(s) 4 . . . e4 is not so attractive as in cols. 29 and 32: 5 f3 exf3 6 exf3 Nf6 7 Bg2 g6 8 Nge2 Bg7 9 0-0 0-0 10 Be3 Re8 11 Qd2 Be6 12 b3 $\pm$, Benko–Formanek, US 1968. Without the e-pawns, Black's formation is not coherent.

(t) 11 0-0 Re8 12 Rad1 Bc7 13 Nh4, Taimanov-Vaganian, Leningrad 1977. White has a minute advantage.

ENGLISH OPENING

1 c4 e5

	37	38	39	40	41	42
2	(Nc3)..................		g3		Qc2.........	Nf3(m)
	(Nf6) ....Bb4(c)		Nf6		Nf6	e4(n)
3	e3	g3(d)	Bg2		e3	Nd4
	Bb4(a)	Bxc3	c6(g)		Nc6	Nc6
4	Nge2	bxc3	d4	Nf3	a3	Nxc6(o)
	0-0	Nc6	exd4	e4	g6	dxc6
5	a3	Bg2	Qxd4	Nd4	b4	Nc3
	Be7!	Nge7(e)	d5	d5	Bg7	Nf6
6	d4	c5	Nf3(h)	cxd5	Bb2	e3
	exd4	b6	Be7(i)	Qxd5!	d6	Bf5
7	Qxd4(b)	Ba3	cxd5	Nb3	Nc3	b3
	Nc6	Bb7	cxd5	Qh5	0-0	Bc5
8	Qd1	Nf3(f)	0-0	h3	d3	Bb2 ∞
	Ne5	0-0	0-0	Qg6	a5	
9	Nf4	d4 ±	Be3	Nc3	b5	
	c6 =		Nc6(j)	Nbd7(k)	Ne7 = (l)	

(a) (A) 3 . . . d6 may lead to a King's Indian or Old Indian after 4 d4 Nbd7. (B) 3 . . . Nc6 4 a3 see col. 41. (C) 3 . . . c6 4 Nf3 e4 5 Nd4 d5 6 cxd5 cxd5 7 d3 exd3 8 Qxd3 Nc6 9 g3 Bb4 10 Bg2 0-0 11 Nxc6 bxc6 12 0-0 with chances for both sides, Quinteros–Tarjan, Los Angeles 1983. The column is J. Watson–Browne, Berkeley 1976.

(b) (A) 7 Nxd4 d5 is similar to col. 10 but White has played a3. (B) 7 exd4 d5 8 c5 b6 9 b4 a5 10 Bb2 axb4 11 axb4 Rxa1 12 Qxa1 bxc5 13 bxc5 Ba6 =.

(c) 2 . . . f5 3 d4 with (A) 3 . . . e4 4 Nh3 Nf6 5 Bg5 Be7 6 a3 d6 7 Be1 ±. (B) 3 . . . exd4 4 Qxd4 Nc6 5 Qe3† Kf7!? 6 Nh3 Nf6 7 Qd2 (preventing 7 . . . d5) ±.

(d) (A) 3 Nd5 Be7 4 d4 d6 5 b3 Nf6 6 Nxe7 Qxe7 7 Bb2 c5! 8 dxe5 dxe5 and Black has good counterplay, Karner–Gavrikov, Tbilisi 1983. (B) 3 Nf3 Bxc3 4 bxc3 d6 5 d3 Nc6 6 g3 f5 7 Bg2 Nf6 8 0-0 0-0 =. (C) 3 Qb3 Ba5 (Bc5!?) 4 Qa3! Bxc3 (4 . . . Nc6 5 Nd5) 5 Qxc3 is pleasant for White, Miles–Timman, Reggio Emilia 1984–85.

(e) 5 . . . d6 would have prevented White's next move (Timman).

(f) 8 d4 d5! 8 cxd5 cxd5 10 dxe5 dxe5 11 Qa4 0-0! ∓, Speelman–Timman, Taxco 1985. 8 Nf3 is a suggestion by Sosonko.

(g) 3 . . . Nc6 is ill-timed: 4 Nc3 Bb4 5 Nd5! (A) 5 . . . Bc5 6 e3 0-0 7 Ne2 ±. (B) 5 . . . Nxd5 6 cxd5 Ne7 7 Nf3 Nd6 (7 . . . d6 Qa4†) 8 e4 c6 9 d4 with a distinct advantage, Geller–Debarnot, Las Palmas 1976.

(h) 6 cxd5 cxd5 7 Nf3 Nc6 8 Qa4 (8 Qd1 Bc5 ∓) 8 . . . Bc5 9 0-0 0-0 10 Bg5 Re8 11 e3 h6 12 Bxf6 Qxf6 13 Nc3 Be6 14 Rad1 Rad8 15 Rd2 Bb6 16 Rfd1 d4! with level chances, Larsen–Chandler, London 1986.

(i) 6 . . . dxc4 7 Qxc4 Be7 8 0-0 0-0 9 Qc2 Na6 with approximate equality, Larsen–Hübner, Tilburg 1981.

(j) 10 Qa4 Re8 11 Nc3. The variation has almost transposed to a Tarrasch Defense to the Queen's Gambit: 1 d4 d5 2 c4 e6 3 Nc3 c5 4 cxd5 exd5 5 Nf3 Nc6 6 g3 Nf6 7 Bg2 Be7 8 0-0 0-0 9 Bg5 cxd5 10 Nxd4 h6 11 Be3 Re8. Both sides have chances.

(k) 10 Qc2 e3 11 Qxg6 exf2† 12 Kxf2 hxg6 ∞, Larsen–Korchnoi, Leningrad 1973.

(l) 10 Nf3 Nd7 11 Be2 Nc5 (or 11 . . . f5!?) 12 0-0 ±, Miles–Sosonko, Tilburg 1984.

(m) 2 b3 g6 (2 . . . Nc6 3 Bb2, see Misc. Flank Openings, col. 13) 3 Bb2 Bg7 4 g3 c5 (a setup similar to that of col. 103) 5 Bg2 Ne7 6 Nc3 Nbc6 7 d3 (7 e3 d6 8 Nge2 Be6 9 Nd5? Bxd5 10 cxd5 Nb4 is strong) 7 . . . d5 8 e3 Be6 9 Nd5 Bxd5 (9 . . . Qd7 planning . . . Bh3, looks better) 10 cxd5 Nb4 11 e4 Qa5 12 Bc3 Qb5 13 Bf1 Qd7 14 Nf3 0-0 (14 . . . h6!?) 15 a3 Na6 16 h4! Nc7 17 a4 b5?! (17 . . . Qe8) 18 h5 bxa4 19 Bh3 Qe8 20 Rxa4 Nc8 (20 . . . Nexd5? 21 exd5 e4 22 Bxg7 exf3 23 Re4 +) 21 hxg6 hxg6 22 Kf1 Nb6 23 Ra5 Qe7 24 Nh4 Nd7 25 Bd2 Rfb8 26 Kg2 Rb7 27 Qc2 Rab8 28 Rb1 Nf8 29 Nf3 Bf6 30 Qa2 Ne8 31 Qa4 Nh7 32 Ra1 Rxb3 33 Rxa7 Qf8 (33 . . . R3b7 34 Rxb7 Rxb7 35 Qc6) 34 Qc4 Bd8 35 R1a6 Rb2 36 Rc6 Nef6 37 Qa6 R2b6 38 Qa4 Rb3 39 Rc8! Rxc8 40 Qxb3 Re7 41 Ra8 Re7 42 Bh6! Qxh6 43 Rxd8† Kg7 44 Rxd6 and White won, Larsen–Seirawan, Nikšić 1983.

(n) (A) 2 . . . d6 transposes to cols. 32–34. (B) 2 . . . Nc6 3 d4 (3 Nc3 transposes to other columns) 3 . . . exd4 4 Nxd4 Bc5 (4 . . . Bb4†?! 5 Bd2 Bxd2† 6 Qxd2 ±) 5 Nc2 (5 Nxc6 Qf6 =) 5 . . . Nf6 6 Nc3 0-0 7 e3 Nb4!? ∞, Dlugy–Smyslov, New York 1987.

(o) 4 e3 Nxd4 5 exd4 Qf6! 6 d5 Bc5 7 Qe2 Qg6 8 Nc3 Nf6 9 d3 0-0 10 dxe4 Ng4!, Murei–Udov, Moscow 1966. Black has enough for the pawn. The column is analysis by J. Watson.

ENGLISH OPENING

1 c4 Nf6 2 Nc3 e6 3 Nf3

	Nimzo-Indian English				Queen's Indian English	
	43	44	45	46	47	48
	Bb4				b6	
4	Qc2		g3	Qb3	e4	
	0-0	c5	0-0(i)	c5(l)	Bb7	
5	a3	a3	Bg2	a3	Qe2	Bd3
	Bxc3	Ba5	d5!?	Ba5	Bb4(n)	d6(p)
6	Qxc3	g3(e)	a3(j)	g3	e5	Bc2
	b6(a)	0-0	Be7	Nc6	Ng8	c5
7	b4(b)	Bg2	d4	Bg2	g3(o)	d4
	Bb7(c)	Nc6(f)	Nbd7	d5(m)	Nc6	cxd4
8	Bb2	0-0	b3	0-0	Bg2	Nxd4
	a5	Qe7	c6	Bxc3!	Nd4	Be7
9	e3	d3	0-0	Qxc3	Qd3	0-0
	Qe7	h6(g)	b6	d4	Bxf3	0-0
10	Be2(d)	e3	Bb2	Qc2	Bxf3	b3
	axb4	d6	Bb7(k)	a5	Nxf3†	a6
11	axb4	b3		d3	Qxf3 ±	Bb2(q)
	Na6 ∞	Bd7(h)		e5 =		

(a) Also critical is 6 . . . d6 7 g3 e5 8 Bg2 Nc6 9 b4 Bg4. Black's aggressive development and center control compensate for the two bishops.

(b) (A) 7 e3 Bb7 8 Be2 Ne4 9 Qc2 Ng5 =. (B) 7 g3 Bb7 8 Bg2 d5 9 cxd5 exd5 10 0-0 Re8 11 Re1 c5 12 d4 Ne4 $\mp$, Speelman–Seirawan, match 1987. (C) 7 b3 Bb7 8 Bb2 d6 9 e3 Nbd7 10 Be2 e5 11 d4 Ne4 12 Qc2 Qe7 (12 . . . Ng5 is safer) 13 Rd1 Rad8 14 Ba1 Rfe8 15 0-0 a5 16 Rfe1 h6 17 Bd3 f5 with an exciting battle in prospect, Seirawan–Christiansen, U.S. Chp. 1980.

(c) 7 . . . a5 8 Bb2 axb4?! seems premature: 9 axb4 Bxa1† 10 Bxa1 c5 11 e3 Nc6 12 b5 Ne7 13 Be2 d5 14 0-0 Bb7 15 d3 Nf5 16 Qe5! with a strong initiative, Timman–Nikolić, Belgrade 1987.

(d) 10 d3? axb4 11 axb4 Na6 12 b5 Nc5 13 Ba3 Ra4! 14 Bxc5 (14 Be2 Rfa8 15 Bb2 Rxa1† 16 Bxa1 Ra2 +) 14 . . . Rxa1† 15 Qxa1 Qxc5, Hebert–Korchnoi, Toronto 1985. Black's lead in development gives him a lasting advantage.

(e) 6 e3 Nc6 7 d4 d6 8 Bd3 e5 (more cautious is 8 . . . 0-0 9 0-0 Qe7) 9 dxe5 Nxe5 10 Nxe5 dxe5 ±, Larsen–Gheorghiu, Winnipeg 1967.

(f) 7 . . . d5 8 Na4! b6 (or Nbd7) 9 0-0 planning d4 is strong (Razuvaev).

(g) 9 . . . a6 10 Rb1 (Polugaevsky–Hübner, Palma de Mallorca 1970) 10 . . . Bc7 with the idea of . . . Rb8 and . . . b5 is more active.

(h) 12 Bb2 Rab8 13 d4 $\pm$, Lombardy–Polugaevsky, Reykjavik 1978.

(i) 4 . . . b6 is the other main line: 5 Bg2 Bb7 6 0-0 0-0 7 Qc2 d5 8 cxd5 $\pm$, Strauss–Christiansen, Los Angeles 1985.

(j) 6 0-0 dxc4! 7 Qa4 Na6 8 a3 Bd7 keeps the pawn.

(k) 11 Nd2 Rc8 12 e4 $\pm$, Ribli–Korchnoi, Wijk aan Zee 1983. The position has transposed to a Catalan, except for White's pawn on a3.

(l) 4 . . . Nc6 5 d4! is a Nimzo-Indian favorable for White.

(m) 7 . . . 0-0 8 0-0 a6 9 d3 Rb8! is also a good plan. But not 8 . . . d5 9 d3 d4? 10 Na4 b6 11 Ne5 Nxe5 12 Bxe8 Qe8 13 Bg2 (Speelman–Seirawan, match 1987), and now if 13 . . . Bd7 14 Qa2! Bxa4 15 b4!, maintaining White's material advantage.

(n) (A) 5 . . . c5 6 e5 Ng8 7 d4 Bxf3?! (7 . . . cxd4 8 Nxd4 $\pm$) 8 Qxf3 Nc6 9 d5! Nxe5 10 Qg3 d6 11 Bf4 with powerful pressure on the center, Korchnoi–Petrosian, match 1974. (B) 5 . . . d6? 6 d4 Be7 7 Qc2 with an obvious advantage.

(o) The older 7 d4 is met by Karpov's 7 . . . Ne7! and (A) 8 Bd2 0-0 9 0-0 d5 (Korchnoi–Karpov, match 1974, game 3), and if 10 cxd5? Bxc3 11 Bxc3 Ba6! takes control of the light squares (Hartston). (B) 8 Qd3 d5 9 exd6 cxd6 10 a3 Bxc3† 11 Qxc3 0-0 12 b4 Nd7 13 Be2 Rc8 =, Korchnoi–Karpov, match 1974, game 7. The column is Korchnoi–Portisch, match 1983.

(p) (A) 5 . . . c5 6 e5!? Ng4 7 h3 Bxf3 8 Qxf3 Nxe5 9 Qxa8 Nxd3† 10 Ke2 Nf4† (10 . . . Nb4!? gives some attacking chances) 11 Kf1 Nc6 12 Qxd8† $\pm$, Korchnoi–Polugaevsky, match 1977, game 1. (B) 5 . . . d5 is wild: 6 cxd5 exd5 7 e5 Nfd7 8 Bc2 d4 9 Be4 c6 10 e6! dxc3 11 exf7† Kxf7 12 Qb3† Ke8 13 d4 ∞.

(q) White has good attacking chances in this Sicilian-like position. 11 . . . Nc6 12 Nxc6 Bxc6 13 Qd3 g6 14 a4 Qc7 15 f4 Rad8 16 Qe2 Rfe8 17 Rad1 Bb7 18 Kh1 Qc5? (18 . . . Nd7) 19 e5 Nd7? 20 Be4 Bc8 21 exd6 Bf8 (21 . . . Bxd6 22 Bg6 hxg6 23 Ne4) 22 Bf3 f5 23 b4! Qxb4 24 Nd5 Qc5 25 Nc7 Nb8 26 Nxe8 Rxe8 27 Qd3, Resigns, Polugaevsky–Petrosian, USSR Team Chp. 1982.

ENGLISH OPENING

1 c4 Nf6 2 Nc3 e6

	49	50	51	52	53	54
3	(Nf3) e4					
	(b6)	c5		d5		
4	g3	e5(f)		cxd5........e5		
	Bb7	Ng8		exd5	Ne4........d4(s)	
5	Bg2	Nf3.........d4		e5	Nf3(q)	exf6
	Be7(a)	Nc6	cxd4	Ne4(n)	Nc6	dxc3
6	0-0(b)	d4	Qxd4	Nf3(o)	Be2	bxc3(t)
	0-0	cxd4	Nc6	Bf5!(p)	Be7	Qxf6
7	Re1(c)	Nxd4	Qe4	Qb3	d4	d4
	d5	Nxe5	d6(j)	Nc5	0-0	c5(u)
8	cxd5	Ndb5(g)	Nf3	Qxd5	0-0	Nf3
	Nxd5(d)	a6(h)	dxe5(k)	Nc6 =	b6!	cxd4(v)
9	Nxd5(e)	Nd6†	Nxe5		Qc2	Bg5!
	exd5	Bxd6	Bd7(l)		Nxc3	Qf5
10	d4 =	Qxd6	Nxd7		bxc3	cxd4
		f6(i)	Qxd7(m)		Ba6(r)	Bb4†(w)

(a) 5 . . . c5 is a Hedgehog Defense, cols. 85–90.

(b) 6 d4 is a Queen's Indian.

(c) 7 b3 d5 8 e3 is similar to a Reti Opening, 8 . . . dxc4 9 bxc4 c5 10 Qe2 Nc6 11 Rd1 Rc8 =, Portisch–Smyslov, Monte Carlo 1969.

(d) 8 . . . exd5 9 d4 is similar to some Queen's Indian positions: 9 . . . Nbd7 10 Qb3 c5 11 dxc5 Nxc5 12 Qd1 $\pm$, Petrosian–Gulko, 43rd USSR Ch., 1975.

(e) More enterprising is 9 e4. The text is Portisch–Karpov, Milan 1975.

(f) Other moves are less challenging: (A) 4 Nf3 Nc6 5 d4 (5 e5 Ng4) 5 . . . cxd4 6 Nxd4 Bb4 is an equal variation of the Sicilian Defense. (B) 4 g3 Nc6 (4 . . . d5 5 cxd5 exd5 6 e5 Ne4! 7 Bg2 Nc6!) 8 f4 Bf5 is also good for Black) 5 Bg2 d4! is a sound gambit.

(g) 8 Bf4 is the main alternative: 8 . . . Ng6 (8 . . . d6 is also possible) 9 Bg3 (A) 9 . . . a6 10 Qa4 Nf6 11 Ndb5 e5 12 0-0-0 (12 Bd3 Bc5 13 0-0 0-0 is interesting) 12 . . . Bc5 13 Nd6† Bxd6 14 Rxd6 0-0, Reshko–Bonch-Osmolovsky, Moscow–Leningrad 1966. White has fair compensation for the pawn. (B) 9 . . . Nf6 10 Ndb5 e5 11 Nd6† Bxd6 12 Qxd6 Qe7 13 Nb5 Qxd6 14 Nxd6† Ke7 15 0-0-0 Ne8 16 c5 b5? (16 . . . Nxd6 17 cxd6† Kf6 is better) 17 f4! with great pressure, Spassky–Ivanov, Toluca 1982.

(h) 9 . . . d6? 10 c5! a6 (10 . . . dxc5 11 Bf4 +) 11 Nxd6† Bxd6 12 cxd6 Nf6 13 Bf4 Ng6 14 Bg3 Bd7 15 h4 with a big advantage, Timman-Najdorf, Haifa 1976.

(i) 11 Be3 (11 Bf4 Nf7 12 Qa3 Ne7 13 Be2 0-0 14 Rd1 d5 15 cxd5 Nxd5 16 Bf3 Qe8! $\overline{\overline{+}}$, Timman–Karpov, Las Palmas 1977) 11 . . . Ne7 12 Bb6 Nf5 13 Bxd8 Nxd4 14 Bc7 Ke7 15 c5 Ne8 16 Bb6 d5 17 cxd6† Nxd6 18 0-0-0, and now (1) 18 . . . Bd7 19 Bc5 Nef7 ∞,

Miles–Karpov, London 1977. (2) 18 . . . Nec4?! 19 Bd4 (19 Bc5 b6 $\mp$) e5 20 Bc5 $\pm$. (3) 18 . . . Nef7 may be best.

(j) Plausible but less natural are: (A) 7 . . . f5 8 Qe2 a6 9 Bd2 Qc7 10 f4 Nh6 11 Nf3 Nf7 12 g3 d6 13 exd6 Bxd6, Bagirov–Abakarov, Baku 1959. (B) 7 . . . Bb4 8 Bd2 d6 9 Qg4!? dxe5 10 Qxg7 Qf6 11 Qg3 Nh6 =, Seirawan–Hort, Bad Kissingen 1981. (C) 7 . . . Qa5 8 Nf3 f5?! (8 . . . d6 is note k) 9 exf6 Nxf6 10 Qc2 Ne5? 11 Be2 Nxf3† 12 Bxf3 Qe5† 13 Qe2, Christiansen–Kudrin, U.S Chp. 1981. White's lead in development is overwhelming.

(k) 8 . . . Qa5 is also common: 9 exd6 Bxd6 10 Qd3 (or 10 Bd2 Nf6 11 Qd3 Qd8 or 10 Bd3 Nf6 11 Qe2) Be7 11 Bd2 with a cramped game for Black, Seirawan–Peters, US Chp. 1980.

(l) 9 . . . Nf6 10 Nxc6 Qb6 11 Qf3 bxc6 12 Be2 Bb7 13 0-0 c5, Korchnoi–Karpov, World Chp. 1978 (game 29). Black's divided pawns give White a minimal advantage.

(m) 11 Bg5 Bb4 12 Be2 Nf6 13 Qe3 Qd4 14 0-0 0-0 (14 . . . Qxe3 15 Bxe3 0-0-0!, U. Andersson) 15 Nb5 $\pm$, Seirawan–Andersson, Mar del Plata 1982.

(n) (A) 5 . . . d4 6 exf6 dxc3 7 Qe2† Be6 8 dxc3 Qxf6 9 Nf3 $\pm$. (B) 5 . . . Nfd7, see note (s).

(o) (A) 6 Nxe4 dxe4 7 Qa4† Nc6 8 Qxe4 Qd4 =. (B) 6 d4 Bb4 7 Qa4† Nc6 8 Bb5 Bd7 9 Nge2 0-0! =.

(p) 6 . . . Nc6 is also strong: 7 Bb5 (7 d3 Nxc3 8 bxc3 d4) 7 . . . Be7 8 Bb5 Nc5! 9 Bxc6† Kf8 10 Qc2 bxc6 11 d4 Ne6 12 0-0 Bd7 13 Be3 h5! 14 Ne2 g6 =, Diesen–Mednis, New York 1977.

(q) 5 Nxe4 dxe4 6 Qg4 Bd7 7 Qxe4 Bc6 (7 . . . Na6?!, Christiansen) 8 Qe3 Na6 9 d4 Nb4 ∞, Seirawan–Timman, Wijk aan Zee 1090.

(r) 11 Bd3 h6 12 cxd5 Bxd3 13 Qxd3 with an aggressive position, Christiansen–Reshevsky, US 1981.

(s) 4 . . . Nfd7 5 d4 c5 6 cxd5 exd5 7 Nf3 Nc6 8 Bb5! a6 (8 . . . cxd4 9 Nxd4 Ndxe5 10 Qe2 +, Quinteros–Nunn, London 1977) 9 Bxc6 bxc6 10 0-0 Be7 11 dxc5 Nxc5 12 Nd4 with a clear plus, Smyslov–Farago, Hastings 1976–77.

(t) 6 fxg7 cxd2† 7 Qxd2 Qxd2† 8 Bxd2 Bxg7 9 0-0-0 Nc6 10 Nf3 b6 11 g3 Bb7 12 Bg2 0-0-0 =, Paulsen–van Scheltinga, Stockholm 1937.

(u) (A) 7 . . . e5!? 8 Nf3 (8 Qe2 Be7! 9 Qxe5 Qxe5 10 dxe5 Nc6 11 f4 f6 gives Black good counterplay) 8 . . . exd4 9 Bg5 Qe6† 10 Be2 (1) 10 . . . f6 11 Nxd4 Qf7 12 Bf4 c6 13 0-0 Be7 14 Re1 0-0 15 Rb1 Na6 16 Bf3 (threatening 17 Nxe6) Rd8 17 Qe2 Bc6 18 Rbd1 leaves White with the initiative, Campillo–Frank, US Corr. Chp. 1984–87. (2) 10 . . . Be7! 11 Bxe7 d3! 12 0-0! Qxe7 13 Bxd3 0-0 =, Adorjan–Speelman, Banja Luka 1983. (B) 7 . . . b6 8 Nf3 Bb7 9 Bd3 h6 (9 . . . Bd6?! 10 Bg5 Bxf3 11 Qd2 Bf4 12 Bxf4 +, Miles–Sosonko, Amsterdam 1977) 10 Qe2 Bd6 11 Be4 $\pm$, Hübner–Unzicker, Bad Kissingen 1980.

(v) 8 . . . h6 9 Bd3 (A) 9 . . . Nc6 10 0-0 cxd4 11 cxd4 Nxd4 12 Nxd4 Qxd4 13 Rb1 Qd8 14 Qf3 Be7 15 Rd1 Qc7 16 Rb6 $\pm$. Dvoretsky–Agzamov, Alma Ata 1976. (B) 9 . . . cxd4 10 cxd4 Bb4† 11 Kf1! Nc6 12 Bb2 Bc5 13 Bc2 0-0 14 Qd3 Rd8 15 Rd1 with a strong attack, Seirawan–Korchnoi, Wijk aan Zee 1980.

(w) 11 Bd2 Nc6 12 Bxb4! Nxb4 13 Rb1! Qa5 14 Qd2 Nc6 15 Bd3 Qxd2† (15 . . . 0-0—or 15 . . . Ke7—16 Be4!) 16 Kxd2 with a difficult endgame for Black, Miles–Sosonko, Tilburg 1977.

ENGLISH OPENING

King's Indian English

1 c4 Nf6 2 Nc3 g6 3 g3(a) Bg7 4 Bg2 0-0

	55	56	57	58	59	60
5	Nf3					e4(m)
	d6					d6
6	0-0					Nge2
	Nc6...				e5	e5
7	d3				d3	0-0
	Nh5 ....e5				c6(k)	Nbd7(n)
8	d4(b)	Rb1			Rb1	f4
	e5(c)	a5 ....Nh5(i)			Re8	c6
9	d5	a3		b4	Bg5	h3
	Ne7	Nd4 ....h6(g)		f5	Nbd7	b5
10	e4	b4(e)	b4	Nd5	b4	d3
	f5	axb3	axb3	h6	h6	Qb6†
11	ef	axb3	axb3	b5	Bxf6	Kh1
	gf	c6	Be6	Ne7	Nxf6	Bb7
12	Ng5	b5	b5	Qc2	b5	g4
	Nf6(d)	Bg4(f)	Ne7(h)	g5(j)	d5(l)	exf4(o)

(a) 3 e4 is often played, to transpose to a King's Indian after 3 . . . d6 or 3 . . . Bg7 4 d4 while avoiding the Grünfeld and other defenses to 1 d4. 3 . . . c5 4 Nf3 becomes a Sicilian Defense Maróczy Bind.

(b) 8 Rb1!? f5! 9 Bd2 f4 10 b4 e5 11 Qb3 Bg4 12 Ne4 Kh8 13 b5 Nd4 14 Nxd4 exd4 15 Rae1 Be5 ∓, Andersson–Tal, Sochi 1973.

(c) 8 . . . f5!? 9 d5 Na5 (or . . . Ne5) is worthy of attention.

(d) 13 f4 e4 14 h3!? h6 15 Ne6 is promising for White (J. Watson).

(e) (A) 10 Nxd4 exd4 11 Nb5 Ng4! 12 h3 c6 13 hxg4 Bxg4! ∓. (B) 10 Nd2 c6 11 b4 axb4 12 axb4 d5 13 Bb2 Re8 14 e3 Nf5 15 cxd5 cxd5 16 Nb3 h5, Smejkal–Smyslov, Biel 1976; Black has an excellent game.

(f) 13 Bg5! Bxf3 14 Bxf3 h6 15 Bxf6 Bxf6 (15 . . . Qxf6!?) 16 bxc6 bxc6 17 Rb7! ±, Andersson–Nunn, Johannesburg 1981.

(g) 9 . . . Re8 is solid: 10 Nd2 (10 b4 axb4 11 axb4 e4 =) (A) 10 . . . Ne7 11 Qc2! d5 12 cxd5 Nexd5 13 Nxd5 14 Ne4 ±. (B) 10 . . . Be6 11 b4 (11 Nd5 Bxd5 12 cxd5 Ne7 13 Qb3 c6 =) 11 . . . axb4 12 axb4 d5 13 b5 Ne7 14 cxd5 Nexd5 15 Bb2 Nxc3 16 Bxc3 Bd5 =, Benko–van Riemsdyk, Sao Paulo 1977.

(h) 13 Qb3 Nd7 14 Ba3 f5 15 Bb4 ±, is less committal than 15 Nd5 Kh7 16 Nd2 Ra7 17 b6 ∞, Deze–Vukić, Novi Sad 1976.

(i) (A) 8 . . . Bd7 9 b4 Qc8 10 b5 Ne7 11 Re1 Bh3 12 Bh1 h6 gives chances to both sides. (B) 8 . . . h6 9 b4 Be6 10 b5 Ne7 11 a4 Qd7 (11 . . . Qc8?! 12 Ba3 Nd7 13 Nd2 Rb8 14 Nd5

Re8 15 Ne4 f5 16 Nec3 ±, Miles–Beliavsky, Hastings 1974–75) 12 Re1 Bh3 13 Bh1 ±.

(j) 12 . . . f4?! 13 Nd2 ± (Taimanov). Black should wait to play f4 until White cannot take advantage of the hole at e4, as in note (b).

(k) 7 . . . Nbd7 8 Rb1 a5 9 a3 c6! (9 . . . Re8 10 Nd2 c6 11 b4 axb4 12 axb4 ±, Andersson–van der Sterren, Wijk aan Zee 1978) 10 Nd2 Nb6! 11 b4 axb4 12 axb4 d5 13 cxd5 cxd5 14 Nb3 d4 ∓, Ree–Polugaevsky, Amsterdam 1970. To improve, White can consider 8 Bd2 followed by 9 Rc1, or 8 Bg5.

(l) 13 bxc6 bxc6 14 Nd2 Bf5 15 Qa4 ±, U. Andersson–Kavalek, Manila 1974.

(m) 5 e3 is flexible: 5 . . . d6 6 Nge2 e5 7 0-0 Re8 8 d3 Nbd7 9 Rb1 Nf8! (9 . . . a5 10 a3 Nb6 11 e4 a4 12 f4 exf4 13 gxf4 Bg4 14 Be3 with a powerful center, Karlsson–Tukmakov, Las Palmas 1982) 10 b4 h5 11 h3 Be6!? 12 Bxb7 Bxh3 13 Bxa8 Qxa8 14 e4 Bxf1 =, Dvoretsky–Vasiukov, Vilnius 1975.

(n) (A) 7 . . . Be6 is worse than useless: 8 d3 Qd7 9 f4 Bh3 10 f5 Bxg2 11 Kxg2 Nc6 12 h3 Ne7 13 g4 with a strong attack, Stoyko–Weeramantry, New Jersey 1987. (B) 7 . . . c6 8 d3 (1) 8 . . . Nh5?! 9 Be3 f5 10 Qd2 Be6 11 exf5 gxf5 12 f4 Nd7 13 Rae1 ±, Bilek–Tisdall, Lone Pine 1975; White's blockade cannot be broken. (2) 8 . . . a6 9 h3 b5 is equal, Popov–Kavalek, Wijk aan Zee 1975.

(o) 13 Bxf4 Rfe8 14 cxb5! cxb5 15 Ng3 with attacking chances on the kingside, Seirawan–Sigurjonsson, Wijk aan Zee 1980.

ENGLISH OPENING

1 c4 Nf6

	61	62	63	64	65	66
2	(Nc3)................Nf3					
	d5(a)(Grünfeld English)	b6................................				e6
3	cxd5		g3			g3
	Nxd5		Bb7			a6
4	g3 ....Nf3		Bg2			Bg2(s)
	g6(b)	g6	c5			b5
5	Bg2	Qa4†(g)	0-0(j)			Ne5(t)
	Nb6(c)	Bd7	g6(k)			Ra7
6	d3(d)	Qh4(h)	d4 ....Nc3.........d3(q)			cxb5
	Bg7	Bc6	cxd4	Bg7	Bg7	axb5
7	Be3	Qd4	Qxd4	d4	e4	Qb3
	0-0(e)	f6	Bg7	cxd4(o)	d6	Bb7!
8	Qc1	e3	Nc3	Nxd4	Nc3	0-0
	Re8	Bg7	d6(l)	Bxg2	0-0	Bxg2
9	Bh6	Be2	Be3(m)	Kxg2(p)	Nh4	Kxg2
	Bh8(f)	e5(i)	Nbd7(n)		Nc6(r)	c6 =

(a) 2 . . . c6 3 e4 (A) 3 . . . e5 4 Nf3 Bb4!? (4 . . . d6, see Old Indian) 5 Nxe5 0-0 6 Be2 Re8 7 Nd3 Bxc3 8 dxc3 Nxe4 9 0-0 d5 10 cxd5 Qxd5 11 Be3 ±. (B) 3 . . . d5 4 cxd5 cxd5 5 e5 d4 6 exf6 dxc3 7 bxc3 gxf6 8 d4 ±.

(b) (A) 4 . . . e5 is cols. 15–16. (B) 4 . . . c5 is covered in the Symmetrical Variation.

(c) The older line is 5 . . . Nxc3 6 bxc3 Bg7 (A) 7 Nf3 0-0 8 0-0 c5 9 Rb1 Nc6 10 Qa4 Na5 11 d3 b6! 12 Qh4 Bb7 13 Bh6 Bxh6 14 Qxh6 Bxf3 15 Bxf3 Rc8, Karpov–Korchnoi, World Chp. 1978; White's kingside attack has been defanged. (B) 7 Rb1 Nd7 8 Nf3 0-0 9 0-0 e5 10 d4 c6 11 e4 Qa5 12 Qc2 exd4 13 cxd4 Nb6 14 Bd2 Qa4?! (14 . . . Qh5 may be equal) 15 Qxa4 Nxa4 16 Rfc1 ±, Botvinnik–Smyslov, World Chp. 1958.

(d) 6 Nf3 is also reasonable: 6 . . . Bg7 7 0-0 0-0 8 d3 Nc6 9 Bd2 h6 10 Rc1 Kh7 11 Qc2 Bg4 12 Qb1 ±, Portisch–Uhlmann, Amsterdam 1971.

(e) 7 . . . Nc6?! 8 Bxc6† bxc6 9 Qc1 h6 10 Nf3 Bh3 11 Rg1 Bg2 12 Nd2 Nd5 13 Nxd5! cxd5 14 Nb3 with a firm grip on d4 and c5, Petrosian–Schmidt, Skopje 1972.

(f) 10 h4 Nc6 11 h5 Nd4 12 Nf3 Nxf3† 13 Bxf3 c6 14 hxg6 hxg6 15 Kf1! with prospects of an attack on the h-file, Seirawan–I. Sokolov, Sarajevo 1987.

(g) (A) 5 Qb3 Nb6 6 d4 Bg7 7 Bg5 h6 8 Bh4 Be6 9 Qc2 0-0 =. (B) 5 e4!? Nxc3 6 dxc3 Qxd1† 7 Kxd1 may not be as easy to defend as it looks: 7 . . . Bg7 8 Kc2 Nd7 9 Bf4 c6 10 Nd2! 0-0 11 f3 planning Nc4 and Na5 ±, Hort–Smejkal, Czechoslovakia 1983. (C) 5 g3 Bg7 6 Bg2 0-0 7 0-0 Nc6 8 d4 is a Neo-Grünfeld.

(h) 6 Qb3 Nb6 7 d4 Bg2 8 e4 0-0 9 Be3 a5 10 Rd1 a4 11 Qc2 Bg4 12 Be2 Bxf3 13 gxf3 Nc6 14 d5 Ne5 15 Nb5 ±, Fedorowicz–London, New York 1984.

650

(i) 10 Qc4 Nxc3 11 Qe6†! Qe7 12 Qxe7† Kxe7 13 bxc3 $\pm$, Polugaevsky–Mecking, match 1977.

(j) White gains nothing by delaying castling with 5 d4 cxd4 6 Qxd4 g6 7 b3 Nc6 8 Qd1 Ne5 9 0-0 Nxf3† 10 exf3 Bg7 =, Andersson–Adorjan, Indonesia 1983.

(k) 5 . . . e6 6 Nc3 Nc6 transposes to the Hedgehog Defense, col. 86.

(l) 8 . . . Nc6 9 Qf4 (9 Qh4 h6!) 9 . . . Rc8 10 Rd1 (A) 10 . . . Nh5 11 Qe3 Nb4 12 Rb1 Rxc4 13 Ne5 Bxe5 14 Qxe5 f6 15 Qb5 Ba6 16 Qa4 ∞, Panno–Ljubojević, Petropolis 1973. (B) 10 . . . 0-0!? 11 Qh4 Na5 12 b3 Nh5 13 Nd4 Bxg2 14 Kxg2 Nc6 15 Be3 d6 16 Rac1 Qd7 17 Nf3 f5 =, Benjamin–Chandler, Hastings 1987–88.

(m) 9 Rd1 Nbd7 10 b3 Rc8 (if 10 . . . 0-0 11 Qh4, planning 12 Bh6, is inconvenient) 11 Bb2 0-0 12 Qe3 Re8 13 Rc1 a6 with chances for both sides, Karpov–Kasparov, World Chp. 1986.

(n) 10 Rac1 0-0 11 Qd2 Ne4 12 Nxe4 Bxe4 13 Rfd1 Qc7 14 Bh3 Rab8 15 Nd4 Ba8 (15 . . . a6!?) 16 Nb5 Qb7 17 f3 a6 18 Nc3 b5 19 Nd5! with complications favoring White, Korchnoi–Seirawan, Zagreb 1987.

(o) 7 . . . Ne4 8 Nxe4 9 d5 0-0 10 Bh3 Bxf3 (White threatened 11 Nd2) 11 exf3 ∞.

(p) (A) 9 . . . Qc8 10 b3 Qb7† 11 f3 d5 12 cxd5 Nxd5 13 Nxd5 Qxd5 14 Be3 Nc6 15 Nxc6 Qxc6 16 Rc1 Qe6 17 Qd3 0-0 18 Rfd1 $\pm$, Black must struggle to draw. (B) 9 . . . 0-0! 10 e4 Qc7 11 b3 (11 Qe2!?) Nxe4 12 Nxe4 Qd5 13 Qf3 Qxd4 14 Rb1 Qe5 15 Bf4, Draw, Karpov–Kasparov, World Chp. 1984.

(q) 6 b3 Bg7 7 Bb2 0-0 8 Nc3 Na6 9 d4 d5! =.

(r) 10 f4 a6 (A) 11 f5 b5! with attacks on opposite wins, Alburt–Speelman, match 1986. (B) 11 Be3 Nd7 12 Qd2 Nd4 13 f5 b5 14 b3 e6 15 Bh6 Re8 16 Bxg7 Kxg7 17 f6!†, Schneider–Conquest, Schmallenberg 1986.

(s) 4 Nc3 d5 5 cxd5 exd5 6 d4 is about equal.

(t) 5 b3 Bb7 6 Nc3?! (6 0-0 c5 =) 6 . . . b4 7 Na4 d6! 8 d4 Nbd7 9 0-0 Be7 10 a3 a5 11 Bd2 c5 12 dxc5 dxc5 $\pm$, Anderson–Korchnoi, Tilburg 1987. The column is Vaganian–Korchnoi, London 1984.

651

ENGLISH OPENING

Symmetrical Four Knights' Variation

1 c4 c5 2 Nf3 Nf6 3 Nc3 Nc6 4 d4 cxd4 5 Nxd4 e6(a)

	67	68	69	70	71	72
6	Ndb5		g3(k)			
	d5	Bb4(f)	Qb6		Bc5(t)	
7	Bf4(b)	Bf4(g)	Nb3(l)		Nb3	
	e5	0-0	Bb4	d5(p)	Bb4	Be7
8	cxd5	Bd6(h)	Bg2	cxd5(q)	Bg2	Bg2
	exf4	Bxd6	Qa6(m)	Nxd5	d5	0-0
9	dxc6	Nxd6	c5(n)	Bg2(r)	cxd5	0-0
	bxc6	Ne8	b6	Nxc3	Nxd5	d6
10	Qxd8†	e3(i)	0-0(o)	bxc3	0-0(u)	Bf4(x)
	Kxd8	Qb6	bxc5	Be7	Nxc3	Nh5
11	Rd1†(c)	Rb1	a3	0-0	bxc3(v)	Be3
	Bd7	Qb4(j)	Bxc3	e5	Qxd1	Nf6(y)
12	Nd6	Nxe8	bxc3	Be3	Rxd1	Rc1
	Bxd6(d)	Rxe8	0-0	Qc7	Bxc3	Ng4
13	Rxd6	Be2	Nxc5	Nc5	Rb1(w)	Bf4
	Rb8(e)	Rd8 ±	Qc4 ∞	0-0(s)		g5(z)

(a) 5 . . . g6 can lead to a Sicilian Defense, Maróczy Bind, after 6 e4.

(b) 7 cxd5 Nxd5 8 Nxd5 exd5 9 Qxd5 Bb4† =, but not 9 . . . Qxd5? 10 Nc7†.

(c) 11 Nd4 (A) 11 . . . Kc7 12 g3 Bc5 13 Rc1! fxg3 14 hxg3 Ba6? 15 Nxc6! Bb7 (15 . . . Kxc6 16 Na4 Nd7 17 Nxc5 Nxc5 18 Rh5) 16 Na4! (16 Bg2 Bxc6 17 Bxc6 Nxf2†! 18 Kxf2 Ng4 † =) 16 . . . Bxf2† (16 . . . Bxc6 17 Rxc5 Kd6 18 Rxc6† Kxc6 19 Bg2†) 17 Kxf2 Ne4† 18 Kg1 Bxc6 19 Bg2 Rae8 20 Rh4! f5 21 g4 f4 (21 . . . g6 22 gxf5 gxf5 23 Rh6) 22 Bxc6† Kxc6 23 Nc3 Kc5 24 Bxe4 Kd4 25 Bf3 Rb8 26 Na4 Rb4 27 Rh5! Rd8 (27 . . . Rxa4 28 Rd5† Kc4 29 b3†) 28 b3 h6 29 Kf2 Rd6 30 Rf5 g5 31 Rf7 Ke5 32 Rxa7 Rd2 33 Nc5 Rbd4 34 Ra6 Rd6 35 Ra5! Resigns, Korchnoi–Portisch, match 1983 (game 3). (B) 11 . . . Bd7 12 g3 fxg3 13 hxg3 Bb4! 14 Bg2 Bxc3† 15 bxc3 Kc7 =, Timman–Gligorić, Belgrade 1984.

(d) 12 . . . Kc7 13 Nxf7 Rg8 14 Ne5 Rb8 15 Nxd7 Nxd7 16 g3 Rxb2 ∞, Korchnoi–Portisch, match 1983 (game 5).

(e) 14 Rd2 Re8 15 g3 f3! 16 Kd1 fxe2† 17 Bxe2 Kc7 18 Bc4 Bg4† 19 Kc2 Re7 is equal, Karpov–Polugaevsky, London 1984.

(f) (A) 6 . . . d6 7 Bf4 e5 8 Bg5 a6 9 Bxf6 gxf6 10 Na3 f5 is analogous to a Sicilian Defense, Pelikan Variation. (B) 6 . . . Bc5!? 7 Bf4 0-0 8 Bc7 (8 Bd6 Qb6! 9 Bxc5 Qxc5 =, Grünfeld–Yates, Kecskemet 1927) 8 . . . Qe7 9 Bd6 Bxd6 transposes to note (h).

(g) 7 a3 Bxc3† 8 Nxc3 d5 9 e3 0-0 10 cxd4 exd5 11 Be2 Bf5 =, Reshevsky–Benko, Amsterdam 1964.

(h) 8 Bc7 Qe7 9 Bd6 Bxd6 10 Qxd6 Qd8 11 e4 b6 12 Be2 a6 13 Na3 Ne8 14 Qd2 Bb7 15 Rd1 d6, Johansson–de Firmian, London 1982; Black's game is cramped but without weaknesses.

(i) 10 Qd2 Ne8 11 Nxe8 Rxe8 12 e3 Rd8 13 Be2 d6 14 0-0 Bd7 15 Rfd1 Be8 with only mild pressure for White, Korchnoi–Polugaevsky, match 1980.

(j) 11 . . . Ne5?! 12 Nxe8 Rxe8 13 Be2 Qc6 14 Qd4! (14 0-0 Nxc4 15 Rc1 d5 ±, Nimzowitsch–Tarrasch, Karlovy Vary 1923) 14 . . . Qxg2 15 Kd2 Nf3† 16 Bxf3 Qxf3 17 Rhg1 Qxf2† 18 Kd3 e5 19 Qg4 Qf6 (Schmid–Tringov, Siegen 1970) 20 Nd5! Qh6 21 Rbf1 d6 22 Qxg7† + (Schmid). The column is Korchnoi–Andersson, Johannesburg 1981.

(k) (A) 6 e3 Bb4 7 Bd2 0-0 8 Be2 d5 =. (B) 6 Bf4 d5!? 7 cxd5 (7 Nbd5 is col. 67) 7 . . . Nxd5 8 Nxc6 bxc6 9 Bd2 Bb4 10 Nxd5 Bxd2† 11 Qxd2 cxd5 with equal chances, Korchnoi–Timman, match 1982. (C) 6 a3 d5 7 cxd5 exd5 8 Bg5 Bc5 = (Speelman).

(l) (A) 7 Ndb5?! Ne5 8 Bg2 a6 9 Na3 Bxa3 10 bxa3 Nxc4 and White has doubtful compensation for the pawn. (B) 7 Nc2 Bc5 8 e3 0-0 9 Bg2 Qa6 10 Qe2 Rd8 ∓; White cannot prevent . . . d5.

(m) (A) 8 . . . Ne5? 9 Be3 Qc7 10 c5 Nc4 11 Bg5! Bxc5 12 Nxc5 Qxc5 13 Bxf6 gxf6 14 Rc1 ±, Christiansen–Leverett, US 1977. (B) 8 . . . d5 9 cxd5 Nxd5 10 0-0! (1) 10 . . . Nxc3 11 bxc3 Bxc3? 12 Be3 Qc7 13 Rc1 Bf6 14 Bc5 +; (2) 10 . . . Bxc3 11 bxc3 Nxc3? 12 Qd2 Nd5 13 Ba3 +.

(n) 9 0-0 Qxc4 10 Bd2 d5 11 Rc1 Qa6 12 e4 ∞ (Bagirov).

(o) 10 cxb6 axb6 11 0-0 0-0 12 Bg5 Be7 13 e4 (van Dyck–Bernard, XV World corr. chp. prelims. 1979–82) may give White a slight edge, but the gambit is more in the spirit of the position. The column is D. Gurevich–Dlugy, Berkeley 1984.

(p) 7 . . . Ne5 8 e4 Bb4 9 Qe2 (A) 9 . . . 0-0 10 f4 Nc6 11 Be3 Qc7 12 Bg2 d5 13 e5 Ne4 14 0-0 ±, Korchnoi–Spassky, match game 3, 1977–78. (B) 9 . . . a5 10 Be3 Qc6 11 f3 0-0 12 Nd4 Qa6 13 Nb5 d5!? 14 Nc7, Karpov–Miles, Tilburg 1977. Black does not get enough for the rook. (C) 9 . . . d5 10 f4 Nc6 11 Be3 Bxc3† 12 bxc3 Qc7 13 Bg2 0-0 =, Timman–Sax, Reykjavik 1988. d6

(q) 8 Be3 Qb4 9 cxd5 Nxd5 10 Bd2 Nxc3 11 Bxc3 Qe4 12 f3 Qe3 13 Qd2 =.

(r) 9 Nxd5 exd5 10 Bg2 (10 Qxd5 Be6) 10 . . . Bb4† 11 Bd2 a5! 12 0-0 Bxd2 13 Qxd2 a4 14 Nc1 0-0 =, Roger–Tringov, Lucerne 1982.

(s) 14 Qa4 Bxc5 15 Bxc5 Rd8 16 Rfd1 Be6 17 h3 with some pressure, Kasparov–Karpov, World Chp. 1984–85.

(t) (A) 6 . . . Bb4 7 Bg2 0-0 (7 . . . d5 8 Nxc6 bxc6 9 Qa4) 8 0-0 Qe7?! (8 . . . d5 9 cxd5 exd5 10 Be3 ±) 9 Nc2 Bxc3 10 bxc3 Rd8 11 Ba3 d6 12 Nd4 Ne5 13 Qb3 Nfd7 14 f4! Nc5 15 Bxc5 dxc5 16 fxe5 cxd4 17 cxd4 Rxd4 18 Rad1 +, K. Burger–Leverett, Gausdal 1982. (B) 6 . . . Be7 7 Bg2 d5 8 cxd5 Nxd5 (8 . . . exd5 is a Queen's Gambit Declined, Tarrasch Defense) 9 Nxc6 bxc6 10 Bd2 ±.

(u) The older move is 10 a3 Bxc3† 11 bxc3 0-0 12 Qc2!? Qc7 13 c4 Ne5 14 Nd2 b5 15 c5 Bb7 16 0-0 Rac8 17 Nb3 a5 18 Bd2 (Korchnoi–Spassky, match 1977–78, game 1) 18 . . . Nc6 =.

(v) 11 Qxd8† Nxd8 12 bxc3 Bxc3 13 Rb1 a5?! (13 . . . 0-0 or 13 . . . f6 planning 14 . . . Rf8 and 15 . . . Rf7) 14 Rd1 f6 15 a3! ±, Reshevsky–Kogan, US Chp. 1982.

(w) 13 . . . 0-0 (13 . . . a5!?, Browne) 14 Nc5 Rd8! (14 . . . Nd8? 15 Ba3 Re8 16 Na6! Ba5 17 Rb5 bxa6 18 Rxa5 ±, Christiansen–Radulov, Surakarta 1982) 15 Be3 Ba5 16 Rxd8† Nxd8 = (Ftáčnik).

(x) 10 Nd4 Bd7 11 Ndb5 (11 b3 a6 12 Bb2 Rb8) Qb8 12 Bf4 $\pm$, Vukić–Minić, Vinkovči 1977.

(y) 11 ... Ne5 12 c5 d5 13 Bd4 Nc6 14 e4! $\pm$.

(z) 14 Bd2 Ng5 15 Nb5 Ng6 16 c5! d5 17 e4 d4 18 Nd6 with the initiative, Adorjan–Hulak, Toluca 1982.

ENGLISH OPENING

Symmetrical Four Knights' Variation

1 c4 c5 2 Nf3 Nf6 3 Nc3 Nc6 4 g3 g6(a) 5 Bg2 Bg7 6 0-0

	73	74	75	76	77	78
	d5 0-0					
7	cxd5	d4				
	Nxd5	cxd4(e)				
8	Nxd5	Nxd4				
	Qxd5	Qa5 . . . . .Nxd4(h)				
9	d3	Nb3(f)	Qxd4			
	0-0	Qh5	d6			
10	Be3(b)	e4	Bg5(i) Qd3			
	Bd7(c)	Qxd1	Be6(j)	Bf5 . . . . .Be6 . . . . .a6(p)		
11	Nd4	Rxd1	Qf4	e4	Bxb7(n)	Be3(q)
	Qd6	d6	Qa5	Be6	Rb8	Ng4
12	Nxc6	c5(g)	Rac1	b3	Bg2	Bd4
	Bxc6	dxc5	Rab8	a6	Qa5	Na5
13	Bxc6	Nxc5	b3	Bd2(l)	b3	Qd1
	Qxc6(d)	Rb8 =	Rfc8(k)	Nd7(m)	Rxb3(o)	Rb8(r)

(a) 4 . . . d5 5 cxd5 Nxd5 6 Bg2 can transpose to col. 73 after 6 . . . g6 7 0-0 Bg7. 6 . . . Nc7 and 6 . . . e6 can also lead to other lines.

(b) Less forcing is 10 a3 b6 11 Rb1 Bb7 12 Be3 Rfd8 13 b4 cxb4 with chances for both sides, Portisch–Olafsson, 1978.

(c) (A) 10 . . . Qd6 11 Rc1 Nd4 12 Nxd4! cxd4 13 Bd2 Bg4 14 h3 Be6 15 Qa4 ± (Gufeld). (B) 10 . . . Bxb2 11 Rb1 Bf6 12 Qa4 Nb4 (12 . . . Qd6!?, Watson) 13 a3 Na2 14 Ng5, Jansa–Přibyl, Luhačovice 1973. White will regain the pawn with interest.

(d) 14 Rc1 Qe6 15 Rxc5 Qxa2 16 Rb5! b6 17 Qa1 Qe6 (17 . . . Qxa1 18 Rxa1 Rfb8 19 Ra6 ±, Ribli–Karpov, Amsterdam 1980) 18 Qa6 Qd7 19 Ra1 ±, Ivanov–Timman, Lucerne 1982.

(e) 7 . . . d6 8 dxc5 transposes to the King's Indian Defense, col. 56.

(f) Alternatives are 9 Nc2 and 9 e3.

(g) 12 Nd5 Nxd5 13 cxd5 Nb4 14 Bg5! Bxb2? (14 . . . Re8 ±, Pomar) 15 Bxe7 Bxa1 16 Rxa1! ±, Pomar–Smejkal, Wijk aan Zee 1972. The column is Sunye–Tukmakov, Las Palmas 1982.

(h) (A) 8 . . . d6?! 9 Nxc6 bxc6 10 Bxc6 Rb8 (10 . . . Bh3 11 Bxa8 Qxa8 12 f3 Bxf1 13 Kxf1 ±) 11 Bg2 Qa5 12 Qc2 Be6 13 b3 and Black has too little for the pawn, Espig–Markland, Polanica Zdroj 1973. (B) 8 . . . Ng4 9 e3 d6 10 b3 (if 10 Nxc6 bxc6 11 Bxc6 Rb8 planning 12 . . . Ne5) 10 . . . Nxd4 11 exd4 Nh6 12 Bb2 Nf5 13 d5 Bd7 14 Rb1 a6 15 Ne4 (Taimanov). (C) 8 . . . a6 9 e3 ±.

(i) 10 Bd2 is similar to note (j) but does not provoke Black to play . . . h6.

(j) 10 . . . h6 11 Bd2 Be6 12 Qd3 Qd7 (or 12 . . . Nd7) with even chances.

(k) 14 Qd2 a6 15 Be3 b5? (15 . . . Bd7 16 Ba7 Ra8 17 Bd4 Bc6 18 e4 b5 is all right for Black) 16 Ba7 bxc4 17 Bxb8 Rxb8 18 bxc4 Bxc4 19 Rfd1 Nd7? 20 Nd5 +, Fischer–Spassky, World Chp. 1972.

(l) Also possible is 13 Bb2 Nd7 14 Qd2 Nc5 15 f4 ±, Smyslov–Timman, Moscow 1981.

(m) 14 Qe2 Nc5 15 Rac1 b5 16 cxb5! axb5 17 Rc2! b4 18 Nd5 Bxd5 19 exd5 ±, Smejkal–L. Popov, Wijk aan Zee 1975.

(n) 11 Bd2 Qd7 12 Rac1 Rac8 13 b3 Bh3 14 Nd5 (14 e4 ±, Keene) Bxg2 15 Kxg2 Nxd5 =, Reshevsky–Stein, Amsterdam 1964.

(o) 14 axb3 Qxa1 15 Bd2 Qa6 16 Nb5 ±, Quinteros–Jimenez, Cienfuegos 1972.

(p) 10 . . . Nd7 11 Qc2 Nc5 12 Bg5 h6 13 Be3 Bf5 14 Qd2 Kh7 15 Bd4 ±, Hort–Unzicker, Venice 1969.

(q) 11 Bd2 Rb8 12 Rac1 (12 a4 Nd7 13 Qc2 a5 =) 12 . . . Nd7 13 e4 Ne5 14 Qe2 Bg4! 15 f3 Be6 16 b3 b5 17 cxb5 axb5 18 Nd5 Bxd5 19 exd5 Re8 20 Kh1 Rb7! 21 Rc2 Qa8 22 Rfc1 Rbb8 =, Kavalek–Grefe, US Chp. 1975.

(r) 14 Rc1 Be6 15 Nd5 b5 16 cxb5 Bxd5 17 Bxd5 axb5 =, Tal–Torre, Leningrad 1973.

ENGLISH OPENING

1 c4 c5 2 Nf3 Nf6 3 Nc3

	79	80	81	82	83	84
	d5................................e6					
4	cxd5			d4		
	Nxd5			cxd4		
5	d4.........e4(f)			Nxd4		
	Nxc3(a)	Nxc3 ......Nb4(k)		Bb4 ....d5		
6	bxc3	dxc3(g)	Bc4(l)	g3(p)		cxd5
	g6	Qxd1†	Nd3†(m)	Ne4.........0-0		Nxd5
7	e3(b)	Kxd1	Ke2	Qd3	Bg2	Bd2
	Bg7	Nc6	Nf4†	Qa5	d5	Be7
8	Bd3(c)	Be3(h)	Kf1	Nb3(q)	Qb3(t)	e4
	0-0	b6(i)	Ne6	Nxc3(r)	Bxc3†	Nb4
9	0-0	Nd2	b4	Bd2	bxc3	Be3
	Qc7	Bb7	cxb4	Ne4	dxc4(u)	0-0
10	Rb1(d)	f3	Ne2(n)	Qxe4	Qa3(v)	Be2
	b6(e)	g6(j)	Nc7(o)	Bxd2†(s)	Nbd7(w)	N8c6(x)

(a) 5 ... cxd4 6 Qxd4 Nxc3 7 Qxc3 Nc6 8 e4: (A) 8 ... Bg4 9 Bb5 Rc8 10 Be3! Bxf3 11 gxf3 $\pm$, Portisch–Hübner, Montreal 1979; (B) 8 ... e6 9 Bb5 Bd7 10 0-0 Qb6 11 Ba4 Qc5! 12 Qd3 Qd6! 13 Qe2 a6 =, Miles–Ribli, Baden-Baden 1981.

(b) 7 e4 transposes to the Grünfeld Defense.

(c) 8 Bb5† achieved nothing after 8 ... Bd7 9 a4 Qa5! 10 Bxd7† Nxd7 =, Polugaevsky–Vaganian, USSR 1983.

(d) 10 Ba3 b6!? 11 dxc5 Bb7 12 cxb6 axb6 13 Bb2 Nd7 ∞, Furman–Timoshchenko, USSR 1977.

(e) 11 Qe2 Rd8 12 Be4! Ba6! 13 c4 Nc6 14 d5 f5! with counterplay against White's strong center, Karpov–Kasparov, World Chp. 1987.

(f) (A) 5 g3 transposes to col. 73. (B) 5 e3 is similar to col. 79 after 5 ... Nxc3 6 bxc3. If 5 ... Nc6 6 Bb5 gives White a position from cols. 67–72 with colors reversed.

(g) 6 bxc3 Bg7 7 d4 is a Grünfeld Defense.

(h) 8 Bf4 may be even stronger, e.g., 8 ... g6?! (8 ... b6) 9 Kc2 Bg7 10 Rd1 Bd7 11 Bc4 f6 12 Bf7† Kxf7 13 Rxd7 $\pm$, Miles–Vaganian, London 1984.

(i) 8 ... e6 9 Kc2 Bd7 10 Be2 Be7 11 Rbd1 0-0-0 12 Rd2 f6 13 Rad1 $\pm$, Cvetković–Palatnik, Yugoslavia–USSR match 1976.

(j) 11 Kc2 h5 12 a4 Bh6 13 Bxh6 Rxh6 14 h4, with good winning chances in the endgame, Vaganian–Mikhalchishin, Lvov 1984. Mednis's idea of 10 ... 0-0-0, hoping to play ... e6, ... Bd6, and ... Bc7, may be Black's best in this line.

(k) 5 ... Nc7 6 d4 cxd4 7 Nxd4 e5 8 Ndb5 Qxd1† 9 Kxd1 Nxb5 10 Nxb5 Na6 11 Be3 Be6 =, Timman–Miles, Nikšić 1983. But 7 Qxd4! gives White the superior game.

657

(l) 6 Bb5† N8c6 7 d4 cxd4 8 a3 dxc3 (8 . . . Qb6 9 Bxc6† bxc6 10 axb4 dxc3 11 bxc3 ±, Ribli–Ftáčnik, Baile Herculane 1982) 9 axb4 cxb2 10 Qxd8† Kxd8 11 Bxb2 e6 12 0-0 f6 is about equal.

(m) 6 . . . Be6?! 7 Bxe6 Nd3† 8 Kf1 fxe6 requires precise play: 9 Ng5 Qb6 10 Qa4† (but not 10 Qc2? c4 11 b3 h6 12 Nf3 Nc6 13 bxc4 0-0-0 with a strong bind, Polugaevsky–Tal, Riga 1979) 10 . . . Nd7 11 Qc4 N7e5 12 Qxe6 ±, Chekhov–Kharitonov, Riga 1980.

(n) 10 Nd5 g6 11 Bb2 Bg7 12 Bxg7 Nxg7 13 Nxb4 0-0 14 h3 e5! 15 g3 Be6 16 Rc1 gave White a small advantage in Seirawan–Sax, Linares 1983.

(o) 10 . . . g6? 11 Bb2 Bg7 12 Bxe6 Bxb2 13 Bxf7†. After 10 . . . Nc7 11 d4 e6 12 h4 Bd6 13 h5 h6 14 Bb2. White's strong center clearly compensates for the pawn, Hübner–Tukmakov, Wijk aan Zee 1984.

(p) 6 Qb3 Na6 7 Bg5 Qa5 =. But not 7 . . . h6?! 8 Bxf6 Qxf6 9 e3 Qg6 10 Rc1 ±, Gunawan–Romanishin, Indonesia 1983.

(q) 8 Nc2?! Bxc3† 9 bxc3 Nc5 10 Qd2 b6 11 Bg2 Bb7 ∓, Lombard–Rogoff, Biel 1976.

(r) 8 . . . Qf5 is an important alternative, but after 9 Qe3 Nxc3 10 bxc3 Be7 11 Bg2 Nc6 12 0-0 0-0 13 c5 White has an edge.

(s) 11 Nxd2 0-0 12 Bg2 Nc6 13 Qe3 d5 14 0-0 d4 15 Qd3 e5 with chances for both sides, Padevsky–Semkov, Bulgaria 1981.

(t) (A) 8 cxd5 Nxd5 9 Bd2 offers White little: 9 . . . Bxc3 10 bxc3 e5 11 Nb3 Nc6 12 0-0 Nde7 =, Kogan–Lein, US Chp. 1983. (B) 8 0-0!? dxc4 9 Qa4 Na6 10 Nbd5 Nd5!? 11 Rd1 Bd7 12 Nxd5 exd5 13 Rxd5 Qc8 14 a3 Be7 15 Bf4 Bf6 ∞, Karpov–Portisch, Tilburg 1986.

(u) 9 . . . Nc6!? 10 cxd5 Na5 11 Qc2 Nxd5 12 Qd3 Bd7 13 c4 ∞, Kasparov–Karpov, World Chp. 1986. 12 . . . b6!? (Korchnoi) prepares to answer 13 c4 with 13 . . . Ba6.

(v) 10 Qxc4 e5 11 Nb5 a6! 12 Nc7 Ra7! =, Holzl–Portisch, Lucerne 1982.

(w) 10 . . . Nbd7 11 Nb5 Nb6 12 0-0 Bd7 13 Rd1 Nfd5 14 Nd6 Qf6 15 Rd4 Bc6 with a balanced position, Karpov–Portisch, Lucerne 1985.

(x) 11 Nxc6 Nxc6, Quinteros–Kasparov, Moscow 1982; it is hard for White to maintain his initiative.

ENGLISH OPENING

Hedgehog Defense

1 c4 c5 2 Nf3 Nf6 3 Nc3 e6 4 g3 b6

	85	86	87	88	89	90
5	e4	Bg2				
	Bb7	Bb7				
6	d3(a)	0-0				
	d6(b)	Nc6........	Be7......................		d6	
7	Bg2	d4(e)	d4(g)		d4(q)	
	Be7	Nxd4	cxd4		cxd4	
8	0-0	Nxd4	Qxd4(h)		Qxd4	
	0-0	Bxg2	0-0	d6	a6	
9	Re1	Kxg2	Rd1	Bg5(m)	e4	Rd1(s)
	Nc6	cxd4	Nc6(i)	a6	Be7	Be7
10	b3(c)	Qxd4	Qf4	Bxf6	Qe3	b3(t)
	a6	Be7	Qb8	Bxf6	Nbd7	Nbd7
11	Bb2	Rd1	e4(j)	Qf4(n)	Nd4	e4(u)
	Rb8	0-0	Qxf4(k)	Bxf3(o)	Qc7	Qc8(v)
12	d4	Bf4	Bxf4	Qxf3	b3	Bb2
	cxd4(d)	Qc8(f)	Rfd8(l)	Ra7(p)	0-0(r)	0-0(w)

(a) 6 Qe2!? Nc6 7 Bg2 d6 8 0-0 Be7 9 Rd1 Nd4? (9 . . . e5) 10 Nxd4 cxd3 11 Nb5 e5 12 Nxd4!, Seirawan–van der Wiel, Wijk aan Zee 1983.

(b) 6 . . . d5 7 cxd5 exd5 8 e5 Nfd7 9 d4 $\pm$.

(c) On 10 d4, Black may play 10 . . . cxd4 as in the column, or 10 . . . e5 11 dxe5 dxe5 12 Nd5 Ne8 followed by 13 . . . Nc7 and 14 . . . Ne6.

(d) 13 Nxd4 Nxd4 14 Qxd4 (A) 14 . . . Qc7 15 Rac1 Rfd8 16 Rfd1 Bf8 ∞, Portisch–Andersson, Wijk aan Zee 1978. (B) 14 . . . b5!? 15 cxb5 axb5 16 Nxb5 Bxe4 17 Bxe4 Rxb5 18 Rac1 Qb8 19 Bd3 Rb4 =, Larsen–Browne, Las Palmas 1983.

(e) (A) 7 e4!? attempts to save a tempo on col. 85. Black may try 7 . . . Qb8!? 8 d4 cxd4 9 Nxd4 Nxd4 10 Qxd4 Bd6! 11 Bg5 Be5 12 Qd2 h6 13 Be3 0-0 14 Bd4 Bxd4 15 Qxd4 e5! =, Smejkal–Larsen, Biel 1976. (B) 7 b3 Be7 8 Bb2 0-0 9 e3 Rc8 10 d3 a6 11 Rc1 Ba8 12 Qe2 d5 =, Salov–Seirawan, Rotterdam 1989.

(f) 13 b3 d6 14 Qd3 Rd8 15 Qf3 a6 16 Rd3 Qc7 17 Rad1 Rac8 18 g4!, Nikolić–de Firmian, Vrsać 1983; in spite of the exchanges, Black has not equalized.

(g) 7 Re1 d5 (7 . . . d6, see note p) 8 cxd5 exd5 (8 . . . Nxd5 9 e4 $\pm$) 9 d4 0-0 10 Bg5 Na6 11 Qa4 Ne4 12 Bxe7 Nxc3 13 bxc3 Qxe7 14 Ne5 Rfc8 15 e4 with a slight initiative, Karlsson–Suba, Eksjö 1982.

(h) 8 Nxd4 Bxg2 9 Kxg2 Qc8 10 Qd3 (10 Bf4 0-0! is no better) 10 . . . Nc6 11 Nxc6 Qxc6† 12 e4 0-0 13 Bd2 Rac8 14 b3 Rfd8 =. Black's development is ideal.

659

(i) 9 . . . Qc8 (A) 10 e4 d6 (10 . . . Nc6!?) 11 b3 Nc6 12 Qd2 Rd8 13 Qe2 Nd7?! (13 . . . Ne8 or 13 . . . Rd7 are better tries) 14 Ba3 Qb8 15 Rd2 Nc5 16 Rad1 ±, Korchnoi–Gipslis, Stockholm 1962. (B) 10 Bf4 Nc6 11 Qd2 Na5 12 b3 Bb4 13 Be5 Ne4 14 Qb2 Bxc3 15 Bxc3 Nxc3 16 Qxc3 d5 17 Rac1 ±, Andersson–Giardelli, Buenos Aires 1980.

(j) (A) 11 Qxb8 is less precise, though Black must avoid many traps: 11 . . . Raxb8 12 Bf4 Rac8! (12 . . . Rbd8 13 Nb5 d5 14 Ne5) 13 Ne5 d6! (13 . . . Rfd8 14 Nb5 d5 15 Nxc6 Rxc6 16 Rac1! a6 17 Na7 Rc5 18 b4 +, Gipslis) 14 Nxc6 Bxc6 15 Bxd6 Bxd6 16 Rxd6 Bxg2 17 Kxg2 Rxc4 18 Rad1 g5! with active play, Portisch–Pachman, Amsterdam 1967. (B) 11 b3 Rd8 12 Bb2 a6 (12 . . . d6 13 e4 a6 14 Qe3 Nd7) 13 Na4! b5 14 Nb6 ±, Christiansen–Peters, Los Angeles 1989.

(k) 11 . . . d6 12 b3 Rd8 13 Bb2 a6 14 Qe3 ±, Taimanov–Kholmov, USSR Chp. 1967.

(l) 13 e5 Ne8 14 Nd4 Na5 15 b3 Bxg2 16 Kxg2 g5 (16 . . . d6 17 exd6 Bxd6 18 Bxd6 Nxd6 19 Rd2 ±, Karpov–Petrosian, Milan 1975) 17 Be3 Kg7 18 f4 gxf4 19 gxf4 Nc6 20 Nce2 +, Petrosian–Portisch, Palma de Mallorca 1974.

(m) 9 e4, 9 Rd1, and 9 b3 are similar to cols. 89 and 90.

(n) 11 Qd3 allows 11 . . . Ra7! 12 Rad1 Be7 13 Ne4 0-0! =, and if 14 Nxd6? Bxf3 15 Bxf3 Rd7 +.

(o) 11 . . . 0-0 12 Rad1 Be7 13 Ne4 Bxe4 14 Qxe4 Ra7 15 Nd4 Qc8 16 b3 Qc5 17 a4 Rc7 18 Rd2 Qe5 (18 . . . Qh5!?) 19 Qb1 Rfc8 20 Rfd1 Nd7 21 b4! g6 22 b5! axb5 23 cxb5 d5 24 Nc6 +, Kavalek–Velikov, Solingen–Slavia club match 1984.

(p) 13 Rfd1 0-0 14 Rd2 Rd7 15 Rc1 Qc7 16 b3 with a pull, Andersson–Browne, Tilburg 1982.

(q) (A) 7 Re1 Be7 8 e4 (1) 8 . . . Nc6 9 d4 is similar to col. 85 but White has saved a tempo with his d-pawn. (2) 8 . . . Nbd7 9 d4 cxd4 is similar to this column but White is saving time with his queen. (3) 8 . . . e5!? is playable. (B) 7 b3 a6 8 d4 cxd4 9 Nxd4 Qc7 =, Korchnoi–Hjartarson, Reykjavik 1988.

(r) 13 Bb2 Rfe8 14 Rfe1 Bf8 15 h3 Rac8 16 Re2 Qb8 17 Rae1 g6 18 Qd2 Bg7 19 Kh2 Nc5 =, Hübner–Polugaevsky, Tilburg 1983.

(s) 9 Bg5 is ineffective due to 9 . . . Nbd7 and 10 . . . Qc7. Compare col. 88.

(t) 10 Ng5 Bxg2 11 Kxg2 Nc6 12 Qf4 Re7 13 b3 Rd7 14 Bb2 0-0 15 Nce4 Ne8 16 Nf3 Qa8 17 Kg1 ±, Adorjan–Schneider, Hungarian Chp. 1984.

(u) 11 Bb2 0-0 (A) 12 Ng5 Bxg2 13 Kxg2 Qc7 14 Nge4 Qc6 15 f3 Rfd8 =, Hort–Browne, Buenos Aires 1980. (B) 12 Qe3 Qc7 13 Nd4 Bxg2 14 Kxg2 Qb7† =.

(v) 11 . . . Qc7 12 Ba3 Nc5 13 e5! dxe5 14 Qxe5 Rc8 15 Qxc7 Rxc7 16 Bc1! gives White a comfortable edge, Gutman–de Firmian, Lone Pine 1981.

(w) 13 Nd2 Qc7 14 Rac1 Rac8 15 h3 Rfe8 16 a3 Qb8 17 b4 Red8 18 Qe3 Ba8 19 Qe2 Ne8 20 Nf1 Bb7 21 Kh2 Nef6 22 Nd2 Ne8 23 Re1 Ba8 24 Nb3 Bg5 25 Rc2 Rc7 26 f4 Bf6 27 Rec1 Rdc8 28 Nd1 Bb7 29 Qd3 Bxb2 30 Nxb2 Qa8 31 Nd1 a5 32 Nd4 Rd8 33 Nb5 Rcc8 34 Ndc3 Qb8 35 Rd1 Ndf6 36 Rcd2 h6 37 Qe2 Ba8 38 Kg1 Bc6 39 Kh2 e5 40 f5 Qa8 41 g4! (41 Nxd6 Nxd6 42 Rxd6 Rxd6 43 Rxd6 axb4 44 axb4 Qa3) 41 . . . Qb8 42 h4 Qb7 43 Bf3! (43 Nxd6 Nxd6 44 Rxd6 Rxd6 45 Rxd6 Qe7 46 c5 Ne8) 43 . . . Qe7 44 Kg3 axb4 45 axb4 d5! 46 cxd5 Bxb5 47 Nxb5 Qxb4? (47 . . . Nd6) 48 g5 hxg5? 49 hxg5 Nh7 50 d6! Rxc5 51 Rb2 Qc4 52 Qh2 Rxb5 53 Qxh7† Kxh7 54 Rh2† Kg8 55 Rhd1 f6 56 Rh8† Resigns, Karpov–Ribli, Dubai 1986.

ENGLISH OPENING

Symmetrical Variation, Keres Defense

1 c4 c5 2 Nf3 Nf6 3 Nc3 e6 4 g3 d5 5 cxd5 Nxd5(a) 6 Bg2 Nc6 7 0-0 Be7

	91	92	93	94	95	96
8	Nxd5............................d4					
	exd5(b)			0-0		
9	d4			e4		
	0-0			Nxc3 ....Nb6 ....Nb4		
10	Be3........dxc5			bxc3	d5	d5(q)
	c4(c)	Bxc5		cxd4	exd5	exd5
11	Ne5(d)	Bg5........Qc2(h)		cxd4	exd5	exd5
	Bf5	f6	Bb6	Bf6(l)	Nb4	Nd4
12	Qa4(e)	Bd2(f)	Ng5	Bb2	Ne1(n)	a3
	Nxe5	Be6?!(g)	g6	b6	Bf6(o)	Nxd5(r)
13	dxe5	e3	Qd1(i)	Rb1	Be3	Nxd4
	d4	d4	Nd4(j)	Bb7	Bxc3	Nxc3
14	Bf4	exd4	Be3	d5	bxc3	bxc3
	g5	Nxd4	Ne6	exd5	N4xd5	cxd4
15	Bd2	Be3 ±	Nxe6	exd5	Bxc5	cxd4
	Qc7 ∞		Bxe6(k)	Na5(m)	Re8(p)	Rb8(s)

(a) 5 . . . exd5 6 d4 is a Queen's Gambit Declined, Tarrasch Defense.

(b) 8 . . . Qxd5 (A) 9 d3 Bb7 10 Be3 Rc8 11 de ±. (B) 9 d4!? Nxd4 10 Nxd4 Qxd4 11 Qc2 0-0 12 Be3 Qf6 ∞.

(c) 10 . . . Bf6 11 dxc5 Bxb2 12 Rb1 Bf6 13 Nc1 d4 14 Bf4 Qa5?! (14 . . . Re8 planning 15 . . . Bg4 should equalize) 15 Nd3 Qxa2 16 Bd5 Re8 17 Nf4 Bf5 18 Rxb7 Be4 19 Bxe4 Rxe4 20 Qb1! Qxb1 21 Rfxb1 +, Portisch–Keres, Petropolis 1973.

(d) 11 b3 cxb3 12 axb3 Be6 13 Ne5 Qb6 14 Qd2 Rad8 15 Nxc6 bxc6 16 Qa5 ±, E. Meyer–Shamkovich, New York 1983.

(e) (A) 12 Qd2 Rc8 13 Nxc6 Rxc6 14 f3 Re8 15 a3 Re6 16 Rf31 h5 ±, Bass–Dlugy, Bermuda 1984. (B) 12 b3?! Rc8 13 bxc4 Nxe5 14 dxe5 dxc4, Tal–Alburt, USSR Chp. 1975, when Black's passed pawn is strong. The column is analysis by Tal.

(f) 12 Rc1 Bd6 13 Bd2 Bg4 14 Qb3 Kh8 15 e3 Qd7! (15 . . . d4 16 exd4 Bxf3 17 Qxf3 Nxd4 18 Qh5 with the initiative, Portisch–Keres, San Antonio 1972) 16 Bc3 Rad8 =, Christiansen–Tarjan, US Chp. 1978.

(g) 12 . . . Re8 13 Rc1 Bb6 14 e3 Bf5 15 Bc3 Be4 16 Qb3 ±, Larsen–Agdestein, Gausdal 1985. The column is Larsen–Yusupov, Reykjavik 1985.

(h) (A) 11 Ng5 h6! 12 Qc2 Bxf2† 13 Rxf2 hxg5 14 Qd2 d4 15 Qxg5 Qxg5 16 Bxg5 Bg4 ±. (B) 11 a3 Bf5 12 b4 Bb6 13 Ra2 Be4 14 Rd2 Qe7 15 Bb2 Rfe8 16 Qa1 f6 =, Portisch–Spassky,

Bugojno 1978l. (C) 11 b3 Bf5 12 Bb2 Be4 13 Rc1 Qe7 14 Qd2 Bb6 15 Rfd1 Rfe8 16 e3 Rad8 17 Ba1 f6 18 Qe2 Kh8 =, Quinteros–Alburt, New York 1983.

(i) 13 Qd2 d4! 14 Nf3 Qe7 15 Qh6 f6 16 e3 d3 17 Bd2 Bf5 18 Bc3 Be4 19 Rad1 Rad8 =, Agzamov–Tal, USSR 1981.

(j) 13 . . . Bd4 14 Qb3 Bf6 15 Qxd5 Nd4 16 Qxd8 Nxe2† 17 Kh1 Rxd8 18 Ne4 with complications favoring White, Benko–Peters, US Chp. 1975.

(k) 16 Bd4 Rc8 17 e3 Qd6 18 Qd2 Bxd4 19 Qxd4 Rc2 (A) 20 Qxa7 Rxb2 21 Qd4 Rb4 =, Adorjan–Gruenfeld, Dortmund 1984. (B) 20 Rfd1 Qb6 21 Qxb6 axb6 22 b3 ± (Ribli).

(l) 11 . . . b6 12 d5 exd5 13 exd5 Nb4 14 Ne5 Bf6 15 Re1 Bb7 16 Ba3 Re8 17 Rxb4 Rxe5 18 Rc1, Yusupov–Tukmakov, USSR 1979; Black has not solved the problem of blockading the d-pawn.

(m) 16 Ne5 Bxe5?! (16 . . . Rc8 17 Re1 Re8 is more natural) 17 Bxe5 Rc8 18 Rc1 with a distinct advantage, Christiansen–Portisch, Linares 1981.

(n) 12 Ne5 Bd6! 13 Nd3 Bg4! 14 Qxg4 Nxd3 15 Bg5 f5! 16 Qh5 Qd7 17 Qe2 c4 and Black has the upper hand, Dorfman–Tukmakov, USSR 1981.

(o) (A) 12 . . . Nc4 13 a3 Na6 14 Ne4 Bf5 15 Nc2 (Korchnoi–Kuzmin, Moscow 1973) 15 . . . Bf6 =. (B) 12 . . . c4 13 a3 Na6 14 Bf4 Bd6 15 Bxd6 Qx6 16 Qd4! Bf5 17 Nf3 Rfd8?! (17 . . . Rfe8 ±) 18 Nd2 Qc5 19 Qf4 Bd3 20 Rfe1 ±, Gulko–Alburt, USSR Chp. 1975.

(p) 16 Bd4 Be6 17 Nd3 Qd6 18 Rc1 Rc8 19 Re1 Rfd8 20 Be4 Nd7 21 Ne5 N7f6 22 Bb1 b6 ∞, Chernin–Petursson, World Junior Chp. 1979.

(q) (A) 10 a3 cxd4 11 axb4 dxc3 12 bxc3 b6 13 Bf4 Bb7 14 Qb3 Qc8 15 Rfd1 Rfd8 16 Nd3 a5 ±, Ftáčnik–Tarjan, Malta 1980. (B) 10 dxc5 Bxc5 11 e5 Be7 12 a3 Nd3 13 Qe2 Nxc1 14 Raxc1 Qa5 15 Rfd1 Rd8 16 Nb5 Qa6 17 Bf1 Bd7 18 Qe3 Qb6 19 Qxb6 axb6 20 Nd6 ±, Korchnoi–Hübner, Johannesburg 1982.

(r) 12 . . . Nbc2 13 Nxd4! Nxd4 (13 . . . Nxa1 14 Ndb5) 14 b4 cxb4 15 axb4 Nf5 16 Qb3 ±, Vaganian–Hartston, Tallinn 1979.

(s) 16 Rb1 b5 17 Qd3 a6 18 Re1 Bd6 19 Bd2 Bd7 20 Bb4 Bxb4 21 axb4 a5 22 Bxa5 Qxa5, Draw, Gheorghiu–Unzicker, Lucerne 1982.

ENGLISH OPENING

1 c4 c5 2 Nf3 Nf6

	97	98	99	100	101	102
3	(Nc3)......d4					
	b6	cxd4				
4	e4(a)	Nxd4				
	d6(b)	b6.....................e5			e6	
5	d4	Nc3		Nb5	g3	
	cxd4	Bb7		d5(h)	Qc7........Bb4†(p)	
6	Nxd4	Bg5........f3		cxd5	Nc3	Bd2
	Bb7	a6!(e)	e6	Bc5	a6(m)	Qb6(q)
7	Bd3(c)	Bxf6	e4	N5c3(i)	Bg5(n)	Bxb4
	Nbd7	gxf6	d6	0-0	Be7	Qxb4†
8	0-0	e3	Be2	e3	Rc1	Nc3
	g6	e6	Be7	Qe7(j)	d6	Nc6(r)
9	Re1	Qh5	0-0	a3	Bg2	Nb5
	Bg7	Qc7	0-0	e4(k)	Nbd7	0-0
10	Bf1	Nf3	Be3	b4	0-0	e3
	0-0(d)	Qc5(f)	Nbd7(g)	Bd6(l)	h6(o)	d5(s)

(a) (A) 4 d4 cxd4 5 Nxd4 is cols. 98–9. (B) 4 e3 g6 5 d4 Bg7 6 Be2 0-0 7 0-0 Na6 = , but not 7 . . . Bb7? 8 d5!.

(b) (A) 4 . . . Bb7 5 e5 Ng8 6 d4 (6 Bd3 e6 7 0-0 f5!, Korchnoi–Lein, Sao Paulo 1979) 6 . . . Bxf3 (6 . . . cxd4 7 Nxd4 g6 8 Bf4 Bg7 9 Qe2 Nc6 10 Nf3 Nh6 11 h4 Nf5 12 h5 0-0 13 0-0-0 with a strong attack, Mestel–Miles, London 1984) 7 Qxf3 Nc6 8 dxc5 bxc5 9 Qe4 g6 10 Bd3 Bg7 11 f4 f5 12 Qe3 d6 13 Bc2 Nd4 14 Ba4† Kf8 ∞, Portisch–Quinteros, Mar del Plata 1981. (B) 4 . . . Nc6 5 d4 cxd4 6 Nxd4 Bb7 7 Bf4! (7 Be2 Qb8!) 7 . . . d6 8 Nf3 g6 9 Qd2 Bg7 10 Be2 Rc8 11 Bh6 ±, Tal–Winants, Brussels 1987.

(c) (A) 7 f3 is col. 99. (B) 7 Qe2 (1) 7 . . . e6 8 g3 a6 9 Bg2 Qc7 10 0-0 Be7 11 Be3 Nbd7 12 Rac1 Rc8 13 b3 Qb8 14 Bd2 0-0 15 g4 ±, Korchnoi–Csom, Rome 1981. (2) 7 . . . g6 8 g3 Bg7 9 Bg2 0-0 10 0-0 Nd7 ±. (3) 7 . . . Nbd7 8 g3 Rc8 =, Kasparov–Salov, Barcelona 1989.

(d) 11 Bg5 a6 12 Qd2 Nc5 13 f3 ±. Compare cols. 85–90.

(e) (A) 6 . . . Ne4 7 Nxe4 Bxe4 8 f3 Bb7 9 e4 ±. Alekhine–Sämisch, Baden-Baden 1925. (B) 6 . . . d6 7 Bxf6 gxf6 8 e3 e6 9 Qh5! Qc8 (or 9 . . . Qe7) 10 Be2!, Kavalek–Kudrin, Berkeley 1984.

(f) 11 Qh4 f5 12 Be2 Bg7 13 0-0 Nc6 ±, Lerner–Psakhis, Riga 1985. If 10 Be2 Qe5!.

(g) 11 Qd2 a6 12 Rfd1 Rc8 13 Rac1 Qc7 14 Bf1 Qb8 with a complex struggle ahead, Hort–Ljubojević, Wijk aan Zee 1973. Compare col. 97 and cols. 85–90.

(h) 5 . . . Bb4† 6 Bd2 Bc5 7 Bc3 Qb6 8 e3 a6 9 N5a3 Nc6 ±, Dake–Fine, New York 1933. Fine's 9 b4!? is stronger: 9 . . . axb5 10 bxc5 Qxc5 11 cxb5 0-0 12 Qb3 d6 13 Bb4 ±.

(i) (A) 7 d6 0-0! 8 Nc7? Ne4 9 e3 Bb4† 10 Nd2 Qxd6 11 Nxa8 Rd8 +. (B) 7 e3 0-0 8 N5c3 e4 9 a3 Qe7 10 Nd2 Rd8 = Krasenkov–Smirin, Vilnius 1988.

(j) 8 . . . e4 may transpose to the column; 9 Be2 Qe7 10 Nd2 Rd8 11 a3 Nxd5 12 Nxd5 (12 Ncxe4? Nxe3! 13 fxe3 Bxe3) Rxd5 13 Qc2 Bf5 14 b4 Bb6 15 Bb2 Nc6 with chances for both sides, Mikhalchishin–Kasparov, Moscow 1981.

(k) 9 . . . a5!? 10 Nd2 e4 11 Qc2 Bf5 12 Be2 Nbd7 13 g4!? ∞.

(l) 11 Bb2 a5 12 bxa5 Rxa5 13 Nd2 Be5 14 Qb3, de Firmian–Alburt, Los Angeles 1987; Black must make serious concessions to regain the pawn. 11 . . . Rd8 may be better.

(m) (A) 6 . . . Qxc4 7 e4 Qb4 8 a3 Qb6 9 Be3 ±. (B) 6 . . . Bb4 7 Qd3 Nc6 8 Nb5 Qb8 9 Bf4 Ne5 10 Qd4 d6 11 Nxd6† Bxd6 12 0-0-0 Nxc4 13 Qxc4 Bxf4† 14 gxf4 0-0 15 Rg1 ±, Polugaevsky–Seirawan, London 1984.

(n) (A) 7 Bg2 Qxc4 8 Bf4 Nc6 9 Nxc6 bxc6 10 Rc1 Qb4 11 a3 Qb7 12 Bd6 Bxd6 13 Qxd6 Qb8 14 Qc5 Qa7 15 Qd6, Draw, Sosonko–Kavalek, Wijk aan Zee 1978. (B) 7 Qd3 Nc6 8 Nxc6 Qxc6 9 e4 b6 10 Bg2 Bb7 11 Bd2 Bc5 12 0-0 0-0 13 Rac1 Ng4 =, Olafsson–Ljubojević, Wijk aan Zee 1987.

(o) 11 Be3 0-0 and White's queen bishop is awkwardly placed, Yusupov–Psakhis, Erevan 1982.

(p) (A) 5 . . . d5 transposes to the Catalan Opening. (B) 5 . . . Nc6 6 Bg2!? (6 Nc3 transposes to cols. 69–72) 6 . . . Qb6 7 Nc2 d5 8 0-0! dxc4 9 Nca3 Qa6 10 b3 Be7 11 bxc4 0-0 12 Nb5 Qa5 13 Bd2 Qd8 14 Bf4 e5 15 Bg5 ±, Alburt–de Firmian, New York 1985. (C) 5 . . . Qb6 6 Bg2 Bc5 7 e3 Nc6 8 0-0!? Nxd4 9 exd4 Bxd4 10 Nc3 e5 11 Qc7 0-0 =, Manor–Psahis, West Berlin 1988.

(q) 6 . . . Be7 7 Bg2 Nc6 8 Bc3 0-0 9 0-0 d5 10 Nd2 Bd7 11 cxd5 Nxd5 12 Bxd5 exd5 13 N2f3 ±, Seirawan–Benjamin, Philadelphia 1986.

(r) (A) 8 . . . Qxb2 9 Ndb5 Qb4 10 Nc7† Kd8 11 Qd2 Ne4 12 Nxe6† fxe6 13 Nxe4 Qxd2† 14 Kxd2 with a small pull, Zilberstein–Vasiukov, USSR 1972. (B) 8 . . . Qxc4 9 e4 Qc5 10 Nb3 Qc7 11 e5 ±, Kapengut–Alburt, Odessa 1972.

(s) 11 a3 Qa5 12 b4 Qd8 13 cxd5 exd5 14 Bg2 Bg4 15 Qd2 Ne5 with approximate equality, Hausner–Pinter, Skara 1980.

ENGLISH OPENING

1 c4 c5 2 Nf3

	103	104	105	106	107	108
	(Nf6)...				Nc6	
3	(d4)........g3				d4.........Nc3	
	(cxd4)	d5..........e6..........g6(j)			cxd4	g6?!
4	(Nxd4)	cxd5	Bg2	b3	Nxd4	e3
	g6(a)	Nxd5	d5	Bg7	g6	Bg7(o)
5	Nc3	Bg2	cxd5	Bb2	Nc3	d4
	d5(b)	Nc6	Nxd5	0-0	Bg7	d6
6	Bg5	d4(e)	0-0	Bg2	Nc2(m)	Be2(p)
	dxc4	cxd4(f)	Nc6	d6	Bxc3†	Nf6
7	e3	Nxd4	d4	0-0	bxc3	d5
	Bg7(c)	Ndb4	Be7	e5(k)	Qa5	Na5
8	Bxc4	Nxc6	dxc5(h)	Nc3	e4!	e4
	0-0	Qxd1†	Bxc5	Nc6	Nf6	0-0(q)
9	0-0	Kxd1	Qc2	d3	f3	
	Bd7(d)	Nxc6(g)	Qe7(i)	Nh5(l)	Qxc3†(n)	

(a) (A) 4 ... Nc6 5 g3 (5 Nc3 is the Symmetrical Four Knights' Variation, cols. 67–72) 5 ... Qb6 (or 5 ... e6) 6 Nb5!? (6 Nb3 Ne5 =) 6 ... a6 7 N5c3 e6 8 Bg2 Ne5 9 Qb3 Qb4 =, Miles–Gligorić, Bugojno 1984. (B) 4 ... d5!? may also arise from the Queen's Gambit Declined and is not easy to refute: 5 cxd5 Nxd5 6 e4 and not (1) 6 ... Nf6 7 Bb5†! Bd7 8 Qe2! a6 9 Bxd7† Nbxf7 10 0-0 e6 11 Nc3 Qc7 (Udovčić–Karaklajić, Yugoslav Chp. 1951) 12 Be3 ±, but (2) 6 ... Nc7!? 7 Nc3 e5 =, Timman–Miles, col. 81, note (1). (C) 4 ... a6!? 5 Nc3 d5 6 Nb3!? e6 7 cxd5 exd5 8 g3 Nc6 9 Bg2 Be6 10 0-0 ±, Rashkovsky–Chekhov, USSR Chp. 1976. (D) 4 ... e5 5 g3 d5 6 Bg2 arrives at a Catalan Opening.

(b) 5 ... Nc6 (or 5 ... Bg7) 6 e4 is a Maróczy Bind Sicilian Defense.

(c) 7 ... Qa5 8 Bxf6 exf6 9 Bxc4?! (9 ... Bg7 ±) 10 Rc1 a6 11 0-0 Nd7 (11 ... 0-0 12 Nd5) 12 a3 Be7? 13 b4! Qe5 (13 ... Qxa3 14 Nd5) 14 f4! Qb8 15 Bxf7†! Kxf7 16 Qb3† Ke8 17 Nd5 Bf6 18 Ne6 b5 19 Ndc7† Ke7 20 Nd4! Resigns, Petrosian–Korchnoi, Curaçao 1962.

(d) 10 Qd2 Nc6 11 Rfd1 Ne5 12 Bb3 Rc8 13 Qe2 ± (Portisch).

(e) 6 Nc3 g6 7 0-0 Bg7 transposes to col. 72.

(f) (A) 6 ... e6 is col. 105. (B) 6 ... Bf5 7 0-0 e6 8 a3! Be7 9 dxc5 Bxc5 10 b4 Be7 11 Bb2 Bf6 12 Qb3 ±, P. Nikolić–Razuvaev, Novi Šad 1982. (C) 6 ... Nb6!? 7 dxc5 Qxd1† 8 Kxd1 Na4 9 Nc3 Nxc5 10 Be3 Ne6 =, Andersson–Seirawan, Wijk aan Zee 1983.

(g) (A) 10 Nc3 Bd7 11 Be3 e5 (11 ... Rc8 is safer) 12 Rc1 0-0-0 13 Kc2! Bf5† 14 Kb3! Be6† 15 Ka4! with pressure on the queenside, Speelman–Alburt, match 1986. (B) 10 Bxc6† bxc6 gives White just the shadow of an advantage after 11 Be3 a5 12 Nd2 Be6 13 Kc2 Bf5†, Miles–Ljubojević, Nikšić 1983.

(h) 8 Nc3 transposes to the Keres Defense (cols. 91–96).

(i) 9 . . . Be7 allows White a dangerous spatial advantage: 10 Rd1 Bd7 11 e4 Nb6 12 Nc3 0-0 13 Bf4 $\pm$. The text is more enterprising: (9 . . . Qe7) 10 a3 0-0 11 b4 Bb6 12 Bb2 Bd7 13 Nc3 Nxc3 14 Nxc3 Rfc8 15 Rfd1 Rc7 =, Ribli–Unzicker, West German club match 1985.

(j) 3 . . . b6 and 3 . . . Nc6 will transpose to other columns.

(k) 7 . . . Nc6 8 d4 cxd4 9 Nxd4 Bd7 10 Nc3 Qa5 11 e3 Rab8 12 Re1 Rfc8 13 h3 a6 14 a3 $\pm$, Romanishin–Gulko, USSR 1978.

(l) 10 Nd2 f5 11 Nd5 Ne7 12 b4 Nxd5 13 Bxd5† Kh8 14 bxc5 dxc5 15 Nb3 Nf6 16 Bg2 Qc7 17 Ba3 Nd7 18 e3 with a slight initiative, I. Ivanov–D. Gurevich, New York 1982.

(m) 6 e3 Nf6 7 Be2 0-0 8 0-0 d5 =.

(n) 10 Bd2 Qe5 11 Rb1 0-0 12 Rb5 Qc7, Szabó–Matulović, Kapfenberg 1970; White has lasting pressure for the pawn.

(o) It's too late to challenge the center: 4 . . . Nf6 5 d4 cxd4 6 exd4 d5 7 Bg5! Ne4 8 cxd5 Nxc3 9 bxc3 Qxd5 10 Be2 Bg7 11 0-0 0-0 12 c4! Qd6 13 d5! with threats, Rogoff–Zaltsman, Lone Pine 1979.

(p) 6 d5 Ne5!? 7 Nd2 f5 8 Be2 Nf6 9 h3 0-0 10 f4 Nf7 ∞, Korchnoi–Fischer, Sousse, 1967.

ENGLISH OPENING
Rubinstein/Botvinnik Variation

1 c4 c5 2 Nc3 Nf6 3 g3 d5(a) 4 cxd5 Nxd5 5 Bg2 Nc7(b)

	109	110	111	112	113	114
6	d3 .... Nf3					
	e5	Nc6				
7	Nh3(c)	b3 .... 0-0(h)				
	Be7	e5	g6 .... e5			
8	0-0	Bb2	d3(i)	Ne1 .... d3		
	0-0	Be7	Bg7	Bd7(j)	Be7	
9	f4	Rc1	Be3	Nd3	Nd2(l)	
	Nc6	Ne6(e)	b6	f6	Bd7	
10	Be3	0-0	Qd2	f4	Nc4	
	Rb8	0-0	0-0	c4	f6 .... 0-0!?	
11	Rc1	Ne1	Bh6	Nf2	f4	Bxc6(n)
	b6(d)	Bd7	e5	exf4	b5	Bxc6
12	Nf2	Nd3	Rfc1	gxf4	Ne3	Nxe5
	exf4	b6!?(f)	f6 =	f5	Rab8	Be8
13	Bxf4	Nd5		b3	f5	Be3
	Nd4 =	Bd6(g)		cxb3(k)	0-0(m)	Ne6(o)

(a) On 3 . . . e6 4 Nf3 transposes to other columns, and for 4 Bg2 d5 5 cxd5 Nxd5 6 Nf3 Nc6 7 d4 Be7 8 0-0 0-0 =, see Queen's Gambit, Tarrasch Defense.

(b) 5 . . . e6! 6 Nxd5 exd5 7 Qb3 ±.

(c) 7 Qb3 (A) 7 . . . Nd7 8 Nf3 Be7 9 Nd2 0-0 10 0-0 Nb6 11 Nc4 Be6 12 Qc2 Nxc4 13 dxc4 ±, Karlsson–Alburt, Hastings 1983–84. (B) 7 . . . Nc6!? 8 Bxc6† bxc6 9 Qa4 e5! is col. 107. Though colors are reversed, White is not a tempo ahead because his queen has moved twice.

(d) 11 . . . Bg4?! 12 Nf2 exf4 13 gxf4 Bh5 14 Nce4 f5 15 Ng3 Bg6 16 Bxc5 +. The column is Wexler–Redolfi, Mar del Plata 1960.

(e) 9 . . . f6 10 0-0 0-0 11 Na4 Na6 12 e3 Be6 13 d4 ±, Furman–Witkowski, Polanica Zdroj 1969.

(f) 12 . . . f6 is passive: 13 Nd5 b6 14 f4 ±. The text allows 13 Bxc6 Bxc6 14 Nxe5 Bb7 ∞; compare col. 114.

(g) 14 f4 exf4 15 gxf4 Rc8 16 e3 f6 =, Speelman–Sax, Plovdiv 1983.

(h) (A) 7 Qa4 Bd7 8 Qe4 g6 9 Ne5 Bg7 10 Nxd7 Qxd7 11 0-0 0-0 =, Kasparov–Kapengut, Minsk 1978. (B) 7 a3 e6 8 0-0 Be7 9 d3 0-0 10 Be3 Nd5 11 Rc1 Nxe3 12 fxe3 Bd7 13 Ne4 Qb6! 14 Qc2 c4! 15 d4 Rac8 =, Vaganian–Ljubojević, Tilburg 1983.

(i) On 8 Ne4 Black should not play 8 . . . b6 9 d4 cxd4 10 Bf4 Bg7 11 Nxd4 Nxd4 12 Bxc7 Qxc7 13 Bxa8 ±, Polugaevsky–Taimanov, USSR Chp. 1967, but 8 . . . Ne6 with equality. The column is Langeweg–Timman, Amsterdam 1978.

(j) 8 ... Be6 9 Bxc6† (9 Nd3 f6 10 f4?! c4 11 Nf2 exf4 12 gxf4 Qd7 13 d3 Rd8 $\mp$,
Smyslov–Hübner, match 1983) 9 ... bxc6 10 Qa4 Qd7 11 Nd3 f6 12 b3 $\pm$, Watson–
Gruenberg, Gausdal 1980.

(k) 14 d4! Bd6 15 e4 with a strong attack, I. Ivanov–Chow, Chicago 1986.

(l) 9 Be4 is often played, but it is less sharp than the text: 9 ... 0-0 10 Nd2 Bd7 11 Rc1
(Dake–Rogoff, Lone Pine 1976) 11 ... Rc8 =.

(m) 14 Bd2 Nd4 15 Rc1 c4 with chances for both sides, Smejkal–Sax, New York Open 1986.

(n) White can decline the gambit by 11 f4 or 11 a4!? with a level game.

(o) 13 ... Bf6, 13 ... Nd5, and 13 ... f6 are also possible. After 13 ... Ne6 14 Rc1 Bf6 15
Nc4 Nc6 16 Ne4 Bd4 17 Bxd4 cxd4 18 Ne5 Bd5 19 Qa4 Re8 20 Nf3 Qb6 21 Rc2 Rad8 22
Rfc1 h6 White is hard put to improve his position, Dorfman–Kapengut, USSR 1976.

ENGLISH OPENING

Ultra-Symmetrical Variation

1 c4 c5 2 Nc3 Nc6 3 g3 g6 4 Bg2 Bg7

	115	116	117	118	119	120
5	Nf3.........	......e4	e4	e3	a3	......a3
	e5	e6(d)	Nf6(h)	e6(k)	a6	e6(r)
6	0-0	0-0	Nge2	Nge2	Rb1	Rb1(s)
	d6	Nge7	0-0	Nge7	Rb8	a5(t)
7	a3(a)	d3(e)	0-0	0-0(l)	Qa4(o)	e4
	Nge7	0-0	d6	0-0	Nd4(p)	d6
8	Rb1	a3(f)	d3(i)	d4	b4	d3
	a5	d5	Ne8	cxd4	b5	Nge7
9	d3	Bg5	Be3	Nxd4	cxb5	Nge2
	0-0	h6	Nd4	Nxd4	Nxb5	0-0
10	Bg5(b)	Bd2	Qd2	exd4	Nxb5	0-0
	f6	b6	Rb8	d5	Rxb5	Rb8
11	Be3	Rb1	Rb1	cxd5	Nf3	Nb5
	Be6	Bb7	Bg4	Nxd5	Bb7	b6(u)
12	Ne1	b4!?	f3	Nxd5(m)	Bb2	d4 ±
	Qd7(c)	cxb4(g)	Bd7(j)	exd5(n)	Bxb2(q)	

(a) 7 d3 Nge7 8 Ne1 Be6 9 Nc2 d5?! (9 . . . 0-0) 10 cxd5 Nxd5 11 Ne3! Nde7 (11 . . . Nxe3 12 Bxe3 Nd4? 13 Bxb7 +) 12 Nc4 ±, Youngworth–Shirazi, Pasadena 1983.

(b) (A) 10 Ne1 Be6 11 Nd5 (11 Nc2!? d5 12 cxd5 13 Ne3 resembles note a) Rb8 12 Nc2 b5 =. (B) 10 Bd2 Rb8 (10 . . . h6 11 Ne1 Be6 12 Nd5 Rb8 13 b4 ±) 11 Ne1 Be6 12 Nc2 d5 =, Evans–Karpov, San Antonio 1972.

(c) 13 Nc2 a4!? (13 . . . Rab8 14 b4 axb4 15 axb4 ±) 14 b3 axb3 with roughly equal chances, Andersson–Seirawan, Linares 1983.

(d) 5 . . . Nf6 is cols. 73–78. 5 . . . Nh6!?, 5 . . . Nh6!?, and 5 . . . a6 are playable alternatives.

(e) (A) 7 e3 is similar to col. 118. (B) 7 d4 (6 d4 was also possible) 7. . . Nxd4 8 Nxd4 cxd4 9 Nb5 Nf5 10 e4 dxe3 11 fxe3 0-0 12 Nd6 gives White enough for the pawn but no more, Denker–Browne, Florida 1981. (C) 7 e4!? 0-0 8 d3 d5 9 cxd5 exd5 10 h3 Be6 11 Bf4 ±, Romanishin–Hulak, Indonesia 1983.

(f) 8 Rb1 d5 9 Bg5 h6 10 cxd5 exd5 11 Bxe7 Nxe7 12 d4 cxd4 13 Nxd4 Nc6 14 Nxc6 bxc6 15 Qc2 Rb8 16 Rfd1 Qa5 17 e4 dxe4 18 Bxe4 Be6 =, Larsen–Tukmakov, Las Palmas 1982.

(g) 13 axb4 dxc4 14 dxc4 Rc8 15 c5 bxc5 16 bxc5 Na5 17 Nb5! (17 Na4 Bc6 18 Qc2 Nb7 $\mp$, Petrosian–Fischer, USSR vs. Rest of the World 1970, but without White's Bg5 and Black's h6) 17 . . . Rxc5 18 Qa4 a6 19 Bxa5 Qe8 20 Qa3 Rxb5 21 Rxb5 axb5 22 Bb4 with a strong bind, Larsen–Psakhis, Hastings 1987–88. In the column, for 6 d4 see col. 121, note (a–C).

(h) (A) 5 . . . e5 is plausible but seldom played. (B) 5 . . . e6 is not bad: 6 Nge2 Nge7 7 0-0 0-0 8 d3 d6 9 Rb1 a6 10 a3 Rb8 =, Bilek–Bednarski, Bath 1973.

(i) 8 a3 a5 9 Rb1 Ne8 10 d3 Nc7 11 Be3 Nd4 12 b4 axb4 13 axb4 b6 offers White little, Evans–Fischer, New York 1967.

(j) 13 b4 Nc7 14 f4 b6 15 h3 f5 16 Kh2 Bc6 =, Filip–Gligorić, Moscow 1956. Neither side can easily be budged.

(k) 5 . . . e5, as in col. 115, is playable here: 6 Nge2 Nge7 7 0-0 0-0 8 b3 d6 9 Bb2 Rb8 10 d3 a6 11 Qd2 b5 12 Rad1, although White is preferable, Lein–Polugaevsky, Tbilisi 1967.

(l) (A) 7 d4 cxd4 8 Nxd4 d5 (8 . . . Nxd4, attempting to transpose to the column, may be more reliable) 9 cxd5 Nxd5 10 Nxd5 Nxd4 11 Nc3 Nc6 12 Qxd8† Nxd8 13 Bd2 at least took the game out of symmetrical channels, Andersson–Miles, Tilburg 1981. (B) 7 Nf4 0-0 8 0-0 and now 8 . . . a6, 8 . . . b6, or 8 . . . d6 all lead to a playable game.

(m) 12 Qb3 is no better: 12 . . . Bxd4 (or 12 . . . Ne7) 13 Nxd5 exd5 14 Bh6 Bg7 15 Bxg7 Kxg7 16 Bxd5 a5! 17 Rac1 a4! 18 Qc3† Qf6 =, Andersson–Gheorghiu, Moscow 1981.

(n) 13 Qb3 Be6 14 Be3 Qd7 =.

(o) 7 b4 cxb4 8 axb4 b5 9 cxb5 axb5 =. See also col. 121, note (a).

(p) 7 . . . d6!? 8 b4 Bf5 9 Bxc6† bxc6 10 Qxc6† Bd7 11 Qxc6 (11 Qg2!?) Bxc3 12 dxc3 Nf6 $\overline{\overline{+}}$, Seirawan–Timman, Montpellier 1985.

(q) 13 Rxb2 Nf6 14 0-0 Qa8 15 Rc1 cxb4 16 Rxb4 0-0 =, Seirawan–Wl. Schmidt, Indonesia 1983.

(r) Of course Black has many other moves. Noteworthy is 5 . . . b6 6 Rb1 Bb7 7 b4 cxb4 8 axb4 Qc8 9 f3!? Nh6 10 Nh3 Nf3 11 Nf2 0-0 ∞, Seirawan–Adorjan, New York Open (playoff, 5-minute game) 1987.

(s) 6 b4? Nxb4! (6 . . . cxb4? 7 axb4 Nxb4 8 Ba3 with obvious compensation) 7 axb4 cxb4 8 d4 bxc3 9 e3 Ne7 $\overline{\overline{+}}$.

(t) 6 . . . Ng7 7 b4 d6 is another reasonable choice.

(u) 11 . . . d5?! 12 cxd5 exd5 13 Bf5 ± (Smejkal). The column is Smejkal–Andersson, Biel 1976.

ENGLISH OPENING

1 c4

	121	122	123	124	125	126
	(c5)....................g6........................b6..........Nc6(p)					
2	(Nc3)......b3 (Nc6)	Nf6(d)	e4.........g3 e5	Bg7	Nc3(n) e6	d4 e5
3	(g3) (g6)	Bb2 g6?!(e)	d4(h) Nf6	Bg2 e5	e4 Bb7	d5 Nce7
4	(Bg2) (Bg7)	Bxf6 exf6	Nf3 Bb4†(i)	Nc3 f5(k)	Nf3 Bb4	e4 Nf6
5	b3(a) Nf6(b)	Nc3 Bg7(f)	Bd2 Bxd2†	e3(l) d6	Qb3 Bxc3(o)	Nc3 Ng6
6	Bb2 0-0	g3 Nc6	Qxd2 Nxe4	Nge2 Nf6	Qxc3 Bxe4	Bd3 d6
7	d3 e6	Bg2 f5	Qe3 d5	0-0 0-0	Qxg7 Qf6	Nge2 ± (q)
8	Bxc6!? bxc6(c)	e3 0-0(g)	dxe5 Nc6(j)	b4!? c6(m)	Qxf6 Nxf6 ±	

(a) (A) 5 d3 may transpose to other columns, such as col. 73 or col. 116. Black must not fall asleep: 5 ... e6 6 Nh3 Nge7 7 Nf4 d6?! 8 Qd2 Rb8 9 b3 0-0 10 Bb2 Qa5 11 0-0, Larsen–Hartston, Hastings 1972–73; here White's formation is noticeably more aggressive than Black's. (B) 5 a3 a6 6 e3 Rb8 7 Nge2 h5 =. Seirawan–Ftáčnik, Thessaloniki 1988. (C) 5 Nf3 e6 6 d4 (for 6 0-0 see col. 116) and now (1) 6 ... cxd4 7 Nb5 d5 8 cxd5 Qa5† 9 Qd2 ± or (2) 6 ... Nxd4 7 Nxd4 cxd4 8 Ne4! Ne7 9 Nd6† ±, D. Gurevich–Dlugy, New York Open 1989.

(b) 5 ... e6 is also important: 6 Bb2 Nge7 7 Qc1!? d6 (7 ... d5 8 Nxd5) 8 f4 0-0 9 Ne4 e5 10 fxe5 Nxe5 11 Nf3 f5 12 Nf2 N7c6 13 Nxe5 dxe5 ∞ Hort–Gulko, Nikšić 1978.

(c) 9 Qd2 e5! (9 ... d6? 10 f4 ±, Larsen–Betancourt, Lanzarote 1976) 10 0-0-0 d6 11 Kb1 Qe7 12 f3 Be6 13 h4 h6 14 Nh3 Nd7, J. Watson–Browne, Los Angeles 1982.

(d) 2 ... Nc6 3 Bb2 e5 4 g3 d6 5 Bg2 g6 6 Nc3 Bg7 7 d3 is similar to col. 115. Also compare note (m) in col. 42.

(e) 3 ... Nc6 is safer: 4 Nf3 e6 5 e3 d5 6 cxd5 exd5 7 Be2 a6 8 d4 is similar to the Queen's Gambit Declined, Petrosian–Beliavsky, USSR Chp. 1973. Black can also play 3 ... b6 or 3 ... e6, aiming for a symmetrical setup.

(f) (A) 5 ... b6 6 e3 Bb7 7 Nge2 d5 8 cxd5 Bxd5 9 Nxd5 Qxd5 10 Nf4 (Watson) does not solve Black's problems. (B) 5 ... d6 6 g3 Nc6 7 Bg2 h5! 8 h4 Bh6 9 Nf3 Bg4 is at least more active than the text, Keene–Bellon, Cala Galdana 1974.

(g) 9 Nge2 a6 10 Rc1 b5 11 d3 ±, Karpov–Browne, San Antonio 1972.

(h) (A) 3 Nf3?! Bg7 4 d4 exd4 5 Nxd4 Nf6 6 Nc3 0-0 7 Be2 Re8 8 f3 c6! with no problems, Bobotsov–Adorjan, Vrnjačka Banja 1972. Black will play d7-d5 and be a tempo ahead of the King's Indian Defense because his d-pawn gets to d5 in only one move. (B) 3 Nc3 Bg7 4 g3 will transpose into col. 24 or col. 124. (C) In reply to 3 d4, if 3 . . . d6 4 Nf3 see Robatsch Defense, col. 10 (l)

(i) 4 . . . exd4!? 5 e5 Ne4 6 Qxd4 Nc5 7 Nc3 Nc6 8 Qe3 b6! 9 Nd5 Bg7 10 Kf6† Kf8 =, J. Watson–Martz, Vancouver 1976.

(j) 9 Na3! Bf5 10 Nc2 ±, with the strong threat of 0-0-0, Portisch–Sax, Rio de Janeiro 1979.

(k) 4 . . . Nc6 is the Closed Variation (cols. 19–24). 4 . . . Ne7 5 d3 c6 6 e4! makes Black's development awkward.

(l) 5 d4!? exd4 6 Nb5 Nc6 7 Nf3 Nf6 8 0-0 Ne4 9 Nbxd4 =, Benko–Petrosian, Curaçao 1962.

(m) 9 b5 Be6 10 Qa4 (or 10 Qb3) creates complications favoring White.

(n) For 2 d4 (which is more common), see Queen's Pawn Games.

(o) 5 . . . Na6 (A) 6 d3 f5! 7 exf5 Bxf3 8 gxf3 exf5 =. (B) 6 Be2 Ne7 7 0-0 0-0 8 d3 f5 9 e5 is interesting. The column is Smejkal–Miles, Reykjavik 1978.

(p) (A) 1 . . . e6 2 Nf3 d5 may lead to the Queen's Gambit Declined, to the Catalan, or to the Reti Opening. (B) 1 . . . c6 may transpose to note (a) of col. 61 or to the Reti Opening. An independent variation is 2 Nf3 d5 3 e3 Nf6 4 Nc3 e6 5 b3 Nbd7 6 Bb2 Be7 7 d4 with a kind of Queen's Gambit Declined, Korchnoi–Petrosian, match 1980. (C) 1 . . . g5!? (Basman's Defense) is not without merit. (D) 1 . . . f5 will usually transpose to a Dutch Defense, but a more "English" setup, restraining White's d-pawn, is also dangerous: 2 Nc3 e6 3 g3 Nf6 4 Bg2 c6 5 d3 Na6 6 a3 Be7 7 e3 0-0 8 Nge2 Nc7 9 0-0 d5 10 b3 Qe8?! (10 . . . e5) 11 Bb2 Qf7 12 Rc1 Bd7 13 e4! fxe4 14 dxe4 Rad8 15 e5 Nfe8 16 f4 ± dxc4 17 bxc4 Bc5† 18 Kh1 Be3 19 Rb1 g6?! 20 Qb3 Bc8 21 Ne4 Bb6 22 Rad1 Na6 23 Qc3 Rxd1 24 Rxd1 Nc5 25 Nd6 Qc7 26 Qc2 Ng7 27 g4! Qe7 28 Bd4 Qc7 29 a4 (threatening 30 a5) 29 . . . Na6 (29 . . . a5 30 Rb1) 30 c5 Ba5 31 Qb3 b6 32 Ne4 bxc5 (32 . . . Nxc5? 33 Bxc5 bxc5 34 Nf6† Kh8 35 Qh3 Ne8 36 Rd7!) 33 Nf6† Kh8 34 Qh3 Ne8 35 Ba1 Nxf6 36 exf6 Kg8 37 Be5 Qb7 38 Be4 Qf7 39 Ng1! Bd8 40 g5 Bb7 41 Nf3 Re8 42 Bd6 Bxf6 43 gxf6 Qxf6 44 Ng5 Qg7 45 Be5 Qe7 46 Bxg6 Resigns, Staunton–Horwitz, London 1851. (E) 1 . . . Nf6 2 Nf3 b6 results in a Queen's Indian Defense.

(q) This column arises also from the Queen's Knight Defense, col. 24: 1 d4 Nc6 2 c4 etc.

RETI OPENING

1 Nf3 d5 2 c4 (Incorporating the Barcza System, 1 Nf3 d5 2 g3)

Diagram 91

W HEN ALEKHINE LEGITIMIZED THE RETI OPENING in the 1920s, it included almost any game that began with White's moves Nf3 and c4. Reti popularized this sequence against all defenses, demonstrating the hypermodern strategies of flexible restraint of the center pawns and the fianchetto of both bishops. In recent years, the revival of the English Opening has brought about a reclassification of many variations. Following the usual practice, we now include under Reti's name only variations in which (1) Black plays d5 and (2) White plays c4, fianchettoes at least his king bishop, and does not transpose to a Catalan or Neo Grünfeld by playing an early d4.

White's setup lacks direct aggression and thus allows Black the choice of many comfortable defensive postures. Compared with the Slav Defense, the Orthodox Queen's Gambit Declined, and the Catalan, Black appears to have the best of two worlds: he easily develops his minor pieces, especially the queen bishop, and he need not pay the price of surrendering the center. White's initiative of the first move does not vanish, however, but takes subtler forms, with pressure and possibilities of expansion in all sectors of the board.

The highly critical *Benoni Reversed* (cols. 1–2) is Black's only method of injecting sharpness into this otherwise slow opening. White's extra tempo is a mixed blessing in some lines, such as the "normal" Benoni variation of note (d), in which Black easily equalizes by avoiding ... c5. The *Reti Accepted* (col. 3) seems too compliant, but offers opportunities for further exploration. It is also called the Reti Gambit Accepted. The *London System* (cols. 4–5), championed by Lasker, is a reliable defense. Black's development is easy, though the bishop on f5 bites on granite. The closely related system of Lasker's great rival Capablanca (col. 6) develops the bishop to g4, and Black must be prepared to exchange it for a knight. Black's kingside fianchetto (col. 7) is equally solid. White's gambit of col. 8 is sharp but hardly terrifying. The *Neo-Catalan* (cols. 9–10), or Reti Catalan, is often reached by transposition from the English. The notes to col. 9 show that by avoiding various hazards, Black's strong central phalanx may give the game a double-edged character.

In the BARCZA SYSTEM (cols. 11–12), White delays c4 so as to use it as a lever to pry open the queenside by exchanging pawns on d5. This is effective against ... Bf5 (col. 11), but ... Bg4 confounds this strategy, leaving White with nothing better than to transpose to Capablanca's system. The same initial moves also typify the King's Indian Attack but without Reti's c4 at all, and the same opening moves may also be found in col. 1 of the Miscellaneous Flank Openings.

RETI OPENING

1 Nf3 d5 2 c4

	1	2	3	4	5	6
	d4...................dxc4........c6					
3	b4 ....g3(d)		Na3	b3		
	f6(a)	g6(e)	c5(h)	Nf6(j)		
4	e3	b4	Nxc4	g3		
	e5	Bg7	Nc6	Bf5 (London System) ...Bg4		
5	Qb3(b)	d3	b3	Bg2(k)		Bg2(p)
	c5	e5	f6	e6		e6
6	bxc5	Bg2	Bb2	0-0		0-0
	Bxc5	Ne7	e5	Nbd7		Bd6
7	exd4	0-0	g3	Bb2		Bb2
	exd4	0-0	Nge7	Bd6........Be7(n)		0-0
8	Ba3	Nbd2	Bg2	d3(l)	d3	Na3!?(q)
	Qe7†	c6(f)	Nd5	0-0	h6	Nbd7
9	Be2	a4	0-0	Nbd2	Nbd2	d3
	Nc6(c)	Nd7(g)	Be7(i)	e5(m)	0-0(o)	a5(r)

(a) (A) 3 . . . c5!? (the move that 3 b4 was intended to prevent) 4 e3 (4 g3 is note e) 4 . . . dxe3 5 fxe3 cxb4 6 d4 g6 7 Bd3 Bg7 8 0-0 Ng6! 9 Nbd2 0-0 10 Qe2 Bf5! 11 Ne4 Nc6 ∓, Seirawan–Nikolić, Sarajevo 1987. (B) 3 . . . g6 4 e3?! (4 g3 is col. 2) 4 . . . e5! 5 Bb2 Bg7 =.

(b) (A) 5 exd4 e4! 6 Qe2 Qe7 7 Ng1 Nc6 ∓. (B) 5 Bb2 c5 6 exd4 cxd4 7 a3 (7 c5!?) 7 . . . Nh6 8 Bd3 a5 9 0-0!? axb4 10 Re1 Nc6 11 Be4 Nf7 12 Qe2 Bc5 13 Bd5 Kf8 14 d3, Kramer–Tartakower, 1937; White has a dangerous initiative for the pawn.

(c) 10 0-0 b6 11 Re1 Qd6 ∞, Napolitano–Balogh, corr. 1960–62. 7 Ba3!? is worthy of investigation.

(d) 3 e3 Nc6! (A) 4 b4?! dxe3 5 fxe3 Nxb4 6 d4 e5! ∓, Keres–Stahlberg, match 1938. (B) 4 exd4 Nxd4 5 Nxd4 Qxd4 6 Nc3 e5 7 d3 Ne7 (7 . . . Bc5 8 Qe2 ∞) 8 Be3 Qd8 9 d4 exd4 10 Qxd4 Qxd4 11 Bxd4 Nc6 12 Be3 Bb4 =, Langeweg–Hort, Amsterdam 1976.

(e) (A) 3 . . . c5 4 b4 (4 Bg2 Nc6 5 d3 e5, see King's Indian Attack) 4 . . . cxb4 5 Bg2 Nc6 6 0-0 e5 7 d3 Nf6 8 a3 a5 ∓. The position is a Benko Gambit. The colors are reversed, but White is not a tempo ahead because Black's e-pawn has only moved once. (B) 3 . . . Nc6 4 Bg2 e5 5 0-0 Nf6 6 d3 Nd7 (6 . . . Be7 7 b4!; 6 . . . a5!?) 7 e3 Be7 8 Na3 0-0 ∞.

(f) 8 . . . a5 9 b5 c5 10 bxc6 Nexc6 11 Ba3 Nb4 12 Qb3 N8a6 13 Bxb4 axb4 14 a3 bxa3 15 Qxa3 ±, Larsen–Chandler, Hastings 1987–88.

(g) 10 Nb3 Qc7 11 Ba3 Rb8 12 Qc2 Re8 13 Nfd2 Nf6 14 b5 ±, Korchnoi–Pachman, Buenos Aires 1960.

(h) (A) 3 . . . e5?! 4 Nxe5 Bxa3 5 Qa4† (5 bxa3 Qd4) b5 6 Qxa3 Bb7 7 e3 Qd6 8 Qxd6 cxd6 9 Nf3 Nc6? (9 . . . a6 ±) 10 b3 d5 11 bxc4 dxc4 12 a4 ±, Tartakower–Spielmann,

675

Moscow 1925. (B) 3 . . . Nf6 4 Nxc4 e6 5 g3 b6 6 Bg2 Bg7 7 0-0 Be7 8 d3 0-0 9 a3 c5 10 Bd2 Nc6 11 Rb1 ±, Andersson–Radulov, Nice 1974.

(i) 10 Nh4! 0-0 11 Qb1! Rf7 12 Nf5 with pressure on the kingside, Botvinnik–Fine, Nottingham 1936.

(j) For 3 . . . dxc4 4 bxc4 e5 see note (o).

(k) 5 Ba3!? g6 6 d3 Bg7 7 Nbd2 Qb6?! (7 . . . 0-0 ±) 8 Bg2 Ng4 9 d4! ±, Petrosian–Tal, Curaçao 1962.

(l) 8 d4 transposes into a type of Queen's Pawn game, e.g. 8 . . . 0-0 9 Nc3 h6 10 Nd2 planning 11 e4.

(m) 10 cxd5 cxd5 (A) 11 Rc1 Qe7 12 Rc2 a5 13 a4 h6 14 Qa1 Rfe8 15 Rfc1 Bh7 ($\overline{\mp}$) 16 Nf1 Nc5 17 Rxc5 Bxc5 18 Nxe5 Rac8 19 Ne3 Qe6 20 h3!? Bd6? (20 . . . b6) 21 Rxc8 Rxc8 22 Nf3? (22 N5g4! Nxg4 23 hxg4 ±) 22 . . . Be7 23 Nd4 Qd7 24 Kh2? h5 25 Qh1 h4 26 Nxd5 hxg3† 27 fxg3 Nxd5 28 Bxd5 Bf6 29 Bxb7 Rc5 30 Ba6 Bg6 31 Qb7 Qd8 32 b4 (32 e3 Bxd4 33 Bxd4 Rc2† 34 Kh1 Qd6) 32 . . . Rc7 33 Qb6 Rd7 34 Qxd8† Rxd8 35 e3 (35 Nc6 Rd6 36 Bxf6 Rxc6) 35 . . . axb4 36 Kg2 Bxd4 37 exd4 Bf5 38 Bb7 Be6 39 Kf3 Bb3 40 Bc6 Rd6 41 Bb5 Rf6† 42 Ke3 Re6† 43 Kf4 Re2 44 Bc1 Rc2 45 Be3 Bd5 46 Resigns, Reti–Lasker, New York 1924. Notes based on Alekhine's. (B) 11 e4! dxe4 (11 . . . Bg4 12 exd5 Nxd5 13 Nc4 is strong) 12 Nxe4 Bxe4 13 dxe4 Qe7 (13 . . . Nxe4 14 Nh4 Ndf6 15 Qe2 with strong pressure) 14 Qe2 Rfd8 15 Rfd1 a5 16 Nd2 followed by Nc4 and Ne3 with a comfortable advantage, Ribli–Lengyel, Hungarian Chp. 1975.

(n) 7 . . . Bc5 provokes 8 d4 Be7 9 Nc3 0-0 10 Nd2 as in note (k).

(o) 10 a3 a5 11 Rc1 Bh7 12 Rc2 Bd6 (or 12 . . . Ne8 13 Qa1 Bf6 14 Ne5, Andersson–Chekhov, Banja Luka 1976) 13 Qa1 Qe7 14 Bb3 e5 15 cxd5 cxd5 16 Nh4 =, Stein–Platonov, USSR Chp. 1971.

(p) 5 Ne5 Bh5 6 Bg2 e6 7 Bb2 Be7 8 0-0 Nbd7 9 Nxd7 Qxd7 10 d3 0-0 11 Nd2 Qc7 12 Rc1 Rfd8 =, Reti–Capablanca, Moscow 1925.

(q) (A) 8 d4 Nbd7 9 Nbd2 Qe7 10 a3 a5 11 Re1 Rfd8 12 e4 dxe4 13 Nxe4 Nxe4 14 Rxe4 Nf6 15 Re3 Qc7 16 Qe1 c5 17 d5!? with a pull, Ribli–Campora, Lucerne 1982. (B) 8 d3 Nbd7 9 Nd2 e5 10 cxd5 cxd5 11 h3 Bxf3 12 Bxf3 Re8 =, Larsen–Gligorić, Bugojno 1984.

(r) 10 Nc2 a4 11 b4 Bxf3 12 Bxf3 dxc4 13 dxc4 Be5 14 Bxe5 Nxe5 15 Ne3, Larsen–Timman, Brussels 1987; White was able to organize some pressure against Black's queenside.

RETI OPENING

1 Nf3 d5

	7	8	9	10	11	12 ✓
2	(c4)	....			g3 (Barcza System)	
	(c6)	....	e6 (Neo-Catalan)		Nf6	........Bg4
3	(b3)........g3		g3		Bg2	Bg2
	(Nf6)	Nf6(d)	Nf6		Bf5	c6
4	(g3)	Bg2	Bg2		c4	c4
	g6(a)	dxc4	Be7........dxc4		c6(q)	e6(t)
5	Bb2	0-0(e)	0-0	Qa4†(m)	cxd5	cxd5
	Bg7	Nbd7(f)	0-0	Nbd7(n)	cxd5	Bxf3(u)
6	Bg2	Na3	b3	Qxc4	Qb3	Bxf3
	0-0	Nb6	c5(h)	c5	Qc8(r)	cxd5
7	0-0	Qc2	Bb2(i)	0-0	Nc3	Nc3
	Bg4(b)	Qd5	Nc6	a6(o)	e6	Nf6
8	d3	Nh4	e3	Qb3	d3	0-0
	Bxf3	Qe6	b6(j)	Bd6	Nc6	Nc6
9	Bxf3	e4	Nc3(k)	a4	Bf4	d3
	Nbd7(c)	g6(g)	Bb7(l)	0-0(p)	Be7(s)	Be7 =

(a) (A) 4 . . . Qb6!? 5 Bg2 e5 6 0-0 e4 7 Ne1 h5 ∞, Larsen–Korchnoi, Brussels 1987. (B) 4 . . . dxc4!? 5 bxc4 e5 6 Bb2 e4 7 Nd4 Bc5 8 Nb3 Bb6 =, Markland–Keene, England 1973.

(b) 7 . . . Nbd7 8 d3 (8 d4 is a Neo-Grünfeld) Re8 9 Nbd2 e5 10 cxd5 Nxd5 11 Nc4 Qc7 12 Qd2 b5 13 Ne3 Nxe3 14 Qxe3 Bb7 =, Kostich–Spielmann, Bled 1931.

(c) 10 Nd2 e6 with a solid position, Larsen–Uhlmann, match 1971.

(d) 3 . . . dxc4 4 Bg2 b5? (4 . . . Nf6 is the column) 5 a4 Bb7 6 b3 cxb3 7 Qxb3 a6 8 axb5 axb5 (8 . . . cxb5? 9 Ne5 wins) 9 Rxa8 Bxa8 10 Ne5 e6 11 Na3 ±, Schmidt–Schaufelberger, Switzerland 1970.

(e) 5 Na3 b5 6 Ne5 (A) 6 . . . Nd5 7 d3 cxd3 8 Qxd3 e6 9 e4 Qa5† 10 Bd2 Nb4 11 Qe2 (11 Qf3 Qc7 12 Bf4 Bd6 13 Nxf7 Bxf4 14 Nxh8 Be5 ∞) 11 . . . Qc7 12 Nf3 Be7 13 0-0 0-0 ∞, Portisch–Donner, Bled 1961. (B) 6 . . . Qc7! 7 d4 Bb7 8 0-0 e6 9 b3 c3 ∓. M. Tseitlin–Sveshnikov, USSR 1975.

(f) Sharpest is 5 . . . b5 6 a4 Bb7 7 b3 cxb3 8 Qxb3 a6 9 Ba3 Nbd7 10 Nc3 Qb6 11 d4 e6 12 Bxf8 Kxf8 (Plaskett–I. Ivanov, Brighton 1983) when White's most aggressive continuation is 13 Qa3†! Kg8 (13 . . . b4 14 a5 bxa3 15 axb6 ±) 14 Qd6 ∞ (Plaskett).

(g) (A) 10 b3 Bg7 11 Bb2 cxb3 12 axb3 0-0 =, Salov–Beliavsky, USSR Chp. 1987. (B) 10 Re1 Nfd7 11 b3 Bg7 12 Bb2 Bxb2 13 Qxb2 0-0 14 bxc4 Ne5 15 d4 Nexc4 16 Nxc4 Nxc4 17 Qc3 Nd6 =, Salov–Torre, Leningrad 1987.

(h) 6 . . . b6 7 Bb2 Bb7 8 e3 Nbd7 9 Nc3 and now: (A) 9 . . . c5 10 d3 Qc7 11 Nc3 Rac8 12 Rac1 Qb8 13 Rfd1 Rfd8 14 e4 dxe4 15 dxe4 ±, Malich–Kholmov, Tbilisi 1969. (B) 9 . . . Ne4 10 Ne2 a5 11 d3 Bf6 12 Qc2 Bxb2 13 Qxb2 Nd6 14 cxd5 Bxd5 15 d4 ±, Kasparov–Karpov, World Chp. 1987.

(i) 7 cxd5 exd5 8 Bb2 d4 9 Na3 Nc6 10 e3 Bg4 11 b3 Bf5 12 exd4 cxd4 13 Re1 Qd7 14 Nc4 Be4 15 d3 Bxf3 16 Qxf3 Bb4 ∞, Larsen–Tal, Nikšić 1983.

(j) 8 . . . d4 9 exd4 cxd4 10 Re1 Re8 11 d3 Bc5 12 a3 a5 13 Nbd2 e5 (13 . . . h6 may equalize) 14 Ng5 Bg4 15 Bf3!? Bxf3 16 Qxf3 h6 17 Nge4 ±, Miles–Geller, Lone Pine 1980. White set up a strong blockade and kingside attack by h4, h5, and g4.

(k) 9 Qe2 Bb7 10 Rd1 Qc7 11 Nc3 Rad8 12 cxd5 exd5 with chances for both sides, but if 12 . . . Nxd5?! 13 Nxd5 Rxd5 14 d4! cxd4 15 Nxd4 Nxd4 16 Bxd4 White is better, Vaganian–Karpov, 39th USSR Chp. 1971.

(l) (A) 10 d3 dxc4 11 bxc4 a6 (11 . . . Nb4 12 Qb3!) 12 Qc2 Qc7 13 Rab1 Rab8 14 Ba1 Na7 15 Rfc1 Rfc8 =, Vaganian–Tal, Erevan 1980. (B) 10 cxd5! Nxd5 (10 . . . exd5 11 d4 ±) 11 Nxd5 Qxd5 (11 . . . exd5!) 12 d4 Qd8 13 dxc5 Bxc5 14 Ne5 Qc7 15 Nd7 Bd4 16 exd4 Qxd7 17 d5 exd5 18 Qxd5 Qxd5 19 Bxd5 with pressure, Adorjan–de Firmian, Stara Pazova 1983.

(m) 5 Na3?! Bxa3 6 bxa3 b5 7 Rb1 a6 8 a4 Bb7! 9 axb5 Be4! ∓, Smyslov–Sveshnikov, USSR Chp. 1976.

(n) (A) 5 . . . Bd7 6 Qxa4 Bc6 7 0-0 Nbd7 (7 . . . Bd5 8 Qc2 and 9 Nc3 ±) 8 Qc2 e5 9 Nc3 Bc5 10 d3 0-0 11 e4 Re8 12 Be3 Qe7 13 Rac1 ±, Smyslov–Suetin, USSR Chp. 1952. (B) 5 . . . Qd7 6 Qxc4 Qc6 7 b3 ±.

(o) 7 . . . b5! is tactically sound: 8 Nd4?! Ne5 9 Nc6 Nxc4 10 Nxd8 Nd5 11 Nc3 Kxd8 12 Nxd5 Bb7 13 Nxb6 Bxg2 14 Nxc4 Bxf1 with advantage, Taimanov–Sveshnikov, Wijk aan Zee 1981. To avoid this, White might try 7 Qb3.

(p) 10 Na3 ±, Miles–Timman, Tilburg 1985.

(q) (A) 4 . . . dxc4 5 Na3 Be6!? 6 Ng5 Bd5 7 e4 Bc6 ∞, Dizdar–Korchnoi, Sarajevo 1984; 6 Qc2 is better. (B) 4 . . . e6 5 Qb3 Na6! 6 cxd5 exd5 7 Nd4 Bc8 8 Nc3 c6 9 0-0 Bc5 10 Nf3 0-0 =, Romanishin–Polugaevsky, USSR 1980.

(r) 6 . . . Qb6 7 Qxb6 axb6 8 Nc3 e6 9 d3 Nc6 10 Nb5 Bb4† 11 Bd2 Ke7 12 Nfd4 Bxd2† 13 Kxd2 Bg6 14 f4 ±, Portisch–Smyslov, Wijk aan Zee 1974.

(s) 10 0-0-0-0 11 Rac1 (A) 11 . . . a6?! 12 Ne5 Nd7 13 Nxc6 bxc6 14 e4 dxe4 15 dxe4 ±. (B) 11 . . . Qd7 12 e4 dxe4 13 dxe4 Nxe4 14 Nxe4 Bxe4 15 Ne5 Nxe5 16 Bxe4 Nc6 17 Rfd1 Qc8 18 Qa4 ±, Barcza–Smyslov, Moscow 1956. (C) 11 . . . Bg6 12 Ne5 Nd7 13 Nxg6 hxg6 14 h4! Nc5 15 Qd1 Qd8 16 d4 Nd7 17 e4 Nb6 18 e5 and Black is in difficulties, Korchnoi–Karpov, match 1974.

(t) 4 . . . Nf6 5 cxd5 cxd5 (5 . . . Bxf3 is similar to the column) 6 Ne5!? Bc8 7 0-0 e6 8 Nc3 Be7 9 d4 0-0 10 Bf4 ±, Smyslov–Darga, Amsterdam 1964.

(u) 5 . . . exd5 (5 . . . cxd5? 6 Qa4†) 6 0-0 Nf6 7 d3 Nbd7 8 h3 Bxf3 9 Bxf3 Bc5 =. The column is Larsen–Ivkov, Bled 1965.

KING'S INDIAN ATTACK

1 Nf3, 2 g3, 3 Bg2, 4 0-0, 5 d3, 6 Nbd2, 7 e4

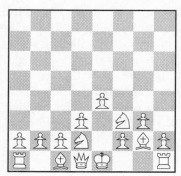

Diagram 92

T HE KING'S INDIAN ATTACK is not, strictly speaking, an opening, but a path for White to follow that leads to different openings depending on Black's play. The diagram depicts White's basic structure. Because White's formation is rather passive, like Black's in the King's Indian Defense, his opponent cannot prevent him from setting it up. For the same reason, however, White should not expect to retain the initiative of the first move. The King's Indian Attack as we know it is a creature of modern times. In the United States it was popularized by Evans and Fischer. The rise of the Sicilian Defense has brought the King's Indian Attack to prominence, for White can force transposition to the King's Indian Attack with 2 Nf3, 3 d3, 4 Nbd2, 5 g3, etc., avoiding the fearsome Sicilian. The French Defense may be likewise avoided with 2 d3, 3 Nd2, etc.

When Black plays . . . d5 and . . . c5, the opening becomes a genuine King's Indian Defense with colors reversed. Curiously, the sharpest and most popular variations of this type (cols. 1 and 10) correspond to obscure side variations of the King's Indian Defense. The King's Indian Attack includes not only the *King's Indian Reversed*, but also reversed-color variations of the English Opening and the Pirc Defense, and lines that are not reversed forms of anything at all. Column 1 is the most double-edged and difficult variation, and can be considered the main line (to the extent that there is one). Black's queenside attack balances White's on the kingside, but both players must walk a tightrope. Some of the other lines, especially columns 4, 6, 7, and 10, are best interpreted as attempts by Black to steer the game away from this problematical struggle. By contrast, columns 2 and 3 are placid lines related to the Reti Opening and the Barcza System, where they are dealt with in conjunction with Reti's c4 (see also Grünfeld Reversed). In columns 4 and 10, Black develops his knight to e7, a safer if less active square than f6. White's pawn push to e5 loses some of its effect. In columns 5 and 9, Black occupies the center, following White's play in popular variations of the King's Indian Defense. This aggressive strategy can backfire, but Black should hold his own.

Black can follow a middle course, neutralizing or preventing the advance of White's king pawn without overextending his own center. The resulting openings are complex but give Black chances that are in no way inferior. The blockade of col. 6 gives Black a satisfactory game despite the loss of a tempo. If White transposes to the King's Indian Attack from the French Defense, he must reckon with this variation. Col. 7 shows an interesting subtlety that is available when Black holds back his queen pawn. Cols. 8 and 11 are related to the English Opening (with colors reversed), while col. 12 is a Pirc Defense with colors reversed.

KING'S INDIAN ATTACK

1 Nf3 d5

	1	2	3	4	5	6
2	g3 .... d3					
	Nf6	c6		c5(j)		Nf6
3	Bg2	Bg2		Bg2		Nbd2
	c5(a)	Bf5 .... Bg4		Nc6		e6
4	0-0	0-0	0-0(g)	0-0(k)		e4(r)
	Nc6	Nf6	Nf6	e6 .... e5		Nc6
5	d3	d3	d3	d3	d3(n)	g3
	e6(b)	e6	e6	Bd6	Be7(o)	dxe4
6	Nbd2	Nbd2(e)	Qe1(h)	Nbd2	e4	dxe4
	Be7	h6	Nbd7	Nge7	d4(p)	e5
7	e4	Qe1	e4	e4	Nbd2	Bg2
	0-0(c)	Bh7	dxe4	0-0	Nf6	Bc5
8	e5	e4	dxe4	Nh4(l)	Nc4	0-0
	Nd7(d)	Be7(f)	e5(i)	f5(m)	Nd7(q)	0-0(s)

(a) An interesting but seldom-seen plan is 3 ... b6 4 0-0 Bb7 5 d3 e6 6 Nbd2 Nbd7 (6 ... Nc6 and 7 ... Be7 transposes to note c) 7 Re1 Bc5!?, Portisch–Karpov, Moscow 1977.

(b) (A) 5 ... e5 is col. 5. (B) 5 ... g6 is col. 9. (C) 5 ... Bf5 and (D) 5 ... Bg4 are playable, but are not so safe as cols. 2 and 3.

(c) 7 ... Qc7 8 Re1 b6 9 e5 Nd7 10 Qe2 Bb7 11 c4!? (too slow is 11 c3 0-0-0 12 d4 h6! 13 h4 Rdg8!) 11 ... dxc4 12 Nxc4 b5 13 Nd6! Bxd6 14 exd6 Qxd6 15 Bf4 Qe7 16 d4 with a promising attack, Schlenker–Lovass, Kecskemet 1986.

(d) 9 Re1 b5 (9 ... Qc7 10 Qe2 is an important alternative) 10 Nf1 a5 11 Bf4 b4 12 Ne3 Ba6 13 h4 a4 14 a3! (Fischer's move) Bb5! =, Damjanović–Uhlmann, Monaco 1968. Powerful attacks are shaping up on opposite wings.

(e) 6 b3 Be7 7 Bb2 0-0 8 Nbd2 h6 and now: (A) 9 e3 a5 10 a3 Bh7 11 Qe2 Qb6!? ∞, Haugli–Tisdall, Gausdal 1983. (B) 9 Qe1 Bh7 10 e4 c5 11 Ne5 Nc6?! 12 Nxc6 bxc6 13 Qe2 ±, Smejkal–Ivanchuk, New York Open 1988.

(f) 9 e5 Nfd7 10 Qe2 c5! 11 Re1 Nc6 12 Nf1 g5 13 h3 Qc7 14 a3 0-0-0 with equal chances, Vaganian–Beliavsky, USSR 1983.

(g) 4 b3 Nd7 5 Bb2 Ngf6 6 0-0 e6 7 d3 Bc5 8 Nbd2 0-0 9 e4 dxe4 10 dxe4 e5 11 h3 Bxf3 12 Qxf3 Qe7 13 Rad1 b5 =, Ribli–Tal, Montpellier 1985. 13 Nc4 planning 14 Ne3 should give White a small edge.

(h) 6 Nbd2 Nbd7 7 h3 Bxf3 8 Nxf3 Be7 (8 ... dxe4 9 dxe4 e5 is similar to the column) 9 e3 0-0 10 Qe2 a5 11 e4 a4 12 e5 Ne8 13 a3 b5 14 d4 ±, Portisch–Hort, Lugano 1968.

(i) 9 Nbd2 Bc5 10 Nc4 Qe7 11 Ne3 h5!? 12 a3 0-0-0 =, Korchnoi–Flear, Lugano 1986.

(j) Moves such as 2 ... Nd7 and 2 ... g6 usually transpose to other columns. 2 ... Nc6 allows a Queen's Pawn opening after 3 d4, or transposes to a Pirc Reversed after 3 Bg2 e5 4 d3.

(k) 4 d4 is a Grünfeld Defense Reversed (col. 1 of Miscellaneous Flank Openings).

(l) 8 Re1 Bc7 9 c3 a5 10 a4 b6 11 exd5 exd5 12 Nb1!? (12 d4 Bg4 =) 12 . . . Bg4 13 Na3 d4 14 Nb5 dxc3 15 bxc3 Rc8 $\pm$, Vaganian–Sokolov, Minsk 1986.

(m) 9 f4 Bc7 10 c3 Kh8 11 exf5 Nxf5! =. Less committal alternatives for Black are: (A) 8 . . . b6 9 f4 dxe4 (9 . . . f6) 10 dxe4 Ba6 11 Re1 c4 12 c3 Na5? (12 . . . Rc8) 13 e5 Bc5† 14 Kh1 Nd5 15 Ne4 Bb7 16 Qh5 $\pm$, Fischer–Ivkov, Santa Monica 1966. (B) 8 . . . Qc7 9 f4 f6 10 c3 Bd7 11 Qh5 Be8 12 Qe2 Bf7 ∞, Rigo–Sax, Hungarian Chp. 1976.

(n) 5 c4 d4 6 d3 Bd6 7 e3 Ng7 8 exd4 cxd4 9 b3 0-0 10 Ba3 Rb8 11 Bxd6 Qxd6 12 a3 b5 $\overline{\mp}$, Keffer–Kavalek, Las Vegas 1984. The position resembles a Benoni Defense with colors reversed. 9 a3 or 9 Na3 may be better. 8 e4 transposes to note (o).

(o) 5 . . . Bd6 (or 5 . . . f6) 6 e4 d4 7 Nbd2 Nge7 8 c4 f6 9 Nh4 Be6 10 f4 exf4?! 11 gxf4 Qc7 12 e5! fxe5 13 f5 Bf7 14 Ne4 0-0-0 15 Qg4 $\pm$, Botvinnik–Pomar, Varna 1962.

(p) (A) 6 . . . dxe4 7 dxe4 Qxd1 8 Rxd1 Bg4 9 c3 $\pm$, Larsen–Kraidman, Manila 1974. White often avoids this exchange with 6 Nbd2. (B) 6 . . . Nf6 7 Nbd2 0-0 8 c3 Re8 9 exd5 Nxd5 10 Re1 Bf8 11 Nc4 Qc7 12 Ng5 Rd8 13 Qe2 Nb6 14 Qe4 g6 15 Qh4 $\pm$, Planinc–Rubinetti, Nice 1974; White has made good use of his extra tempo.

(q) 9 a4 0-0 10 Bh3 (10 c3) 10 . . . Qc7 11 Nfd2 Nb6 12 Bxc3 Qxc8!? 13 f4 exf4! 14 gxf4 f5! with a comfortable position, Rizzitano–Dlugy, New York 1983.

(r) This position is most often reached from the French Defense: 1 e4 e6 2 d3 d5 3 Nd2 Nf6 4 Ngf3 Nc6. In that variation, 4 . . . Nc6 is a handy alternative to 4 . . . c5, which tranposes into col. 1 of the King's Indian Reversed.

(s) (A) 9 c3 a5! 10 Qc2 Be6 11 Ng5 Bd7 =, Csom–Fuchs, Berlin 1968. (B) 9 Qe2 a5 10 Nc4 (10 a4? b6 $\overline{\mp}$) 10 . . . Qe7 11 c3 or 11 Ne3 is Hort's recommendation.

KING'S INDIAN ATTACK

1 Nf3

	7	8	9	10	11	12
	c5				Nf6	g6
2	g3				g3	g3
	Nc6				g6	Bg7
3	Bg2				Bg2	Bg2
	e6	g6			Bg7	e5
4	0-0	0-0			0-0	d3
	Nf6	Bg7			0-0	d5
5	d3	d3			d3	0-0
	Be7	d6	Nf6	e6	d6(k)	Ne7
6	e4	d3	e4	e4	e4	c3
	0-0	e5	d5	Nge7	c5(l)	Nc6
7	Nbd2(a)	c3	Nbd2	Re1	Nbd2	e4
	d6	Nge7	0-0	d5(h)	Nc6	0-0
8	c3(b)	a3(d)	c3(f)	Nbd2(i)	a4	Nbd2
	e5(c)	0-0(e)	d4?!(g)	b6(j)	Rb8(m)	b6(n)

(a) 7 Nc3 d5! and White's queen-knight is misplaced compared with col. 1.

(b) 8 Re1 Qc7 9 Nf1 Rb8 = .

(c) 9 Nc4 h6 with equal chances.

(d) 8 Nbd2 0-0 9 a4 h6 10 Nc4 Be6 11 Qe2 Qc7, Saidy–Evans, US Chp. 1968.

(e) 9 b4 h6 10 Nbd2 Be6 11 Rb1 Qd7 12 Bb2 b5 13 Re1 (Andersson–Gheorghiu, Orense 1975): now 13 . . . cxb4 14 axb4 a5 is equal.

(f) 8 exd5 Nxd5 9 Nc4 e5 10 Re1 Re8 11 a4 h6 12 c3 $\pm$; White has pressure on the queenside and center.

(g) 9 cxd4 cxd4 10 a4 e5 11 Nc4 Ne1 12 b4! $\pm$, Plachetka–Přibyl, USSR 1974. White's last move establishes ownership of the queenside. 8 . . . e5 transposing into note (h) is more enterprising.

(h) 7 . . . d6 8 c3 0-0 (8 . . . e5 is more testing) 9 d4 cxd4 10 cxd4 d5 11 e5 Bd7 12 Nc3 $\pm$, Fischer–Panno, Buenos Aires 1970; Black has no compensation for White's large advantage in territory.

(i) 8 e5!? h6 9 h4 Qc7 10 Qe2 Nd4?! 11 Nxd4 cxd4 12 c3 Nc6 13 Bf4 g5 14 Qg4 Nxe5 15 Bxe5 Bxe5 16 cxd4 Bf6 17 hxg5 hxg5 18 Bxd5 wins, Glueck–Damjanović, Philadelphia 1987. 10 . . . b6! is calmer. Compare note (l) (A).

(j) (A) 9 e5?! Ba6 10 Nf1 Qc7 11 Bf4 h6 12 h4 g5! 13 hxg5 hxg5 14 Bxg5 Ng6 $\mp$. (B) 9 c3 h6?! (9 . . . 0-0) 10 e5 Qd7 11 d4 cxd4 12 cxd4 Ba6 13 a3 g5 14 Nf1 Nf5 15 g4! Nge7 16 Ng3 $\pm$, Yurtaev–Dolmatov, USSR 1983. (C) Another plan for White is illustrated by 8 . . . h6 9 h4 b6 10 c3 a5 11 a4 Ba6 12 exd5 exd5 13 Nb3 0-0 14 d4 c4 15 Nbd2 Bc8 16 Nf1 Be6 17 Bf4 Qd7 18 b3 cxb3 19 Qxb3 $\pm$, Benjamin–Eingorn, Saint John 1988.

683

(k) 5 . . . d5 may transpose to col. 9 or, after 6 Nbd2 Nc6!? 7 e4 e5 8 exd5 Nxd5, to col. 12.

(l) (A) 6 . . . e5 7 Nbd2 Nbd7 8 a4 a5 9 Nc4 Nc5 10 Be3 Ne6 11 Nbd2 planning 12 f4 is better for White (Evans). But not 11 h3?! b6 12 Qd2 Ba6 13 b3 Nh5 $\mp$, Filip–Petrosian, Amsterdam 1956.

(m) 9 Re1 b6 10 Nc4 Bb7 11 h4 Qc7 12 Bd2 Rbd8 13 Qc1 d5 14 Bf4!? Qc8 15 exd5 Nxd5 16 Bh6 $\pm$, Larsen–Gligorić, Vinkovči 1970.

(n) 9 Re1 Bb7 10 exd5 Nxd5 11 Nc4 Re8 12 Qb3 Qd7 13 Bd2 Rad8 =, Benjamin–Bisguier, Lone Pine 1981. The position is a Pirc Defense with colors reversed.

MISCELLANEOUS FLANK OPENINGS

O F THE OPENINGS IN THIS CHAPTER, some are quite important but others have no more than surprise value. Bird's Opening, formerly found here, now has its own chapter, but in compensation a new section of openings formerly classified under the Reti Opening has been added.

THE GRÜNFELD REVERSED

1 Nf3 d5 2 g3 c5 3 Bg2 Nc6 4 d4 (col. 1).

Black must take this into account if he wishes to play aggressively against the King's Indian Attack. Aside from the transposition into the Catalan, a reliable method of meeting White's central pressure is hard to find. (For the first three moves see also Reti Opening, cols. 11–12, and King's Indian Attack, cols. 1–5).

Diagram 93

THE NIMZOWITSCH ATTACK

1 Nf3 d5 2 b3 (cols. 2–5)—see diagram.

This is related to Bird's and Larsen's openings, and transpositions among the three are common. Using hypermodern restraint of his center pawns (cols. 2–3), White may create subtle pressure on Black's center as in the Reti Opening. Col. 4 shows that this strategy should not be allowed to degenerate to careless neglect of the center.

THE POLISH DEFENSE DEFERRED

1 Nf3 Nf6 2 g3 b5 (col. 6).

This defense was revived by Spassky in his 1966 World Championship match with Petrosian. Black avoids transposition to the English, and has little to fear from White's King's Indian Attack setup (note q). White's attack on the loosened queenside is critical. Also see Queen's Pawn Games for the same defense after 1 d4.

THE LISITSIN GAMBIT

1 Nf3 f5 2 e4 (col. 7).

This is a lively way for White to avoid transposing to a Dutch Defense. Black is probably required to return the pawn immediately, but this does not solve his problems. Lisitsin employed the gambit against Botvinnik in Leningrad 1934.

THE KING'S FIANCHETTO OPENING

    1 g3 (cols. 8–12)

    This can, and usually does, transpose to almost any other opening in which White fianchettoes the king bishop. This section gives only variations in which the move order beginning with 1 g3 is the most natural or the most common. Col. 8 is a Pirc, while col. 9 is a Pirc Reversed, related to col. 12 of the King's Indian Attack. Col. 10 is an irregular Queen's Pawn Game, and col. 11 is an Indo-Sicilian Defense—neither a Closed Sicilian nor a King's Indian Attack, but related to both. Col. 12 is akin to the Panno Variation of the King's Indian Defense, with colors reversed.

Diagram 94

LARSEN'S OPENING

    1 b3 (cols. 13–18)

    This opening was championed by the Rev. Owen in the nineteenth century, by Nimzowitsch in the 1920s, and in the modern era by Larsen and Ljubojević. Some variations, particularly the classical occupation of the center by Black (cols. 13–14), lead to exciting, double-edged positions. But Black has powerful equalizing methods in other lines. In many King's Indian-like positions, Black can take advantage of the unprotected state of White's queen bishop (col. 16), while against the double fianchetto, he can make that bishop an awkward bystander by placing pawns on c5, d6, and e5 (col. 17). Unless these defenses are undermined, Larsen's Opening will not gain the respect accorded the classical openings.

MISCELLANEOUS FLANK OPENINGS

1 Nf3

	1	2	3	4	5	6
	d5 ....Nf6					
2	g3	c4	b3		b3(l)	g3
	c5	e6	Bg4........c5		b6	b5
3	Bg2	b3	Bb2	Bb2?!(j)	Bb2	Bg2(o)
	Nc6	Nf6	Nf6	f6!	Bb7	Bb7
4	d4	Bb2	e3	c4	e3	0-0(p)
	Nf6(a)	Be7	e6	d4	e6	e6
5	0-0	e3(e)	h3	d3	c4(m)	c3(q)
	Bg4(b)	0-0	Bh5(h)	e5	c5	c5
6	dxc5(c)	Be2(f)	d3	e3	Nc3(n)	d3(r)
	e5	c5	Nbd7(i)	Ne7	Nc6	Be7
7	c4	0-0	Nbd2	Be2	d4	Qb3
	Bxc5	Nc6	c6	Nec6	cxd4	Qb6
8	cxd5	cxd5	Be2	Nbd2	Nxd4	a4
	Qxd5(d)	Nxd5(g)	a5 =	Be7 ∓(k)	Qb8 =	bxa4(s)

(a) 4 ... e6 5 0-0 cxd4 6 Nxd4 Bc5 7 Nb3 Bb6 8 c4 Nge7 9 cxd5 Nxd5 10 Nc3! Nxc3 11 Qxd8† Nxd8 12 bxc3 Bd7 13 c4 Bc6 14 Ba3 Bxg2 15 Kxg2 Nc6 16 Rfd1 ±, Speelman–Mestel, Hastings 1979–80. White's lead in development persists to the endgame.

(b) (A) 5 ... e6 6 c4 dxc4 is a Catalan, while 6 ... Be7 may transpose to an English Opening or into a Queen's Gambit Declined, Tarrasch Defense. (B) 5 ... Bf5 6 c4 dxc4 7 Qa4 Nd7 8 dxc5 e6 9 Qxc4 Bx5 10 Nc3 Rc8 11 Rd1 Nb4?! (11 ... Qe7 ∞) 12 Be3! ±, Dzindzichashvili–Ljubojević, Thessaloniki 1984.

(c) 6 Ne5 cxd4 7 Nxg4 Nxg4 8 e3 Nf6 9 exd4 e6 10 Be3 Be7 =, Ribli–Kapengut, Kecskemet 1972.

(d) 9 Nc3 Qxd1 10 Rxd1 h6 11 Na4 Be7 12 Be3 e4 13 Nd4 Nxd4 14 Rxd4 Bxe2 15 Nc3 Bf3 16 Nxe4 Bxg2 17 Kxg2 ±, Petrosian–Sosonko, Las Palmas 1980.

(e) 5 g3 is a Reti Opening (see col. 9 of that chapter).

(f) 6 Nc3 c5 7 cxd5 Nxd5 8 Nxd5 Qxd5 9 Bc4 Qd8 and now: (A) 10 0-0 Nc6 11 Qe2 Bf6 12 Bxf6 Qxf6 13 Rac1 b6 14 Bb5 Ne5 =, Botvinnik–Levenfish, match 1937. (B) 10 Ne5 Nd7 11 0-0 Nxe5 12 Bxe5 Bf6 13 d4 cxd4 14 exd4 Bd7 15 Qh5 Bc6 =, Smyslov–Trifunović, Zagreb 1955.

(g) 9 a3 (9 Nc3 Bf6 10 Rc1 Ndb4 ∓) 9 ... Qc7 10 Nc3 Nxc3 11 Bxc3 e5 12 Qb1! a5 13 Qe4! Bf6 14 h4! with the initiative, Dzindzichashvili–Beliavsky, Thessaloniki 1984.

(h) 5 ... Bxf3 6 Qxf3 Nbd7 7 g3!? Bd6 8 Bg2 0-0 9 0-0 b5 10 Qe2 c6 with equal chances, Karlsson–Sunye, Las Palmas 1982.

(i) 6 ... c5 is not bad: 7 g4 Bg6 8 Ne5 Nbd7 9 Nxg6 hxg6 10 Bg2 Qb6 ∞, Korchnoi–Mecking, match 1974. The column is Dzindzichashvili–Alburt, US Chp. 1983.

(j) 3 e3 may transpose into a Bird's Opening after 3 . . . Nf6 (also 3 . . . a6 4 a4—4 c4 d4!—4 . . . Nc6 =) 4 Bb2 Nc6 (or 4 . . . g6) 5 Bb5! Bd7 6 0-0 e6 7 d3 Be7 8 Bxc6! Bxc6 9 Ne5 Rc8 10 Nbd2 0-0 11 f4 $\pm$.

(k) 9 0-0 0-0 10 e4 a6 11 Ne1 b5 $\mp$, Petrosian–Fischer, match 1971. 6 g3 is a slight improvement.

(l) A related and important line is 2 g3 g6 3 Bg2 Bg7 4 b3 c5 5 Bb2 d5 6 c4 d4 7 b4 0-0 8 0-0 Nfd7! 9 d3 e5 10 Nbd2 Na6 $\mp$, Wirthensohn–Gheorghiu, Vraca 1975. Also see Larsen's Opening, col. 17, note (o-B). 2 c4 is the English Opening.

(m) 5 Be2 c5 6 d3 d5 7 Nbd2 Be7 8 Ne5 0-0 9 0-0 Re8?! 10 f4! Bf8?! 11 Qe1 a5 12 g4 a4 13 Rc1 axb3 14 axb3 Ra2 15 Ba1 Na6 16 g5 Nd7 17 Bh5 Nxe5 18 Bxe5 Nb4 19 Qh4 Nxc2 20 Rf3 Nxe3 21 Rxe3 Rxd2 22 Rh3 c4 23 Bf6! Bc5† 24 Kf1 Bf2 25 Bxf7† Kf8 26 Qxh7 gxf6 27 Bg6 Resigns, W. Stanley Davis–Fedorowicz, U.S. Open 1980.

(n) 6 Be2 Be7 7 0-0 0-0 8 d4 d5 9 dxc5 Bxc5 10 Nbd2 Nc6 11 cxd5 Qxd5 =, Petrosian–Saidy, San Antonio 1972. The column is Korchnoi–Karpov, Brussels 1986.

(o) 3 a4 b4 4 d3 Bb7 5 e4 d6 6 Bg2 Nbd7 7 0-0 e6 8 a5 Rb8 9 Nbd2 Be7 10 Nc4 0-0 =, Petrosian–Spassky, World Chp. 1966.

(p) 4 Na3!? a6 5 c4 b4 6 Nc2 c5 with: (A) 7 0-0 e6 8 b3 Be7 9 Bb2 0-0 10 d4 d6 11 Ne3 Nbd7 ∞, Larsen–Ljubojević, 1972. (B) 7 d4 cxd4 (7 . . . e6 8 d5! exd5 9 Nh4 $\pm$) 8 0-0 e6 9 Nxcd4 Be7 10 Bf4 0-0 11 Rc1 ($\pm$) Qb6 12 Nb3 Rc8?! 13 c5! $\pm$, Vaganian–P. Popović, Sarajevo 1987.

(q) 5 d3 Be7 (5 . . . d5 6 Nbd2 Be7 7 e4 0-0 8 Re1 c5 transposes to the King's Indian Attack, col. 1) 6 e4 0-0 7 Nd4?! a6 8 Nb3 Nc6 9 e5 Nd5 10 Re1 d6 11 d4 a5 $\mp$, Bilek–Portisch, Hungary 1985.

(r) 6 Qb3 Bc6?! (6 . . . Qb6) 7 d3 d6 8 Bg5 Be7 9 Nfd2 Bxg2 10 Kxg2 a6 11 Bxf6 Bxf6 12 a4 $\pm$, Gutman–Grünfeld, Beersheba 1985.

(s) 9 Qxa4 0-0 10 Nbd2 d5 11 Ne5 $\pm$, Gutman–Gallagher, England 1985.

MISCELLANEOUS FLANK
OPENINGS

	7	8	9	10	11	12
1	(Nf3) ......g3 (King's Fianchetto Opening)					
	f5	Nf6.........e5 ....c5 ....g6				
2	e4!?(a)	Bg2	d3	Bg2		Bg2
	fxe4	g6	d5	Nc6		Bg7
3	Ng5	e4	Bg2	Nf3.........e4		Nc3
	Nf6(b)	d6	Nf6	g6	g6	c5(o)
4	d3	d4	Nf3	c3	d3	d3
	e3(c)	Bg7	Nc6	Bg7	Bg7	Nc6
5	Bxe3	Ne2	0-0(f)	d4	f4	Nf3
	Nc6	0-0	Be7	cxd4	d6(l)	e6
6	d4	0-0	c3(g)	cxd4	Nf3	0-0
	e5	e5(d)	0-0(h)	d5	Nf6(m)	d5
7	d5	Nbc3	Qc2	Nc3	0-0	a3
	Ne7	c6	Bf5	e6	0-0	Nge7
8	Bd3	a4	Nbd2	0-0(j)	c3	Rb1
	d6 ∞	Nbd7(e)	Qd7(i)	Nge7(k)	Rb8(n)	0-0(p)

(a) The Lisitsin Gambit. For (A) 2 d4, see the Dutch Defense. (B) 2 b3 Nf6 3 c4 b6: (1) 4 g3 Bb7 5 Bg2 e6 6 Nc3 Bb4 7 Bb2 0-0 8 0-0 Bxc3 9 Bxc3 d6 10 d3 Qe8 11 e3 Nbd7 (11 ... Qh5 12 Ne1) 12 b4 Qe7 13 a4 ±, Korchnoi–Spassky, match 1977–78; (2) 4 e3 Bb7 5 Be2 e6 6 Bb2 Bd6 7 0-0 0-0 8 d3 Nc6 with equal chances, Andersson–Larsen, match 1975. Compare English Opening, col. 126, note (p) (D).

(b) 3 ... d5 4 d3 Qd6!? 5 Nc3 (5 dxe4 h6) 5 ... h6 6 Nb5 Qc6 (6 ... Qb4† 7 c3 Qxb5 8 Qh5† Kd7 9 Qg4† Kd8 10 Nf7† Ke8 11 Qg6 +) 7 dxe4! hxg5 8 exd5 Qb6 9 Be3 c5 10 d6! exd6 11 Bc4 with a strong attack (Christiansen).

(c) 4 ... exd3? 5 Bxd3 g6 6 f4 ± is Bird's Opening, col. 6, note (m) (B). The column is Pachman–Clemens, Hamburg 1980.

(d) 6 ... Nbd7 7 Nbc3 c6 8 a4 a5 9 b3 Re8 10 Ba3 Qc7 11 Qd2 e5 12 Rad1 exd4 13 Nxd4 Nc5 14 f3 ±, Benko–Tal, Candidates 1962.

(e) 9 a5! exd4 10 Nxd4 Nc5 11 h3 Re8 12 Re1 Nfd7 13 Be3 Qc7 14 f4 ±, Benko–Fischer, Curaçao 1962; safer is 8 ... a5 as in note (d). The opening has transposed to a type of Pirc Defense.

(f) 5 a3!? Be7 6 b4 e4 7 Nfd2 e3 8 fxe3 Ng4 9 Nf3 Bf6 10 d4 h5 ∞, Suttles–Miles, Vancouver 1981.

(g) 6 c4 0-0 7 cxd5 Nxd5 8 Nbd2 (8 Nc3 is an English Opening, Four Knights' Variation) 8 ... Be6 9 a3 a5 10 Nc4 f6 11 Bd2 a4 12 Rc1 Qd7 13 e4 Nb6 14 Nxb6 cxb6 15 Be3 ±, Bilek–Portisch, Budapest 1986.

(h) Black chooses not to prevent 7 b4. Also 6 . . . a5 is possible: 7 a4 0-0 8 Nbd2 Re8 9 e4 Bf8 10 Qb3 $\pm$.

(i) 9 e4 Bh3 10 Re1 Bxg2 11 Kxg2 Rfe8 12 b4 a6 $\pm$, Dzindzichashvili–Ljubojević, Tilburg 1985.

(j) 8 Bf4 Nge7 9 Qd2 Nf5 10 Nb5 0-0 11 g4 Nge7 12 h3 Bd7 13 0-0 a6 =, Miles–Sosonko, Tilburg 1981.

(k) 9 Bf4 0-0 10 Qd2 Nf5 11 e3 f6 12 h4 h6 13 g4 Nd6 14 g5! $\pm$, Dzindzichashvili–Browne, New York 1984.

(l) 5 . . . e6 (A) 6 Nd2 Nge7 7 Nh3! d5 8 0-0 0-0 9 e5 with a small plus, Petrosian–Pachman, Moscow 1967. (B) 6 Nh3 Nge7 7 Nf2 f5 8 Nd2 Rb8 9 g4 d5 10 0-0 0-0 =, Lombardy–Mednis, New York 1968.

(m) 6 . . . e6 7 0-0 Nge7 8 c3 e5 9 Nbd2 $\pm$, DeFotis–Reshevsky, US Chp. 1972.

(n) Compare also Sicilian Defense, f4 attack. After the text follows (A) 9 Qe2 Ne8 10 Be3 Nc7 11 d4 cxd4 12 cxd4 Bg4 13 Rd1 d5 14 e5 Qd7 15 Nc3 $\pm$, Korchnoi–Karpov, match 1978. (B) 9 Na3 b5 10 Nc2 b4 11 c4 e5 12 f5 b3!? 13 Ne3 Nd4 ∞, Speelman–Alburt, match 1986.

(o) 3 . . . e5 4 d3 Nc6 5 f4 d6 6 Nf3 Nge7 7 0-0 0-0 8 e4 h6 9 Be3 Nd4 10 Qd2 Kh7 is equal, Larsen–Panno, Palma de Mallorca 1969.

(p) 9 Bd2 Rb8 10 b4 cxb4 11 axb4 b5 12 e4 a5 =, Larsen–Mecking, Palma de Mallorca 1969.

MISCELLANEOUS FLANK OPENINGS

Larsen's Opening

1 b3

	13	14	15	16	17	18
1	e5..Nf6........b6(q)					
2	Bb2				Bb2	Bb2
	Nc6			d6(k)	g6	Bb7
3	c4.........e3			e3(l)	e4(o)	f4
	Nf6	d5.........Nf6		Nf6(m)	d6	e6(r)
4	e3(a)	Bb5	Bb5(i)	c4	g3	e3
	Be7(b)	Bd6(e)	d6	g6	Bg7	Nf6
5	a3	Nf3(f)	Nf3(j)	Nf3	Bg2	Nf3
	0-0	Bg4(g)	Bd7	Nc6	0-0	c5(s)
6	Qc2(c)	h3	0-0	d4	Ne2	Bd3!?
	d5	Bxf3	Be7	Bg7	e5	Nc6
7	cxd5	Qxf3	Be2	dxe5	0-0	0-0
	Nxd5	Nge7	0-0	Nd7(n)	c5	Qc7
8	Nf3	d4	c4 =	Nc3	d3	Nc3
	Bf6(d)	0-0(h)		dxe5 ∞	Nc6(p)	a6(t)

(a) 4 Nf3?! e4 5 Nd4 Bc5 6 Nxc6 dxc6 7 e3 Bf5 $\mp$, Larsen–Spassky, USSR vs. Rest of the World, 1970.

(b) 4 . . . d5!? 5 cxd5 Nxd5 6 a3 Bd6! 7 Qc2 0-0 8 Nf3 Qe7 9 Bd3!? Kh8 produced an unclear position, Petrosian–Balashov, USSR 1978.

(c) 6 d3 d5 7 cxd5 Qxd5 8 Nc3 Qd6 9 Nf3 Bf5 10 Qc2 Rfd8 11 Rd1 h6 12 h3 Qe6 13 Nd2 Nd7 with equal chances, Fischer–Tukmakov, Buenos Aires 1970.

(d) 9 d3 g6 10 Nbd2 Bg7 11 Rc1 g5 =, Petrosian–Sosonko, Tilburg 1981.

(e) 4 . . . f6 5 d4! e4 6 Ne2 a6 7 Bxc6† bxc6 8 c4 f5, Larsen–Balinas, Manila 1975. The position resembles a French Defense, Winawer variation, with colors reversed. Keene's 9 Qc2 and 10 Ba3 (instead of 10 Nbc3 as played) gives White a strong game.

(f) 5 f4!? Qh4† 6 g3 Qe7 7 Nf3 Bg4 8 h3 Bxf3 9 Qxf3 Nf6 10 Nc3 0-0! 11 0-0 (11 Nxd5? Nxd5 12 Qxd5 Nb4) 11 . . . e4 12 Qf2 a6 =, Barczay–Hardicsay, Budapest 1978.

(g) 5 . . . Qe7 6 c4 Nf6 7 c5 Bxc5 8 Nxe5 $\pm$.

(h) 9 cxd5 Nb4 10 Qd1 Nbxd5 with chances for both sides, Frederick–Sisniega, Syosset 1984.

(i) 4 c4 d6 5 Nf3 g6 transposes into col. 16.

(j) 5 Ne2 Bd7 6 0-0 a6! 7 Bxc6 Bxc6 8 d4 Qe7 9 c4 g6 is equal, Bellon–S. Garcia, Palma de Mallorca 1971. The column is Larsen–Andersson, Teesside 1972.

(k) 2 . . . f6?! (the Löwenthal Variation) 3 e4! (3 e3 d6 4 c4 Be6 5 Nc3 Nc6 6 Nf3 Nh6 7 Be2 Ne7 8 0-0 Qd7 9 d4 ±, Owen–Skipworth, match 1873, is also good) 3 . . . Bc5 4 Bc4 Ne7 5 Nf3 planning d4 is very strong (Keene).

(l) 3 g3 Nf6 4 Bg2 g6 5 c4 Bg7 6 Nc3 0-0 7 d3 c6! 8 e4 Be6 9 Nf3 d5! =, Ribli–Beliavsky, Las Palmas 1974. If 10 Nxe5?? d4! 11 Ne2 Qa5† +.

(m) (A) 3 . . . f6 is note (j). (B) 3 . . . g6 and (C) 3 . . . f5 are also playable.

(n) 7 . . . Ng4 8 Nc3 Ngxe5 9 Nxe5 Bxe5 10 Be2 0-0 11 Qd2 Be6 12 0-0 Qe7 13 f4 Bg7 14 Bf3 f5 15 Nd5 ±, Timman–Padevsky, Amsterdam 1972. The column is Ljubojević–Savon, Wijk aan Zee 1972.

(o) (A) 3 g4!? Bg7 4 g5 Nh5 5 Bxg7 Nxg7 6 Qc1 0-0 is unclear, Kholmov–Oplachkin, Kirgiz 1966. (B) 3 Nf3 Bg7 4 g3 0-0 (4 . . . d6 might be better) 5 Bg2 d6 6 d4 e5 7 dxe5 Ng4 8 h3 Nxe5 9 Nxe5 dxe5?! 10 Qxd8 Rxd8 11 Nd2 and 12 0-0-0 ±, Smyslov–Polugaevsky, Palma de Mallorca 1970. (C) Moves such as 3 c4, 3 d4, 3 f4, and 3 g3 can transpose to other variations or other openings.

(p) 9 a4 d5 10 Nd2 d4 11 h3 ±, Bellon–Tarjan, Örense 1975.

(q) (A) 1 . . . c5 2 c4, see English Opening, cols. 121–122. (B) 1 . . . d5 may transpose into the Nimzowitsch Attack, cols. 2–5, or to Bird's Opening.

(r) (A) 3 . . . f5 4 e3 Nf6 (4 . . . e6 5 Qh5† g6 6 Qh3 Nf6 8 Be2 Bg7 8 Bf3 ±, Soltis) 5 Bxf6! exf6 6 Nf3 Be7 7 Nc3 g6 8 h3! planning an eventual g4 with advantage, Larsen–Colón, San Juan 1969. (B) 3 . . . Nf6 4 e3 g6 5 Nf3 Bg7 6 Be2 c5 7 0-0 0-0 8 a4 Nc6 9 Na3 d5 =, Ljubojević–Keene, Örense 1975.

(s) 5 . . . Be7 6 Be2 0-0 7 0-0 a5 8 Nc3 Na6 with an equal game, Nurmi–Speelman, Mexico 1978.

(t) 9 a3 d5 10 Ne2 b5 11 Bxf6!? gxf6 ∞, Larsen–Wade, Hastings 1972–73.

BIRD'S OPENING

1 f4

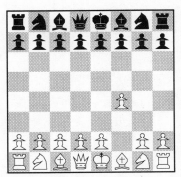

Diagram 95

THE ENGLISH MASTER H. E. Bird demonstrated the aggressive potential of this opening in the second half of the nineteenth century. Tartakower revived it, Nimzowitsch won several beautiful games with it in the 1920s, and in modern times Larsen and Soltis have attempted to popularize it. But Bird's Opening has never attracted a large following; White's strategy of dark-square control is too monothematic for consistent success.

Against 1 . . . d5, White may play a Dutch Defense with colors reversed (col. 3, note f, and col. 4), but these setups offer little more than equality. Instead, White will usually fianchetto his queen bishop and blockade on the a1-h8 diagonal while attacking Black's center with the c-pawn. This strategy is relatively effective against routine development (col. 1), and Black's sacrifice of the minor exchange (col. 2) does not solve all his problems. In col. 3, Black meets hypermodern with hypermodern, neutralizing White's fianchetto with his own.

Black may play *From's Gambit* (1 . . . e5), obtaining strong pressure against White's weakened king's field, especially in conjunction with the unorthodox but brutal 4 . . . g5. Col. 5 is a heavily analyzed countersacrifice of White's knight. In col. 6 White simply tries to hold the pawn, with unclear results.

BIRD'S OPENING

1 f4

	1	2	3	4	5	6
	d5 ....e5(m)					
2	Nf3				fxe5	
	Nf6				d6	
3	e3................................g3				exd6	
	c5 ....Bg4.........g6			c5(j)	Bxd6	
4	b3	h3(c)	b3(f)	Bg2	Nf3	
	Nc6(a)	Bxf3	Bg7	Nc6	g5(n)	
5	Bb5	Qxf3	Bb2	0-0	d4 ....g3	
	Bd7	Nbd7	0-0	g6	g4	g4
6	Bb2	Nc3	Be2	d3	Ng5(o)	Nh4
	e6	e6(d)	c5(g)	Bg7	f5(p)	Ne7
7	0-0	g4	0-0	c3(k)	e4	d4
	Be7	Bb4	Nc6(h)	0-0	h6	Ng6
8	d3	g5	Ne5	Qc2	e5	Nxg6(r)
	0-0(b)	Bxc3(e)	Qc7(i)	d4(l)	Be7(q)	hxg6(s)

(a) (A) 4 ... a6!? 5 Bb2 e6 6 Be2 Be7 7 0-0 Nc6 8 Ne5 Qc7 9 d3 (9 Bf3 0-0?! 10 Nxc6! Qxc6 11 c4! ±, Soltis) 9 ... 0-0 10 Nd2 Nd7 11 Ndf3 f6 12 Nxc6 Qxc6 13 Qe1 b5 =, Bird–Tarrasch, Manchester 1890. (B) 4 ... e6 5 Bb2 Be7 6 Ne5! Nbd7 7 Qf3 0-0 8 Bd3 Nxe5 9 fxe5 Ne8 10 0-0 with pressure on the kingside.

(b) 9 Bxc6 Bxc6 10 Ne5 Rc8 11 Nd2 Nd7 12 Qg4! Nxe5 13 Bxe5 Bf6 14 Rf3 Bxe5 (14 ... Qe7 15 Raf1 a5 16 Rg3 Bxe5 17 fxe5 f5 18 exf6 Rxf6 19 Qxg7†! ±, Fischer–Mecking, Palma de Mallorca 1970) 15 fxe5 Qc7 16 Qh5 h6?! (16 ... Be8 17 Rh3 h6 18 Nf3 f5 ±—Nimzowitsch) 17 Raf1 g6 18 Qxh6 Qxe5 19 Rf6 ±, Nimzowitsch–Spielmann, New York 1927.

(c) 4 Be2 Bxf3! 5 Bxf3 Nbd7 6 c4 e6 7 cxd5 exd5 8 Nc3 c6 9 0-0 Be7 10 d3 Nb6 11 e4 dxe4 12 dxe4 Bc5† =, Tartakower–Grünfeld, Vienna 1917.

(d) On 6 ... c6!? 7 d4 e6 8 g4 c5 9 g5 Ng8 10 dxc5 Bxc5 11 Bd3 and 12 e4 is promising (Soltis).

(e) 9 bxc3 Ne4 10 d3! Nd6 11 c4 c6 and now 12 e4?! is premature (Nimzowitsch–Kmoch, Kecskemét 1927) but 12 Be2 gives White a pull.

(f) "Dutch Defense Reversed" variations include: (A) 4 d4 Bg7 5 Bd3 0-0 6 Nbd2 c5 7 c3 b6 8 Qe2 Bb7 9 0-0 Ne4 (Tartakower–Teichmann, Teplice Šanov 1922) 10 c4!? Nxc2 11 Bxd2 dxc4 12 Bxc4 cxd4 ∞. (B) 4 Be2 Bg7 5 0-0 0-0 6 d3 c5 7 Qe1 Nc6 8 c3 Re8 9 Qg3 e5! =.

(g) 6 ... b6 7 0-0 Bb7 8 Ne5 Nbd7 9 Bf3 Nxe5 10 fxe5 Nd7 11 d4 f6 is unclear.

(h) 7 ... b6 8 a4 Nc6 9 Ne5 Bb7 10 Bf3 Rc8 11 d3 Nd7 12 d4 ±, Larsen–Keene, Palma de Mallorca 1971.

(i) 9 Nc3 a6 10 Nxc6 Qxc6 11 Bf3 $\pm$, Pirc–Golombek, Bognor Regis 1956.

(j) 3 . . . e6 4 Bg2 Bc5!? 5 e3 Nbd7 6 b3 b6 7 Bb2 Bb7 8 Qe2 Qe7 is roughly equal, Kan–Leverett, Hong Kong 1981.

(k) (A) 7 Nc3 d4 8 Na4 Nbd7 9 c4 Qc7 10 b4 Rd8 =, Horvath–Farago, Hungarian Chp. 1976. (B) 7 Qe1 and (C) 7 e3 are other tries.

(l) (A) 9 e4?! dxe3 10 Bxe3 Bf5 $\mp$. Compared with the Dutch Defense, White's extra move (Qc2) is a liability. (B) 9 Na3 Nd5 10 Bd2 Bf5 11 Nc4 Re8 12 a4 Qd7 =, Gerzadowicz–Eckert, corr. 1985–87.

(m) Moves such as 1 . . . c5, 1 . . . Nf6, 1 . . . g6, and 1 . . . d6 may transpose to the Closed Sicilian, Pirc Defense, or King's Fianchetto. Uniquely "Bird" lines are: (A) 1 . . . c5 2 Nf3 g6 3 e3 Bg7 4 c4!? Nf6 5 Nc3 0-0 6 g3 (6 b3? d5 $\mp$) 6 . . . Nc6 7 Bg2 d6 ∞. (B) 1 . . . f5 2 e4! (2 Nf3 Nf6 3 e3 e6 4 Be2 Be7 5 0-0 0-0 6 b3 d6 =, Kolisch–Anderssen, London 1861) fxe4 3 d3 e3 (3 . . . exd3 4 Bxd3 Nf6 5 Nf3 e6 6 Ng5! g6 7 h4 with a strong attack, Bird–Gelbfuss, Vienna 1873) 4 Bxe3 Nf6 5 d4 e6 6 Bd3 Nc6 7 a3 Ne7 8 Nh3 b6 9 0-0 Bb7 10 Nd2 g6 11 Bf2 Bg7 12 c3 0-0 13 Qe2 a5 14 g4 $\pm$, Pelikan–Alekhine, Poděbrady 1936. White has all the play. A "Bird Deferred" might arise after Larsen's 1 b3; e.g. 1 . . . b6 (or . . . d6, or . . . c5) 2 f4.

(n) 4 . . . Nf6 (A) 5 g3 h5?! (5 . . . Nc6 6 Bg2 Bg4 7 d3 0-0 8 0-0 $\pm$) 6 d4 h4 7 gxh4! Ne4 8 Qd3 Bf5 9 Bh3! Bg6 10 Rg1 Qe7 11 Rxg6! fxg6 12 Nc3 $\pm$, Tartakower–Prins, Zandvoort 1936. (B) 5 d4 Ng4 6 Qd3 c5 7 Nc3 cxd4 8 Qxd4 0-0 9 Bg5 $\pm$, Heemsoth–Röthgen, corr. 1961–62.

(o) 6 Ne5 Bxe5 7 dxe5 Qxd1† 8 Kxd1 Nc6 =.

(p) 6 . . . Qe7 7 Qd3 f5 8 h3 Nc6 (8 . . . g3 9 Nc3! Nf6 10 e4!, Soltis) 9 hxg4 Nf6 10 c3 Ne4 11 Nxe4 fxe4 12 Qe3 Bxg4 13 Nd2 Bf5 14 Nc4 $\pm$, Röthgen–Cording, corr. 1961–62.

(q) 9 Nh3 gxh3 10 Qh5† Kf8 11 Bc4 Rh7! (11 . . . Qe8 12 Qxh3 Qg6 13 0-0 Nc6 14 c3 with good compensation) when 12 Be3 is unclear, but not 12 Qg6? Bb4†! 13 Ke2 (13 c3 Qh4†) 13 . . . Rg7 14 Bxh6 Nxh6 15 Qxh6 Qg5 $\pm$. Black can also try 8 . . . Bxe5 9 dxe5 Qxd1† 10 Kxd1 hxg5 11 Bxg5 Rh5 (11 . . . Be6 12 Nc3) 12 h4 gxh3 13 Bf4 $\pm$ (Soltis).

(r) 8 Ng2 Nc6 9 c3 h5 10 e4 h4 11 e5 Be7 (11 . . . hxg3!?, Schwarz) 12 Rg1 hxg3 13 hxg3 Rh2 =, Larsen–Zuidema, Beverwijk 1964.

(s) 9 Qd3 Nc6 10 c3 Bf5 11 e4 Qe7 12 Bg2 0-0-0 13 0-0?! (13 Bf4 is better) 13 . . . Ne5! 14 Qd1 Nf3† 15 Bxf3 gxf3 16 Qxf3 Rxh2! +, Antoshin–Panchenko, Leningrad–Moscow 1983.

UNUSUAL FLANK OPENINGS

THE REASONS FOR DEPARTURE from orthodox lines have been dealt with in the remarks to the Unusual King's Pawn Defenses. White has even more opportunities than Black to "take the opponent out of the book." Thus these openings have received attention from analysts such as Benjamin, Harding, Kapitaniak, Myers, Soltis, and others.

Diagram 96

Grob's Attack, 1 g4 (cols. 1–2), also called the "Spike" (note c), was described in MCO-12 as reaching for originality but failing to be effective (see diagram). It owed its reputation to countless postal games successfully conducted by Henri Grob with readers of his Swiss newspaper column. While the force of the attack is still unproved, it has gained respectability through its use by Britain's Basman and Greece's Skembris.

Diagram 97

The Queen's Knight Attack, 1 Nc3 (cols. 3–4), allows transposition to the Vienna Game (after 1 . . . e5 2 e4), or into several fianchetto or Queen's Pawn games (see diagram). Both players are wise to remain alert to such possibilities.

Diagram 98

The Sokolsky Opening, 1 b4 (cols. 5–6), also called the "Polish Attack," underwent its baptism in the game Tartakower–Maróczy, New York 1924, and was thoroughly scrutinized by the Russian Sokolsky in 1963 (see diagram). Tartakower jestingly named it the *Orangutan*. It has unexpected ramifications and is at times chosen by players seeking tactics outside the norm. Again, postal players often utilize this debut. If the move b4 is deferred, it might transpose to or from some of the Indian defenses. The move 2 . . . f6 (col. 5) aims at creating an early blockage of the fianchetto but leaves Black restricted. 1 . . . c6 (col. 6) creates counterpressure on the queen's wing; 2 . . . e6 (col. 7) is Black's most flexible response.

UNUSUAL FLANK OPENINGS

	Grob's Attack		Queen's Knight Attack		Sokolsky Opening	
	1	2	3	4	5	6
1	g4		Nc3		b4(p)	
	d5(a)		d5 . . . . c5(l)		e5 . . . . Nf6(w)	
2	Bg2 . . . . h3		e4(i)	Nf3(m)	Bb2(q)	Bb2(x)
	c6(b)	e5	dxe4(j)	Nc6	f6(r)	e6!
3	h3(c)	Bg2	Nxe4	d4	e4(s)	b5
	h5	c6(f)	e5	cxd4	Bxb4	b6
4	g5	d4	Nf3	Nxd4	Bc4	e3
	h4(d)	e4	Nf6	g6	Nc6(t)	Bb7
5	e4	c4	Nc3	Be3(n)	f4(u)	Nf3
	dxe4	Bd6(g)	Bg5	Bg7	Qe7	Be7
6	Nc3	Nc3	Be2	Nxc6	f5	Be2
	Qa5	Ne7	Nc6	bxc6	g6	0-0
7	Ne4	Bg5	d3	Bd4	Nc3	0-0
	Bf5(e)	f6(h)	Bb4(k)	Nf6(o)	Bxc3(v)	d5!(y)

(a) Or 1 . . . e5 2 h3, transposing to col. 2, but not 2 Bg2 h5! 3 gxh5 Qg5! 4 Bf3 Qh4! 5 Nc3 Nf6 6 e4 Bc5 7 d4 Bxd4 8 Qe2 Bxc3† 9 bxc3 Nxh5 ∓, Skembris–Mariotti, Budapest 1983.

(b) 2 . . . e5 3 c4 c6 4 cxd5 cxd5 5 Qb3 Ne7 6 Nc3 Nbc6 7 h3 Nd4 8 Qd1 a6 9 e3 Ndc6 10 d4 ± (Grob).

(c) (A) 3 e4 dxe4 4 Nc3 Nf6 5 h3 ?! (Skembris). (B) 3 c4 dxc4 4 b3 cxb3 5 Qxb3 e5 6 Nc3 Qb6 ∓. (C) 3 g5 (The "Spike") 3 . . . h6! 4 h4 hxg5 5 hxg5 Rxh1 6 Bxh1 Qd6 7 Nf3 Bg4 8 d3 e5 ∓.

(d) 4 . . . e5 5 d4 e4 6 Nc3 ∞.

(e) 8 Nc3 e6 9 Be4 Nd7 10 Qe2 Bb4 11 Bxf5 Qxf5 12 Ne4 0-0-0 13 a3! Bf8 14 d3 Kb8 15 Bd2 Ne7 16 Nf3 Ng6 17 0-0-0 Nb6 18 Nc3 Bc5 19 Rdg1 Nd5 20 Rg4 Bb6 (Skembris–Gheorghiu, Skopje 1984) 21 Kb1 ±.

(f) 3 . . . Nc6 4 dxc4 (4 d3!?) 4 . . . dxc4 5 Qa4 Nge7 6 Nf3 Ng6 7 Nc3 (7 Qxc4 ±) 7 . . . Be6 8 h4 Nf4 = (Harding).

(g) 5 . . . Na6 6 Nc3 Nc7 7 f3 f5 8 cxd5 cxd5 9 Qb3 Bd6 10 Kf1 Ne7 11 g5 Rb8 12 h4 b5 13 Na3 Bd7 =, Basman–King, British Chp. 1984.

(h) 8 Bd2 0-0 9 Qb3 Kh8 10 Rc1 Na6 11 e3 f5 12 Nge2 Nb4 13 Nxe4 Nxa2! ∓, Basman–Kudrin, Manchester 1981.

(i) (A) 2 d4 Nf6 3 Bg5 see Richter–Veresov Attack. (B) 2 e3 e5 becomes a Van't Kruijs. (C) 2 Nf3 c5 (2 . . . Nf6 3 d4 ±) 3 d4 cxd4 4 Qxd4 Nf6 5 e4 Nc6 6 Bb5 Bd7 7 Bxc6 Bxc6 8 exd5 Nxd5 9 Ne5 Nxc3 10 Nxc6 Qd5 11 Qxd5 Nxd5 12 Ne5 Nb4 13 Kd1 f6 14 Bd2 e6 15 c3 Nd5 =, Ermenkov–Ghinda, Prague 1985.

(j) 2 . . . d4 3 Nce2 (3 Nb1!?, Euwe) 3 . . . e5 4 f4 exf4 5 Nxf4 Bd6 6 d3 Ne7 7 c3 Ng6 8 Nxg6 hxg6 9 Qa4† Nc6 10 Nf3 Bg4 11 Bg5 f6 12 Bd2 Bg3† 13 hxg3 Rxh1 14 Nxd4 Qd7 15 Nxc6 Qxc6 16 Qxc6† bxc6 17 Be3 0-0-0 =, Hector–Hjartarson, Reykjavik 1984.

(k) 8 Bg5 0-0 9 0-0 Bxc3 10 bxc3 h6 =, Eising–Capelan, Solingen 1968.

(l) (A) 1 . . . e5 2 Nf3 Nc6 3 d4 exd4 4 Nxd4 g6 5 Nxd5 a6 Bg5 ± (van Geet). (B) 1 . . . g6 2 Nf3 d5 3 e3. (C) 1 . . . Nf6 2 e3 g6 3 b3 (Larsen), or 3 f4 (Bird's Opening), or 3 Nf3 (Reti) are all feasible, but after 3 d4?! d5 White's knight on c3 is misplaced. (D) 1 . . . f5? 2 e4 fxe4 3 d3 exd3 4 Bxd3 Nf6 5 g4! is a From's Gambit reversed, combined with an auspicious Grob's Attack.

(m) (A) 2 Ne4 e6 3 Ng3 d5 4 Nf3 Nf6 5 e3 Be7 6 d4 0-0 7 c3 Nc6 8 Bd3 Qc7 9 0-0 e5 10 dxe5 Nxe5 =, Mestrović–Sunye, Lone Pine 1978. (B) 2 d4 exd4 3 Qxd4 Nc6 4 Qh4 g6 5 Bd2 Bg7 6 e4 d6 7 0-0-0 Be6 8 Nd5 Bxd5 9 exd5 Qb6 = (Benjamin).

(n) 5 Bf4 d6! (Hartston), or 5 . . . Nf6 (Larsen).

(o) 8 Ne4 Rb8 9 Nxf6† Bxf6 10 Nxf6 exf6 11 d4 d5 12 0-0-0 Qe7 = (Korn). The Queen's Knight Attack has also been known as the "Dunst Opening." Many sidelines have been analyzed by Myers.

(p) Other "Unorthodox" first moves are: (A) 1 a3, a waiting move employed by Adolf Anderssen in three match games against Morphy. It allows White, with a move in hand, to defend against Black's choice of an available King's Pawn opening. He can also play a reversed Sicilian (or a "Delayed English") upon 1 . . . e5 2 c4. (B) Juncosa's (1920) Saragossa Opening 1 c3, when a regular Queen's Pawn Game with 1 . . . d5 is natural, as is 1 . . . b6. Harding proposes 1 . . . f5 2 d4 Nf6 and Myers suggests the risky 2 e4!? fxe4 (2 . . . d6! Korn) 3 d3 exd3 4 Bxd3 Nf6 5 Qc2 e5 6 Bg5. (C) 1 e3 (The Van't Kruijs) 1 . . . e5 2 Nc3 d5 3 d4 exd4 = (Blackburne, 1883); or 2 b3!: Nc6 3 Bb7 d6, e.g. 4 Nc3 Be7 5 Nf3 Bg4 6 Be2 Nf6 7 0-0 0-0 8 d3 Qd7 9 Qd2 a6 10 a4 d5! 11 Nd1 d4 ∞. Other experiments such as 1 h3, 1 h4, 1 a4, 1 Na3 (The Durkin), or 1 Nh3 (The Paris Gambit) are dealt with in monographs on irregular openings.

(q) 2 a3 a5 (2 . . . c5?! 3 Bb2 e4?! 4 e3 Nf6 5 bxc5 Bxc5 6 Bxf6 Qxf6 7 Nc3 Qe5 8 Bc4 was the erratic sequence in Ermenkov–Adorjan, Riga 1981) 3 Bb2 e4 4 c4 Nf6 5 Qb3 Na6 =.

(r) Black may exchange pawns at once by 2 . . . Bxb4 3 Bxe5 Nf6 and now: (A) 4 e3 0-0 5 Be2 d5 6 Nf3 Nc6 7 Bb2 Re8 8 0-0 Bg4 9 c3 Bd6 10 d4 Qe7 11 Nbd2 Ne4 =, Grund–de Visser, corr. (ICCF theme tourney) 1980–83. (B) 4 c4 Be7! (4 . . . 0-0 5 Qb3 ±) 5 Bb2, retreating immediately to effectively meet Black's choice of 5 . . . c5 or 5 . . . d6. In the column, . . . Bxb4 is a gambit in exchange for space.

(s) 3 c4!? c6 4 b5 cxb5 5 cxb5 d5 6 e3 Be6 7 Nf3 Bd6 8 Nc3 Nd7 9 Be2 Ne7! (Diener, but see col. 2).

(t) Of older standing is 4 . . . Ne7, which can continue: (A) 5 f4 d5! 6 exd5 exf4 7 Qf3 Bd6 8 Ne2 Ng6 9 d4 Qe7 10 Bc1 Bf5 11 Bd3! Bxd3 12 Qxd3 0-0 13 0-0 Re8 14 Nxf4 Nxf4 15 Bxf4 ±, Tartakower–Colle, Bartfeld 1926. (B) 5 Qh5† Ng6 6 f4 exf4 7 Nf3 Nc6 8 Nc3 Bxc3 9 Bxc3 d6 10 Nh4 Nce7 11 Nf5 Kf8 12 0-0 Qe8 13 Bxf6! Bxf5 14 exf5 d5? (14 . . . Nge5! =) 15 fxg6 gxf6 16 Qh6† Kg8 17 g7 Resigns, Fischer–Gloger, Cleveland 1964 (simul.).

(u) 5 Ne2 Nge7 6 a3 Ba5 7 0-0 d6 8 Nc3 Bg4 9 f3 Bh5 10 Ng3 Bf7 11 Bxf7† Kxf7 12 f4 Qd7 (12 . . . exf4 13 Nh5) 13 f5 Rag8 ∞ (Korn).

(v) 8 Bxc3 Qc5 9 Qe2 Nfe7 10 0-0-0 b5! 11 Bd5 Nxd5 12 exd5 Qxd5 13 d4 e4 ∓, Sadler–Veczey, corr. 1969.

(w) A curious line is 1 . . . c6 2 Bb2 Qb6 3 a3 a5 4 c4 axb4 5 c5! Qc7 (5 . . . Qxc5? 6 axb4 wins) 6 axb4 Rxa1 7 Rxa1 d6 8 e3 b5 9 Nf3 Bg4 10 Be2 Nd7 11 0-0 e5 12 h3 Bh5 13 Nh2 Bxe2 14 Qxe2 Ngf6 =, Nekrasov–Lyuborsky, USSR 1970.

(x) 2 Nf3 (or rather 1 Nf3 Nf6 2 b4) constitutes "Santasiere's Folly." He successfully practiced it for decades, e.g. 2 . . . e6 3 a3 a5 4 b5 d5 5 e3 c5 6 Bb2 Nbd7 7 c4 Bd6 8 d4 0-0
9 Nbd2 b6 10 Be2 Bb7 11 0-0 Rc8 12 Rc1 Qe7 13 Qb3 Bb8 14 Ne5 Nxe5 15 dxe5 Nd7 16
f4 f6 =, Santasiere–Gonzalez, Florida 1969.

(y) 8 d3 c5 9 Nbd2 Nbd7 10 c4 Bd6 11 Re1 Qc7 =, Miles–Ribli, London 1984.

INDEX

Abrahams-Noteboom Variation, 416, 438–40
Accelerated Counterthrust Variation, 27, 79–80
Accelerated Dragon, 246–47, 279–83
  Maróczy Bind, 247, 282–83
Accelerated Fianchetto (Carls' Bremen System), 626, 634–35
Advance Variations:
  Caro-Kann Defense, 172, 183–84
  French Defense, 200, 238–40, 323
Alapin's Opening, 152–54
Albin Counter Gambit, 362, 442, 451–52
Alekhine-Chatard Attack, 198, 203–4
Alekhine's Defense, 157–70, 340
  Exchange Variation, 157–58, 162–64
  Four Pawns' Attack, 158, 165–69
  Modern Variation, 157, 159–63
  Nimzowitsch Defense, 351–52
  Two Pawns' Attack, 158, 167–68
  unusual lines, 155, 169–70
Allgaier Gambit, 5
Anti-Marshall Lines, 26, 59–60
Anti-Meran Variation, 414–15, 430–33
Anti-Queen's Indian system, 471
Austrian Attack, 327, 329–34, 340
Averbakh Variation, 572, 581, 596–97

Baker's Defense, 353, 355–56
Balogh's Defense, 464
Barcza System, 674, 677–79
Basman's Defense, 353, 355–56
Belgrade Gambit, 90, 95–96
Benko Gambit, 596, 618–22
Benoni Defense, 470, 515, 571, 588, 604–17
  Czech Benoni, 605, 616–17
  Four Pawns Attack, 572, 598, 605, 614–15
  Knight's Tour Variation, 605, 610–13
  Mikenas Attack, 605, 614–15
  Old Benoni, 605, 616–17
  Reversed Benoni, 673, 675–76

Taimanov's Variation, 605, 616–17
Berlin Defense, 24–25, 31–32
Bird's Defense, 25, 33–34
Bird's Opening, 685, 688–89, 693–95
  Deferred, 695
  From's Gambit, 693–95
Bishop's Opening, 143–45
Blackmar-Diemer Gambit, 441, 443–44
Blumenfeld Counter Gambit, 442, 451–52
Bogolyubov (Bogo-) Indian Defense, 490–94, 530, 543
Boleslavsky Variation, 248, 308–9
Breyer Gambit, 4, 11–12
Breyer Variation, 26, 45–46
Browne's System, 254
Budapest (Counter) Gambit, 453–55
  Fajarowicz Variation, 453–55
Burn's Variation, 198, 203–4
Byrne Variation, 327–28, 337–39

Cambridge Springs Defense, 359–60, 373–74
Canal Variation:
  Giuoco Piano, 98, 103–4
  Two Knights' Defense, 114
Carls' Bremen System (Accelerated Fianchetto), 626, 634–35
Caro-Kann Defense, 171–96, 340
  Advance Variation, 172, 183–84
  Exchange Variation, 172, 193–94
  Fantasy Variation, 172, 193–94
  King's Indian Attack style of, 172, 195–96
  Main Line, 172–82
  Panov Attack, 345, 348–49
  Panov-Botvinnik Attack, 172, 189–92
  Two Knights' Variation, 172, 185–88
Catalan Opening, 491, 493, 498, 530–47, 550, 673, 685
  Classical Line, 531, 533–36
  Closed Variation, 532, 545–47
  with English flavor, 531, 543–44
  Open Variation, 531, 533–44
  Reti Neo-Catalan, 674, 677–78

Center Counter Defense, 146–48,
343, 345–49
Mieses-Kotrč Gambit, 346
Nimzowitsch Defense, 352
Center Game, 146–48
Center Variation, Ruy Lopez, 26, 63–
64
Chigorin Defense:
Queen's Gambit, 415, 428–29
Queen's Gambit Declined, 362,
402–3
Chigorin Variation, Ruy Lopez, 26,
49–54
Classical (Cordel) Defense, 24, 29–30
Colle System, 441, 444–46
Compromised Defense, 98, 105–6
Cordel (Classical) Defense, 24, 29–30
Cozio Defense, 25, 33–34
Cracow Variation, 101
Cunningham's Variation, 4, 9–10
Czech Benoni, 605, 616–17

Damiano's Defense, 154
Danish Gambit, 118, 125, 149–51
Declined, 149–51
Dilworth Attack, 27, 67–69
Döry Defense, 446
Double Fianchetto Defense, 627,
650–51
Dragon Variation, see Sicilian De-
fense, Dragon Variation
Dunst Opening (Queen's Knight At-
tack), 696, 698–700
Duras Variation, 79–80
Durkin's Opening, 699
Dutch Defense, 456–65, 625, 685–86,
693–95
Balogh's Defense, 464
Classical (Ilyin-Genevsky) System,
457, 462–63
Dutch-Nimzo-Indian, 457, 464–65
Leningrad Variation, 457–59
Reversed, 694
Staunton Gambit, 457, 464–65
Stonewall Formation, 457, 460–61
Dutch-Nimzo-Indian, 457, 464–65
Dutch Variation, Queen's Gambit
Declined, 360, 373–74

English Opening, 289, 448, 450,
530–31, 550, 625–72, 674, 679–
80, 687–89
Carls' Bremen System, 626, 634–
35
Closed Variation, 626–27, 636–39
Delayed, 699

Double Fianchetto Defense, 627,
650–51
Four Knights' Variation, 626–27,
630–33, 689
Grünfeld English, 627, 650–51
Hedgehog Defense, 625, 628, 651,
659–60, 663–64
hybrid variation, 627, 644–47
Keres Defense, 628, 661–62, 665
Keres Variation, 626, 634–35
King's Indian English, 627, 648–
49
Nimzo-Indian English, 627, 644–
45
Queen's Indian English, 627, 644–
47
Romanishin Variation, 627
Rubinstein/Botvinnik Variation,
628, 667–68
Slav Defense English, 627, 650
Symmetrical Four Knights' Varia-
tion, 627, 650–56
Symmetrical Variations, 625, 627–
29, 650–70
Ultra-Symmetrical Variation, 625,
628–29, 669–70
Englund Gambit, 450
Evans Gambit, 107, 128
Accepted, 105–6
Giuoco Piano, 98, 105–6

Fajarowicz Variation, 453–55
Falkbeer Counter Gambit, 4, 13–14,
144
Fantasy Variation, 172, 193–94
f4 Attack, Sicilian Defense, 249,
320–21, 690
Fianchetto Defenses, 354
Double, 627, 650–51
King's Fianchetto Defense, 441,
447–48
King's Indian Defense, 572, 589–
95
Fianchetto Systems:
Accelerated Fianchetto, 626, 634–
35
Classical Variation, 572, 589–91
King's Fianchetto Opening, 686,
689–90, 695
Larsen Opening, 685–86, 691–92
Yugoslav Line, 572, 594–95
Fianchetto Variations:
Pirc Defense, 328, 337–39
Ruy Lopez, 26, 43–44
Fischer Variations:
King's Gambit, 7

Nimzo-Indian Defense, 497, 516–17
Four Knights' Defense, 90–96, 135
Four Knights' Game, 87
    Belgrade Gambit, 90, 95–96
    Rubinstein Variation, 90, 93–96
    Scotch Four Knights' Game, 90, 95–96
    Spanish Four Knights' Game, 90, 93–94
    Svenonius Variation, 93
    Symmetrical Variation, 90–92
Four Knights' Variations:
    English Opening, 626–27, 630–33, 689
    Sicilian Defense, 247, 294–95
Four Pawns' Attack:
    Alekhine's Defense, 158, 165–69
    Benoni Defense, 572, 598, 605, 614–15
    King's Indian Defense, 572, 598–99
Franco-Indian Defense, 448
French Defense, 170, 194, 197–242, 679–80
    Advance Variation, 200, 238–40, 323
    Alekhine-Chatard Attack, 198, 203–4
    Burn's Variation, 198, 203–4
    Classical Variation, 198, 201–4
    Exchange Variation, 200, 236–37
    Guimard Variation, 200, 234–35
    King's Indian Attack, 200, 241–42
    MacCutcheon Variation, 198, 205–6
    Rubinstein Variation, 198, 209–10
    Steinitz Variation, 198, 207–8
    Tarrasch Variation, 199–200, 223–35
    Two Knights' Variation, 200, 241–42
    Winawer Variation, 198–99, 211–22, 691
Fried Liver Attack, 112
Fritz Variation, 111–12
From's Gambit, 693–95
    Reversed, 699

Giuoco Pianissimo, 97–98, 103–4
Giuoco Piano (Italian Opening), 97–106, 118, 124, 143
    Canal Variation, 98, 103–4
    Compromised Defense, 98, 105–6
    Cracow Variation, 101
    Evans Gambit, 98, 105–7

Möller Attack, 97, 99–100, 107
Göring Gambit, 118, 125–27, 129, 151
Göteborg Variation, 254
Greco Counter (Latvian) Gambit, 140–42
Grob's Attack, 696, 698–700
    Basman Defense, 353, 355–56
Grünfeld (Indian) Defense, 548–69, 657
    Classical Line, 549–50, 559–62
    Exchange Variation, 548–49, 551–56
    Neo-Grünfeld, 550, 567–69, 673
    Prins Variation, 549–50, 561–62
    Reversed, 682, 685, 687–88
    Smyslov Variation, 549, 559–60
Grünfeld English, 627, 650–51
Guimard Variation, 200, 234–35

Hamppe-Allgaier Gambit, 17, 22–23
Hanham Variation, 137–39
Hanstein Gambit, 5–6
Hedgehog Defense, see English Opening, Hedgehog Defense
Heinrich Wagner Gambit, 446
Hennig-Schara Gambit, 362, 398–99
Howell Attack, 27, 71–72
Hübner Variation, 469, 497, 518–20
Hungarian Defense, 152–54

Ilyin-Genevsky (Classical) System, 457, 462–63
Italian Opening, see Giuoco Piano

Jaenisch Gambit (Schliemann Defense), 25, 35–36

Kan (Paulsen) Variation, 247, 290–93, 628
Keres Attack, Sicilian Defense, 245, 266–67
Keres Defense, English Opening, 628, 661–62, 665
Keres Variations:
    English Opening, 626, 634–35
    Ruy Lopez, 26, 53–54
Kevitz-Trajković Defense, 350–51, 442, 449–50
Kieseritzky Gambit, 3, 5–6
King's Bishop Gambit, 4, 11–12
King's Fianchetto Defense, 441, 447–48
King's Fianchetto Opening, 686, 689–90, 695

King's Gambit, 1–16, 140, 143
  Accepted, 140
  Allgaier Gambit, 5
  Breyer Gambit, 4, 11–12
  Cunningham's Variation, 4, 9–10
  Declined, 4, 15–16
  Delayed, 17, 20–21
  Falkbeer Counter Gambit, 4, 13–
    14, 144
  Fischer's Variation, 7
  Hanstein Gambit, 5–6
  Kieseritzky Gambit, 3, 5–6
  King's Bishop Gambit, 4, 11–12
  Muzio Gambit, 5–6
  Philidor Gambit, 5–6
King's Indian Attack, 674, 679–85,
    688
  Caro-Kann Defense, 172, 195–96
  French Defense, 200, 241–42
King's Indian Defense, 28, 457, 550,
    570–604, 625, 642, 655, 679–80
  Averbakh Variation, 572, 596–97,
    581
  Classical Variation, 571–72, 574–
    81, 589–91, 602
  Fianchetto System, 572, 589–95
  Four Pawns' Attack, 572, 598–99
  Old Indian Defense, 573, 602–3,
    641–42
  Orthodox Variation, 571–72, 582–
    83
  Panno Variation, 571–72, 584–85,
    594
  Robatsch Defense, 340, 343–44
  Sämisch Attack, 571–72, 582–88
  Yugoslav Line, 572, 594–95
King's Indian English, 627, 648–49
King's Indian Reversed, 679
Knight's Tour Variation, 605, 610–13

Larsen's (Queen's Fianchetto) Open-
    ing, 685–86, 691–92
Larsen Variation, Sicilian Defense,
    248, 308–9
Lasker's Defense, 359–60, 375
Latvian (Greco Counter-) Gambit,
    140–42
Leningrad Variations:
  Dutch Defense, 457–59
  Nimzo-Indian Defense, 497, 526–
    27
Levenfish Variation, 246, 278–79
Lisitsin Gambit, 685–86, 689–90
London System, 673, 675–76
Löwenthal Variation, 692
  Sicilian Defense, 248, 296–97

MacCutcheon Variation, 198, 205–6
Manhattan Variation, 359
Maróczy Bind:
  Accelerated Dragon, 247, 282–83
  Sicilian Defense, 247, 282–83, 344,
    628, 648, 652, 665
Marshall (Counter) Attack, 26, 61–
    62
Marshall Gambit:
  Queen's Gambit, 416, 438–40
  Queen's Gambit Declined, 362,
    398–99
Marshall Lines, Anti-, 26, 59–60
Max Lange Attack, 107, 113–14
Meran Variation, 414–27
  Anti-Meran Variation, 414–15,
    430–33
Mieses-Kotrč Gambit, 346
Mikenas Attack, 605, 614–15
Milner-Barry Variation, 496, 501–2
Modern (Robatsch) Defense, 326,
    340–44
Modern Steinitz Defense, 28, 81–86
  Siesta Variation, 28, 83–84
Modern Variation, Alekhine's De-
    fense, 157, 159–63
Möller Attack, 97, 99–100, 107
Morra Gambit, 249, 322–23
Muzio Gambit, 5–6

Najdorf-Dragon, 278
Najdorf Variation:
  Poisoned Pawn, 244, 250–51, 415
  Sicilian Defense, 244, 250–61, 415
Neo-Catalan, Reti, 674, 677–78
Neo-Grünfeld, 550, 567–69, 673
Nimzo-Indian English, 627, 644–45
Nimzowitsch Attack, 685, 687–88,
    692
Nimzowitsch Defense, 350–52
  Alekhine's Defense, 351–52
  Center Counter Defense, 352
  Queen's Knight Defense, 442, 449–
    50, 672
Nimzowitsch (Nimzo-) Indian De-
    fense, 448, 490, 495–530, 543,
    626–27
  Classical Variation, 496, 499–504
  Dutch-Nimzo-Indian, 457, 464–65
  Fischer Variation, 497, 516–17
  Gligorić Variation, 497, 510–13
  Hübner Variation, 469, 497, 518–
    20
  Leningrad Variation, 497, 526–27
  Milner-Barry Variation, 496, 501–2
  Queen's Gambit Declined, 361

704

Rubinstein Variation, 469, 496–97, 505–19
Sämisch Variation, 497, 519–25
Spielmann Variation, 497–98, 526–27

Old Benoni, 605, 616–17
Old Indian Defense, 573, 602–3, 641–42
Old Steinitz Defense, 25, 28, 37–38
Opočenský System, 564
Orangutan, 697
Owen's Defense, 354–56

Panno Variation, 571–72, 584–85, 594
Panov Attack, 345, 348–49
Panov-Botvinnik Attack, 172, 189–92
Paris Gambit, 699
Paulsen (Kan) Variation, 247, 290–93, 628
Pelikan Variation, 248, 294, 298–301, 652
Petrosian System, Queen's Indian Defense, 470–79
Petrosian Variation, Queen's Gambit Declined, 359–60, 369–72
Petrov's Defense, 131–36, 143
Philidor Defense, 137–39, 141
  Hanham Variation, 137–39
Philidor Gambit, King's Gambit, 5–6
Pierce Gambit, 17, 22–23
Pincus Variation, 112
Pirc Defense, 170, 326–40, 342, 679–80, 695
  Austrian Attack, 327, 329–34, 340
  Byrne Variation, 327–28, 337–39
  Classical System, 327, 335–36
  Fianchetto Variation, 328, 337–39
  4 Be3 System, 328, 337–39
  4 f3 System, 328, 337–39
  Reversed, 681
  unusual systems, 328, 337–39
Poisoned Pawn Variations:
  Najdorf, Sicilian, 244, 250–51, 415
  Winawer, French, 198–99, 211–22, 691
Polish Attack, 697–700
Polish Defense, 353, 355, 441–42, 449–50
  Deferred, 685, 687–88
Polish Gambit, 443
Ponziani's Opening, 128–30
Prins Variation, 549–50, 561–62

Queen's Bishop Attack, 441, 443–44
Queen's Fianchetto (Larsen's Opening), 685–86, 691–92
Queen's Gambit Accepted, 172, 401, 404–13
Queen's Gambit Declined, 359–404, 441, 470, 530, 625, 665
  Abrahams-Noteboom Variation, 416, 438–40
  Albin Counter Gambit, 362, 442, 451–52
  Anti-Meran Variation, 414–15, 430–33
  Cambridge Springs Defense, 359–60, 373–74
  Chigorin's Defense, 362, 402–3, 415, 428–29
  Classical Variation, 360–61, 371–74, 382–85
  Dutch Variation, 360, 373–74
  Exchange Variation, 359–61, 378–81
  Hennig-Schara Gambit, 362, 398–99
  Lasker's Defense, 359–60, 375
  Manhattan Variation, 359
  Marshall Gambit, 362, 398–99, 416, 438–40
  Meran Variation, 414–27
  Nimzo-Indian Defense, 361
  Orthodox Defense, 360, 363–68, 673
  Petrosian Variation, 359–60, 369–72
  Ragozin System, 359, 361, 386–87, 490
  Reynolds Variation, 415, 421–23
  Romih Variation, 415, 428–29
  Rubinstein Variation, 362, 394–97
  Semi-Slav Defense, 400, 414–33, 438–40
  Semi-Tarrasch Defense, 172, 190, 361, 388–93, 628
  Slav Defense, 400, 414–16, 434–40, 530, 627, 650, 673
  Slav Exchange Variation, 414, 416, 438–40
  sundry lines, 414–16, 428–29, 438–40
  Swedish Variation, 362, 398–99
  Tarrasch Defense, 359, 362, 394–99, 564, 628, 643, 653, 661, 687
  Tartakower Variation, 360, 376–77
  Vienna Variation, 359, 401

Queen's Indian Defense, 469–90,
530, 628
  earlier version of, 471, 488–89
  less common lines in, 471, 482–83
  old main line of, 471, 480–81
  Petrosian System, 470–79
Queen's Indian English, 627, 644–47
Queen's Knight Attack (Dunst Open-
ing), 696, 698–700
Queen's Knight Defense, 442, 449–
50, 672
Queen's Pawn Counter Gambit, 152–
54
Queen's Pawn Games, 676, 696, 699
  Blackmar-Diemer Gambit, 441,
443–44
  Blumenfeld Counter Gambit, 442,
451–52
  Budapest Gambit, 453–55
  Colle System, 441, 444–46
  Döry Defense, 446
  Dutch Defense, 456–65, 625, 685–
86, 693–95
  Englund Gambit, 450
  Franco-Indian Defense, 448
  Heinrich Wagner Gambit, 446
  Kevitz-Trajković Defense, 350–51,
442, 449–50
  King's Fianchetto Defense, 441,
447–48
  Polish Defense, 353, 355, 441–42,
449–50
  Queen's Bishop Attack, 441, 443–
44
  Queen's Knight Defense, 442, 449–
40, 672
  Richter-Veresov Attack, 441, 443–
44
  Ruth-Trompowski Attack, 441,
447–48
  Staunton Gambit, 457, 464–65
  Stonewall Variation, 441, 443–44
  Torre Attack, 441, 445–48
Quiet Game, see Giuoco Plano

Ragozin System, 359, 361, 386–87,
490
Rauzer-Richter Attack, 248, 256,
302–9
Reti Gambit Accepted, 673, 675–76
Reti Opening, 442, 448, 530, 646,
685, 687
  Barcza System, 674, 677–79
  Benoni Reversed, 673, 675–76
  Classical Variation, 673, 675–76
  London System, 673, 675–76

Reti Accepted, 673, 675–76
Reti Neo-Catalan, 674, 677–78
Reverse Openings:
  Benoni, 673, 675–76
  From's Gambit, 699
  Grünfeld (Indian) Defense, 682,
685, 687–88
  King's Indian Defense, 172, 679
  Pirc Defense, 681
  Sicilian Defense, 625, 699
Reynolds Variation, 415, 421–23
Richter-Rauzer Attack, 248, 256,
302–9
Richter-Veresov Attack, 441, 443–44
Robatsch (Modern) Defense, 326,
340–44
Romanishin Variation, 627
Romih Variation, 415, 428–29
Russian Game, 131
Ruth-Trompowski Attack, 441, 447–
48
Ruy Lopez, 24–86, 98, 128, 157
  Accelerated Counterthrust Varia-
tion, 27, 79–80
  Anti-Marshall Lines, 26, 59–60
  Berlin Defesne, 24–25, 31–32
  Bird's Defense, 25, 33–34
  Breyer Variation, 26, 45–46
  Center Variation, 26, 63–64
  Chigorin Variation, 26, 49–54
  Closed Systems, 25–26, 43–59
  Cordel (Classical) Defense, 24, 29–
30
  Counterthrust Variation, 27, 75–
76, 79–80
  Cozio Defense, 25, 33–34
  Dilworth Attack, 27, 67–69
  Duras Variation, 79–80
  Exchange Variation, 25, 39–42
  Exchange Variation Deferred, 79–
80
  Exchange Variation Doubly De-
ferred, 26, 65–66
  Fianchetto Variation, 26, 43–44
  Howell Attack, 27, 71–72
  Keres Variation, 26, 53–54
  Marshall (Counter) Attack, 26, 61–
62
  Modern Steinitz Defense, 28, 81–
86
  Old Steinitz Defense, 25, 28, 37–
38
  Open Defense, 27, 67–74
  Schliemann Defense, 25, 35–36
  Schliemann Deferred, 25, 35–36
  Siesta Variation, 28, 83–84

Smyslov Variation, 26, 47–48
unusual lines, 26, 59–60
Wormald Variation, 79–80
Worrall Attack, 26, 63–64

St. George Defense, 353
Sämisch Attack:
  King's Indian Defense, 571–72,
    582–88
  Orthodox Variation, 571–72, 582–
    83
  Panno Variation, 571–72, 584–85,
    594
Sämisch Variation, Nimzo-Indian
  Defense, 497, 519–25
Santasiere's Folly, 700
Saragossa Opening, 699
Scandinavian Defense, see Center
  Counter Defense
Scheveningen Variation:
  Keres Attack, 245, 266–67
  Sicilian Defense, 245, 259, 261–69,
    286, 292, 633
Schliemann Defense (Jaenisch Gam-
  bit), 25, 35–36
  Deferred, 25, 35–36
Scotch Four Knights' Game, 90, 95–
  96
Scotch Gambit, 118, 123–24
Scotch Game, 117–24
Semi-Slav Defense, see Queen's
  Gambit Declined, Semi-Slav De-
  fense
Sicilian Counter Attack, 247, 294–95
Sicilian Defense, 157, 243–324, 581,
  646, 679
  Accelerated Dragon, 246–47, 279–
    83
  Boleslavsky Variation, 248, 308–9
  Browne's System, 254
  Classical Dragon Variation, 246,
    276–77
  Closed Variations, 249, 316–19,
    626, 695
  Dragon Variation, 246–47, 270–83,
    626
  f4 Attack, 249, 320–21, 690
  Four Knights' Variation, 247, 294–
    95
  Göteborg Variation, 254
  Keres Attack, 245, 266–67
  Larsen Variation, 248, 308–9
  Levenfish Variation, 246, 278–79
  Löwenthal Variation, 248, 296–97
  Maróczy Bind, 247, 282–83, 344,
    628, 648, 652, 665

Morra Gambit, 249, 322–23
Najdorf-Dragon, 278
Najdorf Variation, 244, 250–61,
  415
Paulsen Variation, 247, 290–93,
  628
Pelikan Variation, 248, 294, 298–
  301, 652
Polugaevsky Variation, 244, 254–
  55
Reversed, 625, 699
Richter-Rauzer Attack, 248, 256,
  302–9
Scheveningen Variation, 245,
  259, 261–69, 286, 292, 633
Sicilian Counter Attack, 247, 294–
  95
Sozin Variation, 248–49, 256, 312–
  13
Taimanov Variation, 247, 284–89,
  292, 295
unusual lines, 249, 324–25
variations with 3 Bb5, 249, 314–
  15
variations with 2 c3, 249, 322–
  23
Velimirović Attack, 248–49, 310–
  11
Wing Gambit, 249, 324
Yugoslav Attack, 246, 270–75
Siesta Variation, 28, 83–84
Slav Defense:
  Abrahams-Noteboom Variation,
    438–40
  Exchange Variation, 438–40
  Marshall Gambit, 438–40
  sundry lines, 438–40
Slav-Grünfeld Formation, 564
Sokolsky Opening, 697–700
Sozin Variation, 248–49, 256, 312–
  13
Spanish Four Knights' Game, 90,
  93–94
Spanish Game, see Ruy Lopez
Spanish torture, see Ruy Lopez
Spielmann Variation, 497–98, 526–
  27
Spike, The, 696, 698–700
Staunton Gambit, 457, 464–65
Steinitz Defense:
  Modern, 28, 81–86
  Old, 25, 28, 37–38
Steinitz Gambit, Vienna Game, 17,
  22–23
Steinitz Variation, French Defense,
  198, 207–8

Stonewall Formation, Dutch Defense, 457, 460–61
Stonewall Variation, Queen's Pawn Games, 441, 443–44
Svenonius Variation, 93
Swedish Variation, 362, 398–99
Symmetrical Four Knights' Variation, 627, 650–56

Tarrasch Defense, *see* Queen's Gambit Declined, Tarrasch Defense
Tarrasch Variation, French Defense, 199–200, 223–35
Tartakower Variation, 360, 376–77
Three Knights' Defense, 87–89
Torre Attack, 441, 445–48
Traxler Variation, 107, 111–12
Two Knights' Defense, 97, 107–16, 118, 124, 135, 144
  Canal Variation, 114
  Fried Liver Attack, 112
  Fritz Variation, 111–12
  Max Lange Attack, 107, 113–14
  Pincus Variation, 112
  Ulvestad Variation, 111–12
  Wilkes-Barre Variation, 107, 111–12
Two Knights' Variations:
  Caro-Kann Defense, 172, 185–88
  French Defense, 200, 241–42

Ufimtsev Defense, *see* Pirc Defense
Ulvestad Variation, 111–12

Velimirović Attack, 248–49, 310–11
Veresov (-Richter) Attack, 441, 443–44
Vienna Gambit, 20–21
Vienna Game, 17–23, 143, 170, 696
  Hamppe-Allgaier Gambit, 17, 22–23
  King's Gambit Delayed, 17, 20–21
  Pierce Gambit, 17, 22–23
  Steinitz Gambit, 17, 22–23
  Vienna Gambit, 20–21
Vienna Variation, Queen's Gambit Declined, 359, 401
Volga Gambit, 618

Wagner, Heinrich, Gambit, 446
Wilkes-Barre Variation, 107, 111–12
Winawer (Poisoned Pawn) Variation, 198–99, 211–22, 691
Wing Gambit, 249, 324
Wormald Variation, 79–80
Worrall Attack, 26, 63–64

Yugoslav Attack, Sicilian Defense, 246, 270–75
Yugoslav Defense, *see* Pirc Defense
Yugoslav Line, Fianchetto System, 572, 594–95

NOTES

NOTES

NOTES

NOTES

NOTES

NOTES

NOTES

NOTES